PROFESSIONAL GOLF
2015

Written by Daniel Wexler

Published by MT III Golf Media
1100 East Imperial Ave.   Suite B
El Segundo, CA   90245
Midd23@aol.com

Also by Daniel Wexler:

The Missing Links: America's Greatest Lost Golf Courses and Holes

Lost Links: Forgotten Treasures From Golf's Golden Age

The Golfer's Library: A Reader's Guide to Three Centuries of Golf Literature

The Book of Golfers: A Biographical History of the Royal & Ancient Game

The World Atlas of Golf (with Michael Clayton, Ran Morrissett, et al)

The Black Book

The American Private Golf Club Guide

The American Golf Resort Guide

The Tropical Golf Guide

The New York Metro Area Golf Guide

The Southern California Golf Guide

The Southeast Florida Golf Guide

The Phoenix Area Golf Guide

Copyright © 2014 Daniel Wexler

ALL RIGHTS RESERVED.

No part of this book may be reproduced in any manner without the prior written consent of the publisher, except in the case of brief excerpts utilized for purposes of review or promotion.

MT III Golf Media

In addition to producing Professional Golf 2015, and our series of comprehensive national and regional golf course guidebooks ("The Black Book"), MT III Golf Media also offers customized public relations and promotional materials for public courses, resorts and private clubs. Please visit us at www.danielwexler.com.

TABLE OF CONTENTS

Section One: 2014

Future Major Championship Sites	4
Major Championships	5
2014's Rounds Of The Year	14
Official World Ranking Tables	18
PGA Tour	24
European Tour	70
Japan Tour	116
Asian Tour	131
Sunshine Tour	141
Australasian Tour	153
OneAsia Tour	161
Web.com Tour	165
European Challenge Tour	175
Special Events	185
Smaller Developmental Tours	189

Section Two: 2015

PGA/European Tour Schedules	196
PGA/European Tour Priority Lists	198
2015 Major Championship Previews	200
Miscellaneous PGA Tour Information	204
PGA Tour Event-By-Event Previews	208
European Tour Event-By-Event Previews	225
Projected Top 50 Players In The World, 2015	238
Top 25 Rising/Falling	240
Top 100 Prospects In The World, 2015	242
Scouting The Rookies	245

Section Three: Player Profiles

Legend/Glossary	248
Player Profiles	249

AUTHOR'S NOTE

Professional Golf 2015 is, as its cover suggests, an annual guidebook comprehensively covering the men's professional game in a manner designed to appeal – and be useful – to fans, media, and fantasy game players around the globe. Its roots lie in player-oriented historical materials that I began putting together for my 2005 volume *The Book of Golfers* – materials which became entirely contemporary over the past few years as I began doing research for ESPN, Golf Channel and Fox Sports. The result is a book which provides tournament records/recaps, individual player records and profiles, and a wide range of statistical and prognosticative materials for seven major tours, two major developmental circuits and more than 600 players worldwide.

It is a book that would have been impossible to create – at least in a reasonably professional manner – until recent years, partially because internet technology allows us to mine vast arrays of competitive information previously unavailable around the golfing world (save, perhaps, from the American PGA Tour). But equally significant – indeed, a good portion of the book's *raison d'être* – is the ever-increasing integration of the various professional tours combined with the game's rapid competitive globalization, circumstances which, to cite one obvious example, make top young prospects in Korea or China vastly more relevant to western golf fans than they have ever been before.

There are, of course, limitations to any printed volume, and as anyone who has ever used (or compiled) a major tour media guide can attest, there is simply never enough room to adequately portray all of the accomplishments of the Woods, Els and Mickelsons of the world. But those, of course, are the exceptions; I think that on balance, readers will find the materials assembled on everyone from Warren Abery to Lian-Wei Zhang to be useful, thorough and clear enough to paint an accurate picture of each man's past, present and future.

A goal of this volume is to be comprehensive, but one must acknowledge the realities of modern professional golf schedules as they relate to producing the book in a timely fashion. Specifically, the Sunshine Tour (as well as one or two developmental circuits) do not complete their schedules in time for our printing deadline, with the former actually running all the way into March. Consequently, their statistical information cannot be final as the book goes to press, though such numbers will be updated to reflect 2014's final results in future editions. Meanwhile, with the PGA Tour and European Tour both commencing their seasons prior to the start of the new calendar year, there is the slightly awkward circumstance of multiple new-year events having already been completed prior to the book's publication. Neither Tour shows signs of changing this practice, and there are, alas, limits to everything.

Several new features have been added to this 2015 edition, the most obvious being event-by-event previews of all tournaments officially scheduled by the PGA and European Tours. In addition, a section has been added chronicling the best/most significant rounds recorded worldwide during the 2014 season, with scorecard information included. Among the less obvious changes, Major championship previews have been expanded, several event-strength tables from the Official World Ranking have been added, developmental tour coverage has grown to include the European Challenge Tour's four satellite circuits and, most notably, all PGA Tour rookies (and a majority of the E Tour's top newcomers) now have full entries in the Player Profiles section in addition to being assessed on a new Scouting The Rookies page. Also, within each player's profile, a notation has been added indicating the highest ranking they've reached in the Official World Ranking through 2014, and when - often a handy number to have when assessing the evolution of the golfer's career.

And finally a point regarding statistics. *Professional Golf 2015* provides letter grades within each player's profile for five primary statistical categories (Driving Distance, Driving Accuracy, Greens In Regulation, Short Game and Putting) and frequently cites additional categories when the information is available and relevant. Because the degree to which major professional tours gather statistical information varies greatly, the letter grades are not based entirely on a strict formula but are instead derived by utilizing a player's actual numerical rankings over the past two or three seasons, then marginally adjusting these results as needed to reflect longer term numbers that differ greatly, and to acknowledge the talent differentials which exist among the various tours. In general then, these grades should be used not has hard numbers but rather as general guideposts to a player's particular abilities. Further, as the PGA Tour provides statistical information miles greater than the other circuits, it is their data that is utilized wherever possible. Thus it is inevitable that the accuracy of these grades may lessen slightly for players whose numbers were drawn exclusively from overseas tours – and this accuracy may diminish significantly for players whose statistical samplings (which are labeled "LTD") are smaller than the two- or three-year norm.

And lastly, three final procedural points of modest relevance. First, for reasons of space and graphic simplicity, all lists of prize money won feature numbers rounded to the nearest dollar, euro, etc. Second, these same lists are generally taken verbatim from the results pages of each tour's respective website. Thus with the exception of reversing many Asian names to western form (or the occasional abbreviating of first names for spatial reasons), they appear as listed by the tours themselves, with whatever inconsistencies in spelling, nicknames, etc. appeared therein. And third, while the event's actual name is The Open Championship, for reasons of both space and clarity, it is generally referred to within these pages as the "British Open." A necessary concession to the format, then, and not simple Yankee ignorance.

It is my hope that in an era when professional golf has truly become a worldwide game, fans, media, and fantasy game players far beyond just those in America will find *Professional Golf 2015* a useful and informative volume.

Thanks, as ever, for giving it a look.

DW

WARMING UP

It seems almost quaintly amusing to reflect upon the fact that one year ago at this time, there were many of us who wondered just where the career of then-world number six Rory McIlroy might be headed. McIlroy, after all, had ended the 2012 season by winning the PGA Championship, taking two of four events in the FedEx Cup Playoffs, and then putting a cherry on top by claiming the European Tour's DP World Tour Championship in Dubai in his final start. He thus began 2013 as the world's number one-ranked golfer, armed with a new mega-contract from Nike and, for all intents and purposes, sitting atop the golfing world. There is little point in rehashing the specifics of his 2013 plunge, except to note that it was only a "plunge" by the very highest of standards; in truth, he still managed nine top-10 finishes worldwide and avoided being shut out of the win column by defeating a hot Adam Scott at December's Australian Open. Still, in a year when he was supposed to be building on his number one status and beginning a long-term assault on various career records, the bottom – at least relatively speaking – fell out.

But what a difference a year makes.

For millions of viewers who are not personal acquaintances of McIlroy, we will likely never know to what extent his tumultuous relationship with tennis star Caroline Wozniacki was negatively affecting his golf game, nor should we. But coincidental or not, history will record that while he logged five top 10s in seven early 2014 American starts, McIlroy's golfing clouds truly lifted in the very same May week that the relationship ended – at the European Tour's marquee event, the BMW PGA Championship. A closing 66 at Wentworth did the trick here, and suddenly the world was looking at his prospects more optimistically. But it would be six weeks later that his career truly crossed back into the fast lane as he played three days of inspiring, overpowering golf, then hit all the key Sunday shots that he needed to cruise home to his third career Major championship in the British Open at Hoylake. Two weeks later, he returned to America and strung together closing rounds of 64-66-66 at Firestone to claim his first World Golf Championship title in the WGC-Bridgestone Invitational, and then it was on to Louisville where, with a late rush to overtake Mickelson, Stenson and Fowler, he charged home to his second career PGA Championship. The upshot? He cemented world Player Of The Year status, put a stranglehold on the top spot in the Official World Ranking and, most impressively, joined Jones, Nicklaus and Woods as the only men in over a century to win four Major championships by age 25.

One unintended aspect of McIlroy's dominance was that some spectacular late-spring golf played by Germany's Martin Kaymer ended up almost lost in the shuffle. Kaymer, a former world number one who had struggled at times over the previous three seasons, entered 2014 somewhat under the radar relative to the game's elite, and his early season form in America (nothing better than a T18 in eight starts) showed little to suggest that change was in the air. But the 29-year-old from Dusseldorf opened the Player's Championship with a record-tying round of 63, then hung on with rounds of 69-72-71 to win the game's biggest non-Major title by one. His form peaked five weeks later, however, when he opened with a pair of spectacular 65s at Pinehurst to take control of the U.S. Open, and eventually marched methodically home in 69 to clinch an eye-popping eight-shot victory, and his second career Major championship. The rest of Kaymer's year was a bit less productive, however, and by the time he'd logged two top 10s in his 13 remaining PGA and E Tour starts, McIlroy had turned up the jets and was stealing all of the limelight.

And then there was the year's other Major championship winner, American Gerry Lester "Bubba" Watson Jr., who remained as complex a golfer (and person) as ever during what would prove an impressively resurgent season. Winless since his 2012 Masters victory, Watson got the ball rolling via back-to-back bogey-free 64s at Riviera to win the Northern Trust Open, then scored an impressive second win at Augusta during which his range of shotmaking skills gave one the distinct impression that his second Green Jacket would likely not be his last. Though never a factor in the remaining three Majors (two MCs and a T64 at the PGA), Watson also logged a victory at China's WGC-HSBC Champions event in November – an event played late enough to count towards the 2015 PGA Tour schedule.

It is interesting to note that while McIlroy's performance was hardly shocking, each of these three players achieved rather more than was realistically expected of them as the year began. Yet despite their respective rises, there was actually relatively little change atop the OWR in 2014 – which speaks eloquently to the high caliber of golf played by Mssrs. Scott, Stenson and Rose, who won only four PGA or E Tour events among them, yet remained at lofty levels within the OWR throughout the campaign, as the below tables suggests.

	OWR Top 10 - Week 52, 2013			OWR Top 10 - Week 50, 2014	
1	Tiger Woods	11.695	1	Rory McIlroy	11.346
2	Adam Scott	9.6969	2	Henrik Stenson	8.3962
3	Henrik Stenson	9.1577	3	Adam Scott	8.0139
4	Justin Rose	7.1635	4	Bubba Watson (28)	7.4747
5	Phil Mickelson	7.0596	5	Justin Rose	6.9393
6	Rory McIlroy	6.4989	6	Sergio Garcia	6.9231
7	Matt Kuchar	6.1526	7	Jim Furyk (19)	6.8526
8	Steve Stricker	5.7235	8	Jason Day (11)	6.0553
9	Zach Johnson	5.4467	9	Jordan Spieth	5.9035
10	Sergio Garcia	5.3059	10	Rickie Fowler (40)	5.6264

(Numbers in parenthesis are player's Week 52, 2013 ranking)

Of course, at age 44, Phil Mickelson's fall from the top five cannot realistically be called surprising – and yet he held things together well enough during a markedly down year to remain a fixture among the top 15 at the time of this December writing. All of which left the most precipitous drop to the struggling Tiger Woods, who began the year number one - and was barely hanging on to a spot in the top 25 as we approached Christmas. One hates to dwell upon the negative here, but there can be no ignoring the disaster that was Woods' 2014, a season which began with a T80 in San Diego and a T41 in Dubai, suffered through back-oriented withdrawals at the Honda Classic and the WGC-Bridgestone, and, eventually, back surgery that would sideline him for the rest of the season. His every step scrutinized to a degree seldom seen in the golf world, Woods ended the season with a departed swing coach (the fired Sean Foley), a questionable body, a game in disarray, and the sense on the part of some that the second sometimes seemed the result of the third, and not vice versa.

On the more positive side, mention must be made of several younger players who took significant steps forward in 2014. Chief among these must be Rickie Fowler who, in his first year working with swing coach Butch Harmon, leaped from 40th to 10th in the OWR, doubled his PGA Tour top 10s (from five to 10) and earned the impressive-yet-dubious distinction of becoming the first man in history to log top-5 finishes in all four Major championships without winning one. But more wins, be they majors or otherwise, would now seem imminent.

And then there is the quintet of players ranked by the 2014 edition of this publication as the top five under-24 prospects in the game: Jordan Spieth, Hideki Matsuyama, Matteo Manassero, Brooks Koepka and Patrick Reed. Oddly it was Manassero, the most established of the group, who had (easily) the most disappointing year, but the other four carried the ball quite effectively. Early on it was Reed who stood tallest, winning twice on the PGA Tour, including the WGC-Cadillac at Doral. And in the later going, Reed again shined, this time distinguishing himself as the U.S. Ryder Cup team's lone real bright spot. Though a bit brash at times, he certainly walked the walk in 2014. Matsuyama also validated his selection relatively early, winning the Memorial Tournament in a playoff with Kevin Na, and thus cementing a place in the OWR top 20 - pretty good work for a 22 year old. Koepka, who split time playing in both the U.S. and Europe, took a bit longer to announce himself before eventually doing so in November by winning the penultimate event in the E Tour's Final Series, the Turkish Airlines Open. All of which left number one pick Spieth (who contended into Sunday at Augusta and finished T4 at The Players) somehow seeming like the surprise underachiever in the bunch - that is, until he ran away with late November's Australian Open behind a dazzling final round 63, then recorded an almost surreal 10-shot triumph over a star-packed field at Tiger Woods' unofficial Hero World Challenge event in Orlando. And thus, in the end, order was restored.

And then there was the business side of things.

In addition to facing the very real possibility that the Tiger Woods era may be drawing to a close, the PGA Tour continues to embrace change of a different sort as it went through year two of both a wraparound schedule and a Q School-free qualifying system that funnels the great majority of potential prospects through the developmental Web.com circuit. On balance, it would not at this point seem accurate to call the wraparound schedule highly popular – though one presumes that for the sponsors of these late-season events, the moderately stronger fields generated by making them count on the following year's schedule must be considered a good thing. The problem here is that the strengthening is indeed just moderate – and how can it be anything but? Because aside from the fact that the game's elite are affluent enough not to shorten their vacations just to jump into next year's Fedex Cup points race, several of these autumn events go head-to-head with the European Tour's Final Series, a run of four tournaments which draws most of the European elite – whose ranks presently include about half of the PGA Tour's most marketable stars. So it's highly unlikely that many marquee names are going to show up in the fall, and beyond that sort of sea change, does it really matter if these events' OWR ratings go from 150 to 175?

Of course it must always be remembered that the Commissioner is employed by the players, and while Rory, Tiger and Phil may be satisfied with making 18 or 20 American starts, the rank and file are always looking for more opportunities to play. Thus the Commissioner would appear to be in the rather tricky position of trying to balance keeping the troops happy with not oversaturating the market and watering down his product. Under the old construct, where the fall was largely reserved for second-tier players trying to keep their cards, that seemed less an issue since the audience (such as it was) seemed to understand the nature of what they were watching. So if there is a fan dissatisfaction with the wraparound approach, perhaps it lies more with the attempt to make the fall schedule "important" – at which point the feeling of oversaturation seems to become more relevant.

Whether or not these changes represent a net positive for the Tour will, of course, be sorted out over time. More immediately obvious are their operational impact, most notably on how players are able to gain status on the world's top circuit. The initial storyline was that the only viable avenue would be to play the Web.com Tour and qualify either by finishing among the top 25 regular season money winners, or by playing one's way through the overly complex mechanism of the Web.com Finals. Such a circumstance may not have seemed fair to overseas stars whose spirits were not lifted by thoughts of spending a full year on a developmental circuit, but such players have, perhaps inevitably, found a more palatable route. Indeed, by earning at least as many dollars (or FedEx Cup points) as the Tour's 125th-ranked player, such men gain status in Category 21 – which falls just behind the top 125 in FedEx Cup points and, in a recent development, the top 125 on the money list through the regular season-ending Wyndham Championship. Combine this with the opportunity to play on Special Temporary Membership status (with its unlimited sponsor exemptions) upon earning as much as the 150th man on the previous year's money list and, for a 2015 class that includes American Brooks Koepka, Italy's Francesco Molinari, France's Victor Dubuisson and Wales' Jamie Donaldson, it was the only way to travel.

But beyond such nuts and bolts issues (which are generally only of interest to the players themselves), the PGA Tour motors lucratively onward, offering a 2015 schedule totaling 47 events, including a season-ending four-event playoff series. Secondary or "opposite" events are scheduled in the weeks of the HSBC-WGC Champions (Sanderson Farms), the WGC-Cadillac Championship (Puerto Rico) and the WGC-Bridgestone Invitational (Barracuda Championship), as well as during British Open week, when the new Barbasol Championship will make its debut in Alabama. Purses remain by far the world's largest, sponsors are obviously still willing to pay the freight, and TV ratings – which are far less of a consideration to golf advertisers than in most other sports – show signs of spiking around Rory McIlroy, always a good omen. The Commissioner may have his critics then, but few can argue the notion that from a business perspective, he helped the Tour to survive the worst economy in eight decades relatively unscathed. And if, in fact, the Tiger Woods era has come to a close, the Tour will weather that storm just as surely as it weathered the departures of Nicklaus, Palmer, Hogan and many others in days gone by. The re-blossoming of McIlroy took place at the perfect time, of course, but the PGA Tour will march affluently onward regardless.

The European Tour, on the other hand, operates on a less consistent business model, reportedly earning substantial profits in Ryder Cup years, then operating at a deficit during non-Ryder Cup campaigns. They also continue to experience a far more volatile sponsorship climate than the PGA Tour – but part of that, to be sure, stems from the fact that they are operating in more than 20 different countries instead of just one. The E Tour will say goodbye – at least temporarily – to six events in 2015 (the Nelson Mandela Championship, the Volvo Golf Champions, the NH Collection Open, The Championship at Laguna National, the Wales Open and the Perth International) while a seventh, the long-running World Match Play, is in sponsorship limbo at the time of this writing, but may yet be plugged into a vacant October slot. Coming aboard, on the other hand, are four brand new events – the Thailand Classic, the Shenzhen International (China), the Mauritius Open and a Scottish match play event hosted by Paul Lawrie – as well as the Indian Open (which will be co-sanctioned by the E Tour for the first time) and the revived European Open, which hasn't been played since 1969. Toss in the continued presence of three bigger-money tournaments in the Middle East, the flagship BMW PGA and the lucrative four-tournament Final Series (even if one of those is actually a WGC event) and the E Tour remains easily the game's most international circuit – and one whose biggest concern currently seems to be finding ways to convince its native stars to play a few more events at home.

Things are rather more fluid around the Far East, where the Japanese Golf Tour represents a true model of stability but most everything else is fragmented beyond all sense of logic. This, after all, is a region which houses the Asian Tour, the Australasian Tour and the fledgling OneAsia circuit (whose schedule is made up almost completely of other tours' events which they co-sanction), as well as a Korean PGA Tour with enough financial backing to deserve far more standing than it has, and the PGA Tour's newest international venture, the PGA Tour China. How players throughout the region are able to chart a course through this maze is a fair question, and one wonders how long it will be before one regional super tour (the original goal of OneAsia's creation) is established to simplify things, and to compete on a more level basis with the PGA and European circuits. The Australasian Tour, for one, seems in great need of such an occurrence – but the fact that the PGA Tour only just opened their China outfit in 2014 suggest that they're likely not anticipating any imminent changes to the landscape.

As ever, stories to follow all over the globe in what continues to become an increasingly worldwide game.

2014

FUTURE MAJOR CHAMPIONSHIP SITES

THE U.S. OPEN

2015	Chambers Bay – University Place, WA	June 18-21
2016	Oakmont Country Club – Oakmont, PA	June 16-19
2017	Erin Hills – Erin, WI	June 15-18
2018	Shinnecock Hills Golf Club – Southampton, NY	June 14-17
2019	Pebble Beach Golf Links – Pebble Beach, CA	June 13-16
2020	Winged Foot Golf Club – Mamaroneck, NY	June 18-21
2021	Torrey Pines Golf Club – San Diego, CA	June 17-20
2023	Los Angeles Country Club – Los Angeles, CA	TBA

THE OPEN CHAMPIONSHIP

2015	Old Course at St Andrews – St Andrews, Scotland	July 16-19
2016	Royal Troon Golf Club – Troon, Scotland	July 21-24
2017	Royal Birkdale Golf Club – Southport, England	July 20-23
2018	Carnoustie Golf Links – Carnoustie, Scotland	July 19-22

THE PGA CHAMPIONSHIP

2015	Whistling Straits (Straits) – Kohler, WI	August 13-15
2016	Baltusrol Golf Club (Lower) – Springfield, NJ	July 28-31
2017	Quail Hollow Club – Charlotte, NC	TBA
2018	Bellerive Country Golf Club – St. Louis, MO	TBA
2019	Bethpage State Park (Black) – Farmingdale, NY	TBA
2020	TPC Harding Park – San Francisco CA	TBA
2022	Trump National Golf Club – Bedminster, NY	TBA

THE RYDER CUP

2016	Hazeltine National Golf Club – Chaska, MN	Sept 30-Oct 2
2018	Le Golf National – Paris, France	TBA
2020	Whistling Straits (Straits) – Kohler, WI	TBA
2022	TBD	TBA
2024	Bethpage State Park (Black) – Farmingdale, NY	TBA

THE PRESIDENTS CUP

2015	Jack Nicklaus Golf Club – Incheon, South Korea	October 8-11
2017	Liberty National Golf Club – Jersey City, NJ	TBA
2025	TPC Harding Park – San Francisco, CA	TBA

THE MAJORS
2014

Masters Tournament

April 10 - April 13

Augusta National Golf Club - Augusta, GA
Champion: Bubba Watson

7,435 yards   Par 72
Purse: $8 Million

Conventional wisdom has long held that there are two keys to playing the Augusta National Golf Club successfully; a golfer must possess great length and, perhaps more importantly in an era when *everyone* is long, the ability to reliably move the ball right-to-left. Toss in a sense of shotmaking imagination to counter Augusta's unique undulations and green contouring and you have.......Bubba Watson.

Indeed, of all the events in professional golf's rich international spectrum, The Masters would seem the one most ideally suited to Watson's distinctive brand of power/finesse golf - and for the second time in three years, he proved this point emphatically by cruising uneventfully home on Sunday to claim his second career Green Jacket.

It was a Masters week which arrived with negative overtones, first with the winter storm loss of Augusta National's famed Eisenhower Tree, the massive loblolly pine whose 17th-hole presence was prominent enough to occasionally effect one or two ill-struck Masters tee shots. And then there was the absence of world number one Tiger Woods, gone for the foreseeable future following back surgery after what had been, even by mortal standards, a very disappointing beginning to his 2014 campaign.

Woods' absence may well have affected betting handles in Las Vegas and abroad but given the state of his game, it seemed of only moderate importance as the various other pre-tournament favorites began play on Thursday. While five-time PGA Tour winner Bill Haas set the pace with a four-under-par 68, more wagered-upon entries included defending champion Adam Scott, who opened with a 69 that might well have been far lower had he not reached the 12th tee at four under par, then suffered a momentum-crushing double-bogey after splashing his tee shot into the tributary of Rae's Creek. Also starting with 69 was Watson (who was bogey-free) and 2010 British Open champion Louis Oosthuizen, while the seven players grouped on two-under-par 70 included Jimmy Walker, Brandt Snedeker, K.J. Choi and long-hitting Gary Woodland. Two more favorites, Northern Ireland's Rory McIlroy and 20-year-old Jordan Spieth headed the group at 71, which also included 54-year-old Fred Couples and 50-year-old Spaniard Miguel Ángel Jiménez. On the down side of the ledger, perennial Augusta favorite Phil Mickelson triple-bogeyed the 12th en route to an opening 76 - a number exceeded by stars like reigning PGA champion Jason Dufner (80), frequent Masters contender Angel Cabrera (78) and a player who seemingly ought to be one, Dustin Johnson (77).

With scores remaining high despite ideal weather conditions, Watson stepped to the fore on Friday, taking the halfway lead via a 68 which included a run of five straight birdies at holes 12-16, and might well have been lower; he narrowly missed a hole-in-one at the par-3 16th and missed a four-footer for par at the last. Tied with John Senden, Jim Furyk and Thomas Bjørn for low round of the day, Watson's four-under-par effort not only staked him to a three-stroke halfway lead, it also meant that a slew of stars who otherwise likely would have seen the weekend via the 10-shot rule were sent packing. This group included Mickelson, Luke Donald, Ernie Els, Charl Schwartzel, Sergio García, Ryan Moore and Webb Simpson, all of whom would have survived had Watson shot 70 or higher. Senden, a two-time PGA Tour winner, was Watson's closest pursuer, three strokes back at 140, while the group at 141 included Scott (72) and Spieth (70). The ageless Couples carded a second straight 71 to sit on 142, five shots back, and for the fifth straight year was within the top 10 headed into the weekend.

Saturday began rather oddly as Rory McIlroy, who made the cut on the number and was the 51st player left in the field, required a non-competing marker as a playing partner. That marker, Augusta National member Jeff Knox, proceeded to fire a cool two-under-par 70 - and actually beat McIlroy by a shot. But with the undercard out of the way, the main event began seriously to take shape with Jordan Spieth birdieing the 14th and 15th en route to posting a two-under-par 70, good enough the gain a share of the 54-hole lead when Watson stumbled to the turn in 38 and eventually carded a disappointing 74. And while conditions remained relatively demanding, at least a few low numbers were out there for the taking, as demonstrated by the next four players atop the leaderboard. One shot behind Watson and Spieth were Matt Kuchar and Sweden's Jonas Blixt, Kuchar on the strength of a 68 which included six birdies, Blixt after posting his third straight sub-par round, a four-birdie, three-bogey 71. Two shots behind were Rickie Fowler and the remarkable Jiménez, Fowler riding his retooled swing to a five-under-par 67, while the ponytailed Jiménez carded the week's low round, a blazing 66. Among those relegated to the wings for Sunday, Adam Scott shot an outgoing 40 on his way to a disastrous 76, Senden recorded three bogeys and a double bogey over his first seven holes en route to a 75, and Oosthuizen posted his second consecutive 75 after his oft-painful back began acting up again on Friday.

Thus Sunday dawned with a prospect of seeing a youngest-ever Masters champion (Spieth) or an oldest-ever Major champion (Jiménez – or even Couples) or, very possibly, one of many contenders who fell in between. The first of these contenders to fall by the wayside was Fowler, who roared out of the gate with an opening birdie, then promptly three-putted from eight feet for a bogey at the 2nd to lose all his momentum. He would later bogey the 10th and 11th, birdie the 14th and post a 73, good enough to tie for fifth. Also starting fast was Kuchar, who birdied both the 2nd and 3rd to look like a very serious contender before a four-putt double-bogey at the par-3 4th scuttled his charge. But as one of the game's more consistent players, Kuchar would hang tough for much of the afternoon, lingering on the edge of contention until bogeys at the 17th and 18th dropped him to a 74, and a tie with Fowler. While Couples electrified the crowd with early birdies at the 1st and 2nd before eventually falling back to a 75, Jiménez struggled directly out of the box (three bogeys in his first five holes) but righted the ship to eventually come home in 33, his 71 good enough to claim solo fourth. Blixt, meanwhile, twice got it to six-under-par, most meaningfully with a birdie at the 16th. But a crucial bogey at the 17th dropped him back to minus five and a tie for second – his second straight Major top five following the 2013 PGA Championship.

So in the end, as for much of the day, it came down to Watson and the 20-year-old phenom Spieth. And indeed, Spieth got the better of the action in the early going, making birdie at the 2nd to move one in front, extending the lead to two when Watson bogeyed the 3rd, and keeping it there by spectacularly holing a long bunker shot for birdie after Watson had stiffed his approach at the par-3 4th. A Spieth bogey at the 5th was quickly offset by fine birdies at the 6th and the demanding 7th, but the young man from Dallas then lost the lead with a three-putt bogey at the 8th and another bogey at the 9th, all while Watson birdied both to suddenly grab a two-shot lead. Spieth briefly closed the gap with a par at the demanding 10th (to Watson's bogey) but aside from a scrambling bogey after hitting his tee shot into the water at the 12th, the rest of his day was a story of missed putts, with meaningful opportunities squandered at the 11th, 13th and 15th. By this time, Watson had logged a two-putt birdie at the 13th to extend his margin to three and, save for a brief nervous moment when Spieth nearly holed a difficult chip at the 17th, it was smooth sailing for Bubba from Bagdad (Florida) thereafter.

Weather

Thursday: Sunny with a high of 77 degrees. Winds SSW 5-10 mph.
Friday: Mostly sunny with a high of 79 degrees. Winds SW 10-15 mph.
Saturday: Sunny with a high of 82 degrees. Winds S 5-10 mph.
Sunday: Sunny with a high of 82 degrees. Winds SSE 8-14 mph.

Masters Tournament   April 10 - April 13

1	2	3	4	5	6	7	8	9	10	11	12	13	14	15	16	17	18
445	575	350	240	455	180	450	570	460	495	505	155	510	440	530	170	440	465
4	5	4	3	4	3	4	5	4	4	4	3	5	4	5	3	4	4
4.30	4.73	4.07	3.41	4.11	3.14	4.25	4.75	4.10	4.24	4.48	3.26	4.70	4.21	4.75	2.96	4.24	4.22

Pos	Player	Rounds	Total	Prize
1	Bubba Watson	69-68-74-69	280	$1.62 mil
2=	Jonas Blixt	70-71-71-71	283	$792,000
	Jordan Spieth	71-70-70-72	283	$792,000
4	Miguel Jiménez	71-76-66-71	284	$432,000
5=	Rickie Fowler	71-75-67-73	286	$342,000
	Matt Kuchar	73-71-68-74	286	$342,000
7	Lee Westwood	73-71-70-73	287	$301,500
8=	Bernhard Langer	72-74-73-69	288	$234,000
	Jimmy Walker	70-72-76-70	288	$234,000
	Rory McIlroy	71-77-71-69	288	$234,000
	John Senden	72-68-75-73	288	$234,000
	Kevin Stadler	70-73-72-73	288	$234,000
	Thomas Bjørn	73-68-73-74	288	$234,000
14=	Stewart Cink	73-72-76-68	289	$148,500
	Jamie Donaldson	73-70-76-70	289	$148,500
	Henrik Stenson	73-72-74-70	289	$148,500
	Adam Scott	69-72-76-72	289	$148,500
	Justin Rose	76-70-69-74	289	$148,500
	Jim Furyk	74-68-72-75	289	$148,500
20=	Bill Haas	68-78-74-70	290	$101,160
	Chris Kirk	75-72-71-72	290	$101,160
	Jason Day	75-73-70-72	290	$101,160
	Ian Poulter	76-70-70-74	290	$101,160
	Fred Couples	71-71-73-75	290	$101,160
25	Louis Oosthuizen	69-75-75-72	291	$79,200
26=	Joost Luiten	75-73-77-67	292	$66,600
	Hunter Mahan	74-72-74-72	292	$66,600
	Steven Bowditch	74-72-74-72	292	$66,600
	Gon. Fdez-Castaño	75-69-74-74	292	$66,600
	Gary Woodland	70-77-69-76	292	$66,600
31=	Martin Kaymer	75-72-73-73	293	$55,800
	Russell Henley	73-70-75-75	293	$55,800
	Steve Stricker	72-73-73-75	293	$55,800
34=	Stephen Gallacher	71-72-81-70	294	$48,600
	K.J. Choi	70-75-78-71	294	$48,600
	José María Olazábal	74-74-73-73	294	$48,600
37=	Brandt Snedeker	70-74-80-71	295	$40,500
	Brendon de Jonge	74-72-76-73	295	$40,500
	Thongchai Jaidee	73-74-75-73	295	$40,500
	Billy Horschel	75-72-75-73	295	$40,500
	Vijay Singh	75-71-74-75	295	$40,500
42=	Lucas Glover	75-69-77-75	296	$34,200
	Kevin Streelman	72-71-74-79	296	$34,200
44=	Mike Weir	73-72-79-73	297	$27,972
	Sandy Lyle	76-72-76-73	297	$27,972
	Nick Watney	72-75-76-74	297	$27,972
	Thorbjørn Olesen	74-72-76-75	297	$27,972
	Darren Clarke	74-74-73-76	297	$27,972
49	Oliver Goss (a)	76-71-76-75	298	-
50	Francesco Molinari	71-76-76-76	299	$11,340
51	Larry Mize	74-72-79-79	304	$11,340

Out Of The Money: **149**: Ryan Moore, Sang-Moon Bae, Sergio García, Luke Donald, Marc Leishman, Victor Dubuisson, Phil Mickelson, Ernie Els, Webb Simpson, Charl Schwartzel, Matthew Fitzpatrick (a) **150**: D.A. Points, Harris English, Ian Woosnam, Graeme McDowell, Zach Johnson **151**: Ken Duke, Dustin Johnson, John Huh, Hideki Matsuyama **152**: Matt Jones, Graham DeLaet, Derek Ernst, Mark O'Meara, David Lynn, Angel Cabrera, Matteo Manassero, Patrick Reed **153**: Branden Grace, Trevor Immelman, Keegan Bradley, Roberto Castro, Chang-woo Lee (a) **154**: Y.E. Yang, Jason Dufner **155**: Jordan Niebrugge (a), Scott Stallings, Matt Every **156**: Garrick Porteous (a), Boo Weekley **157**: Tim Clark **159**: Peter Hanson, Craig Stadler, Tom Watson **161**: Michael McCoy (a) **168**: Ben Crenshaw

Eagles (Crystal Goblets)

Sang Moon Bae — Rd 1, 15th hole	Matt Jones — Rd 1, 13th hole	Justin Rose — Rd 3, 13th hole
Sang Moon Bae — Rd 2, 15th hole	Martin Kaymer — Rd 4, 13th hole	Brandt Snedeker — Rd 4, 13th hole
Steven Bowditch — Rd 4, 2nd hole	Bernhard Langer — Rd 4, 2nd hole	Jordan Spieth — Rd 2, 15th hole
Ken Duke — Rd 1, 13th hole	Sandy Lyle — Rd 4, 13th hole	Nick Watney — Rd 2, 15th hole
Derek Ernst — Rd 2, 13th hole	Louis Oosthuizen — Rd 2, 13th hole	Bubba Watson — Rd 3, 2nd hole
Billy Horschel — Rd 2, 2nd hole	Justin Rose — Rd 2, 8th hole	Gary Woodland — Rd 3, 2nd hole
Billy Horschel — Rd 3, 15th hole	Justin Rose — Rd 3, 3rd hole	

FIRST ROUND
Bill Haas	68 (-4)
Adam Scott	69 (-3)
Louis Oosthuizen	69 (-3)
Bubba Watson	69 (-3)
Kevin Stadler	70 (-2)
Jonas Blixt	70 (-2)
Gary Woodland	70 (-2)
Jimmy Walker	70 (-2)
K.J. Choi	70 (-2)
Brandt Snedeker	70 (-2)
Marc Leishman	70 (-2)

SECOND ROUND
Bubba Watson	137 (-7)
John Senden	140 (-4)
Thomas Bjørn	141 (-3)
Jonas Blixt	141 (-3)
Adam Scott	141 (-3)
Jordan Spieth	141 (-3)
Fred Couples	142 (-2)
Jimmy Walker	142 (-2)
Jim Furyk	142 (-2)
Jamie Donaldson	143 (-1)
Stephen Gallacher	143 (-1)
Russell Henley	143 (-1)
Kevin Stadler	143 (-1)
Kevin Streelman	143 (-1)

THIRD ROUND
Jordan Spieth	211 (-5)
Bubba Watson	211 (-5)
Matt Kuchar	212 (-4)
Jonas Blixt	212 (-4)
Miguel A. Jiménez	213 (-3)
Rickie Fowler	213 (-3)
Lee Westwood	214 (-2)
Jim Furyk	214 (-2)
Thomas Bjørn	214 (-2)
Justin Rose	215 (-1)
Kevin Stadler	215 (-1)
Fred Couples	215 (-1)
John Senden	215 (-1)

OWR: 49 of top 50 entered - Rating: 766 - Points to 51st - Scott: 100 points, to 4th in OWR

United States Open

Pinehurst Resort & Country Club (No.2 Course) - Pinehurst, NC
Champion: Martin Kaymer

June 12 - June 15

7,562 yards   Par 70
Purse: $8 Million

In a unique experiment which saw the U.S. Women's Open contested over the very same golf course only four days later, the United States Open returned to the No.2 Course at Pinehurst in 2014 - but to rather a different layout than the one which had previously hosted the Open in 1999 and 2005. This was because of a significant restoration/renovation performed by Bill Coore and Ben Crenshaw, a major undertaking that included the rebuilding of greens and bunkers, and the replacement (with native sand and wire grass) of the rough which had usurped Donald Ross's splendid sand-strewn playing corridors over the decades. The result was a striking layout which, it could be boasted, utilizes nearly 75% less water than before - a wonderful environmental advancement certainly, but really only a drop in the bucket relative to so many extra acres of maintained turf required of most championship courses due to the USGA's failure to regulate modern equipment.

Especially in its enhanced state, Pinehurst's 7,562-yard, par-70 layout would prove rather a different sort of Open site, with its wide fairways (and lack of punishing rough) encouraging more aggressive driving, and the often steep pitch of its greens mandating a somewhat more lenient setup in terms of speed and firmness. In theory, it was a golf course that might produce a wider-than-usual array of contenders.

But in the event, it was strictly a one man show.

Martin Kaymer took control of this U.S. Open on Thursday when, after watching some lower-than-expected scoring on television in the morning, he methodically took Pinehurst apart in the afternoon with a stunning round of five-under-par 65. He opened with a birdie at the 402-yard 1st and, save for a bogey at the 424-yard 7th, never looked back, eventually playing Pinehurst's vaunted final five holes in three-under par, logging birdies at the 473-yard 14th, the 528-yard par-4 16th and the 202-yard par-3 7th. And it would be this late run which separated him from the field as his lead was three strokes over 2010 Open winner Graeme McDowell, Brendon de Jonge, the recently hot Kevin Na and 49-year-old journeyman Fran Quinn, whose last U.S. Open start came way back in 1996. More imposing, however, was the collection of talent sitting on one-under-par 69, a stellar group which included presumed contenders like world number two Henrik Stenson and 20-year-old phenom Jordan Spieth, as well proven PGA Tour winners like Dustin Johnson, Brandt Snedeker and Matt Kuchar. Phil Mickelson – who remained a U.S. Open shy of claiming the career Grand Slam – opened with a 70, while more disappointed with their rounds were men like world number one Adam Scott (73), Lee Westwood (75), Bubba Watson (76) and Luke Donald (77).

In broadcaster parlance Saturday is "moving day," but it was on Friday that Kaymer simply left the rest of the field behind, posting a second consecutive 65 (this time bogey-free) to set a new 36-hole Open scoring record and, more importantly, extend his lead to an imposing six shots. This margin itself tied a record (set by Tiger Woods in 2000 and Rory McIlroy in 2011) and in the process Kaymer became only the sixth player in the event's 114 playings ever to reach double digits under par. Alone in second was recent Byron Nelson Championship winner Brendon Todd (with impressive rounds of 69-67) while seven shots adrift and tied for third were Snedeker (68) and Na (69), the latter observing of Kaymer's uniquely great play: "Is four or five under out there? Yes. Is ten under out there? I don't think so." Among those who surely concurred with Na after missing the cut were Luke Donald, Bubba Watson, Charl Schwartzel, current PGA Champion Jason Dufner, Hunter Mahan and the ageless Miguel Ángel Jiménez, all of whom finished on 146, one shot off the number.

Though scoring was not dramatically low overall, Kaymer's barrage may have inspired the USGA to toughen things up on Saturday, with two-time Open winner Retief Goosen (who shot 71) suggesting that "Some of the pins look like they're about to fall off the greens." And on a day when scores did indeed climb, Kaymer suffered through several anxious moments early, bogeying the long 2nd before having to take an unplayable lie off a wayward drive at the par-4 4th, then ultimately holing a clutch 15-footer for bogey. But if so one-sided an event could have anything resembling a turning point, Kaymer provided it at the par-5 5th when, after driving into a native area, he laced a 7 iron inside six feet, then converted the putt for an eagle to regain both of his lost shots. Three more bogeys would follow but with his lead trimmed to four, Kaymer recorded a clutch birdie at the 451-yard 18th, thus ending the day with his cushion relatively intact at five strokes. But now lying in second were a pair of players who shared Saturday's low score (67), Rickie Fowler and two-time heart transplant recipient Erik Compton - and while these two might be hard-pressed to repeat such heroics on Sunday, the two players sitting immediately behind them at two-under-par 208, Henrik Stenson and Dustin Johnson, both seemed poised to mount a final round charge.

But as it turned out, among the leaders only Kaymer was ready to advance on Sunday, as his 69 was the sole sub-70 round turned in by anyone in the final eight pairings. And while nobody ever moved closer than four strokes throughout the day, there were at least a few moments of semi-suspense in the latter stages of the front nine. This came about when Kaymer, who had already birdied the driveable par-4 3rd, made bogey after driving into the native sand at the 7th, then lay shy of the green at the 502-yard par-4 8th after again missing the fairway off the tee. With Compton at that moment sitting on four under par, the potential for the lead to dwindle to three was apparent. But Kaymer got it up-and-down at the 8th, Compton bogeyed the 9th, and Kaymer promptly birdied the 9th by stuffing an eight iron to within four feet, pushing the lead back to five and, for all intents and purposes, slamming the door.

Kaymer further cemented his lead with back-to-back birdies at the 13th and 14th, by which time it was apparent that everyone else was simply playing for second. Neither Stenson (73) nor Johnson (73) ever made a meaningful move, leaving Compton and Fowler to slug it out down the stretch, with the former standing four under through 10 before carding bogeys at the 11th, 12th and 15th, ultimately finishing on 279. Fowler had removed himself from the edges of contention early with a double-bogey at the 4th, but later birdied the 12th and 13th (and secured a remarkable par at the long 16th) before a late bogey at the 17th left him tied with Compton for runner-up honors.

The 29-year-old Kaymer's stroll home was thus an easy one, and when he holed a 15-footer for par at the last, he emerged as both the first German and the first continental European ever to claim the American championship. He also became only the seventh wire-to-wire winner in the Open's history and joined Tiger Woods, Rory McIlroy, Seve Ballesteros and Ernie Els as the only players to win two Major championships before their 30th birthday since the onset of the Official World Ranking in 1986. Indeed, only a late bogey at the tough 16th kept Kaymer from matching Woods and McIlroy as the only players to complete a U.S. Open in double digits under par – though McIlroy graciously opined that given the rain-softened conditions that aided his own 16-under-par total in 2011, Kaymer's performance was "nearly more impressive than what I did at Congressional."

But perhaps it was Fowler who stated it best when observed that: "Martin was playing his own tournament." And so he was.

Weather

Thursday: Mostly cloudy. High of 88. Winds SSW 6-12 mph.
Friday: Partly cloudy. High of 88. Winds WSW 5-10 mph.
Saturday: Mostly sunny. High of 88. Winds NE 4-8 mph.
Sunday: Mostly sunny. High of 88. Winds ESE 4-8 mph.

United States Open   June 12 - June 15

1	2	3	4	5	6	7	8	9	10	11	12	13	14	15	16	17	18
402	507	387	529	576	219	424	502	191	617	483	484	382	473	202	528	205	451
4	4	4	4	5	3	4	4	3	5	4	4	4	4	3	4	3	4
4.11	4.34	3.92	4.26	4.80	3.37	4.14	4.34	3.08	5.00	4.32	4.23	4.00	4.14	3.26	4.34	3.21	4.20

1	Martin Kaymer	65-65-72-69	271	$1.62 mil
2=	Erik Compton	72-68-67-72	279	$789,330
	Rickie Fowler	70-70-67-72	279	$789,330
4=	Keegan Bradley	69-69-76-67	281	$326,310
	Jason Day	73-68-72-68	281	$326,310
	Brooks Koepka	70-68-72-71	281	$326,310
	Dustin Johnson	69-69-70-73	281	$326,310
	Henrik Stenson	69-69-70-73	281	$326,310
9=	Adam Scott	73-67-73-69	282	$230,900
	Jimmy Walker	70-72-71-69	282	$230,900
	Brandt Snedeker	69-68-72-73	282	$230,900
12=	Jim Furyk	73-70-73-67	283	$156,679
	Marcel Siem	70-71-72-70	283	$156,679
	Kevin Na	68-69-73-73	283	$156,679
	Justin Rose	72-69-70-72	283	$156,679
	Matt Kuchar	69-70-71-73	283	$156,679
17=	Brendon Todd	69-67-79-69	284	$118,234
	Ian Poulter	70-70-74-70	284	$118,234
	J.B. Holmes	70-71-72-71	284	$118,234
	Jordan Spieth	69-70-72-73	284	$118,234
21=	Cody Gribble	72-72-72-69	285	$98,598
	Steve Stricker	70-71-73-71	285	$98,598
23=	Billy Horschel	75-68-73-70	286	$79,968
	Aaron Baddeley	70-71-73-72	286	$79,968
	Shiv Kapur	73-70-71-72	286	$79,968
	Rory McIlroy	71-68-74-73	286	$79,968
	Francesco Molinari	69-71-72-74	286	$79,968
28=	Daniel Berger	72-71-78-66	287	$59,588
	Graeme McDowell	68-74-75-70	287	$59,588
	Kenny Perry	74-69-74-70	287	$59,588
	Phil Mickelson	70-73-72-72	287	$59,588
	Victor Dubuisson	70-72-70-75	287	$59,588
	Brendon de Jonge	68-70-73-76	287	$59,588
	Chris Kirk	71-68-72-76	287	$59,588
35=	Patrick Reed	71-72-73-72	288	$46,803
	Ernie Els	74-70-72-72	288	$46,803
	Sergio García	73-71-72-72	288	$46,803
	Bill Haas	72-72-71-73	288	$46,803
	Hideki Matsuyama	69-71-74-74	288	$46,803
40=	Louis Oosthuizen	71-73-78-67	289	$37,753
	Zac Blair	71-74-73-71	289	$37,753
	Zach Johnson	71-74-72-72	289	$37,753
	Lucas Bjerregaard	70-72-72-75	289	$37,753
	Garth Mulroy	71-72-70-76	289	$37,753
45=	Danny Willett	70-71-78-71	290	$30,827
	Webb Simpson	71-72-73-74	290	$30,827
	Retief Goosen	73-71-71-75	290	$30,827
48=	Matt. Fitzpatrick (a)	71-73-78-69	291	-
	Billy Hurley III	71-74-75-71	291	$26,504
	Harris English	69-75-75-72	291	$26,504
	Ryan Moore	76-68-71-76	291	$26,504
52=	Seung-Yul Noh	70-72-76-74	292	$24,513
	Gary Woodland	72-71-75-74	292	$24,513
54=	Stewart Cink	72-72-74-75	293	$23,534
	Scott Langley	72-71-75-75	293	$23,534
56=	Fran Quinn	68-74-79-73	294	$22,649
	Paul Casey	70-75-74-75	294	$22,649
	Nicholas Lindheim	72-73-72-77	294	$22,649
59	Justin Leonard	75-70-75-75	295	$22,090
60=	Russell Henley	70-74-82-71	297	$21,564
	Kevin Tway	72-72-81-72	297	$21,564
	Alex Cejka	73-71-77-76	297	$21,564
63=	Kevin Stadler	77-68-78-75	298	$20,775
	Clayton Rask	73-71-77-77	298	$20,775
	Bo Van Pelt	72-72-75-79	298	$20,775
66	Boo Weekley	71-73-80-75	299	$20,249
67	Toru Taniguchi	72-73-88-76	309	$19,985

Out Of The Money: **146**: Andres Echavarria, Hudson Swafford, Casey Wittenberg, Mark Wilson, Shane Lowry, Luke Donald, Charl Schwartzel, Bubba Watson, Jason Dufner, Hunter Mahan, Rod Pampling, Cory Whitsett (a), Hunter Stewart (a), Kyoung-Hoon Lee, Matt Jones, Angel Cabrera, Thongchai Jaidee, Miguel Ángel Jiménez, Joost Luiten, Matt Dobyns, Brian Campbell (a)   **147**: Nicolas Colsaerts, Ken Duke, John Senden, Darren Clarke, Geoff Ogilvy, Ryan Blaum, Luke Guthrie, Chris Doak, Jim Renner, Andrea Pavan, Stephen Gallacher, David Toms   **148**: Lucas Glover, Ryan Palmer, David Gossett, Sam Love (a), Cameron Wilson (a), Chad Collins, Brian Stuard, Roberto Castro, Matt Every, Lee Westwood, Nick Watney, Wen-Chong Liang, Justin Thomas   **149**: Oliver Fisher, Joe Ogilvie, Henrik Norlander, Pablo Larrazábal, Craig Barlow, Tom Lewis, Smylie Kaufman   **150**: Niclas Fasth, Graham DeLaet, Hyung-Sung Kim, Bernd Wiesberger, Kevin Sutherland, Maximilian Kieffer, Maverick McNealy (a), Anthony Broussard   **151**: David Oh, Graeme Storm, Y.E. Yang, Jamie Donaldson, Brett Stegmaier, D.A. Points, Brady Watt   **152**: Steve Alker, Gonzalo Fernández-Castaño, Kevin Streelman, Simon Griffiths, Rob Oppenheim, Kevin Kisner, Robert Allenby, Aron Price   **153**: Jonas Blixt, Jeff Maggert, Robby Shelton (a), Nick Mason   **154**: Chris Thompson, Oliver Goss (a)   **155**: Bobby Gates, Donald Constable, Brandon McIver (a)   **157**: Will Grimmer (a)   **159**: Andrew Dorn (a)   **160**: Azuma Yano   **162**: Kiyoshi Miyazato

FIRST ROUND		SECOND ROUND		THIRD ROUND	
Martin Kaymer	65 (-5)	**Martin Kaymer**	130 (-10)	**Martin Kaymer**	202 (-8)
Kevin Na	68 (-2)	Brendon Todd	136 (-4)	Rickie Fowler	207 (-3)
Graeme McDowell	68 (-2)	Kevin Na	137 (-3)	Erik Compton	207 (-3)
Brendon de Jonge	68 (-2)	Brandt Snedeker	137 (-3)	Henrik Stenson	208 (-2)
Fran Quinn	68 (-2)	Brooks Koepka	138 (-2)	Dustin Johnson	208 (-2)
Brandt Snedeker	69 (-1)	Dustin Johnson	138 (-2)	Brandt Snedeker	209 (-1)
Henrik Stenson	69 (-1)	Brendon de Jonge	138 (-2)	Matt Kuchar	210 (E)
Matt Kuchar	69 (-1)	Keegan Bradley	138 (-2)	Brooks Koepka	210 (E)
Brendon Todd	69 (-1)	Henrik Stenson	138 (-2)	Kevin Na	210 (E)
Jordan Spieth	69 (-1)	Matt Kuchar	139 (-1)	Justin Rose	211 (+1)
Hideki Matsuyama	69 (-1)	Rory McIlroy	139 (-1)	Jordan Spieth	211 (+1)
Dustin Johnson	69 (-1)	Chris Kirk	139 (-1)	Chris Kirk	211 (+1)
Harris English	69 (-1)	Jordan Spieth	139 (-1)	Brendon de Jonge	211 (+1)
Keegan Bradley	69 (-1)				
Francesco Molinari	69 (-1)				

OWR: 48 of top 50 entered - Rating: 789 - Points to 67th - Kaymer: 100 points, to 11th in OWR

The Open Championship

Royal Liverpool Golf Club - Hoylake, England
Champion: Rory McIlroy

July 17 - July 20

7,312 yards Par 72
Purse: € 5.4 Million

How many times can a star be born?

Since Rory McIlroy first burst upon the scene as the hugely talented teen who shot 61 at Royal Portrush, he was marked for greatness. Logging top-5 finishes in his second and third E Tour starts as an 18-year-old professional, then winning the Dubai Desert Classic at 19, told the world that he was for real, and a victory at the PGA Tour's 2010 Quail Hollow Championship (behind a stunning final round 62) indicated he might be rather more than that. In 2011 there was the famous meltdown over the final nine at Augusta, yet two months later he was leaving the field in the dust in an eight-shot U.S. Open triumph at Congressional, proving categorically, it seemed, that he was made of championship timber. In 2012 there was another resounding Major triumph, this time an eight-shot runaway in the PGA Championship which, combined with two subsequent FedEx Cup playoff wins and a year-end world number one ranking, cemented his status as the game's next superstar. But then, puzzlingly, there was 2013, a year in which a new equipment contract and a tumultuous relationship with tennis star Caroline Wozniacki seemed to deflate him – and which ended with him mired in a slump and ranked number six in the world. Amidst rampant speculation as to the direction of his career, the cancellation of wedding plans in May of 2014 seemed to light a spark; indeed, McIlroy won the E Tour's flagship BMW PGA Championship that very week. And thus the stage was set for a victory which seems destined to lift him among the game's all-time greats at the tender age of 25: an utterly dominant victory at the 2014 British Open at Royal Liverpool.

One could reasonably fancy McIlroy's chances at Hoylake, for he entered play with nine top 10s in calendar 2014, including the BMW win. But it was clear that as the Open returned to one of England's most historic clubs for the first time since 2006, the competition would be fierce, for top-10 players like Adam Scott, Henrik Stenson, Justin Rose and Sergio García were all arriving in top form, and there was no shortage of additional world-class players nipping closely at their heels. And then, of course, there was Tiger Woods, rebounding – perhaps a bit too soon – from spring back surgery, seemingly physically fit, and returning to the place of his last British triumph eight years earlier.

In order to clear the stage for the more prominent members of the cast, Woods' week could be summarized thusly: He opened with a 69 which left him three off the lead, an impressive round in that his back appeared fine and – equally revealingly – he seemed capable of consistently drawing the ball in a manner unseen in many moons. Thus igniting a hail of hopeful commentary among the pundits, he promptly began round two double-bogey, bogey, then later triple-bogeyed the 17th en route to a 77 that required a birdie at the last just to make the cut. From that point forward he represented little more than marquee filler for the early hours of ESPN's wall-to-wall coverage, playing far from the leaders on Saturday and Sunday and carding erratic rounds of 73-75 that left him alone in 69th – and with more than one observer noting that dramatic improvement in his driver would be required before he'd seriously contend at this level again.

On the more positive side, McIlroy sent a message bright and early on Thursday, carding a bogey-free 66 in ideal morning conditions to grab a one-shot lead over Italian Matteo Manassero, with a group of seven players – including Scott, García and Jim Furyk – sitting two back. Among the biggest names, Stenson and Rose settled for even-par 72s, Rickie Fowler and Japan's Hideki Matsuyama posted 69s, and defending champion Phil Mickelson continued a disappointing season with an afternoon 74.

The McIlroy lead quickly led to another offbeat storyline: whether he would be able to avoid stumbling badly on Friday, an odd malady that had recently submarined his chances at The Masters (77), Wells Fargo (76), Memorial (78 – after leading with 63) and the Scottish Open (78 - after leading with 64). It was a bizarre hex indeed, and one which perhaps seemed unbeatable when he opened Friday with a bogey at the par-4 1st. But in true championship form, McIlroy stopped the bleeding forthwith and went on to card seven birdies to record his second consecutive 66, good enough to move four shots clear of long-hitting Dustin Johnson (65) and six ahead of a blue-chip sixsome composed of García (70), Fowler (69), Francesco Molinari (70), Louis Oosthuizen (68), Charl Schwartzel (67) and Ryan Moore (68). Cut casualties included Lee Westwood (147), Masters champion Bubba Watson (148) and Ernie Els (152), while a notable survivor was 64-year-old Tom Watson, who made it on the number with consecutive 73s to extend his own record as the oldest man to play on the weekend at a Major.

If there was a defining day to this championship, it was Saturday – a day in which the R&A set a precedent by knuckling under to ominous weather forecasts (which largely failed to pan out) and sent the field off early, off both tees, and in threesomes. McIlroy, for his part, seemed like a man trying to get himself to Sunday as quickly as possible, once again opening with a bogey (which allowed Johnson, who birdied the 1st, to move within two), then plodding around in even par figures through 13 holes. Though he was hardly playing badly, his relative stagnation left the door open to his pursuers and while Johnson bogeyed holes 7-9 to slip a bit, Fowler made an impressive move, posting seven birdies over his first 12 holes and actually drawing even. But it was then that McIlroy put his indelible stamp on the Open, for as Fowler played his final five holes in two over par, Rory proceeded to play his in four under, spearheaded by overpowering eagles at both the 577-yard 16th and the 551-yard 18th – the only eagles recorded on either hole all day.

Thus off these spectacular fireworks, McIlroy went into a Sunday with a six-shot lead which would indeed prove insurmountable, though not before there were a few moments of at least marginal interest. Fowler, for his part, initially played steady golf, logging two birdies over his first 10 holes – not quite a full-fledged charge as McIlroy recovered from minor stumbles at the 5th and 6th to play the same stretch in one under. Instead the charge came from 34-year-old Sergio García, who began the day seven back before turning in three-under-par 32, then eagling the par-5 10th to pull within three. A McIlroy bogey at the 13th briefly narrowed the lead to one but moments later, García left his second in a greenside bunker at the 161-yard 16th and a bit of breathing room was restored. García made obligatory birdies at both the 16th and 18th (numbers matched by Fowler, who also birdied the 15th) but when McIlroy carded his own four at the 16th, then got deftly up-and-down from right of the green at the 458-yard 17th, there was little left for him to do but record a safe par at the last to win by two.

For García, now four times a Major bridesmaid, his performance at Hoylake surely felt like a sign of good things to come; he clearly seemed a more focused and measured player on the biggest of stages. Following work with swing coach Butch Harmon, Fowler (who logged his third top-5 Major finish of 2014) also appeared to raise his stock significantly going forward. But in the end, the glory was reserved primarily for McIlroy, who joined Jack Nicklaus and Tiger Woods as the only men to claim three legs of the career Grand Slam by age 25, and once again demonstrated to the golfing world that he is both a player of transcendent skill and a man very much at home in the idol's limelight.

For the third time in his brief but illustrious career, a star was born.

Weather

Thursday: Mostly sunny. Winds 7-10 mph. High of 78.
Friday: Partly cloudy, with light sprinkles in the morning. Winds SE 15-25. High of 80.
Saturday: Overcast and rainy, with temperatures in the lower 80s. Winds N/NW 8-15 mph. Due to expected inclement weather in the afternoon, players teed off Nos. 1 and 10 in threesomes between 9:00 a.m.- 11:01 a.m.
Sunday: Mostly sunny with highs in the mid-80s. Winds N/NW 10-15 mph.

The Open Championship — July 17 - July 20

1	2	3	4	5	6	7	8	9	10	11	12	13	14	15	16	17	18
458	454	426	372	528	201	480	431	197	532	391	447	194	454	161	577	458	551
4	4	4	4	5	3	4	4	3	5	4	4	3	4	3	5	4	5
4.21	4.26	4.08	3.97	4.62	3.15	4.37	4.14	3.10	4.58	3.99	4.17	3.10	4.28	3.06	4.80	4.14	4.78

Pos	Player	Rounds	Total	Money		Pos	Player	Rounds	Total	Money
1	Rory McIlroy	66-66-68-71	271	$1,665,788			Jordan Spieth	71-75-67-73	286	$46,271
2=	Sergio García	68-70-69-66	273	$785,910			Branden Grace	71-72-69-74	286	$46,271
	Rickie Fowler	69-69-68-67	273	$785,910		39=	Brendon Todd	73-73-74-67	287	$36,253
4	Jim Furyk	68-71-71-65	275	$478,380			Koumei Oda	69-77-74-67	287	$36,253
5=	Marc Leishman	69-72-70-65	276	$359,639			Henrik Stenson	72-73-73-69	287	$36,253
	Adam Scott	68-73-69-66	276	$359,639			Hideki Matsuyama	69-74-73-71	287	$36,253
7=	Charl Schwartzel	71-67-72-67	277	$263,536			Thongchai Jaidee	72-72-72-71	287	$36,253
	Edoardo Molinari	68-73-68-68	277	$263,536			Gary Woodland	75-69-72-71	287	$36,253
9=	Shane Lowry	68-75-70-65	278	$192,492			Kevin Stadler	73-72-71-71	287	$36,253
	Graeme McDowell	74-69-68-67	278	$192,492			Marc Warren	71-68-72-76	287	$36,253
	Victor Dubuisson	74-66-68-70	278	$192,492		47=	Stewart Cink	71-75-73-69	288	$27,358
12=	Ryan Moore	70-68-73-68	279	$144,654			Grégory Bourdy	75-69-74-70	288	$27,358
	Robert Karlsson	69-71-70-69	279	$144,654			Paul Casey	74-71-73-70	288	$27,358
	Dustin Johnson	71-65-71-72	279	$144,654			Zach Johnson	71-75-71-71	288	$27,358
15=	Francesco Molinari	68-70-75-67	280	$117,318		51=	Tom Watson	73-73-75-68	289	$25,030
	Stephen Gallacher	70-72-70-68	280	$117,318			Jason Dufner	70-74-74-71	289	$25,030
	David Howell	72-70-70-68	280	$117,318			Bill Haas	70-72-73-74	289	$25,030
18	George Coetzee	70-69-74-68	281	$105,073		54=	Matt Kuchar	73-71-74-72	290	$23,791
19=	Angel Cabrera	76-69-70-67	282	$93,968			Matt Jones	71-74-72-73	290	$23,791
	Keegan Bradley	73-71-69-69	282	$93,968			Kevin Na	76-70-70-74	290	$23,791
	Chris Kirk	71-74-68-69	282	$93,968			Kevin Streelman	72-74-69-75	290	$23,791
	Matteo Manassero	67-75-68-72	282	$93,968		58=	Jamie McLeary	73-73-75-70	291	$22,808
23=	Chris Wood	75-70-73-65	283	$78,876			Ryan Palmer	74-71-76-70	291	$22,808
	Phil Mickelson	74-70-71-68	283	$78,876			John Senden	71-74-75-71	291	$22,808
	Justin Rose	72-70-69-72	283	$78,876			Jason Day	73-73-74-71	291	$22,808
26=	Thomas Bjørn	70-71-76-67	284	$65,350			Chris Rodgers	73-71-73-74	291	$22,808
	Ben Martin	71-73-70-70	284	$65,350			Brandt Snedeker	74-72-71-74	291	$22,808
	Brian Harman	72-73-68-71	284	$65,350		64=	Billy Hurley III	73-72-76-71	292	$22,040
	Byeong-Hun An	72-71-69-72	284	$65,350			Thorbjørn Olesen	75-71-73-73	292	$22,040
	Jimmy Walker	69-71-71-73	284	$65,350			Luke Donald	73-73-71-75	292	$22,040
	Darren Clarke	72-72-67-73	284	$65,350		67=	Charley Hoffman	74-72-76-71	293	$21,613
32=	D.A. Points	75-69-72-69	285	$52,964			Brooks Koepka	68-77-74-74	293	$21,613
	Hunter Mahan	71-73-72-69	285	$52,964		69	Tiger Woods	69-77-73-75	294	$21,356
	David Hearn	70-73-71-71	285	$52,964		70	Martin Kaymer	73-72-72-79	296	$21,185
	Kristoffer Broberg	70-73-70-72	285	$52,964		71	Matt Every	75-71-73-78	297	$21,015
36=	Louis Oosthuizen	70-68-76-72	286	$46,271		72	Rhein Gibson	72-74-74-78	298	$20,844

Out Of The Money: **147**: Hiroshi Iwata, Shawn Stefani, Nick Watney, Graham DeLaet, Lee Westwood, Rafael Cabrera-Bello, Oliver Fisher, Dawie van der Walt, Kiradech Aphibarnrat, Ashley Chesters (a), Justin Leonard, K.J. Choi, Ian Poulter, Paul McKechnie, Oscar Floren, Yoshinobu Tsukada **148**: Brendon de Jonge, Cheng-Tsung Pan (a), Boo Weekley, Danny Willett, Miguel Ángel Jiménez, Bubba Watson, Billy Horschel, Ryo Ishikawa, John Daly, Ross Fisher, Paul Dunne (a), Cameron Tringale, Erik Compton, Hyung-Sung Kim, Fredrik Jacobson, Ben Curtis, Mikko Ilonen, Harris English, Brett Rumford, John Singleton, Hyung-Tae Kim **149**: Scott Stallings, Yusaku Miyazato, George McNeill, Rhys Enoch, Patrick Reed, Juvic Pagunsan **150**: Jonas Blixt, Gonzalo F'dez-Castaño, Tommy Fleetwood, Matthew Baldwin, Anirban Lahiri **151**: Victor Riu, Y.E. Yang, Ashun Wu, J.B. Holmes, Jamie Donaldson, Chesson Hadley, Justin Walters, Masanori Kobayashi, Bernd Wiesberger, Todd Hamilton **152**: Tyrrell Hatton, Pablo Larrazábal, Ernie Els, Richard Sterne, David Duval, Padraig Harrington **153**: Webb Simpson, Nick Faldo, Tomohiro Kondo **154**: Brendan Steele, Scott Jamieson, Paul Lawrie **155**: Roberto Castro, Russell Henley, Yeon-Jin Jeong, Bradley Neil (a), Chris Hanson **156**: Matthew Southgate, Chris Stroud, Peter Uihlein **157**: Dong-Kyu Jang, Joost Luiten, Mark Wiebe **166**: Sandy Lyle **170**: Bryden MacPherson **WD**: Michael Hoey (75)

FIRST ROUND		SECOND ROUND		THIRD ROUND	
Rory McIlroy	66 (-6)	**Rory McIlroy**	132 (-12)	**Rory McIlroy**	200 (-16)
Matteo Manassero	67 (-5)	Dustin Johnson	136 (-8)	Rickie Fowler	206 (-10)
Brooks Koepka	68 (-4)	Francesco Molinari	138 (-6)	Sergio García	207 (-9)
Edoardo Molinari	68 (-4)	Ryan Moore	138 (-6)	Dustin Johnson	207 (-9)
Francesco Molinari	68 (-4)	Rickie Fowler	138 (-6)	Victor Dubuisson	208 (-8)
Jim Furyk	68 (-4)	Sergio García	138 (-6)	Edoardo Molinari	209 (-7)
Sergio García	68 (-4)	Charl Schwartzel	138 (-6)	Matteo Manassero	210 (-6)
Adam Scott	68 (-4)	Louis Oosthuizen	138 (-6)	Adam Scott	210 (-6)
Shane Lowry	68 (-4)	George Coetzee	139 (-5)	Robert Karlsson	210 (-6)
9 Players	69 (-3)	Jim Furyk	139 (-5)	Jim Furyk	210 (-6)
		Marc Warren	139 (-5)	Charl Schwartzel	210 (-6)

OWR: 49 of top 50 entered - Rating: 902 - Points to 72nd - McIlroy: 100 points, to 2nd in OWR

PGA Championship

Valhalla Golf Club - Louisville, KY
Champion: Rory McIlroy

August 7 - August 10

7,458 yards   Par 71
Purse: $10 Million

"I'm not eating my words, but I'm certainly starting to chew on them right now."

So said fellow Northern Irishman Graeme McDowell, who one month earlier had suggested that despite Rory McIlroy's impressive victory at July's British Open, professional golf was not yet on the verge of seeing McIlroy dominate in a manner akin to Tiger Woods. But as the clock wound down on McIlroy's equally impressive triumph in the PGA Championship, McDowell - like the rest of the golfing world - was perhaps starting to see things in a different light. For this, to be sure, was a Major championship performance for the ages.

McIlroy, of course, was coming in hot, having backed his victory at Hoylake with a two-shot triumph at the WGC-Bridgestone Invitational in his next start, climbing back into the number one spot in the Official World Ranking in the process. Thus he arrived at Louisville's Valhalla Golf Club as the strongest Major championship favorite since Woods himself - and seemingly very much at home with the expectations.

McIlroy's performance in Thursday's opening round did little to suggest that the oddsmakers were wrong, for playing over a rain-softened Valhalla layout that would yield low scores all week, he posted a five-under-par 66 that left him one shot off the lead held by England's Lee Westwood and a pair of Americans, Kevin Chappell and Ryan Palmer. What made McIlroy's round notable, however, was that it might have been quite a bit lower, for after turning in three-under-par 32, he hooked his second at the par-5 10th out-of-bounds en route to a double-bogey, then followed that with a bogey at the 210-yard 11th. But where many a golfer might have lost their momentum entirely after falling back to even, McIlroy instead responded with four straight birdies at holes 12-15, then added one more at the par-5 closer to push himself resiliently back into the mix. Among the tri-leaders, Palmer would hang around all week to ultimately tie for fifth, Chappell struggled to a Friday 74 but bounced back to tie for 13th, and Westwood (who'd began his day with a double-bogey before adding nine subsequent birdies) never seriously contended thereafter, tying for 15th. McIlroy, meanwhile had some strong company on 66, including world number four Henrik Stenson, Jim Furyk, Italy's Edoardo Molinari and England's Chris Wood.

Friday saw McIlroy play in the morning and it was then that he began taking control of the tournament, piecing together an up-and-down 67 that included four birdies and an eagle (at his ninth hole, the par-5 18th) and finishing with a tournament-leading nine-under-par 133 total. His margin was only one, however, for hot on his heels were the ever-competitive Furyk (68) and three-time Major championship runner-up Jason Day, who posted the day's low round (65) by logging five birdies, plus an eagle at the 597-yard 7th. Two back were Palmer, Finland's Mikko Ilonen and Rickie Fowler, while three in arrears were Phil Mickelson (69-67) and Austria's Bernd Wiesberger, a two-time European Tour winner who posted a pair of solid 68s. Notable casualties of Friday evening's cut included reigning U.S. Open champion Martin Kaymer (144), 64-year-old Tom Watson (145), Keegan Bradley (146), Jordan Spieth (148) and four-time PGA winner Tiger Woods (148). Woods' story, of course, requires a moment's amplification, for he arrived having withdrawn from the final round of the WGC-Bridgestone while playing terrible golf, citing back spasms which were not immediately visible to many observers. But only three days later, he pronounced himself pain-free and fit at Valhalla before posting a disappointing 74 on Thursday, then staggering badly (including missing several short putts) for seven holes on Friday before suddenly coming up lame again. Undoubtedly wary of further criticism he soldiered on, eventually posting a second straight 74 and being largely forgotten as the weekend's drama unfolded.

Following more morning rain, Saturday would prove to be the lowest scoring round in PGA Championship history, ultimately producing a 54-leaderboard that was both deep and star-studded. McIlroy may not have loved his round of 67 but on a day when a number of stars might well have shot past him, he gamely rallied late in the back nine to birdie the 15th, 16th and 18th and maintain a one-shot lead. Now his closest pursuer was the upstart Wiesberger, who carded a flawless 65 that included birdies on the final three holes, and moved him into air far more rarified than anything he'd experienced on the European circuit. Two back was Fowler (playing with great confidence as he sailed around with a bogey-free 67) while three behind were Mickelson (67) and Day, who played uneven golf en route to a 69. And while McIlroy's form seemed to all but eliminate the remainder of the field, it was hard not to notice Stenson (67) in a group four back.

Sunday morning witnessed still more rain and with play delayed nearly 90 minutes, questions emerged as to whether the round could be completed before darkness. As things ultimately unfolded, players like Ernie Els (who birdied six of his first 11 holes), Jimmy Walker (who matched Els' closing 65) and Furyk (66) all made some early noise, but the real challengers proved to be Mickelson, Stenson and Fowler. Trying gamely to salvage an otherwise disappointing year, Mickelson charged to an outgoing 31 and by the 12th tee stood 15 under par. Stenson, for his part, turned in 30 and, with a birdie at the island green 13th, joined Mickelson at -15. Fowler, meanwhile, bogeyed the 2nd but bounced back with four birdies in five holes and, with one more at the par-5 10th, also stood on 15 under. McIlroy, meanwhile, had stumbled to an outgoing 36, leaving him, quite surprisingly, three off the pace. But at a moment when almost any sane golfing mind might well have concluded that his run of form was cooling, McIlroy instead mounted an epic charge, ripping a 281-yard 3 wood to seven feet en route to eagling the 10th, then adding a birdie at the 13th which, combined with each of his opponents carding one untimely bogey, saw him nose improbably back ahead. A wayward drive at the 17th threatened to pull him back, but a 9 iron from a fairway bunker dropped 11 feet from the hole, with the ensuing birdie putt extending the lead to two. Yet there was still some drama left.

With darkness rapidly setting in, Mickelson and Fowler followed standard Tour etiquette in allowing McIlroy and Wiesberger to drive off quickly behind them at the last, guaranteeing all four players the option to finish even if the horn sounded. McIlroy's tee ball narrowly missed right-side water before things became confusing when PGA of America officials then instructed Mickelson and Fowler to stand aside while the final pair hit their second shots - an odd suggestion in any circumstance. In the end, Mickelson narrowly missed holing a long pitch to tie, Fowler missed his long eagle putt as well, and when McIlroy took two putts from 33 feet for his five, the championship was his.

Fowler, for his part, became the only player in history to finish among the top five in all four of a season's Major championships without winning one. McIlroy, meanwhile, deeply solidified his hold on world number one status, and also became only the fourth player in the last century (joining Jones, Nicklaus and Woods) to win four Majors by age 25. Most importantly, however, he seemed now to have moved across a grand threshold: from competing against his everyday opponents to competing against history.

Weather

Thursday: Mostly cloudy early, turning to partly sunny in the afternoon. High of 83. Winds E 6-12 mph.
Friday: Mostly cloudy with intermittent rain throughout the morning. High of 80. Winds E 6-12 mph. Play was suspended due to heavy rain at 7:50 a.m. and resumed at 8:35 a.m.
Saturday: Mostly cloudy with scattered showers throughout the day. High of 82. Winds ESE 6-12 mph.
Sunday: Mostly cloudy with scattered showers throughout the day. High of 82. Winds E 6-12 mph. Play was suspended due to heavy rain at 12:53 p.m. and resumed at 2:44 p.m.

PGA Championship August 7 - August 10

1	2	3	4	5	6	7	8	9	10	11	12	13	14	15	16	17	18
446	500	205	372	463	495	597	174	415	590	210	467	350	217	435	508	472	542
4	4	3	4	4	4	5	3	4	5	3	4	4	3	4	4	4	5
4.02	4.36	3.02	3.73	4.06	4.35	4.77	2.96	3.93	4.82	3.07	4.24	3.95	3.20	4.23	4.31	4.06	4.49

1	Rory McIlroy	66-67-67-68	268	$1.8 mil		Jonas Blixt	71-70-68-72	281	$42,520
2	Phil Mickelson	69-67-67-66	269	$1.08 mil		Sergio García	70-72-66-73	281	$42,520
3=	Henrik Stenson	66-71-67-66	270	$580,000	40=	Koumei Oda	74-68-71-69	282	$32,000
	Rickie Fowler	69-66-67-68	270	$580,000		Jason Bohn	71-71-71-69	282	$32,000
5=	Jim Furyk	66-68-72-66	272	$367,500		Brendon de Jonge	70-70-72-70	282	$32,000
	Ryan Palmer	65-70-69-68	272	$367,500		Luke Donald	70-72-68-72	282	$32,000
7=	Ernie Els	70-70-68-65	273	$263,000		Brian Harman	71-69-69-73	282	$32,000
	Jimmy Walker	69-71-68-65	273	$263,000		Ryan Moore	73-68-67-74	282	$32,000
	Victor Dubuisson	69-68-70-66	273	$263,000	46=	Shane Lowry	68-74-74-67	283	$24,792
	Hunter Mahan	70-71-65-67	273	$263,000		Robert Karlsson	71-69-74-69	283	$24,792
	Steve Stricker	69-68-68-68	273	$263,000		Marc Leishman	71-71-72-69	283	$24,792
	Mikko Ilonen	67-68-69-69	273	$263,000		Graeme McDowell	73-70-71-69	283	$24,792
13=	Brandt Snedeker	73-68-66-67	274	$191,000		Pat Perez	71-71-71-70	283	$24,792
	Kevin Chappell	65-74-67-68	274	$191,000		Fabrizio Zanotti	70-71-71-71	283	$24,792
15=	Charl Schwartzel	72-68-69-66	275	$127,889		Matt Jones	68-71-72-72	283	$24,792
	Brooks Koepka	71-71-66-67	275	$127,889		Scott Brown	71-70-70-72	283	$24,792
	Marc Warren	71-71-66-67	275	$127,889		Geoff Ogilvy	69-71-71-72	283	$24,792
	Lee Westwood	65-72-69-69	275	$127,889		Branden Grace	73-70-68-72	283	$24,792
	Adam Scott	71-69-66-69	275	$127,889		Edoardo Molinari	66-73-71-73	283	$24,792
	Graham DeLaet	69-68-68-70	275	$127,889		Chris Wood	66-73-70-74	283	$24,792
	Jason Day	69-65-69-72	275	$127,889	58=	Brendan Steele	71-70-73-70	284	$20,417
	Louis Oosthuizen	70-67-67-71	275	$127,889		Gon. F'dez-Castaño	71-70-72-71	284	$20,417
	Bernd Wiesberger	68-68-65-74	275	$127,889		Francesco Molinari	71-71-71-71	284	$20,417
24=	Justin Rose	70-72-67-67	276	$84,000		Ian Poulter	68-73-71-72	284	$20,417
	Jamie Donaldson	69-70-66-71	276	$84,000		Patrick Reed	70-71-70-73	284	$20,417
26	Joost Luiten	68-69-69-71	277	$78,000		Billy Horschel	71-68-69-76	284	$20,417
27=	Jerry Kelly	67-74-70-67	278	$71,000	64=	Chris Stroud	70-73-73-71	287	$18,700
	Kenny Perry	72-69-69-68	278	$71,000		Bubba Watson	70-72-73-72	287	$18,700
	Bill Haas	71-68-68-71	278	$71,000		Kevin Stadler	71-70-72-74	287	$18,700
30=	Thorbjørn Olesen	71-71-70-67	279	$62,000		J.B. Holmes	68-72-69-78	287	$18,700
	Alexander Levy	69-71-68-71	279	$62,000	68	Shawn Stefani	68-75-72-73	288	$18,200
	Danny Willett	68-73-66-72	279	$62,000	69=	Fredrik Jacobson	72-69-73-75	289	$17,900
33=	Daniel Summerhays	70-72-68-70	280	$53,000		Colin Montgomerie	70-72-72-75	289	$17,900
	Nick Watney	69-69-70-72	280	$53,000		Zach Johnson	70-72-70-77	289	$17,900
35=	Hideki Matsuyama	71-72-70-68	281	$42,520	72	Brendon Todd	70-73-75-75	293	$17,700
	Vijay Singh	71-68-73-69	281	$42,520	73	Rafael Cabrera-Bello	69-71-74-80	294	$17,600
	Richard Sterne	70-69-72-70	281	$42,520					

Out Of The Money: **144**: Charley Hoffman, Erik Compton, Gary Woodland, Scott Piercy, Martin Kaymer, Tommy Fleetwood, Tim Clark, Padraig Harrington, Ryan Helminen, Russell Henley **145**: Anirban Lahiri, Tom Watson, Davis Love III, Seung-Yul Noh, Johan Kok, Ben Martin, Russell Knox, Brian Stuard, Matt Every, Kevin Streelman **146**: Ryo Ishikawa, Rory Sabbatini, Stuart Deane, David Hearn, Keegan Bradley, Y.E. Yang, Chris Kirk, Hideto Tanihara, Paul Casey, Kevin Na, Steven Bowditch, Roberto Castro, Jamie Broce, Ross Fisher, Harris English **147**: Eric Williamson, Webb Simpson, Chesson Hadley, Charles Howell III, George Coetzee, Stewart Cink, Stephen Gallacher **148**: Darren Clarke, Pablo Larrazábal, Jordan Spieth, John Daly, Tiger Woods, Hyung-Sung Kim, George McNeill **149**: Scott Stallings, John Senden, Rod Perry, Miguel Ángel Jiménez **150**: Bob Sowards, Will MacKenzie, Steve Schneiter, Thongchai Jaidee, Thomas Bjørn **151**: Michael Block, Shaun Micheel, K.J. Choi, John Huh, Jason Kokrak **152**: Brian Norman **153**: Rich Beem, Rob Corcoran **157**: Matteo Manassero, Jim McGovern, Mark Brooks, David McNabb **158**: Dave Tentis, David Hronek, Jerry Smith **161**: Frank Esposito, Aaron Krueger **163**: Dustin Volk **168**: Matt Pesta **WD**: Kiradech Aphibarnrat (72), Ben Crane (74), Boo Weekley (80), Angel Cabrera (82), Jason Dufner **DQ**: Cameron Tringale (280)

FIRST ROUND		SECOND ROUND		THIRD ROUND	
Lee Westwood	65 (-6)	**Rory McIlroy**	133 (-9)	**Rory McIlroy**	200 (-13)
Kevin Chappell	65 (-6)	Jason Day	134 (-8)	Bernd Wiesberger	201 (-12)
Ryan Palmer	65 (-6)	Jim Furyk	134 (-8)	Rickie Fowler	202 (-11)
Jim Furyk	66 (-5)	Ryan Palmer	135 (-7)	Phil Mickelson	203 (-10)
Edoardo Molinari	66 (-5)	Rickie Fowler	135 (-7)	Jason Day	203 (-10)
Henrik Stenson	66 (-5)	Mikko Ilonen	135 (-7)	Louis Oosthuizen	204 (-9)
Rory McIlroy	66 (-5)	Phil Mickelson	136 (-6)	Henrik Stenson	204 (-9)
Chris Wood	66 (-5)	Bernd Wiesberger	136 (-6)	Mikko Ilonen	204 (-9)
Mikko Ilonen	67 (-4)	Graham DeLaet	137 (-5)	Ryan Palmer	204 (-9)
Jerry Kelly	67 (-4)	Steve Stricker	137 (-5)	Jamie Donaldson	205 (-8)
		Henrik Stenson	137 (-5)	Graham DeLaet	205 (-8)
		Joost Luiten	137 (-5)	Steve Stricker	205 (-8)
		Victor Dubuisson	137 (-5)		
		Lee Westwood	137 (-5)		
		Louis Oosthuizen	137 (-5)		

OWR: 47 of top 50 entered - Rating: 890 - Points to 74th - McIlroy: 100 points, to remain 1st in OWR

2014 ROUNDS OF THE YEAR

The criteria for selecting the 20 most significant rounds of 2014 are built around simply that: their significance. And while there is a bit of wiggle room in defining the word (e.g., we assume a positive connotation and will not include disastrous rounds - however "significant" they may have been), what is generally being measured here is a blend of the player's score with the magnitude of the occasion, the caliber of the golf course, and, of course, potential long-term historical implications. As regards score, the raw number is obviously of greatest significance, but also of importance can be the margin by which a given round beat the field. To wit: A round of 62 may not have been all that special if three other players shot 63, whereas someone shooting 66 and beating the field by, say, four shots, would be infinitely more newsworthy. As for the magnitude of the occasion, the preponderance of Major championship rounds near the top of the list should speak eloquently as to where our priorities - and, historically, those of the game - must lie.

1) Rory McIlroy — 66 — The Open Championship - 2nd Rd — Jul 18, 2014
Royal Liverpool GC — 7,312 yds Par 72 — 2:27 p.m. - 1st tee

McIlroy had taken the Thursday lead at Hoylake with an opening 66, but having recently been plagued by a series of Friday disasters, this was make-or-break day. A bogey at the 1st augured poorly, but after three steady pars, the 25-year-old reeled off four birdies over six holes, then closed with three more over his final four, destroying the Friday hex and grabbing a four-shot halfway lead en route to victory.

	1	2	3	4	5	6	7	8	9	10	11	12	13	14	15	16	17	18
Par	4	4	4	4	5	3	4	4	3	5	4	4	3	4	3	5	4	5
Yards	458	454	426	372	528	201	480	431	197	532	391	447	194	454	161	577	458	551
Score	5	4	4	4	4	2	4	3	3	4	4	4	3	4	2	5	3	4

2) Rory McIlroy — 68 — The PGA Championship - 4th Rd — Aug 10, 2014
Valhalla CC — 7,458 yds Par 71 — 2:55 p.m. - 1st tee

A round which may someday be looked upon as the most important of McIlroy's career. Gunning for his fourth career Major championship, and having led after the second and third rounds, he turned in one-over-par 36 to fall three behind Mickelson, Fowler and Stenson. But facing agonizing defeat, he promptly eagled the 10th and birdied the 13th before ultimately clinching the title with a birdie at the par-4 17th.

	1	2	3	4	5	6	7	8	9	10	11	12	13	14	15	16	17	18
Par	4	4	3	4	4	4	5	3	4	5	3	4	4	3	4	4	4	5
Yards	446	500	205	372	463	495	597	174	415	590	210	467	350	217	435	508	472	542
Score	4	4	2	4	4	5	4	3	4	3	3	4	3	3	4	4	3	5

3) Martin Kaymer — 65 — The U.S. Open - 1st Rd — Jun 12, 2014
Pinehurst Resort & CC (No.2) — 7,214 yds Par 70 — 1:47 p.m. - 1st tee

One could have chosen Kaymer's first or second round at Pinehurst, for they were both 65s which combined to spring him to a runaway six-shot lead and, eventually, a stunning eight-shot victory. In point of fact, the second round was bogey-free and thus more aesthetically pure - but Thursday afternoon's 65 produced a rare three-shot first round lead in a Major and set the tone for the entire championship.

	1	2	3	4	5	6	7	8	9	10	11	12	13	14	15	16	17	18
Par	4	4	4	4	5	3	4	4	3	5	4	4	4	4	3	4	3	4
Yards	402	507	387	529	576	219	424	486	191	617	483	484	382	473	202	528	205	451
Score	3	4	4	4	4	3	5	4	3	4	4	4	4	3	3	3	2	4

4) Bubba Watson — 68 — The Masters - 2nd Rd — Apr 11, 2014
Augusta National GC — 7,435 yds Par 72 — 1:15 p.m. - 1st tee

A four-under-par 68 is hardly lights-out golf at most venues, and Bubba Watson's 68 during the second round of The Masters was matched by three players that day. But for Watson, the round - which was driven by a run of five straight birdies at holes 12-16 - was the key to winning his second Green Jacket in three years, moving him from one stroke behind to three ahead - a lead he would not relinquish.

	1	2	3	4	5	6	7	8	9	10	11	12	13	14	15	16	17	18
Par	4	5	4	3	4	3	4	5	4	4	4	3	5	4	5	3	4	4
Yards	445	575	350	240	455	180	450	570	460	495	505	155	510	440	530	170	440	465
Score	4	5	4	3	4	3	3	5	4	4	4	2	4	3	4	2	4	5

5) Kevin Streelman — 64 — Travelers Championship - 4th Rd — Jun 22, 2014
TPC River Highlands — 6,841 yds Par 72 — 1:30 p.m. - 1st tee

Kevin Streelman began the final round of the Travelers Championship four shots behind leader Ryan Moore, and with bogeys at the 2nd and 7th holes, seemed to disappear altogether. But after birdieing the 9th, he mounted a dazzling charge home which included birdies at his last seven holes to take the title - and break Mike Souchak's 58-year-old record for the most consecutive closing birdies by a tournament winner.

	1	2	3	4	5	6	7	8	9	10	11	12	13	14	15	16	17	18
Par	4	4	4	4	3	5	4	3	4	4	3	4	5	4	4	3	4	4
Yards	434	341	431	481	223	574	443	202	406	462	158	411	523	421	296	171	420	444
Score	4	5	4	4	3	5	5	3	3	4	3	3	4	3	3	2	3	3

6) Rory McIlroy — 66 — BMW PGA Championship - 4th Rd — May 25, 2014
Wentworth C — 7,302 yds Par 72 — 12:50 p.m. - 1st tee

In the week which saw him end his relationship with tennis star Caroline Wozniacki, Rory McIlroy began his ascent back to world number one status by closing with a 66 to win the flagship BMW PGA Championship. Beginning the day seven shots behind 54-hole leader Thomas Bjørn, McIlroy got help from Bjørn (who shot 75) but clinched the title with a back nine 32, including closing birdies at the 17th and 18th.

	1	2	3	4	5	6	7	8	9	10	11	12	13	14	15	16	17	18
Par	4	3	4	5	3	4	4	4	4	3	4	5	4	3	4	4	5	5
Yards	473	154	465	552	203	418	396	391	449	184	416	521	470	179	489	383	610	539
Score	4	3	4	3	3	3	4	2	2	4	4	3	3	4	4	4	4	4

7) Martin Kaymer — 63 — Players Championship - 1st Rd — May 8, 2014
TPC Sawgrass — 7,215 yds Par 72 — 12:57 p.m. - 10th tee

The round that jumpstarted the revival of Kaymer's career. Arriving at the Players in quietly strong form, he began day one on the 10th hole and turned in an unremarkable two-under-par 34. But on his second nine, the 29-year-old caught fire, carding seven birdies (including on his last four holes) to come home in 29, tying the TPC Sawgrass course record previously shared by Couples, Norman & Roberto Castro.

	1	2	3	4	5	6	7	8	9	10	11	12	13	14	15	16	17	18
Par	4	5	3	4	4	4	4	3	5	4	5	4	3	4	4	5	3	4
Yards	423	532	177	384	471	393	442	237	583	424	558	358	181	481	449	523	137	462
Score	3	4	3	3	4	3	3	2	4	4	4	4	3	4	3	5	3	4

8) Sergio García — 61 — WGC-Bridgestone Inv - 2nd Rd — Aug 1, 2014
Firestone CC — 7,400 yds Par 70 — 2:20 p.m. - 1st tee

Sergio García would finish second (two behind a streaking Rory McIlroy) at the WGC-Bridgestone Invitational, but not before matching Firestone's course record with a second round 61. Remarkably, García turned at only one under par before picking up a birdie at the 10th - and then birdieing the final seven holes! In the process, he became only the ninth man in PGA Tour history to shoot 27 on a single nine.

	1	2	3	4	5	6	7	8	9	10	11	12	13	14	15	16	17	18
Par	4	5	4	4	3	4	3	4	4	4	4	3	4	4	3	5	4	4
Yards	399	526	442	471	200	469	219	482	494	410	418	180	471	467	221	667	400	464
Score	4	4	4	4	3	4	3	4	4	3	4	2	3	3	2	4	3	3

9) Jordan Spieth — 63 — Australian Open - 4th Rd — Nov 30, 2014
The Australian GC — 7,245 yds Par 71 — 12:00 p.m. - 1st tee

Ending an otherwise winless 2014 on a high note, Jordan Spieth emerged from the pack atop a crowded leaderboard with a dazzling Sunday 63 to win the Australian Open by six shots. His near-flawless round (which beat the field by three, and was the week's best by two) came over a firm, breezy and demanding Australian Golf Club layout and was, by Spieth's own description, the best of his young career.

	1	2	3	4	5	6	7	8	9	10	11	12	13	14	15	16	17	18
Par	4	3	4	3	5	4	4	4	4	4	3	4	4	5	3	4	4	5
Yards	470	217	372	211	605	413	429	481	464	439	188	416	396	501	206	470	436	531
Score	4	3	3	3	4	3	3	4	4	4	3	4	4	4	2	4	3	4

10) Felipe Aguilar — 62 — Champ at Laguna National - 4th Rd — May 4, 2014
Laguna National G&CC — 7,204 yds Par 72 — 9:20 a.m. - 1st tee

After starting the final round four shots off the lead, Chile's Felipe Aguilar won the E Tour's inaugural Championship at Laguna National with a stunning final round 62, that including a dazzling 2-2 finish when he holed a 142-yard pitching wedge at the last. Aguilar turned in a modest two-under-par 34 before reeling off his incoming 28. He also managed the comparatively rare feat of birdieing all four par 3s.

	1	2	3	4	5	6	7	8	9	10	11	12	13	14	15	16	17	18
Par	4	5	4	4	3	4	5	3	4	4	5	3	4	4	5	4	3	4
Yards	383	567	363	392	193	436	616	181	452	437	547	210	383	451	563	445	202	386
Score	4	5	4	4	2	4	5	2	4	3	4	2	3	4	4	4	2	2

11) Dustin Johnson — 63 — WGC-HSBC Champions - 2nd Rd — Nov 1, 2013
Sheshan International GC — 7,266 yds Par 72 — 10:35 a.m. - 1st tee

Dustin Johnson extended to seven the number of consecutive seasons in which he'd won on the PGA Tour directly out of college by claiming the WGC-HSBC Champions, an event which officially counted in 2014 due to the new wraparound schedule. Johnson took control on Friday via this near-flawless 63, a round which began with six birdies in seven holes - and which beat a powerhouse world-class field by four shots.

	1	2	3	4	5	6	7	8	9	10	11	12	13	14	15	16	17	18
Par	4	5	4	3	4	3	4	5	4	4	4	3	4	5	4	4	3	5
Yards	459	550	362	200	456	200	346	603	486	401	456	217	411	594	487	288	212	538
Score	3	4	4	2	3	2	3	5	4	4	3	3	4	4	3	3	3	4

12) Paul Casey — 63 — Byron Nelson Championship - 2nd Rd — May 16, 2014
TPC Four Seasons Resort — 7,166 yds Par 70 — 8:20 a.m. - 1st tee

Several years removed (partially by injury) from the world's elite, Paul Casey at least caught fire for a day - or, more accurately, for nine holes. For having played the front nine in one-over-par 36, he proceeded to reel off six birdies and an eagle over the TPC Four Seasons Resort inward half to become only the eighth player to card a nine-hole score of 27 in PGA Tour history. He would tie for 15th overall.

	1	2	3	4	5	6	7	8	9	10	11	12	13	14	15	16	17	18
Par	4	3	4	4	3	4	5	4	4	4	4	4	5	4	4	5	3	4
Yards	458	221	528	431	174	448	542	461	427	435	323	455	180	406	504	546	198	429
Score	4	3	5	4	4	4	3	4	3	3	3	4	2	3	3	3	3	3

13) Adam Scott — 62 — Arnold Palmer Invitational - 1st Rd — Mar 20, 2014
Bay Hill Club & Lodge — 7,419 yds Par 72 — 8:23 a.m. - 1st tee

Starting on the 10th hole, Scott got his week off to a blazing start by carding a 10-under-par 62 - good enough to beat the field by three. He stood six under par through his first seven holes before recording his lone bogey at the tough 18th, then logged three more birdies and his second eagle of the day on the front side. Unfortunately a Sunday 76 would ultimately see him home to a third-place finish.

	1	2	3	4	5	6	7	8	9	10	11	12	13	14	15	16	17	18
Par	4	3	4	5	4	5	3	4	4	4	4	5	4	3	4	5	3	4
Yards	461	231	434	561	390	555	199	460	474	400	438	574	370	215	457	511	221	458
Score*	4	3	3	3	4	4	2	4	4	3	4	4	2	3	3	3	5

14) Rory McIlroy — 63 — Memorial Tournament - 1st Rd — May 29, 2014
Muirfield Village GC — 7,392 yds Par 72 — 1:16 p.m. - 1st tee

Rory McIlroy wasted little time getting rolling at the Memorial Tournament, carding a 63 that was even more remarkable due to its including a sloppy double-bogey at the short par-4 14th. McIlroy was eight under par at the time but rather than being derailed, he promptly eagled the 15th and birdied the 16th to recover. Unfortunately, a Friday 78 did derail him, and he would ultimately end up tying for 15th.

	1	2	3	4	5	6	7	8	9	10	11	12	13	14	15	16	17	18
Par	4	4	4	3	5	4	5	3	4	4	5	3	4	4	5	3	4	4
Yards	470	455	401	200	527	447	563	185	412	471	567	184	455	363	529	201	478	484
Score	4	3	4	2	5	4	3	3	3	3	3	3	6	3	2	4	4

15) Rashid Khan — 61 — SAIL-SBI Open - 2nd Rd — Feb 28, 2014
Delhi GC — 6,963 yds Par 72 — 7:40 a.m. - 1st tee

Twenty-three-year-old Rashid Kahn's 11-under-par 61 jumpstarted his maiden victory on the Asian Tour (he eventually defeated Siddikur Rahman in sudden death) and came while playing in the fourth group of the morning over his home course at the Delhi Golf Club. Most remarkably, it beat the entire field by a resounding five shots - and that is one very rare accomplishment indeed.

	1	2	3	4	5	6	7	8	9	10	11	12	13	14	15	16	17	18
Par	5	4	4	4	3	4	3	5	4	4	4	3	4	5	4	4	3	5
Yards	518	377	445	418	182	401	230	518	445	474	437	208	386	516	353	412	171	545
Score	4	3	4	4	3	4	2	4	4	4	3	3	3	3	3	3	3	4

16) Tom Watson — 68 — The Open Championship - 4th Rd — Jul 18, 2014
Royal Liverpool GC — 7,312 yds Par 72 — 8:55 a.m. - 1st tee

Sixty-four-year-old Tom Watson finished T51 at Hoylake, but the five-time Open champion (and 2014 Ryder Cup captain) greatly impressed with his final round 68. Watson opened with a bogey but played extremely steady golf thereafter, and while no clear records were available for such things, this must surely rate among the finest Major championship scores ever posted by a player of anywhere near this age.

	1	2	3	4	5	6	7	8	9	10	11	12	13	14	15	16	17	18
Par	4	4	4	4	5	3	4	4	3	5	4	4	3	4	3	5	4	5
Yards	458	454	426	372	528	201	480	431	197	532	391	447	194	454	161	577	458	551
Score	5	3	4	4	4	3	3	4	3	5	4	4	3	4	3	4	4	4

17) Michio Matsumura — 60 — The Crowns - 1st Rd — May 1, 2014
Nagoya GC — 6,545 yds Par 70 — 11:20 a.m. - 1st tee

While observing that Michio Matsumura's 10-under-par 60 was the lowest round shot on a major tour in 2014, it must be noted that the Nagoya GC's 6,545-yard Wago Course was also the site of Ryo Ishikawa's final round 58 in 2010 - so Pine Valley this isn't. Impressively, Matsumura beat the field by a robust four shots this day. Less impressively, he then added rounds of 71-74-76, to finish in a tie for 19th.

	1	2	3	4	5	6	7	8	9	10	11	12	13	14	15	16	17	18
Par	4	5	4	3	4	4	3	4	4	4	4	3	4	5	4	4	3	4
Yards	370	523	449	170	426	370	181	398	374	366	337	360	200	444	591	376	175	435
Score	3	5	3	2	3	4	3	4	3	3	3	4	2	4	4	3	3	4

18) Kris Blanks	62	Chitimacha Louisiana Open - 4th Rd	Mar 30, 2014
Le Triomphe CC		7,006 yds Par 71	9:47 a.m. - 1st tee

PGA Tour veteran Kris Blanks entered the final round of the Web.com Tour's Chitimacha Louisiana Open seven shots out of the lead, then proceeded to fire a bogey-free, nine-under-par 62 to tie Brett Stegmaier atop the leaderboard at 270. Having already beaten the Sunday field by a remarkable five shots, Blanks then wasted no time in birdieing the first playoff to clinch his first Web.com victory.

	1	2	3	4	5	6	7	8	9	10	11	12	13	14	15	16	17	18
Par	5	4	3	4	5	3	5	3	5	4	3	5	4	4	4	3	4	4
Yards	555	366	225	392	560	190	544	172	485	400	181	559	446	485	445	182	378	441
Score	4	3	3	4	5	2	4	2	4	4	3	4	3	4	4	2	3	4

19) Bubba Watson	64	Northern Trust Open - 4th Rd	Feb 16, 2014
Riviera CC		7,349 yds Par 71	10:04 a.m. - 1st tee

Bubba Watson played flawless weekend golf in breaking a two-year victory drought at the Northern Trust Open - but then he sort of had to after standing nine shots off the lead through 36 holes. Watson shot a bogey-free Saturday 64 at Riviera to pull within four, then made six birdies in his first 11 holes on Sunday to charge into the lead, eventually clinching a two-shot victory with one final birdie at the famed 18th.

	1	2	3	4	5	6	7	8	9	10	11	12	13	14	15	16	17	18
Par	5	4	4	3	4	3	4	4	4	4	5	4	4	3	4	3	5	4
Yards	503	471	434	236	434	199	408	460	458	315	583	479	459	192	487	166	590	475
Score	4	4	3	2	4	2	4	3	4	4	4	4	4	3	4	3	5	3

20) John Hahn	58	European Tour Q School - 4th Rd	Nov 18, 2014
PGA Catalunya Resort		6,610 yds Par 70	10:20 a.m. - 10th tee

With a 61 at the 2014 Africa Open already under his belt, American John Hahn had already proven he could go low - but 58? Yes, preferred lies (but not lift, clean and place) were allowed due to wet conditions, Hahn was playing the much easier of the two qualifier courses, he was "only" 12 under par (not 14) and, remarkably, he followed this with a fifth round 78 and ultimately failed to qualify. But seriously, a 58?

	1	2	3	4	5	6	7	8	9	10	11	12	13	14	15	16	17	18
Par	4	3	4	4	4	4	5	3	4	5	3	4	4	3	4	3	4	5
Yards	378	201	367	460	507	344	564	182	360	491	192	396	406	203	481	143	412	523
Score	3	2	4	4	3	4	4	3	3	4	2	3	3	2	4	3	3	4

25 ADDITIONAL ROUNDS OF DISTINCTION

PLAYER	EVENT (RD)	SCORE	COMMENT
Christiaan Basson	Lombard Insurance Classic (3rd)	62	Shot 10 under par to come from 2 shots behind and win by 5
Thomas Bjørn	BMW PGA Championship (1st)	62	Set a new Wentworth course record and beat the field by 2
Paul Casey	KLM Open (3rd)	62	8-under-par round jumpstarted his run to victory
Greg Chalmers	Australian PGA Championship (4th)	64	Beat field by 4; set up epic 7-hole playoff win over Adam Scott
Nicolas Colsaerts	Portugal Masters (1st)	60	Narrowly missed the first 59 in E Tour history; beat the field by 3
Jon Curran	Brasil Champions (1st)	61	10-under-par round drove him to his first Web.com Tour victory
Tommy Fleetwood	Dunhill Links Championship (3rd)	62	Record-tying 10 under par at St Andrews in ideal conditions
Stephen Gallacher	Dubai Desert Classic (3rd)	63	The keystone round as Gallacher became first to repeat in Dubai
Rhein Gibson	Indonesia PGA Championship (4th)	62	Shot 10 under par to beat a relatively light field by 3
Branden Grace	Alfred Dunhill Championship (1st)	62	Shot 10 under par to beat a middling field by 3
John Hahn	Africa Open (2nd)	61	Shot 10 under par over the 6,616-yard East London GC layout
Miguel Ángel Jiménez	The Masters (3rd)	66	It's not often that a 50-year-old cards the week's lowest round
Martin Kaymer	U.S. Open (1st)	65	Listed here only because his round 2 was even more impressive
Brooks Koepka	Turkish Airlines Open (4th)	65	Shot 7 under par en route to claiming his first E Tour win
Antonio Lascuña	Selangor Masters (4th)	64	Beat the Sunday field by 4 before losing in a playoff
Anirban Lahiri	Macau Open (1st)	61	Jumpstarted a victory.....but Scott Hend shot 62 the same day
Rory McIlroy	Honda Classic (1st)	63	He would lead for three days before losing in a four-man playoff
George McNeill	Greenbrier Classic (4th)	61	To finish 2nd as his sister was tragically dying of cancer
Phil Mickelson	Abu Dhabi HSBC Championship (3rd)	63	Beat field by 3; arguably the high point of a disappointing year
Ryuichi Oda	Mynavi ABC Cup (4th)	62	9-under-par round separated him from the field for a 5-shot win
Louis Oosthuizen	Dunhill Links Championship (3rd)	62	Record-tying 10 under par at St Andrews (same day as Fleetwood)
Hennie Otto	Open d'Italia (2nd)	62	Otto wins in his second start after back surgery, led by this 62
Ryan Ruffels	BetEasy Australian Masters (2nd)	68	16-year-old Ruffels matches partner Adam Scott shot-for-shot
John Senden	Valspar Championship (3rd)	64	7-under-par beat field by 3, keyed his second PGA Tour victory
Robert Streb	McGladrey Classic (4th)	63	7-under-par round lifted him from 5 shots behind to his first win

2013-14 Week-By-Week OWR Event Ratings

	PGA Tour	European Tour	Japan Tour	Asian Tour	Sunshine Tour	Austral. Tour	OneAsia Tour	Web.com Tour
Week 1 1/5	T of C 259							
Week 2 1/12	Sony Open 232	Volvo 174						
Week 3 1/19	Humana 212	Abu Dhabi 291		King's Cup 11				
Week 4 1/26	Farmers Ins. 371	Qatar 242						
Week 5 2/2	Phoenix 367	Dubai 307						
Week 6 2/9	AT&T Pro-Am 246	Joburg Open 70			< E Tour	Vic PGA 0		
Week 7 2/16	N. Trust 433	Africa Open 25			< E Tour	QLD PGA 2		Colombia 2
Week 8 2/23	WGC-Match 689				Dimension 14	Vic Open 2		
Week 9 3/2	Honda 494	Tshwane 65		SAIL-SBI 7	< E Tour	NZ Open 2		
Week 10 3/9	WGC CA 770	< Puerto Rico 32						Chile 3
Week 11 3/16	Valspar 305	Hassan II 57		Solaire 7				Brasil 5
Week 12 3/23	Bay Hill 377				Investec 17			Panama 0
Week 13 3/30	Texas 211		Indonesia 23				< J Tour	Louisiana 2
Week 14 4/6	Houston 461	NH Coll 22			Telkom PGA 16			
Week 15 4/13	Masters 766				Zimbabwe 2			El Bosque 2
Week 16 4/20	Heritage 332	Malaysia 154	Token Home. 23					
Week 17 4/27	New Orleans 190	China Open 158	Tsuruya 30	Ind. Masters 65				WNB Classic 4
Week 18 5/4	Wells Fargo 341	The Champ 77	Crowns 28					S. Georgia 5
Week 19 5/11	Players 771	Madeira 0			Swazi Open 02		Maekyung 12	
Week 20 5/18	Byron Nelson 250	Open España 148		Philippines 11	Zambia 2		SK Telecom 14	BMW Pro-Am 4
Week 21 5/25	Colonial 396	BMW PGA 361	Kansai Open 19		Lombard 5			Rex Hospital 4
Week 22 6/1	Memorial 541	Nordea 183	Mizuno 26					
Week 23 6/8	FedEx 240	Lyoness 35	Japan PGA 32	Queens Cup 7	Zambia Sug 4			Cleveland 2
Week 24 6/15	US Open 789							
Week 25 6/22	Travelers 314	Irish Open 115	Tour Champ 32					Air Cap 5
Week 26 6/29	Quicken 305	BMW Int'l 238			V-Euphoria 5			Utd Leasing 6

2013-14 Week-By-Week OWR Event Ratings (Cont'd)

	PGA Tour		European Tour	Japan Tour	Asian Tour	Sunshine Tour	Austral. Tour	OneAsia Tour	Web.com Tour
Week 27 7/6	Greenbrier 234		French 188	SegaSammy 54		Sun City 4			Nova Scotia 0
Week 28 7/13	John Deere 166		Scottish 366						Utah Champ 4
Week 29 7/20	British Open 902								Boise 4
Week 30 7/27	Canadian 186		Russian 3						Midwest 4
Week 31 8/3	WGC-Bridge 804	<RenoTahoe 33		Fukushima 18		V-St Fran 2			Stonebrae 2
Week 32 8/10	PGA Champ 890								Price Cutter 5
Week 33 8/17	Wyndham 172		Denmark 52				Fiji Int'l 9		Knoxville 4
Week 34 8/24	Barclays 735		Czech Mas 62						Portland 7
Week 35 8/31	Deutsche 630		Italian 87	KBC Augusta 21		Wild Waves 2	QLD Open 0		Hotel Fit. 21
Week 36 9/7	BMW Champ 642		Euro Masters 142	Fujisankei 23	< E Tour	V-Port Ed 2			Chiquita 16
Week 37 9/14	Tour Champ 439		Dutch 123		Yeangder 5		South Pacific 0		Nationwide 18
Week 38 9/21			Wales Open 144	ANA Open 30	Selangor 5				Tour Champ 14
Week 39 9/28				Diamond 37	< J Tour				
Week 40 10/5			Dunhill Links 252	Tokai Classic 23	Taiwan Mas 5	V-Parys 0			
Week 41 10/12	Frys.com 191		Portugal Mas 107	Toshin 23		Boardwalk 0		China Mas 0	
Week 42 10/19	Shriners 195	Hong Kong> 44	Match Play 131	Japan Open 95	< E Tour	BMG Classic 4	WA Open 0		
Week 43 10/26	McGladrey 162		Perth Int'l 81	Bridgestone 39	Macau 54		< E Tour	Korean Open 26	
Week 44 11/2	CIMB 228		BMW Mas 278	Mynavi ABC 35	< PGA Tour	V-Final 0	WA PGA 0		
Week 45 11/9	WGC-HSBC 612	<Sanderson 40	< PGA Tour	Heiwa PGM 35	Pan. India 0	Nedbank Aff 0			
Week 46 11/16	Mayakoba 68		Turkey 294	Taiheiyo 102	Chiangmai 49		NSW Open 0		
Week 47 11/23			Tour Champ 413	Dunlop 109	Manila Mas 11		Aus Masters 75		
Week 48 11/30				Casio 49	Kings Cup 11	Cape Town 14	Aus Open 175		
Week 49 12/7			Nedbank 196	Nippon 51	Ind. Open 12	< E Tour	NSW PGA 0		
Week 50 12/14			Dunhill 77	Thailand 176		< E Tour	Aus PGA 96		
Week 51 12/21				Dubai Open 19					
Week 52 12/28									

TOP OWR EVENTS WORLDWIDE

#	Top OWR Events - 2013-14		#	Top OWR Events - 2013-14	
1	British Open	902	46	Shriners Hospitals For Children Open (PGA)	195
2	PGA Championship	890	47	Frys.com Open (PGA)	191
3	WGC-Bridgestone Invitational	804	48	Zurich Classic of New Orleans (PGA)	190
4	U.S. Open	789	49	Alstom Open de France (Eur)	188
5	Players Championship	771	50	RBC Canadian Open (PGA)	186
6	WGC-Cadillac Championship	770	51	Nordea Masters (Eur)	183
7	The Masters	766	52	Thailand Golf Championship (Asia)	176
8	The Barclays (PGA)	735	53	Emirates Australian Open (Aus)	175
9	WGC-Accenture Match Play	689	54	Volvo Golf Champions (Eur)	174
10	BMW Championship (PGA)	642	55	Wyndham Championship (PGA)	172
11	Deutsche Bank Championship (PGA)	630	56	John Deere Classic (PGA)	166
12	WGC-HSBC Champions	612	57	McGladrey Classic (PGA)	162
13	Memorial Tournament (PGA)	541	58	Volvo China Open (Eur)	158
14	Honda Classic (PGA)	494	59	Maybank Malaysian Open (Eur)	154
15	Shell Houston Open (PGA)	461	60	Open de España (Eur)	148
16	Tour Championship (PGA)	439	61	ISPS Handa Wales Open (Eur)	144
17	Northern Trust Open (PGA)	433	62	Omega European Masters (Eur)	142
18	DP World Tour Championship (Eur)	413	63	Volvo World Match Play Championship (Eur)	131
19	Arnold Palmer Invitational (PGA)	406	64	KLM Open (Eur)	123
20	Crowne Plaza Invitational at Colonial (PGA)	396	65	Irish Open (Eur)	115
21	Farmers Insurance Open (PGA)	371	66	Dunlop Phoenix (Jap)	109
22	Waste Management Phoenix Open (PGA)	367	67	Portugal Masters (Eur)	107
23	Aberdeen Asset Management Scottish Open (Eur)	366	68	Mitsui Sumitomo Visa Taiheiyo Masters (Jap)	102
24	BMW PGA Championship (Eur)	361	69	Japan Open (Jap)	95
25	Wells Fargo Championship (PGA)	341	70	71st Open d'Italia (Eur)	87
26	Valspar Championship (PGA)	335	71	ISPS Handa Perth International (Eur)	81
27	RBC Heritage (PGA)	332	72	Championship at Laguna National (Eur)	77
28	Travelers Championship (PGA)	314	73	BetEasy Masters (Aus)	75
29	Omega Dubai Desert Classic (Eur)	307	74	Joburg Open (Eur)	70
30	Quicken Loans National (PGA)	305	75	OHL Classic at Mayakoba (PGA)	68
31	Turkish Airlines Open (Eur)	294	76	Tshwane Open (Eur)	65
32	Abu Dhabi HSBC Golf Championship (Eur)	291	77	CIMB Niaga Indonesian Masters (Asia)	65
33	BMW Masters (Eur)	278	78	D+D Real Czech Masters (Eur)	62
34	Hyundai Tournament of Champions (PGA)	259	79	Trophée Hassan II (Eur)	57
35	Alfred Dunhill Links Championship (Eur)	252	79	Nagashima Shigeo Inv Sega Sammy Cup (Jap)	54
36	HP Byron Nelson Championship (PGA)	250	81	Venetian Macau Open (Asia)	54
37	AT&T Pebble Beach National Pro-Am (PGA)	246	82	Made In Denmark (Eur)	52
38	Commercial Bank Qatar Masters (Eur)	242	82	Golf Nippon Series JT Cup (Jap)	51
39	FedEx St Jude Classic (PGA)	240	84	Chiangmai Golf Classic (Asia)	49
40	BMW International Open (Eur)	238	85	Casio World Open (Jap)	49
41	Greenbrier Classic (PGA)	234	86	Hong Kong Open (Eur)	44
42	Sony Open in Hawaii (PGA)	232	87	Sanderson Farms Championship (PGA)	40
43	CIMB Classic (PGA)	228	88	Bridgestone Open (Jap)	39
44	Humana Challenge (PGA)	212	89	Asia-Pacific Diamond Cup Golf (Jap)	37
45	Valero Texas Open (PGA)	211	90	Lyoness Open (Eur)	35

PGA TOUR OWR TABLES

	Top OWR Events - 2013/14			Top OWR Events - Last 5 Years	
1	British Open	902	1	PGA Championship	903.4
2	PGA Championship	890	2	British Open	869.6
3	WGC-Bridgestone Invitational	804	3	U.S. Open	817.4
4	U.S. Open	789	4	The Masters	803.8
5	Players Championship	771	5	WGC-Bridgestone Invitational	797.0
6	WGC-Cadillac Championship	770	6	Players Championship	783.0
7	The Masters	766	7	WGC-Cadillac Championship	772.5
8	The Barclays	735	8	WGC-Accenture Match Play	738.5
9	WGC-Accenture Match Play	689	9	The Barclays	707.4
10	BMW Championship	642	10	Deutsche Bank Championship	675.8
11	Deutsche Bank Championship	630	11	BMW Championship	638.0
12	WGC-HSBC Champions	574	12	WGC-HSBC Champions (4 Yrs)	574.3
13	Memorial Tournament	541	13	Memorial Tournament	569.8
14	Honda Classic	494	14	Northern Trust Open	475.6
15	Shell Houston Open	461	15	Arnold Palmer Invitational	465.6
16	Tour Championship	439	16	Tour Championship	446.4
17	Northern Trust Open	433	17	Wells Fargo Championship	424.6
18	Arnold Palmer Invitational	406	18	Honda Classic	394.8
19	Crowne Plaza Invitational at Colonial	396	19	Valspar Championship	387.4
20	Farmers Insurance Open	371	20	Shell Houston Open	381.2
21	Waste Management Phoenix Open	367	21	Crowne Plaza Invitational at Colonial	359.0
22	Wells Fargo Championship	341	22	Waste Management Phoenix Open	355.8
23	Valspar Championship	335	23	RBC Heritage	330.0
24	RBC Heritage	332	24	Farmers Insurance Open	298.8
25	Travelers Championship	314	25	Quicken Loans National	286.8
26	CIMB Classic	309	26	Hyundai Tournament of Champions	277.3
27	Quicken Loans National	305	27	Travelers Championship	271.6
28	Hyundai Tournament of Champions	259	28	Sony Open in Hawaii	259.2
29	HP Byron Nelson Championship	250	29	AT&T Pebble Beach National Pro-Am	242.6
30	AT&T Pebble Beach National Pro-Am	246	30	Zurich Classic of New Orleans	236.6
31	FedEx St Jude Classic	240	31	RBC Canadian Open	219.4
32	Greenbrier Classic	234	32	HP Byron Nelson Championship	214.0
33	Sony Open in Hawaii	232	33	Greenbrier Classic	213.4
34	Humana Challenge	212	34	CIMB Classic	210.0
35	Valero Texas Open	211	35	FedEx St Jude Classic	207.4
36	Zurich Classic of New Orleans	190	36	Humana Challenge	203.8
37	Shriners Hospitals For Children Open	187	37	Wyndham Championship	199.8
38	RBC Canadian Open	186	38	John Deere Classic	170.0
39	Wyndham Championship	172	39	McGladrey Classic	163.3
40	John Deere Classic	166	40	Valero Texas Open	158.0
41	McGladrey Classic	152	41	Shriners Hospitals For Children Open	150.6
42	Frys.com Open	125	42	Frys.com Open	102.6
43	OHL Classic at Mayakoba	84	43	OHL Classic at Mayakoba	43.4
44	Barracuda Championship	33	44	Puerto Rico Open	30.0
45	Puerto Rico Open	32	45	Barracuda Championship	25.2

EUROPEAN TOUR OWR TABLES

	Top OWR Events - 2013/14				Top OWR Events - Last 5 Years	
1	WGC-HSBC Champions	612		1	WGC-HSBC Champions	574.3
2	DP World Tour Championship	413		2	DP World Tour Championship	425.2
3	Scottish Open	366		3	BMW PGA Championship	417.0
4	BMW PGA Championship	361		4	Abu Dhabi HSBC Golf Championship	387.8
5	Omega Dubai Desert Classic	307		5	BMW Masters (3 Yrs)	340.0
6	Turkish Airlines Open	294		6	Turkish Airlines Open (2 Yrs)	332.0
7	Abu Dhabi HSBC Golf Championship	291		7	Scottish Open	321.8
8	BMW Masters	278		8	Commercial Bank Qatar Masters	309.4
9	Nedbank Golf Challenge	263		9	Omega Dubai Desert Classic	287.8
10	Alfred Dunhill Links Championship	252		10	Alfred Dunhill Links Championship	284.2
11	Commercial Bank Qatar Masters	242		11	Alstom Open de France	257.0
12	BMW International Open	238		12	Volvo World Match Play Championship (3 Yrs) *	217.0
13	Alstom Open de France	188		13	BMW International Open	192.0
14	Nordea Masters	183		14	Nedbank Golf Challenge **	186.8
15	Volvo Golf Champions	174		15	Volvo Golf Champions (4 Yrs)	184.5
16	Volvo China Masters	158		16	Maybank Malaysian Open	165.6
17	Maybank Malaysian Open	154		17	Omega European Masters	163.8
18	Open de España	148		18	Portugal Masters	154.2
19	ISPS Handa Wales Open	144		19	Championship at Laguna National	150.5
20	Omega European Masters	142		20	Irish Open	150.2
21	Volvo World Match Play Championship	131		21	KLM Open	146.6
22	KLM Open	123		22	ISPS Handa Wales Open (NLE)	142.4
23	Irish Open	115		23	Volvo China Open	141.6
24	Portugal Masters	107		24	Hong Kong Open	128.0
25	Open d'Italia	87		25	Nordea Masters	122.0
26	ISPS Handa Perth International	81		26	Open de España	116.8
27	Alfred Dunhill Championship	77		27	Open d'Italia	85.4
27	Championship at Laguna National	77		28	Joburg Open	74.0
29	Joburg Open	70		29	ISPS Handa Perth International (3 Yrs)	73.7
30	Tshwane Open	65		30	South African Open Championship	72.6
31	D+D Real Czech Masters	62		31	Alfred Dunhill Championship	64.8
32	Trophée Hassan II	57		32	D+D Real Czech Masters (1 Yr)	62.0
33	Made in Denmark	52		33	Tshwane Open (3 Yrs)	59.0
34	South African Open Championship	46		34	Made in Denmark (1 Yr)	52.0
35	Hong Kong Open (2014)	44		35	Trophée Hassan II	50.6
36	Hong Kong Open (2013)	40		36	Nelson Mandela Championship (2 Yrs - NLE)	46.5
37	Lyoness Open	35		37	Africa Open	40.4
38	Nelson Mandela Championship	30		38	Lyoness Open	25.2
39	Africa Open	25		39	NH Collection Open (1 Yr)	22.0
40	NH Collection Open	22		40	M2M Russian Open (2 Yrs)	6.0
41	M2M Russian Open	3		41	Madeira Islands Open	1.8
42	Madeira Islands Open	0		42		

* Event was not rated in 2012, and was not played in 2010
** Became an E Tour event in 2013-14; was solely a Sunshine Tour event previously

TOP OWR EVENTS - OTHER TOURS

	Japan - Top OWR Events - 2014	
1	Dunlop Phoenix	109
2	Mitsui Sumitomo Visa Taiheiyo Masters	102
3	Japan Open	95
4	Nagashima Shigeo Inv Sega Sammy Cup	54
5	Golf Nippon Series JT Cup	51
6	Casio World Open	49
7	Bridgestone Open	39
8	Asia-Pacific Diamond Cup Golf	37
9	Mynavi ABC Championship	35
9	Heiwa PGM Championship	35
11	PGA Championship Nissin Cupnoodle Cup	32
11	Japan Golf Tour Championship	32
13	Tsuruya Open	30
13	Ana Open	30
15	The Crowns	28

	Japan - Top OWR Events - Last 5 Years	
1	Dunlop Phoenix	132.0
2	Mitsui Sumitomo Visa Taiheiyo Masters	77.4
3	Golf Nippon Series JT Cup	65.0
4	Casio World Open	61.2
5	Japan Open	59.8
6	PGA Championship Nissin Cupnoodle Cup	56.4
7	Bridgestone Open	55.0
8	Nagashima Shigeo Inv Sega Sammy Cup	53.6
9	Gateway To The Open Mizuno Open	52.6
10	Japan Golf Tour Championship	52.4
11	Mynavi ABC Championship	52.0
12	Asia-Pacific Diamond Cup Golf	51.6
13	Ana Open	50.6
14	Tsuruya Open	50.6
15	Token Homemate Cup	50.0

	Asia - Top OWR Events - 2014	
1	Thailand Golf Championship	176
2	CIMB Niaga Indonesian Masters	65
3	Venetian Macau Open	54
4	Chiangmai Golf Classic	49
5	King's Cup (1st)	11
5	ICTSI Philippine Open	11
5	Resorts World Manila Masters	11
5	King's Cup (2nd)	11
9	SAIL-SBI Open	7
9	Queen's Cup	7

	Asia - Top OWR Events - Last 5 Years	
1	Thailand Golf Championship (4 Yrs)	178.5
2	CIMB Niaga Indonesian Masters (4 Yrs)	60.3
3	Chiangmai Golf Classic (2 Yrs)	46.5
4	Venetian Macau Open (4 Yrs)	26.0
5	Indian Open (4 Yrs)	17.3
6	King's Cup (4 Yrs)	9.3
7	Queen's Cup	9.2
8	ICTSI Philippines Open (4 Yrs)	9.0
9	Resorts World Manila Masters (2 Yrs)	7.5
9	Panasonic Open India (4 Yrs)	6.0

*Includes only those events not co-sanctioned by the European or PGA Tours

	Sunshine - Top OWR Events - 2014	
1	Investec Cup	30
2	Telkom Business PGA Championship	16
3	Dimension Data Pro-Am	14

	Sunshine - Top OWR Events - Last 5 Years	
1	Investec Cup (2 Yrs)	22.5
2	Telkom Business PGA Championship	13.8
3	Dimension Data Pro-Am	11.0

*Includes only those events not co-sanctioned by the European Tour

	Australia - Top OWR Events - 2014	
1	Emirates Australian Open	175
2	Australian PGA Championship	96
3	BetEasy Masters	75

	Australia - Top OWR Events - Last 5 Years	
1	Emirates Australian Open	154.4
2	BetEasy Masters	111.4
3	Australian PGA Championship	101.2

*Includes only those events not co-sanctioned by the European Tour

PGA TOUR INCIDENTALS

PGA TOUR TOP 60 CAREER MONEY WINNERS

1	Tiger Woods	$109,612,414	21	Geoff Ogilvy	$28,440,710	41	Tom Lehman	$21,495,878
2	Phil Mickelson	$75,298,510	22	Mike Weir	$27,870,873	42	Carl Pettersson	$21,227,059
3	Vijay Singh	$68,576,122	23	Hunter Mahan	$27,857,040	43	Fred Funk	$21,130,324
4	Jim Furyk	$61,911,633	24	Rory Sabbatini	$27,817,395	44	Nick Price	$20,576,104
5	Ernie Els	$47,744,740	25	Charles Howell III	$27,623,015	45	Bill Haas	$20,416,477
6	Davis Love III	$42,796,746	26	Scott Verplank	$27,474,543	46	Billy Mayfair	$20,244,211
7	Steve Stricker	$40,674,840	27	Robert Allenby	$27,127,382	47	Bo Van Pelt	$19,830,885
8	David Toms	$40,313,294	28	Jerry Kelly	$26,128,629	48	Stephen Ames	$19,710,547
9	Sergio García	$37,773,319	29	Bubba Watson	$25,055,896	49	Jeff Maggert	$19,364,566
10	Adam Scott	$37,297,653	30	Mark Calcavecchia	$24,216,436	50	Ben Crane	$19,311,408
11	Zach Johnson	$33,675,219	31	Dustin Johnson	$24,157,093	51	David Duval	$18,947,092
12	Justin Leonard	$33,363,488	32	Rory McIlroy	$23,440,098	52	John Senden	$18,867,849
13	Stewart Cink	$32,818,873	33	Brandt Snedeker	$23,068,691	53	Tim Herron	$18,781,482
14	Luke Donald	$32,242,519	34	Tim Clark	$22,803,821	54	Ryan Moore	$18,566,241
15	Kenny Perry	$31,980,740	35	Chris DiMarco	$22,656,443	55	Webb Simpson	$18,542,390
16	Matt Kuchar	$31,111,543	36	Fred Couples	$22,595,874	56	Scott Hoch	$18,530,156
17	K.J. Choi	$30,025,453	37	Padraig Harrington	$22,526,233	57	Jeff Sluman	$18,165,266
18	Justin Rose	$29,204,533	38	Chad Campbell	$22,262,675	58	Steve Flesch	$18,153,356
19	Stuart Appleby	$28,774,161	39	Nick Watney	$22,123,311	59	John Rollins	$18,098,041
20	Retief Goosen	$28,667,416	40	Bob Estes	$21,536,179	60	Brian Gay	$17,795,366

PGA TOUR TOP 30 CAREER TOURNAMENT WINNERS

1	Sam Snead	82	12	Gene Sarazen	38	23=	Tommy Armour	25
2	Tiger Woods	79	13	Lloyd Mangrum	36		Johnny Miller	25
3	Jack Nicklaus	73	14	Vijay Singh	34	25=	Gary Player	24
4	Ben Hogan	64	15	Jimmy Demaret	31		Macdonald Smith	24
5	Arnold Palmer	62	16	Horton Smith	30	27=	Johnny Farrell	22
6	Byron Nelson	52	17=	Harry Cooper	29		Raymond Floyd	22
7	Billy Casper	51		Gene Littler	29	29=	Willie Macfarlane	21
8	Walter Hagen	45		Lee Trevino	29		Lanny Wadkins	21
9	Phil Mickelson	42	20=	Leo Diegel	28		Craig Wood	21
10=	Cary Middlecoff	39		Paul Runyan	28		James Barnes	21
	Tom Watson	39	22	Henry Picard	26			

PGA TOUR EVENT / SPONSOR / VENUE UPDATES

The 2014-15 PGA Tour represents year two of the marginally well-received wraparound schedule, with seven October/November 2014 events counting towards the 2015 season and Q School now serving only to decide places on the Web.com Tour. One significant change to this early section of the calendar is the move of Mississippi's **Sanderson Farms Championship** (formerly the Viking Classic) from a slot opposite July's British Open to the first week of November, placing it directly up against the WGC-HSBC Champions event in China. The Sanderson Farms is also moving from its only previous venue, the Annandale Golf Club, to the nearby Country Club of Jackson.

An even more significant schedule change sees the **WGC-Match Play** leave both its familiar late February time slot and its Tucson area venue, moving to May (the week before the Players Championship) and San Francisco's municipal Harding Park Golf Course. For the moment, the new date is likely to be a one-time thing, as is a new 2015 sponsor, Cadillac, which is already committed long-term to the WGC event at Doral. There will also be a brand new event added to the schedule opposite the British Open, the **Barbasol Championship**, which will offer a $3.5 million purse to an obviously light field at the Lakes Course of the Robert Trent Jones Golf Trail Grand National facility.

As for venue changes, regularly rotating events include the **Canadian Open** (returning from Royal Montreal to its most frequent site, Ontario's Glen Abbey Golf Club) and a pair of FedEx Cup playoff events, **The Barclays** (from the classic Ridgewood to the equally classic Plainfield Country Club) and the **BMW Championship** (née the Western Open), which returns to Chicago's Conway Farms Country Club after a one-year stop at Denver's iconic Cherry Hills. Also on the move in 2015 are the **Frys.com Open** (from CordeValle to Napa's famed Silverado Resort - with rumors continuing of a future switch to the 7,952-yard Institute Golf Course, built by Frys.com's owner) and the **Quicken Loans National**, which heads for the Robert Trent Jones Golf Club (a four-time Presidents Cup site) after a three-year run at Congressional. Also noteworthy is the Waste Management Phoenix Open, which remains at the TPC Scottsdale Stadium Course, a popular venue recently lengthened and re-bunkered by one of its two original architects, Tom Weiskopf.

PGA TOUR 2014

And so began a genuinely new era in PGA Tour golf.

Following a path traveled by the European Tour since the dawn of the millennium, the U.S. circuit began playing a "wraparound" schedule in 2014 - that is, they began their official 2014 schedule in October of 2013, with six events being played before a six-week break was taken through the holidays. Was this new approach successful? That would depend upon what criteria we employ in judging. It was, for example, an undeniable fact that all six tournaments enjoyed noticeably stronger fields as beginning-of-the-season events than they did as part of a post-Tour Championship "Fall Series," the latter only being relevant to less-successful players scrambling to keep their cards for the following year. But at the same time, it would be difficult to argue that this upgraded fall slate had any major impact on a viewing audience which has largely seen enough golf following the Majors and the FedEx Cup playoffs, and who by this time have turned their collective gaze to football, or something else. It is a tricky scenario and one for which, short of contracting the Tour by at least four or five events, there is no easy answer. For multiple reasons, the fall is just a much more challenging time for the PGA Tour to do business.

So far as the golf itself went, that can be distilled down to two words: Rory McIlroy.

Bouncing back from a hugely disappointing 2013 plagued by business/legal issues, new clubs and, seemingly, problems in his personal life, McIlroy began the year with seven top 10s in his first nine worldwide appearances before exploding, first winning the E Tour's flagship BMW PGA Championship, then laying waste to the competition by claiming the British Open, the WGC-Bridgestone Invitational and the PGA Championship in successive starts. It was enough, in fact, not only to reestablish McIlroy as the world's best but also to draw all eyes completely away from the stellar campaigns enjoyed by the year's two other Major championship winners, Martin Kaymer (who added an impressive triumph at the Players Championship to his runaway win at the U.S. Open) and Bubba Watson, who won impressively in Los Angeles (and at the late season WGC-HSBC Champions) in addition to claiming his second Masters. Even with the prolonged absence of Tiger Woods due to back surgery, it made for a highly compelling golfing year.

Player Of The Year: Rory McIlroy

There was a time in late spring when Martin Kaymer, with Players and U.S. Open trophies firmly in hand, looked a good bet to win this award - but by Labor Day, McIlroy's spectacular summer form had made Kaymer's run all but forgotten. Indeed, McIlroy's was truly an epic season, as he recorded victories in four top-shelf events, logged 15 top-10 finishes (including four runner-ups) in 22 worldwide starts, and joined Bobby Jones, Jack Nicklaus and Tiger Woods as the only men in over a century to win four Major titles by age 25. Further, he sparked a level of buzz and excitement not seen since Woods' ascension. He was, by any measure, the obvious Player Of The Year.

2014 PGA Tour Top 60 Money Winners

#	Player	Money	#	Player	Money	#	Player	Money
1	Rory McIlroy	$8,280,096	21	Ryan Moore	$3,098,263	41	Graeme McDowell	$2,077,387
2	Bubba Watson	$6,336,978	22	Hunter Mahan	$3,097,983	42	Tim Clark	$2,066,344
3	Jim Furyk	$5,987,395	23	Harris English	$2,947,322	43	George McNeill	$2,014,357
4	Jimmy Walker	$5,787,016	24	Ryan Palmer	$2,924,300	44	Charl Schwartzel	$1,997,482
5	Sergio García	$4,939,606	25	John Senden	$2,856,685	45	Charles Howell III	$1,997,044
6	Chris Kirk	$4,854,777	26	Bill Haas	$2,841,521	46	Charley Hoffman	$1,977,296
7	Billy Horschel	$4,814,787	27	Hideki Matsuyama	$2,837,477	47	Matt Jones	$1,928,154
8	Rickie Fowler	$4,806,117	28	Keegan Bradley	$2,828,638	48	Freddie Jacobson	$1,901,789
9	Matt Kuchar	$4,695,515	29	Gary Woodland	$2,734,153	49	Henrik Stenson	$1,894,235
10	Martin Kaymer	$4,532,537	30	Graham DeLaet	$2,616,518	50	Angel Cabrera	$1,868,559
11	Jordan Spieth	$4,342,748	31	Russell Henley	$2,590,493	51	Will MacKenzie	$1,853,822
12	Dustin Johnson	$4,249,180	32	Marc Leishman	$2,558,657	52	Brian Stuard	$1,852,531
13	Adam Scott	$4,098,588	33	Matt Every	$2,540,370	53	Chris Stroud	$1,826,399
14	Patrick Reed	$4,026,076	34	Brian Harman	$2,414,334	54	Geoff Ogilvy	$1,809,632
15	Justin Rose	$3,926,768	35	J.B. Holmes	$2,365,204	55	Ernie Els	$1,799,569
16	Jason Day	$3,789,574	36	Kevin Stadler	$2,300,307	56	Erik Compton	$1,796,143
17	Webb Simpson	$3,539,601	37	Cameron Tringale	$2,169,723	57	Steven Bowditch	$1,734,693
18	Brendon Todd	$3,396,747	38	Phil Mickelson	$2,158,019	58	Chesson Hadley	$1,703,316
19	Zach Johnson	$3,353,417	39	Seung-Yul Noh	$2,115,234	59	K.J. Choi	$1,677,848
20	Kevin Na	$3,153,107	40	Kevin Streelman	$2,107,994	60	Brandt Snedeker	$1,652,380

2013-2014 PGA Tour Week-By-Week

	Tournament	Purse	Winner/Score		Notes
Week 41 10/13	Frys.com Open	$5 mil	Jimmy Walker	267	Eight-year veteran Walker claims his first win in his 188th PGA Tour start, edging 50-year-old Vijay Singh by two.
Week 42 10/20	Shriners Hospitals for Children Open	$6 mil	Webb Simpson	260	Simpson records his fourth PGA Tour triumph in a six-shot runaway over Jason Bohn & Ryo Ishikawa.
Week 43 10/27	CIMB Classic	$7 mil	Ryan Moore	274	After opening with a 63, Moore pockets his third career PGA Tour win in a Monday morning playoff with Gary Woodland.
Week 44 11/3	WGC-HSBC Champions	$8.5 mil	Dustin Johnson	264	Johnson beats Ian Poulter by three in China, winning for the seventh straight season since joining the PGA Tour.
Week 45 11/10	McGladrey Classic	$5.5 mil	Chris Kirk	266	As Briny Baird faded late, local resident Chris Kirk claimed his second career win. beating Baird and Tim Clark by one.
Week 46 11/17	OHL Classic at Mayakoba	$6 mil	Harris English	263	English wins for the second time in calendar 2013, his closing 65 giving him a four-shot margin over Brian Stuard.
Week 47 11/24					
Week 48 12/1					
Week 49 12/8					
Week 50 12/15					
Week 51 12/22					
Week 52 12/28					
Week 1 1/5	Hyundai Tournament of Champions	$5.7 mil	Zach Johnson	273	The Tour's hottest player at the end of 2013, Johnson wins his 11th PGA Tour title, edging Jordan Spieth by one.
Week 2 1/12	Sony Open in Hawaii	$5.6 mil	Jimmy Walker	263	Walker wins for the second time in three months, closing with a 63 to beat Chris Kirk by one.
Week 3 1/19	Humana Challenge	$5.6 mil	Patrick Reed	260	Reed sets all-time 54-hole relative-to-par scoring record by opening with three straight 63s, hangs on to win by two.
Week 4 1/26	Farmers Insurance Open	$6.1 mil	Scott Stallings	279	Stallings claims his third career win by birdieing the 72nd hole to edge five players by one.
Week 5 2/2	Waste Management Phoenix Open	$6.2 mil	Kevin Stadler	268	Playing on his home course, Stadler wins for the first time when Bubba Watson bogeys the 72nd hole to lose by one.
Week 6 2/9	AT&T Pebble Beach National Pro-Am	$6.6 mil	Jimmy Walker	276	Walker wins for third time in eight starts, nearly blowing a six-shot final nine lead before winning by one.
Week 7 2/16	Northern Trust Open	$6.7 mil	Bubba Watson	269	Watson edges Dustin Johnson by two, carding back-to-back bogey-free weekend rounds of 64-64 at Riviera.
Week 8 2/23	WGC-Accenture Match Play Championship	$9 mil	Jason Day	23rd	Day scores a breakthrough victory, beating Victor Dubuisson at the 23rd hole to claim his second PGA Tour win.
Week 9 3/2	Honda Classic	$6 mil	Russell Henley	272	Henley wins a four-man playoff over Russell Knox, Rory McIlroy & Ryan Palmer by birdieing the first extra hole.
Week 10 3/9	WGC-Cadillac Champ. & Puerto Rico Open	$9 mil $3.5 mil	Patrick Reed Chesson Hadley	284 267	Reed hangs on late to claim his third win in 14 starts. Hadley takes his first PGA Tour win, by two over Danny Lee.
Week 11 3/16	Valspar Championship	$5.7 mil	John Senden	277	Senden ends an eight-year victory drought, edging Kevin Na by one with late birdies at the 70th and 71st holes.
Week 12 3/23	Arnold Palmer Invitational	$6.2 mil	Matt Every	275	Trailing by nine after 36 holes, Every closes 66-70 to edge Keegan Bradley by one, claiming his first PGA Tour victory.
Week 13 3/30	Valero Texas Open	$6.2 mil	Steven Bowditch	280	Bowditch lands his first PGA Tour win despite posting the highest final round winning score (76) in a decade.
Week 14 4/6	Shell Houston Open	$6.4 mil	Matt Jones	273	Jones is the second straight Australian to win, beating Matt Kuchar (with a 42-yard chip-in) on the first extra hole.

2013-2014 PGA Tour Week-By-Week (Cont'd)

	Tournament	Purse	Winner/Score		Notes
Week 15 4/13	The Masters	$8 mil	Bubba Watson	273	Watson holds steady on Sunday as the other contenders falter, beats Jordan Spieth & Jonas Blixt by three.
Week 16 4/20	RBC Heritage	$5.8 mil	Matt Kuchar	273	After contending for several weeks, Kuchar lands his first 2014 title, holing a bunker shot at the last to win by one.
Week 17 4/27	Zurich Classic of New Orleans	$6.8 mil	Seung-Yul Noh	269	A touted prospect in Asia, the 22-year-old Noh lands his first U.S. win, by two over Andrew Svoboda & Robert Streb.
Week 18 5/4	Wells Fargo Championship	$6.9 mil	J.B. Holmes	274	Long-hitting Holmes completes his comeback from brain and ankle surgery to claim his third PGA Tour victory.
Week 19 5/11	Players Championship	$10 mil	Martin Kaymer	275	Kaymer ends a long victory drought, edging Jim Furyk by two after holing a clutch 28-foot par putt at the 71st hole.
Week 20 5/18	HP Byron Nelson Championship	$6.9 mil	Brendon Todd	266	In his 77th career start, Todd claims his first PGA Tour win, closing with a bogey-free 66 to edge Mike Weir by two.
Week 21 5/25	Crowne Plaza Invitational at Colonial	$6.4 mil	Adam Scott	271	Six days after reaching #1 in the OWR, Scott validates his position by beating Jason Dufner in a three-hole playoff.
Week 22 6/1	Memorial Tournament	$6.2 mil	Hideki Matsuyama	275	At age 22, Matsuyama breaks through for his maiden PGA Tour win, beating Kevin Na on the first extra hole.
Week 23 6/8	FedEx St Jude Classic	$5.8 mil	Ben Crane	270	Crane opens with a 63 en route to claiming his fifth PGA Tour win, holding off Troy Merritt by one.
Week 24 6/15	The U.S. Open	$8 mil	Martin Kaymer	271	In a record-setting performance, Kaymer opens 65-65 en route to an eight-shot runaway triumph at Pinehurst
Week 25 6/22	Travelers Championship	$6.2 mil	Kevin Streelman	265	Streelman sets a new PGA Tour record by birdieing the last seven holes to beat K.J. Choi & Sergio García by one.
Week 26 6/29	Quicken Loans National	$6.5 mil	Justin Rose	280	On a wild Sunday afternoon, Rose defeats Shawn Stefani on the first extra hole for his sixth PGA Tour victory.
Week 27 7/6	Greenbrier Classic	$6.5 mil	Angel Cabrera	264	Cabrera holes an 8 iron at the 67th en route to his first non-Major PGA Tour win, beating George McNeill by two.
Week 28 7/13	John Deere Classic	$4.7 mil	Brian Harman	262	Ex-USGA Junior champion Harman lands his first PGA Tour victory, and a last-minute trip to the British Open
Week 29 7/20	The Open Championship	$8 mil	Rory McIlroy	271	McIlroy joins Nicklaus & Woods as winners of three legs of the career Grand Slam by age 25 in a wire-to-wire triumph.
Week 30 7/27	Canadian Open	$5.7 mil	Tim Clark	263	Clark closes 64-65 to edge Jim Furyk by one, claiming his second career PGA Tour win and his first since 2010.
Week 31 8/3	WGC-Bridgestone Inv. & Reno-Tahoe Open	$9 mil $3 mil	Rory McIlroy Geoff Ogilvy	265 49 pts	McIlroy returns to OWR #1 with his second straight victory. Ogilvy breaks a four-year drought with a 5 point win.
Week 32 8/10	The PGA Championship	$10 mil	Rory McIlroy	268	McIlroy rallies on the final nine to win his second straight (and fourth career) Major, edging Phil Mickelson by one.
Week 33 8/17	Wyndham Championship	$5.3 mil	Camilo Villegas	263	Villegas takes a big step towards reviving his career, closing with a 63 to edge Bill Haas & Freddie Jacobson by one.
Week 34 8/24	The Barclays	$8 mil	Hunter Mahan	270	Mahan ends a 30-month drought, closing with a 65 to beat Stuart Appleby, Jason Day & Cameron Tringale by one.
Week 35 9/1	Deutsche Bank Championship	$8 mil	Chris Kirk	269	Kirk closes with bogey-free rounds of 64-66 to take his third PGA Tour win, beating a trio of players by two shots.
Week 36 9/7	BMW Championship	$8 mil	Billy Horschel	266	After losing on the 72nd-hole loss a week earlier, Horschel bounces back to beat Bubba Watson by two.
Week 37 9/14	Tour Championship	$8 mil	Billy Horschel	269	Horschel wins for the second straight week - and clinches the jackpot $10 million FedEx Cup playoffs prize.
Week 38 9/21					
Week 39 9/28					
Week 40 10/5					

Frys.com Open

CordeValle Golf Club - San Martin, CA
Champion: Jimmy Walker

Oct 10 - Oct 13
7,368 yards   Par 71
Purse: $5 Million

It took 188 starts for eight-year veteran Jimmy Walker to break through for his first PGA Tour victory but his timing was immaculate; instead of solidifying his earnings for 2013 by claiming the Frys.com Open, he instead recorded the first official victory of the 2014 season (and with it a Masters invite) as the event was the first in the Tour's new calendar-crossing wraparound schedule. Though the field boasted few of the stars that it was suggested might play under the new arrangement, it produced a final-round leaderboard dotted with both up-and-coming names (American Brooks Koepka and Japan's Hideki Matsuyama) as well as veterans like Walker, Kevin Na and even 50-year-old Vijay Singh. For much of the week, it looked like Koepka – recent winner of a three-victory battlefield promotion from the European Challenge Tour to the E Tour, and here on sponsor exemption – might break through for a lightning-bolt debut victory, particularly after rounds of 67-64-67 staked him to a two-shot 54-hole lead. The lead actually grew to four during Sunday's front nine but as the pressure mounted Koepka wilted, bogeying the 9th and 11th, and then, after a bounce-back birdie at the 12th, both the 16th and 17th to blow himself out of contention. Walker, meanwhile, had been miles off the halfway lead with rounds of 70-69, then exploded with a Saturday 62 that included 10 birdies. Thus entering the final round three strokes behind Koepka, he proceeded to post a six-birdie, one-bogey 66 which, though lacking any fireworks, was good enough to provide a two-shot margin over the surprising Singh (who carded rounds of 65-68 on the weekend) and three over a quartet that included Na, Matsuyama (who also closed with 66), Koepka and Scott Brown.

1	Jimmy Walker	70-69-62-66	267	$900,000		Luke Guthrie	69-70-68-71	278	$19,000
2	Vijay Singh	69-67-65-68	269	$540,000		Daniel Summerhays	72-68-69-69	278	$19,000
3=	Scott Brown	68-67-71-64	270	$240,000		T. Van Aswegen	69-72-68-69	278	$19,000
	Kevin Na	75-67-64-64	270	$240,000		Jason Bohn	70-70-69-69	278	$19,000
	Hideki Matsuyama	70-66-68-66	270	$240,000		Heath Slocum	71-71-69-67	278	$19,000
	Brooks Koepka	67-64-67-72	270	$240,000	46=	John Rollins	74-68-66-71	279	$13,860
7=	Brian Harman	65-74-67-65	271	$161,250		Will Claxton	70-72-67-70	279	$13,860
	George McNeill	68-70-62-71	271	$161,250		Morgan Hoffmann	70-72-67-70	279	$13,860
9=	Billy Hurley III	69-66-69-68	272	$135,000		Charlie Beljan	73-66-71-69	279	$13,860
	Max Homa	69-68-66-69	272	$135,000		Kevin Chappell	70-69-65-75	279	$13,860
	Will MacKenzie	69-70-64-69	272	$135,000	51=	Lee Williams	68-71-68-73	280	$11,767
12=	Charlie Wi	67-68-69-69	273	$101,250		Brice Garnett	71-67-70-72	280	$11,767
	Spencer Levin	71-65-68-69	273	$101,250		Robert Streb	70-70-68-72	280	$11,767
	Robert Garrigus	70-63-68-72	273	$101,250		Josh Teater	71-70-67-72	280	$11,767
	Jason Kokrak	67-65-68-73	273	$101,250		Jonas Blixt	69-72-69-70	280	$11,767
16=	J.J. Henry	67-71-68-68	274	$75,000		Chez Reavie	73-69-69-69	280	$11,767
	Andres Gonzales	74-62-69-69	274	$75,000	57	Jerry Kelly	69-72-67-73	281	$11,300
	Jeff Overton	64-72-69-69	274	$75,000	58=	Scott Langley	71-68-71-72	282	$11,050
	Justin Hicks	68-68-68-70	274	$75,000		Johnson Wagner	68-73-71-70	282	$11,050
	Ben Martin	69-68-66-71	274	$75,000		Brian Stuard	71-71-70-70	282	$11,050
21=	David Hearn	73-68-66-68	275	$52,000		Pat Perez	72-70-70-70	282	$11,050
	Trevor Immelman	70-69-68-68	275	$52,000	62=	Ben Crane	69-71-68-75	283	$10,500
	James Driscoll	74-67-65-69	275	$52,000		Michael Putnam	67-71-74	283	$10,500
	John Peterson	68-70-68-69	275	$52,000		Davis Love III	69-69-71-74	283	$10,500
	Ryo Ishikawa	69-67-67-72	275	$52,000		Bryce Molder	72-69-69-73	283	$10,500
26=	Russell Knox	71-68-69-68	276	$35,500		Mike Weir	72-70-69-72	283	$10,500
	Sean O'Hair	71-70-65-70	276	$35,500		Jamie Lovemark	70-71-71-71	283	$10,500
	Brendon Todd	71-70-69-66	276	$35,500		Robert Allenby	68-73-71-71	283	$10,500
	Briny Baird	71-68-65-72	276	$35,500	69	Mark Hubbard	69-71-72-73	285	$10,100
	Jason Gore	73-69-68-66	276	$35,500	70	John Huh	70-69-73-75	287	$10,000
	Camilo Villegas	68-66-77-65	276	$35,500	71	Bud Cauley	69-69-74-76	288	$9,900
	Jim Herman	67-66-70-73	276	$35,500		Tim Clark	73-67-73	213	$9,600
33=	Charles Howell III	72-70-65-70	277	$25,857		Chesson Hadley	72-68-73	213	$9,600
	Danny Lee	73-68-66-70	277	$25,857		Chad Collins	72-68-73	213	$9,600
	Kyle Stanley	66-69-72-70	277	$25,857		Justin Thomas	72-70-71	213	$9,600
	Brian Davis	70-69-66-72	277	$25,857		Geoff Ogilvy	76-66-71	213	$9,600
	Y.E. Yang	71-68-71-67	277	$25,857		Stewart Cink	72-69-73	214	$9,250
	Kevin Kisner	73-69-68-67	277	$25,857		Alex Aragon	68-73-73	214	$9,250
	Ricky Barnes	71-69-64-73	277	$25,857		Justin Leonard	70-72-73	215	$9,100
40=	Kevin Tway	70-65-72-71	278	$19,000		Jeff Maggert	73-69-76	218	$9,000

Out Of The Money: **143**: Chad Campbell, Freddie Jacobson, Marc Leishman, Brian Gay, John Senden, Scott Gardiner, David Carr, Lucas Glover, Carl Pettersson, Billy Horschel, Tim Wilkinson, Paul Goydos, Andrew Svoboda, Hudson Swafford **144**: Stuart Appleby, William McGirt, Tommy Gainey, Chris Williams **145**: Fred Funk, Retief Goosen, Aaron Baddeley, Patrick Reed, Ben Curtis, Stephen Ames, Jim Renner **146**: Erik Compton, Cameron Tringale, Edward Loar, Gary Woodland, Peter Malnati **147**: Angel Cabrera, Cameron Beckman, Doug LaBelle II, Ted Potter, Jr., Brendan Steele, Troy Matteson **148**: Chris Stroud, Nicholas Thompson, Derek Ernst, Rocco Mediate, Bronson La'Cassie, Andrew Loupe **149**: Robert Gates **150**: Scott Verplank, Blake Adams **151**: Jhonattan Vegas, Troy Merritt **154**: Rory Sabbatini **156**: Jose Coceres **158**: Seung-Yul Noh **WD**: Steven Bowditch (75)

FIRST ROUND		SECOND ROUND		THIRD ROUND	
Jeff Overton	64 (-7)	Brooks Koepka	131 (-11)	Brooks Koepka	198 (-15)
Brian Harman	65 (-6)	Jason Kokrak	132 (-10)	George McNeill	200 (-13)
Kyle Stanley	66 (-5)	Robert Garrigus	133 (-9)	Jason Kokrak	200 (-13)
6 Players	67 (-4)	Jim Herman	133 (-9)	4 Players	201 (-12)
Jimmy Walker	70 (-1)	**Jimmy Walker**	139 (-3)	**Jimmy Walker**	201 (-12)

OWR: 3 of top 50 entered   -   Rating: 125   -   Points to 32nd   -   Walker: 28 points, to 45th in OWR

Shriners Hospitals For Children Open

TPC Summerlin - Las Vegas, NV
Champion: Webb Simpson

Oct 17 - Oct 20
7,223 yards   Par 71
Purse: $6 Million

It had been nearly 16 months since Webb Simpson's breakthrough triumph at the 2012 U.S. Open, but during a week in Las Vegas in which the scores were exceptionally low, Simpson posted by far the lowest, returning to the winners circle at the Shriners Hospitals For Children Open. He began with a Thursday 64 over the friendly TPC Summerlin layout but surprisingly sat well off the lead – that because J.J. Henry managed to card an 11-under-par 60, while Argentina's Andrés Romero nearly matched him with a 61. Neither would factor into the action late, however, and in Romero's case, the decline was spectacular: he carded a second-round 81, with the 20-stroke differential being both mind-boggling and enough to make him miss the cut. Simpson, on the other hand, fired a Friday 63 to move out to a four-shot lead, then added a Saturday 67 to maintain that cushion going into the final round. On a golf course obviously prone to yielding low numbers, a round anywhere near par would surely have left him ripe to be overtaken, but Simpson instead gained momentum early with birdies at the 2nd and 3rd holes, then added one more at the 9th to go out in 32 and blow things wide open. A three-birdie, one-bogey inward half made things largely a formality, leaving Simpson to coast home with a 66 and a six-shot victory. Japan's Ryo Ishikawa – fresh off retaining his playing privileges via the Web.com Finals – tied for second with Jason Bohn, while third place was taken by Charley Hoffman, who closed with a 64. Also notable was rookie Chesson Hadley, who began the day in second but fell to a tie for fifth despite shooting a one-under-par 70.

#	Player	Scores	Total	Money		#	Player	Scores	Total	Money
1	Webb Simpson	64-63-67-66	260	$1.08 mil			Chad Campbell	71-66-70-68	275	$30,225
2=	Ryo Ishikawa	67-66-68-65	266	$528,000			David Toms	68-68-69-70	275	$30,225
	Jason Bohn	67-64-69-66	266	$528,000			Briny Baird	70-69-65-71	275	$30,225
4	Charley Hoffman	66-70-67-64	267	$288,000		40=	Zach Johnson	69-70-70-67	276	$25,800
5=	Luke Guthrie	69-64-71-64	268	$210,750			Harris English	69-67-70-70	276	$25,800
	Troy Matteson	67-69-68-64	268	$210,750			Jhonattan Vegas	68-67-68-73	276	$25,800
	Charles Howell III	67-69-67-65	268	$210,750		43=	Justin Hicks	71-65-72-69	277	$21,000
	Chesson Hadley	65-66-67-70	268	$210,750			Kevin Penner	71-65-72-69	277	$21,000
9=	Freddie Jacobson	67-67-71-64	269	$162,000			Cameron Tringale	66-71-69-71	277	$21,000
	Ryan Moore	69-63-69-68	269	$162,000			Richard Lee	70-69-67-71	277	$21,000
	Jeff Overton	63-68-68-70	269	$162,000			Morgan Hoffmann	67-67-71-72	277	$21,000
12=	Carl Pettersson	68-67-69-66	270	$126,000		48=	Ben Curtis	71-68-72-67	278	$15,864
	Jimmy Walker	71-68-64-67	270	$126,000			Brian Harman	70-67-69-72	278	$15,864
	Brendon Todd	67-68-67-68	270	$126,000			Billy Hurley III	69-70-66-73	278	$15,864
15=	Ken Duke	73-65-68-65	271	$90,000			Nick Watney	73-66-66-73	278	$15,864
	Greg Chalmers	67-68-69-67	271	$90,000			Stephen Ames	65-68-71-74	278	$15,864
	Ricky Barnes	66-71-67-67	271	$90,000		53=	Spencer Levin	69-69-72-69	279	$14,070
	Brian Stuard	68-65-70-68	271	$90,000			Brice Garnett	67-68-73-71	279	$14,070
	Andrew Svoboda	68-67-67-69	271	$90,000			Marc Turnesa	68-69-71-71	279	$14,070
	J.J. Henry	60-71-70-70	271	$90,000			John Senden	65-66-71-77	279	$14,070
	Sean O'Hair	66-72-63-70	271	$90,000		57=	Ted Potter, Jr.	69-68-73-70	280	$13,440
	Will MacKenzie	70-68-68-65	271	$90,000			Jim Herman	70-69-71-70	280	$13,440
23=	Vijay Singh	67-69-70-66	272	$57,600			Brendan Steele	67-67-74-72	280	$13,440
	Brian Davis	68-66-71-67	272	$57,600			Seung-Yul Noh	69-65-72-74	280	$13,440
	Robert Garrigus	69-70-66-67	272	$57,600			Jonathan Byrd	63-72-70-75	280	$13,440
	Stuart Appleby	70-68-65-69	272	$57,600		62=	Davis Love III	69-70-70-72	281	$12,960
	Daniel Summerhays	66-68-68-70	272	$57,600			Ben Crane	68-68-72-73	281	$12,960
28=	James Driscoll	63-72-71-67	273	$45,300			George McNeill	70-67-71-73	281	$12,960
	William McGirt	71-66-64-72	273	$45,300		65=	T. Van Aswegen	70-69-71-72	282	$12,660
30=	John Huh	69-70-69-66	274	$38,150			John Merrick	71-67-70-74	282	$12,660
	Max Homa	69-70-68-67	274	$38,150		67=	Bryce Molder	65-73-72-73	283	$12,420
	Hudson Swafford	68-69-70-67	274	$38,150			Kyle Reifers	69-68-71-75	283	$12,420
	Kevin Stadler	70-65-69-70	274	$38,150		69	Geoff Ogilvy	71-67-75-71	284	$12,240
	Jose Coceres	67-70-67-70	274	$38,150		70	Josh Teater	69-69-74-74	286	$12,120
	Russell Knox	67-65-69-73	274	$38,150		71	Will Claxton	66-73-73-75	287	$12,000
36=	Chris Kirk	68-70-70-67	275	$30,225						

Out Of The Money: **140**: Graham DeLaet, Kyle Stanley, Tim Clark, Heath Slocum, David Duval, Erik Compton, Andres Gonzales, Alex Prugh, Martin Laird, Russell Henley, Robert Allenby, Tommy Gainey, Charlie Beljan, Y.E. Yang, Ryan Palmer, John Peterson **141**: Matt Jones, Camilo Villegas, Chad Collins, Scott Stallings, Derek Ernst, Woody Austin, Martin Flores **142**: Bill Lunde, Scott Brown, Michael Putnam, Danny Lee, Kris Blanks, Mark Wilson, Andrés Romero, Edward Loar **143**: Chez Reavie, Chris Smith, Mike Weir, Alex Aragon, Tim Wilkinson, Jason Kokrak, Charlie Wi, Kevin Na, James Hahn, Scott Gardiner **144**: Kevin Kisner, Trevor Immelman, Brendon de Jonge, Angel Cabrera **145**: David Lingmerth, Jeff Maggert, Scott Langley, Lucas Glover, Bud Cauley, Brooks Koepka **146**: Paul Goydos, Scott Piercy **147**: Ben Martin, Pat Perez **149**: Bob Estes, Don Littrell **150**: David Hearn, Rory Sabbatini **151**: Harrison Frazar **WD**: Patrick Reed

FIRST ROUND		SECOND ROUND		THIRD ROUND	
J.J. Henry	60 (-11)	**Webb Simpson**	127 (-15)	**Webb Simpson**	194 (-19)
Andrés Romero	61 (-10)	J.J. Henry	131 (-11)	Chesson Hadley	198 (-15)
James Driscoll	63 (-8)	John Senden	131 (-11)	Jeff Overton	199 (-14)
Jonathan Byrd	63 (-8)	Jeff Overton	131 (-11)	Jason Bohn	200 (-13)
Jeff Overton	63 (-8)	Chesson Hadley	131 (-11)	6 Players	201 (-12)
Webb Simpson	64 (-7)	Jason Bohn	131 (-11)		

OWR: 7 of top 50 entered - Rating: 187 - Points to 42nd - Simpson: 36 points, to 17th in OWR

CIMB Classic

Kuala Lumpur Golf & Country Club - Kuala Lumpur, Malaysia
Champion: Ryan Moore

Oct 24 - Oct 27
6,951 yards   Par 72
Purse: $7 Million

Thirty-one-year-old Ryan Moore had to work overtime to claim his third career PGA Tour victory, but in the end he emerged victorious in Malaysia's CIMB Classic on the first hole of a Monday morning playoff with fellow American Gary Woodland. An official part of the Tour schedule for the first time, the event drew a limited field of 77 players from the PGA and Asian circuits, and initially saw Keegan Bradley jump out to a commanding four-shot lead at the halfway point behind rounds of 65-65. But after turning in 35 on Saturday, Bradley stumbled badly on the back nine, carding three bogeys and a double bogey en route to a 41 and, eventually, 10th place. That left the door open for Moore and Chris Stroud to share the 54-hole lead on 12-under-par 204 as the field embarked on a long Sunday of golf that was twice interrupted by rain delays totaling over three and a half hours in length. Early on, the spotlight belonged to 24-year-old Kiradech Aphibarnrat, the Asian Tour's runaway Order of Merit leader, who made four quick birdies in a bid to become the first native of Thailand to win an official PGA Tour event. A bogey at the par-5 10th derailed Aphibarnrat's run, however, and he would ultimately share third place with Stroud, who narrowly missed holing a birdie chip at the 634-yard 18th to get to the magic number of 14 under par. Moore managed a clutch up-and-down at the same green to remain at 14 under, leaving Woodland to narrowly miss a 10-foot birdie putt that would have won the title in regulation. But with floodlights already in use as the players finished, officials ruled that the playoff would wait until Monday morning, when Moore promptly birdied the 18th to claim victory.

1	Ryan Moore	63-72-69-70	274	$1.26 mil
2	Gary Woodland	68-70-67-69	274	$756,000
3=	K. Aphibarnrat	67-69-69-70	275	$406,000
	Chris Stroud	67-69-68-71	275	$406,000
5	Aaron Baddeley	73-67-70-66	276	$280,000
6	Jimmy Walker	74-68-67-68	277	$252,000
7=	Charles Howell III	69-72-69-68	278	$218,167
	Harris English	71-67-71-69	278	$218,167
	Graham DeLaet	72-67-68-71	278	$218,167
10	Keegan Bradley	65-66-76-72	279	$189,000
11=	Billy Horschel	72-69-72-67	280	$161,000
	Sergio García	66-71-71-72	280	$161,000
	Stewart Cink	70-68-69-73	280	$161,000
14=	K.J. Choi	68-71-70-72	281	$129,500
	Bryce Molder	73-69-67-72	281	$129,500
16=	Jeff Overton	73-67-72-70	282	$112,000
	Bill Haas	72-67-71-72	282	$112,000
	Shiv Kapur	69-70-71-72	282	$112,000
19	Rickie Fowler	71-72-73-67	283	$81,900
	Kevin Stadler	71-69-73-70	283	$81,900
	Bo Van Pelt	72-77-69-65	283	$81,900
	Phil Mickelson	71-70-68-74	283	$81,900
	Kyle Stanley	73-67-68-75	283	$81,900
	Jerry Kelly	71-69-66-77	283	$81,900
25=	Siddikur Rahman	75-70-69-70	284	$53,433
	Brendan Steele	74-70-72-68	284	$53,433
	Kevin Chappell	73-71-72-68	284	$53,433
	Chris Kirk	67-71-72-74	284	$53,433
	Hideki Matsuyama	70-68-7274	284	$53,433
	Jonas Blixt	72-70-68-74	284	$53,433
31=	Bubba Watson	78-69-65-73	285	$44,450
	Tim Clark	72-69-70-74	285	$44,450
33=	Boo Weekley	67-74-72-73	286	$40,425
	Gaganjeet Bhullar	72-70-71-73	286	$40,425
35=	Michael Thompson	75-71-68-73	287	$34,510
	Richard Lee	70-73-72-72	287	$34,510
	Roberto Castro	74-70-70-73	287	$34,510
	Nick Watney	75-69-70-73	287	$34,510
	Anirban Lahiri	74-70-75-68	287	$34,510
40=	Matt Jones	73-71-71-73	288	$28,000
	Nicholas Thompson	69-71-76-72	288	$28,000
	Scott Hend	74-72-71-71	288	$28,000
	Patrick Reed	74-71-72-71	288	$28,000
44=	Marc Leishman	72-65-77-75	289	$23,100
	Camilo Villegas	70-71-73-75	289	$23,100
	Prayad Marksaeng	74-71-71-73	289	$23,100
47=	Retief Goosen	72-74-69-75	290	$18,223
	Berry Henson	74-71-72-73	290	$18,223
	Ernie Els	76-71-69-74	290	$18,223
	Brian Gay	72-72-74-72	290	$18,223
	Matt Every	72-77-68-73	290	$18,223
	Scott Stallings	73-70-78-69	290	$18,223
53=	Charley Hoffman	69-72-74-76	291	$15,908
	Ryan Palmer	76-68-71-76	291	$15,908
	John Huh	71-74-69-77	291	$15,908
	Brendon de Jonge	72-71-73-75	291	$15,908
	Rory Sabbatini	67-74-75-75	291	$15,908
	Kevin Streelman	72-73-71-75	291	$15,908
	Daniel Summerhays	75-69-73-74	291	$15,908
	Josh Teater	74-66-72-79	291	$15,908
61=	Martin Laird	68-70-76-78	292	$15,190
	Russell Henley	71-74-72-75	292	$15,190
63	Nicholas Fung	74-78-71-70	293	$14,980
64=	David Lynn	75-70-71-79	295	$14,630
	John Merrick	77-75-69-74	295	$14,630
	Lucas Glover	71-75-75-74	295	$14,630
	David Lingmerth	73-78-73-71	295	$14,630
68=	David Hearn	72-70-73-81	296	$14,070
	Wade Ormsby	70-69-74-83	296	$14,070
	D.A. Points	71-76-73-76	296	$14,070
	Sang-Moon Bae	80-71-74-71	296	$14,070
72	Scott Brown	77-72-75-74	298	$13,720
73	Cameron Tringale	79-77-71-75	302	$13,580
74	Martin Flores	73-79-74-78	304	$13,440
75=	Brian Davis	79-75-74-78	306	$13,230
	Rashid Ismail	73-76-80-77	306	$13,230
77=	John Rollins	74-76-77-82	309	$12,950
	Seuk-Hyun Baek	80-72-82-75	309	$12,950

FIRST ROUND		SECOND ROUND		THIRD ROUND	
Ryan Moore	63 (-9)	Keegan Bradley	131 (-13)	**Ryan Moore**	204 (-12)
Keegan Bradley	65 (-7)	**Ryan Moore**	135 (-9)	Chris Stroud	204 (-12)
Sergio García	66 (-6)	Chris Stroud	136 (-8)	Gary Woodland	205 (-11)
5 Players	67 (-5)	Kiradech Aphibarnrat	136 (-8)	Kiradech Aphibarnrat	205 (-11)
		2 Players	137 (-7)	Jerry Kelly	206 (-10)

OWR: 16 of top 50 entered - Rating: 302 - Points to 52nd - Moore: 48 points, to 31st in OWR

Eligibility for the 2013 CIMB Classic

The top 60 available players from the 2013 final FedEx Cup Points list; The top 10 available money leaders from the Asian Tour Order of Merit as of October 7, 2013; Eight sponsor exemptions: One designated for the defending champion, if needed, and five restricted to players who are PGA TOUR members. Two Malaysians will qualify – one via the SapuraKencana National Qualifier (held August 26 – 28, 2013) and one via the Official World Golf Ranking. If necessary to fill the field to 78 players, additional players from 2013 final FedEx Cup Points list.

WGC-HSBC Champions

Sheshan International Golf Club - Shanghai, China
Champion: Dustin Johnson

Oct 31 - Nov 3
7,266 yards   Par 72
Purse: $8.5 Million

Twenty-nine-year-old Dustin Johnson didn't wait long to extend his impressive streak of claiming at least one PGA Tour victory in every season since joining the Tour directly out of college. Having previously logged a total of seven victories since 2008, he grabbed his first 2014 triumph while the calendar still read 2013, riding some inspired golf - and a well-timed eagle at the 70th hole - to a three-shot triumph at the newest of the World Golf Championship events, the WGC-HSBC Champions in China. After opening with a 69, Johnson seized the halfway lead on the back of a Friday 63, then appeared on the verge of running away on Saturday before double-bogeys at both the 10th and the par-5 18th clipped a potential seven-shot lead down to three. An opening bogey on Sunday added another brief flash of doubt, and on a day where benign conditions allowed a number of world-class players to make a run, Johnson actually trailed Ian Poulter by one through 12. Back-to-back birdies at the 13th and 14th put him back on top, however, setting up the coup de grâce: a chip-in eagle at the short par-4 16th, where a smart 3 iron off the tee had left him little more than 30 yards from the pin. Poulter, meanwhile, played nearly flawless golf during a seven-birdie round of 66, save for an untimely bogey at the par-4 15th. Nonetheless, the defending champion managed to hold solo second, one shot ahead of Graeme McDowell (whose own 66 might have been better had his putter not cooled down the stretch) and two up on Sergio García, who closed with a Sunday-low round of 63. Also a winner was Rory McIlroy, whose tie for 6th went a long way in assuring him a spot in the lucrative Tour Championship, scheduled to be played two weeks hence in Dubai.

1	Dustin Johnson	69-63-66-66	264	$1.4 mil			David Lynn	74-70-69-71	284	$58,000
2	Ian Poulter	71-67-63-66	267	$850,000			Chris Wood	71-71-73-69	284	$58,000
3	Graeme McDowell	69-69-64-66	268	$480,000			Thomas Bjørn	74-72-70-68	284	$58,000
4	Sergio García	70-68-69-63	270	$365,000			Hao-Tong Li	72-71-74-67	284	$58,000
5	Justin Rose	68-71-65-68	272	$300,000			Gon. F'dez-Castaño	67-71-70-76	284	$58,000
6=	Graham DeLaet	71-68-65-69	273	$231,500			Richard Sterne	74-73-74-63	284	$58,000
	Rory McIlroy	65-72-67-69	273	$231,500		46=	Jimmy Walker	73-73-69-70	285	$52,500
8=	Jamie Donaldson	67-74-66-67	274	$161,667			Thongchai Jaidee	76-68-68-73	285	$52,500
	Martin Kaymer	70-74-62-68	274	$161,667			Ken Duke	70-72-73-70	285	$52,500
	Bubba Watson	68-69-69-68	274	$161,667			Brian Gay	71-72-72-70	285	$52,500
11=	Ernie Els	69-69-71-66	275	$116,667		50=	Hiroyuki Fujita	75-70-68-73	286	$49,000
	Keegan Bradley	71-68-68-68	275	$116,667			Michael Thompson	74-72-68-72	286	$49,000
	Boo Weekley	70-67-69-69	275	$116,667			Ryan Moore	70-74-69-73	286	$49,000
14	Phil Mickelson	71-68-72-65	276	$100,000			Masahiro Kawamura	73-72-70-71	286	$49,000
15=	Wen-Chong Liang	72-67-72-66	277	$93,500			Michael Hendry	72-73-73-68	286	$49,000
	Louis Oosthuizen	70-70-70-67	277	$93,500		55=	K. Aphibarnrat	69-78-68-72	287	$46,250
17	Jordan Spieth	68-71-70-69	278	$90,000			Rickie Fowler	74-70-70-73	287	$46,250
18=	Yeon-Jin Jeong	70-69-71-69	279	$87,000			Lee Westwood	71-73-68-75	287	$46,250
	Tommy Fleetwood	68-70-69-72	279	$87,000			John Merrick	72-75-69-71	287	$46,250
20	Paul Casey	69-73-69-69	280	$84,000			Brandt Snedeker	73-74-70-70	287	$46,250
21=	Bill Haas	72-72-69-68	281	$75,100			Peter Uihlein	71-73-73-70	287	$46,250
	Scott Piercy	72-73-68-68	281	$75,100		61=	Derek Ernst	71-72-73-72	288	$44,250
	Jaco Van Zyl	72-73-68-68	281	$75,100			Darren Fichardt	70-74-75-69	288	$44,250
	Mikko Ilonen	72-69-72-68	281	$75,100		63=	Gaganjeet Bhullar	69-71-75-74	289	$43,500
	Peter Hanson	70-73-70-68	281	$75,100			Stephen Gallacher	73-73-72-71	289	$43,500
	Matteo Manassero	72-70-70-69	281	$75,100			Jonas Blixt	70-75-74-70	289	$43,500
	Francesco Molinari	72-69-70-70	281	$75,100		66=	Daniel Popovic	77-71-69-73	290	$42,875
	Grégory Bourdy	75-68-67-71	281	$75,100			Ryo Ishikawa	81-72-68-69	290	$42,875
	Bo Van Pelt	77-67-66-71	281	$75,100		68=	D.A. Points	72-74-70-75	291	$42,375
	Scott Hend	69-74-66-72	281	$75,100			A Shun Wu	74-75-70-72	291	$42,375
31=	Nick Watney	75-74-67-66	282	$68,000		70	David Howell	72-75-73-72	292	$42,000
	Luke Donald	70-71-70-71	282	$68,000		71	Seuk-Hyun Baek	81-68-69-75	293	$41,750
	Henrik Stenson	74-76-67-65	282	$68,000		72	Miguel A. Jiménez	75-76-70-74	295	$41,500
34=	Wen-Yi Huang	70-74-69-70	283	$64,000		73	Raphaël Jacquelin	81-70-71-74	296	$41,250
	Mark Brown	72-68-72-71	283	$64,000		74	George Coetzee	75-77-74-71	297	$41,000
	Billy Horschel	71-69-72-71	283	$64,000		75	Mu Hu	76-75-73-75	299	$40,750
	Kevin Streelman	70-73-72-68	283	$64,000		76	Brett Rumford	75-77-79-72	303	$40,500
	Jason Dufner	73-67-71-72	283	$64,000		77	Ming Jie Huang	83-77-80-83	323	$40,250
39=	Branden Grace	77-71-67-69	284	$58,000						

Out Of The Money: WD: Hideki Matsuyama (71)

FIRST ROUND		SECOND ROUND		THIRD ROUND	
Rory McIlroy	65 (-7)	**Dustin Johnson**	132 (-12)	**Dustin Johnson**	198 (-18)
Gon. F'dez-Castaño	67 (-5)	Rory McIlroy	137 (-7)	Ian Poulter	201 (-15)
Jamie Donaldson	67 (-5)	Bubba Watson	137 (-7)	Graeme McDowell	202 (-14)
4 Players	68 (-4)	Boo Weekley	137 (-7)	3 Players	204 (-12)
Dustin Johnson	69 (-3)	5 Players	138 (-6)		

OWR: 39 of top 50 entered - Rating: 574 - Points to 60th - Johnson: 66 points, to 12th in OWR

Eligibility for the 2013 WGC- HSBC Champions

Approximately 78 players, consisting of tournament winners from around the world and the best players from the International Federation of PGA Tours, as dictated by each Tour's money list, order of merit, etc.

McGladrey Classic

Sea Island Golf Club (Seaside) - Sea Island, GA
Champion: Chris Kirk

Nov 7 - Nov 10
7,055 yards Par 70
Purse: $5.5 Million

Former University of Georgia star and Sea Island resident Chris Kirk won for the second time on the PGA Tour, holding his game together over an exciting back nine to edge a charging Tim Clark and a fading Briny Baird by one at the McGladrey Classic. In truth, the finish was more about Baird's late-round struggles, which began at the par-5 15th where, having birdied the 13th and 14th, he stood poised to take complete command as he faced a 40-footer for eagle. Instead, Baird three-putted for par, Kirk rolled in a 20-footer for a scrambling par of his own, and what seemed destined to become a two- or three-stroke lead remained only one. Kirk would eventually tie with a clutch birdie at the par-3 17th, leaving the outcome to be determined at the 470-yard finisher, where Baird promptly topped his second out of a fairway bunker en route to a bogey, allowing Kirk to clinch the title with a routine par. Waiting on the range for a possible playoff was Clark, who'd began Sunday's round five strokes off the lead before uncorking a nine-birdie round of 62 that was marred only by a bogey at the par-4 14th. Scott Brown, Australian John Senden and first-round leader Brian Gay tied for fourth, two shots back. For Kirk, the hometown victory was especially sweet in that it also earned him his first bid to The Masters. For Baird, who failed to win for a Tour-leading 365th straight start, the pain was tempered somewhat by his $484,000 paycheck – more than enough to help him beat the odds and clear a Medical Extension dating to 2012 surgeries on both of his shoulders.

1	Chris Kirk	66-66-68-66	266	$990,000		Ted Potter, Jr.	67-67-72-72	278	$26,469
2=	Tim Clark	67-67-71-62	267	$484,000		Chad Campbell	70-70-71-67	278	$26,469
	Briny Baird	63-70-67-67	267	$484,000	40=	Aaron Baddeley	68-71-70-70	279	$19,800
4=	Scott Brown	66-68-68-66	268	$227,333		Lucas Glover	69-72-68-70	279	$19,800
	Brian Gay	63-72-66-67	268	$227,333		Woody Austin	68-73-68-70	279	$19,800
	John Senden	66-67-68-67	268	$227,333		David Hearn	74-66-70-69	279	$19,800
7=	Matt Every	67-68-69-66	270	$171,417		Will Claxton	65-71-71-72	279	$19,800
	Webb Simpson	65-68-71-66	270	$171,417		Troy Matteson	71-69-70-69	279	$19,800
	Matt Kuchar	68-68-68-66	270	$171,417		Danny Lee	70-71-70-68	279	$19,800
10=	Greg Chalmers	68-68-72-64	272	$121,917		Camilo Villegas	66-74-72-67	279	$19,800
	Robert Karlsson	68-68-71-65	272	$121,917	48=	Mark Wilson	70-71-68-71	280	$13,671
	Brian Harman	67-68-70-67	272	$121,917		Eric Axley	71-70-68-71	280	$13,671
	Daniel Summerhays	69-66-69-68	272	$121,917		Pat Perez	68-71-72-69	280	$13,671
	Jason Kokrak	69-65-69-69	272	$121,917		J.J. Henry	67-72-72-69	280	$13,671
	Kevin Stadler	68-68-65-71	272	$121,917		James Hahn	69-72-73-66	280	$13,671
16=	Brendon de Jonge	67-71-70-65	273	$85,250		Michael Putnam	68-73-72-67	280	$13,671
	Heath Slocum	67-71-69-66	273	$85,250		Josh Broadaway	72-68-75-65	280	$13,671
	Zach Johnson	70-68-68-67	273	$85,250	55=	Kyle Stanley	68-71-70-72	281	$12,320
	Brendon Todd	68-67-67-71	273	$85,250		Mike Weir	70-71-68-72	281	$12,320
20=	Trevor Immelman	67-72-70-65	274	$68,750		Spencer Levin	69-70-71-71	281	$12,320
	Kevin Kisner	65-73-70-66	274	$68,750		Jonathan Byrd	66-69-72-74	281	$12,320
22=	Boo Weekley	67-69-73-66	275	$52,800		Martin Flores	70-68-72-71	281	$12,320
	Charley Hoffman	66-73-68-68	275	$52,800		Blake Adams	73-68-73-67	281	$12,320
	George McNeill	62-76-68-69	275	$52,800		Carl Pettersson	66-74-75-66	281	$12,320
	Robert Garrigus	65-74-67-69	275	$52,800	62=	Steven Bowditch	68-73-68-73	282	$11,880
	Scott Langley	66-71-68-70	275	$52,800	63=	Scott Piercy	67-73-71-72	283	$11,715
27=	Harris English	68-70-71-67	276	$39,050		Erik Compton	68-73-76-66	283	$11,715
	David Toms	68-73-68-67	276	$39,050	65=	Retief Goosen	68-71-69-76	284	$11,385
	Seung-Yul Noh	65-70-73-68	276	$39,050		Darren Clarke	69-70-71-74	284	$11,385
	Cameron Tringale	70-69-68-69	276	$39,050		Russell Henley	69-71-71-73	284	$11,385
	Charles Howell III	69-70-66-71	276	$39,050		Justin Leonard	71-70-73-70	284	$11,385
32=	Ben Curtis	68-69-72-68	277	$31,831	69	Andrés Romero	70-69-72-74	285	$11,110
	Kevin Chappell	65-68-74-70	277	$31,831	70=	D.H. Lee	67-70-71-78	286	$10,945
	John Rollins	65-76-66-70	277	$31,831		Rory Sabbatini	66-73-73-74	286	$10,945
	Russell Knox	70-71-69-67	277	$31,831	72=	Paul Goydos	68-71-76-72	287	$10,725
36=	Stuart Appleby	68-70-71-69	278	$26,469		Y.E. Yang	68-71-76-72	287	$10,725
	Brice Garnett	67-72-67-72	278	$26,469					

Out Of The Money: **142:** Robert Allenby, Jose Coceres, Brian Davis, Chris DiMarco, Luke Guthrie, Fredrik Jacobson, Ben Martin, William McGirt, Kevin Na, Jeff Overton, Vijay Singh, Lee Williams **143:** Mark Calcavecchia, Joe Durant, Fred Funk, Jim Herman, Andrew Svoboda, Hudson Swafford **144:** Bud Cauley, Ben Crane, Harrison Frazar, Tommy Gainey, Justin Hicks, Steve Marino, Sean O'Hair, John Peterson, Scott Stallings, Tyrone Van Aswegen **145:** Jason Bohn, Stewart Cink, Scott Gardiner, Richard H. Lee, Will MacKenzie, Chris Stroud, James Vargas **146:** Stephen Ames, Charlie Beljan, Chad Collins, James Driscoll, David Duval, Chesson Hadley, Troy Merritt, Wes Roach, Scott Verplank **147:** Morgan Hoffmann, Brian Stuard **148:** Brad Fritsch, Billy Hurley II, Kyle Reifers, Justin Thomas, Kevin Tway **149:** Davis Love III **150:** Johnson Wagner **151:** Edward Loar **152:** Hunter Hamrick **153:** Nicholas Thompson **159:** Craig Stevens **WD:** Kris Blanks (74), Jerry Kelly (75)

FIRST ROUND		SECOND ROUND		THIRD ROUND	
George McNeill	62 (-8)	**Chris Kirk**	132 (-8)	**Chris Kirk**	200 (-10)
Brian Gay	63 (-7)	Kevin Chappell	133 (-7)	Briny Baird	200 (-10)
Briny Baird	63 (-7)	Webb Simpson	133 (-7)	Kevin Stadler	201 (-9)
7 Players	65 (-5)	John Senden	133 (-7)	Brian Gay	201 (-9)
Chris Kirk	66 (-4)	Briny Baird	133 (-7)	John Senden	201 (-9)

OWR: 5 of top 50 entered - Rating: 152 - Points to 39th - Kirk: 32 points, to 56th in OWR

OHL Classic at Mayakoba

El Camaleon - Riviera Maya, Mexico
Champion: Harris English

Nov 14 - Nov 17
6,987 yards   Par 71
Purse: $6 Million

Though it officially counted as a part of the new, wraparound 2014 schedule, 24-year-old Harris English claimed his second PGA Tour victory of calendar 2013 at the OHL Classic at Mayakoba, riding a final round 65 to a four-shot victory over Brian Stuard in Playa Del Carmen, Mexico. In an event plagued by enough rain to cause both Friday and Saturday's rounds to be finished the following mornings (and lift, clean and place rules to be in effect), English opened with a 68 before pressing into contention with a weather-interrupted, bogey-free second round 62. A third round 68 then left him one behind 54-hole leader Robert Karlsson, and an early bogey at the par-4 2nd got his final round off to a disappointing start. But having gained valuable experience from winning the FedEx St. Jude Classic back in June, English was able to retain his focus and quickly mount a charge, birdieing four of his next six to join the heart of the battle, then opening a multi-shot lead with additional birdies at the 10th, 11th and 13th. Despite battling his driver much of the day, Karlsson still remained in contention at this point (largely due an earlier eagle at the par-5 5th) but soon wilted under the sort of back nine pressure that a swing-related slump had recently kept him isolated from. Indeed, a bogey, bogey, double-bogey run at holes 12-14 ultimately dropped him to a tie for sixth, leaving third-year player Stuard to claim solo second (via a closing 65), while Jason Bohn, Chris Stroud and Rory Sabbatini shared third.

1	Harris English	68-62-68-65 263	$1.08 mil		Camilo Villegas	70-67-67-73 277	$25,833
2	Brian Stuard	65-70-65-67 267	$648,000		Erik Compton	67-69-71-70 277	$25,833
3=	Jason Bohn	67-68-65-68 268	$312,000		Scott Gardiner	70-70-69-68 277	$25,833
	Chris Stroud	66-68-66-68 268	$312,000		Kevin Na	71-70-71-65 277	$25,833
	Rory Sabbatini	68-65-65-70 268	$312,000		Tim Clark	71-70-63-73 277	$25,833
6=	Justin Leonard	70-67-65-67 269	$194,250	45=	Joe Durant	70-68-71-69 278	$18,060
	Justin Hicks	69-67-66-67 269	$194,250		William McGirt	70-68-74-66 278	$18,060
	Charles Howell III	67-67-66-69 269	$194,250		Jhonattan Vegas	66-68-71-73 278	$18,060
	Robert Karlsson	63-67-67-72 269	$194,250		Brian Gay	70-71-67-70 278	$18,060
10=	Bob Estes	68-69-65-69 271	$156,000	49=	T. Van Aswegen	69-69-71-70 279	$14,660
	Tim Wilkinson	70-63-71-67 271	$156,000		Len Mattiace	69-68-69-73 279	$14,660
12=	Will MacKenzie	69-69-69-65 272	$126,000		Brendon Todd	71-66-70-72 279	$14,660
	Fredrik Jacobson	70-69-67-66 272	$126,000		Jose Coceres	68-69-72-70 279	$14,660
	Kevin Stadler	67-63-68-74 272	$126,000		Morgan Hoffmann	69-71-72-67 279	$14,660
15	Peter Malnati	69-69-70-65 273	$108,000		Oscar Fraustro	72-68-69-70 279	$14,660
16=	Robert Allenby	70-68-66-70 274	$84,171	55=	Spencer Levin	70-68-65-77 280	$13,560
	Álvaro Quirós	67-70-66-71 274	$84,171		Cameron Beckman	72-67-71-70 280	$13,560
	Brendan Steele	70-66-68-70 274	$84,171		Seung-Yul Noh	69-70-71-70 280	$13,560
	Jay McLuen	67-69-69-69 274	$84,171		Luke Guthrie	71-70-70-69 280	$13,560
	Jeff Maggert	69-66-69-70 274	$84,171		Lee Williams	73-68-67-72 280	$13,560
	Scott Brown	69-66-67-72 274	$84,171	60=	Greg Chalmers	70-70-66-75 281	$12,960
	Pat Perez	66-68-71-69 274	$84,171		Ben Curtis	72-68-70-71 281	$12,960
23=	John Huh	70-68-71-66 275	$49,350		Kevin Kisner	65-75-67-74 281	$12,960
	Jeff Overton	68-70-70-67 275	$49,350		Ryan Palmer	70-71-67-73 281	$12,960
	Wes Roach	67-70-68-70 275	$49,350		Kyle Stanley	73-68-67-73 281	$12,960
	J.J. Henry	72-65-70-68 275	$49,350	65=	Billy Hurley III	69-69-72-72 282	$12,420
	Chad Collins	69-67-70-69 275	$49,350		Jamie Lovemark	68-69-70-75 282	$12,420
	Tommy Gainey	71-65-68-71 275	$49,350		Lucas Glover	70-70-70-72 282	$12,420
	Josh Teater	68-73-67-67 275	$49,350		John Senden	73-68-72-69 282	$12,420
	Ryan Moore	67-67-71-70 275	$49,350	69=	Derek Ernst	69-70-72-72 283	$12,000
31=	Matt Jones	69-69-68-70 276	$35,580		Tag Ridings	70-69-74-70 283	$12,000
	Russell Knox	67-70-68-71 276	$35,580		Brian Davis	71-70-71-71 283	$12,000
	James Driscoll	69-68-68-71 276	$35,580	72=	Martin Flores	69-71-74-71 285	$11,700
	Ben Martin	69-70-68-69 276	$35,580		Richard H. Lee	75-65-72-73 285	$11,700
	Charley Hoffman	73-68-68-67 276	$35,580	74	Y.E. Yang	74-67-70-75 286	$11,520
36=	Michael Putnam	69-69-69-70 277	$25,833	75=	David Duval	67-73-75-73 288	$11,340
	Matt Every	71-67-68-71 277	$25,833		Mike Weir	72-69-72-75 288	$11,340
	Davis Love III	69-68-68-72 277	$25,833	77	Darren Clarke	71-68-73-78 290	$11,160
	Tim Petrovic	71-68-70-68 277	$25,833				

Out Of The Money: 142: Blake Adams, Briny Baird, Brice Garnett, Robert Garrigus, Brian Harman, Jerry Kelly, Scott Langley, Andrew Loupe, Steve Marino, Joe Ogilvie, Jim Renner, Scott Stallings **143**: Miguel Ángel Carballo, Bud Cauley, Will Claxton, Brooks Koepka, Danny Lee, Dicky Pride, Alex Prugh, Heath Slocum, Daniel Summerhays, Hudson Swafford, Esteban Toledo, Cameron Tringale, Mark Wilson **144**: Stephen Ames, Trevor Immelman, Jose de Jesus Rodriguez, Kevin Tway **145**: Ricky Barnes, Harrison Frazar, Chesson Hadley **146**: David Lingmerth, Troy Matteson, John Rollins, Scott Verplank, Johnson Wagner **147**: Jordi García Pinto, James Hahn, D.H. Lee, Sean O'Hair, Andrew Svoboda **149**: Alex Aragon, Steven Bowditch **150**: Bobby Gates, Bronson La'Cassie **153**: Roberto Diaz **154**: Edward Loar **WD**: Jim Herman (71), Stuart Appleby (74), Fred Funk (75), George McNeill (75), Scott Piercy (76), Andrés Romero

FIRST ROUND		SECOND ROUND		THIRD ROUND	
Robert Karlsson	63 (-8)	Robert Karlsson	130 (-12)	Robert Karlsson	197 (-16)
Brian Stuard	65 (-6)	Kevin Stadler	130 (-12)	**Harris English**	198 (-15)
Kevin Kisner	65 (-6)	**Harris English**	130 (-12)	Rory Sabbatini	198 (-15)
3 Players	66 (-5)	Rory Sabbatini	133 (-9)	Kevin Stadler	198 (-15)
Harris English	68 (-3)	Tim Wilkinson	133 (-9)	4 Players	200 (-13)

OWR: 2 of top 50 entered - Rating: 84 - Points to 30th - English: 24 points, to 54th in OWR

Hyundai Tournament of Champions

Jan 3 - Jan 6

Plantation Course at Kapalua - Kapalua, HI
Champion: Zach Johnson

7,411 yards Par 73
Purse: $5.7 Million

The PGA Tour's hottest player at the close of 2013 didn't miss a beat in opening the new year, as Zach Johnson recovered from a disappointing third-round 74 by firing a closing 66 to win the season-opening Hyundai Tournament of Champions in Hawaii. After taking a strong three-shot lead at the halfway mark, Johnson struggled to get anything going in the third round, posting two late bogeys en route to the 74 which left him two in arrears of Dustin Johnson, Jordan Spieth and Webb Simpson. But in the scheduled Monday finale, the 37-year-old from Cedar Rapids, Iowa methodically took apart the par-73 Plantation Course, eventually pulling away from a crowded list of pursuers first by birdieing the 12th, then by adding three straight birdies at holes 14-16. Among the overnight leaders, only Spieth remained in serious contention, holding the lead prior to Johnson's back nine explosion, then carding late birdies at the 17th and 18th to make the final margin of victory only one. Third place was shared by Kevin Streelman (who closed with 67) and the 2012 U.S. Open champion Simpson, who carded early Monday bogeys at the 3rd and 4th to blow himself from contention before adding five subsequent birdies to close with 70. Defending champion Dustin Johnson, meanwhile, opened with bogeys at the 1st and 2nd, then largely buried his hopes with one more bogey at the par-4 6th before ultimately tying for sixth with a closing 73. The victory was Johnson's third in his last six starts (counting the unofficial Northwestern Mutual World Challenge) and the 11th of his career; since his rookie season of 2004, only Tiger Woods, Phil Mickelson and Vijay Singh have won more times on the PGA Tour.

1	Zach Johnson	67-66-74-66	273	$1.14 mil		16=	Michael Thompson	66-71-73-72	282	$100,250
2	Jordan Spieth	66-70-69-69	274	$665,000			Ken Duke	70-69-71-72	282	$100,250
3=	Kevin Streelman	67-71-70-67	275	$382,000			Chris Kirk	66-75-68-73	282	$100,250
	Webb Simpson	66-71-68-70	275	$382,000			Patrick Reed	70-72-67-73	282	$100,250
5	Jason Dufner	67-72-69-69	277	$276,000		20	Martin Laird	71-72-70-70	283	$87,000
6=	Billy Horschel	72-72-68-66	278	$198,750		21=	Jonas Blixt	76-70-69-70	285	$79,333
	Matt Kuchar	68-68-75-67	278	$198,750			Sang-Moon Bae	69-73-71-72	285	$79,333
	Adam Scott	70-70-69-69	278	$198,750			Jimmy Walker	73-73-67-72	285	$79,333
	Dustin Johnson	70-66-69-73	278	$198,750		24=	Bill Haas	71-73-69-74	287	$71,500
10	Ryan Moore	67-71-72-69	279	$170,000			Scott Brown	71-73-68-75	287	$71,500
11=	Harris English	70-71-70-69	280	$155,000		26	Boo Weekley	71-74-70-73	288	$68,000
	Brandt Snedeker	70-69-69-72	280	$155,000		27	Russell Henley	72-72-70-75	289	$66,000
13=	Brian Gay	70-76-65-70	281	$130,000		28=	D.A. Points	72-74-73-73	292	$63,000
	Woody Austin	72-70-68-71	281	$130,000			John Merrick	71-76-71-74	292	$63,000
	Gary Woodland	71-70-67-73	281	$130,000		30	Derek Ernst	79-76-76-70	301	$61,000

FIRST ROUND		SECOND ROUND		THIRD ROUND	
Michael Thompson	66 (-7)	**Zach Johnson**	133 (-13)	Webb Simpson	205 (-14)
Chris Kirk	66 (-7)	Dustin Johnson	136 (-10)	Jordan Spieth	205 (-14)
Jordan Spieth	66 (-7)	Matt Kuchar	136 (-10)	Dustin Johnson	205 (-14)
Webb Simpson	66 (-7)	Jordan Spieth	136 (-10)	**Zach Johnson**	207 (-12)
4 Players	67 (-6)	2 Players	137 (-9)	4 Players	208 (-11)
Zach Johnson	67 (-6)				

OWR: 13 of top 50 entered - Rating: 259 - Points to 30th - Johnson: 46 points, to 7th in OWR

2013 PGA Tour Winners (Players Eligible For Hyundai T of C Field)

Hyundai Tournament of Champions:	Dustin Johnson	HP Byron Nelson Championship:	Sang-Moon Bae
Sony Open In Hawaii:	Russell Henley	Crowne Plaza Invitational at Colonial:	Boo Weekley
Humana Challenge:	Brian Gay	Memorial Tournament:	Matt Kuchar
Farmers Insurance Open:	Tiger Woods *	FedEx St Jude Classic:	Harris English
Waste Management Phoenix Open:	Phil Mickelson *	U.S. Open:	Justin Rose *
AT&T Pebble Beach National Pro-Am:	Brandt Snedeker	Travelers Championship:	Ken Duke
Northern Trust Open:	John Merrick	AT&T National:	Bill Haas
WGC-Accenture Match Play:	Matt Kuchar	Greenbrier Classic:	Jonas Blixt
Honda Classic:	Michael Thompson	John Deere Classic:	Jordan Spieth
WGC-Cadillac Championship:	Tiger Woods *	Open Championship:	Phil Mickelson *
Puerto Rico Open:	Scott Brown	Sanderson Farms Championship:	Woody Austin
Tampa Bay Championship:	Kevin Streelman	RBC Canadian Open:	Brandt Snedeker
Arnold Palmer Invitational:	Tiger Woods *	WGC-Bridgestone Invitational:	Tiger Woods *
Shell Houston Open:	D.A. Points	Reno-Tahoe Open:	Gary Woodland
Valero Texas Open:	Martin Laird	PGA Championship:	Jason Dufner
The Masters:	Adam Scott	Wyndham Championship:	Patrick Reed
RBC Heritage:	Graeme McDowell *	The Barclays:	Adam Scott
Zurich Classic of New Orleans:	Billy Horschel	Deutsche Bank Championship:	Henrik Stenson *
Wells Fargo Championship:	Derek Ernst	BMW Championship:	Zach Johnson
Players Championship:	Tiger Woods *	Tour Championship:	Henrik Stenson *

* Eligible winners not in the Hyundai Tournament of Champions field

Sony Open in Hawaii

Waialae Country Club - Honolulu, HI
Champion: Jimmy Walker

Jan 9 - Jan 12
7,068 yards   Par 70
Purse: $5.6 Million

It took Jimmy Walker seven years to land his first PGA Tour victory at the 2013 Frys.com Open but only three months to claim his second, as he tore through the field with a closing 63 to win the Sony Open in Hawaii, in Honolulu. Walker began the day two strokes behind 54-hole leader Chris Kirk and on a day when scoring was predictably low at the Waialae Country Club, did little more than stay in the mix after carding three birdies in his first 10 holes. But following another birdie at the par-4 13th and a clutch up-and-down for par at the 14th, Walker then poured in three straight birdies to seemingly take command, gaining the lead when Harris English made bogey at the 15th, then stretching it to three with additional birdies at the 16th (from seven feet) and the seaside par-3 17th (from six feet). A birdie at the par-5 finisher would have salted away the victory but when Walker could do no better than five, he had to look on nervously as Kirk made a late charge, birdieing the 17th and leaving himself a makeable 30-foot eagle chip at the last that would have forced a playoff. But Kirk missed, leaving him alone in second place and Walker as the champion. Third place was claimed by 47-year-old Jerry Kelly (who closed with the day's second lowest round, a 65) while fourth went to English who, like both Walker and Kirk, was looking or his second win of the season within the PGA Tour's new wraparound schedule.

1	Jimmy Walker	66-67-67-63	263	$1.008 mil		Ben Martin	67-69-68-70	274	$22,400
2	Chris Kirk	64-69-65-66	264	$604,800		Brice Garnett	67-71-67-69	274	$22,400
3	Jerry Kelly	67-67-66-65	265	$380,800		Charlie Beljan	68-70-69-67	274	$22,400
4	Harris English	66-66-67-67	266	$268,800		Charlie Wi	69-70-68-67	274	$22,400
5	Marc Leishman	67-64-71-65	267	$224,000		Peter Malnati	69-69-70-66	274	$22,400
6	Brian Stuard	65-65-71-67	268	$201,600	46=	Tim Wilkinson	71-67-67-70	275	$15,523
7	Jeff Overton	68-68-65-68	269	$187,600		Chad Collins	71-67-68-69	275	$15,523
8=	Charles Howell III	71-67-66-66	270	$119,000		James Hahn	67-68-71-69	275	$15,523
	Adam Scott	67-66-71-66	270	$119,000		Daniel Summerhays	66-71-70-68	275	$15,523
	Matt Kuchar	68-68-68-66	270	$119,000		William McGirt	67-72-68-68	275	$15,523
	Kevin Na	70-67-67-66	270	$119,000	51=	Tim Herron	68-70-66-72	276	$12,902
	Matt Every	69-65-69-67	270	$119,000		Y.E. Yang	73-66-66-71	276	$12,902
	Hudson Swafford	70-64-69-67	270	$119,000		Greg Chalmers	68-66-69-73	276	$12,902
	Ryan Palmer	65-70-67-68	270	$119,000		D.A. Points	70-69-67-70	276	$12,902
	Zach Johnson	68-67-66-69	270	$119,000		Russell Henley	73-65-69-69	276	$12,902
	Hideto Tanihara	66-65-70-69	270	$119,000		John Rollins	69-68-70-69	276	$12,902
	Retief Goosen	66-69-66-69	270	$119,000		Steven Bowditch	72-66-69-69	276	$12,902
	Pat Perez	68-67-66-69	270	$119,000		Mark Wilson	68-68-71-69	276	$12,902
	Will Wilcox	69-66-64-71	270	$119,000		Justin Hicks	69-69-70-68	276	$12,902
20=	Ryuji Imada	67-69-68-67	271	$54,818		Brendon de Jonge	68-71-69-68	276	$12,902
	Stewart Cink	69-69-66-67	271	$54,818	61=	Seung-Yul Noh	70-66-69-72	277	$12,040
	K.J. Choi	67-69-69-66	271	$54,818		T. Van Aswegen	69-69-66-73	277	$12,040
	Jason Kokrak	66-67-70-68	271	$54,818		John Senden	72-67-68-70	277	$12,040
	Chris Stroud	68-65-70-68	271	$54,818		Paul Goydos	74-64-70-69	277	$12,040
	Heath Slocum	69-69-65-68	271	$54,818	65=	Hyung-Sung Kim	70-68-66-74	278	$11,648
	John Peterson	68-69-65-69	271	$54,818		Morgan Hoffmann	68-69-71-70	278	$11,648
	Brendon Todd	70-66-66-69	271	$54,818		Stuart Appleby	70-68-71-69	278	$11,648
	Robert Allenby	68-68-65-70	271	$54,818	68=	Robert Streb	70-69-67-73	279	$11,368
29=	Boo Weekley	67-67-70-68	272	$38,080		Scott Brown	71-67-70-71	279	$11,368
	Spencer Levin	69-69-66-68	272	$38,080	70=	Derek Tolan	70-66-70-76	282	$11,144
	Jason Dufner	67-68-67-70	272	$38,080		Tommy Gainey	72-67-70-73	282	$11,144
32=	Brian Harman	69-66-69-69	273	$30,987	72=	Miguel A. Carballo	68-70-72	210	$10,696
	John Daly	66-73-64-70	273	$30,987		Ken Duke	68-71-71	210	$10,696
	Michael Putnam	70-68-68-67	273	$30,987		Kevin Foley	67-72-71	210	$10,696
	Sang-Moon Bae	63-70-70-70	273	$30,987		John Huh	71-67-72	210	$10,696
	Brian Gay	71-68-67-67	273	$30,987		Toshinori Muto	70-69-71	210	$10,696
	Justin Leonard	68-66-69-70	273	$30,987		Scott Verplank	71-67-72	210	$10,696
38=	Ricky Barnes	68-69-68-69	274	$22,400	78	Eric Dugas	70-68-73	211	$10,304
	David Hearn	68-70-67-69	274	$22,400	79	Joe Durant	68-71-73	212	$10,192
	Billy Hurley III	67-69-69-69	274	$22,400					

Out Of The Money: 140: Briny Baird, Bo Van Pelt, Johnson Wagner, Scott Piercy, Troy Merritt, Kevin Kisner, Yuta Ikeda, Frank Lickliter II, Matt Bettencourt, Daniel Chopra, Will MacKenzie, Derek Ernst, Bobby Gates, Jim Herman, Russell Knox, Masahiro Kawamura **141**: Jonathan Byrd, Jordan Spieth, Jeff Maggert, David Lingmerth, Danny Lee, Alex Prugh, D.H. Lee, Martin Trainer **142**: Erik Compton, Cameron Tringale, Josh Teater, Nicholas Thompson, Woody Austin, Roberto Castro, Ted Potter Jr., Vijay Singh, Rory Sabbatini, Scott Langley, Edward Loar, Yusaku Miyazato, Andrew Svoboda, Mark Anderson **143**: Michael Thompson, Ryo Ishikawa, Bronson La'Cassie, Shane Bertsch, Will Claxton **144**: Fred Funk, Scott Gardiner, Kevin Tway, Chesson Hadley, Jim Renner, Alex Aragon, Jamie Lovemark, Wes Roach **145**: Mike Weir, Carl Pettersson, Kenny Perry, Brad Fritsch **146**: Yan-Wei Liu, Andrew Loupe, Lee Williams **148**: Sean O'Hair, Guan Tianlang (A) **150**: Jared Sawada **151**: Bud Cauley **152**: Troy Matteson **154**: Kirk Nelson **WD**: Tim Clark (73)

FIRST ROUND		SECOND ROUND		THIRD ROUND	
Sang-Moon Bae	63 (-7)	Brian Stuard	130 (-10)	Chris Kirk	198 (-12)
Chris Kirk	64 (-6)	Marc Leishman	131 (-9)	Will Wilcox	199 (-11)
Brian Stuard	65 (-5)	Hideto Tanihara	131 (-9)	Harris English	199 (-11)
Ryan Palmer	65 (-5)	Harris English	132 (-8)	Jerry Kelly	200 (-10)
Jimmy Walker	66 (-4)	**Jimmy Walker**	133 (-7)	**Jimmy Walker**	200 (-10)

OWR: 8 of top 50 entered - Rating: 232 - Points to 50th - Walker: 42 points, to 32nd in OWR

Humana Challenge   Jan 16 - Jan 19

PGA West (Palmer) - La Quinta, CA — 6,950 yards Par 72
PGA West (Nicklaus Private) - La Quinta, CA — 6,924 yards Par 72
La Quinta Country Club - La Quinta, CA — 7,060 yards Par 72
Champion: Patrick Reed — Purse: $5.7 Million

Twenty-three-year-old Patrick Reed labeled himself one of American golf's up-and-coming stars by winning for the second time in his first 46 PGA Tour starts, cruising to a two-shot victory at the Humana Challenge in La Quinta, California. Though Reed's closing round of 71 left the door ajar enough for a few moments of semi-excitement down the stretch, the victory margin was misleadingly close, for he had begun Sunday's final round with an imposing seven-shot lead, and runner-up Ryan Palmer eagled the 72nd hole to pull within two. Reed's first three days, however, were epic, as he became the first man ever to better 64 for three straight PGA Tour rounds by carding a trio of 63s over the event's three course rota. His 189 total not only built what proved to be an insurmountable lead but also set a Tour record for the lowest 54-hole score relative to par at an eye-popping 27 under. Under ideal playing conditions, when Reed barely bettered par on Sunday, both Zach Johnson (who closed with a scorching 62) and veteran Justin Leonard (65) were able to at least creep within shouting distance.

Pos	Player	Scores	Total	Money
1	Patrick Reed	63-63-63-71	260	$1.026 mil
2	Ryan Palmer	64-65-70-63	262	$615,600
3=	Zach Johnson	65-68-68-62	263	$330,600
	Justin Leonard	66-67-65-65	263	$330,600
5	Brian Stuard	67-66-66-65	264	$228,000
6=	Bill Haas	65-66-67-67	265	$198,075
	Brendon Todd	65-63-68-69	265	$198,075
8	Chad Collins	68-68-65-65	266	$176,700
9=	Stuart Appleby	66-69-67-65	267	$148,200
	Charlie Beljan	68-64-68-67	267	$148,200
	Ben Crane	70-64-65-68	267	$148,200
	Charley Hoffman	64-66-66-71	267	$148,200
13=	Russell Knox	65-70-67-66	268	$103,740
	Matt Every	65-68-69-66	268	$103,740
	Jerry Kelly	69-65-68-66	268	$103,740
	Will MacKenzie	67-66-66-69	268	$103,740
	Matt Jones	66-67-66-69	268	$103,740
18=	Brendon de Jonge	69-68-66-66	269	$74,328
	Luke Guthrie	69-67-67-66	269	$74,328
	Scott Langley	69-68-65-67	269	$74,328
	Keegan Bradley	69-66-65-69	269	$74,328
	James Driscoll	68-63-66-72	269	$74,328
23=	Webb Simpson	69-70-67-64	270	$57,000
	Charlie Wi	65-69-69-67	270	$57,000
25=	Ryo Ishikawa	66-69-69-67	271	$41,681
	T. Van Aswegen	69-67-67-68	271	$41,681
	Martin Flores	69-65-69-68	271	$41,681
	Johnson Wagner	72-66-68-65	271	$41,681
	Martin Laird	69-66-68-68	271	$41,681
	Hudson Swafford	65-71-70-65	271	$41,681
	Billy Horschel	72-65-70-64	271	$41,681
	Roberto Castro	68-73-66-64	271	$41,681
33=	Harris English	67-66-71-68	272	$30,780
	Camilo Villegas	70-66-68-68	272	$30,780
	Josh Teater	68-68-70-66	272	$30,780
	Rickie Fowler	68-71-67-66	272	$30,780
	Jason Bohn	70-65-66-71	272	$30,780
38=	Bryce Molder	69-72-63-69	273	$21,660
	Gary Woodland	69-71-65-68	273	$21,660
	Andrew Svoboda	69-69-66-69	273	$21,660
	Cameron Tringale	68-66-70-69	273	$21,660
	Jeff Overton	70-67-67-69	273	$21,660
	Brian Davis	69-71-66-67	273	$21,660
	Spencer Levin	69-68-66-70	273	$21,660
	Rory Sabbatini	68-67-67-71	273	$21,660
	Seung-Yul Noh	68-66-66-73	273	$21,660
	James Hahn	70-68-69-66	273	$21,660
48=	Justin Hicks	64-71-70-69	274	$13,817
	Kevin Kisner	66-70-69-69	274	$13,817
	John Merrick	66-70-69-69	274	$13,817
	Scott Brown	67-68-70-69	274	$13,817
	Brad Fritsch	67-70-67-70	274	$13,817
	Bo Van Pelt	70-68-67-69	274	$13,817
	Brice Garnett	67-69-68-70	274	$13,817
	Kevin Na	68-68-68-70	274	$13,817
	Steven Bowditch	71-67-68-68	274	$13,817
	Michael Putnam	68-69-70-67	274	$13,817
58=	Harrison Frazar	69-68-68-70	275	$12,198
	Pat Perez	69-70-66-70	275	$12,198
	Brandt Snedeker	72-64-69-70	275	$12,198
	Davis Love III	69-68-69-69	275	$12,198
	Daniel Summerhays	64-69-73-69	275	$12,198
	Kevin Chappell	70-70-63-72	275	$12,198
	Charles Howell III	73-68-65-69	275	$12,198
	Scott Stallings	68-69-69-69	275	$12,198
	Jonathan Byrd	68-69-65-73	275	$12,198
	Stewart Cink	73-63-71-68	275	$12,198
	Lee Williams	70-68-69-68	275	$12,198
69=	Erik Compton	70-66-70-70	276	$11,172
	Blake Adams	70-70-66-70	276	$11,172
	Jim Herman	67-68-68-73	276	$11,172
	Ken Duke	71-70-65-70	276	$11,172
	Nicholas Thompson	71-69-67-69	276	$11,172
	Chad Campbell	71-68-68-69	276	$11,172
	John Senden	71-70-66-69	276	$11,172
76=	William McGirt	70-70-64-73	277	$10,659
	Fredrik Jacobson	71-68-68-70	277	$10,659
78=	David Lingmerth	69-68-69-72	278	$10,431
	Kevin Stadler	69-66-72-71	278	$10,431
80	Brett Quigley	66-73-68-72	279	$10,260
81	Scott McCarron	72-69-66-73	280	$10,146
82=	J.J. Henry	71-70-65-75	281	$9,975
	Brian Harman	69-66-72-74	281	$9,975
84	Jhonattan Vegas	69-71-67-76	283	$9,804

Out Of The Money: **208**: Sang-Moon Bae, Daniel Chopra, Joe Durant, Jeff Maggert, Sean O'Hair, John Peterson, Scott Piercy, Justin Thomas, David Toms **209**: Aaron Baddeley, Ricky Barnes, Will Claxton, Nicolas Colsaerts, Robert Garrigus, Brian Gay, Lucas Glover, Jason Kokrak, Bronson La'Cassie, Brendan Steele, Chris Stroud **210**: John Daly, Morgan Hoffmann, Danny Lee, Jamie Lovemark, Peter Malnati, Ted Potter Jr. **211**: Stephen Ames, Ben Martin, Troy Merritt, Jesper Parnevik, John Rollins, Scott Verplank **212**: Chris DiMarco, Billy Hurley III, Lee Janzen, Andrew Loupe, John Mallinger, Geoff Ogilvy, Carl Pettersson, Wes Roach, Mike Weir **213**: Briny Baird, Jonas Blixt, Scott Gardiner, David Hearn, Edward Loar, Troy Matteson, Heath Slocum, Tim Wilkinson, Mark Wilson, Y.E. Yang **214**: Bud Cauley, Retief Goosen, Richard H. Lee, Kevin Tway **215**: Robert Allenby, Alex Aragon, Greg Chalmers **216**: Paul Goydos, Dudley Hart **217**: Mark Brooks, Ben Curtis **218**: Peter Jacobsen **219**: Will Wilcox **220**: Chesson Hadley **222**: Derek Ernst, Tommy Gainey, Bobby Gates, Alan Scheer **223**: Trevor Immelman, D.J. Trahan **WD**: Boo Weekley

FIRST ROUND		SECOND ROUND		THIRD ROUND	
Patrick Reed	63 (-9)	**Patrick Reed**	126 (-18)	**Patrick Reed**	189 (-27)
Ryan Palmer	64 (-8)	Brendon Todd	128 (-16)	Charley Hoffman	196 (-20)
Justin Hicks	64 (-8)	Ryan Palmer	129 (-15)	Brendon Todd	196 (-20)
Daniel Summerhays	64 (-8)	Charley Hoffman	130 (-14)	James Driscoll	197 (-19)
Charley Hoffman	64 (-8)	2 Players	131 (-13)	2 Players	198 (-18)

OWR: 9 of top 50 entered - Rating: 212 - Points to 47th - Reed: 40 points, to 41st in OWR

Farmers Insurance Open
Jan 24 - Jan 27

Torrey Pines (South Course) - La Jolla, CA — 7,698 yards Par 72
Torrey Pines (North Course) - La Jolla, CA — 7,052 yards Par 72
Champion: Scott Stallings — Purse: $6.1 Million

On a Sunday which, for the first time in two decades, included neither Phil Mickelson nor Tiger Woods, 28-year-old Scott Stallings charged from a three-stroke 54-hole deficit to claim his third PGA Tour win at the Farmers Insurance Open in San Diego. Stallings made up much of his ground with a run of three birdies from the 11th through the 14th before nearly being derailed by a bogey at the par-3 16th. But under the gun, he logged the critical birdie he needed at the par-5 18th by reaching the pond-fronted green with a 4 iron, then two-putting from 40 feet. This last birdie then held up as the margin of victory when a long list of erstwhile contenders – at one point nine players were tied for the lead - eventually fell by the wayside. This list was headed by Gary Woodland, who stood eight-under-par before a crushing double-bogey at the 17th left him unable to utilize his length to tie at the last. Australian Marc Leishman then came up one shy when he could only birdie the last – a circumstance matched earlier by Jason Day, Graham DeLaet and area native Pat Perez. Also sharing second was K.J. Choi, who finished well before the leaders with a 66, the week's low South Course round. Less happy with their week were Mickelson (who withdrew Friday night with a back injury) and Woods, who failed to make the 54-hole cut after crashing to an ugly Saturday 79.

Pos	Player	Scores	Total	Money		Player	Scores	Total	Money
1	Scott Stallings	72-67-72-68	279	$1.098 mil		T. Van Aswegen	66-76-76-69	287	$26,840
2=	K.J. Choi	74-70-70-66	280	$366,000	43=	Stuart Appleby	74-69-72-73	288	$20,740
	Jason Day	66-73-73-68	280	$366,000		Bill Haas	74-70-71-73	288	$20,740
	Graham DeLaet	70-73-69-68	280	$366,000		Justin Hicks	71-68-75-74	288	$20,740
	Pat Perez	67-71-72-70	280	$366,000		Matt Jones	75-65-77-71	288	$20,740
	Marc Leishman	66-71-72-71	280	$366,000	47=	Jim Herman	66-75-74-74	289	$15,479
7=	Charley Hoffman	69-70-75-67	281	$190,117		John Merrick	69-74-72-74	289	$15,479
	Ryo Ishikawa	72-70-69-70	281	$190,117		Lee Westwood	73-68-75-73	289	$15,479
	Will MacKenzie	72-69-70-70	281	$190,117		David Lingmerth	72-70-75-72	289	$15,479
10=	Trevor Immelman	68-74-71-69	282	$135,217		Ian Poulter	75-67-71-76	289	$15,479
	Seung-Yul Noh	68-73-72-69	282	$135,217		Kevin Chappell	73-66-73-77	289	$15,479
	Russell Knox	71-67-74-70	282	$135,217		Hunter Mahan	72-72-73-72	289	$15,479
	Justin Thomas	68-73-72-69	282	$135,217		Andrés Romero	72-72-67-78	289	$15,479
	Brad Fritsch	69-70-72-71	282	$135,217	55=	Mark Calcavecchia	70-74-71-75	290	$13,847
	Gary Woodland	65-73-70-74	282	$135,217		David Lynn	68-73-75-74	290	$13,847
16=	Hideki Matsuyama	72-72-70-69	283	$97,600		Blake Adams	75-69-72-74	290	$13,847
	Keegan Bradley	69-72-71-71	283	$97,600		Tag Ridings	73-70-73-74	290	$13,847
	Morgan Hoffmann	72-66-72-73	283	$97,600	59=	Victor Dubuisson	72-69-74-76	291	$13,176
19=	Erik Compton	69-69-74-72	284	$76,555		Chris Williams	71-72-72-76	291	$13,176
	Robert Streb	73-69-70-72	284	$76,555		D.A. Points	67-74-75-75	291	$13,176
	Nicolas Colsaerts	69-67-75-73	284	$76,555		Jhonattan Vegas	68-75-74-74	291	$13,176
	Jordan Spieth	71-63-75-75	284	$76,555		Nick Watney	70-74-74-73	291	$13,176
23=	Luke Guthrie	76-68-71-70	285	$54,290		Harrison Frazar	68-74-77-72	291	$13,176
	J.B. Holmes	71-68-75-71	285	$54,290		D.H. Lee	73-71-75-72	291	$13,176
	Billy Horschel	70-67-77-71	285	$54,290	66=	Cameron Tringale	71-71-76-74	292	$12,627
	Bubba Watson	70-73-73-69	285	$54,290		Matt Bettencourt	71-73-74-74	292	$12,627
	Rory Sabbatini	74-68-69-74	285	$54,290	68=	Ben Crane	77-67-73-76	293	$12,383
28=	Stewart Cink	64-71-79-72	286	$38,023		Jonathan Byrd	70-72-77-74	293	$12,383
	Jamie Lovemark	72-67-76-71	286	$38,023	70	Bryce Molder	77-65-77-75	294	$12,200
	Justin Leonard	74-69-73-70	286	$38,023	71=	Nicholas Thompson	72-70-76-77	295	$12,017
	Sang-Moon Bae	67-76-71-72	286	$38,023		Charlie Wi	72-70-77-76	295	$12,017
	Robert Garrigus	71-71-72-72	286	$38,023	73	Greg Owen	70-74-74-82	300	$11,834
	Brendan Steele	76-67-74-69	286	$38,023	74	Aaron Baddeley	71-73-76	220	$11,712
	Chad Collins	78-66-73-69	286	$38,023	75=	Steven Bowditch	68-76-77	221	$11,346
	Y.E. Yang	76-67-74-69	286	$38,023		Will Claxton	71-73-77	221	$11,346
	Brian Stuard	70-73-69-74	286	$38,023		Brice Garnett	75-68-78	221	$11,346
37=	Martin Laird	69-71-74-73	287	$26,840		Tim Herron	70-74-77	221	$11,346
	Brendon Todd	69-73-72-73	287	$26,840		Camilo Villegas	72-71-78	221	$11,346
	Michael Putnam	69-73-75-70	287	$26,840	80=	Bobby Gates	69-72-81	222	$10,919
	Kevin Tway	69-70-73-75	287	$26,840		Tiger Woods	72-71-79	222	$10,919
	Charles Howell III	70-72-70-75	287	$26,840	82	Michael Block	74-69-86	229	$10,736

Out Of The Money: **145**: James Driscoll, Martin Flores, Spencer Levin, Jimmy Walker, Hideto Tanihara, Alex Aragon, Danny Lee, Ben Martin, Troy Matteson, Johnson Wagner, Chesson Hadley, Chris Riley, Fabián Gómez, Andrew Svoboda **146**: J.J. Henry, Peter Malnati, Heath Slocum, Brendon de Jonge, Tommy Gainey, Jonas Blixt, Geoff Ogilvy, Chris Smith **147**: Roberto Castro, Scott Brown, Rickie Fowler, Vijay Singh, Ben Curtis, Tim Wilkinson, Robert Allenby, Paul Goydos **148**: David Hearn, John Huh, Lucas Glover, Chad Campbell, Hudson Swafford, Kevin Foley, Bronson La'Cassie, Alex Prugh **149**: Billy Mayfair, Dicky Pride, Andrew Loupe, Troy Merritt, Brandt Snedeker, Kyle Stanley, James Hahn, Miguel Ángel Carballo, Edward Loar, Wes Roach, Will Strickler **150**: Daniel Chopra, Joe Durant, Davis Love III, Derek Ernst, Russell Henley, Michael Kim **151**: Max Homa, Richard H. Lee, Jim Renner, Shawn Stefani, Kevin Kisner, John Peterson **152**: Charlie Beljan, Will Wilcox, Josh Teater **154**: Mark Anderson **155**: Gonzalo F'dez-Castaño, Scott Gardiner, Lee Williams **156**: John Rollins **157**: Riley Wheeldon **WD**: Rocco Mediate (74), Mike Weir (77), Fredrik Jacobson (81)

FIRST ROUND		SECOND ROUND		THIRD ROUND	
Stewart Cink	64 (-8)	Jordan Spieth	134 (-10)	Gary Woodland	208 (-8)
Gary Woodland	65 (-7)	Stewart Cink	135 (-9)	Jordan Spieth	209 (-7)
3 Players	66 (-6)	Nicolas Colsaerts	136 (-8)	Marc Leishman	209 (-7)
Scott Stallings	72 (E)	2 Players	137 (-7)	2 Players	210 (-6)
		Scott Stallings	139 (-5)	**Scott Stallings**	211 (-5)

OWR: 14 of top 50 entered - Rating: 371 - Points to 54th - Stallings: 52 points, to 53rd in OWR

Waste Management Phoenix Open

Jan 30 - Feb 2

TPC Scottsdale (Stadium Course) - Scottsdale, AZ
Champion: Kevin Stadler

7,216 yards   Par 71
Purse: $6.2 Million

Thirty-three-year-old Kevin Stadler claimed his first PGA Tour victory in 239 starts at the Waste Management Phoenix Open, his 268 aggregate proving good enough to edge 54-hole leader Bubba Watson by one. Stadler, a local resident and the son of 1982 Masters champion Craig Stadler, initially moved into the final round lead with a birdie at the par-4 9th but fell behind again with a double bogey at the 11th. Playing over his home course at the TPC Scottsdale,, he remained one back through the par-5 15th (where both he and Watson scrambled for par after hitting it in the water), then drew even when Watson bogeyed the short 16th from a front-left bunker. The pair each carded two-putt birdies at the driveable par-4 17th before Watson handed Stadler the victory by bogeying the 438-yard 18th after driving in the rough. The final bogey dropped Watson into a tie for second with Canada's Graham DeLaet (who closed with a pair of weekend 65s), while Hunter Mahan and 21-year-old Japanese rookie Hideki Matsuyama (who might have won with a slightly more cooperative putter) shared fourth. Though he is a four-time winner on the Web.com Tour, this was Stadler's first major circuit triumph since taking the European Tour's Johnnie Walker Classic (played in Australia) in 2006. The victory made the Stadlers the ninth father-son pair to win on the PGA Tour and, with Kevin's resulting ticket to Augusta, set them up to be the first father-son team ever to appear in the same Masters.

1	Kevin Stadler	65-68-67-68	268	$1.116 mil		Matt Every	72-66-67-75 280	$27,900
2=	Graham DeLaet	67-72-65-65	269	$545,600		Ricky Barnes	71-67-67-75 280	$27,900
	Bubba Watson	64-66-68-71	269	$545,600	42=	Chris Smith	70-69-71-71 281	$21,080
4=	Hunter Mahan	66-71-65-68	270	$272,800		Phil Mickelson	71-67-72-71 281	$21,080
	Hideki Matsuyama	66-67-68-69	270	$272,800		James Driscoll	67-70-73-71 281	$21,080
6=	Charles Howell III	70-69-67-65	271	$207,700		David Lingmerth	72-68-68-73 281	$21,080
	Brendan Steele	66-74-62-69	271	$207,700		K.J. Choi	71-70-69-71 281	$21,080
	Ryan Moore	66-71-64-70	271	$207,700		Ben Crane	69-69-69-74 281	$21,080
9	Harris English	65-67-69-71	272	$179,800	48=	Erik Compton	67-72-71-72 282	$15,773
10	Webb Simpson	68-72-67-66	273	$167,400		Ryan Palmer	76-64-70-72 282	$15,773
11	Pat Perez	65-68-70-71	274	$155,000		David Lynn	72-66-70-74 282	$15,773
12=	Cameron Tringale	71-67-69-68	275	$130,200		Aaron Baddeley	68-70-73-71 282	$15,773
	John Mallinger	67-72-67-69	275	$130,200		Jhonattan Vegas	71-66-75-70 282	$15,773
	Matt Jones	65-65-72-73	275	$130,200	53=	Robert Garrigus	70-70-70-73 283	$14,285
15=	Scott Piercy	67-67-75-67	276	$102,300		Brendon de Jonge	66-73-70-74 283	$14,285
	Morgan Hoffmann	69-66-70-71	276	$102,300		Brian Stuard	73-68-69-73 283	$14,285
	Greg Chalmers	65-67-71-73	276	$102,300		Martin Kaymer	69-71-71-72 283	$14,285
	Jason Kokrak	66-69-68-73	276	$102,300		Kevin Streelman	71-68-74-70 283	$14,285
19=	John Merrick	75-65-69-68	277	$63,302	58=	David Hearn	68-70-73-73 284	$13,764
	Michael Thompson	72-68-70-67	277	$63,302		Nicolas Colsaerts	69-68-74-73 284	$13,764
	Kevin Na	70-70-68-69	277	$63,302		J.B. Holmes	73-68-70-73 284	$13,764
	William McGirt	65-69-73-70	277	$63,302	61=	Charley Hoffman	70-71-69-75 285	$13,206
	Justin Hicks	71-70-69-67	277	$63,302		Jonathan Byrd	68-73-69-75 285	$13,206
	Martin Laird	67-68-71-71	277	$63,302		Brandt Snedeker	70-64-72-79 285	$13,206
	John Rollins	72-67-67-71	277	$63,302		Brian Gay	69-71-71-74 285	$13,206
	Roberto Castro	72-69-70-66	277	$63,302		Sang-Moon Bae	67-73-71-74 285	$13,206
	Patrick Reed	67-67-71-72	277	$63,302		John Peterson	68-70-74-73 285	$13,206
	Chris Stroud	70-67-68-72	277	$63,302	67=	K. Aphibarnrat	66-71-73-76 286	$12,710
29=	Geoff Ogilvy	71-70-68-69	278	$40,300		Fred Funk	69-71-76-70 286	$12,710
	Ken Duke	70-67-72-69	278	$40,300	69=	Y.E. Yang	64-73-75-75 287	$12,276
	Bryce Molder	67-71-70-70	278	$40,300		Mark Calcavecchia	70-71-71-75 287	$12,276
	Spencer Levin	67-69-70-72	278	$40,300		Scott Langley	71-70-71-75 287	$12,276
	Nick Watney	69-68-68-73	278	$40,300		Steven Bowditch	71-69-75-72 287	$12,276
34=	Bill Haas	69-68-71-71	279	$33,480		Derek Ernst	72-69-72-74 287	$12,276
	Jason Bohn	70-70-70-69	279	$33,480	74=	Ben Curtis	68-72-73-75 288	$11,842
	Jonas Blixt	68-71-72-68	279	$33,480		Joe Ogilvie	71-70-77-70 288	$11,842
37=	Camilo Villegas	70-71-68-71	280	$27,900	76	Chris Kirk	65-73-75-76 289	$11,656
	Gary Woodland	67-72-72-69	280	$27,900	77	Vijay Singh	69-72-75-76 292	$11,532
	Brian Davis	72-69-70-69	280	$27,900				

Out Of The Money: **142**: Charlie Beljan, Martin Flores, Luke Guthrie, Padraig Harrington, Daniel Summerhays, Josh Teater, Lee Westwood **143**: Kris Blanks, Kevin Chappell, Rickie Fowler, Retief Goosen, Russell Henley, Billy Horschel, John Huh, Richard H. Lee, Justin Leonard, D.A. Points, Michael Putnam, Nicholas Thompson, Kevin Tway, Charlie Wi **144**: Angel Cabrera, James Hahn, Danny Lee, Marc Leishman, Ted Potter Jr., Ian Poulter, Scott Stallings, Scott Verplank **145**: Tommy Gainey, Lucas Glover, Paul Goydos, Brian Harman, Mike Weir **146**: Robert Allenby, Woody Austin, Keegan Bradley, D.H. Lee, George McNeill, Jeff Overton, Carl Pettersson, Rory Sabbatini, David Toms, Bo Van Pelt, J.J. Henry, Ki Taek Lee **148**: Stephen Ames, Jeff Maggert, Mark Wilson **149**: Ryo Ishikawa **151**: Andrés Romero **152**: Gonzalo F'dez-Castaño **153**: Kyle Stanley, Paul Trittler **159**: Joey Snyder III

FIRST ROUND		SECOND ROUND		THIRD ROUND	
Y.E. Yang	64 (-7)	Matt Jones	130 (-12)	Bubba Watson	198 (-15)
Bubba Watson	64 (-7)	Bubba Watson	130 (-12)	**Kevin Stadler**	200 (-13)
7 Players	65 (-6)	Greg Chalmers	132 (-10)	Ryan Moore	201 (-12)
Kevin Stadler	65 (-6)	Harris English	132 (-10)	Harris English	201 (-12)
		3 Players	133 (-9)	Hideki Matsuyama	201 (-12)
		Kevin Stadler	133 (-9)		

OWR: 22 of top 50 entered - Rating: 367 - Points to 52nd - Stadler: 52 points, to 57th in OWR

AT&T National Pebble Beach Pro-Am — Feb 6 - Feb 9

Pebble Beach Golf Links - Pebble Beach, CA — 6,816 yards   Par 72
Spyglass Hill Golf Club - Pebble Beach, CA — 6,858 yards   Par 72
Monterey Peninsula Country Club (Shore Course) - Pebble Beach, CA — 6,838 yards   Par 70
Champion: Jimmy Walker — Purse: $6.6 Million

It took PGA Tour veteran Jimmy Walker 187 PGA Tour starts to claim his first victory, but once he got the hang of it, the wins started ringing up like clockwork. Indeed, Walker claimed his third title in eight starts on the 2013-14 wraparound schedule at the AT&T Pebble Beach National Pro-Am, charging out to a six-stroke 54 hole lead behind rounds of 66-69-67 before barely hanging on over a bumpy final nine at Pebble Beach. Walker seemed in firm command over his first 11 holes on Sunday, coming to the 12th tee with his entire six-shot margin intact. But while Dustin Johnson and Tour rookie Jim Renner charged home ahead of him with rounds of 66 and 67 respectively, Walker stumbled, first bogeying both the par-3 12th (after missing the green) and the par-4 13th (by three-putting). But even as Johnson and Renner charged, Walker still reached the 17th tee two ahead before again three-putting. Then, with two putts to win from 25 feet at the last, he ran his first effort five feet past the hole before coolly holing the comebacker to avoid a playoff. While Johnson and Renner shared second, Jordan Spieth tied Kevin Na for fourth after sharing the 36-hole lead with Walker, then struggling to a windblown third round 78 at Pebble Beach which, due to inclement weather, was actually completed on Sunday morning.

1	Jimmy Walker	66-69-67-74	276	$1.188 mil
2=	Dustin Johnson	68-73-70-66	277	$580,800
	Jim Renner	65-73-72-67	277	$580,800
4=	Jordan Spieth	67-67-78-67	279	$290,400
	Kevin Na	72-68-70-69	279	$290,400
6	Hunter Mahan	68-68-72-72	280	$237,600
7=	Graeme McDowell	71-71-72-67	281	$205,700
	Pat Perez	69-70-71-71	281	$205,700
	Tim Wilkinson	67-72-69-73	281	$205,700
10=	Bryce Molder	72-71-69-70	282	$165,000
	Chesson Hadley	71-70-70-71	282	$165,000
	Richard H. Lee	65-72-72-73	282	$165,000
13=	Will MacKenzie	69-74-70-70	283	$116,600
	Cameron Tringale	70-73-71-69	283	$116,600
	Patrick Reed	69-70-75-69	283	$116,600
	Victor Dubuisson	73-67-74-69	283	$116,600
	Brian Davis	68-74-70-71	283	$116,600
	Scott Gardiner	65-73-77-68	283	$116,600
19=	Steven Bowditch	68-70-75-71	284	$71,775
	Seung-Yul Noh	72-71-71-70	284	$71,775
	Daniel Summerhays	69-69-74-72	284	$71,775
	Jason Kokrak	74-68-70-72	284	$71,775
	Roberto Castro	70-73-71-70	284	$71,775
	Brice Garnett	75-68-68-73	284	$71,775
	Michael Thompson	71-68-72-73	284	$71,775
	Phil Mickelson	66-73-71-74	284	$71,775
27=	Padraig Harrington	72-69-72-72	285	$46,860
	Andrew Loupe	63-73-76-73	285	$46,860
	Russell Knox	70-72-70-73	285	$46,860
	Jim Herman	70-70-71-74	285	$46,860
	Robert Garrigus	67-71-73-74	285	$46,860
32=	Robert Streb	67-75-72-72	286	$39,050
	Ryan Palmer	72-66-72-76	286	$39,050
	Wes Roach	67-74-72-73	286	$39,050
35=	James Driscoll	69-71-73-74	287	$29,139
	Jim Furyk	70-70-73-74	287	$29,139
	David Duval	72-68-74-73	287	$29,139
	Dudley Hart	71-68-73-75	287	$29,139
	Bronson La'Cassie	70-72-72-73	287	$29,139
	Dicky Pride	66-72-74-75	287	$29,139
	Kevin Chappell	73-68-73-73	287	$29,139
	Stuart Appleby	65-74-76-72	287	$29,139
	Michael Putnam	69-71-75-72	287	$29,139
	Kevin Foley	68-76-71-72	287	$29,139
45=	Kevin Stadler	67-73-73-75	288	$18,499
	Brian Gay	70-72-72-76	288	$18,499
	Matt Jones	68-74-70-76	288	$18,499
	Woody Austin	73-70-69-76	288	$18,499
	Bud Cauley	73-69-72-74	288	$18,499
	Brendon Todd	70-68-73-77	288	$18,499
	Blake Adams	69-69-72-78	288	$18,499
52=	Doug LaBelle II	70-74-70-75	289	$15,477
	George McNeill	67-74-73-75	289	$15,477
	Andrés Romero	71-70-74-74	289	$15,477
	Russell Henley	73-70-72-74	289	$15,477
56=	Aaron Baddeley	69-70-73-78	290	$14,784
	Ben Kohles	72-73-69-76	290	$14,784
	Alex Cejka	69-71-75-75	290	$14,784
	Sean O'Hair	70-71-74-75	290	$14,784
	Greg Owen	67-74-74-75	290	$14,784
61=	J.B. Holmes	68-75-70-78	291	$14,256
	Chris Kirk	71-68-76-76	291	$14,256
	Kyle Stanley	74-69-72-76	291	$14,256
64=	K. Aphibarnrat	69-74-73	216	$13,200
	Rafael Cabrera-Bello	74-71-71	216	$13,200
	Jason Day	68-77-71	216	$13,200
	Fabián Gómez	72-74-70	216	$13,200
	Retief Goosen	71-73-72	216	$13,200
	Lee Janzen	68-73-75	216	$13,200
	Kevin Kisner	72-69-75	216	$13,200
	Scott Langley	69-75-72	216	$13,200
	Jamie Lovemark	73-69-74	216	$13,200
	John Mallinger	71-71-74	216	$13,200
	John Peterson	70-72-74	216	$13,200
	Rory Sabbatini	67-72-77	216	$13,200
	Will Wilcox	72-69-75	216	$13,200

Out Of The Money: **217**: Lee Williams, Brian Harman, Troy Merritt, Justin Thomas, Jason Bohn, Freddie Jacobson, Will Claxton, Chad Campbell, D.H. Lee, Scott Brown, Jeff Maggert, Peter Malnati, Alex Aragon, Danny Lee **218**: Paul Goydos, Nick Watney, Martin Flores, Ben Martin, Brendan Steele, Ken Duke, Alex Prugh, Chris Williams **219**: Matt Every, K.J. Choi, William McGirt, Vijay Singh, Mike Weir, Mark Wilson, Trevor Immelman **220**: Bo Van Pelt, Kevin Tway, Joe Durant, Sang-Moon Bae, Lucas Glover, John Senden **221**: Paul McGinley, Tag Ridings, Spencer Levin, Matt Bettencourt, John Huh, Miguel Ángel Carballo, Geoff Ogilvy, Rod Pampling, Brandt Snedeker, Hudson Swafford **222**: Justin Hicks, Bobby Gates, James Hahn, Nicholas Thompson **223**: Ted Potter, Jr., Tyrone Van Aswegen **224**: Charlie Wi, Steven Fox **225**: Jerry Kelly, Rod Perry, J.J. Henry, Ricky Barnes, Daniel Chopra, Tommy Gainey, Max Homa **226**: Charlie Beljan, Chad Collins, Troy Matteson **227**: Davis Love III, Edward Loar, Brad Fritsch **228**: Kris Blanks, John Daly, Joe Ogilvie, Andrew Svoboda, Josh Teater **229**: Mark Anderson, Greg Chalmers, Charley Hoffman **230**: Scott McCarron, Heath Slocum **231**: Justin Bolli **236**: David Carr **WD**: Briny Baird (154) **DQ**: D.A. Points (142)

FIRST ROUND		SECOND ROUND		THIRD ROUND	
Andrew Loupe	63 (-8)	**Jimmy Walker**	135 (-9)	**Jimmy Walker**	202 (-13)
Scott Gardiner	65 (-6)	Jordan Spieth	135 (-9)	Tim Wilkinson	208 (-7)
Richard H. Lee	65 (-6)	Hunter Mahan	136 (-8)	Hunter Mahan	208 (-7)
Stuart Appleby	65 (-6)	Andrew Loupe	136 (-7)	Richard H. Lee	209 (-6)
Jimmy Walker	66 (-5)				

OWR: 13 of top 50 entered - Rating: 246 - Points to 51st - Walker: 44 points, to 24th in OWR

Northern Trust Open

Riviera Country Club - Pacific Palisades, CA
Champion: Bubba Watson

Feb 13 - Feb 16
7,349 yards   Par 71
Purse: $6.7 Million

It took nearly two years, some 41 PGA Tour starts and a disappointing meltdown loss two weeks earlier in Phoenix, but Bubba Watson finally broke through for his first victory since the 2012 Masters, riding some spectacular weekend golf to victory at the Northern Trust Open in Los Angeles. Watson reached the 36-hole mark well back in the pack following opening rounds of 70-71 - somewhat mediocre stuff in a week marked by perfect weather and firm, fast fairways. But his was a very different game thereafter, as Watson became the first man in three decades to play the entire weekend at Riviera without a bogey, his flawless back-to-back rounds of 64 vaulting him over the field and, ultimately, to a two-shot victory. Even after his Saturday effort, Watson began Sunday's final round five behind 54-hole leader William McGirt, but that ground was quickly covered via five birdies in his first eight holes en route to an outgoing 30. One more birdie at the par-5 11th moved Watson to 14 under par, a number which none of his long list of pursuers was ever able to reach. A closing birdie at the famed 475-yard 18th would ultimately clinch a two-shot triumph over Dustin Johnson, who shot a closing 66 and finished second for the second straight week. Third place was shared by Watson's fellow ex-Georgia Bulldog Brian Harman and upstart Jason Allred, who'd threatened to become the first Monday qualifier to win a Tour event since Arjun Atwal at the 2010 Wyndham Championship.

1	Bubba Watson	70-71-64-64	269	$1.206 mil		40=	J.J. Henry	70-69-71-72	282	$26,130
2	Dustin Johnson	66-70-69-66	271	$723,600			Francesco Molinari	67-73-71-71	282	$26,130
3=	Jason Allred	73-64-67-68	272	$388,600			Jhonattan Vegas	70-69-71-72	282	$26,130
	Brian Harman	67-69-68-68	272	$388,600			Victor Dubuisson	70-72-68-72	282	$26,130
5	Charl Schwartzel	69-68-68-68	273	$268,000			Luke Guthrie	71-69-67-75	282	$26,130
6=	Bryce Molder	69-69-69-67	274	$216,913		45=	Stuart Appleby	72-71-67-73	283	$18,779
	George McNeill	69-68-66-71	274	$216,913			Justin Rose	70-72-68-73	283	$18,779
	Matt Every	69-69-69-67	274	$216,913			Vijay Singh	75-67-70-71	283	$18,779
	William McGirt	69-67-65-73	274	$216,913			Richard H. Lee	69-72-73-69	283	$18,779
10=	Harris English	70-69-69-67	275	$174,200			Davis Love III	71-71-73-68	283	$18,779
	Brendan Steele	68-71-67-69	275	$174,200			Scott Brown	70-67-74-72	283	$18,779
12=	K.J. Choi	69-72-67-68	276	$127,300			Scott Stallings	67-72-72-72	283	$18,779
	Charley Hoffman	67-71-68-70	276	$127,300		52=	Angel Cabrera	69-71-71-73	284	$15,467
	Sang-Moon Bae	67-66-72-71	276	$127,300			Ken Duke	71-69-69-75	284	$15,467
	Charlie Beljan	67-68-68-73	276	$127,300			Justin Leonard	70-72-70-72	284	$15,467
	Jordan Spieth	72-66-67-71	276	$127,300			J.B. Holmes	67-71-75-71	284	$15,467
	Cameron Tringale	68-70-67-71	276	$127,300			Will MacKenzie	73-69-72-70	284	$15,467
18=	Aaron Baddeley	69-65-72-71	277	$97,150			Hunter Mahan	70-73-71-70	284	$15,467
	John Senden	71-70-66-70	277	$97,150			Billy Hurley III	70-71-74-69	284	$15,467
20=	Lee Westwood	69-70-68-71	278	$80,847		59=	David Lynn	70-71-70-74	285	$14,539
	Jimmy Walker	67-71-67-73	278	$80,847			Matt Jones	67-73-70-75	285	$14,539
	Keegan Bradley	68-70-72-68	278	$80,847			Erik Compton	74-67-71-73	285	$14,539
23=	Kevin Stadler	69-69-74-67	279	$57,955			Ian Poulter	72-70-71-72	285	$14,539
	Jim Furyk	68-68-71-72	279	$57,955			Jason Gore	71-69-74-71	285	$14,539
	Robert Garrigus	67-67-73-72	279	$57,955			Marc Leishman	69-74-71-71	285	$14,539
	Bill Haas	72-67-67-73	279	$57,955		65=	Retief Goosen	73-69-73-71	286	$13,869
	Kevin Chappell	71-70-69-69	279	$57,955			Tim Wilkinson	71-72-73-70	286	$13,869
	Hideki Matsuyama	70-69-69-71	279	$57,955			Jason Dufner	70-72-76-68	286	$13,869
29=	Robert Allenby	71-69-71-69	280	$42,601			Martin Laird	70-73-70-73	286	$13,869
	Geoff Ogilvy	74-68-69-69	280	$42,601		69	Ben Crane	72-70-69-76	287	$13,534
	Daniel Summerhays	71-72-66-71	280	$42,601		70=	Graham DeLaet	70-73-72-73	288	$13,199
	Blake Adams	67-70-71-72	280	$42,601			Martin Flores	72-69-73-74	288	$13,199
	James Hahn	71-72-65-72	280	$42,601			Webb Simpson	70-72-72-74	288	$13,199
	David Lingmerth	70-69-70-71	280	$42,601			Harold Varner III	69-72-72-75	288	$13,199
35=	Ernie Els	71-70-68-72	281	$33,031		74	Michael Putnam	71-72-75-72	290	$12,864
	Gon. F'dez-Castaño	71-70-71-69	281	$33,031		75	Pat Perez	69-72-73-78	292	$12,730
	Kevin Streelman	72-69-73-67	281	$33,031		76	Ben Curtis	70-73-74-78	295	$12,596
	John Huh	71-71-72-67	281	$33,031		77	Scott Piercy	71-69-76-83	299	$12,462
	Brendon Todd	71-70-69-71	281	$33,031						

Out Of The Money: **144**: Fred Couples, Bubba Dickerson, Rickie Fowler, Aaron Goldberg, Paul Goydos, Chesson Hadley, Russell Henley, Kevin Na, Hudson Swafford, Josh Teater, Bo Van Pelt, Charlie Wi **145**: Ricky Barnes, Jonathan Byrd, Nicolas Colsaerts, Padraig Harrington, David Hearn, Max Homa, Joost Luiten, John Merrick, Ryan Moore, Thorbjørn Olesen, Brendon de Jonge **146**: Stewart Cink, James Driscoll, Fred Funk, Brian Gay, Morgan Hoffmann **146**: Charles Howell III, Ryo Ishikawa, Fredrik Jacobson, Jason Kokrak, Spencer Levin, John Mallinger, Brian Stuard, Y.E. Yang **147**: Steven Bowditch, Justin Hicks, Trevor Immelman, Scott Langley, Troy Matteson, Carl Pettersson, Ted Potter Jr., Nicholas Thompson **148**: Briny Baird, Greg Chalmers, Brian Davis, Lucas Glover, Russell Knox, Jeff Maggert, Louis Oosthuizen, John Rollins, Kyle Stanley, Mike Weir **149**: Matt Kuchar, Johnson Wagner **151**: Tommy Gainey, Andrés Romero, David Toms **152**: Derek Ernst, D.H. Lee **155**: Woody Austin **158**: Steve Holmes **WD**: Jim Renner (70), Darren Clarke (78), Scott Verplank **DQ**: John Peterson

FIRST ROUND		SECOND ROUND		THIRD ROUND	
Dustin Johnson	66 (-5)	Sang-Moon Bae	133 (-9)	William McGirt	201 (-12)
11 Players	67 (-4)	Aaron Baddeley	134 (-8)	George McNeill	203 (-10)
Bubba Watson	70 (-1)	Robert Garrigus	134 (-8)	Charlie Beljan	203 (-10)
		Charlie Beljan	135 (-7)	Jason Allred	204 (-9)
		4 Players	136 (-5)	Brian Harman	204 (-9)
		Bubba Watson	141 (-1)	**Bubba Watson**	205 (-8)

OWR: 26 of top 50 entered - Rating: 433 - Points to 58th - Watson: 56 points, to 14th in OWR

WGC-Accenture Match Play Championship

Feb 19 - Feb 23

Golf Club at Dove Mountain - Marana, AZ
Champion: Jason Day
7,833 yards Par 72
Purse: $9 Million

In a nail biting finale that took 23 holes to decide, Jason Day logged his first PGA Tour victory since the 2010 Byron Nelson Championship by defeating France's Victor Dubuisson to capture the WGC-Accenture Match Play Championship. Making his first career start in a WGC event, the 23-year-old Dubuisson did well to extend the playoff the full five holes, a feat he managed by recording spectacular back-to-back up-and-downs from some rocky desert terrain at both the 19th and 20th. He then very nearly won it at the 22nd when a 21-foot birdie putt narrowly missed, but was relegated to second place when Day birdied the driveable par-4 15th from just off the fringe, while Dubuisson could do no better than a four. Dubuisson had shown considerable resilience just reaching extra holes as he stood three down after 12 before winning the 13th and 17th with birdies, then the 18th with a clutch greenside sand save combined with Day's three-putting from 70 feet. Making only his fourth start on American soil, Dubuisson reached the final by edging 44-year-old match play stalwart Ernie Els one up in the semi-finals, after previously vanquishing Kevin Streelman (5&4), Peter Hanson (3&1), Bubba Watson (1 up) and Graeme McDowell (1 up). Day, who raised his career record in the event to 14-3, dispatched Rickie Fowler 3&2 in the Sunday morning semis after beating Thorbjørn Olesen (2 up), Billy Horschel (22 holes), George Coetzee (3&1) and an injured Louis Oosthuizen (3&1) in earlier rounds. In the Sunday afternoon third-place match, Fowler defeated Els at the 19th hole.

FIRST ROUND (Losers earn $48,000)

BOBBY JONES BRACKET

Henrik Stenson def. Kiradech Aphibarnrat 2 & 1
Louis Oosthuizen def. Nick Watney 1 up
Brandt Snedeker def. David Lynn 20th
Webb Simpson def. Thongchai Jaidee 3 & 2

Jason Day def. Thorbjørn Olesen 2 up
Billy Horschel def. Jamie Donaldson 6 & 5
George Coetzee def. Steve Stricker 3 & 1
Patrick Reed def. Graham DeLaet 1 up

BEN HOGAN BRACKET

Rory McIlroy def. Boo Weekley 3 & 2
Harris English def. Lee Westwood 5 & 3
Charl Schwartzel def. Kevin Stadler 3 & 2
Jim Furyk def. Chris Kirk 2 & 1

Sergio García def. Marc Leishman 22nd
Bill Haas def. Miguel A. Jiménez 4 & 3
Rickie Fowler def. Ian Poulter 2 & 1
Jimmy Walker def. Branden Grace 5 & 4

GARY PLAYER BRACKET

Justin Rose def. Scott Piercy 1 up
Ernie Els def. Stephen Gallacher 19th
Jason Dufner def. Scott Stallings 20th
Matteo Manassero def. Luke Donald 5 & 4

Matt Kuchar def. Bernd Wiesberger 3 & 2
Ryan Moore def. Joost Luiten 1 up
Jordan Spieth def. Pablo Larrazábal 2 up
Thomas Bjørn def. Francesco Molinari 2 & 1

SAM SNEAD BRACKET

Richard Sterne def. Zach Johnson 5 & 4
Hunter Mahan def. Gonzalo F'dez-Castaño 3 & 2
Graeme McDowell def. Gary Woodland 19th
Hideki Matsuyama def. Martin Kaymer 2 & 1

Peter Hanson def. Dustin Johnson 4 & 3
Victor Dubuisson def. Kevin Streelman 5 & 4
Bubba Watson def. Mikko Ilonen 2 & 1
Jonas Blixt def. Keegan Bradley 2 & 1

SECOND ROUND (Losers earn $99,000)

Louis Oosthuizen def. Henrik Stenson 4 & 3
Webb Simpson def. Brandt Snedeker 4 & 3
Jason Day def. Billy Horschel 22nd
George Coetzee def. Patrick Reed 21st

Harris English def. Rory McIlroy 19th
Jim Furyk def. Charl Schwartzel 3 & 2
Sergio García def. Bill Haas 3 & 1
Rickie Fowler def. Jimmy Walker 1 up

Ernie Els def. Justin Rose 20th
Jason Dufner def. Matteo Manassero 2 & 1
Matt Kuchar def. Ryan Moore 1 up
Jordan Spieth def. Thomas Bjørn 5 & 4

Hunter Mahan def. Richard Sterne 2 up
Graeme McDowell def. Hideki Matsuyama 1 up
Victor Dubuisson def. Peter Hanson 3 & 1
Bubba Watson def. Jonas Blixt 2 up

THIRD ROUND (Losers earn $148,000)

Louis Oosthuizen def. Webb Simpson 5 & 4
Jason Day def. George Coetzee 3 & 1

Jim Furyk def. Harris English 1 up
Rickie Fowler def. Sergio García 1 up

Ernie Els def. Jason Dufner 1 up
Jordan Spieth def. Matt Kuchar 2 & 1

Graeme McDowell def. Hunter Mahan 21st
Victor Dubuisson def. Bubba Watson 1 up

FOURTH ROUND (Losers earn $289,000)

Jason Day def. Louis Oosthuizen 2 & 1
Rickie Fowler def. Jim Furyk 1 up
Ernie Els def. Jordan Spieth 4 & 2
Victor Dubuisson def. Graeme McDowell 1 up

FIFTH ROUND

Jason Day def. Rickie Fowler 3 & 2
Victor Dubuisson def. Ernie Els 1 up

Day wins $1.53 million - Dubuisson wins $906,000 - Fowler wins $630,000 - Els wins $510,000

FINAL ROUND - Jason Day def. Victor Dubuisson 23rd

	1	2	3	4	5	6	7	8	9	10	11	12	13	14	15	16	17	18
Par	4	5	3	4	4	3	4	5	4	4	5	3	5	4	4	3	4	4
J.Day	3	4	3	5	5	3	3	4	C	4	4	3	5	4	4	3	4	5
V.Dubuisson	5	6	2	4	5	4	5	4	-	4	4	3	4	4	3	3	3	4

	19	20	21	22	23
Par	4	4	4	4	4
J.Day	4	4	5	4	3
V.Dubuisson	4	4	5	4	4

THIRD PLACE MATCH: Rickie Fowler def. Ernie Els 19th

OWR: 47 of top 50 entered - Rating: 689 - Points to 64th - Day: 72 points, to 4th in OWR

Honda Classic
Feb 27 - Mar 2

PGA National Golf Club (Champion) - Palm Beach Gardens, FL
Champion: Russell Henley

7,158 yards Par 70
Purse: $6 Million

In an event which ended up being former world number one Rory McIlroy's to lose, Russell Henley claimed his second PGA Tour victory in 14 months by winning the Honda Classic in a four-man sudden death playoff. McIlroy looked in command after an opening round 63 and remained atop the leaderboard both Friday and Saturday with middle rounds of 66-69. But during a final round which saw stiffer winds and higher scores, McIlroy struggled to a 74, his hopes nearly buried by a double-bogey at the 16th and a bogey at the par-3 17th. Still, he ripped his second to within 12 feet at the par-5 18th and thus had an eagle putt to win – which he missed. Henley's game, meanwhile, was a microcosm of Sunday's wild final nine leaderboard, as he birdied the 13th and 14th (the latter by chipping in), then double-bogeyed the 15th to fall back to the magic number of eight under par. Already in the clubhouse at that figure was Ryan Palmer, who was the only player in the final six groups to break par (and then just barely, with a 69) – though Palmer might well have won it outright had he not missed a spate of shorter putts down the stretch. Also in the playoff was Scotland's Russell Knox, who'd gotten it to 10 under par before recording a double-bogey of his own, at the par-4 14th. The playoff itself was brief, as Henley reached the 18th in two and, with two putts from 40 feet, recorded the only birdie and the victory. Also notable was the departure of Tiger Woods, who barely made the cut, shot a Saturday 65, the withdrew with back pain after 13 holes on Sunday, standing five over par for the day.

1	Russell Henley	64-68-68-72	272	$1.08 mil			Nicholas Thompson	68-70-66-74	278	$30,375
2=	Russell Knox	70-63-68-71	272	$448,000		41=	Jason Kokrak	70-66-70-73	279	$22,200
	Rory McIlroy	63-66-69-74	272	$448,000			Ted Potter Jr.	71-66-67-75	279	$22,200
	Ryan Palmer	68-66-69-69	272	$448,000			Cameron Tringale	69-69-66-75	279	$22,200
5	Billy Hurley III	70-67-67-69	273	$240,000			Camilo Villegas	71-68-69-71	279	$22,200
6=	David Hearn	67-70-70-67	274	$208,500			Boo Weekley	68-67-73-71	279	$22,200
	Will MacKenzie	67-68-69-70	274	$208,500		46=	Thomas Bjørn	69-66-70-75	280	$15,600
8=	Stuart Appleby	69-69-65-72	275	$168,000			James Driscoll	68-71-70-71	280	$15,600
	Luke Donald	67-68-68-72	275	$168,000			Graeme McDowell	70-67-72-71	280	$15,600
	Sergio García	72-68-68-67	275	$168,000			Troy Merritt	68-69-72-71	280	$15,600
	David Lingmerth	69-68-68-70	275	$168,000			Carl Pettersson	72-67-68-73	280	$15,600
12=	Keegan Bradley	69-68-66-73	276	$94,800			John Senden	72-63-73-72	280	$15,600
	Paul Casey	72-68-69-67	276	$94,800			Lee Westwood	68-65-73-74	280	$15,600
	Martin Flores	69-70-68-69	276	$94,800			Charlie Wi	69-71-68-72	280	$15,600
	Fredrik Jacobson	69-69-67-71	276	$94,800			Mark Wilson	67-69-73-71	280	$15,600
	Chris Kirk	69-67-72-68	276	$94,800		55=	Jamie Donaldson	65-69-72-75	281	$13,680
	Matteo Manassero	67-71-71-67	276	$94,800			Charles Howell III	72-68-69-72	281	$13,680
	George McNeill	70-67-69-70	276	$94,800			Tim Wilkinson	70-69-67-75	281	$13,680
	Andrés Romero	70-68-71-67	276	$94,800		58=	Stewart Cink	69-68-69-76	282	$13,320
	Adam Scott	68-69-70-69	276	$94,800			Derek Fathauer	67-71-69-75	282	$13,320
	Chris Stroud	69-66-73-68	276	$94,800			Brian Harman	67-72-69-74	282	$13,320
	Daniel Summerhays	70-65-69-72	276	$94,800		61=	D.A. Points	70-69-70-74	283	$13,020
	Jhonattan Vegas	70-66-66-74	276	$94,800			Hudson Swafford	67-71-68-77	283	$13,020
24=	Matt Every	66-73-65-73	277	$45,400		63=	Ken Duke	68-71-72-73	284	$12,660
	Gon. F'dez-Castaño	71-69-68-69	277	$45,400			Justin Hicks	70-70-71-73	284	$12,660
	Rickie Fowler	69-69-69-70	277	$45,400			Vijay Singh	69-71-68-76	284	$12,660
	Luke Guthrie	67-73-65-72	277	$45,400			Brendon de Jonge	66-64-76-78	284	$12,660
	Chesson Hadley	73-66-69-69	277	$45,400		67=	Trevor Immelman	69-69-72-75	285	$12,300
	Patrick Reed	71-67-70-69	277	$45,400			Jeff Overton	69-71-71-74	285	$12,300
	Brian Stuard	72-68-65-72	277	$45,400		69	Ben Crane	69-68-71-78	286	$12,120
	T. Van Aswegen	67-71-68-71	277	$45,400		71=	Mark Calcavecchia	69-70-73	212	$11,700
	Nick Watney	71-69-70-67	277	$45,400			Erik Compton	70-68-74	212	$11,700
33=	Derek Ernst	66-69-71-72	278	$30,375			Davis Love III	69-71-72	212	$11,700
	Zach Johnson	67-70-68-73	278	$30,375			William McGirt	65-69-78	212	$11,700
	Brooks Koepka	71-68-68-71	278	$30,375		75=	Scott Brown	71-69-73	213	$11,220
	Seung-Yul Noh	69-68-72-69	278	$30,375			Brice Garnett	66-71-76	213	$11,220
	Rory Sabbatini	65-71-68-74	278	$30,375			Jamie Lovemark	69-68-76	213	$11,220
	Brendan Steele	69-66-71-72	278	$30,375			Y.E. Yang	71-68-74	213	$11,220
	Josh Teater	70-68-71-69	278	$30,375		79	Heath Slocum	71-68-75	214	$10,920

Out Of The Money: 141: Angel Cabrera, Phil Mickelson, Matt Jones, Ricky Barnes, Jason Allred, Morgan Hoffmann, Harrison Frazar, Scott Langley **142**: Chad Collins, Spencer Levin, Mike Weir, Robert Allenby, Sean O'Hair, Jason Millard, Mark Silvers, Bo Van Pelt, Jason Bohn, Thorbjørn Olesen, Tim Clark, Martin Kaymer, Tommy Gainey, Lucas Glover, Greg Chalmers, Padraig Harrington, Brendon Todd **143**: Stephen Gallacher, John Peterson, Jeff Maggert, Kenny Perry **144**: Robert Garrigus, Steven Bowditch, David Lynn, Jerry Kelly, Charlie Beljan, Johnson Wagner, Woody Austin, J.J. Henry, Jose Coceres, Tim Herron, Peter Uihlein **145**: Retief Goosen, Michael Thompson, Peter Hanson, Brian Davis, Kyle Stanley, Roberto Castro **146**: Billy Horschel, Jim Renner, John Rollins, Ryo Ishikawa, J.B. Holmes, James Hahn **147**: Charl Schwartzel, Geoff Ogilvy **148**: Stephen Ames **149**: Briny Baird, Henrik Stenson **150**: John Merrick **151**: Jesper Parnevik, Alan Morin **152**: Ben Curtis **153**: Troy Matteson **155**: Darren Clarke **WD**: Hideki Matsuyama (70), D.H. Lee (72), Tiger Woods (205)

FIRST ROUND		SECOND ROUND		THIRD ROUND	
Rory McIlroy	63 (-7)	Rory McIlroy	129 (-11)	Rory McIlroy	198 (-12)
Russell Henley	64 (-6)	Brendon de Jonge	130 (-10)	**Russell Henley**	200 (-10)
Rory Sabbatini	65 (-5)	**Russell Henley**	132 (-8)	Russell Knox	201 (-9)
William McGirt	65 (-5)	Lee Westwood	133 (-7)	Jhonattan Vegas	202 (-8)
Jamie Donaldson	65 (-5)	Russell Knox	133 (-7)	4 Players	203 (-7)

OWR: 26 of top 50 entered - Rating: 494 - Points to 57th - Henley: 60 points, to 46th in OWR

WGC-Cadillac Championship

Trump National Doral (Blue Monster Course) - Miami, FL
Champion: Patrick Reed

Mar 6 - Mar 9
7,481 yards   Par 72
Purse: $9 Million

Following the WGC-Cadillac Championship, 23-year-old Patrick Reed answered a reporter's question by affirming that he considers himself one of the five best golfers in the world – and while the confident Reed later re-framed those words to suggest that he's working towards that goal, his impressive victory over a world-class field suggested that he is perhaps already on the cusp. Indeed, Reed triumphed wire-to-wire over the exceedingly rare non-Major championship field to include the entire top 50 in the Official World Ranking, and he did so without wilting under some serious final-nine pressure on Doral's revamped – and dangerous – Blue Monster layout. Reed topped the leaderboard on Thursday following an opening 68, then maintained a share of the lead following a 75 on a windy Friday which saw scores skyrocket. A 69 on Saturday then built him a two-stroke 54-hole lead, and when he quickly extended that lead to four via three early Sunday birdies, his position seemed fairly secure. But as Bubba Watson and Wales' Jamie Donaldson mounted late charges, an untimely Reed bogey at the 14th suddenly left the door slightly ajar – and it got wider when Donaldson birdied the 17th to close within one. Relying on a deft short game, however, Reed saved par from greenside bunkers at the 15th and 16th (having earlier done so at the 11th and 13th) and when Donaldson bogeyed the demanding 471-yard finisher from a greenside bunker, the lead was back to two. Smartly, Reed took the water out of play at the last by laying up with an iron, his "routine" bogey clinching the title. Watson and Donaldson shared second, while also noteworthy was world number one Tiger Woods, who stood three back after a fine Saturday 66, only to implode to Sunday 78 wherein his disappointing play was turbocharged by an aching back. The victory was Reed's third in his last PGA Tour 14 starts, and moved him up to 20th in the OWR – not quite in the top five but, like Reed, the season was still young.

1	Patrick Reed	68-75-69-72	284	$1.53 mil		Lee Westwood	75-79-70-70	294	$68,500
2=	Bubba Watson	73-72-72-68	285	$753,000		Justin Rose	74-77-70-73	294	$68,500
	Jamie Donaldson	74-70-71-70	285	$753,000		Hyung-Sung Kim	72-74-74-74	294	$68,500
4=	Richard Sterne	74-73-70-71	288	$395,000		Hideki Matsuyama	72-77-71-74	294	$68,500
	Dustin Johnson	69-74-73-72	288	$395,000		Graham DeLaet	78-72-70-74	294	$68,500
6=	Thongchai Jaidee	73-74-74-68	289	$248,333	40=	Darren Fichardt	73-78-72-72	295	$63,500
	Stephen Gallacher	75-75-70-69	289	$248,333		Chris Kirk	75-71-76-73	295	$63,500
	Bill Haas	73-76-69-71	289	$248,333		Louis Oosthuizen	72-78-71-74	295	$63,500
9=	Charl Schwartzel	70-76-76-68	290	$151,250		Branden Grace	75-74-69-77	295	$63,500
	Graeme McDowell	73-71-73-73	290	$151,250	44=	Rickie Fowler	76-75-74-71	296	$60,500
	Hunter Mahan	69-74-71-76	290	$151,250		Thomas Bjørn	75-75-73-73	296	$60,500
	Jason Dufner	69-77-68-76	290	$151,250	46	Brandt Snedeker	73-73-75-76	297	$59,000
13=	Joost Luiten	76-72-71-72	291	$110,000	47=	Webb Simpson	80-78-70-70	298	$57,000
	Matt Kuchar	69-74-74-74	291	$110,000		Russell Henley	72-78-75-73	298	$57,000
	Miguel A. Jiménez	70-77-69-75	291	$110,000		Kevin Stadler	77-76-72-73	298	$57,000
16=	Jonas Blixt	79-72-75-66	292	$90,667	50=	Billy Horschel	77-78-71-73	299	$54,500
	Henrik Stenson	73-76-74-69	292	$90,667		Keegan Bradley	74-76-75-74	299	$54,500
	Sergio García	74-76-73-69	292	$90,667	52=	Ernie Els	75-78-73-74	300	$52,500
	George Coetzee	74-74-73-71	292	$90,667		Ian Poulter	71-78-73-78	300	$52,500
	Scott Hend	72-76-73-71	292	$90,667	54=	Gon. F'dez-Castaño	77-77-77-70	301	$51,000
	Gary Woodland	72-78-71-71	292	$90,667		Brendon de Jonge	76-79-74-72	301	$51,000
	Harris English	69-77-74-72	292	$90,667		Boo Weekley	75-75-78-73	301	$51,000
	Phil Mickelson	74-75-69-74	292	$90,667	57	Steve Stricker	77-78-71-76	302	$50,000
	Zach Johnson	70-75-71-76	292	$90,667	58=	Roberto Castro	74-78-78-73	303	$49,250
25=	Luke Donald	70-82-72-69	293	$76,000		Martin Kaymer	75-80-73-75	303	$49,250
	Kevin Streelman	75-74-72-72	293	$76,000	60=	Yeon-Jin Jeong	75-75-78-77	305	$48,250
	Peter Uihlein	73-77-71-72	293	$76,000		Matteo Manassero	76-76-74-79	305	$48,250
	Francesco Molinari	69-75-76-73	293	$76,000	62=	D.A. Points	82-76-74-74	306	$47,000
	Adam Scott	75-73-72-73	293	$76,000		Jim Furyk	78-77-75-76	306	$47,000
	Rory McIlroy	70-74-75-74	293	$76,000		Victor Dubuisson	72-81-75-78	306	$47,000
	Ryan Moore	70-79-69-75	293	$76,000	65	Dawie van der Walt	81-83-71-75	310	$46,000
	Jimmy Walker	73-77-67-76	293	$76,000	66	Brett Rumford	83-79-77-74	313	$45,500
	Tiger Woods	76-73-66-78	293	$76,000	67	K. Aphibarnrat	74-82-79-79	314	$45,000
34=	Jordan Spieth	73-79-73-69	294	$68,500					

WD: Nick Watney (218)

FIRST ROUND		**SECOND ROUND**		**THIRD ROUND**	
Patrick Reed	68 (-4)	**Patrick Reed**	143 (-1)	**Patrick Reed**	212 (-4)
6 Players	69 (-3)	Dustin Johnson	143 (-1)	Jason Dufner	214 (-2)
		Matt Kuchar	143 (-1)	Hunter Mahan	214 (-2)
		Hunter Mahan	143 (-1)	Tiger Woods	215 (-1)
		4 Players	144 (E)	Jamie Donaldson	215 (-1)

OWR: 50 of top 50 entered - Rating: 770 - Points to 59th - Reed: 76 points, to 20th in OWR

Eligibility for the 2014 WGC-Cadillac Championship

The top 50 players, including any players tied for 50th place, from the Official World Golf Ranking as of Monday, February 25, 2013; the top 50 players, including any players tied for 50th place, from the Official World Golf Ranking as of Monday, March 4, 2013; the top 30 players from the final 2012 FedExCup Points List; the top 10 players from the PGA TOUR FedExCup points list as of March 4, 2013; the top 20 players from the final 2012 European Tour order of merit; the top 10 players from the European Tour order of merit as of Monday, February 28, 2013; the top 2 players from the final 2012 Japan Golf Tour order of merit; the top 2 players from the final 2012 Australasian Tour order of merit; the top two players from the final 2012 Sunshine Tour order of merit; the top 2 players from the final 2012 Asian Tour order of merit.

Puerto Rico Open

Trump International Golf Club - Rio Grande, Puerto Rico
Champion: Chesson Hadley

Mar 6 - Mar 9
7,506 yards   Par 72
Purse: $3.5 Million

Ex-Georgia Tech All-American Chesson Hadley took only 13 PGA Tour starts to give some major support to those touting him as a future star, birdieing the final two holes to claim a two-stroke victory at the Puerto Rico Open, in Rio Grande. In an event played opposite the WGC-Cadillac Championship (and thus featuring a light field), Hadley played steady golf for the first 54 holes, his rounds of 68-65-67 staking him to a one-shot lead over 2008 U.S. Amateur champion Danny Lee of New Zealand. But after an admittedly nervous night, Hadley quickly extended his lead by birdieing three of his first five holes on Sunday, with a chip-in four at the par-5 5th proving a turning point. Lee would mount a late charge, however, carding birdies at the 13th, 15th and 16th to make things interesting, and even adding a final birdie at the par-5 18th for good measure. But after reeling off seven straight pars from holes 10-16, Hadley kicked it into gear once more to post his final two birdies and clinch the title. The victory gained the 2013 Web.com Tour graduate a PGA Tour exemption through 2016, while also moving him up to 63rd in the OWR. Lee's strong finish allowed him to clinch solo second, while another recent Web.com grad, Ben Martin, closed with 66 to take solo third, two shots back.

Pos	Player	Rounds	Total	Money
1	Chesson Hadley	68-65-67-67	267	$630,000
2	Danny Lee	67-68-66-68	269	$378,000
3	Ben Martin	68-67-70-66	271	$238,000
4=	Wes Roach	69-66-70-67	272	$131,950
	Richard H. Lee	69-68-68-67	272	$131,950
	David Toms	72-64-67-69	272	$131,950
	Carl Pettersson	71-66-66-69	272	$131,950
	Jason Gore	67-69-66-70	272	$131,950
9=	Chris Stroud	73-67-68-65	273	$94,500
	Ricky Barnes	68-68-69-68	273	$94,500
	Jerry Kelly	69-67-67-70	273	$94,500
12=	Andrew Loupe	70-70-65-69	274	$77,000
	Jonathan Byrd	69-66-67-72	274	$77,000
14=	Peter Malnati	73-68-69-66	276	$59,500
	James Driscoll	69-63-75-69	276	$59,500
	Robert Karlsson	71-67-69-69	276	$59,500
	Robert Streb	69-72-66-69	276	$59,500
	Tim Petrovic	68-72-66-70	276	$59,500
19=	Scott Langley	72-70-70-65	277	$42,420
	Martin Flores	72-69-69-67	277	$42,420
	Brooks Koepka	72-68-69-68	277	$42,420
	Ryo Ishikawa	70-69-69-69	277	$42,420
	George McNeill	69-67-68-73	277	$42,420
24=	Andrew Svoboda	74-66-68-70	278	$29,050
	Greg Owen	69-67-71-71	278	$29,050
	David Hearn	70-68-69-71	278	$29,050
	Eric Axley	68-66-72-72	278	$29,050
	R. Cabrera-Bello	69-67-68-74	278	$29,050
29=	Emiliano Grillo	71-71-71-66	279	$21,306
	Nicolas Colsaerts	70-69-73-67	279	$21,306
	David Skinns	74-66-71-68	279	$21,306
	Rafael Campos	74-69-67-69	279	$21,306
	Bud Cauley	69-67-72-71	279	$21,306
	William McGirt	68-71-69-71	279	$21,306
	Ted Potter Jr.	71-70-65-73	279	$21,306
	Brad Fritsch	71-68-67-73	279	$21,306
37=	Seung-Yul Noh	72-70-71-67	280	$15,400
	Cameron Beckman	69-71-71-69	280	$15,400
	Trevor Immelman	74-66-70-70	280	$15,400
	T. Van Aswegen	69-68-72-71	280	$15,400
	Y.E. Yang	68-70-71-71	280	$15,400
	Steven Bowditch	69-70-67-74	280	$15,400
43=	Will Wilcox	71-71-69-70	281	$11,223
	Brian Stuard	66-71-73-71	281	$11,223
	Lee Williams	71-70-68-72	281	$11,223
	Hudson Swafford	72-68-69-72	281	$11,223
	Ryuji Imada	73-67-68-73	281	$11,223
	Ryan Sullivan	69-70-68-74	281	$11,223
49=	Sean O'Hair	75-67-70-70	282	$8,638
	Brady Watt	71-69-72-70	282	$8,638
	John Daly	74-69-67-72	282	$8,638
	Kevin Kisner	71-69-69-73	282	$8,638
	Jim Herman	69-70-68-75	282	$8,638
54=	Stephen Ames	70-72-71-70	283	$8,015
	Joe Ogilvie	74-67-72-70	283	$8,015
	Alex Cejka	69-73-68-73	283	$8,015
	Michael Thompson	71-69-68-75	283	$8,015
58=	Harrison Frazar	72-71-71-70	284	$7,665
	Daniel Chopra	74-66-74-70	284	$7,665
	Bronson La'Cassie	71-70-72-71	284	$7,665
	Edward Loar	69-70-72-73	284	$7,665
	John Rollins	69-69-71-75	284	$7,665
	Jamie Lovemark	73-65-71-75	284	$7,665
64	Scott Brown	70-73-70-72	285	$7,420
65=	Fred Funk	71-72-71-72	286	$7,245
	Marco Dawson	70-73-71-72	286	$7,245
	Vaughn Taylor	72-71-71-72	286	$7,245
	Jesper Parnevik	69-73-71-73	286	$7,245
69	Jhonattan Vegas	74-68-71-74	287	$7,070
70	Matt Bettencourt	71-71-71-75	288	$7,000
71	Max Homa	73-70-71-75	289	$6,930
72=	Brice Garnett	70-72-73	215	$6,720
	Rod Pampling	70-71-74	215	$6,720
	Tag Ridings	70-72-73	215	$6,720
	Chris Smith	69-74-72	215	$6,720
	Paul Stankowski	73-70-72	215	$6,720
77	Jose Coceres	73-70-73	216	$6,510
78=	Tim Clark	72-70-75	217	$6,370
	Chris DiMarco	75-68-74	217	$6,370
	Lee Janzen	73-70-74	217	$6,370

Out Of The Money: **144**: Johnson Wagner, Troy Matteson, Scott McCarron, Andrés Romero, Álvaro Quirós, Miguel Ángel Carballo, Ben Kohles, Justin Bolli, Kevin Foley **145**: Nathan Green, Dicky Pride, Steve Flesch, Mark Anderson, Tim Wilkinson, Alex Prugh, Chad Collins, Morgan Hoffmann, John Mallinger, Marcel Siem, Doug LaBelle II, Austen Truslow, Marc Turnesa **146**: David Duval, Michael Bradley, Kris Blanks, Nicholas Thompson, Max Alverio, Bobby Gates, Kevin Tway **147**: Glen Day, Derek Lamely, Robert Allenby, Erick Morales, Scott Gardiner **148**: Chad Campbell, Troy Merritt, Joe Durant, Matt Jones, Alex Aragon, Frank Lickliter II **149**: Julian Etulain, Danny Balin, Wes Short Jr., D.J. Trahan **150**: Timothy Puetz, Michael Putnam, Fabián Gómez, Jay Westerlund **151**: Rod Perry **153**: Miguel Suarez **WD**: J.J. Henry (74), Tommy Gainey

FIRST ROUND		SECOND ROUND		THIRD ROUND	
Brian Stuard	66 (-6)	James Driscoll	132 (-12)	**Chesson Hadley**	200 (-16)
Jason Gore	67 (-5)	**Chesson Hadley**	133 (-11)	Danny Lee	201 (-15)
Danny Lee	67 (-5)	Eric Axley	134 (-10)	Jason Gore	202 (-14)
7 Players	68 (-4)	4 Players	135 (-9)	Jonathan Byrd	202 (-14)
Chesson Hadley	68 (-4)			3 Players	203 (-13)

OWR: 0 of top 50 entered - Rating: 32 - Points to 28th - Hadley: 24 points, to 63rd in OWR

Valspar Championship

Innisbrook Resort (Copperhead) - Palm Harbor, FL
Champion: John Senden

Mar 13 - Mar 16
7,340 yards   Par 71
Purse: $5.7 Million

Forty-two-year-old Australian John Senden claimed his first victory anywhere in the world since 2006, logging clutch birdies at the 70th and 71st holes on a tough Innisbrook Copperhead course to win the Valspar Championship by one. One of the PGA Tour's purest ball-strikers, Senden stood far off the lead after opening rounds of 71-72 but began Saturday with four birdies in his first five holes, then later added three more to card the week's low round of 64 and move within two of 54-hole leader Robert Garrigus. Garrigus, for his part, fell apart early on Sunday, logging two double-bogeys and a bogey over a four-hole front nine stretch, leaving him to close with 75 and an eventual tie for fourth. Senden, on the other hand, made two early birdies before struggling in the middle of his round, then eventually scoring decisive blows by holing a 70-foot chip for birdie at the 16th hole, then a 20-footer for his clinching birdie at the par-3 17th. Second place was taken by Kevin Na, who recovered from a double-bogey at the 8th (and an outward 39) to move into contention with late birdies at the 14th and 17th, only to miss a 40-foot tying birdie putt at the last. Scott Langley, the only player to break par in all four rounds, took solo third, two shots off the pace. Both Justin Rose and former world number one Luke Donald briefly flirted with contention on Sunday with Donald, the event's 2012 champion, closing with a 70 to tie for fourth.

Pos	Player	Scores	Total	Money
1	John Senden	72-71-64-70	277	$1.026 mil
2	Kevin Na	70-68-68-72	278	$615,600
3	Scott Langley	71-69-69-70	279	$387,600
4=	Will MacKenzie	73-70-68-69	280	$235,600
	Luke Donald	71-72-67-70	280	$235,600
	Robert Garrigus	69-66-70-75	280	$235,600
7	George McNeill	73-71-67-70	281	$190,950
8=	Graham DeLaet	75-68-71-68	282	$148,200
	Gary Woodland	72-71-70-69	282	$148,200
	Matt Every	68-71-72-71	282	$148,200
	David Hearn	71-70-70-71	282	$148,200
	Matteo Manassero	69-70-71-72	282	$148,200
	Justin Rose	71-68-69-74	282	$148,200
14=	Sang-Moon Bae	72-73-71-67	283	$94,050
	Charles Howell III	71-70-74-68	283	$94,050
	Bill Haas	69-73-72-69	283	$94,050
	Jason Dufner	72-73-68-70	283	$94,050
	Chesson Hadley	75-70-67-71	283	$94,050
	Jason Kokrak	74-68-68-73	283	$94,050
20=	Carl Pettersson	71-70-71-72	284	$64,068
	Jordan Spieth	71-70-71-72	284	$64,068
	Jim Furyk	71-69-71-73	284	$64,068
	Fredrik Jacobson	70-71-70-73	284	$64,068
	Ted Potter Jr.	73-71-67-73	284	$64,068
25=	Ryo Ishikawa	73-72-72-68	285	$42,587
	Cameron Tringale	74-71-70-70	285	$42,587
	Brian Harman	71-70-73-71	285	$42,587
	Morgan Hoffmann	74-69-71-71	285	$42,587
	Josh Teater	73-70-70-72	285	$42,587
	Russell Knox	70-73-70-72	285	$42,587
	Charley Hoffman	70-72-67-76	285	$42,587
32=	Erik Compton	72-73-72-69	286	$31,540
	Robert Allenby	73-71-70-72	286	$31,540
	Justin Hicks	72-72-70-72	286	$31,540
	Ben Crane	70-72-71-73	286	$31,540
	Jonathan Byrd	70-73-70-73	286	$31,540
	John Merrick	70-70-72-74	286	$31,540
38=	Harris English	72-69-74-72	287	$23,940
	Y.E. Yang	73-72-70-72	287	$23,940
	Kevin Streelman	73-69-71-74	287	$23,940
	James Hahn	69-74-70-74	287	$23,940
	Chad Collins	73-71-69-74	287	$23,940
	Matt Kuchar	73-71-69-74	287	$23,940
44=	Woody Austin	71-71-74-72	288	$15,892
	Pat Perez	68-71-77-72	288	$15,892
	Ben Curtis	70-74-71-73	288	$15,892
	Brendon Todd	70-75-70-73	288	$15,892
	Nicholas Thompson	76-69-69-74	288	$15,892
	Tommy Gainey	69-72-72-75	288	$15,892
	Peter Hanson	75-70-69-74	288	$15,892
	K.J. Choi	72-72-69-75	288	$15,892
	Greg Chalmers	68-72-72-76	288	$15,892
	Retief Goosen	72-73-64-79	288	$15,892
54=	J.B. Holmes	71-74-71-73	289	$13,053
	Michael Putnam	69-72-74-74	289	$13,053
	Justin Leonard	71-71-71-76	289	$13,053
	James Driscoll	73-70-68-78	289	$13,053
58=	Stuart Appleby	71-73-74-72	290	$12,426
	Darren Clarke	71-74-73-72	290	$12,426
	David Lingmerth	73-72-71-74	290	$12,426
	Brandt Snedeker	72-73-71-74	290	$12,426
	Jerry Kelly	76-68-71-75	290	$12,426
	D.H. Lee	74-70-70-76	290	$12,426
	Michael Thompson	72-69-72-77	290	$12,426
65=	Nicolas Colsaerts	69-73-76-73	291	$11,742
	Marc Leishman	75-69-74-73	291	$11,742
	Jason Bohn	71-74-73-73	291	$11,742
	Padraig Harrington	75-70-72-74	291	$11,742
	Stephen Ames	72-70-72-77	291	$11,742
70=	Paul Goydos	75-69-73-75	292	$11,229
	Daniel Summerhays	77-68-71-76	292	$11,229
	Davis Love III	74-70-71-77	292	$11,229
	Rory Sabbatini	70-72-72-78	292	$11,229
74	Sean O'Hair	73-71-74-78	296	$10,944
75	John Mallinger	71-73-74-80	298	$10,830
	Eric Axley	72-70-77	219	$10,431
	Ricky Barnes	70-72-77	219	$10,431
	Brian Gay	75-69-75	219	$10,431
	Tim Herron	73-72-74	219	$10,431
	Luke Guthrie	70-70-80	220	$10,146
	Tim Clark	73-72-76	221	$9,975
	Ken Duke	71-71-79	221	$9,975
	Boo Weekley	74-71-77	222	$9,804

Out Of The Money: **146**: William McGirt, Scott Brown, Ernie Els, Bo Van Pelt, Briny Baird, Wes Roach, Kevin Kisner, Andrés Romero, Jonas Blixt, Mike Weir, Camilo Villegas **147**: Webb Simpson, Lucas Glover, Geoff Ogilvy, D.A. Points, Bryce Molder, Brendon de Jonge, Max Homa, Danny Lee, Paul Casey, Jason Gore, Louis Oosthuizen, J.J. Henry, Stewart Cink, John Huh, Steven Bowditch, Martin Flores, Branden Grace, Brooks Koepka, Rod Perry **148**: Brian Stuard, Vijay Singh, Mark Wilson, John Rollins **149**: Kevin Chappell, Scott Stallings, Richard H. Lee, Billy Hurley III, Peter Uihlein, Spencer Levin, Aaron Baddeley, Angel Cabrera, Roberto Castro **150**: David Toms, Derek Ernst, Mark Blakefield, Ben Martin **151**: Jeff Overton, Kyle Stanley, Thorbjørn Olesen, Johnson Wagner, David Lynn, Michael Hebert **152**: Brian Davis **153**: Charlie Wi, John Peterson, Charlie Beljan **156**: Jim Renner **164**: John Daly   **WD**: Blake Adams (78), Mark Calcavecchia (217)

	FIRST ROUND		SECOND ROUND		THIRD ROUND	
	Matt Every	68 (-3)	Robert Garrigus	135 (-7)	Robert Garrigus	205 (-8)
	Pat Perez	68 (-3)	Kevin Na	138 (-4)	Kevin Na	206 (-7)
	Greg Chalmers	68 (-3)	4 Players	139 (-3)	**John Senden**	207 (-6)
	Danny Lee	68 (-3)	**John Senden**	143 (+1)	Justin Rose	208 (-5)
	John Senden	72 (+1)			3 Players	209 (-4)

OWR: 15 of top 50 entered   -   Rating: 335   -   Points to 53rd   -   Senden: 50 points, to 60th in OWR

Arnold Palmer Invitational

Bay Hill Club & Lodge - Orlando, FL
Champion: Matt Every

Mar 20 - Mar 23
7,381 yards   Par 72
Purse: $6.2 Million

In his 92nd career start, native Floridian Matt Every stood nine shots off the pace after 36 holes of the Arnold Palmer Invitational, before finishing with rounds of 66-70 to claim his first PGA Tour victory, edging Keegan Bradley by one. For the first three days, the stage belonged squarely to world number two Adam Scott, who could have reached number one with a victory and opened with a dazzling Thursday 62. A second round 68 saw him standing seven clear of the field at the halfway mark, and if a Saturday 71 was slightly disappointing, Scott still held a three shot lead through 54 holes. Unfortunately, that advantage dissipated early on Sunday when Scott opened with two bogeys in his first three holes, eventually turning in 38. He could do little better on the inward half, and as he staggered home to a 76 (and solo third), both Every and Keegan Bradley were able to move ahead of him for the stretch run. Every, for his part, ran off four birdies from holes 9-13 and, at 15-under-par, might well have cruised home to an easy victory had he not posted late bogeys at the 16th and, after missing a four-footer to clinch, the watery 18th. This allowed Bradley – who'd ably recovered from a double-bogey at the second and a bogey at the third – to move within one via clutch birdies at the par-5 16th and the tough par-3 17th. But when his 30-foot birdie putt at the last slid by, Bradley was second and Every - who'd attended this event regularly as a youth - was hoisting the trophy. Long-hitting Jason Kokrak, who bogeyed both the 14th and the 18th, claimed solo fourth, while world number three Henrik Stenson logged his first high finish of the season by closing 69-68 to head a trio tied for fifth.

1	Matt Every	69-70-66-70	275	$1.116 mil		Bryce Molder	72-72-69-74	287	$28,636
2	Keegan Bradley	71-67-66-72	276	$669,600		Charles Howell III	68-71-72-76	287	$28,636
3	Adam Scott	62-68-71-76	277	$421,600		Aaron Baddeley	70-70-70-77	287	$28,636
4	Jason Kokrak	67-71-67-73	278	$297,600		Morgan Hoffmann	67-71-71-78	287	$28,636
5=	Henrik Stenson	69-73-69-68	279	$226,300	43=	Will MacKenzie	71-75-72-70	288	$18,476
	Erik Compton	72-68-70-69	279	$226,300		Jhonattan Vegas	70-72-75-71	288	$18,476
	Francesco Molinari	67-70-69-73	279	$226,300		John Merrick	65-74-76-73	288	$18,476
8=	Brandt Snedeker	67-71-74-68	280	$186,000		Zach Johnson	71-71-73-73	288	$18,476
	Ryo Ishikawa	65-74-70-71	280	$186,000		Russell Knox	71-71-72-74	288	$18,476
10=	Sean O'Hair	71-75-69-67	282	$148,800		Charlie Beljan	72-72-70-74	288	$18,476
	Graeme McDowell	68-77-67-70	282	$148,800		Billy Horschel	70-74-69-75	288	$18,476
	J.B. Holmes	68-69-72-73	282	$148,800		Jamie Donaldson	67-71-74-76	288	$18,476
	Fredrik Jacobson	71-68-70-73	282	$148,800		Sam Saunders	69-71-71-77	288	$18,476
14=	Harris English	69-71-75-68	283	$102,300	52=	John Senden	72-74-71-72	289	$14,539
	Lucas Glover	72-74-68-69	283	$102,300		David Hearn	70-72-73-74	289	$14,539
	Kevin Chappell	71-70-71-71	283	$102,300		David Lingmerth	75-71-69-74	289	$14,539
	Kevin Na	70-71-71-71	283	$102,300		Patrick Reed	69-73-70-77	289	$14,539
	George McNeill	71-72-69-71	283	$102,300	56=	Cameron Tringale	70-74-75-71	290	$14,012
	Matt Jones	71-71-69-72	283	$102,300		Lee Janzen	72-73-74-71	290	$14,012
20=	Camilo Villegas	71-73-73-67	284	$67,167		Jason Bohn	73-73-72-72	290	$14,012
	Brian Davis	70-74-71-69	284	$67,167		Zachary Olsen (a)	73-71-72-74	290	-
	Gary Woodland	73-71-70-70	284	$67,167	60=	Brian Stuard	72-74-74-71	291	$13,454
	Vijay Singh	72-73-68-71	284	$67,167		Ryan Moore	68-72-78-73	291	$13,454
	Brendan Steele	68-74-70-72	284	$67,167		Paul Casey	67-79-72-73	291	$13,454
	Ian Poulter	68-71-69-76	284	$67,167		Briny Baird	72-71-74-74	291	$13,454
26=	Brooks Koepka	74-70-72-69	285	$45,880		K.J. Choi	70-76-70-75	291	$13,454
	Nicholas Thompson	71-73-71-70	285	$45,880		Chris Kirk	69-72-72-78	291	$13,454
	Trevor Immelman	69-72-71-73	285	$45,880	66	Stewart Cink	71-70-72-79	292	$13,020
	Davis Love III	70-73-69-73	285	$45,880	67=	Rod Pampling	73-72-71-77	293	$12,772
	Chesson Hadley	69-68-69-79	285	$45,880		Padraig Harrington	70-70-73-80	293	$12,772
31=	Danny Lee	71-72-73-70	286	$37,588		Pat Perez	70-70-70-83	293	$12,772
	Marc Leishman	72-74-69-71	286	$37,588	70=	Michael Putnam	70-75-74-75	294	$12,462
	Chris Stroud	73-69-72-72	286	$37,588		Woody Austin	72-71-75-76	294	$12,462
	Retief Goosen	70-75-68-73	286	$37,588	72=	Tim Wilkinson	71-74-77-73	295	$12,214
35=	Gon. F'dez-Castaño	66-77-74-70	287	$28,636		Greg Owen	76-69-74-76	295	$12,214
	Luke Guthrie	71-71-74-71	287	$28,636	74=	Chad Campbell	69-77-73-77	296	$11,966
	Peter Hanson	75-69-71-72	287	$28,636		Justin Hicks	78-68-71-79	296	$11,966
	Seung-Yul Noh	72-68-74-73	287	$28,636	76	Martin Laird	71-72-76-78	297	$11,780

Out Of The Money: **147**: David Lynn, Brian Harman, Stuart Appleby, Angel Cabrera, Ben Martin, Dicky Pride **148**: Rod Perry, Tyrone Van Aswegen, Jim Renner **149**: Tim Herron, Nicolas Colsaerts, Daniel Chopra, Rickie Fowler, Russell Henley, D.A. Points, J.J. Henry, Ken Duke **150**: Justin Rose, David Duval **151**: Daniel Summerhays, Brice Garnett, Boo Weekley, Chad Collins, Scott Stallings, Lee Westwood, Billy Hurley **152**: Greg Chalmers, Robert Garrigus, Brendon Todd, Scott Brown, Matthew Fitzpatrick **153**: Darren Clarke, Paul Goydos **154**: Hudson Swafford, Sang-Moon Bae, William McGirt **155**: Brian Gay, Robert Gamez **158**: Derek Ernst   **WD**: Nathan T. Smith (73), Jeff Overton (75), Rory Sabbatini (81), Bubba Watson (83)

FIRST ROUND		SECOND ROUND		THIRD ROUND	
Adam Scott	62 (-10)	Adam Scott	130 (-14)	Adam Scott	201 (-15)
Ryo Ishikawa	65 (-7)	J.B. Holmes	137 (-7)	Keegan Bradley	204 (-12)
John Merrick	65 (-7)	Chesson Hadley	137 (-7)	**Matt Every**	205 (-11)
Gon. F'dez-Castaño	66 (-6)	Francesco Molinari	137 (-7)	Jason Kokrak	205 (-11)
6 Players	67 (-5)	5 Players	138 (-6)	2 Players	206 (-10)
Matt Every	69 (-3)	**Matt Every**	139 (-5)		

OWR: 20 of top 50 entered - Rating: 377 - Points to 55th - Every: 56 points, to 44th in OWR

Valero Texas Open

TPC San Antonio (AT&T Oaks Course) - San Antonio, TX
Champion: Steven Bowditch

Mar 27 - Mar 30
7,522 yards Par 72
Purse: $6.2 Million

Thirty-year-old Australian Steven Bowditch had only logged two top-10 finishes in eight seasons on the PGA Tour, but in windy, demanding Sunday conditions at the Texas Open, he broke through for career-altering first victory. On a day which saw as many players (two) fail to break 80 as break 70, Bowditch struggled throughout his round, carding four bogeys and one double-bogey en route to a closing 76 – the highest final round by a winner since Vijay Singh's 76 at the 2004 PGA, and the highest in a non-major since Fred Couples shot 77 in winning the 1983 Kemper Open. The halfway and 54-hole leader, Bowditch – a two-time Web.com Tour winner – also recorded two birdies on Sunday, with the second (at the par-5 14th) giving him a two-shot lead which he nursed right up until missing a three-footer for par at the last. Second place was shared by a hot Will MacKenzie (who bogeyed the 1st hole on Sunday before going three-under-par the rest of the way) and Daniel Summerhays, whose closing 71 helped him make up significant ground on the pack. More disappointed was world number 11 Matt Kuchar who could have won outright had he maintained the even par pace of his Sunday front nine, but bogeys at the 10th, 11th and 14th instead saw him home with a 75, and a tie for fourth.

1	Steven Bowditch	69-67-68-76	280	$1.116 mil
2=	Will MacKenzie	69-72-70-70	281	$545,600
	Daniel Summerhays	72-68-70-71	281	$545,600
4=	Matt Kuchar	70-72-65-75	282	$272,800
	Andrew Loupe	67-70-70-75	282	$272,800
6=	Brendon Todd	71-76-68-68	283	$200,725
	Jerry Kelly	71-71-70-71	283	$200,725
	Jim Furyk	70-74-68-71	283	$200,725
	Zach Johnson	70-71-70-72	283	$200,725
10	Jordan Spieth	75-70-68-71	284	$167,400
11=	Charley Hoffman	70-75-70-70	285	$136,400
	Geoff Ogilvy	74-69-69-73	285	$136,400
	Kevin Na	70-70-69-76	285	$136,400
	Pat Perez	68-71-69-77	285	$136,400
15	Justin Hicks	69-73-72-72	286	$111,600
16=	Seung-Yul Noh	69-76-71-71	287	$78,740
	Michael Thompson	70-75-71-71	287	$78,740
	James Hahn	71-70-76-70	287	$78,740
	Brian Harman	70-72-75-70	287	$78,740
	Martin Flores	71-71-73-72	287	$78,740
	Fredrik Jacobson	70-70-73-74	287	$78,740
	Carl Pettersson	70-73-71-73	287	$78,740
	Wes Roach	75-66-72-74	287	$78,740
	Jimmy Walker	76-71-71-69	287	$78,740
	Stephen Ames	74-71-68-74	287	$78,740
26=	Johnson Wagner	73-73-71-71	288	$45,880
	Russell Knox	74-70-71-73	288	$45,880
	Andrew Svoboda	73-73-67-75	288	$45,880
	Bo Van Pelt	69-73-71-75	288	$45,880
	Chad Collins	71-66-73-78	288	$45,880
31=	Justin Leonard	76-69-71-73	289	$36,766
	Trevor Immelman	70-71-74-74	289	$36,766
	William McGirt	72-71-72-74	289	$36,766
	Brice Garnett	70-73-71-75	289	$36,766
	Jason Kokrak	71-71-77-70	289	$36,766
36=	Cameron Beckman	69-70-77-74	290	$28,572
	Scott Brown	70-74-73-73	290	$28,572
	Jamie Lovemark	73-72-72-73	290	$28,572
	Brendon de Jonge	73-72-71-74	290	$28,572
	Brooks Koepka	71-74-73-72	290	$28,572
	Josh Teater	71-70-77-72	290	$28,572
42=	Michael Putnam	72-71-73-75	291	$22,320
	Kevin Foley	74-73-70-74	291	$22,320
	John Senden	72-73-73-73	291	$22,320
	Joe Ogilvie	74-73-71-73	291	$22,320
46=	Cameron Tringale	71-74-72-75	292	$15,934
	Ben Curtis	70-75-72-75	292	$15,934
	Briny Baird	72-72-72-76	292	$15,934
	Bronson La'Cassie	74-73-70-75	292	$15,934
	John Mallinger	74-73-70-75	292	$15,934
	Andrés Romero	71-74-73-74	292	$15,934
	Miguel A. Carballo	69-76-74-73	292	$15,934
	Troy Merritt	73-72-74-73	292	$15,934
	Brian Davis	71-72-76-73	292	$15,934
	Troy Matteson	72-73-74-73	292	$15,934
56=	Brian Gay	73-71-73-76	293	$13,826
	Jeff Maggert	72-74-72-75	293	$13,826
	Chesson Hadley	69-73-71-80	293	$13,826
	Mike Weir	76-71-72-74	293	$13,826
	Ryan Palmer	72-71-68-82	293	$13,826
	Greg Chalmers	73-73-74-73	293	$13,826
62=	Tim Wilkinson	74-70-74-76	294	$13,330
	Richard H. Lee	72-75-73-74	294	$13,330
64=	J.B. Holmes	72-75-72-76	295	$13,020
	Scott Gardiner	74-69-77-75	295	$13,020
	Luke Guthrie	74-72-74-75	295	$13,020
67=	John Peterson	74-72-74-76	296	$12,710
	Aaron Baddeley	70-71-79-76	296	$12,710
69=	Fred Funk	70-72-77-78	297	$12,462
	Charlie Beljan	70-76-74-77	297	$12,462
71	Alex Aragon	70-74-76-78	298	$12,276
72=	Stuart Appleby	70-77-74	221	$11,966
	Alex Prugh	71-73-77	221	$11,966
	Robert Streb	72-72-77	221	$11,966
	Charlie Wi	73-73-75	221	$11,966
76	Jim Herman	73-73-76	222	$11,656
77=	T. Van Aswegen	71-76-77	224	$11,470
	Camilo Villegas	71-73-80	224	$11,470
79=	Branden Grace	72-73-82	227	$11,222
	John Merrick	72-75-80	227	$11,222

Out Of The Money: 148: Sean O'Hair, Robert Allenby, Ernie Els, Harrison Frazar, John Rollins, Edward Loar, Hunter Brown, Nicolas Colsaerts, D.H. Lee, Nicholas Thompson, Mark Wilson, John Huh, Daniel Chopra, Jim Renner **149:** Woody Austin, Kyle Stanley, Matt Bettencourt, Mike Miller, David Lingmerth, Padraig Harrington, Martin Laird, Ted Potter Jr., David Toms, Ben Crane **150:** J.J. Henry, Bud Cauley, Brendan Steele, K.J. Choi, Ryo Ishikawa, Heath Slocum, Kevin Kisner, Derek Lamely **151:** Billy Horschel, Jhonattan Vegas, Billy Hurley III, Benjamin Alvarado, Danny Lee, Peter Uihlein **152:** Jason Bohn, Jay McLuen, Peter Malnati, Joe Durant, Mark Anderson, Kevin Tway, Lee Williams, Ben Martin **153:** Retief Goosen, Kevin Chappell, Jeff Overton **154:** Brad Fritsch, Will Wilcox **155:** Bobby Gates, Scott Verplank **156:** Paul Goydos, Scott Langley, Hudson Swafford **161:** David Von Hoffman **WD:** Erik Compton (71), Tommy Gainey (73), Bryce Molder (74), Dudley Hart (77), Ricky Barnes (77), Phil Mickelson (147)

FIRST ROUND		SECOND ROUND		THIRD ROUND	
Andrew Loupe	67 (-5)	**Steven Bowditch**	136 (-8)	**Steven Bowditch**	204 (-12)
Pat Perez	68 (-4)	Chad Collins	137 (-7)	Matt Kuchar	207 (-9)
Danny Lee	68 (-4)	Andrew Loupe	137 (-7)	Andrew Loupe	207 (-9)
8 Players	69 (-3)	Pat Perez	139 (-5)	Pat Perez	208 (-8)
Steven Bowditch	69 (-3)	Cameron Beckman	139 (-5)	Kevin Na	209 (-7)

OWR: 8 of top 50 entered - Rating: 211 - Points to 45th - Bowditch: 40 points, to 134th in OWR

Shell Houston Open

Golf Club of Houston (Tournament) - Humble, TX
Champion: Matt Jones

Apr 3 - Apr 6
7,457 yards Par 72
Purse: $6.4 Million

For the second straight week, an Australian scored his maiden win on the PGA Tour as 33-year-old Matt Jones holed a 42-yard chip on the first hole of sudden death to defeat Matt Kuchar at the Shell Houston Open. A former collegiate star at Arizona State, Jones opened his week with rounds of 68-68-71 at the rain-softened Golf Club of Houston, which left him six shots behind 54-hole leader Kuchar. Jones then fell further behind by bogeying the 1st hole on Sunday before reeling off a run of six birdies over his next 10 holes, briefly tying for the lead near the turn. By the time he birdied the 16th he stood one behind Kuchar, then appeared to squander his chance with an untimely bogey at the par-4 17th. But with little to lose, Jones then rolled in a 46-foot birdie putt at the last, then looked on as Kuchar hit his approach into the water at the difficult par-4 18th, ultimately scrambling to make bogey and force the playoff. After Jones drove it in a fairway bunker as they played the 18th again, then hit his second shy of the green, Kuchar proceeded to bunker his approach from the fairway, leaving the door open just enough for Jones to hole the chip and claim the title. The victory meant a change in travel plans for Jones who was initially planning on taking the following week off but instead earned the final spot in The Masters. Thirty-six hole leader Sergio García finished third and Cameron Tringale fourth, though equally notable on Sunday was the 65 posted by world number nine Rory McIlroy, which matched the event's low score in McIlroy's final pre-Masters tune-up.

#	Player	Rounds	Total	Prize
1	Matt Jones	68-68-71-66	273	$1.152 mil
2	Matt Kuchar	66-67-68-72	273	$691,200
3	Sergio García	67-65-73-70	275	$435,200
4	Cameron Tringale	68-68-69-71	276	$307,200
5	Shawn Stefani	67-69-73-69	278	$256,000
6	Rickie Fowler	70-70-68-71	279	$230,400
7=	Brice Garnett	68-71-72-69	280	$186,240
	Retief Goosen	68-71-71-70	280	$186,240
	Russell Henley	73-69-72-66	280	$186,240
	Rory McIlroy	70-71-74-65	280	$186,240
	Ryan Palmer	70-68-73-69	280	$186,240
12=	Erik Compton	66-73-73-69	281	$125,440
	Ben Curtis	67-70-71-73	281	$125,440
	J.B. Holmes	66-73-71-71	281	$125,440
	Phil Mickelson	68-70-72-71	281	$125,440
	Chris Stroud	68-72-71-70	281	$125,440
17=	Martin Flores	68-72-72-70	282	$99,200
	Lee Westwood	70-72-71-69	282	$99,200
19=	Jonathan Byrd	68-74-73-68	283	$77,568
	Graham DeLaet	70-71-72-70	283	$77,568
	Jason Gore	67-71-74-71	283	$77,568
	Fredrik Jacobson	68-72-74-69	283	$77,568
	Charl Schwartzel	67-75-70-71	283	$77,568
24=	Luke Donald	71-71-71-71	284	$50,651
	Michael Putnam	68-72-73-71	284	$50,651
	Jim Renner	66-72-74-72	284	$50,651
	Andrés Romero	72-69-70-73	284	$50,651
	Steve Stricker	68-69-76-71	284	$50,651
	Nicholas Thompson	71-69-74-70	284	$50,651
	Jimmy Walker	71-65-77-71	284	$50,651
31=	Kevin Chappell	71-72-76-66	285	$37,952
	Jon Curran	69-72-69-75	285	$37,952
	Ryo Ishikawa	69-74-71-71	285	$37,952
	Hunter Mahan	69-72-71-73	285	$37,952
	Carl Pettersson	69-74-72-70	285	$37,952
36	James Hahn	71-72-73-70	286	$32,960
37=	Bill Haas	65-74-76-72	287	$28,160
	Charley Hoffman	65-76-78-68	287	$28,160
	John Huh	71-71-72-73	287	$28,160
	Jeff Overton	73-69-74-71	287	$28,160
	David Toms	71-71-75-70	287	$28,160
	Brendon de Jonge	71-73-72-71	287	$28,160
43=	Ricky Barnes	70-73-74-71	288	$18,374
	Keegan Bradley	66-77-73-72	288	$18,374
	Angel Cabrera	68-73-75-72	288	$18,374
	Ben Crane	70-74-72-72	288	$18,374
	Ernie Els	68-76-74-70	288	$18,374
	Brian Gay	71-70-71-76	288	$18,374
	Justin Hicks	67-73-74-74	288	$18,374
	Jeff Maggert	69-73-74-72	288	$18,374
	Hudson Swafford	70-74-76-68	288	$18,374
	Brendon Todd	69-74-73-72	288	$18,374
	Camilo Villegas	67-73-73-75	288	$18,374
54=	John Mallinger	72-72-75-70	289	$14,656
	John Merrick	74-68-75-72	289	$14,656
	Kyle Stanley	69-74-74-72	289	$14,656
	Henrik Stenson	71-72-76-70	289	$14,656
58=	Stewart Cink	67-75-74-74	290	$14,208
	Harrison Frazar	71-71-76-72	290	$14,208
	Brian Harman	70-71-74-75	290	$14,208
61=	Robert Garrigus	74-69-73-75	291	$13,760
	Davis Love III	68-73-78-72	291	$13,760
	Webb Simpson	68-73-73-77	291	$13,760
	Michael Thompson	67-73-77-74	291	$13,760
65=	Chris Kirk	68-74-75-75	292	$13,312
	Justin Leonard	70-71-81-70	292	$13,312
	John Rollins	68-76-72-76	292	$13,312
68	Kevin Kisner	71-70-81-71	293	$13,056
69=	Greg Chalmers	69-74-75-76	294	$12,864
	Tommy Gainey	71-72-77-74	294	$12,864
71	T. Van Aswegen	71-73-74-77	295	$12,672
72=	J.J. Henry	72-71-78-75	296	$12,480
	Jhonattan Vegas	67-75-78-76	296	$12,480
74=	Stephen Ames	72-71-78-76	297	$12,224
	Bubba Dickerson	74-70-74-79	297	$12,224
76	Roberto Castro	71-72-83-73	299	$12,032

Out Of The Money: 145: Charlie Wi, Jordan Spieth, Kevin Stadler, D.A. Points, Jim Herman, Ben Martin, Aaron Baddeley, Scott Langley, Joe Ogilvie, Louis Oosthuizen, Robert Allenby, Sang-Moon Bae, Chad Collins, Peter Hanson **146**: Paul Casey, Jonas Blixt, Stuart Appleby, Martin Kaymer, Y.E. Yang, David Hearn, Richard H. Lee, David Lingmerth, Heath Slocum, Jason Kokrak, Brendan Steele, Josh Teater, Lucas Glover, Kevin Streelman, Andrew Loupe, Daniel Summerhays, Matteo Manassero **147**: Trevor Immelman, Ian Poulter, Mike Weir, Ted Potter Jr., D.H. Lee, John Peterson, Andrew Putnam, Paul Goydos, Derek Ernst, Peter Uihlein **148**: Padraig Harrington, Scott Stallings, Charlie Beljan, Brian Stuard, Ted Purdy **149**: Charles Howell III, Luke Guthrie, Morgan Hoffmann, Steven Bowditch **150**: Bryce Molder, Darren Clarke, Geoff Ogilvy, Johnson Wagner, James Driscoll **151**: Bobby Gates, Brian Davis, Tim Clark **152**: Troy Matteson, Branden Grace **154**: Scott Gardiner **155**: Bo Van Pelt, Jamie Lovemark **159**: Brad Lardon **WD**: Seung-Yul Noh (72), Nicolas Colsaerts (76), Dustin Johnson (80)

FIRST ROUND		SECOND ROUND		THIRD ROUND	
Bill Haas	65 (-7)	Sergio García	132 (-12)	Matt Kuchar	201 (-15)
Charley Hoffman	65 (-7)	Matt Kuchar	133 (-11)	Cameron Tringale	205 (-11)
5 Players	66 (-6)	4 Players	136 (-8)	Sergio García	205 (-11)
Matt Jones	68 (-4)	**Matt Jones**	136 (-8)	**Matt Jones**	207 (-9)
				2 Players	208 (-8)

OWR: 23 of top 50 entered - Rating: 461 - Points to 57th - Jones: 58 points, to 41st in OWR

RBC Heritage

Harbour Town Golf Links - Hilton Head, SC
Champion: Matt Kuchar

Apr 17 - Apr 20
7,101 yards   Par 71
Purse: $5.8 Million

Coming off three straight top-five finishes (including contending late at The Masters and losing a playoff in Houston to a 42-yard Matt Jones chip-in), world number six Matt Kuchar seemed a good bet to contend at the RBC Heritage – even after trailing 54-hole leader Luke Donald by four strokes on Saturday night. But on a Sunday which saw the week's first really good golfing weather, Kuchar came out blazing, logging seven birdies over Harbour Town's first 10 holes and eventually taking a one-stroke lead to the tee of the par-3 17th. Looking for a clinching birdie, he ripped a seven iron inside of eight feet, then promptly three putted to fall back into a tie with Donald, who had rebounded with four big birdies after double-bogeying the 6th and bogeying the 10th. Donald, however, would prove unable to break the tie at either the 17th or 18th. Kuchar, for his part, then landed his 5 iron approach to the long par-4 18th in a fronting bunker and, with victory seemingly about to slip through his grasp once more, dramatically proceeded to hole the bunker shot to claim the title. Kuchar's seven-under-par 64 matched Pat Perez for the week's low round, and was just enough to secure his seventh PGA Tour victory, and his first since the 2013 Memorial Tournament. For former world number one Donald, the runner-up finish was his third at Harbour Town, and represented his fifth top-five finish there. Ben Martin, a 2013 Web.com Tour graduate and former Clemson University star, carded a Sunday 67, which was good enough to tie John Huh for third, two shots off the pace.

Pos	Player	Scores	Total	Money		Pos	Player	Scores	Total	Money
1	Matt Kuchar	66-73-70-64	273	$1,044 mil			Spencer Levin	72-74-70-69	285	$23,200
2	Luke Donald	70-69-66-69	274	$626,400			Scott Langley	66-73-75-71	285	$23,200
3=	Ben Martin	69-68-71-67	275	$336,400			Tim Clark	72-71-71-71	285	$23,200
	John Huh	71-68-68-68	275	$336,400			Justin Hicks	75-70-68-72	285	$23,200
5=	Scott Brown	70-69-71-67	277	$220,400			Kevin Kisner	73-72-68-72	285	$23,200
	Brian Stuard	69-72-68-68	277	$220,400			Chesson Hadley	72-67-73-73	285	$23,200
7=	Brian Harman	69-71-69-69	278	$187,050			Kevin Stadler	71-69-72-73	285	$23,200
	Jim Furyk	71-66-71-70	278	$187,050			Charley Hoffman	73-71-68-73	285	$23,200
9=	William McGirt	66-76-71-66	279	$156,600		48=	Chris Stroud	71-71-74-70	286	$15,335
	Rory Sabbatini	69-72-70-68	279	$156,600			Andrew Loupe	70-73-72-71	286	$15,335
	Russell Knox	69-72-68-70	279	$156,600			Patrick Reed	71-72-70-73	286	$15,335
12=	Stuart Appleby	73-73-67-67	280	$110,200			Bo Van Pelt	69-70-73-74	286	$15,335
	Jordan Spieth	69-74-70-67	280	$110,200			Ken Duke	72-71-69-74	286	$15,335
	Matt Every	69-70-70-71	280	$110,200		53=	Boo Weekley	73-73-73-68	287	$13,326
	Jason Kokrak	71-73-66-70	280	$110,200			David Toms	73-73-72-69	287	$13,326
	Charl Schwartzel	70-70-68-72	280	$110,200			Brice Garnett	73-71-72-71	287	$13,326
	Nicholas Thompson	70-70-68-72	280	$110,200			Charles Howell III	69-73-74-71	287	$13,326
18=	Pat Perez	74-69-74-64	281	$75,632			Shawn Stefani	74-69-71-73	287	$13,326
	Paul Casey	74-67-72-68	281	$75,632			Woody Austin	74-71-67-75	287	$13,326
	Ryo Ishikawa	77-68-67-69	281	$75,632			Gon. F'dez-Castaño	74-71-67-75	287	$13,326
	J.B. Holmes	72-71-69-69	281	$75,632			Kevin Streelman	69-72-70-76	287	$13,326
	Ted Potter Jr.	70-69-71-71	281	$75,632		61=	Zach Johnson	71-73-70-74	288	$12,644
23=	Martin Kaymer	73-67-72-70	282	$55,680			Tim Wilkinson	70-71-73-74	288	$12,644
	Graeme McDowell	71-69-72-70	282	$55,680			Stewart Cink	70-72-72-74	288	$12,644
	Robert Allenby	69-72-70-71	282	$55,680		64=	Tommy Gainey	72-74-75-68	289	$12,238
	M. Fitzpatrick (a)	71-71-69-71	282	-			Jeff Maggert	70-76-72-71	289	$12,238
27=	Camilo Villegas	72-71-73-67	283	$43,790			Ernie Els	72-73-73-71	289	$12,238
	Chris Kirk	71-72-71-69	283	$43,790			John Mallinger	69-74-73-73	289	$12,238
	Tim Herron	69-72-72-70	283	$43,790		68=	Mark Anderson	71-75-74-70	290	$11,716
	Geoff Ogilvy	72-68-71-72	283	$43,790			Erik Compton	70-75-73-72	290	$11,716
31=	Jonathan Byrd	71-73-73-67	284	$34,469			Brian Gay	70-74-74-72	290	$11,716
	Harris English	68-73-75-68	284	$34,469			James Hahn	72-74-69-75	290	$11,716
	Steve Marino	72-72-72-68	284	$34,469			Billy Horschel	69-74-72-75	290	$11,716
	Jerry Kelly	76-70-67-71	284	$34,469		73	Robert Garrigus	71-74-71-75	291	$11,368
	Billy Hurley III	70-69-73-72	284	$34,469		74=	Brian Davis	71-75-73-73	292	$11,078
	K.J. Choi	70-67-74-73	284	$34,469			Brandt Snedeker	72-73-74-73	292	$11,078
	Richard H. Lee	70-69-71-74	284	$34,469			Trevor Immelman	74-69-75-74	292	$11,078
38=	Ricky Barnes	72-73-72-68	285	$23,200			Dudley Hart	73-69-75-75	292	$11,078
	Brendon Todd	75-71-71-68	285	$23,200		78	Briny Baird	72-72-74-78	296	$10,788

Out Of The Money: **147**: Aaron Baddeley, Charlie Beljan, Roberto Castro, Kevin Chappell, David Hearn, Hunter Stewart, Josh Teater, Cameron Tringale, Mike Weir, Brendon de Jonge **148**: Chad Collins, Ben Crane, Lucas Glover, Danny Lee, Marc Leishman, Justin Leonard, Hunter Mahan, Kevin Na, John Peterson, Carl Pettersson, Jim Renner, Johnson Wagner, Tom Watson Charlie Wi **149**: John Daly, Glen Day, Vijay Singh, Vaughn Taylor, Mark Wilson **150**: Jason Bohn, Rick Lewallen, Davis Love III, Hideki Matsuyama, Kyle Stanley, Kevin Tway, Scott Verplank **151**: Paul Goydos **152**: Steven Bowditch, Stephen Gallacher, Bryce Molder, Wes Roach, John Rollins, Tyrone Van Aswegen **153**: James Driscoll, Nick Faldo, Martin Laird **154**: Russell Henley, Will MacKenzie, Michael Putnam **155**: Ben Curtis **157**: Stephen Ames, Chris DiMarco **WD**: Bill Haas (72), Greg Chalmers

FIRST ROUND		SECOND ROUND		THIRD ROUND	
Matt Kuchar	66 (-5)	K.J. Choi	137 (-5)	Luke Donald	205 (-8)
Scott Langley	66 (-5)	Jim Furyk	137 (-5)	John Huh	207 (-6)
William McGirt	66 (-5)	Ben Martin	137 (-5)	4 Players	208 (-5)
Harris English	68 (-3)	11 Players	138 (-4)	**Matt Kuchar**	209 (-4)
15 Players	69 (-2)	**Matt Kuchar**	139 (-3)		

OWR: 20 of top 50 entered - Rating: 332 - Points to 37th - Kuchar: 50 points, to 5th in OWR

Zurich Classic of New Orleans

TPC Louisiana - Avondale, LA
Champion: Seung-Yul Noh

Apr 24 - Apr 27
7,425 yards   Par 72
Purse: $6.8 Million

Once among the most highly touted Asian prospects ever as a teenager, Korea's Seung-Yul Noh took a major step towards fulfilling that promise by claiming his first PGA Tour victory at the Zurich Classic of New Orleans. The event's seventh first-time winner in its last 10 playings, Noh wore yellow and black ribbons in memory of the victims of a recent maritime tragedy in his homeland and was right in the mix from the beginning, opening with rounds of 65-68 at the TPC of Louisiana. A third-round 65 (keyed by three straight birdies at holes 14-16) then moved him two strokes ahead of the pack and required Noh to sleep on his first 54-hole PGA Tour lead – the pressure of which was seemingly felt when he opened Sunday's final round with his first bogey of the tournament. A 2nd-hole birdie by 2011 PGA Champion Keegan Bradley brought him into a tie with Noh but perhaps surprisingly, it was Major champion Bradley who wilted under the pressure, missing a two-footer for par at the 5th, then driving into the water at the par-4 6th en route to a crippling triple bogey – and, eventually, a tie for 8th. This left Noh free to play an up-and-down back nine, with his one-under-par 71 proving enough to beat Andrew Svoboda and Robert Streb by two, and Jeff Overton (who briefly moved within one before bogeying the 11th hole) by three.

Pos	Player	Rounds	Total	Money		Pos	Player	Rounds	Total	Money
1	Seung-Yul Noh	65-68-65-71	269	$1.224 mil			Will Wilcox	68-68-71-75	282	$30,785
2=	Andrew Svoboda	64-68-70-69	271	$598,400			Kevin Kisner	69-68-69-76	282	$30,785
	Robert Streb	67-66-68-70	271	$598,400		45=	Chad Collins	66-71-76-70	283	$21,080
4	Jeff Overton	67-68-67-70	272	$326,400			Tag Ridings	71-70-72-70	283	$21,080
5=	Robert Garrigus	73-69-68-64	274	$248,200			Andrés Romero	70-71-70-72	283	$21,080
	Erik Compton	66-68-72-68	274	$248,200		48=	Max Homa	71-71-71-71	284	$17,544
	Charley Hoffman	68-67-68-71	274	$248,200			Kevin Tway	70-72-69-73	284	$17,544
8=	Justin Rose	71-67-69-68	275	$197,200			Y.E. Yang	72-70-69-73	284	$17,544
	Tommy Gainey	71-66-67-71	275	$197,200			Troy Merritt	71-69-70-74	284	$17,544
	Keegan Bradley	69-66-65-75	275	$197,200		52=	Shawn Stefani	69-72-72-72	285	$15,477
11=	Peter Hanson	65-69-71-71	276	$149,600			Andrew Loupe	71-70-71-73	285	$15,477
	J.B. Holmes	71-65-69-71	276	$149,600			Ricky Barnes	70-72-69-74	285	$15,477
	Bud Cauley	71-68-66-71	276	$149,600			Sean O'Hair	71-69-71-74	285	$15,477
	Paul Casey	71-68-64-73	276	$149,600			D.A. Points	73-68-69-75	285	$15,477
15=	David Toms	73-68-67-69	277	$119,000			Briny Baird	71-69-70-75	285	$15,477
	Ben Martin	62-67-73-75	277	$119,000			Brendan Steele	73-67-70-75	285	$15,477
17=	Rory Sabbatini	69-72-69-68	278	$98,600			Kyle Stanley	71-67-71-76	285	$15,477
	Stuart Appleby	67-72-70-69	278	$98,600			Martin Flores	72-68-69-76	285	$15,477
	Cameron Tringale	73-69-66-70	278	$98,600			Tim Wilkinson	70-70-65-80	285	$15,477
	Mark Anderson	72-65-70-71	278	$98,600		62=	John Merrick	69-72-72-73	286	$14,416
21=	Bronson La'Cassie	70-69-69-71	279	$73,440			Wes Roach	74-67-71-74	286	$14,416
	Daniel Summerhays	72-66-68-73	279	$73,440			Lucas Glover	71-71-69-75	286	$14,416
	Brooks Koepka	71-68-67-73	279	$73,440			Vijay Singh	70-71-68-77	286	$14,416
	Retief Goosen	72-65-68-74	279	$73,440			Fabián Gómez	72-69-66-79	286	$14,416
25=	Bo Van Pelt	74-63-73-70	280	$54,230		67=	Padraig Harrington	70-72-71-74	287	$13,872
	David Duval	68-69-70-73	280	$54,230			Michael Thompson	66-71-75-75	287	$13,872
	Robert Allenby	71-68-68-73	280	$54,230			Joe Durant	69-71-67-80	287	$13,872
	Danny Lee	71-69-65-75	280	$54,230		70=	Jim Renner	75-67-71-75	288	$13,396
29=	Boo Weekley	71-70-71-69	281	$44,200			Doug LaBelle II	68-73-72-75	288	$13,396
	John Senden	70-70-69-72	281	$44,200			J.J. Henry	68-69-75-76	288	$13,396
	Graham DeLaet	69-68-71-73	281	$44,200			Troy Matteson	72-68-69-79	288	$13,396
	Alex Prugh	70-68-70-73	281	$44,200		74	John Rollins	74-66-73-76	289	$13,056
	Fredrik Jacobson	72-69-66-74	281	$44,200		75=	Ken Duke	73-68-73	214	$12,648
34=	Greg Chalmers	71-71-71-69	282	$30,785			D.H. Lee	68-71-75	214	$12,648
	Derek Ernst	71-71-71-69	282	$30,785			Scott McCarron	70-71-73	214	$12,648
	David Hearn	71-71-69-71	282	$30,785			Josh Teater	73-69-72	214	$12,648
	Charles Howell III	68-73-70-71	282	$30,785			Nick Watney	69-73-72	214	$12,648
	Sang-Moon Bae	68-72-71-71	282	$30,785		80=	Scott Gardiner	74-68-73	215	$12,104
	Charlie Wi	70-71-69-72	282	$30,785			Luke Guthrie	70-71-74	215	$12,104
	Mark Calcavecchia	71-70-69-72	282	$30,785			Billy Hurley III	71-71-73	215	$12,104
	Morgan Hoffmann	70-68-70-74	282	$30,785		83	Brice Garnett	69-73-75	217	$11,832
	Kevin Chappell	72-67-69-74	282	$30,785		84	Geoff Ogilvy	72-70-78	220	$11,696

Out Of The Money: 143: Will MacKenzie **144:** Jerry Kelly, Stephen Ames, Billy Horschel, Brian Davis, Heath Slocum, Scott Langley, Jim Herman, Ken Looper, William McGirt, Thorbjørn Olesen, Chad Campbell, Carl Pettersson, Harrison Frazar, Woody Austin, Ben Curtis, Rich Beem, Richard H. Lee, John Mallinger, Jamie Lovemark **145:** Jonathan Byrd, Russell Knox, James Driscoll, Hudson Swafford, Tyrone Van Aswegen, Kevin Foley, Mark Wilson, Mike Weir, Roberto Castro, Miguel Ángel Carballo **146:** Camilo Villegas, Trevor Immelman, Matt Bettencourt, Ben Crane, Thomas Aiken, Garrett Osborn, Dicky Pride, Cameron Beckman, Chris DiMarco, Chris Stroud, Benjamin Alvarado **147:** James Hahn, Rickie Fowler, Daniel Chopra, Spencer Levin, John Peterson, Brad Fritsch, David Lingmerth, Martin Laird, Peter Malnati **148:** Scott Stallings, Greg Owen, Alex Aragon, Neal Ajubita, Tim Petrovic, Kevin Stadler **149:** Scott Verplank, George McNeill, Brady Watt **150:** Patrick Reed, Steve Marino **151:** David Bradshaw, Bobby Gates **154:** Dustin Morris **155:** Tim Herron **WD:** Matt Every (76)

FIRST ROUND		SECOND ROUND		THIRD ROUND	
Ben Martin	62 (-10)	Ben Martin	129 (-15)	**Seung-Yul Noh**	198 (-18)
Andrew Svoboda	64 (-8)	Andrew Svoboda	132 (-12)	Keegan Bradley	200 (-16)
Peter Hanson	65 (-7)	**Seung-Yul Noh**	133 (-11)	Robert Streb	201 (-15)
Seung-Yul Noh	65 (-7)	Robert Streb	133 (-11)	3 Players	202 (-14)

OWR: 9 of top 50 entered - Rating: 190 - Points to 44th - Noh: 36 points, to 88th in OWR

		Wells Fargo Championship						**May 1 - May 4**	
		Quail Hollow Club - Charlotte, NC						7,442 yards Par 72	
		Champion: J.B. Holmes						Purse: $6.9 Million	

It had been more than five years since long-hitting J.B. Holmes last tasted victory – a period in which he endured brain surgery, as well procedures on both an elbow and a broken ankle. But fully healthy for the first time in eons, Holmes first manage to salvage his playing privileges a week earlier at the RBC Heritage (earning enough to cover an expiring medical extension), then claimed his third career PGA Tour victory at the Wells Fargo Championship, surviving two late bogeys to beat a hard-charging Jim Furyk by one. After opening with rounds of 70-67, Holmes moved into the 54-hole lead via a Saturday 66, then used a run of four birdies between the 8th and the 15th holes to solidify that position on Sunday. A bogey at the 16th trimmed the lead to two, however, and there were some anxious moments at the watery par-3 17th until an eight-footer holed for par gave Holmes the latitude to make bogey at the difficult 18th and still raise the trophy. Furyk, for his part, had begun Sunday well back in the pack, making himself relevant with a closing 65 that included chipping in for eagle at the par-5 16th. Thirty-six-hole co-leader Martin Flores bogeyed the 18th to fall back to solo third, while Jason Bohn, who stood one behind on the 17th tee before making double-bogey, took fourth. Also noteworthy were the performances of Phil Mickelson and Brendon de Jonge, Mickelson for stumbling home with a closing 76 after a scorching Saturday 63 had launched him strongly into contention, de Jonge for managing a tie for sixth after opening his week with the stunningly disparate rounds of 80-62.

1	J.B. Holmes	70-67-66-71	274	$1.242 mil		38=	Rickie Fowler	74-71-74-67	286	$28,980
2	Jim Furyk	72-69-69-65	275	$745,200			Sang-Moon Bae	72-71-71-72	286	$28,980
3	Martin Flores	67-68-69-72	276	$469,200			Hideki Matsuyama	69-72-72-73	286	$28,980
4	Jason Bohn	73-67-67-70	277	$331,200			Scott Langley	70-71-71-74	286	$28,980
5	Justin Rose	69-67-71-71	278	$276,000			Bud Cauley	71-71-70-74	286	$28,980
6=	Brendon de Jonge	80-62-68-69	279	$239,775			Webb Simpson	68-73-70-75	286	$28,980
	Kevin Kisner	72-66-68-73	279	$239,775		44=	David Hearn	70-74-71-72	287	$20,861
8=	Rory Sabbatini	74-68-71-67	280	$200,100			Bill Haas	75-70-70-72	287	$20,861
	Roberto Castro	71-70-69-70	280	$200,100			Andrew Svoboda	72-72-69-74	287	$20,861
	Rory McIlroy	69-76-65-70	280	$200,100			Shawn Stefani	69-68-75-75	287	$20,861
11=	Kevin Chappell	73-70-70-68	281	$158,700			Ernie Els	76-67-67-77	287	$20,861
	Michael Thompson	71-69-69-72	281	$158,700			Pat Perez	73-71-66-77	287	$20,861
	Phil Mickelson	67-75-63-76	281	$158,700		50=	Ted Potter Jr.	72-73-74-69	288	$16,643
14=	Kevin Streelman	72-69-71-70	282	$120,750			Hunter Mahan	72-73-72-71	288	$16,643
	Zach Johnson	71-70-69-72	282	$120,750			Retief Goosen	70-70-74-74	288	$16,643
	Geoff Ogilvy	72-67-70-73	282	$120,750			Ben Martin	71-73-69-75	288	$16,643
	Jonathan Byrd	68-71-70-73	282	$120,750			Danny Lee	71-71-70-76	288	$16,643
18=	Ryan Moore	70-71-76-66	283	$89,976		55=	Robert Allenby	73-72-73-71	289	$15,801
	Gary Woodland	71-72-68-72	283	$89,976			Daniel Summerhays	70-72-72-75	289	$15,801
	Charles Howell III	69-71-70-73	283	$89,976		57=	Josh Teater	72-73-75-70	290	$15,456
	Kevin Na	69-72-69-73	283	$89,976			Will Wilcox	71-72-73-74	290	$15,456
	Martin Kaymer	69-69-70-75	283	$89,976			Mike Weir	72-71-70-77	290	$15,456
23=	Jason Kokrak	75-68-73-68	284	$58,157		60=	Cameron Tringale	74-68-79-70	291	$14,904
	Y.E. Yang	73-72-71-68	284	$58,157			Brian Davis	74-71-75-71	291	$14,904
	Stewart Cink	68-70-74-72	284	$58,157			Kyle Stanley	74-71-75-71	291	$14,904
	Robert Streb	71-69-71-73	284	$58,157			Heath Slocum	77-68-74-72	291	$14,904
	John Merrick	71-70-70-73	284	$58,157			Michael Putnam	73-69-72-77	291	$14,904
	Wes Roach	71-71-69-73	284	$58,157		65=	Brian Harman	70-74-78-70	292	$14,352
	Mark Wilson	72-72-66-74	284	$58,157			Kevin Tway	73-72-75-72	292	$14,352
30=	Scott Brown	71-73-70-71	285	$40,106			Davis Love III	75-68-74-75	292	$14,352
	Brendan Steele	72-72-69-72	285	$40,106		68	Johnson Wagner	75-70-73-75	293	$14,076
	Martin Laird	69-70-73-73	285	$40,106		69=	Justin Hicks	74-71-74-76	295	$13,800
	Chris Kirk	71-70-71-73	285	$40,106			Jim Renner	71-74-74-76	295	$13,800
	Vijay Singh	69-72-71-73	285	$40,106			Carl Pettersson	73-71-74-77	295	$13,800
	Ricky Barnes	72-72-68-73	285	$40,106		72	Bronson La'Cassie	71-73-77-75	296	$13,524
	Derek Ernst	73-68-70-74	285	$40,106		73	Jim Herman	76-68-72-81	297	$13,386
	Angel Cabrera	66-69-75-75	285	$40,106						

Out Of The Money: **146**: Richard H. Lee, Greg Chalmers, Brian Gay, George McNeill, Jeff Overton, Billy Hurley III, Jamie Lovemark, Fielding Brewbaker, Brian Stuard, Stephen Ames, John Rollins, Jhonattan Vegas, Jonas Blixt, Scott Gardiner **147**: Bo Van Pelt, Spencer Levin, Woody Austin, Lee Westwood, Thorbjørn Olesen, Nicolas Colsaerts, Chris Stroud, James Driscoll, Chad Collins, Scott McCarron, Seung-Yul Noh, Lee Williams, Andrew Loupe **148**: David Lingmerth, Ben Crane, D.H. Lee, Joe Ogilvie, John Peterson, Troy Merritt, Peter Malnati, D.A. Points, Jimmy Walker, Darren Clarke, Brendon Todd, Nick Watney, Robert Karlsson, Nicholas Thompson **149**: Steve Marino, Will MacKenzie, Stuart Appleby, Ben Curtis, Scott Stallings, Trevor Immelman, Tim Wilkinson, Dustin Bray, Lucas Glover, Harrison Frazar, Jason Gore, Jamie Donaldson, Morgan Hoffmann **150**: K.J. Choi, Padraig Harrington, Andrés Romero, Harold Varner III, Gonzalo Fernández-Castaño, Brice Garnett, Charlie Beljan, Charlie Wi, Hudson Swafford, Kevin Foley, Hunter Green **151**: Sean O'Hair, Russell Henley, Rod Perry, Matt Jones **152**: Tommy Gainey, Tyrone Van Aswegen, Camilo Villegas **153**: J.J. Henry, Frank Lickliter II, Kelly Mitchum, Chesson Hadley, Troy Matteson **154**: Paul Goydos **155**: William McGirt, James Hahn **159**: Ben Kohles **WD**: Brad Fritsch (79), Peter Hanson (80)

FIRST ROUND			SECOND ROUND			THIRD ROUND	
Angel Cabrera	66 (-6)		Martin Flores	135 (-9)		**J.B. Holmes**	203 (-13)
Martin Flores	67 (-5)		Angel Cabrera	135 (-9)		Martin Flores	204 (-12)
Phil Mickelson	67 (-5)		Justin Rose	136 (-8)		Phil Mickelson	205 (-11)
3 Players	68 (-4)		Shawn Stefani	137 (-7)		Kevin Kisner	206 (-10)
J.B. Holmes	70 (-2)		**J.B. Holmes**	137 (-7)		2 Players	207 (-9)

OWR: 21 of top 50 entered - Rating: 341 - Points to 54th - Holmes: 50 points, to 68th in OWR

The Players Championship

TPC Sawgrass - Ponte Vedra Beach, FL
Champion: Martin Kaymer

May 8 - May 11
7,215 yards   Par 72
Purse: $10 Million

Having contended into the weekend at the previous week's Wells Fargo Championship, former world number one Martin Kaymer continued his second ascent towards the top of the golfing world by hanging on late for a nerve-wracking wire-to-wire victory at the Players Championship. Kaymer took control of the event early, carding a flawless course record-tying 63 on Thursday to grab the early lead, then backing it up with a 69 that stood him one ahead of 20-year-old Jordan Spieth at the halfway mark. But Spieth was able to catch Kaymer on Saturday with a round of 71 as the 29-year-old German managed only a two-birdie, two-bogey round of 72, setting up a likely two-man battle on Sunday. Coming off a disappointing final round at The Masters, Spieth jumped into a one-shot lead after birdies at the 2nd and 4th – but also like Augusta, he ran into trouble through the middle of the round, dropping himself from contention via a run of five bogeys from holes 5-15. Kaymer at this point held a three-shot lead, but his march to victory was halted by a lengthy delay as thunderstorms rolled across the Jacksonville area. Upon the resumption of play, Kaymer double-bogeyed the 15th off a wayward drive and when he failed to birdie the short par-5 16th, it seemed that a hard-charging Jim Furyk, who was in the clubhouse on 276 after a closing 66, might still have a chance at victory. Furyk's fortunes brightened when a poor chip left Kaymer a 28-footer for par at the TPC Sawgrass's famed par-3 17th – but Kaymer promptly holed the sharply breaking putt, then got up-and-down with his putter from off the front of the 18th green to clinch a one-shot victory.

1	Martin Kaymer	63-69-72-71	275	$1.8 mil		Charley Hoffman	77-67-71-71	286	$38,000
2	Jim Furyk	70-68-72-66	276	$1.08 mil		Angel Cabrera	70-74-71-71	286	$38,000
3	Sergio García	67-71-69-70	277	$680,000		Rory Sabbatini	71-73-69-73	286	$38,000
4=	Jordan Spieth	67-66-71-74	278	$440,000		Adam Scott	77-67-69-73	286	$38,000
	Justin Rose	67-71-71-69	278	$440,000		Justin Leonard	68-73-70-75	286	$38,000
6=	Jimmy Walker	75-68-71-65	279	$313,000		Stewart Cink	70-70-70-76	286	$38,000
	Rory McIlroy	70-74-69-66	279	$313,000	48=	Retief Goosen	72-70-75-70	287	$24,073
	David Hearn	70-71-68-70	279	$313,000		Jeff Maggert	72-71-74-70	287	$24,073
	Lee Westwood	67-71-71-70	279	$313,000		Pat Perez	68-73-75-71	287	$24,073
	Francesco Molinari	72-70-67-70	279	$313,000		Charl Schwartzel	72-67-77-71	287	$24,073
11=	Brian Davis	72-67-73-68	280	$240,000		J.J. Henry	74-70-72-71	287	$24,073
	Gary Woodland	67-71-70-72	280	$240,000		Charlie Beljan	73-69-73-72	287	$24,073
13=	K.J. Choi	74-70-72-65	281	$187,500		Martin Flores	70-71-74-72	287	$24,073
	Chris Kirk	71-73-70-67	281	$187,500		Jason Dufner	69-74-72-72	287	$24,073
	Steve Stricker	71-70-71-69	281	$187,500		Steven Bowditch	72-72-71-72	287	$24,073
	George McNeill	71-68-69-73	281	$187,500		Bubba Watson	69-72-70-76	287	$24,073
17=	Russell Henley	65-71-80-66	282	$135,333		Brandt Snedeker	75-69-67-76	287	$24,073
	Justin Hicks	73-70-71-68	282	$135,333	59=	Ryan Palmer	71-73-71-73	288	$22,000
	Brian Stuard	67-76-69-70	282	$135,333		Dustin Johnson	68-74-72-74	288	$22,000
	Morgan Hoffmann	71-70-70-71	282	$135,333		John Peterson	73-69-72-74	288	$22,000
	Matt Kuchar	71-71-69-71	282	$135,333	62=	Graeme McDowell	69-71-77-72	289	$21,500
	Matt Jones	70-69-69-74	282	$135,333		Scott Brown	68-71-77-73	289	$21,500
23=	Marc Leishman	70-72-74-67	283	$96,000	64	Fredrik Jacobson	70-70-75-75	290	$21,200
	Hideki Matsuyama	70-71-72-70	283	$96,000	65=	Richard H. Lee	71-71-76-73	291	$20,800
	Daniel Summerhays	74-68-69-72	283	$96,000		Ian Poulter	74-69-72-76	291	$20,800
26=	Billy Horschel	72-70-75-67	284	$69,500		Scott Stallings	67-77-71-76	291	$20,800
	Brendan Steele	69-73-75-67	284	$69,500	68	Sang-Moon Bae	66-73-79-74	292	$20,400
	Kevin Chappell	72-68-75-69	284	$69,500	69	Geoff Ogilvy	69-70-76-78	293	$20,200
	Zach Johnson	69-71-72-72	284	$69,500	70	Brendon de Jonge	69-74-75-76	294	$20,000
	Bill Haas	68-71-72-73	284	$69,500	71	Kyle Stanley	73-69-76-77	295	$19,800
	Bo Van Pelt	71-70-70-73	284	$69,500	72=	Ernie Els	68-76-75	219	$19,400
	Ryan Moore	70-74-67-73	284	$69,500		John Huh	69-72-78	219	$19,400
	John Senden	70-69-68-77	284	$69,500		Seung-Yul Noh	76-68-75	219	$19,400
34=	Russell Knox	72-72-73-68	285	$52,750	75=	Jonas Blixt	71-72-77	220	$18,900
	Erik Compton	72-70-74-69	285	$52,750		John Merrick	72-71-77	220	$18,900
	Scott Langley	71-72-72-70	285	$52,750	77=	Stuart Appleby	71-73-77	221	$18,400
	Henrik Stenson	71-70-70-74	285	$52,750		Rickie Fowler	71-72-78	221	$18,400
38=	Luke Donald	73-69-75-69	286	$38,000		John Rollins	73-71-77	221	$18,400
	Gon. F'dez-Castaño	67-77-72-70	286	$38,000	80=	Joost Luiten	68-72-82	222	$17,900
	Kevin Na	70-69-76-71	286	$38,000		Chris Stroud	76-67-79	222	$17,900
	Jamie Donaldson	74-67-74-71	286	$38,000	82	Jeff Overton	70-72-83	225	$17,600

Out Of The Money: **145**: Will MacKenzie, Charlie Wi, Ted Potter Jr., Lucas Glover, Keegan Bradley, Chesson Hadley, Charles Howell III, Derek Ernst, Carl Pettersson, Phil Mickelson, Johnson Wagner **146**: Roberto Castro, Thongchai Jaidee, Brian Harman, Jason Bohn, Kevin Stadler, Martin Laird, James Hahn, Jerry Kelly, Ken Duke, Jonathan Byrd, Camilo Villegas, Graham DeLaet, Robert Garrigus **147**: Luke Guthrie, Kenny Perry, Cameron Tringale, Michael Thompson, Josh Teater **148**: Webb Simpson, Michael Putnam, Bryce Molder, Aaron Baddeley, Kevin Streelman, Harris English, Boo Weekley, David Lingmerth, Stephen Gallacher **149**: Greg Chalmers, Darren Clarke, Shawn Stefani, Thomas Bjørn, Brian Gay, J.B. Holmes, Y.E. Yang **150**: Nick Watney, Andrés Romero, Jason Kokrak **151**: Nicholas Thompson, Hunter Mahan, D.A. Points, Ben Crane **152**: Tim Clark, Louis Oosthuizen **153**: Matt Every, Mark Wilson, James Driscoll, William McGirt, Patrick Reed **154**: Woody Austin **WD**: Briny Baird 977), D.H. Lee (78)

FIRST ROUND		SECOND ROUND		THIRD ROUND	
Martin Kaymer	63 (-9)	**Martin Kaymer**	132 (-12)	**Martin Kaymer**	204 (-12)
Russell Henley	65 (-7)	Jordan Spieth	133 (-11)	Jordan Spieth	204 (-12)
Sang-Moon Bae	66 (-6)	Russell Henley	136 (-8)	John Senden	207 (-9)
8 Players	67 (-5)	5 Players	138 (-6)	Sergio García	207 (-9)
				3 Players	208 (-8)

OWR: 46 of top 50 entered - Rating: 771 - Points to 61st - Kaymer: 80 points, to 28th in OWR

HP Byron Nelson Championship

TPC Four Seasons Resort - Irving, TX
Champion: Brendon Todd

May 15 - May 18
7,166 yards   Par 70
Purse: $6.9 Million

Twenty-eight-year-old Brendon Todd became the fifth former University of Georgia golfer to win on the 2013-2014 PGA Tour, claiming his first career title at the HP Byron Nelson Championship. Making his 77th career Tour start, Todd opened with a 68 before vaulting himself into the halfway lead via a Friday 64, then maintaining a share of the lead (with 2010 British Open champion Louis Oosthuizen) through 54 holes after posting a two-under-par 68 on Saturday. Oosthuizen – who continued to be plagued by a balky back – got off to a slow start on Sunday (turning in 35) before falling out of contention with bogeys at the 10th, 11th and 13th. Todd, meanwhile, holed a bunker shot for birdie at the par-3 2nd, added a birdie at the 5th, then moved securely ahead by posting back-to-back birdies at the 9th and 10th. Closing with a bogey-free 66, his primary late competition came from 2003 Masters champion Mike Weir, who began Sunday one stroke behind before jumping into the lead with four birdies in his first five holes on Sunday. But bogeys at the 6th and 9th would ultimately relegate Weir to second – his first top-25 finish since 2010 after having surgery on a partially torn right elbow ligament that same year. Also notable was the performance of 17-year-old amateur Scottie Scheffler, who finished with three straight sub-70 rounds to tie for 22nd.

Pos	Player	Scores	Total	Money		Player	Scores	Total	Money
1	Brendon Todd	68-64-68-66	266	$1.242 mil		Scott Gardiner	70-69-67-72	278	$30,403
2	Mike Weir	68-66-67-67	268	$745,200		Vijay Singh	69-68-68-73	278	$30,403
3=	Charles Howell III	68-66-69-67	270	$400,200	45=	Michael Putnam	70-70-71-68	279	$22,770
	Marc Leishman	66-68-68-68	270	$400,200		Rory Sabbatini	70-68-71-70	279	$22,770
5=	Boo Weekley	67-68-68-68	271	$262,200		Carl Pettersson	69-71-67-72	279	$22,770
	James Hahn	71-65-65-70	271	$262,200	48=	Bryce Molder	71-70-71-68	280	$17,327
7=	Dustin Johnson	69-69-68-66	272	$207,862		Sean O'Hair	69-72-71-68	280	$17,327
	Matt Kuchar	69-67-68-68	272	$207,862		Chad Campbell	69-72-70-69	280	$17,327
	Graham DeLaet	68-66-68-70	272	$207,862		David Toms	71-68-72-69	280	$17,327
	Gary Woodland	68-67-66-71	272	$207,862		Jason Dufner	70-70-69-71	280	$17,327
11=	John Senden	70-70-68-66	274	$146,280		Kris Blanks	70-69-70-71	280	$17,327
	Charlie Beljan	72-65-70-67	274	$146,280		Ricky Barnes	72-68-68-72	280	$17,327
	Shawn Stefani	74-66-67-67	274	$146,280		Jason Allred	68-70-70-72	280	$17,327
	Charl Schwartzel	73-67-67-67	274	$146,280		Lee Williams	67-71-68-74	280	$17,327
	Louis Oosthuizen	68-68-64-74	274	$146,280	57=	Ken Duke	70-69-72-70	281	$15,663
16=	Kevin Kisner	69-70-70-66	275	$100,050		Brian Gay	71-67-72-71	281	$15,663
	Paul Casey	71-63-73-68	275	$100,050	59=	Brad Fritsch	72-69-71-70	282	$15,180
	T. Van Aswegen	67-68-72-68	275	$100,050		Brian Davis	70-71-70-71	282	$15,180
	Billy Hurley III	70-69-68-68	275	$100,050		Martin Flores	70-71-69-72	282	$15,180
	John Huh	67-71-66-71	275	$100,050		J.J. Henry	70-71-68-73	282	$15,180
	Morgan Hoffmann	68-66-68-73	275	$100,050		Angel Cabrera	73-67-68-74	282	$15,180
22=	Tim Herron	68-66-74-68	276	$64,055	64=	Rod Pampling	68-72-71-72	283	$14,559
	Tim Wilkinson	66-71-71-68	276	$64,055		Jamie Lovemark	73-67-71-72	283	$14,559
	Scottie Scheffler (a)	71-68-69-68	276	-		Chris Thompson	69-69-72-73	283	$14,559
	Ryan Palmer	67-68-71-70	276	$64,055		James Driscoll	70-71-66-76	283	$14,559
	Andrés Romero	71-66-69-70	276	$64,055	68=	Jim Renner	69-71-71-73	284	$14,145
	Greg Chalmers	71-67-65-73	276	$64,055		Josh Teater	71-69-68-76	284	$14,145
	Padraig Harrington	68-68-66-74	276	$64,055	70	Luke Guthrie	69-72-71-73	285	$13,938
29=	Brian Harman	72-69-71-65	277	$43,944	71=	Alex Prugh	67-71-72-76	286	$13,731
	Brendon de Jonge	73-68-67-69	277	$43,944		Patrick Cantlay	70-69-71-76	286	$13,731
	Brice Garnett	69-70-68-70	277	$43,944	73	Jim Herman	70-68-74-76	288	$13,524
	Charlie Wi	73-67-66-71	277	$43,944	74	Steve Marino	70-69-71-79	289	$13,386
	Keegan Bradley	70-68-68-71	277	$43,944	75=	Daniel Chopra	70-68-75	213	$13,110
	Robert Garrigus	74-64-68-71	277	$43,944		Kevin Foley	70-71-72	213	$13,110
	Martin Kaymer	67-67-71-72	277	$43,944		Ryo Ishikawa	73-68-72	213	$13,110
	Aaron Baddeley	68-70-67-72	277	$43,944	78=	Alex Cejka	67-70-77	214	$12,696
37=	Robert Allenby	72-69-70-67	278	$30,403		Jhonattan Vegas	70-71-73	214	$12,696
	Ben Crane	68-70-73-67	278	$30,403		Will Wilcox	72-68-74	214	$12,696
	Jordan Spieth	70-67-73-68	278	$30,403	81=	Mark Anderson	73-68-74	215	$12,282
	Peter Hanson	65-73-69-71	278	$30,403		Eric Axley	68-73-74	215	$12,282
	Jimmy Walker	71-68-68-71	278	$30,403		Johnson Wagner	73-68-74	215	$12,282
	Retief Goosen	70-65-71-72	278	$30,403	84	Kyle Stanley	74-66-76	216	$12,006

Out Of The Money: **142**: David Duval, Ryan Moore, Miguel Ángel Carballo, Bronson La'Cassie, Hudson Swafford, D.J. Trahan, Briny Baird, Edward Loar **143**: John Rollins, Steven Bowditch, Brandt Snedeker, Harrison Frazar, Ben Curtis, Tommy Gainey, Alex Aragon, Greg Owen, Matt Bettencourt, Nicholas Thompson, Harris English, Fredrik Jacobson, Trevor Immelman, Andrew Svoboda, Benjamin Alvarado **144**: Troy Matteson, Chad Collins, Brendan Steele, Dicky Pride, Doug LaBelle II, Kevin Tway, Brooks Koepka, Joe Ogilvie, Ted Potter Jr., Tag Ridings, Gary Christian **145**: Marcel Siem, Cameron Beckman, Scott McCarron, Derek Ernst, Spencer Levin, Chris Smith, Colt Knost **146**: Ryuji Imada, Heath Slocum, John Peterson, Alex Carpenter, Danny Lee, Erik Compton, Steve Flesch, Robert Streb, Bud Cauley, Stuart Deane, Wes Roach **147**: Jonathan Byrd, Tim Petrovic, Brian Stuard, Sang-Moon Bae, Tim Clark, Richard H. Lee, Troy Merritt **148**: Case Cochran, Jeff Overton, Justin Leonard **149**: John Mallinger, Justin Hicks, Bobby Gates **150**: Andrew Loupe, Peter Malnati **151**: D.A. Points **153**: John Daly **154**: Will Strickler **WD**: John Merrick (78), Stephen Ames (142

FIRST ROUND		SECOND ROUND		THIRD ROUND	
Peter Hanson	65 (-5)	**Brendon Todd**	132 (-8)	Louis Oosthuizen	200 (-10)
Marc Leishman	66 (-4)	8 Players	134 (-6)	**Brendon Todd**	200 (-10)
David Duval	66 (-4)			James Hahn	201 (-9)
Tim Wilkinson	66 (-4)			Gary Woodland	201 (-9)
Brendon Todd	68 (-2)			Mike Weir	201 (-9)

OWR: 14 of top 50 entered - Rating: 250 - Points to 47th - Todd: 44 points, to 63rd in OWR

Crowne Plaza Invitational At Colonial

May 22 - May 25

Colonial Country Club - Ft. Worth, TX
Champion: Adam Scott

7,204 yards Par 70
Purse: $6.4 Million

Less than a week after achieving world number one status for the first time in his career, Adam Scott greatly solidified his position atop the Official World Ranking by winning the Crowne Plaza Invitational at Colonial, defeating reigning PGA champion Jason Dufner on the third hole of sudden death. Both Scott and Dufner began Sunday's final round in a seven-way tie for 11th place, yet only two strokes behind leaders David Toms, Chris Stroud, Hideki Matsuyama and Chad Campbell. Campbell (74) fell from contention with back-to-back double-bogeys at the 6th and 7th while Stroud and Matsuyama remained in the mix until getting derailed early in the final nine. Toms, however, maintained a one shot lead at the turn before bogeys at the 10th, 13th and 14th ultimately dashed his hopes. Scott and Dufner, meanwhile, mounted charges, with Scott getting to three under par on the day before double-bogeying the par-4 9th, then bouncing back with a three-under-par 32 on the back to close with 66, and a 271 total. Dufner, meanwhile, stood four under through 10, missed a short par putt at the par-5 11th, then regained that lost stroke with a clutch 25-foot birdie putt at the last. After both men parred the first extra hole (the 18th), Dufner stuffed his approach inside of five feet at the 17th but could do no more than extend the playoff after Scott holed from 14 feet before him. Finally, upon returning to the 18th, Scott made his second straight birdie (this time from seven feet) to clinch the title. It proved a satisfying end to the week given that Scott had ascended to the number one spot in the OWR despite not having played the week before.

#	Player	Scores	Total	Money		#	Player	Scores	Total	Money
1	Adam Scott	71-68-66-66	271	$1.152 mil			Jerry Kelly	70-71-69-68	278	$26,240
2	Jason Dufner	67-69-69-66	271	$691,200			Danny Lee	71-69-68-70	278	$26,240
3=	Fredrik Jacobson	67-71-67-67	272	$371,200			Louis Oosthuizen	72-68-67-71	278	$26,240
	Nicholas Thompson	69-68-69-66	272	$371,200			Michael Putnam	70-71-68-69	278	$26,240
5=	David Lingmerth	72-69-66-66	273	$216,960			Robert Streb	66-68-74-70	278	$26,240
	Ryan Palmer	69-69-68-67	273	$216,960			Josh Teater	68-71-70-69	278	$26,240
	John Senden	71-68-66-68	273	$216,960		45=	Trevor Immelman	69-71-68-71	279	$18,304
	Brendon Todd	69-69-67-68	273	$216,960			Matt Jones	70-67-73-69	279	$18,304
	David Toms	72-66-65-70	273	$216,960			Andrew Loupe	75-65-68-71	279	$18,304
10=	Kevin Chappell	68-73-63-70	274	$153,600			Bryce Molder	70-70-67-72	279	$18,304
	Hideki Matsuyama	69-70-64-71	274	$153,600			Jeff Overton	70-71-70-68	279	$18,304
	Michael Thompson	73-66-69-66	274	$153,600			Brandt Snedeker	70-66-73-70	279	$18,304
	Jimmy Walker	67-68-69-70	274	$153,600		51=	Aaron Baddeley	68-67-71-74	280	$15,061
14=	Brian Davis	68-67-70-70	275	$102,400			Ken Duke	67-72-69-72	280	$15,061
	Graham DeLaet	69-70-68-68	275	$102,400			Jim Furyk	69-69-71-71	280	$15,061
	Dustin Johnson	65-70-74-66	275	$102,400			Charley Hoffman	70-68-69-73	280	$15,061
	Chris Kirk	73-64-67-71	275	$102,400			Daniel Summerhays	69-71-73-67	280	$15,061
	Jordan Spieth	67-69-70-69	275	$102,400			Tim Wilkinson	66-71-69-74	280	$15,061
	Chris Stroud	70-64-69-72	275	$102,400		57=	Brian Gay	71-69-72-69	281	$14,336
	Bo Van Pelt	67-68-70-70	275	$102,400			J.J. Henry	70-70-68-73	281	$14,336
21=	Bud Cauley	70-69-69-68	276	$58,453			Justin Leonard	69-72-70-70	281	$14,336
	Tim Clark	67-68-69-72	276	$58,453		60=	Ricky Barnes	68-71-73-70	282	$13,952
	Bill Haas	70-68-69-69	276	$58,453			Steve Flesch	71-70-69-72	282	$13,952
	David Hearn	67-69-74-66	276	$58,453			Hunter Mahan	66-71-70-75	282	$13,952
	Russell Knox	71-70-66-69	276	$58,453		63=	Jeff Curl	71-69-71-72	283	$13,440
	Marc Leishman	69-68-67-72	276	$58,453			Tim Herron	72-69-71-71	283	$13,440
	Ben Martin	70-68-69-69	276	$58,453			Sean O'Hair	69-69-70-75	283	$13,440
	William McGirt	72-67-67-70	276	$58,453			John Rollins	69-72-69-73	283	$13,440
	George McNeill	68-72-68-68	276	$58,453			Cameron Tringale	70-70-67-76	283	$13,440
30=	Chad Campbell	69-66-68-74	277	$37,200		68=	Scott Langley	71-70-74-69	284	$12,992
	Harris English	66-70-73-68	277	$37,200			Kyle Stanley	73-68-73-70	284	$12,992
	Brice Garnett	67-66-74-70	277	$37,200		70=	Jonathan Byrd	70-70-73-72	285	$12,672
	Brian Harman	69-67-68-73	277	$37,200			Davis Love III	72-69-74-70	285	$12,672
	Billy Hurley III	71-67-70-69	277	$37,200			Vijay Singh	68-73-69-75	285	$12,672
	Martin Laird	70-69-69-69	277	$37,200		73	Zach Johnson	70-71-69-76	286	$12,416
	Heath Slocum	69-69-69-70	277	$37,200		74	Briny Baird	71-70-72-74	287	$12,288
	Brendon de Jonge	70-68-70-69	277	$37,200		75	Boo Weekley	71-69-74-74	288	$12,160
38=	Robert Allenby	68-70-68-72	278	$26,240						

Out Of The Money: **142**: Paul Casey, Ryo Ishikawa, Brian Stuard, Kevin Na, Derek Ernst, Scott Stallings, Corey Pavin, Rod Pampling, Matt Kuchar, Kevin Stadler, Woody Austin, Angel Cabrera **143**: Camilo Villegas, Geoff Ogilvy, Luke Guthrie, Steven Bowditch, Scott Brown, Rory Sabbatini, Spencer Levin, Kevin Kisner **144**: Pat Perez, Justin Hicks, Olin Browne, Nick Watney, Lucas Glover, John Huh **145**: Richard H. Lee, Carl Pettersson, Wes Roach, James Hahn, Jim Renner, Mark Wilson, Franklin Corpening **146**: Chris Williams, Andrew Svoboda, Greg Chalmers, Seung-Yul Noh, Kevin Tway **147**: Matt Every, Chad Collins **148**: John Merrick **149**: Roberto Castro **150**: Y.E. Yang **151**: Jason Bohn **153**: Julien Brun **154**: Chesson Hadley **155**: Rickie Fowler **157**: Keith Clearwater

FIRST ROUND		SECOND ROUND		THIRD ROUND	
Dustin Johnson	65 (-5)	Brice Garnett	133 (-7)	Hideki Matsuyama	203 (-7)
Tim Wilkinson	66 (-4)	Chris Stroud	134 (-6)	David Toms	203 (-7)
Hunter Mahan	66 (-4)	Robert Streb	134 (-6)	Chad Campbell	203 (-7)
Harris English	66 (-4)	7 Players	135 (-5)	Chris Stroud	203 (-7)
Robert Streb	66 (-4)	**Adam Scott**	139 (-1)	6 Players	204 (-6)
Adam Scott	71 (+1)			**Adam Scott**	205 (-5)

OWR: 20 of top 50 entered - Rating: 396 - Points to 56th - Scott: 54 points, remains 1st in OWR

Memorial Tournament				**May 29 - Jun 1**	
Muirfield Village Golf Club - Dublin, OH				7,265 yards Par 72	
Champion: Hideki Matsuyama				Purse: $6.2 Million	

Marked for international stardom since winning back-to-back Asia-Pacific Amateurs (and their associated Masters exemptions) in 2010 and '11, Japan's Hideki Matsuyama went a long way towards validating those predictions by scoring his first PGA Tour win, a playoff triumph over Kevin Na at the Memorial Tournament. It was a wild week at Muirfield Village, beginning with Rory McIlroy's Thursday 63 (which included a double-bogey), a superb round which the streaking Northern Irishman promptly followed with a disastrous 78. But the event's real ups and downs were saved for the final nine on Sunday, when a host of big name contenders held or shared the lead, all to collapse near the close. The biggest crash came from Masters champion Bubba Watson, who seemed well on his way to his third win of the year before bogeying the short par-4 14th, then carding a double-bogey at the par 5 15th after hooking his tee shot miles out of bounds. He could do no better than three pars thereafter, missing the playoff by a shot. World number one Adam Scott also had his chances, grabbing a share of the lead through 11 holes before a watery double-bogey at the par-3 12th (and subsequent bogeys at holes 14-16) ended his hopes. And then there was Matsuyama who, following Watson's collapse, stood two ahead before promptly double-bogeying the 16th (with a water-bound tee shot) and bogeying the 17th. Enter the 30-year-old Na, who'd teed off two hours before the leaders and carded an eight-under-par 64 to get in the clubhouse at 13-under-par 275. Needing a birdie to tie him, Matsuyama stuffed his approach at the 18th inside six feet, holed the putt, then promptly won with an up-and-down par on the first playoff hole (the 18th) after Na pulled his drive left, into a creek.

1	Hideki Matsuyama	70-67-69-69	275	$1.116 mil		Justin Thomas	73-68-72-72	285	$25,420
2	Kevin Na	72-69-70-64	275	$669,600		Aaron Baddeley	69-74-70-72	285	$25,420
3	Bubba Watson	66-69-69-72	276	$421,600		Cameron Tringale	73-70-70-72	285	$25,420
4=	Chris Kirk	66-70-74-68	278	$272,800		Marc Leishman	71-68-73-73	285	$25,420
	Adam Scott	69-70-68-71	278	$272,800		Keegan Bradley	67-75-70-73	285	$25,420
6=	Steve Stricker	71-70-70-68	279	$215,450		Camilo Villegas	71-68-72-74	285	$25,420
	Ben Curtis	69-71-69-70	279	$215,450		Jason Day	72-69-70-74	285	$25,420
8=	Thorbjørn Olesen	71-67-74-68	280	$167,400	46=	Kevin Kisner	69-72-76-69	286	$18,063
	Bill Haas	73-67-72-68	280	$167,400		Dustin Johnson	73-68-72-73	286	$18,063
	Luke Guthrie	75-69-66-70	280	$167,400		Justin Hicks	73-67-71-75	286	$18,063
	Brendon Todd	71-68-69-72	280	$167,400	49=	Stewart Cink	71-73-72-71	287	$15,149
	Charl Schwartzel	72-69-67-72	280	$167,400		Phil Mickelson	72-70-72-73	287	$15,149
13=	Scott Brown	70-69-71-71	281	$124,000		David Lingmerth	72-72-70-73	287	$15,149
	Paul Casey	66-66-76-73	281	$124,000		Luke Donald	71-69-73-74	287	$15,149
15=	Jason Allred	74-68-74-66	282	$102,300		Fredrik Jacobson	71-71-71-74	287	$15,149
	Matt Kuchar	74-69-69-70	282	$102,300		Ben Martin	72-72-65-78	287	$15,149
	Rory McIlroy	63-78-69-72	282	$102,300	55=	Michael Putnam	71-73-73-71	288	$14,198
	Billy Horschel	71-69-68-74	282	$102,300		Nick Watney	69-71-74-74	288	$14,198
19=	Charley Hoffman	69-72-73-69	283	$65,238	57=	Richard H. Lee	76-68-76-69	289	$13,764
	Jim Furyk	73-68-72-70	283	$65,238		Charles Howell III	69-75-71-74	289	$13,764
	Martin Flores	69-68-75-71	283	$65,238		Gary Woodland	71-68-75-75	289	$13,764
	Jason Dufner	71-69-71-72	283	$65,238		Ryo Ishikawa	72-71-71-75	289	$13,764
	Ernie Els	70-72-69-72	283	$65,238		Justin Leonard	68-75-68-78	289	$13,764
	Ryan Moore	68-70-72-73	283	$65,238	62=	John Huh	73-70-75-72	290	$13,268
	Bo Van Pelt	72-72-66-73	283	$65,238		Carl Pettersson	72-72-73-73	290	$13,268
	Andrew Svoboda	72-69-68-74	283	$65,238		K. Aphibarnrat	73-71-70-76	290	$13,268
	Jordan Spieth	69-72-67-75	283	$65,238	65=	Scott Stallings	72-71-77-71	291	$12,834
28=	K.J. Choi	73-71-72-68	284	$38,647		Carlos Ortiz	75-68-76-72	291	$12,834
	David Hearn	71-73-69-71	284	$38,647		Josh Teater	71-72-76-72	291	$12,834
	Robert Garrigus	72-70-70-72	284	$38,647		Hyung-Sung Kim	70-72-76-73	291	$12,834
	Daniel Summerhays	74-70-68-72	284	$38,647	69=	Lucas Glover	70-73-76-73	292	$12,400
	Hunter Mahan	68-70-73-73	284	$38,647		Pat Perez	71-70-77-74	292	$12,400
	Brendon de Jonge	73-69-69-73	284	$38,647		Chris Stroud	74-68-74-76	292	$12,400
	Kevin Stadler	72-71-68-73	284	$38,647	72=	Greg Chalmers	71-72-75-75	293	$12,090
	Robert Streb	72-67-69-76	284	$38,647		Mark Wilson	69-74-74-76	293	$12,090
	Scott Langley	72-66-67-79	284	$38,647	74	Kyle Stanley	74-68-80-76	298	$11,904
37=	Billy Hurley III	73-70-74-68	285	$25,420	75=	J.B. Holmes	67-75-81-76	299	$11,718
	Michael Thompson	67-76-72-70	285	$25,420		Gon. F'dez-Castaño	73-70-79-77	299	$11,718

Out Of The Money: **145**: Kevin Chappell, Bryce Molder, Nicholas Thompson, Brendan Steele, Tim Clark, Rickie Fowler, Mike Weir, Michael Kim, Steven Bowditch, Y.E. Yang, Justin Rose, Russell Henley, D.A. Points, Thomas Aiken **146**: Robert Allenby, Woody Austin, Russell Knox, Matt Every **147**: Brice Garnett, Seung-Yul Noh, Rory Sabbatini, Kevin Streelman, Nicolas Colsaerts, Will MacKenzie, Roberto Castro, Brian Stuard **148**: Erik Compton, Brian Harman **149**: Sean O'Hair, Morgan Hoffmann, Trevor Immelman, Justin Lower, Jason Bohn, George McNeill, Chesson Hadley **150**: Vijay Singh, Ken Duke **151**: Brian Davis, Branden Grace **152**: Martin Laird, Matt Jones **154**: Wil. McGirt **155**: Derek Ernst **WD**: Stuart Appleby (77)

FIRST ROUND		SECOND ROUND		THIRD ROUND	
Rory McIlroy	63 (-9)	Paul Casey	132 (-12)	Bubba Watson	204 (-12)
Paul Casey	66 (-6)	Bubba Watson	135 (-9)	Scott Langley	205 (-11)
Chris Kirk	66 (-6)	Chris Kirk	136 (-9)	**Hideki Matsuyama**	206 (-10)
Bubba Watson	66 (-6)	**Hideki Matsuyama**	137 (-5)	Adam Scott	207 (-9)
3 Players	67 (-5)	Martin Flores	137 (-5)	6 Players	208 (-8)
Hideki Matsuyama	70 (-2)				

OWR: 26 of top 50 entered - Rating: 541 - Points to 56th - Matsuyama: 64 points, to 13th in OWR

FedEx St. Jude Classic
TPC Southwind - Memphis, TN
Champion: Ben Crane

Jun 5 - Jun 8
7,239 yards Par 70
Purse: $5.8 Million

Emerging from a three-year victory drought with a golf swing reconfigured to ease pressure on his oft-injured back, Ben Crane claimed his fifth career PGA Tour victory at the FedEx St Jude Classic, the Tour's final tune-up prior to the U.S. Open. After opening with a bogey-free seven-under-par 63, Crane's win was, in fact, wire-to-wire – though with heavy rains preventing play from finishing on each of the first three days, it did not readily appear that way. But a second round 65 (whose only bogey came at the par-4 18th) cushioned Crane's lead significantly before Saturday's weather sent him home with 12 holes left to play in his third round. He then completed those 12 in par figures on Sunday morning, and thus retained a three-stroke lead over Troy Merritt, which, in turn, allowed a relatively cautious approach to Sunday afternoon's finale. Indeed, Crane's approach proved so cautious that he carded a three-over-par 73 (which included a safe bogey at the last) and held on to edge Merritt by only one – and in the process become the first man to win on the PGA Tour without a final-round birdie since Justin Leonard did it in this same event in 2005. Among the marquee names preparing for the upcoming U.S. Open, 2012 Open champion Webb Simpson (who closed with 66) tied for third with Matt Every (70) and Carl Pettersson (69), while Ian Poulter carded Sunday's low round (a 64) en route to finishing in a five-way tie for sixth. Phil Mickelson, meanwhile, moved into the edges of Sunday contention after birdieing the 11th and 12th holes but ultimately fell back to close with 72, and a tie for 11th.

1	Ben Crane	63-65-69-73	270	$1.044 mil		Ryan Palmer	67-72-72-68	279	$28,842
2	Troy Merritt	67-66-67-71	271	$626,400		Heath Slocum	69-70-70-70	279	$28,842
3=	Webb Simpson	71-66-69-66	272	$301,600		Tim Wilkinson	68-68-70-73	279	$28,842
	Matt Every	69-68-65-70	272	$301,600		Ben Curtis	70-69-71-69	279	$28,842
	Carl Pettersson	67-67-69-69	272	$301,600		Scott Stallings	68-72-68-71	279	$28,842
6=	Ian Poulter	69-68-72-64	273	$181,540		Retief Goosen	66-66-75-72	279	$28,842
	James Hahn	69-70-67-67	273	$181,540	43=	Luke Guthrie	67-72-70-71	280	$20,300
	Andrew Svoboda	69-66-68-70	273	$181,540		Sean O'Hair	69-70-70-71	280	$20,300
	Brian Harman	69-65-67-72	273	$181,540		Davis Love III	65-70-71-74	280	$20,300
	Billy Horschel	67-68-68-70	273	$181,540	46=	Chad Campbell	70-68-71-72	281	$16,443
11=	Phil Mickelson	67-68-67-72	274	$139,200		Boo Weekley	69-70-70-72	281	$16,443
	Camilo Villegas	68-64-71-71	274	$139,200		Gon. F'dez-Castaño	67-71-70-73	281	$16,443
13=	Rickie Fowler	70-68-68-69	275	$102,467		Robert Streb	70-70-72-69	281	$16,443
	Ben Martin	69-67-74-65	275	$102,467	50=	Kevin Kisner	65-72-70-75	282	$14,268
	Chesson Hadley	67-69-72-67	275	$102,467		John Rollins	70-69-69-74	282	$14,268
	J.J. Henry	66-70-71-68	275	$102,467		Ryuji Imada	71-69-71-71	282	$14,268
	Ted Potter Jr.	68-67-70-70	275	$102,467	53=	Zach Johnson	64-74-74-71	283	$13,241
	Austin Cook	67-73-65-70	275	$102,467		Miguel A. Carballo	68-70-74-71	283	$13,241
19=	Brooks Koepka	67-70-72-67	276	$70,296		Stuart Appleby	65-74-72-72	283	$13,241
	Tim Clark	68-69-67-72	276	$70,296		Stewart Cink	70-66-75-72	283	$13,241
	John Peterson	69-68-73-66	276	$70,296		Jeff Overton	68-71-72-72	283	$13,241
	Will Wilcox	70-67-68-71	276	$70,296		Woody Austin	68-71-72-72	283	$13,241
	Peter Malnati	65-68-70-73	276	$70,296		Benjamin Alvarado	68-72-70-73	283	$13,241
24=	Paul Casey	70-67-70-70	277	$49,445	60=	Fredrik Jacobson	67-71-73-73	284	$12,644
	Graeme McDowell	69-68-70-70	277	$49,445		Martin Laird	70-67-76-71	284	$12,644
	Dustin Johnson	68-67-75-67	277	$49,445		Greg Owen	70-70-70-74	284	$12,644
	Jason Bohn	67-68-70-72	277	$49,445	63=	John Merrick	70-68-77-70	285	$12,354
28=	George McNeill	69-69-73-67	278	$40,319		Shawn Stefani	70-67-74-74	285	$12,354
	Charlie Wi	68-71-69-70	278	$40,319	65=	Jerry Kelly	71-67-73-75	286	$12,064
	Steve Marino	69-70-68-71	278	$40,319		Padraig Harrington	68-67-79-72	286	$12,064
	Charles Howell III	71-68-71-68	278	$40,319		Martin Flores	70-70-75-71	286	$12,064
32=	Tommy Gainey	69-68-70-72	279	$28,842	68	Josh Teater	72-67-75-73	287	$11,832
	Cameron Tringale	68-70-70-71	279	$28,842	69=	Justin Leonard	68-71-74-75	288	$11,658
	Danny Lee	72-67-67-73	279	$28,842		David Lingmerth	77-63-71-77	288	$11,658
	Jhonattan Vegas	69-70-70-70	279	$28,842	71	John Daly	72-67-76-76	291	$11,484
	William McGirt	73-66-74-66	279	$28,842					

Out Of The Money: **141**: Ricky Barnes, Chad Collins, Joe Durant, Harris English, Harrison Frazar, Scott Gardiner, David Hearn, Doug LaBelle II, Geoff Ogilvy, Alex Prugh, Tag Ridings, Andrés Romero, John Senden, Kyle Stanley, Kevin Streelman, David Toms, Tyrone Van Aswegen **142**: Eric Axley, Sang-Moon Bae, Roberto Castro, Brad Fritsch, Brice Garnett, Trevor Immelman, Russell Knox, Bronson La'Cassie, Wes Roach **143**: Morgan Hoffmann, J.B. Holmes, Scott Langley, Troy Matteson, Joe Ogilvie, Michael Putnam, Patrick Reed, Michael Thompson, Nicholas Thompson **144**: Stephen Ames, Matt Bettencourt, Gary Christian, Darren Clarke, Grant Leaver, Jamie Lovemark, Jeff Maggert, Thorbjørn Olesen, Lee Williams, Mark Wilson **145**: Robert Allenby, Steven Bowditch, Bobby Gates, Talor Gooch, Russell Henley, Jim Herman, Edward Loar, Tim Petrovic, Hudson Swafford **146**: Alex Aragon, James Driscoll, Brian Gay, Tim Herron, Andrew Loupe, Will MacKenzie, Zachary Olsen, Lee Westwood **147**: John Mallinger, Scottie Scheffler **148**: Jonathan Byrd, Dicky Pride, Kevin Tway **149**: Daniel Chopra, Dustin Morris, Jim Renner **150**: Johnson Wagner **151**: Kevin Foley **153**: Scott Verplank **156**: Kelvin Burgin **167**: Isaac Sanchez **WD**: Bud Cauley (70), Kevin Stadler (71), David Duval (74), D.A. Points (74), Scott McCarron (75), Kris Blanks (75), Cameron Beckman (76), Paul Goydos (77), Charlie Beljan (77), Robert Garrigus (79)

FIRST ROUND		SECOND ROUND		THIRD ROUND	
Ben Crane	63 (-7)	**Ben Crane**	128 (-12)	**Ben Crane**	197 (-13)
Zach Johnson	64 (-6)	Retief Goosen	132 (-8)	Troy Merritt	200 (-10)
4 Players	65 (-5)	Camilo Villegas	132 (-8)	Brian Harman	201 (-9)
		Peter Malnati	133 (-7)	Matt Every	202 (-8)
		Troy Merritt	133 (-7)	Phil Mickelson	202 (-8)

OWR: 12 of top 50 entered - Rating: 240 - Points to 49th - Crane: 42 points, to 101st in OWR

Travelers Championship

Jun 19 - Jun 22

TPC River Highlands - Cromwell, CT
Champion: Kevin Streelman

6,844 yards   Par 70
Purse: $6.2 Million

In a stunning finish which broke a PGA Tour record that had stood for 58 years, Kevin Streelman claimed his second career PGA Tour victory by birdieing his last seven holes at the TPC River Highlands to steal the Travelers Championship by a single shot. The 35-year-old Streelman barely registered as an afterthought heading into the weekend as his opening rounds of 69-68 left him eight shots behind halfway leader Scott Langley. His fortunes improved considerably on Saturday, however, when a six-under-par 64 brought him within four strokes of 54-hole leader Ryan Moore – though much of the ground he'd gained seemed to vanish early on Sunday after two early bogeys left him six in arrears and off the radar screen. But Streelman partially righted the ship with a birdie at the par-4 9th, then caught fire at the 12th, where he began a dash home that ultimately saw him hole a 40-footer for birdie at the 16th and, knowing he had a chance to win, a nine-footer at the last for his second consecutive 64 and a 265 total. The charge allowed Streelman to overtake Sergio García (67) and K.J. Choi (67), as well as Aaron Baddeley (69), all of who had spent the back nine jockeying for the lead until being passed just before the wire. Streelman finished his round with an amazing 10 straight one-putts, and his seven-birdie closing barrage bettered the old record for consecutive closing birdies by a winner (set by Mike Souchak in the 1956 St. Paul Open) by one.

1	Kevin Streelman	69-68-64-64	265	$1.116 mil		Dustin Johnson	66-66-71-71	274	$32,296
2	K.J. Choi	65-65-69-67	266	$545,600		Jamie Lovemark	68-63-70-73	274	$32,296
	Sergio García	65-69-65-67	266	$545,600	42=	Brendon de Jonge	70-66-71-68	275	$22,320
4	Aaron Baddeley	67-66-65-69	267	$297,600		Brian Davis	69-70-68-68	275	$22,320
5=	Brendan Steele	62-69-71-66	268	$235,600		Brian Harman	68-67-69-71	275	$22,320
	Ryan Moore	63-68-66-71	268	$235,600		Eric Axley	64-67-71-73	275	$22,320
7=	Harris English	66-64-72-67	269	$186,775	46=	Ken Duke	65-72-71-68	276	$17,186
	Jeff Maggert	64-70-68-67	269	$186,775		Patrick Rodgers	66-69-71-70	276	$17,186
	Chad Campbell	64-70-67-68	269	$186,775		Ricky Barnes	73-65-68-70	276	$17,186
	Carl Pettersson	68-67-66-68	269	$186,775		Heath Slocum	66-69-70-71	276	$17,186
11=	Brandt Snedeker	65-69-72-64	270	$123,114		Matt Jones	69-69-67-71	276	$17,186
	Marc Leishman	70-68-65-67	270	$123,114	51=	Graham DeLaet	70-68-71-68	277	$14,591
	Angel Cabrera	68-70-65-67	270	$123,114		Greg Owen	72-65-71-69	277	$14,591
	Bud Cauley	63-70-68-69	270	$123,114		Retief Goosen	68-69-71-69	277	$14,591
	Nick Watney	70-66-65-69	270	$123,114		Brooks Koepka	65-72-71-69	277	$14,591
	Scott Langley	64-65-70-71	270	$123,114		Steve Marino	66-72-70-69	277	$14,591
	Michael Putnam	67-63-69-71	270	$123,114		Jonathan Byrd	70-68-69-70	277	$14,591
18=	Miguel A. Carballo	68-68-72-63	271	$78,120	57=	Johnson Wagner	68-66-74-70	278	$13,826
	Stuart Appleby	69-70-68-64	271	$78,120		John Daly	70-68-70-70	278	$13,826
	Jason Day	70-69-67-65	271	$78,120		Billy Hurley III	71-66-70-71	278	$13,826
	Tommy Gainey	70-66-67-68	271	$78,120		Justin Hicks	66-71-69-72	278	$13,826
	Chris Stroud	67-67-68-69	271	$78,120	61=	Seung-Yul Noh	68-69-72-70	279	$13,206
	Tim Wilkinson	66-68-67-70	271	$78,120		Wes Roach	68-70-71-70	279	$13,206
24=	Hudson Swafford	66-71-66-69	272	$57,040		Vaughn Taylor	67-71-71-70	279	$13,206
	Sang-Moon Bae	67-68-67-70	272	$57,040		Doug LaBelle II	65-71-72-71	279	$13,206
26=	Gon. F'dez-Castaño	68-68-71-66	273	$45,880		Russell Knox	66-72-70-71	279	$13,206
	Charley Hoffman	67-68-71-67	273	$45,880		Tim Herron	68-71-69-71	279	$13,206
	John Merrick	67-72-67-67	273	$45,880	67=	Camilo Villegas	71-66-74-69	280	$12,586
	Kevin Tway	71-65-69-68	273	$45,880		Bo Van Pelt	69-68-73-70	280	$12,586
	T. Van Aswegen	68-70-67-68	273	$45,880		Troy Merritt	71-66-72-71	280	$12,586
31=	Joe Durant	64-72-71-67	274	$32,296		Morgan Hoffmann	68-70-69-73	280	$12,586
	Jerry Kelly	70-66-71-67	274	$32,296	71=	Andrew Svoboda	67-71-77-66	281	$12,214
	Fredrik Jacobson	69-69-69-67	274	$32,296		Brian Gay	70-66-72-73	281	$12,214
	Keegan Bradley	66-69-71-68	274	$32,296	73	Kevin Stadler	72-67-72-72	283	$12,028
	Vijay Singh	68-68-70-68	274	$32,296	74	Ben Crane	69-68-68-79	284	$11,904
	Bubba Watson	67-72-67-68	274	$32,296	75=	Billy Mayfair	67-71-71-76	285	$11,718
	Matt Kuchar	66-67-72-69	274	$32,296		Brice Garnett	67-68-72-78	285	$11,718
	William McGirt	71-67-66-70	274	$32,296	77	James Hahn	69-70-76-73	288	$11,532
	Jhonattan Vegas	69-70-65-70	274	$32,296					

Out Of The Money: 140: Jonas Blixt, Andrés Romero, Sean O'Hair, Chad Collins, Y.E. Yang, Scott Brown, Hunter Mahan, Kris Blanks, Bobby Wyatt **141:** Jim Renner, John Rollins, Ted Potter Jr., Patrick Reed, David Lingmerth, Patrick Cantlay, Brad Fritsch, Marc Turnesa, Cameron Beckman, Danny Lee, Lee Janzen, Robert Streb, J.J. Henry, Kevin Chappell, Greg Chalmers, Kevin Foley, Oliver Goss **142:** Dicky Pride, Kyle Stanley, Chesson Hadley, Thorbjørn Olesen, John Mallinger, Jason Allred, Will Wilcox, Derek Ernst, Bryce Molder, John Peterson **143:** Brian Stuard, Michael Thompson, Shawn Stefani, Charlie Wi, James Driscoll, Troy Matteson, John Huh, D.A. Points, Erik Compton, Ryo Ishikawa, Tim Petrovic **144:** Spencer Levin, Mark Wilson, Zach Johnson, Benjamin Alvarado, Edward Loar, Peter Malnati, Justin Bolli, Joey Garber, Charlie Beljan, Paul Goydos, Bronson La'Cassie, Andrew Loupe **145:** Matt Bettencourt, Ryuji Imada, Tim Clark, Adam Rainaud **146:** Jim Herman, Trevor Immelman, Nicholas Thompson **147:** Luke Guthrie **148:** Scott McCarron, Cameron Wilson, Richard H. Lee, Daniel Chopra, Alex Aragon **149:** Alex Prugh, Tag Ridings, Sebastian Saavedra **151:** Bobby Gates, David Duval **152:** Scott Gardiner **WD:** Louis Oosthuizen

FIRST ROUND		SECOND ROUND		THIRD ROUND	
Brendan Steele	62 (-8)	Scott Langley	129 (-11)	Ryan Moore	197 (-13)
Bud Cauley	63 (-7)	Michael Putnam	130 (-10)	Aaron Baddeley	198 (-12)
Ryan Moore	63 (-7)	K.J. Choi	130 (-10)	4 Players	199 (-11)
5 players	64 (-6)	Harris English	130 (-10)	**Kevin Streelman**	201 (-9)
Kevin Streelman	69 (-1)	**Kevin Streelman**	137 (-3)		

OWR: 16 of top 50 entered - Rating: 314 - Points to 50th - Streelman: 48 points, to 36th in OWR

Quicken Loans National

Jun 26 - Jun 29

Congressional Country Club (Blue Course) - Bethesda, MD
Champion: Justin Rose

7,569 yards   Par 71
Purse: $6.5 Million

England's Justin Rose won his first Major championship at the 2013 U.S. Open at Merion, and he logged his next PGA Tour victory on a course which seemed equally ready to host an Open, scoring a playoff triumph over Shawn Stefani at the Quicken Loans National at Congressional. In many ways the conditions were the primary story as slick greens and punishing rough regularly took their toll; indeed, Congressional joined fellow ex-U.S. Open site Torrey Pines as the only 2014 PGA Tour venues where the winner's relative-to-par total (four-under-par 280) was actually higher than that of the quartet of players who shared the 36-hole lead (at six-under-par 136). Seven players held at least a share of the lead during Sunday's wild final round, with the most prominent disappointment belonging to two-time 2014 winner Patrick Reed, who held a two-shot lead at the turn before carding double-bogeys at both the 10th and 11th en route to a closing 76 that dropped him all the way into a tie for 11th. Also stumbling late was Brendan Steele, who would have made it a three-way playoff but for a watery double-bogey at the famed/brutal par-4 18th. The 18th very nearly dashed Rose's hopes as well, but after hitting his second in the front-left water, he holed a clutch 15-footer for bogey to remain alive. Stefani, for his part, managed to par the closer to gain his spot in the playoff — but then promptly hit *his* second into the water when it served as the first playoff, handing the title to Rose. Stefani gained a valuable consolation prize, however, joining Steele, Ben Martin and Charley Hoffmann among the top four finishers not yet exempt, and thus earning a spot in the field at the upcoming British Open at Hoylake.

1	Justin Rose	74-65-71-70	280	$1.17 mil		39=	Brian Davis	72-73-71-73	289	$25,350
2	Shawn Stefani	74-68-68-70	280	$702,000			Matt Every	71-69-72-77	289	$25,350
3=	Charley Hoffman	72-72-68-69	281	$377,000			Retief Goosen	69-71-76-73	289	$25,350
	Ben Martin	72-68-70-71	281	$377,000			J.J. Henry	74-69-74-72	289	$25,350
5=	Andrés Romero	70-72-72-68	282	$237,250			Andrew Loupe	74-70-69-76	289	$25,350
	Brendan Steele	74-66-71-71	282	$237,250			Davis Love III	72-70-74-73	289	$25,350
	Brendon Todd	72-70-69-71	282	$237,250			John Rollins	72-72-71-74	289	$25,350
8=	Billy Hurley III	69-73-70-71	283	$188,500		46=	Stuart Appleby	70-67-76-77	290	$16,900
	Marc Leishman	70-66-73-74	283	$188,500			Erik Compton	68-73-75-74	290	$16,900
	Brendon de Jonge	71-68-71-73	283	$188,500			Ben Curtis	75-69-71-75	290	$16,900
11=	Ricky Barnes	67-69-75-73	284	$125,125			Peter Hanson	72-68-75-75	290	$16,900
	Robert Garrigus	73-70-70-71	284	$125,125			Charles Howell III	71-73-72-74	290	$16,900
	Billy Horschel	70-68-74-72	284	$125,125			Trevor Immelman	74-71-71-74	290	$16,900
	Fredrik Jacobson	67-71-71-75	284	$125,125			John Merrick	74-71-73-72	290	$16,900
	Richard H. Lee	74-68-68-74	284	$125,125			Andrew Svoboda	71-72-76-71	290	$16,900
	Patrick Reed	68-68-71-77	284	$125,125			Gary Woodland	72-71-69-78	290	$16,900
	Jordan Spieth	74-70-69-71	284	$125,125		55=	Kevin Chappell	71-72-76-72	291	$14,430
	Hudson Swafford	69-68-73-74	284	$125,125			Oliver Goss	70-66-76-79	291	$14,430
19=	Stewart Cink	74-69-71-71	285	$87,750			J.B. Holmes	72-72-70-77	291	$14,430
	John Huh	72-72-70-71	285	$87,750			Sean O'Hair	73-71-74-73	291	$14,430
21=	Steven Bowditch	73-71-70-72	286	$72,800			Geoff Ogilvy	70-72-72-77	291	$14,430
	Brandt Snedeker	70-70-75-71	286	$72,800			Ryan Palmer	73-71-70-77	291	$14,430
	T. Van Aswegen	68-74-73-71	286	$72,800			Carl Pettersson	72-69-76-74	291	$14,430
24=	Angel Cabrera	71-74-69-73	287	$52,650			Patrick Rodgers	73-69-73-76	291	$14,430
	Russell Knox	73-67-78-69	287	$52,650			Heath Slocum	72-72-72-75	291	$14,430
	Hunter Mahan	71-73-69-74	287	$52,650		64=	Jason Bohn	71-71-78-72	292	$13,520
	Michael Putnam	69-72-72-74	287	$52,650			K.J. Choi	69-72-75-76	292	$13,520
	Brady Watt	71-71-71-74	287	$52,650			D.H. Lee	73-71-75-73	292	$13,520
	Tim Wilkinson	70-71-72-74	287	$52,650			Spencer Levin	69-74-73-76	292	$13,520
30=	Roberto Castro	71-72-75-70	288	$36,978			Bo Van Pelt	71-71-78-72	292	$13,520
	Greg Chalmers	66-78-72-72	288	$36,978		69=	James Driscoll	71-74-74-74	293	$13,065
	Bill Haas	68-72-71-77	288	$36,978			Kevin Kisner	75-68-78-72	293	$13,065
	George McNeill	69-69-77-73	288	$36,978		71=	Scott Brown	72-72-74-76	294	$12,740
	Seung-Yul Noh	73-70-66-79	288	$36,978			Morgan Hoffmann	70-68-78-78	294	$12,740
	Webb Simpson	72-73-71-72	288	$36,978			Scott Stallings	75-70-68-81	294	$12,740
	Daniel Summerhays	70-72-71-75	288	$36,978		74	Robert Streb	74-71-75-77	297	$12,480
	Cameron Tringale	70-71-73-74	288	$36,978		75	Rory Sabbatini	71-74-77-78	300	$12,350
	Nick Watney	69-75-69-75	288	$36,978						

Out Of The Money: **146**: Camilo Villegas, Troy Merritt, Sang-Moon Bae, Arjun Atwal, Kyle Stanley, Mike Weir, Jason Day, Vijay Singh, Brian Harman **147**: Nicholas Thompson, Josh Teater, Y.E. Yang, Martin Laird, Russell Henley, Aaron Baddeley, Bud Cauley, James Hahn, Danny Lee, Jonathan Byrd, Ted Potter Jr., Chad Collins **148**: Charlie Beljan, Jason Dufner, Will MacKenzie, Bryce Molder, Jhonattan Vegas, Jim Renner **149**: Martin Flores, Woody Austin, Ernie Els, Justin Hicks, Tiger Woods, Charlie Wi **150**: Keegan Bradley, Robert Allenby, Patrick Cantlay **151**: Wes Roach, Mark Wilson, Derek Ernst **152**: David Lingmerth, Chesson Hadley, Harrison Frazar **153**: Brice Garnett **154**: Johnson Wagner **159**: Pat Perez

FIRST ROUND		SECOND ROUND		THIRD ROUND	
Greg Chalmers	66 (-5)	Marc Leishman	136 (-6)	Patrick Reed	207 (-6)
Ricky Barnes	67 (-4)	Oliver Goss	136 (-6)	Seung-Yul Noh	209 (-4)
Freddie Jacobson	67 (-4)	Ricky Barnes	136 (-6)	Freddie Jacobson	209 (-4)
4 Players	68 (-3)	Patrick Reed	136 (-6)	Marc Leishman	209 (-4)
Justin Rose	74 (+3)	2 Players	137 (-5)	**Justin Rose**	210 (-3)
		Justin Rose	139 (-3)		

OWR: 13 of top 50 entered - Rating: 305 - Points to 54th - Rose: 48 points, to 8th in OWR

Greenbrier Classic	**July 3 - Jul 6**
Greenbrier Resort (Old White Course) - White Sulphur Springs, WV	7,287 yards Par 70
Champion: Angel Cabrera	Purse: $6.5 Million

Ending a run of disappointing play that extended all the way back to 2010, 44-year-old Angel Cabrera won the first non-Major event of his career on the PGA Tour, claiming a two-shot triumph at the Greenbrier Classic, in White Sulphur Springs, West Virginia. The 2007 Masters and 2009 U.S. Open champion, Cabrera stood well back in the field after 36 holes (despite opening rounds of 68-68) but pulled to within two shots of 54-hole leader William Hurley III following a seven-birdie, one-bogey round of 64 on Saturday. A newcomer to Saturday night leads, Hurley birdied his opener on Sunday before stumbling to four bogeys over his next five holes, eventually posting a 74 and tying for fourth. But Cabrera's path remained anything but clear due to a dazzling final round posted by George McNeill, who carded seven birdies and a hole-in-one at the 234-yard 8th en route to the week's low score of 61, and the clubhouse lead on 14-under-par 266. At that point, Cabrera had completed 10 holes and trailed by one, but he quickly sped to the front with back-to-back birdies at the 11th and 12th, then extended his lead to three upon holing a 176-yard 8 iron for an eagle at the 492-yard par-4 13th. But now seemingly in command, he promptly bogeyed both the 14th and the par-3 15th, leaving matters unresolved until a two-putt birdie at the 616-yard 17th proved to be the clincher. With places in the upcoming British Open field being awarded to the top four players among the top 12 not already exempt, also leaving the Greenbrier happy were McNeill, Hurley, Chris Stroud (who closed with 69) and Cameron Tringale (69). Less fortunate was Bud Cauley, who aced the par-3 18th en route to a tie fourth, only to lose out on a British open spot due to his lower position in the OWR.

1	Angel Cabrera	68-68-64-64	264	$1.17 mil		Shawn Stefani	73-67-67-69	276	$28,698
2	George McNeill	70-67-68-61	266	$702,000		Brice Garnett	68-66-72-70	276	$28,698
3	Webb Simpson	71-69-67-63	270	$442,000		Michael Putnam	67-72-67-70	276	$28,698
4=	Bud Cauley	69-68-70-64	271	$227,036		Jonas Blixt	64-73-68-71	276	$28,698
	Keegan Bradley	67-69-69-66	271	$227,036		Kyle Stanley	71-68-66-71	276	$28,698
	Brendon Todd	71-67-67-66	271	$227,036		Davis Love III	67-73-65-71	276	$28,698
	Chris Stroud	66-66-70-69	271	$227,036		Steve Stricker	66-68-68-74	276	$28,698
	Cameron Tringale	72-66-64-69	271	$227,036	45=	Chris Kirk	65-69-75-68	277	$18,219
	Will Wilcox	68-69-65-69	271	$227,036		Josh Teater	69-69-70-69	277	$18,219
	Billy Hurley III	68-63-67-73	271	$227,036		Patrick Rodgers	65-75-68-69	277	$18,219
11=	Charlie Beljan	67-69-71-65	272	$137,800		Andrés Romero	72-68-67-70	277	$18,219
	Jason Bohn	65-72-68-67	272	$137,800		Heath Slocum	70-69-68-70	277	$18,219
	Steve Marino	69-70-66-67	272	$137,800		Richard H. Lee	71-68-67-71	277	$18,219
	Joe Durant	65-71-66-70	272	$137,800		Troy Matteson	72-61-71-73	277	$18,219
	Michael Thompson	66-72-64-70	272	$137,800	52=	Stephen Ames	69-68-71-70	278	$15,158
16=	Danny Lee	65-71-71-66	273	$91,186		Kevin Na	66-70-71-71	278	$15,158
	Troy Merritt	66-72-68-67	273	$91,186		Justin Leonard	71-67-69-71	278	$15,158
	Sang-Moon Bae	66-74-66-67	273	$91,186		Charles Howell III	67-71-68-72	278	$15,158
	David Lingmerth	67-68-69-69	273	$91,186		Hudson Swafford	72-67-65-74	278	$15,158
	Bubba Watson	68-67-69-69	273	$91,186	57=	T. Van Aswegen	67-70-72-70	279	$14,300
	Jim Renner	65-70-68-70	273	$91,186		Tim Wilkinson	68-71-70-70	279	$14,300
	Kevin Chappell	67-65-69-72	273	$91,186		Jason Gore	70-70-69-70	279	$14,300
23=	Patrick Cantlay	69-68-69-68	274	$62,400		J.J. Henry	70-70-69-70	279	$14,300
	J.B. Holmes	68-68-69-69	274	$62,400		Wes Roach	69-71-69-70	279	$14,300
	Bill Haas	69-70-65-70	274	$62,400		Bronson La'Cassie	70-66-70-73	279	$14,300
26=	Ted Potter Jr.	70-70-68-67	275	$44,236		Trevor Immelman	69-70-67-73	279	$14,300
	Johnson Wagner	68-68-71-68	275	$44,236	64=	Gon. F'dez-Castaño	68-71-70-71	280	$13,585
	Patrick Reed	67-69-71-68	275	$44,236		Andrew Svoboda	72-68-69-71	280	$13,585
	David Toms	69-69-68-69	275	$44,236		Brendon de Jonge	70-69-68-73	280	$13,585
	Scott Langley	68-71-67-69	275	$44,236		David Hearn	68-68-68-76	280	$13,585
	Robert Allenby	67-70-68-70	275	$44,236	68=	Chad Collins	66-73-70-72	281	$13,130
	Andrew Loupe	69-69-67-70	275	$44,236		Matt Bettencourt	70-68-68-75	281	$13,130
	Luke Guthrie	67-69-68-71	275	$44,236		Oliver Goss	70-68-68-75	281	$13,130
	Camilo Villegas	68-67-67-73	275	$44,236	71	Robert Streb	68-72-69-73	282	$12,870
35=	Carl Pettersson	71-68-70-67	276	$28,698	72	Gary Woodland	69-70-69-75	283	$12,740
	Scott Stallings	70-69-70-67	276	$28,698	73=	Ken Duke	72-67-70-75	284	$12,545
	Tom Watson	71-68-68-69	276	$28,698		Roberto Castro	72-68-69-75	284	$12,545

Out Of The Money: **141**: Nick Watney, Justin Hicks, Bobby Wyatt, Chad Campbell, Marc Leishman, Ricky Barnes, Will MacKenzie, John Peterson, Jim Herman **142**: Jonathan Byrd, John Huh, Vijay Singh, Daniel Chopra, Kevin Foley, Alex Aragon, Ben Curtis, Jhonattan Vegas, Scott McCarron, Edward Loar **143**: Brian Harman, Chesson Hadley, Jeff Curl, Miguel Ángel Carballo, Kevin Tway, Rory Sabbatini, Scott Verplank, Benjamin Alvarado, Brad Fritsch **144**: Ben Martin, Morgan Hoffmann, John Rollins, Alex Prugh, Charlie Wi, William McGirt, Brian Davis, Stuart Appleby, Darren Clarke, Troy Kelly **145**: Harrison Frazar, Kevin Kisner, Mike Weir, Jimmy Walker, Sean O'Hair, Spencer Levin, Doug LaBelle, Y.E. Yang, James Driscoll, Peter Hanson **147**: Tim Clark **148**: Bryce Molder, Nick Faldo, Robert McClellan, Paul Goydos, Thorbjørn Olesen **149**: Daniel Summerhays, Peter Malnati, Tommy Gainey **150**: Nicholas Thompson, Brian Anania, K.J. Choi, Brian Agee **151**: Tag Ridings **153**: Neal Lancaster **154**: Mikey Moyers **158**: Rod Perry **WD**: Brian Gay

FIRST ROUND		SECOND ROUND		THIRD ROUND	
Jonas Blixt	64 (-6)	Billy Hurley III	131 (-9)	Billy Hurley III	198 (-12)
8 Players	65 (-5)	Kevin Chappell	132 (-8)	**Angel Cabrera**	200 (-10)
Angel Cabrera	68 (-2)	Chris Stroud	132 (-8)	Kevin Chappell	201 (-9)
		Troy Matteson	133 (-7)	7 Players	202 (-8)
		3 Players	134 (-6)		
		Angel Cabrera	136 (-4)		

OWR: 12 of top 50 entered - Rating: 234 - Points to 51st - Cabrera: 42 points, to 56th in OWR

John Deere Classic

TPC Deere Run - Silvis, IL
Champion: Brian Harman

Jul 10 - Jul 13
7,257 yards Par 71
Purse: $4.7 Million

Twenty-seven-year-old left-hander Brian Harman claimed his maiden victory on the PGA Tour at the John Deere Classic, saving some of his best golf for the final nine as he battled – and ultimately defeated – local favorite Zach Johnson by one. After sharing the first round lead with an eight-under-par 63, Harman added a Friday 68 and a Saturday 65 (which included two eagles) to claim the 54-hole lead, one shot ahead of three-time John Deere champion Steve Stricker. But while the 47-year-old Sticker uncharacteristically stumbled to a Sunday 72, Johnson – the event's 2012 champion and also twice a runner-up – mounted a charge, ultimately carding seven birdies and posting a bogey-free 64 to finish on 21-under-par 263. Also in the Sunday mix were Tim Clark and Scott Brown, both of whom turned in 32 to jump into contention before coming home in 35 and 36 respectively and falling into ties for 5th. Harman, meanwhile, solidified his position early with an eagle at the par-5 2nd before eventually turning in 33. A birdie at 10 kept him narrowly in front before a run of three straight birdies at holes 14-16 opened up a two shot cushion, allowing him to take a safe three-putt bogey at the pond-guarded 18th to clinch the title. In addition to a two-year exemption and a trip to the 2015 Masters, Harman also earned a spot in the following week's British Open at Hoylake, the final berth to be awarded for the world's oldest event.

Pos	Player	Scores	Total	Prize
1	Brian Harman	63-68-65-66	262	$846,000
2	Zach Johnson	63-67-69-64	263	$507,600
3=	Jhonattan Vegas	69-68-63-65	265	$272,600
	Jerry Kelly	66-68-65-66	265	$272,600
5=	Scott Brown	67-70-61-68	266	$178,600
	Tim Clark	72-63-64-67	266	$178,600
7=	Bo Van Pelt	67-69-67-65	268	$141,588
	Jordan Spieth	71-64-67-66	268	$141,588
	Ryan Moore	66-67-67-68	268	$141,588
	Johnson Wagner	66-65-69-68	268	$141,588
11=	Steven Bowditch	64-67-70-68	269	$112,800
	Steve Stricker	68-65-64-72	269	$112,800
13=	Kevin Na	68-66-71-65	270	$80,571
	Bryce Molder	73-65-67-65	270	$80,571
	Shawn Stefani	73-67-64-66	270	$80,571
	Chad Campbell	69-71-62-68	270	$80,571
	David Toms	65-70-67-68	270	$80,571
	Daniel Summerhays	69-68-65-68	270	$80,571
	Brad Fritsch	70-68-63-69	270	$80,571
20=	Kevin Kisner	68-72-68-64	272	$56,713
	Troy Merritt	68-70-66-68	272	$56,713
	D.H. Lee	72-66-66-68	272	$56,713
23=	John Rollins	72-68-66-67	273	$43,240
	Charlie Beljan	71-68-66-68	273	$43,240
	Charles Howell III	66-68-67-72	273	$43,240
	William McGirt	64-66-69-74	273	$43,240
27=	Luke Guthrie	69-69-69-67	274	$30,628
	Dicky Pride	70-70-66-68	274	$30,628
	Justin Hicks	66-70-70-68	274	$30,628
	Glen Day	72-65-69-68	274	$30,628
	Steven Ihm	73-65-68-68	274	$30,628
	Jordan Niebrugge (a)	71-68-66-69	274	-
	Tommy Gainey	70-68-67-69	274	$30,628
	Russell Henley	70-67-68-69	274	$30,628
	Will MacKenzie	73-65-67-69	274	$30,628
	Scott Langley	69-70-65-70	274	$30,628
37=	Greg Chalmers	70-68-71-66	275	$20,709
	Ben Crane	69-70-69-67	275	$20,709
	Robert Streb	65-69-72-69	275	$20,709
	Davis Love III	69-70-67-69	275	$20,709
	Nicholas Thompson	67-71-68-69	275	$20,709
	Alex Prugh	68-68-69-70	275	$20,709
	Rory Sabbatini	63-70-71-71	275	$20,709
	Brian Davis	72-68-64-71	275	$20,709
45=	David Hearn	71-69-69-67	276	$13,872
	John Senden	68-69-71-68	276	$13,872
	Brice Garnett	68-71-68-69	276	$13,872
	Andrés Romero	71-68-68-69	276	$13,872
	Trevor Immelman	66-71-70-69	276	$13,872
	Camilo Villegas	70-67-69-70	276	$13,872
	Brendon de Jonge	65-75-65-71	276	$13,872
52=	Richard H. Lee	70-70-69-68	277	$10,998
	Stewart Cink	69-66-74-68	277	$10,998
	Jonathan Byrd	74-66-68-69	277	$10,998
	Heath Slocum	69-70-68-70	277	$10,998
	Kevin Chappell	68-69-70-70	277	$10,998
	Kevin Tway	65-69-72-71	277	$10,998
	Bud Cauley	67-67-69-74	277	$10,998
59=	Chris Stroud	69-71-70-68	278	$10,387
	Retief Goosen	71-69-69-69	278	$10,387
	Todd Hamilton	64-69-73-72	278	$10,387
	Wes Roach	67-69-70-72	278	$10,387
63=	Bobby Wyatt	69-71-71-68	279	$9,964
	Kyle Stanley	71-67-72-69	279	$9,964
	Mark Wilson	71-69-69-70	279	$9,964
	Derek Ernst	69-71-68-71	279	$9,964
	J.J. Henry	68-67-72-72	279	$9,964
68=	Ricky Barnes	68-70-72-70	280	$9,635
	Sean O'Hair	67-70-69-74	280	$9,635
70=	Chad Collins	69-71-70-71	281	$9,447
	Paul Goydos	69-71-66-75	281	$9,447
72=	Edward Loar	70-68-72-72	282	$9,259
	Marc Turnesa	69-71-66-76	282	$9,259
74=	Harris English	67-73-74-69	283	$9,071
	Jamie Lovemark	69-71-71-72	283	$9,071
76=	Cameron Beckman	69-69-74-74	286	$8,883
	John Merrick	71-69-71-75	286	$8,883

Out Of The Money: **141**: Charlie Wi, Tag Ridings, John Huh, Brian Stuard, Martin Flores, John Peterson, Tyrone Van Aswegen, Cameron Wilson, Jim Herman, Andrew Loupe, Josh Teater, Robert Allenby, Ted Potter Jr., Billy Mayfair, Ben Martin, Kent Jones, Justin Bolli, Bronson La'Cassie **142**: Daniel Chopra, Jim Renner, D.J. Trahan, Gonzalo Fernández-Castaño, Chris Kirk, Kevin Streelman, Tim Wilkinson, Lee Janzen, Andrew Ruthkoski, Steve Marino, Boo Weekley, Billy Hurley III, Armando Villarreal, Alex Aragon **143**: Troy Kelly, Andrew Svoboda, Robert Garrigus, Danny Lee, Eric Axley, Patrick Rodgers, Tim Herron, Ryuji Imada, Pat Perez, Matt Bettencourt, Tim Petrovic, Ken Duke, Arjun Atwal, Kevin Foley **144**: Sang-Moon Bae, Guy Boros, David Lingmerth, Will Wilcox, Doug LaBelle II, Morgan Hoffmann, Michael Thompson, Joe Ogilvie, Jason Bohn, Nathan Green, Jason Allred **145**: Raymond Knoll, Lucas Glover, Miguel Ángel Carballo **146**: D.A. Points, Frank Lickliter II, Roberto Castro **147**: Scott Stallings, Scott McCarron, Peter Malnati **148**: James Driscoll, David Gossett, Ryan Lenahan, Hudson Swafford **149**: Chris Smith, Len Mattiace **151**: Aaron Krueger **152**: Troy Matteson **157**: Michael Bradley **159**: Paul Stankowski **WD**: Scott Gardiner (78), David Duval (81), Patrick Cantlay

FIRST ROUND
Zach Johnson	63	(-8)
Rory Sabbatini	63	(-8)
Brian Harman	63	(-8)
3 Players	64	(-7)

SECOND ROUND
William McGirt	130	(-12)
Zach Johnson	130	(-12)
Steven Bowditch	131	(-11)
Johnson Wagner	131	(-11)
Brian Harman	131	(-11)

THIRD ROUND
Brian Harman	196	(-17)
Steve Stricker	197	(-16)
Scott Brown	198	(-15)
4 Players	199	(-14)

OWR: 8 of top 50 entered - Rating: 166 - Points to 44th - Harman: 34 points, to 70th in OWR

RBC Canadian Open
Royal Montreal Golf Club (Blue Course) - Ile Bizard, Quebec, Canada
Champion: Tim Clark

Jul 24 - Jul 27
7,153 yards   Par 70
Purse: $5.7 Million

Thirty-eight-year-old Tim Clark ended a victory drought which dated to the 2010 Players Championship by coming from behind to win the RBC Canadian Open, edging Jim Furyk by one at the Royal Montreal Golf Club. For Furyk, a back-to-back champion here in 2006 and 2007, the event appeared a golden opportunity to break a nearly five-year winless streak of his own, as he opened with a 67, then added a course record-tying 63 and a Saturday 65 to build a three-shot 54-hole lead. Clark, for his part, began with rounds of 67-67 before an eagle at the par-4 2nd jumpstarted a third round 64, allowing him to go to sleep Saturday night as Furyk's closest pursuer. On a Sunday which saw players go off both tees, in threesomes, in attempts at beating incoming rain, the status quo was maintained over the first nine as both Clark and Furyk turned even par. But Clark soon found another gear coming home, reeling in birdies at the 11th, 12th, 14th and, after a short rain delay, the 15th to finally move into the lead. He maintained this margin by matching Furyk's birdie at the par-3 17th, then clinched the title by holing a six-footer for par at the last after Furyk missed a 12-foot birdie putt to tie. Clark's 17-under-par 263 total tied the tournament record and the victory was his first on Canadian soil since claiming his first two professional wins on the Canadian circuit in 1998. For Furyk, the loss marked the seventh straight time he has failed to hold a 54-hole lead, another streak dating to 2010.

1	Tim Clark	67-67-64-65	263	$1.026 mil		Danny Lee	69-65-72-70	276	$26,980
2	Jim Furyk	67-63-65-69	264	$615,600		Stewart Cink	68-69-71-68	276	$26,980
3	Justin Hicks	66-67-70-64	267	$387,600		Johnson Wagner	71-67-71-67	276	$26,980
4=	Matt Kuchar	69-65-70-65	269	$235,600		Ken Duke	67-71-72-66	276	$26,980
	Michael Putnam	64-70-69-66	269	$235,600		Ben Crane	71-69-71-65	276	$26,980
	Gon. F'dez-Castaño	67-67-69-66	269	$235,600	43=	J.J. Henry	67-69-71-70	277	$16,986
7=	Dicky Pride	66-71-70-63	270	$183,825		James Hahn	72-68-68-69	277	$16,986
	Graham DeLaet	69-63-70-68	270	$183,825		Taylor Pendrith (a)	65-75-68-69	277	-
9=	Kevin Kisner	70-69-68-64	271	$153,900		Morgan Hoffmann	69-69-70-69	277	$16,986
	Brad Fritsch	72-68-67-64	271	$153,900		Vijay Singh	69-69-70-69	277	$16,986
	Graeme McDowell	68-65-70-68	271	$153,900		Charl Schwartzel	66-72-70-69	277	$16,986
12=	Ben Curtis	67-70-70-65	272	$101,888		Jeff Overton	69-71-69-68	277	$16,986
	Ernie Els	70-67-69-66	272	$101,888		Ricky Barnes	70-70-70-67	277	$16,986
	Nick Watney	66-68-71-67	272	$101,888		Andrew Svoboda	67-66-72-72	277	$16,986
	Retief Goosen	69-67-69-67	272	$101,888		Tim Petrovic	64-66-72-75	277	$16,986
	Troy Matteson	70-68-67-67	272	$101,888	53=	Nathan Green	67-69-71-71	278	$13,034
	Joe Durant	69-66-67-70	272	$101,888		David Hearn	67-70-70-71	278	$13,034
	Jamie Lovemark	69-65-67-71	272	$101,888		D.H. Lee	69-70-69-70	278	$13,034
	Kyle Stanley	65-67-68-72	272	$101,888		D.A. Points	71-68-69-70	278	$13,034
20=	Robert Allenby	66-69-72-66	273	$64,068		Adam Hadwin	70-69-68-71	278	$13,034
	Kevin Chappell	72-67-68-66	273	$64,068		Joel Dahmen	66-72-68-72	278	$13,034
	Andrés Romero	71-68-67-67	273	$64,068		Troy Merritt	66-74-70-68	278	$13,034
	Matt Bettencourt	67-70-68-68	273	$64,068		Tim Wilkinson	67-68-75-68	278	$13,034
	Scott Brown	67-66-69-71	273	$64,068		Edward Loar	72-64-75-67	278	$13,034
25=	William McGirt	69-70-69-66	274	$45,458	62=	Patrick Rodgers	71-66-70-73	280	$12,369
	Scott Piercy	72-65-71-66	274	$45,458		Sean O'Hair	69-70-69-72	280	$12,369
	Will Wilcox	68-68-69-69	274	$45,458	64=	Charlie Beljan	67-72-71-71	281	$12,141
	Brandt Snedeker	69-69-67-69	274	$45,458		Greg Chalmers	66-68-76-71	281	$12,141
29=	Martin Laird	71-66-70-68	275	$37,050	66=	Josh Teater	70-69-68-75	282	$11,799
	Russell Knox	72-66-69-68	275	$37,050		Jerry Kelly	67-71-72-72	282	$11,799
	Steve Marino	69-69-70-67	275	$37,050		Mike Weir	70-70-71-71	282	$11,799
	Woody Austin	68-70-71-66	275	$37,050		K.J. Choi	72-68-73-69	282	$11,799
	Charlie Wi	66-73-66-70	275	$37,050	70=	Derek Ernst	70-69-73-72	284	$11,457
34=	Eric Axley	68-68-71-69	276	$26,980		Ryuji Imada	68-72-75-69	284	$11,457
	Geoff Ogilvy	70-68-70-68	276	$26,980	72	Thomas Aiken	70-69-73-73	285	$11,286
	Roberto Castro	69-67-70-70	276	$26,980	73	Jim Herman	70-70-75-73	288	$11,172
	Tim Herron	69-67-70-70	276	$26,980					

Out Of The Money: **141**: Chad Campbell, Bo Van Pelt, Stuart Appleby, Charley Hoffman, Peter Malnati, Hudson Swafford, Pat Perez, Daniel Chopra, Bryce Molder, Mark Calcavecchia, Luke Guthrie, Timothy Madigan, Alex Prugh, Adam Svensson, Alex Aragon, Bronson La'Cassie **142**: Aaron Baddeley, Seung-Yul Noh, John Peterson, Robbie Greenwell, Doug LaBelle II, Eugene Wong, Jeff Maggert, Mark Wilson, Dustin Johnson, Sang-Moon Bae, Kevin Foley **143**: Tyrone Van Aswegen, Dave Levesque, Brian Davis, John Rollins, Justin Leonard, Hunter Mahan, Carl Pettersson, Martin Flores, Andrew Loupe, Miguel Ángel Carballo, Wes Roach **144**: Robert Garrigus, David Lingmerth, Brian Gay, Luke Donald, Tommy Gainey, Jason Bohn, Jason Allred, Michael Gligic, Benjamin Silverman, Chad Collins, Nicholas Thompson, Tag Ridings, Heath Slocum **145**: Brice Garnett, John Merrick, Beon Yeong Lee, Trevor Immelman, Jonathan Byrd, Kevin Carrigan, Corey Conners (a) **146**: Robert Streb, Eli Cole, Billy Andrade, John Daly, Lucas Glover, Y.E. Yang, John Huh, Jhonattan Vegas, Kevin Tway, Oliver Goss **147**: Cameron Beckman, Ted Potter Jr., Jim Renner, Bill Q. Walsh **148**: Josh Persons, Chris Hemmerich **149**: David Duval **150**: Chris DiMarco, Stephen Ames **151**: Erik Compton **153**: Scott McCarron, Kevin Stinson **WD**: Camilo Villegas (73), Richard H. Lee (74), James Driscoll (78)

FIRST ROUND		SECOND ROUND		THIRD ROUND	
Michael Putnam	64 (-6)	Jim Furyk	130 (-10)	Jim Furyk	195 (-15)
Tim Petrovic	64 (-6)	Tim Petrovic	130 (-10)	**Tim Clark**	198 (-12)
Kyle Stanley	65 (-5)	Graham DeLaet	132 (-8)	Kyle Stanley	200 (-10)
Taylor Pendrith (a)	65 (-5)	Kyle Stanley	132 (-8)	Jamie Lovemark	201 (-9)
11 Players	66 (-4)	4 Players	133 (-7)	4 Players	202 (-8)
Tim Clark	67 (-3)	**Tim Clark**	134 (-6)		

OWR: 9 of top 50 entered - Rating: 186 - Points to 42nd - Clark: 36 points, to 75th in OWR

WGC-Bridgestone Invitational

Jul 31 - Aug 3

Firestone Country Club (South Course) - Akron, OH
Champion: Rory McIlroy

7,400 yards Par 70
Purse: $9 Million

Any notions that Rory McIlroy might be complacent following his dominant victory at the British Open were dispelled quickly at the WGC-Bridgestone Invitational as the 25-year-old Northern Irishman threw his game into gear on the weekend and cruised to a two-shot victory over the same man he battled hardest at Hoylake, Sergio García. McIlroy stood five shots off Marc Leishman's lead after an opening round 69, then posted a 64 that might well have given him the halfway lead under normal circumstances. On this occasion, however, it would only be good enough to trail by four as García uncorked a stunning Friday 61 – a truly remarkable round in that he turned in one-under-par 34, then birdied the 10th and parred the 11th before charging home with seven straight birdies to become the ninth man in PGA Tour history to card a 27 on a par-35-or-greater nine. It also set up what appeared to be a two-man battle on the weekend between García and McIlroy, and that storyline grew as both men turned in 32 on Saturday before García's lead expanded to five prior to rain causing a three-hour delay in play. Upon returning to the course, however, McIlroy birdied both the 17th and 18th to cut the margin to three after 54 holes - a run he would continue on Sunday when he birdied four of his first five holes, moving into the lead when García played the same stretch one over, then playing even-par golf thereafter to march methodically home to victory. The win lifted him back into the number one spot in the OWR for the first time since March of 2013 - a career in direct contrast to the staggering Tiger Woods, who trailed by 15 shots through 54 holes, then collapsed on the Sunday's front nine before withdrawing with back spasms at the turn.

1	Rory McIlroy	69-64-66-66	265	$1.53 mil	37=	Bubba Watson	69-70-73-68	280	$64,500
2	Sergio García	68-61-67-71	267	$900,000		Brendon de Jonge	72-69-70-69	280	$64,500
3	Marc Leishman	64-69-68-67	268	$522,000		Jamie Donaldson	68-70-71-71	280	$64,500
4=	Charl Schwartzel	65-69-73-64	271	$308,000		Seung-Yul Noh	69-69-70-72	280	$64,500
	Patrick Reed	67-68-71-65	271	$308,000	41=	Chris Kirk	69-73-72-67	281	$61,000
	Keegan Bradley	68-67-67-69	271	$308,000		Russell Henley	72-70-71-68	281	$61,000
	Justin Rose	65-67-70-69	271	$308,000		Bill Haas	71-69-69-72	281	$61,000
8=	Graeme McDowell	71-70-66-66	273	$170,000	44	Steven Bowditch	69-71-73-69	282	$59,000
	Rickie Fowler	67-67-72-67	273	$170,000	45=	Brendon Todd	74-70-69-70	283	$57,500
	Ryan Moore	65-73-68-67	273	$170,000		Miguel A. Jiménez	69-69-72-73	283	$57,500
	Adam Scott	69-68-65-71	273	$170,000	47=	Matt Every	74-68-73-69	284	$55,500
12=	Matt Kuchar	71-66-72-65	274	$115,000		Stephen Gallacher	74-71-69-70	284	$55,500
	Hideki Matsuyama	70-71-65-68	274	$115,000	49	Jordan Spieth	71-70-73-71	285	$54,000
	Brandt Snedeker	68-68-68-70	274	$115,000	50=	Tim Clark	72-73-70-71	286	$52,500
15=	Phil Mickelson	71-73-69-62	275	$97,500		Luke Donald	73-70-72-71	286	$52,500
	Hunter Mahan	71-65-71-68	275	$97,500	52=	Ian Poulter	73-73-70-71	287	$49,625
	Jim Furyk	69-68-69-69	275	$97,500		Scott Stallings	72-75-68-72	287	$49,625
	Thomas Bjørn	69-68-69-69	275	$97,500		Thongchai Jaidee	70-74-71-72	287	$49,625
19=	Lee Westwood	72-71-70-63	276	$89,000		David Howell	69-71-71-76	287	$49,625
	Kevin Stadler	71-70-66-69	276	$89,000	56=	Joost Luiten	73-73-71-71	288	$47,750
	Gary Woodland	70-68-68-70	276	$89,000		Martin Kaymer	77-68-72-71	288	$47,750
	Henrik Stenson	71-66-68-71	276	$89,000	58=	Alexander Levy	72-71-77-69	289	$46,500
23=	Kevin Na	71-73-66-67	277	$82,000		Richard Sterne	75-70-73-71	289	$46,500
	Zach Johnson	70-70-68-69	277	$82,000		Jonas Blixt	75-72-69-73	289	$46,500
	Branden Grace	69-71-67-70	277	$82,000	61	Louis Oosthuizen	75-73-67-75	290	$45,500
26=	Ernie Els	71-69-70-68	278	$75,200	62	Gon. F'dez-Castaño	79-71-67-74	291	$45,000
	Jimmy Walker	69-70-70-69	278	$75,200	63=	Pablo Larrazábal	71-74-77-70	292	$44,250
	Fabrizio Zanotti	70-71-68-69	278	$75,200		Steve Stricker	74-73-72-73	292	$44,250
	John Senden	74-66-67-71	278	$75,200	65	Brian Harman	72-70-75-76	293	$43,750
	J.B. Holmes	69-69-67-73	278	$75,200	66=	Mikko Ilonen	75-74-73-72	294	$43,375
31=	Victor Dubuisson	72-70-69-68	279	$69,500		Jason Dufner	70-74-73-77	294	$43,375
	Angel Cabrera	73-68-70-68	279	$69,500	68	Daisuke Maruyama	73-73-73-78	297	$43,000
	Webb Simpson	72-69-70-68	279	$69,500	69=	David Lynn	76-72-75-75	298	$42,625
	Francesco Molinari	67-70-73-69	279	$69,500		Yoshitaka Takeya	74-75-74-75	298	$42,625
	Matt Jones	70-70-69-70	279	$69,500	71	Kevin Streelman	78-71-78-73	300	$42,250
	Harris English	69-69-68-73	279	$69,500	72	Estanislao Goya	76-77-71-78	302	$42,000

WD: Tiger Woods (211), Graham DeLaet (212), Jason Day (145), Ben Crane (143)

FIRST ROUND		SECOND ROUND		THIRD ROUND	
Marc Leishman	64 (-6)	Sergio García	129 (-11)	Sergio García	196 (-14)
Ryan Moore	65 (-5)	Justin Rose	132 (-8)	**Rory McIlroy**	199 (-11)
Charl Schwartzel	65 (-5)	Marc Leishman	133 (-7)	Marc Leishman	201 (-9)
Justin Rose	65 (-5)	**Rory McIlroy**	133 (-7)	3 Players	202 (-8)
Rory McIlroy	69 (-1)	2 Players	134 (-6)		

Eligibility for the 2013 WGC-Bridgestone Invitational

Playing members of the 2012 U.S. and European Ryder Cup teams; the top 50 players, including any tied for 50th place, from the Official World Golf Ranking as of Monday, July 21, 2014; the top 50 players, including any tied for 50th place, from the Official World Golf Ranking as of Monday, July 28, 2014; tournament winners, whose victories are considered official, of tournaments from the Federation Tours since the prior season's Bridgestone Invitational with an Official World Golf Ranking Strength of Field Rating of 115 points or more; the winner of the following tournament from each of the following Tours: 1) Japan Golf Tour: Japan Golf Tour Championship (2014) and Bridgestone Open (2013). 2) Australasian Tour: Australian PGA Championship (2014). 3) Southern Africa Tour: Dimension Data Pro-Am (2014). 4. Asian Tour: Thailand Golf Champions (2013).

OWR: 49 of top 50 entered - Rating: 804 - Points to 60th - McIlroy: 76 points, to 1st in OWR

Barracuda Championship

Montreux Golf & Country Club - Reno, NV
Champion: Geoff Ogilvy

Jul 31 - Aug 3
7,472 yards   Par 72
Purse: $3 Million

In danger of losing his PGA Tour card for the first time in his long and successful career, 37-year-old Australian Geoff Ogilvy instead righted his ship in comprehensive fashion by claiming his eighth PGA Tour title at the newly renamed Barracuda Championship, in Reno. In the Tour's only event to be contested using the modified Stableford scoring system, the 2006 U.S. Open champion played solid golf throughout the week, racking up point totals of 16, 7, 12 and 14 over four days of play to salvage his season, gain entrance to the upcoming PGA Championship and guarantee his exempt status on Tour through 2016. Ogilvy was chased down the stretch by Justin Hicks who, while looking for his first PGA Tour victory, led the entire field on Sunday by carding 18 points. But as Hicks drew close early in the final nine, Ogilvy responded by grabbing five points with an eagle at the 518-yard 13th, then added birdies at the 367-yard 14th and the 616-yard finisher to ultimately stretch his margin of victory to five. Though he'd only previously logged two top-25 finishes in 2014, Ogilvy's form had been on the upswing since before the U.S. Open, and he acknowledged improved putting as reason he was able to convert this into a long-awaited victory. Despite not winning, Hicks held his game together down the stretch to finish a career-best second while John Huh and another player returning from a palpable dip in form, Jonathan Byrd, shared third.

1	Geoff Ogilvy	16-07-12-14	49	$540,000		J.J. Henry	05-04-12-06	27	$15,480
2	Justin Hicks	09-06-11-18	44	$324,000	39=	John Mallinger	04-05-19--2	26	$12,900
3=	John Huh	12-07-07-11	37	$174,000		D.J. Trahan	02-06-09-09	26	$12,900
	Jonathan Byrd	07-06-13-11	37	$174,000		Patrick Rodgers	11-00-11-04	26	$12,900
5	Rod Pampling	11-05-09-11	36	$120,000	42=	Greg Chalmers	03-13-10--1	25	$11,100
6	Martin Laird	13-00-14-12	35	$104,250		Jeff Overton	07-13-00-05	25	$11,100
7	Jason Allred	07-11-14-03	35	$104,250		Kevin Tway	08-01-05-11	25	$11,100
8=	Tim Wilkinson	16-05-01-12	34	$84,000	45=	Oliver Goss	06-03-09-05	23	$9,600
	Kyle Stanley	05-11-06-12	34	$84,000		Mark Wilson	08-09-02-04	23	$9,600
	Ricky Barnes	05-06-12-11	34	$84,000	47=	Michael Putnam	08-03-16--5	22	$7,810
	Nick Watney	18-08-06-02	34	$84,000		Thorbjørn Olesen	10-05--2-09	22	$7,810
12=	Eric Axley	11-04-03-15	33	$66,000		Padraig Harrington	10-07-02-03	22	$7,810
	Hudson Swafford	09-09-06-09	33	$66,000		Troy Matteson	05-03-11-03	22	$7,810
14=	Robert Streb	10-04-09-09	32	$54,000		Marc Turnesa	06-05-06-05	22	$7,810
	Chad Campbell	13--1-07-13	32	$54,000		Kevin Lucas	11-02-03-06	22	$7,810
	Bryce Molder	10-10-06-06	32	$54,000	53=	Arjun Atwal	07-10-06-02	21	$6,980
17=	Miguel A. Carballo	10-01-07-13	31	$43,500		Tim Petrovic	10-02-04-05	21	$6,980
	George Coetzee	11--1-11-10	31	$43,500		Danny Lee	11-04-00-06	21	$6,980
	Joe Durant	09-01-14-07	31	$43,500	56	Nicholas Thompson	10-05--1-06	20	$6,840
	Tommy Gainey	11-10-03-07	31	$43,500	57=	Trevor Immelman	07-01-06-04	18	$6,750
21=	Steve Flesch	01-09-11-09	30	$32,400		Andrew Loupe	08-00-06-04	18	$6,750
	Wes Roach	12-10-00-08	30	$32,400	59=	Jim Herman	10-02-05-00	17	$6,630
	Morgan Hoffmann	06-03-13-08	30	$32,400		Bronson La'Cassie	06-03-02-06	17	$6,630
	David Lingmerth	09-07-12-02	30	$32,400	61=	Ben Curtis	07-05-06--2	16	$6,420
25=	Retief Goosen	05-08-06-10	29	$25,200		John Merrick	03-05-08-00	16	$6,420
	Brendan Steele	09-11-10--1	29	$25,200		Charlie Beljan	06-05-05-00	16	$6,420
27=	Andrés Romero	07-07-04-10	28	$20,400		Cameron Beckman	07-02-04-03	16	$6,420
	Woody Austin	11-08-03-06	28	$20,400		Ryuji Imada	04-05-04-03	16	$6,420
	Johnson Wagner	10-08-04-06	28	$20,400	66=	D.H. Lee	11-05--1-00	15	$6,180
	Derek Ernst	11-00-05-12	28	$20,400		Tim Herron	04-08-03-00	15	$6,180
	Billy Mayfair	03-09-11-05	28	$20,400		John Rollins	12-02-01-00	15	$6,180
	Doug LaBelle II	11-01-13-03	28	$20,400	69=	Rory Sabbatini	-3-13-02-02	14	$6,000
	Lee Janzen	08-07-13-00	28	$20,400		Len Mattiace	-1-09-07--1	14	$6,000
34=	Brice Garnett	-2-10-15-04	27	$15,480		Mike Weir	04-10-00-00	14	$6,000
	Kent Jones	05-11--2-13	27	$15,480	72	Brian Stuard	04-09--2-00	11	$5,880
	Kevin Chappell	12--1-06-10	27	$15,480	73	Chris Smith	08-03-00--1	10	$5,820
	Jamie Lovemark	06-05-10-06	27	$15,480	74	Chad Collins	07-04-03--5	9	$5,760

Out Of The Money: **7 pts**: Glen Day, Steve Marino, Scott Langley, Lucas Glover, Robert Allenby, Bobby Wyatt, Todd Hamilton, Brian Gay, D.A. Points **6 pts**: Nathan Green, Stuart Appleby, Edward Loar, Craig Barlow **5 pts**: Dicky Pride, Richard H. Lee, Matt Bettencourt, Chris Riley, Justin Bolli, Will Wilcox, Brad Fritsch **4 pts**: Tag Ridings, Alex Prugh, Heath Slocum **3 pts**: Alex Cejka, David Gossett, Davis Love III, Roberto Castro, Scott McCarron, Guy Boros **2 pts**: Joe Ogilvie, Jhonattan Vegas, Ken Duke, Charlie Wi, Skip Kendall **0 pts**: Josh Teater **-1pt**: Dean Wilson, Peter Malnati **-2 pts**: Ted Purdy, Kevin Foley **-3 pts**: James Hahn, Jim Renner, Rich Beem, Daniel Chopra, Sebastian Saavedra **-4 pts**: Stuart Smith **-5 pts**: David Carr **-7 pts**: Alex Aragon **-8 pts**: John Peterson, Jesse Schutte **-12 pts**: Chris DiMarco **-15 pts**: Aaron Baddeley, John Daly **-21 pts**: Paul Stankowski **WD**: Richard S. Johnson (5 pts), Tyrone Van Aswegen (2 pts), David Duval (-1 pt) **DQ**: Y.E. Yang

FIRST ROUND		SECOND ROUND		THIRD ROUND	
Nick Watney	+18	Nick Watney	+26	**Geoff Ogilvy**	+35
Geoff Ogilvy	+16	**Geoff Ogilvy**	+23	Jason Allred	+32
Tim Wilkinson	+16	Wes Roach	+22	Nick Watney	+32
Martin Laird	+13	Tommy Gainey	+21	Brendan Steel	+30
Chad Campbell	+13	Tim Wilkinson	+21	3 Players	+28

OWR: 0 of top 50 entered - Rating: 33 - Points to 33rd - Ogilvy: 24 points, to 126th in OWR

Wyndham Championship

Sedgefield Country Golf Club - Greensboro, NC
Champion: Camilo Villegas

Aug 14 - Aug 17
7,130 yards   Par 70
Purse: $5.3 Million

It had been nearly four and a half years since Colombia's Camilo Villegas had found the winner's circle on the PGA Tour, and as he sat five strokes back on a very crowded Saturday night leaderboard, the 2014 Wyndham Classic didn't seem likely to be the event that would end the drought. But Villegas came out firing on Sunday, logging four birdies and an eagle over his first eight holes at the Sedgefield Country Club, turning in 29 and injecting himself very much into the championship mix. The first round leader with a bogey-free 63, the 32-year-old Villegas had played somewhat disappointing golf during middle rounds of 69-68, and that form returned over his final nine when, with a chance to push himself well out in front, he managed but a single birdie over the final nine. Thus in the clubhouse with his second 63 of the week, Villegas waited for 45 minutes in the hope that he might still end up in a playoff – a wait which must have become progressively more optimistic as, one by one, the other contenders all stumbled. Among those who came up shy, the most prominent were Sweden's Freddie Jacobson (who needed only a par 4 at the tough 18th to force a playoff but left his approach short, then three-putted from off the fringe), Nick Watney (who needed a birdie for to tie but instead drove out-of-bounds and carded a double-bogey) and Heath Slocum, who finished two shots back after bogeying both the 17th and 18th. Apparently it was just Villegas's time.

1	Camilo Villegas	63-69-68-63	263	$954,000		Brian Davis	69-65-70-69	273	$21,730
2=	Bill Haas	68-66-66-64	264	$466,400		Johnson Wagner	66-67-70-70	273	$21,730
	Fredrik Jacobson	68-64-66-66	264	$466,400		Doug LaBelle II	72-65-66-70	273	$21,730
4	Heath Slocum	65-65-68-67	265	$254,400		Stuart Appleby	68-69-66-70	273	$21,730
5=	Webb Simpson	64-69-66-67	266	$193,450		Josh Teater	67-69-66-71	273	$21,730
	Brandt Snedeker	68-65-66-67	266	$193,450	45=	Y.E. Yang	69-68-68-69	274	$16,960
	Nick Watney	67-64-65-70	266	$193,450		Steve Marino	66-69-69-70	274	$16,960
8=	William McGirt	64-68-71-64	267	$148,400	47=	Ben Curtis	68-67-73-67	275	$14,257
	Jhonattan Vegas	67-65-69-66	267	$148,400		Robert Garrigus	68-68-72-67	275	$14,257
	Kevin Kisner	69-64-67-67	267	$148,400		Billy Horschel	70-65-72-68	275	$14,257
	Brad Fritsch	69-63-65-70	267	$148,400		Jason Allred	69-66-67-73	275	$14,257
12=	Scott Piercy	70-64-69-65	268	$116,600	51=	Mark Wilson	71-67-72-66	276	$12,473
	Scott Langley	65-65-69-69	268	$116,600		Charlie Wi	70-66-71-69	276	$12,473
14=	Sang-Moon Bae	69-68-66-66	269	$92,750		Shawn Stefani	67-67-71-71	276	$12,473
	Martin Laird	65-66-69-69	269	$92,750		Retief Goosen	69-69-67-71	276	$12,473
	Bo Van Pelt	67-65-68-69	269	$92,750		Troy Merritt	70-68-67-71	276	$12,473
	Andrés Romero	70-66-64-69	269	$92,750		Kevin Foley	69-68-67-72	276	$12,473
18=	Carl Pettersson	67-65-71-67	270	$66,780	57=	Wes Roach	70-68-74-65	277	$11,660
	David Toms	67-69-67-67	270	$66,780		Michael Putnam	68-67-74-68	277	$11,660
	Paul Casey	65-69-68-68	270	$66,780		John Huh	70-68-70-69	277	$11,660
	D.A. Points	67-65-70-68	270	$66,780		Joe Durant	69-67-71-70	277	$11,660
	Robert Streb	69-66-67-68	270	$66,780		James Hahn	69-69-69-70	277	$11,660
	Roberto Castro	71-66-65-68	270	$66,780		Justin Hicks	69-69-69-70	277	$11,660
24=	Luke Guthrie	69-69-68-65	271	$41,009		Steven Bowditch	66-70-70-71	277	$11,660
	Patrick Reed	71-67-67-66	271	$41,009	64=	Peter Malnati	70-67-74-67	278	$11,130
	Francesco Molinari	69-67-68-67	271	$41,009		Ernie Els	68-69-73-68	278	$11,130
	Andrew Loupe	65-68-70-68	271	$41,009		Michael Thompson	70-66-73-69	278	$11,130
	Tim Clark	67-67-69-68	271	$41,009	67=	Hudson Swafford	71-67-73-68	279	$10,812
	Andrew Svoboda	67-64-70-70	271	$41,009		Richard Sterne	69-68-71-71	279	$10,812
	Will Wilcox	67-67-67-70	271	$41,009		Tommy Gainey	66-72-67-74	279	$10,812
	Ricky Barnes	66-69-66-70	271	$41,009	70=	Nicholas Thompson	70-68-73-69	280	$10,441
32=	Brice Garnett	71-67-68-66	272	$29,327		Ryo Ishikawa	70-62-78-70	280	$10,441
	John Merrick	70-67-68-67	272	$29,327		Bobby Wyatt	67-70-73-70	280	$10,441
	J.J. Henry	66-70-68-68	272	$29,327		Tim Herron	70-68-69-73	280	$10,441
	Jeff Overton	70-67-67-68	272	$29,327	74=	David Lingmerth	67-70-73-71	281	$10,123
	Brian Stuard	66-65-71-70	272	$29,327		T. Van Aswegen	72-66-72-71	281	$10,123
	Justin Bolli	67-68-67-70	272	$29,327	76	Lee Janzen	70-68-71-73	282	$9,964
38=	Brooks Koepka	68-68-73-64	273	$21,730	77	Joe Ogilvie	70-68-72-73	283	$9,858
	Derek Ernst	68-69-69-67	273	$21,730					

Out Of The Money: **139**: Scott Brown, Brian Harman, Jonathan Byrd, Matt Bettencourt, Robert Karlsson, David Duval, Richard H. Lee, Bud Cauley, Eric Axley, James Driscoll, Hideki Matsuyama, Dicky Pride, Tim Petrovic, Jim Herman **140**: Will MacKenzie, Len Mattiace, Mike Weir, Robert Allenby, Gonzalo Fernández-Castaño, Chad Collins, Trevor Immelman, Alex Aragon, Jamie Lovemark, Gary Christian, Will Collins, John Daly, Chad Campbell, Boo Weekley, Ken Duke **141**: Martin Flores, Billy Hurley III, Greg Chalmers, John Peterson, Sean O'Hair, D.H. Lee, Scott Stallings, Davis Love III, Bryce Molder, Kevin Tway **142**: Patrick Cantlay, Bronson La'Cassie, Cameron Beckman, Arjun Atwal, Brian Gay, Charlie Beljan, Glen Day, Rafael Cabrera-Bello, Marc Turnesa **143**: Danny Lee, Troy Matteson, Matteo Manassero, Alex Prugh, Fred Couples, Chesson Hadley **144**: Jim Renner, Brendon de Jonge, Charles Howell III, Kyle Stanley, Padraig Harrington, Rocco Mediate, Armando Villarreal, Morgan Hoffmann, Ryuji Imada, Aaron Baddeley, Lucas Glover **145**: Peter Hanson, Miguel Ángel Carballo **146**: Steve Flesch, Daniel Chopra **147**: Todd Hamilton, Stephen Gallacher, Sam Love **148**: John Rollins, Jesse Hutchins **149**: Jeff Maggert **150**: Edward Loar **151**: Kelly Mitchum **WD**: Patrick Rodgers (73)

FIRST ROUND		SECOND ROUND		THIRD ROUND	
Camilo Villegas	63 (-7)	Heath Slocum	130 (-10)	Nick Watney	196 (-14)
William McGirt	64 (-6)	Scott Langley	130 (-10)	Brad Fritsch	197 (-13)
Webb Simpson	64 (-6)	4 Players	131 (-9)	Freddie Jacobson	198 (-12)
5 Players	65 (-5)	**Camilo Villegas**	132 (-8)	Heath Slocum	198 (-12)
				Camilo Villegas	200 (-10)

OWR: 7 of top 50 entered - Rating: 172 - Points to 44th - Villegas: 34 points, to 112th in OWR

The Barclays	**Aug 21 - Aug 24**
Ridgewood Country Club - Paramus, NJ	7,319 yards Par 71
Champion: Hunter Mahan	Purse: $8 Million

Breaking a two-and-a-half-year, 48-tournament drought, Hunter Mahan won the first event of the 2014 FedEx Cup Playoffs, claiming a two-shot victory at The Barclays, played at the Ridgewood Country Club in Paramus, New Jersey. Ultimately prevailing over a crowded leaderboard on Sunday, Mahan began the week in style, trailing first round leader Bo Van Pelt by one after carding a five-under-par 66. His fortunes slipped slightly on Friday following a three-birdie, three-bogey 71, but a 68 on Saturday put him in the clubhouse only one stroke behind co-54-hole leaders Jason Day and Jim Furyk. For Furyk, the final round turned into another frustration-filled Sunday, for even after birdieing the 2nd and 3rd holes, he could manage no better than a closing 70, leaving him alone in eighth place; it was the eighth straight time he had failed to convert a 54-hole lead. Day, for his part, did somewhat better. Looking for his second PGA Tour victory of an injury-slowed 2014, he turned in two-under-par 33, bogeyed the par-4 11th but then added back-to-back birdies at the 13th and 14th to finish with 68 – good enough for a three-way tie for second. Joining him there were Cameron Tringale (who might have tied Mahan with a 72nd-hole birdie, but instead made bogey) and the least likely contender of all, Stuart Appleby, who closed with a sparkling 65 to land his first top-three finish since winning the Greenbrier Classic in 2010. Amidst this crowded competition, Mahan separated himself by logging three straight birdies at holes 15-17, allowing him the luxury of a slightly sloppy bogey at the last to still win by two.

1	Hunter Mahan	66-71-68-65	270	$1.44 mil
2=	Stuart Appleby	73-66-68-65	272	$597,333
	Cameron Tringale	66-68-72-66	272	$597,333
	Jason Day	72-64-68-68	272	$597,333
5=	Ernie Els	68-68-71-66	273	$292,000
	William McGirt	68-71-68-66	273	$292,000
	Matt Kuchar	68-70-68-67	273	$292,000
8	Jim Furyk	66-69-69-70	274	$248,000
9=	Patrick Reed	71-66-73-65	275	$208,000
	Rickie Fowler	68-73-67-67	275	$208,000
	Kevin Na	70-66-70-69	275	$208,000
	Morgan Hoffmann	70-70-66-69	275	$208,000
13=	Gary Woodland	73-66-69-68	276	$160,000
	Bo Van Pelt	65-71-70-70	276	$160,000
15=	Bill Haas	70-70-70-67	277	$132,000
	Adam Scott	69-65-75-68	277	$132,000
	Stewart Cink	69-72-68-68	277	$132,000
	Gon. F'dez-Castaño	70-69-68-70	277	$132,000
19=	Chris Stroud	69-70-69-70	278	$104,000
	Ryo Ishikawa	67-73-68-70	278	$104,000
	Erik Compton	68-69-70-71	278	$104,000
22=	John Senden	68-71-74-66	279	$70,200
	Jordan Spieth	70-70-72-67	279	$70,200
	Zach Johnson	68-70-72-69	279	$70,200
	Steven Bowditch	68-72-70-69	279	$70,200
	Angel Cabrera	71-69-69-70	279	$70,200
	Rory McIlroy	74-65-70-70	279	$70,200
	Charles Howell III	66-75-68-70	279	$70,200
	Paul Casey	66-71-71-71	279	$70,200
30=	Scott Langley	70-68-76-66	280	$46,500
	Shawn Stefani	71-70-71-68	280	$46,500
	Charley Hoffman	73-69-69-69	280	$46,500
	Hideki Matsuyama	68-70-72-70	280	$46,500
	Charl Schwartzel	69-70-71-70	280	$46,500
	Bubba Watson	68-70-71-71	280	$46,500
	Justin Rose	68-70-70-72	280	$46,500
	Kevin Chappell	68-67-71-74	280	$46,500
38=	Henrik Stenson	72-64-77-68	281	$32,000
	John Huh	69-69-74-69	281	$32,000
	Russell Knox	67-69-74-71	281	$32,000
	David Hearn	69-72-69-71	281	$32,000
	Jerry Kelly	74-68-68-71	281	$32,000
	Andrés Romero	72-70-68-71	281	$32,000
	Graeme McDowell	70-68-71-72	281	$32,000
	Danny Lee	67-71-70-73	281	$32,000
46=	Daniel Summerhays	68-72-72-70	282	$21,394
	Troy Merritt	69-71-72-70	282	$21,394
	Ben Martin	66-76-70-70	282	$21,394
	Kevin Stadler	74-67-70-71	282	$21,394
	Kevin Streelman	75-67-69-71	282	$21,394
	Bryce Molder	74-68-68-72	282	$21,394
	Brendon Todd	66-69-71-76	282	$21,394
53=	Jeff Overton	72-71-70-70	283	$18,520
	Chris Kirk	71-68-73-71	283	$18,520
	Keegan Bradley	68-73-70-72	283	$18,520
	Seung-Yul Noh	68-72-70-73	283	$18,520
57=	Lee Westwood	70-73-71-70	284	$17,840
	Brendan Steele	71-71-69-73	284	$17,840
	Brian Harman	69-74-68-73	284	$17,840
	Sergio García	71-68-71-74	284	$17,840
61=	Russell Henley	70-71-73-71	285	$17,120
	Jason Bohn	68-71-74-72	285	$17,120
	Jason Kokrak	70-71-71-73	285	$17,120
	Boo Weekley	72-68-71-74	285	$17,120
	Brendon de Jonge	66-72-72-75	285	$17,120
66=	Retief Goosen	69-69-74-74	286	$16,560
	Jhonattan Vegas	69-74-69-74	286	$16,560
68=	Ricky Barnes	68-75-70-76	289	$16,240
	Vijay Singh	69-73-71-76	289	$16,240
70	Chesson Hadley	74-69-70-78	291	$16,000
71=	K.J. Choi	68-75-72	215	$15,680
	Luke Guthrie	71-72-72	215	$15,680
	Tim Wilkinson	72-71-72	215	$15,680
74=	Brian Davis	73-66-77	216	$15,120
	Ryan Palmer	69-71-76	216	$15,120
	Brian Stuard	73-70-73	216	$15,120
	David Toms	69-73-74	216	$15,120
78	Phil Mickelson	71-72-75	218	$14,720
79	Martin Flores	73-70-76	219	$14,460

Out Of The Money: **144**: Ian Poulter, Andrew Svoboda, Brandt Snedeker, Matt Jones, George McNeill, Aaron Baddeley, Robert Garrigus, Justin Hicks, Billy Hurley III **145**: Luke Donald, Jonas Blixt, Kevin Kisner, Nick Watney, Justin Leonard, Scott Stallings, Graham DeLaet, Jimmy Walker, Michael Putnam, Louis Oosthuizen **146**: Billy Horschel, Scott Brown, Harris English, Webb Simpson, Matt Every, Robert Allenby, Robert Streb, Ben Crane, James Hahn **147**: Carl Pettersson, Ryan Moore, Sang-Moon Bae, Will MacKenzie, Marc Leishman **148**: Fredrik Jacobson, J.B. Holmes, Camilo Villegas, Pat Perez, Martin Kaymer **149**: Geoff Ogilvy, Michael Thompson **150**: Brice Garnett **151**: Rory Sabbatini   WD: Tim Clark (76)

FIRST ROUND		SECOND ROUND		THIRD ROUND	
Bo Van Pelt	65 (-6)	Cameron Tringale	134 (-8)	Jason Day	204 (-9)
6 Players	66 (-5)	Adam Scott	134 (-8)	Jim Furyk	204 (-9)
Hunter Mahan	66 (-5)	Kevin Chappell	135 (-7)	**Hunter Mahan**	205 (-8)
		Brendon Todd	135 (-7)	7 Players	206 (-7)
		Jim Furyk	135 (-7)		
		Hunter Mahan	137 (-5)		

OWR: 37 of top 50 entered - Rating: 735 - Points to 60th - Mahan: 74 points, to 19th in OWR

Deutsche Bank Championship

Aug 29 - Sep 1

TPC Boston - Norton, MA
Champion: Chris Kirk

7,216 yards   Par 71
Purse: $8 Million

Though a winner of the McGladrey Classic back in November of 2013, Chris Kirk arrived at the second event of the 2014 FedEx Cup Playoffs in middling form, having logged but a single top-25 finish (a T19 at the British Open) since late May's Memorial Tournament. An opening 73 in the Deutsche Bank Championship did little to suggest that this week would be different, but Kirk turned things around with a topsy turvy second round 66 which included eagles at the 298-yard 4th and the par-5 18th, and thus moved back to within five of co-36-hole leaders Ryan Palmer (who'd opened with a 63, the week's low round) and Jason Day. He then opened with back-to-back birdies during Sunday's third round and would go on to play blemish-free golf for the duration, initially birdieing both the 17th and 18th to come home in 64 and move within two of 54-hole leader Russell Henley. However, even at this point Kirk was still flying somewhat under the radar, this because he stood tied with Day (who shot 69) and world number one Rory McIlroy, who matched Kirk with a bogey-free 64 and commanded the great majority of post-round attention. But McIlroy never found the right gear in round four, posting four bogeys between holes 5-12 en route to a 70 that would ultimately drop him to a tie for 5th. Instead Monday's news was initially dominated by Geoff Ogilvy, who began the Labor Day finale five shots in arrears before birdieing six of his first 13 holes to sprint into the lead. Unfortunately, Ogilvy couldn't advance any further, carding a disappointing par at the 530-yard 18th to finish on 271. This left the stage clear for Kirk, who methodically reeled off five birdies between the 3rd and 16th holes to move to 15 under, then watched as the lone man with a chance to catch him, Billy Horschel, chunked his second at the 18th into a water hazard, posting a bogey when a birdie had been needed. Kirk then made a routine par to clinch the two-shot victory, with Horschel, Ogilvy and Henley (who quietly closed with 70) sharing second.

Pos	Player	Scores	Total	Money		Pos	Player	Scores	Total	Money
1	Chris Kirk	73-66-64-66	269	$1.44 mil			Vijay Singh	72-68-69-71	280	$36,950
2=	Geoff Ogilvy	70-71-65-65	271	$597,333			Morgan Hoffmann	72-69-68-71	280	$36,950
	Russell Henley	70-66-65-70	271	$597,333		43=	David Hearn	70-74-72-65	281	$28,800
	Billy Horschel	69-66-67-69	271	$597,333			Charl Schwartzel	72-72-68-69	281	$28,800
5=	John Senden	69-71-67-66	273	$304,000		45=	Steven Bowditch	77-68-57-65	282	$23,424
	Rory McIlroy	70-69-64-70	273	$304,000			Phil Mickelson	74-69-72-67	282	$23,424
7=	Martin Kaymer	71-66-70-67	274	$258,000			Chris Stroud	69-69-73-71	282	$23,424
	Jason Day	66-68-69-71	274	$258,000			Will MacKenzie	70-73-67-72	282	$23,424
9=	Carl Pettersson	67-73-69-66	275	$185,143			Gon. F'dez-Castaño	71-69-68-74	282	$23,424
	Jimmy Walker	70-70-68-67	275	$185,143		50=	Ernie Els	72-71-73-67	283	$19,017
	Robert Streb	73-67-67-68	275	$185,143			Brendan Steele	74-71-69-69	283	$19,017
	Bill Haas	67-69-70-69	275	$185,143			Camilo Villegas	72-69-72-70	283	$19,017
	Chesson Hadley	66-73-67-69	275	$185,143			Stewart Cink	71-72-69-71	283	$19,017
	Seung-Yul Noh	69-68-68-70	275	$185,143			Graham DeLaet	71-74-67-71	283	$19,017
	Webb Simpson	66-70-68-71	275	$185,143			Kevin Chappell	68-73-68-74	283	$19,017
16=	Jason Kokrak	68-72-70-66	276	$112,229			Michael Putnam	71-70-68-74	283	$19,017
	Zach Johnson	71-68-70-67	276	$112,229		57=	Luke Donald	69-74-74-67	284	$17,600
	Adam Scott	73-68-68-67	276	$112,229			Jerry Kelly	71-74-70-69	284	$17,600
	Kevin Stadler	71-70-67-68	276	$112,229			Billy Hurley III	68-74-71-71	284	$17,600
	Brian Stuard	72-71-65-68	276	$112,229			Bo Van Pelt	70-73-69-72	284	$17,600
	Keegan Bradley	65-71-69-71	276	$112,229			Andrew Svoboda	71-72-69-72	284	$17,600
	Ryan Palmer	63-71-71-71	276	$112,229			Daniel Summerhays	74-71-67-72	284	$17,600
23=	Ian Poulter	67-73-71-66	277	$76,800			Hideki Matsuyama	73-69-68-74	284	$17,600
	Jim Furyk	72-66-69-70	277	$76,800		64	Hunter Mahan	73-71-73-68	285	$16,960
	Rickie Fowler	70-69-67-71	277	$76,800		65=	Brian Harman	72-70-75-69	286	$16,640
26=	Henrik Stenson	70-70-73-65	278	$61,600			Marc Leishman	73-72-72-69	286	$16,640
	Russell Knox	67-70-71-70	278	$61,600			Scott Langley	71-72-70-73	286	$16,640
	Kevin Streelman	73-67-65-73	278	$61,600		68	Shawn Stefani	69-74-71-73	287	$16,320
29=	Gary Woodland	71-70-73-65	279	$50,867		69=	Jeff Overton	73-69-75-71	288	$15,920
	George McNeill	73-68-72-66	279	$50,867			John Huh	70-75-71-72	288	$15,920
	Bubba Watson	72-71-69-67	279	$50,867			William McGirt	71-74-71-72	288	$15,920
	Matt Kuchar	69-66-73-71	279	$50,867			Cameron Tringale	72-73-71-72	288	$15,920
	Ben Crane	69-68-70-72	279	$50,867		73	Ryan Moore	72-71-74-73	290	$15,520
	Jordan Spieth	67-70-69-73	279	$50,867		74=	Patrick Reed	68-68-82	218	$15,280
35=	Scott Stallings	70-74-72-64	280	$36,950			Brendon de Jonge	77-67-74	218	$15,280
	J.B. Holmes	70-75-68-67	280	$36,950		76	Andrés Romero	76-69-74	219	$15,040
	Danny Lee	74-65-73-68	280	$36,950		77	Scott Brown	75-68-77	220	$14,880
	K.J. Choi	72-70-70-68	280	$36,950		78	Matt Jones	69-75-79	223	$14,720
	Charles Howell III	68-73-71-68	280	$36,950		79	Fredrik Jacobson	72-72-80	224	$14,560
	Jason Bohn	74-68-69-69	280	$36,950		80	Matt Every	68-73-86	227	$14,400

Out Of The Money: 146: Brendon Todd, Harris English, Robert Garrigus **147**: Justin Hicks, Stuart Appleby, Charley Hoffman, Kevin Na **148**: Brandt Snedeker, Angel Cabrera, Erik Compton **149**: Ryo Ishikawa **150**: Ben Martin **WD**: Pat Perez (77), Tim Clark

FIRST ROUND		SECOND ROUND		THIRD ROUND	
Ryan Palmer	63 (-8)	Ryan Palmer	134 (-8)	Russell Henley	201 (-12)
Keegan Bradley	65 (-6)	Jason Day	134 (-8)	Billy Horschel	202 (-11)
Jason Day	66 (-5)	Matt Kuchar	135 (-7)	**Chris Kirk**	203 (-10)
Webb Simpson	66 (-5)	Billy Horschel	135 (-7)	Rory McIlroy	203 (-10)
Chesson Hadley	66 (-5)	5 Players	136 (-6)	Jason Day	203 (-10)
Chris Kirk	73 (+2)	**Chris Kirk**	139 (-3)		

OWR: 32 of top 50 entered - Rating: 630 - Points to 63rd - Kirk: 68 points, to 25th in OWR

BMW Championship

Sep 4 - Sep 7

Cherry Hills Country Club - Cherry Hills Village, CO
Champion: Billy Horschel

7,352 yards   Par 70
Purse: $8 Million

One week after squandering a chance for a playoff following a poor second shot on the final hole of the Deutsche Bank Championship, Billy Horschel rallied to score a major bounce-back win at the BMW Championship, played at Denver's famed Cherry Hills Country Club. The 27-year-old Horschel who, prior to the Deutsche Bank, had logged but a single PGA Tour top-10 finish since January, was around the lead all week, initially trailing first-round pace setters Rory McIlroy, Jordan Spieth and Garry Woodland by one after opening with a 68 that concluded with 11 consecutive pars. Despite a fine second round 66, his 36-hole deficit grew to two due to Sergio García posting a Friday 64 that included five birdies and an eagle, the latter the result of a holed pitch at the 395-yard 7th. But Horschel would take command on Saturday when, after turning relatively quietly in two-under-par 32, he caught fire on the back, eventually birdieing four of the final five holes to post a 63 that staked him to a three-shot 54-hole lead over Ryan Palmer. Sunday would prove something less than a cakewalk, however, as Palmer mounted a charge and twice drew even over the first 11 holes, only to fade after shanking his second out of heavy rough at the 13th on his way to a double bogey. This left Horschel's main challenge to come from García, who'd slipped to a 72 on Saturday before heating up again on Sunday, this time logging four birdies and an eagle (once again at the 7th) over his first 16 holes to pull within two. But at the 545-yard island-green 17th García imploded, actually chipping his fourth shot into the water en route to a triple-bogey eight, and a tie for fourth. That left Bubba Watson (who closed with three straight 66s but never truly threatened the lead) to claim solo second, with third place going to Morgan Hoffman, who was grateful there was no cut after opening 72-72, then tore Cherry Hills up with rounds of 62-63 on the weekend. The victory lifted Horschel into second place in the four-event FedEx Cup Playoffs heading to the finale in Atlanta.

1	Billy Horschel	68-66-63-69	266	$1.44 mil		Harris English	71-71-67-70	279	$48,500
2	Bubba Watson	70-66-66-66	268	$864,000	35	Justin Rose	69-71-70-70	280	$43,200
3	Morgan Hoffmann	72-72-62-63	269	$544,000	36=	Tim Clark	71-69-70-71	281	$36,057
4=	Jim Furyk	70-68-67-66	271	$319,000		Geoff Ogilvy	73-69-69-70	281	$36,057
	Rickie Fowler	71-66-66-68	271	$319,000		Brian Stuard	71-69-71-70	281	$36,057
	Sergio García	68-64-72-67	271	$319,000		Charles Howell III	69-72-71-69	281	$36,057
	Ryan Palmer	69-64-67-71	271	$319,000		Chris Kirk	71-70-71-69	281	$36,057
8=	Rory McIlroy	67-67-72-66	272	$232,000		Brendon Todd	73-67-72-69	281	$36,057
	Adam Scott	71-66-69-66	272	$232,000		Graeme McDowell	73-72-69-67	281	$36,057
	Jordan Spieth	67-70-68-67	272	$232,000	43=	Chris Stroud	69-73-69-71	282	$28,000
11	Graham DeLaet	68-68-69-68	273	$200,000		Zach Johnson	71-71-71-69	282	$28,000
12=	Angel Cabrera	71-72-66-65	274	$162,000		Brian Harman	73-71-71-67	282	$28,000
	Charl Schwartzel	72-66-70-66	274	$162,000	46=	Stuart Appleby	71-71-70-71	283	$22,680
	Chesson Hadley	68-70-68-68	274	$162,000		Kevin Na	74-69-69-71	283	$22,680
	J.B. Holmes	71-68-67-68	274	$162,000		Matt Kuchar	71-73-70-69	283	$22,680
16=	Kevin Chappell	68-72-70-65	275	$124,000		Erik Compton	69-74-73-67	283	$22,680
	Ernie Els	70-69-69-67	275	$124,000	50=	Matt Every	68-73-71-72	284	$19,680
	Bill Haas	72-68-67-68	275	$124,000		Kevin Stadler	74-69-70-71	284	$19,680
	Martin Kaymer	68-70-64-73	275	$124,000		Ryan Moore	80-69-69-66	284	$19,680
20=	Camilo Villegas	70-71-68-67	276	$96,533	53=	Fredrik Jacobson	73-71-66-75	285	$18,347
	Jimmy Walker	72-67-69-68	276	$96,533		Marc Leishman	74-69-69-73	285	$18,347
	Hideki Matsuyama	69-67-71-69	276	$96,533		Webb Simpson	73-72-69-71	285	$18,347
23=	Henrik Stenson	68-69-72-68	277	$69,200		Charley Hoffman	72-71-73-69	285	$18,347
	John Senden	73-66-70-68	277	$69,200		Matt Jones	73-73-70-69	285	$18,347
	Gary Woodland	67-73-68-69	277	$69,200		Patrick Reed	77-70-71-67	285	$18,347
	Ben Crane	70-70-68-69	277	$69,200	59=	Hunter Mahan	75-70-71-71	287	$17,520
	Seung-Yul Noh	70-71-67-69	277	$69,200		Will MacKenzie	75-72-69-71	287	$17,520
	Russell Knox	74-69-72-62	277	$69,200		Russell Henley	68-74-76-69	287	$17,520
29=	Jerry Kelly	71-73-66-68	278	$55,600		Kevin Streelman	75-70-76-66	287	$17,520
	Daniel Summerhays	75-68-71-64	278	$55,600	63=	K.J. Choi	69-74-69-76	288	$17,040
31=	Cameron Tringale	70-73-68-68	279	$48,500		Steven Bowditch	72-77-70-69	288	$17,040
	Carl Pettersson	73-70-68-68	279	$48,500	65	William McGirt	71-71-76-73	291	$16,800
	George McNeill	71-69-69-70	279	$48,500	66	Jason Bohn	74-71-75-72	292	$16,640

WD: Jason Day (70), Keegan Bradley (143), Phil Mickelson (146)

FIRST ROUND		**SECOND ROUND**		**THIRD ROUND**	
Gary Woodland	67 (-3)	Sergio García	132 (-8)	**Billy Horschel**	197 (-13)
Jordan Spieth	67 (-3)	Ryan Palmer	133 (-7)	Ryan Palmer	200 (-10)
Rory McIlroy	67 (-3)	Rory McIlroy	134 (-6)	Martin Kaymer	202 (-8)
9 Players	68 (-2)	**Billy Horschel**	134 (-6)	Bubba Watson	202 (-8)
Billy Horschel	68 (-2)	3 Players	136 (-4)	Rickie Fowler	203 (-7)

OWR: 33 of top 50 entered - Rating: 642 - Points to 58th - Horschel: 70 points, to 23rd in OWR

Tour Championship by Coca-Cola

East Lake Golf Club - Atlanta, GA
Champion: Billy Horschel

Sep 11 - Sep 14
7,154 yards   Par 70
Purse: $8 Million

Perhaps it says something about the nature of the FedEx Cup Playoffs that their 2014 champion, Billy Horschel, logged but a single top 10 PGA Tour finish from January through August, making him the biggest longshot winner in the Playoffs' history. On the other hand, after a chunked 72nd-hole 4 iron cost him a chance at the Deutsche Bank Championship (where he finished second), Horschel won the final two FedEx Cup events in succession and, lest there still be doubters, closed out his Tour Championship victory by playing head-to-head with world number one Rory McIlroy over the final 36 holes. And while McIlroy seemed to be running on fumes after a long summer of spectacular golf, Horschel was just reaching cruising speed at Eastlake, putting together four impressively steady rounds to roll to a three-shot victory. He grabbed a share of the first round lead (with Chris Kirk) by posting a bogey-free four-under-par 66, then matched that (despite two bogeys) on Friday to take a two-shot halfway lead over McIlroy, Kirk and the recently hot Jason Day. Seemingly unfazed by the first of his two pairings with McIlroy, Horschel turned in three-under-par 32 on Saturday, but just as his lead began to look imposing, he bogeyed both the 10th and 13th which, combined with McIlroy eagling the par-5 15th en route to a 67, left the pair tied atop the leaderboard after 54 holes, two ahead of Furyk, who posted a 67 of his own. With birdies at the 4th and 5th, Horschel nosed one ahead in Sunday's early going before McIlroy seemed to abruptly run out of gas, double-bogeying the par-3 6th with a tee shot in the water, then spinning out entirely with bogeys at the 9th, 10th and 11th. He would eventually recover with birdies at the 15th, 16th and 17th, just as Furyk would mount a late charge by birdieing the 12th, 13th and 16th. But in the end, Horschel played steady, even-par golf on the inward half to comfortably claim both his third PGA Tour win and the $10 million top prize for clinching the FedEx Cup.

1	Billy Horschel	66-66-69-68	269	$1.44 mil		16	Bill Haas	68-71-73-70	282	$175,000
2=	Jim Furyk	67-69-67-69	272	$708,000		17=	Brendon Todd	70-75-72-66	283	$168,000
	Rory McIlroy	69-65-67-71	272	$708,000			Jimmy Walker	73-69-69-72	283	$168,000
4=	Chris Kirk	66-68-71-68	273	$343,333		19=	Patrick Reed	67-74-74-69	284	$160,000
	Jason Day	67-67-70-69	273	$343,333			Kevin Na	70-66-75-73	284	$160,000
	Justin Rose	72-66-66-69	273	$343,333		21	Zach Johnson	68-74-72-71	285	$154,000
7	Ryan Palmer	69-67-69-69	274	$275,000		22	Hideki Matsuyama	71-71-71-73	286	$150,000
8	Rickie Fowler	69-68-67-71	275	$260,000		23=	Webb Simpson	74-72-72-70	288	$143,000
9=	Gary Woodland	71-75-63-67	276	$231,667			Hunter Mahan	74-72-71-71	288	$143,000
	Sergio García	69-71-70-66	276	$231,667			Martin Kaymer	73-69-73-73	288	$143,000
	Adam Scott	69-72-65-70	276	$231,667		26	John Senden	72-75-69-74	290	$138,000
12	Russell Henley	70-68-67-72	277	$210,000		27=	Jordan Spieth	71-70-80-71	292	$135,000
13	Matt Kuchar	68-71-69-70	278	$200,000			Morgan Hoffmann	70-73-73-76	292	$135,000
14	Bubba Watson	67-73-67-73	280	$190,000			Geoff Ogilvy	77-77-73-73	300	$132,000
15	Cameron Tringale	68-68-74-71	281	$180,000						

FIRST ROUND		SECOND ROUND		THIRD ROUND	
Chris Kirk	66 (-4)	**Billy Horschel**	132 (-8)	**Billy Horschel**	201 (-9)
Billy Horschel	66 (-4)	Rory McIlroy	134 (-6)	Rory McIlroy	201 (-9)
4 Players	67 (-3)	Jason Day	134 (-6)	Jim Furyk	203 (-7)
		Chris Kirk	134 (-6)	3 Players	204 (-6)
		4 Players	136 (-4)		

OWR: 25 of top 50 entered - Rating: 439 - Points to 29th - Horschel: 58 points, to 14th in OWR

Top 40 In 2013 FedEx Cup Bonus Pool

1	Billy Horschel	$10,000,000	21	Patrick Reed	$220,000
2	Chris Kirk	$3,000,000	22	Gary Woodland	$215,000
3	Rory McIlroy	$2,000,000	23	John Senden	$210,000
4	Jim Furyk	$1,500,000	24	Kevin Na	$205,000
5	Bubba Watson	$1,000,000	25	Webb Simpson	$200,000
6	Hunter Mahan	$800,000	26	Morgan Hoffman	$195,000
7	Jimmy Walker	$700,000	27	Brendon Todd	$190,000
8	Matt Kuchar	$600,000	28	Hideki Matsuyama	$185,000
9	Rickie Fowler	$550,000	29	Geoff Ogilvy	$180,000
10	Jason Day	$500,000	30	Dustin Johnson	$175,000
11	Justin Rose	$300,000	31	Stuart Appleby	$165,000
12	Adam Scott	$290,000	32	Harris English	$155,000
13	Sergio García	$280,000	33	Keegan Bradley	$150,000
14	Ryan Palmer	$270,000	34	Charles Howell III	$145,000
15	Jordan Spieth	$250,000	35	Seung-Yul Noh	$142,000
16	Bill Haas	$245,000	36	Brian Harman	$140,000
17	Martin Kaymer	$240,000	37	Graham DeLaet	$138,000
18	Zach Johnson	$235,000	38	Kevin Stadler	$137,000
19	Russell Henley	$230,000	39	Ryan Moore	$136,000
20	Cameron Tringale	$225,000	40	Russell Knox	$135,000

FINAL 2014 OWR

Rank	2013	Player	Pts Avg	Tot Pts	Events	Pts Lost	Pts Added
1	6	Rory McIlroy, NIR	11.0429	541.10	49	-345.11	567.77
2	3	Henrik Stenson, SWE	8.1334	422.93	52	-334.37	279.26
3	2	Adam Scott, AUS	7.7100	323.82	42	-317.70	248.09
4	28	Bubba Watson, USA	7.2741	349.16	48	-211.61	398.45
5	4	Sergio García, ESP	6.6963	334.81	50	-246.10	315.61
6	10	Justin Rose, ENG	6.6888	327.75	49	-317.52	272.77
7	19	Jim Furyk, USA	6.6230	291.41	44	-206.96	280.17
8	11	Jason Day, AUS	5.8111	232.44	40	-201.58	201.37
9	22	Jordan Spieth, USA	5.7476	298.88	52	-161.57	296.42
10	40	Rickie Fowler, USA	5.4674	284.30	52	-146.66	297.94
11	7	Matt Kuchar, USA	5.1066	265.54	52	-289.13	234.98
12	39	Martin Kaymer, GER	4.8623	252.84	52	-152.06	265.03
13	5	Phil Mickelson, USA	4.4465	200.09	45	-283.04	137.21
14	41	Billy Horschel, USA	4.4776	232.84	52	-120.91	217.90
15	14	Graeme McDowell, NIR	4.1571	199.54	48	-224.51	163.74
16	23	Hideki Matsuyama, JAP	4.1208	210.16	51	-132.67	187.80
17	32	Victor Dubuisson, FRA	4.0228	185.05	46	-108.79	161.64
18	9	Zach Johnson, USA	3.8267	198.99	52	-229.31	145.11
19	16	Dustin Johnson, USA	3.7848	158.96	42	-208.84	137.25
20	60	Chris Kirk, USA	3.7640	195.73	52	-108.84	198.82
21	47	Jimmy Walker, USA	3.7191	193.39	52	-148.38	213.00
22	31	Hunter Mahan, USA	3.6104	187.74	52	-156.51	176.12
23	73	Patrick Reed, USA	3.5132	182.68	52	-103.15	210.97
24	26	Jamie Donaldson, WAL	3.4392	178.84	52	-152.14	151.71
25	233	Kevin Na, USA	3.3096	135.69	41	-61.01	164.07
26	25	Lee Westwood, ENG	3.2786	170.49	52	-175.32	154.18
27	12	Ian Poulter, ENG	3.2320	151.90	47	-196.29	91.52
28	20	Keegan Bradley, USA	3.1637	164.51	52	-205.33	142.96
29	49	Joost Luiten, NED	3.1578	164.21	52	-102.76	147.19
30	33	Ryan Moore, USA	3.0828	154.14	50	-131.90	125.07
31	18	Charl Schwartzel, RSA	3.0249	157.30	52	-209.68	120.21
32	1	Tiger Woods, USA	3.0069	120.28	40	-368.94	9.73
33	17	Luke Donald, ENG	2.9933	146.67	49	-208.47	121.67
34	86	Brooks Koepka, USA	2.9736	154.63	52	-60.75	150.68
35	66	Stephen Gallacher, SCO	2.9134	151.49	52	-115.61	170.12
36	24	Thomas Bjørn, SWE	2.8632	148.88	52	-139.09	96.13
37	46	Thongchai Jaidee, THA	2.8297	147.14	52	-122.49	136.51
38	15	Jason Dufner, USA	2.8207	135.40	48	-214.62	91.18
39	29	Bill Haas, USA	2.8100	146.12	52	-155.35	128.04
40	37	Miguel Ángel Jiménez, ESP	2.8053	129.05	46	-113.28	111.37
41	8	Steve Stricker, USA	2.7413	109.65	40	-181.12	61.84
42	126	Ryan Palmer, USA	2.7379	134.15	49	-84.24	153.49
43	21	Webb Simpson, USA	2.7122	141.03	52	-182.53	104.57
44	76	Shane Lowry, IRE	2.6553	138.08	52	-83.69	132.22
45	34	Louis Oosthuizen, RSA	2.6401	118.41	45	-169.61	134.34
46	72	Marc Leishman, AUS	2.6006	135.23	52	-99.82	140.41
47	84	Mikko Ilonen, FIN	2.5964	129.82	50	-77.82	133.54
48	56	Gary Woodland, USA	2.5564	132.93	52	-90.72	110.50
49	108	John Senden, AUS	2.4823	129.08	52	-89.67	140.53
50	116	Danny Willett, ENG	2.4681	125.87	51	-64.99	123.06

EUROPEAN TOUR INCIDENTALS

EUROPEAN TOUR TOP 60 CAREER MONEY WINNERS

1	Ernie Els	€30,453,388	21	Charl Schwartzel	€13,367,894	41	Søren Hansen	€9,022,087
2	Lee Westwood	€30,364,288	22	David Howell	€12,879,873	42	Thongchai Jaidee	€8,951,933
3	Colin Montgomerie	€24,477,508	23	Bernhard Langer	€12,724,888	43	Gonzalo Fdez-Castaño	€8,880,195
4	Padraig Harrington	€24,064,761	24	José María Olazábal	€12,342,527	44	David Lynn	€8,445,648
5	Rory McIlroy	€23,671,908	25	Francesco Molinari	€12,315,664	45	Sir Nick Faldo	€8,004,560
6	Miguel Ángel Jiménez	€22,526,069	26	Paul Lawrie	€12,128,653	46	Thomas Levet	€7,911,015
7	Ian Poulter	€22,407,415	27	Peter Hanson	€12,083,967	47	Bradley Dredge	€7,847,199
8	Retief Goosen	€21,907,047	28	Anders Hansen	€11,980,071	48	Steve Webster	€7,345,125
9	Sergio García	€21,175,800	29	Michael Campbell	€11,892,642	49	Anthony Wall	€7,334,360
10	Darren Clarke	€20,281,886	30	Louis Oosthuizen	€11,458,274	50	Phillip Price	€7,306,744
11	Thomas Bjørn	€19,889,217	31	Paul McGinley	€11,304,937	51	Álvaro Quirós	€7,221,043
12	Henrik Stenson	€19,653,051	32	Simon Dyson	€10,476,038	52	Marcel Siem	€7,166,710
13	Graeme McDowell	€18,055,128	33	Søren Kjeldsen	€10,404,188	53	Barry Lane	€6,975,306
14	Martin Kaymer	€17,275,374	34	Niclas Fasth	€10,215,767	54	Richard Sterne	€6,948,782
15	Justin Rose	€16,588,424	35	Ross Fisher	€10,172,104	55	Peter O'Malley	€6,802,658
16	Luke Donald	€16,572,760	36	Raphaël Jacquelin	€9,902,839	56	Grégory Havret	€6,666,871
17	Paul Casey	€16,209,535	37	Jamie Donaldson	€9,767,925	57	Ignacio Garrido	€6,661,032
18	Robert Karlsson	€15,641,848	38	Ian Woosnam	€9,607,799	58	Oliver Wilson	€6,544,529
19	Angel Cabrera	€14,770,159	39	Richard Green	€9,310,766	59	Ricardo González	€6,332,479
20	Vijay Singh	€14,143,414	40	Stephen Gallacher	€9,306,847	60	Joost Luiten	€6,323,367

PGA TOUR TOP 30 CAREER TOURNAMENT WINNERS

1	Seve Ballesteros	50		Sandy Lyle	18		Sergio García	11
2	Bernhard Langer	42	14	Mark McNulty	16		Martin Kaymer	11
3	Tiger Woods	40	15	Thomas Bjørn	15	27=	Bernard Gallacher	10
4	Colin Montgomerie	31	16=	Retief Goosen	14		Graham Marsh	10
5	Sir Nick Faldo	30		Padraig Harrington	14		Graeme McDowell	10
6	Ian Woosnam	29		Greg Norman	14	30=	Manuel Piñero	9
7	Ernie Els	28		Darren Clarke	14		Adam Scott	9
8=	José María Olazábal	23	20=	Vijay Singh	13		Phil Mickelson	9
	Lee Westwood	23		Paul Casey	13		Charl Schwartzel	9
10=	Sam Torrance	21	22	Ian Poulter	12		Jack Nicklaus	9
	Miguel A. Jiménez	21	23=	Howard Clark	11		Rory McIlroy	9
12=	Mark James	18		Robert Karlsson	11		Henrik Stenson	9

EUROPEAN TOUR EVENT / SPONSOR/ VENUE UPDATES

Few are the years in which the European Tour doesn't see significant change and 2015 will be no exception. On the negative side, fully six events played in 2014 will be disappearing from the schedule (the **Nelson Mandela Championship**, the **Volvo Golf Champions**, the **NH Collection Open**, The **Championship at Laguna National**, the **Wales Open** and the **Perth International**) while a seventh, the venerable World Match Play, remains without a sponsor at year's end but may yet reappear in a vacant October slot. But in his final juggling act before retiring as the Tour's Chief Executive, George O'Grady managed to fight to a draw, as six new events will be arriving in their places. These include February's **Thailand Classic** (offering a $2 million purse), April's **Shenzhen Classic** (creating a two-event China swing with the Volvo China Open), the **Mauritius Open** (tri-sanctioned with the Asian and Sunshine Tours) and the **Saltire Energy Paul Lawrie Match Play**, an August event to be played in Scotland. The fifth addition, February's **Indian Open**, as been around since the 1960s, but will be co-sanctioned by the European Tour for the first time, while the sixth, the **European Open**, was a prominent Tour event from 1978-2009 before being discontinued.

Further modification exists in a relatively long list of changed, or as yet undetermined, venues. Among those events moving to new sites are the **Tshwane Open** (from Copperleaf to the venerable Pretoria CC), the **Open de España** (from the PGA Catalunya Resort to the Greg Norman-designed Real Club de Golf El Prat), the **Irish Open** (from the Fota Island Resort to the legendary Royal County Down GC), the **BMW International** (returning to the GC Munchen Eichenried from alternate year host CG Gut Larchenhof), the **Scottish Open** (from Royal Aberdeen to the equally famed Gullane GC) and the **Open d'Italia** (from Circolo Golf Torino to the GC Milano). Still uncertain at press time were the venues from the **Indian Open**, the **Volvo China Open** (whose 2014 venue, the Genzon GC, will now become host to the new Shenzhen Classic) and the **M2M Russian Open**, which has previously been played at Le Meridien Moscow CC and the Tseleevo G & Polo Club - and which is not exactly drowning in additional Moscow-area options.

EUROPEAN TOUR 2014

The one-year dominance of Henrik Stenson was impressive, but in 2014 King Rory retook his throne.

Indeed, by any definition 2014 will be remembered as McIlroy's, and very likely for decades to come as his campaign - which started fairly quietly following his disappointing 2012 - was entirely dominant. The winning of two Major championships in a single year is a rare enough feat (though it is perhaps worth interjecting here that the last to do it was a European - Padraig Harrington - and not Tiger Woods) and this is of particular importance in Europe when one of those is the British Open. But McIlroy also managed to claim the circuit's flagship BMW PGA Championship, and he did so in storybook fashion, shooting a final round 66 at Wentworth to steal the title in the very same week that he ended his seemingly tumultuous relationship with tennis star Caroline Wozniacki. We have no idea - nor should we - to what extent this domestic resolution keyed his epic season, but one would be remiss not to note the timing of it in the reporting of his resurgence.

The rest of the Tour, however, was rather less dramatic, with no other player making any sort of sustained case to question McIlroy's dominance. The record will show that Henrik Stenson finished second in the Order of Merit but while he played consistently strong golf throughout the campaign, his lone win (and much of his earnings) came at the season-ending Tour Championship in Dubai. Of course, McIlroy actually only won twice on European soil, and that accomplishment *was* equaled, indeed by three men:

- The ageless and endlessly colorful Miguel Ángel Jiménez posted the Tour's greatest-ever season by a 50-year-old, winning in both Hong Kong (again) and, after lo these many years, at his native Spanish Open, extending his record as the circuit's oldest winner each time.

- Finland's Mikko Ilonen claimed both the Irish Open and the World Match Play, though the remainder of his year was quiet enough that he only finished 18th in the Order of Merit.

- France's Alexander Levy won the Volvo China Open and the Portugal Masters, though the latter was rain-shortened to 36 holes.

And so, in the end, it was easily McIlroy's year. Surprise!

Player Of The Year: Rory McIlroy

It's always a dicey proposition when the European Tour's top player does much of his damage in events played on American soil that are co-sanctioned by the E Tour, since most such tournaments often feel like PGA Tour events in disguise. But while Rory McIlroy's victories at the PGA Championship and the WGC-Bridgestone may feel American, his titles at the BMW PGA and the British Open were about as European as it gets. And besides, when the world number one plays your circuit and has a dominant season, how often is he not Player Of The Year?

2014 European Tour Top 60 Money Winners *

#	Player	Money	#	Player	Money	#	Player	Money
1	Rory McIlroy	7,149,503	21	Miguel A. Jiménez	1,570,215	41	Simon Dyson	978,293
2	Henrik Stenson	4,981,093	22	Thongchai Jaidee	1,545,786	42	Rafa Cabrera-Bello	952,452
3	Justin Rose	3,180,388	23	George Coetzee	1,348,680	43	Richie Ramsay	928,827
4	Jamie Donaldson	3,058,166	24	Charl Schwartzel	1,304,818	44	Emiliano Grillo	910,884
5	Victor Dubuisson	2,966,524	25	Danny Willett	1,304,728	45	Nicolas Colsaerts	905,777
6	Sergio García	2,861,930	26	Marc Warren	1,285,147	46	Hennie Otto	893,014
7	Marcel Siem	2,739,373	27	Lee Westwood	1,254,911	47	Kristoffer Broberg	885,272
8	Brooks Koepka	2,631,873	28	Romain Wattel	1,251,927	48	Richard Sterne	864,173
9	Alexander Levy	2,452,757	29	Pablo Larrazábal	1,221,212	49	Eddie Pepperell	832,563
10	Shane Lowry	2,173,864	30	Jonas Blixt	1,199,111	50	Luke Donald	810,972
11	Joost Luiten	2,158,172	31	Branden Grace	1,190,107	51	Wade Ormsby	790,559
12	Thomas Bjørn	2,122,402	32	Thorbjørn Olesen	1,177,612	52	Darren Fichardt	755,905
13	Ian Poulter	2,092,569	33	Andy Sullivan	1,162,917	53	David Howell	739,940
14	Graeme McDowell	2,049,356	34	Robert Karlsson	1,143,774	54	Oliver Wilson	734,197
15	Martin Kaymer	2,040,550	35	Francesco Molinari	1,096,949	55	Thomas Aiken	730,637
16	Stephen Gallacher	1,863,965	36	Tyrrell Hatton	1,088,446	56	Oliver Fisher	697,972
17	Louis Oosthuizen	1,783,971	37	Ernie Els	1,064,496	57	Michael Hoey	676,775
18	Mikko Ilonen	1,769,997	38	Fabrizio Zanotti	1,046,154	58	David Lipsky	627,780
19	Tommy Fleetwood	1,586,287	39	Bernd Wiesberger	1,033,821	59	Matthew Baldwin	622,101
20	Ross Fisher	1,574,123	40	Edoardo Molinari	1,003,142	60	Matteo Manassero	603,907

* Converted to points for the Final Series

2013-2014 European Tour Week-By-Week

	Tournament	Purse	Winner/Score		Notes
Week 47 11/24	South African Open	€1 mil	Morten O. Madsen	269	25-year-old Madsen claims his first major tour win, closing with 67 to beat Jbe' Kruger & Hennie Otto by 2.
Week 48 12/1	Alfred Dunhill Championship	€1.5 mil	Charl Schwartzel	271	Schwartzel defends his Alfred Dunhill title, shooting four rounds in the 60s to beat Richard Finch by 4.
Week 49 12/8	Hong Kong Open & Nedbank Challenge	$1.3 mil $6.5 mil	Miguel A. Jiménez Thomas Bjørn	268 268	Jiménez wins three-way playoff to defend his title. Bjørn tops 30-man field in event's official E Tour debut.
Week 50 12/15	Nelson Mandela Championship	€1 mil	Dawie van der Walt	195	Van der Walt lands his second E Tour win in an event cut to 54 holes by rain, and played under lift, clean & place.
Week 51 12/22					
Week 52 12/28					
Week 2 1/12	Volvo Golf Champions	$4 mil	Louis Oosthuizen	276	Oosthuizen edges Branden Grace by 1 to win his first event of the calendar year for the fourth consecutive season.
Week 3 1/19	Abu Dhabi HSBC Golf Championship	$2.7 mil	Pablo Larrazábal	274	Larrazábal wins his third career E Tour title, holding off Phil Mickelson & Rory McIlroy by one.
Week 4 1/26	Commercial Bank Qatar Masters	$2.5 mil	Sergio García	272	García cards 12 birdies in his last 21 holes (including three straight in sudden death) to edge Mikko Ilonen in a playoff.
Week 5 2/2	Omega Dubai Desert Classic	$2.5 mil	Stephen Gallacher	272	Gallacher becomes the first man to defend his title in Dubai, led by a nine-under-par 28 on Saturday's back nine.
Week 6 2/9	Joburg Open	€1.3 mil	George Coetzee	268	Frequent contender Coetzee wins his first E Tour title, closing with 66 to edge three players by three.
Week 7 2/16	Africa Open	€1 mil	Thomas Aiken	264	Aiken wins his third career E Tour title but his first on native soil, beating Oliver Fisher on the first hole of sudden death.
Week 8 2/23	WGC-Accenture Match Play Championship	$9 mil	Jason Day	23rd	Day scores a breakthrough victory, beating Victor Dubuisson at the 23rd hole to claim his second PGA Tour win.
Week 9 3/2	Tshwane Open	€1.5 mil	Ross Fisher	268	Fisher claims his fifth career E Tour title, winning by three after holding a commanding five-stroke 54-hole lead.
Week 10 3/9	WGC-Cadillac Champ	$9 mil	Patrick Reed	284	On a rebuilt Doral Blue Monster, Reed hangs on late to win for the third time in his last 14 PGA Tour starts.
Week 11 3/16	Trophée Hassan II	€1.5 mil	Alejandro Cañizares	269	Cañizares ends an eight-year victory drought with a wire-to-wire five-shot victory after opening with a Thursday 62.
Week 12 3/23					
Week 13 3/30					
Week 14 4/6	NH Collection Open	€600,000	Marco Crespi	278	35-year-old rookie Crespi wins for the first time on the E Tour in the inaugural playing of this light-field event.
Week 15 4/14	The Masters	$8 mil	Bubba Watson	273	Watson holds steady on Sunday as the other contenders falter, beats Jordan Spieth & Jonas Blixt by three.
Week 16 4/20	Mayban Malaysian Open	$2.75 mil	Lee Westwood	270	Westwood breaks a two-year victory drought, routing the field by seven to win for the 10th time in Asia.
Week 17 4/27	Volvo China Open	$2.136 mil	Alexander Levy	269	Levy rides a second round 62 to his first E Tour victory, beating Tommy Fleetwood by four.
Week 18 5/4	Championship at Laguna National	$1.5 mil	Felipe Aguilar	266	Aguilar holes a 142-yard wedge at the 72nd for eagle to shoot 62 and claim his second E Tour title by a single shot.
Week 19 5/11	Madeira Islands Open	€600,000	Daniel Brooks	135	With two rounds cancelled due to incessant fog, England's Brooks beats Scott Henry on the first hole of sudden death.
Week 20 5/18	Open de España	€1.5 mil	Miguel A. Jiménez	284	Jiménez becomes the E Tour's first 50-year-old winner, taking a three-way playoff to win his first Spanish Open.
Week 21 5/25	BMW PGA Championship	€4.75 mil	Rory McIlroy	274	Within days of breaking off wedding plans, McIlroy claims his first win of 2014 with a closing 66 at Wentworth.

2013-2014 European Tour Week-By-Week (Cont'd)

	Tournament	Purse	Winner/Score		Notes
Week 22 6/1	Nordea Masters	€1.5 mil	Thongchai Jaidee	272	After closing with 65, Jaidee lands his sixth E Tour victory, beating Victor Dubuisson & Stephen Gallacher in a playoff.
Week 23 6/8	Lyoness Open	€1 mil	Mikael Lundberg	276	Lundberg breaks a six-year drought by defeating local favorite Bernd Wiesberger on the first hole of sudden death.
Week 24 6/15	The U.S. Open	$8 mil	Martin Kaymer	271	In a record-setting performance, Kaymer opens 65-65 en route to an eight-shot runaway triumph at Pinehurst
Week 25 6/22	Irish Open	€2 mil	Mikko Ilonen	271	Ilonen goes wire-to-wire to claim his fourth career victory in his 300th career European Tour start.
Week 26 6/29	BMW International Open	€2 mil	Fabrizio Zanotti	269	After weekend bogey-free rounds of 65-65, Zanotti takes a four-way playoff to become Paraguay's first E Tour winner.
Week 27 7/6	Alstom French Open	€3 mil	Graeme McDowell	279	In miserable final-round weather, McDowell cards a closing 67 and successfully defends his 2013 French Open title.
Week 28 7/13	Aberdeen Asset Mgmt. Scottish Open	€3 mil	Justin Rose	268	Follow his PGA Tour victory at Quicken Loans National, Rose takes his second win in a row going into the British Open.
Week 29 7/20	The Open Championship	$8 mil	Rory McIlroy	271	McIlroy joins Nicklaus & Woods as winners of three legs of the career Grand Slam by age 25 in wire-to-wire triumph.
Week 30 7/27	Russian Open	€1 mil	David Horsey	275	After falling behind late, Horsey eagles the 17th to force a playoff with Damian McGrane, winning on the first hole.
Week 31 8/3	WGC-Bridgestone Inv	$9 mil	Rory McIlroy	265	McIlroy closes 64-66-66 to win his second straight start and return to #1 in the OWR for the first time since 3/2013.
Week 32 8/10	The PGA Championship	$10 mil	Rory McIlroy	268	McIlroy rallies on the final nine to win his second straight (and fourth career) Major, edging Phil Mickelson by one.
Week 33 8/17	Made In Denmark	€1.5 mil	Marc Warren	275	Warren rides a windblown Saturday 66 to secure his first win since 2007, beating Bradley Dredge by two.
Week 34 8/25	D+D Real Czech Masters	€1 mil	Jamie Donaldson	272	Donaldson claims his third E Tour win and clinches a spot on the Ryder Cup team, edging Bradley Dredge by two.
Week 35 9/1	Italian Open	€1.5 mil	Hennie Otto	268	Otto wins his second Italian Open (and third career E Tour title) after grabbing the lead with a second round 62.
Week 36 9/7	Omega European Masters	€2.3 mil	David Lipsky	262	Lipsky, a little-known American playing in Asia, earns E Tour status by defeating Graeme Storm on the first playoff hole.
Week 37 9/14	KLM Open	€1.8 mil	Paul Casey	266	Behind a Saturday 62, Casey comes back from an eight-shot 36-hole deficit to clinch his 13th European Tour win.
Week 38 9/21	ISPS Handa Wales Open	€1.8 mil	Joost Luiten	270	Luiten claims his fourth career E Tour victory, edging Tommy Fleetwood and Shane Lowry by one.
Week 39 9/28					
Week 40 10/5	Alfred Dunhill Links Championship	$5 mil	Oliver Wilson	271	Once highly touted, the 34-year-old Wilson breaks through for his first E Tour win in his 228th career start.
Week 41 10/12	Portugal Masters	€2 mil	Alexander Levy	124	In a rain-shortened event, Levy shoots 63-61 to become the the first Frenchman to win twice in one E Tour season.
Week 42 10/19	World Match Play & Hong Kong Open	€2.25 mil $1.3 mil	Mikko Ilonen Scott Hend	3 & 1 267	Ilonen beats #1 seed Henrik Stenson 3 & 1 in the final. Hend defeats Angelo Que on first hole of sudden death.
Week 43 10/26	ISPS Handa Perth International	AU $1.75 mil	Thorbjørn Olesen	271	Olesen opens with 64 and then goes wire-to-wire, beating Victor Dubuisson by three for his second E Tour win.
Week 44 11/2	BMW Masters	€7 mil	Marcel Siem	272	On a blustery Sunday, Siem wins the first Final Series event beating Ross Fisher & Alexander Levy in sudden death.
Week 45 11/9	WGC-HSBC Championship	€8.5 mil	Bubba Watson	277	Watson claims his first WGC victory after holing a 60-yard bunker shot at the last, then beating Tim Clark in a playoff.
Week 46 11/16	Turkish Airlines Open	€7 mil	Brooks Koepka	271	Koepka cards a clutch Sunday 65 to clinch his first E Tour title after Ian Poulter misses a 5-footer to tie at the last.
Week 47 11/23	DP World Tour Championship	€8 mil	Henrik Stenson	272	As Rafa Cabrera-Bello collapses late, Stenson birdies the last two holes to successfully defend his 2013 title.

South African Open Championship

Glendower Golf Club - Ekurhuleni, South Africa
Champion: Morten O. Madsen

Nov 21 - Nov 24
6,899 yards   Par 72
Purse: €3.5 Million

Denmark's 25-year-old Morten Ørum Madsen broke through for his first major tour victory at the venerable South African Open, and in the process became the first champion of the European Tour's 2014 season – even if five weeks still remained in calendar 2013. Madsen played highly consistent golf all week but after rounds of 67-66-69, he trailed 54-hole lead (and popular pre-tournament favorite) Charl Schwartzel by one going into Sunday. Schwartzel, however, would suffer through a painfully up-and-down final round, tearing out of the box with birdies at the 2nd, 3rd and 4th, then collapsing with a watery double-bogey at the 182-yard 6th, then another double at the 436-yard 10th. He would fight gamely back with three back nine birdies but in the end, it would only be enough to tie recent Q School graduate Marco Crespi for fourth. Madsen, meanwhile, played the steadiest of golf, posting five birdies against no bogeys, and logging three of them in the critical moments at the 13th, 15th and 16th. His 19-under-par 269 total would, in the end, provide a two-shot margin over a pair of South Africans, Jbe' Kruger and Hennie Otto. Coming off a disappointing 2013 campaign, Kruger launched himself into the heart of the action with a closing 65 that included an eagle at the par-5 13th, followed by birdies at the 14th, 15th and 16th. Less happy with his share of second was Otto, who stood a commanding four strokes ahead through 14 before making bogey at the par-5 15th, then a double-bogey at the 403-yard 16th to blow himself out of contention. Also worthy of note was Trevor Fisher Jr., who began Sunday eight shots in arrears but actually took the lead after playing his first 12 holes in nine under par. Unfortunately he could add no more birdies thereafter, and a bogey at the last ultimately saw him home in 64, and a tie for seventh.

1	Morten O. Madsen	67-66-69-67	269	€174,350		34=	Oliver Bekker	70-69-70-73	282	€8,470
2=	Jbe' Kruger	65-70-71-65	271	€101,310			Alastair Forsyth	72-66-71-73	282	€8,470
	Hennie Otto	72-66-65-68	271	€101,310			Matthew Nixon	64-72-72-74	282	€8,470
4=	Marco Crespi	65-67-70-70	272	€49,720		37=	Vaughn Groenewald	70-70-74-69	283	€7,700
	Charl Schwartzel	67-65-69-71	272	€49,720			Christopher Doak	71-68-74-70	283	€7,700
6	Alejandro Cañizares	69-67-69-68	273	€38,940			Darren Fichardt	77-65-69-72	283	€7,700
7=	Trevor Fisher Jr.	70-67-73-4	274	€29,755			Andrea Pavan	67-70-68-78	283	€7,700
	Johan Carlsson	69-70-68-67	274	€29,755		41=	Danie van Tonder	68-70-75-71	284	€6,710
9	Warren Abery	68-71-68-68	275	€23,760			Atti Schwartzel	67-71-73-73	284	€6,710
10=	Garth Mulroy	70-67-70-69	276	€20,625			Heinrich Bruiners	69-72-70-73	284	€6,710
	Christiaan Basson	66-68-71-71	276	€20,625			Keenan Davidse	70-72-68-74	284	€6,710
12=	Jean Hugo	71-67-70-69	277	€16,500			Magnus Carlsson	72-68-66-78	284	€6,710
	Martin Du toit	70-70-68-69	277	€16,500		46=	Allan Versfeld	71-68-74-72	285	€5,720
	Peter Karmis	69-72-67-69	277	€16,500			Neil Schietekat	68-69-74-74	285	€5,720
	Andy Sullivan	71-68-68-70	277	€16,500			Alexander Levy	69-72-69-75	285	€5,720
	Jaco Van Zyl	71-70-66-70	277	€16,500			Adam Gee	73-69-67-76	285	€5,720
17=	Daan Huizing	68-69-73-68	278	€13,486		50=	Kristoffer Broberg	73-67-75-71	286	€5,060
	Peter Whiteford	71-68-70-69	278	€13,486			B. van der Merwe	69-70-75-72	286	€5,060
	Thomas Levet	69-70-70-69	278	€13,486		52=	Charl Coetzee	70-71-75-71	287	€4,180
	Merrick Bremner	73-69-67-69	278	€13,486			Justin Walters	72-70-71-74	287	€4,180
	Thomas Aiken	70-67-71-70	278	€13,486			James Heath	75-66-71-75	287	€4,180
22=	James Morrison	69-66-74-70	279	€11,220			Edoardo Molinari	72-69-70-76	287	€4,180
	Michael Hollick	75-67-68-69	279	€11,220			Simon Dyson	68-74-68-77	287	€4,180
	Tom Lewis	68-68-72-71	279	€11,220			James Kamte	69-67-70-81	287	€4,180
	Ross Fisher	71-69-68-71	279	€11,220		58	Jamie McLeary	74-68-75-71	288	€3,520
	Jorge Campillo	72-70-66-71	279	€11,220		59=	Doug McGuigan	71-70-78-70	289	€3,245
	Ulrich Van Den Berg	70-66-71-72	279	€11,220			David Drysdale	71-71-75-72	289	€3,245
	Retief Goosen	66-71-70-72	279	€11,220			Simon Thornton	70-72-75-72	289	€3,245
29=	Jared Harvey	71-69-70-71	281	€9,372			Louis Taylor (a)	71-70-70-78	289	-
	Anthony Wall	70-70-70-71	281	€9,372			Steve Surry	68-73-70-78	289	€3,245
	Seve Benson	72-70-68-71	281	€9,372		64=	Chris Swanepoel Jr.	70-71-78-71	290	€2,915
	P. H. McIntyre	73-68-69-71	281	€9,372			J.J. Senekal	71-70-70-79	290	€2,915
	Sihwan Kim	72-70-66-73	281	€9,372		66	Lucas Bjerregaard	73-69-76-74	292	€2,750

Out Of The Money: **143**: Estanislao Goya, Lyle Rowe, Justin Harding, Wade Ormsby, Jake Roos, David Frost, Theunis Spangenberg, Wallie Coetsee, Brandon Stone, Andrew Curlewis **144**: Mikael Lundberg, Tyrrell Hatton, Sipho Bujela, Tjaart van der Walt, Christiaan Bezuidenhout (a), Romain Wattel, Tyrone Mordt, Colin Nel, Teboho Sefatsa, Simon Wakefield, Matthew Baldwin, Francois Calmels, Gareth Maybin, Nacho Elvira **145**: Daniel Hammond, Robert Rock, Victor Riu, Drikus Bruyns, Ockie Strydom, Mark Williams, Lindani Ndwandwe, Peter Lawrie, Søren Hansen, Ross Wellington **146**: Neil Cheetham, Francois Coetzee, Craig Lee, Ruan de Smidt, Grant Muller, N.J. Arnoldi (a), Eddie Pepperell, Graeme Storm, Keith Horne, Dean Burmester, Dawie van der Walt, Jaco Ahlers **147**: Andreas Hartø, Jacques Blaauw, Bryce Easton, Richard Finch, J.G. Claassen, Damien McGrane, Michael Hoey **148**: Desvonde Botes, Scott Jamieson, Toto Thimba Jr., David Duval, Tyrone Ferreira, T.I. Mazibuko **149**: Justin Turner, Paul Waring, Matthew Carvell, Thriston Lawrence (a), Shaun Norris, Pieter Moolman **150**: Adrian Otaegui, Titch Moore, Gert Myburgh, Zander Lombard (a), James Kingston **151**: Louis de Jager, Paul McGinley, Brandon Pieters, Andrew Georgiou, Justin Brink **152**: Hendrik Burhmann, Carlos Del Moral, Dion Fourie, Alex Haindl **153**: Lee Slattery, Ryan Cairnes **154**: Wynand Dingle, J.B. Hansen, Pieter Kruger **156**: Niclas Fasth, Gavan Levenson, Steve Webster **157**: Jacobus Mouton, Pablo Martin Benavides   **WD**: Stephen Swanepoel

FIRST ROUND		SECOND ROUND		THIRD ROUND	
Matthew Nixon	64 (-8)	Marco Crespi	132 (-12)	Charl Schwartzel	201 (-15)
Marco Crespi	65 (-7)	Charl Schwartzel	132 (-12)	Marco Crespi	202 (-14)
Jbe' Kruger	65 (-7)	**Morten O. Madsen**	133 (-11)	**Morten O. Madsen**	202 (-14)
Christiaan Basson	66 (-6)	Christiaan Basson	134 (-10)	Hennie Otto	203 (-13)
Retief Goosen	66 (-6)	2 Players	135 (-9)	3 Players	205 (-11)
Morten O. Madsen	67 (-5)				

OWR: 1 of top 50 entered - Rating: 46 - Points to 40th - Madsen: 32 points, to 121st in OWR

Alfred Dunhill Championship

Leopard Creek Country Club - Malelane, South Africa
Champion: Charl Schwartzel

Nov 28 - Dec 1
7,287 yards   Par 72
Purse: €1.5 Million

Having previously recorded two victories and four runner-ups at the Leopard Creek Country Club, and traditionally finding his best form in the late autumn, Charl Schwartzel was an obvious pre-tournament favorite at the Alfred Dunhill Championship, and in the end he did not disappoint. Stringing together consistent rounds of 68-68-67-68 – and playing the final 62 holes without dropping a single shot – Schwartzel stood at or near the top of the leaderboard throughout the week before pulling away on Sunday to beat England's Richard Finch by four. Indeed, had Schwartzel not struggled with the lead during the final round of the previous week's South African Open, there might well have been an air of inevitability about this, as he began the final round two strokes clear of Finch and three ahead of recent Challenge Tour graduate Victor Riu of France. Finch, for his part, pressed Schwartzel early, recording birdies at the 1st and 3rd holes to draw even, then adding birdies at the 6th and the 8th to very nearly keep pace with Schwartzel's birdies at the 5th, 6th and 8th. But a bogey at the 375-yard 11th and a double-bogey at the 413-yard 14th would ultimately be Finch's undoing, allowing Schwartzel to pull away with only a single birdie on the inward half, at the par-5 13th. Riu, for his part, closed with a disappointing 76 to fall into a tie for 11th. Third place was shared by Simon Dyson (who closed with 67),Ross Fisher (69) and Romain Wattel (71), though at seven shots off the pace, this trio spent Sunday playing primarily for a paycheck. The win was Schwartzel's first of calendar year 2013 and his ninth overall on the European Tour.

1	Charl Schwartzel	68-68-67-68	271	€237,750			Adrien Saddier	72-71-72-72	287	€12,656
2	Richard Finch	68-70-67-70	275	€172,500			Jaco Van Zyl	70-72-73-72	287	€ 12,656
3=	Simon Dyson	72-69-70-67	278	€79,800		37=	François Calmels	74-68-75-71	288	€10,350
	Ross Fisher	72-65-72-69	278	€79,800			Johan Carlsson	73-70-79-66	288	€10,350
	Romain Wattel	70-69-68-71	278	€79,800			Ruan de Smidt	69-74-73-72	288	€10,350
6	Søren Hansen	72-65-71-71	279	€53,100			Oliver Fisher	71-73-72-72	288	€10,350
7=	Magnus Carlsson	70-72-72-66	280	€40,575			Matthew Nixon	72-71-71-74	288	€10,350
	Simon Wakefield	74-68-70-68	280	€40,575			Robert Rock	75-69-73-71	288	€10,350
9=	Warren Abery	73-71-69-68	281	€30,900			Tjaart van der Walt	70-74-74-70	288	€10,350
	Danny Willett	69-70-73-69	281	€30,900		44=	Ryan Cairns	70-71-76-72	289	€8,100
11=	David Drysdale	68-72-72-70	282	€25,150			Jorge Campillo	70-70-75-74	289	€8,100
	Andrea Pavan	72-71-74-65	282	€25,150			Michael Hollick	69-70-74-76	289	€8,100
	Victor Riu	68-71-67-76	282	€25,150			Yubin Jung	73-70-73-73	289	€8,100
14=	G. Porteous (a)	71-69-74-69	283	-			Garth Mulroy	76-67-68-78	289	€8,100
	Andy Sullivan	71-72-70-70	283	€22,050			John Parry	70-73-74-72	289	€8,100
16=	Lucas Bjerregaard	72-72-67-73	284	€19,114			Haydn Porteous	72-69-78-70	289	€8,100
	Brendon de Jonge	73-69-68-74	284	€19,114			Graeme Storm	72-68-77-72	289	€8,100
	James Kingston	69-74-70-71	284	€19,114		52=	Jbe' Kruger	74-68-81-67	290	€6,150
	Morten O. Madsen	65-71-79-69	284	€19,114			Alexander Levy	73-68-74-75	290	€6,150
	Ricardo Santos	66-74-72-72	284	€19,114			Gareth Maybin	69-75-71-75	290	€6,150
	T. Van Aswegen	70-68-72-74	284	€19,114			J.J. Senekal	72-72-80-66	290	€6,150
	Allen Versfeld	66-77-69-72	284	€19,114			Lee Slattery	73-71-75-71	290	€6,150
23	Alejandro Cañizares	74-69-68-74	285	€16,650		57=	Chris Doak	69-73-76-74	292	€5,100
24=	Hendrik Buhrmann	72-72-72-70	286	€15,300			Damien McGrane	72-72-74-74	292	€5,100
	Hennie Otto	69-71-69-77	286	€15,300		59	Andrew Curlewis	70-73-72-78	293	€4,800
	Brinson Paolini	73-71-69-73	286	€15,300		60	Jens Dantorp	70-71-75-78	294	€4,650
	Kevin Phelan	70-74-68-74	286	€15,300		61	Jaco Ahlers	71-71-79-74	295	€4,500
	Steve Webster	71-73-73-69	286	€15,300		62=	Jacques Blaauw	76-68-73-80	297	€4,275
29=	Daniel Brooks	70-74-73-70	287	€12,656			Justin Walters	76-68-79-74	297	€4,275
	Carlos Del Moral	73-71-66-77	287	€12,656		64=	J.G. Claassen	70-73-76-79	298	€3,975
	Niclas Fasth	72-68-73-74	287	€12,656			Charl Coetzee	70-72-71-85	298	€3,975
	Alex Haindl	71-73-70-73	287	€12,656		66	Tyrone Ferreira	72-70-81-76	299	€3,750
	Sihwan Kim	70-69-74-74	287	€12,656		67	Mark Williams	76-68-87-71	302	€3,600
	Titch Moore	71-69-73-74	287	€12,656						

Out Of The Money: **146**: Francois Coetzee, Mikael Lundberg, James Heath, Seve Benson, Trevor Fisher Jr., Kristoffer Broberg, Ulrich Van Den Berg, Neil Schietekat, Oliver Bekker, Prinavin Nelson **147**: Dion Fourie, Teboho Sefatsa, Merrick Bremner, James Morrison, Omar Sandys, Emiliano Grillo, M.J. Daffue, Marco Crespi, Jean Hugo, John Daly, P.H. McIntyre, Dawie van der Walt, Wade Ormsby, Matthew Baldwin, Tom Lewis, Pablo Martin Benavides **148**: Scott Jamieson, Peter Lawrie, Stuart Manley, Doug McGuigan, Jake Roos, Theunis Spangenberg, Ignacio Garrido, Adrian Otaegui, Shaun Norris, Heinrich Bruiners, Christiaan Basson **149**: George Coetzee, Vaughn Groenewald, Fabrizio Zanotti, James Kamte, Simon Thornton, Andreas Hart, Colin Nel, J.P. van der Walt **150**: Keith Horne, Brandon Pieters **151**: Juan Langeveld, Craig Lee, Daan Huizing, Jared Harvey, Gary Stal, Ockie Strydom, Bryce Easton **152**: Edoardo Molinari, Matthew Carvell, Thomas Pieters **153**: Desne Van Den Bergh, Louis de Jager, Riekus Nortje, Maximilian Kieffer **154**: Louis Calitz, Francesco Laporta, Peter Karmis **155**: Lyle Rowe, Justin Harding **156**: J.B. Hansen **157**: Mark Murless, Danie van Tonder, Richard Sterne **158**: Andrew George, Thabang Simon **160**: Musolo Nethunzwi **163**: Chris Swanepoel Jr.   **WD**: Thomas Levet, Desvonde Botes (74), Michael Hoey (76)   **DQ**: John Hahn

FIRST ROUND		SECOND ROUND		THIRD ROUND	
Morten O. Madsen	65 (-7)	Morten O. Madsen	136 (-8)	**Charl Schwartzel**	203 (-13)
Allan Versfeld	66 (-6)	**Charl Schwartzel**	136 (-8)	Richard Finch	205 (-11)
Ricardo Santos	66 (-6)	Søren Hansen	137 (-7)	Victor Riu	206 (-10)
4 Players	68 (-4)	Ross Fisher	137 (-7)	Romain Wattel	207 (-9)
Charl Schwartzel	68 (-4)	2 Players	138 (-6)	Søren Hansen	208 (-8)

OWR: 2 of top 50 entered - Rating: 77 - Points to 28th - Schwartzel: 22 points, to 18th in OWR

Hong Kong Open

Hong Kong Golf Club - Fanling, Hong Kong
Champion: Miguel Ángel Jiménez

Dec 5 - Dec 8
6,699 yards   Par 70
Purse: $1.3 Million

The ageless Miguel Ángel Jiménez successfully defended his title at the Hong Kong Open, defeating Stuart Manley of Wales and Thailand's Prom Meesawat on the first hole of sudden death. In doing so, Jiménez extended his record as the European Tour's oldest-ever winner (49 years, 337 days) which he set here a year ago, and also claimed both his 20th career E Tour win and his 13th after turning 40. Playing against a somewhat light field (Jiménez was the only member of the OWR top 50 present), the ponytailed Spaniard trailed halfway leader Manley by four on Friday night before charging into the mix with a Saturday 65 which might well have been lower but for a double-bogey at the 427-yard 15th. He thus began Sunday two in arrears, then initially made only limited progress after turning in one-under-par 33. But upon reaching the easier inward half Jiménez heated up, his four-birdie run home marred only by a bogey at his nemesis 15th. This left him on 268, a number equaled by Manley (with a clutch birdie at the last) and Meesawat, who eagled the 13th, bogeyed the 14th, then strung together four pars thereafter. The playoff was contested over the 410-yard pond-fronted 18th, and while neither Manley (who drove into a hospitality area) nor Meesawat (who missed the green short - but dry) were assured of their pars, Jiménez rendered matters moot by hitting a wedge to 18 feet, then coolly holing the clinching putt.

1	Miguel A. Jiménez	70-67-65-66	268	€159,063	39=	Chris Doak	68-68-73-69	278	€5,726
2=	Stuart Manley	67-67-66-68	268	€82,894		David Drysdale	72-68-71-67	278	€5,726
	Prom Meesawat	66-70-67-65	268	€82,894		Nacho Elvira	67-72-67-72	278	€5,726
4	Robert-Jan Derksen	69-67-68-65	269	€47,720		Daniel Im	71-66-71-70	278	€5,726
5	Javier Colomo	72-66-68-66	272	€34,168		Daisuke Kataoka	68-68-69-73	278	€5,726
	Jose Manuel Lara	69-68-65-70	272	€34,168		Jason Knutzon	70-71-69-68	278	€5,726
	Angelo Que	69-67-68-68	272	€34,168		Chris Paisley	71-70-70-67	278	€5,726
8=	Richard Finch	70-67-68-68	273	€20,472		Anthony Wall	71-70-68-69	278	€5,726
	Wade Ormsby	67-68-66-72	273	€20,472	47=	Andrew Dodt	66-70-72-71	279	€4,009
	Andrea Pavan	65-72-68-68	273	€20,472		Marcus Fraser	68-69-72-70	279	€4,009
	Joel Sjoholm	68-70-65-70	273	€20,472		John Hahn	70-68-73-68	279	€4,009
12=	Alex Cejka	68-67-68-71	274	€14,459		Scott Henry	68-72-71-68	279	€4,009
	Oliver Fisher	68-70-67-69	274	€14,459		Sung Lee	70-70-71-68	279	€4,009
	Shiv Kapur	69-66-66-73	274	€14,459		Alexander Levy	70-70-72-67	279	€4,009
	Anirban Lahiri	68-70-67-69	274	€14,459		Wei-Chih Lu	69-72-70-68	279	€4,009
	David Lipsky	69-68-67-70	274	€14,459		Edoardo Molinari	72-69-68-70	279	€4,009
	Chawalit Plaphol	69-70-69-66	274	€14,459		James Morrison	71-67-69-72	279	€4,009
18=	Byeong-Hun An	69-69-71-66	275	€11,326		Chapchai Nirat	71-70-71-67	279	€4,009
	Seve Benson	66-72-69-68	275	€11,326	57=	T. Chuayprakong	69-72-70-69	280	€2,863
	Johan Carlsson	70-70-66-69	275	€11,326		Antonio Lascuña	72-69-70-69	280	€2,863
	Grégory Havret	71-70-65-69	275	€11,326		Himmat Rai	72-67-68-73	280	€2,863
	Unho Park	71-66-67-71	275	€11,326		Rafael Cabrera-Bello	70-71-69-71	281	€2,481
	Panuphol Pittayarat	69-70-68-68	275	€11,326	60=	Alastair Forsyth	68-72-71-70	281	€2,481
24=	Lucas Bjerregaard	70-67-73-66	276	€9,496		P. Junhasavasdikul	73-68-70-70	281	€2,481
	Jorge Campillo	73-65-69-69	276	€9,496		Thorbjørn Olesen	69-71-70-71	281	€2,481
	Roope Kakko	71-66-69-70	276	€9,496		Gary Stal	70-71-73-67	281	€2,481
	Rikard Karlberg	69-68-72-67	276	€9,496	65=	S.S.P. Chowrasia	68-69-70-75	282	€2,052
	Espen Kofstad	68-68-70-70	276	€9,496		Chih-Bing Lam	66-72-72-72	282	€2,052
	Jbe' Kruger	67-66-73-70	276	€9,496		Juvic Pagunsan	71-70-73-68	282	€2,052
30=	Adilson da Silva	71-70-67-69	277	€7,455		Sujjan Singh	66-73-73-70	282	€2,052
	David Higgins	64-74-71-68	277	€7,455		Joong-Kyung Mo	70-70-76-69	285	€1,780
	Wen-Yi Huang	72-69-68-68	277	€7,455		Brinson Paolini	70-68-70-77	285	€1,780
	Gi-Whan Kim	70-69-69-69	277	€7,455	71=	Wen-Tang Lin	74-64-75-73	286	€1,430
	Jaakko Makitalo	67-71-66-73	277	€7,455		Andy Sullivan	70-71-70-75	286	€1,430
	C. Phadungsil	68-71-68-70	277	€7,455	73	Daniel Brooks	69-71-77-71	288	€1,426
	Jyoti Randhawa	72-67-66-72	277	€7,455	74=	Scott Hend	70-70-75-74	289	€1,422
	Boonchu Ruangkit	69-67-70-71	277	€7,455		Timothy Tang	71-70-72-76	289	€1,422
	Steve Webster	71-66-65-75	277	€7,455					

Out Of The Money: **142**: Joakim Lagergren, Arnond Vongvanij, Wen-Chong Liang, Adam Gee, In-Woo Lee, Mardan Mamat, James Heath, Zaw Moe, Jeev Milkha Singh, Kevin Phelan, Marcus Both **143**: Fredrik Andersson Hed, Sung-Hoon Kang, Berry Henson, Daniel Gaunt, Sihwan Kim, Mikko Korhonen, Gunn Charoenkul, Kristoffer Broberg, J.B. Hansen, Duncan Stewart **144**: Siddikur Rahman, Søren Hansen, Daniel Chopra, James Stewart, Scott Barr, Kalle Samooja **145**: Fabrizio Zanotti, Steven Lam (a), Sam Walker **146**: Phillip Archer, Jack Doherty, John Daly, Tianlang Guan (a) **147**: Mithun Perera, Chi-Huang Tsai, Lian-Wei Zhang, Peter Lawrie, Jens Dantorp, Andreas Hartø **148**: Miguel Tabuena, Jens Fahrbring, Yu Jui Liu (a) **149**: Hyun-Bin Park, Woon Man Wong, Shinichi Mizuno (a), David Gleeson, Shun Yat Hak **150**: Namchok Tantipokhakul **151**: Gaganjeet Bhullar, John Parry, Björn Akesson **152**: Andrew McArthur, C. Muniyappa **153**: Elmer Salvador, Doug Williams (a), Humphrey Wong (a), Max Wong (a) **156**: Yih-Shin Chan **164**: Max Ting (a) **WD**: Kwanchai Tannin (74), Kieran Pratt (79), Ben Fox (82)

FIRST ROUND		SECOND ROUND		THIRD ROUND	
David Higgins	64 (-6)	Jbe' Kruger	133 (-7)	Stuart Manley	200 (-10)
Andrea Pavan	65 (-5)	Stuart Manley	134 (-6)	Shiv Kapur	201 (-9)
7 Players	66 (-4)	Alex Cejka	135 (-5)	Wade Ormsby	200 (-9)
Miguel A. Jiménez	70 (E)	Wade Ormsby	135 (-5)	3 Players	201 (-8)
		Shiv Kapur	135 (-5)	**Miguel A. Jiménez**	202 (-7)
		Miguel A. Jiménez	137 (-3)		

OWR: 1 of top 50 entered - Rating: 40 - Points to 23rd - Jiménez: 20 points, to 38th in OWR

Nedbank Golf Challenge

Gary Player Country Club - Sun City, South Africa
Champion: Thomas Bjørn

Dec 5 - Dec 8
7,831 yards   Par 72
Purse: $6.5 Million

In an event darkened by the Thursday passing of former South African president Nelson Mandela, Denmark's Thomas Bjørn closed with a seven-under-par 65 to win the Nedbank Golf Challenge in the long-running tournament's debut as an official European Tour event. Bjørn began Sunday's final round trailing Jamie Donaldson by two strokes before going out in 33, which was enough to overtake the Welshman (who carded an ill-timed bogey at the par-4 9th) but not enough to stay ahead of Sergio García, who'd continued an up-and-down week by going out in a flawless six-under-par 30. But Bjørn quickly seized the lead with an eagle at the 547-yard 10th, then compounded it with a second eagle (this after his approach skipped through a greenside bunker) at the 601-yard 14th. García gamely fought back with birdies at the 14th and the 471-yard 15th, but his crucial bogey at the 211-yard 17th was one stroke too many, allowing the 42-year-old Bjørn to bogey the 502-yard par-4 18th and still collect his 15th career European Tour victory. García's Sunday 65 lifted him into a tie for second with Donaldson, who closed with a disappointing 70 after losing momentum at the 9th. The world's hottest player, Henrik Stenson, recorded four straight rounds in the 60s en route to taking fourth in his first event back following a three-week layoff.

1	Thomas Bjørn	67-70-66-65	268	€795,338	16=	Martin Kaymer	71-66-74-75	286	€64,423
2=	Jamie Donaldson	67-66-67-70	270	€414,478		Joost Luiten	74-68-75-69	286	€64,423
	Sergio García	66-73-66-65	270	€414,478		D.A. Points	71-67-70-78	286	€64,423
4	Henrik Stenson	69-67-69-67	272	€238,602	19	Luke Donald	68-71-74-74	287	€59,173
5	Brendon De Jonge	70-68-69-66	273	€202,335	20=	Victor Dubuisson	73-72-71-72	288	€56,310
6	Charl Schwartzel	68-70-71-66	275	€167,022		Branden Grace	75-71-69-73	288	€56,310
7=	Ryan Moore	71-65-67-73	276	€131,231	22=	Matteo Manassero	72-74-72-72	290	€53,208
	Justin Rose	73-67-69-67	276	€131,231		Gary Woodland	74-73-75-68	290	€53,208
9	Thongchai Jaidee	69-70-66-72	277	€106,894	24=	Dawie van der Walt	77-72-73-69	291	€51,061
10	Peter Uihlein	70-69-70-70	279	€95,441	25=	David Lynn	73-71-75-74	293	€48,198
11	Gon. F'dez-Castaño	67-72-72-69	280	€87,806		Morten O. Madsen	76-71-68-78	293	€48,198
12=	Darren Fichardt	71-68-69-74	282	€79,455		Thaworn Wiratchant	71-76-70-76	293	€48,198
	Francesco Molinari	76-70-69-67	282	€79,455	28	Kevin Streelman	75-71-77-72	295	€45,334
14=	Louis Oosthuizen	74-69-67-73	283	€71,581	29	Ernie Els	75-71-77-77	300	€43,903
	Richard Sterne	73-73-71-66	283	€71,581	30	Peter Senior	80-68-75-81	304	€42,471

FIRST ROUND		SECOND ROUND		THIRD ROUND	
Sergio García	66 (-6)	Jamie Donaldson	133 (-11)	Jamie Donaldson	200 (-16)
Jamie Donaldson	67 (-5)	Henrik Stenson	136 (-8)	**Thomas Bjørn**	203 (-13)
Gon. F'dez-Castaño	67 (-5)	Ryan Moore	136 (-8)	Ryan Moore	203 (-13)
Thomas Bjørn	67 (-5)	**Thomas Bjørn**	137 (-7)	3 Players	205 (-11)
2 Players	68 (-4)	Martin Kaymer	137 (-7)		

OWR: 14 of top 50 entered - Rating: 263 - Points to 30th - Bjørn : 46 points, to 25th in OWR

Nelson Mandela Championship

Mount Edgecombe Country Club - Durban, South Africa
Champion: Dawie van der Walt

Dec 11 - Dec 14
6,612 yards   Par 70
Purse: €1 Million

It was both fitting and sadly ironic that the Nelson Mandela Championship was played the very week of the great South African leader's passing, with the event's finish being moved to Saturday to avoid conflicting with his Sunday state funeral. But the shift in schedule didn't help the tournament to avoid being deluged by heavy rains for the second straight year – though where the 2012 playing could only manage 36 holes, this year managed to get in 54. The winner was Dawie van der Walt, who began the third round three strokes behind England's Daniel Brooks before posting a closing 66 that was keyed by an eagle at the 558-yard 12th, and a follow-up birdie at the par-4 13th. An additional birdie at the 15th ultimately extended the margin of victory to two, with England's Matthew Baldwin and Spain's Jorge Campillo tying for second. Equally notable was the scoring in a rain-delayed second round which extended from Thursday into Friday, most prominently the matching 59s posted by Campillo and South Africa's Colin Nel. These rounds, however, would not go into the European Tour record book as official as they were shot on a waterlogged layout whose par was lowered to 70, and under lift, clean and place conditions. Both van der Walt and Baldwin posted 62s in round two, though at that point the tournament seemed in the hands of the 26-year-old Brooks, who'd opened with rounds of 62-64 to hold a three-stroke lead before crashing with a final round 76, to fall into a tie for 11th. Curiously, Nel surrounded his 59 with a 77 and a 71, making him the rare player to card a 59 and still tie for 40th.

1	Dawie van der Walt	67-62-66	195	$206,050		Thomas Aiken	70-69-67	206	$9,490
2=	Matthew Baldwin	67-62-68	197	$119,730	40=	Oliver Wilson	70-67-70	207	$7,540
	Jorge Campillo	70-59-68	197	$119,730		Phillip Archer	67-69-71	207	$7,540
4	Romain Wattel	64-67-67	198	$63,830		Lyle Rowe	71-66-70	207	$7,540
5	Oliver Bekker	64-66-69	199	$53,690		Björn Akesson	69-67-71	207	$7,540
6=	John Hahn	69-66-65	200	$36,108		Andrew McArthur	66-72-69	207	$7,540
	Jaco Ahlers	66-68-66	200	$36,108		Colin Nel	77-59-71	207	$7,540
	Adrien Saddier	66-67-67	200	$36,108		Charl Coetzee	67-68-72	207	$7,540
	Branden Grace	64-66-70	200	$36,108		Jens Fahrbring	68-70-69	207	$7,540
10	Merrick Bremner	68-66-67	201	$25,480		Jaco Van Zyl	74-65-68	207	$7,540
11=	Joel Sjoholm	65-70-67	202	$19,704		Robert Rock	72-67-68	207	$7,540
	Jbe' Kruger	67-67-68	202	$19,704	50=	Gary Stal	70-67-71	208	$5,200
	Titch Moore	69-64-69	202	$19,704		Darren Fichardt	66-70-72	208	$5,200
	F. Andersson Hed	68-65-69	202	$19,704		Keith Horne	69-67-72	208	$5,200
	Jacques Blaauw	68-64-70	202	$19,704		Søren Hansen	71-67-70	208	$5,200
	David Higgins	68-64-70	202	$19,704		Bradford Vaughan	67-71-70	208	$5,200
	Daniel Brooks	62-64-76	202	$19,704		Matthew Carvell	67-67-74	208	$5,200
18=	Estanislao Goya	66-71-66	203	$15,392		Michael Hoey	65-69-74	208	$5,200
	Julien Guerrier	68-69-66	203	$15,392		Damien McGrane	71-68-69	208	$5,200
	Oliver Fisher	70-66-67	203	$15,392	58=	Carlos Del Moral	69-67-73	209	$3,835
	Andrew Johnston	68-67-68	203	$15,392		Matthew Nixon	69-69-71	209	$3,835
	Jose-Filipe Lima	70-64-69	203	$15,392		Daniel Im	70-68-71	209	$3,835
23=	Jeppe Huldahl	72-65-67	204	$13,260		Simon Wakefield	70-69-70	209	$3,835
	Scott Jamieson	73-65-66	204	$13,260		P. Martin Benavides	70-69-70	209	$3,835
	Alastair Forsyth	68-67-69	204	$13,260		Vaughn Groenewald	68-71-70	209	$3,835
	Jake Roos	68-70-66	204	$13,260	64=	Byeong-Hun An	67-69-74	210	$3,120
	Francois Calmels	63-70-71	204	$13,260		Chris Hanson	72-66-72	210	$3,120
28=	Shiv Kapur	71-65-69	205	$11,106		Niklas Lemke	73-66-71	210	$3,120
	Victor Riu	66-70-69	205	$11,106		Garth Mulroy	69-70-71	210	$3,120
	Keenan Davidse	67-70-68	205	$11,106		Stuart Manley	71-68-71	210	$3,120
	Anthony Wall	71-66-68	205	$11,106	69	Edouard Dubois	64-71-76	211	$2,427
	Daniel Gaunt	68-70-67	205	$11,106		Alex Haindl	68-71-72	211	$2,427
	Adilson da Silva	67-68-70	205	$11,106		Dean Burmester	70-69-72	211	$2,427
	Tjaart Van der Walt	67-67-71	205	$11,106	72=	James Kamte	70-67-75	212	$1,942
35=	Jens Dantorp	69-67-70	206	$9,490		James Kingston	67-71-74	212	$1,942
	Brandon Stone	68-69-69	206	$9,490		Christiaan Basson	68-71-73	212	$1,942
	Thomas Pieters	73-66-67	206	$9,490	75	Duncan Stewart	68-70-75	213	$1,934
	Lee Slattery	73-66-67	206	$9,490					

Out Of The Money: **140**: Warren Abery, Richard Finch, Andrew Georgiou, Peter Hedblom, P.H. McIntyre, Edoardo Molinari, Adrian Otaegui, Neil Schietekat, Theunis Spangenberg, Simon Thornton, Peter Whiteford, Fabrizio Zanotti, Ruan de Smidt **141**: Ryan Cairns, George Coetzee, Edouard Espana, Jared Harvey, Michael Hollick, Espen Kofstad, Shaun Norris, Haydn Porteous, J.J. Senekal **142**: Andrew Curlewis, Jean Hugo, Thriston Lawrence, Sam Little, Anthony Michael, Grant Muller, Brinson Paolini, Oscar Stark, Ockie Strydom **143**: Louis de Jager, Jack Doherty, Johan Du Buisson, Jamie McLeary, Thomas Norret, Chris Paisley, Allan Versfeld, Justin Walters **144**: Bryce Easton, Mathias Gronberg, Andreas Hartø, Kevin Phelan, Ulrich Van Den Berg **145**: John Bele, Peter Karmis, Alphuis Kelapile, Bernd Ritthammer, Danie van Tonder, Graham Van der Merwe **146**: Heinrich Bruiners, Cliffie Howes, Ryan Tipping **147**: Le Roux Ferreira, Dylan Frittelli, Scott Henry, Thabo Maseko, Brandon Pieters, Chris Swanepoel, Louis Taylor **148**: Drikus Bruyns, Makgetha Mazibuko **149**: Daniel Greene, Tyrone Mordt, Riekus Nortje **150**: J.G. Claassen, Steven Tiley, Sam Walker **151**: Josh Cunliffe, Ben Evans, Dominic Foos (a) **159**: Mark Williams **WD**: David Drysdale (70), Tyrone Ferreira (71), Jose Manuel Lara (71), Desvonde Botes (71), Doug McGuigan (75), Adam Gee (78), Teboho Sefatsa (79) **DQ**: Gary Lockerbie, Justin Harding (69).

FIRST ROUND		SECOND ROUND	
Daniel Brooks	62 (-8)	Daniel Brooks	126 (-14)
Francois Calmels	63 (-7)	Jorge Campillo	129 (-11)
4 Players	64 (-6)	Matthew Baldwin	129 (-11)
Dawie van der Walt	67 (-3)	**Dawie van der Walt**	129 (-11)
		2 Players	130 (-10)

OWR: 0 of top 50 entered - Rating: 30 - Points to 22nd - van der Walt: 20 points, to 196th in OWR

Volvo Golf Champions

Durban Country Club - Durban, South Africa
Champion: Louis Oosthuizen

Jan 9 - Jan 12
6,689 yards Par 72
Purse: $4 Million

Despite still feeling the effects of a back/neck injury dating to the summer of 2013, Louis Oosthuizen managed the rare feat of winning his first event of the new year for the fourth consecutive season, successfully defending his title at the Volvo Golf Champions in Durban, South Africa. Following a disappointing third round 71 that was marred by a triple-bogey at the 417-yard 16th, Oosthuizen began Sunday two behind 54-hole leader Tommy Fleetwood and initially made little headway before an eagle at the par-5 8th moved him briefly into the lead. The 2010 British Open champion played uneven golf thereafter, however, bogeying the par-5 10th, birdieing both the 13th and 14th, then making a crucial bogey at the 16th to fall one behind countryman Branden Grace, who'd birdied both the 16th and the 273-yard par-4 18th en route to a closing 68, and the lead. But rather then wait for the driveable 18th and a chance to tie, Oosthuizen proceeded to stick his approach to two feet at the tumbling 401-yard 17th to draw even, then clinched the title by chipping to a similar distance to birdie the last. Grace, who was looking for his first win since 2012, took solo second, while England's Fleetwood (who closed with a disappointing 72) and Joost Luiten of The Netherlands (71) shared third, two shots off the pace. Oosthuizen's triumph was the eighth time in the E Tour's last 11 events on South African soil that a homestanding player won, and the seventh straight E Tour visit to Durban to produce a native winner.

1	Louis Oosthuizen	68-69-71-68	276	€507,655	19=	G. F'dez-Castaño	74-73-71-69	287	€46,414
2	Branden Grace	74-67-68-68	277	€326,349		Mikko Ilonen	73-73-69-72	287	€46,414
3=	Joost Luiten	70-67-70-71	278	€174,053		Paul Casey	72-75-65-75	287	€46,414
	Tommy Fleetwood	70-67-69-72	278	€174,053	22=	David Lynn	71-74-72-71	288	€43,695
5=	Padraig Harrington	71-71-70-67	279	€116,761		Yeon-Jin Jeong	73-76-68-71	288	€43,695
	Raphaël Jacquelin	67-73-70-69	279	€116,761	24=	K. Aphibarnrat	75-74-71-69	289	€40,431
	Victor Dubuisson	69-69-69-72	279	€116,761		David Howell	76-69-71-73	289	€40,431
8=	Thomas Aiken	72-72-70-67	281	€81,043		Colin Montgomerie	70-74-69-76	289	€40,431
	Julien Quesne	74-73-66-68	281	€81,043		Darren Clarke	69-71-72-77	289	€40,431
10=	Thomas Bjørn	79-68-67-69	283	€64,545	28	Richard Sterne	72-73-73-73	291	€37,711
	Matteo Manassero	72-67-73-71	283	€64,545	29=	Stephen Gallacher	73-74-72-73	292	€36,080
	Brett Rumford	73-70-68-72	283	€64,545		Michael Hoey	72-73-73-74	292	€36,080
13=	Morten Madsen	71-74-69-70	284	€58,380	31	Simon Thornton	70-72-80-71	293	€34,448
	Jamie Donaldson	71-71-68-74	284	€58,380	32	Robert Karlsson	74-72-73-75	294	€33,360
15=	Marcel Siem	70-71-72-72	285	€52,941	33	Dawie van der Walt	71-71-75-78	295	€32,272
	Miguel A. Jiménez	76-70-67-72	285	€52,941	34	Peter Uihlein	70-78-70-78	296	€31,185
	Charl Schwartzel	74-69-68-74	285	€52,941	35	Darren Fichardt	73-71-74-79	297	€30,097
18	Chris Wood	70-71-71-74	286	€48,590	36	José María Olazábal	73-77-77-73	300	€29,009

FIRST ROUND		SECOND ROUND		THIRD ROUND	
Raphaël Jacquelin	67 (-5)	**Louis Oosthuizen**	137 (-7)	Tommy Fleetwood	206 (-10)
Louis Oosthuizen	68 (-4)	Tommy Fleetwood	137 (-7)	Victor Dubuisson	207 (-9)
Darren Clarke	69 (-3)	Joost Luiten	137 (-7)	Joost Luiten	207 (-9)
Victor Dubuisson	69 (-3)	Victor Dubuisson	138 (-6)	**Louis Oosthuizen**	208 (-8)
7 Players	70 (-2)	Matteo Manassero	139 (-5)	Branden Grave	209 (-7)

OWR: 10 of top 50 entered - Rating: 174 - Points to 36th - Oosthuizen: 34 points, to 27th in OWR

2013 European Tour Winners (Players Eligible For the Volvo Golf Champions)

Nelson Mandela Championship	Scott Jamieson *	Najeti Hotels et Golfs Open	Simon Thornton
Alfred Dunhill Championship	Charl Schwartzel	BMW International Open	Ernie Els *
Volvo Golf Champions	Louis Oosthuizen	Irish Open	Paul Casey
Abu Dhabi HSBC Golf Championship	Jamie Donaldson	Alstom Open de France	Graeme McDowell *
Commercial Bank Qatar Masters	Chris Wood	Aberdeen Asset Mgmt Scottish Open	Phil Mickelson *
Omega Dubai Desert Classic	Stephen Gallacher	142nd Open Championship	Phil Mickelson *
Joburg Open	Richard Sterne	M2M Russian Open	Michael Hoey
Africa Open	Darren Fichardt	Johnnie Walker Champ. at Gleneagles	Tommy Fleetwood
Tshwane Open	Dawie van der Walt	ISPS Handa Wales Open	Grégory Bourdy *
Avantha Masters	Thomas Aiken	Omega European Masters	Thomas Bjørn
Maybank Malaysian Open	Kiradech Aphibarnrat	KLM Open	Joost Luiten
Trophée Hassan II	Marcel Siem	70° Open D'Italia Lindt	Julien Quesne
Open de España	Raphaël Jacquelin	Alfred Dunhill Links Championship	David Howell
Ballantine's Championship	Brett Rumford	Portugal Masters	David Lynn
Volvo China Open	Brett Rumford	ISPS Handa Perth International	Jin Jeong
Volvo World Match Play Championship	Graeme McDowell *	BMW Masters	Gon. F'dez-Castaño
Madeira Islands Open - Portugal - BPI	Peter Uihlein	WGC-HSBC Champions	Dustin Johnson *
BMW PGA Championship	Matteo Manassero	Turkish Airlines Open	Victor Dubuisson
Nordea Masters	Mikko Ilonen	DP World Tour Championship	Henrik Stenson *
Lyoness Open	Joost Luiten		

* Eligible winners not in the Volvo Golf Champions field

Also eligible and entered were past winners of the Volvo Golf Champions under 50 years of age (Branden Grace) and players with 10 or more career European Tour wins under 50 years of age (Colin Montgomerie, Padraig Harrington, Darren Clarke, Robert Karlsson and José Maria Olazábal).

Abu Dhabi HSBC Golf Championship

Abu Dhabi Golf Club - Abu Dhabi, U.A.E.
Champion: Pablo Larrazábal

Jan 16 - Jan 19
7,600 yards   Par 72
Purse: $2.7 Million

Battling down to the wire against the two highest ranked players in the field, Spain's Pablo Larrazábal claimed his third career European Tour victory at the Abu Dhabi HSBC Championship, edging Phil Mickelson and Rory McIlroy by one. Though Larrazábal played solid, steady golf en route to a closing 67, he had a bit of help down the stretch, especially from Mickelson who double-hit a recovery shot on the 13th hole and posted a triple-bogey seven, dropping him rather abruptly from the tournament lead to three shots in arrears. The world number five nearly managed a spectacular comeback, however, recording three birdies over the final five holes before ultimately coming up one shy. McIlroy too had chances to win, failing to hole a number of makeable birdie putts on the final nine, then finally carding a birdie at the par-5 finisher when it was an eagle that was required. McIlroy's prospects had already been dimmed on Saturday evening when a two-stroke penalty assessed after the round for an illegal drop at the 2nd hole moved him from one to three shots off the lead, a deficit he was ultimately unable to recover from. His form, however, looked considerably improved from his missed cut here in 2013, and seemed to be pointing him towards a big year ahead. Larrazábal, for his part, proved himself quite capable under pressure, logging birdies at the 11th and 13th to move into the lead, then recording a clutch two-putt birdie to close the door on his pursuers at the 567-yard par-5 18th. South African George Coetzee was also heard from, birdieing six of his first 13 holes on Sunday to move into contention before a run of five closing pars left him in a tie for fourth with Spain's Rafael Cabrera-Bello, two shots back.

1	Pablo Larrazábal	69-70-68-67	274	€328,779
2=	Rory McIlroy	70-67-70-68	275	€171,338
	Phil Mickelson	73-70-63-69	275	€171,338
4=	George Coetzee	68-70-72-66	276	€91,138
	Rafael Cabrera-Bello	67-68-73-68	276	€91,138
6	Joost Luiten	68-70-72-68	278	€69,044
7	Johan Carlsson	73-70-71-65	279	€59,180
8=	Robert Karlsson	73-67-72-68	280	€46,752
	Stephen Gallacher	70-73-68-69	280	€46,752
10=	Darren Fichardt	70-70-75-66	281	€31,168
	Tyrrell Hatton	69-71-70-71	281	€31,168
	Thomas Bjørn	70-67-72-72	281	€31,168
	Peter Hanson	70-70-69-72	281	€31,168
	Michael Hoey	69-71-68-73	281	€31,168
	Thongchai Jaidee	70-70-68-73	281	€31,168
	Miguel A. Jiménez	73-68-67-73	281	€31,168
	Gaganjeet Bhullar	72-68-66-75	281	€31,168
	Craig Lee	68-67-69-77	281	€31,168
19=	Paul McGinley	68-72-72-70	282	€21,765
	Danny Willett	73-63-76-70	282	€21,765
	Sergio García	76-68-70-68	282	€21,765
	Thomas Aiken	70-73-69-70	282	€21,765
	Andy Sullivan	73-70-69-70	282	€21,765
	Brandon Stone	71-71-73-67	282	€21,765
	Tommy Fleetwood	73-65-72-72	282	€21,765
	Hennie Otto	70-71-69-72	282	€21,765
	Matthew Baldwin	67-72-69-74	282	€21,765
28=	Wade Ormsby	69-73-71-70	283	€18,149
	Edoardo Molinari	70-71-71-71	283	€18,149
	Jose-Filipe Lima	68-75-67-73	283	€18,149
31=	Maximilian Kieffer	71-71-72-70	284	€15,584
	Emiliano Grillo	72-72-70-70	284	€15,584
	Matteo Manassero	71-73-70-70	284	€15,584
	Ricardo González	71-66-74-73	284	€15,584
	Álvaro Quirós	71-70-70-73	284	€15,584
	Martin Kaymer	70-71-69-74	284	€15,584
37=	Oliver Fisher	69-72-73-71	285	€12,625
	Raphaël Jacquelin	71-72-70-72	285	€12,625
	Luke Donald	70-73-71-71	285	€12,625
	Marcel Siem	69-70-73-73	285	€12,625
	Marc Warren	68-73-70-74	285	€12,625
	David Howell	73-71-72-69	285	€12,625
	Shiv Kapur	71-72-75-67	285	€12,625
	Paul Waring	73-71-74-67	285	€12,625
45=	Tom Lewis	71-70-72-73	286	€10,258
	Romain Wattel	67-75-70-74	286	€10,258
	Colin Montgomerie	73-68-74-71	286	€10,258
	Eddie Pepperell	70-72-69-75	286	€10,258
49=	Seve Benson	73-70-72-72	287	€8,877
	Alejandro Cañizares	71-69-76-71	287	€8,877
	Jorge Campillo	72-72-73-70	287	€8,877
52=	Branden Grace	73-70-70-75	288	€7,496
	Ricardo Santos	70-72-71-75	288	€7,496
	Darren Clarke	74-69-72-73	288	€7,496
	Julien Quesne	71-72-74-71	288	€7,496
56=	Alexander Levy	74-69-69-77	289	€6,066
	Thorbjørn Olesen	74-70-71-74	289	€6,066
	Eduardo De La Riva	70-74-72-73	289	€6,066
	Jamie Donaldson	73-70-73-73	289	€6,066
60=	Steve Webster	69-73-75-73	290	€5,326
	Peter Whiteford	74-70-73-73	290	€5,326
	Jeev Milkha Singh	69-75-74-72	290	€5,326
63=	Nacho Elvira	72-70-74-75	291	€4,833
	Yeon-Jin Jeong	70-71-76-74	291	€4,833
65=	Paul Casey	72-71-73-76	292	€4,143
	Chris Wood	71-73-72-76	292	€4,143
	Richard Bland	71-73-75-73	292	€4,143
	Magnus A. Carlsson	71-71-77-73	292	€4,143
	Gareth Maybin	73-70-76-73	292	€4,143
70	Damien McGrane	70-72-75-76	293	€3,595
71	Dawie van der Walt	68-73-74-79	294	€2,959

Out Of The Money: 145: Kiradech Aphibarnrat, Mark Foster, Padraig Harrington, David Horsey, John Parry, Adrien Saddier, Peter Uihlein **146**: Francois Calmels, Robert Dinwiddie, Simon Dyson, Ross Fisher, Marcus Fraser, Richard Green, Grégory Havret, Daan Huizing, Søren Kjeldsen, Robert Rock, Lee Slattery, Henrik Stenson, Simon Thornton, Anthony Wall, Bernd Wiesberger **147**: Marco Crespi, Chris Doak, Jbe' Kruger, Peter Lawrie, Shane Lowry, Gary Stal **148**: Niclas Fasth, Morten Madsen, Kevin Phelan, Graeme Storm **149**: Wen-Yi Huang, Mikko Ilonen, Andrea Pavan, Victor Riu **150**: Kristoffer Broberg, Søren Hansen, Brooks Koepka **151**: Matthew Nixon, Adrian Otaegui **152**: Garth Mulroy, Fabrizio Zanotti **153**: Paul Lawrie, Jamie McLeary, Thomas Pieters **154**: J.B. Hansen, Brett Rumford **155**: Carlos Del Moral **156**: Sihwan Kim **157**: Michael Campbell **158**: Thomas Levet **162**: Ahmed Al Musharrekh **WD**: José María Olazábal (217)

FIRST ROUND		SECOND ROUND		THIRD ROUND	
Rafael Cabrera-Bello	67 (-5)	Craig Lee	135 (-9)	Craig Lee	204 (-12)
Romain Wattel	67 (-5)	Rafael Cabrera-Bello	135 (-9)	Rory McIlroy	205 (-11)
Mathew Baldwin	67 (-5)	Danny Willett	136 (-8)	Phil Mickelson	206 (-10)
7 Players	68 (-4)	3 Players	137 (-7)	Gaganjeet Bhullar	206 (-10)
Pablo Larrazábal	69 (-3)	**Pablo Larrazábal**	139 (-5)	**Pablo Larrazábal**	207 (-9)

OWR: 12 of top 50 entered - Rating: 291 - Points to 51st - Larrazábal: 48 points, to 53rd in OWR

Commercial Bank Qatar Masters

Jan 22 - Jan 25

Doha Golf Club - Doha, Qatar
Champion: Sergio García

7,400 yards Par 72
Purse: $2.5 Million

Sergio García spent the first three days of the Qatar Masters flying almost completely under the radar, his opening rounds of 71-67-69 leaving him seven, seven and three shots off the lead respectively. But in a Saturday finale played under ideal conditions, the 34-year-old García raced home with six birdies over his final 12 holes to card the day's co-low round (a seven-under-par 65) and charge into the clubhouse lead. Unfortunately, García missed an eight-footer for birdie at the 72nd, and thus left the door ajar for Finland's Mikko Ilonen, who promptly holed a clutch 18-footer for birdie at the par-5 finisher to join García on 272 and force a playoff. The pair were nearly joined by Denmark's 24-year-old Thorbjørn Olesen, who arrived at the last trailing by two but, after reaching the 589-yarder in two, he narrowly missed a 15-foot eagle putt to tie. Returning to the 18th for sudden death, García too missed a makeable eagle putt on the first playoff hole, and both he and Ilonen birdied the hole on its second playing. But Ilonen was unable to match García's birdie on the third go-round, and with a total of 10 birdies in 21 Saturday holes, the Spaniard clinched his 11th career European Tour victory. Olesen would share third place with third round leader Rafael Cabrera-Bello of Spain, who closed with a more-than-respectable 69. Also noteworthy was 16-year-old German amateur Dominic Foos, who closed with an impressive 68 to tie for 16th. For the second straight year, the week's play was scheduled Wednesday-Saturday to coincide with the Middle Eastern Friday-Saturday weekend.

1	Sergio García	71-67-69-65	272	€305,232		Brooks Koepka	70-70-70-72	282	€12,454
2	Mikko Ilonen	68-67-71-66	272	€203,486		Tom Lewis	68-67-76-71	282	€12,454
3=	Rafa Cabrera-Bello	66-65-73-69	273	€103,109		Hennie Otto	71-71-71-69	282	€12,454
	Thorbjørn Olesen	68-69-68-68	273	€103,109		Anthony Wall	70-66-76-70	282	€12,454
5=	Thomas Aiken	67-68-70-69	274	€60,620	43=	Robert-Jan Derksen	70-72-73-68	283	€9,340
	Alejandro Cañizares	68-68-73-65	274	€60,620		Robert Dinwiddie	71-72-72-68	283	€9,340
	George Coetzee	64-69-73-68	274	€60,620		Ross Fisher	66-72-75-70	283	€9,340
	Steve Webster	65-69-70-70	274	€60,620		Craig Lee	72-67-72-72	283	€9,340
9=	Magnus A. Carlsson	69-71-70-65	275	€38,826		Stuart Manley	69-70-71-73	283	€9,340
	Dawie van der Walt	65-72-70-68	275	€38,826		Ricardo Santos	72-69-73-69	283	€9,340
11=	Paul Lawrie	67-70-69-70	276	€32,599		Marcel Siem	69-73-71-70	283	€9,340
	Romain Wattel	67-68-74-67	276	€32,599		Jeev Milkha Singh	71-71-73-68	283	€9,340
13=	Seve Benson	68-71-69-69	277	€28,142		Simon Thornton	70-68-74-71	283	€9,340
	Carlos Del Moral	72-68-69-68	277	€28,142		Danny Willett	71-72-70-70	283	€9,340
	Branden Grace	67-69-71-70	277	€28,142		Chris Wood	73-70-71-69	283	€9,340
16=	Johan Carlsson	69-65-72-72	278	€23,772	54=	Francois Calmels	66-70-73-75	284	€6,776
	Simon Dyson	68-69-71-70	278	€23,772		Marcus Fraser	74-68-74-68	284	€6,776
	Darren Fichardt	69-70-69-70	278	€23,772		Robert Karlsson	70-73-71-70	284	€6,776
	Dominic Foos (a)	70-70-70-68	278	-	57=	Luke Donald	72-69-74-70	285	€5,632
	Adrien Saddier	70-71-64-73	278	€23,772		Mark Foster	72-71-73-69	285	€5,632
	Peter Uihlein	70-69-69-70	278	€23,772		Martin Kaymer	70-70-73-72	285	€5,632
22=	Matthew Baldwin	68-66-74-71	279	€19,871		Søren Kjeldsen	70-71-74-70	285	€5,632
	Gaganjeet Bhullar	67-70-73-69	279	€19,871	61=	John Daly	67-69-77-73	286	€5,036
	Peter Hanson	69-67-75-68	279	€19,871		Michael Hoey	68-70-74-74	286	€5,036
	Tyrrell Hatton	69-71-71-68	279	€19,871	63=	Paul McGinley	73-70-72-72	287	€4,487
	Robert Rock	70-71-71-67	279	€19,871		James Morrison	68-73-75-71	287	€4,487
	Fabrizio Zanotti	69-69-68-73	279	€19,871		José María Olazábal	69-70-74-74	287	€4,487
28=	Kristoffer Broberg	69-68-70-73	280	€16,849		Eddie Pepperell	69-74-76-68	287	€4,487
	Stephen Gallacher	69-68-75-68	280	€16,849	67=	Chris Doak	69-72-74-73	288	€3,846
	Julien Quesne	71-70-70-69	280	€16,849		Nacho Elvira	66-73-76-73	288	€3,846
	Álvaro Quirós	69-72-69-70	280	€16,849		Wade Ormsby	72-70-74-72	288	€3,846
	Henrik Stenson	68-71-74-67	280	€16,849	70=	Marco Crespi	70-71-77-71	289	€3,414
33=	Richard Bland	69-70-71-71	281	€14,422		Jose-Filipe Lima	72-70-75-72	289	€3,414
	Thongchai Jaidee	68-73-72-68	281	€14,422	72=	Jason Dufner	70-71-78-71	290	€2,746
	Shiv Kapur	68-71-71-71	281	€14,422		Victor Riu	73-70-74-73	290	€2,746
	Gary Stal	69-70-71-71	281	€14,422	74	Emiliano Grillo	72-70-77-72	291	€2,741
37=	Ernie Els	67-76-71-68	282	€12,454	75	Tommy Fleetwood	73-70-74-75	292	€2,738
	Søren Hansen	73-70-68-71	282	€12,454	76	Lee Slattery	73-70-77-73	293	€2,735

Out Of The Money: **144:** David Howell, Miguel A. Jiménez, Sihwan Kim, Shane Lowry, Damien McGrane, Garth Mulroy, Brett Rumford, Richard Sterne, Justin Walters, Paul Waring **145:** Thomas Bjørn, Eduardo De La Riva, Ricardo González, Richard Green, Daan Huizing, Maximilian Kieffer, Jamie McLeary, Edoardo Molinari, Graeme Storm, Peter Whiteford **146:** Jorge Campillo, Richard Finch, Raphaël Jacquelin, Adrian Otaegui, Brandon Stone, Marc Warren **147:** Jens Dantorp, Grégory Havret, Jin Jeong, Pablo Larrazábal, Alexander Levy, Andrea Pavan, Bernd Wiesberger **148:** Saleh Al Kaabi, Andy Sullivan **149:** Niclas Fasth, Morten Madsen, John Parry, Max Williams **150:** John Hahn, Gareth Maybin **151:** Roope Kakko, Matthew Nixon **152:** Jbe' Kruger **153:** Connor Arendell, Thomas Levet **156:** J.B. Hansen, Peter Lawrie **157:** Ali Al-Shahrani **WD:** Michael Campbell

FIRST ROUND		SECOND ROUND		THIRD ROUND	
George Coetzee	64 (-8)	Rafael Cabrera-Bello	131 (-13)	Rafael Cabrera-Bello	204 (-12)
Dawie van der Walt	65 (-7)	George Coetzee	133 (-11)	Steve Webster	204 (-12)
Steve Webster	65 (-7)	Matthew Baldwin	134 (-10)	Thomas Aiken	205 (-11)
4 Players	66 (-6)	Johan Carlsson	134 (-10)	Thorbjørn Olesen	205 (-11)
Sergio García	71 (-1)	Steve Webster	134 (-10)	Adrien Saddier	205 (-11)
		Sergio García	138 (-6)	**Sergio García**	207 (-9)

OWR: 10 of top 50 entered - Rating: 242 - Points to 53rd - García: 44 points, to 9th in OWR

Omega Dubai Desert Classic

Emirates Golf Club - Dubai, U.A.E.
Champion: Stephen Gallacher

Jan 31 - Feb 3
7,316 yards   Par 72
Purse: $2.5 Million

Thirty-nine-year-old Stephen Gallacher became the first man to successfully defend his title at the Dubai Desert Classic, winning the event's 25th anniversary playing in a hotly contested shootout which at one point late in the final round saw 18 players within two shots of the lead. Indeed, the crowded nature of Sunday's competition created much late drama as one man after another posted ever-lower finishing scores, beginning with Finland's Mikko Ilonen, who continued his strong form by closing with 64 to post a 13-under-par clubhouse total. Next came France's Romain Wattel, whose birdie-birdie finish (for a 66) lifted him to 14-under-par - a number soon eclipsed by 21-year-old Argentinean Emiliano Grillo, who reached 15 under via a closing eagle that included an approach ricocheted off the spectator pavilion, followed by a 60-foot putt. But the resolute Gallacher, who began the week with a rock-solid 66 in the company of superstars Rory McIlroy and Tiger Woods, authored the biggest stories on both Saturday and Sunday. In many ways, Gallacher's Saturday work was the most impressive, for after seemingly drifting out of contention through 45 holes, he tied the all-time European Tour record by playing the back nine in nine-under-par 28, a stunning run that included seven birdies and an eagle. Thus vaulting himself into a two-man after posted two-stroke 54-hole lead, Gallacher then staggered out of the gate with two bogeys Sunday and ultimately turned in four-over-par 39. But birdies at the 11th and 13th got the ship righted, and when he added clutch birdies at both the 16th and the driveable 17th, he had climbed back to 16 under, allowing him a routine par 5 at the last to clinch the title. Less happy, certainly, was a recently rejuvenated Rory McIlroy, who played spectacular golf en route to an opening 63 but stumbled thereafter, ultimately closing with a very disappointing 74 to tie for ninth.

1	Stephen Gallacher	66-71-63-72	272	€303,268
2	Emiliano Grillo	71-67-69-66	273	€202,176
3=	Romain Wattel	68-73-67-66	274	€102,446
	Brooks Koepka	69-65-70-70	274	€102,446
5=	Mikko Ilonen	69-72-70-64	275	€60,230
	Robert Rock	67-70-68-70	275	€60,230
	Steve Webster	71-70-64-70	275	€60,230
	Thorbjørn Olesen	71-68-65-71	275	€60,230
9=	Paul Casey	70-72-67-67	276	€35,483
	Bernd Wiesberger	70-70-68-68	276	€35,483
	Edoardo Molinari	65-72-68-71	276	€35,483
	Rory McIlroy	63-70-69-74	276	€35,483
13=	Brett Rumford	69-70-71-67	277	€25,735
	Thomas Bjørn	72-70-68-67	277	€25,735
	Francesco Molinari	69-69-71-68	277	€25,735
	Danny Willett	71-65-73-68	277	€25,735
	Søren Hansen	67-71-71-68	277	€25,735
	Paul Waring	70-70-68-69	277	€25,735
	Darren Fichardt	69-72-66-70	277	€25,735
20=	Simon Dyson	69-69-73-67	278	€21,168
	Damien McGrane	66-70-71-71	278	€21,168
	Jamie Donaldson	69-68-70-71	278	€21,168
23=	Chris Wood	73-69-70-67	279	€18,651
	Morten Madsen	71-67-72-69	279	€18,651
	Jorge Campillo	68-72-70-69	279	€18,651
	Joost Luiten	70-69-70-70	279	€18,651
	Anthony Wall	74-66-69-70	279	€18,651
	Roope Kakko	69-69-68-73	279	€18,651
29=	Kristoffer Broberg	71-69-73-67	280	€14,898
	Henrik Stenson	70-67-75-68	280	€14,898
	Eduardo De La Riva	70-70-72-68	280	€14,898
	Seve Benson	72-70-70-68	280	€14,898
	Fabrizio Zanotti	72-70-70-68	280	€14,898
	Scott Hend	69-72-70-69	280	€14,898
	Søren Kjeldsen	68-71-71-70	280	€14,898
	Dawie van der Walt	72-70-65-73	280	€14,898
37=	Marcel Siem	72-67-73-69	281	€12,374
	Sihwan Kim	70-69-72-70	281	€12,374
	Robert Karlsson	73-67-71-70	281	€12,374
	Hennie Otto	68-73-69-71	281	€12,374
41=	Gary Stal	74-68-73-67	282	€10,372
	Rafa Cabrera-Bello	71-69-71-71	282	€10,372
	Pablo Larrazábal	74-68-69-71	282	€10,372
	Tiger Woods	68-73-70-71	282	€10,372
	Chris Doak	71-68-71-72	282	€10,372
	Matthew Baldwin	66-74-69-73	282	€10,372
	Thongchai Jaidee	68-69-71-74	282	€10,372
48=	Julien Quesne	66-70-77-70	283	€8,006
	Scott Jamieson	73-69-70-71	283	€8,006
	Seung-Yul Noh	69-72-71-71	283	€8,006
	Shiv Kapur	72-70-70-71	283	€8,006
	Colin Montgomerie	70-70-69-74	283	€8,006
	Marco Crespi	69-71-69-74	283	€8,006
54=	Alejandro Cañizares	74-67-74-69	284	€5,376
	Álvaro Quirós	69-72-74-69	284	€5,376
	Michael Hoey	70-72-73-69	284	€5,376
	Fred Couples	70-71-73-70	284	€5,376
	Grégory Havret	70-72-72-70	284	€5,376
	Magnus A. Carlsson	69-69-74-72	284	€5,376
	Grégory Bourdy	71-68-73-72	284	€5,376
	Maximilian Kieffer	71-70-71-72	284	€5,376
	Paul Lawrie	68-71-72-73	284	€5,376
	Jaco Van Zyl	71-68-71-74	284	€5,376
	Richard Sterne	66-73-69-76	284	€5,376
65=	Justin Walters	69-68-75-74	286	€4,094
	Raphaël Jacquelin	69-71-69-77	286	€4,094
67=	Alexander Levy	69-72-76-70	287	€3,639
	Carlos Del Moral	70-72-73-72	287	€3,639
	Lee Slattery	70-71-70-76	287	€3,639
70	Jose-Filipe Lima	71-71-75-72	289	€3,326
71	Tom Lewis	71-69-78-73	291	€2,729

Out Of The Money: **143**: Peter Whiteford, David Drysdale, Shane Lowry, Garth Mulroy, Richard Green, Peter Uihlein, Ross Fisher, Eddie Pepperell **144**: Nacho Elvira, Miguel A. Jiménez, Ernie Els, Jeev Milkha Singh, John Daly, Tyrrell Hatton, Mark Foster, Johan Carlsson, Niclas Fasth, Mark O'Meara, Branden Grace, David Horsey, Peter Hanson, Gareth Maybin, Andy Sullivan **145**: Jbe' Kruger, Matthew Nixon, José María Olazábal, Francois Calmels, Javier Ballesteros (a), David Howell, Craig Lee, Tommy Fleetwood, Ricardo González **146**: Simon Thornton, Ricardo Santos, Yeon-Jin Jeong **147**: Jamie McLeary, Stephen Dodd, J.B. Hansen, Daan Huizing **148**: Robert Dinwiddie, Robert-Jan Derksen, Adrian Otaegui, Matteo Manassero **149**: Richard Bland, Andrea Pavan, Peter Lawrie, Marc Warren, Barry Lane, Jose Coceres, Lee Corfield **150**: Graeme Storm **151**: Gaganjeet Bhullar **152**: Victor Riu, Mustapha El Maouas **153**: Wayne Westner **154**: Thomas Levet, Faycal Serghini **155**: John Parry **WD**: Marcus Fraser (77) **DQ**: Zane Scotland (149), Derek McKenzie (158)

FIRST ROUND

Rory McIlroy	63 (-9)
Edoardo Molinari	65 (-7)
5 Players	66 (-6)
Stephen Gallacher	66 (-6)

SECOND ROUND

Rory McIlroy	133 (-11)
Brooks Koepka	134 (-10)
Danny Willett	136 (-8)
Damien McGrane	136 (-8)
Julien Quesne	136 (-8)
Stephen Gallacher	137 (-7)

THIRD ROUND

Stephen Gallacher	200 (-16)
Rory McIlroy	202 (-14)
Brooks Koepka	204 (-12)
Thorbjørn Olesen	204 (-12)
3 Players	205 (-11)

OWR: 11 of top 50 entered - Rating: 307 - Points to 53rd - Gallacher: 48 points, to 37th in OWR

Joburg Open	**Feb 6 - Feb 9**
Royal Johannesburg & Kensington Golf Club (East) - Johannesburg, South Africa	7,658 yards Par 72
Royal Johannesburg & Kensington Golf Club (West) - Johannesburg, South Africa	7,203 yards Par 71
Champion: George Coetzee	Purse: €1.3 Million

A frequent European Tour contender over the previous two seasons, South Africa's George Coetzee finally landed his first career victory on the circuit, closing with a six-under-par 66 to claim a three-shot win at the eighth playing of the Joburg Open, in Johannesburg. The 27-year-old Coetzee began Sunday's final round four shots behind 54-hole co-leaders Thomas Aiken and Justin Walters but quickly launched himself into the fray via a four-under-par 33 on the outward nine. Two inward birdies (including at the par-4 15th, where his tee shot ricocheted off a tree and back into the fairway) allowed him to set the bar at 19 under par, and in the end only Walters – who needed an eagle at the last but instead bogeyed – had any chance to catch him. In addition to winning, Coetzee was one of three men to land births in the 2014 Open championship, joining Walters and Korean Jin Jeong as the three low finishers among the top 10 not already qualified.

1	George Coetzee	65-68-69-66	268	€205,050		Heinrich Bruiners	71-68-69-71	279	€8,970
2=	Tyrrell Hatton	67-69-69-66	271	€101,097		Lorenzo Gagli	68-71-68-72	279	€8,970
	Yeon-Jin Jeong	65-69-66-71	271	€101,097		Edoardo Molinari	64-68-72-75	279	€8,970
	Justin Walters	64-70-64-73	271	€101,097	42=	Michael Hollick	69-68-73-70	280	€7,410
5=	Andy Sullivan	66-72-69-65	272	€42,510		Alexander Levy	71-67-72-70	280	€7,410
	Álvaro Quirós	69-68-69-66	272	€42,510		Richard Bland	67-71-72-70	280	€7,410
	Matthew Baldwin	68-69-68-67	272	€42,510		Søren Hansen	70-67-72-71	280	€7,410
	Thomas Aiken	70-65-63-74	272	€42,510		Jason Knutzon	67-71-70-72	280	€7,410
9	Danie van Tonder	65-72-69-67	273	€28,080		Erik van Rooyen	69-70-68-73	280	€7,410
10=	Seve Benson	68-68-70-68	274	€21,407		Andrew Georgiou	69-65-72-74	280	€7,410
	Ross Fisher	69-69-68-68	274	€21,407	49=	Eduardo De La Riva	68-68-73-72	281	€5,850
	Robert-Jan Derksen	65-74-67-68	274	€21,407		Wallie Coetsee	70-67-72-72	281	€5,850
	Anthony Wall	69-70-66-69	274	€21,407		Tyrone Ryan	71-65-72-73	281	€5,850
	David Horsey	70-63-70-71	274	€21,407		Christiaan Basson	71-65-71-74	281	€5,850
	Roope Kakko	70-64-67-73	274	€21,407		Craig Lee	65-67-74-75	281	€5,850
16=	Jorge Campillo	67-69-71-68	275	€16,250	54=	Adilson da Silva	69-69-72-72	282	€4,576
	Justin Harding	66-72-69-68	275	€16,250		Garth Mulroy	73-66-71-72	282	€4,576
	Danny Willett	69-65-71-70	275	€16,250		Keith Horne	69-70-71-72	282	€4,576
	Grégory Bourdy	68-67-70-70	275	€16,250		Jean Hugo	66-73-70-73	282	€4,576
	Brandon Stone	68-67-70-70	275	€16,250		Edouard Dubois	65-70-73-74	282	€4,576
	James Morrison	70-66-69-70	275	€16,250	59=	Lucas Bjerregaard	71-68-73-71	283	€3,705
22=	Graeme Storm	71-67-70-68	276	€13,455		Charl Schwartzel	69-70-72-72	283	€3,705
	Adrian Otaegui	71-68-68-69	276	€13,455		Patrik Sjoland	68-71-71-73	283	€3,705
	Drikus Van der Walt	66-71-69-70	276	€13,455		Gaganjeet Bhullar	71-67-71-74	283	€3,705
	Peter Karmis	73-65-68-70	276	€13,455		Ariel Cañete	70-68-69-76	283	€3,705
	Robert Dinwiddie	68-70-68-70	276	€13,455		Byeong-Hun An	69-68-68-78	283	€3,705
	Jaco Van Zyl	70-68-68-70	276	€13,455	65	Colin Nel	68-71-71-74	284	€3,250
28=	Dawie van der Walt	69-68-72-68	277	€11,700	66=	John Hahn	71-67-77-70	285	€2,990
	Emiliano Grillo	68-69-69-71	277	€11,700		Mark Murless	67-72-73-73	285	€2,990
	Gary Stal	66-69-70-72	277	€11,700		Mikael Lundberg	70-69-73-73	285	€2,990
31=	Ricardo Santos	67-71-72-68	278	€10,400	69=	Daniel Brooks	69-69-75-73	286	€2,234
	Wade Ormsby	68-71-70-69	278	€10,400		Daniel Im	69-70-75-72	286	€2,234
	Fabrizio Zanotti	71-68-70-69	278	€10,400		David Drysdale	71-67-74-74	286	€2,234
	Jbe' Kruger	68-71-69-70	278	€10,400		Dean Burmester	72-67-72-75	286	€2,234
	Louis de Jager	68-70-69-71	278	€10,400		Tyrone Mordt	68-71-71-76	286	€2,234
	Alastair Forsyth	64-70-68-76	278	€10,400	74=	Francesco Laporta	69-70-75-74	288	€1,940
37=	Hennie Otto	65-71-74-69	279	€8,970		D. van den Heever	70-68-76-74	288	€1,940
	James Heath	66-68-74-71	279	€8,970	76	Søren Kjeldsen	68-71-76-74	289	€1,935

Out Of The Money: **140**: Jaco Ahlers, Torben Baumann, Francois Calmels, Andre Cruse, Chris Doak, Simon Dyson, Darren Fichardt, Richard Finch, Trevor Fisher Jr., Chris Gane, Ricardo González, Daniel Greene, Scott Henry, Andrew Marshall, Robert Rock, Neil Schietekat, Lee Slattery, Richard Sterne, Peter Whiteford **141**: Ryan Cairns, Louis Calitz, Matthew Carvell, Nacho Elvira, Steven Ferreira, Andreas Hartø, Nic Henning, Damien McGrane, Brinson Paolini, Brandon Pieters, Phillip Price, Adrien Saddier, Steve Surry, Chris Swanepoel, Ulrich van den Berg, Graham van der Merwe, Tjaart van der Walt, Paul Waring **142**: Oliver Bekker, Keenan Davidse, Tyrone Ferreira, Scott Jamieson, James Kamte, Sihwan Kim, Mikko Korhonen, Tom Lewis, Darryn Lloyd, Shaun Norris, Kevin Phelan, Lyle Rowe, Simon Wakefield, Steve Webster **143**: Connor Arendell, Jacques Blaauw, Merrick Bremner, Hendrik Buhrmann, Jack Doherty, Pablo Martin Benavides, Alan McLean, Jamie McLeary, Lindani Ndwandwe, J.J. Senekal, Marc Warren, Mark Williams **144**: Kristoffer Broberg, Johan Carlsson, Jens Dantorp, Oliver Fisher, Dylan Frittelli, Jared Harvey, David Higgins, Titch Moore, Matthew Nixon, Andrea Pavan, Teboho Sefatsa, Sam Walker, Brady Watt **145**: Bryce Bibby, Magnus A. Carlsson, Charl Coetzee, James Kingston, Chris Paisley, Atti Schwartzel, Joel Sjoholm, Ockie Strydom **146**: Stefan Andersen, Marco Crespi, Andrew Curlewis, Rhys Davies, Mark Foster, Stuart Manley, P.H. McIntyre, John Parry, Theunis Spangenberg, Justin Turner **147**: M.J. Daffue, Bryce Easton, T.I. Mazibuko, Thomas Pieters, Victor Riu, Jake Roos, Toto Thimba Jr., Ruan de Smidt **148**: Warren Abery, Carlos Del Moral, Niclas Fasth, Adam Gee, Alex Haindl, Doug McGuigan, Allan Versfeld **149**: Estanislao Goya, J.B. Hansen, Ross McGowan, Anthony Michael, Jake Redman, Allister de Kock **150**: Sipho Bujela, Jamie Elson, Jacques Kruysjwik, Peter Lawrie, Thabo Maseko, C. Mowat **151**: Kenneth Dube, Vaughn Groenewald **152**: Greg Jacobs, Ryan Strauss **153**: Martin Du Toit **154**: Grant Muller **155**: Desvonde Botes, Yubin Jung, Duncan Stewart **157**: John Bele **159**: Michiel Bothma **WD**: Thomas Levet (69), Bradford Vaughan (71)

FIRST ROUND		SECOND ROUND		THIRD ROUND	
Alastair Forsyth	64 (-7)	Edoardo Molinari	132 (-11)	Thomas Aiken	198 (-17)
Justin Walters	64 (-7)	Craig Lee	132 (-11)	Justin Walters	198 (-17)
Edoardo Molinari	64 (-7)	David Horsey	133 (-10)	Jin Jeong	200 (-15)
8 Players	65 (-7)	**George Coetzee**	133 (-10)	Roope Kakko	201 (-14)
George Coetzee	65 (-7)			**George Coetzee**	202 (-13)

OWR: 1 of top 50 entered - Rating: 70 - Points to 27th - Coetzee: 20 points, to 59th in OWR

Africa Open
East London Golf Club - East London, South Africa
Champion: Thomas Aiken

Feb 13 - Feb 16
6,632 yards   Par 73
Purse: €1 Million

Thirty-year-old South African Thomas Aiken claimed his 10th career victory and his third on the European Tour, coming from behind with a closing 67, then defeating England's Oliver Fisher on the first hole of sudden death in the Africa Open at the short but venerable East London Golf Club. Behind opening rounds of 66-65-66, Aiken began Sunday four shots behind Argentina's young Emiliano Grillo, who'd launched himself to the top of the leaderboard with middle rounds of 63-62 over one of the E Tour's easiest scoring courses. Having recently finished second in Dubai, Grillo seemed poised for a breakthrough victory, but those hopes were quickly dashed on Sunday when he stunningly took a nine on the 446-yard 1st hole before limping to the turn in an inglorious 43 strokes. To his great credit, Grillo would ultimately rally to birdie the last five holes en route to tying for fifth, but by this time Aiken had notched key birdies at the 15th and 16th to draw even with the 25-year-old Fisher, who'd carded a second round 63 but on Sunday could manage no better than a 69, which left both players tied on 264. Contested over the downhill 410-yard 18th, the playoff was a brief one as Aiken quickly rolled in a 30-footer for birdie to secure the title. His victory continued a long trend of South African dominance of European Tour events played on home soil, as Aiken was the 10th home-grown winner in the last 13 such tournaments, the 36th overall in 58 all-time E Tour events, and the fifth straight in the five-year history of the African Open. It was, however, his first E Tour triumph in his native land, with his previous victories coming in the 2011 Spanish Open and the 2013 Avantha Masters, in India.

1	Thomas Aiken	66-65-66-67	264	€158,500		Rhys Davies	64-71-70-68	273	€7,000
2	Oliver Fisher	66-63-66-69	264	€115,000		Robert Dinwiddie	69-68-68-68	273	€7,000
3=	John Hahn	65-61-71-68	265	€59,150		Roope Kakko	69-67-69-68	273	€7,000
	David Horsey	66-64-70-65	265	€59,150		James Kamte	69-64-70-70	273	€7,000
5=	Richard Bland	64-69-64-69	266	€32,700		P.H. McIntyre	69-67-70-67	273	€7,000
	Darren Fichardt	66-67-67-66	266	€32,700		Jamie McLeary	69-68-69-67	273	€7,000
	Emiliano Grillo	68-63-62-73	266	€32,700		Garth Mulroy	64-68-70-71	273	€7,000
	Jaco Van Zyl	69-65-67-65	266	€32,700		Danie van Tonder	70-66-69-68	273	€7,000
9=	Lucas Bjerregaard	64-67-69-68	268	€18,950		Mark Williams	67-65-71-70	273	€7,000
	Keith Horne	68-69-66-65	268	€18,950	44=	Jose-Filipe Lima	67-67-69-71	274	€5,500
	Damien McGrane	67-69-67-65	268	€18,950		Neil Schietekat	69-68-70-67	274	€5,500
	Ulrich Van Den Berg	66-68-65-69	268	€18,950		Brandon Stone	66-71-71-66	274	€5,500
13=	Stuart Manley	68-69-65-67	269	€14,867		Dawie van der Walt	68-66-70-70	274	€5,500
	Adrian Otaegui	69-65-68-67	269	€14,867		Simon Wakefield	66-67-72-69	274	€5,500
	Fabrizio Zanotti	65-66-68-70	269	€14,867	49=	Jacques Blaauw	70-65-71-69	275	€4,500
16=	Jens Dantorp	69-63-68-70	270	€12,950		Daniel Brooks	70-67-69-69	275	€4,500
	Jean Hugo	68-66-67-69	270	€12,950		Jorge Campillo	70-65-75-65	275	€4,500
	Wade Ormsby	70-64-69-67	270	€12,950		Sihwan Kim	68-68-71-68	275	€4,500
	J.J. Senekal	66-71-69-64	270	€12,950		Morten Madsen	72-63-68-72	275	€4,500
20=	Grégory Bourdy	65-72-69-65	271	€10,814	54=	Jaco Ahlers	69-68-69-70	276	€3,520
	Daniel Im	69-67-66-69	271	€10,814		Edouard Dubois	69-67-71-69	276	€3,520
	Jbe' Kruger	67-69-67-68	271	€10,814		Adam Gee	66-65-73-72	276	€3,520
	Ricardo Santos	62-66-73-70	271	€10,814		Michael Hoey	68-68-70-70	276	€3,520
	Lee Slattery	67-68-68-68	271	€10,814		Patrik Sjoland	66-65-76-69	276	€3,520
	Justin Walters	66-69-67-69	271	€10,814	59	Adrien Saddier	70-66-76-65	277	€3,100
	Ruan de Smidt	68-66-69-68	271	€10,814	60=	Oliver Bekker	70-67-66-75	278	€2,950
27=	Charl Coetzee	71-66-70-65	272	€8,756		Tjaart Van der Walt	67-68-70-73	278	€2,950
	David Drysdale	65-70-71-66	272	€8,756	62=	Adilson da Silva	68-69-71-71	279	€2,650
	Jared Harvey	67-69-66-70	272	€8,756		Jason Knutzon	71-66-72-70	279	€2,650
	Mikko Korhonen	72-63-71-66	272	€8,756		Victor Riu	66-67-71-75	279	€2,650
	James Morrison	66-69-72-65	272	€8,756		Sam Walker	67-70-70-72	279	€2,650
	Matthew Nixon	66-70-69-67	272	€8,756	66	Heinrich Bruiners	66-71-75-70	282	€2,400
	Mark Tullo	66-71-66-69	272	€8,756	67	Chris Doak	69-67-67-84	287	€2,300
34=	Gaganjeet Bhullar	67-67-68-71	273	€7,000					

Out Of The Money: 138: Fredrik Andersson Hed, Drikus Bruyns, Francois Calmels, Magnus A. Carlsson, Wallie Coetsee, Louis de Jager, Bryce Easton, Richard Finch, Trevor Fisher Jr., Andreas Hartø, David Higgins, Anthony Michael, Thomas Pieters, Jake Redman **139**: Matthew Carvell, Alastair Forsyth, Estanislao Goya, James Kingston, Alexander Levy, Darryn Lloyd, Gareth Maybin, Titch Moore, Kevin Phelan, Phillip Price, Lyle Rowe, Teboho Sefatsa, Duncan Stewart, Rhys West **140**: Warren Abery, Connor Arendell, Merrick Bremner, Ryan Cairns, Marco Crespi, Keenan Davidse, Nacho Elvira, Tyrone Ferreira, Justin Harding, Shiv Kapur, Maximilian Kieffer, Craig Lee, Thabo Maseko, Doug McGuigan, Brinson Paolini, Robert Rock, Atti Schwartzel, Divan Van Den Heever **141**: Dean Burmester, Andrew Curlewis, Eduardo De La Riva, Martin Du Toit, Simon Dyson, Michael Hollick, Mikael Lundberg, Pablo Martin Benavides, Shaun Norris, Allan Versfeld, Brady Watt **142**: Le Roux Ferreira, Ross McGowan, Tyrone Mordt, Steve Surry, Chris Swanepoel, Ryan Tipping, Graham Van der Merwe **143**: Dylan Frittelli, Lorenzo Gagli, Søren Hansen, James Heath, Madalisto Muthiya, Colin Nel, Grant Veenstra, Erik van Rooyen **144**: Matthew Baldwin, Daan Huizing **145**: Desvonde Botes, Alan McLean, Jake Roos **146**: Hendrik Buhrmann, Vaughn Groenewald, Peter Whiteford **147**: Jack Doherty, Brett Liddle **148**: John Parry, Neo Thubisi **149**: Peter Hedblom **152**: Michiel Bothma **154**: Alex Haindl **WD**: J.C. Ritchie **DQ**: Mpho Mafishe (76)

FIRST ROUND		SECOND ROUND		THIRD ROUND	
Ricardo Santos	62 (-9)	John Hahn	126 (-16)	Emiliano Grillo	193 (-20)
Lucas Bjerregaard	64 (-7)	Ricardo Santos	128 (-14)	Oliver Fisher	195 (-18)
Rhys Davies	64 (-7)	Oliver Fisher	129 (-13)	Richard Bland	197 (-16)
Garth Mulroy	64 (-7)	Fabrizio Zanotti	131 (-11)	**Thomas Aiken**	197 (-16)
Richard Bland	64 (-7)	**Thomas Aiken**	131 (-11)	John Hahn	197 (-16)
Thomas Aiken	66 (-5)				

OWR: 0 of top 50 entered - Rating: 25 - Points to 26th - Aiken: 20 points, to 79th in OWR

Tshwane Open
Copperleaf Golf & Country Estate - Centurion, South Africa
Champion: Ross Fisher

Feb 27 - Mar 2
7,964 yards   Par 72
Purse: €1.5 Million

Former Ryder Cup player Ross Fisher enjoyed a hot week on the greens at the second playing of the Tshwane Open and parlayed it into his fifth career European Tour victory, but his first since that Ryder Cup year of 2010. Fisher's early rounds of 66-65-67 staked him to an imposing five-stroke lead over the Copperleaf Golf & Country Estate course which, at 7,964 altitude-enhanced yards, was the longest in E Tour history. But on a Sunday dotted with intermittent rain, he had trouble keeping his momentum up, carding only two birdies and a bogey as he played the outward half in one-under-par 35. This allowed his playing partner, Northern Ireland's Michael Hoey to charge into the mix, and as Hoey had carded three birdies and an eagle through the 11th hole, he briefly pulled to within one. But promptly Hoey double-bogeyed the 462-yard 12th, leaving as Fisher's primary late challengers homestanding Danie van Tonder (who made his move with late birdies at the 16th and 17th en route to a closing 66) and 2013 Q School medalist Carlos Del Moral, who would have matched that number had he not bogeyed both the 14th and 17th. But as both men crept within two in the late going, Fisher responded by holing a 30-foot eagle putt at the par-5 15th - his second eagle on the 632-yarder in three days - essentially salting away the title. With a bogey at the last, his final margin of victory was three over Hoey and van Tonder, with De Moral taking solo fourth, four strokes off the pace.

1	Ross Fisher	66-65-67-70	268	€237,750		Haydn Porteous	70-70-69-74	283	€12,015
2=	Danie van Tonder	66-70-69-66	271	€138,150		Jens Dantorp	70-69-69-75	283	€12,015
	Michael Hoey	69-65-69-68	271	€138,150		Heinrich Bruiners	69-70-69-75	283	€12,015
4	Carlos Del Moral	68-65-71-68	272	€73,650		James Kamte	72-69-67-75	283	€12,015
5	Hennie Otto	71-65-69-68	273	€61,950	39=	Ryan Cairns	70-69-74-71	284	€9,450
6=	Chris Wood	67-68-72-68	275	€44,750		Søren Kjeldsen	72-69-71-72	284	€9,450
	Darren Fichardt	66-68-71-70	275	€44,750		Jaco Van Zyl	71-70-70-73	284	€9,450
	Kevin Phelan	68-69-68-70	275	€44,750		Alex Haindl	72-68-70-74	284	€9,450
9	Merrick Bremner	69-69-67-71	276	€32,400		Jaco Ahlers	71-66-72-75	284	€9,450
10=	Trevor Fisher Jr.	65-69-71-72	277	€27,100		Justin Harding	70-67-72-75	284	€9,450
	Edoardo Molinari	70-65-70-72	277	€27,100		Shane Lowry	68-71-70-75	284	€9,450
	Simon Dyson	65-68-71-73	277	€27,100	46=	Andy Sullivan	69-69-78-69	285	€7,800
13	Morten Madsen	67-65-75-71	278	€23,550		C.J. Du Plessis	71-69-73-72	285	€7,800
14	Robert Rock	70-71-65-73	279	€22,050		Jared Harvey	66-72-74-73	285	€7,800
15=	David Howell	69-69-74-68	280	€19,450		Tyrrell Hatton	70-69-70-76	285	€7,800
	Shiv Kapur	67-74-70-69	280	€19,450	50=	Tyrone Ferreira	72-69-75-70	286	€6,450
	Matthew Baldwin	72-69-68-71	280	€19,450		Erik van Rooyen	66-72-74-74	286	€6,450
	Keith Horne	74-67-67-72	280	€19,450		George Coetzee	70-70-71-75	286	€6,450
	Oliver Bekker	70-67-69-74	280	€19,450		Gaganjeet Bhullar	70-65-74-77	286	€6,450
	Jake Roos	69-65-72-74	280	€19,450		Maximilian Kieffer	68-70-71-77	286	€6,450
21=	Lucas Bjerregaard	67-71-71-72	281	€16,650	55=	Anthony Wall	68-71-76-72	287	€5,138
	Mikko Korhonen	70-68-70-73	281	€16,650		V. Groenewald	71-68-73-75	287	€5,138
	Paul Waring	70-70-68-73	281	€16,650		James Morrison	69-70-72-76	287	€5,138
24=	Jean Hugo	68-68-76-70	282	€14,850		Ricardo Santos	68-71-71-77	287	€5,138
	Kristoffer Broberg	67-74-71-70	282	€14,850	59=	T. van der Walt	69-71-74-74	288	€4,575
	Thomas Aiken	69-71-70-72	282	€14,850		Daan Huizing	68-71-70-79	288	€4,575
	Oliver Fisher	73-68-69-72	282	€14,850	61=	Doug McGuigan	71-70-75-73	289	€4,275
	Ruan de Smidt	69-71-69-73	282	€14,850		Tyrone Mordt	70-71-74-74	289	€4,275
29=	Grégory Bourdy	72-69-73-69	283	€12,015	63=	Louis de Jager	71-69-75-75	290	€3,900
	Callum Mowat	72-69-71-71	283	€12,015		Jack Doherty	69-71-75-75	290	€3,900
	Marc Warren	73-68-71-71	283	€12,015		Warren Abery	71-70-73-76	290	€3,900
	Daniel Brooks	72-67-72-72	283	€12,015	66=	Alejandro Cañizares	70-71-75-75	291	€3,525
	Nacho Elvira	71-67-72-73	283	€12,015		Søren Hansen	70-70-76-75	291	€3,525
	James Kingston	71-69-70-73	283	€12,015	68	Michael Jonzon	72-69-76-76	293	€3,300

Out Of The Money: **142:** Colin Nel, Patrik Sjoland, Peter Whiteford, Jacques Blaauw, Titch Moore, Johan Carlsson, Connor Arendell, Neil Schietekat, Mark Foster, Toto Thimba Jr, Romain Wattel, Michael Hollick, Adrian Otaegui **143:** Pablo Martin Benavides, Divan van den Heever, Jamie McLeary, Simon Wakefield, Wallie Coetsee, Justin Walters, Tyrone Ryan, David Drysdale, Christiaan Basson, Jbe' Kruger, Eddie Pepperell, Joel Sjoholm **144:** Richard Bland, Graeme Storm, Francois Calmels, Jorge Campillo, Magnus A. Carlsson, Tommy Fleetwood, Damien McGrane, Adilson da Silva, P.H. McIntyre, Andrea Pavan, Brandon Pieters, Omar Sandys **145:** Garrick Porteous, Andrew Curlewis, Lyle Rowe, Ross McGowan, Brinson Paolini, Andreas Hartø, Charl Coetzee, Niclas Fasth, Ulrich van den Berg, Robert Dinwiddie **146:** Keenan Davidse, Gert Myburgh, J.J. Senekal, Bryce Easton, Gareth Maybin, Chris Doak, Roberto Lupini **147:** Michiel Bothma, Martin Du Toit, Sam Walker, Alan McLean **148:** Mikael Lundberg, Estanislao Goya, Stuart Manley, Morne Buys, Grant Veenstra, J.B. Hansen, Peter Karmis, Dean Burmester, Shaun Norris, Allan Versfeld, Thomas Pieters, Grant Muller **149:** Grégory Havret, James Heath, Lindani Ndwandwe, Hendrik Buhrmann **150:** Fredrik Andersson Hed, Dylan Frittelli **151:** Sipho Bujela, Graham van der Merwe **152:** Dawie van der Walt, Peter Lawrie, Scott Jamieson **154:** Jose-Filipe Lima **155:** Ryan Strauss, Nic Henning, Chris Swanepoel **WD:** Yubin Jung (83), Danny Willett, Mikhail Tewary

FIRST ROUND		SECOND ROUND		THIRD ROUND	
Simon Dyson	65 (-7)	**Ross Fisher**	131 (-13)	**Ross Fisher**	198 (-18)
Trevor Fisher Jr.	65 (-7)	Morton Madsen	132 (-12)	Michael Hoey	203 (-13)
5 Players	66 (-6)	Simon Dyson	133 (-11)	Simon Dyson	204 (-12)
Ross Fisher	66 (-6)	Carlos Del Moral	133 (-11)	Carlos Del Moral	204 (-12)
		4 Players	134 (-10)	7 Players	205 (-11)

OWR: 0 of top 50 entered - Rating: 65 - Points to 23rd - Fisher: 20 points, to 68th in OWR

Trophée Hassan II	Mar 13 - Mar 16
Golf du Palais Royal - Agadir, Morocco	6,951 yards Par 72
Champion: Alejandro Cañizares	Purse: €1.5 Million

Spain's 31-year-old Alejandro Cañizares ended an eight-year victory drought in impressive style, running away to a five-shot wire-to-wire triumph at the Trophée Hassan II in Morocco. The son of former five-time European Tour winner Jose Maria Cañizares, Alejandro opened with rounds of 62-68 over the 6,951-yard Golf du Palais Royal course, comfortably separating himself from all but England's Seve Benson, who trailed him by one after both the first and second rounds. Benson, for his part, fell back to the field on Saturday via a disappointing 74, allowing Cañizares to build a commanding six-stroke 54-hole lead after posting a relatively uneventful third round 69. A Cañizares bogey at the 203-yard 2nd on Sunday may have extended a ray of hope to his pursuers, but when he reeled of five birdies over his next 11 holes, everyone else was left far in arrears and playing for second; indeed, Cañizares at one point led by eight, and only an irrelevant double-bogey at the 18th kept the winning margin below seven. Though his form had been better of late (notably posting a T5 in Qatar in January), the title was Cañizares' first since the 2006 Russian Open and lifted him to a career-best 89th in the OWR. Second place was claimed by England's Andy Sullivan (who came from miles off the pace with a closing 63 that included 10 birdies) while Benson recovered from his disappointing Saturday to close with 71, tying Magnus Carlsson for third.

1	Alejandro Cañizares	62-68-69-70	269	€250,000	37=	Mikko Ilonen	69-73-73-71	286	€9,900
2	Andy Sullivan	66-73-72-63	274	€166,660		Simon Dyson	73-70-71-72	286	€9,900
3=	Magnus A. Carlsson	65-71-72-68	276	€84,450		Ross Fisher	70-73-71-72	286	€9,900
	Seve Benson	63-68-74-71	276	€84,450		Connor Arendell	65-71-76-74	286	€9,900
5=	Rafael Cabrera-Bello	68-67-75-67	277	€53,700		Danny Willett	72-70-70-74	286	€9,900
	Richard Bland	69-70-70-68	277	€53,700		Alexander Levy	70-72-69-75	286	€9,900
	Wade Ormsby	68-71-70-68	277	€53,700	43=	Simon Wakefield	72-73-70-72	287	€8,250
8=	Tom Lewis	69-74-70-65	278	€33,700		Tyrrell Hatton	73-72-69-73	287	€8,250
	David Horsey	72-64-72-70	278	€33,700		Nacho Elvira	70-75-68-74	287	€8,250
	Paul Waring	72-69-67-70	278	€33,700		David Drysdale	73-67-72-75	287	€8,250
11=	Brett Rumford	73-71-70-66	280	€23,950		Søren Kjeldsen	74-70-68-75	287	€8,250
	Lucas Bjerregaard	69-73-71-67	280	€23,950	48=	Søren Hansen	74-69-75-70	288	€6,900
	George Coetzee	69-69-74-68	280	€23,950		Alexandre Kaleka	72-73-72-71	288	€6,900
	Richie Ramsay	72-71-68-69	280	€23,950		Marco Crespi	71-74-69-74	288	€6,900
	Jorge Campillo	71-69-70-70	280	€23,950		Marcel Siem	69-69-75-75	288	€6,900
	Robert Karlsson	71-67-72-70	280	€23,950	52=	Matthew Baldwin	71-74-77-67	289	€5,700
17=	Jens Dantorp	73-71-69-68	281	€18,425		Eduardo De La Riva	70-74-76-69	289	€5,700
	Stephen Dodd	68-73-71-69	281	€18,425		Grégory Havret	72-71-73-73	289	€5,700
	Grégory Bourdy	68-69-74-70	281	€18,425		Mark Tullo	74-69-70-76	289	€5,700
	Marc Warren	66-73-70-72	281	€18,425	56=	Daan Huizing	74-70-76-70	290	€4,612
	Shiv Kapur	70-71-67-73	281	€18,425		Maximilian Kieffer	71-72-74-73	290	€4,612
	Robert-Jan Derksen	69-70-67-75	281	€18,425		Shane Lowry	72-72-73-73	290	€4,612
23=	James Morrison	69-69-75-69	282	€16,275		Daniel Brooks	72-70-72-76	290	€4,612
	Tommy Fleetwood	66-72-73-71	282	€16,275	60=	Patrik Sjoland	70-74-76-71	291	€3,975
25=	Edoardo Molinari	73-70-74-66	283	€14,700		Roope Kakko	70-73-75-73	291	€3,975
	Kristoffer Broberg	75-70-72-66	283	€14,700		David Howell	72-69-75-75	291	€3,975
	Daniel Im	71-73-69-70	283	€14,700		Gaganjeet Bhullar	67-73-74-77	291	€3,975
	Adrien Saddier	72-72-69-70	283	€14,700	64=	Damien McGrane	70-73-76-73	292	€3,450
	Rhys Davies	68-73-71-71	283	€14,700		Francois Calmels	70-74-73-75	292	€3,450
30=	Michael Hoey	68-70-76-70	284	€12,900		Estanislao Goya	73-69-74-76	292	€3,450
	Florian Fritsch	72-70-70-72	284	€12,900	67	Jose Manuel Lara	72-73-71-79	295	€3,150
	Richard Green	70-73-69-72	284	€12,900	68=	Peter Whiteford	67-78-79-74	298	€2,925
33=	Robert Dinwiddie	71-71-73-70	285	€11,438		Duncan Stewart	71-74-74-79	298	€2,925
	Gary Stal	73-71-70-71	285	€11,438	70	Raphaël Jacquelin	71-71-79-78	299	€2,740
	Bernd Wiesberger	71-73-70-71	285	€11,438	71	Edouard Dubois	68-75-81-77	301	€2,250
	Robert Rock	71-68-71-75	285	€11,438					

Out Of The Money: 146: Chris Wood, Paul McGinley, Niclas Fasth, Adam Gee, Sihwan Kim, Adrian Otaegui, Andrea Pavan, Brinson Paolini, Younes El Hassani, Kevin Phelan, Sam Walker, Jose-Filipe Lima, Marcel Schneider **147**: J.B. Hansen, Simon Thornton, Ricardo Santos, Simon Khan, Craig Lee, Jason Knutzon, José María Olazábal, Jaco Van Zyl, Victor Riu **148**: Masamichi Ito, Thomas Pieters, Mark Foster, Jack Doherty, Alastair Forsyth, Andreas Hartø, James Heath, Johan Carlsson **149**: Romain Wattel, Faycal Serghini, Peter Lawrie, Carl Yuan **150**: Pablo Larrazábal, Graeme Storm, Carlos Del Moral **151**: Eddie Pepperell, John Hahn, Fabrizio Zanotti **152**: David Higgins, James Kingston, Jamie McLeary **153**: Stuart Manley **154**: John Parry **155**: Zane Scotland **156**: Matthew Nixon **157**: Yasin Ali **158**: Morten Madsen, Amine Joudar **159**: Mikael Lundberg **160**: Ayoub Lguirati **WD**: Mikko Korhonen (79), Chris Doak (79), Anthony Wall

FIRST ROUND		SECOND ROUND		THIRD ROUND	
Alejandro Cañizares	62 (-10)	**Alejandro Cañizares**	130 (-14)	**Alejandro Cañizares**	199 (-17)
Seve Benson	63 (-9)	Seve Benson	131 (-13)	Seve Benson	205 (-11)
Connor Arendell	65 (-7)	Rafael Cabrera-Bello	135 (-9)	Robert-Jan Derksen	206 (-10)
Magnus A. Carlsson	65 (-7)	3 Players	136 (-8)	5 Players	208 (-8)
3 Players	66 (-6)				

OWR: 0 of top 50 entered - Rating: 57 - Points to 29th - Cañizares: 24 points to 89th in OWR

NH Collection Open

La Reserva de Sotogrande Club de Golf - Cadiz, Spain
Champion: Marco Crespi

Apr 3 - Apr 6
7,234 yards Par 72
Purse: €600,000

Battling against a particularly light field on the eve of The Masters, Italy's Marco Crespi claimed his first European Tour victory at the inaugural playing of the NH Collection Open, edging homestanding Jordi García Pinto and Scotland's Richie Ramsay in Cadiz, Spain. After opening with rounds of 70-73, Crespi logged six back nine birdies en route to a Saturday 66 that pulled him within one of the 54-hole leader, England's Matthew Nixon. But as Nixon made his way around Sunday's front nine in 37, Crespi birdied the 1st, 5th, 8th and 9th to turn in 32 and vault into the lead. As the pressure mounted, back-to-back bogeys at the 12th and 13th provided a few moments of doubt, but a clutch bounce-back birdie at the 14th righted the ship and, in the end, would prove enough for a two-shot triumph. García Pinto was a late arrival to the party, birdieing four of his last five holes for a closing 66. Ramsay, on the other hand, might well have found the winners circle as he stood at eight under par through 10 holes on Sunday, but could do no better than eight straight pars coming home. The 35-year-old Crespi, who played the Challenge Tour in 2012 and '13, took 11 professional seasons to reach the E Tour but wasted relatively little time in making good – though as the event carried a purse of under €1.5 million, his exemption will only extend through calendar year 2015.

1	Marco Crespi	70-73-66-69	278	€100,000		35=	Johan Edfors	76-72-69-73	290	€4,200
2=	Jordi García Pinto	73-70-71-66	280	€52,110			Mikko Korhonen	71-75-71-73	290	€4,200
	Richie Ramsay	71-72-69-68	280	€52,110			Eduardo De La Riva	72-76-73-69	290	€4,200
4=	Felipe Aguilar	71-69-70-71	281	€27,720			Sihwan Kim	70-76-70-74	290	€4,200
	Matthew Nixon	72-71-65-73	281	€27,720			Lucas Bjerregaard	72-73-70-75	290	€4,200
6=	Oliver Fisher	71-72-71-68	282	€16,860			Mikael Lundberg	71-72-78-69	290	€4,200
	Marc Warren	72-67-75-68	282	€16,860		41=	Daniel Gaunt	75-70-73-73	291	€3,480
	Kristoffer Broberg	76-70-67-69	282	€16,860			Michael Jonzon	74-70-76-71	291	€3,480
	Adrian Otaegui	71-69-72-70	282	€16,860			Chris Paisley	72-72-76-71	291	€3,480
10=	Bradley Dredge	70-69-78-66	283	€11,520			Oliver Wilson	75-72-75-69	291	€3,480
	Ricardo Santos	74-70-67-72	283	€11,520			Scott Jamieson	71-72-70-78	291	€3,480
12=	Gary Stal	72-74-73-65	284	€9,288			Adrien Bernadet	76-71-78-66	291	€3,480
	Phillip Archer	74-70-73-67	284	€9,288		47=	David Drysdale	79-69-70-74	292	€2,700
	Rhys Davies	72-71-72-69	284	€9,288			Victor Riu	73-74-71-74	292	€2,700
	David Horsey	71-68-73-72	284	€9,288			Lorenzo Gagli	71-74-72-75	292	€2,700
	Tjaart Van der Walt	70-73-69-72	284	€9,288			J.B. Hansen	77-69-74-72	292	€2,700
17=	Daniel Im	72-72-71-70	285	€7,920			David Howell	71-75-70-76	292	€2,700
	Damien McGrane	74-69-70-72	285	€7,920			Jeppe Huldahl	72-73-75-72	292	€2,700
19	Matteo Delpodio	71-73-70-72	286	€7,440			Jorge Campillo	72-73-77-70	292	€2,700
20=	John Hahn	74-68-75-70	287	€6,518		54=	Jack Doherty	69-74-77-73	293	€2,100
	Alexander Levy	72-75-72-68	287	€6,518			Grégory Havret	74-70-76-73	293	€2,100
	Lasse Jensen	73-70-74-70	287	€6,518			Nacho Elvira	72-76-73-72	293	€2,100
	Jamie McLeary	73-70-74-70	287	€6,518		57=	Simon Wakefield	74-74-71-75	294	€1,830
	Connor Arendell	72-75-70-70	287	€6,518			Chris Hanson	72-76-77-69	294	€1,830
	Carlos Del Moral	73-72-72-70	287	€6,518		59=	Simon Khan	75-73-73-74	295	€1,710
	Edouard Dubois	73-73-74-67	287	€6,518			Thomas Norret	73-71-80-71	295	€1,710
	Andrew Johnston	73-72-70-72	287	€6,518		61=	Gary Lockerbie	76-70-74-76	296	€1,560
28=	Maarten Lafeber	78-69-73-68	288	€5,520			Pedro Oriol	75-73-75-73	296	€1,560
	Mark Foster	71-77-73-67	288	€5,520			Lloyd Kennedy	75-72-76-73	296	€1,560
	Byeong-Hun An	73-73-76-66	288	€5,520		64=	Jens Dantorp	71-73-73-81	298	€1,410
31=	Daniel Brooks	73-75-70-71	289	€4,890			Oscar Stark	74-71-75-78	298	€1,410
	Kevin Phelan	75-70-73-71	289	€4,890		66	Simon Thornton	74-73-75-77	299	€1,320
	Estanislao Goya	73-75-69-72	289	€4,890		67=	Thomas Levet	72-76-77-77	302	€1,230
	Andrew Marshall	74-73-71-71	289	€4,890			Cyril Bouniol	74-73-80-75	302	€1,230

Out Of The Money: **149:** Jason Barnes, Maximilian Kieffer, Joakim Lagergren, Niklas Lemke, Santiago Luna, Robert Rock, Patrik Sjoland, Duncan Stewart, Brandon Stone **150:** Alejandro Cañizares, Richard Finch, Jordi García del Mora, Andreas Hartø, James Heath, David Higgins, James Morrison, Steven Tiley **151:** Wil Besseling, Julien Guerrier, Anders Hansen, Dodge Kemmer, Espen Kofstad, Thomas Linard, Stuart Manley, Phillip Price, Jake Roos, Lee Slattery, Andy Sullivan, Pontus Widegren, Chris Wood **152:** Jason Knutzon, Tom Lewis, Andrew McArthur, Bernd Wiesberger **153:** Steven Brown, Edouard Espana, Adam Gee, Mathias Gronberg, Daan Huizing, Jose Manuel Lara, Jesus Legarrea, John Parry, Bernd Ritthammer, Adrien Saddier, Zane Scotland, Callum Shinkwin **154:** Carlos Aguilar, Agustin Domingo, Niclas Fasth, Peter Lawrie, Andrea Pavan, Niccolo Quintarelli, Joel Sjoholm, Mark Tullo, Sam Walker, Peter Whiteford **155:** Jamie Elson, Scott Henry, Alvaro Velasco **156:** Alastair Forsyth, Alexandre Kaleka **157:** Rikard Karlberg, Shane Lowry, Eddie Pepperell, Thomas Pieters **158:** Bjørn Akesson, Tim Sluiter **160:** Jens Fahrbring, Brinson Paolini **WD:** Craig Lee (78), Graeme Storm (79), Paul Waring (79), Anthony Wall (81), Marcel Siem (84), Chris Doak (86)

FIRST ROUND		SECOND ROUND		THIRD ROUND	
Jack Doherty	69 (-3)	Marc Warren	139 (-5)	Matthew Nixon	208 (-8)
Marco Crespi	70 (-2)	David Horsey	139 (-5)	**Marco Crespi**	209 (-7)
Bradley Dredge	70 (-2)	Bradley Dredge	139 (-5)	Felipe Aguilar	210 (-6)
Tjaart van der Walt	70 (-2)	Felipe Aguilar	140 (-4)	Ricardo Santos	211 (-5)
Sihwan Kim	70 (-2)	Adrian Otaegui	140 (-4)	4 Players	212 (-4)
		Marco Crespi	143 (-1)		

OWR: 0 of top 50 entered - Rating: 22 - Points to 27th - Crespi: 18 points, to 167th in OWR

Maybank Malaysian Open

Kuala Lumpur Golf & Country Club - Kuala Lumpur, Malaysia
Champion: Lee Westwood

Apr 17 - Apr 20
6,967 yards   Par 72
Purse: $2.75 Million

With 10 previous career victories on the Asian and Japan Tours, Lee Westwood has proven himself a very dangerous man on Asian soil - thus leaving nobody surprised when he claimed a wire-to-wire triumph in his first 2014 visit to the region, at the Maybank Malaysian Open. Having made the long plane flight from the previous week's Masters, Westwood seemed unaffected by the travel while opening with rounds of 65-66 to grab a four-stroke 36-hole lead. A third-round 71 brought him back to the field, however, but his one-stroke 54-hole lead suddenly blossomed to four on Sunday when leading pursuer Andy Sullivan triple-bogeyed the par-4 2nd hole. Sullivan actually clawed gamely back with birdies at the 4th, 5th and 6th, but tumbled once again thereafter, allowing Westwood to expand his lead to six via birdies at the 10th and 13th, the latter following a four-hour and 13 minute weather delay when lightning threatened the Kuala Lumpur Golf & Country Club layout. Cruising home thereafter, he would eventually birdie the 634-yard finisher to stretch the margin of victory to seven. Second place was shared by Louis Oosthuizen (who joined Westwood as the only world top-50s in the field), Bernd Wiesberger and Nicolas Colsaerts. The win came eight weeks after Westwood parted ways with swing instructor Sean Foley and broke a two-year victory drought for the soon-to-be 41-year-old. It also marked his 40th career title worldwide, including a victory in this same event 17 years earlier.

1	Lee Westwood	65-66-71-68	270	€329,615		S.S.P. Chowrasia	71-70-71-74	286	€14,264
2=	Bernd Wiesberger	69-71-70-67	277	€147,477		Bryce Easton	70-74-72-70	286	€14,264
	Louis Oosthuizen	72-68-69-68	277	€147,477		Andrew Dodt	76-67-74-69	286	€14,264
	Nicolas Colsaerts	66-69-72-70	277	€147,477		Francesco Molinari	71-74-73-68	286	€14,264
5=	Danny Willett	70-66-72-70	278	€70,802	41=	Hennie Otto	79-66-71-71	287	€11,866
	Rikard Karlberg	72-69-67-70	278	€70,802		Carlos Pigem	71-71-73-72	287	€11,866
	Julien Quesne	68-69-69-72	278	€70,802		Adilson da Silva	72-72-72-71	287	€11,866
8=	Pablo Larrazábal	74-68-70-67	279	€46,872		Prayad Marksaeng	69-72-70-76	287	€11,866
	Thomas Pieters	75-67-69-68	279	€46,872	45=	Steve Lewton	71-69-74-74	288	€10,680
10=	Anirban Lahiri	72-72-66-70	280	€26,653		Rahil Gangjee	74-68-70-76	288	€10,680
	Eduardo De La Riva	69-68-71-72	280	€26,653	47=	Nicholas Fung	72-71-73-73	289	€8,900
	Garth Mulroy	71-68-69-72	280	€26,653		Simon Dyson	73-71-73-72	289	€8,900
13=	Álvaro Quirós	73-69-71-68	281	€29,151		J.B. Hansen	72-72-73-72	289	€8,900
	Jbe' Kruger	68-71-72-70	281	€29,151		David Drysdale	71-71-75-72	289	€8,900
	Jason Knutzon	75-67-69-70	281	€29,151		Marcel Siem	72-71-74-72	289	€8,900
	Masahiro Kawamura	68-70-70-73	281	€29,151		Kheng Hwai Khor	72-72-74-71	289	€8,900
	Andy Sullivan	70-67-66-78	281	€29,151		Gavin Green (a)	74-70-75-70	289	-
18=	Michael Hoey	67-73-73-69	282	€23,469		Marc Warren	69-75-75-70	289	€8,900
	Scott Hend	70-70-72-70	282	€23,469	55=	Chiragh Kumar	74-70-75-71	290	€7,120
	Richard T. Lee	69-76-67-70	282	€23,469		Marco Crespi	71-73-75-71	290	€7,120
	Grégory Bourdy	73-70-69-70	282	€23,469	57=	Søren Kjeldsen	75-68-71-77	291	€6,197
	Wade Ormsby	70-71-69-72	282	€23,469		Romain Wattel	71-72-75-73	291	€6,197
	Ricardo Santos	67-71-70-74	282	€23,469		Siddikur Rahman	73-70-77-71	291	€6,197
24=	Prom Meesawat	70-71-74-68	283	€19,975	60=	Simon Thornton	74-68-72-78	292	€5,340
	Antonio Lascuña	70-65-77-71	283	€19,975		Peter Whiteford	73-72-72-75	292	€5,340
	Thongchai Jaidee	72-70-70-71	283	€19,975		Craig Lee	69-75-73-75	292	€5,340
	Richard Bland	73-69-69-72	283	€19,975		Robert-Jan Derksen	72-73-75-72	292	€5,340
	Tom Lewis	70-71-68-74	283	€19,975		Magnus A. Carlsson	74-69-80-69	292	€5,340
29=	Edoardo Molinari	69-73-71-71	284	€17,898	65=	N. Tantipokhakul	76-69-71-77	293	€4,549
	Scott Jamieson	68-71-70-75	284	€17,898		J. Janewattananond	73-72-73-75	293	€4,549
31=	Shiv Kapur	76-69-69-71	285	€16,712		Chawalit Plaphol	74-71-76-72	293	€4,549
	Matteo Manassero	71-72-67-75	285	€16,712	68=	Anthony Kang	71-74-75-74	294	€4,054
33=	P. Junhasavasdikul	73-71-70-72	286	€14,264		Rashid Khan	72-72-76-74	294	€4,054
	Justin Walters	71-72-71-72	286	€14,264	70	Thaworn Wiratchant	69-75-75-76	295	€3,758
	Maximilian Kieffer	70-74-69-73	286	€14,264	71	Søren Hansen	69-76-76-76	297	€3,610
	Arnond Vongvanij	70-71-73-72	286	€14,264	72	C. Phadungsil	74-71-77-76	298	€2,967

Out Of The Money: **146**: Chapchai Nirat, Sukree Othman, Jyoti Randhawa, Richie Ramsay, Shane Lowry, Graeme Storm, Sung Lee, Wei-Tze Yeh, Berry Henson, Robert Rock, Raphaël Jacquelin **147**: Ben Leong, Alastair Forsyth, Mardan Mamat, Elmer Salvador, Seve Benson, Masanori Kobayashi, Javi Colomo, Tommy Fleetwood, Morten Madsen, Mithun Perera **148**: Gunn Charoenkul, Matthew Baldwin, Jeev Milkha Singh, Grégory Havret, Thomas Levet **149**: Chan Kim, Terry Pilkadaris, David Howell, Damien McGrane, Digvijay Singh, Danny Chia, Airil Rizman Zahari, Matt Stieger, Arjun Atwal, Kieran Pratt, Peter Uihlein, Scott Barr **150**: Shaifubari Muda, Rafael Cabrera-Bello, Gaganjeet Bhullar, Joong Kyung Mo, Felipe Aguilar, Kenneth De Silva, Gi-whan Kim **151**: Shaaban Hussein, Wei Chih Lu, Sung Kang, Anders Hansen, Arie Irawan, David Horsey, Iain Steel **152**: In-Woo Lee, Ricardo González **153**: Alejandro Cañizares, Eddie Pepperell, Rizal Amin, David Lipsky, Yeon-Jin Jeong, S. Sivachandran **154**: Ervin Chang (a), Himmat Singh Rai, Panupol Pittayarat **155**: Boonchu Ruangkit, Peter Hedblom, Ramasamy Nachimuthu, Samuel Cyr, Wilson Choo **156**: Garrick Porteous, Kemarol Baharin **157**: Unho Park, Emiliano Grillo **159**: Mohd Wafiyuddin (a), Joonas Granberg **160**: Chi-Huang Tsai, Mohd Iylia Jamil **161**: John Parry **162**: Mikko Ilonen **163**: S. Murthy **165**: Solomon E. Rosidin (a) **WD**: Seuk-Hyun Baek (70), Daisuke Kataoka (7), Wen-Tang Lin

FIRST ROUND		SECOND ROUND		THIRD ROUND	
Lee Westwood	65 (-7)	**Lee Westwood**	131 (-13)	**Lee Westwood**	202 (-14)
Nicolas Colsaerts	66 (-6)	Nicolas Colsaerts	135 (-9)	Andy Sullivan	203 (-13)
Ricardo Santos	67 (-5)	Antonio Lascuña	135 (-9)	Julien Quesne	206 (-10)
Michael Hoey	67 (-5)	Danny Willett	136 (-8)	Nicolas Colsaerts	207 (-9)
4 Players	68 (-4)	3 Players	137 (-7)	6 Players	208 (-8)

OWR: 2 of top 50 entered - Rating: 154 - Points to 40th - Westwood: 32 points, to 30th in OWR

Volvo China Open

Genzon Golf Club - Shenzhen, China
Champion: Alexander Levy

Apr 24 - Apr 27
7,145 yards   Par 72
Purse: $2.136 Million

Despite a few anxious moments on the final nine, 23-year-old Frenchman Alexander Levy broke through for his first victory on the European Tour, claiming a four-shot triumph over England's Tommy Fleetwood at the Volvo China Open. After opening with a 68 in the tournament's maiden visit to the Genzon Golf Club, Levy surged to a four-stroke halfway lead via a near-perfect second round in which he recorded eight birdies and an eagle for a career-best 10-under-par 62. After turning in 35 on Saturday, he appeared on the verge of a runaway after birdieing the 11th, 12th and 13th in succession, but late bogeys at the 14th and 16th saw him home in 70, good enough to close Saturday with a three-shot margin. Having slept on his first solo 54-hole lead, Levy then began Sunday playing strong, methodical golf, carding three birdies over his first 13 holes to hold a seemingly commanding five-shot cushion. But a sloppy double-bogey at the par-4 15th gave the field hope, and when Fleetwood birdied the par-5 17th moments later, the outcome for the first time began to seem in doubt. But rather than simply hang on, Levy reached the 17th with a 3-iron second to card a birdie of his own, then clinched the title in style with a final birdie at the 456-yard finisher to win by four. Long-hitting Spaniard Álvaro Quirós, the first round leader, closed with a disappointing 72 to take solo third, while world number three Henrik Stenson, who could have leapfrogged all the way into the number one spot with a victory, overcame a mid-week bout with the flu to post a Sunday 65, good enough only to tie for fifth.

1	Alexander Levy	68-62-70-69	269	€389,151		Robert-Jan Derksen	70-69-71-73	283	€18,388
2	Tommy Fleetwood	70-68-67-68	273	€259,434	36=	Ricardo Santos	71-73-74-66	284	€16,344
3	Álvaro Quirós	67-68-68-72	275	€146,166		Zheng Ou-yang	72-72-73-67	284	€16,344
4	Francesco Molinari	70-70-69-67	276	€116,746		Pablo Larrazábal	71-70-72-71	284	€16,344
5=	Anders Hansen	73-68-73-63	277	€83,590		Oliver Fisher	73-70-69-72	284	€16,344
	Henrik Stenson	71-70-71-65	277	€83,590	40=	Romain Wattel	70-74-74-67	285	€14,010
	Ian Poulter	69-74-67-67	277	€83,590		Tom Lewis	72-69-74-70	285	€14,010
8=	Rafa Cabrera-Bello	70-70-71-67	278	€48,099		Marco Crespi	71-69-74-71	285	€14,010
	Michael Hoey	69-72-69-68	278	€48,099		Grégory Havret	70-73-70-72	285	€14,010
	Andy Sullivan	71-68-69-70	278	€48,099		Jose-Filipe Lima	72-70-71-72	285	€14,010
	Simon Dyson	67-71-69-71	278	€48,099		Matthew Griffin	71-73-69-72	285	€14,010
	Mikko Ilonen	69-68-67-74	278	€48,099	46=	David Drysdale	70-71-75-70	286	€11,675
13=	Eduardo De La Riva	73-71-71-64	279	€36,658		Marcel Siem	71-69-75-71	286	€11,675
	Hennie Otto	70-71-69-69	279	€36,658		Richard Bland	69-75-71-71	286	€11,675
15=	Jbe' Kruger	74-67-72-67	280	€32,222		Masahiro Kawamura	73-69-72-72	286	€11,675
	Il-Hwan Park	68-72-72-68	280	€32,222	50=	Felipe Aguilar	71-71-75-70	287	€9,807
	Nacho Elvira	69-74-68-69	280	€32,222		A Shun Wu	69-74-73-71	287	€9,807
	Chris Doak	71-68-70-71	280	€32,222		Ji-Man Kang	71-72-70-74	287	€9,807
19=	Grégory Bourdy	71-72-70-68	281	€27,225		Hao-Tong Li	73-69-67-78	287	€9,807
	Morten Madsen	73-68-71-69	281	€27,225	54=	Tyrrell Hatton	68-71-75-74	288	€8,172
	Prom Meesawat	72-69-71-69	281	€27,225		Jason Dufner	73-71-69-75	288	€8,172
	Julien Quesne	69-71-70-71	281	€27,225		Wen-Chong Liang	70-74-69-75	288	€8,172
	Adrian Otaegui	68-66-71-76	281	€27,225	57=	Edoardo Molinari	71-73-75-70	289	€7,005
24=	David Horsey	68-76-70-68	282	€22,532		Eddie Pepperell	70-72-75-72	289	€7,005
	Danny Willett	73-71-71-67	282	€22,532		Gaganjeet Bhullar	71-70-73-75	289	€7,005
	Scott Jamieson	71-68-73-70	282	€22,532	60=	Seve Benson	74-69-76-71	290	€6,304
	Emiliano Grillo	70-71-71-70	282	€22,532		Richard Green	70-71-77-72	290	€6,304
	Scott Strange	71-71-70-70	282	€22,532		Søren Kjeldsen	72-72-72-74	290	€6,304
	Mark Brown	75-69-68-70	282	€22,532	63	Brett Rumford	68-75-74-74	291	€5,837
	Raphaël Jacquelin	69-67-75-71	282	€22,532	64	Jorge Campillo	71-70-76-75	292	€5,604
	Terry Pilkadaris	73-71-67-71	282	€22,532	65=	Simon Khan	69-75-77-72	293	€5,254
32=	Maximilian Kieffer	73-71-69-70	283	€18,388		Stuart Manley	70-74-76-73	293	€5,254
	Lee Slattery	72-72-69-70	283	€18,388	67	Kang-Chun Wu	73-70-76-75	294	€4,903
	Richie Ramsay	69-68-74-72	283	€18,388	68	Anthony Wall	72-72-77-74	295	€4,670

Out Of The Money: **145**: Nick Cullen, Niclas Fasth, Ross Fisher, David McKenzie, Matthew Nixon, Dan Woltman **146**: Kristoffer Broberg, Dae-Sub Kim, Craig Lee, Wade Ormsby, Graeme Storm, Peter Uihlein, Peter Whiteford, Chris Wood, Tian Yuan **147**: Matthew Baldwin, Magnus A. Carlsson, Shiv Kapur, Bio Kim, Sihwan Kim, Masanori Kobayashi, Damien McGrane, Guan Tianlang (a) **148**: Johan Edfors, J.B. Hansen, Peter Lawrie, Xin-yang Li, Gareth Maybin, Victor Riu, Zihan She (a), Jeev Milkha Singh, Paul Waring **149**: Ding-gen Chen, Cheng Jin (a), Shane Lowry, Jamie McLeary, James Stewart, Lian-Wel Zhang **150**: Ze-cheng Dou (a), Mark Foster, Ming Jie Huang, Daan Huizing, Yeon-Jin Jeong, Chung-ho Mou, Garth Mulroy, Dong Su, Justin Walters **151**: Alejandro Cañizares, Zhi-peng Fan, Ricardo González, Søren Hansen, Roope Kakko, Yan-Wei Liu (a), Aaron Townsend, Zhi Xie, Jin Zhang (a) **152**: Nicolas Colsaerts, Stephen Dodd, Ze-yu He, David Howell, Wen-Yi Huang, Do Kim, Robert Rock, Marc Warren **153**: Shao-cai He, Da-xing Jin, Guo-wu Zhou **154**: Yi Cao, Johan Carlsson, Rhein Gibson, Jun-Seok Lee, John Parry, Andrea Pavan, Ming-hao Wang, Xu Wang **155**: Sung Kang **156**: Jason Norris **157**: Mu Hu, Guang-Ming Yang, Xin-Jun Zhang **158**: Peter Hedblom, Gareth Paddison **161**: Thomas Levet **162**: Chuan-Bing Feng **163**: Zi-hao Chen (a) **164**: Daniel Popovic   **WD**: Ren Han (79), Sam Yi (90)

FIRST ROUND			SECOND ROUND			THIRD ROUND	
Álvaro Quirós	67 (-5)		**Alexander Levy**	130 (-14)		**Alexander Levy**	200 (-16)
Simon Dyson	67 (-5)		Adrian Otaegui	134 (-10)		Álvaro Quirós	203 (-13)
6 Players	68 (-4)		Álvaro Quirós	135 (-9)		Mikko Ilonen	204 (-12)
Alexander Levy	68 (-4)		Raphaël Jacquelin	136 (-8)		Tommy Fleetwood	205 (-11)
			2 Players	137 (-7)		Adrian Otaegui	205 (-11)

OWR: 3 of top 50 entered - Rating: 158 - Points to 39th - Levy: 32 points, to 137th in OWR

The Championship at Laguna National

Laguna National Golf & Country Club - Tampines, Singapore
Champion: Felipe Aguilar

May 1 - May 4
7,207 yards   Par 72
Purse: $1.5 Million

In one of the more remarkable finishes in European PGA Tour history, Chile's Felipe Aguilar carded a final round 62 – including an eagle at the 386-yard par-4 18th – to steal victory at the inaugural Championship at Laguna National, in Singapore. Aguilar, whose only previous E Tour win came at the 2008 Indonesia Open, began Sunday's final round four shots behind co-leaders Anders Hansen and Thailand's 21-year-old Panuphol Pittayarat, and fell into a six-shot deficit through nine despite going out in two-under-par 34. But with Hansen seemingly on the verge of running away after turning in 32, Aguilar reeled off four straight birdies at holes 10-13 to climb back into it, then added two more at the par-5 15th and the 202-yard 17th to really apply the pressure. Playing three groups ahead of Hansen, Aguilar assumed he'd need a birdie at the last to have a chance at a playoff – and then proceeded to hole his 142-yard pitching wedge approach for a two, capping off his stunning incoming 28. Hansen, who recently returned from a six-month absence to recover from wrist surgery, still had a chance to tie with a birdie at either of the closers, but when he could only manage two pars, he ended up tied for second with 25-year-old American (and former Northwestern University star) David Lipsky, one shot behind. India's Rahil Gangjee birdied his final five holes to claim solo fourth, while co-54-hole leader Pittayarat struggled to a Sunday 74 and a disappointing tie for 11th.

1	Felipe Aguilar	65-67-72-62	266	€180,531			Wade Ormsby	68-71-70-70	279	€7,799
2=	David Lipsky	64-68-70-65	267	€94,079		38=	Gary Stal	70-70-69-71	280	€6,607
	Anders Hansen	67-66-67-67	267	€94,079			Sihwan Kim	69-67-73-71	280	€6,607
4	Rahil Gangjee	66-67-71-65	269	€54,159			Bernd Wiesberger	71-68-70-71	280	€6,607
5	Chris Wood	68-67-68-67	270	€45,927			Boonchu Ruangkit	67-69-73-71	280	€6,607
6=	Anirban Lahiri	67-70-68-66	271	€35,204			Chan Kim	67-68-72-73	280	€6,607
	Grégory Bourdy	66-70-67-68	271	€35,204			Lucas Bjerregaard	68-70-72-70	280	€6,607
8=	David Drysdale	68-70-70-65	273	€24,336			Nicholas Fung	68-71-72-69	280	€6,607
	Raphaël Jacquelin	69-70-68-66	273	€24,336			Jason Knutzon	69-71-71-69	280	€6,607
	Tommy Fleetwood	68-67-69-69	273	€24,336			Victor Riu	67-71-75-67	280	€6,607
11=	Rikard Karlberg	70-68-70-66	274	€17,295		47=	Mithun Perera	65-71-73-72	281	€5,199
	S.S.P. Chowrasia	68-68-71-67	274	€17,295			Rafa Cabrera-Bello	66-71-71-73	281	€5,199
	Antonio Lascuña	68-69-69-68	274	€17,295			Chih-Bing Lam	71-67-72-71	281	€5,199
	Seuk-Hyun Baek	66-67-72-69	274	€17,295			Paul Waring	70-69-73-69	281	€5,199
	Terry Pilkadaris	68-70-66-70	274	€17,295		51=	Brett Rumford	70-67-70-75	282	€4,441
	Panupol Pittayarat	63-68-69-74	274	€17,295			Bio Kim	68-72-71-71	282	€4,441
17=	Prom Meesawat	66-70-72-67	275	€14,009			Jorge Campillo	73-67-73-69	282	€4,441
	Nacho Elvira	68-69-71-67	275	€14,009		54=	Scott Jamieson	64-71-74-74	283	€3,451
	Kristoffer Broberg	65-69-73-68	275	€14,009			Gareth Maybin	71-67-70-75	283	€3,451
20=	Sung Kang	68-68-72-68	276	€12,430			In-Woo Lee	68-69-72-74	283	€3,451
	Simon Thornton	72-67-69-68	276	€12,430			Adrian Otaegui	69-70-70-74	283	€3,451
	Peter Lawrie	68-72-67-69	276	€12,430			Andy Sullivan	69-69-72-73	283	€3,451
	Arnond Vongvanij	65-69-71-71	276	€12,430			Kyong-jun Moon	66-72-73-72	283	€3,451
24=	Ki-Sang Lee	68-69-71-69	277	€10,290			Nick Dougherty	69-70-73-71	283	€3,451
	Francois Calmels	68-69-72-68	277	€10,290		61=	Søren Kjeldsen	68-71-71-74	284	€2,816
	Craig Lee	72-68-66-71	277	€10,290			Chapchai Nirat	71-69-72-72	284	€2,816
	C. Phadungsil	67-71-69-70	277	€10,290			Andrew Dodt	70-70-75-69	284	€2,816
	Scott Hend	67-65-73-72	277	€10,290		64=	Gi-whan Kim	68-71-72-74	285	€2,329
	Alexander Levy	70-66-70-71	277	€10,290			Chiragh Kumar	69-70-72-74	285	€2,329
	Scott Barr	66-72-67-72	277	€10,290			J. Janewattananond	70-69-73-73	285	€2,329
	Johan Edfors	70-67-68-72	277	€10,290			Adilson da Silva	69-71-74-71	285	€2,329
	Robert-Jan Derksen	68-67-67-75	277	€10,290			Jeev Milkha Singh	67-72-74-72	285	€2,329
33=	Marc Warren	69-67-72-70	278	€8,377			Masahiro Kawamura	70-70-75-70	285	€2,329
	Roope Kakko	70-67-71-70	278	€8,377		70	Quincy Quek	64-74-72-77	287	€1,979
	P. Junhasavasdikul	69-69-71-69	278	€8,377		71	Fabrizio Zanotti	70-68-74-76	288	€1,625
36=	Ross Fisher	73-67-68-71	279	€7,799						

Out Of The Money: **141**: Edoardo Molinari, Kiradech Aphibarnrat, Chawalit Plaphol, Justin Walters, Søren Hansen, Hyung-Tae Kim, Yeon-Jin Jeong, John Hahn, In-Hoi Hur, Thomas Levet, Andrea Pavan, Mark Foster, Digvijay Singh, Jbe' Kruger **142**: Carlos Del Moral, Mardan Mamat, Ricardo González, Rashid Khan, Namchok Tantipokhakul, Heung-chul Joo, Zaw Moe, Wei Chih Lu, Kieran Pratt, Matthew Baldwin, Shiv Kapur, Gunn Charoenkul, Tae-Hoon Kim, Joong Kyung Mo **143**: Grégory Havret, Thaworn Wiratchant, Lee Slattery, Samuel Cyr, Soon-Sang Hong, Todd Baek, Angelo Que, Tyrrell Hatton, Graeme Storm, Anthony Wall, Mikael Lundberg **144**: Prayad Marksaeng, Damien McGrane, Javi Colomo, Joon-Eob Son, Phillip Price, Himmat Singh Rai, Matt Stieger, Richard Finch, Matthew Nixon, Richard Bland, Richard T. Lee, Simon Khan, Lam Zhiqun **145**: Matthew Griffin, Simon Dyson, Chang-Yoon Kim, Deng-Shan Koh, Dong Seop Maeng **146**: Joo-Yeob Baek, Jamie McLeary, Stuart Manley, Bryce Easton, Siddikur Rahman, Carlos Pigem **147**: Masanori Kobayashi, Unho Park, Seve Benson **148**: Peter Uihlein, Peter Whiteford, Elmer Salvador, Tae Hee Lee, Johan Carlsson **149**: J.B. Hansen, Jyoti Randhawa, Richie Ramsay, Morten Madsen **150**: Eng-Wah Poh **152**: Dae-Hyun Kim, Chi-Huang Tsai **155**: Seong-Ho Lee **WD**: Sung Lee (71), Berry Henson (74), Chris Doak (75), John Parry (80) **DQ**: Joonas Granberg

FIRST ROUND		SECOND ROUND		THIRD ROUND	
Panuphol Pittayarat	63 (-9)	Panuphol Pittayarat	131 (-13)	Anders Hansen	200 (-16)
David Lipsky	64 (-8)	David Lipsky	132 (-12)	Panuphol Pittayarat	200 (-16)
Quincy Quek	64 (-8)	**Felipe Aguilar**	132 (-12)	Robert-Jan Derksen	202 (-14)
Byung-Jun Kim	64 (-8)	Scott Hend	132 (-12)	David Lipsky	202 (-14)
Scott Jamieson	64 (-8)	3 Players	133 (-11)	2 Players	203 (-13)
Felipe Aguilar	65 (-7)			**Felipe Aguilar**	204 (-12)

OWR: 0 of top 50 entered - Rating: 77 - Points to 32nd - Aguilar: 22 points, to 130th in OWR

Madeira Islands Open - Portugal - BPI

May 8 - May 11

Clube de Golf do Santo da Serra - Madeira, Portugal
Champion: Daniel Brooks

6,826 yards   Par 72
Purse: €600,000

In one of the stranger events in the circuit's history, the European Tour played its landmark 1,500th tournament at the Madeira Islands Open, with England's Daniel Brooks claiming victory in a week marred by repeated fog delays, the cancellation of two rounds and the tragic death of Alistair Forsyth's caddie Ian MacGregor of an apparent heart attack on Sunday. Played opposite the PGA Tour's Players Championship, the event was buffeted by fog delays so bad that the first round wasn't completed until Sunday morning – by which time officials had decided to shorten play to 36 holes, with an 18-hole cut. MacGregor's death came on Forsyth's final hole and caused still another delay, with many players voicing surprise that play was resumed – even after a moment of silence – at all. But Forsyth himself was supportive of the decision and in the end it came down to Brooks (who bogeyed the par-5 16th, then bounced back with a timely birdie at the 17th) and Scotland's Scott Henry, who birdied his final three holes to draw even with Brooks on nine-under-par 135. Their playoff then lasted only one hole as Henry three-putted from 25 feet, allowing Brooks to claim his maiden victory with a routine two-putt par. Because the event (which was co-sanctioned by the Challenge Tour) offers far less than the €1.5 million total purse necessary for full status, Brooks only gained a one-year E Tour exemption with the victory.

1	Daniel Brooks	68-67	135	€75,000		Phillip Price	72-71	143	€3,900
2	Scott Henry	67-68	135	€50,000		Pontus Widegren	71-72	143	€3,900
3=	Jordi García Pinto	69-69	138	€21,375	39=	Carlos Aguilar	70-74	144	€2,655
	Julien Guerrier	69-69	138	€21,375		Connor Arendell	73-71	144	€2,655
	Antonio Hortal	69-69	138	€21,375		Ken Benz	72-72	144	€2,655
	Fabrizio Zanotti	70-68	138	€21,375		Daniel Gaunt	74-70	144	€2,655
7=	Johan Edfors	70-69	139	€11,610		Mikael Lundberg	74-70	144	€2,655
	M. Lorenzo-Vera	71-68	139	€11,610		James Morrison	72-72	144	€2,655
	Martin Wiegele	69-70	139	€11,610		Hugo Santos	73-71	144	€2,655
10=	Jose-Filipe Lima	69-71	140	€8,640		Patrik Sjoland	74-70	144	€2,655
	Steven Tiley	72-68	140	€8,640		Sam Walker	72-72	144	€2,655
12=	Christopher Mivis	71-70	141	€7,121	48=	Byeong-Hun An	74-71	145	€2,070
	Adrien Saddier	71-70	141	€7,121		Filippo Bergamaschi	73-72	145	€2,070
	Anthony Snobeck	74-67	141	€7,121		Sam Hutsby	73-72	145	€2,070
	Tjaart Van der Walt	70-71	141	€7,121		Pierre Relecom	74-71	145	€2,070
16=	Bjorn Akesson	72-70	142	€5,558	52=	Jens Fahrbring	73-73	146	€1,547
	Scott Arnold	71-71	142	€5,558		Michael Jonzon	73-73	146	€1,547
	Jens Dantorp	71-71	142	€5,558		David Law	74-72	146	€1,547
	Bradley Dredge	72-70	142	€5,558		Jesus Legarrea	74-72	146	€1,547
	Edouard Espana	73-69	142	€5,558		Chris Lloyd	72-74	146	€1,547
	Lukas Nemecz	72-70	142	€5,558		Ricardo Santos	72-74	146	€1,547
	Chris Paisley	72-70	142	€5,558		Gareth Shaw	73-73	146	€1,547
	Brinson Paolini	73-69	142	€5,558		Daniel Vancsik	74-72	146	€1,547
24=	Cyril Bouniol	70-73	143	€3,900	60=	Agustin Domingo	72-75	147	€1,215
	Tiago Cruz	73-70	143	€3,900		Edouard Dubois	73-74	147	€1,215
	Rhys Davies	72-71	143	€3,900		Callum Shinkwin	72-75	147	€1,215
	Oliver Fisher	72-71	143	€3,900	63=	Steven Brown	71-77	148	€1,080
	Lorenzo Gagli	72-71	143	€3,900		Joao Carlota (a)	69-79	148	-
	Adam Gee	73-70	143	€3,900		Alastair Forsyth	73-75	148	€1,215
	Estanislao Goya	73-70	143	€3,900		Mathias Gronberg	73-75	148	€1,215
	David Higgins	72-71	143	€3,900	67	George Woolgar	73-76	149	€990
	Lloyd Kennedy	68-75	143	€3,900	68=	Dara Ford	74-76	150	€922
	Tain Lee	72-71	143	€3,900		Thomas Linard	74-76	150	€922
	Andrew Marshall	69-74	143	€3,900	70=	Matteo Delpodio	74-77	151	€838
	Pedro Oriol	69-74	143	€3,900		Damian Ulrich	74-77	151	€838
	Jason Palmer	73-70	143	€3,900	72	Andrea Rota	74-78	152	€675

Out Of The Money: **75**: Phillip Archer, Jamie Elson, Ben Evans, Pedro Figueiredo, Richard Finch, Jordi García del Mora, Chris Hanson, Andreas Hartø, Nuno Henriques, Wen-Yi Huang, Niclas Johansson, Robin Kind, Jérôme Lando Casanova, Gary Lockerbie, Andrew McArthur, George Murray, Thomas Norret, Terry Pilkadaris, Bernd Ritthammer, Juan Antonio Rodriguez Marti, Oscar Stark, Alvaro Velasco **76**: Alexander Bjork, Christophe Brazillier, David Coupland, Jack Doherty, Matt Ford, Jean-Baptiste Gonnet, Jeppe Huldahl, Daniel Im, Andrew Johnston, Niklas Lemke, Sam Little, Richard McEvoy, Ruaidhri McGee, Garrick Porteous, Niccolo Quintarelli, Jocke Rask, Mark Tullo, Jeff Winther **77**: Jamie Abbott, Fredrik Andersson Hed, Jason Barnes, Wil Besseling, Oliver Farr, Dylan Frittelli, Luke Goddard, Dodge Kemmer, Mikko Korhonen, Maarten Lafeber, Pablo Martin Benavide, Jake Roos, Raymond Russell, Joao Pedro Sousa, Duncan Stewart, Simon Wakefield, Guillaume Watremez **78**: Mark Hensby, Joakim Lagergren, Kevin Phelan, Van Phillips, Brandon Stone, Oliver Wilson **79**: James Heath, Paul Maddy, Goncalo Pinto, Tim Sluiter **80**: Daniel Gavins, Mark F. Haastrup, Jesper Kennegard, Tapio Pulkkanen, Jarmo Sandelin, Joel Sjoholm **82**: Pelle Edberg, Marek Novy **83**: Jose Manuel Lara **84**: Oscar Floren, Paul Kinnear (a) **87**: Neil Connolly   **WD**: Lucas Bjerregaard, Robert Coles

FIRST ROUND

Scott Henry	67 (-5)
Daniel Brooks	68 (-4)
Lloyd Kennedy	68 (-4)
8 Players	69 (-3)

OWR: 0 of top 50 entered - Rating: 0 - Points to 23rd - Brooks: 18 points, to 286th in OWR

Open de España

PGA Catalunya Resort - Girona, Spain
Champion: Miguel Ángel Jiménez

May 15 - May 18
7,172 yards   Par 72
Purse: €1.5 Million

The ageless Miguel Ángel Jiménez reached multiple milestones at the Open de Espana, not the least of which was finally winning his own national open after 26 previous attempts had failed to yield a victory. Jiménez opened with rounds of 69-73-69 over the tough PGA Catalunya Resort layout, good enough to stand two strokes behind 22-year-old Belgian Thomas Pieters through 54 holes. He then mounted an early charge on Sunday, making three early birdies to climb into the lead after Pieters bogeyed the 2nd, 3rd and 4th en route to turning in 39. Bogeys at the 10th and 17th would eventually see Jiménez home in 38, for a 73 and a four-under-par 284 total. Meanwhile, Australian Richard Green had also moved into contention by turning in 34, but proceeded to give back all of his gains with a triple-bogey seven at the 443-yard 14th. Green quickly bounced back with a birdie at the par-5 15th, however, allowing him also to finish on 284. And then there was Pieters who, after stumbling early, still put himself in position to win with an eagle at the 15th, then fell back to 284 with a bogey at the 460-yard 17th. Thus it was off to a three-way playoff where the colorful Jiménez was the only man able to par the first extra hole, and with it claim his 21st career E Tour title, extend his own record (for the second time) as the circuit's oldest-ever winner, and become its only 50-year-old champion. His secret to competitive longevity? "Good food, good wine, good cigars - and some exercise."

1	Miguel A. Jiménez	69-73-69-73	284	€250,000		Agustin Domingo	72-76-72-72	292	€8,850
2=	Richard Green	74-69-69-72	284	€130,280		Sergio García	69-74-73-76	292	€8,850
	Thomas Pieters	69-69-71-75	284	€130,280		David Higgins	73-74-72-73	292	€8,850
4	Joost Luiten	70-69-74-72	285	€75,000		Jbe' Kruger	70-78-71-73	292	€8,850
5=	Maximilian Kieffer	75-69-69-73	286	€58,050		M. Lorenzo-Vera	74-72-74-72	292	€8,850
	Richie Ramsay	69-72-71-74	286	€58,050		Edoardo Molinari	73-72-75-72	292	€8,850
7=	Felipe Aguilar	74-70-69-74	287	€34,740		James Morrison	71-76-73-72	292	€8,850
	Alejandro Cañizares	72-76-69-70	287	€34,740		Mark Tullo	72-74-74-72	292	€8,850
	Darren Fichardt	77-66-73-71	287	€34,740		Romain Wattel	73-75-72-72	292	€8,850
	Gareth Maybin	73-70-73-71	287	€34,740		Bernd Wiesberger	80-68-74-70	292	€8,850
	Chris Wood	73-70-69-75	287	€34,740	49=	Seve Benson	74-73-72-74	293	€6,150
12=	Richard Bland	73-68-72-75	288	€24,300		Francois Calmels	74-73-74-72	293	€6,150
	Daan Huizing	71-76-71-70	288	€24,300		Magnus A. Carlsson	72-74-68-79	293	€6,150
	Alvaro Velasco	75-73-68-72	288	€24,300		Gon. F'dez-Castaño	73-75-71-74	293	€6,150
15=	Ross Fisher	70-76-67-76	289	€18,917		Jordi García Pinto	70-73-74-76	293	€6,150
	Emiliano Grillo	74-72-69-74	289	€18,917		Pedro Oriol	75-73-71-74	293	€6,150
	Mikko Korhonen	74-69-73-73	289	€18,917		Robert Rock	72-75-73-73	293	€6,150
	Paul Lawrie	70-72-74-73	289	€18,917	56	Alexander Noren	71-72-73-78	294	€4,950
	Tom Lewis	72-75-69-73	289	€18,917	57=	Adam Gee	72-75-73-75	295	€4,350
	Shane Lowry	72-74-72-71	289	€18,917		J.B. Hansen	75-73-75-72	295	€4,350
	Paul McGinley	72-72-72-73	289	€18,917		Alexander Levy	72-75-73-75	295	€4,350
	Wade Ormsby	72-74-71-72	289	€18,917		Adrian Otaegui	73-71-74-77	295	€4,350
	Danny Willett	70-75-74-70	289	€18,917		Hennie Otto	71-76-76-72	295	€4,350
24=	Niclas Fasth	75-69-77-69	290	€15,375		Renato Paratore (a)	72-75-73-75	295	-
	Raphaël Jacquelin	73-72-71-74	290	€15,375	63=	Kevin Phelan	76-71-71-78	296	€3,825
	Francesco Molinari	73-67-75-75	290	€15,375		Graeme Storm	71-76-72-77	296	€3,825
	Eddie Pepperell	68-71-79-72	290	€15,375	65	Álvaro Quirós	74-67-76-80	297	€3,600
28=	David Drysdale	74-71-76-70	291	€12,315	66=	Thomas Aiken	74-73-74-77	298	€3,225
	Nacho Elvira	75-72-74-70	291	€12,315		Jorge Campillo	71-75-79-73	298	€3,225
	Tyrrell Hatton	73-74-71-73	291	€12,315		Carlos Pigem	73-71-74-80	298	€3,225
	Grégory Havret	71-75-71-74	291	€12,315		Simon Thornton	72-76-76-74	298	€3,225
	Mikael Lundberg	72-74-70-75	291	€12,315	70	Craig Lee	73-75-71-81	300	€2,850
	Matteo Manassero	74-71-74-72	291	€12,315	71=	Eduardo De La Riva	73-72-75-81	301	€2,412
	Brinson Paolini	73-75-73-70	291	€12,315		Carlos Del Moral	74-74-79-74	301	€2,412
	Andrea Pavan	74-72-71-74	291	€12,315		Jose-Filipe Lima	69-79-76-77	301	€2,412
	Julien Quesne	76-71-73-71	291	€12,315	74	Rafael Cabrera-Bello	69-75-74-85	303	€2,244
	Marc Warren	75-70-72-74	291	€12,315	75=	Gaganjeet Bhullar	71-74-78-83	306	€2,240
38=	Robert-Jan Derksen	69-74-72-77	292	€8,850		Ivo Giner	71-74-78-83	306	€2,240

Out Of The Money: **149:** Victor Riu, Nicolas Colsaerts, Søren Kjeldsen, Fabrizio Zanotti, Gary Stal, Andy Sullivan, Pablo Larrazábal, Jeev Milkha Singh, Antonio Hortal, Sihwan Kim, Peter Whiteford **150:** George Coetzee, Juan Francisco Sarasti, Estanislao Goya, Grégory Bourdy, Thomas Levet, Peter Uihlein, Matthew Baldwin, Søren Hansen, Morten Madsen, Adrien Saddier, Daniel Berna Manazanar **151:** Simon Dyson, Oliver Fisher, Pol Bech, Jens Dantorp, Richard Finch, Paul Waring, Kristoffer Broberg, Lee Slattery, Robert Karlsson, Jack Doherty, Jacobo Pastor Lopez **152:** Tommy Fleetwood, Carlos Aguilar, Ricardo González, José María Olazábal, Michael Hoey, Roope Kakko, Alastair Forsyth **153:** Jose Manuel Lara, Matthew Nixon, Chris Doak, Mikko Ilonen, Patrik Sjoland, David Horsey, Thomas Bjørn, Sam Walker, Tjaart Van der Walt, Javi Colomo **154:** Scott Jamieson, Daniel Brooks, Jarmo Sandelin, Jamie McLeary, Simon Wakefield, Ricardo Santos, Damien McGrane, Connor Arendell, Julien Guerrier, Mark Foster, James Kingston **155:** Stuart Manley, Anthony Wall **156:** Kenneth Ferrie **157:** Andreas Hartø, Marco Crespi **158:** Edouard Dubois, Guido Migliozzi, Daniel Im, Johan Edfors, Justin Walters, Xavier Guzman **159:** Alexandre Kaleka **162:** Gonzalo Gancedo Onieva **163:** John Hahn **165:** Scott Henry

FIRST ROUND		SECOND ROUND		THIRD ROUND	
Eddie Pepperell	68 (-4)	Thomas Pieters	138 (-6)	Thomas Pieters	209 (-7)
8 Players	69 (-3)	Eddie Pepperell	139 (-5)	**Miguel A. Jiménez**	211 (-5)
Miguel A. Jiménez	69 (-3)	Joost Luiten	139 (-5)	Richie Ramsay	212 (-4)
		Francesco Molinari	140 (-4)	Richard Green	212 (-4)
		3 Players	141 (-3)	Chris Wood	212 (-4)
		Miguel A. Jiménez	142 (-2)		

OWR: 6 of top 50 entered - Rating: 148 - Points to 37th - Jiménez: 30 points, to 25th in OWR

BMW PGA Championship

May 22 - May 25

Wentworth Club (West) - Virginia Water, England
Champion: Rory McIlroy

7,302 yards Par 72
Purse: €4.75 Million

In a week in which his much-publicized wedding plans with Danish tennis star Caroline Wozniacki were finally cancelled for good, Rory McIlroy seemed to find that bachelorhood indeed suited his golf game, as he roared home with a final round 66 to claim the European Tour's flagship event, the BMW PGA Championship at Wentworth. The victory was his first worldwide in 2014 and put an exclamation point on the on-again, off-again relationship whose tribulations seemed at times over the previous 18 months to affect the performance of the former world number one. McIlroy - like most of the field - seemed largely irrelevant on a Thursday which saw Denmark's Thomas Bjørn break the Wentworth course record with a stunning 62, enough to give him a two stroke lead over Ireland's Shane Lowry and three over Spain's Rafael Cabrera-Bello. And indeed for two more days the event appeared firmly under Bjørn's control, particularly after he reeled off six consecutive back nine birdies en route to posting a Saturday 67, staking him to a five-shot 54-hole lead over Luke Donald and six over the resilient Lowry. But having slept on so huge a lead, Bjørn struggled on Sunday, triple-bogeying the 418-yard 6th en route to an outgoing 39 that allowed numerous players back into the fray. Lowry, for his part, hung close after eagling the 4th and birdieing the 5th, but a double-bogey at the 470-yard 13th, followed by a bogey at the 15th, ultimately relegated him to second. McIlroy, meanwhile, also eagled the 4th on his way to an outgoing 34, then birdied the 10th, 12th and 13th to move into the lead. Finally, with his biggest victory since the 2012 PGA Championship lying within reach, he birdied both of the two closing par-5s to hold off Lowry by one.

1	Rory McIlroy	68-71-69-66	274	€791,660	38=	Mikko Ilonen	71-71-77-69	288	€29,450
2	Shane Lowry	64-70-73-68	275	€527,770		Thongchai Jaidee	72-73-74-69	288	€29,450
3=	Thomas Bjørn	62-72-67-75	276	€267,425		Søren Hansen	73-72-73-70	288	€29,450
	Luke Donald	71-67-68-70	276	€267,425		Robert Rock	73-73-72-70	288	€29,450
5=	Stephen Gallacher	70-75-68-66	279	€183,825		Richie Ramsay	70-72-74-72	288	€29,450
	Simon Dyson	69-74-69-67	279	€183,825		Tyrrell Hatton	75-70-70-73	288	€29,450
7=	Marcel Siem	69-71-72-68	280	€110,010		Mark Hooper	71-71-71-75	288	€29,450
	Thomas Aiken	68-72-70-70	280	€110,010		Gary Stal	66-76-69-77	288	€29,450
	Henrik Stenson	68-71-71-70	280	€110,010	46=	Eduardo De La Riva	71-72-78-68	289	€21,850
	Francesco Molinari	71-74-65-70	280	€110,010		Daan Huizing	72-74-74-69	289	€21,850
	Pablo Larrazábal	69-71-69-71	280	€110,010		Paul Waring	72-72-74-71	289	€21,850
12=	Alexander Levy	71-73-70-67	281	€75,169		Edoardo Molinari	75-70-72-72	289	€21,850
	Martin Kaymer	68-75-69-69	281	€75,169		Tom Lewis	73-72-71-73	289	€21,850
	Chris Doak	69-72-69-71	281	€75,169		Simon Thornton	74-68-73-74	289	€21,850
	Joost Luiten	70-71-67-73	281	€75,169		Bernd Wiesberger	70-71-74-74	289	€21,850
16=	Marc Warren	73-69-71-69	282	€61,655		Raphaël Jacquelin	70-75-70-74	289	€21,850
	Richard Green	70-73-70-69	282	€61,655	54=	Roope Kakko	75-71-72-72	290	€16,625
	Fabrizio Zanotti	67-72-73-70	282	€61,655		Carlos Del Moral	71-75-71-73	290	€16,625
	Rafa Cabrera-Bello	65-73-73-71	282	€61,655		Thorbjørn Olesen	71-73-70-76	290	€16,625
	Jonas Blixt	68-71-72-71	282	€61,655	57=	Ricardo Santos	72-69-79-71	291	€14,012
21=	Paul Lawrie	72-71-73-67	283	€59,962		Grégory Bourdy	72-73-73-73	291	€14,012
	Chris Wood	73-72-69-69	283	€59,962		Álvaro Quirós	73-72-70-76	291	€14,012
	Seve Benson	71-69-73-70	283	€59,962		Richard Finch	71-72-71-77	291	€14,012
	Eddie Pepperell	69-73-68-73	283	€59,962	61=	Padraig Harrington	69-76-74-73	292	€12,588
25	Justin Rose	70-73-70-71	284	€49,400		Branden Grace	70-75-72-75	292	€12,588
26=	Ian Poulter	70-72-74-69	285	€45,838	63=	Adrian Otaegui	72-73-75-73	293	€11,162
	Mark Foster	72-71-70-72	285	€45,838		Damien McGrane	71-75-74-73	293	€11,162
	Andy Sullivan	70-71-69-75	285	€45,838		Danny Willett	73-73-72-75	293	€11,162
	Anthony Wall	67-76-67-75	285	€45,838		Jorge Campillo	73-73-71-76	293	€11,162
30=	Romain Wattel	72-74-73-67	286	€39,425	67=	Peter Hanson	71-72-80-71	294	€9,500
	George Coetzee	75-70-70-71	286	€39,425		Robert-Jan Derksen	70-76-73-75	294	€9,500
	Grégory Havret	69-76-70-71	286	€39,425		Robert Karlsson	74-70-72-78	294	€9,500
	Anders Hansen	71-69-74-72	286	€39,425	70	Graeme Storm	71-73-73-79	296	€8,670
	Jamie Donaldson	73-69-68-76	286	€39,425	71=	Johan Carlsson	71-75-73-78	297	€7,124
35=	Miguel A. Jiménez	72-72-72-71	287	€34,675		Nicolas Colsaerts	77-69-72-79	297	€7,124
	Lee Westwood	71-71-72-73	287	€34,675	73	Oliver Fisher	69-75-84-73	301	€7,119
	David Horsey	68-76-70-73	287	€34,675	74	Kristoffer Broberg	73-72-80-81	306	€7,116

Out Of The Money: **147**: Matthew Baldwin, Masahiro Kawamura, Ross Fisher, Jeev Milkha Singh, Greig Hutcheon, Andrea Pavan, Matthew Nixon, Maximilian Kieffer, Michael Hoey, David Lynn, Ian Ellis, Peter Whiteford **148**: Brooks Koepka, Felipe Aguilar, David Howell, José María Olazábal, Scott Drummond, Johan Edfors, Graham Fox, Justin Walters, Alejandro Cañizares, Daniel Brooks, Craig Lee, Niclas Fasth **149**: Dawie van der Walt, Phillip Price, Jason Levermore, Gaganjeet Bhullar, Shiv Kapur, Jamie McLeary, Victor Riu, Garth Mulroy, Paul McGinley, Darren Clarke, Darren Fichardt, Lee Slattery, Robert Dinwiddie, Francois Calmels **150**: Tommy Fleetwood, Ernie Els, Jbe' Kruger, Scott Jamieson, Julien Quesne **151**: Peter Lawrie, Yeon-Jin Jeong, Kiradech Aphibarnrat Matteo Manassero, Sihwan Kim, David Drysdale, Brett Rumford, Matthew Cort **152**: Emiliano Grillo, Magnus A. Carlsson, Marco Crespi, Thomas Levet, J.B. Hansen **153**: Richard Bland, Simon Khan, Charl Schwartzel, Søren Kjeldsen, Ricardo González **154**: Morten Madsen **155**: Gareth Maybin, Damian Mooney, Nacho Elvira **156**: John Parry, Thomas Pieters, Jose-Filipe Lima **157**: Chris Kelly **161**: Matt Ford **WD**: Sergio García (73), Retief Goosen (74), Alexander Noren (76)

FIRST ROUND		SECOND ROUND		THIRD ROUND	
Thomas Bjørn	62 (-10)	Thomas Bjørn	134 (-10)	Thomas Bjørn	201 (-15)
Shane Lowry	64 (-8)	Shane Lowry	134 (-10)	Luke Donald	206 (-10)
Gary Stal	66 (-6)	Rafael Cabrera-Bello	138 (-6)	Shane Lowry	207 (-9)
3 Players	67 (-5)	Luke Donald	138 (-6)	Joost Luiten	208 (-8)
Rory McIlroy	68 (-4)	Fabrizio Zanotti	138 (-6)	**Rory McIlroy**	208 (-8)
		Rory McIlroy	139 (-5)		

OWR: 17 of top 50 entered - Rating: 361 - Points to 56th - McIlroy: 64 points, to 6th in OWR

Nordea Masters

PGA Sweden National - Malmö, Sweden
Champion: Thongchai Jaidee

May 29 - Jun 1
7,475 yards Par 72
Purse: €1.5 Million

Though not quite as impressive as the irrepressible 50-year-old Miguel Ángel Jiménez, 44-year-old Thongchai Jaidee continued his own measure of agelessness at the Nordea Masters, besting Victor Dubuisson and Stephen Gallacher on the first hole of sudden death to claim his sixth career European Tour title. Following rounds of 69-70-68, Jaidee trailed 54-hole leaders Henrik Stenson and Eddie Pepperell by four shots on Saturday night but wasted little time mounting a charge on Sunday, birdieing his first three holes en route to an outgoing 33, then adding an eagle at the 552-yard 11th and birdies at both the 14th and the par-3 15th on his way to a seven-under-par 65. With both Stenson (71) and Pepperell (72) playing well enough only to linger on the periphery of contention, Jaidee was left to do battle primarily with Dubuisson and Gallacher, with the former having the best chance to win outright. But having birdied five of his first 11 holes to get to 16 under par, Dubuisson could only manage pars over his final seven, eventually three-putting for par from just off the fringe at the par-5 18th. Gallacher, meanwhile, who stood four under on the day and 16 under overall through 16 holes, bogeyed the 209-yard 17th to fall back, then holed a 20-foot birdie putt at the last to fight his way into the playoff. But the extra session would be short-lived as Jaidee managed to birdie the 18th while Dubuisson and Gallacher could only manage pars, and just that quickly it was over.

Pos	Player	Rounds	Total	Prize
1	Thongchai Jaidee	69-70-68-65	272	€250,000
2=	Victor Dubuisson	69-69-67-67	272	€130,280
	Stephen Gallacher	67-72-65-68	272	€130,280
4	Robert-Jan Derksen	70-71-67-65	273	€75,000
5	Henrik Stenson	69-70-64-71	274	€63,600
6=	Robert Karlsson	70-70-72-63	275	€45,000
	Eddie Pepperell	66-72-65-72	275	€45,000
	Álvaro Quirós	71-67-66-71	275	€45,000
9=	Rafael Cabrera-Bello	68-72-67-69	276	€31,800
	David Howell	73-70-67-66	276	€31,800
11=	Maximilian Kieffer	70-74-67-66	277	€25,850
	Julien Quesne	72-71-70-64	277	€25,850
	Romain Wattel	71-70-66-70	277	€25,850
14	Thomas Pieters	73-69-68-68	278	€22,950
15=	Thomas Bjørn	70-71-68-70	279	€21,150
	Darren Fichardt	73-71-68-67	279	€21,150
	Rikard Karlberg	67-75-68-69	279	€21,150
18=	Michael Hoey	69-75-69-67	280	€18,650
	Craig Lee	68-74-71-67	280	€18,650
	Edoardo Molinari	71-69-73-67	280	€18,650
21=	Eduardo De La Riva	72-72-70-67	281	€16,950
	Simon Dyson	69-72-70-70	281	€16,950
	Marcus Kinhult (a)	71-72-69-69	281	-
	Tom Lewis	71-71-68-71	281	€16,950
25=	Jorge Campillo	68-76-70-68	282	€14,700
	Chris Doak	70-69-69-74	282	€14,700
	Bradley Dredge	69-70-67-76	282	€14,700
	Peter Hanson	69-71-73-69	282	€14,700
	Raphaël Jacquelin	72-70-69-71	282	€14,700
	Alexander Levy	72-73-71-66	282	€14,700
	Shane Lowry	71-73-72-66	282	€14,700
32=	Felipe Aguilar	70-75-70-68	283	€11,512
	Jack Doherty	70-74-68-71	283	€11,512
	Nacho Elvira	73-71-68-71	283	€11,512
	Niclas Fasth	71-70-70-72	283	€11,512
	Mikko Ilonen	70-71-71-71	283	€11,512
	Søren Kjeldsen	70-75-70-68	283	€11,512
	Pablo Larrazábal	70-72-68-73	283	€11,512
	Matteo Manassero	74-70-70-69	283	€11,512
40=	Oliver Fisher	69-75-69-71	284	€9,150
	Richard Green	72-69-76-67	284	€9,150
	Peter Lawrie	75-70-72-67	284	€9,150
	James Morrison	70-73-66-75	284	€9,150
	Andrea Pavan	74-71-71-68	284	€9,150
	Kevin Phelan	71-70-73-70	284	€9,150
	Paul Waring	68-76-70-70	284	€9,150
47=	Lucas Bjerregaard	70-75-70-70	285	€7,200
	Francois Calmels	73-70-75-67	285	€7,200
	Johan Carlsson	68-77-71-69	285	€7,200
	Daniel Im	72-72-74-67	285	€7,200
	Jose-Filipe Lima	71-74-69-71	285	€7,200
	Wade Ormsby	69-74-72-70	285	€7,200
53=	Bjorn Akesson	71-73-75-67	286	€5,700
	Scott Jamieson	69-72-73-72	286	€5,700
	James Kingston	72-70-72-72	286	€5,700
	Richie Ramsay	72-72-71-71	286	€5,700
57=	Jens Dantorp	66-73-71-77	287	€4,700
	Edouard Dubois	70-73-68-76	287	€4,700
	Daan Huizing	67-78-70-72	287	€4,700
60=	Kristoffer Broberg	70-74-68-76	288	€4,125
	Shiv Kapur	76-68-72-72	288	€4,125
	Mikael Lundberg	69-75-72-72	288	€4,125
	S. Soderberg	67-74-76-71	288	€4,125
64=	Matthew Baldwin	71-73-73-72	289	€3,600
	Grégory Havret	71-74-70-74	289	€3,600
	Jeev Milkha Singh	71-74-70-74	289	€3,600
67=	F. Andersson Hed	74-70-74-72	290	€3,150
	Emiliano Grillo	73-72-71-74	290	€3,150
	Gareth Maybin	67-75-74-74	290	€3,150
70	Miguel A. Jiménez	69-73-75-74	291	€2,850
71	Ricardo González	69-73-75-75	292	€2,740
72	Stuart Manley	69-74-77-73	293	€2,250
73	Adam Gee	68-75-76-79	298	€2,247

Out Of The Money: **146**: Jamie McLeary, Andy Sullivan, Richard Bland, Tommy Fleetwood, José María Olazábal, Johan Edfors, Thomas Levet, Alejandro Cañizares, Estanislao Goya, Mark Foster, Simon Thornton **147**: Mathias Gronberg, Brett Rumford, Mark Tullo, Grégory Bourdy, Fabrizio Zanotti, Adrian Otaegui, Scott Henry, Tjaart Van der Walt, Brinson Paolini, Fredik Nilehn, Alastair Forsyth, Roope Kakko, Søren Hansen, Jbe' Kruger, Anthony Wall, Joakim Lagergren, Steven Jeppesen **148**: Francesco Molinari, Jonas Blixt, Mikko Korhonen, Paul Lawrie, Niklas Lemke, John Parry, Richard Finch, Simon Khan, Chris Wood, Sam Walker, Magnus A. Carlsson, Victor Riu, Peter Hedblom **149**: Thomas Norret, Patrik Sjoland **150**: Yeon-Jin Jeong, Simon Wakefield, Axel Ostensson, Sihwan Kim, Matthew Nixon **151**: Connor Arendell, Carlos Del Moral, Jason Knutzon, Mike Miller, J.B. Hansen, David Drysdale **152**: Michael Jonzon, Adrien Saddier, Ross Fisher, Anders Hansen, Richard S. Johnson, John Hahn, Marc Warren, Bjorn Hellgren **153**: Justin Walters, Daniel Brooks, Emil Othberg, Marco Crespi **154**: Oscar Stark, Damien McGrane, Lee Slattery **155**: James Heath, Jamie Elson, Tyrrell Hatton, Joakim Haeggman, Fredrik Gustavsson **156**: Alexandre Kaleka, Robert Dinwiddie, Christoffer Wahlgren **157**: Graeme Storm **161**: Andreas Hartø **164**: Mark Hensby **166**: Jarmo Sandelin **WD**: David Higgins (78), Danny Willett

FIRST ROUND		SECOND ROUND		THIRD ROUND	
Jens Dantorp	66 (-6)	Victor Dubuisson	138 (-6)	Henrik Stenson	203 (-13)
Eddie Pepperell	66 (-6)	Álvaro Quirós	138 (-6)	Eddie Pepperell	203 (-13)
5 Players	67 (-5)	Eddie Pepperell	138 (-6)	Stephen Gallacher	204 (-12)
Thongchai Jaidee	69 (-3)	6 players	139 (-5)	Álvaro Quirós	204 (-12)
		Thongchai Jaidee	139 (-5)	Victor Dubuisson	205 (-11)
				Thongchai Jaidee	207 (-9)

OWR: 6 of top 50 entered - Rating: 183 - Points to 46th - Jaidee: 36 points, to 37th in OWR

Lyoness Open
Diamond Country Club - Atzenbrugg, Austria
Champion: Mikael Lundberg

Jun 5 - Jun 8
7,433 yards   Par 72
Purse: €1 Million

Playing against a relatively light field in the week before the U.S. Open, Sweden's Mikael Lundberg ended a six-year victory drought by defeating homestanding Bernd Wiesberger on the first hole of sudden death to claim the Lyoness Open, in Austria. The 43-year-old Lundberg (whose two previous E Tour victories had both come in the Russian Open) began the week in fine form, posting rounds of 67-68 to take a one-shot halfway lead over England's Lee Slattery. He crumbled badly on Saturday, however, double-bogeying the 376-yard 3rd early and later adding four back nine bogeys en route to a seemingly crippling 76. But now trailing 54-hole leader (and defending champion) Joost Luiten by six, Lundberg mounted a major Sunday charge, birdieing four of his first five holes to pull into contention, then ultimately posting four more birdies at holes 11-15 to card a closing 65 and take the early clubhouse lead. In close pursuit were Luiten and Wiesberger, the event's 2012 winner and the clear favorite among the Austrian gallery. Luiten, for his part, played uneven golf on Sunday, matching four birdies with four bogeys through his first 15 holes, then coming up one stroke shy when he couldn't find one more birdie among the final three. But Wiesberger fared better, actually taking the lead (via his fifth birdie of the day) at the 607-yard 15th before bogeying the 591-yard 16th, and ultimately deadlocking with Lundberg on 276. The playoff hole was the par-3 18th where, having watched Wiesberger knock his approach far closer to the hole, Lundberg proceeded to stun the gallery by holing a tricky downhill 40-footer for birdie. Wiesberger then missed from 15 feet and to the home crowd's great disappointment, the trophy was headed for Sweden.

1	Mikael Lundberg	67-68-76-65	276	€166,660		Anders Hansen	73-73-73-69	288	€7,333
2	Bernd Wiesberger	71-70-66-69	276	€111,110		James Morrison	73-70-74-71	288	€7,333
3	Joost Luiten	72-67-66-72	277	€62,600		Garrick Porteous	74-69-72-73	288	€7,333
4	Lee Slattery	70-66-76-66	278	€50,000		Brett Rumford	73-70-71-74	288	€7,333
5=	Miguel A. Jiménez	70-75-68-67	280	€38,700		Jordan Smith (a)	71-72-74-71	288	-
	Fabrizio Zanotti	69-68-72-71	280	€38,700		Tjaart Van der Walt	70-76-68-74	288	€7,333
7=	Eduardo De La Riva	73-69-70-69	281	€27,500	42=	Richard Bland	69-75-74-71	289	€5,800
	Daniel Im	70-73-74-64	281	€27,500		Alex Haindl	72-69-75-73	289	€5,800
9=	David Horsey	73-73-65-71	282	€20,267		Lloyd Kennedy	72-74-72-71	289	€5,800
	Sihwan Kim	70-68-73-71	282	€20,267		Lukas Nemecz	74-71-73-71	289	€5,800
	Simon Wakefield	70-71-70-71	282	€20,267		Florian Praegant	70-73-76-70	289	€5,800
12=	Matthew Baldwin	68-73-70-72	283	€16,650		Victor Riu	69-74-71-75	289	€5,800
	Adam Gee	67-73-70-73	283	€16,650	48=	Robert Dinwiddie	70-75-74-71	290	€4,500
14=	Jason Knutzon	74-72-69-69	284	€14,700		Jack Doherty	75-71-76-68	290	€4,500
	Andrew Marshall	72-71-75-66	284	€14,700		James Heath	76-72-71-71	290	€4,500
	Simon Thornton	71-74-67-72	284	€14,700		Michael Hoey	73-74-71-72	290	€4,500
17=	Rhys Davies	68-71-77-69	285	€12,100		James Kingston	72-71-75-72	290	€4,500
	Florian Fritsch	74-69-74-68	285	€12,100		Ross McGowan	69-74-70-77	290	€4,500
	Tyrrell Hatton	72-74-71-68	285	€12,100		Matthew Nixon	70-76-73-71	290	€4,500
	Berry Henson	68-72-73-72	285	€12,100	55=	Leo Astl	73-72-74-72	291	€3,186
	Jake Roos	73-73-70-69	285	€12,100		Gaganjeet Bhullar	70-78-72-71	291	€3,186
	Anthony Wall	70-73-75-67	285	€12,100		Bradley Dredge	72-73-75-71	291	€3,186
	Romain Wattel	76-69-71-69	285	€12,100		J.B. Hansen	73-71-74-73	291	€3,186
24	Mikko Korhonen	75-67-74-70	286	€10,700		Tain Lee	71-73-76-71	291	€3,186
25=	Kenneth Ferrie	71-77-71-68	287	€9,500		Thomas Levet	69-73-75-74	291	€3,186
	Søren Hansen	74-70-74-69	287	€9,500		Robert Rock	75-70-75-71	291	€3,186
	Peter Hedblom	74-74-70-69	287	€9,500	62=	Phillip Archer	69-73-75-76	293	€2,550
	Scott Henry	69-75-68-75	287	€9,500		Edouard Dubois	74-73-71-75	293	€2,550
	Rikard Karlberg	73-73-66-75	287	€9,500		Thomas Norret	71-75-76-71	293	€2,550
	Ruaidhri McGee	73-70-69-75	287	€9,500		Jeev Milkha Singh	71-76-72-74	293	€2,550
	Gary Stal	73-74-69-71	287	€9,500	66=	Moritz Mayrhauser	75-72-74-73	294	€2,250
32=	Stephen Dodd	70-73-75-70	288	€7,333		Ricardo Santos	75-71-79-69	294	€2,250
	Richard Finch	68-73-75-72	288	€7,333	68	Lukas Lipold (a)	77-71-77-71	296	-
	Daniel Gaunt	75-73-72-68	288	€7,333	69	Daniel Vancsik	71-75-73-78	297	€2,100
	Estanislao Goya	77-69-74-68	288	€7,333	70	Joakim Lagergren	73-72-84-76	305	€2,000

Out Of The Money: 149: Byeong-Hun An, Oliver Bekker, Kristoffer Broberg, Andreas Hartø, David Higgins, Jose Manuel Lara, Peter Lawrie, Jack Wilson **150:** Fredrik Andersson Hed, Connor Arendell, S.S.P. Chowrasia, Alastair Forsyth, Ricardo González, Mathias Gronberg, Dodge Kemmer, Craig Lee, Jamie McLeary, José María Olazábal, Kevin Phelan, Thomas Pieters, Phillip Price, Lukas Tintera, Sam Walker **151:** Francois Calmels, Jens Dantorp, Nacho Elvira, Søren Kjeldsen, Stuart Manley, Andrew McArthur, Damien McGrane, Adrian Otaegui, Peter Whiteford **152:** Javi Colomo, Jbe' Kruger, Jose-Filipe Lima **153:** Keith Horne, Patrik Sjoland **154:** Johan Carlsson, Mark Davis, Mark Foster, Chris Hanson, Uli Weinhandel **155:** Alexander Kleszcz, Brinson Paolini, John Parry **157:** Gerold Folk **158:** Markus Habeler, Sam Straka, Mark Tullo **160:** Charles Davies, Georg Schultes **161:** Evgeni Kafelnikov, Berni Reiter **162:** Rene Gruber **164:** Cyril Bouniol **166:** Petr Gal **167:** Sebastian Wittmann **170:** Andrey Pavlov **WD:** David Drysdale, Alexandre Kaleka (77), Adrien Saddier (77), Johan Edfors (79) **DQ:** Roope Kakko (213)

FIRST ROUND		SECOND ROUND		THIRD ROUND	
Adam Gee	67 (-5)	**Mikael Lundberg**	135 (-9)	Joost Luiten	205 (-11)
Mikael Lundberg	67 (-5)	Lee Slattery	136 (-8)	Bernd Wiesberger	207 (-9)
4 Players	68 (-4)	Fabrizio Zanotti	137 (-7)	Fabrizio Zanotti	209 (-7)
		Sihwan Kim	138 (-6)	Adam Gee	210 (-6)
		2 Players	139 (-5)	5 Players	211 (-5)
				Mikael Lundberg	211 (-5)

OWR: 2 of top 50 entered - Rating: 35 - Points to 31st - Lundberg: 24 points, to 306th in OWR

Irish Open

Fota Island Resort - County Cork, Ireland
Champion: Mikko Ilonen

Jun 19 - Jun 22
7,043 yards   Par 71
Purse: €2 Million

Finland's Mikko Ilonen celebrated the occasion of his 300th European Tour start with his fourth career victory on the circuit, hanging on down the stretch to claim a wire-to-wire triumph at the Irish Open. The 34-year-old Ilonen, who long ago won the 1999 Western Ireland Amateur, grabbed his initial lead on Thursday via a course record-setting 64 that included birdies on five of his last seven holes. The lead was expanded to two strokes after a Friday 68, then shrunk to one through 54 holes when Ilonen added a Saturday 69 while England's Danny Willett set a new course record with a 63 that included a hole-in-one at the 179-yard 7th and birdies over four of his final five holes. Sunday initially shaped up as a battle between these two, with Ilonen going out in 34 and Willet overcoming a bogey at the 165-yard 3rd to turn in 35. Willett, however, failed to mount a back nine charge, coming home in one-over-par 36 to finish in a tie for third. Ilonen too only held his ground down the homestretch, recording pars at holes 10-17. This left the door slightly open for Edoardo Molinari and the 33-year-old Italian indeed made a late move, recording birdies at the 13th, 16th and 18th to finish on 272. Unfortunately this still left him two behind Ilonen, whose cautious bogey at the 532-yard closer saw him home a winner. Molinari's run was not entirely in vain, however, as he, Willett and England's Matthew Baldwin all earned spots in the upcoming British Open field via their high finishes.

1	Mikko Ilonen	64-68-69-70	271	€333,330		Thomas Pieters	72-70-70-69	281	€12,800
2	Edoardo Molinari	67-69-69-67	272	€222,220		Alejandro Cañizares	72-68-71-70	281	€12,800
3=	Matthew Baldwin	67-71-66-69	273	€103,333		Estanislao Goya	70-70-70-71	281	€12,800
	Kristoffer Broberg	69-69-66-69	273	€103,333		Jeev Milkha Singh	68-73-69-71	281	€12,800
	Danny Willett	73-66-63-71	273	€103,333		Daan Huizing	67-71-71-72	281	€12,800
6=	Magnus A. Carlsson	66-71-68-69	274	€65,000	44=	Robert Karlsson	66-76-72-68	282	€10,600
	Graeme McDowell	68-66-69-71	274	€65,000		Jason Knutzon	73-69-71-69	282	€10,600
8=	Ross Fisher	68-72-70-65	275	€39,700		Álvaro Quirós	70-70-72-70	282	€10,600
	Michael Hoey	68-71-70-66	275	€39,700		Steve Webster	70-70-70-72	282	€10,600
	Chris Wood	69-69-70-67	275	€39,700		Richard Bland	73-68-68-73	282	€10,600
	Richard Finch	68-72-67-68	275	€39,700	49=	Wade Ormsby	70-71-75-67	283	€8,600
	Grégory Bourdy	68-71-67-69	275	€39,700		Anthony Wall	71-71-71-70	283	€8,600
	Gary Stal	70-67-69-69	275	€39,700		David Howell	72-67-71-73	283	€8,600
14=	Marcel Siem	66-74-71-65	276	€27,114		David Horsey	72-69-71-71	283	€8,600
	Matthew Nixon	70-65-74-67	276	€27,114		Grégory Havret	70-68-70-75	283	€8,600
	Padraig Harrington	69-67-71-69	276	€27,114	54=	José María Olazábal	69-73-73-69	284	€6,800
	Adam Gee	68-70-69-69	276	€27,114		Chris Doak	69-70-73-72	284	€6,800
	Simon Khan	69-66-70-71	276	€27,114		Andrea Pavan	71-71-70-72	284	€6,800
	Gareth Maybin	71-65-69-71	276	€27,114		Stuart Manley	70-68-72-74	284	€6,800
	Fabrizio Zanotti	70-69-65-72	276	€27,114	58=	Darren Clarke	72-68-73-72	285	€5,600
21=	Roope Kakko	71-66-72-68	277	€22,000		Andrew McArthur	71-67-74-73	285	€5,600
	Marco Crespi	68-67-73-69	277	€22,000		Johan Carlsson	70-70-72-73	285	€5,600
	Ricardo González	69-70-68-70	277	€22,000		Sam Walker	72-68-71-74	285	€5,600
	Anders Hansen	67-70-68-72	277	€22,000		John G. Kelly	71-71-68-75	285	€5,600
	Romain Wattel	69-65-70-73	277	€22,000	63=	Mikael Lundberg	70-71-74-71	286	€4,800
26=	Rafael Cabrera-Bello	72-68-70-68	278	€19,600		Darren Fichardt	68-74-72-72	286	€4,800
	Pablo Larrazábal	72-69-67-70	278	€19,600		Jake Roos	68-73-72-73	286	€4,800
	Oliver Fisher	73-68-66-71	278	€19,600	66=	Francois Calmels	73-69-75-70	287	€4,200
29=	Matthew Fitzpatrick	72-69-70-68	279	€17,500		Adrien Saddier	71-71-74-71	287	€4,200
	Sihwan Kim	69-67-74-69	279	€17,500		Hao-Tong Li	69-72-69-77	287	€4,200
	Marc Warren	71-70-68-70	279	€17,500	69	Alastair Forsyth	71-71-72-75	289	€3,800
	Robert Rock	68-66-74-71	279	€17,500	70=	Jack Doherty	71-71-74-74	290	€3,325
33=	Stephen Dodd	73-69-72-66	280	€15,040		Justin Walters	68-74-74-74	290	€3,325
	Peter Lawrie	69-72-70-69	280	€15,040	72	Tom Lewis	68-72-76-75	291	€2,997
	Graeme Storm	69-70-70-71	280	€15,040	73=	Gary Hurley (a)	72-66-81-73	292	-
	Ricardo Santos	71-71-66-72	280	€15,040		Patrik Sjoland	69-72-77-74	292	€2,994
	Paul Casey	69-69-69-73	280	€15,040	75	Mike Miller	73-67-79-80	299	€2,991
38=	James Heath	70-72-72-67	281	€12,800					

Out Of The Money: **143**: Shane Lowry, Morten Madsen, Richie Ramsay, Victor Riu, Tommy Fleetwood, Paul Lawrie, Rory McIlroy, Matteo Manassero, Simon Dyson, Lee Slattery, Mikko Korhonen, Brinson Paolini, Jens Dantorp **144**: Kevin Phelan, Scott Jamieson, Lucas Bjerregaard, Adrian Otaegui, Duncan Stewart, Jorge Campillo, Stephen Gallacher, Andreas Hartø, Søren Hansen, Jbe' Kruger, Wen-Yi Huang, Mark Foster, Shiv Kapur, Gavin Moynihan **145**: Thomas Levet, Daniel Brooks, Branden Grace, Paul Waring, Craig Lee, Alexander Levy, Cian McNamara, Carlos Del Moral, Ruaidhri McGee **146**: Eddie Pepperell, Paul McGinley, Julien Quesne, Raphaël Jacquelin, David Drysdale, John Parry, Dermot McElroy, Richard Green, Tyrrell Hatton, Damien McGrane, Simon Thornton **147**: Emiliano Grillo, Søren Kjeldsen, Maximilian Kieffer, Simon Wakefield, Nacho Elvira, Eamonn Brady **148**: J.B. Hansen, Robert Dinwiddie, Tjaart Van der Walt, James Morrison, Jamie McLeary, Alexandre Kaleka, Gareth Shaw **149**: Eduardo De La Riva, Peter Whiteford, Edouard Dubois, Garrick Porteous **150**: Felipe Aguilar, Brian McElhinney, David Higgins, Brett Rumford, Gaganjeet Bhullar **151**: Yeon-Jin Jeong, Daniel Sugrue, Andy Sullivan **152**: Daniel Im, Scott Henry **153**: Robert Cannon **154**: Brendan McGovern, John Hahn **155**: Damian Mooney, Mark Staunton **156**: Jose-Filipe Lima **WD**: Hennie Otto (70)

FIRST ROUND		SECOND ROUND		THIRD ROUND	
Mikko Ilonen	64 (-7)	**Mikko Ilonen**	132 (-10)	**Mikko Ilonen**	201 (-12)
Marcel Siem	65 (-6)	Robert Rock	134 (-8)	Danny Willett	202 (-11)
Robert Karlsson	65 (-6)	Graeme McDowell	134 (-8)	Graeme McDowell	203 (-10)
Magnus Carlsson	65 (-6)	Romain Wattel	134 (-8)	4 Players	204 (-9)
4 Players	67 (-4)	3 Players	135 (-7)		

OWR: 3 of top 50 entered - Rating: 115 - Points to 32nd - Ilonen: 26 points, to 51st in OWR

BMW International Open
Golfclub Gut Larchenhof - Koln, Germany
Champion: Fabrizio Zanotti

Jun 26 - Jun 29
7,228 yards   Par 72
Purse: €2 Million

In an exciting finish that ultimately came down to a four-man playoff, 31-year-old Fabrizio Zanotti became the first man from Paraguay ever to win on the European Tour, claiming the BMW International Open in Germany. Zanotti hardly seemed a part of the picture through 36 holes after rounds of 72-67 left him seven shots behind a quartet of halfway leaders, and his chances seemed only little improved after a bogey-free Saturday 65 moved him within five of 54-hole leader Pablo Larrazábal. But with Larrazábal only able to produce an even-par 72 on Sunday, Zanotti responded with his second straight bogey-free 65 to post a 269 total, then watched as France's Grégory Havret (who birdied three of his last six holes), Spain's Rafael Cabrera-Bello (who finished birdie-eagle-birdie) and world number two Henrik Stenson (who carded a back nine 30 and narrowly missed a winning birdie at the last) all tied him. Stenson again missed a chance for victory at the first extra hole but matched Zanotti shot for shot as first Havret (by failing to birdie the second extra hole) and Cabrera-Bello (who failed to par the fourth) dropped from contention. Finally, on the fifth extra hole (the 397-yard 17th), Stenson drove into the water and, following a penalty stroke and drop, hit his third into a greenside bunker. With Zanotti on the putting surface in two, Stenson then failed to hole his bunker shot and promptly conceded, giving Zanotti - who entered played ranked 305th in the world - his maiden E Tour title.

1	Fabrizio Zanotti	72-67-65-65	269	€333,330			Tommy Fleetwood	70-69-69-68	276	€13,617
2=	Rafael Cabrera-Bello	64-68-70-67	269	€149,140			Estanislao Goya	72-67-66-71	276	€13,617
	Grégory Havret	71-65-67-66	269	€149,140			J.B. Hansen	70-70-68-68	276	€13,617
	Henrik Stenson	68-68-66-67	269	€149,140			Craig Lee	69-65-69-73	276	€13,617
5=	Jamie Donaldson	71-67-65-67	270	€71,600			Wade Ormsby	71-67-69-69	276	€13,617
	Simon Dyson	69-66-69-66	270	€71,600			Gary Stal	66-69-70-71	276	€13,617
	Thongchai Jaidee	71-66-68-65	270	€71,600			Andy Sullivan	66-69-75-66	276	€13,617
8=	Thomas Bjørn	70-66-66-69	271	€42,900			Justin Walters	71-69-66-70	276	€13,617
	Emiliano Grillo	66-66-70-69	271	€42,900			Chris Wood	70-70-66-70	276	€13,617
	Pablo Larrazábal	69-63-67-72	271	€42,900		45=	James Heath	75-65-67-70	277	€10,200
	Danny Willett	64-68-71-68	271	€42,900			Miguel A. Jiménez	67-67-73-70	277	€10,200
12=	Alex Cejka	68-66-69-69	272	€27,960			Jbe' Kruger	72-65-69-71	277	€10,200
	Oliver Fisher	72-66-65-69	272	€27,960			Morten Madsen	70-68-69-70	277	€10,200
	Sergio García	71-66-70-65	272	€27,960			Sam Walker	67-69-72-69	277	€10,200
	Richard Green	72-68-62-70	272	€27,960		50	Alejandro Cañizares	70-67-70-71	278	€9,000
	Alexander Levy	70-67-66-69	272	€27,960		51=	Adam Gee	71-69-69-70	279	€8,000
	Shane Lowry	67-68-70-67	272	€27,960			Mikko Ilonen	68-72-71-68	279	€8,000
	Francesco Molinari	71-66-65-70	272	€27,960			Maximilian Kieffer	69-71-67-72	279	€8,000
	Anthony Wall	69-69-68-66	272	€27,960			Graeme Storm	66-73-69-71	279	€8,000
	Paul Waring	72-63-69-68	272	€27,960		55=	Jorge Campillo	67-71-70-72	280	€6,800
	Romain Wattel	67-68-69-68	272	€27,960			Mikko Korhonen	69-71-69-71	280	€6,800
22=	Paul Casey	73-67-63-70	273	€21,100		57=	Victor Dubuisson	71-69-69-72	281	€5,900
	Mark Foster	70-69-65-69	273	€21,100			Damien McGrane	69-71-71-70	281	€5,900
	Anders Hansen	66-72-67-68	273	€21,100			Max. Rohrig (a)	73-67-71-70	281	-
	Tyrrell Hatton	69-67-70-67	273	€21,100			Adrien Saddier	70-70-69-72	281	€5,900
	Michael Hoey	66-69-69-69	273	€21,100			Marcel Siem	70-66-73-72	281	€5,900
	Robert Karlsson	68-66-68-71	273	€21,100		62	Ross Fisher	70-70-71-71	282	€5,400
28=	Jens Dantorp	68-68-67-71	274	€18,400		63=	Johan Carlsson	68-72-67-76	283	€5,000
	Branden Grace	67-67-74-66	274	€18,400			Jason Knutzon	70-69-71-73	283	€5,000
	Matthew Nixon	69-69-67-69	274	€18,400			Tom Lewis	67-72-72-72	283	€5,000
31=	Eddie Pepperell	72-64-72-67	275	€16,900		66=	John Daly	70-67-76-71	284	€4,400
	Julien Quesne	71-68-69-67	275	€16,900			Nacho Elvira	67-68-72-77	284	€4,400
33=	Gaganjeet Bhullar	67-70-69-70	276	€13,617			Andreas Hartø	68-66-77-73	284	€4,400
	Carlos Del Moral	68-68-66-74	276	€13,617		69	Daniel Im	68-70-72-75	285	€4,000
	David Drysdale	72-68-68-68	276	€13,617						

Out Of The Money: **141**: Álvaro Quirós, Jeev Milkha Singh, Felipe Aguilar, Simon Khan, Jack Doherty, Paul Lawrie, Gareth Maybin, Nicolas Colsaerts, Ricardo Santos, Anirban Lahiri, Brinson Paolini, Simon Wakefield, Matthew Baldwin, Richard Bland **142**: David Howell, Roope Kakko, Kevin Phelan, Bernd Wiesberger, Marco Crespi, Shiv Kapur, Marcel Schneider, Søren Hansen, James Morrison, Phillip Price **143**: Peter Hedblom, Paul McGinley, Daan Huizing, Søren Kjeldsen, Edoardo Molinari, Stuart Manley, Thomas Aiken, Wen-Yi Huang **144**: Victor Riu, Robert Rock, Marc Warren, Eduardo De La Riva, Richard Finch, Martin Kaymer, Francois Calmels **145**: Alexandre Kaleka, Connor Arendell, Richie Ramsay, Thomas Levet, Lee Slattery, Magnus A. Carlsson, Johan Edfors, David Lynn, Thorbjørn Olesen, Raphaël Jacquelin, Ricardo González, Jose Manuel Lara **146**: Nick Dougherty, Mikael Lundberg, Darren Fichardt, Thomas Pieters, Sihwan Kim, Adrian Otaegui, Dominic Foos, David Horsey, Chris Doak **147**: Jamie McLeary, Niclas Fasth, Lucas Bjerregaard, Max Glauert **148**: Scott Jamieson, Peter Lawrie, Yeon-Jin Jeong, Andrea Pavan, Max Kramer, Patrik Sjoland **149**: Alastair Forsyth, Jose-Filipe Lima, Kristoffer Broberg **150**: Mathias Gronberg, José María Olazábal, Simon Thornton **151**: Peter Uihlein, Peter Whiteford, George Coetzee, Brett Rumford, Alexander Knappe **153**: Anton Kirstein **154**: John Parry **DQ** Edouard Dubois (75), David Higgins (75), Daniel Brooks (77), Fredrik Andersson Hed (83)

FIRST ROUND		SECOND ROUND		THIRD ROUND	
Rafael Cabrera-Bello	64 (-8)	Rafael Cabrera-Bello	132 (-12)	Pablo Larrazábal	199 (-17)
Danny Willett	64 (-8)	Danny Willett	132 (-12)	8 Players	202 (-14)
7 Players	66 (-6)	Pablo Larrazábal	132 (-12)	**Fabrizio Zanotti**	204 (-12)
Fabrizio Zanotti	72 (E)	Emiliano Grillo	132 (-12)		
		6 Players	134 (-10)		
		Fabrizio Zanotti	139 (-5)		

OWR: 9 of top 50 entered   -   Rating: 238   -   Points to 49th   -   Zanotti: 42 points, to 112th in OWR

Alstom Open de France
Le Golf National - Paris, France
Champion: Graeme McDowell

Jul 3 - Jul 6
7,331 yards Par 71
Purse: €3 Million

Taking full advantage of the cold and miserable weather conditions that characterized the final round, Northern Ireland's Graeme McDowell came from an imposing eight shots behind to successfully defend his title at the Alstom Open de France. Behind rounds of 70-69-73, McDowell began Sunday's finale in a tie for seventh but amidst the difficult conditions, began methodically moving up the board behind outgoing birdies at the 2nd and the par-5 9th. Meanwhile, first, second and third round leader Kevin Stadler began the day with a four-shot advantage but struggled badly on his outward half, racking up three bogeys and a double-bogey (at the long par-4 7th) to turn in an inglorious 41. Two more bogeys at the 10th and 12th might well have ended his hopes but with nearly all of the field faring poorly, Stadler gamely carded birdies at the 11th, the par-5 14th and the 16th to propel himself back into the hunt. Meanwhile McDowell, , calling forth all of the bad weather skills he developed during a youth spent upon the Irish links, added birdies at the 13th, 14th and 16th to tie Stadler at six under par – good enough, he assumed to at least make a playoff. When Stadler could do no better than to leave himself a long birdie putt to win at the 470-yard 18th, that playoff seemed likely. When Stadler missed his three-footer for par, however, it became entirely unnecessary, leaving McDowell to claim his first worldwide win of 2014. Also noteworthy were the finishes of Robert Karlsson (fourth), Michael Hoey (seventh) and Victor Riu (eighth), each of whom earned places in the upcoming British Open at Hoylake.

1	Graeme McDowell	70-69-73-67	279	€500,000		Rafael Cabrera-Bello	70-72-77-71	290	€20,400
2=	Thongchai Jaidee	70-69-69-72	280	€260,565		Steve Webster	73-68-76-73	290	€20,400
	Kevin Stadler	64-68-72-76	280	€260,565		Ricardo Santos	71-74-72-73	290	€20,400
4	Robert Karlsson	73-69-70-69	281	€150,000		David Howell	72-72-72-74	290	€20,400
5=	Jamie Donaldson	67-72-74-69	282	€116,100		Estanislao Goya	75-66-74-75	290	€20,400
	Matthew Baldwin	70-71-70-71	282	€116,100		Roope Kakko	68-74-73-75	290	€20,400
7	Michael Hoey	73-66-73-71	283	€90,000		Alexander Levy	69-72-72-77	290	€20,400
8	Victor Riu	68-67-73-76	284	€75,000	43=	K. Aphibarnrat	77-66-70-78	291	€17,400
9=	Fabrizio Zanotti	73-70-75-67	285	€63,600		Julien Quesne	74-71-68-78	291	€17,400
	Oliver Fisher	69-71-77-68	285	€63,600	45=	Lee Slattery	70-73-75-74	292	€15,900
11	Wade Ormsby	70-75-69-72	286	€55,200		Gareth Maybin	73-68-76-75	292	€15,900
12=	Grégory Bourdy	73-72-72-70	287	€45,450		David Lynn	73-69-72-78	292	€15,900
	Kristoffer Broberg	70-74-72-71	287	€45,450	48=	Victor Dubuisson	76-68-76-73	293	€12,600
	Magnus A. Carlsson	73-72-70-72	287	€45,450		Jason Knutzon	72-72-76-73	293	€12,600
	Matthew Nixon	71-72-70-74	287	€45,450		Simon Dyson	73-71-75-74	293	€12,600
	Damien McGrane	71-69-72-75	287	€45,450		Mikael Lundberg	75-68-74-76	293	€12,600
	Martin Kaymer	72-68-70-77	287	€45,450		Adam Gee	72-72-73-76	293	€12,600
18=	Shiv Kapur	73-69-76-70	288	€34,612		Matteo Manassero	68-73-75-77	293	€12,600
	Gary Stal	74-68-74-72	288	€34,612		Anders Hansen	71-71-73-78	293	€12,600
	David Bobrowski	73-70-73-72	288	€34,612		Matt Ford	70-74-70-79	293	€12,600
	Søren Kjeldsen	72-73-71-72	288	€34,612	56=	Daan Huizing	72-73-74-75	294	€9,400
	Joost Luiten	73-69-73-73	288	€34,612		Richard Sterne	70-75-73-76	294	€9,400
	Stephen Gallacher	66-73-74-75	288	€34,612		J.B. Hansen	72-69-76-77	294	€9,400
	Scott Jamieson	69-70-74-75	288	€34,612	59=	Paul Waring	71-73-78-73	295	€8,400
	Bernd Wiesberger	70-70-71-77	288	€34,612		Nicolas Colsaerts	72-72-77-74	295	€8,400
26=	Felipe Aguilar	67-73-77-72	289	€26,700		Thomas Linard	72-70-73-80	295	€8,400
	Ross Fisher	72-68-77-72	289	€26,700	62=	James Heath	71-73-76-77	297	€7,500
	Matthew Fitzpatrick	69-74-74-72	289	€26,700		Maximilian Kieffer	72-73-75-77	297	€7,500
	Francesco Molinari	70-72-74-73	289	€26,700		Julien Brun	73-72-75-77	297	-
	Andy Sullivan	73-71-72-73	289	€26,700		Andrew McArthur	76-67-76-78	297	€7,500
	Marc Warren	69-73-73-74	289	€26,700	66	Eduardo De La Riva	73-71-75-79	298	€6,900
	Mikko Korhonen	72-72-71-74	289	€26,700	67=	Patrik Sjoland	73-71-82-73	299	€6,450
	Marcel Siem	65-72-77-75	289	€26,700		Søren Hansen	74-70-78-77	299	€6,450
	Mark Foster	69-70-73-77	289	€26,700	69	Alexandre Kaleka	72-73-75-81	301	€6,000
35=	Edoardo Molinari	70-75-75-70	290	€20,400					

Out Of The Money: Sihwan Kim, Alejandro Cañizares, Brooks Koepka, Jorge Campillo, Brinson Paolini, Jeev Milkha Singh, Grégory Havret, Adrian Otaegui, Romain Wattel, Emiliano Grillo, Simon Wakefield, Joel Stalter **147**: Álvaro Quirós, Padraig Harrington, Raphaël Jacquelin, Jens Dantorp, Connor Arendell **148**: Gaganjeet Bhullar, Raphael Marguery, Eddie Pepperell, Morten Madsen, Anthony Wall, Craig Lee, Robert Rock, Justin Walters, Richard Green, Chris Doak, Ricardo González, Andrea Pavan **149**: John Parry, Carlos Del Moral, Andreas Hartø, David Horsey, Johan Carlsson, George Coetzee, Lucas Bjerregaard, Peter Lawrie, Robert-Jan Derksen, Jêrôme Lando Casanova **150**: Darren Fichardt, John Gallagher, Marco Crespi, Stuart Manley, Thomas Bjørn, Francois Calmels, Rhys Davies **151**: Simon Thornton, Julien Guerrier, Anthony Snobeck, Tyrrell Hatton, James Morrison, David Drysdale, Richard Bland, Niclas Fasth, Lionel Weber **152**: Graeme Storm, Jack Doherty, Alastair Forsyth **153**: Daniel Brooks, Jose-Filipe Lima, Nacho Elvira, Paul Dwyer, Thomas Levet, Mark Tullo **154**: Garrick Porteous, Thomas Perrot, Baptiste Chapellan, Sam Walker, Oskar Henningsson **155**: David Higgins, John Hahn, Michael Lorenzo-Vera, Jbe' Kruger, Edouard Dubois **156**: Adrien Saddier, Kevin Phelan, Daniel Im **157**: Leonard Bem, Anthony Grenier **159**: Yeon-Jin Jeong **166**: Petr Gal   **WD**: Tom Lewis, José María Olazábal (73), Richie Ramsay (75), Thomas Aiken (79), Simon Khan (80) **DQ**: Thomas Pieters (75)

FIRST ROUND		SECOND ROUND		THIRD ROUND	
Kevin Stadler	64 (-7)	Kevin Stadler	132 (-10)	Kevin Stadler	204 (-9)
Marcel Siem	65 (-6)	Victor Riu	135 (-7)	Thongchai Jaidee	208 (-5)
Stephen Gallacher	66 (-5)	Marcel Siem	137 (-5)	Victor Riu	208 (-5)
2 Players	67 (-4)	7 Players	139 (-3)	Martin Kaymer	210 (-3)
Graeme McDowell	70 (-1)	**Graeme McDowell**	139 (-3)	**Graeme McDowell**	212 (-1)

OWR: 9 of top 50 entered - Rating: 188 - Points to 42nd - McDowell: 36 points, to 17th in OWR

Aberdeen Asset Management Scottish Open

Royal Aberdeen Golf Club - Aberdeen, Scotland
Champion: Justin Rose

Jun 10 - Jun 13
6,867 yards   Par 71
Purse: €3 Million

Apparently fully recovered from the shoulder tendinitis which delayed the start of his 2014 season, England's Justin Rose won his second consecutive event at the Aberdeen Asset Management Scottish Open, edging Sweden's Kristoffer Broberg by two at Royal Aberdeen. Hot on the heels of his PGA Tour victory at the Quicken Loans National two weeks earlier, Rose opened with rounds of 69-68 to trail a trio of halfway leaders by one, then carded a Saturday 66 to join Marc Warren atop the 54-hole leaderboard at 10-under-par 203. Looking every bit the class of the strong pre-British Open field, Rose then birdied four of his first six holes on Sunday to take command, eventually turning in 31, then motoring smoothly home in 34 for a closing 65 – a performance which left the remainder of the contenders bobbing in his wake. Indeed, more hotly contested was the battle for the final three places in the British open field which took place behind Rose. With Warren's place at Hoylake already secured, the first beneficiary was the 27-year-old Broberg, who'd opened with a Thursday 65, then hung around the lead admirably enough to nail down second. The remaining two spots went to England's Tyrrell Hatton (T4) and Scotland's Scott Jamieson (T8), with the latter nearly falling out of the 10, which would have nullified his berth.

1	Justin Rose	69-68-66-65	268	€627,020		David Howell	68-70-73-71	282	€26,335
2	Kristoffer Broberg	65-71-68-66	270	€418,009	41=	Ernie Els	73-71-73-66	283	€21,820
3	Marc Warren	67-69-67-70	273	€235,509		Jimmy Walker	71-70-73-69	283	€21,820
4=	Stephen Gallacher	72-69-70-63	274	€148,039		Bernd Wiesberger	74-68-72-69	283	€21,820
	Matteo Manassero	69-72-68-65	274	€148,039		O. Schniederjans (a)	71-70-72-70	283	-
	Shane Lowry	72-68-68-66	274	€148,039		George Coetzee	73-70-70-70	283	€21,820
	Tyrrell Hatton	69-71-66-68	274	€148,039		Martin Laird	70-73-70-70	283	€21,820
8=	Scott Jamieson	74-67-70-64	275	€84,522		Søren Kjeldsen	70-70-70-73	283	€21,820
	Rickie Fowler	71-71-68-65	275	€84,522	48=	Niclas Fasth	69-74-73-68	284	€18,434
	Robert Karlsson	71-71-67-66	275	€84,522		Thongchai Jaidee	71-71-73-69	284	€18,434
11=	Phil Mickelson	68-73-70-65	276	€64,834		Mikael Lundberg	71-73-70-70	284	€18,434
	Danny Willett	70-71-68-67	276	€64,834	51=	Wade Ormsby	71-73-74-67	285	€14,296
	Pablo Larrazábal	69-73-66-68	276	€64,834		Gary Stal	68-75-74-68	285	€14,296
14=	Paul Casey	69-71-72-65	277	€56,432		Thomas Aiken	71-70-74-70	285	€14,296
	Rory McIlroy	64-78-68-67	277	€56,432		Graeme Storm	70-72-73-70	285	€14,296
16=	Luke Donald	67-73-72-66	278	€48,832		Joost Luiten	73-70-72-70	285	€14,296
	James Morrison	71-72-69-66	278	€48,832		Richard Bland	67-74-72-72	285	€14,296
	Mikko Ilonen	71-68-69-70	278	€48,832		Ryan Palmer	70-72-71-72	285	€14,296
	Ricardo González	65-71-71-71	278	€48,832		Gareth Maybin	70-74-69-72	285	€14,296
	Craig Lee	72-69-66-71	278	€48,832	59=	Fabrizio Zanotti	70-70-76-70	286	€10,534
21=	Paul Waring	75-66-73-65	279	€42,512		Magnus A. Carlsson	71-72-72-71	286	€10,534
	Alexander Levy	75-69-69-66	279	€42,512		Johan Carlsson	71-73-71-71	286	€10,534
	John Hahn	71-71-68-69	279	€42,512		Michael Hoey	66-76-74-72	286	€10,534
24=	Felipe Aguilar	73-71-73-63	280	€39,126		Darren Clarke	69-73-70-74	286	€10,534
	Adrian Otaegui	71-69-71-69	280	€39,126	64=	Álvaro Quirós	71-71-75-70	287	€8,465
	Thomas Bjørn	70-73-68-69	280	€39,126		Carlos Del Moral	70-73-73-71	287	€8,465
27=	Paul Lawrie	74-70-71-66	281	€32,919		Ricardo Santos	73-71-71-72	287	€8,465
	Padraig Harrington	71-72-71-67	281	€32,919		Greig Hutcheon	70-70-74-73	287	€8,465
	Lucas Bjerregaard	70-69-73-69	281	€32,919		Tom Lewis	70-71-72-74	287	€8,465
	Mark Foster	71-70-71-69	281	€32,919		Matt Ford	75-67-70-75	287	€8,465
	Shiv Kapur	69-75-68-69	281	€32,919	70=	Gaganjeet Bhullar	75-69-76-68	288	€7,004
	Rafael Cabrera-Bello	72-68-71-70	281	€32,919		Maximilian Kieffer	71-73-73-71	288	€7,004
	Marcel Siem	73-69-69-70	281	€32,919	72=	Kevin Phelan	69-73-76-71	289	€5,640
	Russell Knox	68-74-69-70	281	€32,919		Damien McGrane	71-72-74-72	289	€5,640
35=	Alastair Forsyth	70-73-70-69	282	€26,335		J.B. Hansen	71-73-73-72	289	€5,640
	Miguel A. Jiménez	74-68-71-69	282	€26,335	75	Tommy Fleetwood	70-70-74-76	290	€5,634
	Simon Khan	70-71-71-70	282	€26,335	76	Scott Henry	73-71-72-75	291	€5,631
	David Drysdale	67-76-69-70	282	€26,335	77	Jeev Milkha Singh	70-71-74-77	292	€5,628
	Simon Dyson	71-73-68-70	282	€26,335	78	Matt Jones	71-73-71-80	295	€5,625

Out Of The Money: **145**: Steve Webster, Eduardo De La Riva, Simon Thornton, Kevin Stadler, Lee Westwood, Chris Wood, David Lynn, Kiradech Aphibarnrat, Sihwan Kim, Matthew Baldwin, Jbe' Kruger **146**: Peter Whiteford, Daan Huizing, Nick Faldo, Jonas Blixt, Victor Riu, Edoardo Molinari, Roope Kakko, Matthew Cort, Nicolas Colsaerts, Ross Fisher, Louis Oosthuizen, Thomas Levet, Julien Quesne **147**: Paul McGinley, Grégory Bourdy, Branden Grace, Robert-Jan Derksen, Stuart Manley, Ian Poulter, Francesco Molinari, Alejandro Cañizares, Yeon-Jin Jeong, Thomas Pieters **148**: Brett Rumford, Victor Dubuisson, Raphaël Jacquelin, Nacho Elvira, Jose-Filipe Lima, Jamie Donaldson, Matthew Fitzpatrick, Richie Ramsay, Romain Wattel, Richard Green **149**: Emiliano Grillo, Andy Sullivan, Mike Miller, Grégory Havret, Morten Madsen, Anthony Wall, Matthew Nixon, Simon Wakefield, Jorge Campillo, Eddie Pepperell **150**: David Horsey, Daniel Brooks, Marco Cresp, Peter Hanson, Richard Sterne, Jens Dantorp, David Law, Adam Gee **151**: Peter Lawrie, Dawie van der Walt **152**: Brooks Koepka, Jamie McLeary **153**: Darren Fichardt, Adrien Saddier **154**: Robert Rock, John Parry **157**: Alexander Culverwell (a) **158**: José María Olazábal   **WD**: Andrea Pavan (71), Peter Uihlein (73), Chris Doak (75), Francois Calmels (76), Lee Slattery (83)   **DQ**: Justin Walters

FIRST ROUND		SECOND ROUND		THIRD ROUND	
Rory McIlroy	64 (-7)	Ricardo González	136 (-6)	**Justin Rose**	203 (-10)
Kristoffer Broberg	65 (-6)	Kristoffer Broberg	136 (-6)	Marc Warren	203 (-10)
Ricardo González	65 (-6)	Marc Warren	136 (-6)	Kristoffer Broberg	204 (-9)
Michael Hoey	66 (-5)	**Justin Rose**	137 (-5)	Tyrrell Hatton	206 (-7)
Justin Rose	69 (-2)	David Howell	138 (-4)	2 Players	207 (-6)

OWR: 18 of top 50 entered - Rating: 366 - Points to 58th - Rose: 52 points, to 3rd in OWR

M2M Russian Open

Tseleevo Golf & Polo Club - Moscow, Russia
Champion: David Horsey

Jul 24 - Jul 27
7,491 yards   Par 72
Purse: €1 Million

England's David Horsey endured an up-and-down closing stretch on Sunday afternoon to ultimately claim his third career European Tour title, beating Damien McGrane on the first hole of sudden death at the M2M Russian Open. The 29-year-old Horsey held or shared the lead after each of the first three rounds at Moscow's Tseleevo Golf & Polo Club, leading by one after an opening 65, by two after tacking on a Friday 68, and sharing the top spot with Scotland's Peter Whiteford after posting a Saturday 70 which included two bogeys over his final six holes. Meanwhile, hoping to record his first victory since the 2008 Volvo China Open, McGrane began Sunday six back but his fortunes began turning quickly as two early birdies, combined with Horsey bogeys at the 5th and 6th brought him briefly within two of the lead. That margin returned to three by the turn, then two when McGrane birdied the 10th – and then, rather suddenly, they were tied after Horsey double-bogeyed the 470-yard par-4 12th. A Horsey bogey at the 374-yard 14th then put McGrane in front, and the Irishman promptly added a run of three straight birdies which, on most occasions, would have been enough to salt away the title. But his untimely bogey at the 448-yard 18th left the door slightly ajar, and once again there was Horsey, rising from the ashes to chip in for eagle at the par-5 17th – just enough to force a playoff which he would win (via a routine par) after McGrane's approach found a back bunker at the 18th.

1	David Horsey	65-68-70-72	275	€166,660		Adrian Otaegui	70-73-68-75	286	€7,733
2	Damien McGrane	69-71-69-66	275	€111,110		Kevin Phelan	69-70-74-73	286	€7,733
3	Scott Jamieson	66-72-69-69	276	€62,600	36=	David Drysdale	73-69-77-68	287	€7,200
4	Sam Hutsby	72-67-70-68	277	€50,000		Daniel Im	73-72-70-72	287	€7,200
5	Peter Whiteford	66-71-66-75	278	€42,400	38=	Gunn Charoenkul	73-68-74-73	288	€6,500
6=	Krister Ericsson	72-68-71-68	279	€32,500		S.S.P. Chowrasia	76-70-72-70	288	€6,500
	Thomas Pieters	67-68-72-72	279	€32,500		Roope Kakko	71-73-70-74	288	€6,500
8=	Maximilian Kieffer	67-71-73-69	280	€23,700		Rikard Karlberg	67-76-74-71	288	€6,500
	Andrea Pavan	73-70-64-73	280	€23,700		Jordan Smith	75-70-74-69	288	€6,500
10=	Carlos Del Moral	70-71-73-67	281	€19,200		Simon Wakefield	70-76-70-72	288	€6,500
	Sam Walker	69-71-73-68	281	€19,200	44=	Bradley Dredge	70-74-75-70	289	€5,600
12=	F. Andersson Hed	70-69-77-66	282	€15,150		Edouard Dubois	72-68-72-77	289	€5,600
	Daan Huizing	72-74-69-67	282	€15,150		Rhys Enoch	70-73-74-72	289	€5,600
	Mikko Korhonen	74-71-68-69	282	€15,150		Carlos Pigem	70-71-78-70	289	€5,600
	Brinson Paolini	72-71-70-69	282	€15,150	48=	Andreas Andersson	70-73-72-75	290	€4,900
	Haydn Porteous	72-71-70-69	282	€15,150		Jack Doherty	67-73-78-72	290	€4,900
	Adrien Saddier	69-73-70-70	282	€15,150		Simon Thornton	70-73-73-74	290	€4,900
18=	Seuk-Hyun Baek	74-70-69-70	283	€11,867	51=	Johan Carlsson	74-69-78-70	291	€4,300
	Gary Boyd	69-68-72-74	283	€11,867		Andrea Maestroni	72-71-75-73	291	€4,300
	Jorge Campillo	68-76-68-71	283	€11,867		James Morrison	71-73-71-76	291	€4,300
	Alastair Forsyth	75-70-70-68	283	€11,867	54=	Louis de Jager	67-74-75-76	292	€3,700
	JB Hansen	69-73-71-70	283	€11,867		Craig Lee	72-70-74-76	292	€3,700
	James Heath	71-72-71-69	283	€11,867		Morten Madsen	71-73-73-75	292	€3,700
24=	Søren Hansen	72-69-69-74	284	€10,550	57=	Joakim Mikkelsen	74-69-78-72	293	€3,200
	Jamie McLeary	68-72-70-74	284	€10,550		Matthew Nixon	69-76-74-74	293	€3,200
26=	Oliver Bekker	67-76-72-70	285	€9,200	59=	Merrick Bremner	79-65-71-79	294	€2,950
	Gaganjeet Bhullar	67-71-75-72	285	€9,200		Jack Wilson	67-74-80-73	294	€2,950
	Javi Colomo	72-68-71-74	285	€9,200	61=	Richard Finch	71-73-71-80	295	€2,750
	Nacho Elvira	69-69-77-70	285	€9,200		Mathias Gronberg	70-70-75-80	295	€2,750
	Adam Gee	70-75-69-71	285	€9,200	63	John Hahn	72-74-75-75	296	€2,600
	Andreas Hartø	73-70-73-69	285	€9,200	64=	Peter Erofejeff	74-72-72-79	297	€2,450
	Stuart Manley	71-73-71-70	285	€9,200		Phillip Price	70-75-73-79	297	€2,450
33=	Oskar Henningsson	68-76-73-69	286	€7,733	66	Liam Bond	73-73-76-76	298	€2,300

Out Of The Money: **147**: Poom Saksansin, Alexandre Kaleka, Søren Kjeldsen, Chinnarat Phadungsil **148**: Jose M. Lara **149**: Jaco Ahlers, Jonathan Fly **150**: Luis Claverie, Andrey Pavlov, Henri Satama, Nick Dougherty **151**: Jazz Janewattananond, Van Phillips, Berry Henson **152**: David Higgins, Vladimir Osipov, Daniel Suchan, Marc Dobias, Wen-Yi Huang, James Reiss **153**: Masahiro Kawamura, Julien Clement, Mark Suursalu, Ted Innes Ker **154**: Petr Gal, Jake Roos **155**: Daniel Vancsik, Rene Gruber, Nikolaj Nissen **156**: Arnond Vongvanij, Pavel Goryainov **157**: Petr Dedek **158**: Roland Steiner **160**: Fabian Becker, Mark Nichols, Peter Gustafsson, Benjamin Palanszki **161**: Ari Savolainen **162**: Nikita Ponomarev **166**: Mikhail Morozov **167**: James Ferraby **168**: Samuel Pereltsveyg **170**: Evgeny Volkov **172**: Evgeni Kafelnikov, Iskandar Tursunov **178**: Ilya Kurochkin

FIRST ROUND		SECOND ROUND		THIRD ROUND	
David Horsey	65 (-7)	**David Horsey**	133 (-11)	Peter Whiteford	203 (-13)
Scott Jamieson	66 (-6)	Thomas Pieters	135 (-9)	**David Horsey**	203 (-13)
Peter Whiteford	66 (-6)	Gary Boyd	137 (-7)	Andrea Pavan	207 (-9)
8 Players	67 (-5)	Peter Whiteford	137 (-7)	Scott Jamieson	207 (-9)
		4 Players	138 (-6)	Thomas Pieters	207 (-9)

OWR: 0 of top 50 entered - Rating: 3 - Points to 32nd - Horsey: 24 points, to 118th in OWR

Made In Denmark
Aug 14 - Aug 17

Himmerland Golf & Spa Resort - Aalborg, Denmark
Champion: Marc Warren

7,033 yards Par 71
Purse: €1.5 Million

Marc Warren's form had certainly been on the upswing coming into the inaugural Made In Denmark tournament, for his last three starts had included a third at the Scottish Open, a T39 at the Open Championship and a T15 at the PGA Championship. But in Denmark, the 33-year-old Scot finally put it all together, playing some outstanding weekend golf to claim his third career European Tour victory, and his first since the 2007 Johnnie Walker Championship. Warren initially stood seven shots off the pace at the halfway mark but made a major move in the third round when, in winds gusting as high as 30 mph, he birdied four of his final six holes to post a Saturday-low 66, good enough to join Wales' Bradley Dredge atop the leaderboard, three shots ahead of the pack. Sunday thus essentially shaped up into a two-man battle, but with Dredge bogeying three of his first five holes, Warren was quickly in the driver's seat, gaining a three-shot lead by the turn and playing steady enough golf that Dredge was never able to move closer than two thereafter. Before impressively large galleries, native sons Thomas Bjørn, Thorbjørn Olesen and Lasse Jensen all logged top-10 finishes, as did Swedish veterans Rikard Karlberg and Mikael Lundberg.

1	Marc Warren	71-70-66-68	275	€250,000		Robert-Jan Derksen	74-68-74-72	288	€9,300
2	Bradley Dredge	66-68-73-70	277	€166,660		Adrien Saddier	74-68-73-73	288	€9,300
3	Phillip Archer	70-70-71-69	280	€93,900	45=	Moritz Lampert	74-70-77-68	289	€7,500
4=	Thomas Bjørn	66-73-73-69	281	€63,700		Robert Rock	73-71-75-70	289	€7,500
	Oliver Fisher	75-65-72-69	281	€63,700		Sihwan Kim	70-75-73-71	289	€7,500
	Eddie Pepperell	73-68-71-69	281	€63,700		Grégory Havret	74-69-74-72	289	€7,500
7=	Lasse Jensen	72-69-74-67	282	€41,250		Scott Jamieson	71-75-71-72	289	€7,500
	Thorbjørn Olesen	69-70-72-71	282	€41,250		Johan Carlsson	71-70-75-73	289	€7,500
9=	Rikard Karlberg	73-70-71-69	283	€27,350	51=	Michael Jonzon	75-70-76-69	290	€5,700
	Mikael Lundberg	72-69-71-71	283	€27,350		Brandon Stone	73-73-74-70	290	€5,700
	S.S.P. Chowrasia	70-71-71-71	283	€27,350		Mikko Korhonen	71-73-75-71	290	€5,700
	Stuart Manley	73-69-69-72	283	€27,350		Jack Doherty	74-71-73-72	290	€5,700
	Simon Wakefield	71-67-72-73	283	€27,350		Garrick Porteous	71-68-78-73	290	€5,700
	Gareth Maybin	75-67-68-73	283	€27,350		Kenneth Ferrie	72-70-74-74	290	€5,700
15=	David Lipsky	72-71-73-68	284	€19,543	57=	Andrea Pavan	71-75-79-66	291	€4,425
	David Drysdale	71-68-76-69	284	€19,543		Felipe Aguilar	66-74-79-72	291	€4,425
	Roope Kakko	70-71-73-70	284	€19,543		Peter Hedblom	74-67-75-75	291	€4,425
	Tom Lewis	72-70-72-70	284	€19,543		Chris Doak	72-70-74-75	291	€4,425
	Søren Kjeldsen	71-73-70-70	284	€19,543	61=	Graeme Storm	75-70-78-69	292	€3,450
	Craig Lee	73-72-69-70	284	€19,543		Richard Green	76-69-77-70	292	€3,450
	Richard Bland	71-74-68-71	284	€19,543		Andrew Marshall	70-76-75-71	292	€3,450
22=	Andreas Hartø	70-72-75-68	285	€15,825		Jorge Campillo	73-72-74-73	292	€3,450
	Daniel Im	72-68-76-69	285	€15,825		Tyrrell Hatton	74-72-73-73	292	€3,450
	Andrew McArthur	72-72-72-69	285	€15,825		Mark Foster	73-73-73-73	292	€3,450
	Simon Dyson	77-69-70-69	285	€15,825		Peter Lawrie	70-75-73-74	292	€3,450
	Shiv Kapur	73-68-74-70	285	€15,825		Adrian Otaegui	74-72-72-74	292	€3,450
	Paul Waring	75-66-72-72	285	€15,825		Morten Madsen	71-70-76-75	292	€3,450
28=	Patrik Sjoland	71-70-76-69	286	€13,125	70=	Gary Stal	72-72-79-70	293	€2,370
	Kristoffer Broberg	75-67-75-69	286	€13,125		Richie Ramsay	75-70-75-73	293	€2,370
	Matthew Nixon	73-67-76-70	286	€13,125		Rasmus H. Nielsen	73-73-74-73	293	€2,370
	Damien McGrane	73-70-73-70	286	€13,125		Jamie McLeary	74-70-73-76	293	€2,370
	James Morrison	76-70-70-70	286	€13,125	74=	Gaganjeet Bhullar	73-70-75-76	294	€2,240
	Emiliano Grillo	71-69-74-72	286	€13,125		Nicolas Colsaerts	70-72-76-76	294	€2,240
34=	Wade Ormsby	71-72-76-68	287	€10,950	76=	Nicolai Kristensen	75-70-79-71	295	-
	Estanislao Goya	77-69-73-68	287	€10,950		Lee Slattery	71-75-78-71	295	€2,235
	Adam Gee	76-70-71-70	287	€10,950	78=	Carlos Del Moral	75-71-77-73	296	€2,228
	Romain Wattel	73-71-72-71	287	€10,950		Andrew Johnston	77-69-76-74	296	€2,228
	Steve Webster	76-69-68-74	287	€10,950		Simon Thornton	76-70-75-75	296	€2,228
39=	Chris Hanson	72-73-74-69	288	€9,300		Peter Uihlein	74-72-72-78	296	€2,228
	David Horsey	76-70-73-69	288	€9,300	82	James Heath	77-69-74-77	297	€2,220
	Daniel Gaunt	70-73-74-71	288	€9,300	83	Jonas Magnusson	75-69-78-76	298	€2,217
	Alexandre Kaleka	78-66-73-71	288	€9,300	84	Victor Riu	73-72-77-78	300	€2,214

Out Of The Money: **147**: Peter Vejgaard, Raphaël Jacquelin, Chris Wood, Ricardo González, Andy Sullivan, Merrick Bremner, J.B. Hansen, David Howell, Sam Walker, Fredrik Andersson Hed, James Kingston, Eduardo De La Riva, Ignacio Garrido, Kevin Phelan, Edouard Dubois **148**: Lucas Bjerregaard, Simon Griffiths, John Hahn, Daniel Lokke, John Parry, Magnus A. Carlsson, Ricardo Santos, David Higgins, Jeev Milkha Singh, Phillip Price **149**: Jason Knutzon, Mike Miller, Brett Rumford, Grégory Bourdy, Mads Sogaard, Jose-Filipe Lima, Jamie Elson, Jesper Billing **150**: Steven Jeppesen, Mark F. Haastrup, Nacho Elvira, Niclas Fasth, Daniel Gavins, Daan Huizing, Jesper Gaardsdal, Oscar Zetterwall, Mathias Gronberg, Christian Gloet **151**: Marco Crespi, Matthew Baldwin, Jacob Glennemo **152**: Richard Finch, Alastair Forsyth, Francois Calmels, Thomas Norret, Berry Henson **153**: Justin Walters, Peter Gustafsson, Joel Sjoholm, Anders Hansen, Keith Horne, Haydn Porteous **154**: Jose Manuel Lara **156**: Thriston Lawrence, Daniel Brooks, Krister Eriksson **157**: Thomas Levet, Brinson Paolini, Martin Leth Simonsen **160**: Oliver Bekker **161**: Petr Gal **WD**: Stephen Dodd (74), Julien Quesne (77), Anthony Wall (78), Jens Dantorp (78), Maximilian Kieffer

FIRST ROUND		SECOND ROUND		THIRD ROUND	
Felipe Aguilar	66 (-5)	Bradley Dredge	134 (-8)	**Marc Warren**	207 (-6)
Thomas Bjørn	66 (-5)	Simon Wakefield	138 (-4)	Bradley Dredge	207 (-6)
Bradley Dredge	66 (-5)	4 players	139 (-3)	Gareth Maybin	210 (-3)
Thorbjørn Olesen	69 (-2)	**Marc Warren**	141 (-1)	Simon Wakefield	210 (-3)
Marc Warren	70 (-1)			3 Players	212 (-1)

OWR: 1 of top 50 entered - Rating: 52 - Points to 27th - Warren: 24 points, to 68th in OWR

D+D Real Czech Masters

Albatross Golf Resort - Prague, Czech Republic
Champion: Jamie Donaldson

Aug 21 - Aug 24
7,466 yards Par 72
Purse: €1 Million

Wales' Jamie Donaldson won for the third time on the European PGA Tour – and clinched a spot on his first Ryder Cup team – at the inaugural playing of the D+D Real Czech Masters, outside of Prague, closing with Sunday 68 to edge countryman Bradley Dredge by two. Donaldson needed a top-seven finish to clinch the coveted Ryder Cup berth and demonstrated his determination early, taking the first round lead with an eight-birdie, two-bogey 66, then maintaining a slim one-shot margin over France's Grégory Bourdy after posting a Friday 69. He then began his third round with an eagle at the 538-yard 1st, but a double-bogey at the long par-4 8th and two late back nine bogeys eventually saw him home in 71 – good enough only to stand two shots behind Dredge, who followed opening rounds of 68-70 with a bogey-free 66 on Saturday. But in a final round which also saw Denmark's Søren Kjeldsen and South Africa's Merrick Bremner factor into the mix, Donaldson quickly retook the lead by birdieing the first three holes, leaving him two ahead of Dredge at the turn. Both men then played the final nine in 35, and with neither Kjeldsen nor Bremner being able to match that number, Donaldson walked home to raise the trophy.

Pos	Player	Scores	Total	Prize
1	Jamie Donaldson	66-69-71-68	274	€166,660
2	Bradley Dredge	68-70-66-72	276	€111,110
3=	Merrick Bremner	70-68-70-69	277	€56,300
	Søren Kjeldsen	68-70-68-71	277	€56,300
5=	Eddie Pepperell	70-72-71-67	280	€38,700
	Tommy Fleetwood	72-65-73-70	280	€38,700
7=	Sam Walker	69-71-70-71	281	€27,500
	Stephen Gallacher	70-67-71-73	281	€27,500
9=	Scott Jamieson	71-73-74-64	282	€19,500
	James Heath	73-70-71-68	282	€19,500
	Garrick Porteous	70-67-72-73	282	€19,500
	Peter Hedblom	70-68-73-71	282	€19,500
13=	Danny Willett	68-75-72-68	283	€14,433
	Javi Colomo	69-71-71-72	283	€14,433
	Craig Lee	69-71-71-72	283	€14,433
	Kenneth Ferrie	68-71-71-73	283	€14,433
	James Morrison	70-68-72-73	283	€14,433
	Matthew Baldwin	72-71-67-73	283	€14,433
19=	Peter Uihlein	70-73-72-69	284	€11,825
	Tim Sluiter	69-73-70-72	284	€11,825
	David Lipsky	69-71-69-75	284	€11,825
	Paul Waring	68-71-70-75	284	€11,825
23=	Stuart Manley	71-72-74-68	285	€10,100
	Kevin Phelan	72-69-73-71	285	€10,100
	Felipe Aguilar	73-71-70-71	285	€10,100
	Daan Huizing	69-74-70-72	285	€10,100
	Paul Lawrie	70-70-71-74	285	€10,100
	Rikard Karlberg	70-72-68-75	285	€10,100
	Grégory Bourdy	69-67-71-78	285	€10,100
30=	Lee Slattery	68-69-77-72	286	€7,811
	Tyrrell Hatton	70-73-71-72	286	€7,811
	Edouard Dubois	71-73-70-72	286	€7,811
	Duncan Stewart	70-69-74-73	286	€7,811
	Zane Scotland	74-70-69-73	286	€7,811
	Phillip Archer	69-72-71-74	286	€7,811
	Adrian Otaegui	70-70-72-74	286	€7,811
	JB Hansen	70-69-72-75	286	€7,811
	Mikael Lundberg	67-76-68-75	286	€7,811
39=	Dodge Kemmer	71-70-78-68	287	€5,500
	Hennie Otto	70-71-76-70	287	€5,500
	Tom Lewis	74-70-73-70	287	€5,500
	Gary Stal	71-73-72-71	287	€5,500
	Simon Wakefield	70-74-72-71	287	€5,500
	Anthony Wall	72-72-71-72	287	€5,500
	Oscar Stark	71-67-76-73	287	€5,500
	Adrien Saddier	71-72-70-74	287	€5,500
	Joel Sjoholm	74-70-69-74	287	€5,500
	Tain Lee	72-68-72-75	287	€5,500
	Francois Calmels	70-72-70-75	287	€5,500
	Andrea Pavan	72-70-69-76	287	€5,500
	S.S.P. Chowrasia	68-75-68-76	287	€5,500
52=	Chris Hanson	74-70-75-69	288	€3,438
	Damien McGrane	73-70-74-71	288	€3,438
	Shiv Kapur	71-70-75-72	288	€3,438
	Patrik Sjoland	72-72-71-73	288	€3,438
	Joost Luiten	70-71-73-74	288	€3,438
	Alastair Forsyth	73-71-70-74	288	€3,438
	John Hahn	68-69-76-75	288	€3,438
	Andy Sullivan	69-73-69-77	288	€3,438
60=	Gary Boyd	72-70-75-72	289	€2,400
	Peter Lawrie	72-72-73-72	289	€2,400
	Keith Horne	68-74-74-73	289	€2,400
	F. Andersson Hed	72-68-75-74	289	€2,400
	Richard Bland	71-70-74-74	289	€2,400
	Roope Kakko	70-70-74-75	289	€2,400
	Nacho Elvira	72-71-70-76	289	€2,400
	Andreas Hartø	73-71-69-76	289	€2,400
	Haydn Porteous	74-70-69-76	289	€2,400
69	Gaganjeet Bhullar	72-71-71-76	290	€1,900
70=	Ben Evans	74-70-76-71	291	€1,562
	Dylan Frittelli	72-70-75-74	291	€1,562
	Emiliano Grillo	72-72-73-74	291	€1,562
	Jason Knutzon	70-71-74-76	291	€1,562
	Sihwan Kim	74-67-73-77	291	€1,562
75=	Brandon Stone	71-73-75-73	292	€1,484
	Jack Doherty	73-69-76-74	292	€1,484
	Peter Whiteford	70-70-72-80	292	€1,484
	Steve Webster	70-72-68-82	292	€1,484
79=	Gareth Maybin	72-72-77-72	293	€1,474
	James Kingston	76-68-72-77	293	€1,474
81=	Mark Foster	74-69-74-77	294	€1,468
	Joakim Lagergren	71-68-76-79	294	€1,468
83	Matthew Nixon	68-74-76-77	295	€1,464

Out Of The Money: **145**: Daniel Brooks, Simon Thornton, Jens Dantorp, Lucas Bjerregaard, Thomas Pieters, Robert Rock, Bernd Wiesberger, Ruaidhri McGee, Ricardo Santos, Daniel Im, Florian Praegant **146**: Mikko Korhonen, Jbe' Kruger, Jeev Milkha Singh, Stanislav Matus, Eduardo De La Riva, Adam Gee, David Higgins, Bernd Ritthammer, Simon Dyson, David Drysdale, John Parry, Chris Doak, Stephen Dodd, Mathias Gronberg, Jose Manuel Lara **147**: Nathan Holman, David Horsey, Carlos Del Moral, Richard Finch, Jose-Filipe Lima, Anders Hansen, Michael Jonzon, Alexandre Kaleka, Gary Lockerbie, Jamie McLeary, Nick Dougherty **148**: Rhys Davies, Jamie Elson, Søren Hansen, Oliver Bekker, Ales Korinek, Vitek Novak, Thomas Norret, Lukas Tintera **149**: Chris Paisley, Estanislao Goya, Victor Riu, Nicolas Colsaerts, Graeme Storm, Sam Little **150**: Jorge Campillo, Krister Eriksson, Oskar Henningsson **151**: Justin Walters, Phillip Price, Thomas Levet **152**: Wade Ormsby, Oliver Fisher, Lloyd Kennedy **153**: Berry Henson **154**: Marek Novy **155**: Andrey Pavlov, Roland Hahn, Brinson Paolini **156**: Xavier Ruiz Fonhof **157**: Adam Rajmont **159**: Petr Gal, Petr Dedek **160**: Daniel Suchan, Evgeni Kafelnikov **167**: Rene Gruber **WD**: Ricardo González (213)

FIRST ROUND		SECOND ROUND		THIRD ROUND	
Jamie Donaldson	66 (-6)	**Jamie Donaldson**	135 (-9)	Bradley Dredge	204 (-12)
Mikael Lundberg	67 (-5)	Grégory Bourdy	136 (-8)	Søren Kjeldsen	206 (-10)
10 Players	68 (-4)	5 players	137 (-7)	**Jamie Donaldson**	206 (-10)
				Grégory Bourdy	207 (-9)
				2 Players	208 (-8)

OWR: 3 of top 50 entered - Rating: 62 - Points to 29th - Donaldson: 24 points, to 27th in OWR

71° Open D'Italia

Circolo Golf Torino - Turin, Italy
Champion: Hennie Otto

Aug 28 - Aug 31
7,208 yards Par 72
Purse: €1.5 Million

In only his second tournament since returning from back surgery, South African Hennie Otto spent much of the week atop the leaderboard before ultimately nailing down his third European Tour victory and his second career triumph in the Italian Open. The 38-year-old Otto opened with a bogey-free round of 67, which proved good enough to place him one behind co-leaders Bernd Wiesberger and homestanding Francesco Molinari. But Otto then took command on Friday, carding six outbound birdies to turn in 30, then adding an eagle at the 531-yard 12th and birdies at the both the par-3 13th and the 593-yard 15th to move to 10 under par on the day. Any chance of 59 was dashed with a bogey at the 465-yard 17th, but a birdie at the last brought Otto home in 62, staking him to a three-shot lead. Thereafter his play cooled and it was a matter of hanging on, particularly after a double-bogey at the par-5 9th slowed his Saturday progress - though his 71 still managed to hold a two-shot 54-hole lead. But on a Sunday in which his closest pursuers, Wiesberger and Scotland's Richie Ramsey, could manage no better than 70 and 72 respectively, Otto played solid methodical golf, birdieing the 1st and the 7th to turn in 34, then adding two more birdies at the 12th and 15th that would ultimately proved the margin of victory. Second place was claimed by England's David Howell, who carded seven birdies between holes 7-15 on his way to a closing 63 - a round which was just enough to bump Stephen Gallacher (who closed gamely with a 65) to third, when even a tie for second would have clinched an automatic spot on the European Ryder Cup team. Happily, Gallacher's strong 2013-14 seasons were rewarded when he was named as one of Paul McGinley's captain's picks two days later.

Pos	Player	Scores	Total	Prize		Player	Scores	Total	Prize
1	Hennie Otto	67-62-71-68	268	€250,000		Peter Whiteford	73-67-71-70	281	€9,750
2	David Howell	73-67-67-63	270	€166,660		Marcel Siem	73-68-70-70	281	€9,750
3	Stephen Gallacher	72-65-69-65	271	€93,900		F. Andersson Hed	74-67-70-70	281	€9,750
4=	Joost Luiten	69-68-70-65	272	€69,300		James Heath	73-68-70-70	281	€9,750
	Richie Ramsay	67-69-66-70	272	€69,300		Craig Lee	70-72-68-71	281	€9,750
6	Bernd Wiesberger	66-66-71-72	275	€52,500		Merrick Bremner	71-68-70-72	281	€9,750
7=	Andreas Hartø	70-69-70-67	276	€36,525		Daan Huizing	69-71-69-72	281	€9,750
	Simon Dyson	71-68-69-68	276	€36,525		Marc Warren	69-70-69-73	281	€9,750
	Ross Fisher	69-66-70-71	276	€36,525	46=	Oliver Fisher	74-67-75-66	282	€7,050
	Lee Slattery	70-68-67-71	276	€36,525		Benjamin Rusch (a)	73-66-75-68	282	-
11=	James Morrison	70-66-72-69	277	€25,850		Gareth Maybin	67-73-74-68	282	€7,050
	Andy Sullivan	70-72-66-69	277	€25,850		Felipe Aguilar	68-69-76-69	282	€7,050
	Romain Wattel	73-68-67-69	277	€25,850		J.B. Hansen	69-71-72-70	282	€7,050
14=	David Horsey	71-69-72-66	278	€21,600		Adrien Saddier	70-70-72-70	282	€7,050
	Sam Walker	70-72-68-68	278	€21,600		Anthony Wall	71-70-69-72	282	€7,050
	Shiv Kapur	73-69-68-68	278	€21,600		Seve Benson	70-67-72-73	282	€7,050
	Mikko Korhonen	70-67-71-70	278	€21,600	54=	Thomas Pieters	70-68-79-66	283	€5,250
18=	Kristoffer Broberg	73-68-72-66	279	€17,800		Jorge Campillo	71-71-73-68	283	€5,250
	Álvaro Quirós	70-72-68-69	279	€17,800		Maximilian Kieffer	68-70-76-69	283	€5,250
	Darren Clarke	72-70-67-70	279	€17,800		Matteo Manassero	73-69-71-70	283	€5,250
	Darren Fichardt	68-69-71-71	279	€17,800		Søren Hansen	71-66-72-74	283	€5,250
	Carlos Del Moral	70-68-70-71	279	€17,800	59=	Jason Knutzon	70-70-74-70	284	€4,200
	Francesco Molinari	66-72-69-72	279	€17,800		Magnus A. Carlsson	72-70-72-70	284	€4,200
24=	Tom Lewis	71-69-73-67	280	€13,800		Alessandro Tadini	72-69-72-71	284	€4,200
	Robert Rock	69-70-73-68	280	€13,800		Rafael Cabrera-Bello	73-63-75-73	284	€4,200
	Sihwan Kim	70-72-69-69	280	€13,800		Edoardo Molinari	71-69-71-73	284	€4,200
	Estanislao Goya	71-70-69-70	280	€13,800	64	Ed. Lipparelli (a)	68-70-71-76	285	-
	David Lipsky	69-67-73-71	280	€13,800	65=	Damien McGrane	71-71-73-71	286	€3,675
	Morten Madsen	68-68-73-71	280	€13,800		Roope Kakko	69-72-71-74	286	€3,675
	Richard Bland	67-71-71-71	280	€13,800	67=	Daniel Im	71-71-70-75	287	€3,375
	Francesco Laporta	68-72-69-71	280	€13,800		Alexander Levy	73-68-68-78	287	€3,375
	Tommy Fleetwood	72-70-67-71	280	€13,800	69=	Eduardo De La Riva	72-70-73-73	288	€3,075
	Ricardo González	74-66-68-72	280	€13,800		Filippo Bergamaschi	72-69-72-75	288	€3,075
	S.S.P. Chowrasia	69-72-66-73	280	€13,800	71=	Garrick Porteous	71-71-74-74	290	€2,795
35=	John Hahn	67-73-76-65	281	€9,750		Nacho Elvira	75-67-72-76	290	€2,795
	David Drysdale	73-69-71-88	281	€9,750	73	Gregory Molteni	70-70-74-78	292	€2,250
	Wade Ormsby	74-68-70-69	281	€9,750					

Out Of The Money: **143**: Thomas Aiken, Gaganjeet Bhullar, Grégory Bourdy, Alessio Bruschi, Nicolas Colsaerts, Chris Doak, Jack Doherty, Alexandre Kaleka, Stuart Manley, Jamie McLeary, Thomas Norret, Victor Riu, Gary Stal, Graeme Storm **144**: Edouard Dubois, Richard Finch, Mark Foster, Richard Green, Keith Horne, Raphaël Jacquelin, Jbe' Kruger, Renato Paratore, Andrea Pavan, Eddie Pepperell **145**: George Coetzee, Marco Crespi, Emiliano Grillo, Paul McGinley, José María Olazábal, Andrea Rota, Simon Thornton, Steve Webster **146**: Robert-Jan Derksen, Alastair Forsyth, Tyrrell Hatton, Moritz Lampert, Jose Manuel Lara, Matthew Nixon, Adrian Otaegui, Julien Quesne, Brett Rumford, Ricardo Santos, Simon Wakefield **147**: Phillip Archer, Marco Bernardini, Nino Bertasio, Johan Carlsson, Enrico Di Nitto, Guido Migliozzi, Nicolo Ravano, Jeev Milkha Singh, Chris Wood **148**: Daniel Brooks, Michele Cea, Padraig Harrington, Berry Henson, James Kingston, Peter Lawrie, Brinson Paolini, Pierre Relecom **149**: Nick Dougherty, Niclas Fasth, David Higgins, Thomas Levet, Jose-Filipe Lima, Federico Maccario **150**: Lorenzo Gagli, Patrik Sjoland, Justin Walters **151**: Francois Calmels, Yeon-Jin Jeong **152**: Jens Dantorp, John Parry, Andrea Romano **153**: Emanuele Canonica, Mathias Gronberg **154**: Ignacio Garrido, Michael Jonzon **WD**: Peter Hanson (140), Simon Khan (142) **DQ**: Daniel Vancsik (145), Adam Gee (281), Lucas Bjerregaard (293)

FIRST ROUND		SECOND ROUND		THIRD ROUND	
Bernd Wiesberger	66 (-6)	**Hennie Otto**	129 (-15)	**Hennie Otto**	200 (-16)
Francesco Molinari	66 (-6)	Bernd Wiesberger	132 (-12)	Richie Ramsay	202 (-14)
5 Players	67 (-5)	Ross Fisher	135 (-9)	Bernd Wiesberger	203 (-13)
Hennie Otto	67 (-5)	5 Players	136 (-8)	Ross Fisher	205 (-11)
				Lee Slattery	205 (-11)

OWR: 3 of top 50 entered - Rating: 87 - Points to 34th - Otto: 24 points, to 97th in OWR

Omega European Masters

Crans-sur-Sierre Golf Club - Crans Montana, Switzerland
Champion: David Lipsky

Sep 4 - Sep 7
6,848 yards Par 70
Purse: €2.3 Million

Twenty-six-year-old American David Lipsky, a full-time player on the Asian Tour, scored a breakthrough victory at the Omega European Masters, a longtime E Tour event currently co-sanctioned with the Asian circuit. A graduate of Northwestern University, Lipsky arrived with four straight top-25 E Tour finishes dating back to May but remained largely under the radar upon opening with a three-under-par 67 over the alpine Crans-sur-Sierre layout, a bogey-free round which placed him tied for 27th, five shots behind Scotland's Richie Ramsey. Lipsky hit stride on Friday, however, recording seven birdies en route to a 64 which jumped him up to fifth, then backed that up with a Saturday 66 to trail 54-hole leader Graeme Storm by three. On a Sunday which saw multiple contenders jockeying atop the leaderboard, Lipsky caught fire on the front nine, posting three birdies and an eagle from holes 3-7 to get into the mix, then played par golf through the 17th before birdieing the 402-yard 18th to post 262. Among the other contenders, only Storm (who closed with 68) could match him, setting up a playoff which Lipsky won with a scrambling par at the first extra hole, claiming both the title and a two-exemption on the European circuit.

Pos	Player	Scores	Total	Prize
1	David Lipsky	67-64-66-65	262	€383,330
2	Graeme Storm	64-66-64-68	262	€255,550
3=	Tyrrell Hatton	67-66-65-65	263	€129,490
	Brooks Koepka	65-65-66-67	263	€129,490
5=	Tommy Fleetwood	64-68-63-69	264	€89,010
	Danny Willett	67-70-64-63	264	€89,010
7	Jamie Donaldson	65-64-69-67	265	€69,000
8	Richie Ramsay	62-66-70-68	266	€57,500
9=	Gareth Maybin	64-67-69-67	267	€46,613
	Lee Slattery	68-68-65-66	267	€46,613
	Romain Wattel	68-69-65-65	267	€46,613
12	Richard Green	71-64-67-66	268	€39,560
13=	Seve Benson	65-67-70-67	269	€31,912
	Nicolas Colsaerts	68-67-69-65	269	€31,912
	Anirban Lahiri	70-67-68-64	269	€31,912
	Shane Lowry	66-65-68-70	269	€31,912
	Edoardo Molinari	62-70-68-69	269	€31,912
	Brett Rumford	69-65-71-64	269	€31,912
	Marc Warren	69-63-71-66	269	€31,912
	Bernd Wiesberger	66-70-67-66	269	€31,912
21=	Ricardo González	70-68-68-64	270	€25,645
	Grégory Havret	68-69-68-65	270	€25,645
	David Lynn	65-68-69-68	270	€25,645
	Jyoti Randhawa	72-65-65-68	270	€25,645
25=	Emiliano Grillo	66-68-69-68	271	€22,885
	James Morrison	66-69-67-69	271	€22,885
	Adrien Saddier	69-67-68-67	271	€22,885
	Peter Whiteford	68-65-70-68	271	€22,885
29=	Felipe Aguilar	66-68-70-68	272	€19,123
	Marco Crespi	69-69-62-72	272	€19,123
	Robert-Jan Derksen	66-67-71-68	272	€19,123
	Victor Dubuisson	65-67-68-72	272	€19,123
	Søren Hansen	69-67-68-68	272	€19,123
	Matthew Nixon	66-69-70-67	272	€19,123
	Julien Quesne	69-66-68-69	272	€19,123
36=	Scott Jamieson	70-69-66-68	273	€16,100
	Jason Knutzon	70-69-68-66	273	€16,100
	Thorbjørn Olesen	69-69-67-68	273	€16,100
	Peter Uihlein	72-67-65-69	273	€16,100
40=	Thomas Bjørn	66-72-68-68	274	€13,570
	Richard Bland	70-69-68-67	274	€13,570
	Mikko Ilonen	73-66-65-70	274	€13,570
	Raphaël Jacquelin	65-69-69-71	274	€13,570
	Peter Lawrie	69-70-62-73	274	€13,570
	Morten Madsen	70-69-67-68	274	€13,570
	Adrian Otaegui	68-70-67-69	274	€13,570
47=	Mark Foster	69-68-67-71	275	€10,350
	J.B. Hansen	72-67-65-71	275	€10,350
	David Howell	69-70-68-68	275	€10,350
	Matteo Manassero	68-71-66-70	275	€10,350
	Chapchai Nirat	66-70-73-66	275	€10,350
	Wade Ormsby	67-67-70-71	275	€10,350
	Ricardo Santos	67-70-72-66	275	€10,350
54=	Matthew Baldwin	68-68-72-68	276	€7,636
	Michael Hoey	65-68-73-70	276	€7,636
	Rikard Karlberg	68-68-70-70	276	€7,636
	Craig Lee	66-70-69-71	276	€7,636
	Jamie McLeary	66-70-69-71	276	€7,636
59=	Nacho Elvira	70-68-68-71	277	€6,555
	Anders Hansen	67-71-69-70	277	€6,555
61=	Francois Calmels	70-68-67-73	278	€5,750
	Bradley Dredge	70-69-70-69	278	€5,750
	David Drysdale	66-73-68-71	278	€5,750
	Mikael Lundberg	67-71-66-74	278	€5,750
	Hennie Otto	68-69-68-73	278	€5,750
66=	Peter Hanson	66-68-73-72	279	€4,612
	Sihwan Kim	72-66-71-70	279	€4,612
	Paul Lawrie	70-68-69-72	279	€4,612
	Martin Rominger	68-70-69-72	279	€4,612
	Gary Stal	71-66-67-75	279	€4,612
71=	John Parry	71-68-69-72	280	€3,448
	Álvaro Quirós	69-68-69-74	280	€3,448
73=	Seuk-Hyun Baek	69-70-68-74	281	€3,441
	Padraig Harrington	66-71-72-72	281	€3,441
	Robert Rock	69-69-71-72	281	€3,441
76=	Johan Carlsson	70-69-74-70	283	€3,430
	Rahil Gangjee	72-67-71-73	283	€3,430
	Jose-Filipe Lima	71-68-72-72	283	€3,430
	Prom Meesawat	66-73-71-73	283	€3,430
80=	Adilson da Silva	73-65-70-76	284	€3,422
	Justin Walters	70-68-73-73	284	€3,422
82	Yeon-Jin Jeong	71-68-77-72	288	€3,417

Out Of The Money: **140**: Søren Kjeldsen, Miguel Ángel Jiménez, George Coetzee, Victor Riu, Paul Waring, Chris Doak, Darren Clarke, Alexander Levy, Joonas Granberg, Andy Sullivan **141**: Pablo Larrazábal, Mithun Perera, Ross Fisher, Shiv Kapur, Daniel Brooks, Carlos Pigem, Chris Wood, Roope Kakko **142**: Masahiro Kawamura, Sven Struver, José María Olazábal, Damian Ulrich, Jorge Campillo, Matthew Fitzpatrick, Kristoffer Broberg, Maximilian Kieffer, Thomas Pieters, Magnus A. Carlsson **143**: Robert Karlsson, Thomas Aiken, Daan Huizing, Niclas Fasth, Moritz Lampert, Gi-Whan Kim **144**: Gaganjeet Bhullar, Darren Fichardt, Digvijay Singh, Fabrizio Zanotti, Grégory Bourdy **145**: Jbe' Kruger, Andrea Pavan, Joel Girrbach, Raphael De Sousa, Mardan Mamat, Jeev Milkha Singh, Angelo Que, Thomas Levet, Simon Thornton **146**: Anthony Wall, Stuart Manley, Andreas Hartø, Eduardo De La Riva, Kieran Pratt **147**: Filippo Campigli, Berry Henson, Carlos Del Moral, Pariya Junhasavasdikul, S.S.P. Chowrasia, Marcus Both **149**: Dominic Foos (a) **150**: Federico Zucchetti, Mathias Gronberg, Arnond Vongvanij **151**: Manuel Quirós, Rodrigo Lacerda Soares **154**: Fredrik Svanberg **155**: Jeff Lucquin **169**: Edouard Amacher **WD**: Steve Webster (70), Rashid Khan (72), Marcel Siem (74), Siddikur Rahman (75), Thaworn Wiratchant (76), Richard T. Lee (78)

FIRST ROUND		SECOND ROUND		THIRD ROUND	
Richie Ramsay	62 (-8)	Richie Ramsay	128 (-12)	Graeme Storm	194 (-16)
Edoardo Molinari	62 (-8)	Jamie Donaldson	129 (-11)	Tommy Fleetwood	195 (-15)
Tommy Fleetwood	64 (-6)	Brooks Koepka	130 (-10)	Brooks Koepka	196 (-14)
Gareth Maybin	64 (-6)	Graeme Storm	130 (-10)	**David Lipsky**	197 (-13)
Graeme Storm	64 (-6)	3 Players	131 (-9)	3 Players	198 (-12)
David Lipsky	67 (-3)	**David Lipsky**	131 (-9)		

OWR: 5 of top 50 entered - Rating: 142 - Points to 35th - Lipsky: 30 points, to 154th in OWR

KLM Open

Kennemer Golf & Country Club - Zandvoort, The Netherlands
Champion: Paul Casey

Sep 11 - Sep 14
6,626 yards   Par 70
Purse: €1.8 Million

Paul Casey's chances of winning the KLM Open didn't seem especially good after two rounds, as the 37-year-old Englishman, making his first start since becoming a father, stood tied for 32nd, eight shots behind halfway leader Pablo Larrazábal. Indeed, Casey was far enough back that he actually started on the 10th tee on Saturday - from which he wasted little time lifting himself back into the fray, carding five back nine birdies (including on all three of the loop's par 3s) to turn in 29, then adding four more on the front to reach the 9th at nine under par. Remarkably, his approach at the 418-yard par 4 nearly went in the hole (which would have meant shooting 59) before spinning back off the green, leading to an unlucky bogey and a round of 62 - good enough to stand in third, four shots behind 54-hole leader Romain Wattel. But Wattel would stumble to a 74 on Sunday, paving the way for Casey (who closed with 66, but left the door slightly ajar with an untimely bogey at the par-3 15th) to win by one when three-time KLM winner Simon Dyson could manufacture only one birdie over the final four holes in attempts at catching him. Notably, third place went to England's Andy Sullivan, who nosed ahead of countryman Eddie Pepperell behind a late hole-in-one at the 15th - an ace which won him a trip into space courtesy of XCOR Space Expeditions, a tournament sponsor.

1	Paul Casey	68-70-62-66	266	€300,000		Magnus A. Carlsson	68-71-70-67	276	€12,420
2	Simon Dyson	70-66-66-65	267	€200,000		Tom Lewis	70-69-70-67	276	€12,420
3	Andy Sullivan	67-68-66-67	268	€112,680	41=	Marc Warren	68-68-71-70	277	€9,900
4	Eddie Pepperell	69-68-66-66	269	€90,000		Nicolas Colsaerts	72-68-66-71	277	€9,900
5=	Johan Carlsson	70-67-70-63	270	€59,580		Adam Gee	69-70-69-69	277	€9,900
	Pablo Larrazábal	68-62-75-65	270	€59,580		Grégory Bourdy	73-67-69-68	277	€9,900
	Joost Luiten	65-70-67-68	270	€59,580		Wade Ormsby	70-69-67-71	277	€9,900
	Romain Wattel	67-65-64-74	270	€59,580		David Howell	68-69-73-67	277	€9,900
9=	Oliver Fisher	70-66-70-65	271	€38,160		Mark Foster	70-67-73-67	277	€9,900
	Richie Ramsay	69-65-65-72	271	€38,160		Alexandre Kaleka	72-67-72-66	277	€9,900
11=	Tyrrell Hatton	68-67-72-65	272	€27,495		Andrea Pavan	66-70-67-74	277	€9,900
	Raphaël Jacquelin	71-68-68-65	272	€27,495	50=	James Heath	69-67-71-71	278	€7,920
	Robert-Jan Derksen	71-67-68-66	272	€27,495		Thorbjørn Olesen	69-71-69-69	278	€7,920
	Jbe' Kruger	73-67-70-66	272	€27,495	52=	Miguel A. Jiménez	71-69-66-73	279	€7,020
	Mikko Ilonen	69-66-70-67	272	€27,495		Craig Lee	69-69-68-73	279	€7,020
	Brooks Koepka	69-66-70-67	272	€27,495		Simon Thornton	68-69-75-67	279	€7,020
	Paul Waring	69-71-65-67	272	€27,495	55=	John Hahn	71-66-70-73	280	€5,805
	Edoardo Molinari	66-66-71-69	272	€27,495		Nacho Elvira	71-67-69-73	280	€5,805
19=	Richard Bland	70-70-67-66	273	€21,600		Søren Kjeldsen	70-70-71-69	280	€5,805
	Robert Rock	73-67-65-68	273	€21,600		Jose-Filipe Lima	70-67-74-69	280	€5,805
	Gary Stal	66-71-65-71	273	€21,600	59=	Jack Doherty	69-71-68-73	281	€5,040
22=	Thomas Aiken	67-68-71-68	274	€18,990		Søren Hansen	68-66-75-72	281	€5,040
	Chris Wood	69-67-70-68	274	€18,990		John Parry	71-69-69-72	281	€5,040
	Emiliano Grillo	72-66-67-69	274	€18,990		J. Krietemeijer (a)	71-69-70-71	281	
	Maximilian Kieffer	67-68-68-71	274	€18,990	63	Gaganjeet Bhullar	70-69-75-68	282	€4,680
	Thomas Pieters	70-66-67-71	274	€18,990	64	Inder Van Weerelt	69-70-73-71	283	€4,500
	Peter Uihlein	66-68-67-73	274	€18,990	65=	Darren Clarke	73-67-70-74	284	€4,050
28=	Tommy Fleetwood	70-67-71-67	275	€15,232		Wil Besseling	68-72-71-73	284	€4,050
	Daniel Im	67-70-70-68	275	€15,232		Julien Quesne	70-69-71-74	284	€4,050
	Padraig Harrington	70-68-70-67	275	€15,232		Byeong-Hun An	72-68-72-72	284	€4,050
	Reinier Saxton	71-67-70-67	275	€15,232	69=	Roope Kakko	69-69-71-76	285	€3,510
	Shane Lowry	70-69-67-69	275	€15,232		Damien McGrane	71-68-73-73	285	€3,510
	Robert Karlsson	69-69-68-69	275	€15,232	71	Niclas Fasth	70-70-70-76	286	€3,280
	James Morrison	73-67-65-70	275	€15,232	72=	Marco Crespi	71-69-70-77	287	€2,697
	J.B. Hansen	72-66-67-70	275	€15,232		Jeev Milkha Singh	72-68-72-75	287	€2,697
36=	Chris Doak	69-70-68-69	276	€12,420		Daan Huizing	72-68-76-71	287	€2,697
	Mikko Korhonen	71-69-67-69	276	€12,420	75	Estanislao Goya	67-73-76-72	288	€2,691
	Gon. F'dez-Castaño	71-69-66-70	276	€12,420	76	Jamie McLeary	67-72-74-76	289	€2,688

Out Of The Money: **141**: José María Olazábal, Álvaro Quirós, Carlos Del Moral, Kristoffer Broberg, Robin Kind, Matthew Nixon **142**: Moritz Lampert, Victor Riu, Alastair Forsyth, Stuart Manley, Anders Hansen, Anthony Wall, Peter Lawrie, Matteo Manassero, Peter Whiteford, Matthew Baldwin, David Horsey, Dominic Foos (a), Darius Van Driel **143**: Darren Fichardt, Scott Jamieson, Jason Knutzon, Ben Collier, Kevin Phelan, Ricardo Santos, Lee Slattery, Morten Madsen, Adrian Otaegui, Graeme Storm **144**: Simon Wakefield, Grégory Havret, Gareth Maybin, Paul Lawrie, Michael Hoey, Maarten Lafeber, Brett Rumford, Sam Walker, Duncan Stewart, Matthew Fitzpatrick, Connor Arendell **145**: Severiano Prins, Thomas Bjørn, Richard Green, Fredrik Andersson Hed **146**: Shiv Kapur, David Higgins, Patrik Sjoland, Jorge Campillo, Sihwan Kim, Brinson Paolini, David Drysdale, Jonas Blixt, Taco Remkes **147**: Ross Fisher, Jesper Billing **148**: Floris De Vries, David Lipsky, Mikael Lundberg, Daniel Brooks **149**: Hennie Otto, Lucas Bjerregaard **150**: Eduardo De La Riva, Francois Calmels **151**: Yeon-Jin Jeong, James Kingston, Vince van Veen, Jose Manuel Lara **152**: Andreas Hartø, Tim Sluiter **153**: Edouard Dubois, Sven Struver **155**: Jens Dantorp **157**: Kevin Reints, Lars Keunen   **WD**: Fabrizio Zanotti, Felipe Aguilar, Thomas Levet, Ricardo González, David Lynn (75), Adrien Saddier (82)

FIRST ROUND		SECOND ROUND		THIRD ROUND	
Joost Luiten	65 (-5)	Pablo Larrazábal	130 (-10)	Romain Wattel	196 (-14)
Peter Uihlein	66 (-4)	Romain Wattel	132 (-8)	Richie Ramsay	199 (-11)
Andrea Pavan	66 (-4)	Edoardo Molinari	132 (-8)	**Paul Casey**	200 (-10)
Gary Stal	66 (-4)	3 Players	134 (-6)	Andy Sullivan	201 (-9)
Edoardo Molinari	66 (-4)	**Paul Casey**	138 (-2)	Peter Uihlein	201 (-9)
Paul Casey	68 (-2)				

OWR: 2 of top 50 entered   -   Rating: 123   -   Points to 35th   -   Casey: 28 points, to 62nd in OWR

ISPS Handa Wales Open

Celtic Manor Resort (2010) - Newport, Wales
Champion: Joost Luiten

Sep 18 - Sep 21
7,352 yards   Par 71
Purse: €1.8 Million

Having finished fifth in his homeland a week earlier, 28-year-old Dutchman Joost Luiten came loaded for bear at the ISPS Handa Wales Open, and by week's end he would be raising the trophy for the fourth time in his relatively young European Tour career. Luiten nearly was a wire-to-wire winner, though his opening round 65 was a backloaded affair as he stood even par through eight holes before reeling off seven birdies (against one bogey) over his final 10 holes. He followed this up with a Friday 69 (which left him one stroke off Shane Lowry's halfway lead) before unleashing a second 65 on Saturday - this time bogey-free - to return to the top of the leaderboard by two shots. But on a Sunday in which none of the contenders would be able to go notably low, Luiten bogeyed his first two holes, allowing Lowry to briefly draw even with a birdie at the par-3 3rd. But Luiten would retake control with birdies at the 11th and 12th, and while he could do no better than even par golf down the stretch, this would ultimately prove enough to see him home one ahead of both Lowry (who birdied the 613-yard closer when an eagle was needed) and 23-year-old Englishman Tommy Fleetwood, who played his final five holes in six under par en route to a closing 67. In this, the final event prior to the Ryder Cup, only three European team members participated: Jamie Donaldson (easily showing the best form by closing 68-67 to finish 4th), Thomas Bjørn (who closed with a disappointing 74 to tie for 58th) and captain's pick Lee Westwood, whose Sunday 76 included an inglorious six bogeys and one double bogey, leaving him tied for 60th.

#	Player	Scores	Total	Prize
1	Joost Luiten	65-69-65-71	270	€375,780
2=	Tommy Fleetwood	68-68-68-67	271	€195,831
	Shane Lowry	68-65-68-70	271	€195,831
4=	Nicolas Colsaerts	66-68-71-67	272	€82,251
	Jamie Donaldson	70-67-68-67	272	€82,251
	Eddie Pepperell	68-74-63-67	272	€82,251
	Marc Warren	70-67-67-68	272	€82,251
	Edoardo Molinari	72-63-68-69	272	€82,251
9=	Robert Rock	67-71-70-65	273	€45,695
	Andrea Pavan	72-69-65-67	273	€45,695
	Romain Wattel	69-72-64-68	273	€45,695
12=	Bernd Wiesberger	71-67-71-65	274	€34,902
	Seve Benson	71-69-68-66	274	€34,902
	Graeme Storm	71-69-65-69	274	€34,902
	Anthony Wall	69-71-65-69	274	€34,902
	Steve Webster	68-72-64-70	274	€34,902
17=	Nathan Holman	70-70-70-65	275	€28,138
	Francesco Molinari	71-71-68-65	275	€28,138
	Richie Ramsay	69-70-70-66	275	€28,138
	Andy Sullivan	74-66-66-69	275	€28,138
	Thongchai Jaidee	68-67-67-73	275	€28,138
22=	Sihwan Kim	70-70-70-66	276	€24,463
	Ricardo Santos	68-68-69-71	276	€24,463
	J.B. Hansen	69-71-65-71	276	€24,463
	Grégory Havret	69-67-66-74	276	€24,463
26=	Søren Kjeldsen	69-71-73-64	277	€22,096
	Patrik Sjoland	69-67-71-70	277	€22,096
	Peter Uihlein	71-68-68-70	277	€22,096
29=	Emiliano Grillo	70-71-70-67	278	€20,067
	Raphaël Jacquelin	76-65-69-68	278	€20,067
	Victor Riu	72-71-64-71	278	€20,067
32=	Thorbjørn Olesen	71-70-71-67	279	€16,769
	Kristoffer Broberg	71-70-70-68	279	€16,769
	Ross Fisher	70-72-68-69	279	€16,769
	Julien Quesne	74-68-68-69	279	€16,769
	James Morrison	71-69-69-70	279	€16,769
	Gaganjeet Bhullar	71-70-68-70	279	€16,769
	Phillip Price	71-66-71-71	279	€16,769
	Danny Willett	72-67-67-73	279	€16,769
40	Oliver Fisher	69-72-69-70	280	€14,655
41=	Robert Karlsson	71-72-70-68	281	€13,528
	John Hahn	70-70-72-69	281	€13,528
	Edouard Dubois	73-70-67-71	281	€13,528
	Bradley Dredge	71-70-68-72	281	€13,528
45=	Mark Foster	69-69-74-70	282	€11,499
	Magnus A. Carlsson	76-67-69-70	282	€11,499
	Thomas Pieters	72-68-71-71	282	€11,499
	Simon Wakefield	68-72-70-72	282	€11,499
	David Lynn	72-69-67-74	282	€11,499
50=	Johan Carlsson	69-73-71-70	283	€9,019
	Wade Ormsby	70-71-70-72	283	€9,019
	Adrian Otaegui	70-69-71-73	283	€9,019
	Robert-Jan Derksen	73-66-71-73	283	€9,019
	Simon Thornton	71-69-70-73	283	€9,019
	Daan Huizing	73-69-68-73	283	€9,019
56=	Ricardo González	74-69-71-70	284	€7,215
	Lucas Bjerregaard	71-68-72-73	284	€7,215
58=	Paul Casey	70-70-73-72	285	€6,651
	Thomas Bjørn	71-69-71-74	285	€6,651
60=	Andrew McArthur	66-74-75-71	286	€5,862
	Lee Slattery	73-70-72-71	286	€5,862
	Phillip Archer	71-71-72-72	286	€5,862
	Daniel Im	70-72-71-73	286	€5,862
	Lee Westwood	73-69-68-76	286	€5,862
65=	Paul Lawrie	72-71-74-70	287	€4,848
	Jamie McLeary	68-73-77-69	287	€4,848
	Damien McGrane	71-72-72-72	287	€4,848
	Nacho Elvira	71-70-71-75	287	€4,848
69=	Chris Wood	73-68-72-75	288	€4,196
	Greig Hutcheon	72-70-71-75	288	€4,196
71	Craig Lee	68-72-73-76	289	€3,382
72	Niclas Fasth	69-74-69-78	290	€3,379
73	Adam Gee	72-71-72-78	293	€3,376
74	Maximilian Kieffer	71-70-74-80	295	€3,373

Out Of The Money: **144**: Jorge Campillo, Roope Kakko, David Howell, Rafael Cabrera-Bello, James Kingston, Richard Bland, Nick Dougherty, Adam Gee, Matthew Nixon **145**: Daniel Brooks, Daniel Gaunt, Adrien Saddier, Grégory Bourdy, Søren Hansen, Matthew Baldwin, Michael Hoey, Justin Walters, David Drysdale, Alexandre Kaleka **146**: Andreas Hartø, Brinson Paolini, Richard Finch, Lam Zhiqun, David Boote, Gareth Maybin, Mike Hearne, Estanislao Goya, Pablo Larrazábal, John Parry, Hirofumi Miyase **147**: Scott Jamieson, Jeev Milkha Singh, Mikko Korhonen, Stuart Manley, Eduardo De La Riva, James Heath, Tom Lewis, Thomas Norret, Jack Doherty, Sam Walker, Peter Whiteford **148**: Mathias Gronberg, Stephen Gallacher, Jose-Filipe Lima **149**: Liam Bond, Simon Khan, Francois Calmels, Kevin Phelan, Brett Rumford, Joe Ferguson, Alastair Forsyth **150**: David Higgins, Paul Waring, Tyrrell Hatton **151**: Evan Griffith, Peter Lawrie **152**: Fredrik Andersson Hed, Darren Fichardt, Matthew Cort, Marco Crespi **153**: Carlos Del Moral **154**: Morten Madsen **156**: Yeon-Jin Jeong, Ted Innes Ker **157**: Mikael Lundberg **158**: José María Olazábal **163**: Lee Rooke **WD**: Hennie Otto (74), Álvaro Quirós (75), Rikard Karlberg **DQ**: Jason Knutzon (156), Chris Doak

FIRST ROUND		SECOND ROUND		THIRD ROUND	
Joost Luiten	65 (-6)	Shane Lowry	133 (-9)	**Joost Luiten**	199 (-14)
Nicolas Colsaerts	66 (-5)	**Joost Luiten**	134 (-8)	Shane Lowry	201 (-12)
Andrew McArthur	66 (-5)	Nicolas Colsaerts	134 (-8)	Grégory Havret	202 (-11)
3 Players	67 (-4)	Thongchai Jaidee	135 (-7)	Thongchai Jaidee	202 (-11)
		Edoardo Molinari	135 (-7)	Edoardo Molinari	203 (-10)

OWR: 7 of top 50 entered - Rating: 144 - Points to 39th - Luiten: 30 points, to 36th in OWR

Alfred Dunhill Links Championship

Oct 2 - Oct 5

The Old Course - St Andrews, Scotland — 7,279 yards — Par 72
Carnoustie - Carnoustie, Scotland — 7,412 yards — Par 72
Kingsbarns Golf Links - St Andrews, Scotland — 7,150 yards — Par 72
Champion: Oliver Wilson — Purse: $5 Million

Once among the more touted prospects in modern British golf, 34-year-old Oliver Wilson had spent the better part of his career struggling on the European Tour, but all of that ended with an exciting breakthrough victory - while playing on a sponsor exemption - at the Alfred Dunhill Links Championship. Wilson led after two of the first three rounds at this multi-site event, keyed by a Thursday 64 at Carnoustie and a third round 65 (which included five birdies and an eagle) at St Andrews. This stood him three strokes ahead of a quartet of players headed by world number one Rory McIlroy, and Wilson responded by playing steady Sunday golf, turning in 37, then birdieing the 10th, 11th and 16th to come home with a safe 72, and a 271 total. But he had help in winning, as Scotland's Richie Ramsay finished one behind after bogeying the 16th and 17th, and England's Tommy Fleetwood missed a six-foot birdie putt at the last to tie. And also lamenting a lost opportunity was McIlroy, who tied for second despite double-bogeying the first (when his approach spun back into the Swilcan Burn) and bogeying the 17th, when a putt from off the green found the Infamous Road bunker.

1	Oliver Wilson	64-72-65-70	271	€625,787		Pablo Larrazábal	71-73-68-68	280	€27,147
2=	Richie Ramsay	69-68-68-67	272	€279,990		Lucas Bjerregaard	74-68-70-68	280	€27,147
	Rory McIlroy	73-67-64-68	272	€279,990		Stephen Gallacher	68-70-69-73	280	€27,147
	Tommy Fleetwood	69-73-62-68	272	€279,990		Jbe' Kruger	75-71-66-68	280	€27,147
5	Chris Doak	70-67-70-66	273	€159,200		Gary Stal	69-75-68-68	280	€27,147
6=	Richard Sterne	73-66-68-67	274	€112,642	42=	Matthew Nixon	70-70-70-71	281	€19,900
	Shane Lowry	66-70-71-67	274	€112,642		Ryan Evans	67-74-69-71	281	€19,900
	Louis Oosthuizen	70-74-62-68	274	€112,642		Jamie McLeary	67-72-70-72	281	€19,900
9=	Brooks Koepka	70-73-64-68	275	€79,600		Brandon Stone	72-67-70-72	281	€19,900
	Chris Wood	70-69-66-70	275	€79,600		Grégory Bourdy	67-71-71-72	281	€19,900
11=	Mark Foster	68-72-70-66	276	€64,706		Craig Lee	71-71-69-70	281	€19,900
	Marcel Siem	69-71-68-68	276	€64,706		Paul McGinley	72-70-69-70	281	€19,900
	Robert-Jan Derksen	73-70-63-70	276	€64,706		Grégory Havret	74-71-66-70	281	€19,900
14=	David Howell	70-72-68-67	277	€54,068		Emiliano Grillo	72-73-66-70	281	€19,900
	Bernd Wiesberger	71-71-67-68	277	€54,068	51=	Oliver Fisher	74-69-66-73	282	€13,892
	Robert Karlsson	72-68-68-69	277	€54,068		Paul Casey	69-73-66-74	282	€13,892
	Ryan Palmer	69-68-68-72	277	€54,068		Alejandro Cañizares	72-71-65-74	282	€13,892
18=	Richard Green	68-71-71-68	278	€43,930		Francesco Molinari	74-70-68-70	282	€13,892
	Paul Lawrie	69-72-68-69	278	€43,930		Andy Sullivan	70-71-71-70	282	€13,892
	Søren Hansen	72-68-69-69	278	€43,930		Maximilian Kieffer	72-70-70-70	282	€13,892
	Peter Uihlein	73-69-69-67	278	€43,930		Jason Scrivener	72-72-68-70	282	€13,892
	Thomas Pieters	73-73-65-67	278	€43,930	58=	Ricardo González	69-70-72-72	283	€10,889
	Padraig Harrington	66-70-71-71	278	€43,930		Nick Dougherty	72-69-71-71	283	€10,889
	Raphaël Jacquelin	65-70-69-74	278	€43,930		Thorbjørn Olesen	71-70-71-71	283	€10,889
25=	Branden Grace	76-65-69-69	279	€35,670	61=	Graeme Storm	68-72-70-74	284	€9,575
	Darren Fichardt	73-72-65-69	279	€35,670		Adrian Otaegui	67-75-67-75	284	€9,575
	John Parry	68-73-68-70	279	€35,670		Ross Fisher	73-73-65-73	284	€9,575
	Marc Warren	73-70-68-68	279	€35,670		Edoardo Molinari	73-68-70-73	284	€9,575
	Richard Bland	71-71-70-67	279	€35,670	65	Felipe Aguilar	71-67-72-75	285	€8,636
	George Coetzee	71-67-68-73	279	€35,670	66=	Thomas Aiken	71-70-69-76	286	€7,527
	Alexander Levy	68-68-68-75	279	€35,670		Robert Rock	67-76-67-76	286	€7,527
32=	Ernie Els	71-74-65-70	280	€27,147		Niclas Fasth	72-71-69-74	286	€7,527
	Thongchai Jaidee	71-71-68-70	280	€27,147		Adrien Saddier	72-73-67-74	286	€7,527
	Magnus A. Carlsson	74-70-67-69	280	€27,147		Shiv Kapur	70-72-70-74	286	€7,527
	Nacho Elvira	71-72-68-69	280	€27,147	71	Hennie Otto	69-70-70-78	287	€5,632
	Michael Hoey	72-70-65-73	280	€27,147	72	Garrick Porteous	74-67-71-79	291	€6,629

Out Of The Money: **213**: Nick Cullen, Eduardo De La Riva, Nick Faldo, Ashley Hall, Anders Hansen, Sam Hutsby, Mikko Ilonen, Scott Jamieson, Simon Khan, Peter Lawrie, Tom Lewis, Damien McGrane, James Morrison, Julien Quesne, Brett Rumford, Anthony Wall, Justin Walters, Romain Wattel, Danny Willett, Fabrizio Zanotti **214**: Merrick Bremner, Marco Crespi, Richard Finch, Nathan Holman, Andrew Johnston, Joost Luiten, David McKenzie, Colin Montgomerie, Haydn Porteous, Peter Whiteford **215**: Victor Dubuisson, Simon Dyson, Tyrrell Hatton, Simon Wakefield **216**: Jens Dantorp, David Drysdale, Roope Kakko, Rikard Karlberg, Moritz Lampert, Matteo Manassero, Gareth Maybin, Kevin Phelan, Charl Schwartzel, Paul Waring **217**: Rafael Cabrera-Bello, Martin Kaymer, Morten Madsen, Andrea Pavan, Álvaro Quirós, Steve Webster, Ruan de Smidt **218**: Trevor Fisher Jr., Justin Harding, Keith Horne, Sandy Lyle **219**: Johan Carlsson, J.B. Hansen, Eddie Pepperell, Simon Thornton, Ulrich Van Den Berg **220**: Matthew Baldwin, Darren Clarke, Louis de Jager, Estanislao Goya, David Horsey, Daan Huizing, Wade Ormsby **221**: Mark Anguiano, Jorge Campillo, David Duval, John Hahn, Søren Kjeldsen, Thriston Lawrence, Lee Slattery **222**: Seve Benson, Daniel Brooks, Francois Calmels, Stuart Manley, Ricardo Santos **223**: Sihwan Kim, James Kingston, Danie van Tonder, Jack Wilson **224**: Carlos Del Moral, Joonas Granberg, Matthew Griffin, Andreas Hartø, Jeev Milkha Singh **225**: Victor Riu **226**: Oliver Bekker **227**: Thomas Levet **229**: Mikael Lundberg **232**: Yeon-Jin Jeong, Brody Ninyette **237**: Dimitrios Papadatos **WD**: Kristoffer Broberg

FIRST ROUND		SECOND ROUND		THIRD ROUND	
Oliver Wilson	64 (-8)	Raphaël Jacquelin	135 (-9)	**Oliver Wilson**	201 (-15)
Raphaël Jacquelin	65 (-7)	Shane Lowry	136 (-8)	Tommy Fleetwood	204 (-12)
Padraig Harrington	66 (-6)	Padraig Harrington	136 (-8)	Rory McIlroy	204 (-12)
Shane Lowry	66 (-6)	**Oliver Wilson**	136 (-8)	Alexander Levy	204 (-12)
6 Players	67 (-5)	Alexander Levy	136 (-8)	Raphaël Jacquelin	204 (-12)

OWR: 9 of top 50 entered - Rating: 252 - Points to 50th - Wilson: 44 points, to 156th in OWR

Portugal Masters

Oceanico Victoria Golf Course - Vilamoura, Portugal
Champion: Alexander Levy

Oct 9 - Oct 12
7,209 yards   Par 71
Purse: €2 Million

In an event shortened to 36 holes by unremitting rains, 24-year-old Alexander Levy became the first Frenchman to win two European Tour events in the same season by claiming a three-shot victory at the Portugal Masters. Levy began the week in fast form, birdieing five of his first seven holes on the soft Oceanico Victoria course en route to a front nine 30, then came home in 33 to join Scotland's Scott Jamieson and Spain's Adrian Otaegui on 63 – which, surprisingly found them a full three strokes off of the lead. This was because former Ryder Cup player Nicolas Colsaerts simply overpowered the golf course, posting seven birdies over his first 12 holes, then adding eagles at the 315-yard 15th and the 589-yard 17th before narrowly missing an 18-foot birdie putt at the last for 59; instead of becoming the E Tour's first man to break 60, he instead became the 19th man to equal it. The rains then came hard on Friday and now it was Levy's turn for heroics. Playing early, he methodically carded five birdies on each nine on his way to a 10-under-par 61, posting his 18-under-par 124 total before play was called for the day. Colsaerts would complete a somewhat less glorious second round 67 on Saturday morning to trail by three, and in the end, save for one initial hole on Sunday before the skies opened up yet again, that would be all the golf that either man would play for the duration. With a total of 75 millimeters worth of rain falling during tournament week, the decision was initially made to play only 54 holes, then, after Sunday's early deluge, that was revised to 36, with Levy being declared the winner.

	Player	Scores	Total	Prize		Player	Scores	Total	Prize
1	Alexander Levy	63-61	124	€250,000		Johan Carlsson	67-70	137	€9,911
2	Nicolas Colsaerts	60-67	127	€166,660		Niclas Fasth	69-68	137	€9,911
3	Felipe Aguilar	65-64	129	€93,900		Joachim B Hansen	68-69	137	€9,911
4=	Romain Wattel	67-64	131	€63,700		Peter Whiteford	68-69	137	€9,911
	Morten O. Madsen	65-66	131	€63,700		Ross Fisher	67-70	137	€9,911
	Rich Bland	66-65	131	€63,700		Shane Lowry	71-66	137	€9,911
7=	Grégory Bourdy	67-65	132	€34,740		Pablo Larrazábal	68-69	137	€9,911
	Scott Jamieson	63-69	132	€34,740		Peter Uihlein	69-68	137	€9,911
	Danny Willett	65-67	132	€34,740		Adrien Saddier	70-67	137	€9,911
	Chris Wood	68-64	132	€34,740		Jbe' Kruger	66-71	137	€9,911
	Michael Hoey	65-67	132	€34,740		Steve Webster	71-66	137	€9,911
12=	Rafael Cabrera Bello	64-69	133	€23,220		Gary Stal	69-68	137	€9,911
	Adrian Otaegui	63-70	133	€23,220	47=	Daniel Brooks	68-70	138	€6,150
	Paul Waring	67-66	133	€23,220		Søren Kjeldsen	72-66	138	€6,150
	Thomas Aiken	66-67	133	€23,220		Padraig Harrington	72-66	138	€6,150
	Tommy Fleetwood	68-65	133	€23,220		Fabrizio Zanotti	71-67	138	€6,150
17=	John Hahn	67-67	134	€19,050		Marco Crespi	68-70	138	€6,150
	Ricardo González	69-65	134	€19,050		Andy Sullivan	70-68	138	€6,150
	Thongchai Jaidee	67-67	134	€19,050		Robert-Jan Derksen	70-68	138	€6,150
	Graeme Storm	69-65	134	€19,050		Roope Kakko	68-70	138	€6,150
21=	Branden Grace	66-69	135	€15,600		David Horsey	69-69	138	€6,150
	Marcel Siem	67-68	135	€15,600		Eduardo De La Riva	66-72	138	€6,150
	Thorbjørn Olesen	71-64	135	€15,600		Lucas Bjerregaard	68-70	138	€6,150
	George Coetzee	68-67	135	€15,600	58=	Jeev Milkha Singh	72-67	139	€3,825
	Nacho Elvira	67-68	135	€15,600		David Lynn	65-74	139	€3,825
	Marc Warren	69-66	135	€15,600		Robert Karlsson	69-70	139	€3,825
	Magnus Carlsson	69-66	135	€15,600		Tom Lewis	72-67	139	€3,825
	Justin Walters	68-67	135	€15,600		Tyrrell Hatton	70-69	139	€3,825
	Emiliano Grillo	67-68	135	€15,600		Paul McGinley	67-72	139	€3,825
30=	Pedro Figueiredo	67-69	136	€12,900		Ricardo Gouveia	70-69	139	€3,825
	Ryan Evans	68-68	136	€12,900		Matthew Nixon	73-66	139	€3,825
	David Drysdale	68-68	136	€12,900		Eddie Pepperell	70-69	139	€3,825
33=	Simon Khan	67-70	137	€9,911		Matthew Baldwin	69-70	139	€3,825
	Victor Riu	64-73	137	€9,911					

Out Of The Money: **140**: Julien Quesne, Mikko Ilonen, Oliver Wilson, Francesco Molinari, Seve Benson, Maximilian Kieffer, Ricardo Santos, Anthony Wall, Chris Doak, Paul Lawrie, Lee Slattery, John Parry **141**: Hennie Otto, David Howell, Søren Hansen, Matteo Manassero, Álvaro Quirós, Grégory Havret, Carlos Del Moral, Sihwan Kim, Gareth Maybin **142**: Francois Calmels, Darren Clarke, Simon Wakefield, Bernd Wiesberger, Kevin Phelan, Darren Fichardt, Jorge Campillo, Kristoffer Broberg **143**: Peter Lawrie, Tiago Cruz, James Morrison, Alejandro Cañizares **144**: Joao Carlota, Mikael Lundberg, Hugo Santos, Oliver Fisher, Tomas Silva, Andrea Pavan **145**: Simon Dyson, Damien McGrane, Jamie McLeary, Craig Lee **146**: Thomas Pieters, Shiv Kapur, Daan Huizing, Simon Thornton **147**: Moritz Lampert **148**: Yeon-Jin Jeong, Robert Rock **151**: Goncalo Pinto **166**: Chenxiao Duan **WD**: Richie Ramsay (70), Mark Foster (71), Thomas Levet (77) **DQ**: Stuart Manley (71), José María Olazábal (72), Raphaël Jacquelin (72), Richard Green (75)

FIRST ROUND

Nicolas Colsaerts	60 (-11)
Alexander Levy	63 (-8)
Adrian Otaegui	63 (-8)
Scott Jamieson	63 (-8)
2 Players	64 (-7)

OWR: 2 of top 50 entered - Rating: 107 - Points to 29th - Levy: 24 points, to 74th in OWR

Hong Kong Open

Hong Kong Golf Club - Fanling, Hong Kong
Champion: Scott Hend

Oct 16 - Oct 19
6,699 yards   Par 70
Purse: $1.3 Million

Beyond the scheduling quirk of having both its 2013 and 2014 editions count as part of a single official European Tour season, the venerable Hong Kong has recently borne the misfortune of being scheduled opposite star-drawing limited-field events, in 2013 going head-to-head against South Africa's lucrative Nedbank Golf Challenge, while in 2014 losing stars to the World Match Play Championship. But if only a handful of elite names were present this time around, one of them at least injected some life into things over the first 36 holes as Hall-of-Famer Ernie Els opened 66-65 to take a two-stroke halfway lead. Saddled with an ongoing hip problem, however, Els shot 71 on Saturday to fall to sixth, then a Sunday 69 to ultimately tie for fifth. This left room for a pair of Australians with solid Asian Tour pedigrees to move atop the Saturday leaderboard, with Marcus Fraser bouncing back from an opening bogey to post a 66 and grab the lead on 11-under-par 199, while long-hitting Scott Hend carded his second 67 in three days to trail by one. Fraser would struggle to a closing 72 and fall off the pace, and Hend also stumbled somewhat in the early going, turning in even-par 34. But Hend would settle down on the inward half, adding three birdies to close with another 67 and a 267 total, good enough to tie Filipino Angelo Que, who'd birdied four of his last seven holes to finish with a solid 66. Que, however, made bogey on the first playoff hole (the 410-yard 18th), leaving Hend to become the event's first Australian champion since Greg Norman in 1983, and to gain exempt status on the E Tour throughout 2015.

1	Scott Hend	67-66-67-67	267	€171,843	34=	Seuk-Hyun Baek	66-73-69-69	277	€7,321
2	Angelo Que	65-69-67-66	267	€114,562		Grégory Bourdy	67-68-71-71	277	€7,321
3	Kevin Phelan	69-67-67-66	269	€64,546		Adilson da Silva	69-67-74-67	277	€7,321
4	Mark Foster	67-68-66-69	270	€51,555		Wen-Chong Liang	70-69-68-70	277	€7,321
5=	Lucas Bjerregaard	69-68-67-67	271	€34,129		Julien Quesne	67-67-72-71	277	€7,321
	S.S.P. Chowrasia	69-65-70-67	271	€34,129		Anthony Wall	68-71-68-70	277	€7,321
	Ernie Els	66-65-71-69	271	€34,129		Jeung-Hun Wang	72-67-69-69	277	€7,321
	Marcus Fraser	67-67-65-72	271	€34,129	41=	J. Janewattananond	69-69-72-68	278	€6,187
9=	Eduardo De La Riva	68-67-70-67	272	€20,897		Søren Kjeldsen	71-68-70-69	278	€6,187
	Raphaël Jacquelin	66-67-69-70	272	€20,897		Wade Ormsby	67-67-72-72	278	€6,187
	Cameron Smith	68-65-69-70	272	€20,897		Thaworn Wiratchant	69-68-71-70	278	€6,187
12=	Seve Benson	68-66-71-68	273	€16,704	45=	Nacho Elvira	66-69-71-73	279	€4,949
	Javier Colomo	68-70-64-71	273	€16,704		Alastair Forsyth	69-66-72-72	279	€4,949
	Wei-Chih Lu	66-68-71-68	273	€16,704		J.B. Hansen	70-66-73-70	279	€4,949
15=	Richard Bland	70-65-70-69	274	€13,940		Andreas Hartø	69-69-68-73	279	€4,949
	Rahil Gangjee	68-68-72-66	274	€13,940		James Heath	66-73-74-66	279	€4,949
	Adam Groom	67-68-68-71	274	€13,940		Sihwan Kim	67-72-72-68	279	€4,949
	Jyoti Randhawa	64-70-68-72	274	€13,940		Tom Lewis	71-68-71-69	279	€4,949
	Lee Slattery	68-66-73-67	274	€13,940		Stuart Manley	68-71-70-70	279	€4,949
20=	Daan Huizing	66-68-71-70	275	€10,733	53=	Jack Doherty	68-67-72-73	280	€3,815
	Daniel Im	69-68-70-68	275	€10,733		Nicholas Fung	69-70-73-68	280	€3,815
	P. Junhasavadiskul	69-68-68-70	275	€10,733		Mardan Mamat	71-67-71-71	280	€3,815
	Shiv Kapur	68-68-70-69	275	€10,733	56=	Chan Kim	67-70-73-71	281	€3,114
	Rikard Karlberg	67-70-72-66	275	€10,733		Craig Lee	71-65-70-75	281	€3,114
	Mikko Korhonen	69-67-70-69	275	€10,733		James Morrison	71-68-73-69	281	€3,114
	Jbe' Kruger	66-69-66-74	275	€10,733		Martin Rominger	72-67-73-69	281	€3,114
	Prom Meesawat	71-66-68-70	275	€10,733		Paul Waring	73-64-70-74	281	€3,114
	Joong-Kyung Mo	68-71-66-70	275	€10,733	61=	Jason Knutzon	68-68-73-73	282	€2,732
	Peter Whiteford	67-70-71-67	275	€10,733		David Lipsky	68-70-72-72	282	€2,732
	Charlie Wi	70-68-69-68	275	€10,733	63	Marco Crespi	71-68-69-75	283	€2,578
31=	Marcus Both	67-67-71-71	276	€8,558	64	Jamie McLeary	69-69-77-69	284	€2,475
	Matthew Nixon	70-67-69-70	276	€8,558	65	Chi-Huang Tsai	71-68-74-72	285	€2,372
	Andrea Pavan	70-66-71-69	276	€8,558	66	Sam Cyr	67-69-71-79	286	€2,268

Out Of The Money: **140**: Unho Park, Peter Lawrie, Victor Riu, Steve Lewton, Kieran Pratt, Damien McGrane, Shih-Chang Chan, Matthew Stieger, Jake Higginbottom, Mithun Perera **141**: Zane Scotland, Brinson Paolini, Berry Henson, Scott Jamieson, David Drysdale, Scott Barr, Ricardo Santos, Anthony Kang, Paul Peterson, Joonas Granberg, Jamie Elson, Andrew Dodt **142**: Steve Webster, Yanwei Liu, Chiragh Kumar, Sam Walker, Danny Chia, Chapchai Nirat, Mikael Lundberg, Sung Lee, Kiradech Aphibarnrat, Miguel Ángel Jiménez, Brett Rumford, John Parry, Jose Manuel Lara, Boonchu Ruangkit, Antonio Lascuña **143**: Richard T. Lee, Anirban Lahiri, Justin Walters, Matthew Griffin, Gi-Whan Kim, Simon Yates **144**: Ricardo González, Arnod Vongvanij, Adrian Otaegui, Jeev Milkha Singh, Himmat Rai, Wen Teh Lu, Gunn Charoenkul, Bryce Easton, Roope Kakko, Philip Archer, Chinnarat Phadungsil, Adam Gee, Søren Hansen, Lian-Wei Zhang **145**: Rashid Khan, Carlos Pigem, Nicolas Colsaerts, Robert-Jan Derksen **146**: Michael Regan Wong, Sam Brazel, Y.E. Yang, James Stewart, Timothy Tang, Elmer Salvador, Fredrik Andersson Hed, Dimitrios Papadatos, Chih-Bing Lam, Jens Dantorp **147**: Shinichi Mizuno, Panupol Pittayarat, Sujjan Singh **148**: Rich Beem **149**: Simon Wakefield, Roderick Staunton, In-Woo Lee **150**: Shun Yat Jason Hak, Wen-Tang Lin, Doug Williams **151**: Woon Man Wong, Chawalit Plaphol **152**: Namchok Tantipokakul **153**: Niklas Lemke, Wilson Choy **154**: Adrien Saddier, Martin Liu **WD**: Carlos Del Moral (76), Sung Kang (79)

FIRST ROUND		SECOND ROUND		THIRD ROUND	
Jyoti Randhawa	64 (-6)	Ernie Els	131 (-9)	Marcus Fraser	199 (-11)
Angelo Que	65 (-5)	Raphaël Jacquelin	133 (-7)	**Scott Hend**	200 (-10)
9 Players	66 (-4)	**Scott Hend**	133 (-7)	Jbe' Kruger	201 (-9)
Scott Hend	67 (-3)	Cameron Smith	133 (-7)	Angelo Que	201 (-9)
		11 Players	134 (-6)	Mark Foster	201 (-9)

OWR: 1 of top 50 entered - Rating: 44 - Points to 30th - Hend: 19 points, to 133rd in OWR

Volvo World Match Play Championship

Oct 15 - Oct 19

The London Golf Club - Ash, Kent, England
Champion: Mikko Ilonen

7,026 yards   Par 72
Purse: €2.25 Million

The Volvo World Match Play Championship celebrated its 50th birthday first by returning to England after a four-year absence (its first 45 playings having taken place at Wentworth), then by making a minor format change that saw pool play produce an eight-man knockout field instead of 16, reducing the overall number of rounds played by one. The eight players who reached the quarter-finals included several top international stars, but two such entries were upset forthwith, as France's Victor Dubuisson lost two down to Finland's Mikko Ilonen, while Ryder Cup star Patrick Reed (the only American in the field) was upended by South African George Coetzee (the last man invited) 2 & 1. Meanwhile, the Netherlands' Joost Luiten, still on strong form after a recent win at the Wales Open, cruised past Spain's Pablo Larrazábal 6 & 5, while the event's top overall seed, world number five Henrik Stenson of Sweden, locked down the final semi-final spot with a two up victory over countryman Jonas Blixt. The semi-finals produced a bit more drama with Ilonen and Luiten squaring off in a match which saw the Finn jump out to an early two-hole lead, then fall behind as Luiten birdied the 8th, 11th and 13th to climb back on top. But Ilonen responded with a run of his own – a winning par at the par-3 14th, then birdies at the 15th and 17th – to clinch victory. Meanwhile, on the other side of the draw, Stenson each time drew even after falling behind on four separate occasions, ultimately closing out Coetzee with a birdie at the par-5 18th to win one up. In Sunday afternoon's all-Scandinavian final, Stenson then jumped to a one-up lead with a birdie at the 4th but soon fell deeply in the hole after Ilonen captured the 5th, 8th, 11th and 12th (only two with birdies) to move three up. Stenson tried gamely to rally by birdieing the par-5 13th and 15th, but in the end he still reached the par-4 17th two down, then saw Ilonen slam the door by carding one last birdie to claim his fifth career E Tour triumph by a 3 & 1 margin.

POOL I (Stage Losers earn €33,862 / €43,875)

Graeme McDowell def. Alexander Levy   3 & 2
Joost Luiten def. Mikko Ilonen   1 up
Henrik Stenson halved w/ George Coetzee
Thongchai Jaidee def. Francesco Molinari   2 up
Paul Casey def. Jamie Donaldson   2 & 1
Jonas Blixt def. Patrick Reed   2 & 1
Victor Dubuisson def. Pablo Larrazábal   2 & 1
Shane Lowry def. Stephen Gallacher   3 & 2

POOL II (Stage Losers earn €33,862 / €43,875)

Victor Dubuisson def. Shane Lowry   3 & 2
Pablo Larrazábal def. Stephen Gallacher   1 up
Mikko Ilonen def. Graeme McDowell   2 & 1
Joost Luiten def. Alexander Levy   4 & 3
Henrik Stenson def. Francesco Molinari   2 & 1
George Coetzee def. Thongchai Jaidee   2 & 1
Jamie Donaldson def. Jonas Blixt   3 & 2
Patrick Reed def. Paul Casey   2 & 1

POOL III (Stage Losers earn €33,862 / €43,875)

Patrick Reed def. Jamie Donaldson   3 & 2
Jonas Blixt halved w/ Paul Casey
Stephen Gallacher def. Victor Dubuisson   2 & 1
Pablo Larrazábal def. Shane Lowry   2 & 1
Joost Luiten def. Graeme McDowell   2 up
Mikko Ilonen def. Alexander Levy   1 up
Henrik Stenson def. Thongchai Jaidee   2 & 1
Francesco Molinari def. George Coetzee   2 & 1

QUARTER FINALS (Losers earn €74,475)

George Coetzee def. Patrick Reed   2 & 1
Mikko Ilonen def. Victor Dubuisson   2 up
Joost Luiten def. Pablo Larrazábal   6 & 5
Henrik Stenson def. Jonas Blixt   2 up

SEMI FINALS

Mikko Ilonen def. Joost Luiten   2 & 1
Henrik Stenson def. George Coetzee   2 & 1

Ilonen wins €375,000   -   Henrik Stenson wins €250,000   -   Luiten wins €140,850   -   Coetzee €112,500

FINAL ROUND - Mikko Ilonen def. Henrik Stenson   3 & 1

	1	2	3	4	5	6	7	8	9	10	11	12	13	14	15	16	17	18
Par	5	4	4	3	4	5	4	3	4	4	4	3	5	3	5	3	4	5
M.Ilonen	5	4	4	3	4	5	4	2	4	3	3	3	5	2	5	3	3	-
H.Stenson	5	4	4	2	5	5	4	3	4	3	4	4	3	4	3	4	-

THIRD PLACE MATCH: Joost Luiten def. George Coetzee   19th

OWR: 9 of top 50 entered   -   Rating: 131   -   Points to 16th   -   Ilonen: 28 points, to 37th in OWR

ISPS Handa Perth International
Lake Karrinyup Country Club - Perth, Australia
Champion: Thorbjørn Olesen

Oct 23 - Oct 26
7,143 yards   Par 72
Purse: AU$1.75 Million

Dramatically reshaping what had otherwise been rather a disappointing year, 24-year-old Dane Thorbjørn Olesen weathered a concerted Sunday charge by France's Victor Dubuisson to hang on and win the ISPS Handa Perth International by three shots. Having logged but a single European Tour top-10 finish since January, Olesen started the week in strong form, posting eight birdies during a bogey-free 64 that tied him for the Thursday lead with Australian John Wade. A second round 69 left him one behind England's Peter Whiteford at the halfway mark before Olesen heated up again on Saturday, making six birdies over his first 14 holes to extend the lead to four before a bogey at the 533-yard 15th ultimately saw him home in 67, good enough to hold a three-stroke 54-hole lead over South Korean Sihwan Kim. But while Kim (and his immediate pursuers, James Morrison and Peter Uihlein) would all fade on Sunday, world number 22 Dubuisson mounted a charge. Beginning the day eight shots in arrears, the 24-year-old birdied the 1st and the 7th to turn in 34, then reeled off four birdies at the 11th, 12th, 14th and 15th en route to a bogey-free 66 and a 274 total. Playing well behind him, Olesen struggled somewhat with his driver but scrambled well when he needed to, most notably on a pair of par 5s, the 612-yard 7th and the 553-yard 11th, where he recovered from wayward tee shots to record much-needed birdies. An Olesen bogey at the par-3 12th allowed Dubuisson to creep within one before the touted Dane responded with a bounce-back birdie at the 453-yard 13th and, eventually, the clinching birdie at the 533-yard 15th, eventually marching pleasantly home over the final three holes to capture his second career European Tour title.

Pos	Player	Scores	Total	Prize
1	Thorbjørn Olesen	64-69-67-71	271	€198,300
2	Victor Dubuisson	71-67-70-66	274	€132,200
3	Mark Foster	67-73-67-69	276	€74,483
4=	Lucas Bjerregaard	71-70-66-70	277	€43,405
	Steve Dartnall	68-71-68-70	277	€43,405
	David Drysdale	67-68-71-71	277	€43,405
	Matthew Griffin	67-73-70-67	277	€43,405
	James Morrison	72-63-69-73	277	€43,405
9=	Ryan Fox	69-70-72-67	278	€21,695
	Richard Green	68-68-70-72	278	€21,695
	Sihwan Kim	66-68-69-75	278	€21,695
	Wade Ormsby	72-68-72-66	278	€21,695
	Andrea Pavan	71-70-67-70	278	€21,695
	Peter Uihlein	69-71-65-73	278	€21,695
15=	Marcus Fraser	68-70-71-70	279	€16,420
	Mikko Korhonen	71-70-67-71	279	€16,420
	Charl Schwartzel	68-69-70-72	279	€16,420
	Jason Scrivener	67-74-70-68	279	€16,420
19=	Nathan Green	71-71-66-72	280	€14,516
	Brett Rumford	67-72-73-68	280	€14,516
21=	Richard Bland	68-72-70-71	281	€13,624
	JB Hansen	71-68-69-73	281	€13,624
23=	Jason Dufner	70-70-69-73	282	€12,374
	Nick Gillespie	71-71-67-73	282	€12,374
	Matthew Nixon	70-71-69-72	282	€12,374
	Jason Norris	71-69-68-74	282	€12,374
	Gary Stal	69-71-67-75	282	€12,374
28=	Grégory Bourdy	69-72-71-71	283	€11,125
	Peter O'Malley	72-69-70-72	283	€11,125
30=	Greg Chalmers	70-73-69-72	284	€9,876
	Carlos Del Moral	71-72-69-72	284	€9,876
	Rhein Gibson	70-70-70-74	284	€9,876
	Jamie McLeary	70-71-69-74	284	€9,876
	James Nitties	69-69-72-74	284	€9,876
35=	Anthony Brown	68-75-72-70	285	€8,448
	Magnus A. Carlsson	67-76-69-73	285	€8,448
	Ryan Haller	71-69-74-71	285	€8,448
	Kevin Phelan	72-69-72-72	285	€8,448
	Peter Whiteford	66-66-75-78	285	€8,448
40=	Steven Bowditch	73-70-72-71	286	€6,901
	Ricardo González	68-74-72-72	286	€6,901
	Søren Hansen	72-71-71-72	286	€6,901
	James Heath	72-71-70-73	286	€6,901
	Stuart Manley	73-68-72-73	286	€6,901
	Damien McGrane	70-70-73-73	286	€6,901
	David McKenzie	70-70-74-72	286	€6,901
	Brody Ninyette	69-74-72-71	286	€6,901
48=	Jack Doherty	69-72-72-74	287	€5,354
	Søren Kjeldsen	69-71-74-73	287	€5,354
	Julien Quesne	67-73-72-75	287	€5,354
	Paul Spargo	70-70-74-73	287	€5,354
	Simon Wakefield	72-67-75-73	287	€5,354
53=	John Parry	69-72-73-74	288	€4,164
	Nacho Elvira	71-71-74-72	288	€4,164
	Roope Kakko	72-71-74-71	288	€4,164
	Craig Lee	73-69-75-71	288	€4,164
	John Wade	64-72-75-77	288	€4,164
58=	Oliver Goss	68-74-75-72	289	€3,332
	David Bransdon	69-72-73-75	289	€3,332
	Steven Jeffress	74-69-69-77	289	€3,332
	Clint Rice	68-72-70-79	289	€3,332
	Josh Younger	69-70-74-76	289	€3,332
63=	Daan Huizing	68-73-73-76	290	€2,915
	Tom Lewis	66-74-76-74	290	€2,915
65=	Michael Long	69-74-73-75	291	€2,677
	Michael Sim	66-77-74-74	291	€2,677
67=	Nathan Holman	73-68-75-76	292	€2,439
	Daniel Nisbet	71-72-74-75	292	€2,439
69	Scott Jamieson	69-74-71-81	295	€2,261

Out Of The Money: 144: Jorge Campillo, Nick Cullen, Adam Gee, Matt Jager, Steven Jones, Jason Knutzon, Gareth Maybin, Max McCardle, Brinson Paolini, Mahal Pearce, Andre Stolz **145**: Ben Campbell, Peter Cooke, Oliver Fisher, Jake Higginbottom, Raphaël Jacquelin, Maximilian Kieffer, Bryden MacPherson, Geoff Ogilvy, Adrian Otaegui, Scott Strange, Aaron Townsend, Anthony Wall, Michael Wright **146**: Chris Campbell, Chris Doak, Alastair Forsyth, Andreas Hartø, David Klein, Stephen Leaney, Andrew Martin, Edoardo Molinari, Lee Slattery, Anthony Summers, Justin Walters **147**: Fredrik Andersson Hed, Peter Fowler, Yeon-Jin Jeong, Daniel Popovic, Victor Riu, Adam Stephens **148**: Grégory Havret, Simon Houston, Alexandre Kaleka, Richard Lee, Matthew Millar, Ricardo Santos **149**: David Horsey, Manuel Im, Jose Manuel Lara, Scott Laycock, Craig Parry **150**: Josh Geary, Leigh McKechnie, Callan O'Reilly, Matthew Perry, Jack Wilson **151**: Matthew Giles, Ryan Lynch, David McKendrick **152**: Matthew Ballard, Leigh Deagan, Rick Kulacz, Peter Lawrie, Gareth Paddison, Thomas Pieters **153**: Rohan Blizard, Mark Brown, Ashley Hall **154**: Eduardo De La Riva, Adrien Saddier **155**: Lam Zhiqun **156**: Steve Webster **158**: Tom Bond **WD**: Danny Willett (73)

FIRST ROUND		SECOND ROUND		THIRD ROUND	
John Wade	64 (-8)	Peter Whiteford	132 (-12)	**Thorbjørn Olesen**	200 (-16)
Thorbjørn Olesen	64 (-8)	**Thorbjørn Olesen**	133 (-11)	Sihwan Kim	203 (-13)
4 Players	66 (-6)	Sihwan Kim	134 (-10)	James Morrison	204 (-12)
		James Morrison	135 (-9)	Peter Uihlein	205 (-11)
		David Drysdale	135 (-9)	2 Players	206 (-10)

OWR: 3 of top 50 entered - Rating: 81 - Points to 27th - Olesen: 22 points, to 89th in OWR

BMW Masters

Lake Malaren Golf Club - Shanghai, China
Champion: Marcel Siem

Oct 30 - Nov 2
7,607 yards   Par 72
Purse: $7 Million

In one of the wilder finishes of the 2014 season, Germany's Marcel Siem claimed his fourth career European Tour title at the BMW Masters in China, defeating France's Alexander Levy and England's Ross Fisher on the first hole of sudden death. For three days conditions were benign in Shanghai, and Siem was something of an afterthought on a crowded leaderboard, trailing by four shots at the halfway mark, then falling five behind on Saturday after Levy uncorked a bogey-free 63 to move four shots ahead of the field. But heavy winds arrived on Sunday and just that quickly, the week's proceedings were turned on their head. Indeed, on a day when the venerable Miguel Ángel Jiménez carded an eye-popping 88, Levy stumbled badly, going out in 38, then adding a double-bogey at the par-5 13th and three subsequent bogeys to post a 78 – and yet remarkably he wasn't dead. Having gone out several groups earlier, Siem managed four birdies over his first 11 holes, and he stood two ahead through the 16th before finishing bogey-bogey to join Levy on 272. And earlier still there had been Fisher, who began the day a robust 11 shots back, then made five early birdies to turn in 31 en route to the day's low round, an impressive 67 – and he too stood on 272. Had Levy won the playoff, it would have been his third victory of the season. Had Fisher won, he would have set a new tour record for the largest fourth-round comeback. But with rather less history at stake, Siem promptly chipped in for birdie on the first playoff hole and quietly carried away the trophy.

1	Marcel Siem	68-66-65-73	272	€1.66 mil			Richard Bland	72-68-73-72	285	€61,625
2=	Ross Fisher	70-67-68-67	272	€872,050			Tommy Fleetwood	78-71-67-69	285	€61,625
	Alexander Levy	65-66-63-78	272	€872,050			Ze-yu He	73-71-69-72	285	€61,625
4=	Jamie Donaldson	68-68-62-75	273	€462,750		43=	Matthew Baldwin	73-71-69-73	286	€52,100
	Justin Rose	72-65-64-72	273	€462,750			Gon. F'dez-Castaño	72-68-69-77	286	€52,100
6=	Nicolas Colsaerts	66-64-73-71	274	€325,900			Hao-Tong Li	69-71-74-72	286	€52,100
	Romain Wattel	66-67-71-70	274	€325,900			Paul McGinley	71-73-71-71	286	€52,100
8=	Emiliano Grillo	66-68-69-72	275	€240,000			Marc Warren	70-72-72-72	286	€52,100
	Ryan Palmer	70-67-68-70	275	€240,000		48=	Shao-cai He	71-71-68-77	287	€41,600
10=	George Coetzee	71-67-67-71	276	€186,233			Chris Kirk	73-72-68-74	287	€41,600
	Mikko Ilonen	70-66-69-71	276	€186,233			Brooks Koepka	73-72-70-72	287	€41,600
	Fabrizio Zanotti	70-68-69-69	276	€186,233			Wen-Chong Liang	72-70-73-72	287	€41,600
13=	Darren Fichardt	69-68-69-71	277	€152,533			Ian Poulter	74-69-70-74	287	€41,600
	Joost Luiten	72-69-64-72	277	€152,533		53=	Mu Hu	69-71-74-74	288	€34,400
	Bernd Wiesberger	72-69-66-70	277	€152,533			Francesco Molinari	69-74-71-74	288	€34,400
16=	Branden Grace	68-66-71-73	278	€131,400		55	José María Olazábal	71-70-73-75	289	€31,300
	Robert Karlsson	69-70-66-73	278	€131,400		56=	Simon Dyson	75-72-71-72	290	€27,600
	Shane Lowry	70-66-71-71	278	€131,400			Zheng Ouyang	72-66-77-75	290	€27,600
	Graeme McDowell	67-69-68-74	278	€131,400			Oliver Wilson	68-73-69-80	290	€27,600
	Richard Sterne	68-70-70-70	278	€131,400		59=	Felipe Aguilar	70-74-71-76	291	€23,350
21=	Victor Dubuisson	70-70-68-71	279	€116,267			Kristoffer Broberg	73-69-73-76	291	€23,350
	Richie Ramsay	70-68-68-73	279	€116,267		61=	Morten Madsen	69-74-71-78	292	€19,533
	Danny Willett	71-70-67-71	279	€116,267			Kevin Stadler	73-71-72-76	292	€19,533
24=	Thomas Bjørn	68-67-71-74	280	€107,500			Graeme Storm	75-70-72-75	292	€19,533
	David Howell	74-71-66-69	280	€107,500		64=	Alejandro Cañizares	78-71-73-72	294	€16,900
26=	Ernie Els	69-68-69-75	281	€100,750			Rafael Cabrera-Bello	74-66-70-84	294	€16,900
	Eddie Pepperell	72-69-70-70	281	€100,750			Ashun Wu	75-70-70-79	294	€16,900
28=	Oliver Fisher	71-69-70-72	282	€87,900		67=	Yi Cao	72-71-76-76	295	€15,150
	Tyrrell Hatton	73-67-71-71	282	€87,900			Andy Sullivan	76-72-70-77	295	€15,150
	Thongchai Jaidee	71-70-69-72	282	€87,900		69=	Mark Foster	75-71-75-75	296	€13,800
	Edoardo Molinari	70-71-69-72	282	€87,900			Maximilian Kieffer	71-69-75-81	296	€13,800
	Thorbjørn Olesen	70-70-70-72	282	€87,900		71=	David Horsey	73-75-71-78	297	€12,750
	Dong Su	70-69-68-75	282	€87,900			Pablo Larrazábal	76-72-69-80	297	€12,750
34=	Michael Hoey	70-68-72-73	283	€76,250		73	Zi-Hao Chen	77-76-73-76	302	€12,000
	Seung-Hyuk Kim	70-71-69-73	283	€76,250		74	Chenxiao Duan	78-73-70-82	303	€11,500
36=	Magnus A. Carlsson	73-72-68-71	284	€70,000		75	Yan-Wei Liu	75-76-78-76	305	€11,100
	Stephen Gallacher	72-69-72-71	284	€70,000		76	Matteo Manassero	74-78-74-80	306	€10,800
	Hennie Otto	71-71-70-72	284	€70,000		77	Miguel A. Jiménez	77-70-72-88	307	€10,600
39=	Thomas Aiken	72-68-72-73	285	€61,625		78	Tianyi Wu	76-83-80-81	320	€10,400

FIRST ROUND			SECOND ROUND			THIRD ROUND	
Alexander Levy	65 (-7)		Nicolas Colsaerts	130 (-14)		Alexander Levy	194 (-22)
Romain Wattel	66 (-6)		Alexander Levy	131 (-13)		Jamie Donaldson	198 (-18)
Nicolas Colsaerts	66 (-6)		Romain Wattel	133 (-11)		**Marcel Siem**	199 (-17)
Emiliano Grillo	66 (-6)		3 Players	134 (-10)		Justin Rose	201 (-15)
Graeme McDowell	67 (-5)		**Marcel Siem**	134 (-10)		2 Players	203 (-13)
Marcel Siem	68 (-4)						

OWR: 13 of top 50 entered - Rating: 278 - Points to 52nd - Siem: 46 points, to 70th in OWR

WGC-HSBC Champions

Sheshan International Golf Club - Shanghai, China
Champion: Bubba Watson

Nov 6 - Nov 9
7,199 yards   Par 72
Purse: $8.5 Million

With Phil Mickelson not making the journey to Shanghai this year, it was up to Bubba Watson to provide a degree of golfing excitement/unpredictability for far eastern fans and this he did spectacularly, winning the WGC-HSBC Champions in near-miraculous style. Watson stood in contention throughout the week but did so in a decidedly up-and-down manner, trailing Graeme McDowell by four after an opening 71 that included five birdies, two bogeys and a double-bogey, then remaining four behind McDowell at the halfway mark following a more orthodox seven-birdie, two-bogey 67. McDowell's third round 71 allowed the top of the leaderboard to tighten considerably, with Watson pulling within two via a 69 which included five birdies, two bogeys and a double-bogey - on the back nine alone. This set up a wild Sunday afternoon which saw no less than six world-class players have a chance to win down the stretch under conditions challenging enough that among the realistic contenders, only South African Tim Clark could break 70. McDowell, for his part, never got going, playing even par golf through 13 holes before a bogey at the par-5 14th dropped him back to 10 – one shot shy of what would ultimately be needed. By this time, however, it seemed to be Watson's tournament; indeed, with six birdies and three bogeys on his card, he arrived at the 16th with a two-shot lead. But after laying up at the driveable par-4, he missed the green with a lob wedge and made bogey, then left his ball in a greenside bunker at the 212-yard 17th en route to a double bogey, dropping him to nine under par and seeming extinction. But utilizing his immense power, Watson reached a greenside bunker at the 538-yard 18th in two, then miraculously holed the ensuing 60-yard blast for a closing eagle and an 11-under-par finish. Of all the stars giving chase, only Clark could find the birdie needed at the last to match him, but the ensuing playoff would last only one hole as Watson birdied the 18th from 20 feet to clinch a victory whose final scorecard included 26 birdies, one eagle, 10 bogeys and four double-bogeys over 73 holes. Remarkable stuff.

1	Bubba Watson	71-67-69-70	277	$1.4 mil
2	Tim Clark	69-70-69-69	277	$850,000
3=	Rickie Fowler	69-70-69-70	278	$381,667
	Hiroshi Iwata	73-65-68-72	278	$381,667
	Graeme McDowell	67-67-71-73	278	$381,667
6=	Ian Poulter	70-67-72-71	280	$213,667
	Thorbjørn Olesen	72-68-69-71	280	$213,667
	Martin Kaymer	69-72-66-73	280	$213,667
9	Marc Leishman	72-71-69-69	281	$158,000
10=	Jason Dufner	72-70-72-68	282	$135,500
	Brandt Snedeker	69-74-69-70	282	$135,500
12=	George Coetzee	72-73-69-69	283	$108,000
	Adam Scott	70-72-71-70	283	$108,000
14=	Pablo Larrazábal	75-72-69-68	284	$89,833
	Alexander Levy	74-68-71-71	284	$89,833
	A-Shun Wu	74-70-69-71	284	$89,833
	Louis Oosthuizen	70-70-72-72	284	$89,833
	Chris Kirk	69-74-69-72	284	$89,833
	Jonas Blixt	71-68-71-74	284	$89,833
20=	Kevin Na	71-68-79-67	285	$81,000
	Lee Westwood	70-73-69-73	285	$81,000
22=	Ryan Palmer	74-72-72-68	286	$77,000
	Patrick Reed	71-73-71-71	286	$77,000
24=	Tommy Fleetwood	69-75-74-69	287	$73,500
	Jamie Donaldson	71-77-68-71	287	$73,500
	Stephen Gallacher	72-72-71-72	287	$73,500
	Henrik Stenson	70-71-81-65	287	$73,500
28=	Anirban Lahiri	74-70-74-70	288	$68,500
	Sergio García	74-72-73-69	288	$68,500
	Joost Luiten	77-71-69-71	288	$68,500
	Ryan Moore	74-71-72-71	288	$68,500
	J.B. Holmes	70-71-73-74	288	$68,500
	Hunter Mahan	74-68-71-75	288	$68,500
34	Shane Lowry	78-69-74-68	289	$65,000
35=	John Senden	73-73-72-72	290	$61,500
	Jimmy Walker	73-69-75-73	290	$61,500
	Russell Henley	71-75-74-70	290	$61,500
	Marc Warren	75-72-69-74	290	$61,500
	Jordan Spieth	70-74-72-74	290	$61,500
	Hao-tong Li	75-72-76-67	290	$61,500
41=	Thomas Bjørn	72-75-72-72	291	$56,000
	Dawie van der Walt	70-72-75-74	291	$56,000
	Luke Donald	74-72-74-71	291	$56,000
	Hideki Matsuyama	74-69-73-75	291	$56,000
	Thongchai Jaidee	71-76-75-69	291	$56,000
46=	Ernie Els	74-70-74-74	292	$52,500
	Mikko Ilonen	75-76-71-70	292	$52,500
48=	Justin Rose	72-71-76-74	293	$49,300
	Marcel Siem	72-72-76-73	293	$49,300
	Felipe Aguilar	76-74-71-72	293	$49,300
	Bill Haas	70-74-72-77	293	$49,300
	WC Liang	75-74-73-71	293	$49,300
53=	Matt Jones	75-76-71-72	294	$47,000
	Hennie Otto	74-72-75-73	294	$47,000
	Scott Stallings	74-76-77-67	294	$47,000
56=	Kevin Streelman	77-72-71-75	295	$45,250
	Matt Every	75-72-75-73	295	$45,250
	Gary Woodland	73-75-74-73	295	$45,250
	David Lipsky	78-73-72-72	295	$45,250
60=	Brendon Todd	71-74-73-78	296	$43,875
	Mu Hu	78-71-74-73	296	$43,875
62	Darren Fichardt	74-72-74-77	297	$43,500
63	Hyung-Sung Kim	70-74-75-79	298	$43,250
64=	Oliver Wilson	71-70-79-80	300	$42,500
	Keegan Bradley	72-73-77-78	300	$42,500
	Lian-Wei Zhang	73-76-74-77	300	$42,500
	Mike Hendry	76-75-73-76	300	$42,500
	Charl Schwartzel	74-76-77-73	300	$42,500
69=	Ze-cheng Dou	76-73-74-78	301	$41,625
	Antonio Lascuña	76-79-73-73	301	$41,625
71	Miguel Jiménez	78-75-73-76	302	$41,250
72	Jason Knutzon	78-74-75-77	304	$41,000
73=	Jaco Van Zyl	70-75-83-78	306	$40,500
	Yoshitaka Takeya	77-78-75-76	306	$40,500
	Billy Horschel	80-77-79-70	306	$40,500
76	Jin Jeong	85-79-75-80	319	$40,000

WD: Victor Dubuisson (153), Kevin Stadler, Graham DeLaet   **DQ**: Brody Ninyette (176)

FIRST ROUND		**SECOND ROUND**		**THIRD ROUND**	
Graeme McDowell	67 (-5)	Graeme McDowell	134 (-10)	Graeme McDowell	205 (-11)
6 Players	69 (-3)	Ian Poulter	137 (-7)	Hiroshi Iwata	206 (-10)
Bubba Watson	71 (-1)	**Bubba Watson**	138 (-6)	Martin Kaymer	207 (-9)
		Hiroshi Iwata	138 (-6)	**Bubba Watson**	207 (-9)
		4 Players	139 (-5)	2 Players	108 (-8)

OWR: 40 of top 50 entered - Rating: 612 - Points to 59th - Watson: 68 points, to 3rd in OWR

Turkish Airlines Open

The Montgomerie Maxx Royal - Antalya, Turkey
Champion: Brooks Koepka

Nov 13 - Nov 16
7,132 yards   Par 72
Purse: $7 Million

Despite having gained Special Temporary Membership status on the PGA Tour (and exempt status for 2015), American Brooks Koepka remained a European Tour player long enough to return for the penultimate event in the circuit's lucrative Final Series, and in the process claimed his first major tour victory at the Turkish Airlines Open, in Antalya. Initially Koepka – along with 76 other members of the strong 78-man field – seemed an afterthought, as 50-year-old Miguel Ángel Jiménez topped the first-round leaderboard with a 63 before Ian Poulter stormed out to a massive six-shot halfway lead behind rounds of 64-66. Koepka, however, was among the six players closest to Poulter, and thus factored more greatly into the 54-hole mix after the flashy Englishman posted three bogeys and a double-bogey en route to a disappointing Saturday 75. Thus Koepka began Sunday two behind surprise leader Wade Ormsby of Australia, and one behind Poulter, a hot Marcel Siem and England's Lee Westwood, who had charged into contention behind middle rounds of 68-67. But during a final round which, in its opening half, saw Siem, Jiménez, Danny Willett and even a late-charging Henrik Stenson all creep into contention, play eventually boiled down to Koepka and Poulter, with the American breaking a deadlock with an eagle at the 564-yard 13th, then hanging on via a clutch 17-foot par putt at the 337-yard 15th and a deft up-and-down at the 392-yard 17th. Poulter was not without his chances to tie, however, as he missed a 12-footer for birdie at the 15th and, following a superb long bunker shot, a five-footer for birdie at the last. For the talented Koepka – who dominated the European Challenge Tour in 2013 – it was a major early career win that still felt a long time in coming.

1	Brooks Koepka	69-67-70-65	271	€1.666 mil			Scott Jamieson	70-72-72-70	284	€58,893
2	Ian Poulter	64-66-75-67	272	€1.115 mil			Matthew Baldwin	73-68-72-71	284	€58,893
3	Henrik Stenson	70-70-70-64	274	€629,100			Rich Bland	71-69-73-71	284	€58,893
4=	Miguel Jiménez	63-73-71-68	275	€394,625			Darren Fichardt	68-73-71-72	284	€58,893
	Andy Sullivan	67-75-66-67	275	€394,625			Marc Warren	67-74-75-68	284	€58,893
	Danny Willett	67-70-69-69	275	€394,625			Edoardo Molinari	67-72-71-74	284	€58,893
	Wade Ormsby	65-71-68-71	275	€394,625		46=	Rafael Cabrera Bello	72-68-73-72	285	€49,400
8=	Marcel Siem	70-69-66-71	276	€240,450			Robert Karlsson	71-71-70-73	285	€49,400
	Lee Westwood	70-68-67-71	276	€240,450		48=	David Howell	71-71-71-73	286	€43,100
10	Eddie Pepperell	70-71-67-69	277	€200,850			Magnus Carlsson	69-70-75-72	286	€43,100
11=	Alexander Levy	68-71-73-66	278	€168,375			Robert-Jan Derksen	69-74-72-71	286	€43,100
	Emiliano Grillo	68-72-71-67	278	€168,375			David Lynn	69-74-72-71	286	€43,100
	Romain Wattel	67-71-73-67	278	€168,375		52=	Bernd Wiesberger	71-71-74-71	287	€35,783
	Peter Uihlein	73-65-70-70	278	€168,375			Pablo Larrazábal	70-74-73-70	287	€35,783
15=	Victor Dubuisson	77-68-70-64	279	€137,900			Nicolas Colsaerts	80-71-70-66	287	€35,783
	Brendon de Jonge	65-73-73-68	279	€137,900		55=	Simon Dyson	68-71-75-74	288	€28,100
	David Lipsky	69-73-69-68	279	€137,900			Raphaël Jacquelin	68-72-78-70	288	€28,100
	Stephen Gallacher	67-71-71-70	279	€137,900			George Coetzee	76-71-71-70	288	€28,100
19=	Jamie Donaldson	72-72-70-66	280	€118,683			Matteo Manassero	70-77-72-69	288	€28,100
	Fabrizio Zanotti	72-71-69-68	280	€118,683			Graeme Storm	75-77-69-67	288	€28,100
	Christopher Doak	69-73-69-69	280	€118,683		60=	Martin Kaymer	68-72-75-74	289	€20,725
	Branden Grace	67-69-73-71	280	€118,683			Oliver Fisher	67-81-71-70	289	€20,725
	Tyrrell Hatton	65-72-72-71	280	€118,683			Oliver Wilson	76-70-73-70	289	€20,725
	Hennie Otto	67-69-72-72	280	€118,683			Richard Sterne	74-77-73-65	289	€20,725
25=	Joost Luiten	70-73-71-67	281	€96,307		64=	Mikko Ilonen	69-72-74-75	290	€17,000
	Ross Fisher	74-70-70-67	281	€96,307			Thomas Aiken	70-72-75-73	290	€17,000
	Francesco Molinari	70-71-71-69	281	€96,307			Felipe Aguilar	72-74-71-73	290	€17,000
	Sergio García	75-71-65-70	281	€96,307			Darren Clarke	75-70-73-72	290	€17,000
	Jonas Blixt	68-71-72-70	281	€96,307		68=	Kristoffer Broberg	72-75-72-72	291	€14,900
	John Daly	69-72-67-73	281	€96,307			Mark Foster	70-72-78-71	291	€14,900
	Shane Lowry	70-66-72-73	281	€96,307		70	Colin Montgomerie	76-72-72-72	292	€13,950
32=	Grégory Bourdy	68-73-72-69	282	€79,500		71	Richie Ramsay	76-70-72-76	292	€13,450
	Dawie van der Walt	72-72-68-70	282	€79,500		72	Thorbjørn Olesen	77-71-73-74	295	€12,950
	Luke Donald	74-73-68-67	282	€79,500		73	Morten O. Madsen	72-76-79-70	297	€12,450
	Tommy Fleetwood	69-71-77-65	282	€79,500		74	Julien Quesne	77-76-75-70	298	€11,950
36=	Alejandro Cañizares	69-71-73-70	283	€70,450		75	Michael Hoey	82-75-73-73	303	€11,550
	David Horsey	74-70-72-67	283	€70,450		76	Ali Altuntas (a)	79-84-80-76	319	-
	Thongchai Jaidee	69-68-74-72	283	€70,450		77	Ediz Kemaloglu (a)	81-79-86-74	320	-
39=	Richard Green	71-74-69-70	284	€58,893		78	Alihan Afsar (a)	82-86-87-75	330	-

FIRST ROUND		SECOND ROUND		THIRD ROUND	
Miguel Ángel Jiménez	63 (-9)	Ian Poulter	130 (-14)	Wade Ormsby	204 (-12)
Ian Poulter	64 (-8)	6 Players	136 (-8)	Ian Poulter	205 (-11)
Tyrrell Hatton	65 (-7)	**Brooks Koepka**	136 (-8)	Lee Westwood	205 (-11)
Wade Ormsby	65 (-7)			Marcel Siem	205 (-11)
Brendon de Jonge	65 (-7)			2 Players	206 (-10)
Brooks Koepka	69 (-3)			**Brooks Koepka**	206 (-10)

OWR: 13 of top 50 entered - Rating: 294 - Points to 51st - Koepka: 48 points, to 35th in OWR

DP World Tour Championship, Dubai

Nov 20 - Nov 23

Jumeirah Golf Estates (Earth) - Dubai, U.A.E.
7,675 yards   Par 72
Champion: Henrik Stenson
Purse: $8 Million

In an exciting climax to the 2014 European Tour season, Henrik Stenson came through with some late fireworks to successfully defend his 2013 title at the DP World Tour Championship. For most of the week Stenson did as he had done for much of 2014, lingering around the edges of contention but not necessarily looking like a winner. And indeed, the event seemed to be following the season's general trend when world number one Rory McIlroy, returning from a six-week break, began his first round with birdies on four of his first five holes and eventually posted a 66, good enough to tie for the Thursday lead with Shane Lowry. McIlroy's play would be somewhat uneven thereafter, however, with a Friday 70 leaving him tied with Scotland's Richie Ramsay and England's Danny Willett, two shots behind Stenson, who added a 66 of his own to an opening 68. The 38-year-old Swede remained atop the board after carding a Saturday 68, only now he was tied with Spain's Rafa Cabrera-Bello, who'd opened with a 73 before charging back with middle rounds of 64-65, the former sparked by a run of five straight birdies to open the day. But the story of this week was told mostly on Sunday as a wide range of world-class players found themselves squarely in the mix in the late going. Initially it looked to be Cabrera-Bello's day, particularly after Stenson double-bogeyed the 401-yard 11th to fall two behind. But the 30-year-old from the Canary Islands then missed a short par putt at the 476-yard 12th and, like Stenson, failed to birdie both the par-5 14th and the 371-yard 15th. This allowed McIlroy (who birdied both of those scoring holes), Rose (who birdied those, plus the 16th), France's Victor Dubuisson (who came home in 33) and even a hard-charging Robert Karlsson (who collapsed by three-putting from three feet at the last) all back into the fray – a fray which soon excluded Cabrera-Bello after he logged watery double-bogeys at both the 16th and 17th. But with a high-powered multi-man playoff looming, Stenson stepped up, stiffing his approach at the par-3 17th, then adding another birdie at the par-5 closer to win by two.

1	Henrik Stenson	68-66-68-70	272	€1.666 mil
2=	Rory McIlroy	66-70-70-68	274	€748,323
	Justin Rose	71-66-68-69	274	€748,323
	Victor Dubuisson	71-68-67-68	274	€748,323
5	Shane Lowry	66-71-72-66	275	€424,700
6=	Louis Oosthuizen	69-71-70-66	276	€307,167
	Robert Karlsson	71-68-68-69	276	€307,167
	Tyrrell Hatton	70-68-68-70	276	€307,167
9=	Branden Grace	72-67-68-70	277	€208,870
	Joost Luiten	70-69-68-70	277	€208,870
	Rafael Cabrera Bello	73-64-65-75	277	€208,870
12=	Sergio García	73-69-69-67	278	€162,165
	Tommy Fleetwood	69-74-67-68	278	€162,165
	Jamie Donaldson	72-70-67-69	278	€162,165
	Thorbjørn Olesen	67-70-69-72	278	€162,165
16=	Richie Ramsay	67-69-75-68	279	€136,004
	Francesco Molinari	73-69-69-68	279	€136,004
	Simon Dyson	73-70-67-69	279	€136,004
	Bernd Wiesberger	72-70-68-69	279	€136,004
	Pablo Larrazábal	71-69-69-70	279	€136,004
21=	Ian Poulter	75-69-70-66	280	€117,442
	Hennie Otto	71-68-70-71	280	€117,442
	Andy Sullivan	73-69-67-71	280	€117,442
	Danny Willett	69-67-71-73	280	€117,442
	Marc Warren	71-71-65-73	280	€117,442
26=	Oliver Fisher	72-70-73-66	281	€100,500
	Alexander Levy	71-72-71-67	281	€100,500
	Luke Donald	76-66-71-68	281	€100,500
	Eddie Pepperell	76-69-66-70	281	€100,500
	George Coetzee	70-70-69-72	281	€100,500
31=	Nicolas Colsaerts	73-72-70-67	282	€85,168
	Darren Fichardt	72-68-72-70	282	€85,168
	Stephen Gallacher	72-68-71-71	282	€85,168
	Thongchai Jaidee	72-72-67-71	282	€85,168
	Kristoffer Broberg	70-67-72-73	282	€85,168
36=	Thomas Aiken	76-66-72-69	283	€74,670
	Romain Wattel	71-70-71-71	283	€74,670
	Thomas Bjørn	71-69-69-74	283	€74,670
39=	Martin Kaymer	72-69-74-69	284	€67,403
	Marcel Siem	76-66-72-70	284	€67,403
	Ernie Els	75-67-70-72	284	€67,403
42=	Brooks Koepka	78-68-70-69	285	€58,920
	Miguel Jiménez	71-73-69-72	285	€58,920
	Edoardo Molinari	69-74-69-73	285	€58,920
	David Howell	71-67-73-74	285	€58,920
	Ross Fisher	69-73-67-76	285	€58,920
47=	Lee Westwood	70-71-74-71	286	€49,470
	Graeme McDowell	72-70-72-72	286	€49,470
	Charl Schwartzel	72-71-70-73	286	€49,470
	Wade Ormsby	73-71-69-73	286	€49,470
51=	Richard Sterne	71-74-71-71	287	€42,130
	Fabrizio Zanotti	73-72-72-70	287	€42,130
	Jonas Blixt	70-74-70-73	287	€42,130
54	Emiliano Grillo	68-75-72-73	288	€37,980
55=	Oliver Wilson	75-72-72-73	292	€34,875
	Mikko Ilonen	74-76-68-74	292	€34,875
57	David Lipsky	76-75-70-72	293	€32,170
58	Matthew Baldwin	75-74-71-75	295	€30,500
59	Matteo Manassero	75-72-75-75	297	€28,830
60	Michael Hoey	73-78-70-77	298	€27,170

FIRST ROUND		SECOND ROUND		THIRD ROUND	
Shane Lowry	66 (-6)	**Henrik Stenson**	134 (-10)	Rafa Cabrera-Bello	202 (-14)
Rory McIlroy	66 (-6)	Danny Willett	136 (-8)	**Henrik Stenson**	202 (-14)
Richie Ramsay	67 (-5)	Richie Ramsay	136 (-8)	Justin Rose	205 (-11)
Thorbjørn Olesen	67 (-5)	Rory McIlroy	136 (-8)	Victor Dubuisson	206 (-10)
Henrik Stenson	68 (-4)	5 Players	137 (-7)	Tyrrell Hatton	206 (-10)
Emiliano Grillo	68 (-4)			Thorbjørn Olesen	206 (-10)
				Rory McIlroy	206 (-10)

OWR: 19 of top 50 entered - Rating: 413 - Points to 53rd - Stenson: 56 points, to 2nd in OWR

2014 Race To Dubai Bonus Pool

1	Rory McIlroy	$1,250,000			
2	Henrik Stenson	$800,000	9	Alexander Levy	$170,000
3	Justin Rose	$530,000	10	Shane Lowry	$150,000
4	Jamie Donaldson	$400,000	11	Joost Luiten	$140,000
5	Victor Dubuisson	$350,000	12	Thomas Bjørn	$130,000
6	Sergio García	$300,000	13	Ian Poulter	$120,000
7	Marcel Siem	$250,000	14	Graeme McDowell	$110,000
8	Brooks Koepka	$200,000	15	Martin Kaymer	$100,000

JAPAN TOUR INCIDENTALS

JAPAN TOUR TOP 60 CAREER MONEY WINNERS

#	Name	Amount	#	Name	Amount	#	Name	Amount
1	Masashi Ozaki	¥2,688,836,653	21	Tateo Ozaki	¥772,435,399	41	Teruo Sugihara	¥633,188,689
2	Shingo Katayama	¥1,931,494,661	22	Kiyoshi Murota	¥768,350,125	42	Satoshi Higashi	¥631,369,341
3	Tommy Nakajima	¥1,662,639,766	23	Tetsuji Hiratsuka	¥761,523,871	43	Todd Hamilton	¥631,351,667
4	Toru Taniguchi	¥1,543,558,617	24	Koumei Oda	¥755,862,211	44	Yosh. Yamamoto	¥627,215,929
5	Naomichi Ozaki	¥1,542,501,813	25	Toru Nakamura	¥755,580,792	45	Nobuhito Sato	¥606,760,518
6	Hiroyuki Fujita	¥1,353,893,900	26	Kaname Yokoo	¥737,703,773	46	Brian Watts	¥593,194,439
7	Mas. Kuramoto	¥1,019,915,189	27	Hirofumi Miyase	¥732,425,279	47	Kat. Takahashi	¥591,310,072
8	Toshimitsu Izawa	¥1,007,855,886	28	David Smail	¥722,644,543	48	Prayad Marksaeng	¥590,774,173
9	Isao Aoki	¥980,652,048	29	Nobumitsu Yuhara	¥703,957,263	49	Katsuyoshi Tomori	¥589,365,213
10	Kat. Miyamoto	¥930,517,266	30	Kaz. Hosokawa	¥688,658,062	50	Tsu. Yoneyama	¥579,725,848
11	Taichi Teshima	¥919,970,964	31	Ryo Ishikawa	¥685,540,948	51	Hidemichi Tanaka	¥577,070,603
12	Brendan Jones	¥861,767,424	32	S.K. Ho	¥682,196,450	52	Tze-Chung Chen	¥558,328,835
13	Toru Suzuki	¥817,490,801	33	Frankie Minoza	¥680,377,753	53	Graham Marsh	¥553,811,477
14	David Ishii	¥814,695,905	34	Hideki Kase	¥664,157,397	54	Yoshinori Kaneko	¥548,170,165
15	Hajime Meshiai	¥814,330,660	35	Nobuo Serizwa	¥660,760,145	55	Kat. Kuwabara	¥522,648,904
16	Shigeki Mauruyama	¥805,095,921	36	Saburo Fujiki	¥660,536,413	56	Daisuke Maruyama	¥521,664,438
17	Tomohiro Kondo	¥802,572,668	37	Ryoken Kawagishi	¥657,038,597	57	Yoshi Mizumaki	¥519,687,853
18	Hideto Tanihara	¥801,084,698	38	Kenichi Kuboya	¥653,083,679	58	Kyung-Tae Kim	¥512,709,136
19	Keiichiro Fukabori	¥786,717,012	39	Yasuharu Imano	¥652,543,174	59	Tad. Takayama	¥508,586,643
20	Tsukasa Watanabe	¥783,507,861	40	Yuta Ikeda	¥640,684,714	60	Kiyoshi Maita	¥498,217,607

JAPAN TOUR TOP 30 CAREER TOURNAMENT WINNERS

#	Name	Wins	#	Name	Wins	#	Name	Wins
1	Masashi Ozaki	94	12=	Norio Suzuki	16		Ryo Ishikawa	11
2	Isao Aoki	51		Toshimitsu Izawa	16		Brian Jones	11
3	Tsuneyuki Nakajima	48	14	Tateo Ozaki	15		Seiichi Kanai	11
4	Naomichi Ozaki	32	15=	Saburo Fujiki	14		Hajime Meshiai	11
5	Masahiro Kuramoto	30		David Ishii	14		Takashi Murakami	11
6=	Teruo Sugihara	28	17=	Brendan Jones	13	28=	Shigeki Maruyama	10
	Shingo Katayama	28		Yoshi. Yamamoto	13		Katsunari Takahashi	10
8=	Graham Marsh	20	19=	Brian Watts	12		Hidemichi Tanaka	10
	Toru Nakamura	20		Yuta Ikeda	12		Kat. Miyamoto	10
10	Toru Taniguchi	19	21=	Todd Hamilton	11		Hideto Tanihara	10
11	Hiroyuki Fujita	18		Hsieh Min-Nan	11			

JAPAN TOUR EVENT / SPONSOR/ VENUE UPDATES

Usually the most stable of the world's major circuits, the Japan Golf Tour will witness an uncommon degree of change in 2015, with the biggest story being the expansion of the schedule from 24 to 27 tournaments. In point of fact, two established stops, the 21-year-old **Tsuruya Open** and the five-year-old **Toshin Golf Tournament**, are not scheduled for renewal this year, requiring the Tour to add five events in order to achieve its net gain of three. One of these five, the **Thailand Open**, is actually returning to the schedule following a one-year absence, but in something of a coup given the mediocre state of the world's golfing economy, the other four additions are all brand new and include the **ISPS Handa Global Cup** (6/25-6/28 in Yamanashi Prefecture), the **Musee Platinum Open** (7/9-7/12 in Hyogo), the **Vascory Classic** (8/20-8/23 in Malaysia - presumably co-sanctioned with the Asian Tour) and the **Honma Tourworld Cup**, whose early October dates (in Ibaraki) will make it the last event before the more lucrative eight-tournament run which annually closes the season. And indeed, none of these new stops will exceed ¥100,000,000 in prize money, so they will not be pushing to join the hierarchy of the Tour.

In terms of additional changes to the schedule, three events will be making significant date changes, led by the **Indonesia PGA Championship**, which leaves a season-opening pre-Masters slot for a week ending on August 2nd. Also migrating is the **Japan PGA Championship** (from the first week in June to the third week of May) and the **Japan Golf Tour Championship**, whose move is a bit narrower, coming forward two slots from the third week in June. Among venue changes, the rotating **Japan Open** will move from the Chiba Country Club to the East Course of Hyogo's Rokku Kokusai Golf Club, the more deeply rooted **Kansai Open** jumps from Hyoko's Rokku Country Club to Shiga's Meishin Yokaichi Country Club, and the **Heiwa PGM Championship** moves from Ibaraki's Miho Golf Club to Chiba's Sobhu Country Club.

Any way one looks at it, by Japan Golf Tour standards, definitely a season of significant change.

JAPAN TOUR 2014

Suppose that for the last decade Tiger Woods and Phil Mickelson had opted to play on the European Tour.

A crazy thought for PGA Tour fans no doubt, but this essentially is the issue faced by the Japan Golf Tour circa 2014. Because while Japan has historically produced relatively few players capable of competing at the highest levels in Europe and America, they currently have two such talents, both of whom rate among the elite young prospects in the game: 22-year-old Hideki Matsuyama and 23-year-old Ryo Ishikawa. In each case, the player first cut his teeth on the Japan Golf Tour, with Matsuyama dominating the circuit as a 21-year-old rookie in 2013 and Ishikawa recording a remarkable nine domestic victories before his 21st birthday. But while the Japan Tour (and myriad off-the-course endorsement opportunities) have long been lucrative enough to keep stars like Jumbo Ozaki and Tommy Nakajima anchored firmly at home, both Matsuyama and Ishikawa have clearly embraced the idea of competing regularly on the world's biggest stages, with each taking up what figures to be long-term residency on the PGA Tour in 2014. Matsuyama, at least, came home in the fall for just long enough to win the prestigious Dunlop Phoenix event and Ishikawa claimed the Sega Sammy Cup back in July. But between them, the two stars made a total of 12 Japan Tour starts in 2014 - and where would American golf have been had Woods and Mickelson been such strangers?

In the frequent absence of their two leading guns, the Japan circuit soldiered on in 2014, and a glance at the top of the Order of Merit shows a preponderance of established stars with one or two newer names tossed in. The former category treads familiar ground, as Hiroyuki Fujita, Tomohiro Kondo, Koumei Oda, Katsumasa Miyamoto and, of course, Shingo Katayama, boast a total of 70 domestic victories among them. On the younger side, 29-year-old Yuta Ikeda (himself a 12-time champion) rates the most established, while mid-30s players like Hiroshi Iwata and Korea's Hyung-Sung Kim have emerged in recent years as potential stars.

But if Matsuyama and Ishikawa played full-time at home, the picture here would be very different.

Player Of The Year: Koumei Oda

With the nation's two leading players, Hideki Matsuyama and Ryo Ishikawa, spending most of the year in America, the Player Of The Year battle came down to the circuit's top two money winners, Koumei Oda and Hiroyuki Fujita. Each man won twice and the magnitude of their victories (Oda's strong Bridgestone Open and light-field Kansai Open vs. Fujita's stronger Diamond Cup and lighter KBC Augusta) was almost indistinguishable. But our choice is Oda based on a modest differential in consistency: he finished with nine top 10s while Fujita only had six.

2014 Japan Tour Top 60 Money Winners

#	Player	Earnings	#	Player	Earnings	#	Player	Earnings
1	Koumei Oda	¥130,287,266	21	Satoshi Kogaira	¥47,914,628	41	Sang-Hyun Park	¥28,132,644
2	Hiroyuki Fujita	¥116,275,130	22	I.J. Jang	¥46,388,089	42	Yosuke Tsukada	¥27,590,393
3	Tomohiro Kondo	¥107,089,056	23	Ryuichi Oda	¥46,084,125	43	S.K. Ho	¥26,512,000
4	Hiroshi Iwata	¥97,794,191	24	Kyoung-Hoon Lee	¥43,500,608	44	Han Lee	¥26,428,990
5	Kat. Miyamoto	¥91,048,150	25	Michio Matsumura	¥43,097,968	45	Shunsuke Sonoda	¥25,369,942
6	Shingo Katayama	¥85,535,243	26	Hideki Matsuyama	¥42,770,000	46	Ashun Wu	¥24,473,373
7	Yuta Ikeda	¥77,552,862	27	Tad. Takayama	¥42,232,041	47	Hidemasa Hoshino	¥23,541,764
8	Hideto Tanihara	¥77,492,097	28	Sang-Hee Lee	¥40,609,395	48	Young-Han Song	¥22,922,807
9	Hyung-Sung Kim	¥73,696,675	29	Brad Kennedy	¥39,134,534	49	Yasuharu Imano	¥22,267,700
10	Yoshitaka Takeya	¥64,538,290	30	Kaz. Yamashita	¥36,174,377	50	Toru Taniguchi	¥22,192,133
11	Yusaku Miyazato	¥64,299,792	31	Hyun-Woo Ryu	¥35,494,392	51	Michael Hendry	¥21,306,402
12	Yoshinori Fujimoto	¥61,285,279	32	Wen-Chong Liang	¥33,071,750	52	Nobuhiro Masuda	¥21,066,199
13	Dong-Kyu Jang	¥58,753,618	33	Juvic Pagunsan	¥32,191,873	53	Daisuke Kataoka	¥20,025,649
14	Taichi Teshima	¥58,703,792	34	Jung-Gon Hwang	¥31,453,889	54	Akio Sadakata	¥19,484,657
15	In-Hoi Hur	¥56,913,416	35	Kyung-Tae Kim	¥30,814,350	55	Hiroo Kawai	¥19,085,828
16	Seung-Hyuk Kim	¥55,392,226	36	Satoshi Tomiyama	¥30,252,637	56	Ryuji Masaoka	¥18,374,182
17	Prayad Marksaeng	¥54,807,380	37	Brendan Jones	¥30,143,617	57	Kodai Ichihara	¥17,105,442
18	David Oh	¥53,076,501	38	Adam Bland	¥29,496,007	58	K. Aphibarnrat	¥16,975,000
19	Ryo Ishikawa	¥52,856,504	39	K.T. Kwon	¥29,465,715	59	Than. Khrongpha	¥16,207,666
20	Toshinori Muto	¥48,180,455	40	Min-Gyu Cho	¥28,397,436	60	Hyung-Tae Kim	¥16,205,000

Indonesia PGA Championship

Mar 27 - Mar 30

Damai Indah Golf (Bumi Serpong Damai Course) - Serpong, Indonesia
Champion: Michio Matsumura

6,545 metres   Par 72
Purse: ¥103,640,000

In one of the more dramatic finishes in recent Japan Tour history, Michio Matsumura fired a closing 68 to claim the season-opening Indonesia PGA Championship by a single shot over Australian Rhein Gibson and Juvic Pagunsan of the Philippines. The initial drama was provided by the 28-year-old Gibson, who gained fame by shooting a non-competitive 16-under-par 55 during a 2012 round, and seemed on his way to more fireworks when standing 11-under-par through 15 holes on Sunday. A three-putt bogey at the par-4 16th then slowed his momentum, but his 10-under-par 62 was good enough to take the clubhouse lead. Enter Matsumura, who began Sunday one shot behind 54-hole leader Sang-Hyun Park before falling well off the pace after going out in 38. The three-time Japan Tour winner righted the ship coming home, however, making three birdies through the 14th to pull back within two, then reeling off clutch birdies at the 16th, 17th and 18th to steal the title. Pagunsan also mounted a late charge, birdieing the 15th, 17th and 18th to sneak into his share of second place.

1	Michio Matsumura	65-67-67-68	267	¥18,655,200		David Smail	67-68-71-68 274	¥1,777,426
2=	Rhein Gibson	69-65-72-62	268	¥9,068,500		Dong-Kyu Jang	67-69-69-69 274	¥1,777,426
	Juvic Pagunsan	67-64-68-69	268	¥9,068,500	17=	Yuki Kono	70-66-70-69 275	¥1,254,044
4	Ashun Wu	69-68-64-69	270	¥5,182,000		Kunihiro Kamii	65-70-70-70 275	¥1,254,044
5	Dong-Seop Maeng	67-69-70-65	271	¥4,352,880		Masahiro Kawamura	72-68-64-71 275	¥1,254,044
6=	Sung-Hoon Kang	67-68-70-67	272	¥3,694,766		Toshinori Muto	71-68-64-72 275	¥1,254,044
	Hiroshi Iwata	70-66-69-67	272	¥3,694,766		Sang-Hyun Park	67-64-67-77 275	¥1,254,044
8=	Xin-Jun Zhang	72-67-68-66	273	¥2,675,984	22=	Il-Hwan Park	69-67-71-69 276	¥1,088,220
	Yoshikazu Haku	69-66-71-67	273	¥2,675,984		Matthew Griffin	68-69-73-66 276	¥1,088,220
	Wen-Chong Liang	67-69-70-67	273	¥2,675,984		Jun-Seok Lee	73-68-69-66 276	¥1,088,220
	Bio Kim	68-67-70-68	273	¥2,675,984	25=	Nathan Holman	69-67-71-70 277	¥901,668
	Young-Han Song	69-66-67-71	273	¥2,675,984		Thaworn Wiratchant	69-70-72-66 277	¥901,668
13=	Seung-Hyuk Kim	70-68-70-66	274	¥1,777,426		Akio Sadakata	69-71-66-71 277	¥901,668
	Hao-Tong Li	67-67-72-68	274	¥1,777,426		Danny Chia	69-69-68-71 277	¥901,668

In The Money: **278**: Mamo Osanai, Yoshinori Fujimoto, Terry Pilkadaris, Michael Hendry, Stephen Leaney, David McKenzie, Mu Hu, Satoshi Kodaira **279**: George A Gandranata, Ryn Haller, Mardan Mamat, Jason Norris **280**: Jack Wilson, Hiroyuki Fujita, Scott Strange, Yasuki Hiramoto, Y.E. Yang, Yoshinobu Tsukada, Jung-Gon Hwang **281**: Tae-Hoon Kim, Yusaku Miyazato, Gi-Whan Kim, Masamichi Uehira, Ryuko Tokimatsu, Adam Bland **282**: Arnond Vongvanij, David Oh, Prom Meesawat, Brad Kennedy **283**: Joo-Yeob Baek, Joon-Eob Son, Do-Hoon Kim (#753), Min-Gyu Cho, Sung-Joon Park, Tae-Hee Lee, Tadahiro Takayama **284**: Gareth Paddison, Jin Zhang (a), Yuta Iked **286**: Zheng Ouyang, Daniel Popovic, Hidemasa Hoshino, Ze-Yu He **291**: Andik Mauludin **292**: I.J. Jang

OWR: 0 of top 50 entered - Rating: 23 - Points to 16th - Matsumura: 12 points, to 249th in OWR

Token Homemate Cup

Apr 17 - Apr 20

Token Tado Country Club - Nagoya, Japan
Champion: Yusaku Miyazato

7,081 yards   Par 71
Purse: ¥130,000,000

Little known beyond the Japan Golf Tour over his first 11 competitive seasons, 33-year-old Yusaku Miyazato jumped into the limelight by winning 2013's season-ending Golf Nippon Series JT Cup, then began the Tour's 2014 domestic schedule in similar style, claiming the Token Homemate Cup in Nagoya. Following rounds of 71-66-68, Miyazato began the final round as one of five players trailing 54-hole leader Daisuke Maruyama by a single stroke, but he quickly seized the lead in grand style by birdieing his first five holes and turning in 30. A three-putt bogey at the par-4 10th briefly slowed his momentum before Miyazato again caught fire with birdies at the 11th, 12th and 14th to surge back to a three-stroke advantage. Another three-putt bogey at the par-3 16th ultimately saw him home in 65, good enough for a two-shot triumph over Hiroshi Iwata, who only pulled that close via three birdies over his final five holes. Six-time Japan Tour winner Koumei Oda took solo third, three shots back, while Saturday leader Maruyama posted a disappointing 74 to tie for 14th.

1	Yusaku Miyazato	71-66-68-65	270	¥26,000,000	14=	Toru Taniguchi	66-71-75-66 278	¥2,106,000
2	Hiroshi Iwata	68-70-67-67	272	¥13,000,000		Yoshitaka Takeya	71-65-73-69 278	¥2,106,000
3	Koumei Oda	71-69-68-65	273	¥8,840,000		Kunihiro Kamii	70-71-67-70 278	¥2,106,000
4=	Nobuhiro Masuda	69-66-72-67	274	¥5,720,000		Tomohiro Kondo	68-72-65-73 278	¥2,106,000
	Adam Bland	69-68-68-69	274	¥5,720,000		Daisuke Maruyama	67-68-69-74 278	¥2,106,000
6	Tadahiro Takayama	70-66-69-70	275	¥4,680,000	19=	Ryuji Masaoka	71-69-71-69 280	¥1,360,666
7=	Kat. Miyamoto	69-72-71-64	276	¥3,831,750		Yujiro Ohori	66-67-77-70 280	¥1,360,666
	Yuta Ikeda	67-68-74-67	276	¥3,831,750		Hiroyuki Fujita	71-66-73-70 280	¥1,360,666
	Seung-Hyuk Kim	70-67-72-67	276	¥3,831,750		Toshinori Muto	67-66-77-70 280	¥1,360,666
	Hidemasa Hoshino	68-69-70-69	276	¥3,831,750		Seung-Eun Lim	69-71-73-67 280	¥1,360,666
11=	Michael Hendry	69-68-72-68	277	¥2,886,000		Ashun Wu	69-69-72-70 280	¥1,360,666
	Satoshi Kodaira	71-68-70-68	277	¥2,886,000		Kiyoshi Miyazato	66-72-72-70 280	¥1,360,666
	Kyung-Tae Kim	68-70-70-69	277	¥2,886,000				

In The Money: **281**: Kiyoshi Murota, Sung-Yoon Kim, Steven Conran, I.J. Jang, Scott Strange, Kodai Ichihara, Seung-Su Han, Ho-Sung Choi, Shingo Katayama, David Smail **282**: Katsuya Nakagawa, Joon-Woo Choi, Sang-Hyun Park, Hiroo Kawai **283**: Yosuke Tsukada, Keiichiro Fukabori, Yasukazu Idono, Kyoung-Hoon Lee **284**: Hyun-Woo Ryu, Hyung-Sung Kim **285**: Jay Choi, Jinichiro Kozuma, Tetsuji Hiratsuka, Fumihiro Ebine, Atomu Shigenaga **286**: Akio Sadakata, In-Hoi Hur, Yasuki Hiramoto, Hideto Tanihara **287**: Keisuke Sato, Ryutaro Nagano **288**: Min-Gyu Cho, Taichi Teshima, Mamo Osanai, Jung-Gon Hwang, Naomichi Joe Ozaki **289**: Kurt Barnes **293**: Shinji Tomimura **295**: Ryuichi Kondo

OWR: 0 of top 50 entered - Rating: 23 - Points to 27th - Miyazato: 16 points, to 147th in OWR

Tsuruya Open

Yamanohara Golf Club - Hyogo, Japan
Champion: Hiroyuki Fujita

Apr 24 - Apr 27
6,726 yards   Par 72
Purse: ¥110,000,000

Forty-four-year-old Hiroyuki Fujita claimed his 16th career victory on the Japan Golf Tour at the Tsuruya Open, defeating Korea's hard-charging Sang-Hyun Park on the first hole of a sudden death playoff. Fujita began Sunday's final round two shots behind 54-hole leader Atomu Shigenaga before carding a closing 67 that included late birdies at the 13th, 15th and 16th, putting him in the clubhouse on 13-under-par 271. Park, meanwhile, began the day five off the pace before turning in 31 to move himself into contention. After carding two birdies and a bogey between holes 13-15, he then recorded a clutch eagle at the par-5 17th to also finish on 271. But Fujita's considerable experience came to the fore in the playoff as he methodically parred the 415-yard 18th hole to raise the trophy. Hideto Tanihara (who closed with 64) and New Zealand's Michael Hendry tied for third, while the 25-year-old Shigenaga held it together for eight holes before a run of four bogeys from the 9th-14th saw him stumble home with a 75, dropping him into a tie for 11th.

1	Hiroyuki Fujita	66-72-66-67	271	¥22,000,000		Han Lee	69-69-67-72 277	¥2,244,000
2	Sang-Hyun Park	72-67-68-64	271	¥11,000,000		Atomu Shigenaga	68-66-68-75 277	¥2,244,000
3=	Hideto Tanihara	67-71-70-64	272	¥6,380,000	16=	Shunsuke Sonoda	70-68-71-69 278	¥1,672,000
	Michael Hendry	67-70-66-69	272	¥6,380,000		Ryuji Masaoka	71-71-66-70 278	¥1,672,000
5=	Tomohiro Kondo	72-69-68-65	274	¥3,836,250		Kyoung-Hoon Lee	72-69-65-72 278	¥1,672,000
	Hyung-Sung Kim	74-68-65-67	274	¥3,836,250	19=	Yoshinori Fujimoto	70-70-73-66 279	¥1,216,285
	I.J. Jang	71-66-69-68	274	¥3,836,250		Jay Choi	71-71-67-70 279	¥1,216,285
	Shingo Katayama	66-68-70-70	274	¥3,836,250		Seung-Su Han	69-69-70-71 279	¥1,216,285
9=	K.T. Kwon	68-71-69-68	276	¥2,992,000		Kazuhiro Yamashita	71-70-66-72 279	¥1,216,285
	Koumei Oda	70-69-68-69	276	¥2,992,000		Akio Sadakata	68-67-70-74 279	¥1,216,285
11=	Adam Bland	73-69-70-65	277	¥2,244,000		Azuma Yano	70-68-68-73 279	¥1,216,285
	Ryoma Iwai	68-70-73-66	277	¥2,244,000		Do-Hoon Kim	68-67-69-75 279	¥1,216,285
	David Oh	67-71-71-68	277	¥2,244,000				

In The Money: **280**: Michio Matsumura, Shinichi Yokota, Hyun-Woo Ryu, Ryo Ishikawa, In-Hoi Hur **281**: Kunihiro Kamii, Katsumasa Miyamoto, Jung-Gon Hwang, Satoshi Tomiyama **282**: Kyung-Tae Kim, Tadahiro Takayama, Yoshikazu Haku, Sang-Hee Lee, Shintaro Kai, Ruichi Oda **283**: Yosuke Asaji, Yosuke Tsukada, Hiroshi Iwata, Min-Gyu Cho **284**: S.K. Ho, Toshinori Muto, Tetsuya Haraguchi, Keiichiro Fukabori **285**: Ippei Koike, Kurt Barnes, Juvic Pagunsan **286**: Katsunori Kuwabara, Nobuhiro Masuda, Kiyoshi Murota, Brad Kennedy **287**: Sung-Yoon Kim **288**: Masamichi Uehira, Ryosuke Kinoshita, Keisuke Sato **289**: Hiroo Kawai **290**: Sung-Joon Park **291**: Katsuya Nakagawa **292**: Young-Han Song **293**: Steven Jeffress, Fumihiro Ebine **295**: Ryoken Kawagishi **299**: Keisuke Kondo

OWR: 0 of top 50 entered - Rating: 30 - Points to 25th - Fujita: 16 points, to 157th in OWR

The Crowns

Nagoya Golf Club (Wago) - Aichi, Japan
Champion: Hyung-Sung Kim

May 1 - May 4
6,545 yards   Par 70
Purse: ¥120,000,000

Celebrating his 34th birthday one week early, Korea's Hyung-Sung Kim won for the third time on the Japan Golf Tour at the long-running Crowns, posting a methodical final round 68 to claim a four-shot victory over countryman I.J. Jang at the Nagoya Golf Club. Kim initially rode rounds of 64-67 into a share of the halfway lead, then posted an even-par 70 on Saturday which, surprisingly, proved enough to give him a two-stroke 54-hole advantage. On a Sunday which saw none of the leaders make a major move, Kim turned in 34, then added another birdie at the 12th to move four ahead – a margin he would maintain (with a bogey at the 14th and a birdie at the last) to the finish. Jang, for his part, had climbed into the fray with three outgoing birdies, but bogeys at the 11th, 13th and 17th ultimately derailed his bid. Also noteworthy was defending champion Michio Matsumura, who opened the event with a 10-under-par 60, a stunning round which beat the field by four. Unfortunately, he then staggered home with rounds of 71-74-76 to plummet all the way into a tie for 19th.

1	Hyung-Sung Kim	64-67-70-68	269	¥24,000,000	14=	Sang-Hyun Park	68-73-71-68 280	¥1,944,000
2	I.J. Jang	64-68-72-69	273	¥12,000,000		Yusaku Miyazato	67-74-69-70 280	¥1,944,000
3	Yasuharu Imano	67-69-69-69	274	¥8,160,000		Atomu Shigenaga	68-68-73-71 280	¥1,944,000
4	Hiroshi Iwata	65-69-72-69	275	¥5,760,000		Katsunori Kuwabara	73-69-66-72 280	¥1,944,000
5=	Brad Kennedy	65-73-71-67	276	¥4,360,000		Tomohiro Kondo	66-68-69-77 280	¥1,944,000
	Koumei Oda	72-65-70-69	276	¥4,360,000	19=	Kyung-Tae Kim	69-68-76-68 281	¥1,368,000
	Ryo Ishikawa	66-68-70-72	276	¥4,360,000		Wen-Chong Liang	69-68-75-69 281	¥1,368,000
8	Kyoung-Hoon Lee	72-66-73-66	277	¥3,660,000		Satoshi Tomiyama	70-68-73-70 281	¥1,368,000
9=	Toshinori Muto	68-71-70-69	278	¥3,024,000		Shingo Katayama	72-70-67-72 281	¥1,368,000
	Steven Conran	68-68-72-70	278	¥3,024,000		Yoshinori Fujimoto	69-68-71-73 281	¥1,368,000
	Hideto Tanihara	72-67-70-69	278	¥3,024,000		Michio Matsumura	60-71-74-76 281	¥1,368,000
	Toru Taniguchi	67-69-69-73	278	¥3,024,000	25=	Young-Han Song	70-73-68-71 282	¥1,056,000
13	Toru Suzuki	70-72-66-71	279	¥2,424,000		S.K. Ho	73-68-69-72 282	¥1,056,000

In The Money: **283**: Juvic Pagunsan, Ashun Wu, Ryuichi Oda, Dong-Kyu Jang **284**: Naomichi Ozaki, K.T. Kwon, Michael Hendry, David Smail, Yoshikazu Haku **285**: Sang-Hee Lee, Scott Strange, Katsumasa Miyamoto, Akio Sadakata **286**: Tadahiro Takayama, David Oh, Yuki Kono, Kazuhiro Yamashita, Hiroo Kawai, Ho-Sung Choi, Jung-Gon Hwang, Makoto Inoue, Shinji Tomimura **287**: Kunihiro Kamii, Yoshinobu Tsukada, Min-Gyu Cho **288**: Hyun-Woo Ryu **289**: Hidemasa Hoshino, Daisuke Kataoka **290**: Yoshitaka Takeya **291**: Ryuichi Kondo, Katsufumi Okino **293**: Ryutaro Nagano **295**: Yuji Iagarashi **296**: Yosuke Tsukada, Keiichiro Fukabori

OWR: 0 of top 50 entered - Rating: 28 - Points to 24th - Kim: 16 points, to 70th in OWR

Kansai Open Golf Championship

Aug 22 - Aug 25

Rokko Country Club - Hyogo, Japan
Champion: Koumei Oda

7,061 yards Par 72
Purse: ¥60,000,000

After beginning the final round four shots off the lead, 35-year-old Koumei Oda roared home with a closing 67 to claim his seventh career Japan Tour title - and in dramatic fashion - at the Kansai Open. Oda began the week quietly with a 71 before lifting himself into a 54-hole tie for third via middle rounds of 66-69. Paired with the two men in front of him - leader Yoshinori Fujimoto and Tetsuji Hiratsuka - on Sunday, he closed to within three shots at the turn via an outgoing 34, then drew within one of Fujimoto with birdies at the 12th and 14th. Both players bogeyed the 475-yard 15th, and when Fujimoto followed that by bogeying the 204-yard 16th, the pair were deadlocked. Fours at the 17th brought them to the 72nd tee still square at which point Oda called forth his most brilliant golf, reaching the 563-yard 18th in two and holing his putt for eagle, pulling away to win by two. Despite his closing 73, Fujimoto still managed to claim second all by himself.

1	Koumei Oda	71-66-69-67	273	¥12,000,000		Jung-Gon Hwang	73-68-70-68	279	¥1,012,000
2	Yoshinori Fujimoto	67-69-66-73	275	¥6,000,000		Kyung-Tae Kim	71-70-68-70	279	¥1,012,000
3=	Brad Kennedy	70-67-71-68	276	¥3,120,000		Ashun Wu	67-72-69-71	279	¥1,012,000
	Hiroo Kawai	69-69-69-69	276	¥3,120,000		Daisuke Kataoka	67-69-70-73	279	¥1,012,000
	Dong-Kyu Jang	69-66-72-69	276	¥3,120,000		Tomohiro Kondo	69-70-68-72	279	¥1,012,000
6	Tetsuji Hiratsuka	67-68-69-73	277	¥2,160,000	19=	Shigeru Nonaka	70-70-72-68	280	¥663,428
7=	Yasuharu Imano	71-69-70-68	278	¥1,643,000		I.J. Jang	68-72-70-70	280	¥663,428
	Hiroshi Iwata	69-71-69-69	278	¥1,643,000		Min-Gyu Cho	70-71-69-70	280	¥663,428
	Tadahiro Takayama	68-69-71-70	278	¥1,643,000		Ryuko Tokimatsu	70-72-66-72	280	¥663,428
	S.K. Ho	69-69-70-70	278	¥1,643,000		K.T. Kwon	71-68-69-72	280	¥663,428
	Hideto Tanihara	69-72-67-70	278	¥1,643,000		Yoshitaka Takeya	69-72-67-72	280	¥663,428
	Kat. Miyamoto	71-70-66-71	278	¥1,643,000		Adam Bland	71-67-69-73	280	¥663,428
13=	Akio Sadakata	70-68-73-68	279	¥1,012,000					

In The Money: **281**: Ippei Koike, Daisuje Maruyama, Kazuhiro Yamashita **282**: Shintaro Kobayashi, Shinji Tomimuera, Sang-Hee Lee, Seung-Hyuk Kim, Michio Matsumura **283**: Azuma Yano, Katsufumi Okino **284**: Ryuichi Kondo, Satoshi Tomiyama, Stephen Leaney, Matthew Guyatt, Ryutaro Nagano, Nobuhiro Masuda **285**: Makoto Inoue, Shoji Kawai, Steven Jeffress, Kaname Yokoo, Masamichi Uehira, Taichi Teshima, Thaworn Wiratchant **286**: Do-Hoon Kim, Michael Hendry, Hisaki Sahashi, Yasuki Hiramoto **287**: Sung-Yoon Kim, Hyun-Woo Ryu, Yosuke Tsukada, Ryuji Masaoka **288**: Wen-Chong Liang, Nobuhiro Tsujimura Koki Shiomi, Keisuke Kondo **289**: Yuki Ishikawa, Yoshikazu Haku, Jinichiro Kozuma **290**: Ryoma Iwai, Thanyakon Khrongpha **291**: Issei Suenaga **292**: Richard Tate **293**: Yasukazu Idono **294**: Akira Teranishi (a)

OWR: 0 of top 50 entered - Rating: 19 - Points to 18th - Oda: 16 points, to 66th in OWR

Gateway To The Open Mizuno Open

May 29 - Jun 1

JFE Setonaikai Golf Club - Okayama, Japan
Champion: Dong-Kyu Jang

7,356 yards Par 72
Purse: ¥110,000,000

In an event which in recent years has become as noteworthy for the British Open berths it awards as for the intrinsic value of its title, South Korea's Dong-Kyu Jang claimed both with a three-shot victory at the Mizuno Open. The 25-year-old Jang stood two shots off the halfway lead following rounds of 70-67, then jumped into a two-shot 54-hole lead of his own following a third round 67. With four Open Championship spots up for grabs, winning was not an absolute necessity, but Jang went out in 33 before being slowed by bogeys at the par-5 11th and the 13th. But with his lead now trimmed to one, Jang rallied to birdie both the 17th and 18th to pull away at the wire. His closest third round pursuer, Juvic Pagunsan of the Philippines, finished with a 70 to nail down the second Open slot, while a pair of players who mounted strong Sunday charges, South Korea's Hyung-Tae Kim (66) and Japan's Tomohiro Kondo (67) tied for third to claim the final berths. Also gaining places in the Royal Liverpool field were Japan's Yusaku Miyazato and South Korea's Hyung-Sung Kim, who stood first and second in the Japan Tour Order of Merit after the completion of play.

1	Dong-Kyu Jang	70-67-67-69	273	¥22,000,000		Nobuhiro Masuda	68-74-68-72	282	¥2,772,000
2	Juvic Pagunsan	68-73-65-70	276	¥11,000,000	13=	Kurt Barnes	69-75-72-67	283	¥1,974,500
3=	Hyung-Tae Kim	72-71-68-66	277	¥6,380,000		Atomu Shigenaga	73-73-69-68	283	¥1,974,500
	Tomohiro Kondo	69-71-70-67	277	¥6,380,000		Kyung-Tae Kim	74-70-69-70	283	¥1,974,500
5	In-Hoi Hur	69-69-72-70	280	¥4,400,000		Ashun Wu	69-74-70-70	283	¥1,974,500
6=	Yui Ueda	66-72-73-70	281	¥3,648,333	17=	Steven Conran	71-74-70-69	284	¥1,433,666
	Michael Hendry	69-73-68-71	281	¥3,648,333		Michio Matsumara	70-71-74-69	284	¥1,433,666
	Hiroshi Iwata	66-69-73-73	281	¥3,648,333		Koki Shiomi	73-73-68-70	284	¥1,433,666
9=	Tadahiro Takayama	69-70-74-69	282	¥2,772,000		Jung-Gon Hwang	69-71-74-70	284	¥1,433,666
	Young-Han Song	72-71-70-69	282	¥2,772,000		Yusaku Miyazato	72-70-71-71	284	¥1,433,666
	Taichi Teshima	67-68-75-72	282	¥2,772,000		K.T. Kwon	73-68-71-72	284	¥1,433,666

In The Money: **285**: Wen-Chong Liang, Yoshinobu Tsukada, Kyoung-Hoon Lee **286**: Ryuji Masaoka, Yoshinori Fujimoto **287**: Ryuko Tokimatsu, Shunsuke Sonoda, Seung-Hyuk Kim, Yasuharu Imano, Hiroyuki Fujita, Yuki Kono **288**: Toru Taniguchi, Adam Bland, Han Lee, Hyun-Woo Ryu, Shingo Katayama, Min-Gyu Cho, Sung-Yoon Kim **289**: Daisuke Kataoka, Keiichiro Fukabori, Tetsuji Hiratsuka, Keisuke Kondo, Jay Choi, Yuta Ikeda **290**: Ryoma Iwai, Brad Kennedy, Yoshitaka Takeya **291**: Hirohito Koizumi, Mamo Osanai, Kodai Ichihara, Katsunori Kuwabara, Ho-Sung Choi, Akio Sadakata, Toru Suzuki **292**: Ryutaro Nagano, Takashi Kanemoto **293**: Ryuichi Oda, Makoto Inoue, Satoshi Kodaira, Yohei Haga **294**: Fumihiro Ebine, Ryoken Kawagishi, Yuki Ishikawa **295**: Joon-Woo Choi **296**: Yosuke Asaji, Yasuki Hiramoto **298**: Richard Tate, Shohei Hasegawa (a)

OWR: 0 of top 50 entered - Rating: 26 - Points to 26th - Jang: 16 points, to 257th in OWR

Japan PGA Championship

Jun 5 - Jun 8

Golden Valley Golf Club - Hyogo, Japan
Champion: Taichi Teshima

7,233 yards   Par 72
Purse: ¥150,000,000

Forty-five-year-old Taichi Teshima's last victory on the Japan Golf Tour came in 2007, yet despite this seven-year lull, he held together nicely during an up-and-down finale to claim his seventh career title at the Japan PGA Championship. Teshima, who finished 70th in 2013 earnings and seemed in the twilight of his career, opened with rounds of 70-68-69 at the Golden Valley Golf Club, good enough to take a one-shot 54-hole lead over a hot Koumei Oda and South Korea's Kyung-Hoon Lee. He then solidified his position by opening with two birdies on Sunday before bogeys at the 8th and 10th slowed his momentum. Timely birdies at the 12th and 14th rebuilt his lead, however, ultimately allowing Teshima to bogey the 472-yard 16th and still win by one. While both Oda and Lee matched Teshima's closing 71, neither had any real chance at victory, Oda falling away after bogeying the 14th, 15th and 16th and Lee fading with bogeys at the 15th and 16th.

1	Taichi Teshima	71-68-69-71	279	¥30,000,000		Scott Strange	74-71-74-70	289	¥2,292,857
2=	Kyoung-Hoon Lee	72-69-68-71	280	¥12,600,000		Hiroyuki Fujita	73-69-76-71	289	¥2,292,857
	Koumei Oda	71-71-67-71	280	¥12,600,000		Yuta Ikeda	71-75-75-68	289	¥2,292,857
4	Dong-Kyu Jang	79-69-67-68	283	¥7,200,000		Shinji Tomimura	72-76-68-73	289	¥2,292,857
5=	Hyung-Tae Kim	69-69-72-74	284	¥5,700,000		Ho-Sung Choi	72-74-69-74	289	¥2,292,857
	Yusaku Miyazato	73-69-71-71	284	¥5,700,000		Keiichiro Fukabori	72-69-73-75	289	¥2,292,857
7=	Kat. Miyamoto	75-72-72-66	285	¥4,762,500	21=	I.J. Kang	75-69-75-71	290	¥1,590,000
	Toru Taniguchi	68-71-76-70	285	¥4,762,500		Tomohiro Kondo	78-70-74-68	290	¥1,590,000
9=	Yoshinori Fujimoto	74-70-75-68	287	¥4,080,000		Jung-Gon Hwang	78-69-70-73	290	¥1,590,000
	K.T. Kwon	74-74-68-71	287	¥4,080,000		Michael Hendry	76-72-69-73	290	¥1,590,000
11=	David Oh	77-69-74-68	288	¥3,330,000	25=	Hiroo Kawai	76-67-76-72	291	¥1,290,000
	Hideto Tanihara	75-72-71-70	288	¥3,330,000		Hidemasa Hoshino	74-73-75-69	291	¥1,290,000
	Michio Matsumura	70-73-72-73	288	¥3,330,000		Steven Conran	74-68-73-76	291	¥1,290,000
14=	Han Lee	75-71-74-69	289	¥2,292,857					

In The Money: **292:** Yoshinobu Tsukada, Kazuhiro Yamashita, Keisuke Sato, Hiroshi Iwata, Kiradech Aphibarnrat, Hirotaro Naito, Taichiro Kiyota, Tadahiro Takayama, Kyung-Tae Kim **293:** Takanori Konishi, Hideto Kobukuro, Jay Choi, Yosuke Tsukada, Young-Han Song **294:** Kiyoshi Murota, Yasuharu Imano, Yoshikazu Haku, David Smail, Akio Sadakata, Hirotake Sugano **295:** Sung-Yoon Kim, Keisuke Otawa, Ryutaro Nagano, Nobuhiro Masuda, Kodai Ichihara **296:** Ryoken Kawagishi, Hyun-Woo Ryu, Min-Gyu Cho, Koichi Kitamura **298:** Naoyuki Tamura, Kaname Yokoo **299:** In-Hoi Hur **300:** J.B. Park **303:** Sachio Sugiyama, Naomi Ohta **304:** Hirohito Koizumi, Richard Tate **305:** Katsumune Imai **306:** Satoshi Tomiyama **308:** Shohei Karimata

OWR: 0 of top 50 entered - Rating: 32 - Points to 20th - Teshima: 16 points, to 318th in OWR

Japan Golf Tour Championship

Jun 19 - Jun 22

Shishido Hill Country Club (West) - Ibarakii, Japan
Champion: Yoshitaka Takeya

7,402 yards   Par 72
Purse: ¥150,000,000

Yoshitaka Takeya, who'd never previously finished a season ranked higher than 134th in annual earnings, claimed his first Japan Tour victory at the Japan Golf Tour Championship, in Ibaraki. The 34-year-old Takeya had never posted even a single top 10 on the circuit but wasted little time in taking charge this week, carding opening rounds of 69-65 to share the halfway lead with one of the tour's hottest players, Dong-Kyu Jang of South Korea. Both players then added Saturday 69s to share a three-stroke 54-hole lead over Sang-Hee Lee and Kyung-Tae Kim, setting up a finale which saw Jang tumble from contention with a closing 73 marred by a triple-bogey eight at the 519-yard 2nd. Takeya, meanwhile, reached the 9th tee one under par on the day, then proceeded to reel off five consecutive birdies, building a lead large enough that bogeys at the 71st and 72nd did little more than cut the margin of victory to two strokes over Lee, who closed with 67.

1	Yoshitaka Takeya	69-65-69-68	271	¥30,000,000	16=	Ho-Sung Choi	71-73-71-69	284	¥2,148,000
2	Sang-Hee Lee	71-68-67-67	273	¥15,000,000		Hyung-Sung Kim	67-72-73-72	284	¥2,148,000
3=	Hideto Tanihara	67-72-69-68	276	¥8,700,000		Hidemasa Hoshino	67-72-73-72	284	¥2,148,000
	Dong-Kyu Jang	68-66-69-73	276	¥8,700,000		Masahiro Kawamura	70-69-72-73	284	¥2,148,000
5	Prayad Marksaeng	67-70-70-71	278	¥6,000,000		Hyun-Woo Ryu	71-74-67-72	284	¥2,148,000
6	Kyung-Tae Kim	71-68-67-73	279	¥5,400,000	21=	Tadahiro Takayama	70-71-76-68	285	¥1,590,000
7=	K.T. Kwon	71-70-72-67	280	¥4,421,250		Yasuharu Imano	68-72-73-72	285	¥1,590,000
	Daisuke Maruyama	71-71-70-68	280	¥4,421,250		Taichi Teshima	68-72-73-72	285	¥1,590,000
	Hiroshi Iwata	76-68-65-71	280	¥4,421,250		Scott Strange	70-73-69-73	285	¥1,590,000
	Tetsuji Hiratsuka	72-67-70-71	280	¥4,421,250	25=	Shota Akiyoshi	72-73-70-71	286	¥1,230,000
11	T. Khrongpha	68-68-72-73	281	¥3,630,000		Sang-Hyun Park	74-70-70-72	286	¥1,230,000
12=	I.J. Jang	69-72-73-68	282	¥3,180,000		Seung-Hyuk Kim	71-70-72-73	286	¥1,230,000
	Kazuhiro Yamashita	71-72-68-71	282	¥3,180,000		Yoshinori Fujimoto	70-71-72-73	286	¥1,230,000
14=	Juvic Pagunsan	71-73-69-70	283	¥2,655,000		Masamichi Uehira	68-70-71-77	286	¥1,230,000
	Ryuji Masaoka	71-71-70-71	283	¥2,655,000					

In The Money: **287:** Jung-Gon Hwang, Ryutaro Nagano, Ashun Wu **288:** Kodai Ichihara, Jinichiro Kozuma, Akio Sadakata **289:** Kurt Barnes, Katsunori Kuwabara, Yuta Ikeda, Xin-Jun Zhang, Hiroyuki Fujita **290:** Yoshikazu Haku, Ippei Koike, Kazuhiko Hosokawa **291:** Ryosuke Kinoshita, David Smail, Shunsuke Sonoda, Dimitrios Papadatos **292:** Daisuke Kataoka, Shigeru Nonaka **293:** Hirohito Koizumi **294:** Yoshinobu Tsukada, Ryuichi Oda, Yuki Kono, Michael Hendry, Hyung-Tae Kim, Keisuke Kondo **295:** Nobuhiro Masuda **296:** Keiichiro Fukabori, Yosuke Tsukada, Steven Conran, Han Lee **298:** Kunihiro Kamii **303:** Jay Choi **304:** Yuji Igarashi

OWR: 0 of top 50 entered - Rating: 32 - Points to 20th - Takeya: 16 points, to 366th in OWR

Negashima Shigeo Invitational Sega Sammy Cup

Jul 3 - Jul 6

North Country Club - Hokkaido, Japan
Champion: Ryo Ishikawa

7,127 yards Par 72
Purse: ¥200,000,000

Ending a victory drought dating back to 2012, Japan's Ryo Ishikawa took a break from the U.S. PGA Tour to return to his homeland and win the Sega Sammy Cup, defeating Koumei Oda on the third hole of a playoff. The 22-year-old Ishikawa began Sunday two shots behind Oda, who opened the week with rounds of 69-67-69 and produced a sturdy final effort, closing with a bogey-free two-under-par 69. Ishikawa, meanwhile, began Sunday by three-putt bogeying the par-3 2nd, immediately recovering that stroke at the par-5 3rd, then moving within one of Oda by adding birdies at both the 8th and 9th. Adding two more birdies and a bogey through the 15th, he found himself trailing Oda by one going to the 560-yard 18th before logging the crucial birdie needed to force a playoff, then claiming the title on the third extra hole. It was Ishikawa's third domestic appearance of 2014 and the first homeland event of the year for world number 14 Hideki Matsuyama, who closed with a 68 to tie for 17th. And lest there be any doubt as to the revised power structure of Japanese golf, ex-phenom Ishikawa noted afterwards that: "I have to practice more and more so I can catch up with Hideki."

1	Ryo Ishikawa	69-71-67-67	274	¥40,000,000		Daisuke Kataoka	72-69-70-69	280	¥4,513,333
2	Koumei Oda	69-67-69-69	274	¥20,000,000		Prayad Marksaeng	73-71-67-69	280	¥4,513,333
3=	K.T. Kwon	69-74-69-65	277	¥11,600,000		Han Lee	67-71-70-72	280	¥4,513,333
	Kazuhiro Yamashita	67-69-70-71	277	¥11,600,000	17=	Hideki Matsuyama	71-71-71-68	281	¥2,770,000
5	David Oh	65-74-73-66	278	¥8,000,000		Kyung-Tae Kim	69-69-74-69	281	¥2,770,000
6=	Shunsuke Sonoda	72-69-71-67	279	¥6,900,000		Brad Kennedy	70-73-67-71	281	¥2,770,000
	Kodai Ichihara	71-68-72-68	279	¥6,900,000		Yoshinori Fujimoto	67-69-72-73	281	¥2,770,000
8=	Koki Shiomi	73-70-71-66	280	¥4,513,333	21=	Hiroo Kawai	73-69-70-70	282	¥2,280,000
	Toru Taniguchi	69-68-76-67	280	¥4,513,333		Tadahiro TakayaMA	70-72-70-70	282	¥2,280,000
	Kurt Barnes	69-74-71-66	280	¥4,513,333	23=	Hideto Tanihara	73-70-71-69	283	¥1,860,000
	Ryutaro Nagano	72-72-69-67	280	¥4,513,333		Hyun-Woo Ryu	72-71-73-67	283	¥1,860,000
	I.J. Jang	71-72-70-67	280	¥4,513,333		Kiyoshi Murota	72-70-71-70	283	¥1,860,000
	Scott Strange	68-72-71-69	280	¥4,513,333		Yosuke Tsukada	68-74-70-71	283	¥1,860,000

In The Money: **284**: David Smail, Yoshikazu Haku, Kunihiro Kamii, Jung-Gon Hwang, Tetsuji Hiratsuka **285**: Yoshitaka Takeya, Dong-Kyu Jang, Ryuichi Oda, Ryuji Masaoka, Tomohiro Kondo, Akio Sadakata **286**: Shinji Tomimura, Kyoung-Hoon Lee, Seung-Hyuk Kim, Masaya Tomida, Masamichi Uehira, Ryoken Kawagishi **287**: Keisuke Sato, Atomu Shigenaga, Juvic Pagunsan, Nobuhiro Masuda, Brendan Jones, Ashun Wu, Michio Matsumura **288**: Daisuke Matsubara (a), Hidemasa Hoshino **289**: Daichi Morisugi, In-Hoi Hur, Yuta Ikeda **290**: Katsunori Kuwabara, Daisuke Maruyama, Stephen Leaney, Hiroshi Iwata, Ippei Koike, Sung-Joon Park, Shohei Hasegawa (a) **291**: Katsuya Nakagawa, Jay Choi, Mamo Osanai **293**: Wen-Chong Liang, Seung-Su Han **294**: Masayuki Kawamura **296**: Takashi Kanemoto

OWR: 1 of top 50 entered - Rating: 54 - Points to 20th - Ishikawa: 18 points, to 76th in OWR

Dunlop Srixon Fukushima Open

Jul 31 - Aug 3

Grandee Nasushirakawa Golf Club - Fukushima, Japan
Champion: Satoshi Kodaira

6,961 yards Par 72
Purse: ¥50,000,000

Twenty-four-year-old Satoshi Kodaira landed his second career Japan Tour victory at the Dunlop Srixon Fukushima Open, closing with a workmanlike 68 to overcome a three-shot 54-hole deficit and claim the title. The winner of the 2013 Japan Tour Championship, Kodaira began his week disappointingly, trailing by eight after an opening-round 72. A second round 68 still left him six behind a trio of halfway leaders before Kodaira lifted himself back into the mix on Saturday with a stellar 64, a round which included seven birdies, one bogey and an eagle at the 526-yard par-5 7th. Now standing three back of Ryutaro Nagano and Thailand's Thanyakon Khrongpha, Kodaira methodically posted three front nine birdies to turn in 33 on Sunday, allowing him to catch Khrongpha and pull within one of Nagano. A birdie at the par 5 13th then got him to 16 under par, a number which, after Kodaira closed with five straight routine pars, proved enough to win by two.

1	Satoshi Kodaira	72-68-64-68	272	¥10,000,000		T. Khrongpha	69-65-67-75	276	¥1,060,000
2=	Yuki Inamori	72-69-67-66	274	¥2,920,000	15=	Kodai Ichihara	66-70-73-68	277	¥718,571
	Hiroshi Iwata	70-64-73-67	274	¥2,920,000		Adam Bland	72-70-66-69	277	¥718,571
	Kazuhiro Yamashita	74-67-66-67	274	¥2,920,000		K.T. Kwon	68-69-70-70	277	¥718,571
	Ryosuke Kinoshita	68-69-67-70	274	¥2,920,000		Sung-Joon Park	73-69-65-70	277	¥718,571
	Ryutaro Nagano	68-66-67-73	274	¥2,920,000		Yasuki Hiramoto	68-71-68-70	277	¥718,571
7=	Kazuhiko Hosokawa	74-67-70-64	275	¥1,473,750		Koumei Oda	72-65-69-71	277	¥718,571
	K. Miyamoto	74-63-71-67	275	¥1,473,750		Yuki Kono	70-69-67-71	277	¥718,571
	Daisuke Kataoka	71-67-68-69	275	¥1,473,750	22=	Taichi Teshima	64-71-74-69	278	¥482,000
	Naomi Ohta	71-70-63-71	275	¥1,473,750		Tadahiro Takayama	68-68-72-70	278	¥482,000
11=	Satoshi Tomiyama	70-70-72-64	276	¥1,060,000		S.K. Ho	69-71-67-71	278	¥482,000
	Atomu Sigenaga	68-69-70-69	276	¥1,060,000		Yuichiro Nishi	70-68-68-72	278	¥482,000
	Wen-Chong Liang	65-75-67-69	276	¥1,060,000		Azuma Yano	72-64-68-74	278	¥482,000

In The Money: **279**; Kunihiro Kamii, Nobuhiro Masuda, Ryuko Tokimatsu, Daisuke Shiraishi, Stephen Leaney, Katsufumi Okino, Masahiro Kawamura **280**: Norio Shinozaki, Ippei Koike, Dong-Woo Kang, Yoshinori Fujimoto **281**: Takanori Konishi, Joon-Woo Choi **282**: Masamichi Uehira, Han Lee, Masayuki Omiya, Yui Ueda, Masashi Ishimaru **283**: Hideto Tanihara, Jun Kikuchi, Brendan Jones **284**: Steven Jeffress, Yuta Ikeda, Satoshi Sakamoto, Shunsuke Sonoda, Hiroyuki Fujita, Tatshuko Takahashi, Hiroo Kawai **285**: Kazuhiro Shimuzu **286**: Katsunori Kuwabara, Takuya Fuji, Nobuhiro Tsujimura **287**: Kazuya Koura (a), Shota Akiyoshi **288**: Daijiro Izumida, Michio Matsumura, Yusaku Miyazato **289**: Dae-Jun Lee **290**: Mamo Osanai, Ryuji Masaoka, Tomokazu Yoshinaga, Fumihiro Ebine

OWR: 0 of top 50 entered - Rating: 18 - Points to 21st - Kodaira: 16 points, to 200th in OWR

RZ Everlasting KBC Augusta

Keya Golf Club - Fukuoka, Japan
Champion: Hiroyuki Fujita

Aug 28 - Aug 31
7,144 yards   Par 72
Purse: ￥110,000,000

Veteran Hiroyuki Fujita claimed his second Japan Golf Tour title of 2014 and the 17th of his career with a come-from-behind playoff triumph at the RZ Everlasting KBC Augusta. With opening rounds of 71-66, Fujita found himself very much in the mix at the halfway mark, trailing 36-hole leader Hyung-Sung Kim by three, before a disappointing Saturday 74 dropped him all the way to 17th place, six behind Kim. His hole deepened further after bogeying the par-4 2nd on Sunday before the 45-year-old Fujita got hot, logging eight birdies over his final 17 holes (built around nine consecutive one-putts at holes 9-17) to post a 276 total. Though a slew of players had chances to catch him down the stretch, this number was eventually matched only by 36-year-old Chinese star Wen-Chong Liang, who closed with rounds of 67-69. But Liang, who has never won in Japan, couldn't quite get over the bar in the playoff, with Fujita closing him out on the fifth extra hole.

1	Hiroyuki Fujita	71-66-74-65	276	￥22,000,000		Yuki Inamori	66-73-69-72 280	￥1,800,857
2	Wen-Chong Liang	70-70-67-69	276	￥11,000,000		Shigeru Nonaka	69-69-68-74 280	￥1,800,857
3=	Yosuke Tsukada	72-69-70-66	277	￥5,280,000	20=	Jung-Gon Hwang	69-70-72-70 281	￥1,298,000
	Toshinori Muto	69-72-68-68	277	￥5,280,000		Prayad Marksaeng	72-69-70-70 281	￥1,298,000
	Yusaku Miyazato	74-67-67-69	277	￥5,280,000		Tetsuji Hiratsuka	69-71-69-72 281	￥1,298,000
	Hyung-Sung Kim	65-69-71-72	277	￥5,280,000	23=	Yoshikazu Haku	68-73-72-69 282	￥865,000
7=	Adam Bland	71-70-72-65	278	￥3,242,250		Kazuhiro Yamashita	73-69-72-68 282	￥865,000
	Sang-Hyun Park	68-71-72-67	278	￥3,242,250		Ryosuke Kinoshita	72-70-70-70 282	￥865,000
	Yuta Ikeda	69-69-72-68	278	￥3,242,250		In-Hoi Hur	71-70-71-70 282	￥865,000
	Ryutaro Nagano	71-69-70-68	278	￥3,242,250		Azuma Yano	74-66-72-70 282	￥865,000
11=	Hiroshi Iwata	71-68-74-66	279	￥2,552,000		Kyoung-Hoon Lee	71-71-73-67 282	￥865,000
	Michael Hendry	72-67-69-71	279	￥2,552,000		K. Miyamoto	70-69-76-67 282	￥865,000
13=	Shota Akiyoshi	71-68-73-68	280	￥1,800,857		Jinichiro Kozuma	70-70-71-71 282	￥865,000
	Seung-Hyuk Kim	69-70-73-68	280	￥1,800,857		Juvic Pagunsan	69-70-71-72 282	￥865,000
	Kunihiro Kamii	70-72-70-68	280	￥1,800,857		Keiichiro Fukabori	71-70-68-73 282	￥865,000
	Tomohiro Kondo	69-71-75-65	280	￥1,800,857		Yoshitaka Takeya	71-68-68-75 282	￥865,000
	Toru Suzuki	69-70-71-70	280	￥1,800,857				

In The Money: **283**: Hidemasa Hoshino, Kodai Ichihara, Young-Han Song **284**: Keisuke Sato **285**: Joon-Woo Choi, Yoshinori Fujimoto, Thanyakon Khrongpha, Shinji Tomimura, Yoshitsuda Tsukada, Taigen Tsumagari, Hirohito Koizumi, Sang-Hee Lee **286**: Yuki Kono, Dong-Kyu Jang **287**: Kurt Barnes, Kazuhiko Hosokawa, K.T. Kwon, Steven Conran **288**: Yujiro Ohori **289**: Tadahiro Takayama, Shintaro Kai **290**: Yasuharu Imano, Hiroo Kawai, Hidezumi Shirakata **291**: Sung-Yoon Kim, Shingo Katayama, Ryoken Kawagishi **292**: David Oh **294**: Kiyoshi Murota

OWR: 0 of top 50 entered   -   Rating: 21   -   Points to 19th   -   Fujita: 16 points, to 179th in OWR

Fujisankei Classic

Fujizakura Country Club - Yamanashi, Japan
Champion: Hiroshi Iwata

Sep 4 - Sep 7
7,437 yards   Par 71
Purse: ￥110,000,000

Thirty-three-year-old Hiroshi Iwata entered 2014 winless on his native Japan Tour, and he hadn't cracked the top 25 in official earnings since finishing 21st in 2008. But his form made a precipitous climb from the start of the year as he logged seven top 10s in his first 11 domestic starts, setting the stage for him to break through and land his maiden victory in the 42nd playing of the Fujisankei Classic. Iwata's golf leaned far more towards the steady than the spectacular this week as each of his first two rounds of 69 included four birdies and two bogeys, and he followed these with a Saturday 70 to stand two shots behind 54-hole leader Yuta Ikeda. Iwata found a higher gear on Sunday, however, turning in three-under-par 32 before eventually reaching the 18th tee four under on the day and tied for the lead with Korean In-Hoi Hur. But while Hur could do no better than a closing par, Iwata birdied the 465-yard finisher to steal the trophy.

1	Hiroshi Iwata	69-69-70-66	274	￥22,000,000		Kyoung-Hoon Lee	73-68-71-71 283	￥1,974,500
2	In-Hoi Hur	71-64-72-68	275	￥11,000,000		Toru Taniguchi	66-76-70-71 283	￥1,974,500
3	Brendan Jones	71-70-68-67	276	￥7,480,000		Tomohiro Kondo	69-70-70-74 283	￥1,974,500
4=	Daisuke Kataoka	69-71-69-70	279	￥4,546,666	17=	Ippei Koike	75-68-71-70 284	￥1,523,500
	Yuta Ikeda	68-69-69-73	279	￥4,546,666		Akio Sadakata	71-69-73-71 284	￥1,523,500
	Hyung-Sung Kim	68-71-69-71	279	￥4,546,666		I.J. Jang	73-68-71-72 284	￥1,523,500
7=	Ryuji Masaoka	72-70-72-66	280	￥3,362,333		Scott Strange	69-71-71-73 284	￥1,523,500
	Yosuke Tsukada	69-74-68-69	280	￥3,362,333	21=	Toru Suzuki	68-73-73-71 285	￥1,100,000
	Yoshinobu Tsukada	72-67-69-72	280	￥3,362,333		Han Lee	70-71-73-71 285	￥1,100,000
10	Yoshinori Fujimoto	70-70-72-69	281	￥2,882,000		Satoshi Kodaira	70-73-71-71 285	￥1,100,000
11=	Hyun-Woo Ryu	67-68-75-72	282	￥2,552,000		Kazuhiro Yamashita	75-68-73-69 285	￥1,100,000
	Seung-Hyuk Kim	70-64-75-73	282	￥2,552,000		Yoshikazu Haku	69-72-75-69 285	￥1,100,000
13=	Taichi Teshima	73-69-71-70	283	￥1,974,500		Adam Bland	69-69-72-75 285	￥1,100,000

In The Money: **286**: Kodai ICchihara, Yuki Kono, Koumei Oda, Ryuko Tokimatsu, Hyung-Tae Kim **287**: Prayad Marksaeng, Jung-Gon Hwang, Koichiro Kawano, Tadahiro Takayama, Satoshi Tomiyama, Hiroyuki Fujita **288**: Yusaku Miyazato, Norihiko Furusho, Keiichiro Fukabori, Shinji Tomimura, Wen-Chong Liang **289**: Koki Shiomi, Yuji Igarishi, Steven Conran, Kurt Barnes **290**: Ashun Wu, Tetsuji Hiratsuka, Min-Gyu Cho, Kyung-Tae Kim **291**: J.B. Park, Makoto Inoue **292**: Do-Hoon Kim, Hyung-Joon Lee, Brad Kennedy, Takashi Iwamoto, S.K. Ho **293**: David Smail, Dong-Kyu Jang, Kaname Yokoo **294**: Ryuichi Oda, Hiroki Abe **295**: Shigeru Nonaka **296**: Daisuke Maruyama, Katsuya Nakagawa **298**: Sang-Hyun Park, Sung-Yoon Kim **302**: Shinsuke Yanagisawa

OWR: 0 of top 50 entered   -   Rating: 23   -   Points to 20th   -   Iwata: 16 points, to 127th in OWR

ANA Open

Sep 18 - Sep 21

Sapporo Golf Club (Wattsu) - Hokkaido, Japan
Champion: Katsumasa Miyamoto

7,063 yards   Par 72
Purse: ￥110,000,000

Forty-one-year-old Katsumasa Miyamoto ended a four-year victory drought by claiming his ninth career Japan Golf Tour victory at the ANA Open, beating fellow Tour veteran Hideto Tanihara on the first hole of a sudden death playoff. Miyamoto began his week with a solid 67 that was marred only by a double-bogey at the 4th hole (his 13th), and he followed that with rounds of 67-68, each of which included an eagle. His 54-hole total of 203 proved enough to share a one-shot lead with Tanihara, who opened with 66-68 and might well have held the lead by himself had he not bogeyed two of his final three holes during a Saturday 69. Both players then put together solid five-under-par 67s on Sunday, with Tanihara leading down the stretch before Miyamoto carded a clutch birdie at the 579-yard 17th to match his aggregate of 270. Third place was shared by China's Wen-Chong Liang (who came home in 32 en route to a closing 67) and a pair of players who birdied the 410-yard final hole to catch him, South Korea's Hyung-Sung Kim (68) and Japan's Yoshinori Fujimoto (68).

1	Kat. Miyamoto	68-67-68-67	270	￥22,000,000
2	Hideto Tanihara	66-68-69-67	270	￥11,000,000
3=	Wen-Chong Liang	71-69-65-67	272	￥5,720,000
	Hyung-Sung KIM	65-71-68-68	272	￥5,720,000
	Yoshinori Fujimoto	70-65-69-68	272	￥5,720,000
6	Sang-Hee Lee	66-69-69-69	273	￥3,960,000
7	Nobuhiro Masuda	69-72-63-70	274	￥3,630,000
8=	I.J. Jang	69-70-69-67	275	￥2,777,500
	Kyung-Tae Kim	71-69-67-68	275	￥2,777,500
	Taichi Teshima	69-67-70-69	275	￥2,777,500
	Prayad Marksaeng	68-70-69-68	275	￥2,777,500
	Kyoung-Hoon Lee	70-69-66-70	275	￥2,777,500
	Hiroyuki Fujita	70-72-63-70	275	￥2,777,500
14	Hidemasa Hoshino	74-69-68-66	277	￥2,002,000
15=	Sang-Moon Bae	71-71-69-67	278	￥1,580,857
	Ho-Sung Choi	69-70-71-68	278	￥1,580,857
	Ryo Ishikawa	69-71-70-68	278	￥1,580,857
	Tomohiro Kondo	65-74-70-69	278	￥1,580,857
	Tadahiro Takayama	75-67-67-69	278	￥1,580,857
	Yuta Ikeda	68-73-67-70	278	￥1,580,857
	Ippei Koike	65-70-70-73	278	￥1,580,857
22=	Brendan Jones	71-73-67-68	279	￥1,034,000
	Hyung-Tae Kim	69-75-68-67	279	￥1,034,000
	Kazuhiko Hosokawa	69-72-68-70	279	￥1,034,000
	Shinji Tomimura	67-71-70-71	279	￥1,034,000
	Yasuki Hiramoto	71-73-71-64	279	￥1,034,000
	Masamichi Uehira	70-66-70-73	279	￥1,034,000

In The Money: **280**: S.K. Ho, Brad Kennedy, Hideto Kobukuro, Shingo Katayama **281**: Michio Matsumura, Sang-Hyun Park, David Oh, Hyun-Woo Ryu, Ryuko Tokimatsu **282**: Yoshitaka Takeya, Atomu Shigenaga, Keiichiro Fukabori, Thanyakon Khorngpha, Koumei Oda, Yoshinobu Tsukada **283**: Koki Shiomi, Katsuyuki Sakurai, Scott Strange, Fumihiro Ebine, Ryutaro Nagano, Ryuji Masaoka **285**: Hiroo Kawai, Dong-Kyu Jang, David Smail **286**: Hirotaro Naito, Shigeru Nonaka, Toshinori Muto, Kiyoshi Murota **287**: Hirohito Koizumi **288**: Azuma Yano, Masayoshi Nakayama, Naoyuki Kataoka (a), Adam Bland, Ryosuke Kinoshita **291**: Takanori Konishi, Kunihiro Kamii **292**: Yosuke Asaji, Kaname Yokoo

OWR: 0 of top 50 entered   -   Rating: 30   -   Points to 21st   -   Miyamoto: 16 points, to 255th in OWR

Asia-Pacific Diamond Cup Golf

Sep 25 - Sep 28

Otone Country Club (West Course) - Ibaraki, Japan
Champion: Hiroyuki Fujita

7,024 yards   Par 72
Purse: ￥150,000,000

In an event co-sanctioned by the Asian Tour, 45-year-old Hiroyuki Fujita claimed his 18th career Japan Golf Tour title at the Asia-Pacific Diamond Cup, storming home with a closing 66 to beat a trio of players by two. The 2012 Japan Order of Merit winner, Fujita lingered quietly around the lead for much of the week, initially trailing first round leader Cameron Smith by two, then sitting in a tie for fourth at the halfway mark, two back of Australian Adam Bland. Fujita stumbled a bit on Saturday however, with bogeys at the 17th and 18th pushing him to a 73 and leaving him in a 10-way tie for 14th, four strokes behind 54-hole pacesetter Wen-Chong Liang of China. But Liang would fall apart with three early bogeys on Sunday, and while other contenders played steady, unspectacular golf, Fujita caught fire, birdieing five of his first 15 holes to move into contention before bogeying the long par-4 17th, then birdieing 575-yard closer to clinch a two-shot victory.

1	Hiroyuki Fujita	68-71-73-66	278	￥30,000,000
2=	K. Aphibarnrat	71-72-70-67	280	￥11,850,000
	Jason Knutzon	71-71-70-68	280	￥11,850,000
	S.K. Ho	68-70-73-69	280	￥11,850,000
5=	Kyoung-Hoon Lee	72-68-72-69	281	￥4,987,500
	Seuk-Hyun Baek	70-69-73-69	281	￥4,987,500
	Yoshitaka Takeya	73-67-70-71	281	￥4,987,500
	Yoshinobu Tsukada	71-71-68-71	281	￥4,987,500
9=	Cameron Smith	66-74-72-70	282	￥2,313,750
	Adam Bland	69-68-74-71	282	￥2,313,750
	Juvic Pagunsan	69-72-70-71	282	￥2,313,750
	Shigo Katayama	71-71-69-71	282	￥2,313,750
	Scott Strange	70-71-70-71	282	￥2,313,750
	Yusaku Miyazato	71-73-66-72	282	￥2,313,750
	Kazuhiro Yamashita	72-69-68-73	282	￥2,313,750
	Wen-Chong Liang	70-69-69-74	282	￥2,313,750
17=	Hideto Tanihara	73-70-71-69	283	￥1,431,000
	Javi Colomo	70-70-73-70	283	￥1,431,000
	Prayad Marksaeng	69-69-75-70	283	￥1,431,000
	Arjun Atwal	69-72-72-70	283	￥1,431,000
	Panuphol Pittayarat	70-72-70-71	283	￥1,431,000
22=	Michio Matsumura	74-68-71-71	284	￥1,185,000
	I.J. Jang	70-69-73-72	284	￥1,185,000
	Adilson da Silva	73-67-72-72	284	￥1,185,000
	Masanori Kobayashi	71-69-78-66	284	￥1,185,000
	Hyung-Sung Kim	71-70-70-73	284	￥1,185,000
	N. Tantipokakul	68-74-69-73	284	￥1,185,000

In The Money: **285**: Kazuhiro Kida, Dimitrios Papadatos, Kyung-Tae Kim, Jyoti Randhawa, Akio Sadakata **286**: Anirban Lahiri, Koumei Oda, Wei-Chih Lu **287**: Kieran Pratt, Ryo Ishikawa, Prom Meesawat, Thaworn Wiratchant, Tadahiro Takayama **288**: Kunihiro Kamii, Masahiro Kawamura, Naoyuki Kataoka (a), Dong-Kyu Jang, Kiyoshi Murota, Angelo Que, Hiroshi Iwata **289**: Shinji Tomimura, Marcus Both, Berry Henson **290**: Seung-Hyuk Kim, Pariya Junhasavasdikul **291**: Scott Hend, Yuta Ikeda, Michael Hendry **292**: Joong-Kyung Mo, David Lipsky, S.S.P. Chorasia **293**: Atomu Shigenaga, Keiichiro Fukabori **300**: Chawalit Plaphol

OWR: 0 of top 50 entered   -   Rating: 37   -   Points to 21st   -   Fujita: 15 points, to 127th in OWR

Top Cup Tokai Classic

Miyoshi Country Club (West) - Aichi, Japan
Champion: Seung-Hyuk Kim

Oct 2 - Oct 5
7,315 yards   Par 72
Purse: ¥110,000,000

Twenty-seven-year-old Korean Tour veteran Seung-Hyuk Kim claimed his first title on the Japan Golf Tour, scrambling home to a one-stroke triumph at the Top Cup Tokai Classic. With only one career top-10 finish under his belt (a T7 at this year's Token Homemate Cup) in 26 previous J Tour starts, Kim hardly began the week rated among the favorites. But he served notice that his fortunes might be changing by carding nine birdies en route to an opening 66 that tied him for the Thursday lead, then remaining near the top of the board following less special middle rounds of 73-72. Thus beginning the final round three behind countryman Hyung-Sung Kim, Seung-Hyuk crept slightly forward via a chip-in birdie at the par-4 6th, then moved well past Hyung-Sung (who stumbled home with a 74) with birdies at the 14th and 16th. Now holding a two-stroke lead, he promptly bogeyed the 470-yard 18th, but hung on to win when runners-up Hyung-Sung and a third Korean, Jung-Gon Hwang both failed to birdie either the 17th or the 18th to catch him.

1	Seung-Hyuk Kim	66-73-72-70	281	¥22,000,000
2=	Jung-Gon Hwang	73-70-69-70	282	¥9,240,000
	Hyung-Sung Kim	69-70-69-74	282	¥9,240,000
4	In-Hoi Hur	72-71-67-73	283	¥5,280,000
5=	Yuta Ikeda	72-71-74-67	284	¥3,996,666
	Yoshinori Fujimoto	69-68-77-70	284	¥3,996,666
	Kazuhiko Hosokawa	71-70-72-71	284	¥3,996,666
8=	Yoshitaka Takeya	77-69-70-69	285	¥3,000,250
	Sang-Hyun Park	74-67-73-71	285	¥3,000,250
	Taichi Teshima	70-74-70-71	285	¥3,000,250
	Hideto Tanihara	70-70-72-73	285	¥3,000,250
12=	Do-Hoon Kim	73-73-72-68	286	¥2,002,000
	Prayad Marksaeng	72-75-68-71	286	¥2,002,000
	Koumei Oda	71-67-75-73	286	¥2,002,000
	I.J. Jang	71-75-67-73	286	¥2,002,000
	Nobuhiro Masuda	71-68-73-74	286	¥2,002,000
	Tomohiro Kondo	71-68-72-75	286	¥2,002,000
18=	Hiroo Kawai	74-68-73-72	287	¥1,474,000
	Ryuichi Oda	70-70-74-73	287	¥1,474,000
	Hidemasa Hoshino	72-72-70-73	287	¥1,474,000
21=	Tadahiro Takayama	75-71-71-71	288	¥1,254,000
	Yuki Inamori	71-74-72-71	288	¥1,254,000
23	Min-Gyu Cho	69-70-73-77	289	¥1,122,000
24=	Satoshi Kodaira	72-71-75-72	290	¥924,000
	Sang-Hee Lee	73-74-71-72	290	¥924,000
	Brad Kennedy	71-76-71-72	290	¥924,000
	Han Lee	67-74-76-73	290	¥924,000
	Hiroyuki Fujita	71-72-74-73	290	¥924,000
	Akio Sadakata	72-74-70-74	290	¥924,000

In The Money: **291**: Atomu Sigenaga **292**: Kenta Konishi (a), Ryuji Masaoka, Shingo Katayama, Yusaku Miyazato, Ryosuke Kinoshita, Dong-Kyu Jang, Kunihiro Kamii **293**: S.K. Ho, David Oh, Shunsuke Sonoda, Jay Choi, Yasuki Hiramoto, Scott Strange, J.B. Park, Hyun-Woo Ryu **294**: Brendan Jones, David Smail, Yosuke Tsukada, Shinji Tomimura, Yoshikazu Haku **295**: Satoshi Tomiyama **296**: Jinichiro Kozuma, Ryoma Iwai **297**: Yasuharu Imano **298**: Yoshinobu Tsukada, Daisuke Kataoka, Steven Conran **299**: Keisuke Sato, Kurt Barnes, Daisuke Maruyama **300**: Sung-Yoon Kim, Yuki Kitagawa, Masahiro Kawamura, Yamato Shiraishi (a) **301**: Ryutaro Nagano, Masanori Kobayashi, Makoto Inoue, Toshinori Muto **302**: Ren Okazaki (a), Katsumasa Miyamoto **303**: Yuji Igarishi, Ippei Koike

OWR: 0 of top 50 entered - Rating: 23 - Points to 20th - Kim: 16 points, to 211th in OWR

Toshin Golf Tournament

Toshin Golf Club (Central) - Gifu, Japan
Champion: In-Hoi Hur

Oct 9 - Oct 12
7,004 yards   Par 72
Purse: ¥100,000,000

South Korea's 27-year-old In-Hoi Hur claimed his first career victory on the Japan Tour in grand style, completing a record-setting wire-to-wire triumph at the Toshin Golf Tournament in Gifu. Hur put his stamp on the event early, recording but a single bogey during opening rounds of 64-63, which staked him to a three-shot halfway lead. He then added a bogey-free 66 on Saturday to extend his lead to four - and it was only that close because Seung-Hyuk Kim, a winner of the previous week's Tokai Classic, carded a dazzling 61 to move within shouting distance. Kim put on a bit of Sunday pressure by closing with a 67 but Hur was not to be headed, opening with three birdies over his first six holes en route to turning in 33, then methodically coming home in 34 (punctuated by a birdie at the par-5 closer) to win by four.

1	In-Hoi Hur	64-63-66-67	260	¥20,000,000
2	Seung-Hyuk Kim	68-68-61-67	264	¥10,000,000
3	Tomohiro Kondo	68-65-68-65	266	¥6,800,000
4=	Hiroshi Iwata	70-69-64-64	267	¥3,925,000
	Yoshitaka Takeya	69-65-68-65	267	¥3,925,000
	Min-Gyu Cho	68-67-65-67	267	¥3,925,000
	Dong-Kyu Jang	68-66-65-68	267	¥3,925,000
8=	Sang-Hee Lee	69-65-68-66	268	¥2,830,000
	Kazuhiro Yamashita	71-64-66-67	268	¥2,830,000
	Young-Han Song	69-67-65-67	268	¥2,830,000
11	Ashun Wu	66-69-69-65	269	¥2,420,000
12=	Toru Suzuki	67-70-70-63	270	¥2,020,000
	Hidemasa Hoshino	70-64-70-66	270	¥2,020,000
	Do-Hoon Kim	69-67-67-67	270	¥2,020,000
15=	Ryuji Imada	68-67-68-68	271	¥1,620,000
	Kunihiro Kamii	67-63-71-70	271	¥1,620,000
	Yoshinori Fujimoto	64-67-69-71	271	¥1,620,000
18=	S.K. Ho	68-71-67-66	272	¥1,340,000
	Koumei Oda	69-68-68-67	272	¥1,340,000
	Ryuichi Oda	65-66-70-71	272	¥1,340,000
21=	Hiroo Kawai	68-71-67-67	273	¥1,060,000
	Juvic Pagunsan	65-71-69-68	273	¥1,060,000
	Hyung-Sung Kim	68-68-68-69	273	¥1,060,000
	Ryuji Masaoka	67-73-64-69	273	¥1,060,000
25=	Ho-Sung Choi	68-68-72-66	274	¥800,000
	Wen-Chong Liang	69-69-70-66	274	¥800,000
	Akio Sadakata	71-67-68-68	274	¥800,000
	T. Yoshinaga	70-69-67-68	274	¥800,000
	Satoshi Tomiyama	66-69-69-70	274	¥800,000
	Daisuke Kataoka	68-69-66-71	274	¥800,000

In The Money: **276**: Thanyakon Khrongpha, Shinji Tomimura, Yosuke Tsukada, Brendan Jones, Jay Choi, Ryosuke Kinoshita, Shohei Hasegawa (a) **277**: Keisuke Sato, Yuta Ikeda, Kurt Barnes, Katsumasa Miyamoto, Jung-Gon Hwang **278**: Yasuki Hiramoto, Yoshikazu Haku, Jinichiro Kozuma **279**: Makoto Inoue, Kodai Ichihara, David Smail **280**: Azuma Yano **281**: Yuki Kono, Daisuke Maruyama, Yoshinobu Tsukada, Han Lee, Toshinori Muto **282**: J.B. Park, Hiroki Abe **283**: Yasuharu Imano **284**: Ryuichi Kondo **285**: Hyung-Tae Kim **288**: Seung-Su Han

OWR: 0 of top 50 entered - Rating: 23 - Points to 20th - Hur: 16 points, to 174th in OWR

Japan Open

Oct 16 - Oct 19

Chiba Country Club (Umesato Course) - Chiba, Japan
Champion: Yuta Ikeda

7,081 yards Par 70
Purse: ¥200,000,000

Back in 2009 and '10, Yuta Ikeda was emerging as an elite player on the Japan Tour, winning four times in each season and looking very much like an up-and-coming player of international importance. But Ikeda's stock slipped a bit over three subsequent one-win seasons and if his victory in 2014 Japan Open was, once again, his lone triumph of the year, it must also rate as the most prestigious of his career to date. Ikeda began the week in fine form, posting an opening six-under-par 64 to trail Prayad Marksaeng by one, and remained one back at the halfway point after both men added 68s on Friday. But while Marksaeng carded two late bogeys to slip to a 70 on Saturday, Ikeda shot a 66 to jump out to a three-shot lead over both Marksaeng and 27-time Japan Tour winner Shingo Katayama – a cushion he would ultimately need all of on Sunday when, seemingly in good shape, he bogeyed the 14th and double-bogeyed the par-3 16th to make things close. But with neither Katayama nor Marksaeng mounting a meaningful charge, Ikeda managed to add two closing pars to win by one.

1	Yuta Ikeda	64-68-66-72	270	¥40,000,000		Ryuko Tokimatsu	65-71-68-73 277	¥2,856,000
2=	Satoshi Kodaira	68-68-69-66	271	¥18,700,000	16=	Koumei Oda	68-72-70-68 278	¥2,000,000
	Shingo Katayama	68-66-67-70	271	¥18,700,000		Sang-Hyun Park	68-71-69-70 278	¥2,000,000
4	Prayad Marksaeng	63-68-70-72	273	¥10,000,000		Koichi Kitamura	70-69-68-71 278	¥2,000,000
5	Tomohiro Kondo	68-69-69-68	274	¥8,400,000		Masanori Kobayashi	68-70-69-71 278	¥2,000,000
6=	Kiyoshi Murota	70-72-66-67	275	¥6,500,000		Sung-Joon Park	68-69-67-74 278	¥2,000,000
	Brad Kennedy	68-70-69-68	275	¥6,500,000	21	Hidemasa Hoshino	69-71-70-69 279	¥1,740,000
8=	Shintaro Kai	70-74-67-65	276	¥4,466,666	22=	Makoto Inoue	72-72-70-66 280	¥1,640,000
	Hiroo Kawai	69-71-69-67	276	¥4,466,666		Yasuharu Imano	66-74-71-69 280	¥1,640,000
	Yoshinori Fujimoto	71-70-67-68	276	¥4,466,666		Ryuichi Kondo	70-72-68-70 280	¥1,640,000
11=	Yoshitaka Takeya	68-71-70-68	277	¥2,856,000	25=	Stephen Leaney	71-72-69-69 281	¥1,520,000
	Min-Gyu Cho	68-71-69-69	277	¥2,856,000		Sang-Hee Lee	67-73-70-71 281	¥1,520,000
	Hideto Tanihara	69-68-70-70	277	¥2,856,000		Seung-Hyuk Kim	70-72-68-71 281	¥1,520,000
	Dong-Kyu Jang	68-69-68-72	277	¥2,856,000				

In The Money: **282**: Azuma Yano, Masahiro Kawamura, Michio Matsumura, Yusaku Miyazato, Hiroshi Iwata, Ashun Wu **283**: Hiroyuki Fujita, David Oh, Akio Sadakata, Nobuhiro Masuda **284**: Adam Scott, Ryuichi Oda, Daisuke Kataoka, I.J. Jang **285**: Adam Bland, Ryutaro Nagano, Kazuya Koura (a) **286**: Shinji Tomimura, Tadahiro Takayama, Ren Okazaki (a) **287**: Daisuke Matsubara (a), K.T. Kwon, Kyoung-Hoon Lee, Koki Shiomi **288**: Kazuhiro Yamashita, Michael Hendry, Juvic Pagunsan, Daisuke Maruyama **289**: Takahiro Hataji (a), Naoyuki Tamura, Kyung-Tae Kim **290**: Toshiki Ishitoku (a) **291**: Jung-Gon Hwang **292**: J.B. Park, Taichi Teshima, Tae-Hee Lee **294**: Kenichi Kuboya **295**: Taichi Nabetani **297**: Shota Kishimoto, S.K. Ho

OWR: 1 of top 50 entered   -   Rating: 95   -   Points to 37th   -   Ikeda: 32 points, to 104th in OWR

Bridgestone Open

Oct 23 - Oct 26

Sodegaura Country Club (Sodegaura Course) - Chiba, Japan
Champion: Koumei Oda

7,119 yards Par 71
Purse: ¥150,000,000

In a pitched battle which ultimately came down to the final hole, 36-year-old Koumei Oda claimed his eighth career Japan Tour title with a one-shot victory at the Bridgestone Open. Oda was in the heart of the hunt all week, taking a one-stroke halfway lead with rounds of 67-65, then posting a Saturday 69 to extend the 54-hole margin to three over Azuma Yano. But things would become interesting on Sunday as Oda turned in 35, while 18-time J Tour winner Hiroyuki Fujita was roaring home with a 64 to post a 270 total. Thus trailing by one entering the homestretch, Oda pulled ahead with clutch birdies at the 15th and the par-5 16th, then fell back even with an untimely bogey at the 231-yard 17th. But with everything at stake, he then recorded the decisive birdie at the 569-yard 18th to edge Fujita by one.

1	Koumei Oda	67-65-69-68	269	¥30,000,000		Hideto Tanihara	71-66-69-69 275	¥2,355,000
2	Hiroyuki Fujita	73-68-65-64	270	¥15,000,000		Ryuichi Oda	71-67-67-70 275	¥2,355,000
3=	Yoshitaka Takeya	66-71-69-66	272	¥7,800,000		Azuma Yano	65-68-71-71 275	¥2,355,000
	K. Miyamoto	69-68-69-66	272	¥7,800,000	19=	Han Lee	72-69-68-67 276	¥1,830,000
	Shunsuke Sonoda	69-70-66-67	272	¥7,800,000		Tadahiro Takayama	68-70-70-68 276	¥1,830,000
6=	Shingo Katayama	73-70-65-65	273	¥4,788,750		Kurt Barnes	66-73-69-68 276	¥1,830,000
	Adam Bland	70-69-68-66	273	¥4,788,750		Hyun-Woo Ryu	71-68-68-69 276	¥1,830,000
	Kyung-Tae Kim	69-69-67-68	273	¥4,788,750	23=	Yoshinobu Tsukada	69-72-68-68 277	¥1,267,500
	Hiroshi Iwata	69-69-68-67	273	¥4,788,750		Yosuke Tsukada	71-70-68-68 277	¥1,267,500
10=	Yasuharu Imano	68-69-71-66	274	¥3,330,000		Hidemasa Hoshino	69-69-71-68 277	¥1,267,500
	Koki Shiomi	74-69-66-65	274	¥3,330,000		David Oh	68-72-71-66 277	¥1,267,500
	Kodai Ichihara	66-73-68-67	274	¥3,330,000		Akio Sadakata	69-72-67-69 277	¥1,267,500
	Brad Kennedy	69-68-68-69	274	¥3,330,000		Hyung-Sung Kim	71-69-66-71 277	¥1,267,500
	Prayad Marksaeng	70-65-71-68	274	¥3,330,000		Daisuke Kataoka	70-69-66-72 277	¥1,267,500
15=	Sang-Hee Lee	66-69-72-68	275	¥2,355,000		Min-Gyu Cho	72-66-67-72 277	¥1,267,500

In The Money: Taichi Teshima, Ryoma Iwai, Yui Ueda, Kyoung-Hoon Lee **279**: Jung-Gon Hwang, Thanyakon Khrongpha, Ryuji Masaoka, J.B. Park, Yasuki Hiramoto **280**: Steven Conran, Yusaku Miyazato, David Smail **281**: Takashi Ogiso (a), I.J. Jang, Ryosuke Kinoshita, Keiichiro Fukabori **282**: Shinji Tomimura, Hiroo Kawai **283**: Toshinori Muto, Atomu Shigenaga, Ippei Koike, Dong-Kyu Jang, Juvic Pagunsan **284**: Achi Sato **285**: Shigeru Nonaka, K.T. Kwon, Kenichi Kuboya, Jinichiro Kozuma, Tomokazu Yoshinaga **286**: Naomichi Ozaki, Masamichi Uehira **288**: Michio Matsumura **290**: Motoki Ito, Ryoken Kawagishi **293**: Yuta Ikeda

OWR: 1 of top 50 entered   -   Rating: 39   -   Points to 22nd   -   Oda: 16 points, to 55th in OWR

Mynavi ABC Championship

Oct 30 - Nov 2

ABC Golf Club - Hyogo, Japan
Champion: Ryuichi Oda

7,130 yards Par 71
Purse: ¥150,000,000

Thirty-seven-year-old Ryuichi Oda ended a five-year drought to claim his second career Japan Tour victory, a five-shot triumph at the Mynavi ABC Championship in Hyogo. Oda stood two shoots off the pace on both Thursday and Friday after opening with rounds of 68-67, then charged into a share of the lead (with veteran South Korean star S.K. Ho) behind a Saturday 66 that included birdies on five of his first 10 holes. On a Sunday which saw very low scoring, Ho made two early bogeys and never quite righted the ship, coming home in a 71 which dropped him into a tie for sixth. Better challenges were fielded by the season's leading money winner Koumei Oda (who birdied three of his last four holes on his way to a closing 64), veteran Hideto Tanihara (65) and recent Japan Open champion Yuta Ikeda (65). But in the end these were all rendered moot by Oda, who made three outgoing birdies to turn in 32, then heated up on the final nine with four birdies and an eagle (at the par-5 15th), all of which added up to a dazzling 62 and the runaway victory.

1	Ryuichi Oda	68-67-66-62	263	¥30,000,000		Hyun-Woo Ryu	68-70-67-69 274	¥3,180,000
2=	Koumei Oda	69-65-70-64	268	¥12,600,000	15=	Hiroshi Iwata	70-66-71-68 275	¥2,430,000
	Hideto Tanihara	69-66-68-65	268	¥12,600,000		Tadahiro Takayama	71-70-67-67 275	¥2,430,000
4=	Yuta Ikeda	66-70-70-65	271	¥6,600,000		Young-Han Song	71-65-70-69 275	¥2,430,000
	Tomohiro Kondo	67-71-66-67	271	¥6,600,000	18=	Prayad Marksaeng	71-71-69-65 276	¥1,950,000
6=	Brendan Jones	70-66-68-68	272	¥5,175,000		Yosuke Tsukada	75-67-67-67 276	¥1,950,000
	S.K. Ho	66-69-66-71	272	¥5,175,000		Hiroyuki Fujita	68-70-71-67 276	¥1,950,000
8=	Kyoung-Hoon Lee	66-67-76-64	273	¥4,245,000		David Oh	69-70-67-70 276	¥1,950,000
	Akio Sadakata	66-69-69-69	273	¥4,245,000	22=	Ho-Sung Choi	70-69-71-67 277	¥1,530,000
	Jung-Gon Hwang	69-67-68-69	273	¥4,245,000		Min-Gyu Cho	72-71-67-67 277	¥1,530,000
11=	Yoshinori Fujimoto	68-70-70-66	274	¥3,180,000		Yusaku Miyazato	69-69-73-66 277	¥1,530,000
	K. Aphibarnrat	69-72-67-66	274	¥3,180,000	25=	Hyung-Sung Kim	71-71-67-69 278	¥1,320,000
	Taichi Teshima	69-68-69-68	274	¥3,180,000		Yuki Inamori	70-71-68-69 278	¥1,320,000

In The Money: **279**: Do-Hoon Kim, Juvic Pagunsan, Koki Shiomi, Kiyoshi Miyazato, Sang-Hee Lee, Satoshi Kodaira **280**: Toshinori Muto, Toru Taniguchi **281**: Toru Suzuki, J.B. Park, Daisuke Maruyama **282**: I.J. Jang, Michael Hendry, K.T. Kwon **283**: Steven Conran, Makoto Inoue, Jinichiro Kozuma, Keiichiro Fukabori, Adam Bland **284**: Kaname Yokoo, Hyung-Tae Kim, Hidemasa Hoshino, Kyung-Tae Kim, Kazuhiko Hosokawa, Han Lee **285**: Daisuke Kataoka, Yoshitaka Takeya **286**: Dong-Kyu Jang, Ryutaro Nagano, Yoshinobu Tsukada, Shingo Katayama **287**: Yuki Kono **288**: Naoyuki Kataoka (a), Kenichi Kuboya, Azuma Yano, Shunsuke Sonoda **289**: Shigeru Nonaka, Masamichi Uehira **291**: Nobuhiro Masuda

OWR: 0 of top 50 entered - Rating: 35 - Points to 21st - Oda: 16 points, to 342nd in OWR

Heiwa PGM Championship in Kasumigaura

Nov 6 - Nov 9

Miho Golf Club - Ibaraki, Japan
Champion: Tomohiro Kondo

7,506 yards Par 72
Purse: ¥200,000,000

Breaking a three-year victory drought, 37-year-old Tomohiro Kondo claimed his sixth career Japan Tour title by cruising to a four-shot victory at the Heiwa PGM Championship in Kasumigaura. Kondo opened his week relatively quietly with a three-under par 68 on Thursday, good enough only to stand tied for 14th, four behind a trio of leaders. Among this trio, only Hideto Tanihara would remain atop the board on Friday, his 68 tying him with Korean Hyun-Woo Ryu on 10 under par, while Kondo added a 66 to edge within two. However, Kondo would make his real move on Saturday, carding six back nine birdies en route to a 64 which pushed him two strokes ahead of Tanihara, Brad Kennedy and Yoshinori Fujimoto, who also shot 64. Two early birdies padded Kondo's Sunday lead, and after giving them back with bogeys at the 5th and 7th, he pushed his engine into another gear, logging five subsequent birdies to come home in 66 and win going away.

1	Tomohiro Kondo	68-66-64-66	264	¥40,000,000	17=	I.J. Jang	67-72-72-65 276	¥2,445,000
2=	Hideto Tanihara	64-68-68-68	268	¥14,400,000		Jung-Gon Hwang	68-66-74-68 276	¥2,445,000
	Hyun-Woo Ryu	67-65-69-67	268	¥14,400,000		Han Lee	71-71-69-65 276	¥2,445,000
	Yoshinori Fujimoto	68-68-64-68	268	¥14,400,000		Steven Conran	70-70-68-68 276	¥2,445,000
5	Brad Kennedy	64-72-64-70	270	¥8,000,000		Prayad Marksaeng	69-72-67-68 276	¥2,445,000
6	Taichi Teshima	68-67-70-66	271	¥7,200,000		Yasuharu Imano	66-72-68-70 276	¥2,445,000
7=	Min-Gyu Cho	68-69-69-66	272	¥5,895,000		Shugo Imahira	71-68-67-70 276	¥2,445,000
	Adam Bland	70-65-70-67	272	¥5,895,000		Satoshi Tomiyama	67-66-72-71 276	¥2,445,000
	K. Miyamoto	69-65-71-67	272	¥5,895,000	25=	Shingo Katayama	73-70-68-66 277	¥1,560,000
	Shunsuke Sonoda	64-69-68-71	272	¥5,895,000		Tadahiro Takayama	67-71-70-69 277	¥1,560,000
11=	J.B. Park	68-69-71-65	273	¥4,640,000		Toshinori Muto	69-73-66-69 277	¥1,560,000
	Koumei Oda	66-69-69-69	273	¥4,640,000		Kodai Ichihara	71-65-70-71 277	¥1,560,000
13=	Hiroyuki Fujita	69-67-70-68	274	¥4,040,000		Nobuhiro Masuda	73-69-71-64 277	¥1,560,000
14=	Atomu Shigenaga	68-70-72-65	275	¥3,440,000		Keiichiro Fukabori	68-70-68-71 277	¥1,560,000
	Daisuke Kataoka	68-69-72-66	275	¥3,440,000		Toru Taniguchi	70-68-67-72 277	¥1,560,000
	Yosuke Tsukada	71-68-68-68	275	¥3,440,000				

In The Money: **278**: Jay Choi, Yusaku Miyazato, Koki Shiomi, Azuma Yano, Dong-Kyu Jang **279**: Kiradech Aphibarnrat, David Smail, Shigeru Nonaka, Yoshinobu Tsukada **280**: Kenichi Kuboya, Jinichiro Kozuma, Hiroo Kawai, Kaname Yokoo, Makoto Inoue, Hyung-Tae Kim **281**: Kurt Barnes, Masahiro Kawamura, Yuki Kono, Kazuhiko Hosokawa, Katsunori Kuwabara **282**: Ryo Ishikawa, S.K. Ho, Kyoung-Hoon Lee, Juvic Pagunsan, Hidemas Hoshino **283**: Shinichi Yokota, Yoshikazu Haku, Scott Strange, Shinji Tomimura, David Oh **284**: Ryuji Masaoka **285**: Brendan Jones, Takashi Ogiso (a), Sang-Hee Lee **286**: Masamichi Uehira **287**: Daisuke Kamon **289**: Ryuichi Oda **290**: Rikuya Hoshino (a)

OWR: 0 of top 50 entered - Rating: 35 - Points to 24th - Kondo: 16 points, to 117th in OWR

Mitsui Sumitomo VISA Taiheiyo Masters

Nov 13 - Nov 16

Taiheiyo Club (Gotemba Course) - Shizuoka, Japan
Champion: David Oh

7,246 yards Par 72
Purse: ¥150,000,000

Thirty-three-year-old American David Oh was a quiet presence on the Japan Golf Tour in 2012 and '13, going winless and finishing 94th and 31st in earnings. But his relative anonymity disappeared at the 2014 Taiheiyo Masters, where Oh overcame an ill-timed bogey at the 71st hole to rally for his first victory in the Land Of The Rising Sun. The former USC Trojan opened with rounds of 70-68 to trail Hiroyuki Fujita by two on Friday night before charging home in 32 on Saturday to post a third round 68, good enough to take a one-shot 54-hole lead over fellow American Han Lee and China's Wen-Chong Liang. But Lee could do no better than 71 on Sunday while Liang drifted to a 72, leaving a seemingly open path for Oh who, with back-to-back birdies at the 13th and 14th, held a one-shot lead over Toshinori Muto. Oh briefly stumbled by bogeying the 228-yard 17th, but then bounced back to birdie the 517-yard 18th to clinch his first major tour victory.

1	David Oh	70-68-68-70	276	¥30,000,000		Ryuichi Oda	74-68-71-69	282	¥2,355,000
2	Toshinori Muto	71-68-69-69	277	¥15,000,000		Min-Gyu Cho	73-71-68-70	282	¥2,355,000
3=	Tomohiro Kondo	71-71-69-67	278	¥8,700,000		Yuta Ikeda	71-70-68-73	282	¥2,355,000
	Han Lee	74-66-67-71	278	¥8,700,000	19=	S.K. Ho	71-70-74-68	283	¥1,830,000
5	Wen-Chong Liang	72-67-68-72	279	¥6,000,000		Hiroshi Iwata	72-71-71-69	283	¥1,830,000
6=	Tadahiro Takayama	72-71-69-68	280	¥4,788,750		J.B. Park	70-72-71-70	283	¥1,830,000
	Michio Matsumura	77-67-66-70	280	¥4,788,750		Toru Taniguchi	72-70-71-70	283	¥1,830,000
	Kazuhiro Yamashita	68-71-70-71	280	¥4,788,750	23=	Kyoung-Hoon Lee	73-72-70-69	284	¥1,530,000
	Ashun Wu	71-68-69-72	280	¥4,788,750	24=	Satoshi Tomiyama	75-72-67-71	285	¥1,260,000
10=	Yosuke Tsukada	67-73-76-65	281	¥3,330,000		Bubba Watson	67-70-77-71	285	¥1,260,000
	Hidemasa Hoshino	73-70-70-68	281	¥3,330,000		Kazuhiko Hosokawa	72-71-73-69	285	¥1,260,000
	Sang-Hee Lee	70-73-69-69	281	¥3,330,000		Yuki Kono	71-72-71-71	285	¥1,260,000
	Yusaku Miyazato	70-73-67-71	281	¥3,330,000		Hideto Tanihara	71-74-69-71	285	¥1,260,000
	Hyun-Woo Ryu	71-70-68-72	281	¥3,330,000		Jung-Gon Hwang	72-70-70-73	285	¥1,260,000
15=	Daisuke Maruyama	71-71-74-66	282	¥2,355,000					

In The Money: 286: Akio Sadakata, Brad Kennedy, Do-Hoon Kim, Yoshinori, Fujimoto, Hiroyuki Fujita **287**: Shingo Katayama, Taichi Teshima **288**: Katsumasa Miyamoto, Brendan Jones **289**: Kiyoshi Murota, I.J. Jang, Kyung-Tae Kim, Keiichiro Fukabori **290**: Prayad Marksaeng, Masahiro Kawamura, David Smail, Ho-Sung Choi, Yoshikazu Haku, Ryutaro Nagano, Kunihiro Kamii **291**: Seung-Hyuk Kim, Kiyoshi Miyazato, Hiroo Kawai **292**: Makoto Inoue, Kenichi Kuboya, Steven Conran, In-Hoi Hur, Tommy Nakajima, Masamichi Uehira, Young-Han Song **293**: Shunsuke Sonoda, Ryo Ishikawa **294**: Shigeru Nonaka **296**: Scott Strange, Kurt Barnes **298**: Yuji Igarashi **300**: Dong-Kyu Jang

OWR: 1 of top 50 entered - Rating: 102 - Points to 29th - Oh: 24 points, to 214th in OWR

Dunlop Phoenix

Nov 20 - Nov 23

Phoenix Country Club - Miyazaki, Japan
Champion: Hideki Matsuyama

7,027 yards Par 71
Purse: ¥200,000,000

In an event which clearly saw youth come to the fore, 22-year-old PGA Tour star Hideki Matsuyama made his first domestic start since July and won the prestigious Dunlop Phoenix, edging countryman Hiroshi Iwata in a playoff. A winner at Jack Nicklaus's Memorial Tournament earlier in the year, Matsuyama started here with a relatively quiet 68 before jumping into the halfway lead behind a Friday 64 which included six birdies, plus an eagle at the par-5 18th. Thus standing one ahead of four pursuers (one of whom was 21-year-old American star Jordan Spieth), Matsuyama then posted a bogey-free 67 on Saturday to extend the lead to two over Spieth and three over Australian Brendan Jones. But neither Spieth (69) nor Jones (68) could mount a major charge on Sunday, while the red-hot Iwata certainly did, coming home with five late birdies for a 63, and a 269 total. As Matsuyama stumbled with bogeys at both the 15th and 16th, Iwata looked a likely winner - until Matsuyama recorded clutch birdies at the 185-yard 17th and the 560-yard 18th to tie, then closed Iwata out on the first extra hole.

1	Hideki Matsuyama	68-64-67-70	269	¥40,000,000		Masahiro Kawamura	67-74-69-68	278	¥3,240,000
2	Hiroshi Iwata	68-69-69-63	269	¥20,000,000		Seung-Hyuk Kim	70-71-69-68	278	¥3,240,000
3=	Brendan Jones	65-69-68-68	270	¥11,600,000		Hiroyuki Fujita	70-71-68-69	278	¥3,240,000
	Jordan Spieth	69-64-68-69	270	¥11,600,000		Min-Gyu Cho	69-68-69-72	278	¥3,240,000
5	In-Hoi Hur	67-66-70-69	272	¥8,000,000	19=	Hyung-Sung Kim	68-71-71-69	279	¥2,680,000
6=	Yusaku Miyazato	68-72-69-64	273	¥6,900,000	20=	Gon. Fdez-Castaño	74-69-68-69	280	¥2,440,000
	Toshinori Muto	68-69-68-68	273	¥6,900,000		Yuta Ikeda	69-65-73-73	280	¥2,440,000
8	Chris Stroud	67-70-71-66	274	¥6,100,000	22=	Steven Conran	67-71-72-71	281	¥1,880,000
9=	Tadahiro Takayama	74-66-70-66	276	¥5,440,000		Prayad Marksaeng	70-71-71-69	281	¥1,880,000
	Shingo Katayama	70-66-73-67	276	¥5,440,000		Jung-Gon Hwang	70-70-70-71	281	¥1,880,000
11=	Brad Kennedy	70-68-69-70	277	¥4,440,000		Ryuichi Oda	71-70-68-72	281	¥1,880,000
	Yuki Inamori	64-74-68-71	277	¥4,440,000		David Smail	69-67-70-75	281	¥1,880,000
	Koumei Oda	66-71-68-72	277	¥4,440,000		J.B. Park	69-70-68-74	281	¥1,880,000
14=	Yosuke Tsukada	70-69-71-68	278	¥3,240,000					

In The Money: 282: Michio Matsumura, Kazuhiro Yamashita, Nobuhiro Masuda **283**: Masamichi Uehira, Yoshitaka Takeya, Daisuke Maruyama, Hideto Tanihara, Hidemasa Hoshino, Satoshi Tomiyama, Tommy Nakajima, Ryo Ishikawa, Hiroo Kawai, Ho-Sung Choi, Sung-Yoon Kim **284**: Tomohiro Kondo, Kyoung-Hoon Lee **285**: Masanori Kobayashi, Young-Han Song, Sung-Joon Park, Ryuji Masaoka **286**: David Oh, Taichi Teshima **287**: Satoshi Kodaira, Ashun Wu, Han Lee **288**: Thanyakon Khrongpha **289**: Keiichiro Fukabori **290**: I.J. Jang, Webb Simpson, Yoshikazu Haku **291**: Azuma Yano, Yoshinobu Tsukada **292**: Makoto Inoue, Toru Taniguchi **293**: Hyun-Woo Ryu

OWR: 3 of top 50 entered - Rating: 109 - Points to 30th - Matsuyama: 26 points, to 16th in OWR

Casio World Open

Kochi Kuroshio Country Club - Kochi, Japan
Champion: Shingo Katayama

Nov 27 - Nov 30
7,275 yards   Par 72
Purse: ¥200,000,000

In an up-and-down week that twice saw him fail to break 70 while also posting the event's two lowest rounds, Shingo Katayama claimed his 28th career Japan Tour title at the Casio World Open, in Kochi. The 41-year-old Katayama, who last won at the 2013 Tokai Classic, stood tied for 28th after opening with a 70, then pushed into the halfway lead on Friday behind a bogey-free eight-under-par 64. But such strong form deserted him on Saturday and he needed two late birdies to shoot 72, leaving him tied for second, one shot behind Satoshi Kodaira, Shugo Imahira and Yasuki Hiramoto. Not one of these tri-leaders would break 70 on Sunday, however – though in the end the point might have moot as Katayama came loaded for bear. Indeed, after turning in two-under-par 34, he ran off four straight birdies at holes 12-15 to pull clear, then added a final birdie at the 530-yard finisher to post a 271 aggregate and a three-stroke margin of victory. Second place went to Satoshi Tomiyama, who labored quietly within a pack of players six shots in arrears before running off three closing birdies to elevate himself. The remainder of that pack - fully six players deep - collectively tied for third.

1	Shingo Katayama	70-64-72-65	271	¥40,000,000	Kyung-Tae Kim	72-71-68-68 279	¥2,970,000
2	Satoshi Tomiyama	67-70-70-67	274	¥20,000,000	Ashun Wu	70-70-71-68 279	¥2,970,000
3=	Tomohiro Kondo	70-69-71-67	277	¥8,516,666	Ryuji Masaoka	73-68-70-68 279	¥2,970,000
	Young-Han Song	71-69-69-68	277	¥8,516,666	Koumei Oda	69-67-74-69 279	¥2,970,000
	Hyung-Sung Kim	69-70-69-69	277	¥8,516,666	Sang-Hyun Park	66-72-72-69 279	¥2,970,000
	T. Khrongpha	69-69-69-70	277	¥8,516,666	Yoshitaka Takeya	71-70-69-69 279	¥2,970,000
	Satoshi Kodaira	68-70-67-72	277	¥8,516,666	Tadahiro Takayama	67-70-72-70 279	¥2,970,000
	Yasuki Hiramoto	68-69-68-72	277	¥8,516,666	22= Yusaku Miyazato	72-70-70-68 280	¥1,880,000
9=	Hiroyuki Fujita	71-72-69-66	278	¥4,840,000	Yuta Ikeda	70-72-69-69 280	¥1,880,000
	I.J. Jang	71-70-70-67	278	¥4,840,000	Brendan Jones	72-71-69-68 280	¥1,880,000
	Shinichi Yokota	66-70-72-70	278	¥4,840,000	Kyoung-Hoon Lee	70-65-73-72 280	¥1,880,000
	Toshinori Muto	71-70-67-70	278	¥4,840,000	Brad Kennedy	73-68-67-72 280	¥1,880,000
	Kenichi Kuboya	67-70-69-72	278	¥4,840,000	Shugo Imahira	66-71-68-75 280	¥1,880,000
14=	Min-Gyu Cho	73-69-70-67	279	¥2,970,000			

In The Money: **281**: Ryuji Imada, Do-Hoon Kim, Toru Suzuki, Makoto Inoue, Yasuharu Imano, Steven Conran **282**: Ryo Ishikawa, Prayad Marksaeng, Seung-Hyuk Kim, Atomu Shigenaga, Hyun-Woo Ryu, Ho-Sung Choi, In-Hoi Hur **283**: Hidemasa Hoshino, Yoshinori Fujimoto, Kosei Maeda, Taro Hiroi, Jay Choi **284**: Daisuke Maruyama, David Oh, Akio Sadakata, Sang-Hee Lee, Hiroo Kawai **285**: Ryuichi Oda, Kunihiro Kamii, Toru Taniguchi, Koki Shiomi, Shunsuke Sonoda **286**: Azuma Yano, Yui Ueda, Taichi Teshima, Kazuhiko Hosokawa, Yosuke Tsukada, Takashi Ogiso (a) **287**: Sung-Joon Park, David Smail, Ryosuke Kinoshita, Tatsunori Nukaga **288**: Kodai Ichihara, Shinji Tomimura, Juvic Pagunsan, J.B. Park **289**: Hyung-Tae Kim **290**: Keiichiro Fukabori **292**: Kaname Yokoo, K.T. Kwon **293**: Jinichiro Kozuma **295**: Koichiro Ishika (a)

OWR: 0 of top 50 entered - Rating: 49 - Points to 21st - Katayama: 16 points, to 78th in OWR

Golf Nippon Series JT Cup

Tokyo Yomiuri Country Club - Tokyo, Japan
Champion: Katsumasa Miyamoto

Dec 4 - Dec 7
7,023 yards   Par 70
Purse: ¥130,000,000

Recording his first multi-win season since 2001, 42-year-old Katsumasa Miyamoto claimed his 10th career Japan Tour title with a come-from-behind victory at the season-ending Golf Nippon Series JT Cup. Miyamoto rode something of a roller coaster throughout the week trailing first round leader Koumei Oda by four after opening with 68, tying for the halfway lead (with Yusaku Miyazato and Korean Sang-Hee Lee) following a Friday 67, then falling into a tie for sixth (three behind Lee) after a moderately disappointing Saturday 71. But Lee could do no better than a 71 of his own on Sunday, and while several pursuers stepped up to challenge, none could keep up with Miyamoto, who birdied three of his first six holes to jump firmly into contention. A bogey at the par-4 11th briefly slowed his momentum, but back-to-back birdies at the 13th and 14th drew him even with Prayad Marksaeng before a Marksaeng bogey at the 15th ultimately proved the deciding factor. In addition to marking an early 40s resurgence, the victory was Miyamoto's third in this lucrative year-end event. Marksaeng claimed second-place money while Koumei Oda, whose finish locked away his first career Japan Tour money title, tied for third.

1	K. Miyamoto	68-67-71-65	271	¥40,000,000		Dong-Kyu Jang	68-71-70-69	278 ¥2,467,593
2	Prayad Marksaeng	70-68-67-67	272	¥15,000,000	15	Ryo Ishikaw	70-67-73-69	279 ¥2,207,593
3=	Koumei Oda	64-72-72-66	274	¥6,508,695	16	Hideto Tanihara	70-70-69-71	280 ¥2,077,593
	Michio Matsumura	67-72-69-66	274	¥6,508,695	17=	Tadahiro Takayama	74-73-69-66	282 ¥1,882,593
	Sang-Hee Lee	68-67-68-71	274	¥6,508,695		Tomohiro Kondo	70-72-70-70	282 ¥1,882,593
	Toshinori Muto	68-71-65-70	274	¥6,508,695	19=	Yoshitaka Takeya	70-72-72-69	283 ¥1,609,592
7	Yoshinori Fujimoto	71-68-70-66	275	¥4,261,593		Kyoung-Hoon Lee	71-71-71-70	283 ¥1,609,592
8	In-Hoi Hur	70-69-68-69	276	¥3,936,593		Taichi Teshima	72-71-70-70	283 ¥1,609,592
9=	Shingo Katayama	72-70-69-66	277	¥3,247,593	22=	I.J. Jang	70-73-72-71	286 ¥1,297,592
	Seung-Hyuk Kim	69-67-70-71	277	¥3,247,593		Yuta Ikeda	72-71-71-72	286 ¥1,297,592
	Satoshi Kodaira	66-72-67-72	277	¥3,247,593		David Oh	69-70-71-76	286 ¥1,297,592
	Yusaku Miyazato	67-68-69-73	277	¥3,247,593	25	Hiroshi Iwata	70-70-73-74	287 ¥1,141,592
13=	Hyung-Sung Kim	69-72-70-67	278	¥2,467,593				

In The Money: **288**: Ryuichi Oda **289**: Kazuhiro Yamashita **291**: Hiroyuki Fujita **292**: Brad Kennedy **298**: Hyun-Woo Ryu

OWR: 0 of top 50 entered - Rating: 51 - Points to 21st - Miyamoto: 17 points, to 154th in OWR

HOW THE OWR WORKS

Official Events from 14 professional tours are eligible for ranking points which are awarded according to the tournament's strength of field and the player's finishing position. In addition to the PGA Tour, European Tour, Japan Golf Tour, Asian Tour, Sunshine Tour, PGA Tour of Australasia and the OneAsia Tour, also eligible are seven smaller or developmental circuits: the Web.com Tour, European Challenge Tour, PGA Tour Canada, PGA Tour China, PGA Tour Latinoamérica, Korean Golf Tour and the Asian Development Tour.

World Ranking Points

Each player's world ranking points are accumulated over a two year "rolling" period with the points awarded for each event retaining their full value for a 13-week period to place greater emphasis on recent performance. Ranking points are then reduced in equal increments for the remaining 91 weeks of the two year ranking period. Each player's rank is calculated by his average points earned per tournament, which is determined by dividing his total number of points earned by the number of tournaments he has played in over that two-year period. In order to assure that each player's ranking is based on a representative number of events (i.e., not one hot week), there is a minimum divisor of 40 tournaments over the two-year ranking period and a maximum divisor of a player's last 52 events.

Strength of Field

The Strength of Field for each event is determined by combining a World Rating and a Home Tour Rating. The World Rating is based on the number of Top-200 ranked players competing in the event and a value is allocated to their position within the Top 200. The Home Tour Rating is based on the number of participating players rated among that tour's top 30 at the end of the previous season, with a value allocated to their position within that top 30. Using the values in the chart below, the World and Home Ratings are added together to produce the Strength of Field rating. The number of points allocated to an event is then determined by a Rating Points Structure table, which determines an overall point value, how many competing players will receive points, and how those points will be awarded.

Ranking Pos.	Rating Value	Ranking Pos.	Rating Value	Ranking Pos.	Rating Value
1st	45	10th	17	39th-43rd	8
2nd	37	11th	16	44th-50th	7
3rd	32	12th	15	51st-55th	6
4th	27	13th	14	56th-60th	5
5th	24	14th	13	61st-70th	4
6th	21	15th	12	71st-80th	3
7th	20	16th-30th	11	81st-100th	2
8th	19	31st-34th	10	101st-200th	1
9th	18	35th-38th	9		

Home Rating: Previous year's 1st player = 8 pts, 2nd = 7 pts, 3rd = 6 pts, 4th = 5 pts, 5th = 4 pts, 6th-15th = 3 pts, 16th-30th = 1 pt
Note: The total Home Tour Rating is limited to 75% of the total World Rating value

Minimum Points Level

Each tour has a minimum 1st-place points level which comes into effect should the 1st place points based on the Strength of Field rating be lower than that awarded to each tour in the chart below:

Tour	Minimum 1st-Place Pts	Tour	Minimum 1st-Place Pts
Major Championships	100	European Challenge Tour	12
PGA Tour	24	Australia State Events	6
European Tour	24	PGA Tour Canada	6
Japan Golf Tour	16	PGA Tour China	6
PGA Tour of Australasia	16	PGA Tour Latinoamérica	6
Web.com Hybrid Events	16	OneAsia	6
Sunshine Tour	14	Korean PGA Tour	6
Asian Tour	14	Asian Development Tour	6
Web.com Tour	14	Sunshine Tour Winter (72 Holes)	6
European Challenge Tour - Finals	13	Sunshine Tour Winter (54 Holes)	4

Strength of Field for WGC events is calculated by using the World Rating and an additional World Rating based on the Top-30 World Ranked players with the following values applied: 1st-ranked player = 8 pts, 2nd = 7 pts, 3rd = 6 pts, 4th = 5 pts, 5th = 4pts, 6th-15th = 3 pts, 16th-30th = 1 pt.
Note: The minimum points level for co-sanctioned events are determined using the "average" of each tours minimum 1st-place points level.

Flagship Events

The six leading tours (the PGA Tour, European Tour, Japan Golf Tour, PGA Tour of Australasia, Sunshine Tour and the Asian Tour) as well as two developmental tours (the Web.com and European Challenge) have a designated flagship event which is allocated a higher minimum number of winner's points, as follows: PGA Tour: Players Championship (80 pts), European Tour: BMW PGA Championship (64), Japan Golf Tour: Japan Open (32), PGA Tour of Australasia: Australian Open (32), Sunshine Tour: South African Open (32), Asian Tour: Thailand Golf Championship (20), Web.com Tour: Tour Championship (20), European Challenge Tour: Grand Final (17).

Limited Field Events

Limited field events are defined as less than 30 qualified players. The Strength of Field for such events is set by using the World Rating only. Points are capped to 2.40 maximum points for last place or first round losers in match play events of less than 30 qualified players.

ASIA TOUR 2014

Completing its 11th season, the modern Asian Tour stepped away from its use of a wraparound schedule in 2014 - though its final event of the year, the brand new Dubai Open, ended decidedly late, on December 21st. The Tour sanctioned 22 non-Major/WGC events in 2014, though among these were six co-sanctioned by a trio of overseas tours, five of which are covered in other sections: the Asia-Pacific Open Diamond Cup (Japan Tour) and the Maybank Malaysian Open, the Championship at Laguna National, the Omega European Masters and the Hong Kong Open, all of which appear within the European Tour's pages. One additional event, Malaysia's CIMB Classic, is included here as it is considered a part of the 2014-15 PGA Tour schedule and thus would otherwise not appear in this volume.

Though the Dubai event still remained at the time of this writing, the Tour's Order of Merit title had already been clinched by 26-year-old American David Lipsky, a former Northwestern University star who began playing in Asia in 2012. Having made 13 starts here in 2014, he can hardly be called an interloper, but it is certainly worth noting that nearly 90% of his earnings were accumulated in lucrative back-to-back events co-sanctioned by the European Tour, the Championship at Laguna National (where he tied for 2nd) and Omega European Masters, which he won. Rather more consistent was the season turned in by India's Anirban Lahiri, whose second-place Order of Merit ranking was fueled by nine top-10 finishes, highlighted by victories at April's Indonesian Masters and October's Macau Open, the latter boasting one of the Tour's strongest fields among non-co-sanctioned events. Thirty-year-old Thai veteran Prom Meesawat won once and finished third in earnings (his total boosted significantly by a $180,000 eighth-place check at the PGA Tour co-sanctioned CIMB Classic), while closely bunched together in fourth and fifth place were long-hitting Australian Scott Hend (who topped the earnings list in 2013) and his promising young countryman, 21-year-old Cameron Smith, who amassed his $427,426 in only nine official starts.

This was also the first season of a 10-year broadcast deal with Golf Channel which guarantees the circuit significant long-term exposure in America and the West – though much of that exposure is centered around a handful of marquee fall and winter events whose fields are boosted by western stars. Nonetheless, the deal represents an important component in the Tour's long-term financial stability.

Player Of The Year: Anirban Lahiri

Though American David Lipsky led the 2014 Asian Tour in earnings, selecting India's Anirban Lahiri as the circuit's Player Of The Year was actually fairly easy. Lipsky, after all, was a one-time winner (albeit of a very big event) who earned nearly all of his money in this and one additional European Tour co-sanctioned tournament. Lahiri, on the other hand, was the Tour's best golfer week in and week out, logging nine top-10 finishes and winning in both Indonesia and Macau. Yes, it was a breakout year for Lipsky, but Lahiri more deserves the award.

2014 Asia Tour Top 60 Money Winners

#	Player	Earnings	#	Player	Earnings	#	Player	Earnings
1	David Lipsky	$713,901	21	Jeung-Hun Wang	$158,727	41	Mithun Perera	$89,014
2	Anirban Lahiri	$602,833	22	Paul Peterson	$151,331	42	Scott Barr	$86,826
3	Prom Meesawat	$532,471	23	Lionel Weber	$148,191	43	Terry Pilkadaris	$85,714
4	Scott Hend	$428,820	24	Adilson da Silva	$129,298	44	Masahiro Kawamura	$85,008
5	Cameron Smith	$427,476	25	Arjun Atwal	$124,682	45	Panuphol Pittayarat	$83,385
6	Angelo Que	$383,330	26	Shiv Kapur	$117,453	46	Danny Chia	$80,855
7	Thaworn Wiratchant	$296,852	27	Unho Park	$116,433	47	Chien-Yao Hung	$80,302
8	Kiradech Aphibarnrat	$255,285	28	Richard T. Lee	$114,735	48	Chawalit Plaphol	$79,834
9	Antonio Lascuña	$253,163	29	Marcus Both	$111,120	49	Nicholas Fung	$79,739
10	Rashid Khan	$243,249	30	Andrew Dodt	$111,062	50	Kalem Richardson	$77,505
11	S.S.P Chowrasia	$235,085	31	Jazz Janewattananond	$105,119	51	Arnond Vongvanij	$76,549
12	Mardan Mamat	$219,972	32	Jbe' Kruger	$104,580	52	Nathan Holman	$74,064
13	Steve Lewton	$215,005	33	Pariya Junhasavadiskul	$97,184	53	Jake Higginbottom	$68,626
14	Jason Knutzon	$209,121	34	Adam Groom	$95,115	54	Kieran Pratt	$68,133
15	Rikard Karlberg	$205,427	35	Berry Henson	$94,957	55	Bryce Easton	$67,075
16	Seuk-Hyun Baek	$191,670	36	Siddikur Rahman	$93,509	56	Chinnarat Phadungsil	$66,166
17	Jyoti Randhawa	$187,589	37	Miguel Tabuena	$91,600	57	Wei-Chih Lu	$65,824
18	Chapchai Nirat	$183,131	38	Sam Brazel	$91,552	58	R. Wannasrichan	$61,544
19	Rahil Gangjee	$179,440	39	Carlos Pigem	$91,316	59	Sattaya Supupramai	$61,278
20	Thanyakon Khrongpha	$178,295	40	Javi Colomo	$91,265	60	N. Tantipokhakul	$58,954

King's Cup Golf Hua Hin   Jan 16 - Jan 19

Black Mountain Golf Club - Hua Hin, Thailand
Champion: Prayad Marksaeng
7,550 yards   Par 72
Purse: $1 Million

Local Hua Hin native Prayad Marksaeng scored a popular hometown victory by rallying from a three-shot 54 hole deficit to win the King's Cup behind Sunday's low round (a six-under-par 66) in a January event that closed out the Asian Tour's official 2013 schedule. Also a winner of his nation's Queen's Cup earlier in the 2013 season, Marksaeng's completion of the Thai royalty double also represented his eighth career victory on the Asian circuit and his 12th major tour victory overall. After making the Sunday turn in two-under-par 34 but still trailing Sweden's Rikard Karlberg by two, Marksaeng birdied the par-4 10th and chipped in for eagle at the par-5 13th, the latter combining with a Karlberg bogey to finally move the 47-year-old Marksaeng into the lead. He would later add an insurance birdie at the 17th, a gained stroke that would prove important when Karlberg finished birdie-birdie to pull within one. Third place was shared by India's Anirban Lahiri and two more well-known Thai stars, Chapchai Nirat and co-first round leader Prom Meesawat.

1	Prayad Marksaeng	68-71-71-66	276	$180,000		Poosit Supupramai	73-68-72-72	285	$14,590
2	Rikard Karlberg	65-71-74-67	277	$110,000		Antonio Lascuña	71-70-72-72	285	$14,590
3=	Anirban Lahiri	69-71-71-68	279	$51,333		Rahil Gangjee	71-71-71-72	285	$14,590
	Chapchai Nirat	68-73-68-70	279	$51,333	17=	N. Tantipokhakul	69-72-77-68	286	$11,850
	Prom Meesawat	65-71-72-71	279	$51,333		Johan Edfors	70-69-77-70	286	$11,850
6	Mardan Mamat	71-70-71-68	280	$33,300		Thaworn Wiratchant	74-71-71-70	286	$11,850
7=	Scott Hend	72-71-69-69	281	$26,500		S.S.P Chowrasia	70-73-72-71	286	$11,850
	Angelo Que	66-75-67-73	281	$26,500	21=	Jyoti Randhawa	70-75-73-69	287	$10,300
9	Daisuke Kataoka	73-69-72-69	283	$21,400		P. Junhasavasdikul	72-70-74-71	287	$10,300
10=	Andrew Dodt	71-73-71-69	284	$18,275		Chih Bing Lam	70-74-72-71	287	$10,300
	Joong Kyung Mo	69-68-70-77	284	$18,275		Gunn Charoenkul	72-73-70-72	287	$10,300
12=	Alex Cejka	70-69-74-72	285	$14,590		Wen-Tang Lin	66-72-76-73	287	$10,300
	Carlos Pigem	71-69-73-72	285	$14,590					

In The Money: **288**: Danthai Boonma (a), Sam Brazel, Pavit Tangkamolprasert, Siddikur Rahman, Jeung-Hun Wang, Sung-Hoon Kang **289**: Chien-Yao Hung, Joonas Granberg, Seuk-Hyun Baek, Darren Beck, Arnond Vongvanij, Kieran Pratt, Wen-Teh Lu, Jazz Janewattananond **290**: Chawalit Plaphol, Poom Saksansin, Piya Swangarunporn, Gi-Whan Kim, Marcus Both, Thitiphun Chuayprakong, Somkiat Srisa-Nga **291**: Sung Lee, Javi Colomo, Adam Groom, Kodai Ichihara **292**: Boonchu Ruangkit **293**: Chan Kim, Wei-Chi Lu, Unho Park, Richard T. Lee, Atthaphon Sriboonkaew, Pelle Edberg **294**: Juvic Pagunsan, Pijit Petchkasem **295**: Simon Yates, Zaw Moe, Jakraphan Presirigorn **297**: Anura Rohana, Berry Henson, Kalle Samooka, Yih-Shin Chan, Fredrik Andersson Hed **298**: Scott Barr **299**: Steve Lewton **303**: Rory Hie **308**: Somchai Pongpaew

OWR: 0 of top 50 entered - Rating: 11 - Points to 20th - Marksaeng: 14 points, to 124th in OWR

SAIL-SBI Open   Feb 26 - Mar 1

Delhi Golf Club - New Delhi, India
Champion: Rashid Khan
7,036 yards   Par 72
Purse: $300,000

As a 22-year-old rookie, India's Rashid Khan lost the 2013 SAIL-SBI Open in a playoff with Anirban Lahiri, coming within a whisker of claiming his maiden Asian Tour title over his home course, the Delhi Golf Club. One year later he returned to the same event and, in a storybook finish, emerged triumphant, beating Siddikur Rahman on the first hole of sudden death. Khan began his week in style with a dazzling first round 61 before rounds of 69-69 pushed him to a two-stroke 54-hole lead. But facing the stifling pressure of playing before a home crowd, Khan stood one over par through 16 holes of the Saturday finale, and thus trailed the charging Siddikur by one. He then got a potential career-altering break when his missed approach to the par-4 17th skipped over a frontal bunker to within tap-in birdie range, then matched Siddikur's birdie at the par-5 18th before birdieing the 18th once more to claim the playoff.

1	Rashid Khan	61-69-69-71	270	$54,000		Akinori Tani	66-71-71-72	280	$4,280
2	Siddikur Rahman	67-67-67-69	270	$33,000		Scott Barr	67-70-72-71	280	$4,280
3	Rikard Karlberg	71-70-67-68	276	$18,900	18=	T. Khrongpha	69-73-69-70	281	$3,475
4=	Carlos Pigem	69-71-69-68	277	$12,430		David Lipsky	70-70-71-70	281	$3,475
	S.S.P Chowrasia	68-69-72-68	277	$12,430		George Gandranata	68-70-71-72	281	$3,475
	Martin Rominger	72-63-70-72	277	$12,430	21=	Simon Griffiths	72-68-69-73	282	$3,225
7	Steve Lewton	68-70-68-72	278	$8,550		Sanjay Kumar	68-70-72-72	282	$3,225
8=	Abhijit Chadha	68-73-69-69	279	$6,184	23=	Chawalit Plaphol	70-71-70-72	283	$2,775
	Jyoti Randhawa	71-69-70-69	279	$6,184		Thaworn Wiratchant	69-73-71-70	283	$2,775
	Anirban Lahiri	70-66-69-74	279	$6,184		Anura Rohana	73-66-69-75	283	$2,775
	Mithun Perera	66-68-73-72	279	$6,184		Zamal Hossain	71-72-68-72	283	$2,775
12=	Rahil Gangjee	71-70-68-71	280	$4,280		Javi Colomo	71-67-71-74	283	$2,775
	Chiragh Kumar	69-73-70-68	280	$4,280		Shamim Khan	68-70-71-74	283	$2,775
	Arnond Vongvanij	74-69-67-70	280	$4,280		Pawan Kumar	72-71-70-70	283	$2,775
	S. Kooratanapoisan	71-72-69-68	280	$4,280		Berry Henson	73-71-69-70	283	$2,775

In The Money: **284**: Chikka S, Adam Groom, Angelo Que, Prom Meesawat, Seuk-Hyun Baek, Mukesh Kumar, Unho Park **285**: Thammanoon Sriroj, Shankar Das, Shubhankar Sharma, Himmat Rai, Chinnarat Phadungsil, Thitiphun Chuayprakong **286**: Wasim Khan, Vikrant Chopra **287**: Gi-Whan Kim, Jeung-Hun Wang, Manav Jaini, Iain Steel, Kwanchai Tannin **288**: Namchok Tantipokhakul **289**: Masahiro Kawamura, Marcus Both, Chapchai Nirat, Tae-Hee Lee, Digvijay Singh **290**: Shakhawat Sohel, Vijay Kumar **291**: Hyk-Chul Shin, M. Dharma **292**: Lionel Weber, Pariya Junhasavasdikul **293**: Ryan McCarthy **295**: Kapil Kumar **300**: Rattanon Wannasrichan **303**: Ali Sher

OWR: 0 of top 50 entered - Rating: 7 - Points to 17th - Khan: 14 points, to 302nd in OWR

Solaire Open
The Country Club - Manila, Philippines
Champion: Richard T. Lee
Apr 11 - Apr 14
7,256 yards   Par 72
Purse: $300,000

Canadian Richard T. Lee claimed his first career Asian Tour victory by coming from behind to take the Solaire Open with a final round 69 at The Country Club, in Manila. Lee began the day four shots behind Angelo Que, and his chances looked even dimmer after double bogeying the 4th hole. But three straight birdies at holes 8-10 righted the ship, and on a day when most of the top contenders failed to gather much momentum, two more birdies at the 12th and 15th ultimately proved enough for Lee to edge Thailand's Chawalit Plaphol by one. The homestanding Que endured an epic early meltdown on Sunday when he hit three balls out-of-bounds en route to a 12 at the par-5 2nd, and he would ultimately shoot an 82, tumbling to a tie for 21st. Also notable was 19-year-old Filipino prospect Miguel Tabuena, who trailed Que by one through 54 holes before bogeying seven of his first eight on Sunday, ultimately carding a 76 to fall into a tie for seventh.

1	Richard T. Lee	68-70-70-69	277	$54,000		Jeung-Hun Wang	71-67-68-77	283	$4,585
2	Chawalit Plaphol	68-72-68-70	278	$33,000	15=	Poom Saksanin	71-69-74-70	284	$3,975
3	Carlos Pigem	69-70-71-69	279	$18,900		Zanie Boy Gialon	68-70-74-72	284	$3,975
4=	Masahiro Kawamura	71-69-75-65	280	$12,430		Simon Griffiths	70-69-71-74	284	$3,975
	Steve Lewton	74-69-70-67	280	$12,430	18=	Siddikur Rahman	70-70-71-74	285	$3,475
	Paul Peterson	72-68-71-69	280	$12,430		Nick Cullen	68-73-70-74	285	$3,475
7=	Andrew Dodt	70-71-70-70	281	$7,440		Sam Cyr	72-69-69-75	285	$3,475
	Clyde Mondilla	71-70-67-73	281	$7,440	21=	Elmer Salvador	72-69-75-70	286	$3,135
	Miguel Tabuena	67-68-70-76	281	$7,440		Kalem Richardson	76-66-72-72	286	$3,135
10=	Sam Brazel	66-75-70-71	282	$5,483		Terry Pilkadaris	70-70-72-74	286	$3,135
	David Lipsky	71-68-71-72	282	$5,483		Angelo Que	70-65-69-82	286	$3,135
12=	Bryce Easton	69-68-74-72	283	$4,585	25=	Dimitrios Papadatos	70-69-77-71	287	$2,865
	Akinori Tani	69-72-67-75	283	$4,585		Matthew Griffin	68-69-73-77	287	$2,865

In The Money: **288**: S.S.P. Chowrasia, Antonio Lascuña, Jazz Janewattananond, Prom Meesawat, Thanyakon Khrongpha **289**: Shih-Chang Chan, Prayad Marksaeng, Ryan McCarthy **290**: Rikard Karlberg, Scott Barr, Daisuke Kataoka **291**: Rahil Gangjee, Jay Bayron, Carl Santos-Ocampo, Javi Colomo **292**: Kieran Pratt, Unho Park, Craig Hancock, Frankie Minoza, Orlan Sumcad, Gerald Rosales, Thaworn Wiratchant, Alex Kang **293**: Nicholas Fung, Nathan Holman, Seuk-Hyun Baek, Toru Nakajima **294**: Jhonnel Ababa **295**: Thammanoon Sriroj, Richard Abaring, Hyung-Joon Lee, Chien-Yao Hung, Wen-Teh Lu **296**: Guy Woodman, James Ryan Lam **297**: Mathiam Keyser, Joong Kyun Mo **298**: Tae-Hee Lee, Edward Reyes **300**: Sattaya Supupramai, Pawin Ingkhapradit **301**: Jessie Balasabas **302**: Thitiphun Chuayprakong

OWR: 0 of top 50 entered - Rating: 7 - Points to 17th - Lee: 14 points, to 272nd in OWR

CIMB Niaga Indonesian Masters
Royale Jakarta Golf Club - Jakarta, Indonesia
Champion: Anirban Lahiri
Apr 24 - Apr 27
6,697 yards   Par 72
Purse: $750,000

Twenty-six-year-old Anirban Lahiri claimed his first Asian Tour victory outside of his native India and his fourth overall, winning the CIMB Niaga Indonesian Masters in dramatic style in Jakarta. Lahiri stood five shots off the 36-hole lead with opening rounds of 70-69 before vaulting himself up the board with a spectacular bogey-free 64 on Saturday, then opening with birdies at the 2nd, 3rd and 4th holes on a rain-interrupted Sunday. Having pressed himself further into the heart of the action with a birdie at the 12th, Lahiri bounced back from a potentially disastrous double-bogey at the par-4 13th with another birdie at the 14th. Meanwhile, Korea's Seuk-Hyun Baek had turned in 31 en route to the closing 65 which made him the leader in the clubhouse, leaving Lahiri in need of a birdie at the par-5 18th to force a playoff. But instead, Lahiri reached the green in two and coolly holed a 20-footer for eagle to steal the trophy. Twenty-year-old Australian Cameron Smith, the 54-hole leader, closed with a 70 to tie for second in only his second start as a professional.

1	Anirban Lahiri	70-69-64-68	271	$135,000		Chan Kim	69-69-70-69	277	$10,863
2=	Seuk-Hyun Baek	71-68-68-65	272	$64,875		Jyoti Randhawa	72-68-67-70	277	$10,863
	Cameron Smith	68-67-67-70	272	$64,875	16	Marcus Both	69-70-68-72	279	$9,938
4	K. Aphibarnrat	71-69-65-68	273	$37,500	17=	Jake Higginbottom	68-72-73-67	280	$8,888
5=	Thongchai Jaidee	71-72-67-64	274	$23,869		N. Tantipokhakul	71-72-69-68	280	$8,888
	J. Janewattananond	68-70-69-67	274	$23,869		Danny Chia	69-73-68-70	280	$8,888
	Wen-Tang Lin	70-64-72-68	274	$23,869		Chih Bing Lam	72-68-69-71	280	$8,888
	S.S.P Chowrasia	71-66-69-68	274	$23,869	21=	Nicholas Fung	67-69-74-71	281	$8,175
9	Rashid Khan	70-70-64-71	275	$16,050	22=	Tae-Hee Lee	69-73-72-68	282	$7,613
10=	Chapchai Nirat	68-68-72-68	276	$13,200		Thaworn Wiratchant	71-70-72-69	282	$7,613
	Bernd Wiesberger	68-71-69-68	276	$13,200		Rahil Gangjee	70-70-72-70	282	$7,613
	Gunn Charoenkul	70-69-67-70	276	$13,200		Antonio Lascuña	73-72-66-71	282	$7,613
13=	Dimitrios Papadatos	73-72-66-66	277	$10,863					

In The Money: **283**: Steve Lewton, Arnond Vongvanij, Matthew Stieger **284**: Joong Kyung Mo, Miguel Tabuena, Bruce Easton, Adilson da Silva, Wolmer Murillo, Matt Jager **285**: Jason Knutzon, Elias Bertheussen, Boonchu Ruangkit, Jeung-Hun Wang **286**: Berry Henson, Iain Steel, Arjun Atwal, Chinnarat Phadungsil, Sam Brazel **287**: George Gandranata, Gi-Whan Kim, Mardan Mamat **288**: Sutijet Kooratanapisan, Chien-Yao Hung, Pariya Junhasavadikul, Andrew Dodt **289**: Seb Gros, Ryan McCarthy **290**: Scott Barr, Hyung-Joon Lee **291**: Adam Groom, Wrn-Hong Lin, Carlos Pigem **292**: Sam Cyr, Anthony Kang, David Lipsky **293**: Wen-Teh Lu, Poom Saksansin **294**: Richard T. Lee **295**: Tae-Woo Kim, Purilarp Euammongkol **297**: Sujjan Singh **301**: Soon-Sang Hong **WD**: Louis Oosthuizen (140), Victor Dubuisson (143)

OWR: 2 of top 50 entered - Rating: 65 - Points to 25th - Lahiri: 20 points, to 67th in OWR

ICTSI Philippine Open

Wack Wack Golf & Country Club (East Course) - Manila, Philippines
Champion: Marcus Both

May 15 - May 18
7,222 yards   Par 72
Purse: $300,000

Australian Marcus Both, whose fortunes had sunk so low that he lost his Asian Tour card after the 2013 season, scored a redemptive two-shot victory at the Philippine Open after gaining entry on a sponsor exemption. Both came somewhat out of nowhere to grab the halfway lead with rounds of 70-66 over the demanding East course at the Wack Wack Golf & Country Club, then fell one behind 54-hole leader Chan Kim after three late bogeys brought him home in 76 on Saturday. But on a Sunday which saw only one player among the contenders break 70, Both turned in 34, then built a significant cushion via back-to-back birdies at the 15th and 16th – a buffer he would need as it turned out, for he bogeyed both the 17th and 18th but won by two. The runner-up spot was shared by five players: Bangladesh's Siddikur Rahman (who closed with 69), Australia's Nathan Holman, Thailand's Arnond Vongvanij and homestanding Antonio Lascuña and Jay Bayron.

1	Marcus Both	70-66-76-70	282	$54,000		Chapchai Nirat	79-67-69-72 287	$4,813
2=	Siddikur Rahman	66-73-76-69	284	$17,838		Chan Kim	66-72-73-76 287	$4,813
	Nathan Holman	71-71-72-70	284	$17,838	16=	Shih-Chang Chan	75-71-73-69 288	$3,795
	Antonio Lascuña	74-71-69-70	284	$17,838		Settee Prakongvech	70-74-74-70 288	$3,795
	Arnond Vongvanij	74-72-68-70	284	$17,838		Gunn Charoenkul	73-70-74-71 288	$3,795
	Jay Bayron	71-72-69-72	284	$17,838	19=	Lionel Weber	72-70-75-72 289	$3,360
7	Tung-Shu Tsieh	77-68-70-70	285	$8,550		Mithun Perera	71-74-73-73 289	$3,360
8=	J. Janewattananond	72-72-72-70	286	$6,885		Anura Rohana	75-70-71-73 289	$3,360
	Jeung-Hun Wang	72-68-72-74	286	$6,885	22=	Unho Park	72-72-75-71 290	$3,000
10=	S.S.P Chowrasia	71-71-76-69	287	$4,813		Anirban Lahiri	75-69-76-70 290	$3,000
	Prayad Marksaeng	70-75-71-71	287	$4,813		Abhijit Chadha	75-72-71-72 290	$3,000
	Daisuke Kataoka	71-75-70-71	287	$4,813		Miguel Tabuena	75-70-72-73 290	$3,000
	Thaworn Wiratchant	74-74-67-72	287	$4,813		Jarin Todd	73-71-71-75 290	$3,000

In The Money: **291**: Pariya Junhasavasdikul, Chia-Jen Hsu, Ryan Yip **292**: Masahiro Kawamura, Chawalit Plaphol, Sam Brazel **293**: Panuphol Pittayarat, Danny Chia, Mao-Chang S Ung, Rufino Bayron, Zanie Boy Gialon, Paul Echavez **294**: George Gandranata **295**: Frankie Minoza, Paul Peterson **296**: Adam Groom, Rupert Saragoza, Elmer Salvador, Berry Henson **297**: Angelo Que, Yih-Shin Chan, Charles Hong **298**: Miguel Ochoa, Poom Saksanin, Rico Depilo, Chinnarat Phadungsil, Lindsay Reynolds, Wen-Tang Lin **299**: Jhonnel Ababa, Mathiam Keyser, Zaw Moe, Robert Pactolerin **300**: Elner Saban, Byung-Joo Park **301**: Matthew Stieger **304**: Zamal Hossain **305**: Michael Tran **307**: Yoshinobu Tsukada **308**; Tze Huang Choo **309**: Rolando Marabe

OWR: 0 of top 50 entered - Rating: 11 - Points to 18th - Both: 14 points, to 396th in OWR

Queen's Cup

Santiburi Samui Country Club - Samui, Thailand
Champion: Thaworn Wiratchant

Jun 5 - Jun 8
6,930 yards   Par 72
Purse: $300,000

Thailand's 47-year-old Thaworn Wiratchant is an established force around Asia and that trend continued in his homeland as Wiratchant notched his 17th career Asian Tour victory with a come-from-behind win at the Queen's Cup. After an opening 71 left him five shots behind countryman Poom Saksansin, Wiratchant fell one shot further back with a second round 68, then crept back within five of Saksansin (and four behind Bangladesh's Siddikur Rahman) following a Saturday 67. He would need some help on Sunday then, and both Saksansin and Siddikur were obliging, each closing with rounds of 72, Siddikur's ending with a crushing bogey at the last. This left the door ajar and Wiratchant promptly charged, turning in 34 before adding birdies at the 11th, 12th and 14th. A bogey at the par-4 17th drew him back to 11 under par but at the par-5 closer, Wiratchant coolly rolled in a five-footer for birdie which, combined with Siddikur's six, secured the title.

1	Thaworn Wiratchant	71-68-67-66	272	$54,000		Jyoti Randhawa	71-73-68-68 280	$4,155
2	Poom Saksansin	66-67-68-72	273	$33,000		R. Wannasrichan	69-71-70-70 280	$4,155
3=	Don. Niyomchon	68-68-70-68	274	$16,950	17	Miguel Tabuena	74-68-71-68 281	$3,795
	Siddikur Rahman	68-70-64-72	274	$16,950	18=	Lionel Weber	72-71-71-68 282	$3,475
5	Seuk-Hyun Baek	69-66-71-70	276	$12,300		T. Kaesiribandit	71-70-71-70 282	$3,475
6=	Tze Huang Choo	67-72-71-68	278	$8,630		T. Khrongpha	75-67-70-70 282	$3,475
	Richard T. Lee	69-71-69-69	278	$8,630	21=	Boonchu Ruangkit	69-76-71-67 283	$3,135
	Jeung-Hun Wang	72-69-68-69	278	$8,630		Joong Kyung Mo	70-72-73-68 283	$3,135
9=	P. Junhasavadiskul	77-68-68-66	279	$5,361		Wolmer Murillo	73-70-69-71 283	$3,135
	Prom Meesawat	71-71-69-68	279	$5,361		Chawalit Plaphol	73-71-68-71 283	$3,135
	Rahil Gangjee	73-70-68-68	279	$5,361	25=	Michael Tran	72-71-74-67 284	$2,865
	Antonio Lascuña	69-71-70-69	279	$5,361		T. Phongphun (a)	73-72-69-70 284	-
	Chapchai Nirat	72-67-69-71	279	$5,361		C. Phadungsil	68-70-75-71 284	$2,865
14=	J. Janewattananond	71-74-71-64	280	$4,155				

In The Money: **285**: Sattaya Supupramai, Vuttipong Puangkaew, Nils Floren, Mars Pucay, Manav Jaini **286**: Bryce Easton, Kasidit Lepkurte (a), Pavit Tangkamolprasaert, Matthew Stieger **287**: Jarin Todd, Rashid Khan, Martin Rominger, Shankar Das, Pawin Ingkhapradit, Anirban Lahiri **288**; Sebastien Grose, Porameth Sonthirato, Namchok Tantipokhakul **289**: Chris Rodgers **290**: Akinori Tani, Zamal Hossain **291**: Poosit Supupramai, Suppakorn Uthaipat, Craig Hinton, Natthapong Niyomchon **292**: Craig Hancock **293**: Jakraphan Premsirigorn, Steve Lewton, Pijit Petchkasem, Somchai Pongpaew, Wongsakorn Choowong, Varut Chomchalam Thitiphun Chuayprakong **294**: Chiragh Kumar, Cameron Smith **295**: Atthaphon Sriboonkaew, wasin Sripattranusorn, Danny Chia, Sorachut Hansapiban **296**: Digvijay Singh **305**: Deng Shan Koh

OWR: 0 of top 50 entered - Rating: 7 - Points to 17th - Wiratchant: 14 points, to 175th in OWR

Yeangder Tournament Players Championship
Sep 11 - Sep 14

Linkou International Golf & Country Club - Linkou, Taiwan
Champion: Prom Meesawat
7,125 yards   Par 72
Purse: $500,000

Thailand's Prom Meesawat won for the second time on the Asian Tour, getting some late help from touted Philippine prospect Miguel Tabuena before defeating Tabuena in a playoff at the Yeangder Tournament Players Championship. Initially, this looked like it might be the 19-year-old Tabuena's breakthrough week, particularly after he followed up a disappointing opening 73 with a bogey-free 68 on Friday and an even better 65 on Saturday, a near-flawless round which included a back nine 30, and which staked him to a one-shot 54-hole lead. Two early bogeys on Sunday quickly took Tabuena out of the top spot but he rallied gamely, carding four birdies between the 9th and 16th to charge back into a one-shot lead. But staring victory directly in the face, the diminutive Tabuena bogeyed the par-3 17th to fall back into a tie with the 30-year-old Meesawat, then lost the playoff by bogeying the par-5 18th, essentially handing Meesawat the title.

1	Prom Meesawat	67-73-68-69	277	$90,000		T. Khrongpha	72-71-67-76	286	$6,925
2	Miguel Tabuena	73-68-65-71	277	$55,000	17=	Lionel Weber	76-67-74-70	287	$5,657
3	Antonio Lascuña	68-69-72-69	278	$31,500		Lian-Wei Zhang	72-69-74-72	287	$5,657
4=	Paul Peterson	71-71-69-69	280	$20,717		Kieran Pratt	72-71-72-72	287	$5,657
	Daniel Chopra	71-68-69-72	280	$20,717		Jake Higginbottom	70-72-72-73	287	$5,657
	Anirban Lahiri	73-66-68-73	280	$20,717		Berry Henson	72-73-69-73	287	$5,657
7	Cameron Smith	70-67-73-73	283	$14,250		Hao-Sheng Hsu	68-73-72-74	287	$5,657
8=	Angelo Que	68-71-76-69	284	$10,306		Danny Chia	68-74-71-74	287	$5,657
	Rashid Khan	71-70-72-71	284	$10,306	24=	Simon Griffiths	73-73-70-72	288	$4,550
	Lu-Sen Lien	67-71-74-72	284	$10,306		Gunn Charoenkul	69-71-75-73	288	$4,550
	Wei-Tze Yeh	72-71-65-76	284	$10,306		S. Kooratanapisan	71-71-73-73	288	$4,550
12=	Ryan Yip	71-69-70-75	285	$7,850		Chih Bing Lam	70-72-73-73	288	$4,550
	Thaworn Wiratchant	70-69-68-78	285	$7,850		Andrew Dodt	73-73-69-73	288	$4,550
14=	Jay Bayron	73-72-69-72	286	$6,925		Carlos Pigem	75-70-69-74	288	$4,550
	Rikard Karlberg	72-72-68-74	286	$6,925		Jack Munro	70-74-69-75	288	$4,550

In The Money: **289**: Chapchai Nirat, Kalem Richardson, Jyoti Randhawa, George Gandranata, Scott Barr, Thitiphun Chuayprakong, Yih-Shin Chan, Rahil Gangjee **290**: Chris Gaunt, Steve Lewton, Shih-Chang Chan, Wei-Chih Lu, Wolmer Murillo **291**: Chien-Bing Lin, Tung-Hung Tsieh, Kwanchai Tannin, Wen-Tang Lin, Seuk-Hyun Baek, Chiragh Kumar **292**: Mong-Nan Hsu, Atthaphon Sriboonkaew, Craig Hancock, Elmer Salvador, Chien-Yao Hung, Panuphol Pittayarat **293**: Ter-Chang Wang, Guy Woodman, Jarin Todd **294**: Adam Groom **295**: Jeung-Hun Wang **296**: Wen-Hong Lin, Bryce Easton **297**: Hao Chuan Fan Chiang **298**: Sam Cyr, Motonari Nakagawa **299**: Kuan-Po Luin **300**: Pariya Junhasavasdikul **301**: Namchok Tantipokhakul, Kai-Jen Tai (a) **DQ**: Richard T. Lee (216)

OWR: 0 of top 50 entered - Rating: 5 - Points to 23rd - Meesawat: 14 points, to 197th in OWR

Worldwide Holdings Selangor Masters
Sep 18 - Sep 21

Seri Selangor Golf Club - Petaling Jaya, Malaysia
Champion: Chapchai Nirat
6,374 metres   Par 72
Purse: $410,000

Thailand's Chapchai Nirat ended a five-year winless drought by capturing his third career Asian Tour victory at the Worldwide Holdings Selangor Masters, edging Antonio Lascuña of the Philippines on the first hole of sudden death. Nirat played extremely steady golf all week, his opening rounds of 68-69-69 placing him one behind 54-hole leader Cameron Smith of Australia. Smith would stumble to a 73 on Sunday, however, leaving Nirat on the verge of running away after logging six birdies between holes 5-16. But ill-timed Nirat bogeys at both the 17th and 18th left just enough room for the 43-year-old Lascuña, who charged home with a stunning 63, to force the playoff.

1	Chapchai Nirat	68-69-69-68	274	$72,671	16=	Jbe' Kruger	71-70-72-69	282	$5,107
2	Antonio Lascuña	70-70-71-63	274	$44,410		Ryan Yip	71-70-69-72	282	$5,107
3	Anirban Lahiri	64-68-76-68	276	$25,435		Kieran Pratt	69-72-68-73	282	$5,107
4=	Scott Barr	70-69-72-67	278	$14,316	19=	Chris Rodgers	72-71-69-71	283	$4,582
	Paul Peterson	69-71-71-67	278	$14,316		Gi-Whan Kim	73-66-71-73	283	$4,582
	S.S.P Chowrasia	66-70-73-69	278	$14,316	21=	Thaworn Wiratchant	70-74-70-70	284	$4,280
	David Lipksy	72-66-69-71	278	$14,316		Mardan Mamat	71-68-74-71	284	$4,280
	Cameron Smith	68-66-71-73	278	$14,316		Rory Hie	75-68-70-71	284	$4,280
9=	Carlos Pigem	71-68-72-68	279	$7,489	24=	Rashid Khan	73-70-72-70	285	$3,674
	J. Janewattananond	70-70-70-69	279	$7,489		Chan Kim	69-74-71-71	285	$3,674
	Jake Higginbottom	72-65-70-72	279	$7,489		Unho Park	71-72-73-69	285	$3,674
	Sattaya Supupramai	68-70-68-73	279	$7,489		Jyoti Randhawa	71-69-73-72	285	$3,674
13=	Kalem Richardson	72-73-68-68	281	$5,847		R. Wannasrichan	69-73-71-72	285	$3,674
	Simon Griffiths	70-68-72-71	281	$5,847		T. Chuayprakong	74-68-70-73	285	$3,674
	Chien-Yao Hung	67-73-67-74	281	$5,847		Lionel Weber	70-70-70-75	285	$3,674

In The Money: **286**: Danny Chia, Joonas Granberg, Sutijet Kooratanapisan, Shih-Chang Chan, Shaaban Hussin **287**: Jay Bayron, Yih-Shin Chan, Angelo Que, Mathiam Keyser, Anthony Kang, Pariya Junhasavasdikul **288**: Chiragh Kumar, Marcus Both, Javi Colomo, Nicholas Fung **289**: George Gandranata, Hyung-Joon Lee, Chris Gaunt, Mithun Perera, Adam Groom, Quincy Quek **290**: Jarin Todd **292**: Ben Leong, Mars Pucay, Guy Woodman **293**: Hans Jamil, Kheng Hwai Khor, Jeung-Hun Wang, Thammanoon Sriroj, Joong Kyung Mo, Wolmer Murillo, Kenneth De Silva **294**: Mohamad A. Basharudin, Zaw Moe, Jack Munro **295**: Zurie Harun, Chawalit Plaphol **298**: Sukree Othman **299**: Byung-Joo Park **300**: Arjun Atwal, Mohd Iylia Jamil **301**: Kunal Bhasin, Wen-Teh Lu

OWR: 0 of top 50 entered - Rating: 5 - Points to 18th - Nirat: 14 points, to 204th in OWR

Mercuries Taiwan Masters

Oct 2 - Oct 5

Taiwan Golf & Country Club - Tam Sui, Taiwan
Champion: Steve Lewton

7,015 yards Par 72
Purse: $650,000

Buoyed by the memory of his father, who died earlier in the year, England's Steve Lewton broke through for his first major tour victory at the Mercuries Taiwan Masters, claiming the title at the Taiwan Golf & Country Club. A former North Carolina State star and runner-up to Rory McIlroy at the 2006 European Amateur, the 31-year-old Lewton played the most consistent golf throughout the week, initially overcoming an early double-bogey to stand second after an opening round 70, then retaining the second spot (this time one back of Brazilian veteran Adilson da Silva) following a Friday 72. A fast start on Saturday led the way to a third round 70, and suddenly Lewton held the 54-hole lead, one ahead of da Silva, as well as the red-hot Antonio Lascuña of the Philippines. Both da Silva and Lascuña would post even-par 72s on Sunday, however, and with neither making a concerted charge, Lewton initially stretched his lead to three at the turn, then bounced his way through an up-and-down back nine, ultimately bogeying the par-4 18th to win by two. The victory gained him an Asian Tour exemption, which includes events co-sanctioned with the European Tour, his onetime - and hopefully future - destination.

1	Steve Lewton	70-72-70-71	283	$130,000		Wen-Teh Lu	74-72-70-75	291	$9,425
2=	Adilson da Silva	75-66-72-72	285	$61,750	16=	Simon Griffiths	74-75-72-71	292	$7,800
	Antonio Lascuña	75-69-69-72	285	$61,750		Wei-Chih Lu	73-74-73-72	292	$7,800
4=	Thaworn Wiratchant	72-73-70-71	286	$29,250		Sam Cyr	71-74-71-76	292	$7,800
	Unho Park	72-72-70-72	286	$29,250	19=	Elmer Salvador	74-71-75-73	293	$6,809
6=	Chapchai Nirat	75-71-72-70	288	$19,500		Mong-Nan Hsu	77-70-73-73	293	$6,809
	Javi Colomo	72-74-69-73	288	$19,500		Prom Meesawat	71-73-74-75	293	$6,809
	Cameron Smith	72-72-70-74	288	$19,500		Jeung-Hun Wang	73-72-75-73	293	$6,809
9=	Angelo Que	75-73-71-70	289	$12,350	23=	Chien-Yao Hung	75-72-75-72	294	$6,110
	Rahil Gangjee	74-71-70-74	289	$12,350		Wei-Tze Weh	72-75-75-72	294	$6,110
11	Andrew Dodt	74-70-73-73	290	$11,050		J. Janewattananond	73-73-74-74	294	$6,110
12=	Wolmer Murillo	76-71-74-70	291	$9,425		Lian-Wei Zhang	74-73-73-74	294	$6,110
	Sam Brazel	72-74-74-71	291	$9,425		S.S.P Chowrasia	72-77-70-75	294	$6,110
	Marcus Both	71-73-73-74	291	$9,425					

In The Money: **295**: Lionel Weber, Arnond Vongvanij, Nicholas Fung, Yih-Shin Chan, Jyoti Randhawa **296**: Kieran Pratt, Chinnarat Phadungsil, Bryce Easton, Mao-Chang Sung, Mardan Mamat, Gunn Charoenkul **297**: Chi-Huang Tsai, Danny Chia, Wen-Hong Lin, Yao-Pin Chang **298**: Anthony Kang, Terry Pilkadaris, Martin Rominger, Paul Peterson, Namchok Tantipokhakul **299**: Boonchu Ruangkit, Adam Groom **300**: Tze-Ming Chen **301**: Hong-Sheng Tseng **302**: Chun-An Yu (a), Chi-Hsien Hsieh **303**: Pariya Junhasavasdikul **304**: Wen-Ting Wu **306**: Chan Kim, Chang-Ting Yeh

OWR: 0 of top 50 entered - Rating: 5 - Points to 18th - Lewton: 14 points, to 288th in OWR

Venetian Macau Open

Oct 23 - Oct 26

Macau Golf & Country Club - Coloane, Macau
Champion: Anirban Lahiri

6,624 yards Par 71
Purse: $900,000

India's 27-year-old Anirban Lahiri claimed his second Asian Tour victory of 2014 and his fifth overall by racing home with a closing 66 to take the Macau Open by a single shot. It initially appeared to be Lahiri's week when he opened with a 61 over the shortish Macau Golf & Country Club course, but this blazing round (which included an eagle at the par-5 18th) was only good enough for a one-shot lead over red-hot Scott Hend, who was coming off a victory in Hong Kong and posted a 62. Conditions toughened on Friday, however, and as Lahiri backed off with a 73, Hend posted a 70 to share the lead with fellow Australian Adam Groom, then added a Saturday 67 to lead Lahiri by two through 54 holes. An early Hend eagle at the par-5 2nd pushed the lead to four, and as he soon added birdies at the 7th and 8th, the powerful Australian looked to be on his way. But Lahiri played near-perfect golf on Sunday, carding a 66 to post a 267 total - an aggregate which proved just enough when Hend missed a four footer for par at the 72nd to miss out on a playoff and hand Lahiri the title.

1	Anirban Lahiri	61-73-67-66	267	$162,000		Martin Rominger	65-68-73-71	277	$13,320
2=	Prom Meesawat	68-70-64-66	268	$77,850	15=	R. Wannasrichan	71-71-73-63	278	$11,403
	Scott Hend	62-70-67-69	268	$77,850		Wei-Tze Yeh	73-69-70-66	278	$11,403
4	Adam Groom	65-67-72-66	270	$45,000		Jeung-Hun Wang	71-68-69-70	278	$11,403
5=	Berry Henson	69-70-68-65	272	$33,435		Jyoti Randhawa	66-74-68-70	278	$11,403
	Unho Park	70-69-68-65	272	$33,435		Shih-Chang Chan	70-64-70-74	278	$11,403
7	Thaworn Wiratchant	67-70-67-69	273	$25,650	20=	Paul Peterson	71-71-70-67	279	$9,795
8	Shiv Kapur	73-67-67-67	274	$22,050		Charlie Wi	69-70-72-68	279	$9,795
9	Kieran Pratt	70-69-68-68	275	$19,260		Sam Brazel	64-73-68-74	279	$9,795
10=	K. Aphibarnrat	71-69-72-64	276	$15,840	23=	Seuk-Hyun Baek	74-68-73-65	280	$9,000
	Thongchai Jaidee	70-70-71-65	276	$15,840		P. Junhasavasdikul	69-67-75-69	280	$9,000
	Chan Kim	70-69-71-66	276	$15,840		Adilson da Silva	69-71-70-70	280	$9,000
13=	Chapchai Nirat	70-68-71-68	277	$13,320					

In The Money: **281**: Namchok Tantipokhakul, Marcus Both, Jeev Milkha Singh, Wei-Chih Lu, Antonio Lascuña, Ernie Els **282**: Sebastien Gros, Angelo Que, S.S.P Chowarsia **283**: Ryan Yip, Jazz Janewattananond, Chawalit Plaphol, Pawin Ingkhapradit, Simon Griffiths **284**: Piya Swangarunporn, Sam Cyr, Chien-Yao Hung, Wen-Chonng Liang, Elmer Salvador, Chinnarat Phadungsil **285**: Daniel Chopra, Rikard Karlberg, Chen-Chih Chiang, Jay Bayron, Jaakko Makitalo, Anthony Kang, Sutijet Kooratanapisan **286**: Mithun Perera, James Bowen, Suppkorn Uthaipat **287**: Joonas Granberg, Lian-Wei Zhang, Sattaya Supupramai **288**: James Byrne, Kwanchai Tannin, Panuwat Muenlek, George Gandranata, Kalem Richardson **291**: Thammanoon Sriroj, Alex Kang **293**: Guy Woodman

OWR: 3 of top 50 entered - Rating: 54 - Points to 22nd - Lahiri: 17 points, to 69th in OWR

CIMB Classic

Kuala Lumpur Golf & Country Club - Kuala Lumpur, Malaysia
Champion: Ryan Moore

Oct 30 - Nov 2
6,951 yards   Par 72
Purse: $7 Million

American Ryan Moore, one year removed from defeating Gary Woodland in a playoff, returned to the Kuala Lumpur Golf & Country Club to successfully defend his title at the CIMB Classic, this time beating Woodland, Sergio García and Kevin Na by three shots. Moore was very much in the mix all week, opening with rounds of 68-69-67 to join Na atop the leaderboard after 54 holes, one stroke ahead of fellow American Billy Hurley III and García. With Hurley fading to a Sunday 73, and García unable to better 69 after a run-in with a palm tree cost him a double-bogey at the par-5 10th, Woodland carded six birdies over his first 17 holes to move into contention before a three-putt bogey at the 634-yard closer left him on 274. Na initially fared better but eventually fell one behind after missing a two-footer at the 16th, then drove into the top of a palm tree at the 17th to end his chances. All of which cleared the road nicely for Moore who, in crunch time, stuffed approaches close to birdie both the 14th and 17th, allowing him an easy walk home at the last.

1	Ryan Moore	68-69-67-67	271	$1.26 mil		Danny Lee	69-69-73-68	279	$123,667
2=	Gary Woodland	71-70-66-67	274	$522,667		Brian Stuard	67-72-72-68	279	$123,667
	Sergio García	69-68-68-69	274	$522,667		Lee Westwood	72-65-74-68	279	$123,667
	Kevin Na	69-68-67-70	274	$522,667		Brendon de Jonge	70-73-65-71	279	$123,667
5=	Cameron Smith	70-69-69-68	276	$266,000		Kevin Chappell	69-68-70-72	279	$123,667
	Sang-Moon Bae	71-68-68-69	276	$266,000	19=	Scott Stallings	69-76-67-68	280	$94,500
7	John Senden	72-68-69-68	277	$234,500		Charl Schwartzel	74-70-68-68	280	$94,500
8=	Rory Sabbatini	70-72-70-66	278	$189,000	21=	Heath Slocum	71-73-70-67	281	$72,800
	Davis Love III	68-71-71-68	278	$189,000		Mike Weir	73-68-72-68	281	$72,800
	Prom Meesawat	68-71-70-69	278	$189,000		Jonathan Byrd	70-74-69-68	281	$72,800
	Angelo Que	67-72-69-70	278	$189,000		Hideki Matsuyama	70-70-72-69	281	$72,800
	Billy Hurley III	67-67-71-73	278	$189,000		Nicholas Thompson	69-73-70-69	281	$72,800
13=	Jonas Blixt	69-69-75-66	279	$123,667					

In The Money: **282**: Ryo Ishikawa, Michael Putnam, Jhonattan Vegas, Jason Dufner, Greg Chalmers, Patrick Reed, Kevin Streelman **283**: Pat Perez, Retief Goosen, Kyle Stanley, Jeff Overton **284**: Billy Horschel, Paul Casey **285**: Charlie Wi, David Lingmerth, Chris Stroud, Rikard Karlberg, Marc Leishman, Luke Guthrie, Seung-Yul Noh **286**: Jason Knutzon, Steven Bowditch **287**: Steve Lewton **288**: Trevor Immelman, Matt Every, J.B. Holmes **289**: Will MacKenzie, Anirban Lahiri, Tim Wilkinson, Matt Jones **290**: Troy Merritt, Brice Garnett, James Hahn, Tim Clark, Stewart Cink **291**: Morgan Hoffmann, Roberto Castro **292**: Robert Allenby, Will Wilcox **293**: Nicholas Fung, Danny Chia, Ricky Barnes, Carlos Ortiz, Chesson Hadley **294**: Boo Weekley **295**: K.J. Choi, Antonio Lascuña **296**: Brian Davis **297**: Guan Tianlang (a) **299**: David Lipsky **301**: Charlie Beljan **303**: Seuk-Hyun Baek **WD**: Graham DeLaet

OWR: 14 of top 50 entered - Rating: 228 - Points to 47th - Moore: 42 points, to 27th in OWR

Panasonic Open India

Delhi Golf Club - New Delhi, India
Champion: S.S.P. Chowrasia

Nov 6 - Nov 9
6,963 yards   Par 72
Purse: $300,000

Playing on home turf in New Delhi, local hero S.S.P. Chowrasia came from far off the pace to win the Panasonic Open India in a three-way playoff with Rahil Gangjee and Sri Lanka's Mithun Perera. Chowrasia stood four off the lead following an opening 70, seven in arrears after a Friday 71, and five back after three late birdies lifted him to a Saturday 69. The pace-setter, meanwhile, was the 36-year-old Gangjee, whose opening rounds of 66-68 gave him a two-shot lead over Australian Wade Ormsby, with that margin slipping to one following a Saturday 71. Gangjee initially stumbled slightly on Sunday but recovered well enough to shoot a 71, for a 272 total – good enough to tie Perera (who made three late birdies to shoot 70) and Chowrasia, who'd posted eight birdies while charging home with the day's low round, a six-under-par 66. Their playoff lasted but a single hole, with Chowrasia quickly holing a 15-foot birdie putt at the 18th to clinch the title.

1	S.S.P Chowrasia	70-71-69-66	276	$54,000	15=	Chiragh Kumar	71-72-72-67	282	$4,065
2=	Mithun Perera	70-67-69-70	276	$25,950		Shamim Khan	72-71-70-69	282	$4,065
	Rahil Gangjee	66-68-71-71	276	$25,950	17	Martin Rominger	73-70-73-67	283	$3,795
4	Shubhankar Sharma	73-65-68-71	277	$15,000	18=	Blair Wilson	70-72-73-69	284	$3,475
5=	Akinori Tani	71-72-67-68	278	$10,280		Manav Jaini	71-71-72-70	284	$3,475
	Unho Park	69-71-68-70	278	$10,280		Tze Huang Choo	68-73-71-72	284	$3,475
	Siddikur Rahman	70-67-69-72	278	$10,280	21=	Abhinav Lohan	72-72-73-68	285	$3,225
8=	J. Janewattananond	69-70-71-69	279	$6,885		Vikrant Chopra	74-68-70-73	285	$3,225
	Panuphol Pittayarat	70-68-69-72	279	$6,885	23=	Terry Pilkadaris	69-68-76-73	286	$3,045
10	Rashid Khan	68-70-71-71	280	$5,730		Chikka S	72-69-71-74	286	$3,045
11=	Shankar Das	69-71-73-68	281	$4,748	25=	Thaworn Wiratchant	75-72-72-69	288	$2,820
	A. Sriboonkaew	73-70-68-70	281	$4,74		Om Prak. Chouhan	69-72-73-74	288	$2,820
	Lionel Weber	73-66-69-73	281	$4,748		Zamal Hossai	68-75-70-75	288	$2,820
	Wade Ormsby	68-68-70-75	281	$4,748					

In The Money: **289**: Vinod Kumar, Angad Cheema, Sanjay Kumar, Anura Rohana **290**: Pawan Kumar, Pratap Atwal (a) **291**: Settee Prakongvech, Shivaram Shrestha, George Gandranata, Rory Hie, K. Prabagaran, Kapil Kumar, Abhishek Jha **292**: Thammanoon Sriroj, Rahul Bajaj, Deng Shan Koh **293**: Carl Santos-Ocampo, Ajeetesh Sandhu, Deepinder Singh Kullar, M.D. Sanju **294**: C. Muniyappa, K.P. Sekhon, Mukesh Kumar **296**: Vishal Singh, Jack Munro **297**: Phachara Khongwatmai, Jarin Todd, Sanjeev Kumar **298**: N. Thangaraja, Scott Barr, Chih Bing Lam, Ajay Baisoya, Arshdeep Tiwana **299**: Wasim Khan, Peter Vejgaard **300**: Thitiphun Chuayprakong, Feroz Ali **301**: Zaw Moe, Akshay Sharma **302**: Abhishek Kuhar **305**: Ashbeer Saini, Rinaldi Adiyandono

OWR: 0 of top 50 entered - Rating: 0 - Points to 17th - Chowrasia: 14 points, to 229th in OWR

Chiangmai Golf Classic

Nov 13 - Nov 16

Alpine Golf Resort - Chiangmai, Thailand
Champion: Rashid Khan

7,471 yards   Par 72
Purse: $750,000

India's 23-year-old Rashid Khan won for the second time on the 2014 Asian Tour, methodically carving out a Sunday 68 to claim a one-shot victory over countryman Jyoti Randhawa and Thailand's Thanyakon Khrongpha at the Chiangmai Golf Classic. Initially, it appeared as though the week might belong to one of the co-runners-up, as Randhawa's opening rounds of 68-65 were good enough to hold a one-shot halfway lead over Khrongpha, with the nearest pursuers – Khan and Australian Scott Barr – another three shots back. Randhawa would post a 70 on Saturday, however, which allowed Khrongpha (67) to assume the top spot, two up on both Randhawa and Khan, as the latter logged five birdies en route to a back nine 31 and a third round 66. But on Sunday Khrongpha could do no better than a 71, and while Randhawa played admirably in posting a 69, Khan went him one better by riding four birdies over his final 10 holes to a 68, and the title.

1	Rashid Khan	68-69-66-68	271	$135,000		Brett Munson	73-70-67-70	280	$10,613
2=	Jyoti Randhawa	68-65-70-69	272	$64,875	16=	Miguel Tabuena	70-72-71-68	281	$8,538
	T. Khrongpha	69-65-67-71	272	$64,875		Javi Colomo	73-72-68-68	281	$8,538
4	K. Aphibarnrat	69-70-66-69	274	$37,500		Chikka S	69-72-71-69	281	$8,538
5=	Mithun Perera	70-70-67-68	275	$27,863		Paul Peterson	70-70-71-70	281	$8,538
	Kalem Richardson	71-69-64-71	275	$27,863		Scott Hend	72-69-70-70	281	$8,538
7=	Jason Dufner	69-69-73-66	277	$17,531		Joong kyung Mo	69-69-72-71	281	$8,538
	Danny Chia	74-68-68-67	277	$17,531		George Gandranata	66-72-72-71	281	$8,538
	Jbe' Kruger	73-66-68-70	277	$17,531		Terry Pilkadaris	70-71-69-71	281	$8,538
	Scott Barr	68-69-67-73	277	$17,531		Wen-Tang Lin	69-71-69-72	281	$8,538
11=	Panuphol Pittayarat	68-75-66-69	278	$12,638	25=	Mardan Mamat	67-72-71-72	282	$7,050
	Chien-Yao Hung	71-68-66-73	278	$12,638		Rory Hie	70-70-70-72	282	$7,050
13	N. Tantipokhakul	71-70-68-70	279	$11,363		Daisuke Kataoka	70-71-66-75	282	$7,050
14=	S. Kooratanapisan	70-69-71-70	280	$10,613					

In The Money: **283**: Martin Rominger, Prom Meesawat, Sung Lee **284**: Chris Rodgers, Chawalit Plaphol, Chiragh Kumar, Suppakorn Uthaipat, Rattanon Wannasrichan **285**: Tze Huang Choo, Piya Swangarunporn, Adam Groom, Jeung-Hun Wang, Simon Yates, Seung-Yul Noh **286**: Charl Schwartzel, Kieran Pratt, Jazz Janewattananond, Michael Tran **287**: Shubhankar Sharma, Chapchai Nirat **288**: Jay Bayron, Ncholas Fung, Unho Park, Sattaya Supupramai, Udorn Duangdecha **289**: Sam Brazel **290**: Wei-Chih Lu, Richard T. Lee, Phiphatphong Naewsuk, Poosit Supupramai, Bryce Easton **291**: Jack Munro **292**: Wolmer Murillo, M Dharma, Mathiam Keyser **293**: Abhijit Chadha **294**: Akinori Tani, Berry Henson **295**: Pijit Petchkasem, Thaworn Wiratchant **296**: Grant Jackson **297**: Wen-Hong Lin, Jarin Todd **299**: Anthony Kang

OWR: 2 of top 50 entered - Rating: 49 - Points to 24th - Khan: 16 points, to 204th in OWR

Resorts World Manila Masters

Nov 20 - Nov 23

Manila Southwoods Golf & Country Club - Manila, Philippines
Champion: Mardan Mamat

7,152 yards   Par 72
Purse: $1 Million

At age 47, winless since 2012 and in danger of losing his Asian Tour card, Singapore's Mardan Mamat was looking at a murky future prior to the Resorts World Manila Masters, but all of that turned around via an impressive wire-to-wire victory at the Manila Southwoods Golf and Country Club. Mamat's week began with a bang as he birdied four of his first seven holes en route to a seven-under-par 65, good enough to hold a share of the lead with Japan's Daisuke Kataoka, who opted to play here over his home circuit's Dunlop Phoenix event. Kataoka would fade to a 73 on Friday, however, leaving Mamat to post a 68 and now share the top spot with South Korean Jeung-Hun Wang, who managed nine birdies in carding a 65. Mamat was not to be headed on the weekend, however, as he opened his third round with four straight birdies and never looked back, eventually returning a 66 that gave him a four-shot lead over Kiradech Aphibarnrat and five over France's Lionel Weber. He then turned in 34 on Sunday before cruising home to a 69, and a runaway six-shot victory.

1	Mardan Mamat	65-68-66-69	268	$180,000		Arie Irawan	71-71-67-71	280	$15,195
2	Lionel Weber	70-70-64-70	274	$110,000		Danny Chia	66-71-71-72	280	$15,195
3	Prom Meesawat	73-72-63-68	276	$63,000		Daisuke Kataoka	65-73-70-72	280	$15,195
4=	Sam Brazel	67-75-67-69	278	$38,200		Jbe' Kruger	70-73-64-73	280	$15,195
	Chien-Yao Hung	67-71-69-71	278	$38,200		Berry Henson	74-68-64-74	280	$15,195
	Paul Peterson	68-70-69-71	278	$38,200	20=	R. Wannasrichan	75-67-71-68	281	$10,738
	K. Aphibarnrat	66-69-68-75	278	$38,200		Sattaya Supupramai	74-68-70-69	281	$10,738
8	Nicholas Fung	69-69-68-73	279	$24,500		George Gandranata	70-70-69-72	281	$10,738
9=	Thaworn Wiratchant	75-70-68-67	280	$15,195		Shiv Kapur	69-73-67-72	281	$10,738
	Akinori Tani	72-69-70-69	280	$15,195	24=	Wen-Teh Lu	68-72-75-67	282	$9,550
	Scott Hend	73-69-69-69	280	$15,195		Chris Rodgers	73-69-69-71	282	$9,550
	Jeung-Hun Wang	68-65-77-70	280	$15,195		Steve Lewton	71-66-73-72	282	$9,550
	Chiragh Kumar	72-71-67-70	280	$15,195		Simon Yates	70-72-67-73	282	$9,550
	T. Chuayprakong	71-68-70-71	280	$15,195					

In The Money: Jazz Janewattananond, Scott Barr, Adilson da Silva, Richard T. Lee, Javi Colomo **284**: Himmat Rai, Elmer Salvador, Unho Park, Arjun Atwal, Jake Higginbottom **285**: Rahil Gangjee, Juvic Pagunsan, Chapchai Nirat **286**: Chih Bing Lam **287**: Shih-Chang Chan, Wei-Chih Lu, Kieran Pratt, Wen-Chong Liang, Kalem Richardson **288**: In-Woo Lee, Chinnarat Phadungsil, Adam Groom, Miguel Tabuena, Bryce Easton **289**: Arnond Vongvanij, Jeev Milkha Singh, Joonas Granberg, Antonio Lascuña **290**: Rashid Khan **291**: Jhonnel Ababa, Clyde Mondilla, Siddikur Rahman, Terry Pilkadaris **292**: Pariya Junhasavasdikul **294**: Benjie Magada, Frankie Minoza, Mithun Perera **295**: Joenard Rates, Anthony Kang

OWR: 0 of top 50 entered - Rating: 11 - Points to 19th - Mamat: 14 points, to 452nd in OWR

King's Cup
Nov 27 - Nov 30

Singha Park Khon Kaen Golf Club - Tambol Taphra, Thailand
Champion: Thaworn Wiratchant

7,502 yards   Par 72
Purse: $500,000

Less than 12 months after Prayad Marksaeng won the event's previous playing, Thaworn Wiratchant became the second late-40s Thai star to win the King's Cup on native soil, claiming his 18th career Asian Tour win by a two-stroke margin. Wiratchant played some very solid golf throughout the week, opening with rounds of 68-67 to trail halfway leader Anirban Lahiri by three, then adding a bogey-free 66 (anchored by five straight birdies at holes 2-6) to narrow the gap to one on Saturday night. Lahiri would get off to a slow start on Sunday, turning in 35, then making two birdies and a bogey coming home to post a 270 aggregate. That number was matched by Australian Andrew Dodt, who charged home with birdies on each of his final three holes to push into contention. But in the end, Wiratchant's domination of the front nine again proved the story as he made birdies on five of his first 10 holes, eventually marching home in 67 to claim the trophy.

1	Thaworn Wiratchant	68-67-66-67	268	$90,000		Steve Lewton	71-68-70-68	277	$7,242
2=	Andrew Dodt	69-65-69-67	270	$43,250		Chan Kim	72-66-70-69	277	$7,242
	Anirban Lahiri	65-67-68-70	270	$43,250	16=	Daniel Chopra	67-72-72-67	278	$5,868
4=	Kalem Richardson	66-72-68-67	273	$20,717		Adam Groom	70-66-74-68	278	$5,868
	Danthai Boonma	66-70-68-69	273	$20,717		Mardan Mamat	68-71-70-69	278	$5,868
	Paul Peterson	69-68-67-69	273	$20,717		S.S.P Chowrasia	65-71-70-72	278	$5,868
7=	R. Wannasrichan	71-68-67-68	274	$13,250		P. Naewsuk	66-71-69-72	278	$5,868
	Panuphol Pittayarat	68-69-66-71	274	$13,250		Carlos Pigem	67-69-69-73	278	$5,868
9=	P. Khongwatmai	71-71-65-68	275	$9,658		S. Kooratanapisan	70-68-65-75	278	$5,868
	Prom Meesawat	68-69-67-71	275	$9,658	23=	Supravee Phatam	69-70-72-68	279	$4,925
	J. Premsirigorn	69-65-69-72	275	$9,658		Antonio Lascuña	68-71-71-69	279	$4,925
12	Jack Munro	69-71-70-66	276	$8,125		C. Phadungsil	70-68-70-71	279	$4,925
13=	Rashid Khan	71-69-71-66	277	$7,242		Mathiam Keyser	68-69-68-74	279	$4,925

In The Money: **280**: Scott Barr, Bryce Easton, Sung Lee, Gi-Whan Kim **281**: Annop Tangkamolprasert, Atthaphon Sriboonkaew, Jeung-Hun Wang, Tirawat Kaewsiribandit, Chawalit Plaphol, Simon Griffiths, Somkiat Srisa-Nga, Itthipat Buranatanyarat **282**: Chris Gaunt, Udorn Duangdecha, Arie Irawan, Porameth Sonthirati, Piya Swanggarunporn, Seuk-Hyun Vaek, Poosit Supupramai, Sam Cyr, Blair Wilson **283**: Sattaya Supupramai **284**: Michael Tran, Pariya Junhasavasdikul, Jazz Janewattananond, Sam Brazel, Teerawat Poipong **285**: Jarin Todd, Angelo Que, Hyung-Joon Lee, Kwanchai Tannin, Arjun Atwal **286**: Pavit Tangkamolprasert, Pigit Petchkasem, Ronnachai Jamnong, Joong Kyung Mo **287**: Varut Chomchalam, Chikka S **288**: Nirun Sae-Ueng, Akinori Tani **289**: Ye Htet Aung (a), Arnond Vonvanij, Craig Hinton **290**: Chris Rodgers **291**: Kieran Pratt **293**: Deng Shan Koh, Ratchaphol Juntavara **294**: James Bowen **298**: Pasavee Lertvilai **300**: Nattapong Putta

OWR: 0 of top 50 entered - Rating: 11 - Points to 22nd - Wiratchant: 14 points, to 172nd in OWR

Bank BRI Indonesia Open
Dec 4 - Dec 7

Damai Indah Golf - Jakarta, Indonesia
Champion: Padraig Harrington

7,120 yards   Par 72
Purse: $750,000

Breaking a drought that dated all the way back to 2010, three-time Major champion Padraig Harrington overcame some early final round nerves to hold on for his second career Asian Tour victory at the Bank BRI Indonesia Open. It was very nearly a wire-to-wire run for Harrington, as his eight-birdie opening round 64 just missed sharing the lead with Australia's Kalem Richardson, who posted a 63. Harrington then made five birdies and an eagle during Friday's second round, with the resulting 66 lifting him into a tie for the lead with Thailand's Thanyakon Khrongpha, who made nine birdies en route to posting a 63 of his own. But while Khrongpha slipped to a 71 on Saturday, Harrington added a smooth 67, and suddenly he held a commanding four-shot 54-hole lead. There was a modest stumble on Sunday, however, as the 43-year-old Irishman bogeyed the par-5 1st and double-bogeyed the par-3 7th. A bounce back birdie at the 8th restored order, however, before birdies on both the back nine par 5s (the 13th and 17th) eventually provided the margin of victory.

1	Padraig Harrington	64-66-67-71	268	$135,000		Jarin Todd	69-64-74-70	277	$11,463
2	T. Khrongpha	67-63-71-69	270	$82,500	15=	Anirban Lahiri	74-66-66-72	278	$9,713
3	Nathan Holman	69-63-70-69	271	$47,250		Andrew Dodt	70-69-69-70	278	$9,713
4	Quincy Quek	71-67-68-66	272	$37,500		Sung Lee	70-72-70-66	278	$9,713
5	Sattaya Supupramai	73-67-67-67	274	$30,750		George Gandranata	69-68-68-73	278	$9,713
6	David Lipsky	72-68-66-69	275	$24,975	19=	S.S.P Chowrasia	68-71-68-72	279	$8,175
7=	Jake Higginbottom	71-69-72-64	276	$16,643		Jordan Irawan	71-67-71-70	279	$8,175
	Terry Pikadaris	69-70-68-69	276	$16,643		Danny Chia	68-69-71-71	279	$8,175
	Jyoti Randhawa	71-68-71-66	276	$16,643		Scott Barr	69-67-70-73	279	$8,175
	Sam Brazel	68-68-69-71	276	$16,643		T. Chuayprakong	69-66-73-71	279	$8,175
	Scott Hend	69-64-75-68	276	$16,643	24=	Mithun Perera	69-71-71-69	280	$7,050
12=	Berry Henson	72-69-70-66	277	$11,463		C. Phadungsil	73-68-68-71	280	$7,050
	Jeung-Hun Wang	70-66-76-65	277	$11,463		Carlos Pigem	68-69-69-74	280	$7,050

In The Money: **281**: Tirawat Kaewsiribandit, Joong Kyung Mo, Masahiro Kawamura, Chawalit Plaphol, Simon Yates **282**: Rattanon Wannasrichan, Chapchai Nirat, Bryce Easton, Chih Bing Lam **283**: Unho Park, Arjun Atwal, Pavit Tangkamolptasert, Chris Gaunt, Fadhli Rahman Soetarso, Kieran Pratt, Mardan Mamat, Nicholas Fung **284**: Panuphol Pittayarat, Sutijet Kooratanapisan, Daniel Chopra **285**: Panuwat Muenlek, Lionel Weber, Paul Peterson, Suppakorn Uthaipat, Miguel Tabuena, Adam Groom Javi Colomo, Kalem Richardson **286**: Tirto Tamardi (a), Chiragh Kumar, Poosit Supupramai, Yoshinobu Tsukada, Wen-Teh Lu **287**: Wolmer Murillo, Gi-Whan Kim **288**: Steve Lewton **289**: Byung-Joo Park, Mao-Chang Sung **290**: Martin Rominger **292**: Shih-Chang Chan, Kunal Bhasin **295**: Shubhankar Sharma **WD**: Johannes Dermawan (143), Settee Prakonvech (143)

OWR: 0 of top 50 entered - Rating: 12 - Points to 18th - Harrington: 14 points, to 260th in OWR

Thailand Golf Championship

Dec 11 - Dec 14

Amata Spring Country Club - Chon Buri, Thailand
Champion: Lee Westwood

7,453 yards Par 72
Purse: $1 Million

Few Western golfers have enjoyed as much success in the Far East as Lee Westwood, and the 41-year-old Englishman added further to that ledger at the Thailand Golf Championship, where he closed with a Sunday-low 67 to beat Martin Kaymer and third-round leader Marcus Fraser by one. Coming to the close of a somewhat disappointing season, Westwood opened with rounds of 70-71-72, good enough to stand only two behind Fraser in a week when steady winds combined with a tough course set-up to produce high scoring. Sunday would see Westwood, Fraser and Kaymer battle throughout with the trio standing tied through the first 16 holes. Westwood, for his part, carded steady pars and the 17th and 18th, while reigning U.S. Open champion Kaymer bogeyed the 17th. That left it up to Fraser to keep pace at the last but under immense pressure, he missed a short par putt to hand Westwood the victory. India's Anirban Lahiri closed with a 73 to tie for sixth, allowing American David Lipsky to clinch the Asian Order of Merit title even with the inaugural Dubai Open left to play.

1	Lee Westwood	70-71-72-67	280	$180,000		Charlie Wi	74-72-71-71	288	$14,483
2=	Martin Kaymer	71-72-70-68	281	$86,500	16=	Kodai Ichihara	78-68-72-71	289	$12,950
	Marcus Fraser	69-72-70-70	281	$86,500		Daisuke Kataoka	74-73-71-71	289	$12,950
4	Tommy Fleetwood	71-69-73-70	283	$50,000	18=	Danny Chia	77-74-72-67	290	$11,413
5	Scott Hend	70-74-71-69	284	$41,000		Berry Henson	73-72-74-71	290	$11,413
6=	Thongchai Jaidee	72-71-74-68	285	$28,767		Jeung-Hun Wang	73-72-73-72	290	$11,413
	Jonathan Moore	71-71-72-71	285	$28,767		Unho Park	76-74-68-72	290	$11,413
	Anirban Lahiri	71-73-68-73	285	$28,767	22=	Ashun Wu	71-75-75-70	291	$10,300
9	Sergio García	71-75-71-69	286	$21,400		Masahiro Kawamura	72-74-74-71	291	$10,300
10=	K. Aphibarnrat	76-72-71-68	287	$17,600		Hiroshi Iwata	72-78-69-72	291	$10,300
	Paul Peterson	71-72-75-69	287	$17,600	25=	Sebastien Gros	75-75-72-70	292	$9,250
	Terry Pilkadaris	77-69-72-69	287	$17,600		Bubba Watson	76-70-77-69	292	$9,250
13=	T. Khrongpha	69-77-73-69	288	$14,483		Mu Hu	72-74-74-72	292	$9,250
	Bernd Wiesberger	76-74-68-70	288	$14,483		Wei-Chih Lu	69-77-73-73	292	$9,250

In The Money: **293**: Anthony Kang, Shingo Katayama, Lionel Weber, Sung-Hoon Kang, Chinnarat Phadungsil, Tian-Lang Guan (a), Andrew Dodt, Matthew Stieger, Simon Griffiths **294**: Nathan Holman, Pavit Tangkamolprasert, Richard T. Lee, Kieran Pratt, David Lipsky, Marcus Both **295**: Chien-Yao Hung **296**: Javi Colomo, Thaworn Wiratchant, Gaganjeet Bhullar, Hao Tong Li, Jazz Janewattananond **297**: Chris Rodgers, Prayad Marksaeng, Darren Clarke, Koumei Oda, Scott Barr **298**: S.S.P. Chowrasia, Chriagh Kumar, Chapchai Nirat, Jakraphan Premsirigorn **299**: Mithun Perera, Wen-Tang Lin, Sam Cyr, Carlos Pigem, Bryce Easton, Joonas Granberg **300**: Arjun Atwal, Mardan Mamat, Yoshinobu Tsukada, Pawin Ingkhapradit **301**: Kalem Richardson, Sutijet Kooratanapisan **302**: Chris Gaunt, Wolmer Murillo, Tirawat Kaewsiribandit **303**: Martin Rominger **304**: Antonio Murdaca (a), Prom Meesawat, Boonchu Ruangkit **305**: Quincy Quek **309**: Joong-Kyung Mo

OWR: 6 of top 50 entered - Rating: 176 - Points to 43rd - Westwood: 34 points, to 26th in OWR

Dubai Open

Dec 18 - Dec 21

Els Golf Club - Dubai, U.A.E.
Champion: Arjun Atwal

7,538 yards Par 72
Purse: $500,000

Ending an injury enhanced drought that dated to 2010, 41-year-old Arjun Atwal birdied the 72nd hole to win the inaugural Dubai Open by a single shot over Korean teenager Jeung-Hun Wang. The week hardly looked to be Atwal's after he opened with a disappointing 73, but the veteran Indian bounced back with middle rounds of 65-68 to pull himself into a four-way tie for the lead through 54 holes. He then charged out in 32 on Sunday, setting up a final nine battle with the talented Wang, who actually stood one ahead through 16 holes. Both men bogeyed the par-3 17th before Wang buckled, bogeying the par-5 finisher, looking on as Atwal birdied to steal the title.

1	Arjun Atwal	73-65-68-66	272	$90,000		R. Wannasrichan	75-70-67-67	279	$6,475
2	Jeung-Hun Wang	71-67-68-67	273	$55,000		T. Chuayprakong	70-71-67-71	279	$6,475
3	Simon Yates	71-67-69-68	275	$31,500		Darren Clarke	72-71-64-72	279	$6,475
4=	Jake Higginbottom	72-71-69-64	276	$22,750	19=	Terry Pilkadaris	71-71-70-68	280	$5,450
	Thaworn Wiratchant	74-69-65-68	276	$22,750		N. Tantipokhakul	71-72-68-69	280	$5,450
6=	Carlos Pigem	70-73-68-66	277	$12,680		P. Pittayarat	69-72-68-71	280	$5,450
	Daisuke Kataoka	73-66-68-70	277	$12,680		Matthew Fitzpatrick	70-71-68-71	280	$5,450
	P. Junhasavasdikul	68-72-67-70	277	$12,680		Javi Colomo	69-73-67-71	280	$5,450
	Chapchai Nirat	71-69-67-70	277	$12,680	24=	Chawalit Plaphol	71-69-72-69	281	$4,550
	Jbe' Kruger	70-72-64-71	277	$12,680		Christopher Cannon	67-74-71-69	281	$4,550
11=	Bryce Easton	69-71-69-69	278	$7,913		Chih Bing Lam	67-74-70-70	281	$4,550
	Joong-Kyung Mo	70-71-68-69	278	$7,913		Poosit Supupramai	72-72-67-70	281	$4,550
	Gaganjeet Bhullar	69-69-69-71	278	$7,913		Thammanoon Sriroj	72-72-67-70	281	$4,550
	Shiv Kapur	71-66-69-72	278	$7,913		Prom Meesawat	71-68-70-72	281	$4,550
15=	Unho Park	75-68-69-67	279	$6,475		Joshua White	71-68-70-72	281	$4,550

In The Money: **282**: Jeev Milkha Singh, Jazz Janewattananond, Joonas Granberg, Nicholas Fung **283**: Daniel Chopra, Danny Chia **284**: Gi-Whan Kim, Craig Hinton **285**: Shih-Chang Chan, Sung Lee, Richard Finch **286**: Pavit Tangkamolprasert, Chinnarat Phadungsil **287**: Ross McGowan, Marcus Both **288**: Carlos Balmaseda, Tylar Hogarty, Hamza Amin, Kalem Richardson, Lee Cornfield **289**: Luke Joy, Kieran Pratt, Dominic Foos. Matthew Stieger, Mardan Mamat **290**: Anthony Kang, Tze Huang Choo **291**: Angelo Que, Scott Barr **292**: Masahiro Kawamura, Stuart Archibald **293**: Simon Griffiths, Zane Scotland **296**: Mehdi Saissai (a), Nathan Holman **299**: Younes El Hassani

OWR: 0 of top 50 entered - Rating: 19 - Points to 18th - Atwal: 14 points, to 432nd

SUNSHINE TOUR
2014

Though hardly the only major tour to utilize a calendar-crossing "wraparound" schedule, the 2014 Sunshine Tour was particularly tricky in this regard – though it was arguably improved from 2013, when the schedule ran into the new year but a December Order of Merit list was marked "Final" regardless. This time, with an apparent desire to see its limited-field Investec Cup (played in mid-March) serve as the circuit's final event, the Tour listed a total of four significant 2015 events as a part of 2014 despite the fact that their actual 2014 playings were initially (though apparently no longer) considered a part of this same schedule. So where does 2014 end and 2015 actually begin? Apparently we'll have to wait for the next Order of Merit list that is marked "Final" in order to find out for certain.

As of the last event of calendar 2014 (December's Alfred Dunhill Championship), the Order of Merit was topped by 23-year-old Danie van Tonder, one of South Africa's more highly rated prospects and the winner of both the Royal Swazi Open (an event contested with Stableford scoring) and the first tournament in the six-event Vodacom Origins of Golf series, at Euphoria. Van Tonder's late climb to the top was significant because it allowed the year to end with an actual full-time Sunshine Tour player leading the Order of Merit – no small accomplishment since the next four men in line (England's Ross Fisher and native stars Thomas Aiken, Branden Grace and George Coetzee) all lacked the requisite number of starts to officially be considered. And here lies an issue which has affected the Tour for a number of years: the difficulty that a less heavily sponsored circuit has in keeping its native stars playing at home. In South Africa, the problem is actually less pressing than elsewhere simply because with the European Tour often co-sanctioning as many as eight tournaments a season, most of these homegrown stars make at least semi-regular appearances on native soil. Still, the discrepancy between these events and the far weaker Winter portion of the schedule is considerable; indeed, the OWR awards less than half as many minimum winner's points to the latter, making this, in effect, two separate tours playing under a single schedule.

And the requisite procedural point: The 2014 South African Open, Alfred Dunhill Championship, Nedbank Golf Challenge, Nelson Mandela Championship, Volvo Golf Champions, Joburg Open, Africa Open and Tshwane Open all appear under the European Tour's section.

Player Of The Year: Danie van Tonder

It is always tempting to name one of South Africa's elite international stars as Sunshine Tour Player Of The Year, but it's a difficult thing to do when they make so few domestic starts beyond E Tour co-sanctioned events. The race among full-time players was close in 2014 but 23-year-old Danie van Tonder - a two time winner and December leader in the Order of Merit - takes the honor by a nose.

2014 Sunshine Tour Top 60 Money Winners

#	Player	Winnings	#	Player	Winnings	#	Player	Winnings
1	Danie van Tonder	R3,827,261	21	Morten Ørum Madsen	R824,463	41	Erik van Rooyen	R476,203
2	Ross Fisher	R3,666,990	22	Jacques Blaauw	R813,149	42	Tyrone Ferreira	R465,856
3	Thomas Aiken	R3,607,017	23	Adilson da Silva	R736,540	43	Michael Hollick	R427,934
4	Branden Grace	R3,347,754	24	Oliver Bekker	R724,316	44	James Kamte	R418,047
5	George Coetzee	R3,339,251	25	Haydn Porteous	R711,198	45	Richard Sterne	R406,418
6	Louis Oosthuizen	R2,469,997	26	Wallie Coetsee	R710,940	46	P.H. McIntyre	R381,945
7	Trevor Fisher Jr	R1,780,128	27	Jared Harvey	R643,053	47	Peter Karmis	R379,085
8	Justin Walters	R1,752,677	28	Lucas Bjerregaard	R622,413	48	Dawie Van der Walt	R364,172
9	Darren Fichardt	R1,645,158	29	Shaun Norris	R619,176	49	Brandon Stone	R345,000
10	Hennie Otto	R1,527,507	30	Tjaart van der Walt	R605,923	50	Charl Schwartzel	R340,357
11	Jean Hugo	R1,405,217	31	Estanislao Goya	R599,097	51	Colin Nel	R330,020
12	Ulrich van den Berg	R1,385,864	32	Ruan de Smidt	R590,125	52	Dean Burmester	R328,646
13	Keith Horne	R1,265,492	33	Grégory Bourdy	R586,189	53	C.J. du Plessis	R324,859
14	Justin Harding	R1,184,396	34	Christiaan Basson	R584,416	54	Andrew Georgiou	R316,720
15	Jbe' Kruger	R1,049,193	35	Heinrich Bruiners	R561,197	55	James Kingston	R311,769
16	Jaco Van Zyl	R1,026,327	36	Alex Haindl	R520,762	56	Dylan Frittelli	R310,497
17	Jaco Ahlers	R1,020,826	37	J.J. Senekal	R520,562	57	Warren Abery	R308,705
18	Merrick Bremner	R904,817	38	Jake Roos	R489,266	58	Vaughn Groenewald	R290,991
19	Titch Moore	R866,352	39	Neil Schietekat	R484,897	59	Jake Redman	R282,006
20	Louis de Jager	R857,271	40	Andrew Curlewis	R477,976	60	Rhys West	R267,247

Dimension Data Pro-Am	**Feb 20 - Feb 23**
Fancourt Golf Estate (Montagu) - George, South Africa	7,342 yards Par 72
Fancourt Golf Estate (Outeniqua) - George, South Africa	6,903 yards Par 72
Fancourt Golf Estate (Links) - George, South Africa	7,579 yards Par 73
Champion: Estanislao Goya	Purse: R4,000,000

With the European Tour taking the week off (in deference to the WGC-Accenture Match Play) between its final two South African stops of 2014, numerous E Tour regulars entered the Sunshine Tour's Dimension Data Pro-Am, with one of them - 25-year-old Argentinean Estanislao "Tano" Goya - emerging as champion. Formerly a winner (at age 20) of the E Tour's light-field 2008 Madeira Islands Open, Goya struggled with his game in 2013 (only regaining E Tour status via Q School) but rediscovered his form this week in Fancourt, opening slowly with a 73 before a pair of 67s left him four behind 54-hole leader Adilson da Silva. The field moved from a three-course rotation onto the Montagu course for Sunday's finale where Goya initially struggled, going out in one-over-par 37. But he heated up on the inward half, logging five birdies - including the coup de grâce at the par-5 18th - to win by one. Denmark's Lucas Bjerregaard (who carded the day's low round, a 66) tied for second along with Sunshine Tour veterans da Silva, Keith Horne and Jean Hugo.

1	Estanislao Goya	73-67-67-68	275	R594,375		Justin Harding	72-66-72-70	280	R55,125
2=	Lucas Bjerregaard	68-73-69-66	276	R257,438		Wallie Coetsee	69-69-72-70	280	R55,125
	Keith Horne	71-66-69-70	276	R257,438		Jake Redman	69-74-65-72	280	R55,125
	Jean Hugo	68-67-70-71	276	R257,438		Trevor Fisher Jr	70-68-67-75	280	R55,125
	Adilson da Silva	67-66-70-73	276	R257,438	18=	Rhys Davies	69-72-69-71	281	R45,875
6=	Jaco Van Zyl	67-73-67-70	277	R121,688		Dawie Van der Walt	69-73-69-70	281	R45,875
	Morten O. Madsen	67-72-66-72	277	R121,688		Francois Coetzee	68-69-69-75	281	R45,875
8	Jack Doherty	68-70-73-67	278	R92,250	21=	Jens Dantorp	69-70-71-72	282	R42,188
9=	Hennie Otto	72-71-66-70	279	R73,875		Oliver Bekker	69-68-74-71	282	R42,188
	Warren Abery	68-72-68-71	279	R73,875	23=	Jacques Kruyswijk	69-71-75-68	283	R39,375
	Rhys Enoch	77-67-66-69	279	R73,875		Jbe' Kruger	72-70-71-70	283	R39,375
12=	Michael Hollick	76-66-71-67	280	R55,125		Charl Coetzee	69-71-70-73	283	R39,375
	Jaco Ahlers	71-69-71-69	280	R55,125					

In The Money: **284**: Phillip Archer, Daniel Greene, Daniel Im **285**: Jacques Blaauw, Kevin Phelan, Dean Burmester, Alex Haindl, Haydn Porteous, Justin Walters **286**: Shaun Norris, Brinson Paolini, Alan Dunbar, Jake Roos, Louis de Jager, Ryan Cairns, Andrew Curlewis **287**: Andrew Marshall, Doug McGuigan **288**: Daniel Brooks, Danie van Tonder, Neil Schietekat, Jared Harvey, Duncan Stewart, Drikus Bruyns, Merrick Bremner **289**: Phillip Price, Peter Karmis, C.J. du Plessis, Van Phillips **290**: Lyle Rowe, Teboho Sefatsa, Ulrich van den Berg, Richard Finch **291**: Ockie Strydom, Thomas Aiken, Chris Lloyd, Juan Langeveld, Colin Nel, Keenan Davidse **293**: James Kingston, Gideon Pienaar, Mark Murless **295**: Oscar Stark, Tyrone Mordt **299**: Sam Walker

OWR: 0 of top 50 entered - Rating: 14 - Points to 17th - Goya: 14 points, to 434th in OWR

Investec Cup	**Mar 20 - Mar 23**
Millvale Private Retreat - Koster, South Africa	7,401 yards Par 72
Lost City Golf Club - Sun City, South Africa	6,983 yards Par 72
Champion: Trevor Fisher Jr.	Purse: R1 Million

Trevor Fisher Jr. survived a last-minute charge from Jacques Blaauw to claim his eighth career Sunshine Tour win – and the R3.5 million bonus pool payday – at the second playing of the select-field Investec Classic, in Sun City. Fisher began the final round one stroke behind 54-hole leader George Coetzee and proceeded to play nearly flawless golf, making eagle at the par-5 4th en route to turning in 33, then adding birdies at 11, 12 and 15 to build what seemed an insurmountable lead. Things got exciting, however, after Blaauw eagled the short par-5 18th to suddenly close the gap from three to one – but Fisher, unaware of the narrowed margin, logged a routine par at the last to close out the victory. Defending champion Jaco Van Zyl charged home with weekend rounds of 65-66 to tie veteran Keith Horne for third, while Coetzee – who made two double bogeys en route to posting Sunday's highest score among the top 10 finishers – took solo fifth.

1	Trevor Fisher Jr	69-70-67-66	272	R163,400		Ulrich van den Berg	70-73-71-69	283	R24,100
2	Jacques Blaauw	67-73-67-66	273	R117,700	15=	Thomas Aiken	74-70-72-68	284	R21,400
3=	Jaco Van Zyl	71-72-65-66	274	R59,950		Morten O. Madsen	74-75-67-68	284	R21,400
	Keith Horne	70-68-69-67	274	R59,950		Lucas Bjerregaard	65-72-75-72	284	R21,400
5	George Coetzee	68-67-70-71	276	R42,600	18	Andrew Curlewis	75-69-74-67	285	R19,800
6=	Jbe' Kruger	68-72-71-66	277	R35,450	19=	Richard Finch	76-71-73-67	287	R19,200
	Dawie Van der Walt	74-70-64-69	277	R35,450		Danie van Tonder	76-70-73-68	287	R19,200
8	Jean Hugo	71-69-70-68	278	R32,400	21=	Justin Harding	74-72-74-69	289	R18,300
9	Darren Fichardt	73-70-66-70	279	R30,300		Oliver Fisher	72-74-71-72	289	R18,300
10	Adilson da Silva	75-70-67-69	281	R28,800	23	Oliver Bekker	76-77-70-67	290	R17,700
11=	Jake Roos	75-68-72-67	282	R26,700	24	Ross Fisher	77-71-73-70	291	R17,300
	Merrick Bremner	69-69-71-73	282	R26,700	25	Warren Abery	78-73-68-73	292	R16,900
13=	Hennie Otto	73-74-68-68	283	R24,100					

In The Money: **293**: Jaco Ahlers **294**: Justin Walters **295**: John Hahn **299**: Titch Moore **302**: Michael Hollick

OWR: 0 of top 50 entered - Rating: 30 - Points to 17th - Fisher: 14 points, to 195th in OWR

Telkom PGA Championship

Country Club Johannesburg - Johannesburg, South Africa
Champion: Titch Moore

Apr 3 - Apr 6
7,546 yards   Par 72
Purse: R3,750,000

Titch Moore ended a six-year Sunshine Tour victory drought in Johannesburg, being the only player to break 70 all four days en route to a marathon playoff victory over Ulrich van den Berg at the Telkom PGA Championship. The long-hitting Moore began Sunday's final round four strokes behind third-round leader Oliver Bekker and had only one cut one from that margin by the time he turned in 34. But Moore carded birdies at the 12th, 14th and 18th to post a 273 total, then watched as Bekker faded (with disastrous bogeys at the 16th and 17th) and van den Berg charged, birdieing the par-5 18th to join him for extra holes. And the playoff would indeed be something, taking place solely on the 18th and seeming initially to favor van den Berg, who missed makeable birdie putts on the second and third playings that would have ended it. But with fatigue setting in, Moore holed a four-foot birdie putt on the fifth go-round to clinch his eighth career Sunshine Tour title. J.J. Senekal posted a 70 to take solo third, while Bekker ended up tied for fourth with Darren Fichardt and Danie van Tonder.

1	Titch Moore	68-69-69-67	273	R594,375
2	Ulrich van den Berg	65-70-70-68	273	R431,250
3	J.J. Senekal	70-68-66-70	274	R259,500
4=	Danie van Tonder	67-69-71-68	275	R157,250
	Darren Fichardt	70-68-68-69	275	R157,250
	Oliver Bekker	65-71-66-73	275	R157,250
7=	Tyrone Ferreira	70-67-72-67	276	R101,438
	Merrick Bremner	67-69-70-70	276	R101,438
9=	Shaun Smith	66-75-70-66	277	R68,625
	Jacques Blaauw	71-70-69-67	277	R68,625
	Haydn Porteous	68-73-68-68	277	R68,625
	Neil Schietekat	72-70-65-70	277	R68,625
	James Kingston	69-69-67-72	277	R68,625
14=	Colin Nel	68-72-73-65	278	R51,375
	Christiaan Basson	67-73-69-69	278	R51,375
	Daniel Greene	69-70-68-71	278	R51,375
	Vaughn Groenewald	70-67-69-72	278	R51,375
	Rhys West	68-68-69-73	278	R51,375
19=	Anthony Michael	70-73-67-69	279	R42,975
	George Coetzee	66-69-74-70	279	R42,975
	Wynand Dingle	69-63-75-72	279	R42,975
	Erik van Rooyen	69-67-71-72	279	R42,975
	Ruan de Smidt	67-74-66-72	279	R42,975
24=	Alex Haindl	71-71-68-70	280	R38,813
	Jean Hugo	69-72-67-72	280	R38,813

In The Money: **281**: Heinrich Bruiners, Jbe' Kruger, Neil Cheetham **282**: Francois Coetzee, Dean Burmester, Adilson da Silva, Trevor Fisher Jr, Mourne Buys **283**: Allan Versfeld, Ross Wellington, Doug McGuigan, Andrew Georgiou, Prinavin Nelson, Eddie Taylor **284**: Jake Redman, Peter Karmis **285**: James Kamte, Pieter Moolman **286**: Dylan Frittelli, Rhys Enoch, Ryan Tipping, Jaco Ahlers, Andrew Curlewis, J.C. Ritchie, Le Roux Ferreira, Francesco Laporta **287**: Steven Ferreira **288**: Steve Surry, Jack Harrison, Keenan Davidse **289**: Stuart Smith, Drikus van der Walt **290**: Lyle Rowe, Ryan Thompson, Callum Mowat, Toto Thimba, Shaun Norris **291**: P.H. McIntyre **292**: Divan van den Heever, Teboho Sefatsa **293**: Alan McLean, Warren Abery **295**: Torben Baumann **WD**: Graham van der Merwe (223)

OWR: 0 of top 50 entered - Rating: 16 - Points to 18th - Moore: 14 points, to 306th in OWR

Golden Pilsener Zimbabwe Open

Royal Harare Golf Club - Harare, Zimbabwe
Champion: Jbe' Kruger

Apr 10 - Apr 13
7,149 yards   Par 72
Purse: R1.8 Million

Twenty-seven-year-old Jbe' Kruger claimed his third career Sunshine Tour victory (and his second in this event) by closing with a blazing 66 to capture the Zimbabwe Open at the venerable Rayal Harare Golf Club. Kruger began Sunday's final round five shots behind Haydn Porteous before carding six birdies in his first 12 holes to lift himself firmly into the fray. His momentum was briefly halted by bogeys at the 13th and 14th, but timely birdies at the 16th and 17th would eventually prove enough to carry him home by one over Jacques Blaauw. Blaauw, who closed strongly with an eagle at the par-5 16th, would surely look back disappointedly at bogeys on both of the front nine's par 5s (the 3rd and 6th) as being difference-makers. Third-round leader Porteous closed with a 73 to hang on for solo third.

1	Jbe' Kruger	67-69-68-66	270	R285,300
2	Jacques Blaauw	66-71-66-68	271	R207,000
3	Haydn Porteous	69-66-64-73	272	R124,560
4	Jaco Ahlers	72-67-69-65	273	R88,380
5	Jean Hugo	66-67-70-71	274	R74,340
6=	Andrew Curlewis	71-68-67-70	276	R58,410
	Andrew Georgiou	70-69-66-71	276	R58,410
8	Le Roux Ferreira	65-71-67-74	277	R44,280
9	Trevor Fisher Jr	73-69-68-68	278	R38,880
10=	Danie van Tonder	70-70-71-68	279	R30,456
	Alex Haindl	72-69-70-68	279	R30,456
	Lindani Ndwandwe	72-68-70-69	279	R30,456
	James Kingston	74-67-67-71	279	R30,456
	T.C. Charamba	67-71-69-72	279	R30,456
15=	Merrick Bremner	71-72-67-70	280	R23,340
	Doug McGuigan	70-70-69-71	280	R23,340
	Steve Surry	71-70-68-71	280	R23,340
	Ulrich van den Berg	68-70-69-73	280	R23,340
	Colin Nel	71-67-68-74	280	R23,340
	Steven Ferreira	69-67-69-75	280	R23,340
21=	Allan Versfeld	69-72-70-70	281	R19,980
	Daniel Greene	67-69-71-74	281	R19,980
	C.J. du Plessis	70-70-66-75	281	R19,980
24=	Scott Vincent (a)	73-70-72-67	282	-
	Titch Moore	70-71-71-70	282	R18,090
	Vaughn Groenewald	69-70-73-70	282	R18,090
	Louis de Jager	70-67-71-74	282	R18,090
	Keith Horne	68-72-68-74	282	R18,090

In The Money: **283**: Wynand Dingle, Shaun Smith, Jake Redman, Jake Roos, P.H. McIntyre **284**: Toto Thimba, Wallie Coetsee, Christiaan Basson **285**: Matthew Carvell, Warren Abery **286**: Heinrich Bruiners, Bryce Easton, Jack Harrison, Stuart Smith **287**: Tyrone Ferreira, Darryn Lloyd, Michael Hollick, Justin Turner, Shaun Norris, Lyle Rowe **288**: Jeff Inglis, Pieter Moolman, Theunis Spangenberg, Neil Schietekat, J.J. Senekal, Madalitso Muthiya, Brandon Stone **289**: Teboho Sefatsa **291**: Alan McLean **293**: Callum Mowat, Alan Michell, J.C. Ritchie, Charl Coetzee, Drikus van der Walt **294**: Roberto Lupini **295**: Ruan de Smidt, Tertius van den Berg, Martin du Toit, Ryan Cairns, Eddie Taylor **297**: J.G. Claassen, Ignatius Mketekete **305**: James Kamte **WD**: Anthony Michael

OWR: 0 of top 50 entered - Rating: 2 - Points to 20th - Kruger: 14 points, to 179th in OWR

Investec Royal Swazi Open

Royal Swazi Spa Country Club - Mbabane, South Africa
Champion: Danie van Tonder

May 8 - May 11
6,715 yards Par 72
Purse: R1 Million

A runner-up in this same event in 2012, 23-year-old South African Danie van Tonder broke through for his maiden Sunshine Tour victory at the Investec Royal Swazi Sun Open, an event annually contested under a Modified Stableford format. Van Tonder ultimately holed an eight-foot birdie putt on the first hole of sudden death to claim the title, winning after neither Jacques Blaauw nor Jared Harvey could do better than par. Harvey made one late final round birdie (at the 17th) to earn his playoff spot while Blaauw made two (at numbers 16 and 17) before leaving a potential clinching birdie putt a centimeter short at the last, thus deadlocking the pair on 48 cumulative points through four days of play. But knowing that he had ground to make up, van Tonder did them one better, carding three straight closing birdies to post 18 final-round points (which added up to a stellar 63 at medal play) and join the playoff. Also notable was the fifth-place finish of touted rookie Haydn Porteous, who was in the heart of the battle for three days before tumbling with a 3 point performance in the final round.

1	Danie van Tonder	4-12-14-18	48	R158,500			C.J. du Plessis	9-1-19-9	38	R15,473
2=	Jared Harvey	4-17-11-16	48	R93,200		16	Jeff Inglis	5-12-8-11	36	R14,306
	Jacques Blaauw	11-14-11-12	48	R93,200		17=	Peter Karmis	5-12-9-9	35	R13,556
4	Ross Wellington	17-11-6-11	45	R50,500			Andrew Curlewis	10-7-13-5	35	R13,556
5	Haydn Porteous	9-14-18-3	44	R42,400		19	Martin du Toit	9-8-4-13	34	R12,906
6	Jaco Ahlers	13-10-15-4	42	R36,300		20=	Desvonde Botes	8-10-9-6	33	R11,981
7	Trevor Fisher Jr	8-11-13-9	41	R30,200			Tyrone Ferreira	10-9-7-7	33	R11,981
8	Le Roux Ferreira	14-5-10-11	40	R25,100			Jean Hugo	6-12-11-4	33	R11,981
9=	Wynand Dingle	11-6-10-12	39	R19,453			Bryce Easton	3-8-13-9	33	R11,981
	Keith Horne	8-18-3-10	39	R19,453		24=	Doug McGuigan	14-3-8-7	32	R10,756
	Keenan Davidse	11-8-7-13	39	R19,453			Allan Versfeld	6-16-11--1	32	R10,756
	James Kingston	14-12-4-9	39	R19,453			Alex Haindl	9-15-10--2	32	R10,756
13=	Dean Burmester	10-6-4-18	38	R15,473			Tyrone Mordt	5-18-16--7	32	R10,756
	Wallie Coetsee	11-7-10-10	38	R15,473						

In The Money: **31**: Ulrich van den Berg **30**: Colin Nel **29**: Rhys Enoch **28**: J.J. Senekal, Andrew Georgiou **27**: Michael Hollick **26**: Warren Abery **25**: Hendrik Buhrmann **24**: Heinrich Bruiners, Derick Petersen, Francesco Laporta **22**: Ryan Cairns, Andrew McLardy **21**: Vaughn Groenewald, Anthony Michael **20**: Neil Schietekat **19**: Alan Michell, P.H. McIntyre **17**: Ryan Tipping **16**: J.G. Claassen **14**: Titch Moore, Charl Coetzee **11**: Michiel Bothma

OWR: 0 of top 50 entered - Rating: 0 - Points to 18th - van Tonder: 14 points, to 212th in OWR

Mopani Copper Mines Zambia Open

Nkana Golf Club - Kitwe, Zambia
Champion: Wallie Coetsee

May 15 - May 18
7,002 yards Par 72
Purse: $250,000

Veteran Wallie Coetsee had to wait 17 years between Sunshine Tour victories, but his drought finally came to an end at the light-field Mopani Copper Mines Zambia Open. The 42-year-old Coetsee - who last won at the 1997 Namibia Open, and was a runner-up at the 2001 Atlantic Beach Classic – held the 54-hole lead after opening with rounds of 65-69-68, and did much to solidify his position by carding three birdies en route to an outgoing 34 on Sunday. After saving a key par from deep rough at the par-5 12th, he bogeyed the 369-yard 16th but bounced right back with a birdie at the 564-yard 17th to reestablish a two shot margin – which, in turn, allowed him the luxury of a 72nd-hole bogey to still win by one. Second place was shared by Justin Harding (who closed with 68) and the previous week's winner Danie van Tonder (71), while fifth was split between Francesco Laporta (67) and veteran Jean Hugo, who might well have been a factor late but for making four bogeys at holes 7-15 en route to a closing 73.

1	Wallie Coetsee	65-69-68-71	273	R410,230		Jared Harvey	67-69-69-75	280	R39,664
2=	Justin Harding	68-71-67-68	274	R238,373	16=	Jacques Blaauw	74-67-72-68	281	R34,164
	Danie van Tonder	69-68-66-71	274	R238,373		Louis de Jager	70-72-68-71	281	R34,164
4=	Francesco Laporta	71-67-70-67	275	R116,987		Allan Versfeld	71-71-65-74	281	R34,164
	Jean Hugo	71-67-64-73	275	R116,987	19=	Gideon Pienaar	73-69-72-68	282	R31,058
6=	Erik van Rooyen	68-69-71-68	276	R83,987		Jacques Kruyswijk	65-72-74-71	282	R31,058
	C.J. du Plessis	70-67-69-70	276	R83,987	21=	J.C. Ritchie	72-69-73-69	283	R28,729
8=	Warren Abery	73-66-69-69	277	R59,787		D. van den Bergh	72-74-68-69	283	R28,729
	T. Spangenberg	62-72-69-74	277	R59,787		Callum Mowat	70-72-68-73	283	R28,729
10=	Jaco Ahlers	72-70-69-67	278	R48,529	24=	Attie Schwartzel	72-71-74-67	284	R25,623
	Keenan Davidse	70-69-68-71	278	R48,529		Jaco Prinsloo	69-77-71-67	284	R25,623
12=	Adilson da Silva	70-73-70-67	280	R39,664		Tyrone Ferreira	72-69-74-69	284	R25,623
	Peter Karmis	71-74-68-67	280	R39,664		Pieter Moolman	69-76-70-69	284	R25,623
	Matthew Carvell	70-72-68-70	280	R39,664		Heinrich Bruiners	70-72-69-73	284	R25,623

In The Money: **285**: Tertius van den Berg, Le Roux Ferreira, Rhys West, Desvonde Botes, Ryan Cairns, Lyle Rowe, Gert Myburgh, Doug McGuigan, Andrew Georgiou **286**: Lindani Ndwandwe, Merrick Bremner, Eddie Taylor, Dayne Moore, Christiaan Basson **287**: Oliver Bekker, Juan Langeveld, Toto Thimba **288**: Torben Baumann, Neil Schietekat, Andrew Light, Wynand Dingle, Ruan de Smidt **289**: Dean Burmester, Stuart Smith, Titch Moore, T.C. Charamba **290**: T.I. Mazibuko, Jake Redman, Bryce Easton **291**: Charl Coetzee, Hendrik Buhrmann **293**: Ryan Tipping, Andrew Curlewis, Justin Turner **294**: Francois Coetzee, Andre Cruse **295**: Grant Veenstra, Drikus Bruyns, Derick Petersen **298**: Shaun Smith, P.H. McIntyre **301**: J.G. Claassen

OWR: 0 of top 50 entered - Rating: 2 - Points to 18th - Coetsee: 14 points, to 355th in OWR

Lombard Insurance Classic	**May 23 - May 25**
Royal Swazi Sun Country Club - Mbebane, South Africa	6,715 yards Par 72
Champion: Christiaan Basson	Purse: R900,000

Thirty-two-year-old Christiaan Basson won for the third time on the Sunshine Tour, posting a remarkable bogey-free 197 total to cruise to a five-shot triumph at the Lombard Insurance Classic. A winner of the 2012 Royal Swazi Open on this same golf course, Basson began the week with a relatively quiet 69 before a second round 66 brought him to within two strokes of 36-hole leader Jake Redman. But Basson's Sunday finale was a round to remember as he made three early birdies to turn in 33, then caught fire on the back nine, making two birdies and an eagle (at the 504-yard 12th) early, then birdieing his final three holes to come home in 29, for a career-best 62. Among those tying for second, Redman held up nicely under the final round pressure, standing four under par through the 13th and ultimately closing with a fine 69 - yet he wasn't even within shouting distance. Joining him in second were Ruan de Smidt (whose closing 64 included a back nine of 30), veteran Adilson da Silva (65) and Neil Schietekat (68) - but in the end, only Basson's story really mattered on Sunday.

1	Christiaan Basson	69-66-62	197	R142,650		Justin Harding	70-68-69	207	R13,663
2=	Ruan de Smidt	67-71-64	202	R62,842		Mark Murless	68-69-70	207	R13,663
	Adilson da Silva	67-70-65	202	R62,842		Francesco Laporta	69-67-71	207	R13,663
	Neil Schietekat	67-67-68	202	R62,842	17=	Oliver Bekker	71-70-67	208	R11,633
	Jake Redman	67-66-69	202	R62,842		Lindani Ndwandwe	69-71-68	208	R11,633
6=	Ulrich van den Berg	70-68-65	203	R27,480		Derick Petersen	71-68-69	208	R11,633
	Jaco Ahlers	69-68-66	203	R27,480		Jacques Blaauw	68-69-71	208	R11,633
	Erik van Rooyen	68-69-66	203	R27,480		Chris Swanepoel	67-67-74	208	R11,633
9=	Vaughn Groenewald	69-69-66	204	R18,855	22=	Attie Schwartzel	72-71-66	209	R10,220
	Danie van Tonder	64-70-70	204	R18,855		Jean Hugo	72-69-68	209	R10,220
11	Trevor Fisher Jr	71-65-69	205	R16,745		Titch Moore	67-71-71	209	R10,220
12	D. van den Heever	70-68-68	206	R15,575		Keenan Davidse	68-69-72	209	R10,220
13=	Riekus Nortje	67-72-68	207	R13,663					

In The Money: **210:** Rhys West, Louis de Jager, Michael Hollick, Matthew Carvell, C.J. du Plessis **211:** Francois Coetzee, Heinrich Bruiners, Colin Nel, Merrick Bremner **212:** Desvonde Botes, Drikus van der Walt, Drikus Bruyns, Grant Muller, Wallie Coetsee, Theunis Spangenberg, Ryan Tipping, Andrew Georgiou **213:** Allan Versfeld, Toto Thimba, Ockie Strydom, Callum Mowat **214:** Hendrik Buhrmann, Morne Buys **215:** Bradford Vaughan **216:** Jared Harvey, Wynand Dingle **217:** Prinavin Nelson **218:** Andrew Curlewis **219:** Steven Ferreira **220:** James Kingston

OWR: 0 of top 50 entered - Rating: 5 - Points to 8th - Basson: 6 points, to 509th in OWR

Zambia Sugar Open	**Jun 5 - Jun 8**
Lusaka Golf Club - Lusaka, Zambia	7,226 yards Par 73
Champion: Lyle Rowe	Purse: R1.2 Million

Less than a week shy of his 28th birthday, South African Lyle Rowe broke through for his maiden Sunshine Tour victory, closing with a five-under-par 68 to claim the Zambia Sugar Open in Lusaka. After opening with a disappointing 76, Rowe played himself into the 54-hole lead via middle rounds of 69-66, then pulled steadily away from the field under cold and windy conditions on Sunday. He began his runaway with birdies at the 1st, 2nd and 4th to turn in 32, then added a fourth birdie at the 531-yard 10th. His momentum was briefly stemmed by a bogey at the short par-3 11th, but Rowe responded by stepping on the gas once more and adding three more birdies, first at the 12th, then on back-to-back par 5s at the 13th and 14th. By this point the lead had grown to five, with only Rowe's irrelevant bogey at the 564-yard closer allowing runner-up Neil Schietekat to pull within four. P.H. McIntyre and Ulrich van den Berg shared third, a full six shots back, while rookie Haydn Porteous (who closed with a disappointing 76) tied for fifth. Rowe's previous best finish was a runner-up at the 2013 Vodacom – Parys event, while his best 2014 result was a tie for 29th, which also came in Zambia at the Mopani Copper Mines Zambia Open.

1	Lyle Rowe	76-69-66-68	279	R190,200		Maritz Wessels	74-71-73-72	290	R16,840
2	Neil Schietekat	70-70-70-73	283	R138,000		Derick Petersen	70-70-77-73	290	R16,840
3=	P.H. McIntyre	69-72-71-73	285	R70,980		Shaun Smith	72-73-72-73	290	R16,840
	Ulrich van den Berg	71-67-72-75	285	R70,980		Le Roux Ferreira	72-70-72-76	290	R16,840
5=	Jared Harvey	68-71-73-75	287	R46,020		Jean Hugo	69-70-74-77	290	R16,840
	Haydn Porteous	70-71-70-76	287	R46,020	19=	Jake Redman	69-74-74-74	291	R14,400
7	Matthew Carvell	78-66-69-75	288	R35,400		Tyrone Mordt	72-71-72-76	291	R14,400
8=	Ryan Cairns	72-70-76-71	289	R24,096	21=	Heinrich Bruiners	74-72-75-71	292	R13,320
	Titch Moore	72-71-74-72	289	R24,096		Wallie Coetsee	66-73-80-73	292	R13,320
	Adilson da Silva	74-71-72-72	289	R24,096		Grant Muller	71-70-74-77	292	R13,320
	Toto Thimba	73-76-67-73	289	R24,096	24=	Christiaan Basson	73-76-71-73	293	R12,420
	Riekus Nortje	70-71-73-75	289	R24,096		Attie Schwartzel	76-69-73-75	293	R12,420
13=	Louis de Jager	73-71-75-71	290	R16,840					

In The Money: **294:** Andrew Light, Jacques Blaauw **295:** Jacques Kruyswijk, Tyrone Ferreira, Ryan Tipping, Pieter Moolman, Merrick Bremner, Andrew McLardy **296:** Danie van Tonder, Andrew Curlewis, Justin Harding, Lindani Ndwandwe, Francois Coetzee **297:** T.I. Mazibuko, J.C. Ritchie, Madalitso Muthiya, Colin Nel **298:** Torben Baumann, Theunis Spangenberg **299:** Rhys West, Bryce Bibby, Alan Michell **300:** Jaco Prinsloo, Eddie Taylor **301:** Gideon Pienaar, Charl Coetzee, Wynand Dingle, Drikus Bruyns, T.C. Charamba, Dayne Moore **302:** Stefan Engell Andersen, Prinavin Nelson **303:** Patrick Mwendapole, Francesco Laporta, Drikus van der Walt, Morne Buys **304:** Timothy Sondashi, Paul de Beer **305:** J.G. Claassen **306:** Christiaan Jonck **307:** Ignatius Mketekete, Arthur Horne **309:** Vaughn Groenewald

OWR: 0 of top 50 entered - Rating: 4 - Points to 18th - Rowe: 14 points, to 423rd in OWR

Vodacom Origins of Golf - Euphoria
Jun 25 - Jun 27

Euphoria Golf Estate - Naboomspruit, South Africa
Champion: Danie van Tonder
7,699 yards   Par 72
Purse: R600,000

Claiming his second Sunshine Tour victory in less than two months, up-and-coming Danie van Tonder held off a hard-charging Tyrone Ferreira to win the Vodacom Origins of Golf event at the Euphoria Golf Estate, the first stop in the six-event Vodacom winter series. Following a pair of opening 67s which included only a single bogey between them, van Tonder entered the Friday finale two strokes ahead of Ulrich van den Berg, but soon fell behind when van den Berg turned in two-under-par 34. An even par back nine slowed van den Berg's progress, however, allowing van Tonder to retake the lead following birdies at the 12th, 13th and 15th. By this time, his primary challenge was coming from Ferreira, who'd began the day three back before bogeys at the 2nd and 6th seemed to bury his hopes. But a run of six straight birdies at holes 7-12 revived Ferreira's chances, and one more at the 164-yard 15th drew him even. An ill-timed bogey at the 16th dropped him one behind, however, and when Ferreira was unable to hole a short birdie putt at the 662-yard 18th, van Tonder was able to claim the title (and the top spot among eligible players in the Order of Merit) with three closing pars.

1	Danie van Tonder	67-67-70	204	R95,100		Bryce Easton	72-71-71	214	R11,213
2	Tyrone Ferreira	72-65-68	205	R69,000		Morne Buys	71-70-73	214	R11,213
3	Ulrich van den Berg	69-67-70	206	R48,000		Le Roux Ferreira	72-69-73	214	R11,213
4	Jared Harvey	72-67-69	208	R37,800		Ross Wellington	68-70-76	214	R11,213
5	Jacques Blaauw	68-69-72	209	R28,200	18=	Ockie Strydom	69-75-71	215	R8,049
6	Adilson da Silva	68-69-73	210	R22,800		Maritz Wessels	74-70-71	215	R8,049
7	Justin Harding	66-73-73	212	R18,900		Jean Hugo	69-73-73	215	R8,049
8=	Callum Mowat	69-71-73	213	R15,600		Oliver Bekker	70-71-74	215	R8,049
	Heinrich Bruiners	73-67-73	213	R15,600		Steven Ferreira	71-70-74	215	R8,049
10=	Anthony Michael	72-73-69	214	R11,213		Andrew Curlewis	72-69-74	215	R8,049
	Keenan Davidse	75-69-70	214	R11,213		Louis de Jager	73-66-76	215	R8,049
	Shaun Norris	69-74-71	214	R11,213	25=	Ruan de Smidt	74-72-70	216	R6,780
	Charl Coetzee	67-76-71	214	R11,213		Chris Swanepoel	69-75-72	216	R6,780

In The Money: **217**: Shaun Smith, Madalitso Muthiya, Peter Karmis, Neil Cheetham, Lindani Ndwandwe **218**: Lyle Rowe, Merrick Bremner, Christiaan Basson, Mark Murless, James Kamte **219**: P.H. McIntyre, Jeff Inglis, C.J. du Plessis **221**: J.J. Senekal, Dean Burmester **223**: Titch Moore, Rhys West

OWR: 0 of top 50 entered - Rating: 5 - Points to 6th - Van Tonder: 6 points, to 168th in OWR

Sun City Challenge
Jul 2 - Jul 4

Lost City Golf Course - Sun City, South Africa
Champion: Dean Burmester
7,310 yards   Par 72
Purse: R700,000

Twenty-five-year-old Dean Burmester claimed his second career Sunshine Tour title at the Sun City Challenge, closing with a final ound 71 to edge a charging Haydn Porteous by one. Burmester was in the mix early at the Lost City Golf Course, trailing little-known first round leader Gert Myburgh by two before moving out to a three-stroke 36-hole lead following a seven-birdie second round of 67. With the 54-hole event ending on Friday, Burmester began fast with an opening birdie before turning in even-par 36. This allowed Porteous to draw even early as he birdied the 4th, 5th and 7th, and he once again took a share of the lead by matching Burmester's 11th-hole birdie with a three at the 363-yard 12th, then moved ahead alone with a birdie at the 16th. But while Burmester carded a seemingly ill-timed bogey at the 470-yard 17th, Porteous crashed to a disastrous double-bogey, then could only par the 530-yard 18th as Burmester got up-and-down from the fringe for a birdie that provided his margin of victory. Despite once again taking his rookie knocks, Porteous held on to solo second. Third place was taken by Merrick Bremner (who's closing 66 included six birdies and an eagle) while fourth was shared by the quintet of P.H. "Power House" McIntyre (who closed with 67), Titch Moore (68), Lindani Nwandwe (69), Ulrich van den Berg (70) and Keith Horne (72).

1	Dean Burmester	68-67-71	206	R110,950		Warren Abery	71-70-73	214	R11,993
2	Haydn Porteous	68-70-69	207	R80,500		Tyrone Ryan	68-70-76	214	R11,993
3	Merrick Bremner	71-71-66	208	R56,000	17=	Madalitso Muthiya	76-67-72	215	R10,122
4=	P.H. McIntyre	69-74-67	210	R28,980		Riekus Nortje	73-70-72	215	R10,122
	Titch Moore	71-71-68	210	R28,980		Trevor Fisher Jr	72-71-72	215	R10,122
	Lindani Ndwandwe	68-73-69	210	R28,980		J.J. Senekal	72-71-72	215	R10,122
	Ulrich van den Berg	70-70-70	210	R28,980		Toto Thimba	70-73-72	215	R10,122
	Keith Horne	70-68-72	210	R28,980	22=	Grant Muller	72-75-69	216	R8,225
9	Adilson da Silva	69-70-72	211	R17,150		Colin Nel	71-75-70	216	R8,225
10=	Jared Harvey	76-69-67	212	R15,225		C.J. du Plessis	72-74-70	216	R8,225
	Louis de Jager	69-69-74	212	R15,225		Tyrone Ferreira	73-73-70	216	R8,225
12=	Matthew Carvell	72-69-72	213	R13,650		Keenan Davidse	72-72-72	216	R8,225
	Jean Hugo	72-68-73	213	R13,650		Christiaan Basson	73-68-75	216	R8,225
14=	Neil Cheetham	71-73-70	214	R11,993					

In The Money: **217**: Attie Schwartzel, Jacques Blaauw **218**: Charl Coetzee **219**: Vaughn Groenewald, Jaco Ahlers **220**: Jake Redman, Drikus van der Walt, Derick Petersen **221**: Rhys West, Drikus Bruyns, Jeff Inglis, Gert Myburgh **222**: Pieter Moolman **223**: Derik Ferreira **224**: Shaun Norris **225**: Anthony Michael **226**: Wallie Coetsee, Theunis Spangenberg

OWR: 0 of top 50 entered - Rating: 4 - Points to 8th - Burmester: 6 points, to 550th in OWR

Vodacom Origins of Golf - Arabella
Arabella Golf Club - Kleinmond, South Africa
Champion: Jean Hugo

Jul 23 - Jul 25
6,976 yards   Par 72
Purse: R600,000

Thirty-eight-year-old Jean Hugo braved the elements to win for the 15th time on the Sunshine Tour, edging rookie Rhys West by one at the Vodacom Origins of Golf event at Arabella. In a week in which gale force winds wiped out the second round, and Friday's finale was drenched by an icy rain, Hugo carded rounds of 68-69, the latter built around three birdies over his final eight holes, including a crucial four at the 563-yard 18th. West actually played a very similar round, turning in even par before bogeying the 10th, than adding two birdies over his final eight - but not the third one needed to tie at the last. Still the 25-year-old claimed solo second (his best Sunshine Tour finish to date), finishing one ahead of an imposing foursome of veterans that included 12-time Tour winner Adilson da Silva, Ulrich van den Berg and Trevor Fisher Jr. The victory moved Hugo into a tie for eighth among all-time Sunshine Tour winners, one win behind Hall-of-Famer Ernie Els. It must be noted, however, that all 15 of Hugo's titles had been claimed on the circuit's far less competitive winter schedule - and fully nine of those (including his last five triumphs) have been 54-hole events in the light-field Vodacom Origins series.

1	Jean Hugo	68-69	137	R95,100	16=	Neil Cheetham	72-73	145	R9,570
2	Rhys West	67-71	138	R69,000		P.H. McIntyre	67-78	145	R9,570
3=	Chris Swanepoel	68-71	139	R34,200	18=	Matthew Carvell	71-75	146	R8,200
	Trevor Fisher Jr	67-72	139	R34,200		Warren Abery	74-72	146	R8,200
	Ulrich van den Berg	69-70	139	R34,200		Michael Hollick	72-74	146	R8,200
	Adilson da Silva	68-71	139	R34,200		Callum Mowat	75-71	146	R8,200
7	Jacques Blaauw	67-74	141	R18,900		Neil Schietekat	69-77	146	R8,200
8=	Wallie Coetsee	70-73	143	R14,900		Tyrone Mordt	72-74	146	R8,200
	Keith Horne	69-74	143	R14,900	24=	Vaughn Groenewald	74-73	147	R6,429
	Jared Harvey	72-71	143	R14,900		James Kamte	70-77	147	R6,429
11=	Christiaan Basson	72-72	144	R11,412		Alex Haindl	71-76	147	R6,429
	Charl Coetzee	74-70	144	R11,412		Heinrich Bruiners	73-74	147	R6,429
	Le Roux Ferreira	71-73	144	R11,412		Jake Redman	72-75	147	R6,429
	Tyrone Ferreira	70-74	144	R11,412		Danie van Tonder	73-74	147	R6,429
	Keenan Davidse	74-70	144	R11,412		Jbe' Kruger	72-75	147	R6,429

In The Money: **148**: Maritz Wessels, Torben Baumann, Omar Sandys, Drikus van der Walt, Titch Moore, Divan van den Heever **149**: Jeff Inglis, Madalitso Muthiya, Peter Karmis, Allan Versfeld, Ryan Tipping, Anthony Michael

OWR: 0 of top 50 entered - Rating: 2 - Points to 6th - Hugo: 4 points, to 289th in OWR

Vodacom Origins of Golf - St. Francis Bay
St. Francis Links - St. Francis Bay, South Africa
Champion: Keith Horne

Jul 30 - Aug 1
7,170 yards   Par 72
Purse: R600,000

Forty-two-year-old veteran Keith Horne won for the sixth time on the Sunshine Tour by cruising to a three-shot victory at the 54-hole Vodacom Origins of Golf event at St. Francis Bay. Horne took control of the tournament early by opening with a course record-setting 65 over the Jack Nicklaus-designed St. Francis Links, a flawless round which included seven birdies and no bogeys, and which staked him to a two-shot lead over Titch Moore. A second round 71 was a bit uneven, however, leaving Horne tied with 24-year-old second-year player Erik van Rooyen, who had posted a pair of fine 68s that included a round one eagle at the 443-yard 18th. Remarkably, the players' 136 total stood them five shots clear of the field, setting up a two-man battle in Friday's finale. Under windy and rainy conditions, Horne bolted out of the gate quickly, recording birdies at the first three holes, then adding another at the 5th before eventually turning with a four-shot cushion over the far less-experienced van Rooyen. The much tougher back nine would extract four bogeys (against a single birdie) from Horne but under difficult conditions, van Rooyen could only manage to do one stroke better, allowing Horne to cruise home to a relatively easy victory. Van Rooyen's solo second was his best-ever Sunshine Tour result, and he finished five ahead of Ulrich van den Berg and Wallie Coetsee, and six ahead of Chris Swanepoel and former University of New Mexico star Madalitso Muthiya of Zambia.

1	Keith Horne	65-71-71	207	R95,100	14=	Peter Karmis	75-70-75	220	R10,050
2	Erik van Rooyen	68-68-74	210	R69,000		Le Roux Ferreira	72-73-75	220	R10,050
3=	Ulrich van den Berg	72-74-69	215	R42,900		Vaughn Groenewald	73-70-77	220	R10,050
	Wallie Coetsee	70-74-71	215	R42,900		Warren Abery	70-73-77	220	R10,050
5=	Chris Swanepoel	74-70-72	216	R25,500	18=	Michael Hollick	74-72-75	221	R8,200
	Madalitso Muthiya	69-74-73	216	R25,500		Doug McGuigan	74-72-75	221	R8,200
7=	Dean Burmester	72-74-71	217	R17,700		Adilson da Silva	75-72-74	221	R8,200
	Ruan de Smidt	72-71-74	217	R17,700		Tyrone Mordt	70-74-77	221	R8,200
9=	Anthony Michael	76-67-75	218	R13,600		Steven Ferreira	73-69-79	221	R8,200
	Jaco Ahlers	74-68-76	218	R13,600		Danie van Tonder	69-73-79	221	R8,200
	Shaun Smith	68-73-77	218	R13,600	24=	Allan Versfeld	69-74-79	222	R7,020
12=	Colin Nel	74-69-76	219	R11,700		Neil Schietekat	68-74-80	222	R7,020
	Titch Moore	67-75-77	219	R11,700					

In The Money: **223**: Mark Williams, Jared Harvey, Jean Hugo, P.H. McIntyre, James Kamte, Trevor Fisher Jr **224**: Christiaan Basson, Shaun Norris **225**: Pieter Moolman, Alex Haindl **226**: Rhys West **227**: J.C. Ritchie, Attie Schwartzel, Gert Myburgh **230**: Desne van den Bergh

OWR: 0 of top 50 entered - Rating: 2 - Points to 6th - Horne: 6 points, to 334th in OWR

Wild Waves Golf Challenge

Aug 27 - Aug 29

Wild Coast Sun Country Club - Port Edward, South Africa
Champion: Colin Nel

6,351 yards Par 70
Purse: R600,000

Previously best known as one of two players (along with Spain's Jose Campillo) to shoot an 11-under-par 59 under lift-clean-and-place conditions at the rain-deluged 2013 Nelson Mandela Championship, 30-year-old Colin Nel broke through for his first career Sunshine Tour victory in another weather-shortened event, the Wild Waves Challenge, in Port Edward. A former second team NAIA All-American at Oklahoma City University, Nel easily played the best golf over the first two days of the mid-week event, birdieing three of his first four holes during Wednesday's opening round en route to a five-under-par 65 which shared the lead with James Kamte. But while Kamte could do no better than a 69 on Thursday, Nel kept it in high gear, again birdieing three of his opening four and again posting a 65, thus building a three shot lead over Jared Harvey and Ulrich van den Berg. Friday opened with winds gusting as high as 40 miles per hour, causing a delay of over three hours and eventually prompting officials - mindful of a similar forecast for the next 48 hours - to cancel play. This left Nel, a local product whose previous best Sunshine Tour finishes were a trio of fourth places, to be declared the somewhat fortunate winner.

1	Colin Nel	65-65	130	R110,950		Warren Abery	67-69	136	R12,164
2=	Jared Harvey	69-64	133	R68,250		D. van den Heever	68-68	136	R12,164
	Ulrich van den Berg	68-65	133	R68,250		Le Roux Ferreira	68-68	136	R12,164
4=	Jaco Ahlers	68-66	134	R28,980		Steven Ferreira	67-69	136	R12,164
	James Kamte	65-69	134	R28,980		Tyrone Ferreira	68-68	136	R12,164
	Ockie Strydom	72-62	134	R28,980	20=	Jake Redman	69-68	137	R8,558
	Tyrone Mordt	67-67	134	R28,980		P.H. McIntyre	69-68	137	R8,558
	Heinrich Bruiners	67-67	134	R28,980		Morne Buys	68-69	137	R8,558
9=	Danie van Tonder	69-66	135	R16,450		Grant Muller	70-67	137	R8,558
	Andrew McLardy	66-69	135	R16,450		Lindani Ndwandwe	73-64	137	R8,558
11=	Alex Haindl	69-67	136	R12,164		Drikus Bruyns	67-70	137	R8,558
	Mark Murless	70-66	136	R12,164		Daniel Greene	69-68	137	R8,558
	Doug McGuigan	69-67	136	R12,164		J.J. Senekal	72-65	137	R8,558
	Charl Coetzee	69-67	136	R12,164					

In The Money: **138**: Stuart Smith, Jacques Blaauw, Louis de Jager, Trevor Fisher Jr, Mark Williams, Attie Schwartzel **139**: Justin Harding, Titch Moore, Keenan Davidse, Stefan Engell Andersen, Adrian Ford, Bryce Bibby, Shaun Smith, Ryan Tipping, Toto Thimba, Anthony Michael, Andrew Curlewis, Shaun Norris, Derick Petersen

OWR: 0 of top 50 entered - Rating: 2 - Points to 8th - Nel: 6 points, to 617th in OWR

Vodacom Origins Of Golf - Port Edward

Sep 3 - Sep 5

Wild Coast Sun Country Club - Port Edward, South Africa
Champion: Louis de Jager

6,351 yards Par 70
Purse: R600,000

Former South African Amateur champion Louis de Jager won for the second time on the Sunshine Tour at the Vodacom Origins of Golf event in Port Edward, barely hanging on to raise the trophy in memorably nerve-wracking style. It seemed to be the 27-year-old de Jager's week from the start after he recorded five birdies and an eagle during a bogey-free 63 on Wednesday, good enough to propel him to an uncommonly large four-shot first round lead. He came back on Thursday with a steady 68, a round that proved good enough to expand his 36-hole lead to five. But standing on the verge of a runaway, de Jager collapsed during Friday's finale, unraveling with a triple-bogey on the 1st hole, then, following a gutsy bounce-back birdie at the 2nd, adding a double at the 421-yard 5th. Still, birdies at the 9th and 13th seemed to lift him clear - until the bottom fell out, as he staggered home with five straight bogeys to post an ugly 77. But as luck would have it, his two primary competitors, Jaco Ahlers and Haydn Porteous, also failed to close, Ahlers finishing bogey-par while Porteous, once again staring his first Sunshine Tour victory in the eye, bogeyed the 18th to leave the trio deadlocked on 208. De Jager's good fortune then continued on the first playoff hole (the 381-yard 18th), where he recorded a routine par and won when neither man could match it.

1	Louis de Jager	63-68-77	208	R95,100		Jean Hugo	71-69-71	211	R11,115
2=	Haydn Porteous	73-68-67	208	R58,500	16=	Ulrich van den Berg	74-70-68	212	R9,195
	Jaco Ahlers	71-65-72	208	R58,500		Jeff Inglis	74-68-70	212	R9,195
4=	Andrew Curlewis	78-65-66	209	R29,600		Wallie Coetsee	74-66-72	212	R9,195
	C.J. du Plessis	72-67-70	209	R29,600		Tyrone Mordt	72-67-73	212	R9,195
	Danie van Tonder	72-66-71	209	R29,600	20=	Heinrich Bruiners	70-69-74	213	R8,040
7=	Jacques Blaauw	73-70-67	210	R15,240		Jared Harvey	67-72-74	213	R8,040
	Christiaan Basson	71-70-69	210	R15,240		Colin Nel	73-66-74	213	R8,040
	Grant Muller	75-66-69	210	R15,240	23=	Andre Cruse	73-72-69	214	R6,790
	Keith Horne	70-69-71	210	R15,240		Bryce Easton	76-69-69	214	R6,790
	Stuart Smith	67-69-74	210	R15,240		Michael Hollick	73-71-70	214	R6,790
12=	Torben Baumann	76-69-66	211	R11,115		Matthew Carvell	71-71-72	214	R6,790
	Warren Abery	72-69-70	211	R11,115		James Kamte	68-73-73	214	R6,790
	Daniel Greene	75-66-70	211	R11,115		Pieter Moolman	72-68-74	214	R6,790

In The Money: **215**: Francois Coetzee, Mark Murless, Keenan Davidse **216**: Anthony Michael, Lyle Rowe, Allan Versfeld, Gideon Pienaar, Trevor Fisher Jr, Neil Schietekat, Shaun Norris **217**: Oliver Bekker, Shaun Smith **221**: Tyrone Ryan, Titch Moore **222**: P.H. McIntyre, Bryce Bibby

OWR: 0 of top 50 entered - Rating: 2 - Points to 11th - de Jager: 7 points, to 536th in OWR

Vodacom Origins of Golf - Parys
Sep 11 - Sep 13
Vaal de Grace Golf Estate - Parys, South Africa
Champion: P.H. McIntyre
7,341 yards   Par 72
Purse: R600,000

Eight-year Sunshine Tour veteran P.H. "Power House" McIntyre claimed his first professional victory at the Vodacom Origins of Golf event played at the Vaal de Grace Golf estate, winning a three-day pitched battle with six-time Sunshine Tour winner Jake Roos which, in the end, required sudden death to decide. McIntyre opened the week with an eight-under-par 64 that might have resulted in a multi-shot lead had Roos not nearly matched it with a 65 which included a remarkable three eagles. The pair then separated themselves from the field during Thursday's second round, taking a joint three stroke lead after Roos bettered McIntyre by a shot, 67 to 68. They then started fast on Friday, effectively eliminating the rest of the field when McIntyre birdied four of his first eight holes while Roos birdied three. But in the end, Roos drew even with a clutch birdie at the 559-yard 17th before McIntyre defied the odds by handing Roos the first sudden death loss of his career (in six playoffs) with a birdie on the third extra hole. For the mercurial McIntyre - a player who has often made eagles and double-bogeys with equal frequency - the win came in his 171st Sunshine Tour start. But better late than never.

1	P.H. McIntyre	64-68-68	200	R95,100		C.J. du Plessis	67-67-73	207	R11,400
2	Jake Roos	65-67-68	200	R69,000	15=	Doug McGuigan	71-68-69	208	R9,408
3=	Shaun Norris	66-72-66	204	R31,140		Roberto Lupini	71-68-69	208	R9,408
	Steven Ferreira	69-67-68	204	R31,140		Tyrone Mordt	70-68-70	208	R9,408
	Jean Hugo	70-66-68	204	R31,140		Christiaan Basson	69-69-70	208	R9,408
	Jaco Ahlers	66-70-68	204	R31,140		Justin Turner	67-68-73	208	R9,408
	Tyrone Ferreira	67-67-70	204	R31,140	20=	Drikus Bruyns	71-70-68	209	R8,040
8	Wallie Coetsee	67-67-71	205	R16,500		Stuart Smith	73-69-67	209	R8,040
9=	Francois Coetzee	69-71-66	206	R13,600		Mark Williams	68-71-70	209	R8,040
	Rhys West	69-68-69	206	R13,600	23=	Heinrich Bruiners	72-68-70	210	R7,160
	Jared Harvey	66-70-70	206	R13,600		Allan Versfeld	69-69-72	210	R7,160
12=	Anthony Michael	66-72-69	207	R11,400		Dean Burmester	66-72-72	210	R7,160
	Jean-Paul Strydom	71-67-69	207	R11,400					

In The Money: **211:** Andrew Curlewis, Lindani Ndwandwe, Titch Moore, Jake Redman **212:** Pieter Moolman, Eddie Taylor, Lyle Rowe, Vaughn Groenewald, J.J. Senekal, Colin Nel, Callum Mowat **213:** Erik van Rooyen, Grant Muller, Alex Haindl, Ockie Strydom **214:** Mark Murless, Desvonde Botes **215:** Madalitso Muthiya, Michiel Bothma, Derik Ferreira, Shaun Smith

OWR: 0 of top 50 entered - Rating: 0 - Points to 7th - McIntyre: 4 points, to 549th in OWR

Sun Boardwalk Golf Challenge
Oct 8 - Oct 10
Humewood Golf Club - Port Elizabeth, South Africa
Champion: Titch Moore
6,988 yards   Par 72
Purse: R600,000

Port Elizabeth area native Titch Moore captured the inaugural playing of the Sun Boardwalk Golf Challenge, birdieing the final hole to claim a one-shot triumph over countryman Roberto Lupini and England's Steve Surry. Originally scheduled for 54 holes, the tournament was shortened to 36 after heavy winds blew away Thursday's second round, meaning that former Big Easy Tour star Lupini began the final round with a two-stroke lead after posting a wild Wednesday 68 that included eight birdies, two bogeys and a double-bogey at the par-4 13th. But facing a chance to log his first Sunshine Tour victory, the 31-year-old Lupini never quite got it going, bogeying the 4th and 5th holes to surrender his lead, then playing one-under-par golf thereafter to finish with a 73, and a 141 total. Moore, meanwhile, moved into the lead with a birdie at the 4th en route to turning in one-under-par 34, then strung together eight straight back nine pars before his timely birdie at the Humewood Country Club's 401-yard finisher saw him home in 140. Surry, for his part, also birdied the last to gain his share of second, while Peter Karmis and Henrich Bruiners both closed with 69 to share fourth, with Bruiners creating the most excitement by birdieing four of his last five holes to do so. Andrew Curlewis, who shared second with Moore after Wednesday, played his first 10 Friday holes in nine over par, eventually staggering home with a second round 80 to fall all the way to a tie for 34th.

1	Titch Moore	70-70	140	R95,100	14=	Justin Harding	74-71	145	R10,280
2=	Steve Surry	71-70	141	R58,500		Steven Ferreira	73-72	145	R10,280
	Roberto Lupini	68-73	141	R58,500		Jake Redman	73-72	145	R10,280
4=	Peter Karmis	73-69	142	R33,000	17=	Louis de Jager	74-72	146	R8,676
	Heinrich Bruiners	73-69	142	R33,000		Justin Turner	74-72	146	R8,676
6=	Ryan Tipping	75-68	143	R19,400		Alex Haindl	74-72	146	R8,676
	Doug McGuigan	73-70	143	R19,400		Colin Nel	74-72	146	R8,676
	Ulrich van den Berg	73-70	143	R19,400		Keith Horne	71-75	146	R8,676
9=	Derik Ferreira	75-69	144	R12,840	22=	Stefan E. Andersen	75-72	147	R7,176
	Adrian Ford	73-71	144	R12,840		Allan Versfeld	74-73	147	R7,176
	Jean Hugo	74-70	144	R12,840		Chris Swanepoel	73-74	147	R7,176
	Danie van Tonder	74-70	144	R12,840		James Kamte	72-75	147	R7,176
	Shaun Norris	72-72	144	R12,840		Bryce Blbby	74-73	147	R7,176

In The Money: **148:** Shaun Smith, Neil Schietekat, Alan Michell, Keenan Davidse **149:** Paul de Beer, Andrew Light, Lindani Ndwandwe **150:** Grant Muller, Andre Cruse, Desvonde Botes, Jean-Paul Strydom, Andrew Curlewis **151:** Tyrone Ferreira, Ruan de Smidt, Dean Burmester, Haydn Porteous **152:** Edwin Kutara, Divan van den Heever, P.H. McIntyre **153:** Francois van Vuuren

OWR: 0 of top 50 entered - Rating: 0 - Points to 5th - Moore: 4 points, to 341st in OWR

BMG Classic

Glendower Golf Club - Johannesburg, South Africa
Champion: Merrick Bremner

Oct 16 - Oct 19
6,899 yards   Par 72
Purse: R800,000

Merrick Bremner won for the fourth time on the Sunshine Tour in highly dramatic fashion, holing a 25-yard bunker shot to birdie the 451-yard 18th hole at the Glendower Golf Club and take the BMG Classic by one. Having spent more time in Europe than on his native South African tour in recent weeks, Bremner wasted little time in making a statement on home soil, birdieing his first two holes on Friday en route to grabbing the first-round lead with a six-under-par 66. A disappointing second round 71 would leave him four strokes behind another South African with E Tour experience, Darren Fichardt, but Fichardt stumbled badly on Sunday, bogeying the par-3 6th and double-bogeying the 522-yard 8th to create a dogfight down the stretch. Fichardt admirably righted himself enough to card birdies at the 10th, 13th and 15th but in the meantime, Bremner had charged, birdieing the 11th, 12th, 15th and 16th to draw even. He then produced his bunker magic at the last to get across the finish line on 204, but still had to wait while Fichardt stuffed his approach at the last to five feet, then missed the putt, capping an obviously frustrating afternoon and giving Bremner the title.

	Player	Scores	Total	Prize		Player	Scores	Total	Prize
1	Merrick Bremner	66-71-67	204	R126,800		Le Roux Ferreira	69-71-71	211	R12,744
2	Darren Fichardt	68-65-72	205	R92,000	16=	Andrew Georgiou	73-66-73	212	R11,244
3	Haydn Porteous	69-70-67	206	R57,120		Christiaan Basson	70-69-73	212	R11,244
4	Justin Harding	72-67-68	207	R40,400	18=	Andre Cruse	70-70-73	213	R10,484
5=	D. van den Heever	74-66-68	208	R31,480		Oliver Bekker	67-71-75	213	R10,484
	Jean Hugo	68-68-72	208	R31,480	20=	Jaco Prinsloo	70-72-72	214	R9,584
7=	Louis de Jager	74-67-68	209	R20,613		Trevor Fisher Jr	69-72-73	214	R9,584
	Jaco Ahlers	70-66-73	209	R20,613		Doug McGuigan	73-68-73	214	R9,584
	Danie van Tonder	70-66-73	209	R20,613		Jacques Blaauw	72-69-73	214	R9,584
10=	Neil Schietekat	71-69-70	210	R15,402	24=	Francesco Laporta	71-73-71	215	R8,604
	Erik van Rooyen	70-70-70	210	R15,402		Jack Harrison	71-72-72	215	R8,604
12=	Jacques Kruyswijk	73-71-67	211	R12,744		Tyrone Mordt	73-69-73	215	R8,604
	J.C. Ritchie	71-72-68	211	R12,744		Thomas Aiken	74-66-75	215	R8,604
	Dylan Frittelli	72-71-68	211	R12,744					

In The Money: **216**: Grant Muller, Jared Harvey, Ross Wellington, Dean Burmester **217**: Shaun Norris, Colin Nel, Anthony Michael **218**: Ruan Huysamen, Madalitso Muthiya, Ulrich van den Berg, Warren Abery, James Kamte, Jeff Inglis **219**: Pieter Moolman, Attie Schwartzel **220**: Allan Versfeld, Mark Murless, Stuart Smith, Brett Liddle, Desvonde Botes **221**: Mark Williams, Ruan de Smidt **222**: Makhetha Mazibuko, Grant Veenstra **226**: Riekus Nortje

OWR: 0 of top 50 entered - Rating: 4 - Points to 9th - Bremner: 7 points, to 265th in OWR

Vodacom Origins of Golf - Final

Pezula Championship Course - Knysna, South Africa
Champion: Keith Horne

Oct 29 - Oct 31
6,951 yards   Par 72
Purse: R650,000

Keith Horne won for the seventh time on the Sunshine Tour and for the second time in 2014 at the Vodacom Origins of Golf Final, the closing event in the six-event tour-within-a-tour that fills much of the circuit's winter schedule. Attributing some of his success to being better rested after not going abroad to play the European Tour early in the year, Horne grabbed the first round lead by carding eight birdies en route to seven-under-par 65 over the Pezula Estate's Championship Course, then trailed 36-hole leader Erik van Rooyen by one after a Thursday 71. However the less-battle-tested van Rooyen faded with a 72 in the Friday finale (eventually finishing in a six-way tie for fourth), leaving Horne to do battle with Ulrich van den Berg, who began the final round three back but played his first 14 holes in seven under par to move into the lead. Horne, meanwhile, bogeyed the 421-yard 2nd but found his stride quite nicely thereafter, methodically posting six birdies over the next 16 holes, including the two he desperately needed at the 311-yard 17th and the 526-yard 18th, the latter off a two-foot tap-in that provided the margin of victory. Van den Berg also birdied the 18th, good enough to clinch solo second.

	Player	Scores	Total	Prize		Player	Scores	Total	Prize
1	Keith Horne	65-71-67	203	R103,025	14=	Danie van Tonder	69-73-67	209	R10,888
2	Ulrich van den Berg	73-66-65	204	R74,750		Jean-Paul Strydom	72-70-67	209	R10,888
3	Dylan Frittelli	69-67-69	205	R52,000		Chris Swanepoel	70-68-71	209	R10,888
4=	Ruan de Smidt	74-69-64	207	R25,079		Doug McGuigan	66-70-73	209	R10,888
	Michael Hollick	69-73-65	207	R25,079	18=	Eddie Taylor	68-73-69	210	R9,555
	Neil Schietekat	69-70-68	207	R25,079		Jean Hugo	66-71-73	210	R9,555
	Alex Haindl	69-70-68	207	R25,079	20=	Wallie Coetsee	72-70-69	211	R8,873
	Madalitso Muthiya	66-71-70	207	R25,079		Steve Surry	75-68-68	211	R8,873
	Erik van Rooyen	69-66-72	207	R25,079	22=	Heinrich Bruiners	69-74-69	212	R7,914
10=	Tyrone Mordt	70-73-65	208	R13,406		Jake Redman	71-70-71	212	R7,914
	Mark Williams	71-71-66	208	R13,406		Shaun Norris	66-74-72	212	R7,914
	Jacques Blaauw	66-74-68	208	R13,406		Jaco Ahlers	72-68-72	212	R7,914
	Dean Burmester	70-69-69	208	R13,406					

In The Money: **213**: Jared Harvey, Steven Ferreira, Haydn Porteous **214**: Jaco Van Zyl, Anthony Michael, Derik Ferreira, Paul de Beer, Tyrone Ferreira, Torben Baumann, Matthew Carvell **215**: Warren Abery, Lindani Ndwandwe, Vaughn Groenewald, Tertius van den Berg **216**: Oliver Bekker, Christiaan Basson, C.J. du Plessis, Louis de Jager **217**: Rhys West **218**: J.J. Senekal **222**: Michiel Bothma

OWR: 0 of top 50 entered - Rating: 0 - Points to 9th - Horne: 4 points, to 343rd in OWR

Nedbank Affinity Cup

Nov 4 - Nov 6

Lost City Golf Course - Sun City, South Africa
Champion: Louis de Jager

7,310 yards   Par 72
Purse: R750,000

After breaking a five-year victory drought in September at the Wild Coast Vodacom Origins of Golf event, 27-year-old Louis de Jager continued his fine form by beating Vaughn Groenewald and Danie van Tonder in a playoff for the Nedbank Affinity Cup. De Jager was actually a late arrival to the party as he trailed first-round leader Dean Burmester by three after an opening 68, then Ruan de Smidt by four after the latter logged a flawless second round 64. But de Smidt would fall to a 74 during Thursday's finisher, leaving the door open for both Vaughn and the touted van Tonder, who each closed in 66, for 212 total. De Jager, meanwhile moved into the hunt with four front nine birdies, but eventually needed clutch birdies at the 470-yard 17th and the 530-yard 18th to join the playoff. Van Tonder was eliminated when he couldn't match his opponents' birdies on the first replay of the 18th hole, leaving de Jager to raise the trophy after holing an eight foot birdie putt on the second go-round – his fourth consecutive birdie under dating back to the last two holes of regulation.

1	Louis de Jager	68-68-68	204	R118,875		Colin Nel	73-68-68	209	R10,287
2=	Danie van Tonder	70-68-66	204	R69,900		Keenan Davidse	73-67-69	209	R10,287
	Vaughn Groenewald	70-68-66	204	R69,900		Rhys West	72-68-69	209	R10,287
4	Jake Redman	69-67-69	205	R37,875		Jeff Inglis	73-66-70	209	R10,287
5=	Dean Burmester	65-72-69	206	R23,400		Christiaan Basson	70-68-71	209	R10,287
	Oliver Bekker	66-71-69	206	R23,400		Morne Buys	66-71-72	209	R10,287
	Trevor Fisher Jr	66-70-70	206	R23,400		Derik Ferreira	69-68-72	209	R10,287
	Ulrich van den Berg	68-66-72	206	R23,400		Titch Moore	71-66-72	209	R10,287
	Ruan de Smidt	68-64-74	206	R23,400	23	Wynand Dingle	68-72-70	210	R8,629
10	Chris Swanepoel	66-74-67	207	R14,925	24=	Jared Harvey	71-71-69	211	R7,954
11=	Madalitso Muthiya	71-70-67	208	R13,467		Tyrone Mordt	71-69-71	211	R7,954
	Peter Karmis	71-69-68	208	R13,467		Jean Hugo	71-68-72	211	R7,954
13=	Neil Schietekat	75-67-67	209	R10,287		James Kamte	69-70-72	211	R7,954
	Alex Haindl	69-72-68	209	R10,287		P.H. McIntyre	69-70-72	211	R7,954

In The Money: **212**: Allan Versfeld, Ross Wellington, Merrick Bremner, Shaun Norris **213**: Jacques Kruyswijk **214**: Attie Schwartzel, Shaun Smith, Divan van den Heever, Wallie Coetsee **215**: Mark Williams, Pieter Moolman, C.J. du Plessis **216**: Thriston Lawrence, Grant Veenstra **217**: Neil Cheetham, Bryce Easton, J.J. Senekal **219**: Justin Harding, Mark Murless, Juan Langeveld **224**: Callum Mowat **WD**: Warren Abery (143)

OWR: 0 of top 50 entered - Rating: 0 - Points to 4th - De Jager: 4 points, to 441st in OWR

Lion of Africa Cape Town Open

Oct 31 - Nov 3

Royal Cape Golf Club - Cape Town, South Africa
Champion: Jaco Ahlers

6,818 yards   Par 72
Purse: R1.5 Million

In one of the more memorable finishes of the 2014 season in South Africa, 32-year-old veteran Jaco Ahlers broke through for his second career Sunshine Tour victory, winning a three-way playoff at the Lion of Africa Cape Town Open. After opening with steadily improving rounds of 71-69-68, Ahlers began Sunday's final round four shots behind co-54-hole leaders Hennie Otto and Danie van Tonder, and on a day which saw the wind pick up during the afternoon, he started slowly, bogeying the long par-4 3rd. But a run of three straight birdies at holes 5-7, then one more at the short par-4 10th, got him going, and he would eventually come home in 68, for a 276 aggregate. This total was matched by England's Ross McGowan (who also closed with a pair of 68s) as well as Otto, who struggled with his putter all day before holing a 15-foot birdie putt at the last to tie. Otto would drop out of the playoff by bogeying the 18th on its first extra playing, but the hole would be played four more times before matters were settled – and then only because McGowan missed a three-footer on the final go-round

1	Jaco Ahlers	71-69-68-68	276	R237,750		Branden Grace	75-64-71-71	281	R21,863
2=	Ross McGowan	69-71-68-68	276	R138,150		Rhys West	71-65-70-75	281	R21,863
	Hennie Otto	66-67-71-72	276	R138,150	17=	Andrew Georgiou	68-76-70-68	282	R16,827
4=	Jbe' Kruger	72-70-70-65	277	R67,800		Peter Karmis	70-72-70-70	282	R16,827
	Thomas Aiken	69-66-71-71	277	R67,800		Jean Hugo	71-68-72-71	282	R16,827
6	David Drysdale	70-69-68-71	278	R53,100		Merrick Bremner	71-68-72-71	282	R16,827
7=	Ryan Tipping	68-70-72-69	279	R35,738		Dean Burmester	71-69-71-71	282	R16,827
	Tjaart van der Walt	71-70-69-69	279	R35,738		David Frost	71-71-69-71	282	R16,827
	Justin Harding	71-68-70-70	279	R35,738		Steven Ferreira	70-73-68-71	282	R16,827
	Danie van Tonder	67-68-69-75	279	R35,738		Jake Redman	69-67-73-73	282	R16,827
11=	Adilson da Silva	69-71-71-69	280	R25,950		Shaun Norris	76-64-69-73	282	R16,827
	Justin Walters	71-67-70-72	280	R25,950		Jacques Blaauw	72-68-68-74	282	R16,827
13=	Christiaan Basson	72-69-71-69	281	R21,863		Titch Moore	67-68-72-75	282	R16,827
	Rhys Enoch	68-71-71-71	281	R21,863					

In The Money: **283**: Michael Hollick, Morne Buys, J.J. Seneka, Alex Haindl, Jack Harrison, Vaughn Groenewald, George Coetzee **284**: Desvonde Botes, Mark Williams, Brandon Stone, Stuart Smith, Ulrich van den Berg, Adrian Ford, Haydn Porteous **285**: Pieter Moolman, Darren Fichardt, Jacques Kruyswijk **286**: Neil Schietekat, Lindani Ndwandwe, Jeff Inglis, Madalitso Muthiya, Tyrone Ferreira **287**: Drikus Bruyns, Omar Sandys, Doug McGuigan, Chris Swanepoel **288**: Darryn Lloyd, Keenan Davidse, Lyle Rowe, Shaun Smith, Derik Ferreira, Wallie Coetsee, Andrew Curlewis **289**: Derick Petersen, Dylan Frittelli, Jared Harvey **290**: Bryce Bibby, Wynand Dingle **291**: Le Roux Ferreira **292**: Nic Henning **293**: Desne van den Bergh, Kevin Stone **294**: Paul de Beer

OWR: 0 of top 50 entered - Rating: 14 - Points to 27th - Ahlers: 14 points, to 227th in OWR

Nedbank Golf Challenge
Dec 4 - Dec 7

Gary Player Country Club - Sun City, South Africa
Champion: Danny Willett
7,831 yards   Par 72
Purse: $6.5 Million

Having closed his 2014 European Tour campaign with a pair of late top 10s, 27-year-old Englishman Danny Willett had to be considered among the favorites at the season-opening Nedbank Golf Challenge, and in the end he justified that standing with a blazing weekend finish to claim his second career E Tour title. Facing a limited but very strong international field, Willett began his week quietly with a three-birdie, two-bogey 71 before turning in even par 36 in round two. But on Friday's back nine he put the engine back into gear, posting four birdies to shoot 68 and climb to fourth place, five shots behind former world number one Luke Donald, who began his week 71-63. Donald continued his strong form on Saturday by carding a 69, but he needed all of it just to maintain his lead as Willett now began to catch fire, birdieing six of his first 11 holes en route to a 65 which beat the field by three shots and lifted him to within one of Donald. As it happened, Sunday was Donald's 37th birthday but his hopes of his celebrating in style were dashed fairly early as he bogeyed the 3rd and 5th, by which time Willett had posted three early birdies and rocketed past him. A former world number one-ranked amateur, Willett turned in 33 and, riding a multi-shot lead, played some very steady golf coming home, methodically birdieing the 547-yard 10th and the 601-yard 14th before providing a final exclamation point by adding one final birdie at the 478-yard 17th. Donald would ultimately finish with a 73, to claim solo third, while second was taken by Ross Fisher, who made seven birdies en route to a closing 68.

1	Danny Willett	71-68-65-66	270	€864,976
2	Ross Fisher	66-70-70-68	274	€576,650
3	Luke Donald	71-63-69-73	276	€324,886
4	Marcel Siem	68-72-71-68	279	€259,493
5	K. Aphibarnrat	72-73-68-68	281	€220,050
6	Miguel A. Jiménez	70-74-69-69	282	€181,645
7=	Jonas Blixt	71-73-70-71	285	€126,373
	Tim Clark	70-71-72-72	285	€126,373
	Thongchai Jaidee	71-70-71-73	285	€126,373
	Louis Oosthuizen	70-73-69-73	285	€126,373
11	Shane Lowry	72-72-71-71	286	€95,494
12=	Brendon Todd	73-68-75-71	287	€86,411
	Stephen Gallacher	70-73-72-72	287	€86,411
14=	Charl Schwartzel	70-71-75-73	289	€77,848
	Tommy Fleetwood	74-67-74-74	289	€77,848
16=	Lee Westwood	72-70-78-70	290	€70,063
	George Coetzee	68-74-76-72	290	€70,063
	Pablo Larrazábal	73-71-71-75	290	€70,063
19=	Brooks Koepka	70-74-75-72	291	€63,316
	Dawie van der Walt	73-72-69-77	291	€63,316
21=	Martin Kaymer	74-75-71-72	292	€58,646
	Jaco Ahlers	74-75-70-73	292	€58,646
	Alexander Levy	68-70-76-78	292	€58,646
24=	Joost Luiten	72-74-73-74	293	€54,753
	Thomas Bjørn	80-72-68-73	293	€54,753

In The Money: **295**: Kevin Na, Marc Warren **298**: Mikko Ilonen **301**: Danie van Tonder **WD**: Jamie Donaldson (74)

OWR: 14 of top 50 entered - Rating: 196 - Points to 29th - Willett: 38 points, to 56th in OWR

Alfred Dunhill Championship
Dec 11 - Dec 14

Leopard Creek Country Club - Malelane, South Africa
Champion: Branden Grace
7,287 yards   Par 72
Purse: €1.5 Million

Claiming his first European Tour victory since 2012, 26-year-old Branden Grace played spectacular, then steady golf en route to a wire-to-wire victory at the Alfred Dunhill Championship. Grace opened the week with a dazzling bogey-free 62 at the Leopard Creek Country Club, then added a Friday 66 to take a five-shot halfway lead over Francesco Molinari. He stumbled slightly on Saturday, however, posting an even-par 72 which allowed Molinari (whose own uninspiring 70 left him three back) and Denmark's 23-year-old Lucas Bjerregaard (68-67-66) back into the mix. With Molinari double-bogeying the 3rd on Sunday (en route to a 76), it quickly became a two-man race, with Grace posting two early birdies to briefly widen his lead. Having bogeyed the 1st, Bjerregaard birdied the 6th to pull back within three, but a difficult chip which trickled into a greenside pond led to a triple-bogey at the par-3 7th, and then the bottom fell out. Bjerregaard staggered around the back nine in a startling 50 strokes to post an 89, dropping him from second all the way to a tie for 49th. His collapse also cleared the way nicely for Grace, who then marched home with a 68, good enough to run away from Louis Oosthuizen and win by seven.

1	Branden Grace	62-66-72-68	268	€237,750
2	Louis Oosthuizen	69-69-68-69	275	€172,500
3	Andrew Johnston	69-67-68-73	277	€103,800
4=	Trevor Fisher Jr.	73-67-69-69	278	€67,800
	Danny Willett	66-69-67-76	278	€67,800
6=	David Drysdale	71-68-71-69	279	€48,675
	Francesco Molinari	68-65-70-76	279	€48,675
8=	Thomas Pieters	71-71-68-70	280	€32,900
	Tjaart Van der Walt	67-67-75-71	280	€32,900
	Shaun Norris	68-67-73-72	280	€32,900
11=	Pedro Oriol	70-72-74-65	281	€25,150
	Justin Harding	71-70-70-70	281	€25,150
	Richard Sterne	71-71-67-72	281	€25,150
14=	Espen Kofstad	70-72-71-69	282	€21,675
	Daniel Brooks	70-72-71-69	282	€21,675
16=	Andrew Curlewis	72-67-74-70	283	€18,750
	Louis de Jager	69-67-76-71	283	€18,750
	Jbe' Kruger	68-69-75-71	283	€18,750
	Thomas Aiken	71-72-69-71	283	€18,750
	Danie van Tonder	70-69-70-74	283	€18,750
	Morten O. Madsen	70-66-72-75	283	€18,750
22=	Hennie Otto	74-67-75-68	284	€15,975
	Dylan Frittelli	70-70-73-71	284	€15,975
	Byeong-Hun An	71-69-72-72	284	€15,975
	Johan Carlsson	70-68-73-73	284	€15,975

In The Money: **285**: Charl Schwartzel, Renato Paratore **286**: Julien Quesne, Darren Fichardt, Craig Lee, Alex Haindl, Benjamin Hebert **287**: Max Orrin, Kevin Phelan, Chris Paisley, Michael Hollick, Lee Slattery, Christiaan Basson, Nacho Elvira **288**: Eduardo De La Riva, Ulrich Van Den Berg, Kevin Stone **289**: Jaco Ahlers, John Hahn, Chris Swanepoel Jr., Jean Hugo, Mark Murless, Scott Jamieson **290**: Magnus Carlsson, Carlos Del Moral, Oliver Bekker, Shiv Kapur Lucas Bjerregaard **291**: Adilson da Silva, Robert Rock, Kristoffer Broberg, Martin Du toit **293**: Alessandro Tadini, Pablo Martin, Ross McGowan **294**: Jake Roos, Tyrone Ferreira **295**: Andrew Georgiou, Bradley Neil (a), Richard McEvoy, Jacques Blaauw **296**: Steve Surry, Rhys West, Desvonde Botes, Søren Hansen **298**: Matt Ford **299**: Jason Barnes **301**: Lasse Jensen **303**: Jason Palmer **305**: James Kamte

OWR: 1 of top 50 entered - Rating: 77 - Points to 25th - Grace: 22 points, to 82nd in OWR

PGA TOUR OF AUSTRALASIA
2014

Playing a 15-event schedule which, allowing for an annual five-month break from early March to mid-August, stretches across all 12 months of the calendar, the 2014 PGA Tour of Australasia was once again the least lucrative of the world's major tours, and it was once again divided into two distinct tiers. The bottom tier was composed of 10 lesser events whose average purse was under AU $125,000, and which generally featured fields of a decidedly lighter caliber. Winners here were of a varied (but generally less-established) nature and included veterans like Matthew Griffin and New Zealand's Gareth Paddison, as well as players with greater apparent international potential like Andrew Dodt (who'll play the European Tour in 2015) and New Zealand's Ryan Fox. In a worldwide sense, these events operate largely under the radar and generally offer OWR points on a scale comparable to that of the European Challenge circuit.

The top tier, however, is another breed of cat entirely, and this year began with a new event, August's $1 million (U.S.) Fiji International, which was won by veteran Steve Jeffress. Next up was October's $1.75 million ISPS Handa Perth International (co-sanctioned by the European Tour and profiled in the E Tour section), where up-and-coming Danish star Thorbjørn Olesen emerged victorious. Then it was on to the Triple Crown of Australian golf: the Masters, the venerable Australian Open and the Australian PGA – with the latter two being separated this year by the second-tier New South Wales PGA Championship. As usual, these events generated a far greater dose of excitement, with Nick Cullen clinching the Masters with a spectacular 72nd-hole bunker shot, American Jordan Spieth running away to a six-shot victory at the Open via a stunning final round 63, and Greg Chalmers winning his second PGA title by outlasting world number three Adam Scott (and, earlier, Wade Ormsby) in an epic seven-hole playoff.

Player Of The Year: Nick Cullen

Thirty-year-old Nick Cullen certainly wasn't the best Australian golfer in the world in 2014; indeed, according to the Official World Ranking, he wasn't even among the top 15. He was, however, among the top Australians who actually played regularly on their home circuit during the year, and he was the only such homebody to win one of the nation's three top-shelf events, the Australian Masters. Last year, Adam Scott's performance in those "majors" was just too strong to ignore. But this time around, there was room for a domestic winner.

2014 PGA Tour of Australasia Top 60 Money Winners

#	Player	Money	#	Player	Money	#	Player	Money
1	Greg Chalmers	$254,525	21	David Bransdon	$68,333	41	Michael Sim	$39,585
2	Steven Jeffress	$213,652	22	Adam Bland	$62,956	42	Peter Cooke	$39,284
3	Nick Cullen	$208,256	23	Paul Spargo	$62,079	43	Josh Geary	$38,562
4	Adam Scott	$207,250	24	David Klein	$61,792	44	Jason Norris	$37,664
5	Ryan Fox	$183,785	25	Jason Scrivener	$60,439	45	Steven Bowditch	$37,445
6	Jake Higginbottom	$164,475	26	Aron Price	$59,750	46	David McKenzie	$36,415
7	Dimitrios Papadatos	$156,745	27	Rhein Gibson	$57,448	47	David Smail	$36,324
8	Matthew Griffin	$138,886	28	Richard Green	$55,759	48	Ryan Haller	$34,340
9	Rod Pampling	$133,100	29	Scott Strange	$55,584	49	Tom Bond	$34,041
10	Brett Rumford	$132,832	30	Matthew Giles	$54,406	50	Nick Gillespie	$32,343
11	Josh Younger	$126,631	31	Daniel Nisbet	$51,191	51	Gareth Paddison	$31,576
12	Stephen Dartnall	$118,001	32	Richard Lee	$50,307	52	Adam Blyth	$31,402
13	Wade Ormsby	$116,658	33	Nathan Green	$47,486	53	Andrew Martin	$30,896
14	James Nitties	$107,549	34	Nathan Holman	$46,872	54	Anthony Houston	$30,197
15	Terry Pilkadaris	$97,254	35	Brad Kennedy	$46,225	55	Marcus Fraser	$29,950
16	Mark Brown	$93,819	36	Rohan Blizard	$41,674	56	Michael Wright	$28,561
17	Andrew Dodt	$85,478	37	Matthew Guyatt	$41,176	57	Alistair Presnell	$27,410
18	Robert Allenby	$79,805	38	Ashley Hall	$40,694	58	Adam Stephens	$27,350
19	Michael Hendry	$76,303	39	Aaron Townsend	$40,038	59	Bryden Macpherson	$26,063
20	Cameron Smith	$70,480	40	Anthony Brown	$39,806	60	Ryan Lynch	$25,573

Lexus of Blackburn Heritage Classic

Heritage Golf & Country Club (St. John Course) - Chirnside Park, Australia
Champion: Gareth Paddison

Feb 6 - Feb 9
6,670 meters   Par 72
Purse: AU$100,000

New Zealand's Gareth Paddison overcame windy conditions and an untimely 71st-hole bogey to win the Victorian PGA Championship, his second victory in this event and his fifth career Australasian Tour triumph. Following opening rounds of 67-68, the 33-year-old from Wellington placed himself in good position on Saturday, posting a 66 that saw him get to seven under par through 15 holes before stumbling with bogeys at the 16th and 17th. Still, he began Sunday with a two-stroke lead and, after playing the first eight holes in even par, appeared to solidify his position with birdies at a pair of par 5s, the 9th and 12th. But a bogey at the 13th gave his pursuers a bit of life, and when countryman Michael Hendry birdied the par-5 15th, the lead had narrowed to one. Paddison then nearly handed Hendry a playoff by bogeying the par-3 17th for the second straight day before rising splendidly to the occasion by ripping his approach to the 455-yard 18th to within five feet, then converting the clinching putt. Australia's Jamie Arnold took solo third, two shots off the pace.

1	Gareth Paddison	67-68-66-71	272	$15,000		Adam Bland	74-71-67-71	283	$1,550
2	Michael Hendry	68-70-66-69	273	$9,500	16=	Michael Long	68-72-74-70	284	$1,275
3	Jamie Arnold	68-67-68-71	274	$7,000		Ryan Fox	70-69-68-77	284	$1,275
4=	Kurt Barnes	67-69-69-71	276	$4,550		Peter O'Malley	70-72-70-72	284	$1,275
	Andrew Martin	71-70-69-66	276	$4,550		Luke Humphries	70-68-69-77	284	$1,275
6=	Mark Brown	65-71-71-70	277	$3,300	20=	Alex Hawley	68-70-66-82	286	$1,110
	Daniel McGraw	70-70-67-70	277	$3,300		Lucas Herbert (a)	70-73-68-75	286	-
8	Ben Eccles (a)	68-69-66-75	278	-		Scott Arnold	70-71-69-76	286	$1,110
9=	Andrew Evans	73-71-65-71	280	$2,483		Aaron Townsend	74-71-65-76	286	$1,110
	Troy Cox	72-72-65-71	280	$2,483	24=	Peter Wilson	70-72-71-74	287	$1,030
	David Bransdon	73-71-68-68	280	$2,483		Adam Blyth	72-69-73-73	287	$1,030
12=	Matthew Ballard	72-70-68-72	282	$1,900		Max McCardle	70-71-66-80	287	$1,030
	Paul Sheehan	68-69-70-75	282	$1,900		Anthony Houston	69-73-71-74	287	$1,030
14=	Kim Felton	72-73-64-74	283	$1,550					

In The Money: **288**: Anthony Brown, Dimitrios Papadatos, Michael Choi **289**: Terry Pilkadaris, Peter Cooke, Kristopher Mueck, Samuel Eaves, Mathew Perry, Jack Wilson **290**: Ben Wharton, Bradley Lamb, Neven Basic, Rohan Blizard, Kieran Muir, Daniel Popovic, Fraser Wilkin, Blake Proverbs (a) **291**: Christopher Thorn, Takuya Taniguchi, Leighton Lyle **292**: Kieran Pratt, Nick Gillespie, Chris Gaunt **293**: Edward Stedman, Tom Bond, Ryan Lynch **294**: Clint Rice **295**: Steven Jones, Ryan Haywood **297**: Adam Fraser **302**: Jared Pender

OWR: 0 of top 50 entered - Rating: 0 - Points to 7th - Paddison: 6 points, to 321st in OWR

Coca-Cola Queensland PGA Championship

City Golf Club - Toowoomba, Australia
Champion: Anthony Summers

Feb 13 - Feb 16
5,805 meters   Par 70
Purse: AU$120,000

Forty-four-year-old Anthony Summers, a 22-year veteran of the Australasian Tour, finally broke through for his maiden victory at the Queensland PGA Championship, capitalizing on a flukish eagle at Sunday's 16th hole to pull away and beat Ryan Fox by three. Summers' stroke of good fortune came after hitting a fairway metal into right-side trees, leaving him with a blind, branch-affected second, the holing of which he became aware of solely due to the greenside crowd's reaction. He then birdied the par-5 17th to put the finishing touches on a closing 63, giving him a 256 aggregate over the short but tree-lined layout of the City Golf Club. Adding to the improbability of Summers' victory was an injured back, which required considerable physical therapy both Saturday night and Sunday morning in order for him even to tee it up in the finale. Second place was claimed by 54-hole leader Ryan Fox while third went to David Bransdon, who'd initially joined both Summers and Fox as first day leaders after posting an opening 61. Notably, Summers' weekday rounds of 61-62 included 17 birdies and nary a bogey, before a Saturday 70 dropped him back into the pack, setting up his Sunday charge.

1	Anthony Summers	61-62-70-63	256	$18,000	14=	Michael Hendry	67-68-70-64	269	$1,626
2	Ryan Fox	61-67-64-67	259	$11,400		Kurt Barnes	67-68-65-69	269	$1,626
3	David Bransdon	61-70-68-62	261	$8,400		Daniel Fox	67-69-68-65	269	$1,626
4=	Stephen Dartnall	66-63-65-68	262	$5,460		Mark Brown	68-68-65-68	269	$1,626
	Brad Kennedy	64-64-67-67	262	$5,460		T. MacDonald (a)	69-69-66-65	269	-
6=	Aaron Townsend	71-65-63-65	264	$3,960	19=	Bradley Hughes	68-65-66-71	270	$1,353
	Ryan Lynch	66-66-65-67	264	$3,960		Scott Laycock	73-65-65-67	270	$1,353
8	Clint Rice	66-66-66-68	266	$3,360		Kevin Conlong	65-68-69-68	270	$1,353
9	Andrew Dodt	67-66-69-65	267	$2,940		Jared Pender	72-63-66-69	270	$1,353
10=	Jamie Arnold	64-73-66-65	268	$2,280	23=	Terry Pilkadaris	69-66-67-69	271	$1,248
	Jason Scrivener	67-65-68-68	268	$2,280		Scott Strange	67-64-71-69	271	$1,248
	Michael Choi	64-68-68-68	268	$2,280		Thomas Petersson	65-67-73-66	271	$1,248
	Adam Stephens	71-66-68-63	268	$2,280					

In The Money: **272**: Matthew Griffin, Tom Bond, Paul Spargo, Peter Wilson, Matthew Guyatt, Edward Stedman **273**: Anthony Brown, Scott Arnold, Brett Rankin, Jamie Hook, Steven Jones, Neven Basic **274**: Matthew Giles, Gareth Paddison, Daniel Nisbet, Max McCardle **275**: Ben Ford, Aaron Wilkin (a), Andrew Evans, Kyu Sim **276**: David McKendrick, Anthony Gilligan **277**: Christopher Wood, Michael Smyth **278**: Alex Edge, Jun Seok Lee, Tim Hart **279**: Peter Welden, Blake McGrory **281**: Brendan Chant **282**: Kim Felton **283**: Daniel McGraw

OWR: 0 of top 50 entered - Rating: 2 - Points to 7th - Summers: 6 points, to 636th in OWR

Oates Victorian Open
Feb 20 - Feb 23

13th Beach Golf Club (Beach Course) - Barwon Heads, Australia — 6,410 meters Par 72
13th Beach Golf Club (Creek Course) - Barwon Heads, Australia — 6,427 meters Par 72
Champion: Matthew Griffin — Purse: AU$150,000

Thirty-year-old Matthew Griffin broke through for his first Australasian Tour victory on home soil at the Victorian Open, closing in 68 before defeating Matthew Stieger on the third of a sudden death playoff. Griffin started slowly with opening rounds of 74-71 over the 36-hole 13th Beach Golf Club before heating up for a pair of weekend 68s, with his final round including clutch birdies at the 15th and 17th. Stieger, meanwhile, closed with a 69 - a slightly bumpy round which saw him double-bogey the par-4 14th before rallying with birdies at both the 16th and the par-5 finisher to tie Griffin on 281. The playoff was contested entirely over the 18th hole and both men birdied it on the first two playings, leaving matters to end with Griffin holing a seven-footer for yet another birdie on the third go-round. Fifty-four-hole leader Brett Drewitt, who closed with 71 and narrowly missed an eagle putt at the last to join the playoff, finished solo third, a single shot back.

1	Matthew Griffin	74-71-68-68	281	$22,500		Samuel Eaves	73-74-72-68	287	$1,838
2	Matthew Stieger	74-68-70-69	281	$14,250		Scott Strange	73-72-71-71	287	$1,838
3	Brett Drewitt	75-66-70-71	282	$10,500		Josh Younger	74-69-73-71	287	$1,838
4=	Andrew Kelly	70-77-70-67	284	$6,825		Dimitrios Papadatos	75-71-70-71	287	$1,838
	Terry Pilkadaris	70-70-73-71	284	$6,825		Kim Felton	74-68-73-72	287	$1,838
6=	Raymond Beaufils	76-70-74-65	285	$4,444	21=	Jun Seok Lee	77-65-74-72	288	$1,590
	Adam Bland	75-71-73-66	285	$4,444		Nick Cullen	71-75-70-72	288	$1,590
	Paul Donahoo	72-73-71-69	285	$4,444		Antonio Murdaca (a)	75-69-73-71	288	-
	Steven Jeffress	72-74-70-69	285	$4,444		Ryan Haller	75-72-72-69	288	$1,590
10=	Peter O'Malley	74-73-69-70	286	$2,730	25=	Wayne Perske	73-75-71-70	289	$1,470
	Brendan Chant	74-73-70-69	286	$2,730		Rohan Blizard	71-75-71-72	289	$1,470
	Jack Wilson	73-75-67-71	286	$2,730		Max McCardle	71-74-73-71	289	$1,470
	Richard Green	78-69-67-72	286	$2,730		David Klein	72-75-68-74	289	$1,470
	Pieter Zwart	76-67-75-68	286	$2,730		C. Campbell	72-73-73-71	289	$1,470
15=	Alex Hawley	77-70-73-67	287	$1,838					

In The Money: **290**: Clint Rice, Mitchell Brown, Ben Eccles (a), Leigh Deagan, Peter Wilson **291**: Aaron Townsend, David McKendrick, Jason Norris, Geoff Drakeford (a), Rhein Gibson **292**: Jordan Cooper (a), Michael Choi, Scott Arnold, Andrew Tampion **293**: Brett Coletta (a), David Bransdon, Peter Cooke, Nathan Holman, Stephen Leaney **294**: Andrew Evans, Callan O'Reilly, Marcus Both, Benjamin Clementson **295**: Kieran Pratt, Jake Stirling, Mahal Pearce **298**: Gareth Paddison **301**: Takuya Taniguchi

OWR: 0 of top 50 entered - Rating: 2 - Points to 9th - Griffin: 6 points, to 236th in OWR

NZ Open
Feb 27 - Mar 2

The Hills Golf Course - Queenstown, New Zealand — 7,213 yards Par 72
Millbrook Golf Course - Queenstown, New Zealand — 7,215 yards Par 72
Champion: Dimitrios Papadatos — Purse: NZD$850,000

Australian Dimitrios Papadatos claimed his first professional victory at the New Zealand Open in a dominant performance which saw him nose ahead of the field through 54 holes, then blow it away in the final round. The 22-year-old from New South Wales opened with rounds of 68-69 before a 67 on Saturday left him one ahead of Mark Brown, who was bidding to become the first New Zealander to claim the title since 2003. But playing before a partisan Kiwi crowd, Papadatos held his lead early by turning in one-under-par 35, then ran away on the final nine by carding five birdies, the last three in succession at the 15th, 16th and 17th. Brown posted late birdies of his own at the 13th, 15th and 17th just to finish four back, while another New Zealander, David Klein claimed solo third with a closing 67.

1	Dimitrios Papadatos	68-69-67-66	270	$141,170	15=	Rohan Blizard	68-77-70-66	281	$10,862
2	Mark Brown	67-72-66-69	274	$79,996		Jack Wilson	72-72-70-67	281	$10,862
3	David Klein	69-70-69-67	275	$52,939		Jake Stirling	66-74-70-71	281	$10,862
4=	Ashley Hall	67-73-66-70	276	$34,508		Adam Bland	73-70-64-74	281	$10,862
	Richard Lee	68-67-70-71	276	$34,508	19	Craig Palmer	72-70-65-75	282	$8,823
6=	Ryan Fox	70-69-69-69	277	$26,665	20=	Nick Gillespie	69-73-73-68	283	$8,117
	Terry Pilkadaris	66-73-69-69	277	$26,665		Steven Jeffress	71-73-69-70	283	$8,117
8=	Andrew Martin	67-75-68-68	278	$21,960		Steven Jones	73-71-68-71	283	$8,117
	Adam Blyth	70-65-73-70	278	$21,960		Daniel Fox	70-71-68-74	283	$8,117
10=	Scott Strange	66-76-68-69	279	$17,516	24=	Jun Seok Lee	70-74-70-70	284	$6,147
	Cameron Smith	70-71-67-71	279	$17,516		Ben Campbell	71-74-69-70	284	$6,147
	Kieran Muir	70-70-67-72	279	$17,516		David Bransdon	67-74-70-73	284	$6,147
13=	Matthew Giles	72-69-70-69	280	$13,725		David Smail	72-71-68-73	284	$6,147
	Gareth Paddison	70-71-66-73	280	$13,725					

In The Money: **285**: Michael Hendry, Matthew Guyatt, Peter Wilson, Stephen Leaney, Andrew Dodt, Aaron Townsend, Hao Tong Li **286**: Takafumi Kawane, Anthony Brown, Bryden Macpherson, Christopher Campbell, Hiroshi Iwata **287**: James Gibellini, Kristopher Mueck, Mathew Perry **288**: Samuel Eaves, Kevin Conlong, Michael Tran, Tom Bond, Brett Drewitt **289**: Aaron Pike, Matthew Stieger, Matthew Griffin **290**: Peter O'Malley, Scott Hend **291**: Callan O'Reilly, Jason Scrivener, Rhein Gibson **292**: Stephen Dartnall, Michael Wright, Michael Long **293**: Dominic Barson, Andrew Tampion **294**: Kazuo Sato, Douglas Holloway **298**: Blake McGrory **299**: Marcus Wheelhouse **300**: Ryan Haller, Brody Ninyette **301**: Leigh Deagan

OWR: 0 of top 50 entered - Rating: 2 - Points to 19th - Papadatos: 16 points, to 304th in OWR

Fiji International

Aug 14 - Aug 17

Natadola Bay Golf Course - Natadola, Fiji
Champion: Steven Jeffress

7,180 yards   Par 72
Purse: AU$1.07 Million

Australian Steve Jeffress managed rather a rare feat at the inaugural playing of the Fiji International, being the first man off the tee on Thursday morning and the last to hole a putt on Sunday afternoon - that final stroke being for a birdie to clinch victory in this lucrative event co-sanctioned by the OneAsia Tour. Jeffress was around the lead all week after beginning the tournament with rounds 69-70-69, good enough to tie him for a two-shot 54-hole lead with 20-year-old Jake Higginbottom. In the Sunday finale, Higginbottom moved out to a two-stroke lead at the turn before bogeying the 10th and 13th to fall back into a tie. Another bogey at the par-3 15th, combined with a clutch Jeffress birdie, buried Higginbottom's chances, with the final margin extending to four strokes when the 38-year-old Jeffress birdied both the 17th and 18th. Third place was shared by Australian veterans Terry Pilkadaris and Andrew Dodt, while the event's biggest name, course designer and national hero Vijay Singh, tied for 10th on 290. Also in the field, making a rare non-Champions Tour appearance, was 57-year-old Hall-of-Famer Nick Price, who never bettered 73 but still managed a very respectable tie for 35th.

1	Steven Jeffress	69-70-69-70	278	$192,143		Cameron Smith	71-68-73-79	291	$19,570
2	Jake Higginbottom	68-69-71-74	282	$108,881	15=	Josh Younger	72-75-76-69	292	$13,779
3=	Terry Pilkadaris	70-76-69-71	286	$61,646		Richard Lee	74-75-74-69	292	$13,779
	Andrew Dodt	68-71-71-76	286	$61,646		Peter Cooke	70-73-77-72	292	$13,779
5	In-Hoi Hur	70-72-70-75	287	$42,699		Brendan Jones	70-73-76-73	292	$13,779
6=	Tae-Hoon Kim	74-74-69-71	288	$34,515		Nathan Holman	69-73-74-76	292	$13,779
	Ryan Fox	69-76-70-73	288	$34,515		Scott Laycock	74-71-71-76	292	$13,779
	Michael Sim	71-70-71-76	288	$34,515	21=	Paul Gow	70-73-76-74	293	$10,728
9	Hyo-Won Park	73-72-76-68	289	$28,822		Dimitrios Papadatos	72-72-75-74	293	$10,728
10=	Vijay Singh	73-74-70-73	290	$25,085		Rohan Blizard	70-74-75-74	293	$10,728
	Brad Kennedy	70-71-70-79	290	$25,085		Lucas Lee	69-71-76-77	293	$10,728
12=	Anirban Lahiri	74-69-75-73	291	$19,570	25=	Ted Oh	75-73-71-75	294	$9,340
	David Smail	76-71-67-77	291	$19,570		Stephen Dartnall	68-78-71-77	294	$9,340

In The Money: **295**: Adam Bland, Adam Blyth, Ryan Haller, Jason Scrivener, Nick Cullen **296**: Michael Hendry, Michael Choi, David McKenzie **297**: Nick Price, Daniel Nisbet, Tom Bond, David Bransdon, Michael Wright **298**: Stephen Leaney, Paul Spargo, Ji-Man Kang, Wen-Chong Liang, Scott Strange **299**: Brady Watt, Richard T. Lee, Josh Geary **300**: Masahiro Kawamura, Callan O'Reilly **301**: Jason Norris, Daniel Fox, Jung-Woong Ko **302**: Rhein Gibson **303**: David Klein, Marcus Cain, Jamie Arnold **305**: Mark Brown **306**: Steven Jones **307**: He Zeyu **308**: Tze-Huang Choo

OWR: 0 of top 50 entered   -   Rating: 9   -   Points to 14th   -   Jeffress: 12 points, to 461st in OWR

Isuzu Queensland Open

Aug 22 - Aug 25

Brookwater Golf & Country Club - Brookwater, Australia
Champion: Andrew Dodt

7,075 yards   Par 72
Purse: AU$110,000

Breaking a drought which dated to a win at the European Tour's 2010 Avantha Masters, 28-year-old Queensland native Andrew Dodt charged home with a final round 67 to claim his second win as a professional at the Isuzu Queensland Open. Dodt was an afterthought for most of the week at the Brookwater Golf & Country Club, playing his first nine in 38 on his way to an opening 72, then double-bogeying the first hole on Saturday en route to another 72, which left him six shots behind Tom Bond after 54 holes. But on a Sunday upon which nobody else bettered 69 (and none of the realistic contenders broke 70), Dodt birdied the opener and added a second birdie at the 8th to turn in 34. A bogey at the 379-yard 10th briefly slowed his momentum but he then mounted a serious charge, first birdieing the par-5 13th and the 436-yard 15th, then - when it mattered most - adding birdies at the 528-yard 17th and the 433-yard 18th to pull away and win by two. Despite a closing 75 (which included four untimely back nine bogeys), Bond held on to claim solo second, while a fivesome of players led by Australian prospect Jake Higginbottom tied for third.

1	Andrew Dodt	72-70-72-67	281	$16,500		David McKendrick	71-72-73-72	288	$1,980
2	Tom Bond	67-73-68-75	283	$10,450	16=	Marcus Cain	76-73-71-69	289	$1,452
3=	Cameron Smith	74-68-73-70	285	$4,994		Scott Laycock	69-74-73-73	289	$1,452
	Michael Long	72-72-71-70	285	$4,994		Daniel McGraw	72-75-68-74	289	$1,452
	Jake Higginbottom	72-67-75-71	285	$4,994		Max McCardle	75-66-73-75	289	$1,452
	Anthony Brown	65-73-74-73	285	$4,994		David Bransdon	67-74-72-76	289	$1,452
	Matthew Griffin	73-70-68-74	285	$4,994	21=	Matthew Guyatt	75-72-72-71	290	$1,221
8=	Kade McBride (a)	66-72-79-69	286	-		Ryan Fox	71-71-76-72	290	$1,221
	Brett Drewitt	73-74-68-71	286	$3,080		Leigh McKechnie	76-74-66-74	290	$1,221
10=	Grant Thomas	77-70-71-69	287	$2,558	24=	Jason Scrivener	74-73-75-69	291	$1,133
	Peter Martin	71-72-72-72	287	$2,558		Michael Sim	76-70-73-72	291	$1,133
12=	Nick Cullen	71-72-76-69	288	$1,980		Jim Cusdin	74-72-73-72	291	$1,133
	T. MacDonald (a)	72-76-71-69	288	-		S. Wools-Cobb (a)	71-72-74-74	291	-
	Adam Stephens	69-74-74-71	288	$1,980		Kim Felton	70-71-73-77	291	$1,133

In The Money: **292**: Rohan Blizard, Jason Norris, Josh Geary, Cameron Davis (a) **293**: Aaron Townsend, Peter Wilson, Viraat Badhwar (a), James Gibellini, Paul Spargo **294**: Aaron Pike, Tim Hart, Blake Proverbs (a), Josh Younger, Kristopher Mueck **295**: Timothy Wood, Steven Jones, Jake McLeod (a), Peter Lee, Rory Bourke, Matt Jager **296**: Pieter Zwart, Daniel Fox **297**: Andrew Evans **298**: David McKenzie, David Klein, Kieran Muir, Gavin Flint, Anthony Quayle (a) **300**: Craig Hancock **301**: Steven Jeffress, Ryan Lynch, Michael Wright **302**: Andy Chu (a), Peter Cooke, Kevin Conlong **304**: Ben Ford **305**: Paul Donahoo

OWR: 0 of top 50 entered   -   Rating: 0   -   Points to 7th   -   Dodt: 6 points, to 424th in OWR

South Pacific Open Championship — Sep 10 - Sep 13

Tina Golf Club - Noumea, New Caledonia
Champion: Adam Stephens
6,442 yards Par 72
Purse: AU$140,000

Twenty-six-year-old Australian Adam Stephens won for the first time on the Australasian Tour, building a big 54-hole lead before eventually marching home to a five-shot victory at the second playing of the South Pacific Open Championship, in New Caledonia. Competing against a relatively light field (world number 304 Matthew Griffin was the top-ranked entry), Stephens opened with rounds of 67-64-68 over the undersize Tina Golf Club layout, numbers which somewhat surprisingly lifted him to a five-shot Saturday night lead. Stephens then three-putt bogeyed the first hole on Sunday, but on a day when his scrambling outpaced his ball-striking, he still managed to turn in 36 before rattling off three birdies between holes 10-14 which effectively secured the title. A late bogey at the par-4 16th reduced Stephens' margin to five strokes over a trio of runners-up: Australians Andrew Kelly and Kota Kagasaki, as well as 21-year-old New Zealand amateur Luke Toomey. Australian prospect Jason Scrivener tied for 5th after a double bogey at the last cost him a solo second-place finish.

1	Adam Stephens	67-64-68-70	269	$21,000	12=	Brady Watt	71-67-73-67	278	$2,520
2=	Luke Toomey (a)	73-64-69-68	274	-		David McKendrick	70-68-70-70	278	$2,520
	Andrew Kelly	74-63-69-68	274	$11,550		Michael Wright	66-68-70-74	278	$2,520
	Kota Kagasaki	72-67-65-70	274	$11,550	15=	Matthew Griffin	71-69-71-68	279	$1,897
5=	Ben. Clementson	71-70-69-65	275	$5,495		Max McCardle	72-69-70-68	279	$1,897
	Jason Scrivener	71-71-67-66	275	$5,495		Brad Shilton	68-65-76-70	279	$1,897
	Peter Lee	71-69-68-67	275	$5,495		Jason Norris	66-67-73-73	279	$1,897
	Daniel Valente	66-69-70-70	275	$5,495	19=	Edward Stedman	68-72-71-69	280	$1,579
9	Tim Hart	68-69-69-70	276	$3,920		Jun Seok Lee	70-70-69-71	280	$1,579
10=	Mitchell A. Brown	72-64-71-70	277	$3,255		Jean-Louis Guepy	70-69-69-72	280	$1,579
	Matthew Guyatt	69-66-70-72	277	$3,255		Josh Geary	72-69-67-72	280	$1,579

In The Money: **281**: Matthew Millar, R.J. Caracella, Anthony Summers, Grant Thomas, Blair Riordan **282**: Pieter Zwart, Paul Spargo, Samuel Eaves, Christopher Wood, Luke Humphries, Jared Pender **283**: Ryan Fox, Kevin Conlong, Theodore Coroneo, Antonio Murdaca (a) **284**: Daniel Nisbet, Daniel Griffin, Neven Basic, Ryan Lynch, Josh Younger, Michael Foster **285**: Taylor Cooper, Andrew Campbell, Steven Jeffress, James Gibellini, Tom Bond **286**: Adam Blyth **287**: Matt Jager **288**: Kieran Muir **289**: Alex Edge **299**: Mitch Davis **300**: Peter Poposki

OWR: 0 of top 50 entered - Rating: 0 - Points to 8th - Stephens: 6 points, to 756th in OWR

Western Australia Open — Oct 16 - Oct 19

Cottesloe Golf Course - Perth, Western Australia
Champion: Ryan Fox
6,716 yards Par 72
Purse: AU$110,000

Twenty-seven-year-old New Zealander Ryan Fox broke through for his first victory on the Australasian Tour, running away from the field to claim the Western Australia Open by a resounding six shots. The son of former rugby star Grant Fox, Ryan did much to justify his reputation as a top (if somewhat late-arriving) Kiwi prospect by carding an opening round 64 at the Cottesloe Golf Club, good enough to join eventual runner-up Steven Dartnall in a tie for second, one behind Victoria's Steven Jones. A second round 66 moved him into the lead, two ahead of South Australian Paul Spargo, and when Fox carded a Saturday 68 and Spargo his third straight 66, the pair were tied atop the 54-hole leaderboard, three shots clear of Queensland's Daniel Nisbet. But while Spargo would crumble to a 74 on Sunday, Fox hit the ground running, logging five birdies (against one bogey) over his first eight holes, then adding to two more at the 10th and the par-5 14th to pull far enough clear that a bogey at the 18th was of no consequence. Dartnall close with 69 to grab second, while Nisbet (71) joined Spargo and globetrotting Rhein Gibson in a tie for third.

1	Ryan Fox	64-66-68-67	265	$16,500		Aaron Townsend	70-67-68-71	276	$1,760
2	Stephen Dartnall	64-69-69-69	271	$10,450	16=	Andre Stolz	70-68-67-72	277	$1,595
3=	Rhein Gibson	71-65-66-70	272	$5,903		David Bransdon	68-70-66-73	277	$1,595
	Daniel Nisbet	65-69-67-71	272	$5,903	18=	Jason Scrivener	69-71-67-71	278	$1,386
	Paul Spargo	66-66-66-74	272	$5,903		Matthew Millar	67-69-70-72	278	$1,386
	Mathew Perry	68-71-69-67	275	$5,903	20=	Kalem Richardson	68-69-71-71	279	$1,240
6=	Josh Younger	71-67-73-64	275	$2,805		Gareth Paddison	69-70-69-71	279	$1,240
	Kim Felton	69-68-69-69	275	$2,805		Tim Hart	70-68-69-72	279	$1,240
	Todd Sinnott (a)	65-67-73-70	275	-		Andrew Tampion	68-69-68-74	279	$1,240
	Daniel Fox	68-68-69-70	275	$2,805	24=	Marcus Cain	68-70-71-71	280	$1,133
	Matt Jager	71-65-68-71	275	$2,805		Peter Lee	68-69-71-72	280	$1,133
	Anthony Houston	73-64-67-71	275	$2,805		David McKenzie	70-71-69-70	280	$1,133
	Steven Jones	63-70-69-73	275	$2,805		Peter O'Malley	66-70-70-74	280	$1,133
14=	Minwoo Lee (a)	73-64-68-71	276	-					

In The Money: **281**: Michael Wright, Jack Wilson, Curtis Luck (a), Josh Geary, Mark Brown, Grant Thomas, Ryan Haller, Mitchell A. Brown **282**: Aaron Pike **283**: Luke Humphries, Brody Ninyette, Clint Rice, Alex Hawley **284**: James Nitties, Matthew Ballard, Jake Stirling, Peter Cooke, Bradley Hughes, Daniel McGraw, Michael Foster **285**: Troy Cox **287**: Michael Choi, Daniel Valente **288**: Jason Norris, Craig Hancock **290**: Scott Laycock **291**: Max McCardle

OWR: 0 of top 50 entered - Rating: 0 - Points to 13th - Fox: 6 points, to 380th in OWR

Western Australia Goldfields PGA Championship

Oct 30 - Nov 2

Kalgoorlie Golf Course - Kalgoorlie, Western Australia
Champion: Ryan Lynch

6,768 metres   Par 72
Purse: AU$110,000

Twenty-five-year-old Victorian Ryan Lynch closed with a five-under-par 67 to record his first Australasian Tour victory, a one-shot triumph at the Western Australia PGA Championship. Lynch played steady golf over the first three days, posting rounds of 68-69-72 but still trailing 54-hole leader Chris Gaunt by an imposing six shots. Thus beginning the final round with lots of distance to cover, he wasted little time in making a move, recording birdies at the 1st, the 6th, the 8th and the 9th to turn in 32 and stand 11 under par – though victory likely still felt like a reach as the 39-year-old Gaunt balanced three birdies against two bogeys to turn in 35, to stand at -14. Birdies by Lynch at the 10th and 13th then narrowed the gap before an untimely Gaunt bogey at the 15th drew the pair even. Both men recorded nervous bogeys at the 17th, but after Lynch parred the three-shot 18th to post a 67, and a 276 total, Gaunt caved in, bogeying the last to hand Lynch the title.

1	Ryan Lynch	68-69-72-67	276	$16,500		Luke Humphries	67-71-71-75	284	$1,980
2=	Peter Cooke	70-66-70-71	277	$9,075	15=	Marcus Cain	69-73-72-71	285	$1,491
	Chris Gaunt	67-67-69-74	277	$9,075		Rhein Gibson	69-74-70-72	285	$1,491
4	Ben Campbell	65-71-71-71	278	$5,500		Andrew Kelly	68-74-69-74	285	$1,491
5=	Daniel Valente	71-68-68-72	279	$4,510		Lincoln Tighe	68-71-71-75	285	$1,491
	Jarryd Felton (a)	71-65-69-74	279	-	19	Tom Bond	71-73-71-71	286	$1,298
7=	Anthony Houston	69-72-72-68	281	$3,630	20=	Michael Choi	71-74-71-71	287	$1,183
	Tim Hart	68-69-71-73	281	$3,630		Callan O'Reilly	70-71-76-70	287	$1,183
9=	Nathan Green	67-71-74-70	282	$2,888		James Nitties	68-72-74-73	287	$1,183
	Peter Lee	71-71-65-75	282	$2,888		Steven Jones	71-74-73-69	287	$1,183
11	Craig Hancock	71-71-73-68	283	$2,420		Gavin Reed	68-73-73-73	287	$1,183
12=	Anthony Brown	69-73-72-70	284	$1,980		Mitchell A. Brown	69-73-72-73	287	$1,183
	Matthew Ballard	70-69-73-72	284	$1,980					

In The Money: **288**: Kieran Muir, Tarquin MacManus, Sven Puymbroeck **289**: Kristopher Mueck **290**: Alex Edge, Nick Gillespie, Daniel Hoeve, Rory Bourke, Grant Thomas, Ashley Hall, James Gibellini **291**: Christopher Brown, Jamie Hook **292**: Bradley Hughes, Aaron Pike, Pieter Zwart, Jordan Sherratt **293**: Kim Felton, Peter Welden, Michael Moore, Jake Stirling **294**: Andrew Martin, Michael Wright, Rika Batibasaga, Ben Ferguson (a) **295**: Matthew Guyatt, Peter Poposki **297**: David Klein **299**: James Betts, Harrison Russell **300**: Luke Whitbread **303**: Ian Esson, Brendan Lee **WD**: Daniel Nisbet (147) **DQ**: Jack Wilson (210)

OWR: 0 of top 50 entered - Rating: 0 - Points to 6th - Lynch: 6 points, to 692nd in OWR

Mazda New South Wales Open

Nov 13 - Nov 16

Stonecutters Ridge Golf Club - Sydney, Australia
Champion: Anthony Brown

6,928 yards   Par 72
Purse: AU$100,000

Thirty-two-year-old Victorian Anthony Brown broke through for his first career Australasian Tour victory at the New South Wales Open, edging New Zealand's Josh Geary on the second hole of sudden death. For the first 54 holes, it looked rather more likely to be Geary's week as he opened with rounds of 66-68-68, his 202 total leaving him tied atop the leaderboard with ex-PGA Tour player James Nitties, and two strokes ahead of reigning U.S. Amateur champion Gunn Yang. Brown, for his part, stood three behind after opening with 71-65-69, and he made little in the way of an early move on Sunday, offsetting an opening birdie with a bogey at the 3rd, and turning in even par – and thus losing ground as both Geary and Nitties went out in one under. But both of the leaders would stumble coming home, Nitties bouncing around to an inward 38 (which included a double-bogey at the par-3 11th), Geary to a slightly less tumultuous 37. This paved the way for Brown, who methodically birdied all three of the homeward par 5s to post a 69 and finish on 274 – a total matched by Geary with a clutch birdie at the last. Both men birdied the 18th on the first replay, but only Brown could do it a second time, and the title was his.

1	Anthony Brown	71-65-69-69	274	$15,000		Jake Stirling	69-72-68-72	281	$1,725
2	Josh Geary	66-68-68-72	274	$9,500		Cameron Davis (a)	73-69-67-72	281	-
3	James Nitties	65-66-71-73	275	$7,000		Ben Campbell	69-75-65-72	281	$1,725
4	Gunn Yang (a)	69-69-66-72	276	-		Matthew Millar	68-67-73-73	281	$1,725
5=	Rohan Blizard	70-70-69-69	278	$4,200	18=	Ewan Porter	72-71-72-67	282	$1,248
	Michael Long	68-68-72-70	278	$4,200		Gavin Reed	77-65-69-71	282	$1,248
	Matthew Giles	70-68-68-72	278	$4,200		Michael Foster	71-71-68-72	282	$1,248
8	Daniel Valente	71-67-66-75	279	$3,100		Gavin Fairfax	71-70-66-75	282	$1,248
9=	Travis Smyth (a)	69-68-71-72	280	-		Nathan Green	67-68-70-77	282	$1,248
	Aaron Pike	71-69-68-72	280	$2,483	23=	Andrew Evans	68-72-73-70	283	$1,083
	Andrew Kelly	68-70-69-73	280	$2,483		Harrison Russell	69-69-72-73	283	$1,083
	Ashley Hall	71-68-68-73	280	$2,483		Ben Eccles (a)	73-66-69-75	283	-
13=	Ryan Lynch	69-68-72-72	281	$1,725		Chris Gaunt	69-68-69-77	283	$1,083

In The Money: **284**: Marcus Cain, Ryan Haller, Peter Lonard, Grant Thomas, Benjamin Clementson, Lincoln Tighe, Justin Warren (a) **285**: Fraser Wilkin, Jason King, Jim Cusdin, Adam Crawford, James Gibellini, Steven Jones **286**: Tarquin MacManus, Daniel Fox, Pieter Zwart, Ryan O'Flaherty, Kristopher Mueck, Harrison Endycott (a), Peter Martin **287**: Sugura Kugai (a), Peter Wilson, Richard Gallichan, Bradley Hughes, Peter Lee **288**: Charles Wright (a), Peter Poposki, Daniel Gale (a), Luke Whitbread, Leigh McKechnie, Dale Brandt-Richards (a) **289**: Jarrod Freeman (a), Kieran Muir, Simon Hawkes, Daniel Pearce **290**: Wayne Perske, Christopher Thorn, William Flitcroft (a), Kota Kagasaki, Andre Stolz **292**: Kim Felton **294**: Mitch Davis **295**: Mitchell Brown **299**: Nick Cochrane (a)

OWR: 0 of top 50 entered - Rating: 0 - Points to 7th - Brown: 6 points, to 646h in OWR

BetEasy Masters
Nov 20 - Nov 23

Metropolitan Golf Club - Oakleigh, Australia
Champion: Nick Cullen

7,170 yards Par 72
Purse: AU$1 Million

In the first of Australia's three major summer events, 30-year-old veteran Nick Cullen ended Adam Scott's quest for a third straight Gold Jacket by coming out of nowhere to edge Scott, Josh Younger and James Nitties at the BetEasy Australian Masters. Cullen entered the week ranked 539th in the world and with only one homeland victory on his résumé, the 2013 Queensland Open. But on a weekend which saw halfway leader Michael Wright shoot 74-80 (plummeting to a T46), Cullen posted a Saturday 66 to pull within two of 54-hole leader Paul Spargo, then jumpstarted an up-and-down final round with an eagle at the par-5 4th. He would ultimately record a wonderful sand save at the 18th to post a 69, then look on as Scott lipped out a birdie putt on the final green that would have forced a playoff.

1	Nick Cullen	73-71-66-69	279	$180,000
2=	Adam Scott	73-68-71-68	280	$72,500
	Josh Younger	70-70-71-69	280	$72,500
	James Nitties	72-71-67-70	280	$72,500
5=	Matthew Griffin	71-69-72-69	281	$34,250
	Aron Price	68-73-71-69	281	$34,250
	Adam Bland	75-68-69-69	281	$34,250
	Paul Spargo	70-67-71-73	281	$34,250
9=	Rhein Gibson	68-74-75-65	282	$26,000
	Robert Allenby	70-73-71-68	282	$26,000
11=	Anthony Houston	71-68-75-69	283	$20,000
	Bryden Macpherson	70-71-72-70	283	$20,000
	Matthew Guyatt	70-69-73-71	283	$20,000
	Lucas Herbert (a)	75-70-65-73	283	-
15=	Boo Weekley	72-72-70-70	284	$16,500
	Brett Rumford	74-68-71-71	284	$16,500
17=	David McKenzie	72-70-74-69	285	$11,975
	Todd Sinnott (a)	67-71-77-70	285	-
	Steven Bowditch	67-75-73-70	285	$11,975
	Ryan Ruffels (a)	75-68-72-70	285	-
	Tom Bond	70-72-72-71	285	$11,975
	Stephen Dartnall	72-73-69-71	285	$11,975
	Peter Wilson	70-71-72-72	285	$11,975
	Chris Campbell	72-74-66-73	285	$11,975
25=	Kristopher Mueck	72-70-76-68	286	$8,290
	Alistair Presnell	75-71-72-68	286	$8,290
	Stephen Leaney	73-71-72-70	286	$8,290
	Nathan Green	73-71-71-71	286	$8,290
	Zac Blair	70-75-69-72	286	$8,290
	Mathew Goggin	71-69-73-73	286	$8,290
	Nick O'Hern	76-69-67-74	286	$8,290
	Geoff Ogilvy	69-71-71-75	286	$8,290

In The Money: **287**: David Bransdon, Richard Green, Marcus Fraser, Kyle Stanley, Rohan Blizard **288**: Stephen Allan, Josh Geary, Benjamin Clementson, Jarrod Lyle, Daniel Valente, Kim Felton **289**: Craig Parry, Ryan Haller, Leigh McKechnie, Michael Wright **290**: Andrew Evans, Nathan Holman, Andrew Martin **291**: Matthew Giles **292**: Riley Wheeldon, Jason Norris **294**: Peter Lonard, Anthony Summers, Jin Jeong **295**: Michael Hendry, Leigh Deagan, David Klein, Richard Caracella **296**: Peter Cooke **297**: Ben Campbell **298**: James Marchesani **300**: Richard Lee

OWR: 1 of top 50 entered - Rating: 75 - Points to 24th - Cullen: 21 points, to 253rd in OWR

Emirates Australian Open
Nov 27 - Nov 30

The Australian Golf Club - Sidney, Australia
Champion: Jordan Spieth

7,245 yards Par 72
Purse: AU$1.25 Million

Twenty-one-year old American Jordan Spieth traveled far abroad hoping to end his year in style and this he did, sprinting to a runaway six-shot victory at the Australian Open. Spieth's victory was made all the more impressive by the manner in which he did it, posting a dazzling Sunday 63 (which beat the field by three shots) to break open a tournament whose scoring was consistently high due to fast greens and steady breezes. Spieth began the final round tied atop the leaderboard with Australians Greg Chalmers and Brett Rumford, and while most of the field struggled to make final round birdies, Spieth reeled off eight of them, carding four on the outward half to build a multi-shot lead. He then padded his margin with additional birdies at the 14th and 15th, then ran away and hid by adding two more at the 17th and the par-5 18th. It was the sort of round that generates a buzz – such as a Tweet from world number one Rory McIlroy, who said simply: "You could give me another 100 rounds today at The Australian and I wouldn't sniff 63. Congratulations Jordan Spieth."

1	Jordan Spieth	67-72-69-63	271	$225,000
2	Rod Pampling	73-67-69-68	277	$127,500
3	Brett Rumford	70-69-69-70	278	$84,375
4	Greg Chalmers	71-66-71-71	279	$60,000
5	Adam Scott	74-66-69-71	280	$50,000
6	Jake Higginbottom	71-69-72-69	281	$45,000
7=	Robert Allenby	71-69-73-70	283	$38,125
	Ryan Fox	72-72-69-70	283	$38,125
9	Daniel Nisbet	74-72-67-71	284	$33,750
10=	Nathan Holman	73-72-73-67	285	$25,500
	Sung-Hoon Kang	73-70-72-70	285	$25,500
	Aaron Townsend	73-70-71-71	285	$25,500
	Josh Younger	71-72-70-72	285	$25,500
	Aron Price	68-75-69-73	285	$25,500
	Stephen Dartnall	72-71-74-69	286	$25,500
15=	Stephen Allan	75-71-70-70	286	$15,320
	Steven Bowditch	70-74-71-71	286	$15,320
	Rory McIlroy	69-69-76-72	286	$15,320
	Richard Green	69-71-74-72	286	$15,320
	Boo Weekley	72-71-71-72	286	$15,320
	Alistair Presnell	74-72-68-72	286	$15,320
	David Bransdon	72-70-71-73	286	$15,320
23=	Conrad Shindler	70-68-81-68	287	$11,594
	Lucas Herbert (a)	75-71-72-69	287	-
	John Senden	73-69-75-70	287	$11,594
	Adam Crawford	69-69-76-73	287	$11,594
	James Nitties	71-73-70-73	287	$11,594

In The Money: **288**: Nick Cullen, Josh Geary, Ryan Ruffels (a), Patrick Rodgers **289**: Jin-ho Choi, Matthew Griffin, Todd Sinnott (a) **290**: Geoff Drakeford, Joon-Wo Choi, Jason Norris **291**: Aaron Pike, David McKenzie, Jason Scrivener, Brendon De Jonge, Nathan Green, Oliver Goss, Callan O'Reilly, Rohan Blizard **292**: Matt Jager, Michael Hendry, Adam Bland, Brad Shilton, Matthew Millar, Antonio Murdaca (a), Leigh McKechnie, Rhein Gibson **293**: Stephen Leaney, Garrett Sapp **294**: Ashley Hall, Jin Jeong, Kyle Stanley, Brady Watt, James Marchesani, Lincoln Tighe **295**: Michael Long, Steven Jeffress, David McKendrick, Bryden Macpherson **296**: Andrew Evans, Craig Parry, Jamie Lovemark, Scott Gardiner, Matthew Giles **297**: Michael Wright, Cameron Smith, Geoff Ogilvy **298**: Taylor MacDonald (a) **299**: Max McCardle **306**: Bradley Hughes

OWR: 4 of top 50 entered - Rating: 175 - Points to 45th - Spieth: 34 points, to 11th in OWR

Nanshan New South Wales PGA Championship

Dec 4 - Dec 7

Riverside Oaks Golf Resort (Gangurru Course) - Cattai, Australia
Champion: Lincoln Tighe

6,311 yards   Par 72
Purse: AU$110,000

Twenty-five-year-old Lincoln Tighe broke through for his first career victory on the Australasian Tour, coming from well off the pace via a sterling final round 64 to capture the New South Wales PGA Championship. A New South Wales native, Tighe grabbed the lead early by opening with a 63 on Thursday, then posted a 70 to stand five behind halfway leader Troy Moses, a local amateur who torched the Riverside Oaks resort layout with a Friday 62 that included eight birdies and an eagle. A third round 72 would take much of the wind out of Moses' sails, though he would ultimately close with 69 (including an eagle at the 1st) to tie for third. With 54-hole leader Scott Arnold having posted another 62 on Saturday, Tighe began Sunday five shots in arrears but quickly recorded five birdies (against one bogey) over his first seven holes, then added three more on the final nine to edge Arnold by one at the wire. The victory gave Tighe a two-year Australasian exemption – a great holiday gift as he'd previously been ticketed for first-stage Q School two weeks hence.

1	Lincoln Tighe	63-70-68-64	265	$16,500		Michael Choi	67-72-65-70	274	$1,760
2	Scott Arnold	65-69-62-70	266	$10,450		Gavin Reed	67-69-68-70	274	$1,760
3=	Kristopher Mueck	71-63-70-66	270	$7,700		Matt Jager	69-68-67-70	274	$1,760
	Troy Moses (a)	67-62-72-69	270	-		David Klein	67-67-69-71	274	$1,760
5=	Clint Rice	66-68-68-69	271	$5,005	19=	Mitchell A. Brown	68-67-73-67	275	$1,279
	Grant Thomas	68-66-67-70	271	$5,005		Josh Younger	67-70-72-66	275	$1,279
7=	Daniel Valente	68-72-67-65	272	$3,630		Matthew Millar	66-67-69-73	275	$1,279
	Peter Cooke	68-68-67-69	272	$3,630		Ryan Lynch	69-65-66-75	275	$1,279
9=	Jamie Arnold	65-71-71-66	273	$2,732	23	Daniel Hoeve	72-65-72-67	276	$1,188
	Travis Smyth (a)	71-68-70-64	273	-	24=	David McKendrick	69-67-71-70	277	$1,122
	Anthony Houston	69-68-69-67	273	$2,732		Aaron Townsend	68-70-71-68	277	$1,122
	Richard Gallichan	69-65-71-68	273	$2,732		Luke Humphries	69-65-71-72	277	$1,122
13=	Bronson La'Cassie	68-69-68-69	274	$1,760		Theodore Coroneo	71-67-67-72	277	$1,122
	Callan O'Reilly	69-69-67-69	274	$1,760		Leigh McKechnie	68-67-76-66	277	$1,122

In The Money: **278**: Samuel Eaves, Michael Foster, Anthony Summers, Andrew Kelly, Jamie Hook **279**: Kieran Muir, Jarryd Felton (a), Fraser Wilkin, Ben Campbell, William Gunn **280**: Peter Martin, Geoff Drakeford **281**: Jin Zhang, Andrew Martin, Jim Cusdin, Harrison Russell, Brendan Smith **282**: Rohan Blizard, Blake McGrory **283**: Simon Hawkes, Alex Edge **284**: Kota Kagasaki, Jason King, Christopher Thorn **285**: Bradley Fasher **288**: Benjamin Clementson **289**: Stuart Meani

OWR: 0 of top 50 entered - Rating: 0 - Points to 6th - Tighe: 6 points, to 760th in OWR

Australian PGA Championship

Nov 7 - Nov 10

RACV Royal Pines - Gold Coast, Australia
Champion: Greg Chalmers

7,378 yards   Par 71
Purse: AU$1 Million

It took an Australian record seven extra holes to do it but PGA Tour veteran Greg Chalmers won his second Australian PGA Championship by beating both Adam Scott and Wade Ormsby in sudden death. The 41-year-old Chalmers began the final round fully seven shots behind the leaders but carded a tournament low 64 on Sunday to roar back into the hunt. Beating the field by four strokes, Chalmers finished two hours before both Scott and Ormsby, who each closed with a 71 to deadlock the trio on 277. Ormsby departed the playoff on the third extra hole after failing to match his opponents' birdies, leaving Chalmers to emerge victorious when Scott three-putted for bogey four holes later. Indeed, the putter was truly the story for the world number three, as Scott missed four potentially clinching birdies during the seven extra holes – though as he observed afterwards, few of them were of the short, highly makeable variety. New Zealand's Michael Hendry took solo fourth, two shots out of the playoff, while visiting Americans Scott Stallings and Boo Weekley claimed fifth and sixth respectively.

1	Greg Chalmers	71-71-71-64	277	$180,000		David Bransdon	73-70-68-74	285	$15,680
2=	Wade Ormsby	68-67-71-71	277	$84,750	18=	Peter Lonard	70-74-72-70	286	$10,607
	Adam Scott	68-69-69-71	277	$84,750		Matthew Guyatt	72-72-70-72	286	$10,607
4	Michael Hendry	70-71-67-71	279	$48,000		Jun Seok Lee	72-68-72-73	286	$10,607
5	Scott Stallings	72-70-68-70	280	$40,000		Michael Wright	71-73-69-73	286	$10,607
6	Boo Weekley	66-72-69-74	281	$36,000		Brett Rumford	72-71-70-73	286	$10,607
7=	Matthew Giles	73-69-70-70	282	$30,500		David Smail	68-71-71-76	286	$10,607
	Scott Strange	69-66-71-76	282	$30,500		Jason Scrivener	73-66-68-79	286	$10,607
9=	John Senden	73-68-73-69	283	$26,000	25=	Adam Crawford	73-70-73-71	287	$7,586
	Cameron Smith	74-68-71-70	283	$26,000		Nathan Green	69-73-73-72	287	$7,586
11=	Marc Leishman	69-71-74-70	284	$21,000		Nick Cullen	68-71-75-73	287	$7,586
	Ryan Fox	70-74-69-71	284	$21,000		Craig Hancock	68-71-75-73	287	$7,586
13=	Brad Kennedy	69-73-75-68	285	$15,680		Josh Geary	70-72-72-73	287	$7,586
	Robert Allenby	72-69-72-72	285	$15,680		Peter Cooke	70-72-71-74	287	$7,586
	Geoff Drakeford	73-68-72-72	285	$15,680		Jarrod Lyle	69-72-70-76	287	$7,586
	Brendon De Jonge	71-71-70-73	285	$15,680					

In The Money: **288**: Ryan Haller, Jin Jeong, Matt Jager, Ryan C.Carter, Jake Higginbottom, Mark Brown, Rod Pampling **289**: Tim Hart, Conrad Shindler, Nick Gillespie, Neven Basic **290**: Alistair Presnell, Garrett Sapp, James Marchesani **291**: Bradley Lamb, Max McCardle, Mathew Goggin, Brady Watt, Rory Hie **292**: Paul Donahoo, Daniel Fox, Steven Jones, Kristopher Mueck **293**: Jason Norris **294**: John Young Kim, Lincoln Tighe, Daniel Popovic **296**: Adam Stephens, Josh Younger **297**: Dimitrios Papadatos, Ratchapol Jantavara

OWR: 3 of top 50 entered - Rating: 96 - Points to 31st - Chalmers: 24 points, to 173rd in OWR

ONEASIA TOUR 2014

Originally planned as a regional supertour which, by joining together parts of the Australasian, Japan and Asian Tours, would potentially be able to stand toe-to-toe with the European circuit in terms of money and prestige, OneAsia has met with only limited success to date. Indeed, while it has nearly doubled the number of events on its schedule since debuting with a slim menu of five tournaments in 2009, the fact is that five of 2014's nine competitions were co-sanctioned with more established tours. Three of these, the European Tour's Volvo China Open and the Australasian circuit's Australian PGA and Australian Open (all profiled in their respective sections), are central events on those Tours, leaving OneAsia's co-sanctioning of them as little more than an asterisk. Another, the Indonesia PGA Championship, is the lead off event on the Japan Golf Tour (and is profiled there) – and while a potentially expanded partnership with the Japan Tour could serve OneAsia well, the loss of a second co-sanctioned event (the Thailand Open) from 2013 hardly bodes well.

And in truth, three of the remaining four events (the Caltex Maekyung Open, the SK Telecom Open and the Kolon Korea Open) are actually marquee stops on the second-tier Korean PGA Tour, and would survive just fine without any OneAsia connection. Thus after six years of doing business, OneAsia has exactly one event - October's Nanshan China Masters - that it can actually call its own.

As a result OneAsia can, in many respects, be viewed as doing little more than stringing together significant events from other tours into a patchwork schedule while possessing little identity of its own. Consequently, while it can still claim noteworthy players like Jordan Spieth, Alexander Levy and up-and-coming Chinese star Hao-Tong Li as 2014 winners, only the 19-year-old Li is likely to think of himself as a OneAsia Tour champion. For the others, that fact is merely a footnote added to a European or Australasian Tour victory.

2014 OneAsia Tour Top 60 Money Winners

#	Player	Money	#	Player	Money	#	Player	Money
1	Seung-Hyuk Kim	$501,990	21	Mark Brown	$54,510	41	Aaron Townsend	$38,982
2	Hao-Tong Li	$219,983	22	Stephen Dartnall	$50,768	42	David Oh	$38,759
3	Jun-Won Park	$205,073	23	Guo-Wu Zhou	$50,000	43	Soon-Sang Hong	$38,401
4	Steve Jeffress	$186,521	24	Garrett Sapp	$49,498	44	Joshua Younger	$37,810
5	Sang-Hyun Park	$161,695	25	Nathan Holman	$47,947	45	Nick Cullen	$36,806
6	Jun Seok Lee	$156,567	26	Jason Scrivener	$46,974	46	Bi-o Kim	$36,688
7	Jake Higginbottom	$147,609	27	Matthew Griffin	$46,381	47	Hyo-Won Park	$35,314
8	Tae-Hee Lee	$144,646	28	Ji-Man Kang	$46,117	48	Ju-Hyuk Park	$34,207
9	Ryan Fox	$117,027	29	Tae-Hoon Kim	$46,027	49	Ryan Haller	$31,352
10	Il-Hwan Park	$113,010	30	Nick Gillespie	$45,919	50	Gareth Paddison	$31,349
11	Rhein Gibson	$109,497	31	Young-Han Song	$45,840	51	Scott Laycock	$29,010
12	Terry Pilkadaris	$99,963	32	Jin-Ho Choi	$45,210	52	Matthew Giles	$28,831
13	Ho-Sung Choi	$87,513	33	In-Hoi Hur	$44,665	53	Joon-Woo Choi	$28,061
14	Sung-Hoon Kang	$86,156	34	Gi-Whan Kim	$44,648	54	Jason Norris	$27,682
15	Michael Sim	$84,092	35	Mu Hu	$42,125	55	Rory Hie	$27,598
16	David Bransdon	$79,553	36	Yi-Keun Chang	$41,859	56	Xin-Jun Zhang	$25,820
17	Dong-Kyu Jang	$71,395	37	Michael Wright	$41,682	57	Zheng Ouyang	$24,142
18	Dong-Seop Maeg	$70,332	38	Wen-Chong Liang	$41,340	58	Geon-Ha Kim	$23,618
19	Scott Strange	$65,990	39	Prom Meesawat	$40,188	59	Rohan Blizard	$22,299
20	Michael Hendry	$58,127	40	David McKenzie	$40,000	60	Josh Geary	$21,863

GS Caltex Maekyung Open Championship

May 8 - May 11

Namseoul Country Club - Seoul, South Korea
Champion: Jun-Won Park
6,964 yards   Par 72
Purse: $918,000

Little-known 27-year-old South Korean Jun-Won Park, who only gained status on the OneAsia circuit on the eve of play, carded a closing 67 to pull away for a surprising first professional victory at the long-running GS Caltex Maekyung Open in Seoul. Park initially moved himself into contention with a Friday 64 (the week's low round), then added a Saturday 70 to share the 54-hole lead with countryman Sang-Hyun Park, with the two standing on 10-under-par 206, two shots ahead of the field. Things initially seemed to favor Hang-Hyun on Sunday when he birdied two of his first five holes, but a bogey at the par-4 8th slowed his momentum just as Jun-Won was heating up, with the less-heralded man promptly birdieing the par-5 9th, then pulling steadily away with additional birdies at the 12th, 14th and 15th holes. Ki-Sang Lee and Jung-Gon Hwang tied for third, six shots back, while the top foreign player was long-hitting Australian Scott Hend, who tied for fifth.

1	Jun-Won Park	72-64-70-67	273	$191,580
2	Sang-Hyun Park	72-66-68-70	276	$114,948
3=	Ki-Sang Lee	70-73-69-67	279	$58,432
	Jung-Gon Hwang	69-73-66-71	279	$58,432
5=	Woo-hyun Kim	69-68-74-70	281	$31,611
	Il-Hwan Park	70-69-71-71	281	$31,611
	Scott Hend	71-66-72-72	281	$31,611
	Dong-Kyu Jang	69-72-69-71	281	$31,611
	Nam-Hun Kim	75-66-69-71	281	$31,611
10=	Young-Han Song	69-71-74-68	282	$20,020
	Ryan Fox	73-71-70-68	282	$20,020
	Dong-Min Lee	72-70-69-71	282	$20,020
13=	Do-Kyu Park	71-70-74-68	283	$13,650
	David Oh	75-70-67-71	283	$13,650
15=	Ho-Sung Choi	68-72-75-69	284	$11,040
	Hyung-Sung Kim	70-72-72-70	284	$11,040
	Seung-Hyuk Kim	68-71-72-73	284	$11,040
	Jeong-Hyup Hyun	70-70-71-73	284	$11,040
19=	Sung-Kug Park	69-72-76-68	285	$9,249
	Hao-Tong Li	70-72-70-73	285	$9,249
	Seng-Yong Kim	70-73-69-73	285	$9,249
	Gareth Paddison	73-69-70-73	285	$9,249
23=	Sung-Hoon Kang	72-70-73-71	286	$8,382
	Hyung-Tae Kim	71-72-70-73	286	$8,382
25=	Gi-Whan Kim	72-74-70-71	287	$7,951
	Jin Jeong	71-72-72-72	287	$7,951
	Tae-Kyu Lee	73-69-73-72	287	$7,951
	Kyung-Tae Kim	71-73-73-70	287	$7,951
	Stephen Dartnall	74-70-70-73	287	$7,951
	Kyoung-Hoon Lee	68-66-78-75	287	$7,951

In The Money: **288**: Jason Norris, Dae-Sub Kim, Joon-Woo Choi, Michael Sim **289**: Geon-Ha Kim, Rohan Blizard, Garrett Sapp, Won-Kyung Heo, Kang-Chun Wu **290**: Wook-Soon Kang, Tae-Hee Park, Ju-Hyuk Park **291**: Hui-Soo Kim, Jae-Hyun An, Soon-Sang Hong, Heung-Chol Joo, In-Choon Hwang **292**: Mark Brown, Bryden MacPherson, Byung-Min Cho, Chang-Woo Lee, Sung-Ho Lee **293**: Ryan Haller **294**: In-Hoi Hur, Yun-Han Jeong (a), Michael Long, Hyun-Woo Ryu **295**: Jun-Seok Lee, Sang-Hee Lee **296**: Jong-Yul Suk, Nathan Holman, Josh Geary **297**: Eun-Ho Yeom (a) **298**: Byung-Jun Kim, Kyong-Jun Moon, Scott Laycock, Joong-Kyung Mo, Seuk-Hyun Baek **299**: Thanyakon Khrongpha, Wei-Huang Wu **301**: Ji-Hoon Lee **303**: Chang-Yoon Kim **304**: Deuk-Hee Park

OWR: 0 of top 50 entered - Rating: 12 - Points to 12th - Park: 10 points, to 416th in OWR

SK Telecom Open

May 15 - May 18

Sky 72 Golf Club (Ocean Course) - Incheon, South Korea
Champion: Seung-Hyuk Kim
6,652 yards   Par 72
Purse: $918,000

Twenty-eight-year-old Seung-Hyuk Kim emerged from a crowded leaderboard to claim his first victory as a professional, winning the long-running SK Telecom Open in Incheon. Kim got off to a fast start with an opening 66, then backed it up with rounds of 74-67 to tie his more internationally experienced countryman Kyung-Tae Kim atop the 54-hole leaderboard on nine-under-par 207. But as four players moved to 10 under early on Sunday, Kim appeared to fall from contention after double-bogeying the 350-yard 4th, only to climb back with birdies at the 5th and the 7th. Despite one more bogey at the 219-yard 8th, he would then charge home in 33 – including sinking a clutch nine-foot birdie putt at the last – to edge Kyung-Tae Kim and Tae-Hee Lee by one. Australian David Bransdon closed with 69 to claim solo fourth, while homestanding hero K.J. Choi finished fifth, three shots back.

1	Seung-Hyuk Kim	66-74-67-70	277	$195,122
2=	Tae-Hee Lee	68-68-73-69	278	$78,049
	Kyung-Tae Kim	70-70-67-71	278	$78,049
4	David Bransdon	71-70-69-69	279	$46,829
5	K.J. Choi	75-67-70-68	280	$39,024
6	Kyoung-Hoon Lee	70-70-69-72	281	$33,951
7=	Dae-Hyun Kim	72-69-75-66	282	$28,098
	Sang-Hyun Park	72-67-73-70	282	$28,098
9=	Nam-Hun Kim (a)	72-73-69-69	283	-
	David Oh	74-70-69-70	283	$22,634
	Dong-Kyu Jang	75-66-70-72	283	$22,634
12=	Michael Wright	71-73-70-70	284	$17,951
	Ho-Sung Choi	71-71-71-71	284	$17,951
	Il-Hwan Park	73-70-69-72	284	$17,951
	Jason Scrivener	72-72-67-73	284	$17,951
16	Gi-Whan Kim	75-68-72-70	285	$14,829
17=	Ryan Fox	74-69-73-70	286	$11,875
	Seong-Man Han	71-70-75-70	286	$11,875
	Ji-Hoon Lee	74-70-72-70	286	$11,875
	Mark Brown	76-68-71-71	286	$11,875
	Hyung-Sung Kim	71-70-73-72	286	$11,875
	Dong-Min Lee	70-72-72-72	286	$11,875
	Sang-Hee Lee	75-68-70-73	286	$11,875
24=	Jason Kang	75-67-74-71	287	$8,780
	Michael Sim	72-71-73-71	287	$8,780
	David McKenzie	73-74-70-70	287	$8,780
	Matthew Griffin	75-70-71-71	287	$8,780
	Garrett Sapp	78-69-68-72	287	$8,780
	Nick Cullen	71-71-72-73	287	$8,780

In The Money: **288**: Adam Bland, Sung-Kug Park, Jung-Gon Hwang, Woo-Lee Bae, Jamie Arnold, Jay Choi **289**: Joon-Woo Choi **290**: Sung-Yoon Kim, Steven Jones, Do-Hoon Kim #752, Seuk-Hyun Baek, Michio Matsumura, Devin Daniels **291**: Soon-Sang Hong, Soo-Min Lee, Tommy Mou, Scott Hend **292**: Terry Pilkadaris, Jung-Hwan Lee, Ryan Galler, Jin-Oh Song, Callan O'Reilly **293**: Min-Gyu Cho, Sung-Yeol Kwan, Ki-Taek Kwon **294**: Lian-Wei Zhang, Streve Jeffress **295**: Woo-Hyun Kim, Michael Long, Hui-Soo Kim, Jason Norris, Dae-Sub Kim, Do-Hoon Kim #753 **296**: Jae-Ho Kim, Jae-Kyung Park, Wisut Artjanawat, Scott Laycock **297**: Rory Hie, Byung-Jun Kim, In-Ho Kim **298**: Kwanchai Tannin. Ki-Sang Lee

OWR: 0 of top 50 entered - Rating: 14 - Points to 15th - Kim: 10 points, to 365th in OWR

Nanshan Chinese Masters
Nanshan International Golf Club (Montgomerie) - Shandong, China
Champion: Hao-Tong Li

Oct 9 - Oct 12
7,508 yards   Par 72
Purse: $1 Million

Nineteen-year-old Hao-Tong Li, a professional on the developmental PGA Tour China, broke through for his first major tour victory at the OneAsia circuit's China Masters, cruising to a four-shot triumph over his home course at the Nanshan International Golf Club. Coming off an eight-shot runaway win on the PGA Tour-sponsored developmental circuit a week earlier, Li tore out to a fast start in Shanghai, following an opening 68 with a bogey-free Friday 65 that opened up a three-shot lead over New Zealand's Nick Gillespie and Garrett Sapp of the United States. Though both pursuers fell off the pace on Saturday, Li's 72 left the door somewhat open as Korean Yi-Keun Chang (65) and Australian Rhein Gibson (69) each closed within one. But on a windy Sunday which saw gusts up to 40 miles per hour, Li played his first 10 holes even par, stumbled briefly with a double-bogey at the par-3 11th, then stepped on the gas with birdies at the 14th, 15th and 17th to pull away to victory. Korean Jun Seok Lee, the only player to break 70 on Sunday, rode his fine 69 to solo second.

1	Hao-Tong Li	68-65-72-70	275	$180,000	15=	Aaron Townsend	75-70-69-73	287	$15,900
2	Jun Seok Lee	69-69-72-69	279	$105,000		Rhein Gibson	67-70-69-81	287	$15,900
3	Todd Baek	73-69-65-74	281	$70,000	17=	David McKenzie	72-75-68-73	288	$13,200
4	Guo-Wu Zhou	68-71-70-73	282	$50,000		Xiong-Yi Zhao	71-72-69-76	288	$13,200
5	Nick Gillespie	68-68-74-73	283	$42,000	19=	Rak Cho	71-76-68-74	289	$11,060
6=	Mu Hu	69-71-72-72	284	$35,650		Scott Laycock	69-73-73-74	289	$11,060
	Michael Sim	70-69-69-76	284	$35,650		Geon-Ha Kim	72-74-67-76	289	$11,060
8=	Sang-Yeop Lee	71-73-71-70	285	$28,367		Jeung-Hun Wang	72-73-68-76	289	$11,060
	Jin-Ho Choi	70-73-67-75	285	$28,367		R. Wannasrichan	70-74-68-77	289	$11,060
	Yi-Keun Chang	70-71-65-79	285	$28,367	24=	Dong Su	70-73-73-74	290	$9,325
11=	Panuwat Muenlek	74-71-71-70	286	$20,200		Rory Hie	72-75-69-74	290	$9,325
	Stephen Dartnall	72-70-71-73	286	$20,200		Ze-Yu He	74-70-73-73	290	$9,325
	Gareth Paddison	69-71-70-76	286	$20,200		Daniel Woltman	67-76-70-77	290	$9,325
	Garrett Sapp	71-65-71-79	286	$20,200					

In The Money: **291**: Lucas Lee, Michael Wright, Jason Scrivener, Michael Long, Nabil Abdul **292**: Tian-Ling Guan, Chris Campbell, Wen-Yi Huang **293**: Nick Cullen, Zhi Xie, Ryan Haller **294**: Bo-Wen Xiao, Martin Kim, Bryden MacPherson, Adam Stephens **295**: Z-Hao Chen, Cheng Jin, Benjamin Lein, Hui-Lin Zhang, Da-Xing Jin, Sattaya Supupramai, Ming-Jie Huang **296**: Tommy Mou, Jordan Krantz, Brad Shilton **297**: Hak-Hyung Kin, Xiao-Jun Zhang, Saho-Cai He **298**: Tian Yuan, Wisut Artjanawat, Lian-Wei Zhang, John Young Kim **299**: Xiao-Ma Chen **300**: Seung-Hwan Jung **301**: Deuk-Hee Park, Seong K. Kim, Kota Kagasaki **302**: Hua-Jun Gu **303**: Hao-Yuan Lu, Richard Lee **304**: Guang-Ming Yang **305**: Wei-Rong Chen **306**: Sung-Hyuk Park

OWR: 0 of top 50 entered - Rating: 0 - Points to 7th - Li: 6 points, to 339th in OWR

Kolon Korea Open
Woo Jeong Hill Country Club - Choongnam, South Korea
Champion: Seung-Hyuk Kim

Oct 23 - Oct 26
7,084 yards   Par 71
Purse: $1.2 million

South Korea's Seung-Hyuk Kim began 2014 ranked 748th in the world, and stood 603rd as recently as May, but he continued his meteoric rise up the world ranking by winning for the second time in four worldwide starts, claiming a two-stroke victory in his native Korea Open. Having already won the circuit's SK Telecom Open, as well as the Japan Tour's Tokai Classic in early October, Kim started slowly here with an up-and-down round of 73 before jumping into the mix via second-round 68 that included an eagle at the 352-yard 12th. He then managed an even-par 71 in a fog-delayed third round not completed until Sunday, before eventually sealing a Monday victory by turning in one-under-par 35, then reeling off nine straight pars coming home - anchored by par putts of 20 and six feet at the 16th and 17th - to edge PGA Tour regular Seung-Yul Noh by two. Korean amateur Jeong-Woo Ham, who held a two-shot lead through 54 holes, remained atop the board until a double bogey at the 12th (plus later bogeys at the 15th and 17th) saw him home in 75, good enough to tie for third.

1	Seung-Hyuk Kim	73-68-71-70	282	$278,678	14=	Rory Hie	72-72-76-69	298	$13,493
2	Seung-Yul Noh	73-71-71-69	284	$111,471		Yi-Keun Chang	74-70-68-77	289	$13,493
3=	Tae-Hee Lee	72-72-72-69	285	$58,522		Jun-Won Park	71-71-73-74	289	$13,493
	Ho-Sung Choi	67-79-67-72	285	$58,522		In-Choon Hwang	73-69-75-72	289	$13,493
	Jeong-Woo Ham (a)	70-68-72-75	285	-	18=	Bi-o Kim	77-67-73-73	290	$10,868
6	Y. E. Yang	72-70-70-74	286	$39,015		Heung-Chol Joo	72-71-76-71	290	$10,868
7=	Dong-Seop Maeng	72-74-74-67	287	$28,332		Tae-Hoon Kim	75-74-69-72	290	$10,868
	Soon-Sang Hong	72-70-73-72	287	$28,332	21=	Dong-Min Lee	74-73-73-71	291	$9,893
	Ju-Hyuk Park	71-70-72-74	287	$28,332		Bong-Sub Kim	72-71-73-75	291	$9,893
	Jun Seok Lee	70-68-78-71	287	$28,332	23=	Seng Yong Kim	76-71-69-76	292	$9,150
	Ji-Man Kang	69-69-77-72	287	$28,332		Jason Kang	74-70-74-74	292	$9,150
12=	Gi-Whan Kim	72-72-70-74	288	$19,043		Jin-Ho Choi	71-71-78-72	292	$9,150
	Sung-Hoon Kang	76-74-68-70	288	$19,043		Yun-Cheol Jeon	67-71-77-77	292	$9,150

In The Money: **293**: Dae-Sub Kim, Hyo-Won Park, In-Ho Kim, Il-Hwan Park **294**: Joon-Woo Choi **295**: Young-Woong Kim **296**: Garrett Sapp, Ki-Sang Lee **297**: Ted Oh, Dae-Hyun Kim, Hyung-Joon Lee, Martin Kim, Do-Hoon Kim 753 **298**: Chang-Yoon Kim, Sang-Hyun Park, Min-Guen Cho, Sung-Min Hong **299**: Jun-Sub Park, Corey Hale **300**: Gwan-Woo Ma, Devin Daniels **301**: Geon-Ha Kim, Woo-Hyun Kim, Jong-Yul Suk **302**: Tommy Mou **303**: Wisut Artjanawat, Benjamin Lein, Jordan Krantz **304**: Sung-Kug Park **306**: Jae-Kyung Park **308**: Deuk-Hee Park **309**: Chan-Joon Park **310**: Ryan Carter

OWR: 1 of top 50 entered - Rating: 26 - Points to 17th - Kim: 12 points, to 122nd in OWR

PGA TOUR CHALLENGE SEASON

Callaway Pebble Beach Invitational - Pebble Beach, CA   November 20-23

In the 43rd playing of this annual event contested over Pebble Beach, Spyglass Hill and Del Monte, 55-year-old Tommy Armour III joined Mark Brooks as the only three-time winner of the Callaway Invitational, beating fellow Champions Tour player Lee Janzen on the first hole of sudden death. Armour forced the playoff with a 72nd-hole birdie on the famed 18th at Pebble Beach despite hitting his tee shot onto the beach. The event includes players from the PGA, LPGA and Champions Tours, competing on an equal basis save for the positioning of tees. Armour took home $60,000 for the victory, but how the remainder of the $300,000 total purse was divided up was not publicly reported.

1	Tommy Armour III	72-69-66-67	274		Robert Streb	72-68-74-71	285
2	Lee Janzen	65-68-72-69	274	23=	Tony Finau	63-79-72-72	286
3	Kevin Sutherland	73-70-68-67	278		Rob Oppenheim	69-74-74-69	286
4=	Tommy Gainey	73-70-65-71	279		Jamie Sindelar	71-69-75-71	286
	Bryce Molder	72-67-76-64	279	26=	Mark Brooks	71-72-70-74	287
	Thomas Pieters	69-71-68-71	279		Jonathan Byrd	72-68-69-78	287
	Andrew Putnam	69-66-70-74	279		Jason Gore	74-68-70-75	287
8=	Arron Oberholser	72-68-72-68	280		Mark Hubbard	71-67-73-76	287
	Michael Putnam	69-71-70-70	280	30	Justin Thomas	75-67-73-73	288
10=	Blake Adams	72-68-73-69	282	31=	Daniel Berger	75-70-68-76	289
	Todd Fischer	70-68-72-72	282		Matt Bettencourt	67-72-76-74	289
	John Rollins	69-69-71-73	282		Bobby Clampett	68-76-69-76	289
13=	Derek Fathauer	68-73-72-70	283		Jeff Gove	72-71-72-74	289
	Scott Langley	68-70-76-69	283		Luke Guthrie	69-68-77-75	289
	Charlie Wi	71-71-73-68	283		Kyle Reifers	67-73-76-73	289
16=	Brandon Harkins	71-70-73-70	284	37=	James Hahn	67-73-74-76	290
	Duffy Waldorf	70-69-73-72	284		Scott McCarron	72-74-71-73	290
	Steve Wheatcroft	71-69-71-73	284	39	Kelly Kraft	71-67-76-77	291
19=	Billy Andrade	65-73-75-72	285	40	Mina Harigae	74-67-75-76	292
	Martin Flores	69-73-70-73	285	41	Andy Miller	74-69-74-78	295
	Adam Hadwin	69-75-71-70	285				

Out Of The Money: **218**: Rich Beem, John Merrick, Gary Christian **219**: John Aber, Harrison Frazar, Joe Horowitz, Stephanie Meadow, Ryan Palmer **220**: Olin Browne, Colt Knost, John Mallinger **221**: Andres Gonzales, Max Homa, Brian Mogg **222**: Mark Brown, Steve Flesch, Tom Purtzer, Kris Tschetter **224**: Olin Browne Jr., Jonathan Randolph, Jamie Sadlowski, Scott Simpson, Joey Sindelar, Annika Sorenstam **225**: Jill McGill, Pat Perez, Michael Schoolcraft, Mike Small, Kirk Triplett **226**: Jeff Hanson, Chesson Hadley, Brooke Pancake **227**: Spencer Fletcher, Mark Wiebe **229**: Mallory Blackwelder **230**: Devin Gee, Tommy Masters **231**: Charlie Gibson, Blair O'Neal **233**: Perry Parker **238**: Taylor Collins **WD**: Andrew Svoboda (143)

Hero World Challenge - Windermere, FL   December 3-7

Twenty-one-year-old Jordan Spieth arrived at the Hero World Challenge having just scored a striking victory (via a final-round 63) at the Australian Open - and fresh off the monumental flight required to get here. But relying upon the boundless energy of youth, he looked anything but tired as he blitzed the stellar 18-man field, running away to a record-setting 10-shot victory. Notably, though unofficial, this event does offer world ranking points. Also notably, event host Tiger Woods began his latest comeback by tying for last place.

1	Jordan Spieth	66-67-63-66	262	$1 mil		Billy Horschel	73-72-67-67	279	$126,667
2	Henrik Stenson	67-68-68-69	272	$400,000	11=	Bubba Watson	69-68-72-71	280	$112,500
3=	Patrick Reed	73-63-69-68	273	$212,500		Graeme McDowell	68-73-68-71	280	$112,500
	Keegan Bradley	72-66-65-70	273	$212,500	13	Hideki Matsuyama	68-73-71-69	281	$109,000
5	Jason Day	71-67-70-66	274	$150,000	14	Steve Stricker	67-73-74-69	283	$108,000
6=	Rickie Fowler	67-70-72-68	277	$142,500	15	Jimmy Walker	68-69-75-72	284	$107,000
	Justin Rose	72-64-70-71	277	$142,500	16	Chris Kirk	70-68-74-73	285	$106,000
8=	Zach Johnson	67-71-72-69	279	$126,667	17=	Tiger Woods	77-70-69-72	288	$102,500
	Matt Kuchar	69-70-70-70	279	$126,667		Hunter Mahan	71-71-71-75	288	$102,500

CVS Caremark Charity Classic - Barrington, RI   June 23-24

1	Steve Stricker/Bo Van Pelt	62-60	122	$300,000		Hunter Mahan/Jason Dufner	64-64	128	$121,667
2	Peter Jacobsen/Jimmy Walker	62-61	123	$200,000		Bill Haas/Billy Andrade	63-64	128	$121,667
3=	Suzann Pettersen/Jonas Blixt	66-61	127	$160,000	8	Lexi Thompson/Billy Horschel	67-62	129	$110,000
	Russell Henley/Harris English	64-63	127	$160,000	9	Zach Johnson/Matt Kuchar	65-68	133	$105,000
5=	Erik Compton/Brad Faxon	65-63	128	$121,667	10	Morgan Pressel/Juli Inkster	67-67	134	$100,000

Franklin Templeton Shootout - Naples, FL   December 11-13

1	Jason Day & Cameron Tringale	55-64-65	184	$385,000	7=	Ch. Howell III & Scott Verplank	61-64-65	190	$83,750
2	Harris English & Matt Kuchar	57-66-62	185	$242,500		Justin Leonard & Rory Sabbatini	60-67-63	190	$83,750
3=	Keegan Bradley & Cam. Villegas	59-67-61	187	$130,000	9	Ryan Palmer & Jimmy Walker	59-68-64	191	$80,000
	Billy Horschel & Ian Poulter	61-65-61	187	$130,000	10	Patrick Reed & Brandt Snedeker	61-65-66	192	$77,500
5=	Gra. McDowell & Gary Woodland	59-63-66	188	$95,000	11	Sean O'Hair & Kenny Perry	60-69-65	194	$75,000
	Jerry Kelly & Steve Stricker	60-68-60	188	$95,000	12	Retief Goosen & Mike Weir	60-74-67	201	$72,500

WEB.COM TOUR
2014

The 2014 Web.com season was the second in which, with the demise of Q School as we knew it, the developmental circuit served as the sole true provider of new talent for the PGA Tour. This it did first by continuing to have its top 25 money winners granted PGA Tour cards, then by playing a four-event Final Series whose fields were made up of the Web.com's top 75 money winners and 75 of the PGA Tour's lower earners – or, more accurately its 126th-200th-place prize winners. The result of this series was a new 50-man priority list for PGA Tour newcomers that appears at the end of this section, a list which, by designation, was topped by combined regular season and Finals money winner Adam Hadwin and leading Finals money winner Derek Fathauer. Unlike the remaining 48 graduates (whose week-by-week status isn't guaranteed, and is subject to the reshuffle), both men will be fully exempt on the 2015 PGA Tour – as will Mexico's Carlos Ortiz, a three-time winner on the 2014 circuit and thus the recipient of a battlefield promotion.

Once again, PGA Tour experience seems to have been a significant advantage for those battling to (re)graduate from the Web.com, with names like Bud Cauley, 2007 U.S. Amateur winner Colt Knost, Jason Gore, Alex Cejka, Greg Owen, Sean O'Hair, Heath Slocum, J.J. Henry and Bill Lunde all likely ringing familiar to regular Tour viewers. But a number of the class's genuine rookies also seem poised to find success on the big Tour, with popular choices to have the most immediate impact including long-hitting Tony Finau, former University of Alabama star Justin Thomas, Auburn All-American Blayne Barber, the aforementioned Hadwin and Ortiz, and something of a ringer, South African veteran (and six-time European Tour winner) Richard Sterne. This 2015 edition of *Professional Golf* includes full profiles of all 50 Web.com graduates in the Player Profiles section, as well as a scouting report on actual PGA Tour rookies on page 245.

Player Of The Year: Carlos Ortiz

Adam Hadwin would lead the "final" Web.com money list (which combined regular season and Finals earnings) and Derek Fathauer won the most money during the Finals themselves. But the 2014 Web.com Player Of The Year has to go to Mexico's Carlos Ortiz, who likely cared little about either one after winning three times in his first 16 starts and earning an immediate battlefield promotion to the PGA Tour.

2014 Web.com Tour Top 60 Regular Season Money Winners

#	Player	Money	#	Player	Money	#	Player	Money
1	Carlos Ortiz	$515,403	21	Byron Smith	$177,172	41	Zachary Blair	$97,799
2	Andrew Putnam	$320,438	22	Bill Lunde	$168,864	42	Chris Wilson	$96,805
3	Zack Sucher	$294,166	23	Fabián Gómez	$162,322	43	Travis Bertoni	$96,741
4	Adam Hadwin	$293,667	24	Roger Sloan	$159,018	44	Ashley Hall	$96,204
5	Justin Thomas	$276,637	25	Kyle Reifers	$146,836	45	Sam Saunders	$95,341
6	Alex Cejka	$276,448	26	Sebastian Cappelen	$145,373	46	Chase Wright	$92,835
7	Blayne Barber	$269,111	27	Greg Owen	$143,631	47	Vaughn Taylor	$92,416
8	Tony Finau	$254,315	28	Aaron Watkins	$143,508	48	Michael Kim	$91,659
9	Jason Gore	$253,046	29	Martin Piller	$120,676	49	Alistair Presnell	$90,750
10	Steven Alker	$249,536	30	Harold Varner III	$119,596	50	Henrik Norlander	$90,648
11	Andres Gonzales	$238,620	31	Ryan Blaum	$114,580	51	Darron Stiles	$90,296
12	Jon Curran	$231,854	32	Matt Weibring	$113,772	52	Manuel Villegas	$87,835
13	Derek Fathauer	$218,052	33	Kris Blanks	$106,894	53	Dawie van der Walt	$87,119
14	Cameron Percy	$217,347	34	Colt Knost	$106,460	54	Tom Gillis	$86,161
15	Daniel Berger	$209,286	35	Brett Stegmaier	$105,548	55	Roland Thatcher	$83,763
16	Jonathan Randolph	$203,676	36	Alex Prugh	$103,864	56	Peter Tomasulo	$83,418
17	Max Homa	$192,350	37	Scott Pinckney	$101,941	57	Richard Johnson	$82,961
18	Mark Hubbard	$187,448	38	Rod Pampling	$101,411	58	Jeff Curl logo	$82,759
19	Steve Wheatcroft	$183,411	39	Steve Allan	$101,097	59	Matt Davidson	$81,612
20	Ryan Armour	$180,856	40	Bronson Burgoon	$100,581	60	Aron Price	$78,128

Pacific Rubiales Colombia Championship

Bogota Country Club - Bogota, Colombia
Champion: Alex Cejka

Feb 13 - Feb 16
7,237 yards   Par 71
Purse: $750,000

Forty-three-year-old Alex Cejka broke a 12-year winless streak at February's Pacific Rubiales Colombia Championship, the season-opening Web.com Tour event whose partially completed final round was washed out by heavy rains. A longtime veteran of both the PGA and European Tours (with a total of four victories on the latter), Cejka charged into a three-shot 54-hole lead via a course record 63 in the weather-delayed third round (completed on Saturday morning), then saw his lead over runner-up Andrew Putnam cut to one early in the finale before the weather intervened once more, forcing the committee to cancel the remainder of play.

1	Alex Cejka	68-68-63	199	$135,000		Sebastian Pinzon	68-71-67	206	$19,500
2	Andrew Putnam	68-66-68	202	$81,000		Vaughn Taylor	69-68-69	206	$19,500
3	Carlos Ortiz	67-69-67	203	$51,000		Peter Tomasulo	67-69-70	206	$19,500
4	Bill Lunde	66-68-70	204	$36,000	14=	Tony Finau	69-69-69	207	$12,000
5=	Sam Saunders	69-67-69	205	$27,375		Jose Garrido	70-69-68	207	$12,000
	Justin Thomas	65-69-71	205	$27,375		Andres Gonzales	69-71-67	207	$12,000
	Chris Wilson	69-66-70	205	$27,375		Matt Hendrix	68-70-69	207	$12,000
8=	Derek Fathauer	72-64-70	206	$19,500		Hugo Leon	66-74-67	207	$12,000
	Adam Hadwin	69-71-66	206	$19,500		Jonathan Randolph	66-70-71	207	$12,000
	Whee Kim	69-70-67	206	$19,500		Manuel Villegas	69-70-68	207	$12,000

OWR: 0 of top 50 entered - Rating: 2 - Points to 20th - Cejka: 14 points, to 317th in OWR

Chile Classic

Prince of Wales Country Club - Santiago, Chile
Champion: Adam Hadwin

Mar 6 - Mar 9
6,681 yards   Par 72
Purse: $650,000

Adam Hadwin became the first Canadian to win on the Web.com Tour since 2009 by birdieing the final two holes to claim a one stroke victory over Australian Alistair Presnell at the Chile Classic in Santiago. The 26-year-old Hadwin, a multi-season Web.com veteran, got up-and-down from a greenside bunker after nearly driving the par-4 17th, then did the same from the rough at the par-5 18th to edge Presnell, whose eagle at the last had, quite remarkably, been his third of the day during a closing 68. Twenty-seven-year-old Japan Tour veteran Sung-Joon Park finished with a 66 to tie for third with former PGA Tour players Henrik Norlander and Kyle Reifers.

1	Adam Hadwin	67-69-67-69	272	$117,000	12=	Tom Hoge	69-69-74-66	278	$10,589
2	Alistair Presnell	70-70-65-68	273	$70,200		Daniel Berger	71-67-73-67	278	$10,589
3=	Sung-Joon Park	67-72-70-66	275	$33,800		Blayne Barber	70-66-74-68	278	$10,589
	Henrik Norlander	64-72-70-69	275	$33,800		Ashley Hall	71-69-69-69	278	$10,589
	Kyle Reifers	68-68-68-71	275	$33,800		Darron Stiles	71-65-72-70	278	$10,589
6=	Bhavik Patel	67-68-72-69	276	$21,775		Justin Thomas	69-68-71-70	278	$10,589
	Andrew Putnam	67-71-68-70	276	$21,775		Martin Ureta	70-69-69-70	278	$10,589
	Scott Pinckney	67-70-67-72	276	$21,775		Andres Gonzales	69-68-70-71	278	$10,589
9=	Mark Hubbard	69-73-67-68	277	$17,550		Jorge F. Valdes	66-66-74-72	278	$10,589
	Franklin Corpening	68-68-70-71	277	$17,550		F. Mechereffe	69-72-65-72	278	$10,589
	Jose D. Rodriguez	70-67-69-71	277	$17,550		Garth Mulroy	64-71-70-73	278	$10,589

OWR: 0 of top 50 entered - Rating: 3 - Points to 22nd - Marksaeng: 14 points, to 336th in OWR

Brazil Champions

Sao Paulo Golf Club - Sao Paulo, Brazil
Champion: Jon Curran

Mar 13 - Mar 16
6,574 yards   Par 71
Purse: $800,000

American Jon Curran won his first career Web.com title in only his fourth start on the developmental circuit, routing a hot Alex Cejka by four at the Brasil Champions in Sao Paulo. The 27-year-old former Vanderbilt star won wire-to-wire and in the process set a tour record with eight consecutive birdies during an opening round 61, while also tying the circuit's lowest-ever 54-hole aggregate of 190. Cejka, already a winner a month earlier in Colombia, earned enough money to clinch a spot on the 2015 PGA Tour only three events into the season.

1	Jon Curran	61-64-65-69	259	$144,000		Jonathan Fricke	69-64-66-70	269	$21,600
2	Alex Cejka	65-66-63-69	263	$86,400	12=	Shane Bertsch	66-68-69-67	270	$16,200
3	Ashley Hall	65-64-65-70	264	$54,400		Andres Echavarria	67-63-70-70	270	$16,200
4	Manuel Villegas	67-66-67-66	266	$38,400		Brad Schneider	66-63-71-70	270	$16,200
5=	Casey Wittenberg	66-71-65-65	267	$30,400		Mathew Goggin	67-67-66-70	270	$16,200
	Oscar Fraustro	67-64-67-69	267	$30,400	16=	Steve Allan	69-65-70-67	271	$12,000
7=	Daniel Berger	64-64-71-69	268	$25,800		Richard S. Johnson	67-69-68-67	271	$12,000
	Tom Gillis	65-66-68-69	268	$25,800		Sam Saunders	72-65-65-69	271	$12,000
9=	Cameron Percy	68-68-69-64	269	$21,600		Jose D. Rodriguez	68-63-69-71	271	$12,000
	Andrew Putnam	69-68-66-66	269	$21,600		Philip Pettitt Jr.	66-68-65-72	271	$12,000

OWR: 0 of top 50 entered - Rating: 3 - Points to 20th - Curran: 14 points, to 419 in OWR

Panama Claro Championship

Mar 20 - Mar 23

Panama Golf Club - Panama City, Panama
Champion: Carlos Ortiz

7,102 yards Par 70
Purse: $625,000

Mexico's Carlos Ortiz, a former collegiate star at North Texas University, closed with a bogey-free six-under-par 64 to claim his first victory on the Web.com Tour, cruising to a four-shot triumph at the Panama Claro Championship in Panama City. PGA Tour veteran Jason Gore shot a Sunday 66 to take solo second, while Americans Daniel Berger and Derek Fathauer, and Australia's Aron Price shared third, five shots off the pace. The win moved Ortiz into second place in Tour earnings, giving him a strong leg up towards gaining PGA Tour status in 2015.

1	Carlos Ortiz	70-68-66-64	268	$112,500		Steve Wheatcroft	68-70-71-67	276	$13,750
2	Jason Gore	70-67-69-66	272	$67,500		Manuel Villegas	69-67-71-69	276	$13,750
3=	Daniel Berger	68-68-70-67	273	$32,500		Alex Cejka	68-69-70-69	276	$13,750
	Derek Fathauer	72-69-65-67	273	$32,500	15=	Justin Thomas	70-67-71-69	277	$10,000
	Aron Price	66-68-69-70	273	$32,500		James Nitties	70-71-66-70	277	$10,000
6=	Nick Taylor	69-69-69-67	274	$21,719		Jonathan Randolph	69-66-71-71	277	$10,000
	Roland Thatcher	73-64-67-70	274	$21,719		Jon Curran	67-68-70-72	277	$10,000
8=	Tim Petrovic	71-67-68-69	275	$18,125		Andrew Putnam	69-68-68-72	277	$10,000
	Mark Hubbard	72-63-70-70	275	$18,125	20=	Steve Alker	69-69-72-68	278	$7,025
	Steve Allan	71-66-67-71	275	$18,125		Will Wilcox	72-67-71-68	278	$7,025
11=	Fabián Gómez	72-68-70-66	276	$13,750		Colt Knost	69-71-68-70	278	$7,025

OWR: 0 of top 50 entered - Rating: 0 - Points to 19th - Ortiz: 14 points, to 333rd in OWR

Chitimacha Louisiana Open

Mar 27 - Mar 30

Le Triomphe Country Club - Broussard, LA
Champion: Kris Blanks

7,004 yards Par 72
Purse: $550,000

Ex-PGA Tour player Kris Blanks began the final round of the Louisiana Open seven shots behind fellow Tour veteran Kyle Reifers, then proceeded to post a spectacular nine-under-par 62 to claim the early clubhouse lead on 270. As Reifers fell of the pace with a closing 70, former University of Florida star Brett Stegmaier came home in 68 to draw even with Blanks, forcing sudden death. But after Stegmaier missed a long birdie putt at the third extra hole, Blanks calmly holed a nine-footer to clinch his second career Web.com title.

1	Kris Blanks	71-66-71-62	270	$99,000		Fabián Gómez	66-67-70-70	273	$12,650
2	Brett Stegmaier	71-66-65-68	270	$59,400		Blayne Barber	69-68-65-71	273	$12,650
3=	Jonathan Randolph	66-65-73-67	271	$31,900	14=	Bronson Burgoon	69-65-73-67	274	$9,900
	Kyle Reifers	65-70-66-70	271	$31,900		Andres Gonzales	69-68-68-69	274	$9,900
5=	Garth Mulroy	70-66-69-67	272	$18,012		Jeff Curl	66-70-69-69	274	$9,900
	Zack Sucher	68-67-69-68	272	$18,012	17=	Jason Gore	68-67-72-68	275	$6,958
	Aaron Goldberg	70-67-67-68	272	$18,012		Jon Curran	71-64-71-69	275	$6,958
	Sebastian Vazquez	69-65-69-69	272	$18,012		Roland Thatcher	73-63-70-69	275	$6,958
	Justin Thomas	69-66-68-69	272	$18,012		Carlos Ortiz	70-66-70-69	275	$6,958
	Steve Saunders	72-66-65-69	272	$18,012		Harold Varner III	69-68-69-69	275	$6,958
11=	Ryan Blaum	65-68-71-69	273	$12,650		Brett Wetterich	69-70-66-70	275	$6,958

OWR: 0 of top 50 entered - Rating: 2 - Points to 24th - Blanks: 14 points, to 401st in OWR

El Bosque Mexico Championship

Apr 10 - Apr 13

El Bosque Golf Club - Leon, Mexico
Champion: Carlos Ortiz

7,701 yards Par 72
Purse: $700,000

Twenty-two-year-old Carlos Ortiz won for the second time on the 2014 Web.com Tour, closing with a 68 to clinch a two-shot triumph on his native soil at the El Bosque Mexico Championship in Leon. After opening with a 74, Ortiz fought his way back into the mix with middle rounds of 67-66, to tie PGA Tour veteran Nathan Green for a share of the 54-hole lead. He then jumped in front by playing his first 15 final round holes in five under par before bogeys at the 16th and 17th made matters close – and a birdie at the par-5 closer proved the clincher.

1	Carlos Ortiz	74-67-66-68	275	$126,000	13=	Oscar Fraustro	74-68-73-68	283	$12,367
2	Justin Thomas	66-70-72-69	277	$75,600		Alex Prugh	74-70-70-69	283	$12,367
3=	Adam Hadwin	73-71-69-68	281	$29,925		Roberto Diaz	72-73-68-70	283	$12,367
	Daniel Berger	71-67-74-69	281	$29,925		Hunter Haas	72-69-71-71	283	$12,367
	Nathan Tyler	71-68-72-70	281	$29,925		Peter Tomasulo	70-69-73-71	283	$12,367
	Jason Gore	72-69-67-73	281	$29,925		Colt Knost	71-70-71-71	283	$12,367
	Jonathan Randolph	69-70-69-73	281	$29,925	19=	Casey Wittenberg	69-73-75-67	284	$8,484
	Nathan Green	67-70-70-74	281	$29,925		Ryan Armour	70-71-74 -9	284	$8,484
9=	Mark Hubbard	72-71-72-67	282	$18,200		Byron Smith	69-75-71-69	284	$8,484
	Cameron Percy	70-72-69-71	282	$18,200		Steven Alker	75-68-71-70	284	$8,484
	Brad Schneider	66-74-69-73	282	$18,200		Kelly Kraft	71-71-69-73	284	$8,484
	D.J. Brigman	73-71-65-73	282	$18,200					

OWR: 0 of top 50 entered - Rating: 2 - Points to 18th - Ortiz: 14 points, to 191st in OWR

WNB Golf Classic

Midland Country Club - Midland, TX
Champion: Andrew Putnam

Apr 24 - Apr 27
7,380 yards   Par 72
Purse: $600,000

Victories achieved following weather-shortened tournaments always carry an unwritten asterisk since the champion didn't have to survive final-round pressure – but in Andrew Putnam's case, his triumph at the wind-shortened WNB Golf Classic might be an exception. This is because following a third round 64 at the Midland Country Club, Putnam held a seven-stroke 54-hole lead, and he actually stood eight ahead through eight Sunday holes when play was cancelled due to high winds. It was the former Pepperdine star's first career Web.com Tour title.

1	Andrew Putnam	66-66-64	196	$108,000		Jeff Klauk	69-70-67	206	$14,400
2=	Richard S. Johnson	68-69-66	203	$52,800		Trevor Murphy	66-71-69	206	$14,400
	Rod Pampling	66-69-68	203	$52,800		Matt Fast	73-68-65	206	$14,400
4=	Tom Gillis	69-64-71	204	$26,400	15=	Roberto Diaz	71-68-68	207	$10,200
	Mathew Goggin	69-68-67	204	$26,400		Andy Pope	73-67-67	207	$10,200
6=	Sam Saunders	70-68-67	205	$20,100		Brett Wetterich	72-70-65	207	$10,200
	Harold Varner III	68-69-68	205	$20,100	18=	Ryan Blaum	68-72-68	208	$8,100
	Jin Park	74-67-64	205	$20,100		Ryuji Imada	70-70-68	208	$8,100
9=	Oscar Fraustro	68-69-69	206	$14,400		Scott Pinckney	71-68-69	208	$8,100
	Carlos Ortiz	67-68-71	206	$14,400		Camilo Benedetti	74-69-65	208	$8,100
	Derek Fathauer	71-67-68	206	$14,400					

OWR: 0 of top 50 entered - Rating: 4 - Points to 17th - Putnam: 14 points, to 208th in OWR

South Georgia Classic

Kinderlou Forest Golf Club - Valdosta, GA
Champion: Blayne Barber

May 1 - May 4
7,781 yards   Par 72
Purse: $650,000

Former Auburn University All-American Blayne Barber won for the first time on the Web.com Tour, closing with a five-under-par 67 to claim a two-shot victory at the South Georgia Classic in Valdosta. PGA Tour veteran Alex Prugh finished second, though the bigger story was Mexico's Carlos Ortiz, who led through 54 holes and was hoping to land both a third victory of the season and an immediate battlefield promotion to the PGA Tour. Unfortunately, Ortiz opened with back-to-back bogeys before ultimately settling for a 72, and solo third.

1	Blayne Barber	68-72-66-67	273	$117,000		Jason Allred	72-69-67-72	280	$14,950
2	Alex Prugh	70-68-70-67	275	$70,200	14=	Daniel Berger	70-68-73-70	281	$11,050
3	Carlos Ortiz	67-65-72-72	276	$44,200		Roger Sloan	70-72-69-70	281	$11,050
4=	Greg Owen	72-69-67-69	277	$26,867		Derek Fathauer	70-73-67-71	281	$11,050
	Ryan Armour	74-66-67-70	277	$26,867		Mike Miller	68-71-70-72	281	$11,050
	Rob Oppenheim	69-66-70-72	277	$26,867		Andrew Putnam	68-69-72-72	281	$11,050
7	Max Homa	67-68-70-73	278	$21,775	19=	Bill Lunde	72-69-74-67	282	$7,096
8=	Trevor Murphy	73-69-71-66	279	$18,850		Andres Gonzales	73-71-69-69	282	$7,096
	Nathan Tyler	71-68-72-68	279	$18,850		Roland Thatcher	70-70-72-70	282	$7,096
	Adam Webb	70-70-65-74	279	$18,850		Jimmy Gunn	70-68-73-71	282	$7,096
11=	Ryan Blaum	72-68-72-68	280	$14,950		Cameron Percy	72-68-71-71	282	$7,096
	Zack Sucher	71-70-70-69	280	$14,950		Kyle Reifers	72-69-70-71	282	$7,096

OWR: 0 of top 50 entered - Rating: 5 - Points to 18th - Barber: 14 points, to 287th in OWR

BMW Charity Pro-Am

Thornblade Club - Greer, SC
Champion: Max Homa

May 15 - May 18
7,024 yards   Par 71
Purse: $650,000

Former University of California All-American Max Homa charged home with an eight-under-par 63 to capture the BMW Pro-Am, his first career Web.com Tour title. Homa began the final round two strokes behind 54-hole leader Blayne Barber, who was looking for his second consecutive Web.com triumph and shot a more-than-respectable closing 67 en route to tying for third. Runner-up honors went to Jonathan Randolph, who matched Homa's 63 shot for shot, and finished one behind.

1	Max Homa	68-65-70-63	266	$117,000		David Skinns	69-66-68-68	271	$16,900
2	Jonathan Randolph	65-70-69-63	267	$70,200	13=	Peter Tomasulo	71-63-72-66	272	$11,830
3=	Jon Curran	68-68-66-66	268	$33,800		Harold Varner III	68-69-69-66	272	$11,830
	Blayne Barber	63-70-68-67	268	$33,800		Kelly Kraft	65-67-72-68	272	$11,830
	Kyle Reifers	68-64-70-66	268	$33,800		Cliff Kresge	65-68-71-68	272	$11,830
6	Zack Sucher	67-70-67-65	269	$23,400		Ryan Blaum	67-66-68-71	272	$11,830
7=	Gavin Coles	68-66-69-67	270	$20,962	18=	Tony Finau	69-68-69-67	273	$8,476
	Matt Davidson	69-65-67-69	270	$20,962		Matt Fast	70-68-68-67	273	$8,476
9=	Dominic Bozzelli	67-69-70-65	271	$16,900		Roger Sloan	68-69-68-68	273	$8,476
	Justin Lower	69-68-70-64	271	$16,900		Bronson Burgoon	68-69-68-68	273	$8,476
	Mark Hubbard	66-67-72-66	271	$16,900		Jimmy Gunn	68-68-68-69	273	$8,476

OWR: 0 of top 50 entered - Rating: 4 - Points to 17th - Homa: 14 points, to 328th in OWR

Rex Hospital Open
May 22 - May 25

TPC Wakefield Plantation - Raleigh, NC
Champion: Byron Smith

7,257 yards   Par 71
Purse: $625,000

Thirty-three-year-old American Byron Smith, who was never able to play his way into a collegiate event while at Pepperdine, claimed his first victory on the Web.com Tour, cruising to a four-stroke triumph at the Rex Hospital Open in Raleigh. Smith moved himself into contention with a tournament-low 63 on Saturday, then ran off four birdies in a five-hole back nine run on Sunday en route to the 66 that would clinch the title. Tied for second were PGA Tour veteran Scott Gardiner and Harold Varner III.

1	Byron Smith	70-69-63-66	268	$112,500		Max Homa	65-68-74-69 276	$14,375
2=	Scott Gardiner	69-66-68-69	272	$55,000		Justin Thomas	69-71-68-68 276	$14,375
	Harold Varner III	67-65-70-70	272	$55,000	14=	Steve Wheatcroft	66-75-69-67 277	$9,688
4=	Brad Fritsch	72-65-70-66	273	$25,833		Derek Fathauer	71-69-69-68 277	$9,688
	Tony Finau	67-71-68-67	273	$25,833		Hugo Leon	72-69-68-68 277	$9,688
	Roberto Diaz	68-68-67-70	273	$25,833		Peter Tomasulo	68-67-73-69 277	$9,688
7	Ryan Blaum	67-69-69-69	274	$20,938		Jin Park	70-69-69-69 277	$9,688
8=	Andres Gonzales	70-66-72-67	275	$18,125		Carlos Sainz Jr.	69-69-69-70 277	$9,688
	Chris Wilson	68-68-72-67	275	$18,125		Alex Prugh	69-70-68-70 277	$9,688
	Hunter Haas	67-68-67-73	275	$18,125		Nathan Tyler	69-68-68-72 277	$9,688
11=	Roland Thatcher	68-69-71-68	276	$14,375				

OWR: 0 of top 50 entered - Rating: 4 - Points to 21st - Smith: 14 points, to 316th in OWR

Cleveland Open
Jun 5 - Jun 8

Lakewood Country Club - Westlake, OH
Champion: Steven Alker

6,824 yards   Par 72
Purse: $600,000

In the longest playoff in Web.com Tour history, New Zealand's Steve Alker defeated South African Dawie van der Walt by birdieing the 11th extra hole to win the Cleveland Open. After deadlocking on 14-under-par 270, the pair notched a combined 20 pars over the first 10 playoff holes before Alker stiffed a 7 iron to close things out at the par-4 18th. Remarkably, the playoff only tied for longest ever in a PGA Tour-sponsored event, matching the 1949 Motor City Open, where Cary Middlecoff and Lloyd Mangrum were named co-winners due to darkness.

1	Steven Alker	70-70-65-65	270	$108,000	14=	Andres Echavarria	72-68-68-68 276	$10,500
2	Dawie van der Walt	70-69-65-66	270	$64,800		Roland Thatcher	69-72-67-68 276	$10,500
3	Si Woo Kim	66-69-71-65	271	$40,800		Scott Harrington	75-66-66-69 276	$10,500
4=	Jon Curran	71-66-67-69	273	$23,625		Aaron Watkins	69-66-70-71 276	$10,500
	Jason Gore	69-68-66-70	273	$23,625	18=	Max Homa	64-76-69-68 277	$6,084
	Jeff Curl	66-67-70-70	273	$23,625		Derek Fathauer	73-66-70-68 277	$6,084
	Ryan Armour	69-68-66-70	273	$23,625		Blayne Barber	69-69-70-69 277	$6,084
8=	Adam Hadwin	72-69-66-67	274	$18,000		Camilo Benedetti	69-68-71-69 277	$6,084
	Byron Smith	71-69-66-68	274	$18,000		Alexandre Rocha	73-68-66-70 277	$6,084
10=	Chase Wright	70-71-66-68	275	$14,400		Scott Parel	69-68-69-71 277	$6,084
	Mark Hubbard	72-64-70-69	275	$14,400		Harold Varner III	70-67-69-71 277	$6,084
	Michael Kim	69-68-69-69	275	$14,400		Sung-hoon Kang	68-71-73-65 277	$6,084
	Meen Whee Kim	68-66-68-73	275	$14,400		Mathew Goggin	71-62-69-75 277	$6,084

OWR: 2 of top 50 entered - Rating: 2 - Points to 17th - Alker: 14 points, to 301st in OWR

Air Capital Classic
Jun 13 - Jun 16

Crestview Country Club - Wichita, KS
Champion: Sebastian Capellen

6,913 yards   Par 71
Purse: $600,000

Twenty-four-year-old Sebastian Capellen of Denmark, a former star at the University of Arkansas, became the 21st Monday qualifier to win on the Web.com Tour by claiming a one-shot victory at the Air Capital Classic in Wichita. Becoming the first Dane ever to win a PGA Tour-sanctioned event, Capellen strung together rounds of 66-65-65-66 over the par-70 Crestview Country Club layout, his 18-under-par total barely nosing out Matt Weibring (who closed with a 64) by a single shot.

1	Sebastian Cappelen	66-65-65-66	262	$108,000		Rod Pampling	68-68-65-67 268	$16,200
2	Matt Weibring	68-65-66-64	263	$64,800		Blayne Barber	65-67-67-69 268	$16,200
3=	Cameron Percy	67-67-70-62	266	$34,800	13	Rob Oppenheim	69-63-67-70 269	$13,800
	Jeff Gove	68-64-68-66	266	$34,800	14=	Tom Hoge	67-67-69-67 270	$11,600
5=	Ryan Armour	69-68-65-65	267	$21,075		Matt Fast	66-68-68-68 270	$11,600
	Paul Claxton	65-68-67-67	267	$21,075		Aaron Watkins	63-66-71-70 270	$11,600
	O. Schniederjans(a)	64-71-65-67	267	-	17=	Vince India	70-68-69-64 271	$9,000
	Sung Joon Park	69-66-64-68	267	$21,075		Shane Bertsch	67-66-70-68 271	$9,000
	Andres Gonzales	65-67-66-69	267	$21,075		Josh Broadaway	67-68-67-69 271	$9,000
10=	Sam Saunders	65-66-70-67	268	$16,200		Oscar Fraustro	70-66-66-69 271	$9,000

OWR: 0 of top 50 entered - Rating: 5 - Points to 21st - Capellen: 14 points, to 461st in OWR

United Leasing Championship — Jun 26 - Jun 29
Victoria National Golf Club - Newburgh, IN
Champion: Greg Owen
7,242 yards Par 72
Purse: $600,000

Recording one of the greatest final round turnarounds in Web.com Tour history, England's Greg Owen began Sunday seven shots behind 54-hole leader Mark Hubbard, then promptly triple-bogeyed his opener to seemingly fall miles out of contention. But the 43-year-old PGA Tour veteran righted the ship thereafter, eventually recording seven birdies and an eagle to finish with a five-under-par 67 – just enough to edge Hubbard (who stumbled to a 75) and Ryan Armour (68) by one for his first Web.com title.

1	Greg Owen	73-67-72-67	279	$108,000		14	Guy Boros	70-71-71-72	284	$11,400
2=	Ryan Armour	70-67-75-68	280	$52,800		15=	David Skinns	73-68-74-70	285	$9,900
	Mark Hubbard	69-68-68-75	280	$52,800			Scott Harrington	76-64-72-73	285	$9,900
4=	Fabián Gómez	69-70-72-70	281	$23,625			Andy Pope	69-72-71-73	285	$9,900
	Justin Thomas	70-71-69-71	281	$23,625			Paul Claxton	76-67-66-76	285	$9,900
	Matt Weibring	74-67-68-72	281	$23,625		19=	Albin Choi	74-68-73-71	286	$6,349
	Tony Finau	71-64-72-74	281	$23,625			Roger Sloan	73-72-69-72	286	$6,349
8=	Henrik Norlander	69-75-68-70	282	$18,000			Glen Day	75-69-69-73	286	$6,349
	Andres Echavarria	68-70-70-74	282	$18,000			Adam Hadwin	68-71-73-74	286	$6,349
10=	Garrett Osborn	71-74-69-69	283	$14,400			Doug LaBelle II	74-71-72-69	286	$6,349
	Chase Wright	73-70-70-70	283	$14,400			Derek Fathauer	74-71-73-68	286	$6,349
	Zack Sucher	70-70-72-71	283	$14,400			Peter Tomasulo	73-70-67-76	286	$6,349
	Chris Smith	70-68-71-74	283	$14,400						

OWR: 0 of top 50 entered - Rating: 5 - Points to 18th - Owen: 14 points, to 290th in OWR

Nova Scotia Open — Jul 3 - Jul 6
Ashburn Golf Club (New Course) - Halifax, Canada
Champion: Roger Sloan
7,014 yards Par 72
Purse: $650,000

In an event delayed (but not shortened) by Hurricane Arthur, Canadian Roger Sloan claimed his first Web.com Tour victory and did so on home soil, winning the inaugural playing of the Nova Scotia Open. A former star at University of Texas-El Paso, Sloan was required to play 36 holes on Sunday to make up for Saturday's washout and responded with rounds of 71-70, good enough to tie Derek Fathauer on 273. Their playoff lasted only one hole as Fathauer made bogey, Sloan holed a five-footer for par, and that was that.

1	Roger Sloan	67-65-71-70	273	$117,000		12=	Ryan Spears	69-71-71-68	279	$13,163
2	Derek Fathauer	70-66-71-66	273	$70,200			Shane Bertsch	69-71-70-69	279	$13,163
3	John Mallinger	70-66-67-73	276	$44,200			Nick Rousey	70-69-71-69	279	$13,163
4=	Kyle Thompson	68-72-68-69	277	$26,867			David Skinns	65-70-72-72	279	$13,163
	Zack Fischer	74-66-70-67	277	$26,867		16=	Scott Pinckney	71-69-70-70	280	$9,119
	Henrik Norlander	66-70-72-69	277	$26,867			Tony Finau	70-69-68-73	280	$9,119
7=	Zac Blair	72-69-67-70	278	$18,915			Kyle Stough	69-73-69-69	280	$9,119
	Adam Hadwin	66-73-74-65	278	$18,915			Vaughn Taylor	67-70-72-71	280	$9,119
	Alex Cejka	71-68-68-71	278	$18,915			Garrett Osborn	67-69-75-69	280	$9,119
	Aaron Goldberg	65-72-68-73	278	$18,915			Peter Tomasulo	68-68-73-71	280	$9,119
	Jose D. Rodriguez	63-69-74-72	278	$18,915			Zack Sucher	69-66-73-72	280	$9,119

OWR: 0 of top 50 entered - Rating: 0 - Points to 22nd - Sloan: 14 points, to 370th in OWR

Utah Championship — Jul 10 - Jul 13
Willow Creek Country Club - Sandy, UT
Champion: Andres Gonzales
7,104 yards Par 71
Purse: $625,000

Andres Gonzales won for the second time on the Web.com Tour, claiming the Utah Championship in a four-shot runaway that began with an opening 62 at the Willow Creek Country Club. In the process, the long-haired Gonzales also became the only man ever to win two Web.com events wire-to-wire, his closing 69 allowing him to duplicate a feat previously accomplished at the 2012 Soboba Classic. PGA Tour veteran Sung-Hoon Kang, Adam Crawford (who posted a second round 61) and Travis Bertoni tied for second, far back in Gonzales' wake.

1	Andres Gonzales	62-67-65-69	263	$112,500		11=	Scott Piercy	68-69-66-68	271	$13,750
2=	Adam Crawford	71-61-69-66	267	$46,667			Kelly Kraft	67-68-66-70	271	$13,750
	Sung-hoon Kang	67-65-67-68	267	$46,667			Zac Blair	68-67-66-70	271	$13,750
	Travis Bertoni	68-63-68-68	267	$46,667			Aaron Goldberg	67-67-64-73	271	$13,750
5	Tony Finau	65-67-68-68	268	$25,000		15=	Max Homa	69-68-69-66	272	$9,688
6	Bill Lunde	67-67-72-63	269	$22,500			Nicholas Lindheim	67-68-68-69	272	$9,688
7=	Chase Wright	68-68-67-67	270	$18,828			Vince India	66-70-67-69	272	$9,688
	Brett Stegmaier	69-67-66-68	270	$18,828			Jason Gore	66-69-67-70	272	$9,688
	Steve Allan	69-65-67-69	270	$18,828			Jonathan Fricke	71-66-64-71	272	$9,688
	Jeff Curl	69-67-63-71	270	$18,828			Jose Toledo	66-66-68-72	272	$9,688

OWR: 0 of top 50 entered - Rating: 4 - Points to 20th - Gonzales: 14 points, to 314th in OWR

Albertsons Boise Open
Hillcrest Country Club - Boise, ID
Champion: Steve Wheatcroft

Jul 17 - Jul 20
6,769 yards   Par 71
Purse: $800,000

PGA Tour veteran Steve Wheatcroft claimed his second career victory on the Web.com Tour, defeating New Zealand's Steven Alker on the first hole of sudden death at the Albertson's Boise Open. Wheatcroft began the final round two behind Alker but quickly lifted his fortunes by starting with two birdies and an eagle on a Hillcrest Country Club prone to yielding very low scores. He stumbled briefly with bogeys at the 12th and 13th before adding three late birdies to match Alker (who closed with 67) on 260.

1	Steve Wheatcroft	64-66-65-65	260	$144,000		F. Mechereffe	71-64-66-67 268	$18,400
2	Steven Alker	62-66-65-67	260	$86,400		Garth Mulroy	66-69-64-69 268	$18,400
3	Justin Thomas	68-65-64-65	262	$54,400	15=	James Nitties	64-72-66-67 269	$12,800
4=	Chase Wright	64-66-69-66	265	$33,067		Nick Taylor	63-68-70-68 269	$12,800
	Andrew Putnam	66-68-65-66	265	$33,067		Matt Weibring	68-64-69-68 269	$12,800
	Zack Sucher	60-67-68-70	265	$33,067		Jamie Lovemark	69-66-66-68 269	$12,800
7=	Matt Davidson	65-70-67-65	267	$24,933		Jeff Curl	65-68-67-69 269	$12,800
	Daniel Berger	69-66-65-67	267	$24,933	20=	Steve Saunders	68-64-70-68 270	$8,992
	Bill Lunde	66-61-70-70	267	$24,933		Luke List	69-65-68-68 270	$8,992
10=	Andres Gonzales	67-66-69-66	268	$18,400		Timothy O'Neal	64-72-66-68 270	$8,992
	Fabián Gómez	65-70-67-66	268	$18,400		Ryan Blaum	66-65-69-70 270	$8,992
	Joey Garber	69-65-67-67	268	$18,400		Jason Gore	67-65-67-71 270	$8,992

OWR: 0 of top 50 entered - Rating: 4 - Points to 19th - Wheatcroft: 14 points, to 356th in OWR

Midwest Classic
Nicklaus Golf Club at LionsGate - Overland Park, KS
Champion: Zack Sucher

Jul 24 - Jul 27
7,237 yards   Par 72
Purse: $600,000

Former Alabama-Birmingham star Zack Sucher won for the first time on the Web.com Tour, closing with a one-over-par 72 to hold on for a three-stroke victory at the Midwest Classic, in Overland Park, Kansas. Sucher basically won the event over the first three days, carding blistering rounds of 66-63-64 over the Nicklaus Golf Club layout to post a 20-under-par 54-hole aggregate of 193. That stood him three ahead of Aaron Watkins who, while paired with Sucher on Sunday, could do no better than a 72 of his own, good enough for solo second.

1	Zack Sucher	66-63-64-72	265	$108,000		Zack Fischer	69-67-70-67 273	$12,300
2	Aaron Watkins	67-65-64-72	268	$64,800		Jarrod Lyle	67-69-68-69 273	$12,300
3	Bill Lunde	69-65-66-69	269	$40,800		Sebastian Cappelen	65-74-66-68 273	$12,300
4	Jonathan Randolph	71-67-65-67	270	$28,800		Nick Rousey	69-69-65-70 273	$12,300
5	Derek Fathauer	66-70-66-69	271	$24,000		Rod Pampling	71-66-64-72 273	$12,300
6=	Andres Gonzales	69-68-67-68	272	$18,780	17=	Chris Smith	67-69-67-71 274	$8,400
	Kyle Reifers	68-67-68-69	272	$18,780		Mark Hubbard	65-71-67-71 274	$8,400
	Aron Price	68-70-63-71	272	$18,780		Harold Varner III	70-67-65-72 274	$8,400
	Tom Hoge	70-71-60-71	272	$18,780		D.J. Trahan	67-72-63-72 274	$8,400
	Jason Gore	68-63-68-73	272	$18,780		Shane Bertsch	65-70-66-73 274	$8,400
11=	Steve Allan	68-67-73-65	273	$12,300				

OWR: 0 of top 50 entered - Rating: 4 - Points to 21st - Sucher: 14 points, to 224th in OWR

Stonebrae Classic
TPC Stonebrae - Hayward, CA
Champion: Tony Finau

Jul 31 - Aug 3
7,100 yards   Par 70
Purse: $600,000

Twenty-four-year-old Tony Finau claimed his first Web.com Tour title by riding middle rounds of 62-63 to a three-shot victory at the Stonebrae Classic, played high up in the hills above Oakland. Finau, who turned pro at age 17 and thus never played collegiate golf, only faced serious trouble at the 315-yard 14th where his drive hit a nearby tree and fell into heavy rough barely 20 yards from the tee. He scrambled gamely for par, however, and thereafter cruised home ahead of a trio that included the previous week's winner Zack Sucher, Argentina's Fabián Gómez (who'd earlier turned heads by shooting a second round 60) and Daniel Berger.

1	Tony Finau	67-62-63-66	258	$108,000	11=	Ryan Blaum	63-70-67-65 265	$13,800
2=	Fabián Gómez	66-60-67-68	261	$44,800		Gregor Main	68-65-67-65 265	$13,800
	Zack Sucher	65-68-62-66	261	$44,800		Bill Lunde	68-66-64-67 265	$13,800
	Daniel Berger	66-65-62-68	261	$44,800	14=	Travis Bertoni	65-65-70-66 266	$10,500
5=	Blayne Barber	63-64-68-67	262	$21,900		Michael Kim	67-64-68-67 266	$10,500
	Ashley Hall	65-65-65-67	262	$21,900		Josh Broadway	64-67-67-68 266	$10,500
	Colt Knost	65-65-64-68	262	$21,900		Aaron Watkins	69-64-65-68 266	$10,500
8=	Max Homa	68-66-63-66	263	$18,000	18=	Michael Hebert	72-65-63-67 267	$8,400
	Nicholas Lindheim	63-67-63-70	263	$18,000		Kelly Kraft	63-70-65-69 267	$8,400
10	Tom Hoge	67-66-66-65	264	$16,200		Bronson Burgoon	66-64-66-71 267	$8,400

OWR: 0 of top 50 entered - Rating: 2 - Points to 17th - Finau: 14 points, to 274th in OWR

Price Cutter Charity Championship

Highland Springs Country Club - Springfield, MO
Champion: Cameron Percy

Aug 7 - Aug 10
7,060 yards   Par 72
Purse: $675,000

Forty-year-old Australian Cameron Percy won for the first time on the Web.com Tour, emerging from a pack of five players with a 72nd-hole birdie to win the Price Cutter Charity Championship. Percy entered Sunday tied for the lead with Martin Piller and Sebastian Cappelen and proceeded to card a five-under-par 67 - though his triumph did not come without a bit of luck, as Michael Kim (who finished in the four-way tie for second) might well have joined Percy on 267 had he not been penalized a stroke for lifting his ball in the rough at the last.

1	Cameron Percy	64-68-68-67	267	$121,500	Mark Hubbard	69-67-66-69	271	$13,838
2=	Brandt Jobe	69-68-66-65	268	$44,550	Daniel Berger	70-67-65-69	271	$13,838
	Zac Blair	66-67-69-66	268	$44,550	J.J. Killeen	67-70-65-69	271	$13,838
	Michael Kim	65-66-70-67	268	$44,550	Scott Pinckney	67-65-69-70	271	$13,838
	Carlos Sainz Jr.	70-66-65-67	268	$44,550	17= Alexandre Rocha	68-64-73-67	272	$8,833
6=	Justin Thomas	72-67-66-64	269	$22,612	Aron Price	70-68-67-67	272	$8,833
	Ryan Spears	69-70-63-67	269	$22,612	Brett Stegmaier	68-67-68-69	272	$8,833
	Sebastian Cappelen	70-63-67-69	269	$22,612	Glen Day	71-67-65-69	272	$8,833
9=	Nick Taylor	67-70-66-67	270	$18,900	Whee Kim	68-66-68-70	272	$8,833
	Dominic Bozzelli	68-68-65-69	270	$18,900	Cory Whitsett	67-68-66-71	272	$8,833
11=	Tony Finau	69-69-69-64	271	$13,838	Martin Piller	65-67-68-72	272	$8,833
	Chris Wilson	68-66-69-68	271	$13,838				

OWR: 0 of top 50 entered - Rating: 5 - Points to 23rd - Percy: 14 points, to 274th in OWR

News Sentinel Open

Fox Den Country Club - Knoxville, TN
Champion: Martin Piller

Aug 14 - Aug 17
7,110 yards   Par 72
Purse: $550,000

On a weekend in which his wife Gerina contended at the LPGA Championship, Martin Piller won for the third time on the Web.com Tour (but for the first time since 2010) at the News Sentinel Open in Knoxville. The 28-year-old Piller opened with rounds of 65-67-67 at the Fox Den Country Club before coming within one shot of the course record with a closing 63. His 22-under-par 262 aggregate was enough to hold off Bronson Burgoon (who did tie the record after roaring home with a Sunday 62) by two shots.

1	Martin Piller	65-67-67-63	262	$99,000	Rob Oppenheim	68-70-66-67	271	$12,650
2	Bronson Burgoon	70-68-64-62	264	$59,400	Fabián Gómez	67-66-67-71	271	$12,650
3	Darron Stiles	72-65-65-64	266	$37,400	14= Bill Lunde	67-67-71-67	272	$9,900
4	Ryan Armour	69-70-63-65	267	$26,400	Zac Blair	72-65-68-67	272	$9,900
5	Vaughn Taylor	68-68-68-64	268	$22,000	Casey Wittenberg	70-69-65-68	272	$9,900
6=	Steve Allan	70-67-65-67	269	$18,425	17= Tyler Duncan	72-67-69-65	273	$7,700
	Aaron Watkins	70-66-65-68	269	$18,425	Adam Crawford	67-72-69-65	273	$7,700
	Josh Broadaway	68-68-65-68	269	$18,425	Camilo Benedetti	67-66-71-69	273	$7,700
9=	Jason Gore	70-70-64-66	270	$15,400	Billy Mayfair	70-67-67-69	273	$7,700
	J.J. Killeen	67-69-64-70	270	$15,400	Derek Fathauer	71-66-65-71	273	$7,700
11=	D.J. Trahan	70-66-69-66	271	$12,650				

OWR: 0 of top 50 entered - Rating: 4 - Points to 21st - Piller: 14 points, to 434th in OWR

WinCo Foods Portland Open

Witch Hollow at Pumpkin Ridge - North Plains, OR
Champion: Carlos Ortiz

Aug 21 - Aug 24
7,017 yards   Par 72
Purse: $800,000

Twenty-three-year-old Mexican star Carlos Ortiz closed the Web.com Tour's regular season in style, claiming his third victory of the year at the Portland Open. Entering play as the Tour's leading money winner, the former North Texas State star began the week with rounds of 66-63, and stood on the verge of a runaway during the final round before three mid-round bogeys and seven closing pars left him only one clear of PGA Tour veteran Jason Gore and Canadian Adam Hadwin. The win gained Ortiz fully exempt status on the 2014-15 PGA Tour.

1	Carlos Ortiz	66-63-70-71	270	$144,000	Nicholas Lindheim	66-64-76-69	275	$20,000
2=	Jason Gore	67-68-70-66	271	$70,400	Chris Wilson	72-65-68-70	275	$20,000
	Adam Hadwin	73-65-63-70	271	$70,400	Gregor Main	66-70-69-70	275	$20,000
4	Colt Knost	69-71-63-70	273	$38,400	14= Alex Cejka	70-71-68-67	276	$12,800
5=	Blayne Barber	67-69-70-68	274	$28,100	Roland Thatcher	69-68-70-69	276	$12,800
	Steven Alker	69-70-65-70	274	$28,100	Matt Hendrix	68-67-71-70	276	$12,800
	James Nitties	66-67-70-71	274	$28,100	Darron Stiles	69-72-64-71	276	$12,800
	Scott Pinckney	67-68-68-71	274	$28,100	Fabián Gómez	70-70-65-71	276	$12,800
9=	Travis Bertoni	70-69-68-68	275	$20,000	Jonathan Randolph	68-72-64-72	276	$12,800
	Aaron Watkins	69-71-67-68	275	$20,000	Mark Hubbard	67-65-70-74	276	$12,800

OWR: 0 of top 50 entered - Rating: 7 - Points to 20th - Ortiz: 14 points, to 121st in OWR

Hotel Fitness Championship
Aug 29 - Sep 1

Sycamore Hills Golf Club - Fort Wayne, IN
Champion: Bud Cauley
7,275 yards   Par 72
Purse: $1 Million

In the first event of the Web.com Tour Finals, 24-year-old Bud Cauley claimed his first professional win at the Hotel Fitness Championship, and in the process secured himself exempt status on the 2014-15 PGA Tour. Forced to play in the Web.com Finals for the second straight year, Cauley began Sunday two shots behind Colt Knost but birdied five of his first six holes to overtake Knost, ultimately posting a 65 to win by one. His $180,000 prize guaranteed that he'd finish among the Finals top 25 money winners, locking in his status for next year.

1	Bud Cauley	66-70-67-65	268	$180,000
2	Colt Knost	67-67-67-68	269	$108,000
3	Greg Owen	67-67-68-70	272	$68,000
4=	David Lingmerth	67-72-71-64	274	$41,333
	Tom Gillis	69-69-70-66	274	$41,333
	Sam Saunders	66-66-70-72	274	$41,333
7=	Dicky Pride	66-69-71-69	275	$32,250
	T. Van Aswegen	68-67-69-71	275	$32,250
9=	Matt Weibring	70-71-71-64	276	$27,000
	Nick Taylor	71-68-71-66	276	$27,000
	Derek Fathauer	66-68-72-70	276	$27,000
12=	Andrew Putnam	70-73-67-67	277	$19,600
	James Driscoll	74-68-68-67	277	$19,600
	Martin Piller	68-67-72-70	277	$19,600
	Scott Gardiner	69-70-68-70	277	$19,600
	John Peterson	70-69-64-74	277	$19,600
17=	Kevin Tway	71-64-72-71	278	$15,500
	Chad Campbell	69-69-67-73	278	$15,500
19=	Rod Pampling	71-70-71-67	279	$11,700
	Will Wilcox	69-73-69-68	279	$11,700
	Tony Finau	66-73-70-70	279	$11,700
	Roland Thatcher	67-73-68-71	279	$11,700

OWR: 0 of top 50 entered - Rating: 21 - Points to 24th - Cauley: 16 points, to 187th in OWR

Chiquita Classic
Sep 4 - Sep 7

River Run Country Club - Davidson, NC
Champion: Adam Hadwin
7,321 yards   Par 72
Purse: $1 Million

Twenty-six-year-old Canadian Adam Hadwin claimed his second victory on the 2014 Web.com Tour, closing with a 68 to edge John Peterson by two in the Chiquita Classic, the second leg of the Web.com Finals. The former University of Louisville star had already clinched his PGA Tour card for 2015 by finishing fourth in regular season Web.com earnings but enhanced his position on the Tour Priority List significantly with the victory. Peterson, who struggled as 2014 PGA Tour rookie, also clinched 2015 playing privileges with his runner-up finish.

1	Adam Hadwin	63-72-67-68	270	$180,000
2	John Peterson	65-70-68-69	272	$108,000
3	Tom Hoge	73-63-69-68	273	$68,000
4=	Oscar Fraustro	67-71-71-66	275	$39,375
	Jim Herman	72-67-69-67	275	$39,375
	Kyle Reifers	67-68-70-70	275	$39,375
	Scott Pinckney	66-68-70-71	275	$39,375
8=	Colt Knost	67-70-69-70	276	$30,000
	Greg Chalmers	69-65-67-75	276	$30,000
10=	Hudson Swafford	66-73-68-70	277	$26,000
	Roberto Castro	72-67-67-71	277	$26,000
12=	Eric Axley	69-74-68-67	278	$20,250
	Will Wilcox	71-70-67-70	278	$20,250
	Spencer Levin	72-65-69-72	278	$20,250
	Carlos Sainz Jr.	70-72-64-72	278	$20,250
16=	Peter Tomasulo	72-71-67-69	279	$13,133
	Roland Thatcher	70-67-71-71	279	$13,133
	Richard S. Johnson	69-69-70-71	279	$13,133
	Derek Fathauer	66-66-75-72	279	$13,133
	Aron Price	72-66-69-72	279	$13,133
	Alex Prugh	72-67-68-72	279	$13,133
	Sam Saunders	71-66-69-73	279	$13,133
	James Nitties	71-66-68-74	279	$13,133
	Heath Slocum	72-69-64-74	279	$13,133

OWR: 0 of top 50 entered - Rating: 16 - Points to 24th - Hadwin: 16 points, to 197th in OWR

Nationwide Children's Hospital Championship
Sep 11 - Sep 14

Ohio State University Golf Club (Scarlet) - Columbus, OH
Champion: Justin Thomas
7,455 yards   Par 72
Purse: $1 Million

Former University of Alabama All-American Justin Thomas claimed his first Web.com Tour victory at the Nationwide Children's Hospital Championship, edging six-time European Tour winner Richard Sterne on the first hole of sudden death. Sterne gave away a three-stroke lead with late bogeys at holes 15-17, but still earned enough money to secure his 2015 PGA Tour card. Thomas, who already earned his card via regular season Web.com earnings, jumped to third place on the 2015 priority list with one Web.com Finals event left to play.

1	Justin Thomas	67-69-72-70	278	$180,000
2	Richard Sterne	72-69-67-70	278	$108,000
3=	Sean O'Hair	68-71-73-67	279	$58,000
	Whee Kim	71-72-67-69	279	$58,000
5	J.J. Henry	74-70-69-67	280	$40,000
6=	Tony Finau	66-72-72-71	281	$34,750
	Blayne Barber	65-74-70-72	281	$34,750
8=	Patrick Rodgers	70-70-73-69	282	$30,000
	Derek Fathauer	63-69-76-74	282	$30,000
10=	Adam Hadwin	71-72-70-70	283	$26,000
	Vaughn Taylor	66-69-74-74	283	$26,000
12=	Sam Saunders	70-70-76-68	284	$22,000
	Tag Ridings	67-73-74-70	284	$22,000
14=	Tom Gillis	70-70-77-68	285	$15,500
	Jason Gore	70-73-73-69	285	$15,500
	David Lingmerth	71-72-72-70	285	$15,500
	Andrew Loupe	64-75-74-72	285	$15,500
	Sebastian Cappelen	71-71-71-72	285	$15,500
	Jim Herman	71-71-70-73	285	$15,500
	Zack Sucher	70-71-71-73	285	$15,500
	Sung Joon Park	69-73-70-73	285	$15,500

OWR: 0 of top 50 entered - Rating: 18 - Points to 21st - Thomas: 16 points, to 129th in OWR

Web.com Tour Championship

Dye's Valley Course - Ponte Vedra Beach, FL
Champion: Derek Fathauer

Sep 18 - Sep 21
6,847 yards   Par 70
Purse: $1 Million

Former University of Louisville All-American Derek Fathauer made his first victory as professional a big one, claiming the season-ending Web.com Tour Championship by a single shot over Zac Blair. Though Fathauer had already secured a 2014-15 PGA Tour card by finishing among the Web.com's top 25 regular season money winners, the victory jumped him to the top of the Web.com Finals standing, giving him much-coveted fully exempt status on the big Tour. Also gaining such status was another ex-Louisville star, Canadian Adam Hadwin, who tied for seventh here but topped the combined regular season and Finals money list. A total of 24 of the 50 players who earned their cards were PGA Tour veterans, including past winners Heath Slocum, Sean O'Hair, Jason Gore, J.J. Henry and Bill Lunde.

Pos	Player	Scores	Total	Money
1	Derek Fathauer	65-66-67-68	266	$180,000
2	Zac Blair	63-65-71-68	267	$108,000
3	Jason Gore	69-65-66-69	269	$68,000
4=	Heath Slocum	67-70-67-68	272	$44,000
	Jim Herman	70-67-65-70	272	$44,000
6	David Lingmerth	68-67-73-65	273	$36,000
7=	Sam Saunders	69-68-70-67	274	$30,125
	Chad Collins	65-69-70-70	274	$30,125
	Travis Bertoni	66-69-68-71	274	$30,125
	Adam Hadwin	66-69-67-72	274	$30,125
11=	John Rollins	70-68-68-69	275	$23,000
	Sung Joon Park	65-68-71-71	275	$23,000
	T. Van Aswegen	66-69-67-73	275	$23,000
14=	Tony Finau	68-72-70-66	276	$16,000
	Alex Prugh	70-69-68-69	276	$16,000
	Michael Kim	71-68-68-69	276	$16,000
	Jamie Lovemark	73-66-67-70	276	$16,000
	Colt Knost	67-69-70-70	276	$16,000
	Richard H. Lee	67-68-70-71	276	$16,000
	Scott Pinckney	65-75-65-71	276	$16,000
21=	Nick Taylor	68-72-74-63	277	$10,800
	Jonathan Byrd	70-69-69-69	277	$10,800
	Justin Thomas	68-71-69-69	277	$10,800
	Tom Gillis	67-67-70-73	277	$10,800
25=	Brett Stegmaier	74-66-71-67	278	$7,772
	Eric Axley	69-71-70-68	278	$7,772
	Shane Bertsch	69-70-70-69	278	$7,772
	Max Homa	74-66-69-69	278	$7,772
	Hudson Swafford	69-70-68-71	278	$7,772
	Chez Reavie	70-67-70-71	278	$7,772
31=	Carlos Sainz Jr.	70-70-68-71	279	$5,975
	Charlie Wi	70-69-69-71	279	$5,975
	Wes Roach	69-66-72-72	279	$5,975
	Mark Hubbard	71-66-68-74	279	$5,975
	Bronson La'Cassie	65-70-70-74	279	$5,975
	Miguel A. Carballo	68-65-71-75	279	$5,975
37=	Blayne Barber	71-69-71-69	280	$4,850
	Peter Malnati	69-69-72-70	280	$4,850
	James Nitties	66-68-73-73	280	$4,850
40=	Cameron Percy	70-70-73-68	281	$3,900
	Whee Kim	68-66-79-68	281	$3,900
	Roberto Castro	71-67-72-71	281	$3,900
	Matt Davidson	69-69-71-72	281	$3,900
	Kyle Reifers	68-71-69-73	281	$3,900
	Tag Ridings	71-67-70-73	281	$3,900
46=	Doug LaBelle II	69-70-72-71	282	$2,992
	Jonathan Randolph	69-71-71-71	282	$2,992
	John Peterson	70-67-74-71	282	$2,992
	Rod Pampling	71-68-70-73	282	$2,992
	Tommy Gainey	73-62-72-75	282	$2,992
	Sebastian Cappelen	69-70-68-75	282	$2,992
52=	Tom Hoge	69-71-73-70	283	$2,727
	Kelly Kraft	70-67-76-70	283	$2,727
	Ben Curtis	73-67-72-71	283	$2,727
	Greg Owen	68-71-73-71	283	$2,727
	Andres Gonzales	66-70-73-74	283	$2,727
	J.J. Henry	70-67-72-74	283	$2,727
58=	Brad Fritsch	74-65-76-69	284	$2,630
	Troy Matteson	72-67-72-73	284	$2,630
60	Andrew Putnam	67-69-72-77	285	$2,600
61=	Vaughn Taylor	69-70-74-73	286	$2,570
	Mathew Goggin	72-66-75-73	286	$2,570
63	Jason Allred	72-67-74-75	288	$2,540
64	Henrik Norlander	69-71-76-73	289	$2,520

OWR: 0 of top 50 entered - Rating: 14 - Points to 24th - Fathauer: 20 points, to 174th in OWR

2014 Web.com Tour Finals PGA Tour Card Earners

#	Player	Age	Country	#	Player	Age	Country
1)	Adam Hadwin	26*	Canada	26)	Cameron Percy	40	Australia
2)	Derek Fathauer	28	United States	27)	Scott Pinckney	25*	United States
3)	Carlos Ortiz	23*	Mexico	28)	Daniel Berger	21*	United States
4)	Bud Cauley	24	United States	29)	Tyrone Van Aswegen	32	South Africa
5)	Justin Thomas	21*	United States	30)	Jonathan Randolph	26*	United States
6)	Colt Knost	29	United States	31)	Sean O'Hair	32	United States
7)	John Peterson	25	United States	32)	Max Homa	23*	United States
8)	Andrew Putnam	25*	United States	33)	Heath Slocum	40	United States
9)	Richard Sterne	33*	South Africa	34)	Mark Hubbard	25*	United States
10)	Jason Gore	40	United States	35)	J.J. Henry	39	United States
11)	Zac Blair	24*	United States	36)	Steve Wheatcroft	36	United States
12)	Tony Finau	24*	United States	37)	Nick Taylor	26*	United States
13)	Sam Saunders	27*	United States	38)	Kyle Reifers	30	United States
14)	Zack Sucher	27*	United States	39)	Hudson Swafford	27	United States
15)	Jim Herman	37	United States	40)	Ryan Armour	38	United States
16)	Blayne Barber	24*	United States	41)	Alex Prugh	30	United States
17)	David Lingmerth	27	United States	42)	Byron Smith	33*	United States
18)	Alex Cejka	43	Germany	43)	Oscar Fraustro	32*	Mexico
19)	Tom Hoge	25*	United States	44)	Bill Lunde	38	United States
20)	Steven Alker	43	New Zealand	45)	Sung-Joon Park	28*	South Korea
21)	Greg Owen	42	England	46)	Roger Sloan	27*	United States
22)	Andres Gonzales	31	United States	47)	Chad Collins	36	United States
23)	Tom Gillis	46	United States	48)	Fabián Gómez	36	Argentina
24)	Jon Curran	27*	United States	49)	Carlos Sainz Jr.	28*	United States
25)	Whee Kim	22*	South Korea	50)	Eric Axley	40	United States

* Players who will be rookies on the PGA Tour (Ages as of Web.com Tour Championship)

CHALLENGE TOUR 2014

The European Challenge Tour must be considered one of the more impressive enterprises in professional golf, because as developmental circuits go, its stability and imposing geographic reach are really quite remarkable. The Tour played a 27-event schedule in 2014, with tournaments crossing the calendar from March until early November, and crossing the globe from Europe south to Africa, and eastward all the way to China. Further, such golfing hotbeds as Kenya, Azerbaijan, Kazakhstan and Oman have become regular stops, and the circuit concludes in the fall with a pair of more lucrative events in China, the Oman stop, and a Tour Championship type of event in – where else – Dubai. If one subscribes to the theory that European Tour players are in some ways better prepared to compete than many Americans due to the immense geographic, cultural and golfing variety of their Tour, then the Challenge circuit must be given real credit as the ideal preparation for that E Tour experience.

This year's edition lacked the star power provided by (and subsequent battlefield promotion provided to) American Brooks Koepka, but it did provide a 15-man graduating class dotted with interesting prospects. Topping the list were a pair of men with a smattering of E Tour experience on their résumés, England's Andrew Johnston (a two-time winner in 2014) and France's Benjamin Hebert, who also won twice, including a five-shot runaway at the season-ending Dubai Festival City Grand Final. But next in line are two more interesting prospects, Korea's Byeong-Hun An and Germany's Moritz Lampert. An came to early fame in 2009 by becoming the youngest-ever winner of the U.S. Amateur, and if his subsequent professional career has been a tad less successful, the talent, it would seem, is still there. The 22-year-old Lampert, however, may be the most intriguing prospect of the bunch as he actually matched Koepka's feat of winning thrice in a single season, and his fourth-place earnings were accumulated in all of 11 starts. Having received a battlefield promotion of his own, he spent the latter weeks of 2014 playing the European Tour, where he'd previously struggled in 2013 as a 20-year-old rookie.

Unlike the Web.com Tour (which has no such "feeder" arrangements), the Challenge circuit offers playing privileges to the top five finishers on each of four European satellite tours, whose seasons are profiled on page 194.

Player Of The Year: Andrew Johnston

With developmental tours, there is always the temptation to only award genuine first-time players and not veterans who've already spent time on the big stage. In the case of England's Andrew Johnston, that time was 20 E Tour starts (and a 163rd-place money ranking) in 2012 - but since his primarily challenger in 2014, Frances Benjamin Hebert, has two E Tour seasons under his belt, Johnston it is.

2014 Challenge Tour Top 60 Money Winners

#	Player	Earnings	#	Player	Earnings	#	Player	Earnings
1	Andrew Johnston	€190,856	21	Lasse Jensen	€71,585	41	Jeppe Huldahl	€51,138
2	Benjamin Hebert	€178,266	22	Max Orrin	€70,888	42	Joakim Lagergren	€50,723
3	Byeong-Hun An	€150,107	23	Alessandro Tadini	€70,645	43	Pedro Oriol	€50,427
4	Moritz Lampert	€137,194	24	Andrew McArthur	€69,646	44	Pelle Edberg	€47,542
5	Mark Tullo	€129,968	25	Scott Henry	€66,576	45	William Harrold	€47,384
6	Sam Hutsby	€128,984	26	Daniel Gaunt	€66,357	46	Connor Arendell	€43,497
7	Jordi García Pinto	€112,317	27	Steven Brown	€63,171	47	Ricardo Gouveia	€43,339
8	Jason Palmer	€108,056	28	Pontus Widegren	€63,106	48	Matthew Fitzpatrick	€43,333
9	Michael Lorenzo-Vera	€106,796	29	Jens Fahrbring	€62,661	49	Terry Pilkadaris	€41,821
10	Oliver Farr	€101,476	30	Alvaro Velasco	€61,375	50	Tim Sluiter	€41,582
11	Edouard Espana	€95,012	31	Thomas Linard	€60,981	51	Julien Guerrier	€39,190
12	Florian Fritsch	€92,943	32	Matteo Delpodio	€60,128	52	Pierre Relecom	€38,530
13	J. Lando Casanova	€88,785	33	Adrien Bernadet	€60,000	53	Chris Hamson	€37,905
14	Jake Roos	€87,431	34	Callum Shinkwin	€59,347	54	Rhys Davies	€37,435
15	Jason Barnes	€77,793	35	Hugues Joannes	€58,667	55	Carlos Aguilar	€36,500
16	Antonio Hortal	€75,864	36	Robert Coles	€55,103	56	Chris Paisley	€35,815
17	Ben Evans	€75,381	37	Niccolo Quintarelli	€54,567	57	Jocke Rask	€34,762
18	Johan Edfors	€74,312	38	Andrew Marshall	€53,936	58	Filippo Bergamaschi	€32,926
19	Cyril Bouniol	€73,330	39	Dave Coupland	€51,910	59	Charlie Ford	€32,529
20	Bernd Ritthammer	€71,898	40	Björn Åkesson	€51,583	60	Maarten Lafeber	€31,229

Barclays Kenya Open

Karen Country Club - Nairobi, Kenya
Champion: Jake Roos

Mar 6 - Mar 9
6,953 yards Par 72
Purse: €200,000

South African Jake Roos took a break from the Sunshine Tour to emerge from a crowded final round leaderboard and win the Barclays Kenya Open in Nairobi. Trailing by one after a bogey at the 16th, Roos was vaulted into the lead when France's Adrien Bernadet double-bogeyed the 17th, and the six-time Sunshine Tour winner then held on with pars at the 17th and 18th to win by one. Bernadet would tie for second with Denmark's Lasse Jensen and Spain's Pedro Oriol, one shot back.

1	Jake Roos	69-68-71-70	278	€32,000		Greg Snow	70-68-71-73	282	€4,067
2=	Adrien Bernadet	70-69-70-70	279	€16,000	13=	Jamie Elson	73-69-73-68	283	€3,300
	Lasse Jensen	67-71-71-70	279	€16,000		Dismas Indiza	73-69-68-73	283	€3,300
	Pedro Oriol	69-69-70-71	279	€16,000		Maarten Lafeber	72-72-69-70	283	€3,300
5=	Steven Brown	70-72-71-68	281	€6,960		Sam Little	75-70-67-71	283	€3,300
	Dodge Kemmer	69-73-71-68	281	€6,960	17=	Cyril Bouniol	70-72-72-70	284	€2,343
	Thomas Linard	71-70-71-69	281	€6,960		Matt Ford	70-70-72-72	284	€2,343
	Danie van Tonder	70-69-70-72	281	€6,960		Sam Hutsby	73-66-70-75	284	€2,343
	Pontus Widegren	69-69-72-71	281	€6,960		Andrew McArthur	71-68-73-72	284	€2,343
10=	Oliver Bekker	71-70-68-73	282	€4,067		Oliver Wilson	69-68-78-69	284	€2,343
	Bernd, Ritthammer	74-69-69-70	282	€4,067		George Woolgar	72-68-75-69	284	€2,343

OWR: 0 of top 50 entered - Rating: 0 - Points to 16th - Roos: 12 points, to 226th in OWR

Challenge de Catalunya

Lumine Golf & Beach Club - Tarragona, Spain
Champion: Antonio Hortal

Apr 24 - Apr 27
6,909 yards Par 71
Purse: €160,000

Twenty-five-year-old Spaniard Antonio Hortal scored a popular homestanding victory at the Challenge de Catalunya, claiming his first Challenge Tour title by three strokes in a 54-hole weather shortened event. Following the cancellation of the second round due to high winds, Hortal tied the Lumine Golf & Beach Club record with an eight-under-par 63 on Saturday, then saw himself home three strokes clear of England's Callum Shinkwin with a closing 68 spurred by key birdies at the 11th, 13th and 15th holes.

1	Antonio Hortal	68-63-68	199	€25,600		M. Lorenzo-Vera	68-69-70	207	€2,960
2	Callum Shinkwin	66-68-68	202	€17,600	14=	Juan A. Bragulat	68-69-71	208	€2,320
3=	Connor Arendell	65-67-72	204	€10,400		Daniel Brooks	69-69-70	208	€2,320
	Andrew Johnston	68-69-67	204	€10,400		Alan Dunbar	66-70-72	208	€2,320
5=	Cyril Bouniol	66-68-71	205	€6,507		J.B. Gonnet	70-67-71	208	€2,320
	Matt Ford	68-70-67	205	€6,507		Niall Kearney	69-65-74	208	€2,320
	J. Lando Casanova	66-68-71	205	€6,507		Mikko Korhonen	70-68-70	208	€2,320
8=	Byeong-Hun An	67-68-71	206	€3,760	20=	Jason Barnes	71-70-68	209	€1,527
	Jordi García Pinto	70-68-68	206	€3,760		Wil Besseling	68-73-68	209	€1,527
	Andrew Marshall	68-69-69	206	€3,760		Lasse Jensen	68-67-74	209	€1,527
	Simon Wakefield	67-70-69	206	€3,760		Adrien Saddier	64-70-75	209	€1,527
12=	Lorenzo Gagli	68-67-72	207	€2,960		Joel Sjoholm	67-72-70	209	€1,527

OWR: 0 of top 50 entered - Rating: 0 - Points to 19th - Hortal: 12 points, to 481st in OWR

Turkish Airlines Challenge

National Golf Club - Antalya, Turkey
Champion: Oliver Farr

May 15 - May 18
7,085 yards Par 72
Purse: €175,000

Wales' Oliver Farr won for the first time on the European Challenge Tour, taking the inaugural Turkish Airlines Challenge by two shots over a trio of players: England's Dave Coupland, Denmark's Jeppe Huldahl and Jérôme Lando Casanova of France. The 26-year-old Farr closed with a 70 to finish on two-under-par 286 – and was the only player in the field to better par over a challenging National Golf Club layout. Farr clinched the title with a closing birdie after sticking his approach to five feet at the 372-yard par-4 18th.

1	Oliver Farr	72-67-77-70	286	€28,000	12	Ruaidhri McGee	73-73-72-74	292	€3,325
2=	Dave Coupland	71-70-73-74	288	€14,000	13=	Byeong-Hun An	70-72-75-76	293	€2,800
	Jeppe Huldahl	76-68-71-73	288	€14,000		Matteo Delpdio	71-75-74-73	293	€2,800
	J. Lando Casanova	71-71-71-75	288	€14,000		Edouard Espana	72-71-78-72	293	€2,800
5=	Bjorn Akesson	71-71-73-74	289	€7,875		Thomas Linard	74-74-74-71	293	€2,800
	Moritz Lampert	74-72-71-72	289	€7,875		Chris Paisley	69-73-74-77	293	€2,800
7=	Chris Hanson	74-71-72-73	290	€4,900	18=	Cyril Bouniol	77-71-72-74	294	€2,034
	Niccolo Quintarelli	72-70-73-75	290	€4,900		Max Orrin	72-74-72-76	294	€2,034
	Bernd Ritthammer	78-66-75-71	290	€4,900		Nicolo Ravano	75-68-73-78	294	€2,034
10=	Adrien Bernadet	73-75-75-68	291	€3,675		Steven Tiley	75-71-75-73	294	€2,034
	Robert Coles	70-75-75-71	291	€3,675					

OWR: 0 of top 50 entered - Rating: 0 - Points to 17th - Farr: 12 points, to 484th in OWR

Kärnten Golf Open
Golfclub Schloss Finkenstein - Gödersdorf, Austria
Champion: Moritz Lampert

Jun 27 - Jun 30
6,931 yards Par 71
Purse: €160,000

Playing on a sponsor's exemption, 22-year-old German Moritz Lampert claimed his maiden Challenge Tour victory at the Kärnten Golf Open, charging home with weekend rounds of 65-65 to edge South Korea's Byeong-Hun An by one. Lampert's closing rounds included 15 birdies (against only three bogeys) and were highlighted by an outgoing 31 on Sunday, which allowed him to move ahead of 54-hole leaders Cyril Bouniol and Jeppe Huldahl. An's closing 66 including birdies on his final three holes to claim solo second.

1	Moritz Lampert	69-66-65-65	265	€25,600		12=	Adrien Bernadet	65-70-71-65	271	€2,720
2	Byeong-Hun An	67-69-64-66	266	€17,600			Jeppe Huldahl	73-60-66-72	271	€2,720
3	Filippo Bergamaschi	69-66-65-67	267	€11,200			Andrew Johnston	67-65-68-71	271	€2,720
4=	Cyril Bouniol	69-67-63-69	268	€8,000			Niccolo Quintarelli	71-67-67-66	271	€2,720
	Florian Fritsch	65-69-66-68	268	€8,000			Daniel Vancsik	67-66-68-70	271	€2,720
	Jake Roos	67-69-66-66	268	€8,000		17=	Benjamin Hebert	70-68-66-68	272	€1,936
7=	Wallace Booth	69-68-68-64	269	€4,240			Chris Lloyd	68-67-71-66	272	€1,936
	Sam Hutsby	72-64-68-65	269	€4,240			Gregory Main	69-69-68-66	272	€1,936
	Paul Maddy	65-68-67-69	269	€4,240			Tom Murray	64-70-68-70	272	€1,936
	Ruaidhri McGee	68-65-69-67	269	€4,240			Max Orrin	64-74-67-67	272	€1,936
	Steven Tiley	72-65-64-69	270	€3,200						

OWR: 0 of top 50 entered - Rating: 0 - Points to 16th - Lampert: 12 points, to 401st in OWR

D+D Real Czech Challenge Open
Golf & Span Kunetica Hora - Dritec, Czech Republic
Champion: Thomas Linard

May 29 - Jun 1
7,337 yards Par 72
Purse: €165,000

France's 26-year-old Thomas Linard claimed his maiden Challenge Tour victory at the Real Czech Challenge, closing with an impressive eight-under-par 64 to pull away to a two-shot triumph. Linard began Sunday two shots behind 54-hole leader Daniel Gaunt, who held up nicely under the pressure with a 68, good enough to claim solo second. But it was clearly to be Linard's day as he reeled off seven birdies over his first 10 holes to vault into the lead, then added two more late birdies and a bogey to cruise to the title.

1	Thomas Linard	70-68-67-64	269	€26,400		12=	Gregor Main	71-71-68-67	277	€2,888
2	Daniel Gaunt	64-69-70-68	271	€18,150			Benjamin Hebert	71-69-68-69	277	€2,888
3	Ross McGowan	70-68-66-69	273	€11,550			Jeppe Huldahl	72-67-68-70	277	€2,888
4=	Pontus Widegren	70-67-66-71	274	€9,075			Edouard Espana	70-67-69-71	277	€2,888
	Chris Lloyd	68-66-69-71	274	€9,075		16=	Wallace Booth	73-67-70-68	278	€2,310
6=	Phillip Archer	70-73-68-65	276	€4,565			Anders Engell	71-72-67-68	278	€2,310
	Steven Brown	73-68-69-66	276	€4,565			Peter Erofejeff	71-69-65-73	278	€2,310
	Ken Benz	77-63-69-67	276	€4,565		19=	Tom Murray	72-68-73-66	279	€1,842
	Lloyd Kennedy	72-69-67-68	276	€4,565			Alvaro Velasco	69-72-69-69	279	€1,842
	Robert Coles	71-70-67-68	276	€4,565			Jeff Winther	70-70-66-73	279	€1,842
	Florian Fritsch	70-68-69-69	276	€4,565						

OWR: 0 of top 50 entered - Rating: 0 - Points to 15th - Linard: 12 points, to 417th in OWR

Fred Olsen Challenge de España
Tecina Golf - Canary Islands, Spain
Champion: Moritz Lampert

Jun 5 - Jun 8
6,937 yards Par 71
Purse: €160,000

Winning for the second time in three Challenge Tour starts, Germany's Moritz Lampert closed with an eight-under-par 63 to claim a two-shot triumph at the Fred Olsen Challenge de España. Lampert's 63 headed a parade of low final round numbers and was led by eight birdies (plus a bogey) over his first 11 holes, though he eventually settled down to add only one more birdie, at the par-5 17th. Runner-up Hugues Joannes also went low on Sunday, posting a 64 which showed four twos on his card, including an eagle at the driveable par-4 9th.

1	Moritz Lampert	69-66-66-63	264	€25,600		12=	David Law	72-66-66-68	272	€2,720
2	Hugues Joannes	68-67-67-64	266	€17,600			Jason Palmer	66-68-69-69	272	€2,720
3=	Luis Claverie	67-69-68-64	268	€10,400			Neil Raymond	71-70-66-65	272	€2,720
	Matteo Delpodio	66-67-66-69	268	€10,400			Matthew Southgate	70-69-64-69	272	€2,720
5=	Andrew Johnston	69-66-66-68	269	€7,200			Alessandro Tadini	70-69-68-65	272	€2,720
	Joel Sjoholm	67-62-72-68	269	€7,200		17=	Sam Hutsby	66-68-71-68	273	€2,160
7=	Agustin Domingo	68-66-68-68	270	€4,240			Damien Perrier	65-72-67-69	273	€2,160
	Nicolo Ravano	68-67-65-70	270	€4,240		19=	William Harrold	72-65-70-67	274	€1,732
	Diego Suazo	70-69-67-64	270	€4,240			Antonio Hortal	68-68-70-68	274	€1,732
	Alvaro Velasco	71-66-66-67	270	€4,240			Lasse Jensen	72-64-69-69	274	€1,732
11	M. Lorenzo-Vera	70-69-66-66	271	€3,200			Pedro Oriol	68-66-69-71	274	€1,732

OWR: 0 of top 50 entered - Rating: 0 - Points to 16th - Lampert: 12 points, to 253rd in OWR

Najeti Hotels et Golfs Open

Jun 13 - Jun 15

AA St. Omer Golf Course - St. Omer, France
Champion: Jordi García Pinto

6,538 yards Par 71
Purse: €200,000

Twenty-four-year-old lawyer-to-be Jordi García Pinto won for the second time on the Challenge Tour, taking the Najeti Hotels et Golfs Open by three shots over countryman Carlos Aguilar in France. García Pinto jumped into the halfway lead via a second round 65, remained two shots up through 54 holes after a Saturday 71, then cruised home with a one-birdie, 17-par performance on Sunday. The victory at this formerly E Tour co-sanctioned event virtually guaranteed García Pinto a spot on the big circuit for 2015.

1	Jordi García Pinto	71-65-71-70	277	€32,000		Pelle Edberg	70-70-71-74	285	€3,200
2	Carlos Aguilar	73-68-68-71	280	€22,000		Benjamin Hebert	71-71-70-73	285	€3,200
3=	Lorenzo Gagli	72-71-68-71	282	€10,080		Lasse Jensen	71-73-69-72	285	€3,200
	Scott Henry	68-74-71-69	282	€10,080		Tain Lee	69-71-70-75	285	€3,200
	Lloyd Kennedy	71-70-70-71	282	€10,080		Ross McGowan	71-71-68-75	285	€3,200
	Andrea Rota	69-69-72-72	282	€10,080		Alessandro Tadini	70-68-74-73	285	€3,200
	Mark Tullo	72-71-71-68	282	€10,080	19=	Bjorn Akesson	74-68-70-74	286	€2,077
8	Berry Henson	72-70-72-69	283	€5,600		Christophe Brazillier	73-68-72-73	286	€2,077
9=	David Law	68-71-72-73	284	€4,400		Pedro Figueiredo	71-71-72-72	286	€2,077
	Daniel Vancsik	72-72-70-70	284	€4,400		Joakim Lagergren	69-75-71-71	286	€2,077
	Pontus Widegren	69-75-71-69	284	€4,400		Chris Paisley	70-73-71-72	286	€2,077
12=	Jack Doherty	73-70-70-72	285	€3,200		Terry Pilkadaris	70-71-72-73	286	€2,077

OWR: 0 of top 50 entered - Rating: 0 - Points to 18th - Pinto: 12 points, to 221st in OWR

Belgian Challenge Open

Jun 19 - Jun 22

Cleydael Golf & Country Club - Aartselaar, Belgium
Champion: William Harrold

6,548 yards Par 71
Purse: €160,000

Twenty-six-year-old Englishman William Harrold won for the first time on the Challenge Tour, defeating Germany's Florian Fritsch on the first hole of sudden death at the Belgian Challenge Open. The 54-hole leader behind rounds of 70-63-67, Harrold closed strongly with a 66 that included a run of eight straight pars to finish. This lack of closing birdies left the door slightly ajar for Fritsch, who carded a clutch birdie at the 17th en route to a Sunday 65, but lost when he bogeyed the first extra hole, the 393-yard 18th.

1	William Harrold	70-63-67-66	266	€25,600	11=	Jason Barnes	73-67-67-66	273	€2,960
2	Florian Fritsch	64-68-69-65	266	€17,600		Rodolfo Cazaubon	65-66-70-72	273	€2,960
3=	Dave Coupland	63-72-67-66	268	€10,400		Edouard Espana	68-69-67-69	273	€2,960
	Jason Palmer	66-63-73-66	268	€10,400		Alvaro Velasco	67-66-72-68	273	€2,960
5	Joel Stalter	68-64-70-67	269	€8,000	15=	Connor Arendell	70-68-69-67	274	€2,160
6=	Filippo Bergamaschi	69-69-68-66	272	€4,672		Robert Coles	74-65-66-69	274	€2,160
	Michael Jonzon	68-69-67-68	272	€4,672		Hugues Joannes	66-71-68-69	274	€2,160
	Tain Lee	68-68-70-66	272	€4,672		Chris Paisley	66-69-69-70	274	€2,160
	Terry Pilkadaris	66-70-67-69	272	€4,672		Nicolo Ravano	66-71-67-70	274	€2,160
	Andrea Rota	66-72-67-67	272	€4,672		Jack Wilson	69-67-68-70	274	€2,160

OWR: 0 of top 50 entered - Rating: 0 - Points to 14th - Harrold: 12 points, to 508th in OWR

Scottish Hydro Challenge

Jun 26 - Jun 29

Macdonald Spey Valley Golf Club - Aviemore, Scotland
Champion: Andrew Johnston

7,100 yards Par 71
Purse: €250,000

Twenty-five-year-old Englishman Andrew Johnston claimed his maiden Challenge Tour victory at the Scottish Hydro Open, riding a blistering 19-under-par 265 aggregate to a three-stroke victory. Opening rounds of 66-65-68 put Johnston two clear of the field through 54 holes and he quickly expanded the lead on Sunday by holing an 83-yard wedge for an eagle at the par-4 2nd hole. It was largely a runaway hereafter, though red-hot Moritz Lampert at least made it interesting by playing the final nine in 29 to tie Australian Terry Pilkadaris for second.

1	Andrew Johnston	66-65-68-66	265	€40,000		M. Lorenzo-Vera	66-69-69-67	271	€4,875
2=	Moritz Lampert	69-67-65-67	268	€22,500	13=	Maarten Lafeber	70-67-66-69	272	€4,375
	Terry Pilkadaris	66-67-68-67	268	€22,500		Taco Remkes	70-65-69-68	272	€4,375
4=	Oliver Farr	68-67-68-66	269	€13,750	15=	Dave Coupland	71-67-69-66	273	€3,500
	Jack Senio	70-66-68-65	269	€13,750		Stephen Dodd	72-66-72-63	273	€3,500
6=	Bjorn Akeson	67-67-68-68	270	€7,300		Bradley Dredge	67-69-68-69	273	€3,500
	Jamie Elson	68-67-67-68	270	€7,300		Xavier Guzman	70-64-68-71	273	€3,500
	Edouard Espana	66-68-69-67	270	€7,300		Lasse Jensen	69-68-69-67	273	€3,500
	Florian Fritsch	69-67-66-68	270	€7,300	20=	Kenneth Ferrie	70-66-69-69	274	€2,515
	Mark Tullo	65-71-69-65	270	€7,300		Benjamin Herbert	70-69-69-66	274	€2,515
11=	Jason Barnes	65-67-69-70	271	€4,875		Greig Hutcheon	67-68-68-71	274	€2,515

OWR: 0 of top 50 entered - Rating: 0 - Points to 14th - Johnston: 12 points, to 271st in OWR

Aegean Airlines Challenge Tour
Hartl Resort - Bad Griesbach, Germany
Champion: Jake Roos

Jul 3 - Jul 6
7,322 yards   Par 72
Purse: €170,000

Six-time Sunshine Tour winner Jake Roos claimed his second title of the 2014 Challenge Tour season, surviving a wild final nine to take the inaugural Aegean Airlines Challenge in Germany. Roos was battling playing partner Chris Hanson when Hanson eagled both the 514-yard 10th and the 368-yard 14th (where he holed his second) to take a seemingly commanding four-stroke lead. But Hanson collapsed with five straight bogeys thereafter, allowing Roos - who birdied both the 16th and 17th - to ultimately steal the title.

1	Jake Roos	69-69-67-70	275	€27,200	12=	Fabian Becker	72-72-69-68-	281	€2,720
2	Jason Barnes	71-71-67-68	277	€18,700		Jeppe Huldahl	71-71-69-70	281	€2,720
3=	Chris Hanson	71-67-67-73	278	€10,200		Michael Jonzon	69-70-71-71	281	€2,720
	Bernd Ritthammer	71-71-71-65	278	€10,200		Moritz Lampert	70-70-73-68	281	€2,720
	Alessandro Tadini	72-66-68-72	278	€10,200		Jaakko Makitalo	71-68-70-72	281	€2,720
6=	Björn Akesson	66-72-67-74	279	€4,964		Pedro Oriol	70-71-68-72	281	€2,720
	Robert Colkes	72-70-68-69	279	€4,964		Max Orrin	69-71-71-70	281	€2,720
	Jens Fahrbring	70-71-70-68	279	€4,964	19=	Jesus Legarrea	69-70-75-68	282	€1,898
	Andrew Johnston	70-68-72-69	279	€4,964		Sam Little	67-72-72-71	282	€1,898
	Nathan Kimsey	71-72-70-66	279	€4,964		Andrew Marshall	69-72-68-73	282	€1,898
11	Florian Fritsch	75-64-72-69	280	€3,400					

OWR: 0 of top 50 entered   -   Rating: 0   -   Points to 18th   -   Roos: 12 points, to 202nd in OWR

D+D Real Czech Challenge Open
Penati Golf Resort - Senica, Czech Republic
Champion: Andrew McArthur

Jul 10 - Jul 13
6,899 yards   Par 72
Purse: €160,000

Scotland's Andrew McArthur may not have been able to play in the European Tour's Scottish Open but he spent his week in the next best fashion, claiming his second Challenge Tour victory at the D+D Real Slovakia Challenge. The victory was accomplished in wire-to-wire style, with rounds of 65-66-68 staking McArthur to a one-shot 54-hole lead, and a methodical bogey-free 68 closing things out on Sunday. England's Sam Hutsby, who began the final round one stroke back, closed with a 69 to take solo second.

1	Andrew McArthur	65-66-68-68	267	€25,600		J. B. Gonnet	72-70-67-67	276	€2,720
2	Sam Hutsby	66-69-65-69	269	€17,600		M. Lorenzo-Vera	69-70-68-69	276	€2,720
3	Oliver Farr	68-67-68-67	270	€11,200		Ross McGowan	66-71-71-68	276	€2,720
4	Alvaro Velasco	68-68-65-70	271	€9,600		Tim Sluiter	68-70-69-69	276	€2,720
5=	Robert Coles	65-68-70-69	272	€7,200		Steven Tiley	68-71-67-70	276	€2,720
	Pedro Oriol	68-65-72-67	272	€7,200		Mark Tullo	70-72-65-69	276	€2,720
7=	Mark Haastrup	67-65-70-72	274	€4,480	18=	Alexander Bjork	71-69-69-68	277	€1,802
	Andrew Johnston	73-68-62-71	274	€4,480		Edouard Espana	66-76-71-64	277	€1,802
	Nathan Kimsey	69-70-69-66	274	€4,480		Cesar Monasterio	71-69-70-67	277	€1,802
10	Brandon Stone	71-67-68-69	275	€3,520		Nicolo Ravano	70-66-72-69	277	€1,802
11=	Florian Fritsch	73-66-68-69	276	€2,720		Anthony Snobeck	70-69-71-67	277	€1,802

OWR: 0 of top 50 entered   -   Rating: 0   -   Points to 17th   -   McArthur: 12 points, to 386th in OWR

Swiss Challenge
Golf Sempachersee - Lucerne, Switzerland
Champion: Pierre Relecom

Jul 17 - Jul 20
7,147 yards   Par 71
Purse: €160,000

Twenty-nine-year-old Belgian Pierre Relecom won for the first time on the Challenge Tour, his victory marked by both a second-round 63 and an up-and-down final nine. Relecom seemed in complete control after holing a 70-yard pitch for eagle at the 14th, then birdieing the 15th, but bogeys at the 17th and 18th soon cut a four-shot lead to two. Italy's Niccolo Quintarelli narrowed the gap to one with a birdie at the par-3 16th but with a chance to tie, Quintarelli missed a six-footer at the 18th, allowing Relecom to raise the trophy. Notable also was the performance of 22-year-old Swiss amateur Mathias Eggenberger, who carded four straight 68s to finish in a three-way tie for third.

1	Pierre Relecom	70-63-68-68	269	€25,600		Manuel Trappel	73-67-70-66	276	€3,520
2	Niccolo Quintarelli	67-66-69-68	270	€17,600	13=	Gary Boyd	70-66-68-73	277	€2,720
3=	Rhys Davies	68-69-67-68	272	€10,400		Sean Einhaus	72-68-72-65	277	€2,720
	M. Eggenberger (a)	68-68-68-68	272	-		Edouard Espana	71-68-68-70	277	€2,720
	George Murray	66-66-70-70	272	€10,400		Ricardo Gouveia	69-69-68-71	277	€2,720
6	Scott Fallon	68-70-67-68	273	€8,000		Bernd Ritthammer	66-66-75-70	277	€2,720
7=	Charlie Ford	67-69-64-74	274	€5,760	18=	S. García Rodriguez	68-71-72-67	278	€1,936
	Jack Senior	67-71-71-65	274	€5,760		Jacobo Pastor	68-70-70-70	278	€1,936
9	Steven Brown	67-70-67-71	275	€4,480		Florian Praegent	69-72-66-71	278	€1,936
10=	Matteo Delpodio	68-68-72-68	276	€3,520		Alessandro Tadini	68-72-68-70	278	€1,936
	Jeppe Huldahl	69-68-69-70	276	€3,520		Lionel Weber	72-69-69-68	278	€1,936

OWR: 0 of top 50 entered   -   Rating: 0   -   Points to 17th   -   Relecom: 12 points, to 500th in OWR

Le Vaudreuil Golf Challenge
Golf PGA France de Vaudreuil - Le Vaudreuil, France
Champion: Andrew Johnston

Jul 24 - Jul 27
6,764 yards   Par 71
Purse: €200,000

Despite starting the final round three shots off the 54-hole lead, England's Andrew Johnston claimed his second Challenge Tour victory in just under a month and did so comfortably, closing with a red-hot 64 to win the Le Vaudreuil Challenge by four. Johnston actually bogeyed the 2nd hole early on Sunday before heating up, adding two birdies and an eagle (at the par-5 8th) to turn in 32, then equaling that number coming home, ultimately pulling away with late birdies at the 16th and 18th.

1	Andrew Johnston	66-69-69-64	268	€32,000		Lionel Weber	68-69-65-72	274	€5,040
2=	Byeong-Hun An	69-70-66-67	272	€16,000	13=	Niall Kearney	67-68-71-69	275	€3,600
	Connor Arendell	67-70-67-68	272	€16,000		Ben Parker	69-70-67-69	275	€3,600
	Jens Fahrbring	66-66-69-71	272	€16,000		Nicolo Ravano	69-68-66-72	275	€3,600
	Clement Sordet (a)	67-74-68-63	272	-	16=	Cristophe Brazillier	71-69-68-68	276	€2,900
6=	Edouard Espana	67-70-69-67	273	€9,000		Jordi García Pinto	75-66-64-71	276	€2,900
	Jason Palmer	66-66-71-70	273	€9,000		Niklas Lemke	74-68-68-66	276	€2,900
8=	Filippo Bergamaschi	66-66-73-69	274	€5,040		Andrew Marshall	67-74-65-70	276	€2,900
	Matthew Fitzpatrick	69-69-67-69	274	€5,040	20=	Ben Evans	69-69-69-70	277	€2,165
	Gareth Shaw	66-68-69-71	274	€5,040		Jack Senior	66-68-73-70	277	€2,165
	Callum Shinkwin	66-72-67-69	274	€5,040					

OWR: 0 of top 50 entered - Rating: 0 - Points to 15th - Johnston: 12 points, to 167th in OWR

Azerbaijan Golf Challenge Open
National Azerbaijan Golf Club - Quba, Azerbaijan
Champion: Moritz Lampert

Jul 31 - Aug 3
7,011 yards   Par 72
Purse: €300,000

Germany's 22-year-old Moritz Lampert earned an immediate battlefield promotion the European Tour by claiming his third Challenge Tour title of 2014, coming from behind to win in Azerbaijan. Having claimed his earlier victories within the previous 10 weeks, Lampert actually began the week with an opening nine of 39, but a remarkable second round 65 included two eagles and a hole-in-one, before a Saturday 69 left him five shots behind Benjamin Hebert. But four birdies in his first 11 holes then keyed a Sunday 66, and a return ticket to the E Tour.

1	Moritz Lampert	72-65-69-66	272	€48,000	13=	Sam Hutsby	71-68-74-66	279	€5,100
2	M. Lorenzo-Vera	68-68-69-69	274	€33,000		Tim Sluiter	67-69-71-72	279	€5,100
3=	Steven Brown	71-68-70-66	275	€19,500		Damian Ulrich	71-71-69-68	279	€5,100
	Andrew Johnston	66-72-69-68	275	€19,500	16=	Johan Edfors	67-70-73-70	280	€4,050
5=	Alexander Björk	68-67-69-72	276	€13,500		Scott Henry	73-69-70-68	280	€4,050
	Andrew Marshall	72-65-69-70	276	€13,500		Maarten Lafeber	69-69-74-68	280	€4,050
7=	Edouard Espana	65-71-74-67	277	€7,950		Kieran Pratt	70-71-68-71	280	€4,050
	Daniel Gaunt	70-68-69-70	277	€7,950	20=	Connor Arendell	73-70-69-69	281	€2,899
	Benjamin Hebert	72-62-67-76	277	€7,950		Dave Coupland	70-73-70-68	281	€2,899
	Alessandro Tadini	70-71-69-67	277	€7,950		Paul McKechnie	72-71-71-67	281	€2,899
11=	Gary Lockerbie	68-68-70-72	278	€5,850		Anthony Snobeck	69-69-71-72	281	€2,899
	Jaaklo Makitalo	69-69-72-68	278	€5,850		Duncan Stewart	71-67-72-71	281	€2,899

OWR: 0 of top 50 entered - Rating: 4 - Points to 15th - Lampert: 12 points, to 149th in OWR

Norwegian Challenge
Miklagard Golf Club - Kløfta, Norway
Champion: Benjamin Hebert

Aug 7 - Aug 10
7,349 yards   Par 72
Purse: €175,000

After blowing a 54-hole lead with a closing 76 in Azerbaijan, France's Benjamin Hebert hardly seemed a sure thing upon taking a three-shot cushion into the final round of the Norwegian Challenge - and his confidence was surely buckled when what had become a four-shot margin vanished when he gave back four strokes at holes 11-14. But showing great heart in the clutch, the 27-year-old from Brive rose to the moment by birdieing the 16th and then, with everything on the line, stiffing his approach at the last to win by two.

1	Benjamin Hebert	65-67-69-72	273	€28,000		Nathan Holman	66-71-71-72	280	€3,062
2	Florian Fritsch	64-67-73-71	275	€19,250		Agustin Domingo	68-70-67-75	280	€3,062
3	Cyril Bouniol	68-68-71-69	276	€12,250		Peter Erofejeff	72-70-69-69	280	€3,062
4=	Mark Tullo	71-67-70-70	278	€8,750		Brandon Stone	71-70-68-71	280	€3,062
	Andrea Hartø	68-69-70-71	278	€8,750		Richard McEvoy	71-66-70-73	280	€3,062
	Wallace Booth	68-73-68-69	278	€8,750	17=	Jacobo Pastor	71-67-72-71	281	€2,050
7=	Scott Arnold	66-74-69-70	279	€4,638		Joel Sjoholm	74-68-66-73	281	€2,050
	Pontus Widegren	70-70-67-72	279	€4,638		Niall Kearney	67-70-72-72	281	€2,050
	Daniel Im	68-70-70-71	279	€4,638		Nicol Ravano	73-66-71-71	281	€2,050
	Max Orrin	72-70-72-65	279	€4,638		William Harrold	70-70-68-73	281	€2,050
11=	Tain Lee	70-67-70-73	280	€3,062		Paul Maddy	69-70-70-72	281	€2,050

OWR: 0 of top 50 entered - Rating: 0 - Points to 16th - Hebert: 12 points, to 414th in OWR

Vacon Open
Kytäjä Golf - Hyvinkää, Finland
Champion: Mark Tullo

Aug 14 - Aug 17
6,961 yards Par 71
Purse: €200,000

Chile's Mark Tullo won for the third time on the Challenge Tour, taking Finland's Vacon Open by three shots on the wings of a closing seven-under-par 64. A full-time E Tour player in 2011 and '13, the 36-year-old Tullo ended a four-year victory drought, jumpstarted by a tap-in eagle at the 305-yard 5th after nearly holing his drive. Another E Tour veteran, Sweden's Pelle Edberg, closed with a 65 to take solo second, while 54-hole leader Charlie Ford of England needed an eagle at the last to finish with a 69, good enough for solo third.

1	Mark Tullo	68-67-65-64	264	€27,200		Maarten Lafeber	67-72-66-68	273	€3,315
2	Pelle Edberg	71-68-63-65	267	€18,700	13=	David Law	69-65-70-70	274	€2,890
3	Charlie Ford	64-68-67-69	268	€11,900		Charles E. Russo	69-68-66-71	274	€2,890
4=	Byeong-Hun An	68-68-67-66	269	€7,735		Zane Scotland	70-66-69-69	274	€2,890
	H.P. Bacher	67-64-70-68	269	€7,735	16=	Max Glauert	70-67-69-69	275	€2,380
	Guillaume Cambis	65-66-70-68	269	€7,735		Jack Hiluta	71-70-67-67	275	€2,380
	Pontus Widegren	68-65-70-66	269	€7,735		Jocke Rask	72-66-68-69	275	€2,380
	Niklas Lemke	68-66-71-67	272	€4,193	19=	Eirik T. Johansen	70-68-69-69	276	€1,898
8=	Andrea Rota	67-68-68-69	272	€4,193		Ruaidhri McGee	69-67-70-70	276	€1,898
	Callum Shinkwin	69-64-70-69	272	€4,193		Erik Myllymaki (a)	69-68-70-69	276	-
11=	Jeppe Huldahl	67-69-67-70	273	€3,315		Max Orrin	71-64-69-72	276	€1,898

OWR: 0 of top 50 entered - Rating: 0 - Points to 15th - Tullo: 12 points, to 307th in OWR

Rolex Trophy
Golf Club de Genève - Geneva, Switzerland
Champion: Byeong-Hun An

Aug 20 - Aug 23
6,727 yards Par 72
Purse: €232,510

Already the youngest golfer ever to win the U.S. Amateur in 2009, Byeong-Hun An became the first Korean ever to win on the Challenge Tour, riding a scorching Sunday finish to a three-shot triumph at the Rolex Trophy. Trailing 54-hole leader Lasse Jensen by seven on Saturday night, An played blemish-free golf on Sunday, logging eight birdies en route to a 64 which beat the field by three. An also posted an 11-birdie 63 on Thursday, but a Saturday 71 (which included a 7 at the 358-yard 16th) had dragged him back into the pack.

1	Byeong-Hun An	63-69-73-64	269	€26,000		Andrew Marshall	71-67-70-69	277	€4,650
2	Benjamin Hebert	67-68-65-72	272	€19,000	13=	Dave Coupland	71-71-67-69	278	€3,900
3=	Lasse Jensen	61-70-67-75	273	€11,650		Edouard Espana	67-71-69-71	278	€3,900
	Callum Shinkwin	69-69-66-69	273	€11,650		Antonio Hortal	68-73-70-67	278	€3,900
5	Sam Hutsby	65-71-71-67	274	€9,000		Damian Ulrich	67-68-69-74	278	€3,900
6=	Steven Brown	68-70-69-68	275	€7,100	17	Andrew Johnston	66-69-72-72	279	€3,400
	Florian Fritsch	68-67-71-69	275	€7,100	18	Carlos Aguilar	74-69-70-67	280	€3,200
	M. Lorenzo-Vera	64-70-71-70	275	€7,100	19=	Matteo Delpodio	70-75-67-69	281	€2,850
9=	Cyril Bouniol	67-68-74-67	276	€5,400		Jordi García Pinto	69-69-72-71	281	€2,850
	J. Lando Casanova	69-70-67-70	276	€5,400		Thomas Linard	71-68-68-74	281	€2,850
11=	Matthew Fitzpatrick	69-68-71-69	277	€4,650		Mark Tullo	69-68-72-72	281	€2,850

OWR: 0 of top 50 entered - Rating: 2 - Points to 16th - An: 12 points, to 191st in OWR

Northern Ireland Open Challenge
Galgorm Castle Golf Club - Antrim, Northern Ireland
Champion: Joakim Lagergren

Aug 28 - Aug 31
6,930 yards Par 71
Purse: €170,000

After opening with a bogey-free nine-under-par 62, then adding rounds of 71-66, 22-year-old Joakim Lagergren of Sweden began the final day of the Northern Ireland Open Challenge with a commanding six shot lead. But bogeys at two of his first three holes gave his pursuers a ray of hope, and by the time Lagergren reached the 72nd, he'd been caught by Adrien Bernadet of France, who turned in 30 (but couldn't add a single birdie on the back) en route to a closing 66. But instead of waiting for a playoff, Lagergren instead holed an eight-footer on the final green for the biggest birdie of his young career, and a one-stroke victory.

1	Joakim Lagergren	62-71-66-72	271	€27,200	12=	Jonathan Caldwell	65-73-69-71	278	€2,890
2	Adrien Bernadet	68-70-68-66	272	€18,700		M. Decottignies	70-74-65-69	278	€2,890
3=	J. Lando Casanova	68-71-69-65	273	€11,050		Dodge Kemmer	66-69-72-71	278	€2,890
	Bernd Ritthammer	68-70-69-66	273	€11,050		Niccolo Quintarelli	69-75-64-70	278	€2,890
5=	Steven Brown	65-69-72-68	274	€6,375		Gareth Shaw	67-72-69-70	278	€2,890
	Kenneth Ferrie	68-68-71-67	274	€6,375	17=	Matt Haines	71-71-65-72	279	€1,992
	Charlie Ford	70-70-66-68	274	€6,375		Scott Henry	72-69-68-70	279	€1,992
	Brandon Stone	69-67-69-69	274	€6,375		Thomas Linard	67-68-72-72	279	€1,992
9	Max Orrin	66-71-68-70	275	€4,080		Richard McEvoy	67-73-68-71	279	€1,992
10=	Paul Maddy	69-70-69-68	276	€3,570		Chris Paisley	72-67-72-68	279	€1,992
	Tim Sluiter	67-70-68-71	276	€3,570		Anthony Snobeck	64-78-68-69	279	€1,992

OWR: 0 of top 50 entered - Rating: 2 - Points to 16th - Lagergren: 12 points, to 476th in OWR

Open Blue Green Cotes D'Armor Bretagne

Sep 4 - Sep 7

Golf Blue Green de Pleneuf Val - Pleneuf, France
Champion: Benjamin Hebert

6,447 yards   Par 70
Purse: €200,000

France's Benjamin Hebert birdied four of his first five holes on his way to a final round 66 and a three-shot victory at the Open Blue Green Cotes d'Armor Bretagne. The victory was Hebert's second Challenge Tour triumph in less than a month (coming on the heels of a win at August's Norwegian Challenge) and the fifth of his career. Scotland's Andrew McArthur claimed solo second (largely on the strength of a fine Saturday 63) while England's Paul Dwyer came home with a Sunday 68 to take third.

1	Benjamin Hebert	66-66-67-66	265	€32,000		Jens Fahrbring	72-67-67-66	272	€3,775
2	Andrew McArthur	67-69-63-69	268	€22,000		N. Loreenzo-Vera	68-65-67-72	272	€3,775
3	Paul Dwyer	67-65-70-68	270	€14,000		Richard McEvoy	70-66-70-66	272	€3,775
4=	Ben Evans	63-73-68-67	271	€8,400		Marl Tullo	66-70-72-64	272	€3,775
	Oliver Farr	66-69-69-67	271	€8,400		Alvaro Velasco	69-69-66-68	272	€3,775
	Hugues Joannes	64-70-69-68	271	€8,400	17=	Carlos Aguilar	68-69-67-69	273	€2,283
	Niccolo Quintarelli	66-69-67-69	271	€8,400		Edouard Espana	68-68-68-69	273	€2,283
	Alessandro Tadini	68-69-62-72	271	€8,400		Pedro Figueiredo	70-67-64-72	273	€2,283
9=	Robert Coles	68-66-69-69	272	€3,775		Lasse Jensen	74-64-66-69	273	€2,283
	Dave Coupland	64-67-71-70	272	€3,775		Joel Sjoholm	67-69-69-68	273	€2,283
	Johan Edfors	67-69-69-67	272	€3,775					

OWR: 0 of top 50 entered - Rating: 2 - Points to 16th - Hebert: 12 points, to 199th in OWR

Kazakhstan Open

Sep 18 - Sep 21

Zhailjau Golf Resort - Almaty, Kazakhstan
Champion: Sam Hutsby

7,197 yards   Par 72
Purse: €450,000

Twenty-five-year-old Englishman Sam Hutsby claimed his maiden professional victory at the Kazakhstan Open, closing with a final round 67 to edge countryman Andrew Johnston by two. Hutsby held a commanding five-shot lead after 54 holes following rounds of 68-63-71, and largely clinched the title with a run of seven Sunday birdies between holes 8-15. This built up enough of a cushion that he could bogey the 458-yard 18th without worrying too much about the charging Johnston, whose closing 64 included 10 birdies over his final 14 holes.

1	Sam Hutsby	68-63-71-67	269	€72,000		Scott Fallon	68-73-71-68	280	€9,000
2	Andrew Johnston	72-70-65-64	271	€49,500		Lasse Jensen	73-69-68-70	280	€9,000
3	Byeong-Hun An	69-67-71-69	276	€31,500		Callum Shinkwin	68-72-70-70	280	€9,000
4=	Jocke Rask	71-69-69-68	277	€24,750	15	Daniel Vancsik	68-74-70-69	281	€7,200
	Alvaro Velasco	67-71-71-68	277	€24,750	16=	Steven Brown	70-71-69-72	282	€5,662
6=	Ben Evans	71-70-68-69	278	€16,200		Guillaume Cambis	72-69-69-72	282	€5,662
	Mark Tullo	68-75-66-69	278	€16,200		Julien Guerrier	72-66-72-72	282	€5,662
8	Matthew Fitzpatrick	70-68-74-67	279	€12,600		Joakim Lagergren	69-74-70-69	282	€5,662
9=	Cyril Bouniol	73-69-66-72	280	€9,000		George Murray	67-71-69-75	282	€5,662
	Matteo Delpodio	68-72-69-71	280	€9,000		Pontus Widegren	68-72-72-70	282	€5,662
	Edouard Espana	69-71-71-69	280	€9,000					

OWR: 0 of top 50 entered - Rating: 2 - Points to 15th - Hutsby: 13 points, to 235th in OWR

EMC Golf Challenge Open 2014

Oct 2 - Oct 5

Olgiata Golf Club - Rome, Italy
Champion: Ricardo Gouveia

7,566 yards   Par 71
Purse: €180,000

Making only his seventh start since turning professional, Portugal's Ricardo Gouveia landed his maiden victory at the EMC Golf Challenge Open, edging Germany's Florian Fritsch in sudden death. A third-team 2014 All-American at the University of Central Florida, Gouveia began Sunday's final round at the famed Olgiata Golf Club two behind Fritsch before ultimately catching him with a run of four birdies at holes 6-11. Eventually moving ahead with a birdie at the 15th, Gouveia nearly gave the title away with a disastrous bogey at the last before rallying to win the playoff with a birdie at the third extra hole. For Fritsch, who is afraid of flying and thus was not headed for the Tour's final four events in China and Middle East, a win would have clinched his E Tour card for 2015 - but finishing second, he would now have to wait.

1	Ricardo Gouveia	68-71-69-67	275	€28,800	11=	Robert Coles	72-73-70-70	285	€3,150
2	Florian Fritsch	70-67-69-69	275	€19,800		Oliver Farr	70-74-68-73	285	€3,150
3=	Edouard Espana	68-73-72-66	279	€11,700		Michael Jonzon	69-73-71-72	285	€3,150
	Benjamin Hebert	71-67-72-69	279	€11,700		Phillip Price	72-70-72-71	285	€3,150
5	Alessandro Tadini	70-71-69-70	280	€9,000		Nicolo Ravano	70-76-68-71	285	€3,150
6	Julien Guerrier	68-71-69-73	281	€7,200		Tim Sluitter	71-72-74-68	285	€3,150
7=	Matteo Delpodio	70-71-71-70	282	€5,400	17	Lasse Jensen	71-70-73-72	286	€2,520
	Matthew Fitzpatrick	75-67-70-70	282	€5,400	18=	Jason Palmer	68-77-72-70	287	€2,160
9=	Pelle Edberg	71-71-71-71	284	€4,140		Niccolo Quintarelli	71-72-74-70	287	€2,160
	Antonio Hortal	68-72-72-72	284	€4,140		Mark Tullo	70-73-71-73	287	€2,160

OWR: 0 of top 50 entered - Rating: 0 - Points to 16th - Gouveia: 12 points, to 504th in OWR

Shankai Classic
Oct 16 - Oct 19

Chongqing Poly Golf Club - Chongquing, China
Champion: Johan Edfors

7,294 yards Par 72
Purse: $350,000

Sweden's Johan Edfors ended a six-year victory drought by claiming a three-shot victory at the rain-shortened Shankai Classic, played in Chongqing, China. A three-time winner on the European Tour during 2008, Edfors had spent recent weeks playing on the Challenge circuit trying to regain E Tour status for 2015, a crusade whose prospects were greatly improved after he birdied the final four holes to pull away from France's Michael Lorenzo-Vera, with Germany's Bernd Ritthammer, the Netherlands' Tim Sluite and China's Mu Hu sharing third.

1	Johan Edfors	69-66-66	201	€44,416		Cyril Bouniol	70-68-69	207	€5,645
2	M. Lorenzo-Vera	72-67-65	204	€30,536	13=	Antonio Hortal	69-65-74	208	€4,858
3=	Bernd Ritthammer	72-66-67	205	€16,656		Joakim Lagergren	70-72-66	208	€4,858
	Tim Sluiter	71-67-67	205	€16,656	15=	David Law	73-70-66	209	€4,164
	Mu Hu	70-68-67	205	€16,656		Lasse Jensen	69-69-71	209	€4,164
6=	Matteo Delpodio	71-66-69	206	€8,606		Yuan Tian	71-69-69	209	€4,164
	Daniel Gaunt	72-67-67	206	€8,606	18=	Zi-Hao Chen (a)	72-68-70	210	-
	Bjorn Akesson	70-68-68	206	€8,606		Jeppe Huldahl	71-68-71	210	€3,227
	Mark Tullo	65-70-71	206	€8,606		Steven Tiley	73-68-69	210	€3,227
10=	Pontus Widegren	70-69-68	207	€5,645		Alvaro Velasco	70-68-72	210	€3,227
	Edouard Espana	69-71-67	207	€5,645		Paul Maddy	65-76-69	210	€3,227

OWR: 0 of top 50 entered - Rating: 2 - Points to 14th - Edfors: 12 points, to 403rd in OWR

Foshan Open
Oct 23 - Oct 26

Foshan Golf Club - Foshan City, China
Champion: Jason Palmer

7,148 yards Par 72
Purse: $350,000

Though he shared the lead on both Thursday and Friday nights, England's Jason Palmer was a wire-to-wire winner in claiming his first Challenge Tour title at the Foshan Open, in China. Standing one ahead of Germany's Bernd Ritthammer through 54 holes, Palmer played methodical golf on Sunday, logging birdies at the 7th and 8th holes going out, then, in the late going, adding two more at the 16th and 17th to build a lead which, even after a bogey at the 18th, proved just enough to see him home victorious.

1	Jason Palmer	65-69-69-69	272	€43,594	12=	Ricardo Gouveia	65-72-70-70	277	€5,041
2	Ben Evans	67-72-68-66	273	€29,971		Terry Pilkadaris	71-70-67-69	277	€5,041
3=	Jason Barnes	66-70-69-70	275	€16,348	14=	Antonio Hortal	71-72-66-69	278	€4,087
	Jens Fahrbring	70-68-69-68	275	€16,348		Hugues Joannes	70-68-68-72	278	€4,087
	Mark Tullo	69-70-68-68	275	€16,348		David Law	70-73-69-66	278	€4,087
6=	Pelle Edberg	70-66-70-70	276	€7,538		Paul Maddy	71-68-69-70	278	€4,087
	Matthew Fitzpatrick	69-70-72-65	276	€7,538		Callum Shinkwin	71-70-67-70	278	€4,087
	Daniel Gaunt	67-69-70-70	276	€7,538	19=	Pedro Oruiol	68-69-74-68	279	€2,883
	Chris Hanson	68-68-69-71	276	€7,538		Max Orrin	68-72-72-67	279	€2,883
	Andrew McArthur	68-70-70-68	276	€7,538		Bernd Ritthammer	66-69-69-75	279	€2,883
	Chris Paisley	68-70-68-70	276	€7,538		Tim Sluiter	70-71-72-66	279	€2,883

OWR: 0 of top 50 entered - Rating: 2 - Points to 18th - Palmer: 13 points, to 353rd in OWR

National Bank of Oman Golf Classic
Oct 30 - Nov 2

Almouj Golf - Muscat, Oman
Champion: Max Orrin

7,310 yards Par 72
Purse: $330,000

Twenty-year-old Englishman Max Orrin, who began the 2014 season with no status on the Challenge Tour, gave himself a chance at earning a 2015 European Tour card by claiming an out-of-left-field victory at the National Bank of Oman Classic. A former Walker Cup player, Orrin stood 68th in the Order of Merit at the start of the week but with the victory climbed to 17th place, thus claiming a spot in the season-ending Dubai Festival City Challenge, after which the top 15 players would be rewarded with E Tour credentials.

1	Max Orrin	71-71-68-71	281	€41,591		Chris Hanson	70-73-74-72	289	€4,679
2	Jason Palmer	69-72-74-68	283	€28,594		Bernd Ritthammer	70-71-75-73	289	€4,679
3=	Jason Barnes	65-75-77-68	285	€16,896	15=	Dave Coupland	73-72-72-73	290	€3,203
	Mark Tullo	73-73-66-73	285	€16,896		Edouard Espana	73-73-73-71	290	€3,203
5=	Byeong-Hun An	72-65-73-76	286	€11,698		Jens Fahrbring	73-74-71-72	290	€3,203
	Michael Jonzon	74-69-75-68	286	€11,698		Pedro Figueiredo	70-75-78-67	290	€3,203
7=	George Murray	70-73-74-70	287	€7,798		Daniel Gaunt	72-75-73-70	290	€3,203
	Niccolo Quintarelli	72-71-73-71	287	€7,798		Andrew McArthur	69-71-73-77	290	€3,203
9=	Robert Coles	75-68-75-70	288	€5,719		Chris Paisley	69-77-73-71	290	€3,203
	Nick Dougherty	74-70-76-68	288	€5,719		Tim Sluiter	71-70-79-70	290	€3,203
	Ricardo Gouveia	69-76-75-68	288	€5,719		Pontus Widegren	70-69-77-74	290	€3,203
12=	Oliver Farr	73-71-73-72	289	€4,679					

OWR: 0 of top 50 entered - Rating: 5 - Points to 23rd - Orrin: 13 points, to 396th in OWR

Dubai Festival City Challenge Tour Grand Finale

Nov 5 - Nov 8

Al Badia Golf Club - Dubai, U.A.E.
Champion: Benjamin Hebert

7,377 yards Par 72
Purse: €350,000

Though already assured of a spot on the 2015 European Tour by the money earned from his two earlier 2014 Challenge Tour victories, France's Benjamin Hebert closed out his campaign in high style by running away to a six-shot victory in the circuit's closing event, the Dubai Festival City Grand Finale. Thrice a Challenge Tour winner in 2011 as well, the 27-year-old Hebert began Saturday's final round with a two-stroke lead after posting opening rounds of 70-69-68, then pulled himself clear by birdieing three of his first six holes on Sunday and never looking back. Indeed, by the time he began the homestretch, attention had long since switched to the race for the top 15 spots on the tour's year-end money list, the occupants of which would be promoted to E Tour for 2015. The biggest winner here was France's Jërôme Lando Casanova, who fought back from an opening round 78, then eventually bogeyed the 71st hole to seemingly fall out before birdieing the 72nd to sneak in under the wire. Big losers included 16th-place Spaniard Antonio Hortal, Denmark's Lasse Jensen (who carded three bogeys and two double-bogeys from the 8th hole in to blow his chances to smithereens) and England's Ben Evans, who stood within the top 15 after Lando Casanova's penultimate bogey – and then on the outside looking in following the colorfully named Frenchman's final birdie.

1	Benjamin Hebert	70-69-68-69	276	€60,085		14=	Jens Fahrbring	71-71-72-74	288	€5,979
2	J. Lando Casanova	78-66-68-69	281	€39,900			Joakim Lagergren	78-69-70-71	288	€5,979
3	Oliver Farr	69-71-69-73	282	€22,517			Mark Tullo	68-70-73-77	288	€5,979
4	Byeong-Hun An	72-71-72-68	283	€18,083			Pontus Widegren	74-73-68-73	288	€5,979
5=	Hugues Joannes	74-71-69-70	284	€14,642		18=	Jason Barnes	71-73-72-73	289	€3,996
	Alessandro Tadini	71-75-67-71	284	€14,642			Daniel Gaunt	76-73-70-70	289	€3,996
7=	Cyril Bouniol	78-68-69-70	285	€12,425			Jeppe Huldahl	76-74-73-66	289	€3,996
	Bernd Ritthammer	72-71-69-73	285	€12,425			Sam Hutsby	76-74-69-70	289	€3,996
9=	Robert Coles	73-69-70-74	286	€9,742			Lasse Jensen	69-75-68-77	289	€3,996
	Edouard Espana	70-68-76-72	286	€9,742			M. Lorenzo-Vera	74-71-73-71	289	€3,996
	Jordi García Pinto	72-69-70-75	286	€9,742			Andrew Marshall	71-70-72-76	289	€3,996
	Andrew Johnston	73-72-69-72	286	€9,742			Pedro Oriol	75-71-72-71	289	€3,996
13	Ben Evans	72-73-70-72	287	€7,700						

OWR: 0 of top 50 entered - Rating: 7 - Points to 25th - Hebert: 17 points, to 120th in OWR

European Tour Final Qualifying Stage

Nov 15 - Nov 20

PGA Catalunya Resort (Stadium Course) - Girona, Spain
PGA Catalunya Resort (Tour Course) - Girona, Spain

7,333 yards Par 72
6,610 yards Par 70

1	Mikko Korhonen	72-65-65-71-68-67	408	€16,000			Seb. Soderberg	67-70-67-74-73-73	424	€750
2	Ricardo González	68-68-65-72-70-67	410	€11,500			J.B. Hansen	71-71-64-74-69-75	424	€750
3	Renato Paratore	67-70-66-69-67-73	412	€9,000			Stuart Manley	66-72-67-71-73-75	424	€750
4	Matt Ford	74-64-65-68-72-70	413	€7,200			Carlos Del Moral	68-74-65-70-70-77	424	€750
5=	Adrian Otaegui	67-71-68-72-70-67	415	€5,240		43=	Duncan Stewart	67-76-71-68-74-69	425	€750
	John Parry	68-68-71-69-72-67	415	€5,240			Sam Walker	66-71-68-75-76-69	425	€750
	Eduardo De La Riva	71-68-69-67-69-71	415	€5,240			Estanislao Goya	71-68-71-73-72-70	425	€750
8	Richard McEvoy	73-65-64-72-70-72	416	€4,440			Nico Geyger	66-74-66-77-69-73	425	€750
9	Rikard Karlberg	67-68-67-73-71-71	417	€4,190			Phillip Archer	68-74-72-67-71-73	425	€750
10=	Andrew Dodt	66-71-68-74-72-67	418	€3,468			Daniel Im	66-73-69-70-74-73	425	€750
	Matthew Fitzpatrick	70-66-67-76-71-68	418	€3,468			Michael Jonzon	69-73-68-72-69-74	425	€750
	Espen Kofstand	72-67-64-74-72-69	418	€3,468		50=	Jason Knutzon	66-76-67-72-76-69	426	€750
	Paul Maddy	67-72-68-69-72-70	418	€3,468			J.B. Gonnet	68-73-70-72-73-70	426	€750
	Tom Murray	76-64-63-73-72-70	418	€3,468			Peter Whiteford	77-66-65-73-75-70	426	€750
	Chris Lloyd	72-66-66-71-73-70	418	€3,468			Andrew Marshall	69-71-69-68-78-71	426	€750
16=	Joakim Lagergren	66-72-69-70-73-69	419	€2,775			Simon Griffiths	76-68-67-72-71-72	426	€750
	Anirban Lahiri	65-68-66-73-75-72	419	€2,775			Jeppe Huldahl	67-79-70-66-72-72	426	€750
18=	Jason Scrivener	77-64-67-74-72-66	420	€2,220			John Hahn	67-79-72-58-78-72	426	€750
	Borja Virto	77-63-67-73-70-70	420	€2,220			David Dixon	68-72-65-74-74-73	426	€750
	Pedro Oriol	70-66-68-69-77-70	420	€2,220		58=	Gareth Maybin	74-71-72-65-74-71	427	€750
	Pelle Edberg	73-62-63-75-76-71	420	€2,220			Antti Ahokas	66-76-71-69-73-72	427	€750
	Chris Paisley	70-69-68-70-69-74	420	€2,220			Björn Akesson	72-68-63-75-75-74	427	€750
	Andrea Pavan	69-67-70-71-69-74	420	€2,220			Emilio C. Blanco (a)	74-65-66-71-77-74	427	-
	Lasse Jensen	69-74-67-66-70-74	420	€2,220		62=	Louis de Jager	73-68-69-73-74-71	428	€750
25=	Alessandro Tadini	72-67-69-71-74-68	421	€1,860			Jens Fahrbring	74-70-71-67-75-71	428	€750
	Daniel Woltman	72-72-71-68-69-69	421	€1,860			Matteo Delpodio	68-68-71-71-75-75	428	€750
	Cyril Bouniol	72-68-67-71-70-73	421	€1,860			Kevin Phelan	69-72-65-72-74-76	428	€750
	----- ----- ----- ----- ----- ----- -----						Christian Gloet	64-74-66-72-75-77	428	€750
28=	Sihwan Kim	73-67-67-75-72-68	422	€750		67=	Adrien Saddier	66-73-71-73-74-72	429	€750
	Wes Homan	77-68-70-65-71-71	422	€750			Gary Lockerbie	76-67-70-69-75-72	429	€750
	Peter Lawrie	71-67-67-74-72-71	422	€750			Max Orrin	69-73-66-70-79-72	429	€750
	Ricardo Gouveia	74-68-64-72-73-71	422	€750			Kenneth Ferrie	66-75-65-72-76-75	429	€750
	Sebastian Gros	67-75-67-74-67-72	422	€750		71=	Scott Henry	70-72-68-73-75-72	430	€750
	Jaakko Makitalo	66-74-71-67-72-72	422	€750		72=	Dave Coupland	76-70-69-68-75-74	432	€750
34=	Justin Walters	73-70-77-62-72-69	423	€750			Marcl Schneider	72-74-72-65-75-74	432	€750
	Simon Thornton	68-69-67-76-72-71	423	€750		74=	Alvaro Velasco	69-74-68-71-78-73	433	€750
36=	Ben Evans	73-68-66-74-73-70	424	€750			Garrick Porteous	80-64-69-69-72-79	433	€750
	Falloon, Scott	72-65-71-74-69-73	424	€750		76	Mads Soegaard	67-73-68-73-76-78	435	€750
	Pontus Widegren	70-71-68-70-72-73	424	€750		77	F. Andersson Hed	76-69-72-66-76-77	436	€750

SPECIAL EVENTS
2014

Ryder Cup
September 26 - September 28
Gleneagles (PGA Centenary Course) - Gleneagles, Scotland   7,243 yards   Par 72

Final Score: Europe 16½ Points -- United States 11½ Points

1	2	3	4	5	6	7	8	9	10	11	12	13	14	15	16	17	18
426	516	431	211	461	201	468	419	618	208	350	445	481	320	463	518	194	513
4	5	4	3	4	3	4	4	5	3	4	4	4	4	4	5	3	5

United States Roster

Player	Residence	Age	Status
Tom Watson	Bucyrus, KS	65	Captain
Keegan Bradley*	Jupiter, FL	28	2nd appearance
Rickie Fowler	Jupiter, FL	25	2nd appearance
Jim Furyk	Ponte Vedra Beach, FL	44	9th appearance
Zach Johnson	St Simons Island, GA	38	4th appearance
Matt Kuchar	Sea Island, GA	36	3rd appearance
Hunter Mahan*	Dallas, TX	32	3rd appearance
Phil Mickelson	Rancho Santa Fe, CA	44	10th appearance
Patrick Reed	Spring, TX	24	Rookie
Webb Simpson*	Charlotte, NC	29	2nd appearance
Jordan Spieth	Dallas, TX	21	Rookie
Jimmy Walker	Boerne, TX	35	Rookie
Bubba Watson	Orlando, FL	35	3rd appearance

European Roster

Player	Residence	Age	Status
Paul McGinley	Ireland	47	Captain
Thomas Bjørn	Denmark	43	3rd appearance
Jamie Donaldson	Wales	38	Rookie
Victor Dubuisson	France	24	Rookie
Stephen Gallacher*	Scotland	39	Rookie
Sergio García	Spain	34	7th appearance
Martin Kaymer	Germany	29	3rd appearance
Graeme McDowell	Northern Ireland	35	4th appearance
Rory McIlroy	Northern Ireland	25	3rd appearance
Ian Poulter*	England	38	5th appearance
Justin Rose	England	34	3rd appearance
Henrik Stenson	Sweden	38	3rd appearance
Lee Westwood*	England	41	9th appearance

* Captain's pick

Friday Morning Four-Balls
Rose/Stenson (Eur) def. Watson/Simpson (USA) 5 & 4
Fowler/Walker (USA) halved w/ Bjørn/Kaymer (Eur)
Spieth/Reed (USA) def. Gallacher/Poulter (Eur) 5 & 4
Bradley/Mickelson (USA) def. García/McIlroy (Eur) 1 up

Friday Afternoon Foursomes
Donaldson/Westwood (Eur) def. Furyk/Kuchar (USA) 2 up
Rose/Stenson (Eur) def. Mahan/Johnson (USA) 2 & 1
Walker/Fowler (USA) halved w/ McIlroy/García (Eur)
Dubuisson/McDowell (Eur) def. Mickelson/Bradley (USA) 3 & 2

Saturday Morning Four-Balls
Rose/Stenson (Eur) def. Watson/Kuchar (USA) 3 & 2
Furyk/Mahan (USA) def. Donaldson/Westwood (Eur) 4 & 3
Reed/Spieth (USA) def. Bjørn/Kaymer (Eur) 5 & 3
Walker/Fowler (USA) halved w/ McIlroy/Poulter (USA)

Saturday Afternoon Foursomes
Donaldson/Westwood (Eur) def. Johnson/Kuchar (USA) 2 & 1
García/McIlroy (Eur) def. Furyk/Mahan (USA) 3 & 2
Spieth/Reed (USA) halved w/ Kaymer/Rose (Eur)
Dubuisson/McDowell (Eur) def. Walker/Fowler (Eur) 5 & 4

Sunday Singles
McDowell (Eur) def. Spieth (USA) 2 & 1
Reed (USA) def. Stenson (Eur) 1 up
McIlroy (Eur) def. Fowler (USA) 5 & 4
Mahan (USA) halved w/ Rose (Eur)
Mickelson (USA) def. Gallacher (Eur) 3 & 1
Kaymer (Eur) def. Watson (USA) 4 & 2
Kuchar (USA) def. Bjørn (Eur) 4 & 3
García (Eur) def. Furyk (USA) 1 up
Simpson (USA) halved w/ Poulter (Eur)
Donaldson (Eur) def. Bradley (USA) 5 & 3
Walker (USA) def. Westwood (Eur) 3 & 2
Johnson (USA) halved w/ Dubuisson (Eur)

The Ryder Cup has gained something of a reputation for unpredictability in recent decades, but in a year in which a homestanding European team was considered a heavy favorite to defend their 2012 victory at Medinah, things largely went according to form. There was no shortage of heroes for a European squad which boasted four of the top six players in the Official World Ranking *plus* additional stalwarts like reigning U.S. Open champion Martin Kaymer, Ryder Cup veteran Graeme McDowell and French up-and-comer Victor Dubuisson. Indeed, it would be difficult to choose a European MVP, though 2013 U.S. Open Champion Justin Rose might well carry a ballot, having gone 3-0-2 for the week, including a trio of Foursomes/Four Ball victories while teamed with Henrik Stenson. McDowell also emerged undefeated, going 3-0-0 behind a pair of Foursomes wins with Dubuisson and a clutch come-from-behind Singles triumph over Jordan Spieth in the always-important opening match on Sunday. And then there was world number one Rory McIlroy and Ryder Cup rookie Jamie Donaldson, the former scoring a key Singles point by routing Rickie Fowler 5 & 4 in match three, the latter marking his first appearance by going 3-1-0 and scoring the clinching point upon stiffing his approach at the 15th hole to close out Keegan Bradley. Meanwhile, with several of Captain Tom Watson's lineup decisions coming under considerable scrutiny, the United States could only draw real solace from the performance of Patrick Reed, who teamed with fellow rookie Spieth to go 2-0-1 in the Foursomes/Four Balls, then took down the imposing Stenson in the Singles. On the downside for the U.S., Bubba Watson, Zach Johnson, Webb Simpson and Fowler all failed to earn a single victory, and Matt Kuchar only avoided joining them by beating Thomas Bjørn in Singles. So in the end, things went reasonably as expected, with the Europeans rather easily dispatching the Americans - and retaining Samuel Ryder's Cup - by a 16½ to 11½ margin.

Eurasia Cup

March 27 - March 29

Glenmarie Golf & Country Club - Kuala Lumpur, Malaysia
7,004 yards   Par 72

Final Score: Europe 10 Points -- Asia 10 Points

1	2	3	4	5	6	7	8	9	10	11	12	13	14	15	16	17	18
390	170	537	429	207	550	394	402	407	410	534	161	421	409	408	566	201	408
4	3	5	4	3	5	4	4	4	4	5	3	4	4	4	5	3	4

European Roster

Player	Country	Age	Status
Miguel A. Jiménez	Spain	50	Playing Captain
Thomas Bjørn	Denmark	43	1st appearance
Jamie Donaldson	Wales	39	1st appearance
Victor Dubuisson	France	24	1st appearance
Gon. F'dez-Castaño	Spain	33	1st appearance
Stephen Gallcher	Scotland	39	1st appearance
Pablo Larrazábal*	Spain	30	1st appearance
Joost Luiten	Netherlands	28	1st appearance
Graeme McDowell	Northern Ireland	34	1st Appearance
Thorbjørn Olesen*	Denmark	24	1st appearance

Asian Roster

Player	Country	Age	Status
Thongchai Jaidee	Thailand	44	Playing Captain
K. Aphibarnrat	Thailand	24	1st appearance
Gaganjeet Bhullar	India	25	1st appearance
Nicholas Fung*	Malaysia	23	1st appearance
Hyung-Sung Kim	South Korea	33	1st appearance
Anirban Lahiri	India	26	1st appearance
Prayad Marksaeng*	Thailand	48	1st appearance
Koumei Oda	Japan	35	1st appearance
Siddikur Rahman	Bangladesh	29	1st appearance
Hideto Tanihara	Japan	35	1st appearance

* Captain's pick

Thursday Four-Balls

Jiménez/Larrazábal (Eur) def. Jaidee/Aphibarnrat (Asia)   2 & 1
Bjørn/Olesen (Eur) def. Oda/Tanihara (Asia)   2 up
Dubuisson/Luiten (Eur) def. Marksaeng/Siddikur (Asia)   3 & 2
F'dez-Castaño/Gallacher (Eur) def. Bhullar/Lahiri (Asia)   4 & 3
McDowell/Donaldson (Eur) def. Kim/Fung (Asia)   3 & 1

Friday Foursomes

Jiménez/Larrazábal (Eur) halved w/ Jaidee/Aphibarnrat (Asia)
Marksaeng/Kim (Asia) def. Bjørn/Olesen (Asia)   4 & 3
F'dez-Castaño/Gallacher (Eur) halved w/ Oda/Tanihara (Asia)
Lahiri/Siddikur (Asia) def. Luiten/Dubuisson (Eur)   1 up
McDowell/Donaldson (Eur) def. Bhullar/Fung (Asia)   2 & 1

Saturday Singles

Jiménez (Eur) def. Fung (Asia)   1 up
Jaidee (Asia) def. McDowell (Eur)   3 & 2
Aphibarnrat (Asia) def. Bjørn (Eur)   2 & 1
Donaldson (Eur) halved w/ Marksaeng (Asia)
Kim (Asia) def. Larrazábal (Eur)   4 & 2
Lahiri (Asia) def. Dubuisson (Eur)   2 & 1
Bhullar (Asia) def. Olesen (Eur)   5 & 3
Luiten (Eur) def. Oda (Asia)   1 up
F'dez-Castaño (Eur) halved w/ Tanihara (Asia)
Siddikur (Asia) def. Gallacher (Eur)   4 & 3

This, the inaugural Eurasia Cup, effectively replaced the Royal Trophy, an earlier team event pitting Europe versus Asia that ran from 2006-2013. The Eurasia Cup included somewhat different team selection criteria with rosters being determined as follows: The Asian team was composed of its playing captain (Thongchai Jaidee), the leading four members of the Asian Tour 2013 Order of Merit opting to play, the three remaining top Asian players in the OWR of February 2, 2014, and two captain's picks. The European side was composed of its playing captain (Miguel Ángel Jiménez), the leading four members of European Tour 2013 Order of Merit opting to play, the three remaining top European players in the OWR of February 2, 2014, and one captain's pick - though on this occasion, as Jiménez also qualified via the OWR, he was allowed a second captain's pick. The golf itself may have proven a bit of a surprise to some observers, though not early on when, as has long been their wont in the Ryder Cup, the Europeans stormed out to a 5-0 lead by sweeping all five of Thursday's Four-Ball matches. The Asian side regrouped somewhat on Friday, however, with the pairings of Prayad Marksaeng & Hyung-Sung Kim and Anirban Lahiri & Siddikur both recording victories, and two other matches being drawn, allowing the Asians to win the session 3-2 - but they still trailed 7-3 overall. Captain Jiménez winning the opening Singles match (over 23-year-old Asian Developmental Tour star Nicholas Fung) appeared only to deepen their plight before the momentum rather comprehensively shifted. Indeed, five of Asia's next six players (Jaidee, Aphibarnrat, Kim, Lahiri and Bhullar) won their matches while the sixth, Marksaeng, halved with Welsh Ryder Cupper Jamie Donaldson, and rather amazingly the sides were now all square. The final three matches then saw Joost Luiten defeat Koumei Oda 1 up, while Bangladesh's Siddikur surprised Stephen Gallacher with a 4 & 3 drubbing. That left the cup hanging on the penultimate match between Spain's Gonzalo Fernandez-Castaño and Japan's Hideto Tanihara - a match which, in the end, was halved, resulting in the two sides sharing the cup.

Dongfeng Nissan Cup
December 5 - December 7
Guangzhou Foison Golf Club - Guangzhou, China

6,649 yards   Par 72

Final Score: Asia-Pacific 15 Points -- China 9 Points

1	2	3	4	5	6	7	8	9	10	11	12	13	14	15	16	17	18
344	383	532	344	499	185	380	160	425	427	435	145	615	331	207	582	276	389
4	4	5	4	5	3	4	3	4	4	4	3	5	4	3	5	4	4

Asia-Pacific Roster

Player	Country	Age	OWR
Peter Thomson	Australia	85	Captain
Mark Brown	New Zealand	39	440
Ryan Fox	New Zealand	27	291
Rhein Gibson	Australia	28	422
Rory Hie	Indonesia	26	792
Keng Hwai Khor	Malaysia	24	816
Hyung-Tae Kim	Korea	37	466
Antonio Lascuña	Philippines	43	157
Scott Laycock	Australia	43	912
Jun Seok Lee	Korea	26	75
Daisuke Maruyama	Japan	43	528
Nobuhiro Masuda	Japan	41	544
Thaworn Wiratchant	Thailand	47	172

China Roster

Player	Country	Age	OWR
Lian-Wei Zhang	China	49	Captain
Zi-Hao Chen	China	18	1244
Mu Hu	China	25	566
Wen-Yi Huang	China	33	1001
Cheng Jin (a)	China	16	666
Hao-Tong Li	China	19	190
Wen-Chong Liang	China	36	166
Dong Su	China	24	1110
Ashun Wu	China	29	184
Bin Yan	China	32	--
Guang-Ming Yang	China	24	--
Tian Yuan	China	32	--
Lian-Wei Zhang	China	49	1074

Friday Four-Balls

Liang & Hu (CHN) def. Laycock & Gibson (AP)	3 & 2
Wu & Su (CHN) def. Brown & Fox (AP)	1 up
Chen & Jin (CHN) def. Wiratchant & Khor (AP)	7 & 5
Maruyama & Masuda (AP) def. Zhang & Li (CHN)	1 up
Yuan & Huang (CHN) def. Kim & Lee (AP)	2 & 1
Hie & Lascuña (AP) def. Yan & Yang (CHN)	5 & 3

Saturday Foursomes

Huang & Yuan (CHN) def. Hie & Lascuña (AP)	1 up
Kim & Lee (AP) def. Wu & Su (CHN)	1 up
Maruyama & Masuda (AP) def. Li & Hu (CHN)	2 & 1
Chen & Jin (CHN) halved with Wiratchant & Khor (AP)	
Fox & Brown (AP) def. Yan & Yang (CHN)	4 & 2
Laycock & Gibson (AP) def. Zhang & Liang (CHN)	3 & 2

Sunday Singles

Liang (CHN) def. Gibson (AP)	4 & 3
Hu (CHN) def. Hie (AP)	1 up
Fox (AP) def. Su (CHN)	2 & 1
Wiratchant (AP) def. Yan (CHN)	6 & 5
Wu (CHN) halved with Brown (AP)	
Laycock (AP) def. Huang (CHN)	4 & 2
Masuda (AP) def. Yang (CHN)	2 & 1
Maruyama (AP) def. Yuan (CHN)	4 & 3
Kim (AP) def. Jin (CHN)	4 & 3
Lascuña (AP) def. Zhang (CHN)	5 & 4
Li (CHN) def. Lee (AP)	3 & 2
Khor (AP) def. Chen (CHN)	4 & 3

Operating far below the western golfing radar, the Dongfeng Nissan Cup pits 12-man teams from China and the larger Asia-Pacific region in a three-day, Ryder Cup-style event which this year was contested over the Neil Haworth-designed course at China's Guangzhou Foison Golf Club. The match has been contested annually since 2011, with the Asia-Pacific side winning the first two playings before the Chinese rose up to claim the cup for the first time in 2013. Notably, it has been lent a greater aura of legitimacy by the presence of 85-year-old Hall-of-Famer (and longtime booster of Asian golf) Peter Thomson, who has captained the Asia-Pacific side in all four playings. In 2014, Thomson's side was an older one, with five players in their 40s, two more above 35 and only one (little-known Indonesian Keng Hwai Khor) under 25. The Chinese, on the other hand, offered a trio of touted teenagers (led by 19-year-old star Hao-Tong Li) and only two players older than 35, Wen-Chong Liang (36) and Lian-Wei Zhang (49). But on this occasion, at least, experience won out, for despite the Chinese side leading 4-2 after Friday's opening Four-Ball matches, the Asia-Pacific team charged back by winning four of six Saturday Foursomes (with one match halved) to take a one point lead, then won eight of Sunday's 12 singles contests to pull away to a comfortable 15-9 victory.

SMALLER DEVELOPMENTAL TOURS
2014

Asian Development Tour

The Asian Development Tour has come a long way in just five years, its schedule expanding from a bare-bones five events in 2010 to a 21-event ledger in 2014, with the latter schedule including stops in Malaysia, Taiwan, Indonesia, India and the Philippines. As in previous years, the top three finishers in the Order of Merit were rewarded with Asian Tour cards, with this year's graduates being 25-year-old Thai star **Pavit Tangkamolprasert**, 28-year-old **Shih-Chang Chan** of Taiwan and 31-year-old **Niall Turner** of Ireland.

In addition to having the trio's most challenging name to pronounce, Tangkamolprasert enjoyed a dominant season in 2014, first winning in Malaysia in August, then claiming two autumn titles in a span of three starts to gain an immediate battlefield promotion to the Asian Tour for the remainder of its season. Overall, he logged an impressive eight top-5 finishes in 17 ADT starts, allowing him to narrowly win the Order of Merit title. But while Tangkamolprasert's season was impressive, it could not quite match that of Chan, who won three times in his first five starts to also earn an immediate spot on the Asian Tour. Consequently he only teed it up in two further ADT events, and while both were top-10 finishes, he was unable to catch Tangkamolprasert for the top spot on the money list - losing all of $252 dollars despite making 10 (!) fewer starts. The real battle, then, was for the third and final Asian Tour berth, and that came down to Turner and 31-year-old Thai prospect Sattaya Supupramai. Supupramai was actually a late arrival to the battle, laboring quietly through the summer before winning twice in his last five starts to suddenly become highly relevant. Turner, on the other hand, was a winner in Indonesia in July, leaving him in a position of being above the line but needing several strong late starts to hold onto his spot. This he managed by finishing 2nd and T4 in his final two appearance, and with that he edged out Supupramai - and earned his Asian Tour card - by the stunning total of $26.

2/26 - 3/1	PGM Sime Darby Harvard Champiomship - Kedah, Malaysia	$60,000	Wisut Artjanawat	266
3/12 - 3/15	PGM CCM Rahman Putra Championship - Kuala Lumpur, Malaysia	$60,000	Brett Munson	208
4/21 - 4/24	PGM Lada Langkawi Championship - Kedah, Malaysia	$80,000	Shih-Chang Chan	269
5/7 - 5/10	PGM Northport Glenmarie Championship - Selangor, Malaysia	$65,000	Danny Chia	275
5/21 - 5/24	PGM Johor Championship - Johor Bahru, Malaysia	$60,000	Shih-Chang Chan	276
5/28 - 5/31	ICTSI Riviera Classic - Manila, Philippines	$60,000	Elmer Salvador	273
6/4 - 6/7	ICTSI Orchard Golf Championship - Dasmarinas, Philippines	$60,000	Rufino Bayron	272
6/11 - 6/14	PGM Vascory Templer Park Championship - Kuala Lumpur, Malaysia	$80,000	Gavin Kyle Green (a)	262
7/15 - 7/18	Linc Group Jakarta Classic - Jakarta, Indonesia	$60,000	Niall Turner	278
7/25 - 7/27	Taifong Open - Chang Hwa, Taiwan	$160,000	Shih-Chang Chan	212
7/31 - 8/3	Ballantine's Taiwan Championship - Kaohsiung, Taiwan	$110,000	Wen-Tang Lin	267
8/14 - 8/17	PGM Terrengganu Championship - Terrengganu, Malaysia	$60,000	Pavit Tangkamolprasert	281
8/21 - 8/24	CIPUTRA Golfpreneur Tournament - Jakarta, Indonesia	$100,000	James Byrne	271
8/27 - 8/30	Aboitiz Invitational - Manila, Philippines	$100,000	Antonio Lascuña	268
9/3 - 9/6	PGM Sabah Championship - Sabah, Malaysia	$80,000	Sattaya Supupramai	274
9/10 - 9/13	PGM MNRB Sarawak Championship - Sarawak, Malaysia	$80,000	Pavit Tangkamolprasert	274
9/24 - 9/27	PGM Port Dickson Championship - Negeri Sembilan, Malaysia	$60,000	Ryan Yip	264
10/16 - 10/19	15th ADT Chang Hwa Open - Chang Hwa, Taiwan	$100,000	Pavit Tangkamolprasert	271
10/29 - 11/1	TAKE Solutions Indian Masters - Bengaluru, India	$70,000	Chikkarangappa S	270
11/5 - 11/8	PGM UMW Championship - Selangor, Malaysia	$60,000	Sattaya Supupramai	201
12/3 - 12/6	PGM MIDF KLGCC Championship - Kuala Lumpur, Malaysia	$80,000	Rizal Amin	276

Big Easy Tour

South Africa's developmental Big Easy Tour had its schedule trimmed from 12 to seven events in 2014, running from late April through mid-September and awarding its top five money winners exempt positions on the 2015 Sunshine Tour. The top slot was claimed by 27-year-old **Gerhardus "Maritz" Wessels**, who played the Sunshine Tour full-time in 2013 and part-time in 2014, and actually made little impact on the Big Easy circuit through his first four 2014 starts. But at the Tour's fifth stop, in Centurion, he broke through to victory when two late birdies nosed him ahead of four other contenders, and he followed this by logging a second win at the season-ending Tour Championship, where he edged **Roberto Lupini** and **Juan Langeveld** by one. Given the much larger purse in the season finale, this victory clinched the Order of Merit for Wessels while also doing much to help the fortunes of those he beat.

The 32-year-old Lupini was boosted into a second-place finish in the Order of Merit by his Tour Championship finish, but such status was clearly well earned, as he never finished worse than 15th in six Big Easy starts and logged four top 10s, including a trio of runner-ups in his last four events. The 31-year-old Langeveld, meanwhile, claimed the third spot in total earnings but was rather less consistent in doing so; indeed, in addition to his Tour Championship finish, he also finished second in the season opener - but only once bettered 48th (an 18th-place finish in the fifth event) in four additional starts in between. The fourth Tour card was awarded to a man quite familiar to the longtime fans, 48-year-old **Carel "Callie" Swart**, who lost his Sunshine status after finishing 120th in the 2013 Order of Merit but regained it behind three top-five 2014 Big Easy finishes, including a victory (via a four-man playoff) in the third event, at Kempton Park. This left the final spot to 39-year-old **Henk Alberts**, another Sunshine Tour veteran who carded two runner-up finishes in seven Big Easy starts.

4/22 - 4/23	Sunshine Big Easy Tour Round 1 - Centurion, South Africa	R100,000	Drikus van der Walt	135
4/29 - 4/30	Sunshine Big Easy Tour Round 2 - Johannesburg, South Africa	R100,000	Andrew Light	135
5/6 - 5/7	Sunshine Big Easy Tour Round 3 - Johannesburg, South Africa	R100,000	Callie Swart	135
5/20 - 5/21	Sunshine Big Easy Tour Round 4 - Pretoria, South Africa	R100,000	Rhys West	141
8/4 - 8/5	Sunshine Big Easy Tour Round 5 - Centurion, South Africa	R100,000	Maritz Wessels	141
8/19 - 8/20	Sunshine Big Easy Tour Round 6 - Johannesburg, South Africa	R100,000	Tyrone Ryan	142
9/15 - 9/17	Sunshine Big Easy Tour Championship - Centurion, South Africa	R200,000	Maritz Wessels	212

PGA Tour Canada

The former Canadian Professional Golf Tour began a new life in 2013, having been acquired by the American PGA Tour (and renamed) in late 2012. Apparently benefiting from the myriad business and marketing strengths that the PGA Tour provides, the circuit managed to expand its schedule by one third in 2014 (from nine to 12 events), all of which continued to offer uniform purses of 150,000 Canadian dollars. Perhaps most importantly, it also continued to award the top five finishers in the Order of Merit fully exempt status onto the following year's Web.com Tour, opening up what, for most players toiling here, is their sole realistic avenue to the PGA Tour.

Standing atop the year-end Order of Merit was 27-year-old American **Joel Dahmen**, a former University of Washington player who pretty well lapped the field in 2014, topping the $80,000 mark in earnings, which placed him more than $20,000 ahead of the pack. Dahmen did most of his damage early, claiming his first professional win at the season-opening PC Financial Open, then cruising to five-shot runaway (after opening with 63) at the Syncrude Boreal Open two events later. He would go on to record only two top 10s thereafter (though one was a T2 at the ATB Financial Classic) but with so big a lead, he'd pretty well clinched the money title by about mid-summer.

Next in the earnings line was 29-year-old American **Matt Harmon** who, like Dahmen, did much of his damage early, logging three top 10s among his first five starts, peaking with his first victory, a three-shot triumph at the SIGA Dakota Dunes Open. Harmon also posted one more timely big finish when, having slipped to fourth in earnings, he lost a playoff to Mark Silvers at the Cape Breton Classic, pocketing enough in the process to clinch his Web.com card. Third place went to New Mexico native **Timothy Madigan**, who never bettered 23rd after July but who logged three top-three finished up to that point (including a win at the Players Cup) to cement his position. Fourth place went to another one-time winner **Brock MacKenzie**, a 33-year-old veteran of the Canadian Tour who, in addition to taking the ATB Financial Classic, also tied for second at the Bayview Place Island Savings Open. And lastly, the final Web.com spot was claimed by the lone non-American to graduate, England's **Greg Eason**, who went winless but logged four top 10s - just enough to secure his card.

5/29 - 6/1	PC Financial Open - Vancouver, British Columbia	$150,000	Joel Dahmen	272
6/5 - 6/8	Bayview Place Island Savings Open - Vancouver, British Columbia	$150,000	Josh Persons	268
6/19 - 6/22	Syncrude Boreal Open - Ft. McMurray, Alberta	$150,000	Joel Dahmen	266
7/3 - 7/6	SIGA Dakota Dunes Open - Saskatoon, Saskatchewan	$150,000	Matt Harmon	264
7/10 - 7/13	The Players Cup - Winnipeg, Manitoba	$150,000	Timothy Madigan	275
7/17 - 7/20	Staal Foundation Open - Thunder Bay, Ontario	$150,000	Wes Homan	271
7/31 - 8/3	ATB Financial Classic - Calgary, Alberta	$150,000	Brock MacKenzie	261
8/7 - 8/10	Forces and Families Open - Ottawa, Ontario	$150,000	Greg Machtaler	267
8/21 - 8/24	Great Waterway Classic - Kingston, Ontario	$150,000	David Brasshaw	267
8/28 - 8/31	Wildfire Invitational - Peterborough, Ontario	$150,000	Nate McCoy	269
9/4 - 9/7	Cape Breton Celtic Classic - Ben Eoin, Nova Scotia	$150,000	Mark Silvers	273
9/11 - 9/14	Tour Championship of Canada - London, Ontario	$150,000	Ryan Williams	274

PGA Tour China

Easily the most ambitious of the United States PGA Tour's recent global undertakings, the PGA Tour China made its debut in 2014, fielding a balanced slate of 12 events (each offering identical purses) spaced out widely across the calendar, with play beginning in April and ending in November. As with the PGA Tour's Canadian and Latinoamérica circuits, the China tour is heavily incentivized by offering exempt status on the next year's Web.com Tour to the top five finishers in its Order of Merit - a huge prize indeed for an up-and-coming Far Eastern prospect.

And if one purpose of the enterprise is to nurture a generation of star golfers in China, the dividends may have begun appearing faster than expected as the Tour's runaway first-year star was 19-year-old **Hao-Tong Li**, whose 2014 campaign was strong enough to actually lift him into the top 200 in the OWR. Li began the year relatively quietly but by the autumn he was on fire, not only winning three of the Tour's final four events (and running away with the Order of Merit title) but also taking time out to win the Nanshan China Masters on the OneAsia Tour. His, undeniably, is a name to watch. Unfortunately, the season produced a second newsworthy name, but this one for more notorious reasons, as Order of Merit runner-up **Xin Jun Zhang** was suspended for six months (through mid-March) by the China Golf Association for twice signing incorrect scorecards. At the time Zhang was the Tour's leading money winner, so his absence was obviously of significance - and it was uncertain at mid-December whether the Web.com Tour would honor the suspension or not. The other three graduates were all from overseas: 24-year-old Australian **Brett Drewitt** (an early season winner with a total of six top 10s) and two more one-time winners, 25-year-old Taiwanese-turned-American **Sam Chien** (a graduate of Northwestern) and **Todd Baek**, a native of South Korea who played collegiately San Diego State. Beyond the cloudiness of the Zhang suspension story, it was a very promising debut season for a tour which, in the years just ahead, may well produce as much major talent as any third-tier circuit in the world.

4/17 - 4/20	Mission Hills Haikou Open - Haiku, China	¥ 1,200,000	J.H. Wang	265
5/1 - 5/4	Buick Open - Guangdong, China	¥ 1,200,000	Sam Chien	272
5/15 - 5/18	United Investment Wuhon Open - Hubei, China	¥ 1,200,000	Brett Drewitt	280
6/5 - 6/8	Lanhai Open - Shanghai, China	¥ 1,200,000	David McKenzie	272
6/12 - 6/15	Earls Beijing Open - Beijing, China	¥ 1,200,000	Xin Jun Zhang	269
8/7 - 8/10	Yulongwan Yunnan Open - Yunnan, China	¥ 1,200,000	Gunn Charoenkul	263
9/4 - 9/7	Chateau Junding Open - Shandong, China	¥ 1,200,000	Todd Baek	271
9/11 - 9/14	Cadillac Championship - Beijing, China	¥ 1,200,000	David McKenzie	272
9/25 - 9/28	Jianye Tianzu Henan Open - Henan, China	¥ 1,200,000	Hao-Tong Li	275
11/13 - 11/16	Nine Dragons Open - Zhejiang, China	¥ 1,200,000	Cheng Jin (2)	281
11/20 - 11/23	Hainan Open - Hainan, China	¥ 1,200,000	Hao-Tong Li	278
11/27 - 11/30	Tour Championship - Guangdong, China	¥ 1,200,000	Hao-Tong Li	277

PGA Tour Latinoamérica

In its third full season since essentially replacing the old Tour de Las Americas, the 2014 PGA Tour Latinoamérica played 17 events in 11 countries from February through December, and once again graduated its top five players ("Los Cinco") to the Web.com Tour. Tops on that list was 26-year-old Argentinian (and Web.com Tour veteran) **Julian Etulain**, who won the final event of the Tour's spring segment (in Panama) and the Peru Open at the beginning of November, but missed the cut in the season-ending Argentine Open, which made for a stressful weekend before he finally emerged as the Order of Merit winner by less than $3,300. Next in line was 25-year-old Colombian (and former Division 2 All-American at Lynn University) **Marcelo Rozo**, who won the circuit's second event (in Mexico) and was later twice a runner-up. He also finished T4 in the Argentine Open when third or better would have jumped him over Etulain. Third place belonged to American **Tyler McCumber**, a former University of Florida star and the son of 10-time PGA Tour winner Mark McCumber. Riding a run of early autumn form, he won twice in a span of three weeks (in Ecuador and Mexico) before also missing a chance at claiming the top spot by finishing T4 in Argentina. Another American, former University of Iowa star **Brad Hopfinger**, was three times a runner-up en route to claiming the fourth Order of Merit slot, while the final Web.com berth went to 22-year-old Argentinian **Jorge Fernandez-Valdes**, who won the Chile Open and was able to claim his spot despite making only 10 Latinoamérica starts - by far the lowest number among all of the main contenders. By any measure, Latin American golf seems on its way to gaining a major lift via the enhanced status of this circuit.

2/20 - 2/23	Arturo Calle Colombian Open - Bucuramanga, Colombia	$ 150,000	David Vanegas	263
3/20 - 3/23	TransAmerican Power Products CRV Open - Guadalajara, Mexico	$ 150,000	Marcelo Rozo	267
3/27 - 3/30	Stella Artois Open - Antigua, Guatamala	$ 150,000	Armando Favela	274
4/3 - 4/6	Mundo Maya Open - Merida, Mexico	$ 150,000	Daniel Mazziotta	278
4/17 - 4/20	Abierto OSDE del Centro - Cordoba, Argentina	$ 150,000	William Kropp	276
4/24 - 4/27	Roberto De Vicenzo Invitational Cup NEC - Montevideo, Uruguay	$ 150,000	Ty Capps	272
5/15 - 5/18	Dominican Republic Open - La Romana, Dominican Republic	$ 150,000	Mike Buttacavoli	276
5/22 - 5/25	Lexus Panama Classic - Rio Hato, Panama	$ 150,000	Julian Etulain	271
9/25 - 9/28	Ecuador Open - Quito, Ecuador	$ 150,000	Tyler McCumber	275
10/2 - 10/5	Arturo Calle Colombian Classic - Bogota, Colombian	$ 150,000	Nicholas Lindheim	269
10/9 - 10/12	TransAmerican Power Products Mazatlan Open - Mazatlan, Mexico	$ 150,000	Tyler McCumber	278
10/16 - 10/19	TransAmerican Power Products Mexican Open - Mexico City, Mexico	$ 150,000	Oscar Alvarez	271
10/30 - 11/2	Lexus Peru Open - Lima, Peru	$ 150,000	Julian Etulain	274
11/6 - 11/9	Abierto do Brasil - Rio de Janeiro, Brazil	$ 150,000	Rafael Becker	262
11/13 - 11/16	Hyundai BBVA Abierto de Chile - Santiago, Chile	$ 150,000	Jorge Fernandez Valdez	271
11/27 - 11/30	Personal Classic - Buenos Aires, Argentina	$ 150,000	Fabián Gómez	192
12/4 - 12/7	Visa Open de Argentina - Buenos Aires, Argentina	$ 150,000	Emiliano Grillo	266

Professional Golf Tour of India

Now completing its fourth season of operation in its modern, revised form, the PGTI is something of a hybrid circuit, operating a varied schedule of 20 events in India, Sri Lanka and Nepal, and filling the calendar from January through December (indeed, its final two events fall after this volume goes to press). The 2014 roster included 18 self-contained tournaments as well as two more that are co-sanctioned with the Asian Tour (covered in that section): the SAIL-SBI Open and the Panasonic Open India. Also noteworthy is the fact that while this circuit's overall talent level and prestige may grade out at the developmental level, it doesn't serve as an official feeder for any other tour - and interestingly, several Indian stars who've been highly successful in both Asia and Europe (notably Rashid Khan and Anirban Lahiri) still make at least semi-regular appearances here. Beyond each of those two claiming a victory, the 2014 season was perhaps most notable for the emergence of the 21-year-old **Seenappa Chikkarangappa**, a former Eisenhower Trophy player generally listed as Chikkarangappa S or, on the Asian Developmental circuit, the more mysterious Chikka S. The youngest-ever winner of the Indian Amateur when he was 16, Chikka won four of his first 12 PGTI starts this year (plus one ADT event) and joined Sri Lanka's Mithun Perera (a regular on the Asian Tour) as the circuit's only multiple winners. Having missed gaining his Asian Tour card by a single shot at February's Q School (but still managing to tie for 23rd at the Panasonic Open India), he looks very much like having an impact outside of his native land in 2015.

1/29 - 2/1	PGTI Ahmedabad Masters - Ahmedabad, India	Anirban Lahiri	274
2/6 - 2/9	Standard Chartered Open - Colombo, Sri Lanka	Mithun Perera	262
2/12 - 2/15	PGTI Eagleburg Open - Bangalore, India	Mithun Perera	266
4/2 - 4/5	PGTI Players Championship - Coimbatore, India	K Prabagaran	279
4/9 - 4/12	PGTI Cochin Masters - Kerala, India	Shubhankar Sharma	135
4/23 - 4/26	Surya Nepal Masters - Kathmandu, Nepal	Chikkarangappa S	273
7/2 - 7/5	PGTI Pehalgam Masters - Pahalgam, India	Om Prakash Chouhan	261
7/9 - 7/12	PGTI Kashmir Masters - Srinagar, India	Chikkarangappa S	269
9/30 - 10/3	PGTI Eagleburg Masters - Bangalore, India	Rashid Khan	269
10/7 - 10/10	Bilt Open - New Delhi, India	Anura Rohana	274
10/14 - 10/17	PGTI Players Championship - Noida, India	Khalin Joshi	281
10/29 - 11/1	TAKE Solutions Indian Masters - Bengaluru, India	Chikkarangappa S	270
11/12 - 11/15	Chief Ministers Meghalaya Open - Shillong, India	Sanjay Kumar	264
11/19 - 11/22	IndianOil Servo Masters - Digboi, India	Shamim Khan	273
12/3 - 12/6	CG Open - Mumbai, India	Chikkarangappa S	263
12/9 - 12/12	PGTI Noida Masters - Noida, India	Amardip Sinh Malik	285

Japan Challenge Tour

The best-established of the world's developmental circuits, the Japan Challenge Tour dates to an abbreviated two-event schedule played in 1985. It grew out soon thereafter, of course, and in 2014 played a 16-event slate beginning in early April and ending in late October. Like its parent Japan Golf Tour, fields remain filled primarily by native players, though also like the Japan Tour, the presence of a growing number of foreigners – primarily South Koreans and Australians – is evident at the top of both leaderboards and the Order of Merit.

This year's Order of Merit winner was 22-year-old **Shugo Imahira**, who began playing the circuit at age 19 and enjoyed a remarkable surge in earnings this year, rocketing from 82nd in 2013 all the way to first. This he accomplished by posting top-10 finishes in eight of 16 starts (spaced fairly evenly throughout the season) and by winning twice, first at the Heiwa PGM Challenge I in May (where he took a three-man playoff) and, much later, at the season-ending JGTO Novil Final, where a one-shot triumph clinched his Order of Merit title. Imahira's closest pursuer was 33-year-old **Shintaro Kai**, who won June's LANDIC Golf Tournament and posted seven top 10s in 16 starts, including a run of five straight in September and October to secure his position. Something of an outlier in the mix was third-place finisher **Peter Wilson**, a 37-year-old Australian who'd never played golf in Japan prior to 2014. Also sporting a somewhat limited record at home, Wilson broke out by winning the season's second event in Fukuoka, then claimed a second victory at September's Madame Shinco Challenge Tournament, where he won a three-man playoff. Fourth place was taken by 39-year-old veteran **Katsufumi Okino**, who split time with the Japan Tour but still managed to post four top 10s and a victory here, the latter coming at October's Ryo Ishikawa Everyone Project Challenge. And lastly, fifth place was secured by a far better-known commodity, 48-year-old eight-time Japan Tour winner **Toru Suzuki**, who made only 10 Challenge starts but won two of them, taking June's Fuji Kani Club Challenge and September's Himari Dragon Cup.

4/4 - 4/6	Novil Cup - Tokushima, Japan	¥15,000,000	Soushi Tajima	213
5/8 - 5/9	Fukuoka Raizen Challenge - Fukuoka, Japan	¥10,000,000	Peter Wilson	136
5/22- 5/23	Heiwa PGM Challenge I - Hyogo, Japan	¥10,000,000	Shugo Imahira	134
6/12 - 6/13	Fuji Kani Club Challenge - Gifu, Japan	¥10,000,000	Toru Suzuki	135
6/26- 6/27	LANDIC Golf Tournament - Fukuoka, Japan	¥10,000,000	Shintaro Kai	132
7/8 - 7/10	ISPS Charity Challenge - Shizuoka, Japan	¥15,000,000	Shota Akiyoshi	194
7/24- 7/25	Heiwa PGM Challenge II - Niigata, Japan	¥10,000,000	Kiyoshi Miyazato	132
7/31 - 8/1	Akita TV Minami Akita CC - Akita, Japan	¥10,000,000	Yasunobu Fukunaga	132
8/20 - 8/22	PGA JGTO Challenge Cup in Boso - Chiba, Japan	¥13,000,000	Taigen Tsumagari	200
9/4 - 9/5	Madame Shinco Challenge Tournament - Hyogo, Japan	¥10,000,000	Peter Wilson	138
9/11 - 9/12	Himari Dragon Cup - Chiba, Japan	¥10,000,000	Toru Suzuki	131
9/18- 9/19	Seven Dreamers Challenge - Chiba, Japan	¥10,000,000	Yuki Inamori	132
9/25 - 9/26	Elite Grips Challenge - Mie, Japan	¥10,000,000	Yuchiro Nishi	133
10/2 - 10/4	Everyone Project Challenge - Tochigi, Japan	¥15,000,000	Katsufumi Okino	194
10/9 - 10/10	Taiheiyo Club Challenge Tournament - Ibaraki, Japan	¥10,000,000	Richard Hattori	131
10/23 - 10/24	JGTO Novil Final - Chiba, Japan	¥10,000,000	Shugo Imahara	137

Korean Tour

The Korean Tour continues to exist in a sort of gray area between the game's better-known first-tier circuits and most of the developmental tours it is grouped with here; its purses are considerably larger than any developmental loop, and while many of its fields are domestic in nature, this was less true of the three 2014 events co-sanctioned by the OneAsia Tour: the Caltex Maekyung Open, the SK Telecom Open and the Kolon Korea Open. These all rate among the circuit's most lucrative events as well.

As a result, the easy winner of the 2013 Order of Merit was 28-year-old **Seung-Hyuk Kim**, an international player who spent much of his year on the Japan Tour, where he won once and logged multiple top-5 finishes. Kim made only seven domestic starts but managed to win two of them, both from among the OneAsia-co-sanctioned trio: the SK Telecom Open (his maiden professional victory) and Korean Open, where he edged PGA Tour winner Seung-Yul Noh by two. With two additional top 10s added to his domestic season, Kim earned nearly $600,000 U.S. dollars, placing him far ahead of runner-up **Sang-Hyun Park** in the Order of Merit. Park was also a two-time winner this year, and while his triumphs came back-to-back, they were also in slightly smaller tournaments: the Vainer-Pineridge Open (where he beat Dong Seop Maeng by one) and the K.J. Choi Invitational, an event previously co-sanctioned with the Asian Tour. Third place in the Order of Merit went to **Jun Won Park**, who played exclusively on home soil in 2014 and lined his pockets by winning the third OneAsia event, the Caltex Maekyung Open, where he came home three strokes better than Sang-Hyun Park. Also notable was the season of fifth-place Order of Merit finisher **Woo-Hyun Kim**, another domestic player who claimed back-to-back victories at a pair of smaller tournaments, the Happiness Songhak Construction Open (a five-shot runaway) and the Bosung Country Club Classic, where he beat Joon-Woo Choi in a playoff.

4/17 - 4/20	Dongbu Insurance Promi Open - Ko Samui, South Korea	$379,000	Dong-Min Lee	279
5/22 - 5/25	Munsingwear Match Play Championship - Pyeongchang, South Korea	$759,000	Ki Sang Lee	
5/29 - 6/1	2nd Happiness Songhak Construction Open - Naju, South Korea	$474,000	Woo-Hyun Kim	264
6/12 - 6/15	Bosung Country Club Classic - Boseong, South Korea	$285,000	Woo-Hyun Kim	276
6/26 - 6/29	Gunsan Country Club Open - Gunsan, South Korea	$285,000	Heung Choi Joo	275
7/10 - 7/13	57th Korean PGA Championship - Incheon, South Korea	$949,000	Matthew Griffin	268
8/7 - 8/10	1st Maeil Dairies Open - Daejeon, South Korea	$285,000	Jung-Gon Hwang	267
8/21 - 8/24	Vainer-Pineridge Open - Gangwon, South Korea	$474,000	Sang-Hyun Park	267
10/9 - 10/12	K.J. Choi Invitational - South Jeolla, South Korea	$474,000	Sang-Hyun Park	267
10/30 - 11/2	Hearld KYJ Tour Championship - Jeju-do, South Korea	$285,000	Hyung-Joon Lee	210
11/6 - 11/9	30th Shinhan Donghae Open - Incheon, South Korea	$949,000	Sang-Moon Bae	275

EUROPEAN SATELLITE TOURS

PGA EuroPro Tour

Playing its 13th season in 2014, England's PGA EuroPro Tour competed over a 17-event schedule, with the first 16 taking place within the United Kingdom and the last, the Tour Championships, being contested in Egypt. Topping the five leading Order of Merit finishers headed for the 2015 Challenge Tour was 32-year-old European Tour veteran **Elliot Saltman** of Scotland, who logged three runner-ups through September before winning the Tour Championship to clinch his spot. Perhaps more impressive was the work of England's **Jack Senior**, already a Challenge Tour regular who made only five starts here, yet won twice and finished second in earnings. And then there was **Peter Tarver-Jones**, who won back-to-back late summer events but also missed four of 13 cuts; he safely finished third. Gaining the final two spots were a pair of one-time winners from England, **James Watts** and 2011 Walker Cup player **Stiggy Hodgson**.

1	Elliot Saltman	£27,990.83	7	Billy Hemstock	£15,696.67
2	Jack Senior	£25,247.50	8	Andrew Cheese	£15,371.90
3	Peter Tarver-Jones	£23,191.67	9	Stuart Archibald	£15,130.71
4	James Watts	£22,106.51	10	Jonathan Caldwell	£14,579.17
5	Stiggy Hodgson	£20,128.20	11	Jack Colegate	£14,237.17
6	James Robinson	£18,720.00	12	Steve Uzzell	£14,218.57

Alps Tour

Playing its 12th season in 2014, the Alps Tour undertook an ambitious international schedule which, in addition to its standard menu of continental stops, also made early visits to Egypt and Guadeloupe, with the great majority of purses set at €40,000 or above. Among the five players graduating to the Challenge Tour, tops was 26-year-old Italian **Nino Bertasio**, who logged back-to-back wins in Guadeloupe and Italy, as well as five additional top 5s to win the Order of Merit points race easily. Next in line was 26-year-old Spaniard **Borja Etchart** (who won in Spain) and 22-year-old Austrian **Tobias Nemecz** (a two-time winner), with both men standing well clear of another young Spanish player, 23-year-old **Borja Virto** – but the latter will only use his Challenge exemption sparingly as he subsequently played his way through E Tour Q School in November. **Thomas Elissalde** of France finished fifth.

1	Nino Bertasio	31,994.20	7	Jean Pierre Verselin	15,704.10
2	Borja Etchart	24,643.81	8	Matthieu Pavon	15,513.08
3	Tobias Nemecz	24,004.57	9	Alessio Bruschi	15,445.13
4	Borja Virto	21,947.23	10	Dominique Nouailhac	15,154.63
5	Thomas Elissalde	20,636.08	11	Andrew Cooley	13,666.28
6	Clement Berardo	19,471.43	12	Brendan McCarroll	13,449.60

EPD Tour

Operated by the PGA of Germany, the EPD Tour dates to 1997 and offered a 20-tournament schedule in 2014, with winter events played in Turkey, Morocco and Egypt before the main body of the schedule was played out in Germany. Per usual, the circuit was dominated by German players, with all five men who graduated to the Challenge Tour being native sons. Tops among these was 24-year-old **Marcel Schneider**, who won twice and logged 13 top 10s in 20 starts, enabling him to easily top the Order of Merit. More closely bunched together were 26-year-old **Sebastian Heisele** (two wins and 11 top 10s in only 13 starts), 24-year-old **Sean Einhaus** (two wins and six top 10s in 19 starts), 30-year-old veteran **Max Kramer** (one win and six top 10s in 20 starts) and 25-year-old **Alexander Knappe**, who won twice and recorded six top 10s in the maximum 20 starts.

1	Marcel Schneider	29665.99	7	Anton Kirstein	16898.00
2	Sebastian Heisele	23883.10	8	Floris DeVries	15444.75
3	Sean Einhaus	22859.03	9	Julian Kunzenbacher	14220.79
4	Max Kramer	21174.27	10	Moritz Lampert	12797.43
5	Alexander Knappe	20645.07	11	Philipp Mejow	12151.38
6	David Antonelli	17833.47	12	Reinier Saxton	11107.04

Nordic Golf League

The Nordic League is composed of three smaller Scandinavian circuits (Denmark's Ecco Tour, Sweden's Nordea Tour and the Finnish Tour) which combine into a single entity for statistical (and Challenge Tour berth) purposes. In 2014 the schedule covered 23 events around Scandinavia and included several with a dash of celebrity attached as regional stars Robert Karlsson, Patrick Sjoland and Peter Hanson each served as a tournament host. Overall, a pair of young Swedish players stood far ahead of the Order of Merit field, **Jacob Glennemo** (who won a tour-leading three times and posted 13 top 10s in 23 starts) and **Jesper Billing**, who nearly matched him stride for stride with identical three-win, 13-top-10s totals. Another Swede, **Steven Jeppesen**, finished third after winning once and logging 11 top 10s, while the final two Challenge Tour spots went to part-time Norwegian Challenge Tour player **Elias Bertheussen** (two wins, two runner-ups in only 10 starts) and Sweden's **David Palm**, who was winless but finished among the top 5 seven times in 23 starts.

1	Jacob Glennemo	64988	7	Rasmus Hjelm Nielsen	26721
2	Jesper Billing	60628	8	Chris Feldborg-Nielsen	25099
3	Steven Jeppesen	39559	9	Mads Sogaard	23062
4	Elias Bertheussen	34398	10	Christian Gloet	22435
5	David Palm	30131	11	Bjorn Hellgren	21639
6	Oscar Zetterwall	27344	12	Fredrik Gustavsson	21010

2015

2014-15 PGA TOUR SCHEDULE

Date	Tournament	Location	Purse
Oct 09 - Oct 12	Frys.com Open	Napa, CA	$6,000,000
Oct 16 - Oct 18	Shriners Hospitals for Children Open	Las Vegas, NV	$6,200,000
Oct 23 - Oct 26	McGladrey Classic	Sea Island, GA	$5,600,000
Oct 30 - Nov 02	CIMB Classic	Kuala Lumpur, Malaysia	$7,000,000
Nov 06 - Nov 09	HSBC-WGC Champions	Shanghai, China	$8,500,000
Nov 06 - Nov 09	Sanderson Farms Championship	Jackson, MS	$4,000,000
Nov 13 - Nov 16	OHL Classic at Mayakoba	Playa del Carmen, Mex	$6,100,000
Jan 09 - Jan 12	Hyundai Tournament of Champions	Kapalua, HI	$5,700,000
Jan 15 - Jan 18	Sony Open in Hawaii	Honolulu, HI	$5,600,000
Jan 22 - Jan 25	Humana Challenge	La Quinta, CA	$5,700,000
Jan 29 - Feb 01	Waste Management Phoenix Open	Scottsdale, AZ	$6,300,000
Feb 05 - Feb 08	Farmers Insurance Open	La Jolla, CA	$6,300,000
Feb 12 - Feb 15	AT&T Pebble Beach National Pro-Am	Pebble Beach, CA	$6,800,000
Feb 19 - Feb 22	Northern Trust Open	Pacific Palisades, CA	$6,700,000
Feb 26 - Mar 01	The Honda Classic	Palm Beach Gardens, FL	$6,100,000
Mar 05 - Mar 08	WGC-Cadillac Championship	Miami, FL	$9,250,000
Mar 05 - Mar 08	Puerto Rico Open	Rio Grande, Puerto Rico	$3,000,000
Mar 12 - Mar 15	Valspar Championship	Palm Harbor, FL	$5,900,000
Mar 19 - Mar 22	Arnold Palmer Invitational	Orlando, FL	$6,200,000
Mar 26 - Mar 29	Valero Texas Open	San Antonio, TX	$6,200,000
Apr 02 - Apr 05	Shell Houston Open	Humble, TX	$6,600,000
Apr 09 - Apr 12	Masters Tournament	Augusta, GA	$9,000,000*
Apr 16 - Apr 19	RBC Heritage	Hilton Head, SC	$5,900,000
Apr 23 - Apr 26	Zurich Classic of New Orleans	Avondale, LA	$6,900,000
Apr 30 - May 03	WGC-Cadillac Match Play	San Francisco, CA	$9,250,000
May 07 - May 10	The Players Championship	Ponte Vedra Beach, FL	$10,000,000
May 14 - May 17	Wells Fargo Championship	Charlotte, NC	$7,100,000
May 21 - May 24	Crowne Plaza Invitational at Colonial	Ft. Worth, TX	$6,500,000
May 28 - May 31	HP Byron Nelson Championship	Irving, TX	$7,100,000
Jun 04 - Jun 07	The Memorial Tournament	Dublin, OH	$6,200,000
Jun 11 - Jun 14	FedEx St. Jude Classic	Memphis, TN	$6,000,000
Jun 18 - Jun 21	U.S. Open	University Place, WA	$9,000,000 *
Jun 25 - Jun 28	Travelers Championship	Cromwell, CT	$6,400,000
Jul 02 - Jul 05	The Greenbrier Classic	White Sulphur Springs, WV	$6,700,000
Jul 09 - Jul 12	John Deere Classic	Silvis, IL	$4,700,000
Jul 16 - Jul 19	The Open Championship	St Andrews, Scotland	$9,200,000*
Jul 16 - Jul 19	Barbasol Championship	Opelika, AL	$3,500,000
Jul 23 - Jul 26	RBC Canadian Open	Oakville, Ontario, Canada	$5,800,000
Jul 30 - Aug 02	Quicken Loans National	Gainesville, VA	$6,700,000
Aug 06 - Aug 09	WGC-Bridgestone Invitational	Akron, OH	$9,250,000
Aug 06 - Aug 09	Barracuda Championship	Reno, NV	$3,100,000
Aug 13 - Aug 16	PGA Championship	Sheboygan, WI	$10,000,000
Aug 20 - Aug 23	Wyndham Championship	Greensboro, NC	$5,400,000
Aug 27 - Aug 30	The Barclays	Edison, NJ	$8,250,000
Sep 04 - Sep 07	Deutsche Bank Championship	Norton, MA	$8,250,000
Sep 17 - Sep 29	BMW Championship	Lake Forest, IL	$8,250,000
Sep 24 - Sep 27	Tour Championship	Atlanta, GA	$8,250,000

Unofficial:

Date	Tournament	Location	Purse
Oct 14 - Oct 15 ('14)	PGA Grand Slam of Golf	Southampton, Bermuda	$1,350,000
Dec 04 - Dec 07 ('14)	Hero World Challenge	Windermere, FL	$3,500,000
Dec 11 - Dec 13 ('14)	Franklin Templeton Shootout	Naples, FL	$3,100,000
Jun 29 - Jun 30	CVS Caremark Charity Classic	Barrington, RI	$1,300,000
Oct 08 - Oct 11	The Presidents Cup	Incheon City, South Korea	

* 2014 Purse (2015 not finalized at press time)

2014-15 EUROPEAN TOUR SCHEDULE

Dates	Tournament	Location	Purse
Dec 04 - Dec 07	Nedbank Golf Challenge	Sun City, South Africa	$6,500,000
Dec 11 - Dec 14	Alfred Dunhill Championship	Malelane, South Africa	€1,500,000
Jan 08 - Jan 11	South African Open Championship	Ekurhuleni, South Africa	€1,100,000*
Jan 15 - Jan 18	Abu Dhabi HSBC Golf Championship	Abu Dhabi, U.A.E.	$2,700,000
Jan 21 - Jan 24	Commercial Bank Qatar Masters	Doha, Qatar	$2,500,000
Jan 29 - Feb 01	Omega Dubai Desert Classic	Dubai, U.A.E.	$2,650,000
Feb 05 - Feb 08	Maybank Malaysian Open	Kuala Lumpur, Malaysia	$3,000,000
Feb 12 - Feb 15	Thailand Classic	Hua Hin, Thailand	$2,000,000
Feb 19 - Feb 22	Hero Indian Open	TBD	$1,500,000
Feb 26 - Mar 01	Joburg Open	Johannesburg, South Africa	€1,300,000*
Mar 05 - Mar 08	WGC-Cadillac Championship	Miami, FL, USA	$9,250,000
Mar 05 - Mar 08	Africa Open	East London, South Africa	€1,000,000*
Mar 12 - Mar 15	Tshwane Open	Waterkloof, South Africa	€1,500,000*
Mar 19 - Mar 22	Madeira Islands Open	Madeira, Portugal	€600,000
Mar 26 - Mar 29	Trophée Hassan II	Agadir, Morocco	€1,500,000
Apr 09 - Apr 12	Masters Tournament	Augusta, GA, USA	$9,000,000*
Apr 16 - Apr 19	Shenzhen international	Shenzhen, China	
Apr 23 - Apr 26	Volvo China Open	Shanghai, China	RMB20 mil*
Apr 29 - May 03	WGC-Cadillac Match Play	San Francisco, CA, USA	$9,250,000
May 07 - May 10	AfrAsia Bank Mauritius Open	Bel Hombre, Mauritius	
May 14 - May 17	Open de España	Barcelona, Spain	€1,500,000*
May 21 - May 24	BMW PGA Championship	Virginia Water, England	€4,750,000*
May 28 - May 31	The Irish Open	Newcastle, Northern Ireland	€2,000,000*
Jun 04 - Jun 07	Nordea Masters	Malmö, Sweden	€1,500,000*
Jun 11 - Jun 14	Lyoness Open	Atzenbrugg, Austria	€1,000,000*
Jun 18 - Jun 21	U.S. Open	University Place, WA, USA	$9,000,000*
Jun 25 - Jun 28	BMW International Open	Munich, Germany	€2,000,000*
Jul 02 - Jul 05	Alstom Open de France	Paris, France	€3,000,000*
Jul 09 - Jul 12	Aberdeen Asset Management Scottish Open	Gullane, Scotland	£3,000,000*
Jul 16 - Jul 19	144th Open Championship	St Andrews, Scotland	$9,200,000*
Jul 23 - Jul 26	Omega European Masters	Crans Montana, Switzerland	€2,300,000*
Jul 30 - Aug 2	Saltire Energy Paul Lawrie Match Play	Aberdeen, Scotland	
Aug 06 - Aug 09	WGC-Bridgestone Invitational	Akron, OH, USA	$9,250,000
Aug 13 - Aug 16	PGA Championship	Sheboygan, WI, USA	$10,000,000*
Aug 20 - Aug 23	Made in Denmark	Aalborg, Denmark	€1,500,000*
Aug 27 - Aug 30	D+D Real Czech Masters	Prague, Czech Republic	€1,000,000*
Sep 03 - Sep 06	M2M Russian Open	TBD	€1,000,000*
Sep 10 - Sep 13	KLM Open	Zandvoort, The Netherlands	€1,800,000*
Sep 17 - Sep 20	72nd Open d'Italia	Milan, Italy	€1,500,000*
Sep 24 - Sep 27	European Open	Bad Griesbach, Germany	
Oct 01 - Oct 04	Alfred Dunhill Links Championship	St Andrews, Scotland	$5,000,000*
Oct 15 - Oct 18	Portugal Masters	Vilamoura, Portugal	€2,000,000*
Oct 22 - Oct 25	Hong Kong Open	Fanling, Hong Kong	$1,300,000*
Oct 29 - Nov 01	BMW Masters	Shanghai, China	$7,000,000*
Nov 05 - Nov 08	WGC-HSBC Champions	Shanghai, China	$8,500,000*
Nov 12 - Nov 15	Turkish Airlines Open	Antalya, Turkey	$7,000,000*
Nov 19 - Nov 22	DP World Tour Championship	Dubai, U.A.E.	$8,000,000*

* 2014 Purse (2015 not finalized at press time)

2014-15 PGA TOUR PRIORITY LIST

1. Winners of PGA Championship or U.S. Open prior to 1970, or in the last five seasons and the current season
2. Winners of The Players Championship in the last five seasons and the current season
3. Winners of the Masters in the last five seasons and the current season
4. Winners of The Open Championship in the last five seasons and the current season
5. Winners of the Tour Championship in the last five seasons and the current season
6. Winners of World Golf Championships events in the last three years and current season
7. Winners of Arnold Palmer Invitational and Memorial Tournament in the last three years and current season, beginning in 2015
8. Leader from the final FedExCup Points List in each of the last five seasons
9. Leader from the final PGA TOUR Money List in each of the last five seasons
10. Winners of PGA TOUR co-sponsored or approved events (except team events) within the last two seasons, or during the current season; winners receive an additional season of exemptions for each additional win, up to five seasons
11. A. Players among the top 50 in career earnings as of the end of the preceding season may elect to use a one-time, exemption for the next season
    B. Players among the top 25 in career earnings as of the end of the preceding season year may elect to use this special one-time exemption for the next season
12. Sponsor Exemptions (a maximum of eight which may include amateurs with handicaps of zero or less) on the following basis:
    A. Not less than two sponsor invitees shall be PGA TOUR members not otherwise exempt.
    B. Not less than two of the 2014 Top Finishers of the Web.com Tour, if not all can otherwise be accommodated. (Note: PGA TOUR members may receive unlimited sponsor invitations. Non-TOUR members may receive a maximum of seven per season).
13. Two international players designated by the Commissioner
14. The current PGA club professional champion for a maximum of six open tournaments (three must be opposite The Open Championship and World Golf Championships events) in addition to any sponsor selections
15. PGA section champion or Player of the Year of the section in which the tournament is played
16. Four low scorers at Open Qualifying which shall normally be held on Monday of tournament week
17. Past champions of the event being contested that week, as follows:
    A. Winners prior to July 28, 1970: Unlimited exemptions for such events
    B. Winners after July 28, 1970 and prior to January 1, 2000: 10 seasons of exemptions for such events
    C. Winners after January 1, 2000: Five seasons of exemptions for such events
18. Life Members (who have been active members of the PGA TOUR for 15 years and have won at least 20 co-sponsored events)
19. Top 125 on the previous season's FedExCup points list
20. Top 125 on previous year's Official Money List through the Wyndham Championship
21. Players who finished in the Top 125 on the 2012 FedEx Cup points or Official Money List as nonmembers
22. Major medical extension: If granted by the Commissioner, if not otherwise eligible and if needed to fill the field
23. Leading money winner from the previous season's Top 25 regular season players using combined money earned on the official Web.com Tour Regular Season money list and Web.com Tour Finals money list, leading money winner from the previous season's Web.com Tour Finals and three-time winners from previous season Web.com Tour.
24. Leading money winner from Web.com Tour medical
25. Top 10 and ties among professionals from the previous open tournament whose victory has official status are exempt into the next open tournament whose victory has official status
26. Finishers 2-25 from the previous season's Top 25 Web.com Tour using combined money earned on the Web.com Tour Regular Season and in the Web.com Tour Finals and the top 25 players and ties on the Web.com Tour Finals money list at the conclusion of the Finals
27. Top finishers from the Web.com Tour medical
28. Players winning three Web.com Tour events in the current year
29. Minor medical extension
30. Twenty-five finishers beyond 125th place on prior year's money list (126-150)
31. Nonexempt, major medical/family crisis
32. Reorder Categories 33-37 (Reordered after Mayakoba & Northern Trust, before the Masters, the Players, U.S. Open and British Open)
33. Past Champions, team tournament winners and veteran members beyond 150 on the money list: If not otherwise eligible and as needed to fill the field, past champion members, team tournament winners and veteran members beyond 150th place on the previous season's money list, in order of their combined official PGA Tour and Web.com Tour earnings in the previous season
34. Past Champion Members: If not otherwise eligible and if needed to fill the field, past Champion members, in order of the total number of co-sponsored or approved events won, excluding team events. If two or more players are tied, the player who is higher on the PGA Tour Career Money List shall be eligible
35. Special Temporary: If during the course of a PGA Tour season, a nonmember of the PGA Tour wins an amount of official money (e.g., by playing in PGA Tour events through sponsor exemptions, Open Qualifying, etc.) equal to the amount won in the preceding year by the 150th finisher on the official money list, he will be eligible for the remainder of the year.
36. Team Tournament Winners: If not otherwise eligible and if needed to fill the field, winners of co-sponsored team championships, in order of the total number of team championship tournament won.
37. Veteran Members: If not otherwise eligible and if needed to fill the field, veteran members (players who have made a minimum of 150 cuts during their career), in order of their standing on the PGA Tour Career Money List.

2014-15 EUROPEAN TOUR PRIORITY LIST

Category 1: Winners of the Open Championship in 2005-2015; winners of the European Tour Order of Merit /Race to Dubai in 2005-2014; winners of the US Open, US PGA Championship and US Masters in 2005-2015

Category 2: Winners of the PGA Championship in 2010-2015; winner of the 2011 Dubai World Championship, the winners of the 2012-2014 DP World Tour Championship, Dubai

Category 3: Winners of the WGC – Accenture Match Play in 2012-2014, Winner of the 2015 WGC-Cadillac Matchplay; winners of the Bridgestone Invitational, Cadillac Championship and WGC-HSBC Champions in 2012-2015; winners of the French Open and Scottish Open in 2012-2015

Category 4: Winners of Race to Dubai Tournaments in Official Seasons 2013-2015 which have a prize fund of 1.5 million Euros and above. Members are ranked within this Category based on the date of their most recent eligible Race to Dubai Tournament win, with the most recent winner being ranked No 1 in this Category.

Category 5: Winners of Race to Dubai Tournaments in Official Seasons 2014-2015 which have a prize fund below 1.5 million Euros. Members are ranked within this Category based on the date of their most recent eligible Race to Dubai Tournament win, with the most recent winner being ranked No 1 in this Category

Category 6: Tournament Invitations

Category 7: National/Regional Orders of Merit

Category 8: Past winners of the tournament in question

Category 9: Members of the last named European Ryder Cup Team. Members are ranked within this Category based on their qualifying position within the 2014 European Ryder Cup Rankings.

Category 10: The top 110 placed players from the final 2014 Race To Dubai

Category 10a: Medical Extension

Category 11: The top 40 from the 2014 Career Money List

Category 12: Winners of 3 European Challenge Tour Ranking tournaments during the 2014 Official Season. Members are ranked within this Category based on the date on which they achieved their 3rd eligible European challenge Tour Ranking tournament win, with the Member who first achieved this being ranked No 1 in this Category

Category 13: Players finishing within positions 1-15 on the final 2014 European Challenge Tour Rankings

Category 14: Winners of three Challenge Tour events during 2014 season

Category 15: European Tour Qualifying School. The top 27 from the 2014 European Tour Qualifying School

Category 16: Players finishing within positions 111-125 on the final 2014 Race to Dubai ranked alternately with Players finishing within positions 16-30 on the Final 2014 European Challenge Tour Rankings

Category 17: Players finishing between positions 126 -145 on the final 2014 Race to Dubai

Category 17a: Membership Extension Category to be determined at the discretion of the Tournament Committee

Category 18: Winners of European Challenge Tour Ranking Tournaments (not invitational) on the 2014 and 2015 European Challenge Tour schedules (one calendar year from date of win exemption)

Category 19: Players finishing within positions 31-45 on the final 2014 European Challenge Tour Rankings

Category 20: European Tour Qualifying School: Players finishing within 28 and 78 at the 2014 European Tour Qualifying School

Masters Tournament

Augusta National Golf Club - Augusta, GA
Defending Champion: Bubba Watson

April 9 - April 12

7,435 yards   Par 72
Purse: $9 Million

Few golf courses anywhere on earth have been altered as significantly - and consistently - as Augusta National has been, more or less from its inception. Yet throughout nearly eight decades of change, conventional wisdom maintains that several aspects of what it takes to excel at Augusta have remained consistent. First, one must be long, for the advantage gained by length (especially on the par 5s) is too significant to ignore. Second, one must be able to move the ball from right to left - and at times we're talking about a big, sweeping hook and not some gentle shotmaker's draw. The advantage gained there - particularly off the tee at the 2nd and the 13th, and on a long-distance approach at the 8th - might well add up to between six and eight shots over 72 holes. And lastly, with so many fast, heavily contoured greens and precarious pin positions, a bit of shotmaking imagination can also come in quite handy. The ideal Masters competitor, then, will possess a strong mix of all of these things - which means that today's ideal Masters competitor is named Bubba Watson.

Watson, of course, claimed his second Green Jacket in three years in 2014, and it is the opinion here that assuming he remains physically healthy and of sound enough mind, he will garner at least one or two more before his career winds down. Yet despite his status as the prototypical Masters golfer, Watson's winning total of 280 was in no way ground-breaking. Indeed - and this may surprise many - his total was bettered or equaled in 48 of the first 77 Masters, making it, in effect, a below average score.

And this brings us back to an annually recurring theme regarding Augusta National: Despite absurd advances in unchecked modern equipment, Augusta has, through a range of new millennium design alterations, restored its challenge to a level very nearly the equal of any in its long and storied past. Doubt it? Consider that Ralph Guldahl bettered Watson's total (279) while winning way back in 1939, Ben Hogan averaged 277 over his two 1950s victories, Arnold Palmer averaged 280.6 during his three 1960s triumphs and Jack Nicklaus averaged exactly 280 over the course of six titles won between 1964-1986.

Masters fans, however, may view this from a slightly different perspective, wondering if course lengthening and alterations have affected the all-or-nothing drama of holes like the 12th, 13th, 15th and 16th, and thus the very tenor of the event on Sunday afternoon. But here again the statistical differences are minimal, with 2014 scoring averages on these holes weighing in only slightly beneath their all-time averages – an almost insignificant number relative to the degree to which equipment and golfers have changed.

Of course, none of this should be interpreted to mean that shorter hitters cannot compete here. Indeed, among the five men who finished immediately behind Watson in 2014, only Rickie Fowler has ever bettered 80th in driving distance over anything close to a full PGA Tour season, while three (Jonas Blixt, Miguel Ángel Jiménez and Matt Kuchar) hadn't recently finished among the top 100. But the advantages that a Bubba Watson brings to Augusta are manifest, and he figures to remain a favorite here for many years to come.

1	2	3	4	5	6	7	8	9	10	11	12	13	14	15	16	17	18
445	575	350	240	455	180	450	570	460	495	505	155	510	440	530	170	440	465
4	5	4	3	4	3	4	5	4	4	4	3	5	4	5	3	4	4

AUGUSTA NATIONAL HOLE-BY-HOLE

1. **445 yds** - A very demanding opener (the 3rd toughest hole in 2014) and the rare Augusta entry to greatly favor a fade off the tee.
2. **575 yds** - Consistently one of the easiest holes (17th toughest in 2014) but the fairway's sharp leftward turn gives the right-to-left player a huge advantage - perhaps as much as two shots for the week.
3. **350 yds** - Theoretically driveable but very few will try it. Pin placement on the elevated green dictates everything.
4. **240 yds** - Easily the toughest of the par 3s (the 2nd toughest overall hole in 2014); everyone will take three and run here.
5. **455 yds** - Less fearsome now than before the equipment revolution. Still, a solid two-shotter played to a tricky, two-tiered green.
6. **180 yds** - Perhaps the front nine's least-dramatic hole despite its Redan-like origins (the green was flattened decades ago).
7. **450 yds** - A long, tree-narrowed test much evolved from its 18th-at-St-Andrews roots. The steeply contoured green makes this the first all-or-nothing approach shot, with trouble everywhere, but well-struck balls often funnel close to several pins.
8. **570 yds** - With its long, uphill, blind approach to a narrow, heavily mounded green, the toughest of the par 5s in 2014. As will become increasingly common from here on, the player who can draw the aggressive second is at a big advantage.
9. **460 yds** - Pin position determines everything on a steeply pitched green. Back pins are often the toughest but most dramatic is Sunday's front location, where the margin between tap-in birdies and balls rolling 30 yards back down the hill can be small.
10. **495 yds** - Modern equipment has made this less dangerous, with properly drawn drives running far down the hill. The approach to another steep green remains a test, however. Tied with the 17th as the 4th toughest par 4 in 2014.
11. **505 yds** - The toughest hole on the golf course, and easily the most demanding par 4. A difficult driving hole but also one of the hardest second shots in golf. Back-left pins perched above the pond are generally only challenged by mistake.
12. **155 yds** - One of the game's elite par 3s, and famous for its swirling winds - which can make club selection to the shallow, creek-fronted green very difficult. Most will not challenge a far-right pin. The 4th toughest hole in 2014.
13. **510 yds** - Viewed in many circles as golf's greatest par 5. Another place where the ability to sweep the ball right-to-left is critical as drives missed right find pine straw. Well-struck approaches can funnel to multiple right-side pins. Long is usually dead.
14. **440 yds** - A wildly contoured Alister MacKenzie green where pin placement is everything. Sunday pin is generally fairly accessible.
15. **530 yds** - The 3rd-easiest hole on the course - but tell that to a contender facing a long Sunday approach over the pond.
16. **170 yds** - Another hole whose difficulty hinges heavily on pin placement. Front-right (on the green's upper level) has historically been a beast. Sunday's back left is another all-or-nothing, with water left but the funnel effect in full force.
17. **440 yds** - Even without the lost Eisenhower tree, tied with the 10th as the 4th most difficult par 4 in 2014.
18. **465 yds** - A demanding closer but perhaps the least strategic hole on the back nine. The one place where the ability to fade the tee ball is a must. The uphill approach is demanding but balls can be funneled to Sunday's front-left pin.

United States Open

June 18 - June 21

Chambers Bay Golf Course - University Place, WA
Defending Champion: Martin Kaymer

7,585 yards   Par 72
Purse: $9 Million

Coming off their 2014 experiment of playing the men's and women's U.S. Opens at Pinehurst in back-to-back weeks, the USGA now embarks on a new type of Open experiment at Chambers Bay, a seven-year-old municipal facility built along the shore of Puget Sound, 24 miles southwest of Seattle. The Robert Trent Jones II-designed layout certainly represents the right sort of municipal golf project as it converted a used-up sand and gravel mine into a faux Scottish links, complete with artificially shaped dunes which somewhat resemble the Old Country and a slew of man-made waste bunkers which, for the most part, do not.

The experimental aspects of the USGA's visit are twofold. First, there is little precedent for bringing the national championship to so untested a facility. Indeed, the last time the Open visited so youthful a site was in 1969 at Hazeltine National – and that is seldom recalled as a halcyon moment. Of course, the USGA learned a lot from their Hazeltine debacle and thus gave Chambers Bay something of a test drive by having it first host the 2010 U.S. Amateur. That event was won by Peter Uihlein and produced enough golf course-related issues to generate a fair number of modifications – few enormous – in the years since.

But there is a larger experimental aspect to all of this, that being the selection of a golf course with so much built-in flexibility that the USGA intends to flip-flop the pars of the 1st and 18th holes (each being playable as a par 4 or a par 5) during tournament. Such flexibility has become a calling card for USGA course set-up man (and Executive Director) Mike Davis, generally manifesting itself in the form of a full-size two-shotter (e.g., the 14th at Torrey Pines or the 3rd at Pinehurst) having its tees thrust forward, creating a driveable par 4 out of a hole which may lack the tactical verve to truly make such a move endearing. Few will be surprised, then, to see such treatment be given to Chambers Bay's 2nd, 6th or 16th - with the driveability of the 304-yard 12th already a given.

One thing about so much flexibility is that it will truly put the onus on Davis and his crew to plan their moves very carefully. For with so many alternate tee possibilities and the huge impact of the wind on this coastal site, the number of potential moving parts is considerable; if most of the right choices aren't made on a given day - or if the wind shifts drastically during play - some awkward moments might well be the result. Of course, Davis & Co. will likely build some forgiveness into their set up regardless, for at nearly 7,600 fescue- and waste bunker-lined yards, a windblown Chambers Bay might producing drastically high scoring were it to be played entirely from the tips.

Lingering also are some nagging agronomical questions exposed during the 2010 Amateur, an event which presumably benefited from being played two months later in growing season than a U.S. Open; given the wind-exposed nature of the site, there seems a very real chance that conditioning - at least to an ultra-elite Major championship level - may well prove an issue.

But with all of that said, Chambers Bay impressed 2010 Amateur contestants as being far more than just a windblown behemoth, with the player's ability to creatively utilize the lay of the land on approach shots and pitches being paramount. It figures to be an interesting Open.

1	2	3	4	5	6	7	8	9	10	11	12	13	14	15	16	17	18
498	404	165	568	490	447	508	602	227	398	500	304	534	521	172	425	218	604
5	4	3	5	4	4	4	5	3	4	4	4	4	4	3	4	3	5

CHAMBERS BAY HOLE-BY-HOLE

1. **498 yds** - The first of two holes whose par will vary during the championship. The mood of a player's entire day may well be set by whether this seaward test is an easy five or a very hard four.
2. **404 yds** - A huge left-side bunker suggests avoiding the driver here – unless the USGA throws the tees forward.
3. **165 yds** - The layout's shortest hole features a green angled above a deep front-left bunker.
4. **568 yds** - Uphill par 5 running directly inland. Reachable for some (depending on wind) but sand flanks the entire right side.
5. **490 yds** - Panoramic, sharply downhill par 4 with a sand-pinched fairway and a boomerang green swung around a central bunker.
6. **447 yds** - Though a strong two-shotter from the tips, alternate tees can shorten (and straighten) this dogleg right considerably, potentially bringing a narrow, elevated, bunker-squeezed green into range under the right conditions.
7. **508 yds** - A brutal uphill par 4 which bends around a massive waste bunker. Leftward bailouts can leave a blind second.
8. **602 yds** - A dead-straight bunkerless par 5 that is among the least engaging – though the fairway does slope from left to right.
9. **227 yds** - A sharply downhill par 3 played to a heavily contoured green angled along front-right sand.
10. **398 yds** - A short par 4 whose fairway narrows progressively between large dunes. A likely lay-up hole for nearly everyone.
11. **500 yds** - The first of three back nine par 4s of at least 500 yards. The fairway twists amidst the dunes to a bunkerless green.
12. **304 yds** - An uphill, driveable par 4 whose long, very narrow Punchbowl-style green is guarded front-left by a prominent bunker. An extremely narrow fairway (this is no easy lay up) suggests that many may go for it here.
13. **534 yds** - Another gargantuan par 4, this time a dogleg right climbing away from the Sound over an extremely wide fairway.
14. **521 yds** - A visually dramatic dogleg-left par 4 where downhill drives must negotiate both an endless left-side waste area and a single centerline bunker. One of Chambers Bay's more memorable – and challenging – holes.
15. **172 yds** - Approaching the shoreline, this is a downhill drop-shot across a wide stretch of sand – and, usually, through lots of wind.
16. **425 yds** - Paralleling the shoreline, this fairway bends gently along a huge right-side bunker en route to a tiny, steeply sloping green. The tightness of the target may tempt the USGA to move these tees well forward once or twice.
17. **218 yds** - The second hole built along the shoreline, with lower and upper teeing grounds offering very different angles of approach.
18. **604 yds** - Climbing steadily as it runs directly inland, this full-size par 5 with a large, heavily contoured green will represent Chambers Bay's last moment of flexibility; it will surely see action as a massive two-shotter at least once or twice during Open week.

AHEAD: **2016**: Oakmont (PA)   **2017**: Erin Hills (WI)   **2018**: Shinnecock Hills (NY)   **2019**: Pebble Beach (CA)
2020: Winged Foot (NY)   **2021**: Torrey Pines (CA)   **2023**: Los Angeles (CA)

The Open Championship

St Andrews (Old Course) - St Andrews, Scotland
Defending Champion: Rory McIlroy

July 16 - July 19
7,305 yards   Par 72
Purse: $9.2 Million

"There is nothing new to say about St Andrews, just as there is nothing new to say about Shakespeare."

Such were the words of the fine British golfer/poet Patric Dickinson in his classic 1951 volume *A Round Of Golf Courses*, and so it is - much like Augusta National - for anyone attempting to preview an Open Championship to be played over the Old Course. After several hundred years of play and 28 Opens, exciting new insights are, by any measure, few and far between. The stories of Bobby Jones storming off the links in frustration (but ultimately coming to love it like no other) have all been told, and the ledger of Hall-of-Fame champions has been recounted. The fact that two of the Open's three greatest champions – Harry Vardon and Tom Watson – never won here is old news, as is the legion of stories reminding us that the Old Course is indeed an acquired taste; many have been the greats who, like Jones, couldn't quite grasp it on first visit. So with great insight at a premium, it must suffice to say that there can be no more special Open Championship - indeed, no more special tournament of any kind - than one contested at St. Andrews.

This time, however, there will be controversy. For the R&A, in its infinite wisdom, has undertaken the first major changes to the Old Course in over a century, hiring Martin Hawtree to oversee work on nine holes that included the moving of bunkers, the recontouring of several green surrounds and, most drastically, the alteration of two of the most famous greens in all of golf, the 11th and the 17th. In both cases, the goal was to lessen some of the steepest sections of putting surface, areas that would be largely unpinable with modern green speeds – and in fairness to the R&A, no less a venue than Augusta National has softened many of its putting surfaces, in several cases within just a few years of opening. But there is something different about altering *anything* at St Andrews – and when it comes to moving bunkers and reconfiguring green surrounds, it is hardly an irrational notion to suggest that the R&A's willingness to change the Old Course in response to its own abject failure to regulate equipment smacks of gross irresponsibility and plain, old-fashioned arrogance.

And yet still there is no greater Major championship venue than the Old Course, with its endless tournament history, its massive double greens, its splendid ambience and, most uniquely, its direct lineage to the game's ancient and mysterious beginnings. For despite the R&A's farcical defacing, there will still be the Swilcan Burn grabbing half-hearted approaches at the 1st, and players will still be looking to pick up strokes within the short par 4s and crossing fairways of The Loop. Legendary bunkers will still be encountered at the 14th (where Hell famously lurks) and 16th (the Principal's Nose), and players will still begin the final dash home at the Road hole, the game's most demanding par 4, complete with the eponymous bunker, perhaps the most dangerous in the game. And players will still make the final walk into the Auld Grey Toun via the driveable 18th, crossing the Swilcan Bridge, then passing Rusacks and Tom Morris's Golf Shop en route to a final green, set adjacent to the famed R&A clubhouse and just beyond the timeless Valley of Sin.

Savor the Valley of Sin, by the way. Rumor has it that the R&A may replace it with a pond before the Open's 2020 return.

1	2	3	4	5	6	7	8	9	10	11	12	13	14	15	16	17	18
376	453	397	480	568	412	371	175	352	386	174	348	465	618	455	423	495	357
4	4	4	4	5	4	4	3	4	4	3	4	4	5	4	4	4	4

ST ANDREWS HOLE-BY-HOLE

1   **376 yds** - The widest fairway - and the most intimidating drive? - in golf. Though one might not expect it of the world's best, the fronting Swilcan Burn will catch its share of approaches, ruining rounds before they've really gotten started.

2   **453 yds** - Tough driving hole with Cheape's bunker left and the whins right. Four is a good score, especially into the wind.

3   **397 yds** - A real birdie opportunity but due to the greenside Cartgate bunker, it is best approached from the right side.

4   **480 yds** - A demanding par 4 defined by Cottage bunker left and a fronting mound which becomes highly relevant into the wind.

5   **568 yds** - The easiest hole here provided one avoids a cluster of right-side bunkers off the tee. Definitely a birdie opportunity.

6   **412 yds** - A blind tee shot, the Coffin bunkers left and a small depression crossing just before the putting surface.

7   **371 yds** - The start of The Loop and another birdie hole. Players must occasionally wait here as the fairway crosses the 11th, with whom it shares a particularly famous double green. The imposing Shell bunker should snare relatively few pros.

8   **175 yds** - The layout's first par 3, and one enlivened by the Short bunker just before the putting surface.

9   **352 yds** - Perhaps the Old Course's least engaging hole. Its bunker-free green can often be driven in the prevailing tailwind.

10   **386 yds** - Another largely basic par 4 but played back into the prevailing wind. Formerly driveable, but not at 386 yards.

11   **174 yds** - Named the High Hole In, but widely copied worldwide under a more colloquial name, the Eden. The green slopes steeply from back to front and is guarded by the dangerous Strath bunker and the ultra-dangerous (12 feet deep) Hill bunker.

12   **348 yds** - The end of The Loop and a driveable par 4 - but a single centerline bunker and the quirky green can cause problems.

13   **465 yds** - A long but usually downwind par 4. This green (shared with the 5th) is believed to be the largest putting surface on earth.

14   **618 yds** - One of the world's great par 5s, with many angles of play and the massive Hell bunker crossing the fairway. Played with the prevailing wind. Its modern Open length comes from a tee that actually sits on the neighboring Eden course.

15   **455 yds** - A relative breather, its length being lessened by the prevailing tailwind.

16   **423 yds** - Another famous entry, with the Principal's Nose bunkers down the middle, the more dangerous (for the pros) Deacon Sime bunker a bit further on, and out-of-bounds (where the old rail line ran) down the right side.

17   **495 yds** - Once a par 5 with blind drive played over the railway sheds, today the world's toughest par 4 with tee ball aimed over part of the Old Course Hotel. A sliver of a green angled between the Road bunker and the road itself. Golfing heaven.

18   **357 yds** - With the prevailing wind, nearly everyone can drive this green, and there will be the odd eagle during the championship. But the Valley of Sin - plus the pressure of the occasion - lurks, making for a fascinating, highly unorthodox finisher.

AHEAD: **2016:** Royal Troon   **2017:** Royal Birkdale   **2018:** Carnoustie

The PGA Championship

August 10 - August 16

Whistling Straits (Straits Course) - Kohler, WI
Defending Champion: Rory McIlroy

7,790 yards   Par 72
Purse: $10 Million

Clearly a popular venue with PGA of America brass, Whistling Straits will be hosting its third PGA Championship of the new millennium in 2015 - or was this third hosting just the price the club had to pay in order to land the 2020 Ryder Cup?

Though the club's somewhat remote Lake Michigan shoreline location has caused some concern in terms of both spectator and media accessibility, the results of the two previous PGAs have done nothing to suggest that Pete Dye's quite remarkable artificial links is anything but a strong championship venue. In 2004, Hall-of-Famer Vijay Singh claimed his third career Major title in a three-way playoff with Chris DiMarco and Justin Leonard while in 2010, Germany's Martin Kaymer broke through in a playoff with Bubba Watson - though that event is perhaps better remembered for Dustin Johnson illegally grounding his club in a waste bunker on the 72nd hole, thus carding a closing double bogey and missing the playoff by one.

Whistling Straits is, in fact, an entirely artificial layout, for it occupies blufftop acreage flush upon Lake Michigan which, in another lifetime, served as a military base. But Dye, who has built strong and engaging courses on far less promising sites, was undaunted, trucking in half of the Sahara desert to cover the property with sand, then shaped it as he pleased, allowing him to create every mound, hazard and green complex precisely as he saw fit. The result was not really a links course (even a fabricated one) in the strictest sense; it occupies more blufftop terrain than waterside, the bunkering is of a far larger scale than one finds in the Old Country, and sizeable sections of reclaimed wetlands form decidedly unlinks-like water hazards at the 603-yard 5th hole. But as modern golf courses go, it is more tactically engaging (not to mention downright memorable) than most high-profile tracks of its period - and as before and after site comparisons go, there can be little in the golfing world to match it.

In order to take the best possible advantage of the shoreline, Dye created a routing that is essentially a figure eight, allowing four holes from each nine to sit directly upon the water. On the outward half, these include a pair of exciting par 3s running in opposite directions (the 188-yard 3rd and the 221-yard 7th) as well as two enormous par 4s, the 494-yard 4th and the 506-yard 8th. Coming home, the 402-yard 13th and the 568-yard 16th follow the coastline, as do a pair of widely varied par 3s, the tiny 163-yard 12th (whose back-right pin placement rates among the game's scariest) and the epic 249-yard 17th, a behemoth of a one-shotter whose deep, narrow green angles along a bulkheaded cliff that falls more then 20 feet to the surf below.

With Whistling Straits measuring nearly 7,800 yards and carrying a course rating of 77.2, there is a good chance that the PGA of America will regularly utilize forward tee markers on a number of holes simply to avoid an unpredictable weather day sending scores into the stratosphere. And therein lies the fundamental rub of playing here; even with shortened holes, relatively wide fairways and magnanimous pin placements, if the wind starts to really blow off Lake Michigan, the entire complexion of a tournament could change on a dime.

1	2	3	4	5	6	7	8	9	10	11	12	13	14	15	16	17	18
493	597	188	494	603	409	221	506	442	391	645	163	402	396	503	568	249	520
4	5	3	4	5	4	3	4	4	4	5	3	4	4	4	5	3	4

WHISTLING STRAITS HOLE-BY-HOLE

1. **493 yds** - A once-basic par 4 which has grown 85 yards since 2010. Especially into the wind, a potentially brutal opener.
2. **597 yds** - A long, slightly twisting par 5. Reachable for some, but a nasty in-fairway pot bunker lurks 35 yard shy of the green.
3. **188 yds** - The first lakeside hole and the first of a memorable set of par 3s. Redan-like in that balls hitting the green's right side will funnel leftward. Players missing the promontory green left (deep bunkers and the lake) won't be upset with bogey.
4. **494 yds** - A huge lakeside par 4 played over a right-to-left-sloping fairway. Once again, approaches missed left equal disaster
5. **603 yds** - A gigantic double dogleg par 5 with large man-made lakes filling each of its corners. Very few will get home in two here.
6. **409 yds** - A gentle dogleg right played to one of the quirkier greens around – a shallow, heavily contoured, boomerang affair nearly cut in half by a truly frightening, grass-walled pot bunker. Has been lengthened 54 yards since 2010.
7. **221 yds** - Another dangerous waterside par 3 but this time the lake is on the right – and there is little bailout room left.
8. **506 yds** - The first of three par 4s that can stretch over 500 yards and the front nine's last lakeside entry. The drive is uphill and blind, the approach slightly downhill to another scary promontory target, this time plunging away off its right edge.
9. **442 yds** - A straight par 4 with a blind drive and a downhill second to a tightly bunkered green perched above Seven Mile Creek.
10. **391 yds** - Drives must avoid a deep centerline bunker as well as a fallaway left of the fairway. The layout's shortest par 4.
11. **645 yds** - Stretched 27 yards since 2010, this massive par 5 is built around a long, deep, railroad-tie buttressed bunker that cuts into the lay-up zone on the left side. Reaching the elevated green will require a helpful wind.
12. **163 yds** - A waterside par 3 played to a long, narrow, heavily contoured green. Balls missed right will plunge 40 feet to the surf. A sliver of back-right putting surface presents one of the more frightening pin locations in all of golf.
13. **402 yds** - Another clifftop par 4 but in the right conditions, this one might well be driveable. Another scary promontory green.
14. **396 yds** - A sharp dogleg left daring a long drive across dunes and bunkers – but most will likely lay up.
15. **503 yds** - The second 500-yard par 4 and a hole which, regardless of wind, figures to yield very few birdies.
16. **568 yds** - The shortest and most reachable of the par 5s, though the approach is uphill with disaster again lying to the left.
17. **249 yds** - As intimidating a par 3 as one is likely to find. With Lake Michigan left, the green is perched above a steep, railroad tie-buttressed hillside which plunges 20+ feet to the water.
18. **520 yds** - An over-the-top closer which first dares a 270-yard carry over dunes to reach a preferred left-side fairway. The approach is downhill and across Seven Mile Creek, to a gigantic, four-spoked green offering numerous tough pin positions.

AHEAD: **2016**: Baltusrol (NJ)   **2017**: Quail Hollow (NC)   **2018**: Bellerive (MO)   **2019**: Bethpage (NY)   **2020**: TPC Harding Park (CA)   **2021**: TBD   **2022**: Trump National (NJ)

MISCELLANEOUS PGA TOUR INFORMATION

PGA Tour Tee Time Categories

Category 1:

PGA TOUR members currently in a tournament winners category. Non-members, who would be in a tournament winners category.
PGA TOUR Life Members (member for 15 years and won 20 events).
Top 25 on Official PGA TOUR Career Money List through the end of the preceding year.
Players within the top 20 positions on the current FedExCup Points List, starting with the event following the U.S. Open.
Players within the top 20 positions on the current Official World Golf Ranking.
One player, on a weekly basis, not otherwise eligible for this category.

Category 1A:

Tournament winners whose victories were considered official that no longer qualify for groupings in category 1 and who played in five or more PGA TOUR co-sponsored or approved events or 10 or more combined PGA TOUR, Champions Tour and Web.com Tour co-sponsored events in previous year.
Former winners of The Players Championship, Masters, U.S. Open, The Open Championship and PGA Championship who no longer qualify for category 1.

Category 2:

PGA TOUR members who play out of the Top 125 and Top 125 Non-members categories.
Players with 50 or more career cuts made in official money PGA TOUR co-sponsored or approved tournaments who played in five or more PGA TOUR co-sponsored or approved events or 10 or more combined PGA TOUR, Champions Tour and Web.com Tour co-sponsored events in the previous year.
Players within the top 21-50 on the current Official World Golf Ranking.

Category 3:

All others.

Toughest Courses On The PGA Tour - 2014

#	Course	Par	Yards	Avg	+/-	Tournament
1	Pinehurst No. 2	70	7546	73.076	+3.076	U.S. Open
2	Augusta National GC	72	7435	73.946	+1.946	Masters Tournament
3	Trump National Doral	72	7481	73.852	+1.852	WGC-Cadillac Championship
4	Torrey Pines (South)	72	7698	73.797	+1.797	Farmers Insurance Open
5	Congressional CC	71	7569	72.546	+1.546	Quicken Loans National
6	Innisbrook Res - Copperhead	71	7340	72.433	+1.433	Valspar Championship
7	Pebble Beach Golf Links	72	6816	73.385	+1.385	AT&T Pebble Beach National Pro-Am
8	TPC San Antonio	72	7435	73.286	+1.286	Valero Texas Open
9	Harbour Town Golf Links	71	7101	72.038	+1.038	RBC Heritage
10	Royal Liverpool GC	72	7312	72.767	+0.767	The Open Championship
11	Spyglass Hill GC	72	6953	72.755	+0.755	AT&T Pebble Beach National Pro-Am
12	TPC Southwind	70	7239	70.718	+0.718	FedEx St. Jude Classic
13	Quail Hollow Club	72	7562	72.546	+0.546	Wells Fargo Championship
14	TPC Four Seasons Resort	70	7166	70.541	+0.541	HP Byron Nelson Championship
15	Valhalla GC	71	7458	71.539	+0.539	PGA Championship
16	Bay Hill Club & Lodge	72	7419	72.473	+0.473	Arnold Palmer Invitational
17	PGA National (Champion)	70	7140	70.408	+0.408	The Honda Classic
18	Firestone CC (South)	70	7400	70.389	+0.389	WGC-Bridgestone Invitational
19	Colonial CC	70	7204	70.273	+0.273	Crowne Plaza Invitational at Colonial
20	East Lake GC	70	7307	70.259	+0.259	Tour Championship by Coca-Cola
21	Seaside Course	70	7005	70.255	+0.255	The McGladrey Classic
22	Monterey Peninsula CC	71	6867	71.252	+0.252	AT&T Pebble Beach National Pro-Am
23	Golf Club of Houston	72	7441	72.245	+0.245	Shell Houston Open
24	Riviera CC	71	7349	71.209	+0.209	Northern Trust Open
25	TPC Sawgrass	72	7215	72.155	+0.155	The Players Championship
26	The Old White TPC	70	7287	70.101	+0.101	The Greenbrier Classic
27	Royal Montreal GC(Blue)	70	7153	70.035	+0.035	RBC Canadian Open
28	Kuala Lumpur Golf & CC	72	6967	71.965	-0.035	CIMB Classic
29	Muirfield Village GC	72	7392	71.898	-0.102	The Memorial Tournament
30	Cherry Hills CC	70	7352	69.840	-0.160	BMW Championship
31	Ridgewood CC	71	7319	70.809	-0.191	The Barclays
32	TPC River Highlands	70	6841	69.685	-0.315	Travelers Championship
33	TPC Scottsdale	71	7152	70.644	-0.356	Waste Management Phoenix Open
34	TPC Boston	71	7216	70.473	-0.527	Deutsche Bank Championship
35	CordeValle GC	71	7379	70.350	-0.650	Frys.com Open
36	Waialae CC	70	7044	69.304	-0.696	Sony Open in Hawaii
37	TPC Louisiana	72	7425	71.211	-0.789	Zurich Classic of New Orleans
38	Sedgefield CC	70	7127	69.209	-0.791	Wyndham Championship
39	El Camaleon	71	6987	70.019	-0.981	OHL Classic at Mayakoba
40	Sheshan International GC	72	7266	70.890	-1.110	WGC-HSBC Champions
41	Trump Intrntl GC - P.R.	72	7506	70.788	-1.212	Puerto Rico Open
42	TPC Deere Run	71	7268	69.764	-1.236	John Deere Classic
43	TPC Summerlin	71	7243	69.546	-1.454	Shriners Hospitals for Children Open
44	Torrey Pines (North)	72	7052	70.242	-1.758	Farmers Insurance Open
45	La Quinta CC	72	7060	69.768	-2.232	Humana Challenge
46	Plantation Course at Kapalua	73	7452	70.583	-2.417	Hyundai Tournament of Champions
47	PGA West (Palmer)	72	6950	68.962	-3.038	Humana Challenge
48	PGA West (Nicklaus)	72	6924	68.819	-3.181	Humana Challenge

150 Toughest Holes On The PGA Tour - 2014

1	Cherry Hills CC	5	4	526	4.483	BMW Championship
2	Congressional CC	11	4	489	4.482	Quicken Loans National
3	Augusta National GC	11	4	505	4.480	Masters Tournament
4	Pebble Beach Golf Links	10	4	446	4.463	AT&T Pebble Beach National Pro-Am
5	Quail Hollow Club	18	4	493	4.452	Wells Fargo Championship
6	PGA National (Champion)	6	4	479	4.442	The Honda Classic
7	Trump National Doral	7	4	471	4.417	WGC-Cadillac Championship
8	Golf Club of Houston	18	4	488	4.412	Shell Houston Open
9	Augusta National GC	4	3	240	3.409	Masters Tournament
10	Spyglass Hill GC	6	4	446	4.400	AT&T Pebble Beach National Pro-Am
11	Pebble Beach Golf Links	12	3	202	3.394	AT&T Pebble Beach National Pro-Am
12	Harbour Town Golf Links	14	3	192	3.393	RBC Heritage
13	Trump National Doral	14	4	484	4.387	WGC-Cadillac Championship
14	Pebble Beach Golf Links	9	4	466	4.376	AT&T Pebble Beach National Pro-Am
15	Riviera CC	12	4	479	4.374	Northern Trust Open
15	Pinehurst No. 2	6	3	219	3.374	U.S. Open
17	TPC San Antonio	4	4	481	4.373	Valero Texas Open
18	Royal Liverpool GC	7	4	480	4.367	The Open Championship
19	Valhalla GC	2	4	500	4.362	PGA Championship
20	Torrey Pines (South)	12	4	504	4.354	Farmers Insurance Open
21	Torrey Pines (North)	12	3	234	3.353	Farmers Insurance Open
22	Valhalla GC	6	4	495	4.351	PGA Championship
23	Harbour Town Golf Links	18	4	472	4.350	RBC Heritage
23	TPC Four Seasons Resort	3	4	528	4.350	HP Byron Nelson Championship
25	TPC Sawgrass	14	4	481	4.349	The Players Championship
26	Trump National Doral	18	4	471	4.343	WGC-Cadillac Championship
27	Quail Hollow Club	17	3	221	3.342	Wells Fargo Championship
28	Pinehurst No. 2	16	4	528	4.341	U.S. Open
29	Trump National Doral	4	3	203	3.339	WGC-Cadillac Championship
29	Pinehurst No. 2	2	4	507	4.339	U.S. Open
31	Muirfield Village G	18	4	484	4.338	Memorial Tournament
32	Pinehurst No. 2	8	4	486	4.336	U.S. Open
33	Spyglass Hill GC	8	4	399	4.335	AT&T Pebble Beach National Pro-Am
34	TPC Summerlin	3	4	492	4.328	Shriners Hospitals for Children Open
35	Torrey Pines (North)	11	4	490	4.327	Farmers Insurance Open
36	Kuala Lumpur Golf & CC	11	3	226	3.324	CIMB Classic
37	Pinehurst No. 2	11	4	483	4.323	U.S. Open
38	Harbour Town Golf Links	8	4	473	4.321	RBC Heritage
39	Muirfield Village G	16	3	201	3.320	Memorial Tournament
40	Valhalla GC	16	4	508	4.313	PGA Championship
41	Innisbrook Res - Copperhead	16	4	475	4.309	Valspar Championship
42	Kuala Lumpur Golf & CC	12	4	479	4.304	CIMB Classic
42	Augusta National GC	1	4	445	4.304	Masters Tournament
44	Torrey Pines (South)	4	4	488	4.299	Farmers Insurance Open
45	Bay Hill Club & Lodge	18	4	458	4.298	Arnold Palmer Invitational
46	PGA West (Palmer)	5	3	233	3.297	Humana Challenge
46	Monterey Peninsula CC	1	4	487	4.297	AT&T Pebble Beach National Pro-Am
46	Monterey Peninsula CC	9	3	187	3.297	AT&T Pebble Beach National Pro-Am
49	Pebble Beach Golf Links	5	3	188	3.294	AT&T Pebble Beach National Pro-Am
50	TPC Four Seasons Resort	15	4	504	4.288	HP Byron Nelson Championship
51	Innisbrook Res - Copperhead	3	4	455	4.287	Valspar Championship
52	Colonial CC	5	4	481	4.285	Crowne Plaza Invitational at Colonial
53	Torrey Pines (South)	11	3	221	3.283	Farmers Insurance Open
53	TPC San Antonio	9	4	474	4.283	Valero Texas Open
55	Trump National Doral	13	3	238	3.277	WGC-Cadillac Championship
55	Royal Liverpool GC	14	4	454	4.277	The Open Championship
57	Quail Hollow Club	9	4	495	4.276	Wells Fargo Championship
58	Congressional CC	2	3	233	3.272	Quicken Loans National
58	TPC Boston	14	4	495	4.272	Deutsche Bank Championship
60	Spyglass Hill GC	9	4	431	4.271	AT&T Pebble Beach National Pro-Am
61	Golf Club of Houston	6	4	464	4.270	Shell Houston Open
61	Royal Montreal GC(Blue)	4	4	501	4.270	RBC Canadian Open
63	El Camaleon	16	4	485	4.268	OHL Classic at Mayakoba
64	TPC Southwind	5	4	485	4.266	FedEx St. Jude Classic
65	TPC Sawgrass	8	3	237	3.262	The Players Championship
65	Pinehurst No. 2	4	4	529	4.262	U.S. Open
67	Quail Hollow Club	16	4	508	4.261	Wells Fargo Championship
68	Kuala Lumpur Golf & CC	13	4	459	4.260	CIMB Classic
68	Seaside Course	14	4	442	4.260	The McGladrey Classic
70	Royal Liverpool GC	2	4	454	4.259	The Open Championship
71	Spyglass Hill GC	16	4	476	4.258	AT&T Pebble Beach National Pro-Am
72	Augusta National GC	12	3	155	3.257	Masters Tournament
72	TPC Sawgrass	5	4	471	4.257	The Players Championship
74	Pinehurst No. 2	15	3	202	3.256	U.S. Open
75	Augusta National GC	7	4	450	4.253	Masters Tournament

150 Toughest Holes On The PGA Tour - 2014 (Cont'd)

Rank	Course	Hole	Par	Yards	Avg	Tournament
76	Monterey Peninsula CC	13	4	434	4.252	AT&T Pebble Beach National Pro-Am
76	Golf Club of Houston	5	4	480	4.252	Shell Houston Open
78	Trump National Doral	9	3	200	3.251	WGC-Cadillac Championship
79	TPC Four Seasons Resort	18	4	429	4.248	HP Byron Nelson Championship
79	Royal Montreal GC(Blue)	11	4	476	4.248	RBC Canadian Open
79	Royal Montreal GC(Blue)	18	4	466	4.248	RBC Canadian Open
82	TPC River Highlands	4	4	481	4.246	Travelers Championship
83	Valhalla GC	12	4	467	4.245	PGA Championship
84	TPC Louisiana	4	4	482	4.243	Zurich Classic of New Orleans
85	Quail Hollow Club	4	4	483	4.241	Wells Fargo Championship
85	East Lake GC	6	3	209	3.241	Tour Championship by Coca-Cola
85	East Lake GC	10	4	469	4.241	Tour Championship by Coca-Cola
88	Augusta National GC	10	4	495	4.240	Masters Tournament
88	Augusta National GC	17	4	440	4.240	Masters Tournament
90	PGA West (Nicklaus)	18	4	455	4.239	Humana Challenge
90	Riviera CC	15	4	487	4.239	Northern Trust Open
90	Bay Hill Club & Lodge	8	4	460	4.239	Arnold Palmer Invitational
93	Torrey Pines (South)	15	4	478	4.238	Farmers Insurance Open
94	TPC Four Seasons Resort	14	4	406	4.237	HP Byron Nelson Championship
94	Sedgefield CC	18	4	507	4.237	Wyndham Championship
96	Sheshan International GC	17	3	212	3.236	WGC-HSBC Champions
96	TPC Deere Run	18	4	476	4.236	John Deere Classic
98	Torrey Pines (South)	7	4	462	4.235	Farmers Insurance Open
99	CordeValle GC	6	4	480	4.234	Frys.com Open
100	Pinehurst No. 2	12	4	484	4.233	U.S. Open
101	Spyglass Hill GC	5	3	197	3.232	AT&T Pebble Beach National Pro-Am
101	Spyglass Hill GC	18	4	408	4.232	AT&T Pebble Beach National Pro-Am
101	Trump National Doral	3	4	436	4.232	WGC-Cadillac Championship
101	Valhalla GC	15	4	435	4.232	PGA Championship
105	Waialae CC	13	4	477	4.231	Sony Open in Hawaii
106	Sheshan International GC	9	4	486	4.227	WGC-HSBC Champions
107	Bay Hill Club & Lodge	3	4	434	4.226	Arnold Palmer Invitational
108	Firestone CC (South)	4	4	471	4.225	WGC-Bridgestone Invitational
109	El Camaleon	12	4	451	4.224	OHL Classic at Mayakoba
109	TPC San Antonio	15	4	464	4.224	Valero Texas Open
111	Cherry Hills CC	8	3	276	3.223	BMW Championship
112	Torrey Pines (North)	6	3	208	3.222	Farmers Insurance Open
113	Augusta National GC	18	4	465	4.220	Masters Tournament
114	Torrey Pines (South)	1	4	450	4.219	Farmers Insurance Open
114	Spyglass Hill GC	13	4	460	4.219	AT&T Pebble Beach National Pro-Am
116	Ridgewood CC	12	4	475	4.217	The Barclays
117	TPC Deere Run	9	4	503	4.216	John Deere Classic
118	TPC Louisiana	6	4	476	4.215	Zurich Classic of New Orleans
118	Congressional CC	18	4	523	4.215	Quicken Loans National
120	TPC San Antonio	13	3	241	3.214	Valero Texas Open
121	Innisbrook Res - Copperhead	6	4	465	4.213	Valspar Championship
121	Augusta National GC	14	4	440	4.213	Masters Tournament
121	Congressional CC	4	4	470	4.213	Quicken Loans National
124	TPC Southwind	17	4	490	4.212	FedEx St. Jude Classic
125	CordeValle GC	11	3	236	3.210	Frys.com Open
126	Pinehurst No. 2	17	3	205	3.209	U.S. Open
127	The Old White TPC	13	4	492	4.207	The Greenbrier Classic
127	East Lake GC	5	4	520	4.207	Tour Championship by Coca-Cola
129	Seaside Course	3	3	204	3.206	The McGladrey Classic
130	Trump Intrntl GC - P.R.	4	4	455	4.204	Puerto Rico Open
130	Royal Liverpool GC	1	4	458	4.204	The Open Championship
132	Pinehurst No. 2	18	4	451	4.202	U.S. Open
133	PGA West (Palmer)	9	4	461	4.201	Humana Challenge
134	Riviera CC	4	3	236	3.200	Northern Trust Open
134	PGA National (Champion)	10	4	508	4.200	The Honda Classic
136	Valhalla GC	14	3	217	3.199	PGA Championship
137	PGA West (Palmer)	10	4	453	4.197	Humana Challenge
138	TPC Southwind	12	4	406	4.194	FedEx St. Jude Classic
139	Congressional CC	14	4	467	4.192	Quicken Loans National
140	Bay Hill Club & Lodge	2	3	231	3.190	Arnold Palmer Invitational
141	Innisbrook Res - Copperhead	8	3	235	3.188	Valspar Championship
141	Innisbrook Res - Copperhead	13	3	200	3.188	Valspar Championship
141	TPC Louisiana	3	3	221	3.188	Zurich Classic of New Orleans
144	Congressional CC	15	4	490	4.187	Quicken Loans National
145	TPC San Antonio	1	4	454	4.184	Valero Texas Open
145	Muirfield Village GC	1	4	470	4.184	Memorial Tournament
147	Golf Club of Houston	17	4	489	4.183	Shell Houston Open
148	PGA National (Champion)	11	4	450	4.182	The Honda Classic
148	Colonial CC	4	3	247	3.182	Crowne Plaza Invitational at Colonial
148	Muirfield Village GC	17	4	478	4.182	Memorial Tournament

75 Easiest Holes On The PGA Tour - 2014

1	Plantation Course at Kapalua	5	5	532	4.150	Hyundai Tournament of Champions
2	PGA West (Palmer)	11	5	512	4.255	Humana Challenge
3	PGA West (Nicklaus)	13	5	528	4.258	Humana Challenge
4	Riviera CC	1	5	503	4.259	Northern Trust Open
5	PGA West (Nicklaus)	4	5	538	4.297	Humana Challenge
6	La Quinta CC	5	5	516	4.329	Humana Challenge
7	Sedgefield CC	5	5	529	4.331	Wyndham Championship
8	PGA West (Nicklaus)	16	5	530	4.335	Humana Challenge
9	Waialae CC	9	5	506	4.339	Sony Open in Hawaii
10	La Quinta CC	6	5	527	4.361	Humana Challenge
11	PGA West (Palmer)	2	5	514	4.368	Humana Challenge
12	Trump Intrntl GC - P.R.	5	5	535	4.392	Puerto Rico Open
13	East Lake GC	15	5	525	4.397	Tour Championship by Coca-Cola
14	Torrey Pines (North)	18	5	516	4.405	Farmers Insurance Open
15	PGA West (Palmer)	18	5	543	4.414	Humana Challenge
16	Spyglass Hill GC	11	5	528	4.419	AT&T Pebble Beach National Pro-Am
17	Bay Hill Club & Lodge	16	5	511	4.427	Arnold Palmer Invitational
18	Plantation Course at Kapalua	9	5	521	4.433	Hyundai Tournament of Champions
19	Waialae CC	18	5	551	4.442	Sony Open in Hawaii
20	Monterey Peninsula CC	16	5	500	4.452	AT&T Pebble Beach National Pro-Am
21	TPC Louisiana	7	5	561	4.458	Zurich Classic of New Orleans
22	Muirfield Village GC	15	5	529	4.476	Memorial Tournament
23	La Quinta CC	11	5	543	4.477	Humana Challenge
23	PGA West (Palmer)	6	5	562	4.477	Humana Challenge
25	Pebble Beach Golf Links	2	5	502	4.482	AT&T Pebble Beach National Pro-Am
26	PGA National (Champion)	3	5	538	4.486	The Honda Classic
27	Valhalla GC	18	5	542	4.490	PGA Championship
28	PGA West (Nicklaus)	8	5	509	4.516	Humana Challenge
29	TPC Summerlin	9	5	563	4.519	Shriners Hospitals for Children Open
30	Sedgefield CC	15	5	545	4.520	Wyndham Championship
30	Sedgefield CC	15	5	545	4.520	Wyndham Championship
30	Sedgefield CC	15	5	545	4.520	Wyndham Championship
33	Harbour Town Golf Links	2	5	502	4.523	RBC Heritage
34	TPC Deere Run	2	5	561	4.528	John Deere Classic
35	Torrey Pines (North)	9	5	547	4.542	Farmers Insurance Open
35	Monterey Peninsula CC	6	5	548	4.542	AT&T Pebble Beach National Pro-Am
37	El Camaleon	13	5	532	4.543	OHL Classic at Mayakoba
37	Trump Intrntl GC - P.R.	2	5	547	4.543	Puerto Rico Open
39	Colonial CC	1	5	565	4.545	Crowne Plaza Invitational at Colonial
40	Plantation Course at Kapalua	15	5	555	4.550	Hyundai Tournament of Champions
40	TPC Deere Run	17	5	569	4.550	John Deere Classic
42	La Quinta CC	13	5	547	4.555	Humana Challenge
43	Torrey Pines (North)	1	5	519	4.556	Farmers Insurance Open
43	Sheshan International GC	14	5	594	4.566	WGC-HSBC Champions
45	Sheshan International GC	2	5	550	4.570	WGC-HSBC Champions
46	Kuala Lumpur Golf & CC	3	5	503	4.577	CIMB Classic
47	Royal Liverpool GC	10	5	532	4.578	The Open Championship
48	Torrey Pines (North)	14	5	523	4.582	Farmers Insurance Open
49	Muirfield Village GC	7	5	563	4.586	Memorial Tournament
50	Quail Hollow Club	5	5	570	4.586	Wells Fargo Championship
51	TPC Southwind	16	5	530	4.590	FedEx St. Jude Classic
52	TPC Summerlin	16	5	560	4.593	Shriners Hospitals for Children Open
53	Spyglass Hill GC	7	5	529	4.594	AT&T Pebble Beach National Pro-Am
54	El Camaleon	5	5	554	4.601	OHL Classic at Mayakoba
55	Muirfield Village GC	5	5	527	4.606	Memorial Tournament
56	Royal Montreal GC (Blue)	12	5	570	4.609	RBC Canadian Open
57	Seaside Course	15	5	565	4.610	The McGladrey Classic
58	TPC Four Seasons Resort	7	5	542	4.613	HP Byron Nelson Championship
58	TPC Deere Run	14	4	361	3.613	John Deere Classic
60	Royal Liverpool GC	5	5	528	4.615	The Open Championship
61	The Old White TPC	12	5	568	4.616	The Greenbrier Classic
62	TPC Boston	4	4	298	3.621	Deutsche Bank Championship
63	TPC Scottsdale	13	5	595	4.629	Waste Management Phoenix Open
64	Plantation Course at Kapalua	14	4	305	3.633	Hyundai Tournament of Champions
65	Golf Club of Houston	13	5	590	4.636	Shell Houston Open
66	TPC Summerlin	15	4	341	3.644	Shriners Hospitals for Children Open
67	Quail Hollow Club	15	5	577	4.651	Wells Fargo Championship
68	Cherry Hills CC	3	4	333	3.658	BMW Championship
69	PGA National (Champion)	18	5	556	4.659	The Honda Classic
70	TPC Boston	18	5	530	4.663	Deutsche Bank Championship
71	Kuala Lumpur Golf & CC	5	5	518	4.679	CIMB Classic
72	Riviera CC	11	5	583	4.679	Northern Trust Open
73	Quail Hollow Club	7	5	532	4.680	Wells Fargo Championship
74	TPC River Highlands	6	5	574	4.681	Travelers Championship
75	Royal Montreal GC (Blue)	6	5	570	4.681	RBC Canadian Open

EVENT PREVIEWS 2015

Event previews cover all official PGA Tour events and all European Tour events which appeared on the schedule and have a venue selected as of press time (absent E Tour events include the Volvo China Open - whose venue had not been selected - and a yet-to-be-announced tournament scheduled for October 8-11). The yardages, pars and scoring averages (as well as notations for which holes ranked among the hardest/easiest on the PGA Tour) are provided by the Tours themselves, though outside sources have occasionally been consulted. With regard to scoring average, numbers shown are from the 2014 playing. For events whose sites rotate, numbers are from the last time the tournament was played at this site provided that was within the last four years. For events which play over multiple courses, the primary or "host" venue appears here. Profiles of PGA Tour events' second and/or third venues appear on page 224. E Tour events whose purses are marked with an asterisk have not yet announced their 2015 purse, thus 2014 numbers are provided.

Event strength is determined primarily by a five-year averaging of its strength-of-field ratings in the Official World Golf Ranking. However, minor adjustments may be made when a single aberrational number unduly skews a five-year average, or for events whose overall history (or flagship status, as designated by the OWR) has imbued them with a generally recognized enhanced level of prestige.

For PGA Tour events, holes marked (+) were among the Tour's 100 toughest in 2014, while those marked (*) were among the 100 easiest.

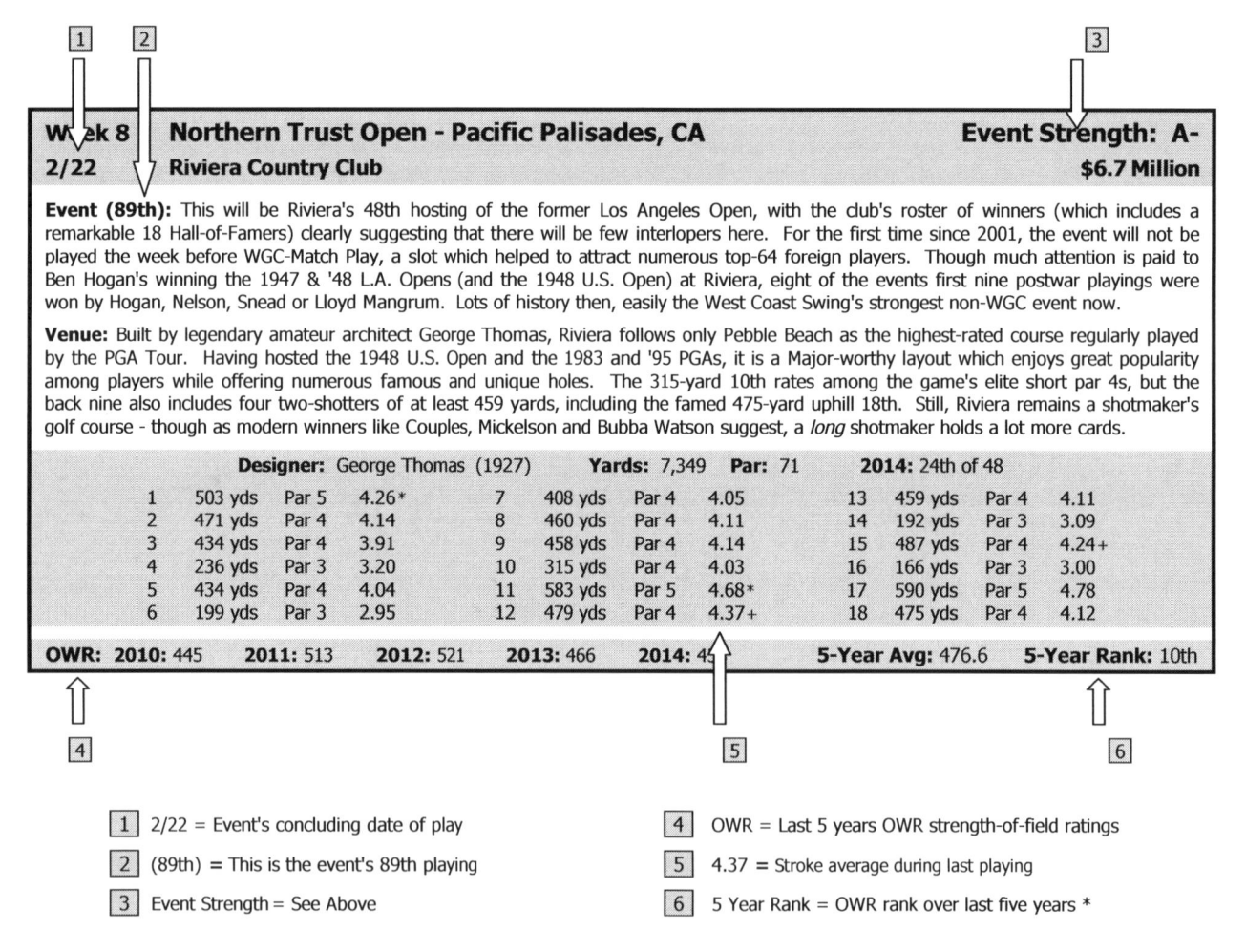

Week 8 — **Northern Trust Open - Pacific Palisades, CA** — **Event Strength: A-**
2/22 — **Riviera Country Club** — **$6.7 Million**

Event (89th): This will be Riviera's 48th hosting of the former Los Angeles Open, with the club's roster of winners (which includes a remarkable 18 Hall-of-Famers) clearly suggesting that there will be few interlopers here. For the first time since 2001, the event will not be played the week before WGC-Match Play, a slot which helped to attract numerous top-64 foreign players. Though much attention is paid to Ben Hogan's winning the 1947 & '48 L.A. Opens (and the 1948 U.S. Open) at Riviera, eight of the events first nine postwar playings were won by Hogan, Nelson, Snead or Lloyd Mangrum. Lots of history then, easily the West Coast Swing's strongest non-WGC event now.

Venue: Built by legendary amateur architect George Thomas, Riviera follows only Pebble Beach as the highest-rated course regularly played by the PGA Tour. Having hosted the 1948 U.S. Open and the 1983 and '95 PGAs, it is a Major-worthy layout which enjoys great popularity among players while offering numerous famous and unique holes. The 315-yard 10th rates among the game's elite short par 4s, but the back nine also includes four two-shotters of at least 459 yards, including the famed 475-yard uphill 18th. Still, Riviera remains a shotmaker's golf course - though as modern winners like Couples, Mickelson and Bubba Watson suggest, a *long* shotmaker holds a lot more cards.

Designer: George Thomas (1927)   **Yards:** 7,349   **Par:** 71   **2014:** 24th of 48

#	Yds	Par	Avg	#	Yds	Par	Avg	#	Yds	Par	Avg
1	503 yds	Par 5	4.26*	7	408 yds	Par 4	4.05	13	459 yds	Par 4	4.11
2	471 yds	Par 4	4.14	8	460 yds	Par 4	4.11	14	192 yds	Par 3	3.09
3	434 yds	Par 4	3.91	9	458 yds	Par 4	4.14	15	487 yds	Par 4	4.24+
4	236 yds	Par 3	3.20	10	315 yds	Par 4	4.03	16	166 yds	Par 3	3.00
5	434 yds	Par 4	4.04	11	583 yds	Par 5	4.68*	17	590 yds	Par 5	4.78
6	199 yds	Par 3	2.95	12	479 yds	Par 4	4.37+	18	475 yds	Par 4	4.12

OWR: **2010:** 445   **2011:** 513   **2012:** 521   **2013:** 466   **2014:** 4?   **5-Year Avg:** 476.6   **5-Year Rank:** 10th

---

[1] 2/22 = Event's concluding date of play
[2] (89th) = This is the event's 89th playing
[3] Event Strength = See Above
[4] OWR = Last 5 years OWR strength-of-field ratings
[5] 4.37 = Stroke average during last playing
[6] 5 Year Rank = OWR rank over last five years *

* For each event's particular tour (either the PGA or the European) only.

Week 41 Frys.com Open - Napa, CA
10/12 Silverado Resort & Spa (North Course)

Event Strength: C
$6 Million

Event (8th): Arriving at the Silverado Resort for what may prove to be a short-term basis, this will be the event's eighth playing, having spent three years at Arizona's Grayhawk GC, then four at the CordeValle Resort in San Martin, California. It has lived its entire existence in a not-so-desirable fall schedule slot, recording its strongest fields in 2008 and '09, and seeing a modest uptick in field strength in 2013, as the debut event in Tour's new wraparound schedule. Among its most memorable playings were the 2009 edition (when Troy Matteson defeated just-out-of-college phenoms Rickie Fowler and Jamie Lovemark in a playoff) as well as 2010, when 47-year-old Rocco Mediate holed a wedge to eagle the par-4 71st hole, edging Alex Prugh and Bo Van Pelt by two.

Venue: Originally designed by Robert Trent Jones in 1966, then renovated by resort part-owner Johnny Miller in 2011, the North Course at Silverado is no stranger to tournament play, having hosted (with its sister South course) the PGA Tour from 1968-1980, counting Nicklaus, Casper, Miller, Watson and Crenshaw among its winners. Also a Champions Tour stop from 1988-2000, it figures to be a layout that will yield relatively low scores, and it is uncertain as to how long the event will remain here - though options exist for 2015 and '16 returns.

Designer: Robert Trent Jones (1966)   **Yards:** 7,171   **Par:** 72   **2014:** New Venue

#	Yards	Par	#	Yards	Par	#	Yards	Par
1	436 yds	Par 4	7	212 yds	Par 3	13	417 yds	Par 4
2	240 yds	Par 3	8	347 yds	Par 4	14	393 yds	Par 4
3	424 yds	Par 4	9	557 yds	Par 5	15	189 yds	Par 3
4	407 yds	Par 4	10	459 yds	Par 4	16	571 yds	Par 5
5	538 yds	Par 5	11	182 yds	Par 3	17	375 yds	Par 4
6	458 yds	Par 4	12	391 yds	Par 4	18	575 yds	Par 5

OWR: 2009: 133   **2010:** 92   **2011:** 80   **2012:** 83   **2013:** 125   **5-Year Avg:** 102.6   **5-Year Rank:** 38th

---

Week 42 Shriners Hospitals For Children Open - Las Vegas, NV
10/19 TPC Summerlin

Event Strength: C
$6.2 Million

Event (32nd): After debuting in 1983, the Tour's Las Vegas stop spent its first 21 years as a pro-am played over five rounds and three courses. Perhaps surprisingly (given the players' dislike of pro-ams) it drew stronger fields in those early days, counting Major winners Zoeller, Norman, Strange, Azinger and Love among its first 15 champions and, famously, being the site of Tiger Woods' first PGA Tour victory in 1996. It has also visited different schedule slots, being stuck in April/May dates (where it lay at the risk of some less-than-ideal desert weather) during the later half of the 1980s. By the time the format was paired to 72 holes in 2004, however, the event was locked into a fall slot, making it non-essential to most top players. One prominent exception was Jim Furyk (a winner here in 1995, '98 and '99), and the event garnered much attention in 2010 when Jonathan Byrd won a three-way playoff with a hole-in-one at the par-3 17th.

Venue: The TPC Summerlin was built in 1991 by Bobby Weed and Fuzzy Zoeller, and has been a part of this event (mostly as a co-host) since 1992. Notably, the three lowest aggregates in tournament history have come in its three years as sole host. Unlike many desert layouts, it does not rely heavily on artificial water hazards - that is, until the final three holes, all of which feature pond-guarded greens.

Designer: Bobby Weed & Fuzzy Zoeller (1991)   **Yards:** 7,243   **Par:** 71   **2014:** 43rd of 48

#	Yards	Par	Avg	#	Yards	Par	Avg	#	Yards	Par	Avg
1	408 yds	Par 4	3.83	7	382 yds	Par 4	3.89	13	606 yds	Par 5	4.74
2	469 yds	Par 4	4.01	8	239 yds	Par 3	3.14	14	156 yds	Par 3	2.89
3	492 yds	Par 4	4.33+	9	563 yds	Par 5	4.52*	15	341 yds	Par 4	3.64*
4	450 yds	Par 4	3.99	10	420 yds	Par 4	3.95	16	560 yds	Par 4	4.59*
5	197 yds	Par 3	2.91	11	448 yds	Par 4	4.15	17	196 yds	Par 3	3.10
6	430 yds	Par 4	4.00	12	442 yds	Par 4	3.88	18	444 yds	Par 4	3.98

OWR: 2009: 211   **2010:** 119   **2011:** 97   **2012:** 139   **2013:** 187   **5-Year Avg:** 150.6   **5-Year Rank:** 37th

---

Week 43 McGladrey Classic - Sea Island, GA
10/26 Sea Island Resort (Seaside Course)

Event Strength: C
$5.7 Million

Event (5th): This will be the fifth playing of this youthful fall tournament - an event which one might expect to draw a slightly stronger field than some other autumn stops based simply on the number of PGA Tour players who reside in proximity to the club. Unfortunately, it has spent its entire four years slotted either immediately before or after the Tour's fall visit to Asia - a tough spot in which to land elite players given the flight time to/from the Far East, and the fact that one of the Asian events is the lucrative WGC-HSBC Champions. Interestingly, over these first four playings, winners have been separated from runners-up by a combined total of only three strokes.

Venue: The Sea Island Resort's Seaside Course traces its roots to a prominent 1929 nine designed by C.H. Alison, and came into its present form when paired with an adjacent Joe Lee-designed loop during a 1999 Tom Fazio renovation. This redesign focused mostly on tree removal and the creation of huge sandy waste areas along many holes - an attractive addition, though not one entirely consistent with the layout's earliest aesthetic. Consequently, today's track is something of a classic-feeling test and one which has proven itself susceptible to low scoring, particularly in less windy conditions. Holes 12, 13 and 16 are especially notable as waterside Alison originals.

Designer: C.H. Alison (1929) / Joe Lee (1974)   **Yards:** 7,005   **Par:** 70   **2014:** 21st of 48

#	Yards	Par	Avg	#	Yards	Par	Avg	#	Yards	Par	Avg
1	417 yds	Par 4	4.08	7	582 yds	Par 5	4.79	13	408 yds	Par 4	4.03
2	415 yds	Par 4	4.09	8	368 yds	Par 4	3.85	14	442 yds	Par 4	4.26+
3	204 yds	Par 3	3.21	9	452 yds	Par 4	4.03	15	565 yds	Par 5	4.61*
4	429 yds	Par 4	4.15	10	418 yds	Par 4	4.06	16	407 yds	Par 4	4.05
5	409 yds	Par 4	3.90	11	425 yds	Par 4	3.99	17	192 yds	Par 3	3.01
6	179 yds	Par 3	2.91	12	223 yds	Par 3	3.15	18	470 yds	Par 4	4.11

OWR: 2009: N/P   **2010:** 149   **2011:** 237   **2012:** 115   **2013:** 152   **5-Year Avg:** 163.3   **5-Year Rank:** 35th

Week 44   CIMB Classic - Kuala Lumpur, Malaysia   Event Strength: B-
11/2   Kuala Lumpur Golf & Country Club (West Course) $7 Million

Event (5th): The first event played in Asia to be eligible for FedEx Cup points, the CIMB Classic spent its first three years at the Mines Resort & Golf Club before moving several miles northwest to the Kuala Lumpur Golf & Country Club in 2013. Partially due to greatly expanding its field, the event made a large strength-of-field jump in 2013 - and figures to sustain that level so long as an Asian WGC event is played the following week. The first three playings (2010-2012) appeared unofficially on the PGA Tour's schedule, and included only 48 players. That number was expanded in 2013, however, with the field of 78 being built around the top 60 available players from the 2013 FedEx Cup points list, the top 10 available players from the Asian Tour Order of Merit, and various sponsor and local exemptions.

Venue: Also the home of the European and Asian Tours' Malaysian Open, the West Course at the Kuala Lumpur Golf & Country Club dates to 1991 but was completely renovated in 2008, with the revised version offering renovated bunkering and water hazards meaningfully affecting play on 10 holes. Nobody has bettered 270 since the renovation - a point which may not impress until one looks at the crazy low scoring previously logged at the par-71 Mines Resort. Notably, three back nine holes rated among the PGA Tour's 100 toughest in 2014.

Designer: Robin Nelson & Neil Haworth (1991)   **Yards:** 6,951   **Par:** 72   **2014:** 28th of 48

#	Yds	Par	Avg	#	Yds	Par	Avg	#	Yds	Par	Avg
1	401 yds	Par 4	4.06	7	386 yds	Par 4	3.95	13	459 yds	Par 4	4.26+
2	444 yds	Par 4	4.09	8	203 yds	Par 3	3.06	14	358 yds	Par 4	3.94
3	503 yds	Par 5	4.58*	9	404 yds	Par 4	4.06	15	199 yds	Par 3	3.09
4	140 yds	Par 3	2.80	10	539 yds	Par 5	4.86	16	318 yds	Par 4	3.92*
5	518 yds	Par 5	4.68*	11	226 yds	Par 3	3.32+	17	336 yds	Par 4	4.00
6	420 yds	Par 4	4.02	12	479 yds	Par 4	4.30+	18	634 yds	Par 5	4.97

OWR: **2009:** N/P   **2010:** 197   **2011:** 141   **2012:** 193   **2013:** 309   **5-Year Avg:** 210   **5-Year Rank:** 30th

Week 45   WGC-HSBC Champions - Shanghai, China   Event Strength: A
11/9   Sheshan International Golf Club $8.5 Million

Event (10th): Initially sanctioned by the European, Asian, Sunshine and Australasian Tours, the HSBC Champions debuted in 2005 and invited all previous-year winners on each tour plus anyone inclined to play from the OWR top 50. But finally finding an overseas sponsor with deep enough pockets, the Federation of Tours answered criticism of their "World" Golf Championship events all being played in America by granting the event WGC status in 2009, causing its already solid fields to take a great leap in quality. Not surprisingly, the list of winners is a strong one, counting Phil Mickelson as its lone two-time champion (his first came in 2007), and names like Els, Westwood and Woods among those who have more than once finished as runner-up. Despite offering $500,000 less in prize money than its three WGC siblings, the event should continue to draw very strong fields given its WGC status and a schedule slot in which there is little worldwide competition.

Venue: The event's host since 2006 (save for 2012), the Nelson & Haworth-designed Sheshan International Golf Club has in recent years yielded some notably low scoring, with the last three winners being 19, 20 and 24 shots under par. There is the potential for some late-round fireworks as well, with the 16th being a 288-yard driveable par 4 and the 538-yard 18th a similarly reachable (if watery) par 5.

Designer: Robin Nelson & Neil Haworth (2004)   **Yards:** 7,266   **Par:** 72   **2014:** 40th of 48

#	Yds	Par	Avg	#	Yds	Par	Avg	#	Yds	Par	Avg
1	459 yds	Par 4	4.02	7	346 yds	Par 4	3.91	13	411 yds	Par 4	3.88
2	550 yds	Par 5	4.57*	8	603 yds	Par 5	4.99	14	594 yds	Par 5	4.57*
3	362 yds	Par 4	3.77	9	486 yds	Par 4	4.23	15	487 yds	Par 4	4.12
4	200 yds	Par 3	2.98	10	401 yds	Par 4	3.91	16	288 yds	Par 4	3.72
5	456 yds	Par 4	4.05	11	456 yds	Par 4	4.13	17	212 yds	Par 3	3.24+
6	200 yds	Par 3	3.06	12	217 yds	Par 3	2.99	18	538 yds	Par 5	4.81

OWR: **2009:** N/A   **2010:** 621   **2011:** N/A   **2012:** 528   **2013:** 574   **5-Year Avg:** 574.3   **5-Year Rank:** 8th

Week 45   Sanderson Farms Championship - Jackson, MS   Event Strength: C-
11/9   Country Club of Jackson $4 Million

Event (28th): Born as the Magnolia State Classic in 1968, today's Sanderson Farms Championship has been an official PGA Tour event since 1994, under names like Deposit Guarantee, Southern Farm Bureau and the Viking Classic. Unfortunately, it has nearly always been an "opposite" stop - indeed, it has gone head-to-head against eight British Opens, four Tour Championships, three WGC-American Express events, two Ryder Cups, a Presidents Cup, and now the WGC-HSBC Champions in China. The most frequent of these were the British and, not surprisingly, trying to lure second-tier players to Mississippi in July seldom proved a winning recipe. Thus as of 2014, the event moves to a late fall slot where it should fare better field-wise - though it must be noted that amidst a list of mid-range names, it has included Luke Donald (2002) and Bill Haas (2010) (as well as Craig Stadler and Payne Stewart in the unofficial years) among its winners.

Venue: After 20 years (1994-2003) at the Jack Nicklaus-designed Annandale Country Club, the event moves to the Country Club of Jackson for 2014. Though the club has existed since 1914, the 27-hole golf course was built by Dick Wilson in 1963 and remodeled by John Fought in 2008. The Tour will play the stronger Dogwood and Azalea nines, a water-dotted combination which figures to yield plenty of birdies.

Designer: Dick Wilson (1963)   **Yards:** 7,334   **Par:** 72   **2014:** New Venue

#	Yds	Par	#	Yds	Par	#	Yds	Par
1	411 yds	Par 4	7	214 yds	Par 3	13	151 yds	Par 3
2	418 yds	Par 4	8	403 yds	Par 4	14	584 yds	Par 5
3	551 yds	Par 5	9	421 yds	Par 4	15	330 yds	Par 4
4	181 yds	Par 3	10	223 yds	Par 3	16	469 yds	Par 4
5	612 yds	Par 5	11	554 yds	Par 5	17	416 yds	Par 4
6	482 yds	Par 4	12	409 yds	Par 4	18	505 yds	Par 4

OWR: **2009:** N/P   **2010:** 71   **2011:** 17   **2012:** 12   **2013:** 21   **5-Year Avg:** 55.3   **5-Year Rank:** 39th

Week 46 OHL Classic at Mayakoba - Playa Del Carmen, Mexico   Event Strength: C-
11/16 El Camaleon   **$6.1 Million**

Event (8th): Another "opposite" event which is now a part of the fall schedule, the former Mayakoba Classic debuted in 2007 and spent its first six years slotted against the WGC-Match Play - thus guaranteeing not a single top-64 player in the field. The move to November clearly helped it in 2013, however, more than doubling the strength of its field. Unfortunately, this mid-November date also conflicts with the latter stages of the European Tour's lucrative Final Series, so the upside relative to foreign players will continue to be limited. But despite its light fields, the event has hardly been devoid of excitement, with three of its seven playings resulting in playoffs, the most notable of which came in 2012 when rookie John Huh defeated Robert Allenby on the eighth extra hole, tying for the second-longest playoff in Tour history.

Venue: El Camaleon is a 6,987-yard Greg Norman-designed layout that anchors an upscale coastal resort just south of Playa Del Carmen. Routed through untamed jungle and, in spots, resort housing, it only twice approaches the oceanfront, with both the 116-yard 7th and the 155-yard 15th backing up against wind-exposed sections of beach. The Tour toughens thing relative to par by playing the 521-yard 16th as a long par 4 but regardless, the *highest* winning score over seven playings (and that by a full four shots) was John Huh's 271 total in 2012.

Designer: Greg Norman (2007)   **Yards:** 6,987   **Par:** 71   **2014:** 39th of 48

#	Yds	Par	Avg	#	Yds	Par	Avg	#	Yds	Par	Avg
1	438 yds	Par 4	4.13	7	554 yds	Par 5	4.73*	13	532 yds	Par 5	4.54*
2	428 yds	Par 4	4.10	8	161 yds	Par 3	2.89	14	452 yds	Par 4	4.15
3	389 yds	Par 4	4.05	9	462 yds	Par 4	3.95	15	155 yds	Par 3	3.00
4	116 yds	Par 3	2.75	10	200 yds	Par 3	3.01	16	485 yds	Par 4	4.27+
5	554 yds	Par 5	4.60*	11	360 yds	Par 4	3.78	17	386 yds	Par 4	3.90
6	416 yds	Par 4	3.85	12	451 yds	Par 4	4.22	18	458 yds	Par 4	4.10

OWR: 2009: 44   **2010:** 25   **2011:** 26   **2012:** 38   **2013:** 84   **5-Year Avg:** 43.4   **5-Year Rank:** 40th

---

Week 2 Hyundai Tournament of Champions - Kapalua, HI   Event Strength: B
1/11 Plantation Course at Kapalua   **$5.7 Million**

Event (63rd): Always a limited-field event restricted to the previous 12 months' PGA Tour winners, the Tournament of Champions dates to 1953, when it debuted at the Wilbur Clark/Moe Dalitz-owned Desert Inn in Las Vegas. After 16 years, it moved to San Diego's new La Costa Resort where it spent three full decades before moving to Hawaii, and Kapalua's Plantation Course, in 1999. The small fields have affected its overall value in the OWR era, and many of game's elite have stayed away in recent years. But the winners-only format still guarantees a solid field, and how many events can claim 14 Hall-of-Famers (including Nicklaus five times) among its champions?

Venue: Kapalua's Plantation Course is a huge, highly strategic test built on a ravine-dotted hillside high above the Pacific. Making major use of several of the jungle-filled chasms within its routing, the layout plays to a par of 73, features par 4s ranging in length from 305-520 yards, and relies upon the ever-present tradewinds to boost its challenge. The rigorous terrain can be a factor here, with the 508-yard par-4 17th and the 663-yard 18th both plunging more than 150 feet as they skirt a huge left-side ravine. But lest the scorecard suggest that this is a bomber's paradise, four of the event's last five winners - Ogilvy, Byrd, Stricker and Zach Johnson - are relatively short off the tee.

Designer: Bill Coore & Ben Crenshaw (1991)   **Yards:** 7,411   **Par:** 73   **2014:** 46th of 48

#	Yds	Par	Avg	#	Yds	Par	Avg	#	Yds	Par	Avg
1	520 yds	Par 4	4.13	7	516 yds	Par 4	4.03	13	407 yds	Par 4	4.08
2	218 yds	Par 3	3.04	8	203 yds	Par 3	3.07	14	305 yds	Par 4	3.63*
3	380 yds	Par 4	3.83	9	521 yds	Par 5	4.43*	15	555 yds	Par 5	4.55*
4	382 yds	Par 4	3.88	10	354 yds	Par 4	3.91	16	365 yds	Par 4	3.81
5	532 yds	Par 5	4.15*	11	164 yds	Par 3	3.13	17	549 yds	Par 4	4.16
6	398 yds	Par 4	4.03	12	420 yds	Par 4	3.88	18	663 yds	Par 5	4.83

OWR: 2010: 262   **2011:** 316   **2012:** N/A   **2013:** 272   **2014:** 259   **5-Year Avg:** 277.3   **5-Year Rank:** 22nd

---

Week 3 Sony Open In Hawaii - Honolulu, HI   Event Strength: B-
1/18 Waialae Country Club   **$5.6 Million**

Event (54th): One of the PGA Tour's oldest events, the Hawaiian Open was first played in 1928 - though for two significant periods (1930-1946 and 1948-1964) it was contested as a local tournament not recognized as a part of the Tour. Like several of the West Coast's older stops, Hawaii drew stronger fields during the 1960s and '70s but after a steady decline towards the new millennium, it experienced a jump in field strength following the Tournament of Champions 1999 move to the Islands, as many better players heading for Kapalua have opted to make it a two-week stay. Those gains have not been retained in recent years, however, with fields slipping noticeably since 2010.

Venue: Quite remarkably, the Waialae Country Club is, since 1928, the only course upon which the PGA Tour has ever contested the Hawaiian Open - a run that is only approached by The Masters (1934) in Tour history. Of course, the layout has changed significantly since Seth Raynor originally planned it for the Royal Hawaiian Hotel, with virtually all of today's front nine (the back during tournament week) having been redesigned, save for the 186-yard 8th, an oceanside Redan. The inward half retains several Raynor remnants (e.g., elements of a Biarritz at the 199-yard 13th and traces of a Short at the 167-yard 16th) but by any measure, pure Golden Age stuff this isn't.

Designer: Seth Raynor (1926)   **Yards:** 7,044   **Par:** 70   **2014:** 36th of 48

#	Yds	Par	Avg	#	Yds	Par	Avg	#	Yds	Par	Avg
1	480 yds	Par 4	4.11	7	176 yds	Par 3	2.93	13	477 yds	Par 4	4.23
2	423 yds	Par 4	4.13	8	454 yds	Par 4	4.02	14	430 yds	Par 4	3.93
3	422 yds	Par 4	4.00	9	506 yds	Par 5	4.34*	15	398 yds	Par 4	3.26
4	204 yds	Par 3	3.14	10	351 yds	Par 4	3.80	16	417 yds	Par 4	4.03
5	467 yds	Par 4	4.05	11	194 yds	Par 3	3.06	17	194 yds	Par 3	4.01
6	460 yds	Par 4	4.10	12	440 yds	Par 4	3.93	18	551 yds	Par 5	4.44*

OWR: 2010: 334   **2011:** 298   **2012:** 229   **2013:** 203   **2014:** 232   **5-Year Avg:** 259.2   **5-Year Rank:** 24th

Week 4	Humana Challenge - La Quinta, CA	Event Strength: C+
1/25	PGA West (Palmer Course), etc.	$5.7 Million

Event (64th): Dating to a 1952 event at the Thunderbird Country Club, the Humana Challenge has existed under a variety of names and sponsors, but was long affiliated with legendary comedian Bob Hope, whose name remained a part of the event for 46 years (1965-2011), eight of those posthumously. Prior to 2012, this was a five-round pro-am affair played over four courses, with a total of 12 Coachella Valley clubs having been utilized at least once. But beginning in 2012, when President Bill Clinton's foundation began partnering with Humana as sponsors, play was shortened to 72 holes and the scope of amateur play scaled back, resulting in a quick rise in the caliber of the field.

Venue: This will be the last year in which the event's three-course rotation includes the La Quinta Country Club and both the Palmer and Nicklaus Private Courses at PGA West - this due to PGA West's pulling the plug on the use of its private facilities. The Palmer Course is historically notable, having been the event's Sunday host 12 times, including in 1999 when David Duval carded his famous closing 59. While the La Quinta CC plans to remain involved, organizers will announce two replacement courses in early 2015, with favorites including the municipally owned SilverRock Resort (a Humana venue from 2008-2011) and PGA West's famed Stadium Course, which was used in 1987.

Designer: Arnold Palmer (1986)   **Yards:** 6,950   **Par:** 72   **2014:** 47th of 48

1	426 yds	Par 4	3.89	7	439 yds	Par 4	4.05	13	447 yds	Par 4	4.00
2	514 yds	Par 5	4.37*	8	358 yds	Par 4	3.75	14	569 yds	Par 5	4.73*
3	180 yds	Par 3	2.86	9	461 yds	Par 4	4.20	15	156 yds	Par 3	2.93
4	396 yds	Par 4	3.91	10	453 yds	Par 4	4.20	16	364 yds	Par 4	3.77
5	233 yds	Par 3	3.30+	11	512 yds	Par 5	4.26*	17	130 yds	Par 3	2.83
6	562 yds	Par 5	4.48*	12	207 yds	Par 3	3.04	18	543 yds	Par 5	4.41*

OWR: 2010: 150   **2011:** 163   **2012:** 253   **2013:** 241   **2014:** 212   **5-Year Avg:** 203.8   **5-Year Rank:** 32nd

---

Week 5	Waste Management Phoenix Open - Scottsdale, AZ	Event Strength: B
2/1	TPC Scottsdale (Stadium Course)	$6.3 Million

Event (77th): Another very well-established West Coast stop, the Phoenix Open has been played annually (save for briefly during the 1930s, plus World War II) since 1932. Prior to settling at the TPC Scottsdale in 1987, it was contested 38 times at the Phoenix Country Club and made 10 visits to the Arizona Country Club, with the two alternating years from 1955-1973. As a measure of the event's early prestige, 20 of its first 26 playings were won by eventual Hall-of-Famers, and five men have won the title back-to-back: Ben Hogan, Jimmy Demaret, Lloyd Mangrum and Johnny Miller, with Arnold Palmer threepeating from 1961-1963. Today Phoenix generally falls opposite the European Tour's lucrative Desert Swing, drawing away many foreign stars. It also embraces a date which few would covet - Super Bowl weekend - and if the result is larger crowds on Saturday than Sunday, that doesn't stop Phoenix from being the Tour's most attended event - by miles.

Venue: Recently renovated by Tom Weiskopf, the TPC Scottsdale is an engaging but relatively easy layout, having yielded two of the Tour's five lowest all-time 72-hole totals (256s posted by Calcavecchia in 2001 and Mickelson in 2013). It is best known for the 162-yard 16th (where up to 20,000 fans surround the players) though both the 552-yard 15th and the 332-yard 17th are more exciting in tactical terms.

Designer: Tom Weiskopf & Jay Morrish (1986)   **Yards:** 7,261   **Par:** 71   **2014:** 33rd of 48

1	403 yds	Par 4	3.99	7	215 yds	Par 3	3.17	13	558 yds	Par 5	4.63*
2	442 yds	Par 4	3.98	8	475 yds	Par 4	4.05	14	490 yds	Par 4	3.97
3	558 yds	Par 5	4.72*	9	453 yds	Par 4	3.99	15	553 yds	Par 5	4.76
4	183 yds	Par 3	2.93	10	428 yds	Par 4	4.01	16	163 yds	Par 3	3.12
5	470 yds	Par 4	4.12	11	472 yds	Par 4	4.18	17	332 yds	Par 4	3.71*
6	432 yds	Par 4	4.06	12	192 yds	Par 3	3.16	18	442 yds	Par 4	4.12

OWR: 2010: 408   **2011:** 317   **2012:** 331   **2013:** 356   **2014:** 367   **5-Year Avg:** 355.8   **5-Year Rank:** 18th

---

Week 6	Farmers Insurance Open - La Jolla, CA	Event Strength: B
2/8	Torrey Pines (South & North Courses)	$6.3 Million

Event (65th): The Farmers Insurance Open dates to 1952 and soon witnessed hometown hero Gene Littler winning the 1954 edition while still an amateur, then, during the 1960s, each of the Big Three (as well as area native Billy Casper) raising the trophy. In more recent years, San Diego gained a reputation as the stop where both Tiger Woods and Phil Mickelson (both Southern California natives) began their PGA Tour seasons - and, quite remarkably, the pair won 10 of 20 playings from 1993-2013. Actually, a number of SoCal players have fared well here: from 1988-2008, fully 15 of 21 winners were natives of Los Angeles, Orange or San Diego Counties.

Venue: Though Thursday and Friday play is split between its South and North courses, golf at Torrey Pines is defined by the South which, in addition to being a part of 47 straight Farmers Insurance events, also hosted Tiger Woods' playoff victory over Rocco Mediate at the 2008 U.S. Open - and will entertain the national championship again in 2021. Originally built by William F. Bell in 1957, then toughened by Rees Jones in 2001, the South is one of the stronger tournament venues in America, though tactically intricate it isn't, nor does it make much use of the huge coastal canyons that dot the site. The difference in difficulty between South and North? Nearly 3.6 stroke per round in 2014.

Designer: William F. Bell (1957)   **Yards:** 7,568   **Par:** 72   **2014:** 4th of 48

1	450 yds	Par 4	4.22	7	462 yds	Par 4	4.24+	13	614 yds	Par 5	5.04
2	389 yds	Par 4	4.06	8	176 yds	Par 3	3.12	14	437 yds	Par 4	4.04
3	200 yds	Par 3	3.09	9	614 yds	Par 5	4.89	15	478 yds	Par 4	4.24+
4	488 yds	Par 4	4.30+	10	416 yds	Par 4	4.11	16	223 yds	Par 3	3.03
5	454 yds	Par 4	4.15	11	221 yds	Par 3	3.28+	17	442 yds	Par 4	4.15
6	560 yds	Par 5	4.69*	12	504 yds	Par 4	4.35+	18	570 yds	Par 5	4.81

OWR: 2010: 228   **2011:** 292   **2012:** 287   **2013:** 316   **2014:** 371   **5-Year Avg:** 298.8   **5-Year Rank:** 20th

Week 7 AT&T Pebble Beach Nat. Pro-Am - Pebble Beach, CA Event Strength: B-
2/15   Pebble Beach Golf Links, etc. $6.8 Million

Event (74th): Long forgotten is that Bing Crosby played the first six of his pro-am events in Rancho Santa Fe, not moving to Pebble Beach until after World War II - and Pebble's continuing presence still makes the event, for many, a centerpiece of the PGA Tour's West Coast swing. Jack Nicklaus and Johnny Miller both won thrice here, but even more impressive are the résumés of Phil Mickelson (a four-time winner, most recently in 2012) and Mark O'Meara, who won a remarkable five times here from 1985-1997. Though some players cite Pebble Beach's greens or the E Tour's competing Desert Swing as reasons for staying away, their dislike of pro-am play is likely the bigger reason.

Venue: Pebble Beach remains, as ever, Pebble Beach - one of the game's iconic venues with a pair of seaside closers that are ideal for both drama and television. The longer serving of its tri-hosts, the infamous Spyglass Hill, does not strike quite as much fear into the hearts of pros as it once did, but its forest can still devour errant shots and the wind still blows mightily across its duneland openers. The Monterey Peninsula Country Club's Shore course, on the other hand, joined the event in 2010 after being comprehensively renovated by Mike Strantz and has been fairly well-received by players - but why not? It played 2.13 shots easier than Pebble and 1.5 easier than Spyglass in 2014.

Designer: Jack Neville & Douglas Grant (1915)   **Yards:** 6,816   **Par:** 72   **2014:** 7th of 48

#	Yds	Par	Avg	#	Yds	Par	Avg	#	Yds	Par	Avg
1	381 yds	Par 4	4.13	7	106 yds	Par 3	3.11	13	399 yds	Par 4	4.01
2	502 yds	Par 5	4.48*	8	418 yds	Par 4	4.12	14	573 yds	Par 5	4.88
3	390 yds	Par 4	4.08	9	466 yds	Par 4	4.38+	15	397 yds	Par 4	3.94
4	331 yds	Par 4	4.12	10	446 yds	Par 4	4.46+	16	403 yds	Par 4	4.13
5	198 yds	Par 3	3.29+	11	380 yds	Par 4	3.96	17	178 yds	Par 3	3.12
6	513 yds	Par 5	4.90	12	202 yds	Par 3	3.39+	18	543 yds	Par 5	4.88

OWR: 2010: 308   **2011:** 227   **2012:** 210   **2013:** 222   **2014:** 246   **5-Year Avg:** 242.6   **5-Year Rank:** 25th

Week 8 Northern Trust Open - Pacific Palisades, CA Event Strength: A-
2/22   Riviera Country Club $6.7 Million

Event (89th): This will be Riviera's 48th hosting of the former Los Angeles Open, with the club's roster of winners (which includes a remarkable 18 Hall-of-Famers) clearly suggesting that there will be few interlopers here. For the first time since 2001, the event will not be played the week before WGC-Match Play, a slot which helped to attract numerous top-64 foreign players. Though much attention is paid to Ben Hogan's winning the 1947 & '48 L.A. Opens (and the 1948 U.S. Open) at Riviera, eight of the event's first nine postwar playings were won by Hogan, Nelson, Snead or Lloyd Mangrum. Lots of history then, easily the West Coast Swing's strongest non-WGC event now.

Venue: Built by legendary amateur architect George Thomas, Riviera follows only Pebble Beach as the highest-rated course regularly played by the PGA Tour. Having hosted the 1948 U.S. Open and the 1983 and '95 PGAs, it is a Major-worthy layout which enjoys great popularity among players while offering numerous famous and unique holes. The 315-yard 10th rates among the game's elite short par 4s, but the back nine also includes four two-shotters of at least 459 yards, including the famed 475-yard uphill 18th. Still, Riviera remains a shotmaker's golf course - though as modern winners like Couples, Mickelson and Bubba Watson suggest, a *long* shotmaker holds a lot more cards.

Designer: George Thomas (1927)   **Yards:** 7,349   **Par:** 71   **2014:** 24th of 48

#	Yds	Par	Avg	#	Yds	Par	Avg	#	Yds	Par	Avg
1	503 yds	Par 5	4.26*	7	408 yds	Par 4	4.05	13	459 yds	Par 4	4.11
2	471 yds	Par 4	4.14	8	460 yds	Par 4	4.11	14	192 yds	Par 3	3.09
3	434 yds	Par 4	3.91	9	458 yds	Par 4	4.14	15	487 yds	Par 4	4.24+
4	236 yds	Par 3	3.20	10	315 yds	Par 4	4.03	16	166 yds	Par 3	3.00
5	434 yds	Par 4	4.04	11	583 yds	Par 5	4.68*	17	590 yds	Par 5	4.78
6	199 yds	Par 3	2.95	12	479 yds	Par 4	4.37+	18	475 yds	Par 4	4.12

OWR: 2010: 445   **2011:** 513   **2012:** 521   **2013:** 466   **2014:** 433   **5-Year Avg:** 476.6   **5-Year Rank:** 10th

Week 9 Honda Classic - Palm Beach Gardens, FL Event Strength: B+
3/1   PGA National Golf Club (Champion Course) $6.1 Million

Event (43rd): Dating to 1972, the Honda Classic traces its roots to the old Jackie Gleason Inverrary event, and visited five venues prior to settling at PGA National in 2007. Early on it was something of a marquee stop, with eight of Inverrary's 11 playing won by eventual Hall-of-Famers. Several less-popular courses affected the event's prestige during the 1980s and '90s (though 10 different Major champions still won during this period) but things have picked up nicely since the move back to Palm Beach Gardens, helped in no small part by the long roster of top domestic and foreign players currently residing in the greater Palm Beach area. In 2015, however, the field may slip a bit as the WGC-Match Play's move to May means that Honda will no longer be slotted between two WGC events, the latter located just down the road.

Venue: The centerpiece of PGA National's five-course facility, the Champion was designed in 1981 by Tom Fazio, completely overhauled by Jack Nicklaus in 1990, and altered periodically by Nicklaus ever since. In recent years its high rough and firm conditions have combined with Florida's seasonal winds to make for a solid challenge. The course's much-marketed highlight is the three-hole stretch (numbers 15-17) known as the "Bear Trap," whose very watery 179-yard 15th and 190-yard 17th can become downright frightening in a stiff breeze.

Designer: Tom Fazio (1981)   **Yards:** 7,140   **Par:** 70   **2014:** 17th of 48

#	Yds	Par	Avg	#	Yds	Par	Avg	#	Yds	Par	Avg
1	365 yds	Par 4	3.93	7	226 yds	Par 3	3.08	13	388 yds	Par 4	3.90
2	464 yds	Par 4	4.09	8	427 yds	Par 4	3.95	14	465 yds	Par 4	4.11
3	538 yds	Par 5	4.49*	9	421 yds	Par 4	3.97	15	179 yds	Par 3	3.10
4	395 yds	Par 4	4.00	10	508 yds	Par 4	4.20	16	434 yds	Par 4	4.13
5	217 yds	Par 3	3.05	11	450 yds	Par 4	4.18	17	190 yds	Par 3	3.17
6	479 yds	Par 4	4.44+	12	438 yds	Par 4	3.96	18	556 yds	Par 5	4.66*

OWR: 2010: 316   **2011:** 403   **2012:** 327   **2013:** 434   **2014:** 494   **5-Year Avg:** 394.8   **5-Year Rank:** 14th

Week 10 WGC-Cadillac Championship - Miami, FL   **Event Strength: A+**
3/8   Trump National Doral (Blue Monster Course)   **$9.25 Million**

Event (16th): Officially this is not the same event that has been played at Doral since 1962, but rather a continuation of the old WGC-American Express tournament which was mostly contested around Europe prior to moving to Miami in 2007. In that event, Tiger Woods is a seven-time winner in four different countries - but to American fans, this certainly *seems* like the tournament which for years kicked off the Florida swing, which favored Bermuda grass putting specialists like Andy Bean and Mark McCumber, which saw Raymond Floyd win thrice, and which witnessed Craig Parry triumph in 2004 by holing a 6 iron at the famed 18th in a playoff with Scott Verplank.

Venue: Doral's Dick Wilson-designed Blue Monster came to fame during the 1960s because in an era of sane equipment, its mix of length, sand and lots of water was indeed a testing one. The course was altered by Raymond Floyd in 1993 and instructor Jim McLean in 1996, but upon Donald Trump's 2011 purchase of the resort, Gil Hanse was hired to perform a major renovation. The result is a test which, even allowing for some freakishly high scoring due to heavy winds, proved a far tougher track during its 2014 WGC debut. Hanse's design was not intended to destroy, however, so it will be interesting to see how it plays if calmer conditions prevail in 2015.

Designer: Dick Wilson (1962) / Gil Hanse (2014) **Yards:** 7,481 **Par:** 72 **2014:** 3rd of 48

1	572 yds	Par 5	4.77	7	471 yds	Par 4	4.42+	13	238 yds	Par 3	3.28+
2	448 yds	Par 4	4.17	8	549 yds	Par 5	4.73*	14	484 yds	Par 4	4.39+
3	436 yds	Par 4	4.23	9	200 yds	Par 3	3.25+	15	153 yds	Par 3	3.09
4	203 yds	Par 3	3.34+	10	614 yds	Par 5	5.03	16	341 yds	Par 4	3.83
5	421 yds	Par 4	4.02	11	422 yds	Par 4	4.03	17	425 yds	Par 4	4.09
6	432 yds	Par 4	4.07	12	601 yds	Par 5	4.79	18	471 yds	Par 4	4.34+

OWR: 2010: 742   **2011:** N/A   **2012:** 816   **2013:** 762   **2014:** 770   **5-Year Avg:** 772.5   **5-Year Rank:** 3rd

---

Week 10 Puerto Rico Open - Rio Grande, Puerto Rico   **Event Strength: D**
3/8   Trump International Golf Club (Championship Course)   **$3 Million**

Event (8th): The Puerto Rico Open has actually been around for a while, having filled a spot on the 1960s Caribbean winter circuit, where it included prominent names like Toski, Knudson, Sifford, Wall and Seve Ballesteros's uncle, Ramon Sota, among its champions. As a PGA Tour event, its presence dates only to 2008, when it was added as an opposite stop slotted next to the WGC-Cadillac Championship. With the world's elite thus already occupied, fields have been extremely light throughout its tenure, with the result being a roster of eclectic winners that has included the young (Chesson Hadley) and the old (Michael Bradley, twice), but little in the way of real star appeal.

Venue: Today's Trump International Golf Club actually began life as the Coco Beach Golf & Country Club, and features 36 holes designed by Tom Kite on a coastal site just outside of Rio Grande. Though it is widely rated the lesser of the two layouts, the Tour utilizes the longer Championship Course, a 7,506-yard track whose centerpiece is a five-hole finish built upon a heavily developed peninsula extending into the Atlantic Ocean. Though this muscular stretch hardly represents a classic close, it has at least produced an interesting finish or two, such as in 2013, when Scott Brown birdied the last to edge Fabián Gómez and a then status-less Jordan Spieth by one.

Designer: Tom Kite (2004) **Yards:** 7,506 **Par:** 72 **2014:** 41st of 48

1	447 yds	Par 4	4.08	7	448 yds	Par 4	4.01	13	410 yds	Par 4	4.10
2	547 yds	Par 5	4.54*	8	236 yds	Par 3	3.02	14	459 yds	Par 4	4.09
3	386 yds	Par 4	3.89	9	450 yds	Par 4	3.97	15	600 yds	Par 5	4.77
4	455 yds	Par 4	4.20	10	430 yds	Par 4	3.96	16	202 yds	Par 3	3.05
5	535 yds	Par 5	4.39*	11	192 yds	Par 3	2.97	17	411 yds	Par 4	3.94
6	203 yds	Par 3	3.02	12	465 yds	Par 4	4.02	18	630 yds	Par 5	4.74

OWR: 2010: 24   **2011:** 22   **2012:** 24   **2013:** 48   **2014:** 32   **5-Year Avg:** 30   **5-Year Rank:** 41st

---

Week 11 Valspar Championship - Palm Harbor, FL   **Event Strength: B+**
3/15   Innisbrook Resort (Copperhead Course)   **$5.9 Million**

Event (15th): Born in 2000, the Valspar Championship has existed under five separate sponsors over 15 years, but it has remained firmly rooted in its venue, having spent the entire time playing over the Innisbrook Resort's well-known Copperhead Course. Always slotted within the middle of the PGA Tour's Florida swing, it has drawn consistently above-average fields for much of its tenure, and the demanding nature of the course has rewarded solid tee-to-green men such as two-time winners K.J. Choi (2002 & '06) and Retief Goosen (2003 & '09), as well as other noted ball-strikers like Vijay Singh (2004), Mark Calcavecchia (2007 - at age 46), Jim Furyk (2010) and John Senden (2014). Perhaps due its location on Florida's west coast, a somewhat overlooked event - at least relative to the WGC Honda and Arnold Palmer.

Venue: The last of the four 18-hole layouts that Larry Packard built for the Innisbrook Resort, the 7,340-yard, par-71 Copperhead Course dates to 1974, and spent some time ranked among *Golf Digest*'s top 100 U.S. courses during the 1980s. It is a difficult tree-lined layout which favors solid ball-striking, and which has occasionally ranked among the PGA Tour's 10 toughest layouts. Its centerpiece comes over a trio of closers marketed as the "Snake Pit," a tricky group led by the dangerous 475-yard 16th, a long and watery dogleg right.

Designer: Larry Packard (1974) **Yards:** 7,340 **Par:** 71 **2014:** 6th of 48

1	560 yds	Par 5	4.72*	7	420 yds	Par 4	4.09	13	200 yds	Par 3	3.19
2	435 yds	Par 4	4.14	8	235 yds	Par 3	3.19	14	590 yds	Par 5	4.77
3	455 yds	Par 4	4.29+	9	430 yds	Par 4	4.11	15	215 yds	Par 3	3.12
4	195 yds	Par 3	3.06	10	445 yds	Par 4	4.17	16	475 yds	Par 4	4.31+
5	605 yds	Par 5	4.95	11	575 yds	Par 5	4.87	17	215 yds	Par 3	3.09
6	465 yds	Par 4	4.21	12	380 yds	Par 4	3.99	18	445 yds	Par 4	4.17

OWR: 2010: 438   **2011:** 358   **2012:** 446   **2013:** 360   **2014:** 335   **5-Year Avg:** 387.4   **5-Year Rank:** 15th

Week 12	**Arnold Palmer Invitational - Orlando, FL**	**Event Strength: A-**
3/22	Bay Hill Club & Lodge	$6.2 Million

Event (50th): Following some relatively humble beginnings as the Florida Citrus Open (played at the Rio Pinar Country Club), the Arnold Palmer Invitational blossomed upon moving to Palmer's Bay Hill resort (and changing its name) in 1979. Multiple Major champions would win during the revised event's first decade, but the most memorable edition to date took place in 1990, when rookie Robert Gamez holed a 171-yard 7 iron on the final hole to steal the title from Greg Norman by one. But if any name has become synonymous with this event, it is that of Tiger Woods who won the title four straight times from 2000-2003, then triumphed again in 2008 & '09, and yet again in 2012 & '13, the latter victory tying Sam Snead (at Greensboro) as the only men in PGA Tour history to win a single event eight times.

Venue: Bay Hill was built by Dick Wilson and Joe Lee in 1961 as a standard flat, watery Florida course of the period. Having been tweaked by club owner Palmer on numerous occasions since, it remains a typically water-oriented test, but the caliber of its best holes rises well above "typical." This is particularly true of the 555-yard 6th (where John Daly memorably recorded an 18 in 1998) and a trio of exciting closers: the 511-yard pond-fronted 16th, the 221-yard 17th and the 458-yard 18th, whose narrow green curls rightward along a lake.

Designer: Dick Wilson & Joe Lee (1961) **Yards:** 7,419 **Par:** 72 **2014:** 16th of 48

1	461 yds	Par 4	4.17	7	199 yds	Par 3	3.02	13	370 yds	Par 4	4.03
2	231 yds	Par 3	3.19	8	460 yds	Par 4	4.24+	14	215 yds	Par 3	3.17
3	434 yds	Par 4	4.23	9	474 yds	Par 4	4.05	15	467 yds	Par 4	4.16
4	561 yds	Par 5	4.72*	10	400 yds	Par 4	4.05	16	511 yds	Par 5	4.43*
5	390 yds	Par 4	4.03	11	438 yds	Par 4	4.09	17	221 yds	Par 3	3.11
6	555 yds	Par 5	4.77	12	574 yds	Par 5	4.73*	18	458 yds	Par 4	4.30+

OWR: 2010: 489   2011: 454   2012: 411   2013: 568   2014: 406   **5-Year Avg:** 465.6   **5-Year Rank:** 11th

---

Week 13	**Valero Texas Open - San Antonio, TX**	**Event Strength: C**
3/29	TPC San Antonio (AT&T Oaks Course)	$6.2 Million

Event (85th): Tied with the Shell Houston Open as the third oldest non-Major championship event on the PGA Tour, the Texas Open dates to 1922, with the early years seeing it played primarily at San Antonio's Brackenridge Park, and Hall-of-Fame names galore appearing on the trophy prior to World War II. The 1940s saw Hogan and Snead (twice) add their names before a 1950s return to Brackenridge witnessed Mike Souchak shooting 257, a Tour scoring record that would stand for 46 years until broken in this same event by Tommy Armour III (who shot 254 at the La Cantera Golf Club) in 2003. Arnold Palmer claimed three straight wins from 1960-1962 but by the 1970s the tournament was buried in an autumn time slot and far less relevant. In recent years it has been moved to a spot shortly before or after The Masters, but this hasn't stopped it from becoming firmly rooted as a second-tier event - with little on the horizon to suggest a comeback.

Venue: The host of the Texas Open since its 2010 opening, the AT&T Oaks Course is a Greg Norman-designed test which has presented a vastly stiffer challenge than its immediate predecessor (La Cantera), where Armour broke the all-time scoring record. Modified somewhat (mostly around the greens) since its opening, it also presents a rugged aesthetic which nicely matches the surrounding Texas landscape.

Designer: Greg Norman (2010) **Yards:** 7,435 **Par:** 72 **2014:** 8th of 48

1	454 yds	Par 4	4.18	7	207 yds	Par 3	3.18	13	241 yds	Par 3	3.21
2	602 yds	Par 5	4.84	8	604 yds	Par 5	5.07	14	567 yds	Par 5	4.72*
3	213 yds	Par 3	3.16	9	474 yds	Par 4	4.28+	15	464 yds	Par 4	4.22
4	481 yds	Par 4	4.37+	10	447 yds	Par 4	4.08	16	183 yds	Par 3	3.06
5	342 yds	Par 4	3.88	11	405 yds	Par 4	4.02	17	347 yds	Par 4	3.77
6	403 yds	Par 4	4.16	12	410 yds	Par 4	4.13	18	591 yds	Par 5	4.96

OWR: 2010: 111   2011: 130   2012: 97   2013: 241   2014: 211   **5-Year Avg:** 158   **5-Year Rank:** 36th

---

Week 14	**Shell Houston Open - Humble, TX**	**Event Strength: B+**
4/5	Golf Club of Houston (Tournament Course)	$6.6 Million

Event (76th): Joining the Texas Open as the third oldest non-Major championship event on the PGA Tour, the Shell Houston Open also dates to 1922, when it began as a 36-hole event played at the Houston Country Club. The tournament spend considerable time at the municipal Memorial Park from 1951-1963, and later visited the Champions Club five times between 1966-1971. By the mid-1970s, it moved to a new development at The Woodlands where it would remain for 28 uninterrupted years before finally opting for its present site in 2004. Surprisingly, among the great postwar Texas trio of Nelson, Hogan and Mangrum, only Nelson won here - though local hero Jack Burke Jr. fared better, taking the title in both 1952 and '59. After spending decades in a late April/early May time slot, the event moved to the week before The Masters in 2007, and quickly began drawing a much stronger field by matching its conditions closely to Augusta National.

Venue: The Tournament Course at the Golf Club of Houston (née Redstone Golf Club) is a big Rees Jones design built specifically to host this event. Any resemblance to Augusta National lies purely in its tournament week conditioning, but the layout is also noteworthy for being the rare Tour site whose 9th green does not return to the clubhouse and, despite having a private sibling, for being open to the public.

Designer: Rees Jones (2005) **Yards:** 7,441 **Par:** 72 **2014:** 23rd of 48

1	397 yds	Par 4	3.91	7	174 yds	Par 3	2.96	13	590 yds	Par 5	4.64*
2	429 yds	Par 4	4.01	8	557 yds	Par 5	4.82	14	216 yds	Par 3	3.12
3	398 yds	Par 4	3.99	9	238 yds	Par 3	3.06	15	608 yds	Par 5	4.90
4	566 yds	Par 5	4.78	10	380 yds	Par 4	3.96	16	188 yds	Par 3	3.06
5	480 yds	Par 4	4.25+	11	441 yds	Par 4	4.09	17	489 yds	Par 4	4.18
6	464 yds	Par 4	4.27+	12	338 yds	Par 4	3.84	18	488 yds	Par 4	4.41+

OWR: 2010: 366   2011: 352   2012: 318   2013: 409   2014: 461   **5-Year Avg:** 381.2   **5-Year Rank:** 16th

Week 16   RBC Heritage - Hilton Head, SC   Event Strength: B
4/19   Harbour Town Golf Links   **$5.9 Million**

Event (47th): This will be the 47th playing of the RBC Heritage, and the 33rd consecutive year (save for 2011) in which the event has been slotted immediately after The Masters - a spot which has surely limited field quality somewhat, but seemingly not to the degree that one might think. Also surprising is that despite a long history of great champions and a marquee venue, the event has suffered sponsorship issues in recent years, though the present Royal Bank of Canada contract is a five-year deal which currently extends through 2016. Sixteen of the event's first 26 winners are today Hall-of-Famers, and men like Davis Love III (a remarkable five victories), Hale Irwin (three, spaced over some 23 years), Payne Stewart, Tom Watson, Fuzzy Zoeller, Johnny Miller and Hubert Green are all multiple winners here.

Venue: One of the most significant courses in the history of golf design, the Harbour Town Links single-handedly turned period architecture away from long, strategically bland creations upon its 1969 debut. This it accomplished by setting forth Pete Dye's pot bunker-and-railroad-ties retro-modern style while remaining both strategically engaging and palpably challenging even to the world's best. How challenging? Despite then measuring only 6,655 yards, Harbour Town induced the Tour's fourth highest winning score of 1969 in its inaugural playing.

Designer: Pete Dye & Jack Nicklaus (1969)   **Yards:** 7,101   **Par:** 71   **2014:** 9th of 48

#	Yds	Par	Avg	#	Yds	Par	Avg	#	Yds	Par	Avg
1	410 yds	Par 4	4.10	7	195 yds	Par 3	3.06	13	373 yds	Par 4	4.00
2	502 yds	Par 5	4.52*	8	473 yds	Par 4	4.32+	14	192 yds	Par 3	4.14+
3	469 yds	Par 4	4.12	9	332 yds	Par 4	3.94	15	588 yds	Par 5	3.26
4	200 yds	Par 3	3.01	10	451 yds	Par 4	4.04	16	434 yds	Par 4	4.34
5	540 yds	Par 5	4.81	11	436 yds	Par 4	4.03	17	185 yds	Par 3	3.21
6	419 yds	Par 4	4.14	12	430 yds	Par 4	4.08	18	472 yds	Par 4	4.20+

OWR: 2010: 291   2011: 320   2012: 332   2013: 375   2014: 332   **5-Year Avg:** 330   **5-Year Rank:** 19th

---

Week 17   Zurich Classic of New Orleans - Avondale, LA   Event Strength: C+
4/26   TPC Louisiana   **$6.9 Million**

Event (67th): The Zurich Classic of New Orleans dates to 1938, when Harry Cooper won the first of 14 editions played at the municipal City Park Golf Course - whose tenure as host straddled the discontinuation of the event from 1949-1957. In 1963 the tournament began a 26-year run at the Lakewood Country Club, a period in which it moved among March, April and May dates but claimed a list of marquee winners headed by Nicklaus, Player, Trevino, Casper, Crenshaw, Tom Watson (twice) and even Seve Ballesteros. The Nicklaus-designed English Turn Golf & Country Club would then host 16 straight playings (plus one more in 2006) before the tournament moved westward to the Pete Dye-designed TPC Louisiana in 2005, remaining there (in a relatively quiet late-April time slot) ever since.

Venue: Occupying a flat, wetlands- and cypress-laden site across the Mississippi River from New Orleans, the TPC Louisiana is a daily fee facility built by Pete Dye specifically to host this event. As such, it is a predictably long and challenging layout - but the need to appeal to everyday golfers also necessitated a track which demands little in the way of scary forced carries, mega-deep bunkers or island greens. This is seldom rated among Dye's best, but a recent run of high quality ball-strikers (Watson, Dufner and Horschel) lifting the trophy speaks well.

Designer: Pete Dye (2004)   **Yards:** 7,425   **Par:** 72   **2014:** 37th of 48

#	Yds	Par	Avg	#	Yds	Par	Avg	#	Yds	Par	Avg
1	399 yds	Par 4	3.96	7	561 yds	Par 5	4.46*	13	403 yds	Par 4	3.80
2	548 yds	Par 5	4.81	8	372 yds	Par 4	3.86	14	216 yds	Par 3	2.91
3	221 yds	Par 3	3.19	9	207 yds	Par 3	3.10	15	490 yds	Par 4	4.02
4	482 yds	Par 4	4.24+	10	390 yds	Par 4	3.95	16	355 yds	Par 4	4.01
5	438 yds	Par 4	3.90	11	575 yds	Par 5	4.80	17	215 yds	Par 3	3.15
6	476 yds	Par 4	4.22	12	492 yds	Par 4	4.14	18	585 yds	Par 5	4.72*

OWR: 2010: 131   2011: 266   2012: 347   2013: 249   2014: 190   **5-Year Avg:** 236.6   **5-Year Rank:** 26th

---

Week 18   WGC-Cadillac Match Play - San Francisco, CA   Event Strength: A+
5/3   TPC Harding Park   **$9.25 Million**

Event (17th): After eight years in the Tucson area, and its entire 16-year history spent as a 64-man single-elimination event, big change comes to the WGC-Match Play in 2015. The biggest is to the format, as the field will still include 64 players but will be divided into 16 four-man groups, each playing a round-robin format on Wednesday, Thursday and Friday. The top player from each group will then advance to single-elimination match play on the weekend, with two matches scheduled on both Saturday and Sunday. The event will also see changes to its schedule slot and host venue this year, the former likely being a one-time move away from its traditional end-of-February dates. However, the new venue, San Francisco's city-owned TPC Harding Park, may well continue to host the event going forward. The bottom line is that Tiger Woods and Phil Mickelson were both healthy absences in 2014 - and that alone seems enough to spark major change.

Venue: The site of the PGA Tour's Lucky International from 1959-1969, the TPC Harding Park dates to 1925 but underwent a major 2003 renovation prior to hosting the 2005 WGC-American Express and, more prominently, the 2009 Presidents Cup. Today a solid tree-lined test on its rolling site above Lake Merced, it is also set to host the 2020 PGA Championship and a return visit from the Presidents Cup in 2025.

Designer: William Watson (1925)   **Yards:** 7,169   **Par:** 70   **2014:** New Venue

#	Yds	Par	#	Yds	Par	#	Yds	Par
1	395 yds	Par 4	7	344 yds	Par 4	13	428 yds	Par 4
2	449 yds	Par 4	8	230 yds	Par 3	14	467 yds	Par 4
3	183 yds	Par 3	9	525 yds	Par 4	15	405 yds	Par 4
4	606 yds	Par 5	10	562 yds	Par 5	16	336 yds	Par 4
5	429 yds	Par 4	11	200 yds	Par 3	17	175 yds	Par 3
6	473 yds	Par 4	12	494 yds	Par 4	18	468 yds	Par 4

OWR: 2010: 723   2011: N/A   2012: 781   2013: 761   2014: 689   **5-Year Avg:** 738.5   **5-Year Rank:** 4th

Week 19	The Players Championship - Ponte Vedra Beach, FL	Event Strength: A+
5/10	TPC Sawgrass (Stadium Course)	$10 Million

Event (42nd): While there are, and always will be, only four Major championships, some 41 playings later, the Players Championship has certainly cemented its status as the Best Of The Rest. Now in its ninth year since being moved from March to May, it has become a perfect halfway fixture between the year's first Major and its second, and continues to draw a field regularly bettered only by the Majors. And while the odd Jodie Mudd or Craig Perks has enjoyed an occasional week of glory here, the pedigree of the event's champions is second to none. To wit: Since its move to the TPC Sawgrass in 1982, 22 of 33 winners were (or would thereafter become) Major champions. Toss in the fact that seven former world number ones have claimed the title and this is, without a doubt, *the* non-Major win to add to one's golfing résumé.

Venue: The rare modern era golf course to establish itself as a truly iconic tournament venue, Pete Dye's TPC Sawgrass also rates among the most stylistically copied, with its island-green 17th - hardly the world's first island target, but likely its most severe - becoming almost Redan-like in the magnitude of its imitators. Sadly, today's layout is far more neatly manicured than Dye's original, and its greens are now a tad more receptive to missed shots. But short of Augusta and St Andrews, is there a more recognized tournament venue anywhere?

Designer: Pete Dye (1980) **Yards:** 7,215 **Par:** 72 **2014:** 25th of 48

1	423 yds	Par 4	3.97	7	442 yds	Par 4	4.08	13	181 yds	Par 3	3.15
2	532 yds	Par 5	4.70*	8	237 yds	Par 3	3.26+	14	481 yds	Par 4	4.35+
3	177 yds	Par 3	3.01	9	583 yds	Par 5	4.70*	15	449 yds	Par 4	4.02
4	384 yds	Par 4	4.12	10	424 yds	Par 4	4.02	16	523 yds	Par 5	4.71*
5	471 yds	Par 4	4.26+	11	558 yds	Par 5	4.79	17	137 yds	Par 3	2.99
6	393 yds	Par 4	4.00	12	358 yds	Par 4	3.87	18	462 yds	Par 4	4.16

OWR: 2010: 753 **2011:** 790 **2012:** 776 **2013:** 825 **2014:** 771 **5-Year Avg:** 783 **5-Year Rank:** 2nd

Week 20	Wells Fargo Championship - Charlotte, NC	Event Strength: A-
5/17	Quail Hollow Club	$7.1 Million

Event (13th): A big money, star-studded event at the time of its 2003 inception, the Wells Fargo Championship has seen its fortunes slip of late, particularly in 2013 & '14 when the strength of its field took a noticeable dip despite the event maintaining its now-standard slot the week before the Players Championship. In 2015 it will make what appears to be a one-time move to the week immediately following the Players, though the field still figures to be a well-above average one. Particularly during the stronger (pre-2013) years, there have been some very significant winners here, with Vijay Singh, Jim Furyk and Tiger Woods claiming the title from 2005-2007, and both Rory McIlroy (with a closing 62) and Rickie Fowler (in a playoff that included McIlroy) landing their first PGA Tour victories in 2010 and 2012 respectively.

Venue: The Quail Hollow Club's original George Cobb-designed layout hosted the PGA Tour's old Kemper Open from 1969-1979, but large-scale Tom Fazio redesigns in 1997, 2003 and 2013 created an entirely different golf course here - a brawny test built (several times) with a specific eye towards hosting both the Tour and the 2017 PGA Championship. The layout's centerpiece is the "Last Mile," a trio of strong closers that includes the 508-yard par-4 16th, the 221-yard over-water 17th and the 493-yard 18th, a creek-menaced par 4.

Designer: Tom Fazio (1997) **Yards:** 7,562 **Par:** 72 **2014:** 13th of 48

1	418 yds	Par 4	4.04	7	532 yds	Par 5	4.68*	13	210 yds	Par 3	3.06
2	178 yds	Par 3	3.06	8	350 yds	Par 4	3.82	14	345 yds	Par 4	3.79
3	453 yds	Par 4	4.18	9	495 yds	Par 4	4.28+	15	577 yds	Par 5	4.65*
4	483 yds	Par 4	4.24+	10	598 yds	Par 5	4.73*	16	508 yds	Par 4	4.26+
5	570 yds	Par 5	4.59*	11	426 yds	Par 4	4.09	17	221 yds	Par 3	3.34+
6	250 yds	Par 3	3.18	12	456 yds	Par 4	4.12	18	493 yds	Par 4	4.45+

OWR: 2010: 530 **2011:** 445 **2012:** 449 **2013:** 358 **2014:** 341 **5-Year Avg:** 424.6 **5-Year Rank:** 13th

Week 21	Crowne Plaza Invitational at Colonial - Fort Worth, TX	Event Strength: B+
5/24	Colonial Country Club	$6.5 Million

Event (68th): One of the PGA Tour's longest running single-site events, the Crowne Plaza Invitational began life in 1946, and its place in the game was quickly defined by hometown hero Ben Hogan, who won the first and second playings. Hogan would later add titles in 1952, '53 and '59 to emerge as the event's only five-time champion, but well over half of the tournament's winners (39 of 67, through 2014) have been Major champions as well. Though its schedule slot has essentially remained unchanged for several decades, the event's ability to attract top-shelf fields has clearly slipped - though it remains a far better draw than its Texas partner, the Byron Nelson Championship.

Venue: The Dean of Texas Golden Age courses, the Colonial Country Club's John Bredemus design dates to 1936 - though its most famous stretch of holes, the "Horrible Horseshoe" (numbers 3-5) were actually built by Perry Maxwell in preparation for the club's hosting of the 1941 U.S. Open. The original 8th hole (a waterside par 3) was lost to the flood control-oriented straightening of the Trinity River in the late 1960s, but beyond lengthening and minor tweaking, the remainder of the golf course remains reasonably intact. Well known as a shotmaker's track, it counts absolute non-bombers Steve Stricker, David Toms and Zach Johnson (twice) among its recent champions.

Designer: John Bredemus (1936) **Yards:** 7,204 **Par:** 70 **2014:** 19th of 48

1	565 yds	Par 5	4.55*	7	440 yds	Par 4	3.95	13	190 yds	Par 3	3.09
2	389 yds	Par 4	3.92	8	194 yds	Par 3	3.03	14	464 yds	Par 4	4.10
3	483 yds	Par 4	4.15	9	407 yds	Par 4	4.13	15	430 yds	Par 4	4.06
4	247 yds	Par 3	3.18	10	408 yds	Par 4	3.99	16	192 yds	Par 3	3.00
5	481 yds	Par 4	4.29+	11	635 yds	Par 5	4.83	17	387 yds	Par 4	3.98
6	406 yds	Par 4	3.90	12	445 yds	Par 4	4.07	18	441 yds	Par 4	4.07

OWR: 2010: 498 **2011:** 283 **2012:** 340 **2013:** 278 **2014:** 396 **5-Year Avg:** 359 **5-Year Rank:** 17th

Week 22	HP Byron Nelson Championship - Irving, TX		Event Strength: C+
5/31	TPC Four Seasons Resort		$7.1 Million

Event (62nd): The second half of May's annual Texas Swing, the Byron Nelson Championship (née the Dallas Open) actually predates Colonial as an official PGA Tour event by two years, yet it has long played second fiddle in terms of prestige. This was not true in the early years, when Nelson, Snead and Hogan won the first three official playings, or even after a nine-year absence (1947-1955) when Australian Hall-of-Famer Peter Thomson claimed his lone win on U.S. soil in 1956. But in recent years, despite a surprisingly bountiful purse, the event has taken on a distinctly second-tier status - a circumstance only hastened by Byron Nelson's 2006 passing. Indeed, the tournament's Strength of Field rating in the OWR has fallen from 559 and 462 in 2005 & '06 to an average of 214 from 2010-2014 - though these recent playings have produced maiden victories for Jason Day and Keegan Bradley, and a second career win for Jason Dufner.

Venue: The TPC Four Seasons Resort has served as at least a co-host of the Byron Nelson Championship since 1983, and as the event's sole site since 2008. The course was built in 1982 by Jay Morrish (with reported input from Nelson and Ben Crenshaw) but was remodeled extensively by D.A. Weibring in 2008, resulting in solid-if-unspectacular track but one with a record for producing quality champions.

Designer: Jay Morrish (1982) **Yards:** 7,166 **Par:** 70 **2014:** 14th of 48

1	458 yds	Par 4	4.00	7	542 yds	Par 5	4.63*	13	180 yds	Par 3	2.92
2	221 yds	Par 3	3.04	8	461 yds	Par 4	4.12	14	406 yds	Par 4	4.24+
3	528 yds	Par 4	4.35+	9	427 yds	Par 4	4.01	15	504 yds	Par 4	4.29+
4	431 yds	Par 4	4.06	10	435 yds	Par 4	3.92	16	546 yds	Par 5	4.74
5	174 yds	Par 3	2.94	11	323 yds	Par 4	3.89	17	198 yds	Par 3	3.10
6	448 yds	Par 4	4.03	12	455 yds	Par 4	4.05	18	429 yds	Par 4	4.25+

OWR: 2010: 197 **2011:** 198 **2012:** 208 **2013:** 217 **2014:** 250 **5-Year Avg:** 214 **5-Year Rank:** 28th

---

Week 23	Memorial Tournament - Dublin, OH		Event Strength: A
6/7	Muirfield Village Golf Club		$6.2 Million

Event (40th): From its inception in 1976, Jack Nicklaus's deep involvement in the Memorial Tournament gave it a cachet enjoyed by few events on the PGA Tour. That Jack himself won the title in 1977 and 1984 certainly helped get the ball rolling, but as a ledger of 25 Major champions in 39 playings suggests, this remains one of golf's biggest non-Major stages. Additional notable victories here have included Paul Azinger memorably holing from a greenside bunker at the 72nd to claim the 1993 title, Tom Watson ending a nine-year victory drought by scoring an emotional win in 1996, and Tiger Woods claiming three straight titles from 1999-2001. With five overall victories Woods is easily the event's winningest player - an imposing ledger given that the Memorial annually draws one of the game's strongest non-Major fields.

Venue: One of America's highest ranked modern courses, the Jack Nicklaus & Desmond Muirhead-designed Muirfield Village Golf Club has hosted a Ryder Cup (1987), Solheim Cup (1998), Presidents Cup (2013) and U.S. Amateur (1992) in addition to the Memorial Tournament. Tweaked a bit by Jack over the decades (most notably at the now-watery 16th and the 478-yard 17th), it remains a tactically testing layout with lots of memorable holes, yet it is also demanding enough to consistently rank among the 20 toughest on Tour.

Designer: Jack Nicklaus & Desmond Muirhead (1974) **Yards:** 7,392 **Par:** 72 **2014:** 29th of 48

1	470 yds	Par 4	4.18	7	563 yds	Par 5	4.59*	13	455 yds	Par 4	4.12
2	455 yds	Par 4	4.10	8	185 yds	Par 3	2.95	14	363 yds	Par 4	4.02
3	401 yds	Par 4	4.00	9	412 yds	Par 4	3.99	15	529 yds	Par 5	4.48*
4	200 yds	Par 3	3.10	10	471 yds	Par 4	4.10	16	201 yds	Par 3	3.32+
5	527 yds	Par 5	4.60*	11	567 yds	Par 5	4.81	17	478 yds	Par 4	4.18
6	447 yds	Par 4	3.88	12	184 yds	Par 3	3.16	18	484 yds	Par 4	4.34+

OWR: 2010: 569 **2011:** 499 **2012:** 609 **2013:** 631 **2014:** 541 **5-Year Avg:** 569.8 **5-Year Rank:** 9th

---

Week 24	FedEx St. Jude Classic - Memphis, TN		Event Strength: C+
6/14	TPC Southwind		$6 Million

Event (58th): Since its 1958 debut, the FedEx St. Jude Classic (née the Memphis Open) has been particularly consistent venue-wise, spending its first 31 playings at the Colonial Country Club before moving to the TPC Southwind, where it has remained since 1989. Bolt, Middlecoff, Lema and Nicklaus were among the event's early winners, but play would soon be dominated by a pair of period stars, Dave Hill (who won it four times from 1967-1973) and Lee Trevino, who raised the trophy in 1971, '72 and '80. Of course, most significant from the Colonial years was the legendary 59 shot by Al Geiberger during the second round in 1977, a landmark score recorded with persimmon woods and steel shafts on a golf course measuring well over 7,200 yards. Since 2007, the event has been played immediately before the U.S. Open, a date which it has not been able to parlay into stronger fields in a manner similar to the Houston Open prior to Augusta.

Venue: The TPC Southwind was built by Ron Prichard specifically to host this event and while it is seldom ranked among the elite of the TPC franchise, it has proven itself a versatile track. To wit: It has hosted victories by bombers like Couples, Norman and Dustin Johnson, but also crowned as champions a more expansive list of shorter hitters led by two-time winners Nick Price, Justin Leonard and David Toms.

Designer: Ron Prichard (1988) **Yards:** 7,239 **Par:** 70 **2014:** 12th of 48

1	434 yds	Par 4	4.01	7	482 yds	Par 4	4.08	13	472 yds	Par 4	4.09
2	401 yds	Par 4	3.91	8	178 yds	Par 3	3.00	14	239 yds	Par 3	3.09
3	554 yds	Par 5	4.84	9	457 yds	Par 4	4.07	15	395 yds	Par 4	4.00
4	196 yds	Par 3	3.03	10	465 yds	Par 4	4.11	16	530 yds	Par 5	4.59*
5	485 yds	Par 4	4.27+	11	157 yds	Par 3	3.08	17	490 yds	Par 4	4.21
6	445 yds	Par 4	3.99	12	406 yds	Par 4	4.19	18	453 yds	Par 4	4.16

OWR: 2010: 241 **2011:** 201 **2012:** 175 **2013:** 180 **2014:** 240 **5-Year Avg:** 207.4 **5-Year Rank:** 31st

Week 26   Travelers Championship - Cromwell, CT   Event Strength: B-
6/28   **TPC River Highlands**   **$6.4 Million**

Event (64th): The Travelers Championship debuted in 1952, at the Wethersfield Country Club, as the Insurance City Open, but by the late 1960s, its name would be changed to the Greater Hartford Open, a moniker under which it enjoyed a long affiliation with Sammy Davis Jr. from 1973-1988. Always a late spring or summer event for reasons of climate, the tournament began being played in the week immediately following the U.S. Open in 2007 - a slot which, somewhat surprisingly, has not negatively affect its strength of field. Hall-of-Famers were regular winners here over the event's first two decades (led by Billy Casper's four triumphs between 1963-1973) and if their numbers slipped a bit over time, names like Strange, Wadkins, Price, Norman and Mickelson (twice) still managed to hoist the trophy. Notably, since the 2007 schedule switch, five of eight champions (Mahan, Watson, Jacobson, Leishman & Duke) were first-time PGA Tour winners.

Venue: Born in 1928 as the Edgewood Country Club, the TPC River Highlands was first called the TPC of Connecticut upon being rebuilt by Pete Dye in 1984. Ex-Dye associate Bobby Weed later modified it further in 1991, resulting in one of the Tour's shorter venues, but also one with a trio of fairly engaging closers wedged tightly around a central lake. Predictably low numbers are regularly recorded here.

Designer: Pete Dye (1984)   **Yards:** 6,841   **Par:** 70   **2014:** 32nd of 48

#	Yds	Par	Avg	#	Yds	Par	Avg	#	Yds	Par	Avg
1	434 yds	Par 4	3.90	7	443 yds	Par 4	4.11	13	523 yds	Par 5	4.72*
2	341 yds	Par 4	3.88	8	202 yds	Par 3	3.16	14	421 yds	Par 4	3.95
3	431 yds	Par 4	3.93	9	406 yds	Par 4	3.89	15	296 yds	Par 4	3.82
4	481 yds	Par 4	4.25+	10	462 yds	Par 4	4.15	16	171 yds	Par 3	3.09
5	223 yds	Par 3	3.12	11	158 yds	Par 3	2.89	17	420 yds	Par 4	4.11
6	574 yds	Par 5	4.68*	12	411 yds	Par 4	3.93	18	444 yds	Par 4	4.11

OWR: 2010: 198   **2011:** 253   **2012:** 278   **2013:** 315   **2014:** 314   **5-Year Avg:** 271.6   **5-Year Rank:** 23rd

Week 27   Greenbrier Classic - White Sulphur Springs, WV   Event Strength: C+
7/5   **The Old White TPC**   **$6.7 Million**

Event (6th): Debuting in 2010, the Greebrier Classic represented the first regular PGA Tour visit to one of America's earliest golf destinations since the old Greenbrier Open (1949-1961), a star-studded event which, inexplicably, is not recognized as official in the Tour record book. This new event is a part of billionaire Jim Justice's attempts at revitalizing the venerable resort and it gained great attention in its inaugural when Stuart Appleby shot a Sunday 59 to steal the title by one. More significant, however, was a 2012 schedule shift from the end of July to two weeks before the British Open, allowing it serve as an Open qualifier (for four spots) and thus draw much stronger fields.

Venue: Originally known as the resort's No.1 Course, today's Old White TPC dates to 1914, when it was built by the legendary design team of Charles Blair Macdonald and Seth Raynor. Site of the ancient White Sulphur Springs Open in 1921 & '22, then the unofficial Greenbrier Open from 1949-1961 (when tournament host Sam Snead won six of 13 playings), the layout underwent an extensive 2006 renovation by Lester George, making it tournament ready for the modern game. The result was a track which differs significantly from Macdonald's original, but which features his aesthetic stylings and a number of his favored replica holes, led by the 175-yard Short 18th.

Designer: C.B. Macdonald & Seth Raynor (1914)   **Yards:** 7,287   **Par:** 70   **2014:** 26th of 48

#	Yds	Par	Avg	#	Yds	Par	Avg	#	Yds	Par	Avg
1	449 yds	Par 4	4.01	7	430 yds	Par 4	3.97	13	492 yds	Par 4	4.21
2	488 yds	Par 4	4.10	8	234 yds	Par 3	3.07	14	401 yds	Par 4	3.98
3	205 yds	Par 3	3.14	9	404 yds	Par 4	3.90	15	217 yds	Par 3	3.13
4	427 yds	Par 4	4.06	10	385 yds	Par 4	3.87	16	444 yds	Par 4	4.10
5	388 yds	Par 4	3.98	11	493 yds	Par 4	4.11	17	616 yds	Par 5	4.76
6	471 yds	Par 4	4.17	12	568 yds	Par 5	4.16*	18	175 yds	Par 3	2.94

OWR: 2010: 165   **2011:** 152   **2012:** 286   **2013:** 230   **2014:** 234   **5-Year Avg:** 213.4   **5-Year Rank:** 29th

Week 28   John Deere Classic - Silvis, IL   Event Strength: C
7/12   **TPC Deere Run**   **$4.7 Million**

Event (45th): Today's John Deere Classic began life in 1971 as the Quad Cities Open, an autumn event that drew light fields and saw both its first and second playings won by future PGA Tour commissioner Deane Beman. Yet if players like Sam Adams, John Lister, Mike Morley and Victor Regalado were among the early winners, so were Dave Stockton, Scott Hoch (twice) and Payne Stewart, who claimed his maiden Tour win here in 1982. But the event's biggest hero over its first few decades was Quincy, IL native D.A. Weibring, who claimed the title in 1979, '91 and '95 - and even built the tournament's current venue, the TPC Deere Run. In recent years the main man has been another Midwesterner Steve Stricker, who scored threepeat wins from 2009-2011. Importantly, a schedule slot just before the British Open is now paying strength-of-field dividends as the R&A has taken to using it as a last-minute qualifier - though in 2014, it was only allotted one spot.

Venue: The D.A. Weibring-designed TPC Deere Run measures 7,268 yards (par 71) but has regularly ranked among the easiest on the PGA Tour, its *highest* winning score being a 16-under-par 268 since becoming host in 2000. Built on a wooded site above the Rock River, its close includes two holes which parallel the river (the 484-yard 15th and the 158-yard 16th) as well as the pond-guarded 476-yard 18th.

Designer: D.A. Weibring (1999)   **Yards:** 7,268   **Par:** 71   **2014:** 42nd of 48

#	Yds	Par	Avg	#	Yds	Par	Avg	#	Yds	Par	Avg
1	395 yds	Par 4	3.89	7	226 yds	Par 3	2.98	13	424 yds	Par 4	4.00
2	561 yds	Par 5	4.53*	8	428 yds	Par 4	3.92	14	361 yds	Par 4	3.61*
3	186 yds	Par 3	2.93	9	503 yds	Par 4	4.22	15	484 yds	Par 4	4.17
4	454 yds	Par 4	4.02	10	596 yds	Par 5	4.71*	16	158 yds	Par 3	2.91
5	433 yds	Par 4	4.00	11	432 yds	Par 4	4.08	17	569 yds	Par 5	4.55*
6	367 yds	Par 4	3.96	12	215 yds	Par 3	3.05	18	476 yds	Par 4	4.24+

OWR: 2010: 167   **2011:** 150   **2012:** 182   **2013:** 185   **2014:** 166   **5-Year Avg:** 170   **5-Year Rank:** 34th

Week 29	**Barbasol Championship - Auburn, AL**	**Event Strength: New**
7/19	Robert Trent Jones Golf Trail - Grand National (Lakes Course)	$3.5 Million

Event (1st): The PGA Tour has scheduled an event opposite the British Open virtually every year since World War II, a practice which made eminent sense during the decades when only the American elite were making the trip across the Atlantic, but which stands on shakier ground today. Mississippi's Sanderson Farms event, perhaps tired of filling out its 132-man field with seemingly the entire Past Champions category on the Tour priority list, wangled a move into a fall schedule slot, leaving no event to be played opposite Britain in 2014. Enter the new Barbasol Championship, a $3.5 million stop which will represent the Tour's first visit to Alabama since the 1990 PGA Championship, and which may be around for a while, having signed a four-year sponsorship agreement. But strength of field still figures to be on the light side.

Venue: A part of the 11-facility, 26-course Robert Trent Jones Golf Trail, the Lake Course at Grand National is actually the easier half of this 36-hole venue, weighing in at 7,149 yards and a par of 72. The property's main feature is the expansive Lake Saugahatchee, which directly affects play on eight holes, often quite invasively. This is especially apparent down the stretch at a pair of dramatic entries, the 230-yard 15th (all carry to a peninsula green jutting far into the lake) and the 334-yard 16th, which dares an aggressive drive across a wide inlet.

Designer: Robert Trent Jones (1992)   **Yards:** 7,149   **Par:** 72   **2014:** New Venue

1	380 yds	Par 4	7	557 yds	Par 5	13	427 yds	Par 4
2	428 yds	Par 4	8	213 yds	Par 3	14	545 yds	Par 5
3	197 yds	Par 3	9	411 yds	Par 4	15	230 yds	Par 3
4	527 yds	Par 5	10	434 yds	Par 4	16	334 yds	Par 4
5	423 yds	Par 4	11	445 yds	Par 4	17	205 yds	Par 3
6	442 yds	Par 4	12	522 yds	Par 5	18	429 yds	Par 4

OWR: 2010: N/A   **2011:** N/A   **2012:** N/A   **2013:** N/A   **2014:** N/A   **5-Year Avg:** N/A   **5-Year Rank:** N/A

Week 30	**RBC Canadian Open - Oakville, Ontario, Canada**	**Event Strength: C+**
7/26	Glen Abbey Golf Club	$5.8 Million

Event (106th): First played in 1904, the Canadian Open trails only the U.S. and British Opens as the oldest event on the PGA Tour. Though limited greatly by it unfavorable schedule slot today, this was, for decades, an elite event on the world stage, with nine Hall Of Fame members being multi-time winners, led by Leo Diegel (a four-time champion) and Tommy Armour, Sam Snead and Lee Trevino, each of whom won it thrice. As recently as the 1980s and '90s (when names like Price, Norman and Strange all won twice) it remained highly significant, though a move to a September date in 1988 began a decline in field strength which was only exacerbated by a 2007 switch to the week after the British Open and before both the WGC-Bridgestone and the PGA. As a notable aside, this was also the biggest event not won by Jack Nicklaus, who logged seven runner-up finishes and 13 top 10s in 25 attempts, but never quite got across the finish line.

Venue: Despite never winning here, Nicklaus did design the event's most frequent venue, Glen Abbey, which will be hosting for the 26th time in 2015. The layout's central feature is Sixteen Mile Creek, which affects holes 11-14, with the 452-yard 11th drawing top billing. Also notable is the 524-yard lake-guarded 18th, which Tiger Woods famously reached from a fairway bunker to clinch his victory in 2000.

Designer: Jack Nicklaus (1976)   **Yards:** 7,253   **Par:** 72   **2013:** 28th of 43

1	417 yds	Par 4	3.94	7	156 yds	Par 3	3.05	13	558 yds	Par 5	4.66*
2	527 yds	Par 5	4.60*	8	485 yds	Par 4	4.22+	14	457 yds	Par 4	4.25+
3	437 yds	Par 4	4.09	9	414 yds	Par 4	3.98	15	141 yds	Par 3	2.98
4	197 yds	Par 3	3.00	10	453 yds	Par 4	4.11	16	516 yds	Par 5	4.58*
5	433 yds	Par 4	3.97	11	452 yds	Par 4	4.11	17	436 yds	Par 4	4.07
6	458 yds	Par 4	4.16	12	202 yds	Par 3	3.17	18	524 yds	Par 5	4.66*

OWR: 2010: 180   **2011:** 256   **2012:** 193   **2013:** 282   **2014:** 186   **5-Year Avg:** 219.4   **5-Year Rank:** 27th

---

Week 31	**Quicken Loans National - Gainesville, VA**	**Event Strength: B-**
8/2	Robert Trent Jones Golf Club	$6.7 Million

Event (9th): The Quicken Loans National (originally known as the AT&T National) arrived with much fanfare in 2007, with the event's beneficiary (the Tiger Woods Foundation) assuring Woods' presence - and enough top players joined him to boast the PGA Tour's fifth-best strength of field among regular season non-Major, non-WGC events. But curiously it has plummeted since, falling very much in the middle of the pack from 2008-2013, and then experiencing a barely noticeable uptick in 2014 despite becoming a four-spot qualifying event for the British Open. It is difficult to argue with the quality of the event's champions, however, as Woods himself raised the trophy in 2009 and '12, with Justin Rose joining him as the only other multiple winner by triumphing in 2010 (his maiden PGA Tour win) and again in 2014.

Venue: Unlike most designers who have clubs named after them, Robert Trent Jones was actually the driving force behind the creation of his namesake facility, and while it has never quite supported his claim of being his career masterpiece, it is strong enough to have hosted four Presidents Cups between 1994-2005. The course is routed along Lake Manassas but Jones opted to bring the lake directly into play only at the 215-yard 11th. With its 2017 and '19 sites still undecided, the Quicken Loans may be returning here again in the near future.

Designer: Robert Trent Jones (1991)   **Yards:** 7,425   **Par:** 72   **2014:** New Venue

1	405 yds	Par 4	7	450 yds	Par 4	13	465 yds	Par 4
2	420 yds	Par 4	8	585 yds	Par 5	14	580 yds	Par 5
3	500 yds	Par 4	9	200 yds	Par 3	15	475 yds	Par 4
4	210 yds	Par 3	10	380 yds	Par 4	16	175 yds	Par 3
5	555 yds	Par 5	11	215 yds	Par 3	17	380 yds	Par 4
6	435 yds	Par 4	12	525 yds	Par 5	18	470 yds	Par 4

OWR: 2010: 308   **2011:** 252   **2012:** 289   **2013:** 280   **2014:** 305   **5-Year Avg:** 286.8   **5-Year Rank:** 21st

Week 32	**WGC-Bridgestone Invitational - Akron, OH**		Event Strength: A+
8/9	**Firestone Country Club (South Course)**		$9.25 Million

Event (40th): Though this event seems like a continuation of the old World Series Of Golf (played on the same course, mostly in the same schedule slot, since 1976), the PGA Tour considers the WGC-Bridgestone to have officially begun in 1999 - perfect timing for the career peak of Tiger Woods who proceeded, quite remarkably, to win seven of the first 11 playing. Scheduled the week before the PGA Championship since 2007, it regularly draws as strong a field as there is in non-Major championship golf - a pointed underlined by the fact that only twice in 16 playings has the winner not been a Major champion. The old World Series drew similarly strong fields and boasted multiple Hall-of-Famers among its winners - though few performances could match that of José María Olazábal in 1990, who opened with a nine-under-par 61 (several years before such things became equipment-generated commonplace) en route to a record-setting 12-shot runaway victory.

Venue: One of Trent Jones's most famous works, Firestone's South Course actually dates to the late 1920s, with Jones retaining virtually all of the original routing during his 1960 renovation. Though seldom ranked among the nation's best today, it is a layout offering tons of competitive history (including three PGA Championships), as well as being the Tour's longest par-70 course (save for Pinehurst) in 2014.

		Designer: Robert Trent Jones (1960)			**Yards:** 7,400	**Par:** 70		**2014:** 18th of 48		
1	399 yds	Par 4	4.06	7	219 yds	Par 3	3.01	13	471 yds	Par 4	4.15
2	526 yds	Par 5	4.53*	8	482 yds	Par 4	4.09	14	467 yds	Par 4	4.09
3	442 yds	Par 4	4.11	9	494 yds	Par 4	4.17	15	221 yds	Par 3	3.05
4	471 yds	Par 4	4.23	10	410 yds	Par 4	3.95	16	667 yds	Par 5	4.92
5	200 yds	Par 3	2.97	11	418 yds	Par 4	3.95	17	400 yds	Par 4	3.95
6	469 yds	Par 4	4.12	12	180 yds	Par 3	2.98	18	464 yds	Par 4	4.05

OWR: 2010: 799　**2011:** N/A　**2012:** 788　**2013:** N/A　**2014:** 804　**5-Year Avg:** 797　**5-Year Rank:** 1st

Week 32	**Barracuda Championship - Reno, NV**		Event Strength: D
8/9	**Montreux Golf & Country Club**		$3.1 Million

Event (17th): Known as the Reno-Tahoe Open for its first 16 playings, today's Barracuda Championship has spent its entire life being scheduled opposite the ultra-strong-field WGC-Bridgestone, meaning that it has forever been contested among players occupying the lower rungs of the PGA Tour priority list. Consequently, it is not surprising that fully half of the event's champions have been first-time winners on the Tour; this is, without question, a great opportunity for young talent to break through. Of course, such events tend to lack much in the way of identity, leading tournament organizers to switch to a modified Stableford scoring format in 2012 - an admittedly gimmicky approach but one which raised the bar by producing a pair of second-time winners (J.J. Henry and Gary Woodland) in 2012 and '13. Barracuda, a San Francisco-based computer security and data storage firm, is committed to the event for four years, extending through 2017.

Venue: The Jack Nicklaus-designed Montreux Golf & Country Club may, at first glance, look enormous, but situated at 5,600 feet, it's "real" yardage is actually well below PGA Tour average. Prior to 2012, it generally fell in middle of the Tour pack scoring-wise (save for ranking sixth in 2010) but due to the conversion to Stableford scoring, it is no longer factored into the Tour's annual scoring statistics.

		Designer: Jack Nicklaus (1999)			**Yards:** 7,237	**Par:** 72	**2014:** N/A		
1	494 yds	Par 4		7	183 yds	Par 3	13	518 yds	Par 5
2	584 yds	Par 5		8	636 yds	Par 5	14	367 yds	Par 4
3	186 yds	Par 3		9	429 yds	Par 4	15	439 yds	Par 4
4	355 yds	Par 4		10	413 yds	Par 4	16	220 yds	Par 3
5	491 yds	Par 4		11	171 yds	Par 3	17	464 yds	Par 4
6	477 yds	Par 4		12	429 yds	Par 4	18	616 yds	Par 5

OWR: 2010: 17　**2011:** 19　**2012:** 27　**2013:** 30　**2014:** 33　**5-Year Avg:** 25.2　**5-Year Rank:** 42nd

Week 34	**Wyndham Championship - Greensboro, NC**		Event Strength: C+
8/23	**Sedgefield Country Club**		$5.4 Million

Event (76th): The year's final "regular season" event, the Wyndham Championship (née the Greater Greensboro Open) dates to 1938, and until 1961 it was shared (either as co-hosts or in alternating years) between the Sedgefield and Starmount Forest Country Clubs. Thereafter it spend 16 years at Sedgefield, then 31 years at Forest Oaks before returning to a newly restored Sedgefield in 2008. The inaugural edition was won by Sam Snead, who would go on to set a PGA Tour record (later matched by Tiger Woods at the Arnold Palmer Invitational) by claiming the title a total of eight times, with his final win coming in 1965. For several decades the tournament was slotted just before The Masters (after falling just after it in the late 1950s) before returning to a post-Augusta spot in the 1990s. It eventually was moved to a fall slot in 2003 before being placed in the theoretically desirable final week before the FedEx Cup Playoffs upon their arrival in 2007.

Venue: The Sedgefield Country Club carries a Golden Age Donald Ross pedigree but was renovated by Kris Spence in 2007, toughening it up in anticipation of hosting this event. The revised layout is well thought of in Carolinas golfing circles but has regularly yielded low numbers to the pros, with Carl Pettersson shooting 259 in 2008 and the *highest* winning score being Patrick Reed's 266 in 2013.

		Designer: Donald Ross (1926)			**Yards:** 7,127	**Par:** 70		**2014:** 38th of 48		
1	418 yds	Par 4	4.06	7	223 yds	Par 3	3.15	13	405 yds	Par 4	3.91
2	442 yds	Par 4	3.97	8	374 yds	Par 4	3.77	14	501 yds	Par 4	4.15
3	174 yds	Par 3	2.99	9	416 yds	Par 4	3.96	15	545 yds	Par 5	4.52*
4	428 yds	Par 4	3.97	10	440 yds	Par 4	4.09	16	175 yds	Par 3	2.90
5	529 yds	Par 5	4.33*	11	486 yds	Par 4	4.17	17	406 yds	Par 4	3.95
6	423 yds	Par 4	4.05	12	235 yds	Par 3	3.04	18	507 yds	Par 4	4.24+

OWR: 2010: 129　**2011:** 196　**2012:** 233　**2013:** 249　**2014:** 192　**5-Year Avg:** 199.8　**5-Year Rank:** 33rd

Week 35 — The Barclays - Plainfield, NJ
8/30 — Plainfield Country Club
Event Strength: A+
$8.25 Million

Event (49th): Debuting in 1967 as the Westchester Classic, The Barclays enjoyed a long run at the Westchester Country Club where it remained, uninterrupted, until the PGA Tour began rotating the event among New York area sites in 2008. In the early days it was one of the Tour's more lucrative stops, resulting in strong fields which yielded eight Major champions among the event's first 10 winners. In 1981 it switched from an August date to the week immediately before the U.S. Open, with the golf course being set up to approximate Open conditions. The result was an influx of foreign stars looking to get acclimated - and a list of champions that included two-time winners Seve Ballesteros, Vijay Singh and Ernie Els. The event finally returned to August in 2007 to serve as the opening event of the FedEx Cup Playoffs.

Venue: The Plainfield Country Club was originally built by Tom Bendelow, but comprehensively renovated by Donald Ross in 1921, and later underwent a significant new millennium restoration by Gil Hanse. The course plays today as a strong 7,091-yard par 72 layout - numbers which were reduced to 6,984 yards (with a par of 71) for the 2011 Barclays via the conversion of the 519-yard 8th to a 480-yard par 4, and reducing the 407-yard 18th (an early turning dogleg left) to a 285-yard driveable test in order to maximize corporate tent space.

Designer: Donald Ross (1921) **Yards:** 6,964 **Par:** 71 **2014:** New Venue

#	Yards	Par	#	Yards	Par	#	Yards	Par
1	432 yds	Par 4	7	471 yds	Par 4	13	482 yds	Par 4
2	443 yds	Par 4	8	480 yds	Par 4	14	228 yds	Par 3
3	196 yds	Par 3	9	368 yds	Par 4	15	372 yds	Par 4
4	360 yds	Par 4	10	411 yds	Par 4	16	582 yds	Par 5
5	527 yds	Par 5	11	148 yds	Par 3	17	427 yds	Par 4
6	164 yds	Par 3	12	588 yds	Par 5	18	285 yds	Par 4

OWR: 2010: 664 **2011:** 649 **2012:** 746 **2013:** 743 **2014:** 735 **5-Year Avg:** 707.4 **5-Year Rank:** 5th

Week 36 — Deutsche Bank Championship - Norton, MA
9/6 — TPC of Boston
Event Strength: A
$8.25 Million

Event (13th): A PGA Tour event since 2003, the Deutsche Bank Championship has spent its entire existence being played on Labor Day weekend, a schedule slot which made it a convenient fit for the FedEx Cup Playoffs upon their arrival in 2007. Interestingly, though its fields were far lighter in those pre-Playoffs days, early winners included Adam Scott, Vijay Singh and Tiger Woods. But with virtually all of the PGA Tour's elite (both domestic and foreign) participating in the Playoffs, its strength of field has gone through the roof in recent years.

Venue: Though originally built by Arnold Palmer and Ed Seay, the TPC of Boston underwent a trend-setting renovation by Gil Hanse in 2007, keeping all of its original routing but being re-fashioned from Palmer's modern stylings into a classic-feeling old New England-style test that looks like it's been there since the Golden Age. Far more popular with the players and TV audiences, it is now a tactically rich track which will yield to smart shotmaking. To wit: only one champion (Olin Browne in 2005) has failed to better 270 over 72 holes. It also features a trio of potentially dramatic holes down the homestretch: the 161-yard pondside 16th, the 412-yard 17th (whose split fairway dares one to drive close to the green) and the 528-yard 18th, which plays across wetlands to an angled, elevated putting surface.

Designer: Arnold Palmer (2002) **Yards:** 7,214 **Par:** 71 **2014:** 34th of 48

#	Yards	Par	Avg	#	Yards	Par	Avg	#	Yards	Par	Avg
1	365 yds	Par 4	3.92	7	600 yds	Par 5	4.74	13	451 yds	Par 4	3.99
2	542 yds	Par 5	4.73	8	213 yds	Par 3	3.08	14	495 yds	Par 4	4.23+
3	208 yds	Par 3	3.17	9	472 yds	Par 4	4.00	15	421 yds	Par 4	3.90
4	298 yds	Par 4	3.65*	10	425 yds	Par 4	3.93	16	161 yds	Par 3	3.03
5	466 yds	Par 4	4.12	11	231 yds	Par 3	3.15	17	412 yds	Par 4	3.97
6	465 yds	Par 4	4.14	12	461 yds	Par 4	4.06	18	528 yds	Par 4	4.50*

OWR: 2010: 672 **2011:** 647 **2012:** 727 **2013:** 751 **2014:** 582 **5-Year Avg:** 675.8 **5-Year Rank:** 6th

Week 38 — BMW Championship - Lake Forest, IL
9/20 — Conway Farms Golf Club
Event Strength: A
$8.25 Million

Event (112th): Trailing only the U.S. Open as the oldest event played on the PGA Tour, the BMW Championship existed as the Western Open for 107 years before corporate money finally crushed tradition, and it was reformatted and rebranded as a part of the FedEx Cup Playoffs in 2007. Widely viewed as one of professional golf's four biggest events in the years before The Masters, it spent its first 75 years moving among sites ranging from New York to California, though its geographic epicenter was always Illinois, with numerous clubs in the Chicago district having hosted it. In 1974 it finally settled at a permanent stop - the demanding Butler National Golf Club, where it would remain until 1990. It then moved to the public Cog Hill for a 17-year run prior to being rotated among various Midwestern venues ever since. How historic an event is this? Virtually every great American golfer for more than a century has won here. Enough said.

Venue: A well-thought-of Tom Fazio design dating to 1991, Conway Farms began life at just over 6,700 yards before being lengthened substantially prior to hosting the BMW Championship in 2013. Though torched by Jim Furyk for a second-round 59 on that occasion, it was well enough received overall to earn a return engagement in 2015. The numbers/statistics below were drawn from the 1913 playing.

Designer: Tom Fazio (1991) **Yards:** 7,149 **Par:** 71 **2013:** 27th of 43

#	Yards	Par	Avg	#	Yards	Par	Avg	#	Yards	Par	Avg
1	360 yds	Par 4	4.05	7	352 yds	Par 4	3.79	13	463 yds	Par 4	4.24+
2	196 yds	Par 3	3.03	8	600 yds	Par 5	4.76	14	585 yds	Par 5	4.63*
3	402 yds	Par 4	3.88	9	405 yds	Par 4	4.01	15	334 yds	Par 4	3.74*
4	485 yds	Par 4	4.10	10	458 yds	Par 4	4.01	16	465 yds	Par 4	4.19
5	469 yds	Par 4	4.24+	11	162 yds	Par 3	3.05	17	207 yds	Par 3	3.11
6	217 yds	Par 3	4.01	12	419 yds	Par 4	3.93	18	570 yds	Par 5	4.91

OWR: 2010: 633 **2011:** 564 **2012:** 660 **2013:** 691 **2014:** 642 **5-Year Avg:** 638 **5-Year Rank:** 7th

Week 39 **Tour Championship - Atlanta, GA** **Event Strength: A-**
9/27 **East Lake Golf Club** **$8.25 Million**

Event (29th): Since its 1987 inception, the Tour Championship has served as one final jackpot payday for the PGA Tour's top 30 money winners - though in recent years the $10 million check that goes with winning the FedEx Cup Playoffs has lifted that concept into a new dimension. After debuting at San Antonio's Oak Hills Country Club, the event spent a decade moving among some very high-profile venues, including two stops each at Pinehurst, Olympic and Southern Hills, as well as single visits to Pebble Beach and Harbour Town. Houston's Champions Golf Club also hosted multiple editions, eventually alternating with Atlanta's East Lake prior to the latter's becoming full-time host in 2004. A field limited to the Tour's top earners has produced many famous champions, but it is interesting to note that through 2014, 11 of 28 winners were not Major champions, and outlying names like Mudd, Mayfair, Jim Gallagher Jr. and Bart Bryant periodically appear.

Venue: Famed for being the childhood home of Bobby Jones, the East Lake Golf Club features the remains of a relatively early Donald Ross design - a solid track which has been altered both by George Cobb (prior to the club's hosting of the 1963 Ryder Cup) and, more recently, Rees Jones. Classic Ross this isn't, but with its challenge ranking in the middle of the PGA Tour pack, it has settled in as a steady venue.

Designer: Donald Ross (1913) **Yards:** 7,154 **Par:** 70 **2014:** 20th of 48

#	Yards	Par	Avg	#	Yards	Par	Avg	#	Yards	Par	Avg
1	424 yds	Par 4	3.91	7	434 yds	Par 4	4.14	13	476 yds	Par 4	4.18
2	214 yds	Par 3	3.04	8	405 yds	Par 4	4.01	14	442 yds	Par 4	3.85
3	390 yds	Par 4	3.85	9	600 yds	Par 5	4.72*	15	525 yds	Par 5	4.40*
4	440 yds	Par 4	4.12	10	469 yds	Par 4	4.24+	16	481 yds	Par 4	4.15
5	520 yds	Par 4	4.21	11	197 yds	Par 3	3.09	17	455 yds	Par 4	4.10
6	209 yds	Par 3	3.24+	12	391 yds	Par 4	3.93	18	235 yds	Par 3	3.09

OWR: 2010: 395 **2011:** 396 **2012:** 519 **2013:** 483 **2014:** 439 **5-Year Avg:** 446.4 **5-Year Rank:** 12th

PGA TOUR SECOND/THIRD COURSES

Week 4 — PGA West (Nicklaus Private Course) — Humana Challenge

Venue: A well-thought-of course in Southern California golf circles, the Nicklaus Private Course joined the Humana rotation in 2009 and has played surprisingly easy, ranking as the easiest course on the PGA Tour four times in six years. Set to be removed from the event's rota after 2015, it does include two tough par 4s (the 443-yard 5th and the 455-yard 18th) but offers birdie opportunities nearly everywhere else.

Designer: Jack Nicklaus (1987) **Yards:** 6,924 **Par:** 72 **2014:** 48th of 48

#	Yds	Par	Avg	#	Yds	Par	Avg	#	Yds	Par	Avg
1	374 yds	Par 4	3.83	7	140 yds	Par 3	2.76	13	528 yds	Par 5	4.26*
2	414 yds	Par 4	4.08	8	509 yds	Par 5	4.52*	14	375 yds	Par 4	3.96
3	177 yds	Par 3	3.00	9	410 yds	Par 4	3.79	15	415 yds	Par 4	3.87
4	538 yds	Par 5	4.30*	10	412 yds	Par 4	3.88	16	530 yds	Par 5	4.34*
5	443 yds	Par 4	4.03	11	191 yds	Par 3	3.05	17	204 yds	Par 3	3.08
6	406 yds	Par 4	3.99	12	403 yds	Par 4	3.87	18	455 yds	Par 4	4.24+

Week 4 — La Quinta Country Club — Humana Challenge

Venue: A part of the Humana rota since 1964, the La Quinta Country Club has been lengthened and modernized over the years, and while it annually joins its PGA West partners among the PGA Tour's easier layouts, it usually rates the toughest of the three. Water affects play (moderately) on seven holes, and though birdies abound, two solid par 4s mark the late going, the 469-yard 14th and the 469-yard 16th.

Designer: Lawrence Hughes (1959) **Yards:** 7,060 **Par:** 72 **2014:** 45th of 48

#	Yds	Par	Avg	#	Yds	Par	Avg	#	Yds	Par	Avg
1	382 yds	Par 4	3.86	7	168 yds	Par 3	3.14	13	547 yds	Par 5	4.56*
2	434 yds	Par 4	4.07	8	389 yds	Par 4	3.94	14	469 yds	Par 4	4.18
3	202 yds	Par 3	3.11	9	399 yds	Par 4	3.88	15	206 yds	Par 3	2.97
4	384 yds	Par 4	3.88	10	405 yds	Par 4	3.91	16	454 yds	Par 4	4.17
5	516 yds	Par 5	4.33*	11	543 yds	Par 5	4.48*	17	421 yds	Par 4	3.83
6	527 yds	Par 5	4.36*	12	202 yds	Par 3	3.12	18	412 yds	Par 4	3.96

Week 6 — Torrey Pines (North Course) — Farmers Insurance Open

Venue: Torrey Pines' North Course has long played second fiddle to the more famous South. Indeed the discrepancy in challenge has been such that it played 3.56 strokes easier per round in 2014, a staggering number. Phil Mickelson is set to begin a long-awaited renovation in 2015, but Mickelson swears he won't be making it tougher, only better - but we'll see if that 3.56 margin remains in 2016 and beyond.

Designer: William F. Bell (1957) **Yards:** 7,052 **Par:** 72 **2014:** 44th of 48

#	Yds	Par	Avg	#	Yds	Par	Avg	#	Yds	Par	Avg
1	519 yds	Par 5	4.56*	7	399 yds	Par 4	4.02	13	471 yds	Par 4	3.95
2	329 yds	Par 4	3.72*	8	436 yds	Par 4	3.95	14	523 yds	Par 5	4.58*
3	184 yds	Par 3	2.96	9	547 yds	Par 5	4.54*	15	397 yds	Par 4	3.80
4	434 yds	Par 4	3.99	10	417 yds	Par 4	3.99	16	366 yds	Par 4	3.87
5	411 yds	Par 4	4.01	11	490 yds	Par 4	4.33+	17	171 yds	Par 3	2.99
6	208 yds	Par 3	3.22	12	234 yds	Par 3	3.35+	18	516 yds	Par 5	4.41*

Week 7 — Monterey Peninsula CC (Shore Course) — AT&T Pebble Beach National Pro-Am

Venue: Mike Strantz's 2002 renovation of the Monterey Peninsula Country Club's Shore Course kept Bob Baldock's original 1961 routing but otherwise completely rebuilt Baldock's stunningly bland design. The result was a tactically strong but somewhat over-the-top test - and one which, despite an obvious lack of size, has managed to rate in the middle of the PGA Tour pack scoring-wise since joining the event in 2010.

Designer: Mike Strantz (2002) **Yards:** 6,867 **Par:** 71 **2014:** 22nd of 48

#	Yds	Par	Avg	#	Yds	Par	Avg	#	Yds	Par	Avg
1	487 yds	Par 4	4.30+	7	226 yds	Par 3	3.07	13	434 yds	Par 4	4.25+
2	391 yds	Par 4	3.97	8	454 yds	Par 4	3.96	14	190 yds	Par 4	3.17
3	155 yds	Par 3	3.01	9	187 yds	Par 3	3.30+	15	415 yds	Par 3	3.97
4	401 yds	Par 4	4.17	10	544 yds	Par 5	4.96	16	500 yds	Par 4	4.45*
5	349 yds	Par 4	3.85	11	176 yds	Par 3	3.16	17	430 yds	Par 3	3.87
6	548 yds	Par 5	4.54*	12	599 yds	Par 5	5.16	18	381 yds	Par 4	4.12

Week 7 — Spyglass Hill Golf Club — AT&T Pebble Beach National Pro-Am

Venue: In its early years, Spyglass Hill was likely the most feared regular stop on the PGA Tour, its mix of wind, water, dunes, woods and scary greens striking genuine concern into the hearts of the pros. But unchecked equipment advances long ago tamed it, leaving it a fairly manageable test today. It's first five holes among the dunes, however, are among the most unique (and wind-exposed) in American golf.

Designer: Robert Trent Jones (1966) **Yards:** 6,953 **Par:** 72 **2014:** 11th of 48

#	Yds	Par	Avg	#	Yds	Par	Avg	#	Yds	Par	Avg
1	595 yds	Par 5	4.88	7	529 yds	Par 5	4.59*	13	460 yds	Par 4	4.22
2	349 yds	Par 4	4.12	8	399 yds	Par 4	4.34+	14	560 yds	Par 5	4.97
3	165 yds	Par 3	3.01	9	431 yds	Par 4	4.27+	15	130 yds	Par 3	2.92
4	370 yds	Par 4	3.97	10	407 yds	Par 4	4.04	16	476 yds	Par 4	4.26+
5	197 yds	Par 3	3.23	11	528 yds	Par 5	4.42*	17	325 yds	Par 4	3.87
6	446 yds	Par 4	4.40+	12	178 yds	Par 3	3.01	18	408 yds	Par 4	4.23

Week 49 Nedbank Golf Challenge - Sun City, South Africa **Event Strength: C+**
12/7 Gary Player Country Club **$6.5 Million**

Event (34th): Largely intended to promote the Sun City Resort, today's Nedbank Challenge began life as a five-man invitational event in 1981 and made an immediate splash for its purse, the first $1 million payout in the game's history. Johnny Miller won that first playing (in a nine-hole playoff with Seve Ballesteros), after which the field was expanded to 10 players, then 12, and eventually to 30 in 2014. But for all of its money and glitz over the decades, the event only began being co-sanctioned by the E Tour in 2013, on that occasion drawing a long list of stars away from the concurrent Hong Kong Open. One thing that has remained constant is the event's lucrative nature; indeed, its 2014 purse of $6.5 million (for a limited field) was the largest on the E Tour outside of its four-event Final Series.

Venue: Built as the recreational centerpiece to developer Sol Kerzner's then-groundbreaking Sun City Resort, the Gary Player Country Club has long been a popular venue for regular Sunshine Tour events in addition to the Nedbank Challenge. Though lengthened beyond 7,800 yards in 2006, the club's 3,700 feet of altitude make the course something less than backbreaking. Quite imposing, however, is a pair of long and dangerous closers, the 478-yard 17th (played around and across a large lake) and the 502-yard 18th, a huge, pond-crossing par 4.

Designer: Gary Player (1979) **Yards:** 7,831 **Par:** 72

#	Yds	Par	Avg	#	Yds	Par	Avg	#	Yds	Par	Avg
1	441 yds	Par 4	4.10	7	225 yds	Par 3	3.03	13	444 yds	Par 4	4.13
2	569 yds	Par 5	4.83	8	492 yds	Par 4	4.33	14	601 yds	Par 5	4.40
3	449 yds	Par 4	4.23	9	596 yds	Par 5	4.67	15	471 yds	Par 4	3.87
4	213 yds	Par 3	2.80	10	547 yds	Par 5	4.53	16	211 yds	Par 3	3.00
5	491 yds	Par 4	3.93	11	458 yds	Par 4	4.03	17	478 yds	Par 4	4.00
6	424 yds	Par 4	3.83	12	219 yds	Par 3	3.23	18	502 yds	Par 4	4.30

OWR: 2009: 142 **2010:** 171 **2011:** 208 **2012:** 150 **2013:** 263 **5-Year Avg:** 185.8 **5-Year Rank:** 14th

---

Week 50 Alfred Dunhill Championship - Malelane, South Africa **Event Strength: C-**
12/14 Leopard Creek Country Club **€1.5 Million**

Event (49th): Born in 1966 as the South African PGA Championship, today's Alfred Dunhill Championship has been co-sanctioned by the E Tour since 1995, taking on Alfred Dunhill as a sponsor a year later. Initially its fields were primarily domestic, with Americans Tom Weiskopf and Hale Irwin being the only non-Africans to claim the title over its first 15 playings. Harold Henning and Dale Hayes each raised the trophy three times before 1980 (Hayes in succession) and Charl Schwartzel has matched that total in E Tour era. But the event's winningest player is Hall-of-Famer Ernie Els, whose four triumphs (including three in the E Tour era) include titles claimed at three different venues.

Venue: Lying adjacent to the sprawling Kruger National Park wildlife preserve, the Leopard Creek Country Club is one of Gary Player's most highly thought of designs, being both fairly long (it sits at less than 1,000 feet of altitude) and impressively scenic. Water - in the form of three man-made lakes and several creeks - significantly affects play on 10 holes, most notably at the parallel 476-yard 9th and 541-yard island-green 18th. Though Spain's Pablo Martin won here in 2009 and '10, the club has served as the personal playground of Charl Schwartzel, who has logged three wins (including a 12-shot runaway in 2012) and four seconds since the event arrived here in 2004.

Designer: Gary Player (1996) **Yards:** 7,287 **Par:** 72

#	Yds	Par	Avg	#	Yds	Par	Avg	#	Yds	Par	Avg
1	419 yds	Par 4	4.10	7	215 yds	Par 3	3.15	13	552 yds	Par 5	4.66
2	580 yds	Par 5	4.78	8	480 yds	Par 4	4.06	14	413 yds	Par 4	4.07
3	448 yds	Par 4	4.00	9	476 yds	Par 4	4.15	15	598 yds	Par 5	4.61
4	427 yds	Par 4	4.19	10	432 yds	Par 4	4.01	16	208 yds	Par 3	3.34
5	164 yds	Par 3	3.09	11	375 yds	Par 4	4.00	17	448 yds	Par 4	4.16
6	319 yds	Par 4	3.67	12	192 yds	Par 3	3.15	18	541 yds	Par 5	5.10

OWR: 2009: 46 **2010:** 54 **2011:** 19 **2012:** 128 **2013:** 77 **5-Year Avg:** 64.8 **5-Year Rank:** 31st

---

Week 2 South African Open Champ. - Johannesburg, South Africa **Event Strength: C**
1/11 Glendower Golf Club **€1.1 Million***

Event (104th): The game's third-oldest Open event (trailing only the British and the U.S.), the South African Open has been played continuously (save for wartime) since 1903. Over its first few decades the event drew primarily domestic fields, which surely helped the nation's first truly great player, Sid Brews, to win it eight times between 1927-1952. By the World War II years, the great Bobby Locke had taken the mantle, and his utter dominance of South African golf led him to claim nine titles between 1935-1955. But even more impressive still was Gary Player who, in an era when notable foreigners began to appear, won the title an amazing 13 times between 1956-1981 - a record not likely to ever be equaled. The E Tour began co-sanctioning the event in 1997, though its standard late autumn time slot has not proven conducive to drawing top international players. It will thus be interesting to see how this year's move to January fares.

Venue: Originally built by the globetrotting C.H. Alison, the Glendower Golf Club thus carries an elite design pedigree - though numerous 1980s changes to greens, the expansion of water hazards, etc. limit his fingerprints today. The main result of the changes has been the ability to host modern major events, including four South African Opens since 1989, with Vijay Singh (2007) being the marquee winner.

Designer: C.H. Alison (1937) **Yards:** 7,564 **Par:** 72

#	Yds	Par	Avg	#	Yds	Par	Avg	#	Yds	Par	Avg
1	445 yds	Par 4	4.21	7	486 yds	Par 4	4.06	13	571 yds	Par 5	4.71
2	557 yds	Par 5	4.56	8	522 yds	Par 5	4.29	14	173 yds	Par 3	2.86
3	220 yds	Par 3	3.17	9	401 yds	Par 4	4.17	15	547 yds	Par 5	4.47
4	509 yds	Par 4	4.14	10	477 yds	Par 4	4.17	16	441 yds	Par 4	4.09
5	503 yds	Par 4	4.24	11	433 yds	Par 4	4.11	17	222 yds	Par 3	3.06
6	199 yds	Par 3	3.18	12	407 yds	Par 4	3.98	18	451 yds	Par 4	4.02

OWR: 2009: 77 **2010:** 124 **2011:** 60 **2012:** 56 **2013:** 46 **5-Year Avg:** 72.6 **5-Year Rank:** 30th

Week 3 — Abu Dhabi HSBC Golf Championship - Abu Dhabi, U.A.E. — Event Strength: B+
1/18 — Abu Dhabi Golf Club — $2.7 Million

Event (10th): Despite being the newest of the European Tour's three Desert Swing events, the Abu Dhabi Golf Championship has in recent years emerged as the kingpin, regularly drawing the strongest fields behind appearance fees large enough to corral Tiger Woods in 2012 and '13, and Rory McIlroy every year since 2008. McIlroy, for his part, has been a runner-up here three times, leaving the stage to be dominated by a pair of players with strong desert records, Paul Casey (a winner here in 2007 and '09) and reigning U.S. Open champion Martin Kaymer, who took the title in 2008, '10 and '11 - the latter in an eight-shot runaway. As Abu Dhabi has weathered recent economic turbulence better than its less-oil-rich Emirates neighbors, there is little reason to think that this event won't continue to lead the Desert Swing, particularly if it remains in a schedule slot perfect for drawing American stars going abroad for only one guaranteed winter payday.

Venue: The event's sole venue over 10 years, the Abu Dhabi Golf Club was built by Englishman Peter Harradine in 1989 on a flat, barren desert site on the mainland, just a short drive from the island that houses the capital. Despite stretching to 7,600 yards, it is a track built more for tourists than the pros, with its five man-made lakes seldom threatening competent ball strikers. Scoring, then, is usually quite low.

Designer: Peter Harradine (1998) **Yards:** 7,600 **Par:** 72

#	Yds	Par	Avg	#	Yds	Par	Avg	#	Yds	Par	Avg
1	405 yds	Par 4	4.11	7	200 yds	Par 3	4.14	13	414 yds	Par 4	4.00
2	600 yds	Par 5	4.34	8	597 yds	Par 5	4.34	14	490 yds	Par 4	4.14
3	439 yds	Par 4	3.92	9	456 yds	Par 4	3.08	15	177 yds	Par 3	3.26
4	174 yds	Par 3	4.26	10	582 yds	Par 5	5.00	16	475 yds	Par 4	4.34
5	469 yds	Par 4	4.80	11	417 yds	Par 4	4.32	17	483 yds	Par 4	3.21
6	469 yds	Par 4	3.37	12	186 yds	Par 3	4.23	18	567 yds	Par 5	4.20

OWR: 2010: 379 **2011:** 435 **2012:** 454 **2013:** 380 **2014:** 291 **5-Year Avg:** 387.8 **5-Year Rank:** 4th

---

Week 4 — Commercial Bank Qatar Masters - Doha, Qatar — Event Strength: B
1/24 — Doha Golf Club — $2.5 Million

Event (18th): The second oldest of the three Desert Swing events, the Qatar Masters debuted in 1998, when England's Andrew Coltart became the first of several early longshot winners (e.g., The Netherlands' Rolf Muntz in 2000 and Sweden's Joakim Haeggman in 2004). But as the prestige (and appearance fees) of the Desert Swing grew, so did the caliber of winner, with Adam Scott (twice), Ernie Els, Henrik Stenson, Retief Goosen, Thomas Bjørn and, most recently, Sergio García all eventually raising the trophy. In recent years, Qatar has moved past Dubai in its ability to draw international players of quality, making it, on balance, the second strongest of the desert events. Notably, it is also the only one of the three that has never had an American winner - or, for that matter, even an American runner-up.

Venue: Though two additional regulation-size courses exist in Qatar, the Doha Golf Club is the only one located in the capital (not to mention the only one to play on grass), and thus has hosted all 17 editions of the Masters. Another desert track designed by England's Peter Harradine, it is shorter than the Abu Dhabi layout but a tad more challenging, with tighter bunkering and water meaningfully affecting five holes. Notably, with a driveable par (the 307-yard 16th), a short par 3 and a par 5 at the close, late fireworks are always a possibility.

Designer: Peter Harradine (1997) **Yards:** 7,400 **Par:** 72

#	Yds	Par	Avg	#	Yds	Par	Avg	#	Yds	Par	Avg
1	591 yds	Par 5	4.53	7	391 yds	Par 4	3.86	13	203 yds	Par 3	3.09
2	433 yds	Par 4	3.83	8	185 yds	Par 3	3.08	14	410 yds	Par 4	3.82
3	223 yds	Par 3	3.22	9	639 yds	Par 5	4.87	15	470 yds	Par 4	4.21
4	413 yds	Par 4	3.89	10	548 yds	Par 5	4.68	16	307 yds	Par 4	3.49
5	452 yds	Par 4	4.09	11	474 yds	Par 4	3.95	17	155 yds	Par 3	3.11
6	488 yds	Par 4	4.04	12	429 yds	Par 4	3.95	18	589 yds	Par 5	4.36

OWR: 2010: 377 **2011:** 338 **2012:** 303 **2013:** 287 **2014:** 242 **5-Year Avg:** 309.4 **5-Year Rank:** 8th

---

Week 5 — Omega Dubai Desert Classic - Dubai, U.A.E. — Event Strength: B-
2/1 — Emirates Golf Club — $2.65 Million

Event (26th): It is hard to imagine today just how groundbreaking the Dubai Desert Classic was upon its 1989 debut, as the European Tour suddenly found itself making an annual visit to a fledgling desert outpost whose golf course was carved from land so barren that it initially contained but a single tree. Perhaps it was the romance of it all (combined with a shortage of winter events to fill out the circuit's growing schedule) but Dubai quickly caught on, as evidenced by names like Ballesteros, Els, Couples and Montgomerie all winning during the first seven playings. Later Els would win twice more, as would Tiger Woods, and it was here in 2009 that a 19-year-old Rory McIlroy scored his first victory as a professional. But as sponsorship deals with Els, Woods and McIlroy have faded, so has the caliber of the event - though it may be encouraging to note an increase in field strength in 2014 following four years worth of steady decline.

Venue: Built by American Karl Litten in 1988, the centrally located Emirates Golf Club kicked off a mini golf boom in Dubai and has served as the event's host for all but two years (1999 and '00). Though hardly a tour de force of strategic design, its very existence seemed a wonder in those early days, and its closer, a 564-yard pond-fronted par 5, has seen plenty of drama over 23 years of professional play.

Designer: Karl Litten (1988) **Yards:** 7,316 **Par:** 72

#	Yds	Par	Avg	#	Yds	Par	Avg	#	Yds	Par	Avg
1	458 yds	Par 4	4.15	7	186 yds	Par 3	3.00	13	550 yds	Par 5	4.54
2	361 yds	Par 4	3.83	8	459 yds	Par 4	4.03	14	434 yds	Par 4	3.94
3	568 yds	Par 5	4.79	9	463 yds	Par 4	4.11	15	190 yds	Par 3	3.14
4	188 yds	Par 3	2.94	10	549 yds	Par 5	4.54	16	425 yds	Par 4	3.83
5	451 yds	Par 4	4.06	11	169 yds	Par 3	2.87	17	359 yds	Par 4	3.46
6	485 yds	Par 4	4.24	12	457 yds	Par 4	4.21	18	564 yds	Par 5	4.65

OWR: 2010: 333 **2011:** 320 **2012:** 291 **2013:** 188 **2014:** 307 **5-Year Avg:** 287.8 **5-Year Rank:** 9th

Week 6 — Maybank Malaysian Open - Kuala Lumpur, Malaysia
2/8 — Kula Lumpur Golf & Country Club

Event Strength: C
$3 Million

Event (17th): The Malaysian Open has spent most of the last few years wedged into a particularly unenviable time slot - the week after The Masters - but has made the most of it, offering significant appearance fees in order to lure names like McIlroy, Westwood, Schwartzel and Oosthuizen into making a very long Sunday night flight. The 2015 playing will move to a theoretically better February slot, but the reality is that it will still be appearance money that draws the big names, particularly as many will be preparing to head for America and the PGA Tour's Florida Swing. Still, lower-ranked E Tour players envisioning a potential big payday can't lick their chops too much; as the event is co-sanctioned by the Asian Tour, a fairly deep roster of that circuit's players are positioned higher up on the priority list.

Venue: Also the home of the PGA Tour's CIMB Classic in November, the West Course at the Kuala Lumpur Golf & Country Club dates to 1991 but was completely renovated in 2008, with the revised version offering tougher bunkering and water hazards meaningfully affecting play on 10 holes. The back nine can cause some exciting leaderboard fluctuations as holes 11, 12 and 13 all rated among the PGA Tour's 100 toughest in 2014, but the closers (two short, watery par 4s and a par 5) are built to provide multiple scoring opportunities.

Designer: Robin Nelson & Neil Haworth (1991) **Yards:** 6,951 **Par:** 72

#	Yds	Par	Avg	#	Yds	Par	Avg	#	Yds	Par	Avg
1	401 yds	Par 4	3.99	7	386 yds	Par 4	3.78	13	459 yds	Par 4	4.31
2	444 yds	Par 4	4.00	8	203 yds	Par 3	3.00	14	358 yds	Par 4	4.04
3	503 yds	Par 5	4.67	9	404 yds	Par 4	3.96	15	199 yds	Par 3	3.21
4	140 yds	Par 3	2.89	10	539 yds	Par 5	4.89	16	318 yds	Par 4	4.11
5	518 yds	Par 5	4.93	11	226 yds	Par 3	3.13	17	336 yds	Par 4	3.86
6	420 yds	Par 4	3.99	12	479 yds	Par 4	4.35	18	634 yds	Par 5	4.86

OWR: 2010: 64 2011: 226 2012: 185 2013: 199 2014: 154 **5-Year Avg:** 165.6 **5-Year Rank:** 16th

---

Week 7 — Thailand Classic - Hua Hin, Thailand
2/15 — Black Mountain Golf Club

Event Strength: New
$2 Million

Event (New): The European Tour returns to Thailand after an eight-year absence with the brand new Thailand Classic, to be played at the scenic Black Mountain Golf Club outside the coastal city of Hua Hin. Co-sanctioned with the Asian Tour (which already plays a late-season event across the Gulf of Thailand at Chon Buri), this event will debut in the traditionally quiet E Tour period between the Desert Swing and the summertime continental schedule - though if the right appearance money is made available, perhaps one or two stars who've already made the trip to Malaysia might perhaps be procured. While sustainability is often an issue with this sort of event, the E Tour has a three-year agreement in place with both organizers and venue, so this figures to stick around at least through 2017.

Venue: Built by Australian architect Phil Ryan in 2007, the Black Mountain Golf Club is attractively situated in a secluded valley, backed up against the base of a 1,400-foot peak. A decidedly modern track, it is built around a network of man-made water hazards which significantly affect nine holes. The course was recently the host of the Asian Tour's King's Cup in early 2014, and had previously entertained that circuit's Black Mountain Masters in 2009 and '10, as well as its own unofficial Black Mountain Invitational (won by Johan Edfors) in 2013.

Designer: Phil Ryan (2007) **Yards:** 7,550 **Par:** 72

#	Yds	Par	#	Yds	Par	#	Yds	Par
1	466 yds	Par 4	7	493 yds	Par 4	13	599 yds	Par 5
2	558 yds	Par 5	8	203 yds	Par 3	14	225 yds	Par 3
3	165 yds	Par 3	9	479 yds	Par 4	15	481 yds	Par 4
4	398 yds	Par 4	10	407 yds	Par 4	16	410 yds	Par 4
5	420 yds	Par 4	11	235 yds	Par 3	17	366 yds	Par 4
6	611 yds	Par 5	12	439 yds	Par 4	18	595 yds	Par 5

OWR: 2010: N/A 2011: N/A 2012: N/A 2013: N/A 2014: N/A **5-Year Avg:** N/A **5-Year Rank:** N/A

Week 8 — Hero Indian Open - New Delhi, India
2/22 — Delhi Golf Club

Event Strength: D
N/A

Event (51st): The India Open is one of Asia's oldest tournaments, dating to 1964, but it will be joining the E Tour for the first time in 2015. As a great supporter of what passed for an Asian Tour in those fledgling days, Australia's Peter Thomson was an early participant, winning two of the first three playings (as well as a third in 1976) and leading a contingent of his mates to regularly compete. By the 1980s, the event took on a more worldwide flavor but strictly as a second-tier stop, with a long list of lesser-known American and Canadian winners who were here because they'd not yet qualified to play closer to home. The tournament became a regular stop on the modern Asian Tour upon that circuit's reformation in 2004 and has since witnessed the standard varied cast of Far Eastern winners, as well as native son Jyoti Randhawa, who won in 2006 and '07. The event was not played in 2014, and will be co-sanctioned with the Asian Tour this year.

Venue: Published reports have the event returning to the Delhi Golf Club, which has hosted all but one playing since 2002. Dating to 1930, the club began life as a municipal facility and came into its present form when Peter Thomson redesigned it during the 1970s. As home of two other 2014 Asian Tour events plus a Ladies European Tour stop, this is one of the more utilized championship layouts anywhere.

Designer: Peter Thomson (1977) **Yards:** 7,036 **Par:** 72

#	Yds	Par	#	Yds	Par	#	Yds	Par
1	518 yds	Par 5	7	230 yds	Par 3	13	386 yds	Par 4
2	377 yds	Par 4	8	518 yds	Par 5	14	516 yds	Par 5
3	445 yds	Par 4	9	445 yds	Par 4	15	353 yds	Par 4
4	418 yds	Par 4	10	474 yds	Par 4	16	412 yds	Par 4
5	182 yds	Par 3	11	437 yds	Par 4	17	171 yds	Par 3
6	401 yds	Par 4	12	208 yds	Par 3	18	545 yds	Par 5

OWR: 2010: 9 2011: 16 2012: 32 2013: 12 2014: N/P **5-Year Avg:** 17.3 **5-Year Rank:** N/A

Week 9 — Joburg Open - Johannesburg, South Africa
3/1 — Royal Johannesburg & Kensington Golf Club (East & West Courses)

Event Strength: C-
€1.3 Million*

Event (9th): Though not yet a decade old, the Joburg Open has carved a niche for itself as one of several late summer (in South Africa) tournaments which, due their E Tour co-sanction, offer far more money (and OWR points) than standard Sunshine Tour events. Having been played at the Royal Johannesburg & Kensington Golf Club throughout, it falls in a time slot in which many of the E Tour's best have headed to Florida, with the result being that beyond early outliers Ariel Cañete (Argentina) and Anders Hansen (Denmark), the trophy has been raised exclusively by South Africans, with Richard Sterne (2008 & '13) and Charl Schwartzel (2010 & '11) each winning twice.

Venue: The first thing one must remember about the courses of the Royal Johannesburg & Kensington Golf Club is that they sit roughly a mile high, so despite appearances, these are actually shortish layouts which regularly yield some very low numbers. Both courses date to before World War II and were built by popular period designer Robert Grimsdell, though each has been modernized considerably over the years. Parkland in style, they are both tree lined, with the property's other primary feature being a creek which traverses its length, and which is flanked by numerous ponds. As the 36 hole splits always demonstrate, the East course is by far the more demanding test.

Designer: Robert Grimsdell (1935)   **Yards:** 7,658   **Par:** 72

#	Yards	Par	Avg	#	Yards	Par	Avg	#	Yards	Par	Avg
1	516 yds	Par 5	4.36	7	459 yds	Par 4	3.99	13	420 yds	Par 4	3.99
2	253 yds	Par 3	3.26	8	553 yds	Par 5	4.47	14	452 yds	Par 4	4.08
3	502 yds	Par 4	4.18	9	425 yds	Par 4	3.99	15	481 yds	Par 4	4.09
4	476 yds	Par 4	4.22	10	518 yds	Par 4	4.30	16	208 yds	Par 3	3.01
5	177 yds	Par 3	3.04	11	500 yds	Par 4	4.26	17	387 yds	Par 4	3.96
6	580 yds	Par 5	4.61	12	200 yds	Par 3	2.99	18	551 yds	Par 5	4.41

OWR: 2010: 81   2011: 49   2012: 81   2013: 89   2014: 70   **5-Year Avg:** 74   **5-Year Rank:** 28th

---

Week 10 — Africa Open - East London, South Africa
3/8 — East London Golf Club

Event Strength: D
€1 Million*

Event (6th): Another late summer South African event which has spent its entire relatively brief existence co-sanctioned by the European Tour, the Africa Open, despite its grand name, is a relatively minor event, paying out a comparatively small purse and drawing generally light fields. The latter issue, at least in part, stems from several times being scheduled the week before the WGC-Match Play - a week in which the nation's top stars have either been traveling to America or already playing there in Los Angeles. Still, its brief ledger of winners includes Charl Schwartzel and Louis Oosthuizen (twice) - but this year it is scheduled head-to-head against the WGC-Cadillac, so...

Venue: The East London Golf Club is one of South Africa's most striking, being situated upon a headland above the Indian Ocean, where it is routed over tumbling, jungle-lined terrain of a sort seldom seen in the U.S. or Europe. Golf has been played here since the 19th century, but the present layout owes mostly to Colonel S.V. Hotchkin, an English military man who turned to golf course design in retirement. At just over 6,600 yards, this will never be backbreaking stuff, leaving scoring to be determined largely by the wind. Consequently numbers have generally been quite low - though things look tougher relative to par since the first hole was converted to a par 4 in 2014.

Designer: S.V. Hotchkin (Unknown)   **Yards:** 6,616   **Par:** 71

#	Yards	Par	Avg	#	Yards	Par	Avg	#	Yards	Par	Avg
1	446 yds	Par 4	4.27	7	386 yds	Par 4	3.78	13	331 yds	Par 4	3.87
2	180 yds	Par 3	2.85	8	366 yds	Par 4	4.01	14	445 yds	Par 4	4.13
3	504 yds	Par 5	4.09	9	470 yds	Par 4	4.19	15	531 yds	Par 5	4.46
4	362 yds	Par 4	3.88	10	175 yds	Par 3	2.85	16	318 yds	Par 4	3.72
5	324 yds	Par 4	3.88	11	477 yds	Par 4	4.06	17	159 yds	Par 3	2.93
6	304 yds	Par 4	3.78	12	428 yds	Par 4	3.96	18	410 yds	Par 4	4.06

OWR: 2010: 25   2011: 79   2012: 47   2013: 26   2014: 25   **5-Year Avg:** 40.4   **5-Year Rank:** 37th

---

Week 11 — Tshwane Open - Waterkloof, South Africa
3/15 — Pretoria Country Club

Event Strength: C-
€1.5 Million*

Event (3rd): The newest of three late summer Sunshine Tour events co-sanctioned by the European Tour, the Tshwane Open spent its first two years in a less-then-enviable schedule slot: wedged into the week which separated the WGC-Match Play and the WGC-Cadillac. As a result, virtually every international player of prominence has been in America during tournament week, meaning that despite the event offering the minimum €1.5 million purse to gain the winner a two-year E Tour exemption (the Joburg and African Open winners only received one), fields have been conspicuously light. Organizers are surely hoping that moving back two calendar weeks will attract more than the four and five OWR top 100 players that appeared in 2013 & '14 - though at least one of them, then #71 Ross Fisher, emerged victorious in 2014.

Venue: The tournament moves to the venerable Pretoria Country Club in 2015, whose doors opened in 1910, but whose present layout dates primarily to a major postwar renovation performed by South Africa's most popular period course designer Robert Grimsdell. However, much of the layout's present aesthetic (particularly the clusters of cookie-cutter bunkers that dot many fairways) owes to alterations by Gary Player's design company in 2005. Notably, at 4,700 feet of altitude, its 7,054 yards will actually play quite short for today's professional.

Designer: Robert Grimsdell (1948)   **Yards:** 7,054   **Par:** 72

#	Yards	Par	#	Yards	Par	#	Yards	Par
1	431 yds	Par 4	7	352 yds	Par 4	13	468 yds	Par 4
2	366 yds	Par 4	8	134 yds	Par 3	14	157 yds	Par 3
3	403 yds	Par 4	9	548 yds	Par 5	15	425 yds	Par 4
4	510 yds	Par 5	10	485 yds	Par 4	16	225 yds	Par 3
5	202 yds	Par 3	11	434 yds	Par 4	17	360 yds	Par 4
6	390 yds	Par 4	12	661 yds	Par 5	18	513 yds	Par 5

OWR: 2010: N/P   2011: N/P   2012: N/P   2013: 53   2014: 65   **5-Year Avg:** 59.0   **5-Year Rank:** 33rd

Week 12 Madeira Islands Open - Portugal - BPI - Madeira, Portugal

Event Strength: D

3/22 Clube de Golf do Santo de Serra

€600,000

Event (23rd): Perhaps because it has long offered on of the lowest purses on the European Tour, the Madeira Islands Open has forever been punted around the circuit's schedule, slotted in one less-desirable week or another. In 2007 & '08 it was played concurrently with the WGC-Cadillac, in 2011 & '13 with the World Match Play, and in 2010, in an all-time moment of scheduling futility, it was slotted head-to-head against The Masters. Combine this with the winner receiving only a one-year E Tour exemption and, predictably, fields have annually been among the weakest on the circuit, with the list of winners being composed mostly of second-tier players. Exceptions have been relatively few and far between, though in recent years Ireland's Michael Hoey (2011) and U.S. prospect Peter Uihlein (2013) have claimed the trophy.

Venue: The Clube do Golf do Santo de Serra actually dates to the 1930s, but it was completely rebuilt in 1991 by Robert Trent Jones, who turned a basic nine-hole track into a modern 27-hole facility. Situated on a 2,000-foot mountaintop in the scenic island's interior, it plays over a notably compact routing and offers numerous panoramic views. The tournament utilizes the Machico and Desertas nines, which add up to a short and relatively easy layout with only three par 4s measuring in excess of 400 yards. Scores, then, are often quite low.

Designer: Robert Trent Jones (1991) **Yards:** 6,826 **Par:** 72

1	398 yds	Par 4	4.01	7	538 yds	Par 5	4.85	13	462 yds	Par 4	4.13
2	441 yds	Par 4	3.89	8	168 yds	Par 3	2.99	14	358 yds	Par 4	3.81
3	521 yds	Par 5	4.64	9	385 yds	Par 4	4.22	15	187 yds	Par 3	3.26
4	202 yds	Par 3	3.14	10	395 yds	Par 4	4.11	16	556 yds	Par 5	4.96
5	412 yds	Par 4	4.21	11	572 yds	Par 5	4.39	17	166 yds	Par 3	2.96
6	364 yds	Par 4	3.97	12	315 yds	Par 4	4.21	18	386 yds	Par 4	4.06

OWR: 2010: 1 **2011:** 1 **2012:** 1 **2013:** 4 **2014:** 0 **5-Year Avg:** 1.8 **5-Year Rank:** 41st

Week 13 Trophée Hassan II - Agadir, Morocco

Event Strength: C-

3/29 Golf du Palais Royal

€1.5 Million

Event (37th): The Trophée Hassan II has only been an official event on the European Tour since 2010, but the tournament has been around since the early 1970s, when noted golf nut King Hassan became a pioneer of the appearance fee game, lavishing gifts upon many of the world's best golfers to appear. After surviving an attack by armed rebels during the inaugural playing, the tournament thrived as an independent event for nearly four decades, with names like Casper, Trevino, Singh, Stewart, Price, Montgomerie and Els all appearing on the trophy. Adding to the event's prestige was the fact that through 2010, it was played at the well known Royal Dar es Salam Golf Club which, during the 1970s, was often rated among the world's best. Its current venue is likely a better a golf course, but in terms of star power at least, fields have actually declined since the E Tour co-sanction began. Still, few events anywhere have enjoyed so colorful a history.

Venue: One of the least known quality golf courses on the planet, the Golf du Palais Royal actually lies within the walls of the Royal Palace, being opened only to host six Moroccan Opens during the 1990s, plus this event since 2011. Built on gently rolling terrain along the Atlantic Ocean, it is a tree-narrowed, heavily bunkered track which would surely rate among Trent Jones's best - if anyone else ever got to play it.

Designer: Robert Trent Jones (1987) **Yards:** 6,951 **Par:** 72

1	530 yds	Par 5	4.59	7	368 yds	Par 4	3.77	13	421 yds	Par 4	3.99
2	208 yds	Par 3	3.25	8	200 yds	Par 3	3.41	14	171 yds	Par 3	3.21
3	433 yds	Par 4	4.31	9	409 yds	Par 4	4.00	15	519 yds	Par 5	4.99
4	467 yds	Par 4	4.18	10	491 yds	Par 5	4.21	16	210 yds	Par 3	2.92
5	580 yds	Par 5	5.04	11	367 yds	Par 4	3.62	17	511 yds	Par 5	4.73
6	371 yds	Par 4	4.07	12	211 yds	Par 3	2.99	18	484 yds	Par 4	4.32

OWR: 2010: 53 **2011:** 53 **2012:** 82 **2013:** 58 **2014:** 57 **5-Year Avg:** 50.6 **5-Year Rank:** 35th

Week 16 Shenzhen International - Shenzhen, China

Event Strength: New

4/19 Genzon Golf Club

N/A

Event (New): Though golf - and, more specifically, the building of golf courses - is officially frowned upon in China, the government there evidently sees nothing hypocritical about hosting multi-million-dollar international tournaments on these supposedly illegal venues. Thus in addition to its well-established Volvo China Open, the European Tour this year adds the Shenzhen International, a 156-man event whose field will be composed of 100 players from the E Tour, 50 from the China Golf Association and six sponsor exemptions. A $2.5 million purse means that things aren't being done on the cheap, and that the winner will receive a full two-year E Tour exemption. The lone negative will be the event's schedule slot - the week immediately following the Masters - which may limit its high-end entrees considerably.

Venue: The Genzon Golf Club can't help but be familiar to E Tour fans as it played host to Alexander Levy's victory in the 2014 Volvo China Open just under a year ago. Built by Neil Haworth in 1995, then renovated (as the club expanded to 36 holes) in 2008, the layout is routed around a huge central lake, which serves as a significant hazard on numerous holes, particularly a final five led by the 470-yard 15th, the 575-yard 17th and the 456-yard 18th. Levy's winning total of 269 was 21 under par, however, so the course will surely yield to quality golf.

Designer: Neil Haworth (1995) **Yards:** 7,145 **Par:** 72

1	358 yds	Par 4	3.85	7	401 yds	Par 4	3.78	13	543 yds	Par 5	4.66
2	547 yds	Par 5	4.75	8	226 yds	Par 3	3.09	14	418 yds	Par 4	3.94
3	186 yds	Par 3	2.90	9	536 yds	Par 5	4.38	15	470 yds	Par 4	4.25
4	437 yds	Par 4	4.04	10	408 yds	Par 4	3.85	16	204 yds	Par 3	3.16
5	475 yds	Par 4	4.29	11	325 yds	Par 4	3.74	17	575 yds	Par 5	4.65
6	375 yds	Par 4	3.94	12	205 yds	Par 3	3.19	18	456 yds	Par 4	4.18

OWR: 2010: N/A **2011:** N/A **2012:** N/A **2013:** N/A **2014:** N/A **5-Year Avg:** N/A6 **5-Year Rank:** N/A

Week 19   AfrAsia Bank Mauritius Open - Bel Hombre, Mauritius   Event Strength: New
5/10   Heritage Golf Club   N/A

Event (New): A new event launched as the rare tri-sanctioned tournament, the AfrAsia Bank Mauritius Open is a joint project of the European, Asian and Sunshine Tours, and will count as an official stop on all three schedules. The field is limited to 138 players composed of 40 players from each of the three tours plus 18 local qualifiers and tournament invitees. Notably, the planned €1 million purse falls well below the E Tour's €1.5 million cutoff line, meaning that the winner will receive only a one-year exemption instead of two - a point which virtually assures that Europe's 40 entries will come from the low end of the deck. This purse is comparably large for the other two circuits, however, so many of their best players are likely to show up. Not surprisingly, this will be the E Tour's first visit to this island nation situated 1,200 miles off the southeast coast of Africa, and it will be interesting to observe the event's longevity in the years ahead.

Venue: The Peter Matkovitch-designed Heritage Golf Club dates to 2004 and is the centerpiece of a resort development along the island's southern coast. Though shortish of stature, the course is well thought of around Africa and utilizes plentiful bunkering and several man-made water hazards at the heart of its challenge. Though the resort is coastal, the golf course is routed entirely inland from the ocean.

Designer: Peter Matkovitch (2004)   **Yards:** 6,685   **Par:** 72

#	Yards	Par	#	Yards	Par	#	Yards	Par
1	438 yds	Par 4	7	527 yds	Par 5	13	167 yds	Par 3
2	494 yds	Par 5	8	208 yds	Par 3	14	526 yds	Par 5
3	181 yds	Par 3	9	312 yds	Par 4	15	168 yds	Par 3
4	407 yds	Par 4	10	396 yds	Par 4	16	427 yds	Par 4
5	318 yds	Par 4	11	387 yds	Par 4	17	429 yds	Par 4
6	403 yds	Par 4	12	357 yds	Par 4	18	540 yds	Par 5

OWR: 2010: N/A   **2011:** N/A   **2012:** N/A   **2013:** N/A   **2014:** N/A   **5-Year Avg:** N/A   **5-Year Rank:** N/A

Week 20   Open de España - Barcelona, Spain   Event Strength: C
5/17   Real Club de Golf El Prat   €1.5 Million*

Event (90th): One of the longer-running stops on the European Tour, the Spanish Open dates to 1912 and will be played for the 90th time in 2015. Other then several incursions by French players (notably three victories by the great Arnaud Massy, including in the inaugural), it honored numerous domestic winners over its first four decades before prominent outsiders like Faulkner, Alliss and Peter Thomson began making inroads after the war. In the modern era, Spain has been well represented by Seve Ballesteros (a three-time champion), though the era's other leading domestic stars haven't fared so well, with Jose-Maria Olazábal never winning here, while men like García, Quirós and, in 2014, Miguel Ángel Jiménez, have raised the trophy only once. In recent years, the event has occupied a May time slot perhaps a tad too close to the flagship BMW PGA - except, of course, for 2013, when it was played immediately after The Masters, assuring a reduced field.

Venue: Having hosted this event nine times, the Real Club de Golf El Prat has been playing golf since before World War I - though the present 45-hole facility is actually the club's third, and was designed by Greg Norman in 2004. As in 2011, the pros will play a long and fairly strong composite course utilizing holes from all three of the club's layouts. The scoring averages below are from the 2011 event.

Designer: Greg Norman (2004)   **Yards:** 7,298   **Par:** 72

#	Yards	Par	Avg	#	Yards	Par	Avg	#	Yards	Par	Avg
1	455 yds	Par 4	4.50	7	545 yds	Par 5	4.86	13	223 yds	Par 3	3.41
2	574 yds	Par 5	4.59	8	160 yds	Par 3	2.92	14	385 yds	Par 4	3.79
3	206 yds	Par 3	2.92	9	466 yds	Par 4	3.98	15	332 yds	Par 4	4.02
4	440 yds	Par 4	4.14	10	582 yds	Par 5	4.88	16	470 yds	Par 4	4.23
5	465 yds	Par 4	4.14	11	182 yds	Par 3	3.09	17	434 yds	Par 4	4.12
6	468 yds	Par 4	4.17	12	369 yds	Par 4	3.95	18	542 yds	Par 5	4.53

OWR: 2010: 100   **2011:** 103   **2012:** 150   **2013:** 83   **2014:** 148   **5-Year Avg:** 116.8   **5-Year Rank:** 26th

Week 21   BMW PGA Championship - Virginia Water, England   Event Strength: B+
5/24   Wentworth Golf Club (West Course)   €4.75 Million*

Event (61st): Today the E Tour's flagship tournament, the BMW PGA actually began life as a closed event, with its first 13 playings being limited to British and Irish PGA members. It remained British-dominated even after opening up (though Arnold Palmer won here in 1975), only becoming more international in flavor after moving to its now-permanent home at Wentworth in 1984. Since that time, the E Tour's elite have had their moments, with names like Montgomerie (thrice), Donald (twice), Ballesteros, Langer and McIlroy all emerging victorious. But perhaps curiously, the trophy is also dotted with names like Way, Harwood, Oldcorn, Drummond and Khan - so one really never knows who might claim victory here. But by any measure, this remains the Tour's top dog, an event that all of its stars annually return home for.

Venue: The West Course at the famed Wentworth Golf Club has long stood among England's elite tournament venues, having hosted the first 44 playings of the World Match Play from 1964-2007. Originally built by the legendary H.S. Colt in 1924, it was long known as a brawny and demanding track, hence its famed nickname "The Burma Road." Heavily renovated by Ernie Els in 2010, however, it is today a far more modern tournament venue whose signature hazard - and Els-added creek fronting the 18th green - does not sing of Golden Age design.

Designer: H.S. Colt (1924)   **Yards:** 7,302   **Par:** 72

#	Yards	Par	Avg	#	Yards	Par	Avg	#	Yards	Par	Avg
1	473 yds	Par 4	4.31	7	396 yds	Par 4	3.99	13	470 yds	Par 4	4.14
2	164 yds	Par 3	3.01	8	391 yds	Par 4	4.11	14	179 yds	Par 3	2.93
3	465 yds	Par 4	4.31	9	449 yds	Par 4	4.26	15	489 yds	Par 4	4.35
4	552 yds	Par 5	4.43	10	184 yds	Par 3	3.11	16	383 yds	Par 4	3.92
5	202 yds	Par 3	2.93	11	416 yds	Par 4	3.95	17	610 yds	Par 5	4.55
6	418 yds	Par 4	4.19	12	531 yds	Par 5	4.65	18	539 yds	Par 5	4.93

OWR: 2010: 413   **2011:** 470   **2012:** 438   **2013:** 403   **2014:** 361   **5-Year Avg:** 417   **5-Year Rank:** 3rd

Week 22	Irish Open - Newcastle, Northern Ireland	Event Strength: C
5/31	Royal County Down Golf Club	€2 Million*

Event (60th): Though the Irish Open debuted in 1927, this will only be its 60th playing, as the event essentially took a quarter-century off (save for 1953) from 1951-1974. Sadly, native players have enjoyed limited success here; indeed, prior to Padraig Harrington and Shane Lowry (as an amateur) winning during the 2000s, only Harry Bradshaw (twice), Christy O'Connor Jr. and John O'Leary had raised the trophy on home soil. Ballesteros, Langer and Montgomerie have all won three times here, though all were clearly outdone by contemporary Nick Faldo, who took the title three times in succession from 1991-1193. Though lacking a primary sponsor in recent years, the event currently carries a greater level of international relevance due to the assumed annual presence of world #1 Rory McIlroy in the field.

Venue: As a special treat for fans, the 2015 the Irish Open will be played at the Royal County Down Golf Club, one of the world's elite links, for the first time since 1939. Originally built by Old Tom Morris but modified by many (including H.S. Colt), this legendary and scenic layout lies beneath the Mountains of Mourne and alongside the Irish Sea, and is notable both for a frequency of blind shots and for being slightly frontloaded, its outward half opening along the water and rating, in many eyes, among the finest nines anywhere in the game.

Designer: Old Tom Morris (1889) **Yards:** 7,186 **Par:** 71

#	Yds	Par	#	Yds	Par	#	Yds	Par
1	539 yds	Par 5	7	144 yds	Par 3	13	446 yds	Par 4
2	444 yds	Par 4	8	429 yds	Par 4	14	212 yds	Par 3
3	475 yds	Par 4	9	483 yds	Par 4	15	468 yds	Par 4
4	229 yds	Par 3	10	196 yds	Par 3	16	337 yds	Par 4
5	440 yds	Par 4	11	442 yds	Par 4	17	433 yds	Par 4
6	396 yds	Par 4	12	525 yds	Par 5	18	548 yds	Par 5

OWR: 2010: 156 **2011:** 127 **2012:** 196 **2013:** 157 **2014:** 115 **5-Year Avg:** 150.2 **5-Year Rank:** 20th

Week 23	Nordea Masters - Malmö, Sweden	Event Strength: C
6/7	PGA Sweden National (Lakes Course)	€1.5 Million*

Event (25th): This will be a milestone year for the event originally known as the Scandinavian Masters, for this will be the tournament's 25th playing - a very strong run for a European Tour event of its vintage. Always slotted in a summer date due to the limited weather window in Sweden, it drew a fair number of top players right from the beginning, with Montgomerie, Faldo, Singh and Westwood joining national hero Jesper Parnevik in claiming spots among the first six winners. Montgomerie, Westwood and Parnevik would become multiple champions here, and the latter's success was emblematic how friendly the event has been to Nordic players over the years, with Joakim Haeggman, Mikko Ilonen (twice), Peter Hanson, Richard S. Johnson and Alexander Noren all carving their names upon the trophy.

Venue: Built by American architect Kyle Phillips, the PGA Sweden National is a modern 36-hole facility whose stronger Lakes Course will be hosting the event for the second straight year. The layout's name comes from the two man-made water hazards which mark its acreage, with the larger of the two greatly affecting a trio of finishers: the 475-yard 9th (whose 4.49 stroke average in 2014 trumpets its difficulty), the demanding, all-carry, 209-yard 17th and the 601-yard 18th, which sweeps leftward along the huge hazard's eastern banks.

Designer: Kyle Phillips (2010) **Yards:** 7,390 **Par:** 72

#	Yds	Par	Avg	#	Yds	Par	Avg	#	Yds	Par	Avg
1	547 yds	Par 5	4.41	7	481 yds	Par 4	4.19	13	443 yds	Par 4	4.04
2	437 yds	Par 4	4.12	8	639 yds	Par 5	4.64	14	334 yds	Par 4	3.59
3	417 yds	Par 4	3.81	9	475 yds	Par 4	4.49	15	170 yds	Par 3	2.93
4	224 yds	Par 3	3.15	10	437 yds	Par 4	3.81	16	476 yds	Par 4	3.96
5	361 yds	Par 4	3.85	11	552 yds	Par 5	4.48	17	209 yds	Par 3	3.10
6	170 yds	Par 3	2.86	12	416 yds	Par 4	3.89	18	601 yds	Par 5	4.85

OWR: 2010: 112 **2011:** 80 **2012:** 113 **2013:** 122 **2014:** 183 **5-Year Avg:** 122.0 **5-Year Rank:** 25th

Week 24	Lyoness Open - Atzenbrugg, Austria	Event Strength: D
6/14	Diamond Country Club	€1 Million*

Event (14th): Few major tour events have witnessed as much change over a quarter-century as the Lyoness Open, which began life as a lower level E Tour event, was played without any major tour affiliation from 1997-2005, then spent several years as a Challenge Tour stop before returning to the big circuit (but as a lower-tier, one-year-exemption event) in 2006. It has also witnessed a plethora of sponsors and operated under at least seven different names, so its now four-year run as the Lyoness Open powered By Greenfinity represents a period of great stability to be sure. Such a history inevitably breeds an eclectic list of winner, and while several lesser players have won here, names like Bernhard Langer, Ryder Cup Captain Paul McGinley and Dutch star Joost Luiten also adorn the trophy. But perhaps most importantly to local fans, Austria's two greatest players, Markus Brier and Bernd Wiesberger, have both claimed the title as well.

Venue: A long and modern layout situated amidst flattish agricultural country, the Diamond Country Club was built in 2000 by American Jeremy Pern, and is routed around a set of large, interconnected man-made lakes. It is noteworthy for its offbeat quartet of finishers: back-to-back par 5s at the 607-yard 15t and 591-yard 16th, followed by the 490-yard dogleg right 17th and a par-3 closer, the 184-yard 18th.

Designer: Jeremy Pern (2000) **Yards:** 7,433 **Par:** 72

#	Yds	Par	Avg	#	Yds	Par	Avg	#	Yds	Par	Avg
1	506 yds	Par 5	4.76	7	411 yds	Par 4	3.83	13	370 yds	Par 4	3.93
2	202 yds	Par 3	3.19	8	468 yds	Par 4	4.19	14	225 yds	Par 3	3.10
3	376 yds	Par 4	3.86	9	479 yds	Par 4	4.14	15	607 yds	Par 5	4.57
4	545 yds	Par 5	4.34	10	504 yds	Par 4	4.17	16	591 yds	Par 5	4.91
5	405 yds	Par 4	4.09	11	437 yds	Par 4	4.10	17	490 yds	Par 4	4.07
6	159 yds	Par 3	2.84	12	474 yds	Par 4	3.97	18	184 yds	Par 3	2.96

OWR: 2010: 36 **2011:** 22 **2012:** 16 **2013:** 27 **2014:** 35 **5-Year Avg:** 25.2 **5-Year Rank:** 38th

Week 26 BMW International Open - Munich, Germany
6/28 Golfclub München Eichenried

Event Strength: C
€2 Million*

Event (27th): Now in its 27th year, the BMW International Open dates to 1989, when the inaugural edition was won by the immortal David Feherty, who routed Fred Couples by five. Feherty's fellow broadcaster Frank Nobilo was also an early winner here (1995), as were other notables like Paul Azinger (twice), Sandy Lyle, Zimbabwe's Mark McNulty and, in the last playing of the old millennium, Colin Montgomerie. In the new century, Thomas Bjørn joined Azinger as the tournament's only two-time winner (2000 and '02) and John Daly (2001) became the second American champion, kicking off a seven-year run that saw elite names like Westwood, Jiménez and Stenson all claim the title. In recent years, a 43-year-old Ernie Els made the event his 28th career E Tour triumph, though no champion could possibly be more popular than Martin Kaymer, who in 2008 became the only German-born player to ever to carve his name on the trophy.

Venue: Since the tournament's inception, it has been played 21 times at the Golfclub Munchen Eichenried, though over the last five years it has alternated between here and the Golfclub Gut Larchenhof. A flattish parkland-style track, Eichenried is frequently tree-lined and offers water meaningfully in play on nine holes, led by the 556-yard pond-fronted 11th and the 319-yard potentially driveable 16th.

Designer: Kurt Rossknecht (1989)   **Yards:** 7,157   **Par:** 72

1	432 yds	Par 4	4.03	7	441 yds	Par 4	4.08	13	372 yds	Par 4	3.81
2	227 yds	Par 3	3.05	8	197 yds	Par 3	2.92	14	490 yds	Par 4	4.38
3	447 yds	Par 4	4.23	9	557 yds	Par 5	4.74	15	464 yds	Par 4	3.92
4	397 yds	Par 4	3.90	10	471 yds	Par 4	4.23	16	319 yds	Par 4	3.62
5	331 yds	Par 4	3.95	11	556 yds	Par 5	4.79	17	189 yds	Par 3	3.04
6	546 yds	Par 5	4.90	12	153 yds	Par 3	2.85	18	568 yds	Par 5	4.26

OWR: 2010: 206   **2011:** 206   **2012:** 147   **2013:** 163   **2014:** 238   **5-Year Avg:** 192.0   **5-Year Rank:** 13th

Week 27 Alstom Open de France - Paris, France
7/5 Le Golf National

Event Strength: B-
€3 Million*

Event (99th): Now fast approaching its 100th playing, the French Open is the rare still-extant event that can boast J.H. Taylor (twice) and James Braid among its champions - and if Harry Vardon didn't join his Triumvirate mates in winning here, the legendary Walter Hagen (1920) isn't a bad alternative. The tournament was initially dominated by the great Arnaud Massy (four victories) and Isle of Jersey native Aubrey Boomer (five), setting the stage for a run of postwar champions that included Hall of Famers Henry Cotton (twice), Roberto de Vicenzo (thrice), Bobby Locke (twice) and even Byron Nelson. In recent years slotted in the run-up to the British Open, the event remains a highlight of the E Tour's summer schedule, still drawing enough international firepower that native champions over the last 40 years have been limited to Jean-Francois Remesy (twice) and Thomas Levet - but Mssrs. Dubuisson, Levy, etc., soon figure to be knocking.

Venue: The site of the 2018 Ryder Cup, Le Golf National is a standard heavily shaped Robert von Hagge design which, like much of the late architect's work, features numerous wildly shaped greens and highly invasive water hazards. This is most apparent down the stretch, where the 399-yard 15th, the 175-yard 16th and the 470-yard 18th all require death-or-glory approaches, often making for eventful finishes.

Designer: Robert von Hagge (1990)   **Yards:** 7,331   **Par:** 71

1	416 yds	Par 4	4.19	7	481 yds	Par 4	4.26	13	427 yds	Par 4	4.16
2	213 yds	Par 3	3.23	8	208 yds	Par 3	3.13	14	607 yds	Par 5	5.01
3	563 yds	Par 5	5.22	9	596 yds	Par 5	4.81	15	399 yds	Par 4	4.25
4	487 yds	Par 4	4.30	10	383 yds	Par 4	4.13	16	175 yds	Par 3	3.19
5	405 yds	Par 4	3.99	11	191 yds	Par 3	3.13	17	484 yds	Par 4	4.19
6	383 yds	Par 4	3.74	12	443 yds	Par 4	4.36	18	470 yds	Par 4	4.86

OWR: 2010: 340   **2011:** 320   **2012:** 282   **2013:** 255   **2014:** 188   **5-Year Avg:** 257.0   **5-Year Rank:** 11th

Week 28 Aberdeen Asset Mgt Scottish Open - Gullane, Scotland
7/12 Gullane Golf Club (Composite Course)

Event Strength: B
€3 Million*

Event (33rd): It may surprise some readers (mostly American) to know that the Scottish Open is not one of the E Tour's older events - in fact, it dates only to 1972. Further, it has not always enjoyed anything resembling the prominence it does today, particularly from 1974-1985, when it wasn't even played. But in our modern era, it has enjoyed a foreigners-get-acclimated time slot immediately before the British Open, with its relevance growing even further following a 2011 move away from Loch Lomond to links layouts at Castle Stuart and Royal Aberdeen. Counting Martin Kaymer, Luke Donald, Phil Mickelson and Justin Rose among its last six winners, the 2014 tournament ranked behind only the season-ending DP World Tour Championship for strength of field among non-Major, non-WGC European Tour events.

Venue: In 2015 the Open will make a first-ever visit to the historic Gullane Golf Club, a much-beloved Scottish links often overshadowed by its near neighbor Muirfield. Gullane has three courses and the Open with primarily play the top-rated Number One layout - but with the added ripples of utilizing several new/temporary tees, as well as a pair of holes (the 7th and 8th) borrowed from the adjacent Number Two course. Consequently, the numbers marked with asterisks below represent Composite course numbers not yet published at press time.

Designer: Unknown (1884)   **Yards:** 7,176*   **Par:** 70*

1	412 yds	Par 4	7	471 yds	Par 4	13	478 yds	Par 4
2	523 yds	Par 5	8	194 yds	Par 3	14	470 yds*	Par 4
3	164 yds	Par 3	9	466 yds	Par 4	15	420 yds*	Par 4
4	450 yds	Par 4	10	471 yds	Par 4	16	610 yds*	Par 5
5	337 yds	Par 4	11	480 yds	Par 4	17	194 yds	Par 3
6	398 yds	Par 4	12	178 yds	Par 3	18	460 yds*	Par 4

OWR: 2010: 359   **2011:** 355   **2012:** 289   **2013:** 240   **2014:** 366   **5-Year Avg:** 321.8   **5-Year Rank:** 7th

Week 30   **Omega European Masters - Crans Montana, Switzerland**   **Event Strength: C**
7/26   Crans-sur-Sierre Golf Club   €2.3 Million*

Event (81st): For those who may wonder why, amidst the roster of national opens which dot the E Tour's continental schedule, so affluent a country as Switzerland is missing, such was not always the case. For the Omega European Masters began life in 1923 as the Swiss Open, and it remained that way all the way through 1982. Over those first six decades, the roster of winners was truly an international one, with many hailing from around the continent and Britain, but many more coming from Australia (Nagle, Marsh, Vines), New Zealand (Charles), South Africa (Locke, Henning, Baiocchi and Hayes) and Zimbabwe (Price). In the modern era, an early September time slot has done little to strengthen fields, but organizers are optimistic that all of that will change this year with a move to the week following the British Open, and early indications suggest that both Rory McIlroy and Adam Scott (who owns a home nearby) may add the event to their schedules.

Venue: Among the more scenic courses in Europe, the Crans-sur-Sierre Golf Club began playing golf as early as 1906, but the present course owes primarily to a post-World War I rebuild, with changes made by Seve Ballesteros during the 1990s. Playing terribly short at nearly 4,800', it annually yields very low scoring - even with the 559-yard (downhill) 15th now played as professional golf's longest par 4.

Designer: Harry Nicholson (1926)   **Yards:** 6,848   **Par:** 70

#	Yds	Par	Avg	#	Yds	Par	Avg	#	Yds	Par	Avg
1	540 yds	Par 5	4.46	7	331 yds	Par 4	3.39	13	195 yds	Par 3	2.94
2	446 yds	Par 4	4.15	8	175 yds	Par 3	3.06	14	559 yds	Par 4	4.23
3	191 yds	Par 3	3.07	9	633 yds	Par 5	4.67	15	516 yds	Par 5	4.49
4	503 yds	Par 4	4.20	10	406 yds	Par 4	4.06	16	235 yds	Par 3	3.34
5	364 yds	Par 5	4.10	11	217 yds	Par 3	3.33	17	394 yds	Par 4	3.99
6	324 yds	Par 4	3.68	12	417 yds	Par 4	4.06	18	402 yds	Par 4	3.96

OWR: 2010: 137   **2011:** 244   **2012:** 156   **2013:** 140   **2014:** 142   **5-Year Avg:** 163.8   **5-Year Rank:** 17th

---

Week 31   **Saltire Energy Paul Lawrie Match Play - Aberdeen, Scotland**   **Event Strength: New**
8/2   Murcar Links Golf Club   €1 Million

Event (New): Coming rather out of left field, this is a brand new event to be contested over another ancient Scottish links - and at match play, no less! Scheduled in the normally quiet week when the elite head back to America for the WGC-Bridgestone Invitational and the PGA Championship, it will host a 64-player field and, unlike the newly revamped WGC Match Play event, will be contested as a single-elimination event - one loss and you're down the road. Given all of the above, a fairly light first-year purse of €1 million, and the winner gaining only a one-year E Tour exemption because of that, it seems unlikely that many of the world's elite (maybe Ian Poulter?) will be here. It will, however, be a treat for TV viewers worldwide, who are given precious few opportunities to see match play, or a professional contest played over a genuine links.

Venue: As with most of Scotland's venerated links, golf at Murcar is an ancient proposition - though dating to "only" to 1909, this is hardly one the region's oldest. The course is palpably short by modern standards (a far less relevant state of affairs in match play) with only the 453-yard dogleg 6th and the 423-yard burn-crossing 7th really measuring up among the par 4s. Further, viewers may be disappointed to find that the seaside holes all come early - but when the wind blows, this figures to be a fascinating venue, particularly at match play.

Designer: Archie Simpson (1909)   **Yards:** 6,516   **Par:** 71

#	Yds	Par	#	Yds	Par	#	Yds	Par
1	322 yds	Par 4	7	423 yds	Par 4	13	386 yds	Par 4
2	404 yds	Par 4	8	383 yds	Par 4	14	540 yds	Par 5
3	401 yds	Par 4	9	323 yds	Par 4	15	383 yds	Par 4
4	489 yds	Par 5	10	400 yds	Par 4	16	172 yds	Par 3
5	176 yds	Par 3	11	367 yds	Par 4	17	367 yds	Par 4
6	453 yds	Par 4	12	155 yds	Par 3	18	372 yds	Par 4

OWR: 2010: N/A   **2011:** N/A   **2012:** N/A   **2013:** N/A   **2014:** N/A   **5-Year Avg:** N/A   **5-Year Rank:** N/A

Week 34   **Made In Denmark - Aalborg, Denmark**   **Event Strength: C-**
8/23   Himmerland Golf & Spa Resort (PGA Backtee Course)   €1.5 Million*

Event (2nd): Only the second major professional golf event ever to be played in Denmark (following the one-off Nordic Open in 2003), the Made In Denmark debuted in 2014 at the Himmerland Resort, ending the game's 11-year absence in a nation where its popularity has grown markedly. And while hardly a high-powered international tournament, the event did arrive with two significant things going for it: a three-year sponsorship agreement (guaranteeing its existence through at least 2016) and a €1.5 million purse - the minimum required to award its winner a two-year European Tour exemption. Consequently its inaugural field was a notch better than many such events - particularly one played in the week following the WGC-Bridgestone and the PGA Championship. Mandatory attendance by Mssrs. Bjørn and Olesen certainly didn't hurt.

Venue: The largest golf resort in northern Europe, the Himmerland Resort & Spa dates to the 1980s, when architect Jan Sederholm built 36 original holes. But the stronger 18 (today's PGA Backtee Course) was significantly renovated in 2013 by one Philip Spogárd, resulting in somewhat more classically styled track that makes surprisingly little use of water for a layout of its vintage. One year is hardly a significant sampling but judging by Marc Warren's nine-under-par 275 winning total in 2014, the layout's hardly a pushover either.

Designer: Philip Spogárd (2013)   **Yards:** 7,033   **Par:** 71

#	Yds	Par	Avg	#	Yds	Par	Avg	#	Yds	Par	Avg
1	368 yds	Par 4	4.14	7	186 yds	Par 3	3.17	13	628 yds	Par 5	5.00
2	203 yds	Par 3	3.13	8	379 yds	Par 4	3.90	14	394 yds	Par 4	3.68
3	342 yds	Par 4	3.80	9	490 yds	Par 4	4.15	15	392 yds	Par 4	3.92
4	549 yds	Par 5	4.70	10	155 yds	Par 3	3.05	16	128 yds	Par 3	3.11
5	433 yds	Par 4	4.21	11	644 yds	Par 5	5.06	17	409 yds	Par 4	3.87
6	471 yds	Par 4	4.21	12	443 yds	Par 4	4.17	18	419 yds	Par 4	4.08

OWR: 2010: N/P   **2011:** N/P   **2012:** N/P   **2013:** N/P   **2014:** 52   **5-Year Avg:** 52.0   **5-Year Rank:** 34th

Week 35 D+D Real Czech Masters - Prague, Czech Republic
8/30 Albatross Golf Resort

Event Strength: C-
€1 Million*

Event (2nd): The D+D Real Czech Masters came into existence in tandem with the Made In Denmark event in 2014, and once again in year two the pair will stick together on the schedule, filling a lean late-August period when the E Tour's elite are likely in America starting the FedEx Cup Playoffs. Still, this debut event in a country devoid of stars and largely devoid of a golfing culture ranked 32nd in field strength - meaning that nine other E Tour events failed to equal it. In point of fact, the Tour had actually been in the Czech Republic fairly recently, spending three official seasons sponsoring the Czech Open from 2009-2011. But generating long-term spectator interest may well remain a challenge in a nation which had not a single player listed in the exhaustive Official World Golf Ranking at the close of 2014.

Venue: Set on a broadly sloping patch of former agricultural land, the Albatross Golf Resort was built by Austrian-based Keith Preston in 2010 and represents the prototypical new millennium course designed for tournament play. It offers considerable length and lots of modern bunkering, though its most memorable holes tend to be those affected by a quintet of man-made water hazards. The water is particularly notable over a trio of closers led by the 217-yard 16th and the 417-yard 18th, both of which play to greens tucked beyond front-left hazards.

Designer: Keith Preston (2010) **Yards:** 7,466 **Par:** 72

#	Yds	Par		#	Yds	Par		#	Yds	Par	
1	538 yds	Par 5	4.77	7	195 yds	Par 3	3.14	13	215 yds	Par 3	3.16
2	394 yds	Par 4	4.02	8	483 yds	Par 4	4.43	14	449 yds	Par 4	4.05
3	219 yds	Par 3	3.34	9	639 yds	Par 5	4.86	15	465 yds	Par 4	4.02
4	379 yds	Par 4	4.25	10	603 yds	Par 5	4.92	16	217 yds	Par 3	3.27
5	451 yds	Par 4	4.07	11	424 yds	Par 4	4.14	17	490 yds	Par 4	4.40
6	348 yds	Par 4	3.83	12	540 yds	Par 5	4.36	18	417 yds	Par 4	4.13

OWR: 2010: N/P 2011: N/P 2012: N/P 2013: N/P 2014: 62 **5-Year Avg:** 62.0 **5-Year Rank:** 32nd

---

Week 36 M2M Russian Open - Moscow, Russia
9/6 Tseleevo Golf & Polo Club

Event Strength: C
€1 Million*

Event (9th): Seemingly one of the least likely tournaments in the world at the time of its creation, the Russian Open dates to 1996, though the European Tour (whose lesser players filled much of the event's early fields) has fluctuated in its degree of official recognition. From 1999-2002, then again from 2009-2012, it was only recognized as a Challenge Tour stop, whereas from 2003-2008, and presently since 2013, it fills an otherwise quiet E Tour schedule slot which today falls head-to-head against the PGA Tour's FedEx Cup playoffs. Add this to a small purse and, perhaps, some general player ambivalence towards playing in Russia and the inevitable result is an event which annually draws among the circuit's weakest fields (only Madeira Islands has rated below it of late), and which has produced rather an eclectic set of champions - though to be sure, recent winners David Horsey and Michael Hoey are legitimate world-class players.

Venue: Though it has not been officially stated by the E Tour, it appears that the Russian Open will return for a third straight year to the Tseleevo Golf & Polo Club, which actually lies 25 miles north of Moscow. A typically strong Jack Nicklaus design, the tree-lined layout offers plenty of water, as well as a noteworthy run of five long par 4s between the 7th-12th, all of which generally average over-par figures.

Designer: Jack Nicklaus (2007) **Yards:** 7,491 **Par:** 72

#	Yds	Par		#	Yds	Par		#	Yds	Par	
1	430 yds	Par 4	4.08	7	454 yds	Par 4	4.05	13	189 yds	Par 3	3.29
2	404 yds	Par 4	3.91	8	564 yds	Par 5	4.42	14	374 yds	Par 4	4.00
3	191 yds	Par 3	2.98	9	452 yds	Par 4	4.18	15	569 yds	Par 5	4.71
4	586 yds	Par 5	4.67	10	480 yds	Par 4	4.23	16	223 yds	Par 3	2.88
5	428 yds	Par 4	4.27	11	477 yds	Par 4	4.14	17	570 yds	Par 5	4.73
6	182 yds	Par 3	3.09	12	470 yds	Par 4	4.32	18	448 yds	Par 4	4.06

OWR: 2010: N/P 2011: N/P 2012: N/P 2013: 9 2014: 3 **5-Year Avg:** 6 **5-Year Rank:** 40th

---

Week 37 KLM Open - Zandvoort, Netherlands
9/13 Kennemer Golf & Country Club

Event Strength: C
€1.8 Million*

Event (91st): Another long-running national open in a nation where golf has seldom been the most popular of games, the Dutch Open (currently using only its sponsor's name, KLM) dates to 1919, when it was claimed by a homegrown player, one D. Oosterweer. Thereafter, only two other little-known Dutchmen would raise the trophy over the next 83 years, a period during which names like Aubrey Boomer (a three-time early winner), Belgian star Flory van Donck (a five-time champion), pioneering black South African Sewsunker Sewgolum (three times) and Seve Ballesteros (ditto) dominated the proceedings. But native son Martin Lefeber ended a 55-year drought by claiming an unlikely victory in 2003 and, after a near miss in 2007, the Netherlands' greatest-ever prospect, Joost Luiten, carried off the trophy in 2013.

Venue: One of 10 courses built by the great H.S. Colt in the Netherlands, the Kennemer Golf & Country Club is widely rated among the very best courses in continental Europe, and will be hosting this event for the 22nd time. Though lying several minutes inland from the sea, Colt's layout is partially routed through some impressive dunes, and it must be noted that the Dutch Open course is actually a composite, making use of holes from three different nines. The 163-yard 15th (whose green sits 50 feet above fronting bunkers) is justifiably famous.

Designer: H.S. Colt (1927) **Yards:** 6,626 **Par:** 70

#	Yds	Par		#	Yds	Par		#	Yds	Par	
1	434 yds	Par 4	4.22	7	562 yds	Par 5	4.68	13	374 yds	Par 4	3.99
2	570 yds	Par 5	4.78	8	222 yds	Par 3	3.01	14	384 yds	Par 4	4.01
3	148 yds	Par 3	2.86	9	418 yds	Par 4	4.05	15	163 yds	Par 3	3.04
4	399 yds	Par 4	4.00	10	447 yds	Par 4	4.03	16	473 yds	Par 4	4.26
5	419 yds	Par 4	4.18	11	158 yds	Par 3	3.28	17	170 yds	Par 3	3.09
6	363 yds	Par 4	3.58	12	525 yds	Par 5	4.55	18	397 yds	Par 4	4.03

OWR: 2010: 164 2011: 211 2012: 142 2013: 93 2014: 123 **5-Year Avg:** 146.6 **5-Year Rank:** 21st

Week 38 72° Open d'Italia - Monza, Italy
9/20 Golf Club Milano

Event Strength: C-
€1.5 Million*

Event (73rd): Though Italy is another European country in which golf took many decades to truly take root, the Italian Open still managed to get up and going relatively early (1926), when it was won by a native son, one F. Pasquali. But unlike some other continental nations slow to embrace the game on a large scale, Italy managed to produce a surprising early crop of home-grown players, with men like Casera, Angelini and Grappasonni all claiming the title in the years following World War II. In the modern era, the event has generally been slotted in either May or September/October, with recent playings being relegated to the latter, often going head-to-head against the PGA Tour's FedEx Cup Playoffs. The result has been predictably light fields - though at least the tournament can presently count on the presence of the Molinari brothers and Matteo Manassero to boost its rating. Both Hennie Otto and Gonzalo Fernandez-Castaño are two-time winners.

Venue: Following a 24-year absence, then Open returns to the Golf Club Milano, a Golden Age layout carved from a forest bordering the famed Monza racetrack - which, thankfully, is only rarely in use. Though a basic layout from a tactical perspective, the course is made at least somewhat more challenging by its tree-lined nature, with the flattish parkland setting widely considered among the most idyllic in Italy.

Designer: Peter Gannon & Cecil Blandford (1928)   **Yards:** 6,814   **Par:** 72

#	Yards	Par	#	Yards	Par	#	Yards	Par
1	497 yds	Par 5	7	193 yds	Par 3	13	451 yds	Par 4
2	418 yds	Par 4	8	400 yds	Par 4	14	497 yds	Par 5
3	189 yds	Par 3	9	554 yds	Par 5	15	409 yds	Par 4
4	343 yds	Par 4	10	213 yds	Par 3	16	500 yds	Par 5
5	416 yds	Par 4	11	381 yds	Par 4	17	377 yds	Par 4
6	383 yds	Par 4	12	148 yds	Par 3	18	445 yds	Par 4

OWR: 2010: 77   **2011:** 67   **2012:** 125   **2013:** 71   **2014:** 87   **5-Year Avg:** 85.4   **5-Year Rank:** 27th

---

Week 39 European Open - Bad Griesbach, Germany
9/27 Golf Resort Bad Griesbach (Beckenbauer Course)

Event Strength: New
N/A

Event (33rd): It is rare that an event billed as one of a tour's most significant shutters its operations only to return several years later, but such is the case with the European Open, whose last playing was in 2009 at the London Golf Club. The tournament dates to 1978 and despite its all-encompassing name, was played exclusively within the British Isles and Ireland during its initial 32-year run - though with venues like Turnberry, Hoylake, Walton Heath and Sunningdale in the early rotation, it's doubtful that many were complaining. Fields were generally strong and while lesser names like Way, Murray, Gilford and even American Bobby Wadkins (who won the inaugural) dot the trophy, also appearing are Hall-of-Famers like Lyle, Aoki, Langer, Norman, Montgomerie and Faldo, as well as contemporary stars including Woosnam, Westwood and Goosen. And if the revived version manages to boast winners of that quality, everybody will be happy.

Venue: Routed over a flat flood plain adjacent to the River Rott, the Bad Griesbach Resort's Beckenbauer course was built by Bernhard Langer but named for an even bigger German sporting legend, soccer hero Franz Beckenbauer. A thoroughly modern track, its most notable holes nearly all involve man-made lakes, led by the 429-yard 9th, the 566-yard dogleg right 12th and the very demanding 468-yard 18th.

Designer: Bernard Langer & Kurt Rossknecht (2002)   **Yards:** 7,092   **Par:** 72

#	Yards	Par	#	Yards	Par	#	Yards	Par
1	421 yds	Par 4	7	225 yds	Par 3	13	369 yds	Par 4
2	374 yds	Par 4	8	578 yds	Par 5	14	183 yds	Par 3
3	547 yds	Par 5	9	429 yds	Par 4	15	437 yds	Par 4
4	217 yds	Par 3	10	514 yds	Par 5	16	353 yds	Par 4
5	455 yds	Par 4	11	378 yds	Par 4	17	178 yds	Par 3
6	400 yds	Par 4	12	566 yds	Par 5	18	468 yds	Par 4

OWR: 2010: N/A   **2011:** N/A   **2012:** N/A   **2013:** N/A   **2014:** N/A   **5-Year Avg:** N/A   **5-Year Rank:** N/A

Week 40 Alfred Dunhill Links Championship - St Andrews, Scotland
10/4 The Old Course, etc.

Event Strength: B-
$5 Million*

Event (15th): A pro-am played over three courses (but always spending Sunday at St Andrews), the Alfred Dunhill Links Championship is strictly a new millennium affair, having made its debut in 2001. The event has always been slotted in the fall, and nowadays finds itself in a potentially nice week between the close of the FedEx Cup Playoffs and the start of the E Tour's Final Series. Perhaps because a trio of links are utilized, players from the United Kingdom and Ireland have long fared well here; indeed, names like Lawrie, Harrington (twice) and Westwood appear upon the trophy, and only three overseas players (Robert Karlsson, Martin Kaymer and Brandon Grace) have found the winners circle over the first 14 playings. Notably, Rory McIlroy finished third here in 2007 - his first event as an 18-year-old pro.

Venue: What is there to say about an event that plays over seven-time British Open host Carnoustie and a great modern links at Kingsbarns - and these are the week's *least desirable* rounds? St Andrews is, as ever, the story here, and despite some recent disfigurement by the same R & A whose abrogation of regulatory responsibility made the course vulnerable in the first place, it remains the game's most timeless venue. The Eden, Hell Bunker, the Principal's Nose, the Road Hole... For golf fans, it just doesn't get much better than this.

Designer: Mother Nature (Unknown)   **Yards:** 7,279   **Par:** 72

#	Yards	Par	#	Yards	Par	#	Yards	Par
1	376 yds	Par 4	7	390 yds	Par 4	13	465 yds	Par 4
2	453 yds	Par 4	8	175 yds	Par 3	14	618 yds	Par 5
3	397 yds	Par 4	9	352 yds	Par 4	15	456 yds	Par 4
4	480 yds	Par 4	10	380 yds	Par 4	16	423 yds	Par 4
5	568 yds	Par 5	11	174 yds	Par 3	17	455 yds	Par 4
6	412 yds	Par 4	12	348 yds	Par 4	18	357 yds	Par 4

OWR: 2010: 310   **2011:** 398   **2012:** 272   **2013:** 189   **2014:** 252   **5-Year Avg:** 284.2   **5-Year Rank:** 10th

Week 42 Portugal Masters - Vilamoura, Portugal
10/18 Oceanico Victoria Golf Club

Event Strength: C
€2 Million*

Event (9th): With the Algarve Portuguese Open discontinued as of 2011, October's Portugal Masters is now this resort-oriented region's lone stop on the European PGA Tour. The event debuted in 2007 and has always been played in the autumn, when colder weather in northern Europe greatly limits the Tour's geographic possibilities (e.g., in its first year, it was surrounded by a trio of events in neighboring Spain). As this tends to be a period of rest for the game's elite, fields here generally fall within the Tour's mid-range, though Lee Westwood did add an element of luster upon winning in 2009. As seems the case since Hall-of-Famer Henry Cotton retired to this region in the 1960s, Britons have fared well here, with four Englishmen (plus Ireland's Shane Lowry) ranking among the first eight champions. Despite the Algarve's usually fine weather, the 2014 edition was nearly washed away, with Alexander Levy being declared the winner after 36 holes.

Venue: Built by Arnold Palmer's design company in 2004, the Oceanico Victoria Golf Club lies a mile inland from the ocean and is a standard Palmer design of the period, blending mostly functional holes with the odd tactically rich entry thrown in. Scoring is generally low here; in the soft conditions of 2014, Alexander Levy shot 63-61 - after runner-up Nicolas Colsaerts opened with an 11-under-par 60 on Thursday.

Designer: Arnold Palmer (2004) **Yards:** 7,209 **Par:** 71

1	446 yds	Par 4	4.11	7	510 yds	Par 5	4.26	13	200 yds	Par 3	2.96
2	358 yds	Par 4	3.58	8	168 yds	Par 3	3.00	14	424 yds	Par 4	3.94
3	481 yds	Par 4	4.18	9	442 yds	Par 4	3.90	15	315 yds	Par 4	3.49
4	407 yds	Par 4	3.82	10	406 yds	Par 4	3.90	16	208 yds	Par 4	3.06
5	579 yds	Par 5	4.36	11	385 yds	Par 4	3.85	17	589 yds	Par 5	4.92
6	218 yds	Par 3	2.85	12	593 yds	Par 5	4.86	18	463 yds	Par 4	4.47

OWR: 2010: 166 **2011:** 167 **2012:** 173 **2013:** 158 **2014:** 107 **5-Year Avg:** 154.2 **5-Year Rank:** 18th

Week 43 Hong Kong Open - Fanling, Hong Kong
10/25 Hong Kong Golf Club

Event Strength: C
$1.3 Million*

Event (55th): A centerpiece of the old Asian Tour in its formative days, the Hong Kong Open dates to 1959 and was dominated over its first 25 years by players from Asia and Australia, with Hall-of-Famers Peter Thomson (thrice) and Greg Norman (twice) both scoring multiple wins. American Orville Moody was the first western winner in 1971, but by the late 1980s a more regular international presence led to men like Tom Watson, Bernhard Langer, Ian Woosnam and David Frost all claiming the title. The E Tour began co-sanctioning the event in 2001 (as an official part of their 2002 schedule) but despite the obvious added prestige therein, the tournament's usual November/December time slot has seldom proved conducive to drawing big fields. A 2015 move to late October may help, however, as this will now be the final regular season event of the E Tour schedule, and will also sit just before the first two Final Series events, which are played in China.

Venue: Long adorned with a "Royal" when the British ruled the roost, the Hong Kong Golf Club began playing the game on its Fanling property in 1911, but that layout was systematically rebuilt over the decades as the club expanded to 54 holes. Scoring is always low on the club's composite tournament course, and many a dramatic moment has occurred at the attractive 18th, a 410-yard pond-fronted finisher.

Designer: Unknown (1911, etc.) **Yards:** 6,699 **Par:** 70

1	468 yds	Par 4	4.42	7	379 yds	Par 4	4.05	13	529 yds	Par 5	4.45
2	149 yds	Par 3	2.79	8	188 yds	Par 3	3.12	14	395 yds	Par 4	4.02
3	551 yds	Par 5	4.71	9	493 yds	Par 4	4.30	15	427 yds	Par 4	4.02
4	288 yds	Par 4	3.73	10	367 yds	Par 4	3.74	16	411 yds	Par 4	4.05
5	192 yds	Par 3	3.09	11	466 yds	Par 4	4.17	17	406 yds	Par 4	3.86
6	436 yds	Par 4	3.95	12	144 yds	Par 3	2.94	18	410 yds	Par 4	4.33

OWR: 2010: 199 **2011:** 196 **2012:** 161 **2013:** 40 **2014:** 44 **5-Year Avg:** 128.0 **5-Year Rank:** 24th

Week 44 BMW Masters - Shanghai, China
11/1 Lake Malaren Golf Club

Event Strength: B
$7 Million*

Event (4th): Initially created in 2012 to front the WGC-HSBC Champions (and thus give the E Tour a two-week stopover in China), the BMW Masters immediately established itself as one of the circuit's marquee fall events - thus making it ideally suited to be plugged into the four-event Final Series (along with its WGC partner) when the Series debuted in 2013. Largely because of its pre-WGC positioning, the event has actually drawn a smattering of American players who have nothing to do with the Final Series, though its initial winners - Hanson, Fernández-Castaño and Siem - have all been full-time E Tour players. For a combination of weather and sponsorship reasons, the E Tour pretty well must be in Asia at this time of the year. So with a high-octane venue and the WGC coming right on its heels, so long as BMW (or someone else) is willing to plunk $7 million in sponsorship money, this figures to remain a prominent stop for the foreseeable future.

Venue: A huge made-for-tournament-play layout situated in fairly developed territory northwest of downtown, the Lake Malaren Golf Club actually represents a Nicklaus redesign of the club's far less-impressive original layout. Predictably, water is a regular presence, with man-made hazards affecting nine holes, but more readily recognized are the several massive waste bunkers that eat up vast areas of acreage.

Designer: Jack Nicklaus (2011) **Yards:** 7,607 **Par:** 72

1	439 yds	Par 4	3.99	7	568 yds	Par 5	4.56	13	544 yds	Par 5	4.97
2	384 yds	Par 4	3.87	8	484 yds	Par 4	4.42	14	483 yds	Par 4	4.24
3	574 yds	Par 5	5.01	9	470 yds	Par 4	4.36	15	612 yds	Par 5	4.50
4	212 yds	Par 3	3.14	10	426 yds	Par 4	3.91	16	420 yds	Par 4	4.36
5	495 yds	Par 4	4.33	11	380 yds	Par 4	3.62	17	201 yds	Par 3	3.54
6	202 yds	Par 3	3.23	12	242 yds	Par 3	3.23	18	471 yds	Par 4	4.63

OWR: 2010: N/P **2011:** N/P **2012:** 415 **2013:** 327 **2014:** 208 **5-Year Avg:** 340.0 **5-Year Rank:** 5th

Week 45 — WGC-HSBC Champions - Shanghai, China
11/8 — Sheshan International Golf Club
Event Strength: A
$8.5 Million

Event (10th): Initially sanctioned by the European, Asian, Sunshine and Australasian Tours, the HSBC Champions debuted in 2005 and invited all previous-year winners on each tour plus anyone inclined to play from the OWR top 50. But finally finding an overseas sponsor with deep enough pockets, the Federation of Tours answered criticism of their "World" Golf Championship events all being played in America by granting the event WGC status in 2009, causing its already solid fields to take a great leap in quality. Not surprisingly, the list of winners is a strong one, counting Phil Mickelson as its lone two-time champion (his first came in 2007), and names like Els, Westwood and Woods among those who have more than once finished as runner-up. Despite offering $500,000 less in prize money than its three WGC siblings, the event should continue to draw very strong fields given its WGC status and a schedule slot in which there is little worldwide competition.

Venue: The event's host since 2006 (save for 2012), the Nelson & Haworth-designed Sheshan International Golf Club has in recent years yielded some notably low scoring, with the last three winners being 19, 20 and 24 shots under par. There is the potential for some late-round fireworks as well, with the 16th being a 288-yard driveable par 4 and the 538-yard 18th a similarly reachable (if watery) par 5.

Designer: Robin Nelson & Neil Haworth (2004) **Yards:** 7,266 **Par:** 72

#	Yds	Par	Avg	#	Yds	Par	Avg	#	Yds	Par	Avg
1	459 yds	Par 4	4.02	7	346 yds	Par 4	3.91	13	411 yds	Par 4	3.88
2	550 yds	Par 5	4.57	8	603 yds	Par 5	4.99	14	594 yds	Par 5	4.57
3	362 yds	Par 4	3.77	9	486 yds	Par 4	4.23	15	487 yds	Par 4	4.12
4	200 yds	Par 3	2.98	10	401 yds	Par 4	3.91	16	288 yds	Par 4	3.72
5	456 yds	Par 4	4.05	11	456 yds	Par 4	4.13	17	212 yds	Par 3	3.24
6	200 yds	Par 3	3.06	12	217 yds	Par 3	2.99	18	538 yds	Par 5	4.81

OWR: 2010: N/A **2011:** 621 **2012:** N/A **2013:** 528 **2014:** 574 **5-Year Avg:** 574.3 **5-Year Rank:** 1st

---

Week 46 — Turkish Airlines Open - Antalya, Turkey
11/15 — Montgomerie Maxx Royal
Event Strength: B
$7 Million*

Event (3rd): One of the newer kids on the European Tour block, the Turkish Airlines Open made quite a splash with its 2013 debut, putting $7 million dollars on the table to buy its way into the penultimate spot in the circuit's lucrative Final series. Given the geopolitical issues affecting Turkey these days, it's hard to say whether such an investment in promoting the nation's tourism sector was a wise one, but it has thus far at least proven a stable one, making this an important and high-profile E Tour stop. Notable over its first two editions were the performances of a pair of young international stars, France's Victor Dubuisson (who claimed his first win here in 2013) and American Brooks Koepka, who split time between the U.S. and Europe in 2014 before also claiming his first major tour victory here in November.

Venue: The centerpiece of a multi-golf course resort complex built along the Mediterranean coast, the Montgomerie Maxx Royal is a mid-size test which has thus far proven susceptible to low professional scoring - Dubuisson, for example, being 24 under par in 2013. The course is built slightly inland but amidst a blend of forest and sand ridges, making for an attractive setting. Also, it's offbeat mix of five par 5s and five par 3s adds great variety, and both the driveable 337-yard 15th and the 558-yard 18th offer chances for some late fireworks.

Designer: Colin Montgomerie (2008) **Yards:** 7,132 **Par:** 72

#	Yds	Par	Avg	#	Yds	Par	Avg	#	Yds	Par	Avg
1	571 yds	Par 5	4.64	7	459 yds	Par 4	4.28	13	564 yds	Par 5	4.72
2	162 yds	Par 3	2.90	8	182 yds	Par 3	2.96	14	176 yds	Par 3	2.90
3	401 yds	Par 4	3.81	9	446 yds	Par 4	4.03	15	337 yds	Par 4	3.72
4	576 yds	Par 5	4.42	10	362 yds	Par 4	3.82	16	180 yds	Par 3	2.95
5	224 yds	Par 3	3.13	11	570 yds	Par 5	4.76	17	392 yds	Par 4	3.96
6	482 yds	Par 4	4.28	12	490 yds	Par 4	4.36	18	558 yds	Par 5	4.47

OWR: 2010: N/P **2011:** N/P **2012:** N/P **2013:** 370 **2014:** 294 **5-Year Avg:** 332.0 **5-Year Rank:** 6th

---

Week 47 — DP World Tour Championship, Dubai - Dubai, U.A.E.
11/22 — Jumeirah Golf Estates (Earth Course)
Event Strength: B+
$8 Million*

Event (7th): Originally created to be a glamorous, big-money wrap up to the European Tour season, the DP World Tour Championship debuted in 2009 as the circuit's second annual stop in Dubai before eventually morphing into the last event in the Tour's annual Final Series beginning in 2013. With the PGA Tour's season over (at least for it's stars) by these late-November dates, the Tour Championship has tended to own the world golfing stage, aided, of course, by the $8.5 million purse-driven loyalty of Europe's marquee names, virtually all of whom show up annually. Given the star-studded nature of the 60-man field, it is hardly surprising that the list of winners is impressive, with particular highlights including Rory McIlroy closing his breakout 2012 campaign with a two-shot victory, and Henrik Stenson hitting 94% of his greens (!) in 2014 as he became the first man to win the FedEx Cup Playoffs and the Final Series in the same year.

Venue: Built by Greg Norman moments before a crashing economy ground Dubai's impressive golf development to a halt, the Jumeirah Estates Earth Course is long and fairly tough, with centerline bunkering often adding challenge off the tee. Water appears only sparingly but it affects the three closers, particularly the 195-yard island green 17th and the 620-yard creek-divided 18th, an exciting finisher.

Designer: Greg Norman (2009) **Yards:** 7,675 **Par:** 72

#	Yds	Par	Avg	#	Yds	Par	Avg	#	Yds	Par	Avg
1	454 yds	Par 4	4.18	7	572 yds	Par 5	4.77	13	204 yds	Par 3	3.00
2	583 yds	Par 5	4.72	8	461 yds	Par 4	4.20	14	626 yds	Par 5	4.63
3	452 yds	Par 4	3.90	9	499 yds	Par 4	4.08	15	371 yds	Par 4	3.68
4	245 yds	Par 3	3.13	10	437 yds	Par 4	3.67	16	486 yds	Par 4	4.10
5	407 yds	Par 4	3.82	11	401 yds	Par 4	3.97	17	195 yds	Par 3	3.07
6	186 yds	Par 3	2.85	12	476 yds	Par 4	4.25	18	620 yds	Par 5	4.67

OWR: 2010: 445 **2011:** 437 **2012:** 445 **2013:** 386 **2014:** 413 **5-Year Avg:** 425.2 **5-Year Rank:** 2nd

PROJECTED TOP 50 PLAYERS IN 2015

Rank	Player	OWR	Comments
1	Rory McIlroy	1	Comprehensively reclaimed the game's top spot with an epic two-Major 2014 season that ranked among the best in recent memory. With off-the-course issues falling into place, extended greatness seems in order.
2	Jordan Spieth	9	After a quieter-than-expected summer regained top form late, running away at both the Australian Open and Tiger Woods' unofficial event. Looks poised to step up to elite status with more wins imminent.
3	Henrik Stenson	2	After a knockout 2013 campaign, was consistently good (but winless) for most of 2014 before successfully defending his Tour Championship title in Dubai. An elite ball striker who shows no sign of slowing down.
4	Adam Scott	3	Like Stenson, he only won once in 2014. Claimed the OWR #1 in May, then validated it by winning the next week at Colonial. Seems able to win more, but few play more consistently excellent golf.
5	Justin Rose	6	Won back-to-back (Quicken Loans and the Scottish Open) on both sides of the Atlantic and stayed among the OWR top 10 all year. Like Stenson and Scott, so good a ball-striker that he's bound not to slip.
6	Sergio García	5	It's remarkable that at age 34 he has A) Accomplished so much, and B) Failed to win a Major. Still, his ball striking remains impressive and his putting has steadied considerably - so he'll be around for a while.
7	Jason Day	8	After winning February's WGC-Match Play, seemed poised to breakout before being slowed by a thumb injury. Closed the year strongly, however, and still looks poised for a major breakthrough any minute now.
8	Bubba Watson	4	Coming of a splendid bounce-back year that saw him win, among other things, a second Masters. His talent is manifest, but questions persist about the stability of his mental game, and the ups and downs therein.
9	Rickie Fowler	10	Took a giant leap in 2014 under Butch Harmon's tutelage, and is another younger (26) player who seems poised for something big. This may be the multi-win breakout year that most have been waiting for.
10	Martin Kaymer	12	Broke his slump in a gigantic way in 2014, winning both the U.S. Open and Players Championship. Lacking, however, was consistency - but his skills are such that a runaway victory is possible any time he tees it up.
11	Victor Dubuisson	17	Though winless in 2014, solidified his position as one of Europe's elite stars. Narrowly missed winning the WGC-Match Play but was stalwart in his first Ryder Cup (2-0-1). Seems one big win away from exploding.
12	Patrick Reed	23	Proved his 2013 debut was no fluke by winning twice more, including at the WGC-Cadillac. Slowed a bit after becoming a father in May but again showed his mettle by standing out on a losing Ryder Cup side.
13	Hideki Matsuyama	16	After dominating in Japan in 2013, announced his PGA Tour presence in 2014 by beating Kevin Na in a playoff at Memorial. Has experienced no bumps in the road to date and appears on track for stardom.
14	Matt Kuchar	11	The most consistent golfer in America rolls onward, winning once in 2014, logging 11 more top 10s and finishing among the top 10 in $$$ for the fourth time in five years. All he needs is that elusive Major.
15	Charl Schwartzel	31	Coming off a disappointing season that saw him go winless worldwide for the first time since 2009. At age 30, he possesses the full package (with a slightly streaky putter) and should have lots of greatness left.
16	Dustin Johnson	19	The toughest player to peg given his uncertain status due to a self-imposed "leave of absence." By any measure he rates among the game's most talented - but will his leave help him to better put it all together?
17	Graeme McDowell	15	The record now suggests that he may never reside among the absolute elite, but no one beyond them holds as consistent a place in the world top 20. Has the tools to win more often - and maybe another Major?
18	Jim Furyk	7	Though winless since 2010, played some wonderfully consistent golf in 2014, recording an imposing 11 top 10s, including four runner-ups. At age 44, some decline could well be imminent, but we'll see...
19	Luke Donald	33	Trying to bounce back from two disappointing years with a re-tooled swing. At present he's showing few signs of catching fire but with his elite short game and putter, and his experience, that could soon change.
20	Keegan Bradley	28	Despite tons of talent and a high ratio of cuts made, hasn't won since 2012. Still he's proven he knows how to raise a trophy; this is another player who could be one big win away from a rapid climb.
21	Brooks Koepka	34	Scored a breakthrough win at the Turkish Airlines Open and begins 2015 with status in both the U.S. and Europe. Hits it a long way and appears capable of competing with the best on both circuits.
22	Jimmy Walker	21	Coming off a breakout year but tellingly, though the wins stopped by springtime, his overall strong play did not. Powerful player who, if he keeps putting like 2013-14, will continue to win on the PGA Tour.
23	Louis Oosthuizen	45	It's all about his health as lingering neck problems have slowed him for much of the last two years. Has the record to prove that when he's right, he's right up among the elite. He just needs a run of pain-free golf.
24	Hunter Mahan	22	After three strong seasons, cooled just a little in 2013 and '14. Remains one of the PGA Tour's top ball strikers, however, and he did rise up to win the 2014 Barclays. Golfers like this seldom fall too far.
25	Billy Horschel	14	Coming off a spectacular season that saw him win two playoff events as well as the $10 million FedEx Cup itself. Should be a force, but he's a rare top-shelf ball strikers to have so up and down a record.

PROJECTED TOP 50 PLAYERS IN 2015 (CONT'D)

Rank	Player	OWR	Comments
26	Zach Johnson	18	Cooled a bit during the latter half of 2014 after closing 2013 on fire, then winning the season-opening Tournament of Champions. A notch below the top tier, but holds his own with anyone when hot.
27	Bill Haas	39	Coming off an oddly quiet year in which he seldom contended but made 27 of 28 cuts while logging an impressive 17 top 25s. Looks ready to win again, perhaps more than once.
28	Gary Woodland	48	An enormously long hitter who's begun to harness his power into a highly consistent game, making 23 of 25 cuts in 2014. A two-time winner who seems capable of adding meaningfully to that.
29	Thomas Bjørn	36	After slumping from 2008-2010, is firmly back among the world top 50. Winless in 2012 and 2014, won twice in 2011 and 2013 - so he's right on schedule to produce a strong 2015.
30	Thorbjørn Olesen	80	Firmly established as a world-class player but has yet to take that big step forward. Hits it a long way for a smaller man and can really stick the irons when he's on. Just needs a hotter putter at the right times.
31	Phil Mickelson	14	At age 44, dealing (quietly) with arthritis, and coming off his worst PGA Tour season in more than a decade, his best years are almost certainly behind him now. But in any given week, look out...
32	Ian Poulter	27	Coming off a sub-par 2014, a season in which he was bothered by a recurring wrist problem. If those issues continue, all bets are off - but if he's healthy, he's still capable of doing world-class stuff.
33	Jamie Donaldson	24	After many years as a steady (but winless) earner, has ranked among the E Tour's very best since 2013, and is coming his first Ryder Cup appearance. Possesses a very solid all-around game.
34	Chris Kirk	20	Stepped up noticeably in 2014, winning twice (including the 2013 McGladrey) and jumping all the way to 6th in PGA Tour $$$. Possesses a complete game and thus figures to be around for a while.
35	Brandt Snedeker	58	Coming off his worst season on Tour - which, to put it in perspective, meant making 80% of his cuts and finishing 60th in $$$. At age 34 he should have lots of good golf left, so a big bounce back is likely.
36	Joost Luiten	29	Won once in Europe in 2014, and logged nine E Tour top 10s, so he's hardly struggling. But a number of observers believe that he's capable of even more...which he is.
37	Jason Dufner	38	It's tough to rate so great a ball-striker (not to mention a recent Major champion) this low but his 2014 was cut short by a neck injury, and he'd only logged four top 10s prior to it. Still, if healthy...
38	Sang-Moon Bae	84	Though his 2014 left a little to be desired, this very sound swinger has already won the Frys.com on the PGA Tour's 2014-15 wraparound schedule, as well as Korea's Shinhan Donghae title in a walkaway.
39	Lee Westwood	26	He won the 2014 Malaysian Open in a runaway, then salvaged his year by adding the Thailand Golf Championship late. Among the elite of his era but at 41, that missing Major is looking less likely.
40	Danny Willett	50	A former world number one amateur who, after five productive European Tour seasons, began to climb noticeably in the latter stages of 2014. Is still only 27, so he has a big window of opportunity ahead.
41	Ryan Moore	30	At age 32 he's playing consistently good golf and, as ever, filling his bank account. Seems like he could/should win more often - but don't bet against him in Malaysia, where he's a two-time defending champ.
42	Harris English	77	Was red hot in the first half of 2014, then much cooler thereafter. But he's a two-time PGA Tour winner at age 25 and possesses a most enviable mix of power and touch. He should continue to climb.
43	Alexander Levy	53	Is something of a wildcard here but had a very strong amateur career before enjoying a breakout two-win E Tour campaign in 2014. Still putting it together at age 24, but has proven he can go low.
44	Webb Simpson	43	Though he won the 2013 Shriners Hospitals (a 2014 wraparound event), played through a mostly quiet year which culminated in a disastrous Ryder Cup. But his overall talent level is a proven commodity.
45	Tim Clark	62	Another semi-wildcard. Is coming off a solid 2014 but the guess here is that as the player who looks to be the most adversely affected by the 2016 anchored-putter ban, he'll be highly motivated in 2015.
46	Edoardo Molinari	103	Appears to now be fully recovered from recent wrist and thumb injuries, and thus able to return to his two-win pre-injuries 2010 form, when he climbed as high as 14th in the OWR.
47	Thongchai Jaidee	37	The ageless, machine-like Jaidee has never relied on length, which likely helps him at a time when he'd otherwise be losing it. Is coming off two of his best E Tour campaigns and figures to keep rolling.
48	Kevin Na	25	Roared back from an injury-shortened 2013 to finish 20th in PGA Tour $$$ and climb back into the top 30 of the OWR. Lost a playoff (to Hideki Matsuyama) at Memorial, but seems ready to win again.
49	Tommy Fleetwood	51	Though winless, enjoyed a very solid third full season on the E Tour, finishing 19th in $$$. Possesses a very strong tee-to-green game and is still only 23, so there's lots of room for growth here.
50	Tiger Woods	32	Actually, 50th is the one place he likely *won't* end up. If everything (including health) somehow comes back together, he'll play with the best; if it doesn't he'll likely crash far lower than this.

25 PLAYERS ON THE RISE IN 2014

Player	OWR	Comments
Sang-Moon Bae	84	Has already won an official 2015 PGA Tour event (the 2014 Frys.com) as well as at home in Korea, and he'll be carrying added motivation this year as October's Presidents Cup will be played in Korea.
Tim Clark	62	Another player with a particular form of motivation in 2015: This will be his final season being able to anchor the putter, which he claims he will not be able to fairly compete without.
Luke Donald	33	This is somewhat by default. Though the changes he's been making to his swing have thus far shown only brief flashes of improvement (e.g., the 54-hole lead at Nedbank), he's too talented overall not to climb.
Victor Dubuisson	17	Has spent most of the year ranked among the OWR top 25, so how much higher can he go? Quite a bit if he can land that next big win to really get the ball rolling. Could be France's best since Arnaud Massy.
Harris English	77	His ability to rise is predicated mostly on the fact that he had a quiet second half in 2014. Thus his "rise" will likely only be back to the levels of his first half, which were world class.
Tony Finau	146	One of the more interesting prospects in recent memory after turning pro at 17 and taking eight years to reach the PGA Tour. One of the game's longest hitters and plenty of skills. Could be force...and soon.
Tommy Fleetwood	51	A former Walker Cup player and top English prospect who possesses a very strong tee-to-green game, and who won on the E Tour at age 22. Looks to be the best of the UK's young crop.
Emiliano Grillo	128	Has existed somewhat under the radar after growing up in Argentina, attending IMG Academy and skipping college. Has already carved a niche on the E Tour at age 22, and should be winning any minute now.
Martin Kaymer	12	How does one move up after winning the U.S. Open and Players Championship? By getting back to the machine-like form that he possessed in 2010-2011, and thus win more regularly. Which he can.
Brooks Koepka	34	After breaking through to win the E Tour's Turkish Airlines Open, has proven he can play at the highest level in Europe - and he's not far away from proving the same thing in the United States.
Alexander Levy	53	Critics will say that he hasn't quite proven it yet (one of his 2014 wins was the 36-hole, rain-shortened Portugal Masters) but among France's young prospects, he's ready to step from Dubuisson's shadow.
Hao Tong Li	192	China's top young prospect, and a three-time winner (in his last four starts) on the 2014 PGA Tour China. He's only 19 and may struggle just to figure out the Web.com Tour.....or he might surprise everybody.
Shane Lowry	44	After looking like a top prospect as an amateur, and winning once (the 2012 Portugal Masters) on the E Tour, began to show signs of stepping up in 2014, including a runner-up at the flagship BMW PGA.
Joost Luiten	29	As a four-time E Tour winner at age 28, he's already proven that he can compete at a very high level. But as The Netherlands' top modern era prospect, he holds the potential to climb further.
Thorbjørn Olesen	80	Like Joost Luiten, he has proven himself a serious E Tour competitor, and his very solid tee-to-green game hints at a lot more. His putting numbers are acceptable, but he needs to make more when it counts.
Louis Oosthuizen	45	Sort of a cheap selection here because we already know that when he's healthy, he's one of the world's very best. Has shown flashes of late so with any medical luck, look for a big 2015.
Patrick Reed	23	Much like Victor Dubuisson (above), he's already shown himself a top-tier talent, and three PGA Tour wins at age 23 was quite impressive. But he's good enough now to be judged by Majors going forward.
Brandt Snedeker	58	Another selection that didn't require a massive degree of insight. Coming off the worst year of his career - but it was still a pretty good year. He figures to be climbing to more familiar ground quickly.
Justin Thomas	122	Joins Tony Finau as the most touted rookies on the PGA Tour in 2015. Was an amateur/collegiate star at Alabama and has won at every level. Thus he may well adjust better than most true rookies.
Cameron Tringale	85	Has established himself as a very solid earner, and climbed to a career-best 37th-place finish in 2014 PGA Tour earnings. His chance to rise, quite obviously, is rooted in the fact that he's now likely ready to win.
Peter Uihlein	143	This former amateur superstar's ability to rise is solely a product of a disastrous 2014. Looked poised for E Tour stardom entering the year, then collapsed. But better form late suggests a far stronger 2015.
Bernd Wiesberger	72	Has quietly lifted himself towards the upper tier of the European Tour since 2012, and gained worldwide attention by contending at the 2014 PGA Championship. Ready to win again - and bigger - in Europe.
Danny Willett	50	Like many a prospect who joins a major tour at a very young age, took some time to get adjusted to the E Tour's level of competition. Appears to have arrived in late 2014, however, and should keep rolling.
Chris Wood	141	An intriguing talent who made two huge British Open splashes as an amateur and has proven himself a solid, workman-like pro. But at 27, and with a strong all-around skill set, there could be something more.
Gary Woodland	48	A powerful player who has made steady progress, particularly since winning the 2013 Reno-Tahoe Open. But well beyond muscle, he has enough all-around game to reach a little higher.

25 PLAYERS WHO MAY FALL IN 2014

Player	OWR	Comments
Steven Bowditch	89	As with others on this list, his likeliness to decline is rooted mostly in the sense that his career-best 2014 (his first PGA Tour win and a 57th-place $$$ rank) was something of an outlier.
Angel Cabrera	73	At age 45, it's strictly about Father Time. He still has his moments - indeed, he won the 2014 Greenbrier Classic - but as that was his lone PGA Tour top 10 of the year, they are now fewer and further between.
K.J. Choi	116	One of many on this list for whom it is primarily about age. Actually enjoyed a career-best year in 2011 but at age 44 those heights will be difficult to repeat. Can still star in Asia if he so chooses.
Stewart Cink	193	Began to slide within a year of winning the 2009 British Open, and while he briefly reversed that course in 2013 (78th in PGA Tour $$$), a declining putting stroke makes it hard to forecast a massive turnaround.
Erik Compton	95	Based on his career body of work, the bet here is that his career-best 2014 (which included a runner-up finish at the U.S. Open and a 56th-place $$$ ranking) will prove something of an outlier.
Jason Dufner	38	This projection is based almost completely upon a neck injury suffered during the defense of his 2013 PGA Championship. If healthy, his ball-striking alone guarantees that he can't fall too far.
Ernie Els	63	Another player slowly falling victim to the passage of time. He's a Hall-of-Famer with more than enough talent to still provide the occasional flashy moment - but at 45, that's increasingly all they are.
Jim Furyk	7	Despite being 44, he has thus far mostly avoided the ravages of time, especially as he ranked an impressive 3rd in PGA Tour $$$ in 2014. But it has to start happening sooner or later...
Scott Hend	96	Has climbed sharply via a great three-win 2013 on the Asian Tour and a win in the E Tour co-sanctioned Hong Kong Open in 2014. But now he has status in Europe, where the competition gets much thicker.
Billy Horschel	13	With his superior ball striking, any drop figures not to be too big, but... 1) It would be hard to maintain his red-hot form of late 2014, and 2) He already appeared to be well off of it by year's end.
Mikko Ilonen	47	This is strictly a percentage bet that based on his complete body of work, he is bound to decline at least somewhat from his 2014 form - but he's a solid player, and this is one of the weaker bets on the board.
Hiroshi Iwata	67	Was a journeyman for the first eight years of his Japan Tour career before taking a quantum leap in form in 2014. But is he really good enough to be contending in WGC events? Some fallback seems inevitable.
Thongchai Jaidee	37	How can he be listed among our top 50 players *and* those most likely to decline? Because age is bound to begin having some affect on him one of these days - but like Mikko Ilonen, this is a chancy 2015 bet.
Matt Jones	78	Was listed here a year ago as well and actually improved his PGA Tour $$$ rank (from 48th to 47th) - but he won in 2014, which represents a career high but also shows that the rest of his earnings were far lower.
Miguel Ángel Jiménez	40	The Most Interesting Golfer In The World is also the most ageless, twice extending his E Tour record for oldest winner with age-50 2014 wins. But even for The Mechanic, it has to start declining eventually...
Jerry Kelly	123	Like several others on this list, the seemingly ageless Kelly relies on great accuracy and near-elite skills around the green to keep his banker very happy - but he just turned 48 in November.
Phil Mickelson	14	He's only 44 and his point about loose, easy swings aging may be valid. But he's got an arthritic issue, and 44 is still 44. Of course, if he can find a way to win a U.S. Open, he won't care if he misses every other cut.
Ryan Palmer	42	Is actually in a five-year up cycle, so his stretch of top-60 $$$ rankings cannot be considered just a good run of form. His eight 2014 top 10s, however, were easily a career best, so some decline may be in order.
Carl Pettersson	173	Another player who will be affected by 2016's anchored putter ban, but his form has been off somewhat since a career-best 2012 anyway. Or perhaps 2012 was more of an outlier than we realized.
John Senden	49	One of the PGA Tour's top ball strikers and at age 43, he's actually coming off the best year of his career - which is precisely why he's a good bet to slip (at least a little) in 2015.
Steve Stricker	41	This is almost an unfair pick as the man is playing so limited a schedule that it will be nearly impossible to find the rhythm to seriously compete - except, of course, that he did it so amazingly in 2013.
Bo Van Pelt	201	We are a year late on this pick as Van Pelt's stellar four-year form of 2009-2012 already cooled noticeably in 2013 and '14. Struck the ball considerably better in 2014 but made little headway, an ominous sign.
Jimmy Walker	21	Another case of a player pegged for decline solely because his 2014 form was so strong that logic just says it it will be too hard to maintain. But he's got plenty of game and isn't likely to fall too sharply.
Boo Weekley	118	A superior ball striker whose numbers slipped slightly, but not much, in 2014. His earnings, however, took a nosedive (22nd to 112th) - and if he's not successful with this level of ball striking, he could be in trouble.
Lee Westwood	26	A final case of an assessment solely due to Father Time. Can clearly still play (as his pair of 2014 wins in Asia clearly shows) but he had only two PGA Tour top 10s. Not likely to fall too far however.

TOP 50 WORLDWIDE PROSPECTS

(Player must be no older than 23 on January 1st, 2015)

Rank	Player (Age)	NAT	Comments
1	Jordan Spieth (21)	USA	After a lights-out rookie year in 2013, consistently contended at the highest levels in 2014 before scoring runaway wins at the Australian Open and the unofficial Hero World Challenge. Looks Major-ready now.
2	Hideki Matsuyama (22)	JAP	After dominating in Japan at age 20, came to America and quickly proved himself the real thing by winning the Memorial Tournament. Looks every bit like Japan's best-ever worldwide prospect.
3	Matteo Manassero (21)	ITA	Coming off a down year in which he failed to win for the first time and finished a career-worst 60th in E Tour $$$, but... Had four wins by age 20! With his putter, very unlikely that he stays down for too long.
4	Ryo Ishikawa (22)	JAP	Hugely touted after winning as a 15-year-old amateur on the Japan Tour. Though initially dominant at home, has found limited success in the West - but begin to show meaningful signs during 2014.
5	Seung-Yul Noh (22)	KOR	Former Asian Tour phenom who won as a professional at age 17, and in Europe at 18. Has gone about his PGA Tour endeavors with limited fanfare but took a big step by winning at New Orleans in 2014.
6	Emiliano Grillo (22)	ARG	Another touted prospect but by coming from Argentina to IMG Academy, then turning pro early, had only a limited amateur résumé. Has already shown he can compete in Europe, and looks ready to win now.
7	Tommy Fleetwood (23)	ENG	Former Walker Cup player who has emerged as Britain's top young prospect. Already has three full E Tour seasons under his belt at 23. A very strong tee-to-greener with the potential to join the ball-striking elite.
8	Justin Thomas (21)	USA	A two-year All-Everything at Alabama who has won - usually without delay - at every level thus far. As a 16-year-old, shot 65 in his first PGA Tour round (2009 Wyndham), so he's already had a taste.
9	Patrick Cantlay (22)	USA	Made a PGA Tour splash in 2011 as an amateur, shooting 60 at Hartford and finishing T9 in Canada. Has been slowed by back problems since turning pro but when healthy, the potential certainly remains.
10	Hao-Tong Li (19)	CHN	Has emerged as China's top prospect after winning three of 12 events on the 2014 PGA Tour China, as well as OneAsia's China Masters. Has Web.com status now - and a big cultural adjustment ahead.
11	Chang-Woo Lee (21)	KOR	In 2013, won the Asia-Pacific and Korean Amateurs, and a Korean Tour event. Also T2 (w/Rory McIlroy, and others) at the Korea Open. Turned pro in 2014 and should begin factoring around the Far East shortly.
12	Ryan Ruffels (16)	AUS	The reigning Junior World and Australian Boys champion, but has already shown he can compete on the professional level. Widely rated Oz's top prospect since Jason Day - but he also has U.S. citizenship.
13	Lucas Herbert (18) (a)	AUS	Another top teenage Australian prospect who turned heads by tying for 11th (behind a dazzling third round 65) at the stronger-field 2014 Australian Masters. Also finished T23 at the 2014 Australian Open.
14	Guan Tianlang (16)	CHN	One of the tougher prospects to judge because, after making the cut at the 2013 Masters at age 14, he has made only sporadic Western appearances, few of them spectacular. But the talent is obviously there.
15	Tyrrell Hatton (23)	ENG	A touted prospect in some British quarters (despite a limited amateur résumé) who began very much to look the part in 2014, finishing 36th in $$$ (with five top 10s) as a European Tour rookie.
16	Romain Wattel (23)	FRA	Hasn't yet won on the European Tour but he's certainly proven his worth at an early age, finishing 28th in earnings in 2014. Poised to join Dubuisson and Levy as a very imposing young French trio.
17	Soo-Min Lee (21)	KOR	Won 2012 Korean Amateur and the KPGA Tour's Gunsan Open in 2013. Played in 4 OneAsia Tour events through 2012-2013, never finishing worse than 35th. Turned pro in 2014 but has been fairly quiet to date.
18	Renato Paratore (18)	ITA	A much-talked-about Italian teen with a fairly limited ledger of amateur wins - but there was no denying the talent when he led 2014 E Tour Q School through five rounds. An intriguing prospect, but it may take time.
19	Todd Sinnott (22) (a)	AUS	Has come to greater attention recently with a T6 at the Western Australia Open and a T17 at the Australian Masters. An exceptionally long hitter - but it may take a little more time to fully harness his power.
20	Matthew Fitzpatrick (20)	ENG	The first Englishman in 102 years to win the U.S. Amateur (2013). Then surprised everyone by turning pro after one semester at Northwestern U. Highly touted despite a short (but strong) ledger of amateur titles.
21	Beau Hossler (19) (a)	USA	A soph at the U of Texas. Best known for a T29 at 2012 U.S. Open after qualifying in at age 16. Was a bit quiet thereafter prior to winning the 2014 Western Amateur and defending his SoCal Amateur title.
22	Rashid Khan (23)	IND	A former caddie who won three times on the Indian Tour from 2011-2013, then starred on the 2014 Asian Tour where he won twice and showed the ability to go low, such as his 61 at the 2013 SAIL-SBI Open.
23	Danny Lee (23)	NZL	An elite prospect after winning the 2008 U.S. Amateur (at age 18) and the E Tour's 2009 Johnnie Walker classic as an amateur. Struggled since but has show signs of late (e.g., T3 at the 2014 Mayakoba Classic).
24	Moritz Lampert (22)	GER	The 2012 German Amateur champion tore up the 2014 Challenge Tour, winning three times in 11 starts to earn a battlefield promotion to the E Tour. More ready than many to make an impact at age 22.
25	Daniel Berger (21)	USA	A somewhat under-the-radar prospect who never played HS golf. Was a first-team All-American in his second season at Florida State before turning pro. #1 in Ball Striking on the 2014 Web.com Tour.

TOP 50 WORLDWIDE PROSPECTS (Cont'd)

(Player must be no older than 23 on January 1st, 2015)

Rank	Player	OWR	Comments
26	Patrick Rodgers (22)	USA	A three-time first-team All-American in three seasons at Stanford, also the rare two-time American Walker Cup player. T15 at 2013 John Deere Classic as an amateur. Lacks PGA Tour status for 2015.
27	Cameron Smith (21)	AUS	Won the 2011 Australian Boys and the 2013 Australian Amateur before turning pro. In 2014, put together seven straight top 10s on three tours, led by a T5 at the PGA Tour co-sanctioned CIMB Classic.
28	Jake Higginbottom (21)	AUS	Won the 2010 China Amateur, then, in 2012, became the first amateur since 1956 to win the New Zealand Open. Turned pro thereafter but has thus far had only modest success in Asia and Australia.
29	Chikkarangappa S (21)	IND	A little-known prospect beyond his native India, where he won the Indian Amateur at age 16. Had little else on his amateur résumé before winning four times and topping the $$$ on the 2014 Indian Tour.
30	Julian Brun (22) (a)	FRA	A senior at Texas Christian U, where he is a three-time first-team All-American. In 2012, T2 at the NCAA Championship and won the Challenge Tour's Allianz Open Tolouse as an amateur. Had a quiet 2014.
31	Jin Cheng (16) (a)	CHN	Won once on the 2014 PGA Tour China and also added a T3. Medalist at the 2014 U.S. Junior Amateur and played on the Chinese side at the professional Dongfeng Nissan Cup matches.
32	Jung-Gon Hwang (22)	KOR	At age 22, already a two-time winner on the Japan Tour, where he claimed the 2011 Mizuno Open (and thus qualified for the British Open) and the 2012 Casio World Open. Won once in Korea in 2014.
33	Adrian Otaegui (22)	ESP	A protégé of Jose Maria Olazábal. Won the 2010 British Boys and the 2011 Spanish Closed Am, played for Spain at the 2010 Eisenhower Trophy. Struggled in 2014 as an E Tour rookie but will be back in 2015.
34	Tom Lewis (23)	ENG	Shot 65 (lowest-ever round by an amateur) in 1st round of 2011 British Open. After turning pro, won the 2011 Portugal Masters & finished 66th in E Tour $$$. Has slipped since but still holds obvious potential.
35	Oliver Goss (23)	AUS	An All-American at U of Tennessee. Lost in 2013 U.S. Amateur final. Won 2012 Western Australian Open as an amateur. Also T20 at 2012 Australian Masters. Has been only middling as a pro thus far.
36	Kyoung-Hoon Lee (23)	KOR	At age 23, has already logged three full seasons on the Japan Tour, winning the 2012 Sega Sammy Cup and ranking among the top 25 in $$$ each year. Seems to have leveled off a bit...for the moment.
37	Dou Ze Cheng (17)	CHN	An ex-Junior World champion (ages 13-14), a 2012 AJGA All-American and a 2014 Eisenhower Trophy. player. After turning pro, competed in five events on the 2014 PGA Tour China, logging two top 10s.
38	Chen-Tsung Pan (23) (a)	USA	A senior at the U of Washington, where he is a two-time All-American. Native of Taiwan who came to America in 2007. Reached quarter-final of 2007 U.S. Amateur, the youngest to do so since Bobby Jones.
39	Carlos Ortiz (23)	MEX	Came from well off the radar to win three times on the 2014 Web.com Tour, and thus become the 10th man to earn a battlefield promotion to the PGA Tour. Thus far, doesn't seem overmatched at this level.
40	Max Orrin (20)	ENG	A Walker Cup player in 2013, turned pro while still a teenager. Seemed headed for a 2015 return to the Challenge Tour but won the penultimate 2014 event to finish 22nd in $$$ and reach the 2015 E Tour.
41	Haydn Porteous (20)	RSA	Won tons of amateur titles in South Africa, including the 2012 South African Amateur. Showed lots of potential as a 2014 Sunshine Tour rookie, contending regularly but several times narrowly failing to win.
42	Byeong-Hun An (23)	KOR	The youngest-ever winner of the U.S. Amateur (age 17) in 2009. Has bounced around among several tours as a pro but finished 3rd in Challenge Tour $$$ in 2014, gaining him full E Tour status in 2015.
43	Si-Woo Kim (19)	KOR	Still something of a mystery man. At age 17, turned pro and played through three stages of Q School to reach the PGA Tour. Was limited to eight starts by age and has been trying to return ever since.
44	Chris Williams (23)	USA	A Four-time All-American, Hogan Award winner and 2011 Walker Cup player while at U of Washington. Won the 2012 Western and Pacific Coast Amateurs. Uses the 10-finger grip. Played in Canada in 2014.
45	Jeung-Hun Wang (19)	KOR	Finished 21st in Asian Tour earnings after losing the season's final event, the Dubai Open, to Arjun Atwal on the final hole. Also won once on the 2014 PGA Tour China in his second year as a professional.
46	Bobby Wyatt (23)	USA	Was a three-time All-American at Alabama. A four-time Alabama state HS champion who famously shot a 57 at the CC of Mobile in 1st round of the 2010 Alabama Junior. Won the 2012 Sunnehanna Amateur.
47	Eddie Pepperell (23)	ENG	Though not the most highly touted amateur prospect, he represented England at the Eisenhower Trophy and, in two full seasons, has established himself as a meaningful presence on the European Tour.
48	Danie van Tonder (23)	RSA	A well-thought-of prospect who in 2011 won 10 out of 18 events on South Africa's IGT mini-tour. Has an odd-looking swing but served notice by winning twice during the Sunshine Tour's lighter winter schedule.
49	Corey Whitsett (23)	USA	A Four-time All-American at Alabama. Won the 2007 U.S. Junior Amateur and the Northeast Amateur in 2013. A member of the 2013 Walker Cup team. Played part-time on the Web.com Tour in 2014.
50	Jordan Niebrugge (21) (a)	USA	A junior at Oklahoma St. In 2013, won the Western Amateur and the U.S. Public Links, plus his native Wisconsin Amateur, and played on the Walker Cup team. Had a somewhat quiet 2014.

50 MORE PROSPECTS TO WATCH

(Player must be no older than 23 on January 1st, 2015)

Player	Age	Country	2014
Lucas Bjerregaard	23	Denmark	European Tour - 90th in $$$ in his rookie season
Sam Burns (a)	18	United States	AJGA All-American, Freshman at Louisiana State
Brian Campbell (a)	21	United States	2nd-team All-American, Senior at University of Illinois
Corey Conners (a)	22	Canada	Senior at Kent State University
Bryson DeChambeau (a)	21	United States	2nd-team All-American, Junior at Southern Methodist University
Paul Dunne (a)	22	Ireland	48th in World Amateur Golf Ranking
Jorge Fernandez-Valdes	22	Argentina	PGA Tour Latinoamérica - 5th in $$$
Pedro Figueiredo	23	Portugal	European Challenge Tour - 98th in $$$
Mario Galiano (a)	19	Spain	18th in World Amateur Golf Ranking
Doug Ghim (a)	18	United States	Freshman at University of Texas
Ricardo Gouveia	23	Portugal	European Challenge Tour - 47th in $$$ (9 events)
Gavin Green (a)	21	Malaysia	19th in World Amateur Golf Ranking
Brandon Hagy (a)	23	United States	1st-team All-American, Senior at University of California
Rico Hoey (a)	20	Philippines	1st-team All-American, Freshman at USC
Nathan Holman	23	Australia	Asian Tour - 52nd in $$$ (8 starts)
Sam Horsfield (a)	17	England	25th in World Amateur Golf Ranking
Chien-Yao Hung	22	Taipei	Asian Tour - 47th in $$$ (9 events)
Jazz Janewattananond	19	Thailand	Asian Tour - 31st in $$$
Masahiro Kawamura	21	Japan	Japan Tour - 80th in $$$
Meen Whee Kim	22	South Korea	Web.com Tour - 72nd in $$$ (played through Finals to PGA Tour)
Woo-Hyun Kim	23	South Korea	Korean PGA Tour - 2-time winner, 5th in $$$
Marcus Kinhult (a)	19	Sweden	5th in World Amateur Golf Ranking
Sang-Hee Lee	22	South Korea	Japan Tour - 28th in $$$
Nick Marsh (a)	20	England	23rd in World Amateur Golf Ranking
Denny McCarthy (a)	21	United States	2nd-team All-American, Senior at University of Virginia
Lee McCoy (a)	20	United States	Honorable Mention All-American, Junior at University of Georgia
Tyler McCumber	23	United States	PGA Tour Latinoamérica - 3rd in $$$
Dermot McElroy (a)	21	Ireland	132nd in World Amateur Golf Ranking
Guido Migliozzi (a)	17	Italy	98th in World Amateur Golf Ranking
Antonio Murdaca (a)	19	Australia	97th in World Amateur Golf Ranking
Bradley Neil (a)	18	Scotland	10th in World Amateur Golf Ranking
Il-Hwan Park	22	South Korea	Korean PGA Tour - 8th in $$$
Thomas Pieters	22	Belgium	European Tour - 83rd in $$$ as a rookie
Panuphol Pittayarat	21	Thailand	Asian Tour - 45th in $$$
Jon Rahm-Rodriguez (a)	20	Spain	Honorable Mention All-American, Junior at Arizona State University
Kristoffer Reitan (a)	16	Norway	264th in World Amateur Golf Ranking
Adrian Saddier	22	France	European Tour - 127th $$$ as a rookie
Xander Schauffele (a)	20	United States	Senior at San Diego State University
Scottie Scheffler (a)	18	United States	Freshman at University of Texas
Oliver Schniederjans (a)	21	United States	Senior at Georgia Tech, 1st in World Amateur Golf Ranking
Matthias Schwab (a)	21	Austria	Sophomore at Vanderbilt University
Robby Shelton (a)	19	United States	1st-team All-American, Sophomore at University of Alabama
Callum Shinkwin	21	England	European Challenge Tour - 34th in $$$
Young-Han Song	23	South Korea	Japan Tour - 48th in $$$
Gary Stal	22	France	European Tour - 89th $$$ as a rookie
Hunter Stewart (a)	21	United States	Senior at Vanderbilt University
Brandon Stone	21	South Africa	Sunshine Tour - 50th in $$$
Miguel Tabuena	20	Philippines	Asian Tour - 37th in $$$
Cameron Wilson	22	United States	1st-team All-American, Senior at Stanford University
Will Zalatoris (a)	18	United States	Freshman at Wake Forest University

THE ROOKIE CLASS - PGA TOUR

Of the 50 players who gained their 2014-15 PGA Tour cards via the Web.com Tour's regular season or Finals (page 174), 26 have previously played the Tour with status, leaving 24 that will officially be considered rookies in the year ahead. Among these, two have enjoyed success on other major circuits, making their rookie status only technical in nature. The more notable of this pair is 33-year-old South African **Richard Sterne**, a six-time winner on the European Tour and a man who has previously cracked the top 30 of the Official World Ranking; he is nobody's rookie. Slightly less established is 27-year-old South Korean **Sun-Joon Park**, who spent 2010-2013 playing the Japan Tour, where he won once and finished fifth in earnings in 2013. He enters 2015 already ranked among the OWR top 200.

Among the more genuine rookies, there may not be a true superstar prospect in the bunch, but there are certainly a handful of players whose talents stand out beyond the rest. Chief among these is 25-year-old **Tony Finau**, a 6'4" mountain of a man who skipped college entirely after winning two Utah State High School titles, turning pro at age 17. Multiple mini-tours, a Golf Channel Big Break and both the PGA Tour Canada and Web.com Tour later, he arrives as one of the game's longest hitters - but as a 2014 Web.com win and two top 10s in five early PGA Tour starts suggest, his talents range well beyond simply driving par 4s. Indeed, Finau looks like someone capable of contending regularly - and exciting fans - for a long time to come. And as an interesting aside, his younger brother Gipper holds the distinction of being the youngest player ever to make a Web.com Tour cut, tying for 58th at the 2006 Utah Energy Solutions Championship at 16 years, 20 days. The brothers are also cousins of NBA star Jabari Parker, so athletic talent is clearly in their genes.

Also ticketed to have an early impact is 21-year-old **Justin Thomas**, a native of Louisville and a two-time All-American in two seasons at the University of Alabama. A former junior superstar, Thomas drew the spotlight when he played the PGA Tour's 2009 Wyndham Championship as a 16-year-old, opened with a 65 and eventually tied for 78th, becoming the third youngest player ever to make a PGA Tour cut. As a 2012 freshman at Alabama, he was first team A-A and swept both the Haskins and Nicklaus Player Of The Year Awards. After falling to second-team A-A as a sophomore, he turned professional, eventually winning on the 2014 Web.com circuit en route to earning his PGA Tour card. Notably, he has made 11 previous PGA Tour starts, making six cuts and tying for 10th at the 2014 Farmers Insurance Open.

The picture becomes slightly more muddled at this point, but next in line may well be 24-year-old **Max Homa**, the University of California-Berkeley's first-ever NCAA champion (2013) and also that season's Pac 12 champion - the latter accomplishment sparked by a remarkable 61 over the North Course at the Los Angeles Country Club, site of the 2023 U.S. Open. Also a member of the victorious 2013 U.S. Walker Cup team, Homa used seven 2013 sponsor exemptions in PGA Tour events trying to gain Special Temporary Member status; upon failing, he turned to the Web.com Tour, where a 17th-place finish on the 2014 regular season money list earned him his PGA Tour card for 2015.

Also in the mix is 27-year-old Canadian **Adam Hadwin**, whose amateur career was limited (he was an honorable mention All-American at the University of Lousville) before his pro career began with two successful campaigns on the Canadian Tour, where he was named Rookie Of The Year in 2010, and claimed titles in both 2010 and '11. Three Web.com seasons later, he has finally earned PGA Tour status for 2015 - but it must be noted that back in 2011, he tied for fourth at the Canadian Open (his top PGA Tour finish to date) and added a T7 at the Frys.com Open 11 weeks later. Despite standing only 5'9", his game is built around power, which always plays well on the big Tour.

But Hadwin is not the only Canadian rookie of note as 26-year-old **Nick Taylor** wasted little time in making his presence loudly felt, winning November's light-field Sanderson Farms Championship in just the fourth start of his rookie year. A two-time All-American at the University of Washington, Taylor won both the 2006 Canadian Junior title (by a record 11 shots) and the 2007 Canadian Amateur before finishing runner-up at both the 2008 NCAA Championship and the 2009 U.S. Public Links. Also the world's number one-ranked amateur for part of 2009, Taylor spent three quite years on the Canadian Tour before playing through the Web.com circuit in 2014.

Two more Americans figure to push the above five prospects, with the better-known being former two-time Auburn University All-American **Blayne Barber**. A 25-year-old native of Tallahassee, FL, Barber won the 2009 Florida Amateur and actually began his collegiate career at the University of Central Florida before transferring. He won once on the 2014 Web.com Tour and clinched his PGA Tour card by finishing 7th in regular season earnings. The lesser-known of the two - indeed, something of a wildcard in this class - is another Floridian, 21-year-old **Daniel Berger**, who skipped high school golf completely before spending two years at Florida State, where he was named first-team All-American as a sophomore. A runner-up (to fellow Max Homa) at the 2013 NCAA championship, he ranked 1st in Ball Striking and 2nd in Total Driving on the 2014 Web.com Tour, so he shouldn't feel outclassed on the big circuit.

Another trio of players capable of having an impact is led by 23-year-old Mexican **Carlos Ortiz**, who has blossomed since concluding an unspectacular collegiate career at the University of North Texas. Playing his second Web.com season in 2014, he became the 10th man ever to gain an in-season battlefield promotion to the PGA Tour by winning three Web.com events - though unfortunately for Ortiz, the third win came virtually at the end of the PGA Tour season. Also in the mix will be 25-year-old **Andrew Putnam**, a former Pepperdine University star and the younger brother of PGA Tour player Michael. Playing his second Web.com season in 2014, Andrew won once and finished second in regular season earnings, easily punching his ticket to the PGA Tour. And then there is the much-traveled **Whee Kim**, a 22-year-old South Korean who won the 2010 Korean Amateur, then played domestically and, briefly, on the OneAsia Tour. His name may ring a bell to serious American fans as he actually led 2012 PGA Tour Q School after the second and third rounds (at age 20) before fading to a T43.

Among the remaining 12 rookies, three who might draw the most attention are **Zac Blair**, **Jon Curran** and **Sam Saunders**. In the case of former Brigham Young star Blair, this is because he played through the fall in hot form, as well as the fact that his father James played briefly on the PGA Tour. Curran, on the other hand, is known as a former Hopkinton (MA) HS teammate of Keegan Bradley, as well as for uncorking the occasional very low round. Saunders, meanwhile, will be one of the first names mentioned anywhere he appears, because regardless of the attention his play might potentially merit, he will first and foremost be known as Arnold Palmer's grandson.

There is also a trio of older players to be considered here, though at least two of them must be viewed as longshots. One, 33-year-old **Byron Smith**, spent two years at Pepperdine without appearing in a collegiate match, and four years in Canada (where he won four times) - but has never played in a PGA Tour event. Another, 29-year-old **Carlos Sainz Jr.**, played collegiately at Mississippi State and gained his PGA Tour status first by finishing 74th in 2014 Web.com regular season earnings (only the top 75 qualify for the Finals), then playing through the Finals to gain the 49th of 50 PGA Tour spots. The third, 32-year-old Mexican **Oscar Fraustro**, played his way from the local Mexican Tour onto the PGA Tour Latinoamérica, then moved up to the Web.com Tour in 2013 before finishing 61st in 2014 regular season earnings, then slipping onto the PGA Tour via a solid performance in the Finals.

Inevitably there will be a pleasant surprise or two among the remaining six players, whose ranks include 25-year-old **Tom Hoge** (Texas Christian University/9th on the Web.com priority list), 25-year-old **Mark Hubbard** (San Jose State/18th in regular season Web.com $$$), 25-year-old **Scott Pinckey** (Arizona State/27th on the Web.com priority list), 26-year-old **Jonathan Randolph** (University of Mississippi/18th in regular season Web.com $$$), 27-year-old Canadian **Roger Sloan** (Texas-El Paso/24th in regular season Web.com $$$) and 28-year-old **Zack Sucher** (Alabama-Birmingham/3rd in regular season Web.com $$$).

THE ROOKIE CLASS - EUROPEAN TOUR

As is often the case, the majority of the 42 men who gained playing privileges for the 2015 European Tour via the Challenge Tour or through Q School have been there before – in this case all of 24 players. And to some degree, a 25th might well be added to that list as 34-year-old South African Q School grad **Jake Roos**, a six-time winner on the Sunshine Tour, has made 43 career E Tour starts, though the great majority of these have been co-sanctioned events played on African soil. Still, a wide-eyed rookie he is not. Similarly, 27-year-old **Anirban Lahiri** of India has won five times on the Asian Tour and ranked as high as 65th in the OWR, so while most of his 31 career E Tour starts have been similarly co-sanctioned events played close to home, he certainly begins the year several steps ahead of the true rookies.

Most watched among this group will surely be England's **Matthew Fitpatrick**, a top 20-year-old prospect who abruptly scrapped his long-term amateur plans by dropping out of Northwestern University after one semester and turning pro in 2014. The rail-thin Fitzpatrick made history in 2012 by becoming the first Englishman to win the U.S. Amateur in 102 years, and was also a star on the 2013 Walker Cup side. A former world number one-ranked amateur, he is surely the rookie who will draw the most attention, and in most eyes his long-term potential will be viewed as the greatest - but one feels a sense of caution not to get too caught up in what remains a short, if impressive, résumé.

Beyond Fitzpatrick, however, this is a class led by several players cited more for potential than a current list of accomplishments. Most intriguing among this group is 18-year-old Italian **Renato Paratore**, who was still 17 at the time of Q School and rather remarkably led the event for five rounds before finishing third following a closing 73. Paratore is a bit of a wildcard given that his biggest victories to date - the 2014 Portuguese Amateur and a gold medal at 2014's Youth Olympic Games - are a far cry from the European Tour. Still, his talent is self-evident, and he clearly has room to grow as he's young enough to count 21-year-old countryman Matteo Manassero as a mentor! Slightly older – but perhaps more ready to compete at this level – is 24-year-old Spaniard **Jordi García Pinto**, a winner on the Challenge Tour in both 2013 and 2014, and the third-place finisher in 2014 Challenge Tour earnings. Also a law student over the past several years, he has skipped Q School each year since 2011 in the belief that he should earn his way onto the big stage via a full season's work - and now he's there. Beyond Roos and Lahiri, García Pinto seems the rookie most likely to contend in 2015. And then there is Australian wildcard **Jason Scrivener**, a 25-year-old who carded the low score of Q School's final round (a back-to-the-wall 66) to sneak under the wire into one of the last qualifying spots. Beyond the 2007 Australian Boys, Scrivener has few titles on his résumé, but there are some in Oz who believe strongly in his international potential regardless. The last addition to this most-likely-to-succeed list is 23-year-old **Byeong-Hun An**, a South Korean whose family moved to Florida when he was 14 so that he could study with David Leadbetter. Known in some quarters as Ben, he became the youngest-ever winner of the U.S. Amateur in 2009, turned pro in 2011 and has spent the last three seasons playing full-time on the Challenge Tour, where he finished third in earnings in 2014. Having also tied for 26th at the 2014 British Open as a qualifier, he perhaps carries a slightly greater element of big game experience than most in this class.

The youngest of the remaining rookies is 23-year-old **Borja Virto**, a Spaniard with plenty of amateur experience (but no major amateur victories) on his résumé. Virto did take something of a step up in 2014, however, by winning twice on the Alps mini-tour and finishing fourth in the satellite circuit's Order of Merit. Another mini-tour veteran is 33-year-old Englishman **Paul Maddy**, a native of Cambridge who can clearly cite persistence among his biggest attributes as he had failed to play through 10 previous Q Schools before running the gauntlet in 2014. Obviously a bit of a longshot then, he is a four-time winner on the EuroPro circuit so given the opportunity, he is capable of closing. Also carrying meaningful mini-tour experience is 26-year-old Welshman **Oliver Farr** (two EuroPro wins in 2013) and 31-year-old Englishman **Jason Barnes** (a two-time Alps Tour winner), but neither seems likely to have a major impact at this level.

Two players with American ties may also figure into the mix, the more prominent being 27-year-old Frenchman **Cyril Bouniol**, the 2010 NCAA Division 2 national champion while attending Abilene (TX) Christian, and a man who birdied the final Q School hole to gain the last spot after double-bogeying the penultimate to seemingly dash his hopes. And then there is Wisconsin native **Daniel Woltman**, a 28-year-old ex-University of Wisconsin star who was ticketed for the 2015 Web.com Tour before surprisingly qualifying here.

Among the remaining five, a pair of Frenchman, 25-year-old **Edouard Espana** and 29-year-old **Jérôme Lando Casanova**, would seem the best bets, followed by a trio of Englishmen: 34-year-old **Matt Ford** (never better than 48th in earnings over four full Challenge Tour seasons), 24-year-old **Tom Murray** (never better than 100th in two) and 30-year-old **Jason Palmer**, the 2006 Italian Amateur champion.

European Tour 2014 Q School Qualifiers (Low 25 and ties received 2015 cards)

1	Mikko Korhonen	72-65-65-71-68-67	408	€16,000		Chris Lloyd	72-66-66-71-73-70	418	€3,468
2	Ricardo González	68-68-65-72-70-67	410	€11,500	16=	Joakim Lagergren	66-72-69-70-73-69	419	€2,775
3	Renato Paratore	67-70-66-69-67-73	412	€9,000		Anirban Lahiri	65-68-66-73-75-72	419	€2,775
4	Matt Ford	74-64-65-68-72-70	413	€7,200	18=	Jason Scrivener	77-64-67-74-72-66	420	€2,220
5=	Adrian Otaegui	67-71-68-72-70-67	415	€5,240		Borja Virto	77-63-67-73-70-70	420	€2,220
	John Parry	68-68-71-69-72-67	415	€5,240		Pedro Oriol	70-66-68-69-77-70	420	€2,220
	Eduardo De La Riva	71-68-69-67-69-71	415	€5,240		Pelle Edberg	73-62-63-75-76-71	420	€2,220
8	Richard McEvoy	73-65-64-72-70-72	416	€4,440		Chris Paisley	70-69-68-70-69-74	420	€2,220
9	Rikard Karlberg	67-68-67-73-71-71	417	€4,190		Andrea Pavan	69-67-70-71-69-74	420	€2,220
10=	Andrew Dodt	66-71-68-74-72-67	418	€3,468		Lasse Jensen	69-74-67-66-70-74	420	€2,220
	Matthew Fitzpatrick	70-66-67-76-71-68	418	€3,468	25=	Alessandro Tadini	72-67-69-71-74-68	421	€1,860
	Espen Kofstad	72-67-64-74-72-69	418	€3,468		Daniel Woltman	72-72-71-68-69-69	421	€1,860
	Paul Maddy	67-72-68-69-72-70	418	€3,468		Cyril Bouniol	72-68-67-71-70-73	421	€1,860
	Tom Murray	76-64-63-73-72-70	418	€3,468					

Top 15 Finishers on the 2014 Challenge Tour Money List

1	Andrew Johnston	€190,856	9	Michael Lorenzo-Vera	€106,796
2	Benjamin Hebert	€178,266	10	Oliver Farr	€101,476
3	Byeong-Hun An	€150,107	11	Edouard Espana	€95,012
4	Moritz Lampert	€137,194	12	Florian Fritsch	€92,943
5	Mark Tullo	€129,968	13	Jérôme Lando Casanova	€88,785
6	Sam Hutsby	€128,984	14	Jake Roos	€87,431
7	Jordi García Pinto	€112,317	15	Jason Barnes	€77,793
8	Jason Palmer	€108,056			

PLAYERS
2015

PLAYER PROFILES

The following player profiles have been designed to provide a maximum amount of career information in the most efficient manner possible, and thus rely heavily on abbreviations and some notably compact formatting. Most of the format's uniquenesses are self-explanatory, at least to the avid golf fan, but several points are perhaps worthy of some amplification, as follows:

-- As their 2014 season will not be completed until March of 2015, all results and statistics from the Sunshine Tour are good through December 31, 2014 only.

-- Within each player's list of career victories, events co-sanctioned by more than one professional tour are listed under the higher-rated circuit only (e.g., events co-sanctioned by the European and Sunshine Tours will be listed as European victories). This is also true for co-sanctioned events listed in each player's 2014 totals (e.g., 19 st / 12 ct / 4 t10). For this purpose, the order of descendancy is the PGA Tour, the European Tour, the Japan Tour, the Asian Tour, the Sunshine Tour, the OneAsia Tour and the Australasian Tour.

-- Because of the ever-evolving nature of tournament sponsorship, it is difficult to maintain the consistency of tournament names within player's lists of career victories. On smaller tours around the world, where both events and sponsors tend change more quickly, events are generally listed exactly as they appeared on the circuit's official schedule. In America and Europe, however, longer-running events which have seen multiple sponsors are generally listed by their original or generic name, with the title sponsor for the year in question appearing in parenthesis afterwards, such as: Los Angeles Open (Nissan)

-- Within the category "Other Wins" (which reflects professional victories outside of the major tours), events are listed with a notation for the country they were played in. Where no such notation appears, the event was contested in the player's home country.

-- As of 2013, the PGA Tour switched from its official money list to FedEx Cup points to determine player's status (e.g., top 125 being exempt) for the following season. This is so referenced within each player's 2014 recap but for reasons of consistency (both historical and with other tours), career ledgers will continue to list money rankings – for now.

-- Though different publications and sources annually produce collegiate All-American teams, All-American designations herein refer strictly to the number of times a player was selected First, Second or Third Team by the Golf Coaches Association of America. Honorable Mention selections, though often noted in a player's bio, are not counted here.

-- For reasons of space, lists of top-10 finishes in players' 2014 ledgers are limited to their five best for the PGA, European and Japan Tours, and to their most relevant two or three ("Incl.") elsewhere.

Within each player's profile, specific abbreviations, symbols and numbers worth noting are as follows:

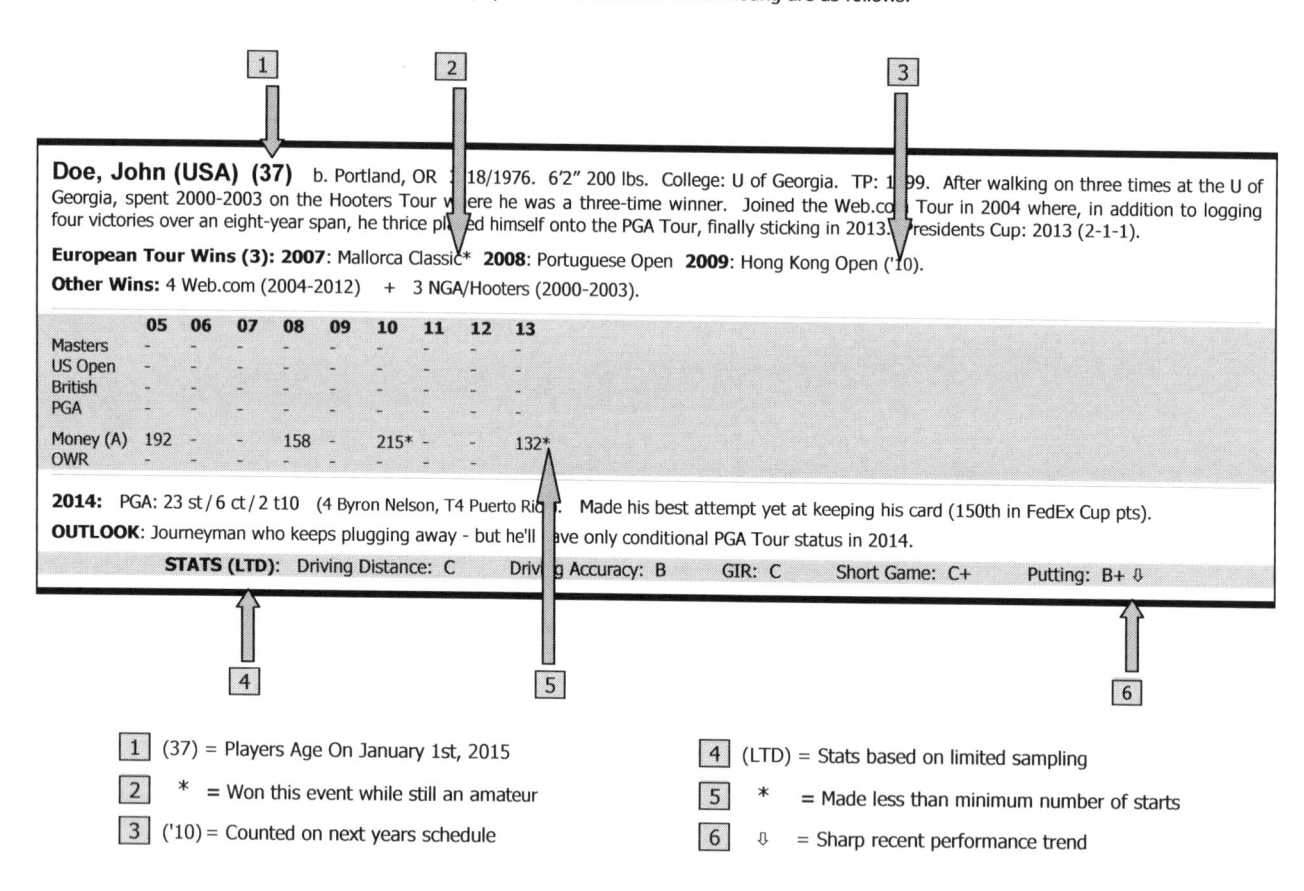

Doe, John (USA) (37) b. Portland, OR 3/18/1976. 6'2" 200 lbs. College: U of Georgia. TP: 1999. After walking on three times at the U of Georgia, spent 2000-2003 on the Hooters Tour where he was a three-time winner. Joined the Web.com Tour in 2004 where, in addition to logging four victories over an eight-year span, he thrice played himself onto the PGA Tour, finally sticking in 2013. Presidents Cup: 2013 (2-1-1).
European Tour Wins (3): 2007: Mallorca Classic* **2008**: Portuguese Open **2009**: Hong Kong Open ('10).
Other Wins: 4 Web.com (2004-2012) + 3 NGA/Hooters (2000-2003).

	05	06	07	08	09	10	11	12	13
Masters	-	-	-	-	-	-	-	-	
US Open	-	-	-	-	-	-	-	-	
British	-	-	-	-	-	-	-	-	
PGA	-	-	-	-	-	-	-	-	
Money (A)	192	-	-	158	-	215*	-	132*	
OWR	-	-	-	-	-	-	-	-	

2014: PGA: 23 st / 6 ct / 2 t10 (4 Byron Nelson, T4 Puerto Rico). Made his best attempt yet at keeping his card (150th in FedEx Cup pts).
OUTLOOK: Journeyman who keeps plugging away - but he'll have only conditional PGA Tour status in 2014.
STATS (LTD): Driving Distance: C   Driving Accuracy: B   GIR: C   Short Game: C+   Putting: B+ ⇓

---

[1] (37) = Players Age On January 1st, 2015
[2] * = Won this event while still an amateur
[3] ('10) = Counted on next years schedule
[4] (LTD) = Stats based on limited sampling
[5] * = Made less than minimum number of starts
[6] ⇓ = Sharp recent performance trend

Statistical grades at the bottom of each profile are derived by utilizing a player's actual numerical rankings over the past two or three seasons, then marginally adjusting these results as needed to reflect longer term numbers that differ greatly, and to acknowledge the talent differentials which exist among the various tours. Most terminology used therein is self-explanatory, though among the most frequently employed, it is worth noting that "SGP" stands for Strokes Gained Putting and "GIR" stands for Greens In Regulation.

Abery, Warren (South Africa) (41)   b. Durban, South Africa 6/28/1973. 5'8" 155 lbs. TP: 1997. The 1995 South African Amateur champion who went on to become a frequent winner on the Sunshine Tour. After beating Richard Sterne by three to claim the 2001 Graceland Challenge, peaked in 2005 and '06 when he twice cracked the Order of Merit top 10 and won both the 2005 Telkom PGA Championship (by one over Charl Schwartzel and Jaco Van Zyl) and the 2006 Nashua Masters. Added a second Nashua Masters title in 2010, when he beat a trio of players (including a young Branden Grace) by two. **Teams:** Eisenhower Trophy: 1996. **OWR Best:** 187 - Mar, 2006.

Sunshine Tour Wins (7): 1998: ABSA Bank Challenge (54H) **2001:** Graceland Challenge (54H) **2005:** Telkom PGA Championship **2006:** Nashua Masters **2007:** Nashua Golf Challenge (54H) **2010:** Nashua Masters **2011:** Nedbank Affinity Cup (54H).

Other Wins: Sun Int'l Touring Pro-Am (SA): 2008.

Amateur Wins: South African Am: 1995   –   Natal Am (2): 1994-95.

	98	99	00	01	02	03	04	05	06	07	08	09	10	11	12	13	14
Masters	-	-	-	-	-	-	-	-	-	-	-	-	-	-	-	-	-
US Open	-	-	-	-	-	-	-	-	-	-	-	-	-	-	-	-	-
British	-	-	-	-	-	-	-	-	MC	-	-	-	-	-	-	-	-
PGA	-	-	-	-	-	-	-	-	-	-	-	-	-	-	-	-	-
Money (E)	-	-	-	-	-	-	-	-	152	232*	-	-	-	-	220*	-	-
Money (SA)	15	20	73	55	51	113*	64	3	7	12	13	35	20	18	40	19	57
OWR	390	405	668	956	-	-	573	392	267	605	571	771	393	461	821	606	713

2014: SUN: 22 st / 15 ct / 2 t10.   (T8 Zambia, T9 Dim Data).   Fell out of the Sunshine $$$ top 50 for the first time in a decade.

OUTLOOK: A steady regional performer who, at age 41, seems to be edging onto the downside - though he can still be a factor at the Sunshine level.

STATS: Driving Distance: --   Driving Accuracy: --   GIR: --   Short Game: --   Putting: --

---

Adams, Samuel Blakely (Blake) (USA) (39)   b. Eatonton, GA 8/27/1975. 6'3" 205 lbs. College: Georgia Southern U. TP: 2001. High school basketball star who played the Hooters Tour from 2002-2004 (1 win) and the Gateway Tour in 2005-2006 (1 win). Qualified for the 2007 Web.com Tour, remaining there for three years (and playing through a late-2008 hip injury) before graduating at the end of 2009 (3rd in $$$). Winless through his first three PGA Tour seasons but cracked the top 100 in earnings all three years, peaking at 73rd in 2012. Missed virtually all of 2013 after undergoing hip surgery in January, then underwent hip replacement surgery in 2014, limiting him to 10 PGA Tour starts over two years. **OWR Best:** 112 - May, 2010.

Other Wins: 1 NGA/Hooters (2005)   1 eGolf Tour (2008)   1 Gateway (2005).

	09	10	11	12	13	14
Masters	-	-	-	-	-	-
US Open	-	-	-	T21	-	-
British	-	-	-	-	-	-
PGA	-	-	-	T7	-	-
Money (A)	-	98	84	73	-	203*
OWR	169	189	209	143	410	1068

2014: PGA: 8 st / 5 ct / 0 t10.   Made eight starts before undergoing hip replacement surgery in July, causing him to miss the rest of the year.

OUTLOOK: Begins 2014 on a 16-event medical extension. A very steady earner prior to injuries, recording nine top 10s in 92 starts (and improving his $$$ each year) from 2010-2012. Solid all-around player whose average rankings were 46.7 in Ball Striking and 19.3 in Total Driving over those seasons, as well as 45 in Strokes Gained Putting. Appeared ready to win in 2012, but his future now seems largely dependent on a replacement hip.

STATS: Driving Distance: B   Driving Accuracy: A   GIR: B+   Short Game: B   Putting: A-

---

Affrunti, Joseph Anthony (USA) (33)   b. Chicago, IL 8/1/1981. 5'7" 155 lbs. College: All-American at U of Illinois (after transferring from Minnesota). TP: 2004. After spending multiple years on mini-tours, played the Web.com Tour in 2010, when a 22nd-place finish in $$$ earned him a PGA Tour card. Had left shoulder surgery after six starts and has been riding a medical extension ever since. **OWR Best:** 286 - Jan, 2011.

	11	12	13	14
Masters	-	-	-	-
US Open	-	-	-	-
British	-	-	-	-
PGA	-	-	-	-
Money (A)	243*	-	217*	-
OWR	583	-	710	1094

2014: Did not make a start while still recovering from 2011 left shoulder surgery.

OUTLOOK: Begins 2015 on a longshot eight-event medical extension which dates to 2011. There is little on his résumé to suggest success at the PGA Tour level, and the length of his layoff surely won't help in that regard. Unlikely to have a major impact upon his return.

STATS (LTD): Driving Distance: B-   Driving Accuracy: B   GIR: C+   Short Game: C   Putting: B

Aguilar Schuller, Felipe (Chile) (40)   b. Valdivia, Chile 11/7/1974. 5'7" 160 lbs. College: U of North Florida. TP: 1999. Played collegiate golf in America and won numerous lesser events in his native Chile before becoming the second player from that nation to play full-time on the European Tour. After falling back to the Challenge Tour for a two-win 2007 campaign, returned to the E Tour for a career-best 2008 in which he finished 41st in $$$ and won the Indonesia Open, where a second round 62 helped to propel him to a one-shot triumph over Jeev Milkha Singh. Soon established himself as a steady $$$ winner, retaining his card (generally comfortably) on an annual basis. Scored his second E Tour win in spectacular fashion in 2014, holing a 142-yard wedge to eagle the 72nd (and shoot 62) as he claimed the inaugural Championship at Laguna National. **Teams:** Eisenhower Trophy (2): 1996-98. World Cup (3): 2003-08-13. **OWR Best:** 99 - Jun, 2008.

European Tour Wins (2): 2008: Indonesia Open **2014:** Championship at Laguna National.

Aguilar Schuller, Felipe, Cont'd

Other Wins: 2 Euro Challenge (2007) + 1 Alps Tour (2004) Chile Open (2): 2002-08.
Amateur Wins: South American Am: 1991 Chile Am (3): 1990-91-92.

	06	07	08	09	10	11	12	13	14
Masters	-	-	-	-	-	-	-	-	
US Open	-	-	-	-	-	-	-	-	
British	-	-	-	-	-	-	-	-	
PGA	-	-	-	-	-	-	-	-	
Money (E)	158	-	41	80	116	54	79	50	62
OWR	277	170	136	268	437	193	242	164	158

2014: E: 21 st / 16 ct / 4 t10. (Won Laguna, T3 Port Masters, T4 NH Collection, T7 Spanish). Enjoyed another solid year, recording half as many top 10s as in 2013 but winning (in spectacular fashion) at Laguna National. Narrowly missed making it to the lucrative Tour Championship in Dubai.
OUTLOOK: Though less consistent overall in 2014, he still seems to be near the top of his game in what are likely the latter stages of his prime. Very straight/solid from tee-to-green, but a lack of length and mediocre putting numbers limit his upside. But he's hardly struggling where he's at...
STATS: Driving Distance: C+   Driving Accuracy: A   GIR: A   Short Game: C+   Putting: C-

---

Ahlers, Johannes ("Jaco") (South Africa) (32)
b. Pretoria, South Africa 11/19/1982. 6'0" 230 lbs. TP: 2006. A steady but unspectacular Sunshine Tour performer who first broke through at the weather-shortened 2009 Vodacom Origins of Golf – Arabella event, which he won in a playoff over Ulrich van den Berg. Maintained a steady upward course in the Sunshine Order of Merit through 2011 before jumping to a career-best 14th in 2012, then largely holding his ground with an 18th-place finish in 2013. Claimed his second career win at the 2014 Cape Town Open, where he beat Hennie Otto and Ross McGowan in sudden death. **OWR Best:** 209 - Dec, 2014.

Sunshine Tour Wins (2): 2009: Vodacom-Arabella (36H) **2014:** Cape Town Open.

	07	08	09	10	11	12	13	14
Masters	-	-	-	-	-	-	-	
US Open	-	-	-	-	-	-	-	
British	-	-	MC	-	-	-	-	
PGA	-	-	-	-	-	-	-	
Money (SA)	81	58	43	43	33	14	18	16
OWR	-	-	-	876	820	369	406	210

2014: SUN: 21 st / 19 ct / 10 t10. (Incl. Won Cape Town, T2 Vodacom-Wild Coast, T3 Vodacom-Vaal de Grace). Ranked among the Sunshine Tour's top 20 $$$ winners for the third straight year, contended several times and claimed his second career win at the Cape Town Open.
OUTLOOK: A steady veteran who has settled into his best golf in his early 30s. Aside from making several 2013 starts on the PGA Tour Canada, has shown little inkling to venture away from his native circuit, but he seems primed for expanding success there.
STATS: Driving Distance: --   Driving Accuracy: --   GIR: --   Short Game: --   Putting: --

---

Aiken, Thomas Edward (South Africa) (31)
b. Johannesburg, South Africa 7/16/1983. 5'8" 150 lbs. TP: 2002. Was named South African Amateur of The Year in 2001 after capturing 10 victories (but not the national title). Began playing the Sunshine Tour at age 19, making a name for himself in 2004 when he won three legs of the six-event Vodacom Origins series, including the Vodacom Final in a seven-shot runaway. Added two more smaller events in 2005 as well as bigger victories at the 2006 Royal Swazi Sun Open and the 2008 Platinum Classic. Claimed his first E Tour win at the 2011 Spanish Open (beating Anders Hansen by two), then backed it up by winning the 2013 Avantha Masters in India, where he edged homestanding Gaganjeet Bhullar by three. Won the 2014 Africa Open, beating Oliver Fisher on the first hole of sudden death at East London. Currently splits time between the E and Sunshine circuits, with the odd foray to America thrown in. **OWR Best:** 73 - May, 2011.

European Tour Wins (3): 2011: Spanish Open **2013:** Avantha Masters **2014:** Africa Open.
Sunshine Tour Wins (7): 2004: Vodacom-Zimbali (54H), Vodacom-Sun City (54H), Vodacom-Final (54H) **2005:** Telkom PGA Pro-Am (54H), Namibia PGA (54H) **2006:** Royal Swazi Sun Open (Stableford) **2008:** Platinum Classic (54H).
Other Wins: Stoke by Nayland (SA): 2003.

	03	04	05	06	07	08	09	10	11	12	13	14
Masters	-	-	-	-	-	-	-	-	-	-	-	
US Open	MC	-	-	-	-	-	-	-	-	-	-	
British	-	-	-	MC	-	T39	T8	T74	MC	T7	MC	-
PGA	-	-	-	-	-	-	-	-	MC	MC	-	
Money (E)	-	-	-	-	-	131	46	58	22	54	44	55
Money (SA)	91	39	14	4	16	3*	21*	2*	4*	6*	18*	3*
OWR	-	680	552	505	724	388	141	138	87	113	159	153

2014: E: 22 st / 16 ct / 5 t10. (Won Africa, T5 Qatar, T5 Joburg, T7 BMW PGA, T8 Volvo Champ). Cracked the top 60 in E Tour $$$ for the sixth straight year and added his third E Tour victory - and unlike many South African E Tour winners (who star only at home), it was his first on native soil.
OUTLOOK: Quietly marches along, earning and winning consistently on two continents. His ball striking (especially off the tee) is the envy of many, and at age 31 he figures to just be entering his prime years. It will be interesting to see if he can find one more gear to either win more consistently in Europe or, alternatively, emerge as a genuinely dominant player at home. At this point, coming to America does not appear to be a priority.
STATS: Driving Distance: B+   Driving Accuracy: A   GIR: A   Short Game: B+   Putting: B-

---

Alker, Steven Craig (New Zealand) (43)
b. Hamilton, New Zealand 9/28/1971. 5'11" 150 lbs. TP: 1995. A former amateur star in New Zealand who enjoyed early success on the Australasian Tour, winning three times in the late 1990s, including a one-shot victory over Wayne Grady at the 1997 Jacobs Creek Open. Aside from a one-year PGA Tour run in 2003, has played in Europe, Canada (winning twice there in 2000) and the Web.com Tour, from which he regained his PGA Tour status in 2014. **Teams:** Eisenhower Trophy (2): 1990-94. **OWR Best:** 120 - Jul, 1997.

Alker, Steven Craig, Cont'd

Australasian Tour Wins (4): 1996: Queensland Open **1997:** Jacobs Creek Open, South Australian Open **2009:** New Zealand PGA.
Other Wins: 3 Web.com (2002-2014) + Fiji Open: 1995 Tahiti Open: 1996 PEI Challenge (Canada): 2000 Bayer Championship (Canada): 2000 Toyota Southern Classic (Aus): 2001.

	98	99	00	01	02	03	04	05	06	07	08	09	10	11	12	13	14
Masters	-	-	-	-	-	-	-	-	-	-	-	-	-	-	-	T45	MC
US Open	-	-	-	-	-	-	-	-	-	-	-	-	-	-	-	-	-
British	MC	-	-	-	-	-	-	-	-	MC	-	-	-	-	T19	-	-
PGA	-	-	-	-	-	-	-	-	-	-	-	-	-	-	-	-	-
Money (A)	-	-	-	-	-	163	-	-	-	-	-	-	-	-	-	-	-
Money (E)	138	249*	-	-	-	-	-	-	-	148	228*	-	-	-	-	-	-
OWR	256	554	346	302	284	375	605	651	774	567	760	504	980	1183	617	397	309

2014: Played the Web.com Tour full-time, winning once and finishing 10th in regular season $$$ to clinch another shot at the PGA Tour.

OUTLOOK: Returns to the PGA Tour (via the Web.com) fully a dozen years after his first try, and statistically speaking he may well be playing the best golf of his career in his early 40s. Would seem a longshot for major success, but he'll be highly motivated as it's now or never.

STATS: Driving Distance: C+   Driving Accuracy: A   GIR: B+   Short Game: B   Putting: B

Allenby, Robert Mark (Australia) (43)
b. Melbourne, Victoria, Australia 7/12/1971. 6'1" 180 lbs. TP: 1991. Won 1991 Victorian Open as an amateur. Competed mostly in Europe upon turning pro, but played enough winter events in Australia to claim five domestic titles between 1992-1995, including the 1994 Australian Open. Blossomed in 1996, winning thrice during the European summer, most notably at the British Masters, where he edged Miguel-Angel Martin in sudden death. Soon thereafter, suffered injuries to his sternum and face in a car accident in Spain. Came to America in 1999 where he won twice in 2000, notably at the Western Open where he beat Nick Price in a playoff. Won 2001 Nissan Open (Los Angeles), claiming a PGA Tour record-tying six-man playoff by hitting a 3 wood to 5 feet (in a freezing rain) at Riviera's famed 18th hole. Multiple winner of the Australian Open (twice), Masters (twice) and PGA (four times), including a sweep of all three in consecutive weeks in 2005 (the only man ever to do so). Closed 2009 with a playoff win over Henrik Stenson at South Africa's Nedbank Challenge as well as his fourth Australian PGA title. Closed out a disappointing 2011 by going 0-4 in the Presidents Cup. Lost a marathon eight-hole playoff to John Huh at the 2012 Mayakoba Classic. **Teams:** Eisenhower Trophy: 1990. Presidents Cup (6): 1994-96-00-03-09-11 (8-17-3). World Cup (3): 1993-95-09. **OWR Best:** 12 - May, 2010.

PGA Tour Wins (4): 2000: Houston Open (Shell), Western Open (Advil) **2001:** Los Angeles Open (Nissan), Pennsylvania Classic (Marconi).
European Tour Wins (4): 1994: Honda Open **1996:** English Open, Open de France, British Masters.
Sunshine Tour Wins (1): 2009: Million Dollar Challenge.
Australasian Tour Wins (12): 1992: Perak Masters, Johnnie Walker Classic **1993:** Optus Players Championship **1994:** Australian Open **1995:** Heineken Classic **2000:** Australian PGA **2001:** Australian PGA **2003:** Australian Masters **2005:** Australian Open, Australian PGA, Australian Masters **2009:** Australian PGA.
Other Wins: Victorian Open (Aus): 1991*.
Amateur Wins: Victorian Am: 1990 – Australian Jr: 1990   Victorian Jr: 1990   Riversdale Cup (2): 1990-91.

	91	92	93	94	95	96	97	98	99	00	01	02	03	04	05	06	07	08	09	10	11	12	13	14
Masters	-	-	-	-	-	-	MC	-	-	-	47	T29	T37	MC	MC	T22	MC	T42	T38	T45	MC	-	-	MC
US Open	-	-	T33	-	-	-	MC	-	T46	-	MC	T12	MC	T7	MC	T16	MC	T18	MC	T29	MC	-	-	-
British	-	-	-	MC	T60	T15	T56	T10	T19	-	T36	T47	MC	T43	MC	T52	T16	MC	T7	T52	T27	T48	MC	-
PGA	-	-	-	MC	-	MC	MC	T49	T13	MC	T19	T16	T10	T39	T9	MC	T20	MC	T31	T24	-	T26	MC	-
Money (A)	-	-	-	-	-	-	-	-	126	16	16	20	24	44	63	56	27	11	42	18	60	111	184	145
Money (E)	-	86	70	17	47	3	55	44	-	-	-	-	-	-	-	-	-	-	21	-	-	-	-	-
OWR	-	84	81	48	64	37	50	84	148	35	22	25	16	33	35	47	51	27	21	21	59	197	552	274

2014: PGA: 29 st / 12 ct / 0 t10. (T16 Mayakoba). Despite missing eight of his last 10 cuts, finished 125th in FedEx Cup points to claim the Tour's final fully exempt spot for 2015 - which is good, because he used his one-time Top 125 Career Money Winners exemption last year.

OUTLOOK: From 2004-2009, he ranked 3, 4, 11, 21, 4 and 7 in total Ball Striking before falling to 126 and 164 in 2012 and '13. But in 2014 he climbed back to 80, while also improving his Driving Accuracy from 141 to 81 and, most importantly, his GIR from 148 to 27. Given his less-impressive putting (even in the best of times), a huge mid-40s resurgence seems unlikely - but a few more relevant years in America now seem a real possibility.

STATS: Driving Distance: C+   Driving Accuracy: B-   GIR: B   Short Game: C+   Putting: C+

Allred, Jason Lee (USA) (34)
b. Ashland, OR 4/6/1980. 6'2" 175 lbs. All-American and Byron Nelson Award winner (2002) at Pepperdine U. TP: 2002. A three-time AJGA All-American and one-time U.S. Junior Amateur prior to college. Struggled for many years as a pro, playing two full seasons (unsuccessfully) on the PGA Tour in 2005 and '08, several years on the Web.com and several more on mini-tours and in Canada. Remains winless as a pro but earned over $600,000 on the 2014 PGA Tour, mostly behind a T3 at the Northern Trust. **OWR Best:** 239 - Aug, 2014.

Amateur Wins: U.S. Junior Am: 1997.

	05	06	07	08	09	10	11	12	13	14
Masters	-	-	-	-	-	-	-	-	-	-
US Open	-	MC	-	-	-	T47	-	-	-	-
British	MC	-	-	-	-	-	-	-	-	-
PGA	-	-	-	-	-	-	-	-	-	-
Money (A)	204	-	-	221	-	-	-	-	-	-
OWR	526	491	629	964	1367	979	1303	847	901	315

2014: PGA: 9 st / 5 ct / 2 t10. (T3 Northern Trust, T6 Barracuda). Made a splash at Northern Trust but still currently lacks PGA Tour status.

OUTLOOK: Despite ranking well within the top 300 of the OWR, has no status on the PGA Tour and only conditional status on the Web.com. He'll probably get several sponsor exemptions, however, so he can try to catch lightning in a bottle once more, as he did in 2014.

STATS (LTD): Driving Distance: B   Driving Accuracy: C   GIR: C   Short Game: B+   Putting: B+

Alvarado, Benjamin (Chile) (29) b. Santiago, Chile 9/2/1985. 5'11" 165 lbs. All-American at Arizona St. TP: 2007. An AJGA All-American. Won the 2003 South American Amateur and the 2003 Chile Open before turning professional. Later played the European Challenge Tour, the Tour de Las Americas (winning a second Chile Open in 2011), the Canadian Tour and the PGA Tour Latinoamérica. Won once on the 2013 Web.com Tour, allowing him to earn a PGA Tour card by finishing 19th in regular season $$$. Spent the latter part of 2013 recovering from a left knee injury, which in turn limited his rookie year on the PGA Tour to six starts. **OWR Best:** 275 - Jul, 2011.

Other Wins: 1 Web.com (2013) + Chile Open (2): 2003*-11.
Amateur Wins: Orange Bowl Jr: 2002   South American Am: 2003.

	08	09	10	11	12	13	14
Masters	-	-	-	-	-	-	-
US Open	-	-	-	-	-	-	-
British	-	-	-	-	-	-	-
PGA	-	-	-	-	-	-	-
Money (A)	-	-	-	-	-	-	246*
OWR	974	1002	1053	322	653	438	1011

2014: PGA: 6 st / 1 ct / 0 t10. (T53 FedEx St Jude). Made only six starts after recovering from surgery on his left knee.
OUTLOOK: Begins 2015 on a precarious four-event medical extension. Seemed a longshot when healthy; it will be really tough now.

STATS (LTD): Driving Distance: C+   Driving Accuracy: C+   GIR: B-   Short Game: B   Putting: C

Ames, Stephen Michael (Trinidad & Tobago/Canada) (50) b. San Fernando, Trinidad 4/28/1964. 6'1" 185 lbs. The first touring pro to emerge from Trinidad & Tobago, but has long resided in Canada. After winning the 1989 Trinidad & Tobago Open, came north and played three Web.com campaigns from 1990-1992 (8th in $$$ in 1991) before beginning a five-year run in Europe in 1993. Scored his first major tour victory at the light-field 1994 Open de Lyon, then his second at the 2006 Benson & Hedges International, the latter heading a year in which he finished 13th in $$$. Came to America in 1998 (at age 33) and enjoyed a long run of success, finishing no worse then 89th in earnings from 1998-2009, and peaking at 8th in 2004. Didn't win a PGA Tour event until the 2004 Western Open (his 166th start) but then backed it up with a six-shot runaway win at the 2006 Players Championship and a season-ending triumph at the 2007 Children's Miracle Network Classic. Won a second Children's Miracle Network title (at age 45) in 2009. **Teams:** Eisenhower Trophy: 1986. World Cup (4): 2000-02-03-06. **OWR Best:** 17 - Jul, 2004.

PGA Tour Wins (4): 2004: Western Open (Cialis) **2006:** Players Championship **2007:** Walt Disney Classic (Children's Miracle) **2009:** Walt Disney Classic (Children's Miracle).
European Tour Wins (2): 1994: Open de Lyon **1996:** Benson & Hedges Int'l.
Other Wins: 1 Web.com (1991) + Trinidad & Tobago Open: 1989   Canadian Skins Game: 1995   Skins Game (2): 2006-07.

	93	94	95	96	97	98	99	00	01	02	03	04	05	06	07	08	09	10	11	12	13	14
Masters	-	-	-	-	-	-	-	-	-	-	-	-	T45	T11	T24	T25	T20	-	-	-	-	-
US Open	-	-	-	T68	-	-	-	-	-	T9	-	MC	T71	MC	T10	T58	T10	MC	-	T68	-	-
British	T51	-	-	T56	T5	T24	-	-	-	T69	-	MC	MC	T41	MC	T7	MC	-	MC	-	-
PGA	-	-	-	-	-	-	T30	-	WD	MC	T9	T72	T55	T12	MC	T24	MC	-	-	-	-	-
Money (A)	-	-	-	-	-	83	84	63	89	46	72	8	83	26	31	27	37	107	139	187	187	194
Money (E)	49	58	77	13	30	-	-	-	-	-	-	-	-	-	-	-	-	-	-	-	-	-
OWR	180	165	192	80	82	82	88	94	157	107	105	17	51	43	33	37	57	118	337	598	756	1028

2014: PGA: 18 st / 6 ct / 0 t10. (T16 Texas). Had only one top-25 finish, his lowest $$$ ranking ever and finished 190 in FedEx Cup points.
OUTLOOK: Despite turning 50 in April, made only two Champions Tour starts (including a T15 at the Senior PGA Championship) in 2014 - but with very few of his numbers suggesting he can still compete effectively on the PGA Tour, that number figures to jump dramatically in the year ahead.

STATS: Driving Distance: C-   Driving Accuracy: B+   GIR: C-   Short Game: B+   Putting: B-

---

An, Byeong-Hun (South Korea) (23) b. Seoul, South Korea 9/17/1991. 6'2" 190 lbs. College: U of California-Berkeley. TP: 2011. An AJGA All-American. Born in South Korea but moved to America in 2005 (age 14) to study at David Leadbetter's Florida academy. In August 2009, became the youngest-ever winner of the U.S. Amateur (age 17) when he defeated Ben Martin 7 & 5 at Southern Hills. Thus appeared at the 2010 Masters, U.S. Open and British Open, missing all three cuts. Had little impact as a professional over his first two seasons but finished third on the 2014 Challenge Tour, gaining full E Tour status for 2015. **OWR Best:** 173 - Nov, 2014.

Amateur Wins: U.S. Amateur: 2009.

	10	11	12	13	14
Masters	MC	-	-	-	-
US Open	MC	-	-	-	-
British	MC	-	-	-	T26
PGA	-	-	-	-	-
Money (E)	-	-	-	-	161*
OWR	1322	-	952	444	179

2014: Played full-time on the Challenge Tour, logging eight top 10s in 21 starts and finishing 3rd in $$$, gaining his 2015 E Tour card.
OUTLOOK: Has been touted since his surprising victory at the 2009 U.S. Amateur, and has shown minor flashes while adjusting to the professional game. Put together a solid 2014 on the Challenge Tour, and figures to enjoy a moment or two as an E Tour rookie in 2015.

STATS (LTD): Driving Distance: A-   Driving Accuracy: B   GIR: B+   Short Game: C   Putting: C

Anderson, Mark Douglas (USA) (28) b. Annapolis, MD 2/14/1986. 6'1" 180 lbs. All-American at U of South Carolina. TP: 2009. Played his first two professional seasons (2010 and '11) on the Web.com Tour, graduating to the PGA Tour after finishing 22nd in $$$ in the latter year. Finished 155th in PGA Tour $$$ in 2012, then returned to the Web.com for 2013 where he won the BMW Charity Pro-Am and finished 8th in $$$ to return to the big stage. Made only eight 2014 PGA Tour starts after injuring his leg falling off a ladder. **OWR Best:** 284 - Aug, 2013.

Anderson, Mark Douglas, Cont'd

Other Wins: 1 Web.com (2013).
Amateur Wins: Players Am: 2008   Oglethorpe Inv: 2008   Master of Amateurs: 2009.

	12	13	14
Masters	-	-	-
US Open	-	-	-
British	-	-	-
PGA	-	-	-
Money (A)	155	-	199*
OWR	465	340	633

2014: PGA: 8 st / 3 ct / 0 t10.   (T17 New Orleans).   Finished 212 in FedEx Cup points in only eight starts, having injured his leg in May.

OUTLOOK: Was highly touted in some quarters in 2012, when he missed earning conditional status by five spots. After a strong 2013 on the Web.com Tour, seemed poised for a strong 2014 return, but now begins 2015 on a medical extension, making his immediate future uncertain at best.

STATS (LTD):   Driving Distance: B+   Driving Accuracy: C   GIR: C+   Short Game: B   Putting: B-

---

Andersson Hed, Fredrik (Sweden) (42)
b. Halmstad, Sweden 1/20/1972. 6'2" 170 lbs. TP: 1992. Played as Fredrik Andersson prior to adding his wife's surname after his 2004 marriage. Bounced back and forth from the Challenge Tour (where he won twice) during the 1990s, playing E Tour Q School on a remarkable 14 occasions. Found form in 2007 when he finished 45th in the Order of Merit. Struggled in 2008 and '09 before breaking through with a career-best 2010, led by a four-shot victory over Nicolas Colsaerts at the Italian Open and a 22nd-place finish in $$$. Remained among the top 40 in $$$ in 2011 and '12 before slipping markedly. **Teams:** Eisenhower Trophy: 1992. **OWR Best:** 68 - Nov, 2010.

European Tour Wins (1): 2010: Italian Open (BMW).
Other Wins: 2 Euro Challenge (1993-2000).
Amateur Wins: Swedish Jr: 1989   European Young Masters: 1990.

	95	96	97	98	99	00	01	02	03	04	05	06	07	08	09	10	11	12	13	14
Masters	-	-	-	-	-	-	-	-	-	-	-	-	-	-	-	-	-	-	-	-
US Open	-	-	-	-	-	-	-	-	-	-	-	-	-	-	-	-	-	-	-	-
British	MC	-	-	-	-	-	T50	-	-	-	T69	-	T65	-	T68	T57	-	-	-	-
PGA	-	-	-	-	-	-	-	-	-	-	-	-	-	-	-	T62	MC	-	-	-
Money (E)	166	-	181	-	-	-	122	113	82	111	132	-	45	121	188	22	39	36	123	183
OWR	-	-	858	-	-	591	344	309	264	451	521	614	159	322	326	72	101	88	192	635

2014: E: 16 st / 5 ct / 0 t10.   (T11 Mandela).   Made only five cuts in falling to 183 in $$$, then came up short at final stage Q School.

OUTLOOK: Enjoyed a career-best three-year run (2010-2012) that was built around decent length off the tee and high-end skills around the greens. But he has struggled since 2013 and will be resigned to the Challenge Tour in 2015. At age 42, his best golf is likely all behind him now.

STATS: Driving Distance: B   Driving Accuracy: C-   GIR: C   Short Game: B+   Putting: A-

---

Aphibarnrat, Kiradech (Thailand) (25)
b. Bangkok, Thailand 7/23/1989. 5'8" 230 lbs. TP: 2008. Was born with the name Anujit Hirunratanakorn but elected to change it. A two-time age group winner at San Diego's Junior World Championships under his original moniker. A regular on both the Asian and Japan Tours since turning pro. Won the 2009 Singha Pattaya Open in his native Thailand by 11 strokes before logging his first major tour title at the Asian circuit's 2011 SAIL Open, edging Siddikur Rahman by one. In something of a breakout year, added the 2013 Malaysian Open (by one over Edoardo Molinari) to gain status on the E Tour, then finished 39th in $$$ there (in only 17 starts) while also easily winning the Asian Tour Order of Merit. **Teams:** World Cup (2): 2011-13. **OWR Best:** 58 - Jan, 2014.

European Tour Wins (1): 2013: Malaysian Open (Maybank)(54H).
Asian Tour Wins (1): 2011: SAIL Open.
Other Wins: Singha Pattaya Open (Thailand): 2009.
Amateur Wins: Junior World (13-14) (2): 2003-04.

	09	10	11	12	13	14
Masters	-	-	-	-	-	-
US Open	-	-	-	-	-	-
British	-	-	-	-	MC	MC
PGA	-	-	-	-	T25	WD
Money (E)	-	-	-	-	39	145*
Money (J)	45	28	62	41	62*	58*
Money (As)	30	10	7	20	1	8
OWR	247	180	177	193	59	134

2014: E: 13 st / 5 ct / 0 t10.   (T24 Volvo Champ).   Had a surprisingly disappointing year, failing to log a top 10 in 13 E Tour starts and falling to 145th in $$$. Also made seven starts in Asia Tour-only events where he fared better, posting one second and a trio of 4ths.

OUTLOOK: A powerful young player whose 2013 performance on larger stages (especially the CIMB Classic) had the feel of one who is ready to move beyond the Far Eastern circuits. That didn't quite pan out in 2014 and now he'll be back to plying his trade primarily around Asia. Would appear to have the power and all-around skills to succeed on the larger stages, so perhaps with a little more time to mature...

STATS: Driving Distance: A-   Driving Accuracy: C+   GIR: B+   Short Game: B   Putting: B+

Appleby, Stuart (Australia) (43)
b. Cohuna, Victoria, Australia 5/1/1971. 6'1" 185 lbs. TP: 1992. Won the 1992 Queensland Open as an amateur, then played three strong seasons in Australia (6th in 1995 $$$). Headed to America in 1995 where a 5th-place finish on the Web.com Tour had him playing the PGA Tour full-time by 1996. Became a steady earner, finishing 18th in $$$ in 1997, then never falling below 55th until 2008. Also

Appleby, Stuart, Cont'd

a regular winner, beginning with 1997's Honda Classic, then continuing on through eight more titles that included a pair of Houston Opens (1999 and 2006) and three successive Mercedes Championships at Kapalua (2004, '05 and '06). Logged only three top 10s in his first 40 Major starts (1997-2006) but did have one close call, being one of the three players (with Thomas Levet and Steve Elkington) to lose to Ernie Els in 4-hole playoff for the 2002 Open Championship at Muirfield. After slipping somewhat in 2009, made history in 2010 by winning the inaugural Greenbrier Classic with a Sunday 59, joining David Duval as the only men to have then broken 60 in a final round. Fell to 129th in earnings in 2011, then 162nd in 2012 and 133rd in 2013 before climbing back to 71st during a much stronger 2014. **Awards:** PGA Tour Comeback Player of the Year: 2010. **Teams:** Presidents Cup (5): 1998-00-03-05-07 (5-14-2). World Cup (3): 1996-03-09. **OWR Best:** 8 - Mar, 2004.

PGA Tour Wins (9): 1997: Honda Classic **1998:** Kemper Open **1999:** Houston Open (Shell) **2003:** Las Vegas Classic (Invensys) (90H) **2004:** Mercedes Championships **2005:** Mercedes Championships **2006:** Mercedes Championships, Houston Open (Shell) **2010:** Greenbrier Classic.
Australasian Tour Wins (3): 1998: Coolum Classic **2001:** Australian Open **2010:** Australian Masters.
Other Wins: 2 Web.com (1995) + Queensland Open (Aus): 1991* CVS Classic: 1999 (w/J.Sluman).
Amateur Wins: Victorian Am: 1991 − Victorian Foursomes: 1992.

	96	97	98	99	00	01	02	03	04	05	06	07	08	09	10	11	12	13	14
Masters	-	T21	MC	MC	MC	MC	T31	MC	T22	T43	T19	T7	T14	T30	-	MC	-	-	-
US Open	-	T36	T10	MC	MC	MC	T37	MC	MC	MC	MC	T26	T36	MC	T29	-	-	-	-
British	-	T20	MC	MC	T11	61	T2P	T15	T36	T41	MC	MC	T51	T65	-	-	-	-	-
PGA	-	T61	MC	MC	T4	T16	T17	T23	T17	T15	T55	T12	T15	MC	T68	-	-	-	-
Money (A)	130	18	40	25	24	55	32	12	13	27	8	45	22	137	38	129	162	133	71
OWR	44	30	35	32	43	32	14	14	13	30	22	36	38	105	75	169	376	272	130

2014: PGA: 29 st / 19 ct / 3 t10. (T2 Barclays, T8 Honda, T9 Humana). Enjoyed a comeback year, finishing 31st in FedEx Cup points in a campaign led by a lucrative T2 at Barclays. Oddly, he declined in every major statistical category save SGP (33 to 12), where he was fairly strong to begin with.
OUTLOOK: As noted above, a decline in nearly all major statistical categories hardly bodes well for a 43-year-old whose driving distance has dropped significantly since his early 30s. While he continues to perform at a high level on and around the green, it must be noted that 40% of his earnings for the entire season came at Barclays. Thus numerically speaking, the future likely looks more like his 2011-2013 than it does his stronger 2014.

STATS: Driving Distance: C+   Driving Accuracy: B   GIR: C+   Short Game: A-   Putting: A-

---

Armour, Ryan Patrick (USA) (38)
b. Akron, OH 2/27/1976. 5'9" 170 lbs. All-American at Ohio St. TP: 1999. Lost to Tiger Woods 1 down in the final of the 1993 U.S. Junior Amateur. Spent several years playing mini-tours before joining the Web.com Tour in 2004. Played there for three seasons before joining the PGA Tour (via Q School) in 2007. Returned to the Web.com after a two-year stint and remained there (save for a non-competitive 2013) until re-qualifying for the PGA Tour via a 20th-place finish in 2014 regular season $$$. **OWR Best:** 285 - Oct, 2007.

	04	05	06	07	08	09	10	11	12	13	14
Masters	-	-	-	-	-	-	-	-	-	-	-
US Open	-	-	-	-	-	-	-	-	-	-	-
British	-	-	-	-	-	-	-	-	-	-	-
PGA	-	-	-	-	-	-	-	-	-	-	-
Money (A)	-	-	-	121	172	-	-	-	-	-	-
OWR	656	560	442	324	565	704	734	650	806	-	402

2014: Played full-time on the Web.com Tour, finishing 20th in regular season $$$ to return him to the PGA Tour for the first time since 2008.
OUTLOOK: Though certainly a more experienced player now, seems a longshot for major success at this level - but stranger things have happened.

STATS: Driving Distance: B+   Driving Accuracy: A-   GIR: B   Short Game: B   Putting: A-

---

Atwal, Arjun Singh (India) (41)
b. Asansol, India 3/20/1973. 6'1" 185 lbs. College: Nassau (NY) Community College. TP: 1995. Attended high school and junior college in the United States. Began his career with a nine-year run on the Asian Tour where he eventually won the 1999 Indian Open. In 2002 and '03, played in both Asia and Europe, winning on each circuit – though all three of his E Tour wins were played on Asian soil. Has won two Honda Masters as well as Hong Kong's Star Alliance Open in 2000. Topped the Asian Tour in $$$ in 2003. Moved to the U.S. in 2004 and played both the PGA and Web.com Tours before becoming the first Indian-born player to win a PGA Tour event at the 2010 Wyndham Championship. At age 41, broke a four-year drought by winning the 2014 Dubai Open on the Asian Tour. **Teams:** World Cup: 2005. **OWR Best:** 106 - Jan, 2011.

PGA Tour Wins (1): 2010: Greater Greensboro Open (Wyndham).
European Tour Wins (3): 2002: Singapore Masters **2003:** Malaysian Open **2008:** Malaysian Open.
Asian Tour Wins (5): 1999: Indian Open **2000:** Honda Masters, Star Alliance Open **2003:** Honda Masters **2014:** Dubai Open.
Other Wins: 1 Web.com (2008) + DCM Open (India): 1995 Chandigarh Open (India): 1995 Southern India Open: 1997.

	96	97	98	99	00	01	02	03	04	05	06	07	08	09	10	11	12	13	14
Masters	-	-	-	-	-	-	-	-	-	-	-	-	-	-	-	MC	-	-	-
US Open	-	-	-	-	-	-	-	-	-	-	-	-	-	-	MC	-	-	-	-
British	-	-	-	-	-	-	MC	-	-	-	-	-	-	-	-	-	-	-	-
PGA	-	-	-	-	-	-	-	MC	-	-	-	-	-	-	MC	-	-	-	-
Money (A)	-	-	-	-	-	-	-	-	146	82	140	207*	-	209*	58*	123	167	235*	256*
Money (E)	-	-	-	-	-	89	63	-	-	-	-	-	-	-	-	-	-	-	-
Money (As)	65	21	29	-	5	5	3	1*	-	-	-	-	-	-	-	-	-	-	25
OWR	688	490	509	680	370	345	354	229	257	159	260	538	206	489	123	246	559	870	432

2014: PGA: 4 st / 1 ct / 0 t10. (T53 Barracuda). With only Past Champion status, played four times, finishing 245th in FedEx Cup points. Also made several late-season starts on the Asian Tour, winning the season-ending Dubai Open in December.
OUTLOOK: Playing on Past Champion status, he will continue to be limited to a handful of PGA Tour and Web.com starts. Could return to the Asian Tour full-time, where his late-season victory was his first since 2010, and where his game obviously remains rather more competitive.

STATS: Driving Distance: C+   Driving Accuracy: B-   GIR: C-   Short Game: C-   Putting: B-

Austin, Albert Woody II (USA) (50) b. Tampa, FL 1/27/1964. 6'0" 190 lbs. All-American at U of Miami (FL). TP: 1986. An AJGA All-American. Spent 1989 and '90 in the Far East, then played on domestic mini-tours before finally reaching the PGA Tour at age 31. Logged strong $$$ seasons in 1995 and '96 before crashing in 1997 and struggling for several years thereafter. Enjoyed a major renaissance beginning in 2003, and beat Tim Herron in a playoff to win the 2004 Buick Championship. Peaked (at age 43) in 2007, winning in Memphis (with a final round 62), finishing 2nd at the PGA Championship and making the President's Cup team – where he gained lasting fame by falling into a lake while trying to blast his ball from the shallows. After several down seasons, came out of nowhere to win the 2013 Sanderson Farms Championship, beating Cameron Beckman and Daniel Summerhays in a playoff. **Awards:** PGA Tour Rookie of the Year: 1995. **Teams:** Presidents Cup: 2007 (1-1-3). **OWR Best:** 29 - Mar, 2008.

PGA Tour Wins (4): 1995: Buick Open **2004:** Buick Championship (Hartford) **2007:** Memphis Classic (Stanford St Jude) **2013:** Sanford Farms Championship.

Other Wins: Waterloo (IA) Open: 1993   Shark Shootout: 2007 (w/M. Calcavecchia).

	95	96	97	98	99	00	01	02	03	04	05	06	07	08	09	10	11	12	13	14
Masters	-	MC	-	-	-	-	-	-	-	-	-	-	-	MC	-	-	-	-	-	-
US Open	-	T23	-	-	-	T37	-	MC	T48	-	-	T32	MC	T71	-	-	-	-	-	-
British	-	MC	-	-	-	-	-	-	-	-	-	-	-	-	T39	-	-	-	-	-
PGA	T23	T69	-	-	-	-	-	-	T27	T62	T66	T16	2	MC	T36	-	-	-	MC	-
Money (A)	24	32	180	-	121	100	125	156	44	45	64	78	15	33	82	129	161	-	130*	171
OWR	64	63	206	474	244	195	267	369	114	112	138	136	31	57	128	266	468	506	292	432

2014: PGA: 22 st / 10 ct / 0 t10. (T13 T of C). Finished 168th in FedEx Cup points but also logged top 10s in all four of his Champions Tour starts.

OUTLOOK: Is fully exempt on the PGA Tour in 2015 due to his 2013 win at Sanderson Farms, but his impressive four-event Champions Tour debut (led by a T2 at Dick's Sporting Goods) suggests where he really belongs. But those $6 million PGA Tour purses remain oh so tempting...

STATS: Driving Distance: C   Driving Accuracy: A-   GIR: B   Short Game: B+   Putting: C ⇩

Axley, Eric (USA) (40) b. Athens, TN 4/22/1974. 6'0" 185 lbs. College: East Tennessee St. TP: 1997. Left-hander who, after spending several years on mini-tours, played his way onto the PGA Tour via a 16th-place $$$ ranking on the 2005 Web.com circuit. Without anything close to a top 10 during his first 23 starts, rode 2nd and 3rd round 63s to a surprise victory at the Texas Open (played opposite the Ryder Cup) in 2006. Save for 2008, never retained his card thereafter prior to playing on Past Champion status in 2014, where he earned a spot in the Web.com Finals, then claimed the 50th and final slot among Web.com graduates. **OWR Best:** 169 - Oct, 2006.

PGA Tour Wins (1): 2006: Texas Open (Valero).

Other Wins: 1 Web.com (2005)   +   2 NGA/Hooters (2002-2203).

	04	05	06	07	08	09	10	11	12	13	14
Masters	-	-	-	-	-	-	-	-	-	-	-
US Open	MC	MC	-	MC	T9	MC	T63	-	-	-	-
British	-	-	-	-	-	-	-	-	-	-	-
PGA	-	-	-	MC	-	-	-	-	-	-	-
Money (A)	-	-	73	156	116	208	232*	-	254*	-	186*
OWR	1155	473	194	374	340	630	1055	1346	1492	1508	627

2014: PGA: 10 st / 7 ct / 0 t10. (T12 Barracuda). Finished 184th in FedEx Cup points but secured the 50th spot in the Web.com Finals.

OUTLOOK: Showed lots of guts playing his way back after a five-year absence, and that sort of desire ought to count for something. His statistical sampling is limited but his putting numbers have always been strong. Thus a longshot - but rolling it at near-elite levels always opens possibilities.

STATS (LTD): Driving Distance: C+   Driving Accuracy: C   GIR: C-   Short Game: B+   Putting: A-

---

Baddeley, Aaron John (Australia) (33) b. Lebanon, NH 3/17/1981. 6'0" 175 lbs. TP: 2000. Born in New Hampshire to Australian parents before family moved back home when he was two. Stunned the golf world by winning the 1999 Australian Open as an unheralded 18-year-old amateur, edging Greg Norman and Nick O'Hern by two at Royal Sydney GC. Returned to defend the title the following year as a pro, beating Robert Allenby by two at Kingston Heath. After finishing 10th in 2002 Web.com Tour $$$, began playing the PGA Tour full-time in 2003 where he established himself as a steady earner prior to breaking through to win the 2006 Heritage Classic. After claiming the 2007 Phoenix Open and the 2007 Australian Masters, became the face of the trendy "Stack & Tilt" golf swing. His fortunes declined during 2009 and 2010, when he fell out of the top 100 in earnings. Returned to his original coach, Dale Lynch, in 2009. Scored his first win in four years at the 2011 Northern Trust Open, beating Vijay Singh by two at Riviera. **Teams:** Eisenhower Trophy (2): 1998-00. Presidents Cup: 2011 (1-3-1). World Cup: 2001. **OWR Best:** 16 - Apr, 2008.

PGA Tour Wins (3): 2006: Heritage Classic (Verizon) **2007:** Phoenix Open (FBR) **2011:** Los Angeles Open (Northern Trust).

European Tour Wins (1): 2007: Australian Masters ('08).

Australasian Tour Wins (3): 1999: Australian Open* **2000:** Australian Open **2001:** Greg Norman Holden Int'l.

Amateur Wins: Riversdale Cup: 1999.

	99	00	01	02	03	04	05	06	07	08	09	10	11	12	13	14
Masters	-	MC	MC	-	-	-	-	-	T52	MC	T17	-	T47	T40	-	-
US Open	-	MC	-	-	-	MC	-	-	T13	T29	-	MC	MC	MC	MC	T23
British	-	-	MC	-	MC	-	MC	MC	MC	-	-	MC	T69	-	-	-
PGA	-	-	-	T57	-	-	T55	MC	T13	MC	-	MC	T42	-	-	-
Money (A)	Am	-	-	-	73	123	78	55	10	49	101	110	20	76	113	102
Ranking	194	129	146	169	108	207	170	87	18	36	139	274	46	78	191	247

2014: PGA: 24 st / 13 ct / 2 t10. (4 Travelers, 5 CIMB). Logged four top 25s for the second straight year while finishing 114th in FedEx Cup points.

OUTLOOK: Righted the ship somewhat after three straight declining years. Remains a below-the-median ball striker (170) with only mid-range length – a circumstance which his always-stellar putter (2 in SGP) tries hard to overcome. But nary a single Major championship top 10 in 30 starts speaks to the difficulty of that recipe, and while his 1st Round Scoring improved to 38, ranking 139 and 166 in 3rd and 4th round average makes it tough.

STATS: Driving Distance: B+   Driving Accuracy: C-   GIR: C-   Short Game: A-   Putting: A+

Bae, Sang-Moon (South Korea) (28)

b. Dae Gu, South Korea 7/21/1986. 5'11" 180 lbs. TP: 2004. One of Korea's strongest-ever prospects who claimed his first domestic win at age 20, then quickly added three additional Korean PGA Tour events. His first major tour win was a KPGA co-sponsored tournament, the Asian Tour's 2007 SK Telecom Open, where he ran away from Aaron Baddeley and Hyung-Tae Kim by six. Also won back-to-back Korean Opens in 2008 and 2009, edging Ian Poulter by one in '08 (an official Asian Tour victory). Won a second SK Telecom Open in 2010, which was by then co-sanctioned by the OneAsia Tour. Dominated the Japan Tour in 2011, winning three times (including the Japan Open) and topping the Order of Merit. Began playing in America regularly in 2012 and claimed his first U.S. win at the 2013 Byron Nelson Championship, where he edged Keegan Bradley by two. Opened the official 2015 PGA Tour season by winning the 2014 Frys.com Open in October, edging Steven Bowditch by two. One month later, added the Korean Tour's Shinhan Donghae Open in a five-shot runaway. Possesses one of the most widely admired swings in the game today. **Teams:** World Cup (2): 2008-13. **OWR Best:** 26 - Nov, 2011.

PGA Tour Wins (2): 2013: Byron Nelson Championship (HP) **2014**: Frys.com Open ('15).
Japan Tour Wins (3): 2011: KBC Augusta, Tokai Classic, Japan Open.
Asian Tour Wins (3): 2007: SK Telecom Open **2008**: Korean Open **2009**: Caltex Maekyung Open.
OneAsia Tour Wins (2): 2009: Korean Open **2010**: SK Telecom Open.
Other Wins: SBS Emerson Pacific Open (KPGA): 2006   KEB Invitational (KPGA): 2008   Korean Open: 2009   Shinhan Donghae Open (KPGA): 2014.

	06	07	08	09	10	11	12	13	14
Masters	-	-	-	-	-	-	T37	-	MC
US Open	-	-	-	MC	-	T42	MC	MC	-
British	-	-	-	-	-	MC	T64	-	-
PGA	-	-	-	-	-	-	T54	MC	-
Money (A)	-	-	-	-	-	-	83	51	124
Money (J)	-	-	-	-	29	1	-	-	-
Money (As)	-	-	7	17	-	-	-	-	-
Money (O)	-	-	-	-	4	28*	-	-	-
OWR	-	403	197	156	149	30	70	139	84

2014: PGA: 24 st / 13 ct / 0 t10. (T12 Northern Trust). Slipped marginally, failing to log a PGA Tour top 10 and falling to 122nd in FedEx Cup points. Won once in his native Korea, however, and heated up the fall, winning the Frys.com Open (officially a 2015 PGA Tour event)

OUTLOOK: Has proven himself a winner in the U.S., Japan and around Asia, and he should just be entering his prime years. Interestingly, despite his classic swing, is statistically a mid-range ball striker (132) who lives and dies by his putter. Also somewhat streaky, with all three of his 2011 Japan Tour wins coming within a six-week period. Seems capable of climbing, but needs to give himself more chances (146 in GIR) to truly excel.

STATS: Driving Distance: B   Driving Accuracy: B-   GIR: C   Short Game: C+   Putting: A-

---

Baek, Seuk-Hyun (South Korea) (24)

b. Seoul, South Korea 10/8/1990. 5'5" 180 lbs. TP: 2009. Aggressive young Korean prospect who moved to Thailand in 2004, and who's recognizable by his bleached-blond hair. Began playing the Asian Tour full-time in 2010 and, though he remains winless, has proven himself a solid $$$ earner, peaking with a 9th-place finish in the 2013 Order of Merit. Has yet to play a major tour event that wasn't at least co-sanctioned by the Asian circuit. **OWR Best:** 185 - May, 2014.

Other Wins: Singha Arthitaya (Thailand): 2010   Singha Challenge (Thailand): 2010.

	10	11	12	13	14
Masters	-	-	-	-	-
US Open	-	-	-	-	-
British	-	-	-	-	-
PGA	-	-	-	-	-
Money (As)	21	51	31	9	16
OWR	535	653	416	210	316

2014: ASIA: 16 st / 12 ct / 3 t10. (Incl. T2 Indonesia Masters, 5 Queens Cup). Held his gains of 2013 nicely, finishing 16th in Asian Tour $$$.

OUTLOOK: As a longer hitter (despite his size) who fails to parlay his length into greens hit – but possesses a deft enough touch around the greens to make it work. Appears to have the tools to compete successfully beyond the Asian circuit, but he needs to land that big breakthrough win.

STATS: Driving Distance: B+   Driving Accuracy: C   GIR: C-   Short Game: B   Putting: A-

---

Baird, Michael Jancey ("Briny") (USA) (42)

b. Miami Beach, FL 5/11/1972. 5'11" 170 lbs. Two-time D-2 Player of the Year (and All-American) at Valdosta (GA) St. TP: 1995. Two-time AJGA All-American. Father, Butch, won twice on both the PGA and Champions Tours. Played two early seasons on the Web.com Tour before reaching the PGA Tour via a 12th-place finish at 1998 Q School. Fell back to the Web.com in 2000 but finished 4th in $$$ and has remained on the PGA Tour ever since. Steady earner who finished no worse than 127th in $$$ through 2011 (best: 22nd in 2003). Never a PGA Tour winner but several times a runner-up, most recently via a late collapse at the 2013 McGladrey Classic, where he lost to Chris Kirk by one. **OWR Best:** 53 - Apr, 2004.

Other Wins: 1 Web.com (2000).

	99	00	01	02	03	04	05	06	07	08	09	10	11	12	13	14
Masters	-	-	-	-	-	MC	-	-	-	-	MC	-	-	-	-	-
US Open	-	-	T40	-	-	MC	-	-	-	-	MC	-	MC	-	-	-
British	-	-	-	-	-	-	-	-	-	-	MC	-	-	-	-	-
PGA	-	-	T22	T43	T39	T37	-	-	-	T42	MC	-	-	-	-	-
Money (A)	186	-	63	82	22	69	126	102	100	37	78	127	95	196*	-	134
OWR	674	478	172	158	68	69	177	250	223	113	184	325	278	503	366	630

2014: PGA: 17 st / 8 ct / 1 t10. (T2 McGladrey). After collapsing late at McGladrey, logged no top 25s and finished 141st in FedEx Cup points.

OUTLOOK: Will begin 2015 on a nine-event medical extension. One of the PGA Tour's more accurate players, always rating far above the median in Driving Accuracy. But now in his early 40s, having struggled after his McGladrey debacle and with health questions, it's tough to be too optimistic.

STATS: Driving Distance: C+   Driving Accuracy: A-   GIR: B   Short Game: B   Putting: C+

Baldwin, Matthew (England) (28) b. Southport, England 2/25/1986. 5'11" 175 lbs. TP: 2008. After turning professional, spent two seasons playing mini-tours before reaching the Challenge circuit full-time in 2011, where a win in Spain led to a 10th-place $$$ ranking and graduation to the European Tour. Was a steady earner immediately, comfortably cracking the top 100 in $$$ in each of his first three seasons, and climbing inside the top 60 in 2014. **OWR Best:** 180 - Jul, 2014.

Other Wins: 1 Euro Challenge (2011).
Amateur Wins: English Under-16s: 2002   European Boys: 2007   Nations Cup (Individual): 2007.

	12	13	14
Masters	-	-	-
US Open	T59	-	-
British	T23	-	MC
PGA	-	-	-
Money (E)	72	87	59
OWR	272	254	237

2014: E: 32 st / 17 ct / 4 t10. (T2 Mandela, T3 Irish, T5 Joburg, T5 French).   Cracked the top 60 in $$$ for the first time.
OUTLOOK: Has thus far shown himself an above-the-median ball striker who may not always make the most of his opportunities once on the putting surface. Ball strikers like this tend to have long careers, but there seems little chance of his climbing markedly until more putts start to fall.

STATS: Driving Distance: B-   Driving Accuracy: B+   GIR: B+   Short Game: B-   Putting: C+

Barber, Blayne Lawrence (USA) (25) b. Tallahassee, FL 12/25/1989. 5'10" 165 lbs. All-American at U of Central Florida, two-time All-American at Auburn. TP: 2012. Starred at Auburn after transferring from UCF, playing in the 2011 Walker Cup and the 2011 and '12 Palmer Cups. Also won the 2009 Florida Amateur. Played the Web.com full-time in 2014, winning once and clinching his PGA Tour card by finishing 7th in regular season earnings. **Teams:** Walker Cup: 2011 (0-2-1). Palmer Cup (2): 2011-12. **OWR Best:** 188 - Nov, 2014.

Other Wins: 1 Web.com (2014).
Amateur Wins: Florida Am: 2009.

	14
Masters	-
US Open	-
British	-
PGA	-
Money (A)	-
OWR	198

2014: Played full-time on the Web.com Tour, where he won once and clinched a 2015 PGA Tour card by finishing 7th in regular season $$$.
OUTLOOK: Coming off a strong Web.com campaign in which he won once and logged six top 10s and 12 top 25s in 20 starts. Is statistically strong on and around the green, and is widely considered one of the stronger prospects in this class. Could make an impact in 2015.

STATS (LTD):   Driving Distance: B-   Driving Accuracy: B   GIR: B+   Short Game: B+   Putting: A-

---

Barnes, Kurt (Australia) (33) b. Muswellbrook, New South Wales, Australia 5/25/1981. 6'0" 215 lbs. TP: 2003. Despite a strong amateur career, was a late-bloomer as a pro who toiled on the Von Nida and Australasian Tours for most of his 20s before briefly joining the OneAsia circuit, then heading off to Japan. Claimed his first major tour win at OneAsia's 2011 SK Telecom Open, where he edged homestanding Kyung-Tae Kim by a stroke. Also won 2012 ANA Open in Japan, beating a trio of Japanese players (including Shingo Katayama) by one. **OWR Best:** 128 - Jan, 2012.

Japan Tour Wins (1): 2012: ANA Open.
OneAsia Tour Wins (1): 2011: SK Telecom Open (54H).
Other Wins: Queensland PGA (Aus): 2004   Victorian Open (Aus): 2005   Meriton Sydney Inv (Aus): 2005   Zongshon IGC Open (China): 2009.
Amateur Wins: Australian Am: 2002   –   New South Wales Stroke Play: 2002   New Zealand Am Stroke Play: 2003   Riversdale Cup: 2003.

	10	11	12	13	14
Masters	-	-	-	-	-
US Open	-	-	-	-	-
British	MC	MC	-	-	-
PGA	-	-	-	-	-
Money (J)	76	26	40	53	72
Money (O)	28*	4	-	-	-
OWR	537	138	171	436	647

2014: JAP: 19 st / 13 ct / 1 t10. (T8 Sega Sammy).   Continued stagnating on the Japan Tour, logging one top 10 and finishing 72nd in $$$.
OUTLOOK: A power-oriented regular who earns a living in Japan but has shown little sign of being able to move up to Europe, or beyond.

STATS: Driving Distance: A   Driving Accuracy: C   GIR: B   Short Game: B-   Putting: C

Barnes, Richard Kyle (Ricky) (USA) (33) b. Stockton, CA 2/6/1981. 6'2" 200 lbs. A three-time All-American, 2002 U.S. Amateur champ (2 & 1 over Hunter Mahan, at Oakland Hills), co-collegiate Player of The Year and co-Hogan Award winner (both 2003, with Mahan) at U of Arizona. TP: 2003. An AJGA All-American. His father, Bruce, was a punter for the New England Patriots (1973-74). After splitting 2004 between the Web.com and Europe, played the Web.com full-time from 2005-2008. Twice cracked the top 25 in $$$ before reaching the PGA Tour in 2009. Narrowly kept his card as a rookie (120th in $$$) but emerged as a steady earner thereafter. T2 at the 2009 U.S. Open, finishing 2 behind Lucas Glover, with a closing 76. Has never won an official event as a professional. **Teams:** Eisenhower Trophy: 2002. **OWR Best:** 58 - Jul, 2010.

Other Wins: CVS/Caremark Charity Classic (w/J.B. Holmes): 2010.

Barnes, Richard Kyle, Cont'd

Amateur Wins: U.S. Amateur: 2002.

	00	01	02	03	04	05	06	07	08	09	10	11	12	13	14
Masters	-	-	-	21	-	-	-	-	-	-	T10	T20	-	-	-
US Open	MC	-	MC	T59	-	-	-	MC	-	T2	T27	-	-	-	-
British	-	-	-	MC	-	-	-	-	-	-	T44	T57	-	-	-
PGA	-	-	-	-	-	-	-	-	-	-	MC	T56	-	-	-
Money (A)	-	-	-	-	-	-	-	-	-	120	43	92	112	131	127
OWR	-	-	-	394	383	770	362	553	439	194	80	134	244	342	356

2014: PGA: 27 st / 19 ct / 2 t10. (T8 Barracuda, T9 Puerto Rico). Logged his first multi-top 10 year since 2011, finished 113th in FedEx Cup points.

OUTLOOK: Reversed a downward trend somewhat in 2014 and is still young enough to have his best years lie ahead. A strong player who, despite missing fairways, annually rates strongly in GIR. Traditionally a below-the-median putter, but his SGP jumped hugely in 2014, from 171 to 63.

STATS: Driving Distance: B+   Driving Accuracy: C+   GIR: B+   Short Game: B-   Putting: B- ⇧

Beckman, Cameron Reid (USA) (44)

b. Minneapolis, MN 2/15/1970. 6'2" 215 lbs. NAIA individual champion (1991) at Texas Lutheran U. TP: 1993. A PGA Tour journeyman who has won three smaller events, beginning with the 2001 Southern Farm Bureau Classic (where he edged Chad Campbell by one) and the 2008 Frys.com Open (in a playoff with Kevin Sutherland). Added the 2010 Mayakoba Classic (at age 40), a light-field event played opposite the WGC Match Play. Lost a three-way playoff (to Woody Austin) at the 2013 Sanderson Farms. **OWR Best:** 75 - Mar, 2002.

PGA Tour Wins (3): 2001: Southern Farm Classic **2008:** Frys.com Open **2010:** Mayakoba Classic.
Amateur Wins: NAIA Individual: 1991.

	99	00	01	02	03	04	05	06	07	08	09	10	11	12	13	14
Masters	-	-	-	-	-	-	-	-	-	-	-	-	-	-	-	-
US Open	-	MC	-	-	-	-	-	-	-	-	MC	-	-	-	-	-
British	-	-	-	-	-	MC	-	-	-	-	-	-	-	-	-	-
PGA	-	-	-	T53	-	-	-	-	-	-	MC	MC	-	-	-	-
Money (A)	172	139	50	72	106	107	152	176	112	82	116	77	144	173	172*	213*
OWR	460	354	122	113	197	177	239	312	241	204	243	253	426	743	543	792

2014: PGA: 12 st / 5 ct / 0 t10. (T36 Texas). Making limited starts on Past Champion status, finished 207th in FedEx Cup points.

OUTLOOK: Having only Past Champion status, will continue getting limited PGA Tour starts - and chose to make only three early-season Web.com starts in 2014. Hasn't approached the top 125 since 2010 but as his 2013 playoff loss at Sanderson Farms suggests, he can catch fire on a dime.

STATS: Driving Distance: C+   Driving Accuracy: B   GIR: C+   Short Game: B-   Putting: C-

---

Beem, Richard Michael (USA) (44)

b. Phoenix, AZ 8/24/1970. 5'8" 165 lbs. College: New Mexico St. TP: 1994. Gave up the game for several years after college, selling cell phones and stereos. Returned to mini-tours in 1998, then played his way through Q School (T8) at year's end. Won the 1999 Kemper Open in his 12th career start, beating Bill Glasson and Bradley Hughes by one. Enjoyed a career year in 2002, first winning at the Stableford-format International, then landing a piece of immortality in his next start by outdueling Tiger Woods to claim the PGA Championship. Finished 7th in 2002 earnings but hasn't bettered 113th since 2003. Has played off Past Champion status since 2010. **OWR Best:** 16 - Jan, 2003.

PGA Tour Wins (3): 1999: Kemper Open **2002:** The International (Stableford), PGA Championship.
Other Wins: Hyundai Team: 2002 (w/P.Lonard)   Wendy's 3-Tour Challenge: 2002 (w/J.Daly & J.Furyk).

	99	00	01	02	03	04	05	06	07	08	09	10	11	12	13	14
Masters	-	-	-	-	T15	MC	MC	T42	54	-	-	-	-	-	-	-
US Open	-	-	MC	-	MC	MC	MC	MC	MC	T78	-	-	-	-	-	-
British	MC	-	-	-	T43	T71	MC	MC	T20	WD	-	-	-	-	-	-
PGA	T70	-	-	Win	MC	MC	MC	T49	MC	MC	T43	-	MC	T36	MC	MC
Money (A)	67	146	109	7	71	183	113	126	119	140	122	198*	207	186*	-	-
OWR	126	198	279	21	47	266	229	217	213	289	324	565	-	657	960	-

2014: PGA: 3 st / 0 ct / 0 t10. His three MCs included the PGA Championship, where he's exempt as a Past Champion.

OUTLOOK: Concentrating more on his broadcasting career and thus can be considered semi-retired now.

STATS (LTD): Driving Distance: C-   Driving Accuracy: B+   GIR: C-   Short Game: C-   Putting: D

Bekker, Oliver (South Africa) (30)

b. Pretoria, South Africa 11/12/1984. 6'2" 210 lbs. College: Lamar U. TP: 2008. An honorable mention All-American at Lamar. As a pro, initially played exclusively on the Sunshine Tour, claiming his first win in a five-shot runaway at the 2011 Northern Cape Classic. Stepped up in class by winning the 2012 Dimension Data Pro-Am (by two over Thomas Aiken and Tyrone Ferreira), then added the Telkom PGA Pro-Am in 2013. Began playing part-time in European Tour events in 2013 and '14 with little success. **OWR Best:** 284 - Mar, 2013.

Sunshine Tour Wins (3): 2011: Northern Cape Classic (54H) **2012:** Dimension Data Pro-Am **2013:** Telkom PGA Pro-Am (54H).
Amateur Wins: Spirit International: 2007   Cotton State Inv: 2007.

	08	09	10	11	12	13	14
Masters	-	-	-	-	-	-	-
US Open	-	-	-	-	-	-	-
British	-	-	-	-	-	-	-
PGA	-	-	-	-	-	-	-
Money (SA)	48	26	28	17	10	9	24
OWR	-	-	701	736	355	468	687

Bekker, Oliver, Cont'd

2014: SUN: 19 st / 13 ct / 2 t10. (T4 Telkom PGA, T5 Nedbank Affinity).   Took a modest step backwards on the Sunshine Tour, logging only two top 10s and falling to 24th in $$$. Also made five starts in non-co-sanctioned lighter-field E Tour events (four MCs and a T26 at the Russian Open).

OUTLOOK: Now hanging around the edges of the upper tier of domestic South African players, he still seems to have eyes on playing more in Europe. Has proven himself capable of winning at home, but has thus far offered little evidence that he holds similar potential abroad.

STATS: Driving Distance: --   Driving Accuracy: --   GIR: --   Short Game: --   Putting: --

---

Beljan, Charlie Benjamin (USA) (30)
b. Mesa, AZ 10/10/1984. 6'4" 230 lbs. All-American at U of New Mexico. TP: 2007. An AJGA All-American. A former U.S. Junior Amateur champion (2002, at the Atlanta AC) and Arizona Amateur winner (2006). Played through 2011 Q School (T13) with very little high-level professional experience, having starred (nine career wins) on the Gateway Tour, but with only two Web.com events and two U.S. Opens (MCs in 2008 and '09) under his belt. After a quiet rookie year, saved his card by winning the 2012 Children's Miracle Network Hospitals Classic after being hospitalized Friday night with acute anxiety. Lost the 1013 Northern Trust Open in a playoff to John Merrick but has been relatively quiet since, failing to crack the top 125 (in $$$ or FedEx Cup points) in 2014. **OWR Best**: 64 - Feb, 2013.

PGA Tour Wins (1): 2012: Walt Disney Classic (Children's Miracle).
Other Wins: 9 Gateway (2007-2009).
Amateur Wins: U.S. Junior Am: 2002   Arizona Am: 2006.

	08	09	10	11	12	13	14
Masters	-	-	-	-	-	-	-
US Open	MC	MC	-	-	-	-	-
British	-	-	-	-	-	-	-
PGA	-	-	-	-	-	MC	-
Money (A)	-	-	-	-	63	90	126
OWR	-	-	-	-	166	188	365

2014: PGA: 26 st / 12 ct / 1 t10. (T9 Humana).   Made less than half his cuts for the second straight year, finishing 130th in FedEx Cup points. Kept his card when, despite missing the cut at the Wyndham Championship, he remained 124th in PGA Tour earnings at the event's close.

OUTLOOK: Long hitting, somewhat inconsistent player who made only 19 of 50 cuts in 2013 and '14. Has a strong mix of strength and accuracy off the tee (34 in Total Driving and 50 in Ball Striking) but is largely inconsistent thereafter. Anxiety issues may potentially be an ongoing concern.

STATS: Driving Distance: A+   Driving Accuracy: B-   GIR: B   Short Game: C   Putting: C+

Benson, Seve (England) (28)
b. Guildford, England 11/4/1986. 6'1" 170 lbs. TP: 2007. Is named after the late Seve Ballesteros. Won twice as a Challenge Tour rookie in 2008, then was the last E Tour player to keep his card (finishing 120th in $$$) in 2009. Was limited by a back injury in 2010 (he failed to keep his card in 2011 on a medical extension) before finally settling in on the E Tour with a productive 2013, then showing incremental improvement in 2014. **OWR Best**: 196 - Sep, 2008.

Other Wins: 3 Euro Challenge (2008-2012)   +   1 EuroPro (2008).
Amateur Wins: Russian Am: 2006   Tailhade Cup (Argentina): 2006   Qatar Am: 2007.

	08	09	10	11	12	13	14
Masters	-	-	-	-	-	-	-
US Open	-	-	-	-	-	-	-
British	-	-	-	-	-	-	-
PGA	-	-	-	-	-	-	-
Money (E)	229*	120	-	163	-	97	82
OWR	221	275	705	683	468	286	253

2014: E: 19 st / 14 ct / 2 t10. (T3 Hassan, T10 Joburg).   Dropped from four to two top 10s, but still climbed (somewhat) to 82nd in $$$.

OUTLOOK: Has established himself as a very reliable ball striker (19 in Driving Distance, 30 in GIR) but his numbers on and around the greens remain around the median. Seemed a longshot based on early career performance, but now he looks like earning a good living for a while.

STATS: Driving Distance: A-   Driving Accuracy: B-   GIR: A-   Short Game: B-   Putting: B-

---

Berganio, David Jr. (USA) (45)
b. Los Angeles, CA 1/14/1969. 5'11" 170 lbs. Three-time All-American at U of Arizona. TP: 1993. After learning the game with a set of clubs given to him by a priest, enjoyed a stellar amateur career while at Arizona but never really got it going on the PGA Tour, due in large part to recurring back problems. Cracked the top 125 in earnings in 2001 and 2002 but never bettered 155th in any other season. **Teams**: Walker Cup: 1993 (1-2-0). **OWR Best**: 99 - Jan, 2002.

Other Wins: 3 Web.com (1996-2000).
Amateur Wins: U.S. Amateur Public Links (2): 1991-93   Pacific Coast Am: 1991.

	92	93	94	95	96	97	98	99	00	01	02	03	04	05	06	07	08	09	10	11	12	13	14
Masters	MC	-	-	-	-	MC	-	-	-	-	-	-	-	-	-	-	-	-	-	-	-	-	-
US Open	-	MC	T47	-	T16	-	-	T28	MC	-	-	-	-	-	MC	-	-	-	-	-	-	-	-
British	-	-	-	-	-	-	-	-	-	-	-	-	-	-	-	-	-	-	-	-	-	-	-
PGA	-	-	-	-	-	-	-	-	-	-	-	-	-	-	-	-	-	-	-	-	-	-	-
Money (A)	-	302*	273*	-	211*	155	300*	228*	-	76	115	197	-	-	263*	251*	-	205	-	-	-	-	-
OWR	-	-	625	603	463	445	584	516	435	190	210	421	868	1182	1309	1375	1381	959	-	-	1492	1508	-

2014: Didn't make a start on either the PGA or Web.com Tour.

OUTLOOK: Has seven events left on a back-related medical extension dating to 2003. Unlikely to play, even less likely to have an impact if he does.

STATS: Driving Distance: --   Driving Accuracy: --   GIR: --   Short Game: --   Putting: --

Berger, Daniel F. (USA) (21)
b. Plantation, FL 4/7/1993. 6'1" 165 lbs. All-American at Florida St. TP: 2013. The son of Jay Berger, director of men's tennis for the USTA. Skipped high school golf but competed at the junior level prior to enrolling for two years at Florida State, where he was named first-team All-American and finished runner-up at the 2013 NCAA Men's championship. Spent 2014 on the Web.com Tour, where he finished 15th in regular season money, earning his PGA Tour card. **Teams:** Palmer Cup: 2013. **OWR Best:** 273 - Aug, 2014.

Amateur Wins: Dixie Am: 2012.

	14
Masters	-
US Open	T28
British	-
PGA	-
Money (A)	-
OWR	301

2014: Played full-time on the Web.com Tour, where he finished 15th in regular season $$$ to secure his PGA Tour card for 2015.

OUTLOOK: An interesting prospect given that his relative lack of high-end competitive experience would seem to be offset by significant results and a skill set which thus far seems imposing (1st in Ball Striking on the 2014 Web.com Tour). A solid dark horse pick to excel among 2015 rookies.

STATS (LTD): Driving Distance: A   Driving Accuracy: B   GIR: B+   Short Game: B   Putting: B

Bettencourt, Matthew Michael (USA) (39)
b. Alameda, CA 4/12/1975. 5'11" 180 lbs. The rare modern American pro never to have played collegiate golf. Was a top amateur prospect, winning the 2000 Northern California Amateur and being named NCGA Player Of The Year in both 2001 and '02. After turning pro, played the Canadian and Web.com Tours with limited success until 2008, when a two-win season saw him finish 1st in Web.com money, graduating him to the PGA Tour. Remained narrowly within the top 125 for three years but did break through to win the 2010 Reno-Tahoe Open, edging Bob Heintz by one when Heintz missed a 3-footer at the last to tie. Has mostly split time between the PGA and Web.com Tours since 2013. **OWR Best:** 112 - Jul, 2009.

PGA Tour Wins (1): 2010: Reno-Tahoe Open.
Other Wins: 2 Web.com (2008).
Amateur Wins: Northern California Am: 2000   Alameda Commuters: 2002.

	08	09	10	11	12	13	14
Masters	-	-	-	-	-	-	-
US Open	-	T10	T70	-	MC	T53	-
British	-	-	-	-	-	-	-
PGA	-	-	MC	-	-	-	-
Money (A)	-	111	114	122	171	203*	205*
OWR	133	192	260	313	678	421	681

2014: PGA: 14 st / 4 ct / 0 t10. (T20 Canada). Split time between the PGA and Web.com Tours (four starts), finishing 211th in FedEx Cup points.

OUTLOOK: As his peak years begin to wind down, he continues to find the middle ground between the PGA and Web.com Tours - and as he'll once again be playing on Past Champion status, that seems unlikely to change in 2015. Long-term issues with bursitis haven't helped.

STATS: Driving Distance: B-   Driving Accuracy: C   GIR: C-   Short Game: C+   Putting: B+

Bhullar, Gaganjeet (India) (26)
b. Kapurthala, India 4/27/1988. 5'7" 185 lbs. TP: 2006. Touted Indian prospect who began making waves with a 2009 victory at the Asian Tour's Indonesia President Invitational – a year in which he also won five times on his home PGTI Tour. Began 2010 by claiming the season-opening Asian Tour International in Thailand. Won two more Asian Tour events in 2012, the Yeangder Tournament Players Championship and the Macau Masters. Claimed his fifth Asian Tour title with a wire-to-wire win at the 2013 Indonesia Open, beating Nicholas Fung and Chapchai Nirat by three. Stepped up to the European Tour full-time in 2014, but finished 139th in $$$ **Teams:** Eisenhower Trophy: 2006. World Cup: 2013. **OWR Best:** 85 - Mar, 2013.

Asian Tour Wins (5): 2009: Indonesia President Inv   **2010:** Asian Tour International   **2012:** Yeangder TPC, Macau Open   **2013:** Indonesia Open.
Other Wins: 1 Euro Challenge (2011)   +   DLF Masters (PGTI): 2009   PGTI Eagleton: 2009   PGTI Aamby Valley: 2009   PGTI Rambagh: 2009   PGTI Panchkula: 2009   PGTI Bombay: 2010   Bangladesh Open: 2011   PGTI RCGC: 2011   PGTI Chandigarh: 2011.

	06	07	08	09	10	11	12	13	14
Masters	-	-	-	-	-	-	-	-	-
US Open	-	-	-	-	-	-	-	-	-
British	-	-	-	MC	-	-	-	-	-
PGA	-	-	-	-	-	-	-	-	-
Money (E)	-	-	-	-	-	201*	148*	102*	139
Money (As)	-	77*	65	6	17	83	5	5	
OWR	619	603	603	168	206	392	89	148	387

2014: E: 24 st / 16 ct / 1 t10. (T10 Abu Dhabi). Made 66% of his cuts but still failed to retain his E Tour card, finishing 139th in $$$.

OUTLOOK: An excellent driver of the ball, hits lots of greens and has a statistically strong short game - but the putter is a question. His first full-time foray into Europe was a disappointment, and he'll have only conditional status in 2015. Might enjoy a big year in Asia, then re-try Europe thereafter.

STATS: Driving Distance: A-   Driving Accuracy: A-   GIR: B+   Short Game: B+   Putting: C+

Bjerregaard, Lucas Justra (Denmark) (23)
b. Frederikshavn, Denmark 8/14/1991. 6'3" 180 lbs. TP: 2011. Enjoyed a fine amateur career, winning the 2010 European Amateur and twice representing Denmark for the Eisenhower Trophy. Signed a letter-of-intent with Florida State in 2011 but instead turned professional. Won twice in the 2012 Nordic League to reach the Challenge Tour, then reached the E Tour for 2014 via Q School before enjoying a solid rookie year, finishing 90th in $$$. **Teams:** Eisenhower Trophy (2): 2008-10. **OWR Best:** 256 - Nov, 2014.

Bjerregaard, Lucas Justra, Cont'd

Other Wins: 3 Nordic League (2011-2013).
Amateur Wins: European Am: 2010 - Danish Am (2): 2007-08   European Boys Team (Individual)(2): 2007-09   Jr World Cup (Individual): 2010.

	11	12	13	14
Masters	-	-	-	-
US Open	-	-	-	T40
British	MC	-	-	-
PGA	-	-	-	-
Money (E)	-	-	-	90
OWR	1401	1492	437	283

2014: E: 26 st / 17 ct / 3 t10. (T4 Perth, T5 Hong Kong, T9 Africa).   Rescued his year with top 5s in his last two starts to finish 90th in $$$.

OUTLOOK: Owned a strong amateur record, then played quickly up the European professional ladder, and kept momentum up with his late top 5s at Perth and Hong Kong to retain his card. Has the requisite length for the modern game, so incremental improvement (at least) in 2015 seems likely.

STATS (LTD):   Driving Distance: A   Driving Accuracy: C+   GIR: B   Short Game: B+   Putting: B

Bjørn, Thomas (Denmark) (43)
b. Silkeborg, Denmark 2/18/1971. 6'2" 195 lbs. TP: 1993. Denmark's greatest-ever golfer who has won regularly, against strong fields, all over the world. Though already a five-time E Tour winner, came to international prominence upon beating Tiger Woods (and Padraig Harrington) head-to-head at the 2001 Dubai Desert Classic. T2 at the 2003 British Open (Royal St. George's) after losing three strokes at the 70th and 71st holes. Also T2 at the 2005 PGA Championship (Baltusrol). Two-time winner of the BMW International (2000 and 2002). A 15-time winner overall in Europe, and twice in Japan (the 1999 and 2003 Dunlop Phoenix) before playing regularly in America in 2004, then returning to Europe in '05. Fell into a long drought from 2007-2009, dropping out of the OWR top 200 before re-emerging with a five-shot win at the 2010 Portuguese Open. Validated this with a banner year in 2011, first taking the 2011 Qatar Masters (by four over Álvaro Quirós), then adding the Johnnie Walker Championship at Gleneagles and the European Masters, in Switzerland. Added a second European Masters in 2013 (defeating Craig Lee on the first hole of sudden death), then closed his year by taking the Nedbank Golf Challenge (officially a 2014 event) in its first playing as a part of the E Tour schedule. **Awards:** E Tour Rookie of the Year: 1996. **Teams:** Eisenhower Trophy: 1992. Ryder Cup (3): 1997-02-14 (O:5-2-2, S: 1-1-1). Seve Trophy (7): 2000-02-03-05-07-11-13 + Capt in 2009. World Cup (5): 1996-97-01-06-13. **OWR Best:** 10 - Jul, 2001.

European Tour Wins (15): 1996: Loch Lomond Inv   **1998:** Heineken Classic, Open de España   **1999:** Sarazen World Open   **2000:** BMW Int'l   **2001:** Dubai Classic   **2002:** BMW Int'l   **2005:** British Masters   **2006:** Irish Open   **2010:** Portuguese Open   **2011:** Qatar Masters, Johnnie Walker Championship, European Masters (Omega)   **2013:** European Masters (Omega), Nedbank Challenge ('14).
Japan Tour Wins (2): 1999: Dunlop Phoenix   **2003:** Dunlop Phoenix.
Other Wins: 3 Euro Challenge (1995).
Amateur Wins: Danish Am Stroke play: 1990   Danish Am: 1991.

	96	97	98	99	00	01	02	03	04	05	06	07	08	09	10	11	12	13	14
Masters	-	-	-	MC	T28	MC	T18	-	MC	T25	T32	MC	-	-	-	-	T37	T46	T8
US Open	-	T68	T25	MC	T46	T22	T37	MC	MC	T52	T48	MC	-	-	-	-	MC	-	-
British	MC	MC	T9	T30	T2	MC	T8	T2	MC	MC	T41	T53	-	-	MC	4	T54	T73	T26
PGA	-	T45	MC	T70	3	T59	MC	MC	-	T2	MC	T62	-	-	-	MC	T48	MC	MC
Money (A)	-	-	-	-	-	-	-	-	73	-	-	-	-	-	-	-	-	-	-
Money (E)	10	15	6	14	5	7	12	8	21	9	14	44	101	91	56	9	31	10	12
OWR	112	73	40	38	20	24	35	19	23	22	46	104	192	250	124	35	45	24	36

2014: E: 26 st / 20 ct / 7 t10. (Won Nedbank, T3 BMW PGA, T4 Denmark, T8 Masters, T8 BMW Int'l, etc.).   Though winless in calendar 2014 (the Nedbank being played in late 2013), he continued rumbling along, finishing 12th in E Tour $$$ and playing in his third Ryder Cup match.

OUTLOOK: Struggled a bit in his late 30s but has experienced a resurgence in his early 40s, fueled largely by top-level skills on and around the greens, as well as above-the-median ball striking (save for power). Highly consistent player who shows little sign of slowing down; indeed, despite his age, his putting numbers have actually improved of late. As long as this continues, he figures to produce a few more world-class seasons.

STATS: Driving Distance: C+   Driving Accuracy: B   GIR: B   Short Game: A-   Putting: A

Blaauw, Jacques (South Africa) (28)
b. Paarl, South Africa 2/12/1986. 6'4" 220 lbs. NAIA All-American at Oklahoma City U. TP: 2008. Swept the 2008 South African Amateur and Amateur Stroke Play titles. Enjoyed limited initial success on the Sunshine Tour over his first four seasons before soaring in 2013, winning twice in three weeks at the Vodacom events at Simola and Selborne, then later adding the Nedbank Affinity Cup with a dramatic final-hole birdie. Went winless in 2014, yet finished 22nd in $$$ again. **Teams:** Eisenhower Trophy: 2008. **OWR Best:** 192 - Jun, 2014.

Sunshine Tour Wins (3): 2013: Vodacom-Simola (54H), Vodacom-Selborne (54H), Nedbank Affinity Cup (54H).
Other Wins: Northern Cape Open (SA): 2008*   Sun Int'l Touring Pro-Am (SA): 2011.
Amateur Wins: South African Am: 2008   -   Cape Province Am: 2003   South African Am Stroke Play: 2008.

	09	10	11	12	13	14
Masters	-	-	-	-	-	-
US Open	-	-	-	-	-	-
British	-	-	-	-	-	-
PGA	-	-	-	-	-	-
Money (SA)	34	54	59	38	22	22
OWR	833	807	955	812	381	264

2014: SUN: 20 st / 18 ct / 8 t10. (Incl. 2 Investec, 2 Zimbabwe, T2 Royal Swazi).   Though failing to follow his three-win 2013 with a 2014 victory, he was thrice a runner-up and played consistently enough to once again finish 22nd in Sunshine Tour $$$.

OUTLOOK: Will obviously be looking to win again soon after failing to in 2014, but there was really little about this past season to suggest that he's not capable of succeeding outside of Africa. His 2014 ledger was rather more consistent than his up-and-down 2013, certainly a positive sign.

STATS: Driving Distance: --   Driving Accuracy: --   GIR: --   Short Game: --   Putting: --

Blair, Zachary James ("Zac") (USA) (24)
b. Salt Lake City, UT 8/20/1990. 5'7" 155 lbs. All-American at Brigham Young U. TP: 2014. The son of former PGA Tour player James Blair. Began 2014 with conditional Web.com status and in only eight starts finished 41st in regular season earnings. In the Web.com Finals, finished 2nd at the Tour Championship to leap to 11th on the priority list. **OWR Best:** 211 - Dec, 2014.

Amateur Wins: Pacific Northwest Am: 2011.

	14
Masters	-
US Open	T40
British	-
PGA	-
Money (A)	-
OWR	213

2014: Spent time in Latin America, then played limited Web.com events before powering through the Finals to gain a 2015 PGA Tour card.

OUTLOOK: Given the meteoric rise that got him his Tour card, an obvious lack of experience at this level and the fact that he doesn't hit it terribly far, there is little on his résumé to suggest immediate PGA Tour stardom. Indeed, keeping his card is probably a reasonable 2015 goal.

STATS: Driving Distance: --   Driving Accuracy: --   GIR: --   Short Game: --   Putting: --

---

Bland, Richard (England) (41)
b. Burton-on-Trent, England 2/3/1973. 6'1" 180 lbs. TP: 1996. A journeyman who has thrice played his way onto the E Tour via the Challenge circuit. Is winless on the E Tour, his closest brush being a T2 at the 2002 Irish Open. In 12 seasons, has only cracked the top 100 in $$$ four times - though one of those was a 66th-place finish during a strong 2014 campaign. **OWR Best:** 214 - Sep, 2002.

Other Wins: 1 Euro Challenge (2001).
Amateur Wins: European Under-21: 1994.

	98	99	00	01	02	03	04	05	06	07	08	09	10	11	12	13	14
Masters	-	-	-	-	-	-	-	-	-	-	-	-	-	-	-	-	-
US Open	-	-	-	-	-	-	-	-	-	-	-	MC	-	-	-	-	-
British	MC	-	-	-	-	-	-	-	-	-	-	-	-	-	-	-	-
PGA	-	-	-	-	-	-	-	-	-	-	-	-	-	-	-	-	-
Money (E)	-	-	217*	260*	73	132	319*	111	72	143	167	112	65	162	119	108	66
OWR	-	-	-	694	435	251	385	475	391	382	478	354	288	279	599	368	389	277

2014: E: 30 st / 22 ct / 3 t10. (T4 Port Masters, T5 Africa, T5 Hassan). Made a solid 22 E Tour cuts en route to finishing a career-best 66th in $$$.

OUTLOOK: His two best seasons have come in the last five years, but overall he has never been able to consistently play at a high E Tour level. Is quite strong on the greens but with only mid-range ball striking, one wonders how many more years like 2015 he'll be able to produce.

STATS: Driving Distance: B   Driving Accuracy: B-   GIR: B-   Short Game: B-   Putting: A-

---

Blanks, Kristoffer Douglas (USA) (42)
b. Warner Robins, GA 11/3/1972. 5'10" 220 lbs. College: Huntingdon (AL) College. TP: 1995. A mini-tour player for nearly a decade following college before finally reaching the Web.com in 2005. Graduated to the PGA Tour (at age 35) after finishing 13th on the 2008 Web.com but ranked 170th on the 2009 money list, mandating a return to Q School where he regained his card. Found his stride in 2010 and '11, climbing to 82nd, then 65th in PGA Tour earnings, before dropping to 161st in 2012. Never a PGA Tour winner but twice a runner-up. Missed much of 2013 due to left shoulder surgery and has struggled to regain his PGA Tour since. **OWR Best:** 142 - Oct, 2011.

Other Wins: 1 Web.com (2008) + 3 NGA/Hooters (1998-2004).

	08	09	10	11	12	13	14
Masters	-	-	-	-	-	-	-
US Open	-	-	-	-	-	-	-
British	-	-	-	-	-	-	-
PGA	-	-	MC	-	-	-	-
Money (A)	-	170	82	65	161	-	243*
OWR	295	440	262	167	307	886	582

2014: PGA: 8 st / 1 ct / 0 t10. Also made 11 Web.com starts, narrowly missing regaining his PGA Tour card by finishing 33rd in regular season $$$.

OUTLOOK: Begins 2015 on a nine-event medical extension after unsuccessfully trying to regain his card via the Web.com Tour.

STATS: Driving Distance: C+   Driving Accuracy: A-   GIR: A   Short Game: C   Putting: C-

---

Blixt, Jonas Fredrik Bergland (Sweden) (30)
b. Nassjo, Sweden 4/24/1984. 5'10" 165 lbs. All-American at Florida St. TP: 2008. A full-time Web.com player from 2009-2011, finishing 43rd, 59th and 5th in earnings, the latter earning him his 2012 PGA Tour card. Broke through for his maiden PGA Tour win at the 2012 Frys.com Open (edging Jason Kokrak by one) en route to finishing 34th in $$$ despite being limited to 21 events by a rib injury. After a slow 2013 start, claimed his second win at the Greenbrier Classic, beating four players by two. Has thus far made only sporadic appearances on the European Tour, but finished 2nd at 2013 Nordea Masters in his native Sweden. After finishing fourth at the 2013 PGA, T2 at the 2014 Masters in his next Major start. **Teams:** Palmer Cup (2): 2007-08. World Cup: 2013. **OWR Best:** 33 - Apr, 2014.

PGA Tour Wins (2): 2012: Frys.com Open **2013:** Greenbrier Classic.

	11	12	13	14
Masters	-	-	-	T2
US Open	-	-	-	MC
British	-	-	T26	MC
PGA	-	-	4	T36
Money (A)	-	34	32	81
Money (E)	-	-	46*	30
OWR	226	74	42	59

Blixt, Jonas Fredrik Bergland, Cont'd

2014: PGA: 21 st / 12 ct / 1 t10. (T2 Masters).   Had his worst year on the PGA Tour: only one top 10 and finished 102nd in FedEx Cup points. Made an additional seven starts in Europe where, with co-sanctioned events included, he ranked 30th in $$$.

OUTLOOK: Trying to bounce back from a quiet (though hardly terrible) year. A short and somewhat wild driver whose tee-to-green game is lifted significantly by a fine short game and some top-shelf putting skills. Likely too short to join the elite but appears capable of being a strong PGA Tour contender for the next decade if his tee-to-green game steadies. In good ball striking weeks, his putter will generally put him in the mix.

STATS: Driving Distance: C+   Driving Accuracy: C   GIR: C   Short Game: A-   Putting: A

Bohn, Jason Duehn (USA) (41)
b. Lewisburg, PA 4/24/1973. 6'0" 180 lbs. College: U of Alabama. TP: 1992. Quit collegiate golf upon winning a $1 million hole-in-one shootout, renouncing his amateur status. Initially played on the Canadian Tour, winning twice. Shot a 13-under-par final round 58 in claiming his second Canadian Tour title, the 2001 Bayer Championship at Ontario's Huron Oaks GC. Graduated to the PGA Tour after finishing 9th on the 2003 Web.com circuit. Claimed first PGA Tour victory (in his 48th career start) at the 2005 B.C. Open, and has been an up-and-down earner since. Had his 2007 shortened by a recurring rib injury. Enjoyed a resurgent 2010 led by a two-shot victory over Jeff Overton at the New Orleans Classic and has been largely a steady (if unspectacular) money earner ever since. **OWR Best:** 60 - Apr, 2010.

PGA Tour Wins (2): 2005: B.C. Open   **2010:** New Orleans Classic (Zurich).
Other Wins: 1 Web.com (2003)   +   1 NGA/Hooters (2003)   Payless Open (Canada): 2000   Bayer Champ (Canada): 2001   Callaway Inv: 2006.

	04	05	06	07	08	09	10	11	12	13	14
Masters	-	-	T39	-	-	-	-	MC	-	-	-
US Open	-	-	-	-	MC	-	-	-	71	-	-
British	-	-	-	-	-	-	MC	-	-	-	-
PGA	-	T34	MC	-	-	-	MC	-	-	-	T41
Money (A)	131	35	43	142	123	81	40	150	114	109	65
OWR	247	84	77	192	178	118	139	329	284	146	137

2014: PGA: 25 st / 15 ct / 3 t10. (T2 Shriners, T3 Mayakoba, 4 Wells Fargo).   Recorded his best PGA Tour season since 2010, finishing 70th in FedEx Cup points and logging five top-25 finishes and a trio of top 5s.

OUTLOOK: A steady veteran with six career runner-ups to go with his two wins. A short-but-accurate driver of the ball whose putting has improved a bit over the last two years, his SGP jumping from 114 to 59 in 2013, then holding steady at 72 in 2014. As his other primary statistics have remained quite consistent into his 40s, this figures to remain the key going forward - and a steady putter is not always a given at this age.

STATS: Driving Distance: C-   Driving Accuracy: A   GIR: B   Short Game: B-   Putting: B+

Bolli, Justin Hans (USA) (38)
b. Portland, OR 3/18/1976. 6'2" 200 lbs. College: U of Georgia. TP: 1999. After walking on at Georgia, spent 2000-2003 on the Hooters Tour where he was a three-time winner. Joined the Web.com Tour in 2004 where he logged four victories over an eight-year span and thrice played himself onto the PGA Tour, finishing 9th, 8th and 9th in $$$ in 2004, 2007 and 2012. **OWR Best:** 181 - Aug, 2007.

Other Wins: 4 Web.com (2004-2012)   +   3 NGA/Hooters (2000-2003).

	05	06	07	08	09	10	11	12	13	14
Masters	-	-	-	-	-	-	-	-	-	-
US Open	-	-	-	-	-	-	-	-	-	-
British	-	-	-	-	-	-	-	-	-	-
PGA	-	-	-	-	-	-	-	-	-	-
Money (A)	192	-	-	158	-	215	-	-	132	234
OWR	513	388	234	420	286	547	667	274	325	860

2014: PGA: 6 st / 1 ct / 0 t10. (T32 Wyndham). Finished 225th in FedEx Cup points. Also made 14 Web.com Tour starts (174th in $$$).

OUTLOOK: Journeyman who keeps plugging away – but he'll have no PGA Tour status going into 2015.

STATS (LTD): Driving Distance: C   Driving Accuracy: B   GIR: C   Short Game: C+   Putting: B+

Botes, Desvonde Pierre Klnever (South Africa) (40)
b. Pretoria, South Africa 11/2/1974. 6'3" 205 lbs. TP: 1992. Youngest ever winner of the South African Amateur (at age 16 in 1991) and turned pro shortly thereafter. Quickly developed into a productive professional, winning nine Sunshine Tour events during the 1990s and 14 titles overall, mostly in smaller winter events, none of which have been E Tour co-sanctioned. Logged three top-5 finishes in the Order of Merit through 2004, peaking at 3rd during the 2003-04 season. Did venture semi-regularly to Europe early in the new millennium (claiming medalist honors at the 2002 E Tour Q School) before being slowed by back problems in 2002 and '03. Briefly returned to Europe in 2004 but remained at home thereafter, and has never played the PGA Tour. **Teams:** World Cup: 2003. **OWR Best:** 257 - Feb, 1999.

Sunshine Tour Wins (14): 1993: Mercedes Benz Challenge (54H)   **1996**: Zambia Open (54H)   **1997**: Bushveld Classic (54H), Vodacom-Western Cape (54H), Platinum Classic   **1998**: Pietersburg Classic (54H), Ellerines Better Ball (w/L.Flanagan)(54H)   **1999**: South African Masters, Vodacom-Free State (54H)   **2000**: Platinum Classic (54H)   **2003**: Parmalat Classic (54H)   **2005**: Vodacom-Pretoria (54H), Vodacom-Pezula (54H)   **2006**: Seeker's Travel Pro-Am (54H).
Other Wins: Royal Swazi Sun Pro-Am (SA): 2000.
Amateur Wins: South African Am: 1991   –   Transvaal Am: 1991   South African Boys: 1990   South African Am Team: 1991   Springbok Am: 1992.

	93	94	95	96	97	98	99	00	01	02	03	04	05	06	07	08	09	10	11	12	13	14
Masters	-	-	-	-	-	-	-	-	-	-	-	-	-	-	-	-	-	-	-	-	-	-
US Open	-	-	-	-	-	-	-	-	-	-	-	-	-	-	-	-	-	-	-	-	-	-
British	-	-	-	-	-	-	T64	-	-	-	-	-	-	MC	-	-	-	-	-	-	-	-
PGA	-	-	-	-	-	-	-	-	-	-	-	-	-	-	-	-	-	-	-	-	-	-
Money (E)	-	-	-	-	-	-	-	105	185	-	161	-	-	-	-	-	-	-	-	-	-	-
Money (SA)	118	83	79	57	5	32	4	18	13	60*	57*	3	57	20	26	25	41	70	45	16	15	91
OWR	711	851	891	899	400	405	289	415	307	565	-	366	643	-	838	-	-	-	739	474	448	954

Botes, Desvonde Pierre Klnever, Cont'd

2014: SUN: 16 st / 8 ct / 0 t10. (T20 Royal Swazi). Struggled through his worst season since his rookie year 21 years ago, finishing 91st in $$$.

OUTLOOK: One of the more experienced 40-year-olds one is likely to encounter on any of the world's tours. He briefly reestablished himself as a Sunshine contender in his late 30s before plunging in 2014. Notably, reestablished or not, he hasn't won since 2006.

STATS: Driving Distance: --   Driving Accuracy: --   GIR: --   Short Game: --   Putting: --

---

Both, Marcus (Australia) (35)
b. Horsham, Australia 6/8/1979. 6'3" 205 lbs. TP: 2003. Joined the Asian Tour soon after turning pro and has remained there ever since, winning as a rookie (at China's Sanya Open) on the old Asian circuit, then settling into a steady career thereafter on the new one. Won the 2009 Cambodian Open, then broke a five-year drought in 2014 by taking the Philippine Open, where he beat a quartet of runners-up by two. **OWR Best**: 215 - Jan, 2010.

Asian Tour Wins (3): **2003**: Sanya Open **2009**: Cambodian Open (Johnnie Walker) **2014**: Philippine Open (ICTSI).

	04	05	06	07	08	09	10	11	12	13	14
Masters	-	-	-	-	-	-	-	-	-	-	-
US Open	-	-	-	-	-	-	-	-	-	-	-
British	-	-	-	-	-	-	-	-	-	-	-
PGA	-	-	-	-	-	-	-	-	-	-	-
Money (As)	31	9	50	52	35	7	20	42	45	74	29
OWR	417	269	488	935	658	220	255	407	716	992	465

2014: ASIA: 13 st / 10 ct / 1 t10. (Won Philippine Open). Jumped from 74th to 29th in $$$ and added his third career Asian Tour win.

OUTLOOK: A lifetime Asian Tour player who is well established there (twice ranking among the circuit's top 10 money winners) and who shows little apparent desire to head elsewhere. His statistics tend to support this, however, as numerically speaking the E Tour might currently be a reach.

STATS: Driving Distance: B   Driving Accuracy: C   GIR: C-   Short Game: B   Putting: B

Bouniol, Cyril (France) (27)
b. Laloubere, France 8/11/1987. 6'2" 180 lbs. Two-time D2 All-American and NCAA individual champion (2010) at Abilene (TX) Christian. TP: 2013. In his first season as a pro, played the Challenge Tour before dramatically claiming the very last card at E Tour Q School by birdieing the final hole - after double-bogeying the penultimate. **OWR Best**: 413 - Dec, 2014.

Amateur Wins: NCAA Div II Individual: 2010.

	14
Masters	-
US Open	-
British	-
PGA	-
Money (E)	-
OWR	420

2014: Played full-time on the Challenge Tour, where he finished 19th in $$$, then played his way through Q School to earn his 2015 E Tour card.

OUTLOOK: Played some of his best golf late in the year but with so limited a level of experience, seems an E Tour longshot in 2015.

STATS: Driving Distance: --   Driving Accuracy: --   GIR: --   Short Game: --   Putting: --

---

Bourdy, Grégory (France) (32)
b. Bordeaux, France 04/25/1982. 5'11" 155 lbs. TP: 2003. Won three times on his domestic Alps Tour. Claimed his first win overseas in 2006, running away with South Africa's Telkom PGA Championship by six shots. Blossomed in 2007 with a victory in the Mallorca Classic, then backed that up by winning the 2008 Portuguese Open and the 2009 Hong Kong Open, where he edged a young Rory McIlroy by two. Remained a steady earner during a six-year victory drought that ended at the 2013 Wales Open, where he birdied the last three holes to beat American Peter Uihlein. **Teams**: Eisenhower Trophy: 2002. Seve Trophy: 2013. World Cup (3): 2008-11-13. **OWR Best**: 75 - Jun, 2011.

European Tour Wins (4): **2007**: Mallorca Classic **2008**: Portuguese Open **2009**: Hong Kong Open **2013**: Wales Open (ISPS Handa).
Sunshine Tour Wins (1): **2006**: Telkom PGA Championship.
Other Wins: 3 Alps (2003-2005).
Amateur Wins: Scottish Youths: 2002.

	05	06	07	08	09	10	11	12	13	14
Masters	-	-	-	-	-	-	-	-	-	-
US Open	-	-	-	-	-	-	-	MC	-	-
British	-	-	T53	T39	-	-	T48	-	T64	T47
PGA	-	-	-	-	-	T58	MC	-	-	-
Money (E)	118	102	39	46	45	55	47	75	25	73
OWR	285	211	138	126	85	96	124	163	100	187

2014: E: 26 st / 19 ct / 3 t10. (T6 Laguna, T7 Port Masters, T8 Irish). Slipped from 25th to 73rd in $$$ during a quieter - but hardly bad - campaign.

OUTLOOK: A shorter, straighter hitter – a recipe which limits his upside in the modern game, but which has also helped to make him a very steady earner. Though he owns four E Tour titles, seems to have become more of a check casher than a winner – but then he's just entering his prime years.

STATS: Driving Distance: C+   Driving Accuracy: A   GIR: A-   Short Game: B   Putting: B

Bowditch, Steven David (Australia) (31)
b. Newcastle, New South Wales, Australia 6/8/1983. 6'0" 200 lbs. TP: 2001. 2000 World Junior runner-up who came to fame in his native Australia upon being paired with Greg Norman in the final round of that season's Australian Open as a 17-year-old amateur. Won the 2001 Australian Stroke play. After turning pro, won the Von Nida Tour's 2004 Queensland Open before coming to

Bowditch, Steven David, Cont'd

America and twice graduating the Web.com Tour (2005 and '10). After finishing 256th in 2006 PGA Tour $$$, returned to the Web.com Tour for 2007-2010, then played on conditional status through 2013, when he finally kept his card. Broke through for his maiden PGA Tour triumph at the 2014 Texas Open, where he edged Will MacKenzie and Daniel Summerhays by one. **OWR Best:** 80 - Oct, 2014.

PGA Tour Wins (1): 2014: Texas Open (Valero).
Australasian Tour Wins (1): 2010: New South Wales PGA.
Other Wins: 2 Web.com (2005-2010) + Queensland Open (Aus): 2004.
Amateur Wins: Australian Stroke Play: 2001.

	03	04	05	06	07	08	09	10	11	12	13	14
Masters	-	-	-	-	-	-	-	-	-	-	-	T26
US Open	-	-	-	-	-	-	-	-	-	-	-	-
British	MC	-	-	-	-	-	-	-	-	-	-	-
PGA	-	-	-	-	-	-	-	-	-	-	-	MC
Money (A)	-	-	-	256	-	-	-	-	132	185	118	57
OWR	571	288	148	503	539	723	681	313	289	616	342	89

2014: PGA: 30 st / 18 ct / 1 t10. (Won Texas).   Logged his first PGA Tour win (his lone top-10 finish) and finished 59th in FedEx Cup points.

OUTLOOK: A very long hitter whose game is built around his power (18 in Par 5 Scoring), while his short game and putting have bounced around a bit. Those numbers make it difficult to predict major continued improvement; indeed, his Texas Open win was his lone top 10 of 2014.

STATS: Driving Distance: A+   Driving Accuracy: C-   GIR: C+   Short Game: B-   Putting: C+

Bradley, Keegan Hansen (USA) (28)
b. Woodstock, VT 6/7/1986. 6'3" 190 lbs. College: St. Johns U. TP: 2008. The nephew of LPGA great and Hall-of-Famer Pat Bradley. Enjoyed a strong nine-win collegiate career at St Johns (NY) University after being passed over by traditional golfing powers. Upon turning pro, spent 2009 on the Hooters Tour (winning twice) before enjoying a solid 2010 on the Web.com, where his 14th-place finish secured 2011 PGA Tour privileges. Broke through to win at the 2011 Byron Nelson Championship in his 16th career start, edging Ryan Palmer on the first hole of sudden death. Ten weeks later, took a giant leap by winning the PGA Championship at the Atlanta Athletic Club, closing a five-stroke gap over the last four holes, then beating Jason Dufner in a three-hole aggregate playoff. Scored a significant third win at the 2012 WGC Bridgestone Invitational, where Jim Furyk's 72nd-hole double bogey allowed him to win by one. Went winless during 2013 and '14 despite logging 13 top 10s (and 28 top 25s) in a combined 51 PGA Tour starts. **Awards:** PGA Tour Rookie of the Year: 2011. **Teams:** Ryder Cup (2): 2012-14 (O: 4-3-0, S: 0-2-0). Presidents Cup: 2013 (2-2-1). **OWR Best:** 10 - Mar, 2013.

PGA Tour Wins (3): 2011: Byron Nelson Championship, PGA Championship **2012**: WGC-Bridgestone.
Other Wins: 2 NGA/Hooters (2009)   PGA Grand Slam: 2011   Shark Shootout: 2011 (w/B.Steele).

	11	12	13	14
Masters	-	T27	T54	MC
US Open	-	T68	MC	T4
British	-	T34	T15	T19
PGA	Win	T3	T19	MC
Money (A)	13	10	11	28
OWR	31	13	20	28

2014: PGA: 26 st / 21 ct / 6 t10. (2 Arnold Palmer, T4 US Open, T4 Greenbrier, T4 WGC-Bridgestone, T8 New Orleans, etc.).   Played consistently good golf despite this being his worst season (33rd in FedEx Cup points) on Tour. The lack of a win, however, was surely a disappointment.

OUTLOOK: Little has changed from a year ago. Is firmly established as one of America's elite young players, utilizing an imposing mix of power and accuracy (8 in Total Driving) and a deft skill set around the greens. Other then having to switch to a non-anchored putting stroke by 2016, there is little to suggest he will not spend a long time among the elite – though to truly be elite, he must begin to win on a regular basis. Plays consistently well all over the country. One of only a handful of players still in their 20s who appear capable of (if not likely to) win multiple Major championships

STATS: Driving Distance: A+   Driving Accuracy: B+   GIR: A-   Short Game: A-   Putting: A-

---

Bremner, Merrick (South Africa) (28)
b. Durban, South Africa 3/26/1986. 6'0" 195 lbs. TP: 2005. Turned professional while still a teenager and in only his second full Sunshine Tour campaign (2008), won both the Lombard Insurance Classic (by three over Kevin Stone) and the Telkom PGA Pro-Am (by one over Jaco Van Zyl and Dean Lambert). Added a second Lombard Insurance Classic during a career-best 2013 (10th in $$$), when he edged P.H. McIntyre by two. Held his gains nicely in 2014, a season anchored by his fourth Sunshine Tour title, a one-shot triumph over Darren Fichardt at the BMG Classic. **OWR Best:** 262 - Oct, 2014.

Sunshine Tour Wins (4): 2008: Lombard Insurance Classic (54H), Telkom PGA Pro-Am (54H) **2013**: Lombard Insurance Classic (54H) **2014**: BMG Classic (54H).

	06	07	08	09	10	11	12	13	14
Masters	-	-	-	-	-	-	-	-	-
US Open	-	-	-	-	-	-	-	-	-
British	-	-	-	-	-	-	-	-	-
PGA	-	-	-	-	-	-	-	-	-
Money (SA)	143*	82	31	57	56	27	23	10	18
OWR	-	-	-	714	-	938	475	329	276

2014: SUN: 19 st / 13 ct / 4 t10. (Incl. Won BMG, 3 Sun City Challenge).   Stepped back slightly from up a stellar 2013 campaign (dropping from 10 top 10s to four) but still managed to win once and remain among the Sunshine Tour's top 20 $$$ winners.

OUTLOOK: Played his most consistently solid golf in 2013 but is on a solid three-year run overall. Has made no attempt thus far to take his game abroad, but might that be coming? Notably, nearly all of his best finishes (and all of his ins) have come during the lighter-field winter season.

STATS: Driving Distance: --   Driving Accuracy: --   GIR: --   Short Game: --   Putting: --

Broberg, Kristoffer (Sweden) (28)
b. Stockholm, Sweden 8/1/1986. 6'0" 165 lbs. TP: 2010. Initially appeared on the Nordic League satellite tour in 2011, winning four times there through 2012. Joined the Challenge circuit in May and promptly won four times in seven starts, cracking the top 100 in the OWR and earning immediate promotion to the E Tour. T2 at the 2012 Alfred Dunhill Championship (E Tour'13) in the second start of a rookie year in which he narrowly retained his card before climbing to 47th in $$$ in 2014. **OWR Best:** 78 - Jan, 2013.

Other Wins: 4 Euro Challenge (2012)   +   4 Nordic League (2011-2012).

	12	13	14
Masters	-	-	-
US Open	-	-	-
British	-	-	T32
PGA	-	-	-
Money (E)	201*	103	47
OWR	79	216	165

2014: E: 31 st / 18 ct / 3 t10. (2 Scottish, T3 Irish, T6 NH Collection). In a strong sophomore season, jumped precipitously from 103rd to 47th in $$$.
OUTLOOK: Though winless over two E Tour seasons, his 2014 campaign suggests that his 2012 Challenge Tour dominance was not just a special run of form. Thus far a sound and accurate (if not long) ball striker who, with a little more seasoning, looks capable of winning at the E Tour level.
STATS: Driving Distance: B-   Driving Accuracy: A-   GIR: B+   Short Game: C+   Putting: B

Brooks, Daniel (England) (27)
b. Basildon, England 1/5/1987. 6'1" 160 lbs. TP: 2007. Won on the 2009 EuroPro Tour before spending 2011 and '12 playing the Challenge Tour (21st in $$$ in '12). Split time between the Challenge and E Tours in 2013 before reaching the 2014 E Tour via Q School. Then made good by winning the fog-shortened Madeira Islands Open in a playoff with Scott Henry. **OWR Best:** 286 - May, 2014.

European Tour Wins (1): 2014: Madeira Islands Open.
Other Wins: 1 EuroPro (2009).

	12	13	14
Masters	-	-	-
US Open	-	-	-
British	-	-	-
PGA	-	-	-
Money (E)	-	215	140
OWR	410	424	419

2014: E: 24 st / 10 ct / 1 t10. (Won Madeira). Won at the rain-shortened Madeira Islands Open to remain exempt despite finishing 140th in $$$.
OUTLOOK: As he logged only one additional top 25 beyond his Madeira Islands win, he remains a major longshot at the E Tour level.
STATS (LTD): Driving Distance: B+   Driving Accuracy: C-   GIR: C-   Short Game: B+   Putting: C

Brown, Samuel Scott (USA) (31)
b. Augusta, GA 5/22/1983. 5'8" 170 lbs. Division 2 Player Of The Year and two-time All-American at U of South Carolina-Aiken. TP: 2006. After leading USC-Aiken to three straight D2 national titles (2004-2006), played the eGolf mini-tour for four seasons before reaching the Web.com in 2010. Finished 70th in $$$ that season but climbed to 8th during 2011, earning his PGA Tour card for 2012. As a rookie, logged three top 10s in 24 starts but finished 148th in $$$. Playing on conditional status, won the 2013 Puerto Rico Open, edging Jordan Spieth and Fabián Gómez by one and securing playing privileges through 2015. **OWR Best:** 128 - Aug, 2014.

PGA Tour Wins (1): 2013: Puerto Rico Open.
Other Wins: 1 Web.com (2001)   +   5 eGolf Tour (2007-2009).

	11	12	13	14
Masters	-	-	-	-
US Open	-	-	-	-
British	-	-	MC	-
PGA	-	-	MC	T47
Money (A)	-	148	81	74
OWR	285	348	162	196

2014: PGA: 30 st / 21 ct / 4 t10. (T3 Frys.com, T4 McGladrey, T5 Heritage, T5 John Deere). Finished a career-best 85th in FedEx Cup points.
OUTLOOK: Measures up fairly well statistically, and saw major 2014 improvement in Driving Accuracy (76 to 26), SGP (138 to 56) and Total Putting (97 to 47). This helped to make him far more consistent (made 21 of 30 cuts), but can such gains be sustained over the log run?
STATS: Driving Distance: B+   Driving Accuracy: B+ ⇧   GIR: B   Short Game: B   Putting: B

Burmester, Dean (South Africa) (25)
b. Bloemfontein, South Africa 6/2/1989. 5'11" 165 lbs. TP: 2010. After three quiet Sunshine Tour seasons, he claimed his maiden win via a four-shot walkaway at the 2013 Polokwane Classic. Validated that victory in 2014 by capturing the Sun City Challenge, where a birdie at the last edged 19-year-old Haydn Porteous by one. **OWR Best:** 402 - Jun, 2013.

Sunshine Tour Wins (2): 2013: Polokwane Classic **2014:** Sun City Challenge (54H).
Amateur Wins: African Int'l Team: 2009.

	10	11	12	13	14
Masters	-	-	-	-	-
US Open	-	-	-	-	-
British	-	-	-	-	-
PGA	-	-	-	-	-
Money (Sa)	105	86	42	28	52
OWR	1322	1401	652	590	669

Burmester, Dean, Cont'd

2014: SUN: 21 st / 14 ct / 3 t10. (Incl. Won Sun City, T5 Nedbank Affinity). Fell to 52nd in $$$ despite claiming his second victory, at Sun City.

OUTLOOK: With wins in both 2013 and '14, he's established himself as a solid domestic player - but succeeding abroad seems a long way off.

STATS: Driving Distance: --   Driving Accuracy: --   GIR: --   Short Game: --   Putting: --

---

Byrd, Jonathan Currie (USA) (36)

b. Anderson, SC 1/27/1978. 5'9" 165 lbs. Two-time All-American at Clemson U. TP: 2000. An Academic All-American and 2009 Walker Cup player while at Clemson. Graduated from a one-year stint on the Web.com Tour (2001) with an 8th-place $$$ ranking. Made a splashy PGA Tour debut in 2002, winning the Buick Challenge in his next-to-last start and being named Rookie Of The Year. Slipped in 2004 and '05 due to late '04 hip surgery, but progressed steadily thereafter, winning for the third time at the 2007 John Deere (nipping Tim Clark by one). Claimed his fourth victory in unique fashion, scoring a hole-in-one on the fourth extra hole to beat Martin Laird and Cameron Percy at the 2010 Justin Timberlake Open (Las Vegas). Won his next start at the 2011 Hyundai Tournament of Champions at Kapalua the following January, beating Robert Garrigus, again in sudden death. Missed the end of 2012 and the beginning of 2013 due to surgery on his left wrist. **Awards**: PGA Tour Rookie of the Year: 2002. **Teams**: Walker Cup: 1999 (1-2-0). Palmer Cup (2): 1999-00. **OWR Best**: 39 - Jun, 2011.

PGA Tour Wins (5): **2002**: Buick Challenge   **2004**: B.C. Open   **2007**: John Deere Classic   **2010**: Shriners Hospital Open (Las Vegas)   **2011**: Hyundai Tournament of Champions.

Other Wins: 1 Web.com (2001).

Amateur Wins: Northeast Am: 1999   Carolinas Am: 1999.

	02	03	04	05	06	07	08	09	10	11	12	13	14
Masters	-	T8	MC	-	-	-	MC	-	-	MC	T27	-	-
US Open	-	T15	MC	-	-	-	MC	-	-	MC	T56	-	-
British	-	-	-	-	-	T23	-	-	-	MC	MC	-	-
PGA	-	MC	MC	-	T20	MC	MC	-	-	MC	MC	-	-
Money (A)	39	47	70	111	63	42	101	67	55	22	50	148	133
OWR	73	69	98	156	98	60	155	148	121	55	92	273	305

2014: PGA: 24 st / 14 ct / 1 t10. (T3 Barracuda). Began the year by clearing a 10-event medical extension but struggled a bit overall, logging only one top 10, finishing 136th in FedEx Cup points and failing to save himself via the Web.com Finals.

OUTLOOK: Begins 2015 with conditional PGA Tour status or must use his one-time career Top 125 Money Winners exemption. Always a strong competitor when healthy, so one wonders if he's still feeling the effects of 2012 wrist surgery. Finished 2 and 20 in GIR in 2009 and '10, improved from 142 to 95 in that category in 2014 - so that's where much of the improvement needs to happen.

STATS: Driving Distance: B   Driving Accuracy: B+   GIR: C   Short Game: B   Putting: B+

Cabrera, Angel Leopoldo (Argentine) (45)

b. Cordoba, Argentina 9/12/1969. 6'0" 210 lbs. TP: 1989. Nicknamed "El Pato" (The Duck). Former caddie who enjoyed success in South America (where he has amassed more than 30 victories) before heading off to Europe and America. First drew major international attention when he missed the Lawrie-Van de Velde-Leonard playoff at 1999 British Open (Carnoustie) by one shot. His three E Tour victories include his homestanding 2001 Argentine Open, the 2002 Benson & Hedges Int'l and the Tour's flagship event, the BMW PGA Championship, where he beat Paul McGinley by two at Wentworth in 2005. Stepped up in class by winning the 2007 U.S. Open at Oakmont, where a superb closing 69 edged Tiger Woods and Jim Furyk by one. Secured a much greater place in history by defeating Kenny Perry and Chad Campbell in sudden death to win the 2009 Masters. Suffered from tendonitis in his thumb and complications from major dental surgery in the latter half of 2010, and slipped further in 2011, save for an out-of-nowhere 7th at Augusta. Similarly quiet in 2012 before awakening in December to win his third career Argentine Open, then re-emerged at the 2013 Masters, making a spectacular 72nd-hole birdie to force a playoff with Adam Scott before losing on the second extra hole. Won his eighth Central Argentina Open a week later, recovering from jetlag to charge from well behind with a closing 64, then win in a playoff. Won his first non-Major PGA Tour event at the 2014 Greenbrier Classic, holing a 176-yard 8 iron to eagle the 493-yard par-4 13th on Sunday en route to beating George McNeill by two. **Teams**: Presidents Cup (4): 2005-07-09-13 (6-8-3). World Cup (9): 1998-99-00-01-02-03-04-05-06. **OWR Best**: 9 - Oct, 2005.

PGA Tour Wins (3): **2007**: U.S. Open   **2009**: The Masters   **2014**: Greenbrier Classic.

European Tour Wins (3): **2001**: Argentine Open   **2002**: Benson & Hedges Int'l   **2005**: BMW PGA.

Asian Tour Wins (1): **2006**: Singapore Open.

Other Wins: San Diego Grand Prix (Arg): 1991   Norpatagonico Open (Arg): 1992   Abierto del Centro (Arg) (8): 1994-97-00-01-05-06-07-13   Abierto del Sur (Arg) (3): 1994-96-04   Villa Gessel Grand Prix (Arg): 1994   Nautico Hacoaj Grand Prix (Arg): 1994   Paraguay Open: 1995   Abierto del Litoral (Arg): 1995   El Rodeo Open (Colombia): 1995   Volvo Masters of Latin America (Brazil): 1996   Santiago del Estero Open (Arg): 1996   Vina del Mar Open (Chile): 1996   Brazil Open (2): 1998-99   Argentine PGA (2): 1998-02 (T w/G.Rojas)   Argentine Masters (4): 1999-01-05-07   Bariloche Match Play (Arg): 2000   Desafio des Maestros (Arg): 2000   Argentine Open (3): 2001-02-12   Ascochingas (Arg): 2001   La Cumbre (Arg): 2001   Rio Cuarto (Arg): 2002   Las Delicias (Arg): 2002   Abierto del Norte (Arg) (2): 2004-05   PGA Grand Slam: 2007   Cordoba PGA (Arg): 2008   Gary Player Inv (SA): 2009 (w/T.Johnstone)   Angel Cabrera #2 (Arg): 2009.

	96	97	98	99	00	01	02	03	04	05	06	07	08	09	10	11	12	13	14
Masters	-	-	-	-	MC	T10	T9	T15	MC	MC	T8	T37	T25	Win	T18	7	T32	2P	MC
US Open	-	-	-	-	T37	T7	T66	T35	16	T33	T26	Win	MC	T54	T22	MC	T46	MC	MC
British	-	T51	-	T4	MC	MC	MC	T22	-	MC	7	34	MC	T24	MC	MC	MC	T11	T19
PGA	-	-	-	T41	T19	T37	T48	T45	MC	-	MC	MC	T20	T63	MC	MC	MC	WD	WD
Money (A)	-	-	-	-	-	-	-	145	-	-	-	-	54	122	21	71	131	174	43	50
Money (E)	72	38	45	10	14	11	11	53	11	5	17	6	57	-	-	-	-	-	-
OWR	309	161	154	60	47	34	14	66	30	12	28	14	42	25	55	139	267	64	73

2014: PGA: 23 st / 12 ct / 1 t10. (Won Greenbrier). Despite making barely half his PGA Tour cuts, claimed his first non-Major American win at the Greenbrier Classic en route to finishing 50th in FedEx Cup points. Made only one non-PGA Tour start (a runner-up in Argentina) all year.

OUTLOOK: At age 45, he proved himself still highly relevant by winning at the Greenbrier Classic. Has long ridden a potent mix of power and an underrated putting stroke, but he's been quite inconsistent since 2010 (due in part to injuries). Despite his age, his power game holds its own with far younger players, meaning that he almost certainly will remain competitive for several more seasons to come.

STATS: Driving Distance: A   Driving Accuracy: C   GIR: B-   Short Game: C+   Putting: B

Cabrera-Bello, Rafael (Spain) (30) b. Las Palmas, Spain 5/25/1984. 6'2" 180 lbs. College: University of Las Palmas. TP: 2005. Grew up in the Canary Islands. His younger sister Emma plays on the Ladies European Tour. Won the Spanish National Championship at every age group level from under-7 through under-18. In 2002, tied for 4th at the Spanish Open as a 17-year-old amateur. Turned pro at age of 20 and played the 2006 Challenge Tour, winning once, and added a second Challenge title in 2008, while splitting time with the E Tour. Reached the E Tour for good in 2009, when he closed with a 60 at the Fontana Golf Club to win the Austrian Open by one. Claimed a much bigger victory at the 2012 Dubai Desert Classic, where he edged Stephen Gallacher and Lee Westwood by one. **Teams:** Eisenhower Trophy: 2004. World Cup: 2013. **OWR Best:** 43 - Aug, 2012.

European Tour Wins (2): 2009: Austrian Open **2012:** Dubai Desert Classic.
Other Wins: 2 Euro Challenge (2006-2008)   +   Canarias Pro Championship (Spain): 2005*.

	06	07	08	09	10	11	12	13	14
Masters	-	-	-	-	-	-	-	-	-
US Open	-	-	-	-	T47	-	MC	-	-
British	-	-	-	-	-	-	T81	T21	MC
PGA	-	-	-	-	-	-	MC	T29	74
Money (E)	-	134	202	39	78	30	17	41	42
OWR	285	586	254	130	211	118	58	140	93

2014: E: 24 st / 20 ct / 7 t10.   (2P BMW Int'l, T3 Qatar, T4 Abu Dhabi, T5 Hassan, T8 Volvo China, etc.).   Nearly closed his year spectacularly before losing the Tour Championship with two late double-bogeys - but he still finished among the top 50 $$$ winners for the fourth straight season.
OUTLOOK: Has long seemed on the verge of big things, and remains a strong ball striker, especially with his irons (12 in GIR). But despite being a productive earner, has only recorded two wins and 19 top 10s in 231 career starts through 2014. Just heading into what should be his best years.

STATS: Driving Distance: B+   Driving Accuracy: B-   GIR: A   Short Game: B-   Putting: B-

---

Campbell, David Chad (USA) (40) b. Andrews, TX 5/31/1974. 6'1" 205 lbs. JC All-American at Midland(TX)JC, All-American at UNLV. TP: 1996. Dominated the Hooters mini-tour for several years (logging 13 victories) before playing the Web.com in 2001, where he won three times and graduated to the PGA Tour. Celebrated ball striker who became the first player to make the season-ending Tour Championship his initial victory, riding a third round 61 at Houston's Champions GC to a three-stroke victory over Charles Howell III in 2003. Also won the 2004 Bay Hill Invitational (in a six-shot runaway over Stuart Appleby), the 2006 Bob Hope Classic and the 2007 Viking Classic. Voted "player most likely to win a Major" by his Tour peers in 2003, and came close at the 2009 Masters, losing in a three-way playoff with winner Angel Cabrera and Kenny Perry. Slipped a bit in 2010, falling to 96th in earnings and, despite a quiet T5 at the British Open, improved only slightly (to 86th) in 2011. Fell further in 2012 before finally dropping out of the top 125 for the first time in 2013. **Teams:** Ryder Cup (3): 2004-06-08 (O: 3-4-2, S: 2-1-0). **OWR Best:** 9 - May, 2004.

PGA Tour Wins (4): 2003: Tour Championship **2004:** Bay Hill Inv **2006:** Bob Hope Classic (90H) **2007:** Viking Classic.
Other Wins: 3 Web.com (2001) + 13 NGA/Hooters (1997-2000).

	99	00	01	02	03	04	05	06	07	08	09	10	11	12	13	14
Masters	-	-	-	-	MC	MC	T17	T3	MC	-	T2P	T45	-	-	-	-
US Open	MC	MC	MC	-	T35	MC	T42	MC	57	T18	MC	-	MC	-	-	-
British	-	-	-	-	T15	MC	MC	65	MC	-	MC	-	T5	T72	-	-
PGA	-	-	-	MC	2	T24	T28	T24	T57	MC	T43	T62	-	-	-	-
Money (A)	-	-	-	81	7	24	20	14	49	24	48	96	83	106	137	149
OWR	741	-	173	165	13	19	38	27	93	65	62	157	173	192	305	397

2014: PGA: 18 st / 10 ct / 1 t10.   (T7 Travelers).   Had his worst year on the PGA Tour, making only 10 cuts and finishing 152nd in FedEx Cup points.
OUTLOOK: Still capable of elite ball striking (1 in GIR, 44 in Total Driving, 16 in Ball Striking) and remains a well-above-average iron player, but his putting remains dicey, a big part of his steady slide since 2011. Unsuccessful in the Web.com Finals, so he will play in 2015 on conditional status for the second straight year. At age 40 there's still time, especially when his ball striking guarantees that he can contend any time his putter heats up.

STATS: Driving Distance: B-   Driving Accuracy: B+   GIR: A+   Short Game: B-   Putting: C

Campbell, Michael Shane (New Zealand) (45) b. Hawera, New Zealand 2/23/1969. 5'10" 200 lbs. TP: 1993. Maori with Scottish bloodlines who first came to international light by leading the 1995 British Open at St Andrews after 54 holes before a closing 76 left him T3. Bothered by a wrist injury for several seasons before breaking through at the E Tour's 1999 Johnnie Walker Classic, where he beat Geoff Ogilvy by one in Taiwan. Blossomed in 2000 by winning four times worldwide, including a six-shot runaway at the E Tour's Heineken Classic (the first of back-to-back victories there), a triumph in his native New Zealand Open and a four-shot walkaway at the prestigious Australian Masters. Following a narrow win at the 2002 European Open and a playoff victory at the 2003 Irish Open at Portmarnock, stunned the golfing world by holding off a charging Tiger Woods to capture the 2005 U.S. Open at Pinehurst, then capped the year by beating Paul McGinley 2 & 1 to claim the World Match Play title. Slipped soon thereafter, struggling badly from 2009-2011 before climbing back to 77th in E Tour $$$ in 2012. Missed nearly all of 2014 with a left ankle injury, making only one start (an MC in Abu Dhabi) worldwide. **Awards:** E Tour Golfer of the Year: 2005. **Teams:** Eisenhower Trophy: 1992. Presidents Cup (2): 2000-05 (3-3-3). World Cup (4): 1995-01-02-03. **OWR Best:** 12 - May, 2001.

PGA Tour Wins (1): 2005: U.S. Open.
European Tour (7): 1999: Johnnie Walker Classic ('00) **2000:** Heineken Classic, German Masters (54H) **2001:** Heineken Classic **2002:** European Open **2003:** Irish Open **2005:** World Match Play.
Australasian Tour Wins (3): 1993: Canon Challenge **2000:** New Zealand Open, Australian Masters.
Other Wins: 3 Euro Challenge (1994) + Dunhill Masters (Indonesia): 1995.
Amateur Wins: Australian Am: 1992   New South Wales Am: 1992.

	93	94	95	96	97	98	99	00	01	02	03	04	05	06	07	08	09	10	11	12	13	14
Masters	-	-	-	MC	-	-	-	MC	MC	MC	MC	-	MC	MC	MC	MC	MC	-	-	-	-	-
US Open	-	-	-	T32	-	-	-	T12	MC	MC	MC	MC	Win	MC	T58	MC	MC	MC	MC	MC	MC	-
British	-	MC	T3	DQ	-	T66	MC	MC	T23	MC	T53	T20	T5	T35	T57	T51	-	-	-	-	-	-
PGA	-	-	-	T17	MC	-	-	MC	MC	T23	T69	T49	T6	MC	MC	T42	MC	-	-	-	-	-
Money (E)	-	-	5	120	133	81	41	4	12	8	15	28	2	31	55	69	249	244	181	77	173	-
OWR	189	209	28	78	418	364	108	14	27	18	44	89	16	25	174	183	445	813	745	285	375	1394

Campbell, Michael Shane, Cont'd

2014: Was sidelined for nearly all of 2014 with a tendon problem in his left ankle, making only one worldwide start (MC at Abu Dhabi).

OUTLOOK: At age 45, and coming of a season all but lost to injury, his competitive future is obviously in question. His mix of limited length and below-the-median putting and short game seems unlikely to improve at this stage, so his days near the top are surely in the rearview now.

STATS: Driving Distance: D   Driving Accuracy: A   GIR: C+   Short Game: C-   Putting: C+

Campillo, Jorge (Spain) (28)
b. Caceres, Spain 6/1/1986. 5'11" 175 lbs. College: Indiana U. TP: 2008. Won a Big 10 individual title at Indiana before turning pro. Joined the Challenge Tour in 2011 where he finished 9th in $$$ to graduate to the E Tour, then established himself as a steady earner by cracking the top 100 in E Tour $$$ in each of his first two seasons. Finished T2 at the 2012 Avantha Masters, two behind winner Jbe' Kruger. **Teams**: Eisenhower Trophy: 2008. Palmer Cup (3): 2007-08-09. **OWR Best**: 236 - Mar, 2014.

Amateur Wins: Biarritz Cup: 2007   Spanish Closed Am: 2008   Big 10 Championship: 2008.

	12	13	14
Masters	-	-	-
US Open	-	-	-
British	-	-	-
PGA	-	-	-
Money (E)	81	96	99
OWR	397	270	461

2014: E: 31 st / 19 ct / 1 t10. (T2 Mandela). Logged only one top 10 but managed to retain his card, finishing 99th in $$$.

OUTLOOK: Has thus far demonstrated a steady all-around game and a strong putter, but has yet to make a major E Tour impact regardless (only five top 10s - and two top 3s - in 104 career starts). With three straight years between 81-99 in $$$, is he on the verge of something better?

STATS: Driving Distance: B+   Driving Accuracy: B-   GIR: B-   Short Game: C   Putting: A-

---

Cañete, Ariel (Argentina) (39)
b. Santa Teresita, Argentina 2/7/1975. 5'7" 160 lbs. TP: 1995. Has spent most of his career competing in South America, first on the old Tour de Las Americas (where he won twice), then on the PGA Tour Latinoamérica, where he won two more times in 2012 and topped the money list. Played five full seasons in Europe between 2006-2011 and scored a significant victory in 2007 at the inaugural Joburg Open, where he beat Andrew McClardy by two. Spent 2013 and '14 playing on both the Web.com Tour and the PGA Tour Latinoamérica, with only limited success. **Teams**: Eisenhower Trophy: 1994. **OWR Best**: 205 - Jan, 2007.

European Tour Wins (1): **2007**: Joburg Open.
Other Wins: Norpatagonico Open (Arg) (2): 2002-12   Abierto del Centro (Arg): 2003   TransAmerican Power Open (PGATLA): 2012   Olivos Classic (PGATLA): 2012
Amateur Wins: South American Cup (3): 1992-93-94.

	05	06	07	08	09	10	11	12	13	14
Masters	-	-	-	-	-	-	-	-		
US Open	-	-	-	-	-	-	-	-		
British	-	-	-	T39	-	-	-	-		
PGA	-	-	-	-	-	-	-	-		
Money (E)	198*	143	70	129	339*	133	224	-	-	-
OWR	417	449	306	547	891	643	947	316	456	859

2014: Played the Web.com Tour part-time, finishing 179th in $$$ in only nine starts.

OUTLOOK: Nearing age 40, seems locked in at the second-tier level. Has demonstrated that he can star in his native South America but aside from 2007, never retained his card in Europe - and that was driven by an outlier win at the Joburg Open. Odds are it won't get too much better than this.

STATS (LTD): Driving Distance: C+   Driving Accuracy: B   GIR: C+   Short Game: B-   Putting: B

Cañizares Gómez, José Alejandro (Spain) (31)
b. Madrid, Spain 1/9/1983. 5'11" 160 lbs. Three-time All-American and NCAA individual champion (2003) at Arizona St. TP: 2006. The son of five-time E Tour winner and four-time Ryder Cup player Jose Maria Cañizares. After starring collegiately in America, won his third career E Tour start at the 2006 Russian Open, where he beat David Drysdale by four. Slumped a bit thereafter before enjoying an up year (38th in $$$) in 2010, and easily retaining his card in 2011 and '12. Broke an eight-year victory drought with a runaway five-shot victory at the 2014 Trophée Hassan II, in Morocco. **Teams**: Palmer Cup (4): 2003-04-05-06. **OWR Best**: 89 - Mar, 2014.

European Tour Wins (2): **2006**: Russian Open   **2014**: Trophée Hassan II.
Amateur Wins: Spanish Am Match Play: 2002   Spanish Under-21: 2002   NCAA Individual: 2003   Puerto Rico Classic: 2005.

	06	07	08	09	10	11	12	13	14
Masters	-	-	-	-	-	-	-	-	
US Open	-	-	-	-	T27	MC	MC	-	-
British	-	-	-	-	-	-	-	-	
PGA	-	-	-	-	-	-	-	-	
Money (E)	109	69	109	130	38	88	57	51	63
OWR	197	125	326	416	112	217	208	150	162

2014: E: 21 st / 13 ct / 4 t10. (Won Hassan, T4 Qatar, 6 South African, T7 Spanish). Extended his strong form through a third season, claiming his second E Tour win at Morocco's Trophée Hassan II and logging four top 10s en route to finishing 63rd in $$$.

OUTLOOK: Stepped up by claiming his second career E Tour win, and has now settled in as a reliable earner, finishing within the top 100 for five straight years. Clearly lacks length but is a highly accurate tee-to-greener and a very strong putter, so more mid-range wins are likely in his future.

STATS: Driving Distance: C   Driving Accuracy: A   GIR: B   Short Game: B   Putting: A

Cantlay, Patrick (USA) (22)   b. Long Beach, CA 3/17/1992. 5'10" 160 lbs. All-American, Nicklaus (2011), Haskins (2011) and Hogan (2012) Awards winner at UCLA. TP: 2012. Two-time AJGA All-American. Lost to Kelly Kraft (2 Down) in final of the 2011 U.S. Amateur (Chambers Bay). Won the 2011 Mark McCormack Medal as the top-ranked amateur in the world. After finishing T21 at the 2011 U.S. Open, shot 60 in the second round of the Travelers Championship (low PGA Tour round ever recorded by an amateur) before finishing T24. One month later tied for 9th at the Canadian Open. Turned pro after two years at UCLA and spent two seasons on the Web.com Tour, the second shortened by a fractured vertebrae in his back, which affected him through much of 2014. **Teams:** Walker Cup: 2011 (2-1-1). Palmer Cup: 2011. **OWR Best:** 176 - Mar, 2013.

Amateur Wins: Southern California Am: 2011   California HS: 2010 .

	11	12	13	14
Masters	-	T47	-	-
US Open	T21	T41	-	-
British	-	-	-	-
PGA	-	-	-	-
Money (A)	Am	-	-	212
OWR	440	311	243	697

2014: PGA: 5 st / 2 ct / 0 t10. (T23 Greenbrier). Limited by lingering effects of a 2013 vertebrae injury, making only five PGA Tour starts.

OUTLOOK: Former world #1 amateur and top prospect hasn't arrived as quickly as anticipated, his progress hampered of late by a back injury. Is a capable ball striker and very effective on and around the green, and stood above the median in nearly all meaningful scoring categories on the Web.com Tour. His health is obviously his first concern - but his 11-event 2015 medical extension will quickly run it a close second.

STATS (LTD): Driving Distance: B+   Driving Accuracy: B+   GIR: B   Short Game: A   Putting: B+

Cappelen, Sebastian (Denmark) (24)   b. Odense, Denmark 4/19/1990. 6'0" 190 lbs. Two-time All-American at U. of Arkansas. TP: 2014. Upon turning pro, Monday qualified (via a seven-man playoff) for the Web.com Tour's Air Capital Classic, then won the tournament in his first-ever Web.com start. **Teams:** Palmer Cup (3): 2011-12-13. **OWR Best:** 360 - Sep, 2014.

Other Wins: 1 Web.com (2014).

	14
Masters	-
US Open	-
British	-
PGA	-
Money (A)	-
OWR	407

2014: After winning in his debut, made 11 more Web.com starts and narrowly missed his PGA Tour card by finishing 26th in regular season $$$.

OUTLOOK: Is a true wildcard as he totaled four top 25s in 12 Web.com starts and looked capable of competing at a high level - but was he just hot? Aside from the Web.com, one assumes he'll make some overseas starts in 2015, where it would not be surprising to see him make an impact.

STATS: Driving Distance: --   Driving Accuracy: --   GIR: --   Short Game: --   Putting: --

---

Carballo, Miguel Ángel (Argentina) (35)   b. Bahia Blanca, Argentina 3/22/1979. 5'10" 175 lbs. TP: 2002. After playing in South America through 2004, spent one year on the Challenge Tour and a full season on the European circuit (166th in 2006 $$$) before settling into the Web.com from 2007-2011, where he won events in his first and last campaigns. After finishing 10th in 2011 $$$, spent 2012 on the PGA Tour where he finished 176th in $$$, and he's bounced back and forth between the two circuits since. **OWR Best:** 285 - Apr, 2012.

Other Wins: 2 Web.com (2007-2011)   +   1 Euro Challenge (2006).

	12	13	14
Masters	-	-	-
US Open	-	-	-
British	-	-	-
PGA	-	-	-
Money (A)	176	-	189
OWR	494	497	682

2014: PGA: 15 st / 5 ct / 0 t10. (T7 Barracuda). Finished 189th in FedEx Cup points. Also made 10 Web.com starts, finishing 162nd in $$$.

OUTLOOK: A successful player in his native South America but has yet to catch on north of the border. His Web.com wins suggest he's not in entirely over his head at this level, but 2014 did little to suggest he's poised for long-term success on the PGA Tour.

STATS (LTD): Driving Distance: B   Driving Accuracy: C+   GIR: B-   Short Game: B-   Putting: C+

Carlsson, Johan Gustav (Sweden) (28)   b. Gothenburg, Sweden 8/29/1986. 6'4" 195 lbs. College: San Diego St. TP: 2011. Finished 2nd in the 2012 Nordic League Order of Merit to reach the Challenge Tour, then won the Kazakhstan Open and finished 5th in $$$ to graduate to the E Tour. A bit of a late-bloomer after a quiet collegiate career in the U.S., but kept his card in a solid 2014 rookie year. **OWR Best:** 166 - Jan, 2014.

Other Wins: 1 Euro Challenge (2013).

	13	14
Masters	-	-
US Open	-	-
British	-	-
PGA	-	-
Money (E)	-	98
OWR	227	291

Carlsson, Johan Gustav, Cont'd

2014: E: 26 st / 16 ct / 3 t10. (T5 KLM, 7 Abu Dhabi, T7 South African). Rode two early T7s to a solid rookie year, finishing 98th in $$$.

OUTLOOK: A late-arriving talent who was quiet as a U.S. collegian but took off on the 2013 Challenge Tour, then made good as an E Tour rookie in 2014. Has plenty of length for the modern game, and thus far appears to possess some short game skills as well - always a strong combination.

STATS (LTD): Driving Distance: A- Driving Accuracy: C+ GIR: B- Short Game: B+ Putting: B

Carlsson, Magnus A. (Sweden) (34)
b. Vasteras, Sweden 8/21/1980. 5'11" 175 lbs. TP: 2001. After turning pro, spent five full seasons on the Challenge Tour before final reaching the E Tour in 2008. Promptly finished T2 at the Joburg Open in his third start en route to a solid rookie campaign which saw him rank 79th in $$$. Has since bounced back and forth between the E and Challenge Tours but despite seldom contending, retained his E Tour card in both 2012 and '13, then finished a solid 68th in $$$ in 2014. **OWR Best**: 176 - Jan, 2008.

Other Wins: 1 Euro Challenge (2007) + 1 Nordic League (2004).

	07	08	09	10	11	12	13	14
Masters	-	-	-	-	-	-	-	-
US Open	-	-	-	-	-	-	-	-
British	-	-	-	-	-	-	-	-
PGA	-	-	-	-	-	-	-	-
Money (E)	-	79	143	201*	134	93*	106	68
OWR	228	249	487	535	353	180	271	323

2014: E: 28 st / 19 ct / 4 t10. (T3 Hassan, T6 Irish, T7 Dunhill Champ, T9 Qatar). Made 19 cuts en route to finishing a career-best 68th in $$$, and thus kept his card without stress for the first time since 2008.

OUTLOOK: A reliably strong ball striker (ranked among the top 5 in GIR for the last three years) who has found less success on and around the greens. Coming off a career-best season and seems likely to hang around a while - but becoming an E Tour winner might be beyond his reach.

STATS: Driving Distance: B Driving Accuracy: B+ GIR: A Short Game: C+ Putting: C+

Casey, Paul Alexander (England) (37)
b. Cheltenham, England 7/21/1977. 5'10" 180 lbs. Three-time All-American at Arizona St. TP: 2000. Two-time English Amateur champion who won all four of his matches at 1999 Walker Cup. Played primarily in Europe from 2001-07 before joining the PGA Tour in 2008. Won 2009 Houston Open in a playoff with J.B. Holmes with a bogey at the first playoff hole (Holmes made a double). His 13 E Tour wins have been led by the Tour's flagship BMW PGA Championship (in 2009, by one over Ross Fisher) and the 2006 HSBC World Match Play (a 10 & 8 route of Shaun Micheel), both at Wentworth. Also won the 2003 Benson & Hedges Int'l (by four over Padraig Harrington) as well as both the 2007 and 2009 Abu Dhabi Championships. Missed much of 2009 with a rib injury. Finished 8th in PGA Tour $$$ and T3 at the British Open during a winless 2010. Battled turf toe for much of 2011 but still won the inaugural Volvo Golf Champions in Bahrain. Began 2012 by dislocating his right shoulder while snowboarding, missing two months and slumping thereafter. Ended a 29-month drought at the 2013 Irish Open, eagling the 72nd to beat Joost Luiten and Robert Rock by three. Added a 13th E Tour win at the 2014 KLM Open, sparked by a third round 62. Became the ninth man ever to shoot 27 for nine holes in a PGA Tour event while carding a 63 in the second round of the 2014 Byron Nelson Championship. **Awards**: E Tour Golfer of the Year: 2006. E Tour Rookie of the Year: 2001. **Teams**: Walker Cup: 1999 (4-0-0). Eisenhower Trophy: 2000. Ryder Cup (3): 2004-06-08 (O: 3-2-4, S: 1-1-1). Seve Trophy (5): 2002-03-05-07-13. World Cup (4): 2001-02-03-04 (won in '04 w/L.Donald). **OWR Best**: 3 - May, 2009.

PGA Tour Wins (1): 2009: Houston Open (Shell).

European Tour Wins (13): 2001: Scottish PGA **2003**: ANZ Championship, Benson & Hedges Int'l **2005**: TCL Classic, China Open (Volvo) ('06) **2006**: Johnnie Walker Championship, World Match Play **2007**: Abu Dhabi Championship **2009**: Abu Dhabi Championship, BMW PGA **2011**: Volvo Golf Champions **2013**: Irish Open **2014**: Dutch Open (KLM).

Other Wins: Shinhan Donghae Open (KPGA): 2011.

Amateur Wins: English Am (2): 1999-00.

	01	02	03	04	05	06	07	08	09	10	11	12	13	14
Masters	-	-	-	T6	MC	-	T10	T11	T20	MC	T38	MC	-	-
US Open	-	-	MC	MC	WD	15	T10	T65	MC	T41	MC	-	T45	T56
British	-	MC	MC	T20	MC	71	T27	T7	T47	T3	T54	MC	-	T47
PGA	-	MC	66	MC	T59	MC	T40	T15	-	T12	T72	MC	T33	MC
Money (A)	-	-	-	-	-	-	95	22	8	136	221*	195*	108	
Money (E)	22	46	6	14	39	2	13	21	5	12	29	74	30	61
OWR	90	104	23	29	52	15	21	41	7	8	20	122	87	75

2014: PGA: 16 st / 12 ct / 0 t10. (T11 New Orleans). Had a flat season in America, failing to log a top 10 and finishing 95th in FedEx Cup points. Also made 10 non-co-sanctioned E Tour starts and fared better, winning the KLM (Dutch) Open and adding T9s in Dubai and the World Match Play.

OUTLOOK: Seems fully recovered from an injury-ridden 2012 but remains far from his halcyon days (#3 in the OWR in the spring/summer of 2009). Builds around his power and a very solid iron game, but he hasn't won 14 times on major tours without putting reasonably well. Is exempt in the U.S. again this year (he was on Past Champion status in 2014) where, at age 37, he still should be capable of competing on a high level.

STATS: Driving Distance: A Driving Accuracy: C GIR: A Short Game: C Putting: B

Castro, Roberto Mario (USA) (29)
b. Houston, TX 6/23/1985. 6'0" 170 lbs. Two-time All-American at Georgia Tech. TP: 2007. An AJGA All-American. Won the 2007 Byron Nelson Award (for golf combined with grades, integrity, etc.) and was also a two-time Academic All-American. A five-time winner on the eGolf mini-tour, while also playing the Hooters Tour, eventually joining the Web.com in 2010. In 2011, finished 23rd in Web.com $$$ to secure his PGA Tour card, then retained it in 2012 by finishing 118th in $$$ as a rookie. Took a quantum leap in 2013, remaining winless but jumping all the way to 29th in PGA Tour $$$. Struggled in 2014, however, making 11 of 27 cuts and falling the 135 in $$$. **Teams**: Palmer Cup (2): 2005-06. **OWR Best**: 64 - Oct, 2013.

Other Wins: 5 eGolf Tour (2007-2010).

Amateur Wins: Georgia HS: 2002.

Castro, Roberto Mario, Cont'd

	12	13	14
Masters	-	-	MC
US Open	MC	-	MC
British	-	-	MC
PGA	-	T12	MC
Money (A)	118	29	135
OWR	281	70	194

2014: PGA: 27 st / 11 ct / 1 t10. (T8 Wells Fargo). Plummeted to 135th in FedEx Cup points, then finished 51st on Web.com Finals priority list.

OUTLOOK: After seemingly establishing himself over two PGA Tour seasons, fell off badly in 2014 behind a dramatic drop from tee to green (31 to 150 in Ball Striking, 44 to 122 in Total Driving, 33 to 169 in GIR). Also hampered by a lack of length, a bad statistical package. Was this tee-to-green free fall a one-time thing? With only conditional status in 2015, he won't have the luxury of many bad starts in trying to turn things around.

STATS: Driving Distance: C+   Driving Accuracy: A-   GIR: B+ ⇩   Short Game: B+ ⇩   Putting: B-

---

Cauley, William Carl III ("Bud") (USA) (24)
b. Daytona Beach, FL 3/16/1990. 5'7" 150 lbs. Two-time All-American at U of Alabama. TP: 2011. Two-time AJGA All-American. Began his career as the top-ranked junior (co-medalist at the 2008 Toyota World Junior) in America before becoming a collegiate star at the University of Alabama. At age 18, beat then-world #1 amateur Rickie Fowler in first round of the 2009 U.S. Amateur. Turned pro upon his 2011 graduation, then earned enough money in eight late-season PGA Tour starts to gain his 2012 card off the Non-Member $$$ list – a path previously taken by only six others including Phil Mickelson and Tiger Woods. Seemed on course for stardom as a 2012 rookie (44th in $$$) before stumbling badly in 2013. Struggled again in 2014 but kept his card after logging his first professional win during the Web.com Finals at the Hotel Fitness Championship. **Teams:** Walker Cup: 2009 (3-0-1). Palmer Cup: 2009. **OWR Best:** 53 - Sep, 2012.

Other Wins: 1 Web.com (2014).
Amateur Wins: Terra Cotta Inv: 2008   Players Am: 2009.

	11	12	13	14
Masters	-	-	-	-
US Open	T63	-	-	-
British	-	-	T32	-
PGA	-	MC	-	-
Money (A)	-	44	146	129
OWR	249	67	217	221

2014: PGA: 19 st / 9 ct / 1 t10. (T4 Greenbrier). Fell to 143rd in FedEx Cup points before playing his way back via the Web.com Finals for the second consecutive year, this time via a victory in the second Finals event, the Hotel Fitness Championship.

OUTLOOK: Failed to reverse the negative momentum of 2013, but saved his card via the Web.com Finals for the second straight year. Continued to struggle with the putter (144 in Total Putting, 155 in SGP) - a real problem since he improved markedly from tee to green in 2014 (126 to 30 in GIR, 144 to 82 in Ball Striking). Still seems capable of succeeding on the PGA Tour, but he's been living very dangerously since a stellar 2012.

STATS: Driving Distance: B+   Driving Accuracy: C+   GIR: A-   Short Game: B+   Putting: C+ ⇩

Cayeux, Marc Elton (Zimbabwe) (36)
b. Lancaster, England 2/22/1978. 5'11" 215 lbs. TP: 1996. Born in England to a South African father and English mother. Raised in Zimbabwe where he turned pro as a teenager and was a touted prospect. Established himself as a regular winner on the Sunshine Tour, claiming one victory each year from 1998-2003, then taking his biggest title at the 2005 Tour Championship, where he ran away from Keith Horne by six. Also claimed the 2008 Nashua Masters, beating Bradford Vaughan by two. Was seriously injured in a 2010 car accident and has been recovering – and away from competition – ever since. **Teams:** Eisenhower Trophy: 1996. **OWR Best:** 191 - Feb, 2005.

Sunshine Tour Wins (9): 1998: Zambia Open **1999**: Stenham Royal Swazi Sun **2000**: Pietersburg Classic **2001**: Botswana Open **2002**: Zambia Open **2003**: Limpopo Classic (54H) **2005**: Vodacom Tour Championship **2007**: Highveld Classic **2008**: Nashua Masters.
Other Wins: 2 Euro Challenge (2004).

	98	99	00	01	02	03	04	05	06	07	08	09	10	11	12	13	14
Masters	-	-	-	-	-	-	-	-	-	-	-	-	-	-	-	-	-
US Open	-	-	-	-	-	-	-	-	-	-	-	-	-	-	-	-	-
British	-	-	-	-	-	-	-	-	-	-	-	MC	-	-	-	-	-
PGA	-	-	-	-	-	-	-	-	-	-	-	-	-	-	-	-	-
Money (SA)	77	8	44	36	14	17	11	5*	67*	8	15	28	38	-	-	-	-
OWR	787	328	430	660	351	610	310	299	545	617	390	307	515	-	-	-	-

2014: Did not compete for the fourth consecutive year due to injuries suffered in 2010 car accident.

OUTLOOK: Was a proven winner prior to his accident, but it's anybody's guess now if he'll be back – and if he'll have anything left in the tank.

STATS: Driving Distance: --   Driving Accuracy: --   GIR: --   Short Game: --   Putting: --

---

Cejka, Alexander (Germany) (44)
b. Marienbad, Czech Republic 12/2/1970. 5'8" 170 lbs. TP: 1989. First Czech-born golfer to make an impact worldwide. Raised in Germany after fleeing native country with his father, and has represented only his adopted country in international play. Played the European Challenge Tour (winning four times) before reaching the European Tour in 1992. Initially had little impact until exploding during a three-win 1995, wherein he triumphed in March at the Andalucia Open, in August at the Austrian Open and, most significantly, in October at the season-ending Volvo Masters (where he edged Colin Montgomerie by two) to finish 6th in $$$. Later added the Trophée Lancôme in 2002, the year in which he finished 2nd at PGA Tour Q School. Has only once bettered 60th in $$$ in over a decade of PGA Tour play (54th in 2004). **Teams:** Seve Trophy (3): 2000-02-03. World Cup (11): 1995-96-97-00-02-03-05-07-08-09-11. **OWR Best:** 33 - Sep, 2003.

European Tour Wins (4): 1995: Turespaña Open Andalucia, Austrian Open, Volvo Masters **2002**: Trophée Lancôme.
Other Wins: 4 Euro Challenge (1991-2002) + Czech Open (2): 1990-92.

Cejka, Alexander, Cont'd

	94	95	96	97	98	99	00	01	02	03	04	05	06	07	08	09	10	11	12	13	14
Masters	-	-	44	-	-	-	-	-	-	-	26	-	-	-	-	-	-	T35	-	-	-
US Open	-	-	T50	-	-	-	-	-	-	T61	T60	-	-	-	-	-	T8	MC	T41	-	T60
British	-	-	T11	MC	-	-	MC	T13	MC	-	-	MC	-	-	MC	-	-	-	-	-	-
PGA	-	-	T52	-	-	T65	-	-	-	4	MC	MC	-	-	-	-	-	-	-	-	-
Money (A)	-	-	-	-	-	-	-	-	-	60	54	140	145	120	117	95	108	163	183*	-	218*
Money (E)	102	6	90	59	34	17	70	51	23	-	38	-	-	-	-	-	-	-	-	-	-
OWR	367	76	93	202	124	94	147	167	55	43	56	163	383	256	219	216	167	281	493	562	296

2014: PGA: 6 st / 5 ct / 0 t10. (T54 Puerto Rico). Also made 14 Web.com starts, finishing 6th in regular season $$$ and regaining his PGA Tour card.

OUTLOOK: At age 44, returns to the PGA Tour in 11th place on the Web.com priority list. An accurate player capable of hitting lots of greens but putting — which seldom improves at this age — remains a question. Can get streaky hot but seems unlikely to have a big PGA Tour impact.

STATS: Driving Distance: C-   Driving Accuracy: A-   GIR: B   Short Game: C+   Putting: C-

---

Chalmers, Gregory John (Australia) (41)
b. Sydney, New South Wales, Australia 10/11/1973. 6'0" 200 lbs. TP: 1995. Upon turning pro, headed off to Europe, where he campaigned in 1996 and 1998 (25th in $$$). Scored his first two major tour wins during these years while playing winter events back in Australia, claiming the 1997 Players Championship and, more significantly, the 1998 Australian Open (by one over Stuart Appleby and Peter Senior at Royal Adelaide). Came to America thereafter where he has battled gamely (though winlessly) for more than a decade, spending time on both the PGA and Web.com Tours. Ended a long victory drought in late 2011, once again back in Australia, when in back-to-back weeks he claimed his second Australian Open (by one over John Senden, with the U.S. President's Cup team in the field), then the Australian PGA, in a playoff with Robert Allenby and Marcus Fraser. Three years later, added a second Australian PGA, this time beating Adam Scott (and Wade Ormsby) in a marathon seven-hole playoff. **Teams**: Eisenhower Trophy: 1995. **OWR Best**: 53 - Sep, 2012.

Australasian Tour Wins (5): 1997: Players Championship (ANZ)   **1998**: Australian Open   **2011**: Australian Open, Australian PGA   **2014**: Australian PGA.

Other Wins: 2 Web.com (2005-2008).

Amateur Wins: Australian Am: 1993   French Am: 1994.

	96	97	98	99	00	01	02	03	04	05	06	07	08	09	10	11	12	13	14
Masters	-	-	-	-	-	MC	-	-	-	-	-	-	-	-	-	MC	-	-	-
US Open	-	-	-	-	-	-	MC	-	-	-	-	-	-	-	-	-	-	-	-
British	-	-	T57	-	-	-	-	-	-	-	-	-	-	-	-	T45	-	-	-
PGA	-	-	MC	-	T4	T44	-	-	-	-	-	-	-	-	-	T32	-	-	-
Money (A)	-	-	-	114	41	75	106	142	156	-	-	-	89	91	105	81	124	139	-
Money (E)	136	-	25	-	-	-	-	-	-	-	-	-	-	-	-	-	-	-	-
OWR	241	171	67	142	100	114	188	299	242	296	343	262	200	144	146	60	64	185	168

2014: PGA: 27 st / 16 ct / 1 t10. (T10 McGladrey). Fell to 132nd in FedEx Cup points, then failed to save himself via the Web.com finals. Did log one more major homeland win, however, beating Adam Scott (and Wade Ormsby) in a seven-hole playoff at December's Australian PGA.

OUTLOOK: At age 41 still chugging along as a mid-range ball striker but an ace around the greens, ranking among the PGA Tour's best in Scrambling and various putting stats. But putting too much pressure on the putter can be dangerous - and he'll be on conditional status in 2015 as a result.

STATS: Driving Distance: C-   Driving Accuracy: B   GIR: C-   Short Game: A+ ⇩   Putting: A+

Chan, Shih-Chang (Taiwan) (28)
b. Hsinchu, Taiwan 6/7/1986. 5'5" 140 lbs. TP: 2008. Diminutive Taiwanese star who has been a regular winner on his domestic circuit in 2010 and a part-time player on the Asian Tour since 2012. Blossomed in 2014, winning twice at home and three times on the Asian Developmental circuit, and cracking the top 250 in the OWR. **OWR Best**: 193 - Aug, 2014.

Other Wins: 4 Asian Developmental (2013-2014) + Taifong Open (Taiwan): 2010   Camry Invitational (Taiwan): 2011   Kaohsiung Open (Taiwan): 2012   Meridigen Technology Cup (Taiwan): 2014   TPGA Championship (Taiwan): 2014.

Amateur Wins: Hong Kong Am: 2004.

	11	12	13	14
Masters	-	-	-	-
US Open	-	-	-	-
British	-	-	-	-
PGA	-	-	-	-
Money (As)	-	110	96*	82
OWR	951	1262	481	256

2014: ASIA: 13 st / 8 ct / 0 t10. (T16 Philippine Open). Split time between the Asian Tour and its developmental circuit, impressively winning three of his first five starts on the latter, then making little impact in 13 appearances on the former.

OUTLOOK: His Development Tour run was impressive, and he held his own on the bigger circuit, but at age 28 stardom is likely beyond his reach.

STATS: Driving Distance: C   Driving Accuracy: B-   GIR: C+   Short Game: B+   Putting: B

Chappell, Kevin Allan (USA) (28)
b. Fresno, CA 7/8/1986. 6'0" 180 lbs. All-American, NCAA individual champion (2008), Nicklaus (2008) and Haskins (2008) Awards winner at UCLA. TP: 2008. After leading UCLA to its first national title since 1988, spent 2009 on the Web.com Tour, where he won the Fresh Express Classic (CA) and finished 9th in $$$, graduating to the PGA Tour. Finished 66th in $$$ as a Tour rookie, a season highlighted by a T3 at the U.S. Open at Congressional (10 shots behind winner Rory McIlroy). Barely retained his card in 2012, finishing 125th in $$$, but roared back with a strong 2013, finishing 56th. **Teams**: Palmer Cup: 2008. **OWR Best**: 85 - Sep, 2014.

Other Wins: 1 Web.com (2009).

Amateur Wins: NCAA Individual: 2008.

Chappell, Kevin Allan, Cont'd

	10	11	12	13	14
Masters	-	-	T44	-	-
US Open	-	T3	T10	T32	-
British	-	-	-	-	-
PGA	-	-	-	MC	T13
Money (A)	-	66	125	56	80
OWR	195	159	220	110	111

2014: PGA: 28 st / 22 ct / 1 t10. (T10 Colonial). Climbed to 55th in FedEx Cup points but logged only one top 10 (barely) in nine top-25 finishes.

OUTLOOK: Seems to be developing into a high-end ball striker, lifting his driving accuracy from 154 to 87 to 41 since 2012 and ranking 6 in Total Driving and 11 in Ball Striking in 2014. The putter remains a question (145 in SGP in 2014 - his *best* season yet) but his Total Putting rank (124) easily beat his SGP for the second straight year. Figures to make a good tee-to-green living for years to come, but winning requires more on the greens.

STATS: Driving Distance: A-   Driving Accuracy: B ⇧   GIR: A-   Short Game: B   Putting: C

Choi, Kyoung-Ju ("K.J.") (South Korea) (44)

b. Wando, South Korea 5/19/1970. 5'8" 185 lbs. TP: 1994. A dominant force in his homeland and the first Korean both to earn a PGA Tour card and to record a victory. Consistent money winner who's logged eight PGA Tour wins and finished no worse than 40th on the money list from 2002-2008, including 5th in 2007. Two-time winner in 2002, claiming his first Tour win at New Orleans, then going wire-to-wire for a seven-shot victory at the Tampa Bay Classic. Also twice a winner in 2007, first at the Memorial (by one over Ryan Moore), then at the AT&T National (by three over Steve Stricker). Also won the 2003 German Masters on the E Tour, a pair of titles during a single abbreviated season (1999) on the Japan Tour and three events on the Asian Tour between 2003-2009. Finished 3rd at the 2004 Masters, where he eagled the par-4 11th during the final round. Enjoyed a career-best 2011, winning the Players Championship (beating David Toms in a playoff) and finishing 4th on the $$$ list. Won the C.J. Invitational on the Asian Tour (an event he hosted) in both 2011 and '12. **Teams:** Presidents Cup (3): 2003-07-11 (6-8-0). World Cup (4): 2002-03-05-13. **OWR Best:** 5 - Mar, 2008.

PGA Tour Wins (8): 2002: New Orleans Classic (Compaq), Tampa Bay Classic **2005:** Greater Greensboro Open **2006:** Chrysler Championship **2007:** Memorial Tournament, AT&T National **2008:** Hawaiian Open (Sony) **2011:** Players Championship.
European Tour Wins (1): 2003: German Masters.
Japan Tour Wins (2): 1999: Ube Kosan Open, Dunlop Open (Kirin) (54H).
Asian Tour Wins (5): 2003: SK Telecom Open **2005:** SK Telecom Open **2009:** Johor Open (54H) **2011:** C.J. Invitational **2012:** C.J. Invitational.
Other Wins: Fantom Open (KPGA) (2): 1995-97   Korean Open (2): 1996-99   Astra Cup PGA (KPGA): 1997   Korea Times Open (KPGA): 1997   Shinhan Donghae Open (KPGA) (2): 2007-08   SK Telecom Open (KPGA): 2008.

	98	99	00	01	02	03	04	05	06	07	08	09	10	11	12	13	14
Masters	-	-	-	-	-	T15	3	T33	MC	T27	41	MC	T4	T8	MC	T46	T34
US Open	-	-	-	MC	T30	MC	T31	T15	MC	MC	MC	T47	T47	MC	T15	T32	-
British	MC	T49	-	-	MC	T22	T16	T41	MC	T8	T16	MC	MC	T44	T39	T44	MC
PGA	-	-	-	T29	MC	T69	T6	T40	T7	T12	MC	T24	T39	T39	T54	T47	MC
Money (A)	-	-	134	65	17	30	26	40	27	5	16	81	93	4	102	85	59
OWR	716	129	212	188	41	21	25	31	29	9	18	88	47	15	48	134	116

2014: PGA: 23 st / 17 ct / 2 t10. (T2 Farmers, T2 Travelers). Enjoyed a steady campaign, twice finishing 2nd and ranking 69th in FedEx Cup points.

OUTLOOK: Hasn't won in America since the 2011 Players Championship so at 44, his best days may be behind him. But he is still a solid enough ball striker (52 in Driving Accuracy, 49 in Proximity to Hole) and he has experienced that rarest of things - a marked improvement in his putting numbers - in his mid 40s. May not play consistently elite golf going forward but with a good tee-to-green week, he can certainly still contend.

STATS: Driving Distance: C   Driving Accuracy: A-   GIR: B-   Short Game: B+   Putting: A-

---

Chopra, Daniel Samir (India) (41)

b. Stockholm, Sweden 12/23/1973. 6'0" 180 lbs. TP: 1992. Born to Swedish mother and Indian father, Raised from age seven in Calcutta. Won three All-India Junior Golf Championships, the first at age 14. Began his career in 1995 on the old Asian Tour, winning the Taiwan Open and being named Rookie Of The Year. Played in Europe from 1996-2000, initially finishing 36th and 51st in earnings before slipping. Eventually joined the PGA Tour via Q School in 2004. Enjoyed a strong three-year run from 2006-2008, finishing no worse than 54th in $$$ and winning twice, first at 2007's late-season Ginn Sur Mer Classic, then at 2008's season-opening Mercedes Championships, where he beat Steve Stricker in a playoff. After a disappointing 2010, has spent time on both the PGA and Web.com Tours. **OWR Best:** 60 - Jan, 2008.

PGA Tour Wins (2): 2007: Ginn Sur Mer Classic **2008:** Mercedes Championships.
Asian Tour Wins (2): 1995: Taiwan Open (54H) **2001:** Taiwan Masters.
Other Wins: 3 Web.com (2004-2011)   +   2 Euro Challenge (1994)   +   Swedish Int'l: 1993   Johor Bahru Open (India): 1993   Indian Masters: 1994   Indian PGA: 1994   Malaysian PGA: 1994.
Amateur Wins: All-India Jr (3): 1988-89-91   Doug Sanders Jr Int'l: 1991.

	95	96	97	98	99	00	01	02	03	04	05	06	07	08	09	10	11	12	13	14
Masters	-	-	-	-	-	-	-	-	-	-	-	-	-	MC	-	-	-	-	-	-
US Open	-	-	-	-	-	-	-	-	-	T24	-	-	T36	-	-	-	-	-	-	-
British	-	-	-	-	-	-	-	-	-	-	-	MC	-	-	-	-	MC	-	-	-
PGA	-	-	-	-	-	-	-	-	-	-	-	T41	MC	MC	-	-	-	-	-	-
Money (A)	-	-	-	-	-	-	-	-	-	108	90	54	48	52	103	176	247*	188	-	240
Money (E)	-	36	51	96	136	223	-	-	-	-	-	-	-	92	-	-	-	-	-	-
OWR	232	163	298	347	441	612	472	616	502	173	176	131	120	130	274	470	247	304	398	743

2014: PGA: 16 st / 2 ct / 0 t10. (T58 Puerto Rico). Finished 249th in FedEx Cup points, failing to qualify for the Web.com Finals.

OUTLOOK: Two-time PGA Tour winner (though in a very brief 2007–2008 span) who, at age 41, will be living off that Past Champion status in 2015. Long but very erratic tee-to-greener whose sometimes up–and–down short game can carry him - though not too often of late. Europe? Asia?

STATS: Driving Distance: B+   Driving Accuracy: D   GIR: C-   Short Game: B-   Putting: B+ ⇩

Chowrasia, Shiv Shankar Prasad ("S.S.P.") (India) (36) b. Calcutta, India 5/15/1978. 5'5" 140 lbs. TP: 1997. Son of the greenkeeper at Royal Calcutta GC who is known as "Chipputtsia" for the caliber of his short game. Won 10 events on the old (pre-2009) Indian PGA Tour, as well as two titles on the current PGTI. Splits time between the European and Asian Tours, with both of his major wins coming in events jointly sponsored by both, the 2008 Indian Masters (where he beat Damian McGrane by two) and the 2011 Avantha Masters. Added a third Asian Tour win at the 2014 Panasonic Open India, beating Rahil Gangjee and Mithun Perera in a playoff. **OWR Best:** 154 - Mar, 2008.

European Tour Wins (2): 2008: Indian Masters **2011:** Avantha Masters.
Asian Tour Wins (1): 2014: Panasonic Open India.
Other Wins: Singhania Open (India) (3): 2001-05-06   Hindustan Times Open (India): 2003   Tata Open (India) (3): 2003-05-06   Hero Honda Open (India): 2003   NGC Open (India): 2003   Hindu Open (India): 2006   Solaris Chemtech Open (PGTI): 2010   PGTI Tour Championship: 2012.

	05	06	07	08	09	10	11	12	13	14
Masters	-	-	-	-	-	-	-	-	-	-
US Open	-	-	-	-	-	-	-	-	-	-
British	-	-	-	-	-	-	-	-	-	-
PGA	-	-	-	-	-	-	-	-	-	-
Money (E)	-	-	-	93	185	135	80	97	145	148*
Money (As)	-	38	32	6	55*	49*	3	27	16	11
OWR	-	412	376	335	616	500	379	454	408	224

2014: ASIA: 17 st / 15 ct / 7 t10. (Incl. Won Panasonic India, T4 SAIL-SBI, T4 Selangor Masters). Played primarily in Asia, where he won once and finished 11th in $$$. Made five additional non-co-sanctioned starts in Europe, led by a T5 at October's Hong Kong Open.

OUTLOOK: Remains a steady, consistent player who has long succeeded nicely in Asia but only sporadically on the bigger European stage. Handicapped significantly by a lack of length, but he remains competitive with his celebrated short game and putting. Figures to remain in his Europe/Asia dual mode into the foreseeable future, while also starring in whatever PGTI events the international schedule allows.

STATS: Driving Distance: D   Driving Accuracy: B   GIR: C+   Short Game: A-   Putting: A-

---

Christian, Gary John (England) (43) b. Carshalton, England 8/7/1971. 5'8" 165 lbs. JC All-American at Wallace (AL) JC/Auburn U. TP: 1998. Englishman who attended college in America, being named a Junior College All-American at Wallace (AL) JC, then playing at Auburn. Has played his entire professional career in the U.S., logging a reported 30+ victories on the Dakotas, All-Star Emerald Coast, DP, Teardrop and Tight Lies Tours. Played six Web.com seasons (best: 42nd in 2009) before finishing 9th in Web.com earnings during a one-win 2011 campaign, graduating him to the 2012 PGA Tour as the rare 40-year-old rookie. Played into 2014 on a medical extension (from a 2013 knee injury) but failed to clear it, leaving him without PGA Tour status. **OWR Best:** 245 - Aug, 2012.

Other Wins: 2 Web.com (2009-2011)   +   4 Gateway (2005).

	11	12	13	14
Masters	-	-	-	-
US Open	-	-	-	-
British	-	-	-	-
PGA	-	-	-	-
Money (A)	-	130	211*	-
OWR	284	307	614	1348

2014: PGA: 3 st / 0 ct / 0 t10. Failed to clear a three-event medical extension, then failed to requalify via the Web.com Finals.

OUTLOOK: Workman-like player who lacks length but is highly consistent tee-to-green. After failing to clear his medical extension, scarcely played on the Web.com Tour and did little in the Finals, leaving him without any PGA Tour status for 2015. Might he give the E Tour a try?

STATS: Driving Distance: C+   Driving Accuracy: A   GIR: B+   Short Game: B-   Putting: B-

---

Chuayprakong, Thitiphan (Thailand) (22) b. Bangkok, Thailand 7/15/1992. 5'9" 155 lbs. TP: 2009. First name is alternatively spelled "Thitiphun." Well-thought-of Thai prospect who was playing the Asian Tour full-time at age 18. Though winless over his first two seasons, challenged in several of the circuit's bigger events, including a T2 (with Bubba Watson, 11 behind runaway winner Charl Schwartzel) at the 2012 Thailand Golf Championship. Took a step back in 2013 (falling from 25th to 65th in Asian Tour $$$) and held that lower level in 2014. **OWR Best:** 281 - Jan, 2013.

Other Wins: Singha All Thailand Challenge: 2010.

	11	12	13	14
Masters	-	-	-	-
US Open	-	-	-	-
British	-	-	-	-
PGA	-	-	-	-
Money (As)	73	25	64	73
OWR	855	282	459	984

2014: ASIA: 14 st / 9 ct / 1 t10. (T9 Manila Masters). Endured s second straight disappointing year, finishing 73rd in Asia Tour $$$.

OUTLOOK: Seemed on his way to good things in 2012 but reversed course thereafter; indeed, he needed strong late finishes in Manila and Dubai to salvage any overall improvement out of 2014. Is largely below the median statistically, though he's still young enough to turn things around.

STATS: Driving Distance: B+   Driving Accuracy: B   GIR: B   Short Game: C+   Putting: B-

---

Cink, Stewart Ernest (USA) (41) b. Huntsville, AL 5/21/1973. 6'4" 205 lbs. Three-time All-American, Nicklaus (1995) and Haskins (1995) Awards winner at Georgia Tech. TP: 1995. Two-time AJGA All-American. A three-time winner (and 1st in $$$) on the 1996 Web.com Tour at age 23, securing a PGA Tour card for 1997. Consistent earner who only once missed the top 50 on the PGA Tour money list from 1997-2009 (73rd in 2002). Won the 1997 Greater Hartford Open, leading to Rookie of the Year honors (the first man to win this award on Web.com and PGA Tours in back-to-back years). Won a second time in Hartford (as the Travelers Championship) in 2008, and is also a two-time winner of the Heritage (2000 and '04) at

Cink, Stewart Ernest, Cont'd

Harbour Town. Justified a somewhat surprising selection to the 2004 Ryder Cup team by handily winning the WGC-NEC Invitational (by four over Rory Sabbatini and Tiger Woods) the same week he was named. Contended in multiple Majors before winning the 2009 British Open at Turnberry, ending the epic bid of 59-year-old Tom Watson in a four-hole playoff. Has declined significantly since, slipping as far as 149th in PGA Tour $$$ (2012) before climbing safely back into the top 125 in 2013 & '14. **Awards:** PGA Tour Rookie of the Year: 1997. **Teams:** Ryder Cup (5): 2002-04-06-08-10 (O: 5-7-7, S: 1-3-1). Presidents Cup (4): 2000-05-07-09 (9-7-2). World Cup (2): 2005-06. **OWR Best:** 5 - Jun, 2008.

PGA Tour Wins (6): 1997: Greater Hartford Open (Canon) **2000:** Heritage Classic (MCI) **2004:** Heritage Classic (MCI), WGC-NEC Inv **2008:** Greater Hartford Open (Travelers) **2009:** British Open.

Int'l Wins (2): 1996: Mexican Open **1999:** Mexican Open.

Other Wins: 3 Web.com (1996) + Wendy's 3-Tour Challenge: 2006 (w/Z.Johnson & S.Verplank) CVS Classic: 2007 (w/J.J.Henry).

Amateur Wins: Rice Planters Am: 1993.

	96	97	98	99	00	01	02	03	04	05	06	07	08	09	10	11	12	13	14
Masters	-	MC	T23	T27	T28	MC	T24	-	T17	T20	10	T17	T3	MC	MC	MC	T50	T25	T14
US Open	T16	T13	T10	T32	T8	3	MC	T28	MC	T15	T37	MC	T14	T27	T33	MC	MC	MC	T54
British	-	-	T66	MC	T41	T30	T59	T34	T14	MC	MC	T6	MC	Win	T48	T30	MC	T26	T47
PGA	-	MC	MC	T3	T15	T59	T10	MC	T17	T28	T24	T32	MC	T67	T18	MC	MC	MC	MC
Money (A)	-	29	31	32	10	26	73	35	5	43	15	25	9	17	52	101	149	78	104
OWR	220	55	45	32	17	31	71	53	10	27	26	24	16	16	46	140	319	165	193

2014: PGA: 25 st / 21 ct / 0 t10. (T11 CIMB). Finished 80th in FedEx Cup points but failed to log a single top 10 despite 21 made cuts.

OUTLOOK: At age 41, still trying to return to his peak days of 2008–2009. Still fairly long but has witnessed a strange reversal in his game over the last four years, seeing his once-modest GIR numbers rise (128, 117, 22, 57) and his once-excellent putting regress (64, 37, 144, 124 in SGP) - though the latter, at least, might be expected with age. Not many players in their 40s improve their putting, so a return to the summit seems a longshot.

STATS: Driving Distance: B+   Driving Accuracy: C+   GIR: B+   Short Game: B-   Putting: B

Clark, Timothy Henry (South Africa) (39)

b. Durban, South Africa 12/17/1975. 5'7" 150 lbs. Three-time All-American at North Carolina St. TP: 1998. Winner of the 1997 U.S. Public Links. After turning pro, played the Canadian Tour (where he won twice) and the Web.com, where a 3rd-place $$$ finish in 2000 graduated him to the PGA Tour. Missed nearly all of his rookie PGA Tour season (2001) after wrist surgery, then won the 2002 South African Open in his first event back en route to claiming the Sunshine Order of Merit (despite making only 7 winter starts). Won a second South African Open in 2004 in a six-shot runaway, again at Durban. Won 2005 Scottish Open and the 2008 Australian Open, the latter over Mathew Goggin in a playoff at Royal Sidney. After finishing eight times a runner-up, finally broke through for his maiden PGA Tour win in 2010, edging Robert Allenby by one at the Players Championship. Finished no worse than 37th in the year-end OWR from 2005-2010 before missing nearly all of 2011 with tendonitis in his right elbow. Recorded his second PGA Tour win at the 2014 Canadian Open, closing 64-65 to beat Jim Furyk by one. **Teams:** Eisenhower Trophy: 1994. Presidents Cup (3): 2003-05-09 (6-7-2). World Cup (2): 2002-05. **OWR Best:** 14 - Apr, 2006.

PGA Tour Wins (2): 2010: Players Championship **2014:** Canadian Open (RBC).

European Tour Wins (3): 2002: South African Open **2005:** South African Open, Scottish Open.

Australasian Tour Wins (1): 2008: Australian Open.

Other Wins: 2 Web.com (2000) + Brunswick Open (Canada): 1998 Canadian PGA: 1998 Nelson Mandela Inv (SA): 2006 (w/V.Tshabalala).

Amateur Wins: Natal Jr (3): 1992-93-94 South African Jr: 1993 U.S. Amateur Public Links: 1997 Cardinal Am: 1997.

	98	99	00	01	02	03	04	05	06	07	08	09	10	11	12	13	14
Masters	MC	-	-	-	-	T13	MC	T39	2	T13	MC	T13	MC	MC	MC	T11	MC
US Open	-	-	-	-	-	-	MC	T13	MC	T17	T48	T40	T12	-	MC	MC	-
British	-	-	-	-	MC	-	MC	T23	T56	-	MC	MC	MC	-	MC	T44	-
PGA	-	-	-	-	T53	3	MC	T17	T24	MC	T55	T16	T39	-	T11	T68	MC
Money (A)	-	-	-	107	53	71	21	32	22	45	29	11	138*	61	64	42	
OWR		591	373	441	56	67	74	20	23	29	28	37	25	94	91	69	62

2014: PGA: 26 st / 14 ct / 3 t10. (Won Canadian, T2 McGladrey, T5 John Deere). Completed his comeback from 2011 elbow problems, claiming his second PGA Tour victory at the Canadian Open and finishing 54th in FedEx Cup points.

OUTLOOK: Remains highly consistent in his late 30s; save for an injury-shortened 2011, hasn't finished worse than 71st in $$$ (with seven top 50s) since 2002. An exceptionally straight driver of the ball (no worse than 5 in Driving Accuracy since 2008, 2 in 2014) but has seen his GIR drop somewhat over the same period. Still in his peak years – but few figure to be adversely affected by the 2016 anchoring ban more than him.

STATS: Driving Distance: C-   Driving Accuracy: A+   GIR: B-   Short Game: A-   Putting: B+

Clarke, Darren Christopher, O.B.E. (Northern Ireland) (46)

b. Dungannon, Northern Ireland 8/14/1968. 6'2" 215 lbs. TP: 1990. Longtime elite European player who logged nine top-10 Order of Merit finishes (including three 2nds) from 1993-2004. Semi-regular competitor in USA from 1999-2007, and has won on four continents. Eleven-time E Tour winner including the 1998 Benson & Hedges International and the 1998 Volvo Masters. Also a three-time English Open winner over a four-year period, from 1999-2002. Became the first player after Tiger Woods to claim two WGC titles with victory at 2003 WGC-NEC Invitational, having already defeated #2 ranked David Duval and #1 Woods in semi-final and final to claim the 2000 WGC-Accenture Match Play. Also won three significant events on the Japan Tour, the 2001 Crowns and the 2004 and '05 Taiheiyo Masters. Played a limited schedule in 2006 and '07 due to his wife's passing from cancer, before returning to win the 2008 BMW Asian Open in Shanghai. Scored one of the more popular British Open victories in recent memory in 2011, coming largely out of nowhere to beat Phil Mickelson and Dustin Johnson by three at Royal St. George's. Awarded an O.B.E. at the end of 2011. Has become something of a part-time player since. **Teams:** Ryder Cup (5): 1997-99-02-04-06 (O: 10-7-3, S: 1-2-2). Seve Trophy: 2000-02-11. World Cup (3): 1994-95-96. **OWR Best:** 8 - Jul, 2001.

PGA Tour Wins (3): 2000: WGC-Match Play **2003:** WGC-NEC Inv **2011:** British Open.

European Tour Wins (11): 1993: Alfred Dunhill Open **1996:** German Masters **1998:** Benson & Hedges Int'l, Volvo Masters **1999:** English Open **2000:** English Open **2001:** European Open **2002:** English Open **2008:** BMW Asian Open, KLM Open **2011:** Iberdrola Open.

Japan Tour Wins (3): 2001: The Crowns **2004:** Taiheiyo Masters **2005:** Taiheiyo Masters.

Sunshine Tour Wins (1): 2001: Dimension Data Pro-Am.

Clarke, Darren Christopher, O.B.E., Cont'd

Other Wins: 1 Euro Challenge (2003)   +   Ulster Pro (N. Ireland): 1992   Irish Pro: 1994.
Amateur Wins: Spanish Am: 1990   –   East of Ireland Am: 1989   Irish Closed: 1990   North of Ireland Am: 1990   South of Ireland Am: 1990.

	91	92	93	94	95	96	97	98	99	00	01	02	03	04	05	06	07	08	09	10	11	12	13	14
Masters	-	-	-	-	-	-	-	T8	MC	T40	24	T20	T28	MC	T17	T22	MC	-	-	-	-	-	MC	T44
US Open	-	-	-	MC	-	MC	T43	T43	T53	T30	T24	T42	MC	-	56	-	-	MC	-	-	-	MC	MC
British	T64	MC	T39	T38	T31	T11	T2	MC	T30	T7	T3	T37	T59	T11	T15	MC	MC	-	T52	T44	Win	MC	T21	T26
PGA	-	-	-	-	-	-	MC	-	MC	T9	MC	MC	MC	T13	MC	-	T42	MC	MC	T48	MC	T54	75	MC
Money (A)	-	-	-	-	249*	202*	87*	175*	176*	-	-	-	85	28	52*	125	215*	-	-	-	-	-	-	-
Money (E)	112	41	8	37	14	8	4	2	8	2	3	22	2	8	20	-	138	13	61	30	11	108	121*	134
OWR	395	146	58	74	88	62	36	17	19	12	9	23	11	14	18	35	225	70	113	98	48	145	296	422

2014: E: 15 st / 11 ct / 0 t10.   (T18 Italian).   Had little impact in 15 starts, finishing 134th in $$$ – but he's still riding his British Open exemption.

OUTLOOK: At age 46, and having won the Open in 2011, has spent the last two seasons playing like he had nothing left to prove to anyone. Has seen declines in most statistical areas in recent years – but his talent is such that in any given week, he might still pop up as a factor.

STATS: Driving Distance: B   Driving Accuracy: B+ ⇩   GIR: C   Short Game: C+   Putting: C

Claxton, Marvin Willis (Will) (USA) (33)
b. Swainsboro, GA 9/14/1981. 5'10" 170 lbs. College: Auburn U. TP: 2006. An AJGA All-American. After a four-year career at Auburn, spent seven years playing mini-tours, primarily the Hooters and eGolf circuits. Having made a career total of one PGA Tour and 10 Web.com starts, took an early lead at 2011 Q School before eventually finishing T18, earning his PGA Tour card for 2012. Then retained his card by finishing 117th in $$$ as a rookie before fading to 182nd in 2013, then having his 2014 campaign cut short by an undisclosed injury. **OWR Best:** 225 - Aug, 2012.

	12	13	14
Masters	-	-	-
US Open	-	-	-
British	-	-	-
PGA	-	-	-
Money (A)	117	182	219*
OWR	266	484	939

2014: PGA: 8 st / 4 ct / 0 t10.   (T40 McGladrey).   Was limited to eight starts due to an undisclosed injury; finished 213th in FedEx Cup points.

OUTLOOK: Will begin 2015 on a 12-event medical extension. Saw his game trend downward in 2013 and, save for jumping from 78 to 35 in GIR, saw little reversal during his limited 2014 starts. May be hard-pressed to clear his medical extension, so the Web.com may lie in his future.

STATS: Driving Distance: B-   Driving Accuracy: A-   GIR: A- ⇩   Short Game: B- ⇩   Putting: C+ ⇩

Coetzee, George Willem (South Africa) (28)
b. Pretoria, South Africa 7/18/1986. 5'10" 210 lbs. College: U of San Diego. TP: 2007. Finished 4th and 8th at 2003 and 2004 Junior World Championships (San Diego), then attended the University of San Diego for one semester. Won the 2005 South African Amateur. After turning pro in 2007, played the Sunshine Tour full-time in 2007 and 2008, claiming victories at the 2007 Vodacom Origins of Golf – Selborne, the 2008 SAA Pro-Am Invitational and the 2008 Vodacom Origins of Golf – Humewood. Has since played primarily in Europe, though he continues to squeeze in several Sunshine events (including those co-sponsored by the E Tour) in the South African autumn. Among these, he won his biggest domestic title yet, the 2011 Telkom PGA Championship, by two over Neil Schietekat. After frequently contending, broke through for his first E Tour victory at the 2014 Joburg Open, where he closed with 66 to win by three. **Teams:** World Cup: 2013.
OWR Best: 41 - Jan, 2013.

European Tour Wins (1): 2014: Joburg Open.
Sunshine Tour Wins (4): 2007: Vodacom-Selborne (54H)   **2008:** SAA Pro-Am Inv (54H), Vodacom-Humewood (54H)   **2011:** Telkom PGA Championship.
Amateur Wins: South African Am: 2005.

	07	08	09	10	11	12	13	14
Masters	-	-	-	-	-	-	MC	-
US Open	-	-	-	-	-	MC	T56	-
British	-	-	-	-	15	MC	T71	18
PGA	-	-	-	-	-	MC	MC	MC
Money (E)	-	-	-	126	26	21	54	23
Money (SA)	16	20	55*	-	3*	2*	23*	5
OWR	-	773	623	412	82	49	98	81

2014: E: 25 st / 17 ct / 6 t10. (Won Joburg, 4 World Match Play, T4 Abu Dhabi, T5 Qatar, T9 WGC-Match Play, etc.). Logged his third top-25 $$$ ranking in four years and, more importantly, won his first E Tour title - although it came on home turf in Johannesburg.

OUTLOOK: A talented South African who has proven his worth in Europe, claiming his first win in 2015. Played only the E Tour (with a handful of South African starts) in 2014. Statistically, he offers an enviable mix of power and a numerically elite touch on the greens, suggesting that the predictions of stardom often placed upon him are hardly a reach. Figures to climb even further in 2015 - but can he win on European soil?

STATS: Driving Distance: A-   Driving Accuracy: C+   GIR: C   Short Game: B+   Putting: A+

Collins, Chad Steven (USA) (36)
b. Indianapolis, IN 9/20/1978. 5'9" 175 lbs. Four-time D3 All-American and three-time NCAA individual champion (1998, '99 and '01) at Methodist (SC) University. TP: 2001. Mini-tour veteran who reached the Web.com circuit in 2005 and the PGA Tour in 2008. Has since played multiple seasons on each circuit, with his 2011 PGA Tour campaign being cut short by a rib injury, earning a 2012 medical extension which he did not clear. Played his way back to the big stage via the 2013 Web.com Finals, then repeated that route in 2014 by finishing T7 at the Web.com Tour Championship. **OWR Best:** 127 - Feb, 2010.

Collins, Chad Steven, Cont'd

Other Wins: 2 Web.com (2005-2009) + 2 NGA/Hooters (2002-2003).
Amateur Wins: Indiana Am: 2000 Indiana Jr Boys: 1997.

	06	07	08	09	10	11	12	13	14
Masters	-	-	-	-	-	-	-	-	-
US Open	T40	-	-	-	-	-	-	-	MC
British	-	-	-	-	-	-	-	-	-
PGA	-	-	-	-	-	-	-	-	-
Money (A)	-	-	174	-	119	194	-	-	157
OWR	347	383	545	171	203	665	-	499	520

2014: PGA: 28 st / 11 ct / 1 t10. (8 Humana). Finished 159th in FedEx Cup points but saved his card (barely) via the Web.com Finals.
OUTLOOK: Might well have hung around after keeping his card in 2010 but for his rib injury. Now healthy but has been unable to get over the hump and retain his PGA Tour card. Quietly finished 17 in SGP but his ball striking (and lack of length) hasn't allowed enough of those putts to be for birdie.
STATS: Driving Distance: D   Driving Accuracy: C   GIR: C-   Short Game: B+   Putting: A-

---

Colsaerts, Nicolas (Belgium) (32)

b. Brussels, Belgium 11/14/1982. 6'1" 165 lbs. TP: 2000. Won the Belgium Amateur Match and Stroke Play titles in 2000. Won a Belgian PGA event in 2000 while still an amateur, and later added the Belgian Match Play (2002) and an Alps Tour event in 2006. From 2001-2010, only twice reached the top 100 in E Tour $$$. Won two Challenge Tour events in 2009 to play his way back to the E Tour, where five top-10 finishes in 2010 set the stage for a career-best 2011. Won the 2011 Volvo China Open, where his 264 total beat four players by four shots. Also lost to eventual champion Ian Poulter at the 19th hole in the semi-finals of the Volvo World Match Play. Returned in 2012 to win the same event, edging Graeme McDowell 1 up in the final. Quieted somewhat in 2013 and '14 but remained a solid earner. **Teams:** Eisenhower Trophy (2): 1998-00. Ryder Cup: 2012 (O: 1-3-0, S: 0-1-0). Seve Trophy (2): 2011-13. World Cup (2): 2011-13. **OWR Best:** 32 - May, 2012.

European Tour Wins (2): 2011: China Open (Volvo) **2012:** World Match Play.
Other Wins: 2 Euro Challenge (2009) + 1 Alps Tour (2006)   World Travel Open (Belgium): 2000*   Belgian Match Play: 2002   Omnium of Belgium: 2003   Mauritius Masters: 2010.
Amateur Wins: Belgium Am: 2000 – Belgium Am Stroke Play: 2000.

	01	02	03	04	05	06	07	08	09	10	11	12	13	14
Masters	-	-	-	-	-	-	-	-	-	-	-	MC	-	-
US Open	MC	-	-	-	-	-	-	-	-	-	MC	T27	T10	MC
British	-	-	-	MC	-	-	-	-	-	-	WD	T7	MC	-
PGA	-	-	-	-	-	-	-	-	-	-	-	MC	MC	-
Money (A)	-	-	-	-	-	-	-	-	-	-	-	114	-	-
Money (E)	172	-	77	120	104	128	201	-	-	67	20	11	38	45
OWR	775	591	365	496	442	561	802	-	132	152	72	36	68	140

2014: E: 19 st / 11 ct / 4 t10. (2 Port Masters, T2 Malaysian, T4 Wales, T6 BMW Masters). Recovered from a relatively slow start to finish 45th in $$$. Also made 11 non-co-sanctioned PGA Tour starts during the winter/spring, but only once cracked the top 25 (T19 at Farmers Insurance).
OUTLOOK: Hugely long hitter who led the E Tour in Driving Distance in 2010, '12 and again in 2014. Has slipped somewhat from his Ryder Cup form of 2012 but still appears skilled enough to make an impact in the U.S. should he play there more regularly. Should bounce back somewhat in 2015.
STATS: Driving Distance: A+   Driving Accuracy: C+   GIR: B+ ⇧   Short Game: C-   Putting: B- ⇩

Compton, Erik Harald Høie. (USA) (35)

b. Miami, FL 11/11/1979. 5'8" 150 lbs. Two-time All-American at U of Georgia. TP: 2001. Two-time AJGA All-American and 1998 AJGA Player of the Year. Because of viral cardiomyopathy, had a heart transplant in 1992, then a second transplant in 2008. After an elite junior career, starred at the University of Georgia before toiling on the Web.com and Canadian Tours during most of the 2000s, winning thrice on the latter. Won the 2005 King Hassan II Trophy in Morocco (prior to it's being an official E Tour event). Finished in 13th-place in 2011 Web.com Tour $$$ to finally earn status on the PGA Tour, which he retained for 2013 via Q School. Secured his PGA status by tying for 2nd at the 2014 U.S. Open, eight shots behind Martin Kaymer. **Teams:** Walker Cup: 2001 (1-1-1). Palmer Cup: 2001. **OWR Best:** 71 - Jul, 2014.

Other Wins: 1 Web.com (2011) + 1 NGA/Hooters (2003)   King Hassan II Trophy (Morocco): 2005   Guadalajara Classic (Canada): 2003   Central Valley Classic (Canada): 2004   MTS Classic (Canada): 2004.
Amateur Wins: Dixie Am: 2000 Monroe Inv: 2001.

	10	11	12	13	14
Masters	-	-	-	-	-
US Open	MC	-	-	-	T2
British	-	-	-	-	MC
PGA	-	-	-	-	MC
Money (A)	-	-	165	122	56
OWR	984	290	451	362	95

2014: PGA: 28 st / 17 ct / 3 t10. (T2 US Open, T5 Arnold Palmer, T5 New Orleans). Logged something of a breakthrough season, finishing a career-best 64th in FedEx Cup points and logging three top 10s including a T2 at the U.S. Open.
OUTLOOK: Suddenly seems capable of doing some damage on the PGA Tour - but can he keep playing at this level? A long but not-too-accurate driver whose GIR (93 to 142) and Ball Striking (110 to 163) slipped during his career-best 2014 - but whose SGP topped out at 39.
STATS: Driving Distance: B+   Driving Accuracy: C+   GIR: C+   Short Game: B   Putting: B+

Couch, Christian Stratton (USA) (41)

b. Fort Lauderdale, FL 5/1/1973. 6'4" 225 lbs. All-American at U of Florida. TP: 1995. Two-time AJGA All-American. Longtime Web.com Tour star who first came to note by qualifying for the PGA Tour's 1990 Honda Classic at age 16 (shot 82-77 to MC). Was the top-rated junior in the U.S. in 1991. His professional career has been spent primarily on the Web.com Tour, where he won five times

Couch, Christian Stratton, Cont'd

between 2001-2005. Has thrice qualified for the PGA Tour, finally breaking through with a victory on his third go-round by taking the 2006 New Orleans Classic, where he edged Fred Funk and Charles Howell III by one. Suffered a significant shoulder injury in 2007, causing him to miss nearly all of 2008 and some of 2009. Suffered a serious back injury in August, 2012 and hasn't made a PGA Tour start since. **OWR Best:** 103 - Apr, 2006.

PGA Tour Wins (1): 2006: New Orleans Classic (Zurich).
Other Wins: 5 Web.com (2001-2005).
Amateur Wins: Orange Bowl Jr: 1990.

	99	00	01	02	03	04	05	06	07	08	09	10	11	12	13	14
Masters	-	-	-	-	-	-	-	-	-	-	-	-	-	-	-	-
US Open	-	-	-	-	-	-	-	-	-	-	-	-	-	-	-	-
British	-	-	-	-	-	-	-	-	-	-	-	-	-	-	-	-
PGA	-	-	-	-	-	-	-	MC	-	-	-	-	-	-	-	-
Money (A)	181	-	-	-	-	217	-	66	167	-	222*	109	99	170	-	-
OWR	422	631	613	-	318	428	33	153	416	982	-	201	228	457	-	-

2014: Missed the entire season due to a back injury suffered in August, 2012.
OUTLOOK: Begins 2015 with a four-event medical extension - but this far removed, it's difficult to envision him having a major impact going forward.

STATS: Driving Distance: A-   Driving Accuracy: A-   GIR: B-   Short Game: B+   Putting: B

Couples, Frederick Steven (USA) (55)

b. Seattle, WA 10/3/1959. 5'11" 185 lbs. Two-time All-American at U of Houston. TP: 1980. Popular player who has won 17 major tour events worldwide. First PGA Tour victory came in five-man playoff at 1983 Kemper Open, a triumph bettered in 1984 when he rode a second round 64 to edge Lee Trevino by a stroke at the Players Championship. Beat Mark Calcavecchia on the third extra hole to win the 1987 Byron Nelson Classic. At the 1990 Nissan Los Angeles Open, used a course-record tying 9-under-par 62 in the third round to cruise to a three-stroke victory at Riviera. After logging two more wins in 1991, enjoyed a career-best 1992 when he led the Tour in $$$, won his second Vardon Trophy and was named PGA Player of the Year after posting three wins. The biggest, his lone Major title at the Masters (by two over Raymond Floyd), capped a remarkable run that included two more wins (Los Angeles and a nine-shot runaway at Bay Hill) and two seconds in a six-event span. Earned his 10th career victory in 1993 at the wind-shortened Honda Classic, beating Robert Gamez in a playoff. In 1995, recorded back-to-back victories on European Tour (at the Dubai Desert and Johnnie Walker Classics), the first American to do so since Charles Coody in 1973. In 1996, closed with a 64 to become first player to win two Players Championships. Won for the last time at the 2003 Shell Houston Open, where he birdied four of the last five holes. Teamed with Davis Love III to win four straight World Cups (1992-1995). Bothered by back trouble beginning in the mid-1990s but never finished worse than 76th on money list from 1981-2000, or worse than 8th in year-end OWR from 1991-1996. Upon arriving on the Champions Tour in 2010, won four times (including three straight events in February/March) and finished 2nd in $$$. Despite continuing back problems, won twice more in 2011, including the Senior Players Championship, where he beat John Cook in a playoff. Added a second senior Major by claiming the 2012 Senior British Open, edging Gary Hallberg by two at Turnberry. **Awards:** World Golf Hall of Fame Member (2013). PGA Tour Player of the Year (2): 1991-92. Vardon Trophy (2): 1991-92. **Teams:** Ryder Cup (5): 1989-91-93-95-97 (O: 7-9-4, S: 2-1-2). Presidents Cup (4): 1994-96-98-05 (9-5-2) + Capt in 2009 & '11. World Cup (4): 1992-93-94-95 (won all four w/D.Love III). **OWR Best:** 1 - Apr, 1992.

PGA Tour Wins (15): 1983: Kemper Open **1984:** Players Championship **1987:** Byron Nelson Classic **1990:** Los Angeles Open **1991:** Memphis Classic (FedEx), B.C. Open **1992:** Los Angeles Open, Bay Hill Inv (Nestle), Masters Tournament **1993:** Honda Classic (54H) **1994:** Buick Open **1996:** Players Championship **1998:** Bob Hope Classic (90H), Memorial Tournament **2003** Houston Open (Shell).
European Tour Wins (2): 1995: Dubai Classic, Johnnie Walker Classic.
Champions Tour Wins (9): 2010-2013 (incl. 2012 Sr British Open).
Other Wins: Washington Open: 1978*   JCPenny Mixed Team: 1983 (w/J.Stephenson)   Shark Shootout (3) 1990 (w/R.Floyd)-94 (w/B.Faxon)-99 (w/D.Duval)   Sazale Classic: 1990 (w/M.Donald)   Johnnie Walker Championship (Jamaica)(2): 1991-95   Kapalua Int'l (2): 1993-94   Dunhill Cup: 1993 (w/P.Stewart & J.Daly)   World Cup (Individual): 1994   Wendy's 3-Tour Challenge (3): 1994 (w/P.Azinger & G.Norman)-96 (w/D.Love III & P.Stewart)-97 (w/T.Lehman & P.Mickelson)   Dunhill Cup: 1993 (w/J.Daly & P.Stewart)   Skins Game (5): 1995-96-99-03-04   Hyundai Team: 2001 (w/M.Calcavecchia)
Amateur Wins: British Columbia Jr: 1978   Washington Am: 1978   British Columbia Am: 1979.

	79	80	81	82	83	84	85	86	87	88	89	90	91	92	93	94	95	96	97	98	99	00	01	02
Masters	-	-	-	-	T32	10	T10	T31	-	T5	T11	5	T35	Win	T21	-	T10	T15	T7	T2	T27	T11	26	T36
US Open	T48	-	-	MC	MC	T9	T39	-	T46	T10	T21	MC	T3	T17	T16	MC	-	T52	T53	MC	T16	MC	-	-
British	-	-	-	-	-	T4	-	T46	T40	T4	T6	T25	T3	MC	T9	-	-	T7	T7	T66	-	6	MC	-
PGA	-	-	-	T3	T23	T20	T6	T36	MC	MC	MC	2	T27	T21	T31	T39	T31	T41	T29	T13	T26	MC	T37	-
Money (A)	Am	-	54	54	19	7	-	38	76	19	21	11	9	3	1	10	23	63	6	55	9	56	47	131	103
OWR									73	46	19	15	11	6	2	5	7	7	5	20	11	20	39	96	145

	03	04	05	06	07	08	09	10	11	12	13	14
Masters	T28	T6	T39	T3	T30	MC	MC	6	T11	T12	T13	T20
US Open	T66	MC	T15	T48	-	-	-	-	-	-	-	-
British	T46	-	T3	MC	-	-	-	-	-	T32	-	-
PGA	T34	-	T70	MC	-	MC	T36	-	-	-	-	-
Money (A)	34	50	38	110	109	75	-	-	-	-	-	-
OWR	37	31	25	62	541	175	108	224	333	445	431	674

2014: PGA: 3 st / 1 ct / 0 t10. (T20 Masters). Spent more time (9 starts) on Champions Tour, winning twice and finishing 5th in $$$.
OUTLOOK: PGA Tour starts are generally limited to Riviera, the Memorial and The Masters now, but he remains surprisingly competitive for a 55-year-old with a chronically bad back. Not as long as he once was but can still move it. An inconsistent putter, however, is his one real sign of age.

STATS (LTD): Driving Distance: B   Driving Accuracy: B   GIR: C+   Short Game: B   Putting: B-

---

Crane, Benjamin McCully (USA) (38)

b. Portland, OR 3/6/1976. 5'11" 165 lbs. College: U of Oregon. TP: 1999. Was a two-time winner on the Web.com Tour (2000 and 2001) before joining the PGA Tour full-time in 2002. Has been plagued by lower back problems, with his 2007 season limited to just nine events. Save for that injury-shortened year, never finished worse than 75th in PGA Tour earnings through 2012. Claimed his first win at the 2003 Bell South Classic, finishing 64-63 after making the cut by a shot. After missing February and March with back issues,

Crane, Benjamin McCully, Cont'd

opened with a 62 en route to a wire-to-wire win at the 2005 U.S. Bank Championship. Enjoyed his best year in 2010, winning January's Farmers Insurance Open, then later claiming the Asia-Pacific Classic, an Asian Tour event co-sponsored (unofficially) by the PGA Tour. Won the 2011 McGladrey Classic before going quiet in 2013, rebuilding his swing (to ease stress on his oft-injured back) and returning to win the 2014 Memphis Classic, where he opened with 63 before ultimately edging Troy Merritt by one. **OWR Best:** 30 - Nov, 2005.

PGA Tour Wins (5): 2003: Atlanta Classic (BellSouth) **2005**: Milwaukee Open (U.S. Bank) **2010**: San Diego Open (Farmers) **2011**: McGladrey Classic **2014**: Memphis Classic (FedEx).
Asian Tour Wins (1): 2010: Asia-Pacific Classic.
Other Wins: 2 Web.com (2000-2001).
Amateur Wins: Pacific Northwest Am: 1997   Pacific Coast Am: 1998.

	02	03	04	05	06	07	08	09	10	11	12	13	14
Masters	-	-	-	-	MC	MC	-	-	T24	MC	T12	-	-
US Open	MC	-	-	-	62	-	T53	MC	MC	MC	MC	-	-
British	-	MC	-	-	T11	-	-	MC	MC	MC	-	-	-
PGA	-	T48	T9	T40	MC	-	MC	T43	T39	T37	-	-	WD
Money (A)	70	48	75	19	58	180*	64	51	23	50	46	105	67
OWR	157	92	118	34	41	205	101	102	39	54	81	236	144

2014: PGA: 25 st / 17 ct / 2 t10. (Won FedEx St Jude, T9 Humana). In an up-and-down year, climbed back to the top by winning in Memphis but logged only one additional top 10 and three top-25s overall. Finished 60th in FedEx Cup points
OUTLOOK: Continues to battle the occasional sore back and a declining four-year GIR trend (68, 105, 121, 130) to remain mainstream competitive. Still a reliably high-end putter, however, with a short game nearly to match. Coming off an inconsistent year but one in which his Memphis win might potentially jumpstart his career. At age 38, he still has time to climb back to the upper reaches - but will his health oblige him?

STATS: Driving Distance: C   Driving Accuracy: A-   GIR: C+   Short Game: B+   Putting: B+

Crespi, Marco (Italy) (36)

b. Monza, Italy 11/5/1978. 5'10" 180 lbs. TP: 2002. Late-bloomer who, save for a three-year Challenge Tour stint from 2006-2008, spent much of his first professional decade on mini-tours. Blossomed in 2012, however, returning to the Challenge Tour after winning the Telenet Trophy on a sponsor exemption, then added a second Challenge title in 2013. Finally reached the 2014 E Tour via Q School in his 11th try, then won the light-field NH Collection Open to become the Tour's oldest-ever rookie winner. **OWR Best:** 167 - Apr, 2014.

European Tour Wins (1): 2014: NH Collection Open.
Other Wins: 2 Euro Challenge (2012-2013)   +   Italian PGA (2): 2005-07.

	07	08	09	10	11	12	13	14
Masters	-	-	-	-	-	-	-	-
US Open	-	-	-	-	-	-	-	-
British	-	-	-	-	-	-	-	-
PGA	-	-	-	-	-	-	-	-
Money (E)	-	-	-	-	-	-	-	105
OWR	786	864	986	1285	1131	392	200	307

2014: E: 26 st / 12 ct / 2 t10. (Won NH Collection, T4 South African). Despite spotty play, finished 105th in $$$ after winning the NH Collection Open.
OUTLOOK: Seldom was a major factor as a 35-year-old rookie but managed to break through and win at the light-field NH Collection Open, which was co-sanctioned by the Challenge Tour. A short-but-accurate type whose upside would seem limited - but he's exempt through 2015.

STATS (LTD):   Driving Distance: C-   Driving Accuracy: A   GIR: C   Short Game: B   Putting: B+

Cullen, Nick (Australia) (30)

b. Adelaide, South Australia 4/10/1984. 5'11" 170 lbs. College: University of South Australia. TP: 2008. A left-hander who began his career on several lesser tours before joining the OneAsia circuit in 2012, where he finished 5th in $$$ and edged David Smail by one to win the Indonesia Open. Claimed his first domestic win at the 2013 Queensland Open, where he ran away by five. Then landed a far bigger triumph in 2014 when he edged Adam Scott and two others by one to claim the Australian Masters. **OWR Best:** 230 - Dec, 2014.

OneAsia Tour Wins (1): 2012: Indonesia Open (Enjoy Jakarta).
Australasian Wins (2): 2013: Queensland Open (Isuzu) **2014**: Australian Masters

	10	11	12	13	14
Masters	-	-	-	-	-
US Open	-	-	-	-	-
British	-	-	MC	-	-
PGA	-	-	-	-	-
Money (O)	-	-	5	6	45
OWR	-	727	287	263	230

2014: OA: 8 st / 5 ct / 0 t10. (T24 SK Telecom). Also played on the Australasian Tour, winning the Australian Masters and finishing 3rd in earnings.
OUTLOOK: Widely considered one of Australia's better prospects who has thus far held his own nicely on the Far East's second-tier tours. His Masters win was certainly a breakthrough, but he still lacks a path (and the résumé) to move significantly westward.

STATS: Driving Distance: --   Driving Accuracy: --   GIR: --   Short Game: --   Putting: --

---

Curran, Jon Lynch (USA) (27)

b. Hopkinton, MA 2/17/1987. 5'9" 165 lbs. College: Vanderbilt U. TP: 2009. Two-time AJGA All-American. Won two state titles at Hopkinton (MA) HS with future PGA Tour star Keegan Bradley. After turning professional in 2009, became a regular on the NGA mini-tour, where he won once and was named Player Of The Year in 2013. Joined the Web.com Tour for 2014, where he won the Brasil Champions in Sao Paulo after opening with a 61. Finished 12th in regular season $$$ to earn his PGA Tour card. **OWR Best:** 263 - Jun, 2014.

Curran, Jon Lynch, Cont'd

Other Wins: 1 Web.com (2014)   +   1 NGA/Hooters (2005).

	10	11	12	13	14
Masters	-	-	-	-	-
US Open	MC	-	-	-	-
British	-	-	-	-	-
PGA	-	-	-	-	-
Money (A)	-	-	-	-	-
OWR	1322	-	-	1311	300

2014: Played full-time on the Web.com Tour, winning once and clinching his 2015 PGA Tour card by finishing 12th in regular season $$$.

OUTLOOK: Is something of streaky player, occasionally going quite low but also prone to hitting bad patches - such as missing 11 of his last 13 Web.com cuts in 2014. Might enjoy a hot week or two but his game seems a tad too mercurial to represent a strong PGA Tour bet in 2015.

STATS: Driving Distance: C   Driving Accuracy: A   GIR: B   Short Game: B-   Putting: B-

---

Curtis, Ben Clifford (USA) (37)

b. Columbus, OH 5/26/1977. 5'11" 175 lbs. Two-time All-American at Kent St. TP: 2000. An AJGA All-American. Former highly-rated amateur who won the Ohio Am in 1999 and '00, the second by 17 shots! Scored one of golf's greatest-ever upsets by coming out of nowhere to win the 2003 British Open at Royal St. George's, beating Vijay Singh and Thomas Bjørn (who lost 3 strokes at the 70th and 71st holes) by one. Re-emerged in 2006 after two years of struggle by routing the field (by five shots) at the rain-delayed Booz Allen Classic, then adding the 84 Lumber Classic, beating Charles Howell III by two. Endured a six-year victory drought before returning to the winner's circle at the 2012 Valero Texas Open, where he edged Matt Every and John Huh by two. **Awards:** PGA Tour Rookie of the Year: 2003. **Teams:** Eisenhower Trophy: 2000. Palmer Cup: 1999. Ryder Cup: 2008 (O: 1-1-1, S: 1-0-0). World Cup: 2008. **OWR Best:** 24 - Nov, 2008.

PGA Tour Wins (4): 2003: British Open **2006:** Booz Allen Classic, 84 Lumber Classic **2012:** Texas Open (Valero).

Other Wins: 1 NGA/Hooters (2002).

Amateur Wins: Ohio Am (2): 1999-00   Players Am: 2000.

	03	04	05	06	07	08	09	10	11	12	13	14
Masters	-	MC	MC	T39	MC	MC	T35	MC	-	-	MC	-
US Open	-	30	MC	57	T45	MC	57	T14	-	-	-	-
British	Win	MC	MC	MC	T8	T7	MC	MC	MC	MC	T64	MC
PGA	MC	MC	T34	T60	MC	T2	T24	MC	-	T11	T66	-
Money (A)	46	141	129	30	126	17	105	120	149	30	154	130
OWR	34	94	190	74	119	24	50	173	310	84	241	377

2014: PGA: 24 st / 14 ct / 1 t10.   (T6 Memorial).   Once again failed to retain his card, logging one top 10 and finishing 131st in FedEx Cup points.

OUTLOOK: Has long been an up-and-down player (four career top-50 $$$ rankings and six outside of the top 125) but has now cracked the top 100 only once since 2008. Still a reliably strong putter but after ranking 150 in GIR and 141 in Ball Striking, it's not too hard to see where the problems are. Will start 2015 with conditional status, which isn't going to help, but his streakiness suggests there may be one or two more wins ahead.

STATS: Driving Distance: C-   Driving Accuracy: A-   GIR: C+   Short Game: B-   Putting: A

Da Silva, Adilson Jose (Brazil) (42)

b. Santa Cruz du Sul, Brazil 1/24/1972. 5'9" 165 lbs. TP: 1994. Brazilian native who moved to Africa while still an amateur. Has won numerous lesser events in Zimbabwe while also establishing himself as a regular winner on the Sunshine Tour – though never in any of the circuit's more lucrative, European Tour co-sanctioned summer events. Though a winner in both 1997 and '98, blossomed in the latter half of his 30s, winning twice in 2007, '10, '11 and '13, cracking the top 10 in the Order of Merit in 2007 and '08, and finishing no worse than 31st from 2004 onward. Began also playing some Asian events in 2013. **Teams:** World Cup (2): 2011-13. **OWR Best:** 215 - Aug, 2013.

Sunshine Tour Wins (12): 1997: Leopard Rock Classic (54H) **1998:** Wild Coast Sun Challenge **2007:** Suncoast Classic (54H), Vodacom-Fancourt (54H) **2009:** Vodacom-Fancourt (54H) **2010:** Zambia Open (54H), Suncoast Classic (54H) **2011:** Nashua Golf Challenge (54H), Vodacom-Sishen (54H) **2012:** Vodacom-Selborne (54H) **2013:** Zambia Open, Sun City Challenge (54H).

Other Wins: SAA Pro-Am Inv (SA): 2009.

Amateur Wins: Brazil Am (2): 1990-91   Zimbabwe Am: 1992

	96	97	98	99	00	01	02	03	04	05	06	07	08	09	10	11	12	13	14
Masters	-	-	-	-	-	-	-	-	-	-	-	-	-	-	-	-	-	-	-
US Open	-	-	-	-	-	-	-	-	-	-	-	-	-	-	-	-	-	-	-
British	-	-	-	-	MC	-	-	-	-	-	MC	-	-	-	-	T69	-	-	-
PGA	-	-	-	-	-	-	-	-	-	-	-	-	-	-	-	-	-	-	-
Money (SA)	37	19*	12	42	25	70*	123	81*	17	27	29	6	10	15	14	23	31	16	23
Money (As)	-	-	-	-	-	-	-	-	-	-	-	-	-	-	-	50*	-	31	24*
OWR	688	431	286	422	743	-	962	-	887	-	743	770	515	496	484	382	356	257	321

2014: SUN: 15 st / 14 ct / 7 t10.   (Incl. T2 Dimension Data, T2 Lombard, T3 Vodacom-Arabella).   Failed to win in South Africa for the first time since 2008 but remained among the top 25 $$$ winners. Also made nine Asia Tour starts, tying for 2nd at the Taiwan Masters.

OUTLOOK: Other than visiting Asia, has never shown the game (nor the inkling) to step too far beyond the Sunshine Tour, but he's certainly established a place for himself there. Might be slowing slightly in his early 40s but is likely good for several more South African wins before he's done.

STATS: Driving Distance: --   Driving Accuracy: --   GIR: --   Short Game: --   Putting: --

---

Daly, John Patrick (USA) (48)

b. Carmichael, CA 4/28/1966. 5'11" 230 lbs. All-American at U of Arkansas. TP: 1987. An AJGA All-American. Stunned the golf world by claiming his first Tour win at the 1991 PGA Championship at Crooked Stick (by three over Bruce Lietzke) after starting the week as ninth alternate. Claimed second Major title by defeating Costantino Rocca in four-hole playoff at the 1995 British Open at St Andrews. In between, won the 1992 B.C. Open (in a six-shot runaway) and the 1994 Atlanta Classic. Fell as far as 188th on the money list during a

Daly, John Patrick, Cont'd

major new millennium slide before resurrecting his career in 2004, winning the Buick Invitational (in a playoff with Luke Donald and Chris Riley) and finishing 21st in earnings. Played the European Tour in 2009 after being suspended for six months in America, and has regularly played around the world throughout his career. Has withdrawn from 38 PGA Tour events through 2013 and racked up several epic meltdown scores, including a legendary 18 at the par-5 6th at Bay Hill (fourth round, 1998) and an 11 at Pinehurst's par-4 8th hole (fourth round of the 1999 U.S. Open) when he batted his ball around like a polo player. Added to this legacy during the first round of the 2011 Australian Open, hitting six balls into the water at the 11th hole at The Lakes GC before walking off. Also shot 90 in the second round of the 2014 Valspar Championship, citing the yips. **Awards:** PGA Tour Rookie of the Year: 1991. PGA Tour Comeback Player of the Year: 2004. **Teams:** World Cup: 1998. **OWR Best:** 23 - Oct, 2005.

PGA Tour Wins (5): 1991: PGA Championship **1992:** B.C. Open **1994:** Atlanta Classic (BellSouth) **1995:** British Open **2004:** San Diego Open (Buick Inv).
European Tour Wins (1): 2001: BMW Int'l.
Asian Wins (1): 2003: Korean Open.
Sunshine Tour Wins (2): 1990: AECI Charity Classic, Royal Swazi Sun Classic.
Other Wins: 1 Web.com (1990)   +   Missouri Open: 1987*   Dunhill Cup: 1993 (w/F.Couples & P.Stewart)   JCPenney Mixed Team: 1999 (w/L.Davies)   Champions Challenge: 2002 (w/P.Perez)   Wendy's 3-Tour Challenge (2): 2002 (w/R.Beem & J.Furyk)-03 (w/M.Calcavecchia & P.Jacobsen)   Callaway Inv: 2003.
Amateur Wins: Arkansas Am Match Play: 1986   Arizona Am Match Play: 1986   Arkansas Am Stroke Play: 1987.

	86	87	88	89	90	91	92	93	94	95	96	97	98	99	00	01	02	03	04	05	06	07	08	09
Masters	-	-	-	-	-	-	T19	T3	T48	T45	T29	-	T33	T52	MC	-	T32	-	MC	MC	MC	-	-	-
US Open	MC	-	-	T69	-	-	MC	T33	MC	T45	T27	WD	T53	68	WD	-	T70	-	-	T75	-	-	-	-
British	-	-	-	-	-	-	75	T14	81	Win	T67	-	MC	-	MC	MC	MC	72	MC	T15	MC	MC	MC	T27
PGA	-	-	-	-	-	Win	82	T51	MC	MC	MC	T29	MC	-	MC	MC	MC	MC	MC	T74	MC	T32	MC	WD
Money (A)	Am	-	-	-	-	17	37	76	49	57	121	165	77	158	188	61	112	171	21	42	193	188	232	215*
OWR	-	-	-	385	224	47	63	96	72	40	91	227	120	203	414	54	91	280	41	29	142	523	736	435

	10	11	12	13	14
Masters	-	-	-	-	-
US Open	-	-	-	-	-
British	T48	MC	T81	-	MC
PGA	WD	MC	T18	-	MC
Money (A)	193	187	146	223*	211
OWR	581	557	195	505	845

2014: PGA: 15 st / 5 ct / 0 t10. (T32 Hawaii). Finished 219th in FedEx Cup points.
OUTLOOK: It's now been 10 years since his last victory but at age 48, he still builds his game around his considerable power. Virtually every other aspect of his game is well below the median, and he will be playing on Past Champion status in 2015 - but this shouldn't matter much as he's been living off sponsor exemptions for quite some time now. Regardless, the Champions Tour likely can't wait for his 2016 arrival.

STATS: Driving Distance: A   Driving Accuracy: D   GIR: C-   Short Game: C   Putting: B-

---

Davies, Rhys Owen (Wales) (29)

b. Edinburgh, Scotland 5/28/1985. 6'1" 170 lbs. Three-time All-American at East Tennessee St. TP: 2007. Scottish native of Welsh descent, who grew up and resides in Wales. Starred collegiately in America and played in two Walker Cups before turning pro and winning twice during a short 2009 Challenge Tour season. Began playing full time on the European Tour in 2010 and won the King Hassan II Trophy in his 8th start. Slipped badly thereafter, finishing 121st in $$$ in 2012, and playing mostly on the Challenge Tour since. **Teams:** Walker Cup (2): 2005-07 (4-3-1). Eisenhower Trophy (2): 2004-06. Palmer Cup (4): 2004-05-06-07. World Cup: 2011. **OWR Best:** 44 - Jun, 2010.
European Tour Wins (1): 2010: King Hassan II Trophy.
Other Wins: 2 Euro Challenge (2009).
Amateur Wins: British Boys: 2003   Scratch Players: 2006.

	07	08	09	10	11	12	13	14
Masters	-	-	-	-	-	-	-	-
US Open	-	-	-	T74	-	-	-	-
British	-	-	MC	MC	MC	-	-	-
PGA	-	-	-	T62	-	-	-	-
Money (E)	-	-	-	18	56	121	182*	181*
OWR	-	339	145	69	149	386	479	610

2014: Played full-time on the Challenge Tour, finishing 54th in $$$. Also made eight E Tour starts, making five cuts and finishing 181st in $$$.
OUTLOOK: What initially seemed a promising E Tour career has hit the rocks over the last three seasons. Possesses a fairly balanced set of mid-range stats and, on paper, would seem to have the game to succeed on the E Tour - but he'll be back on the Challenge Tour again in 2015.

STATS: Driving Distance: B   Driving Accuracy: B-   GIR: C+   Short Game: B+   Putting: B+

Davis, Brian Lester (England) (40)

b. London, England 8/2/1974. 5'11" 185 lbs. TP: 1994. Veteran Englishman who initially played the E Tour full-time from 1997-2004, logging four top-40 Order of Merit finishes between 2000-2004 (including 9th in 2003). Won the 2000 Spanish Open and the 2004 ANZ Championship, an event played in Australia under modified Stableford scoring. Was medalist at the 2004 PGA Tour Q School and has played in America full-time since 2005. Has been a steady earner stateside, particularly in 2009 and 2010 when he finished 43rd and 46th on the PGA Tour money list. A five-time runner-up in America through 2013, most notably at the 2010 Heritage where he lost a playoff to Jim Furyk after calling a penalty on himself for inadvertently touching a loose impediment within the greenside hazard at Harbour Town's 18th. **Teams:** Seve Trophy: 2003. World Cup: 2000. **OWR Best:** 45 - Mar, 2004.
European Tour Wins (2): 2000: Spanish Open **2004:** ANZ Championship.
Amateur Wins: Peter McEvoy Trophy: 1992

Davis, Brian Lester, Cont'd

	97	98	99	00	01	02	03	04	05	06	07	08	09	10	11	12	13	14
Masters	-	-	-	-	-	-	-	MC	-	-	-	-	-	-	-	-	-	-
US Open	-	-	-	-	-	-	T61	MC	-	-	-	-	-	-	MC	-	-	-
British	-	MC	T68	MC	-	-	T6	MC	MC	-	T53	-	-	-	MC	-	MC	-
PGA	-	-	-	-	-	-	-	MC	T13	MC	-	-	MC	T39	T19	MC	-	-
Money (A)	-	-	-	-	-	-	-	98	113	71	96	43	46	71	64	72	110	
Money (E)	53	79	74	29	53	39	9	31	62	-	-	-	-	-	-	-	-	
OWR	313	317	295	121	154	147	60	84	127	221	186	205	161	77	117	136	153	258

2014: PGA: 28 st / 19 ct / 0 t10. (T11 Players). Slipped out of the top 100 in $$$ for the first time since 2006, fell to 110th in FedEx Cup points.
OUTLOOK: Hasn't tasted victory since 2004 (when he won in Australia) and is winless on the PGA Tour overall. At the same time, he has quietly emerged as a very steady money winner, riding top-shelf driving accuracy and a deft touch around the green to regular financial success.

STATS: Driving Distance: C   Driving Accuracy: A+   GIR: C+   Short Game: A   Putting: A-

---

Day, Glen Edward (USA) (49)
b. Mobile, AL 11/16/1965. 5'10" 170 lbs. College U of Oklahoma. TP: 1988. Initially played mini-tours, in Asia (where he won the 1990 Malaysian Open) and the European tour full-time from 1991-93. Returned home in 1994 (via Q School) and made an immediate splash on the PGA Tour, finishing 45th in earnings as a rookie. Enjoyed a strong 10-year run, during which he claimed his lone Tour title at the 1999 Heritage, defeating Jeff Sluman and Payne Stewart in sudden death. **OWR Best:** 30 - Feb, 2000.

PGA Tour Wins (1): 1999: Heritage Classic (MCI).
Asian Tour Wins (1): 1990: Malaysian Open.
Other Wins: Arkansas Open: 1988   Oklahoma PGA: 1993.

	91	92	93	94	95	96	97	98	99	00	01	02	03	04	05	06	07	08	09	10	11	12	13	14
Masters	-	-	-	-	-	-	-	-	MC	T19	-	-	-	-	-	-	-	-	-	-	-	-	-	-
US Open	-	-	-	MC	MC	-	-	T23	MC	MC	MC	-	-	MC	-	-	-	-	-	MC	-	-	-	-
British	-	-	MC	-	-	-	MC	MC	MC	-	-	-	-	-	-	-	-	-	-	-	-	-	-	-
PGA	-	-	-	T15	MC	T41	MC	T29	MC	T51	MC	-	-	-	-	-	-	-	-	-	-	-	-	-
Money (A)	-	-	-	45	91	73	98	15	34	75	71	77	81	138	167	207*	163	155	151	195*	-	230*	186*	237*
Money (E)	61	36	65	-	-	-	-	-	-	-	-	-	-	-	-	-	-	-	-	-	-	-	-	-
OWR	197	127	151	126	192	148	148	43	37	88	148	160	162	240	359	364	485	512	477	660	1139	766	652	869

2014: PGA: 5 st / 1 ct / 0 t10. (T27 John Deere). Also made 11 starts on the Web.com Tour, logging three top-25 finishes.
OUTLOOK: Strictly a part-time player on Past Champion status - for one more year until he becomes Champions Tour eligible.

STATS: Driving Distance: --   Driving Accuracy: --   GIR: --   Short Game: --   Putting: --

---

Day, Jason Anthony (Australia) (27)
b. Beaudesert, Queensland, Australia 11/12/1987. 6'0" 170 lbs. TP: 2006. Former elite Australian prospect whose father is Australian, mother is Filipino and wife is American. Was an elite amateur prospect with a long list of prominent wins. Came directly to America upon turning pro, playing a handful of PGA Tour events in late 2006, then the Web.com Tour in 2007. Became the youngest-ever winner of a PGA Tour-sponsored event by claiming the Web.com Tour's 2007 Legend Financial Group Classic at 19 years, 7 months and 26 days. Made steady progress as a PGA Tour player post-2008, peaking in 2010 when, despite a mysterious illness early in the year, he broke through to win the Byron Nelson Championship, making him the Tour's youngest winner since Tiger Woods (1997). In 2011, T2 (two behind Charl Schwartzel) at The Masters , then finished 2nd (eight strokes back) to Rory McIlroy at the U.S. Open. Held the lead through 69 holes at the 2013 Masters before finishing solo third, then made another late run at the 2013 U.S. Open where he ultimately tied for 2nd. Won the newly emphasized World Cup individual title (and the team title, with Adam Scott) in 2013 at Royal Melbourne, then stepped up to win the 2014 WGC-Match Play, beating Victor Dubuisson on the 23rd hole. **Teams:** Presidents Cup (2): 2011-13 (4-4-2). World Cup: 2013 (won in 2013 w/A. Scott). **OWR Best:** 4 - Feb, 2014.

PGA Tour Wins (2): 2010: Byron Nelson Classic (HP)   **2014**: WGC-Match Play.
Other Wins: 1 Web.com (2007)   +   World Cup (Individual): 2013.
Amateur Wins: Queensland Am (2): 2004-06   Australian Boys: 2004   New Zealand Under 19: 2004   Junior World (15-17): 2004   Dunes Medal: 2005   Australian Am Stroke Play: 2006   Master of the Amateurs: 2006.

	06	07	08	09	10	11	12	13	14
Masters	-	-	-	-	-	T2	WD	3	T20
US Open	-	-	-	-	-	2	T59	T2	T4
British	-	-	-	-	T60	T30	-	T32	T58
PGA	-	-	-	-	T10	MC	MC	T8	T15
Money (A)	-	-	136	69	21	9	88	12	16
OWR	641	175	224	140	38	8	37	11	8

2014: PGA: 15 st / 14 ct / 6 t10. (Won WGC-Match Play, T2 Farmers, T2 Barclays, T4 US Open, T4 Tour Champ, etc.). Logged a big PGA Tour win at the WGC-Match Play and finished 10th in FedEx Cup points despite a springtime thumb injury. Logged top 10s at three of four FedEx Cup Playoffs events.
OUTLOOK: At age 27, he's clearly established among the game's elite young talents – but one still senses that he can win a lot more often than he has. Mixes an elite power game with a deft touch around the greens, and has generally held up well under Sunday afternoon, big-event pressure. Though his iron game lags somewhat behind his other components statistically, his physical tools are matched by few. He enters 2015 in good form and with his big event track record, seems ready to win more regularly - and perhaps at a Major championship? - any minute now.

STATS: Driving Distance: A+   Driving Accuracy: C-   GIR: B-   Short Game: A   Putting: A

De Jonge, Brendon Russell (Zimbabwe) (34)
b. Harare, Zimbabwe 7/18/1980. 6'0" 230 lbs. Two-time All-American at Virginia Tech U. TP: 2003. Winner of the 1999 Zimbabwe Amateur by a record 14 shots (and the nation's #1-ranked amateur) prior to becoming a two-time All-American at Virginia Tech. Upon turning pro, played the Web.com Tour from 2004-2006, then bounced back and forth from the PGA Tour multiple

De Jonge, Brendon Russell, Cont'd

times (T5 at 2009 Q School). Eventually caught on in 2010 and '11 when, though winless, he logged a combined 10 top-10 finishes and ranked 34th and 76th in PGA Tour winnings. Added a combined eight top 10s and 24 top 25s during 2012 and '13, when he remained winless but finished 39th and 42nd in earnings. **Teams:** Eisenhower Trophy: 2000. Presidents Cup: 2013 (2-3-0). World Cup (2): 2011-13. **OWR Best:** 58 - Dec, 2013.

Other Wins: 1 Web.com (2008).

Amateur Wins: Zimbabwe Am: 1999.

	07	08	09	10	11	12	13	14
Masters	-	-	-	-	-	-	-	T37
US Open	-	-	-	T33	-	-	-	T28
British	-	-	-	-	-	-	WD	MC
PGA	-	-	-	T48	T26	T54	T33	T41
Money (A)	155	-	139	34	76	39	42	87
OWR	509	212	319	104	144	83	58	83

2014: PGA: 31 st / 24 ct / 2 t10. (T6 Wells Fargo, T8 Quicken Loans). Slipped marginally, logging only two top 10s (despite making 24 cuts) and dropping from 26th to 91st in FedEx Cup points. Remained a PGA Tour ironman, making a robust 31 starts.

OUTLOOK: One of the PGA Tour's steadiest players and a picture of consistent accuracy, with 2014 numbers that included 17 in Driving Accuracy, 22 in Total Driving, 54 in Ball Striking - though most of these (as well as 86 in Proximity to Hole) were all down slightly. At age 33, he should just be entering his prime years, but at this stage he remains a world-class check casher. A 2014 final round scoring rank of 138 didn't help.

STATS: Driving Distance: B-   Driving Accuracy: A-   GIR: A- ⇩   Short Game: B+   Putting: B

De la Riva, Eduardo (Spain) (32)

b. Barcelona, Spain 6/11/1982. 5'7" 140 lbs. TP: 2001. Two-time Spanish Junior champion who made a brief visit to the European Tour in 2003 before repairing to the Challenge Tour and European mini-tours. Revived his career with a Challenge Tour win in 2012, then joined the E Tour (via Q School) for 2013, where he lost a three-way playoff to Scott Jamieson in his first start, the rain-shortened, 36-hole Nelson Mandela Championship. **Teams:** Eisenhower Trophy: 2000. **OWR Best:** 127 - Jul, 2013.

Other Wins: 1 Euro Challenge (2012)   +   Peugeot Open (France): 2002.

Amateur Wins: Spanish Jr (2): 1997-99.

	03	04	05	06	07	08	09	10	11	12	13	14
Masters	-	-	-	-	-	-	-	-	-	-	-	-
US Open	-	-	-	-	-	-	-	-	-	-	-	-
British	-	-	-	-	-	-	-	-	-	-	T15	-
PGA	-	-	-	-	-	-	-	-	-	-	-	-
Money (E)	222	-	-	-	-	-	-	-	-	-	58	114
OWR	971	-	-	-	-	-	-	595	185	152	321	

2014: E: 27 st / 15 ct / 3 t10. (T7 Lyoness, T9 Hong Kong, T10 Malaysian). Finished 114th in $$$ before regaining his card via Q School.

OUTLOOK: A full decade after taking his first fledgling shot at the E Tour, made good on his second opportunity, but slipped as a sophomore. At this point his 2013 campaign looks like an outlier, but he did play his way through Q School and will get another shot in 2015.

STATS (LTD): Driving Distance: C   Driving Accuracy: A-   GIR: A-   Short Game: B   Putting: C-

---

DeLaet, Graham Norman (Canada) (32)

b. Weyburn, Saskatchewan, Canada 1/22/1982. 5'11" 165 lbs. College: Boise St. TP: 2006. Former top Canadian amateur prospect who first came to professional note in 2009, winning twice (and claiming the Order of Merit title) on the Canadian Tour, while also logging his first major tour win at South Africa's BMG Classic. Tied for 8th at the 2009 PGA Tour Q School, then kept his card in 2010 before missing much of 2011 with back problems. Successfully converted a Medical Exemption in 2012, finishing 95th in PGA Tour $$$, before having a breakout 2013, climbing to 21st in $$$. Followed that up with a 2014 campaign which, though winless, saw him remain firmly entrenched among the world top 50. **Teams:** Presidents Cup: 2013 (3-1-1). World Cup (2): 2008-09. **OWR Best:** 26 - Feb, 2014.

Sunshine Tour Wins (1): 2009: BMG Classic (54H).

Other Wins: Montreal Open (Canada): 2008   ATB Financial Classic (Canada): 2009   Tour Players Cup (Canada): 2009.

Amateur Wins: Saskatchewan Am (2): 2005-06.

	09	10	11	12	13	14
Masters	-	-	-	-	-	MC
US Open	-	-	-	-	-	MC
British	-	-	-	-	83	MC
PGA	-	-	-	-	MC	T15
Money (A)	-	100	-	95	21	30
OWR	213	192	612	177	36	57

2014: PGA: 24 st / 18 ct / 7 t10. (T2 Farmers, T2 Phoenix, T6 WGC-HSBC, T7 CIMB, T7 Byron Nelson, etc.). Slipped from his lofty perch of 2013, but only slightly. Once again logged seven top 10s but slipped from 8th to 37th in FedEx Cup points - and, unfortunately, remained winless.

OUTLOOK: Retained his massive statistical gains of 2013 surprisingly well, ranking 3 in GIR, 9 in Total Driving, 2 in Ball Striking, as well as 10 in the new Strokes Gained Tee To Green category. But his one notable decline came in SGP, from 76 to 118. As noted a year ago, if he can sustain such numbers going forward, he'll be a star for a long time – but he needs a bigger win than a 54-hole Sunshine Tour event atop his résumé.

STATS: Driving Distance: A+   Driving Accuracy: B+   GIR: A+   Short Game: B   Putting: B

Derksen, Robert-Jan (Netherlands) (40)

b. Nijmegen, Netherlands 1/3/1974. 6'1" 175 lbs. TP: 1996. After winning the Dutch Amateur for four years in succession, struggled for five years on the European and Challenge Tours before shocking the golfing world by beating Ernie Els head-to-head to win the 2003 Dubai Classic. Somewhat validated this victory two years later by claiming the 2005 Madeira Islands Open, and has

Derksen, Robert-Jan, Cont'd

remained a steady but unspectacular E Tour $$$ earner since. Announced his retirement at the end of 2014. **Teams:** Eisenhower Trophy: 1994. World Cup (6): 2001-04-05-07-11-13. **OWR Best:** 114 - Jun, 2008.

European Tour Wins (2): 2003: Dubai Classic **2005:** Madeira Islands Open.

Amateur Wins: Dutch Amateur (4): 1993-94-95-96 – Dutch Am Stroke Play: 1996.

	98	99	00	01	02	03	04	05	06	07	08	09	10	11	12	13	14
Masters	-	-	-	-	-	-	-	-	-	-	-	-	-	-	-	-	-
US Open	-	-	-	-	-	-	-	-	-	-	-	-	-	-	-	-	-
British	-	-	-	-	-	MC	-	-	-	-	-	-	-	-	-	-	-
PGA	-	-	-	-	-	-	-	-	-	-	-	-	-	-	-	-	-
Money (E)	166	142	-	-	149	40	63	56	86	36	54	67	54	79	106	74	75
OWR	787	553	614	539	559	211	225	193	303	142	154	154	116	208	401	232	217

2014: E: 22 st / 17 ct / 3 t10. (4 Hong Kong, 4 Nordea, T10 Joburg). Logged three top 10s and retained his card for the 11th straight year.

OUTLOOK: Despite still playing well, announced his retirement at the end of 2014 - but we'll see if he makes sporadic appearances going forward.

STATS: Driving Distance: C- Driving Accuracy: B+ GIR: B Short Game: B- Putting: B-

---

DiMarco, Christian Dean (USA) (46)

b. Huntington, NY 4/23/1968. 6'0" 180 lbs. Two-time All-American at U of Florida. TP: 1990. Spent 1991 and 1993 on the Web.com Tour (while winning the Canadian Tour's Order of Merit in 1992), with 9th-place $$$ in 1993 earning PGA Tour privileges. Finished 85th in $$$ in 1994 as a PGA Tour rookie, fell apart in 1995 and '96 and eventually returned to the Tour via a 3rd-pace season on the Web.com in 1997. Thereafter became one of the PGA Tour's more consistent performers, finishing among the top 20 money winners from 2000-2005 while winning thrice, at the 2000 Pennsylvania Classic, the 2001 Buick Challenge (in a playoff with David Duval) and the 2002 Phoenix Open. Lost two heartbreaking Majors: the 2004 PGA Championship in a three-hole playoff with winner Vijay Singh and Justin Leonard, and the 2005 Masters in sudden-death to Tiger Woods. Also won the 2006 Abu Dhabi Championship on the European Tour. Suffered shoulder problems during a sub-par 2007 and struggled significantly thereafter. Widely recognized as the first high-profile user of the "claw" putting grip, a hands-split style that improved his stroke dramatically. His last medal play top 10 was a T8 at the 2012 John Deere. **Teams:** Ryder Cup (2): 2004-06 (O: 2-4-2, S: 1-1-0). Presidents Cup (2): 2003-05 (6-3-1). **OWR Best:** 6 - May, 2005.

PGA Tour Wins (3): 2000: Pennsylvania Classic (SEI) **2001:** Buick Challenge **2002:** Phoenix Open.

European Tour Wins (1): 2006: Abu Dhabi Championship.

Other Wins: 1 Web.com (1997) + Quebec Open (Canada): 1996 CVS Classic (2): 2002 (w/D.Hart)-05 (w/F.Funk).

Amateur Wins: Western Am: 1988 – Monroe Inv: 1988.

	94	95	96	97	98	99	00	01	02	03	04	05	06	07	08	09	10	11	12	13	14
Masters	-	-	-	-	-	-	-	T10	T12	WD	T6	2P	MC	MC	-	-	-	-	-	-	-
US Open	-	-	-	-	T32	-	-	T16	T24	T35	T9	MC	MC	T45	-	-	-	-	-	-	-
British	-	-	-	-	-	-	MC	T47	T66	MC	T63	T67	2	T23	-	-	-	-	-	-	-
PGA	-	-	-	-	-	T41	T15	T16	T39	56	T2P	MC	T12	MC	T31	-	-	-	-	-	-
Money (A)	85	174	245*	-	111	62	19	12	11	18	12	7	53	107	146	135	165	113	152	192*	258*
OWR	249	376	687	-	304	161	66	20	12	26	15	10	20	79	235	332	491	362	430	668	1182

2014: PGA: 7 st / 1 ct / 0 t10. (T78 Puerto Rico). Playing on Past Champion status, got only three starts and finished 256th in FedEx Cup points.

OUTLOOK: Will again be resigned to playing on Past Champion status – but he may be more focused on a budding broadcasting career anyway.

STATS: Driving Distance: D Driving Accuracy: A GIR: C Short Game: B Putting: C+

Dinwiddie, Robert (England) (32)

b. Dumfries, Scotland 12/29/1982. 6'1" 180 lbs. College: Tennessee St. TP: 2006. Had a solid but unspectacular collegiate career in America but at home, he played in the 2005 Walker Cup and became the rare man to win the English, Scottish and Welsh Amateur Stroke Play titles, holding them simultaneously during 2006. Made a splash on the 2007 Challenge Tour, winning twice and finishing 8th in $$$. But other than finishing 72nd in $$$ in 2008, has yet to truly stick on the E Tour, playing his way back from the Challenge Tour again in 2013. **Teams:** Walker Cup: 2005 (1-1-1). **OWR Best:** 141 - Jul, 2008.

Other Wins: 3 Euro Challenge (2007-2010).

Amateur Wins: Welsh Am Stroke Play: 2005 Scottish Am Stroke Play: 2005 Simon Bolivar Cup: 2005 English Am Stroke Play: 2006.

	07	08	09	10	11	12	13	14
Masters	-	-	-	-	-	-	-	-
US Open	-	T36	-	-	MC	-	-	-
British	-	-	-	-	-	-	-	-
PGA	-	-	-	-	-	-	-	-
Money (E)	-	72	146	170*	141	-	-	-
OWR	172	207	400	264	481	712	339	649

2014: Made only 11 E Tour starts for undisclosed reasons, his best finish being a T22 at the Joburg Open.

OUTLOOK: Continues in that gray area between the E and Challenge Tours, with his status uncertain at the dawn of 2015.

STATS: Driving Distance: -- Driving Accuracy: -- GIR: -- Short Game: -- Putting: --

---

Doak, Christopher (Scotland) (37)

b. Glasgow, Scotland 12/19/1977. 6'0" 195 lbs. TP: 1997. A bit of a late bloomer on the European Tour, having spent most of his 20s as a force on mini-tours and in lesser events in his native Scotland. Logged three top 10s in 101 E Tour events through 2014 (best: 5th at the 2014 Dunhill Links Championship), peaking in the latter year by finishing 71st in $$$. **OWR Best:** 215 - Oct, 2012.

Other Wins: 1 Euro Challenge (2012) + Royal Dornoch Young Masters: 1999 Northern Open (Scotland)(2): 2005-08 Scottish PGA: 2010.

Doak, Christopher, Cont'd

	09	10	11	12	13	14
Masters	-	-	-	-	-	-
US Open	-	-	-	-	-	-
British	-	-	-	-	-	-
PGA	-	-	-	-	-	-
Money (E)	168	288*	240*	183*	101	71
OWR	692	831	439	230	322	317

2014: E: 31 st / 15 ct / 1 t10. (5 Dunhill Links). Logged only one top 10 in 31 starts but easily retained his card, finishing 71st in $$$.

OUTLOOK: In his late 30s, put together his two best seasons back-to-back in 2013 and '14. Is an above-the-media ball striker from tee to green but is held back by his putter. Should be in his peak years - but realistically his résumé suggests that he may have already reached it

STATS: Driving Distance: B+   Driving Accuracy: B+   GIR: B+   Short Game: B   Putting: C

Dodt, Andrew (Australia) (28)

b. Gatton, Queensland, Australia 01/26/1986. 6'1" 185 lbs. TP: 2007. A once-touted prospect who enjoyed a strong amateur career before turning pro at age 20. Initially toiled on the Asian Tour where he claimed a one-shot win over Richard Finch at the E Tour co-sanctioned 2010 Avantha Masters. Largely struggled for several years thereafter before logging two aces in the second round of the E Tour's 2013 Nordea Masters, an estimated 1-in-69 million occurrence. Ended a four-year drought by winning the 2014 Queensland Open, edging Tom Bond by two. Played mostly in Asia in 2014, but graduated E Tour Q School for 2015. **OWR Best**: 105 - Apr, 2010.

European Tour Wins (1): 2010: Avantha Masters.
Australasian Tour Wins (1): 2014: Queensland Open (Isuzu).
Amateur Wins: Australian Am Stroke Play: 2007   Asia-Pacific Nomura Cup (Individual): 2007   Keperra Bowl: 2007   Malaysian Am Stroke Play: 2006   Queensland Jr (2): 2003-04.

	07	08	09	10	11	12	13	14
Masters	-	-	-	-	-	-	-	-
US Open	-	-	-	-	-	-	-	-
British	-	-	-	-	-	-	-	-
PGA	-	-	-	-	-	-	-	-
Money (E)	-	-	-	70	160	118	149	213*
Money (As)	-	43	15	-	-	-	48*	30
OWR	-	310	281	181	507	580	646	303

2014: ASIA: 12 st / 9 ct / 2 t10. (T2 Kings Cup, T7 Solaire). Remained exclusively in the Far East, primarily in Asia but also at home, where he made four Australasian starts, including a win in Queensland. Played successfully through E Tour Q School in the fall.

OUTLOOK: Strong player who, save for his rookie year (in which more than half of his official $$$ came from his lone professional win), has struggled significantly on the European Tour. Played in Asia in 2014 but now returns to Europe again, perhaps slightly better prepared.

STATS: Driving Distance: B+   Driving Accuracy: C+   GIR: B   Short Game: B-   Putting: C+

Donald, Luke Campbell (England) (36)

b. Hempstead, England 12/7/1977. 5'9" 160 lbs. Four-time All-American, NCAA individual champion (1999), Nicklaus (1999) and Haskins (1999) Awards winner at Northwestern U. TP: 2001. Went a combined 7-1 in leading GB & I to back-to-back Walker Cup triumphs in 1999 and '01. Winner as a PGA Tour rookie (at the rain-shortened 2002 Southern Farm Classic) before blossoming with two European Tour triumphs (including a five-shot victory over Miguel Ángel Jiménez at the European Masters) in 2004. Settling regularly into the PGA Tour, he also claimed the 2006 Honda Classic (by two over Geoff Ogilvy) and finished T3 at the 2006 PGA Championship after being tied with Tiger Woods for the 54-hole lead. Missed the second half of 2008 after wrist surgery. Stepped up big in 2010, logging five top-3 finishes in America while also winning the E Tour's Madrid Open one week after a double bogey at the 71st cost him the BMW PGA Championship. Enjoyed an historic 2011, winning twice on both the PGA and European Tours, becoming the first man ever to top both money lists and ascending to number one in the OWR on May 30th. 2011 wins: the WGC Match Play (3 & 2 over Martin Kaymer), the E Tour's BMW PGA Championship (in a playoff with Lee Westwood), the rain-shortened Scottish Open and, with a spectacular closing 64, the season-ending Children's Miracle Network Classic, which clinched the U.S. $$$ title. Also logged a remarkable 20 top-10 finishes worldwide. After being bumped from the number one spot in March of 2012, re-took it two weeks later by winning the Transitions Championship in a four-man playoff. Defended his BMW PGA title in 2012 (in a four-shot runaway) and later took his first victory in Japan, by five shots at the Dunlop Phoenix (a title he would successfully defend in 2013). Slipped significantly in 2013 and '14, however. dropping as far as 72nd in PGA Tour $$$. **Awards**: PGA Tour Player of the Year: 2010. E Tour Golfer of the Year: 2011. Vardon Trophy: 2011. **Teams**: Walker Cup (2): 1999-01 (7-1-0). Eisenhower Trophy (2): 1998-00. Palmer Cup (2): 1998-99. Ryder Cup (4): 2004-06-10-12 (O: 10-4-1, S: 3-1-0). World Cup (3): 2004-05-06 (won in '04 w/P.Casey). **OWR Best**: 1 - May, 2011.

PGA Tour Wins (5): 2002: Southern Farm Classic (54H) **2006**: Honda Classic **2011**: WGC-Match Play, Walt Disney Classic (Children's Miracle) **2012**: Transitions Championship.

European Tour Wins (6): 2004: Scandinavian Masters, European Masters **2010**: Madrid Masters **2011**: BMW PGA, Scottish Open (54H) **2012**: BMW PGA.

Japan Tour Wins (2): 2012: Dunlop Phoenix **2013**: Dunlop Phoenix.

Other Wins: Target World Challenge: 2005.

Amateur Wins: Berkhamstead Trophy: 1996   Sunningdale Foursomes: 1996   Lagonda Trophy: 1997   Midland Am Stroke Play: 1998   NCAA Individual: 1999   Northeast Am (2): 2000-01.

	99	00	01	02	03	04	05	06	07	08	09	10	11	12	13	14
Masters	-	-	-	-	-	-	T3	T42	T10	MC	T38	MC	T4	T32	T25	MC
US Open	-	-	-	T18	-	-	T57	T12	MC	WD	MC	T47	T45	MC	T8	MC
British	MC	MC	-	MC	MC	MC	T52	T35	T63	-	T5	T11	MC	T5	MC	T64
PGA	-	-	-	-	T23	T24	T66	T3	T32	-	T43	MC	T8	T32	MC	T41
Money (A)	Am	Am	-	58	90	35	17	9	29	67*	34	7	1	14	36	72
Money (E)	Am	Am	-	-	115	20	12	7	38	-	55	15	1	7	43*	50
OWR	741	920	585	93	130	26	13	9	17	31	28	9	1	2	17	33

Donald, Luke Campbell, Cont'd

2014: PGA: 17 st / 13 ct / 3 t10. (2 Heritage, T4 Valspar, T8 Honda). Another disappointing year for the former world #1 as he went winless and slipped to 89th in FedEx Cup points. Also made four non-Major/WGC European Tour starts (Best: T3 at BMW PGA Championship - his lone top 10).

OUTLOOK: Begins 2015 in middling form, having been passed over as a Ryder Cup captain's pick, and having failed to log a worldwide top 10 finish from May through November. Has seen statistical declines across the board since his landmark 2011 season, the most damaging being an alarming GIR decline: 41 in 2011, 100 in 2012, 156 in 2013, and 144 in 2014. Though he retains elite skills on and around the green, it's tough to remain at the top when struggling from tee–to–green (e.g., 153 in Ball Striking) - but with his overall talent, plenty of good golf likely still lies ahead.

STATS: Driving Distance: C-   Driving Accuracy: B+   GIR: B-   Short Game: A   Putting: A+

Donaldson, Jamie Ross (Wales) (39)
b. Pontypridd, Wales 10/19/1975. 5'11" 175 lbs. TP: 2000. Following a solid amateur career devoid of major victories, finished 2nd in 2001 Challenge Tour $$$ to reach the E Tour. Returned to the Challenge Tour in 2007, finished 4th in $$$ and returned to the E Tour for good. Scored his maiden E Tour win at the 2012 Irish Open at Portmarnock, closing in 66 to win by four. Backed it up early in 2013 by winning the Abu Dhabi Championship, edging Thorbjørn Olesen and Justin Rose by one. Won for the third straight year in 2014, claiming the inaugural Czech Masters by two over fellow Welshman Bradley Dredge. **Teams:** Eisenhower Trophy: 2000. Ryder Cup: 2014 (O: 3-1-0, S: 1-0-0). Seve Trophy (2): 2011-13. World Cup (2): 2009-11. **OWR Best:** 23 - Nov, 2014.

European Tour Wins (3): 2012: Irish Open   **2013**: Abu Dhabi Championship   **2014**: Czech Masters.

Other Wins: 3 Euro Challenge (2001-2007)   +   Mauritius Open: 2008.

	01	02	03	04	05	06	07	08	09	10	11	12	13	14
Masters	-	-	-	-	-	-	-	-	-	-	-	-	MC	T14
US Open	-	-	-	-	-	-	-	-	-	-	-	-	T32	MC
British	-	-	-	-	-	MC	-	-	-	-	-	T60	T32	MC
PGA	-	-	-	-	-	-	-	-	-	-	MC	T7	WD	T24
Money (E)	-	90	58	179*	79	161	229*	89	59	46	38	19	5	4
OWR	184	286	222	308	264	582	243	261	164	100	86	47	26	24

2014: E: 25 st / 21 ct / 8 t10. (Won Czech Masters, T2 Nedbank, T4 Wales, T4 BMW Masters, T5 BMW Int'l, etc.). Followed up a career-best year with an equally stellar campaign, winning in the Czech Republic, finishing 4th in $$$ and being a captain's pick to his first Ryder Cup side.

OUTLOOK: After several up-and-down years, hit his stride in 2009 and hasn't looked back, winning thrice and logging back-to-back top-5 finishes in the E Tour Order of Merit. Riding a strong and balanced skill set, he is today a frequent E Tour contender and a very steady hand, as evidenced by his 16 top 25s in 2014 (including nine straight to close the year). His formula is working well - and figures continue doing so for several years to come.

STATS: Driving Distance: B+   Driving Accuracy: B-   GIR: B+   Short Game: B+   Putting: A-

---

Dougherty, Nicholas (England) (32)
b. Liverpool, England 5/24/1982. 6'1" 185 lbs. TP: 2001. A protégé of Nick Faldo who enjoyed a strong amateur career, then a promising start on the European Tour. Claimed his first E Tour victory via a five-shot runaway at the 2005 Singapore Masters. Later added the 2007 Dunhill Links Championship (where he edged Justin Rose by two, at St Andrews) and the 2009 BMW International in Germany, where he closed with a 64 to win by one. Suffered a huge loss of form in 2010 and has plummeted since. **Awards:** E Tour Rookie of the Year: 2002. **Teams:** Walker Cup: 2001 (3-1-0). Seve Trophy (3): 2005-07-09. **OWR Best:** 46 - Feb, 2008.

European Tour Wins (3): 2005: Singapore Masters   **2007**: Dunhill Links Championship   **2009**: BMW Int'l.

Amateur Wins: European Under-21s: 1999   World Boys: 1999   Guatamalan Am: 2000   Lake Maquarie Am: 2001.

	02	03	04	05	06	07	08	09	10	11	12	13	14
Masters	-	-	-	-	-	-	T33	-	-	-	-	-	-
US Open	-	-	-	T52	MC	T7	MC	-	-	-	-	-	-
British	-	-	-	-	MC	T42	T78	T38	-	-	-	-	-
PGA	-	-	-	MC	MC	MC	MC	MC	-	-	-	-	-
Money (E)	36	60	97	15	39	11	44	35	121	268	294*	-	-
OWR	174	275	360	75	115	48	78	111	322	984	649	922	1136

2014: Played limited competitive golf, making seven E Tour starts (best: T54 at Laguna National) and three on the Challenge circuit.

OUTLOOK: One assumes the talent is still there – but after his last three years, hopes of a turnaround must be dwindling badly at this point.

STATS (LTD): Driving Distance: B-   Driving Accuracy: D   GIR: C-   Short Game: B   Putting: B

Dredge, Bradley (Wales) (41)
b. Tredegar, Wales 7/6/1973. 6'0" 170 lbs. TP: 1996. Arrived as one of Wales' stronger modern prospects, but took until his early 30s to find his legs on the E Tour. Claimed his first victory in 2003 via an eight-shot runaway at the light-field Madeira Islands Open. Later won the 2005 World Cup with Stephen Dodd before breaking through for a second eight-shot triumph, this time in 2006 over Francesco Molinari and Marcel Siem at the more prestigious European Masters. Has remained a steady earner but less of a contender, logging only one E Tour top 10 from 2011-2013. Was twice a runner-up (in back-to-back weeks) during a solid comeback season in 2014. **Teams:** Walker Cup: 1993 (0-3-0). Eisenhower Trophy: 2002. Seve Trophy (2): 2005-07. World Cup (7): 2002-03-04-05-06-07-08 (won in '05 w/S.Dodd). **OWR Best:** 46 - Sep, 2007.

European Tour Wins (2): 2003: Madeira Islands Open   **2006**: European Masters.

Other Wins: 2 Euro Challenge (1997-1999).

Amateur Wins: Welsh Boys: 1991   Welsh Am: 1993.

	98	99	00	01	02	03	04	05	06	07	08	09	10	11	12	13	14
Masters	-	-	-	-	-	-	-	-	-	T44	-	-	-	-	-	-	-
US Open	-	-	-	-	-	-	-	-	-	-	-	-	-	-	-	-	-
British	MC	-	-	-	T28	MC	-	-	MC	MC	-	-	T27	-	-	-	-
PGA	-	-	-	-	-	-	MC	-	-	MC	MC	-	-	-	-	-	-
Money (E)	157	-	107	72	18	42	60	16	22	23	74	57	63	96	125	259*	81
OWR	700	734	389	239	64	83	198	83	50	53	157	163	154	244	496	888	234

Dredge, Bradley, Cont'd

2014: E: 9 st / 9 ct / 3 t10. (2 Denmark, 2 Czech Masters, T10 NH Collection). Recorded a wild comeback year, making only nine starts on limited status, yet easily regaining playing privileges behind back-to-back runner-ups and an earlier top 10 in the Tour's three first-year events.

OUTLOOK: Returned from an injury-riddled 2013 to roar back into significance. At 41, continued success is hardly a given, but his skill set remains largely intact, and he has a long record as a check casher. Was 2014 a fluke? Perhaps somewhat, but he could stick around a little longer.

STATS: Driving Distance: B   Driving Accuracy: C+   GIR: C+   Short Game: B-   Putting: B+

Driscoll, James Edward (USA) (37)
b. Boston, MA 10/9/1977. 6'0" 190 lbs. College: U of Virginia. TP: 2001. An AJGA All-American. Enjoyed a very strong amateur career including losing to Jeff Quinney in finals of the 2000 U.S. Amateur after upsetting Luke Donald in the semis. Graduated from the Web.com Tour in both 2004 (7th) and 2007 (24th), and has played the PGA Tour full-time ever since. Winless on Tour but lost playoffs at the 2005 New Orleans Classic and the 2009 Texas Open. **Teams:** Walker Cup: 2001 (0-3-0). **OWR Best:** 119 - May, 2005.

Other Wins: 1 Web.com (2004).

Amateur Wins: North & South Am: 1999   —   New England Am: 1995   Western Jr: 1995   Massachusetts Am (2): 1996-98.

	01	02	03	04	05	06	07	08	09	10	11	12	13	14
Masters	MC	-	-	-	-	-	-	-	-	-	-	-	-	-
US Open	-	-	-	-	MC	-	-	-	-	-	-	-	-	-
British	-	-	-	-	-	-	-	-	MC	-	-	MC	-	-
PGA	-	-	-	-	-	-	-	-	-	-	-	-	-	-
Money (A)	-	-	-	-	100	187	-	141	104	157	114	122	101	162
OWR	-	684	740	368	199	401	396	376	362	400	370	338	262	534

2014: PGA: 25 st / 11 ct / 0 t10. (T18 Humana). Finished 155th in FedEx Cup points, then failed to play his way back via the Web.com Finals.

OUTLOOK: Was well established as a steady player – albeit one walking close to the line - prior to losing his status at the end of 2014. A reliably good putter whose tee-to-green game has never ranked above the median. At age 37, he'll try to climb his way back from the Web.com Tour.

STATS: Driving Distance: B   Driving Accuracy: C-   GIR: C-   Short Game: B-   Putting: A-

---

Drysdale, David (Scotland) (39)
b. Edinburgh, Scotland 3/19/1975. 6'0" 165 lbs. TP: 1995. Journeyman who played his way through Q School four times between 2001-2008 and has logged a pair of second-place finishes on the E Tour (the 2006 Russian Open and the 2009 Open de Andalucia). Has retained his card every year since 2008. **Teams:** World Cup: 2009. **OWR Best:** 142 - Oct, 2009.

Other Wins: 2 Euro Challenge (2004-2006).

	02	03	04	05	06	07	08	09	10	11	12	13	14
Masters	-	-	-	-	-	-	-	-	-	-	-	-	-
US Open	-	-	-	-	-	-	-	-	-	-	-	-	-
British	-	-	-	-	-	-	-	T60	-	-	-	-	-
PGA	-	-	-	-	-	-	-	-	-	-	-	-	-
Money (E)	114	148	206*	117	119	195	151	48	73	104	58	80	102
OWR	381	515	508	356	234	599	446	160	220	355	217	311	374

2014: E: 32 st / 19 ct / 2 t10. (T4 Perth, T8 Laguna). Slipped modestly (e.g., only two top 10s) but still retained his card, finishing 102nd in $$$.

OUTLOOK: Despite below-the-median length and putting numbers, has emerged as a steady E Tour earner on the strength of a very accurate tee-to-green game. Given his age, he might be due for one hot, win-producing run before he's finished – but likely be in a lesser (or opposite) event.

STATS: Driving Distance: C+   Driving Accuracy: A-   GIR: B+   Short Game: B   Putting: B-

---

DuBuisson, Victor (France) (24)
b. Cannes, France 4/22/1990. 6'0" 165 lbs. TP: 2010. Top French prospect who came to prominence in 2009 when he won the European Amateur and spent six weeks as the world's #1-ranked amateur beginning in November. Finished T3 in the Challenge Tour's 2009 EurOpen de Lyon while still an amateur. Turned professional after playing in the 2010 British Open and steadily improved his earnings through 2011 and '12. Scored a major breakthrough by winning the 2013 Turkish Airlines Open, holding off a strong field in the penultimate event of the E Tour's inaugural Final Series. Stepped onto the world stage by losing an epic 23-hole final to Jason Day at the 2014 WGC-Match Play, then went on to record his second straight top-10 finish in the E Tour Order of Merit and appear in his first Ryder Cup match. **Teams:** Eisenhower Trophy: 2008. Ryder Cup: 2014 (O: 2-0-1, S: 0-0-1). World Cup: 2013. **OWR Best:** 17 - Nov, 2014.

European Tour Wins (1): 2013: Turkish Airlines Open.

Other Wins: Allianz Finale de Barbaroux (France): 2010.

Amateur Wins: European Am: 2009   —   French Closed Am: 2006   Mexican Am: 2008   Trophée des Regions: 2009.

	10	11	12	13	14
Masters	-	-	-	-	MC
US Open	-	-	-	-	T28
British	MC	-	-	-	**T9**
PGA	-	-	-	-	**T7**
Money (E)	220*	106	52	**6**	**5**
OWR	866	259	132	32	17

2014: E: 23 st / 18 ct / 8 t10. (2P Nordea, 2 WGC-Match Play, 2 Perth, T5 Volvo Champs, T5 World Match Play, etc.). Followed up his breakout year with a season that had everything except a win. Also made three non-co-sanctioned starts on the PGA Tour (best: T13 AT&T Pebble Beach Pro-Am).

OUTLOOK: Was on a sharply upward trajectory over his two full seasons and has now seemingly settled in at the top of the E Tour, riding a game built around major power and some very skillful iron play to two straight top-10 $$$ rankings and an appearance on his first Ryder Cup side. Looks like a long-term force to be reckoned with on the international stage - though it must be noted that he still has only one major tour win through 2014.

STATS: Driving Distance: A   Driving Accuracy: C+   GIR: A-   Short Game: B   Putting: B

Dufner, Jason Christopher (USA) (37)   b. Cleveland, OH 3/24/1977. 5'10" 180 lbs. College: Auburn U. TP: 2000.   Save for one unsuccessful foray onto the PGA Tour (2004), was a Web.com Tour regular from 2001-2006, winning twice. Struggled again on the PGA Tour in 2007 and '08 before hitting stride in 2009 (33rd in $$$), then following it up with a solid 2010 (80th). Nearly achieved immortality at the 2011 PGA Championship at the Atlanta Athletic Club, leading by five shots with four holes to play before being caught by Keegan Bradley, then losing a three-hole aggregate playoff. Broke through for his first PGA Tour victory at the 2012 Zurich Classic of New Orleans, where he beat Ernie Els on the second hole of sudden death. Claimed his second Tour victory just three weeks later, birdieing the 72nd to win the Byron Nelson Championship. Jumped to genuine international stardom upon logging his first Major championship win at the 2013 PGA (Oak Hill), where he put on a tee-to-green clinic in edging Jim Furyk by two. Had a moderately disappointing 2014 season cut short by a neck injury during his defense of his PGA Championship title.
Teams: Ryder Cup: 2012 (O: 3-1-0, S: 1-0-0). Presidents Cup: 2013 (3-1-0).   **OWR Best:** 6 - Sep, 2012.

PGA Tour Wins (3): 2012: New Orleans Classic (Zurich), Byron Nelson Championship (HP)   **2013:** PGA Championship.
Other Wins: 2 Web.com (2001-2006).

	01	02	03	04	05	06	07	08	09	10	11	12	13	14
Masters	-	-	-	-	-	-	-	-	-	T30	-	T24	T20	MC
US Open	MC	-	-	-	-	T40	62	-	-	T33	MC	T4	T4	MC
British	-	-	-	-	-	-	-	-	-	MC	MC	T31	T26	T51
PGA	-	-	-	-	-	-	-	-	MC	T5	2P	T27	Win	WD
Money (A)	-	-	-	164	-	-	140	184	33	80	21	4	16	61
OWR	543	692	464	377	557	286	336	597	66	93	33	9	15	38

2014: PGA: 17 st / 13 ct / 4 t10. (2 Colonial, 5 T of C, T9 WGC-Match play, T9 WGC-Cadillac). In a year that was cut short by a lingering neck injury, slipped to 90th in FedEx Cup points and missed out on a Ryder Cup berth when his WD at the PGA knocked him from the top 10 of the points list.
OUTLOOK: Ball strikers like this tend not to disappear (except when injured), allowing them to regularly contend irrespective of an up-and-down putting stroke. Just entering the prime years of his late 30s, and seems to have the sort of low-key, not-too-full-of-himself temperament to weather the game's obvious ups and downs. Assuming his neck issues are soon heeled, a good bet to keep contending in big events, or anything played on mid-size, Major championship-type set-ups. And should he ever find some magic in that putter (167 in 2014 SGP, 142 in 2013), look out.
STATS: Driving Distance: B-   Driving Accuracy: A-   GIR: A   Short Game: B   Putting: C

Duke, Kenneth Wootson (USA) (45)   b. Hope, AR 1/29/1969. 6'1" 205 lbs. College: Henderson St (AR) U. TP: 1994. After competing on the Web.com Tour in 1995, spent several years playing in Canada (where he finished 1st in $$$ in 1999), South America and Asia. Returned to America in 2003 and finished T12 at Q School, but has bounced between the Web.com and PGA Tours ever since. Hit stride in 2007 and '08, when he finished 37th and 28th in PGA Tour earnings and logged three 2nd-place finishes: 2007 New Orleans, 2008 U.S. Bank and 2008 Ginn Sur Mer. Returned to the Web.com in 2010 and '11 but finished 7th in 2011 earnings to jump back to the big Tour in 2012. Broke through for his first PGA Tour win (at age 44, in his 187th start) at the 2013 Travelers Championship, beating Chris Stroud in a playoff. **OWR Best:** 70 - Jun, 2013.

PGA Tour Wins (1): 2013: Travelers Championship.
Other Wins: 2 Web.com (2006-2011)   +   Shell Payless Open (Canada): 1999   Bayer Championship (Canada): 1999.

	97	98	99	00	01	02	03	04	05	06	07	08	09	10	11	12	13	14
Masters	-	-	-	-	-	-	-	-	-	-	-	-	T35	-	-	-	-	MC
US Open	-	-	-	-	-	MC	-	-	-	-	T23	-	MC	-	-	-	-	MC
British	MC	-	-	-	-	-	-	-	-	-	-	-	MC	-	-	-	T64	-
PGA	-	-	-	-	-	-	-	-	-	-	T18	T13	MC	-	-	T62	T57	-
Money (A)	-	-	-	-	-	166	-	-	-	-	37	28	158	-	-	57	50	150
OWR	570	-	-	586	605	560	564	558	558	170	116	81	238	597	265	153	107	246

2014: PGA: 25 st / 16 ct / 0 t10. (T15 Shriners). Failed to log a top 10 while slipping from 67th to 157th in FedEx Cup points.
OUTLOOK: Though his 2013 Travelers victory proved that he can still win despite reduced length and fewer GIR, struggled a bit in 2014 as his putting numbers dipped (158 in SGP and 154 in Total Putting). Remains exempt through 2015 based on the Travelers win but with the odds hardly favoring a dramatic putting improvement at age 45, it may soon be time to start staying loose for the Champions Tour in 2019.
STATS: Driving Distance: C-   Driving Accuracy: A   GIR: B   Short Game: B+   Putting: B-

---

Durant, Joseph Scott (USA) (50)   b. Pensacola, FL 4/7/1964. 5'10" 170 lbs. Three-time NAIA All-American and individual champion (1987) at Huntington (AL) College. TP: 1987. Played five seasons on the Web.com Tour before latching onto the PGA Tour for good in 1997. Famously fine ball striker whose fate has long been determined by his putter. Debut win came at the 1998 Western Open, where he edged Vijay Singh with three late birdies. Claimed two victories (at the Bob Hope Desert Classic and the Doral Open) in early 2001, when he finished 14th in $$$. Actually placed higher on the money list (13th) during 2006, when he won the season-ending Walt Disney Classic by four. Has only once cracked the top 125 money winners since (124th in 2010). **Awards:** PGA Tour Comeback Player of the Year: 2001.   **OWR Best:** 27 - Feb, 2007.

PGA Tour Wins (4): 1998: Western Open (Motorola)   **2001:** Bob Hope Classic (90H), Doral Open (Genuity)   **2006:** Walt Disney Classic (Funai).
Other Wins: 1 Web.com (1996)   +   3 NGA/Hooters (2000-2004).
Amateur Wins: NAIA Individual: 1987.

	93	94	95	96	97	98	99	00	01	02	03	04	05	06	07	08	09	10	11	12	13	14
Masters	-	-	-	-	-	MC	-	MC	MC	-	-	-	-	-	MC	-	-	-	-	-	-	-
US Open	-	-	-	-	T32	MC	-	T24	MC	MC	-	-	-	-	MC	-	-	-	-	-	MC	-
British	-	-	-	-	-	MC	-	-	MC	T59	MC	-	MC	-	MC	-	-	-	-	-	-	-
PGA	-	-	-	-	-	T40	-	-	T51	T60	T39	MC	T72	-	T18	-	-	-	-	-	-	-
Money (A)	279	-	-	-	100	43	157	76	14	137	66	82	73	13	129	129	182	124	160	156	229*	163
OWR	-	-	-	-	266	85	167	208	39	152	129	120	113	32	85	304	585	321	423	434	542	540

2014: PGA: 15 st / 8 ct / 0 t10. (T11 Greenbrier). Finished 170th in FedEx Cup points; also made eight Champions Tour starts, finishing 31st in $$$.
OUTLOOK: Can play the PGA Tour on Past Champion status in 2015 but may head for the Champions, where he looked quite competitive (six top 10s in eight starts) after turning 50 last April. One of top ball strikers of his time who has waged a quarter-century battle with his putter.
STATS: Driving Distance: C   Driving Accuracy: A+   GIR: A+   Short Game: B-   Putting: D

Duval, David Robert (USA) (43)   b. Jacksonville, FL 11/9/1971. 6'0" 180 lbs. Four-time first-team All-American, Nicklaus (1993) and Haskins (1993) Awards winner at Georgia Tech. TP: 1993. Two-time AJGA All-American and 1989 AJGA Player Of The Year. Son of ex-Champions Tour player Bob Duval. As an amateur, led PGA Tour's 1992 Atlanta Classic through 54 holes before tying for 13th. Failed to secure PGA Tour privileges until 1995, then failed to win until late 1997 when the floodgates opened. Won 11 of 36 events between 10/1997 and 4/1999, claiming the Vardon Trophy in 1998 and the world's #1 ranking during March of 1999. Won three of the final four events of 1997 (the Michelob Championship, the Walt Disney Classic and the Tour Championship) and, following a four-win 1998, two of the first three in 1999 (the Mercedes Championships and the Bob Hope) – plus two more in succession (the Players Championship and the BellSouth Classic) in the spring. Won 1999 Bob Hope by famously closing with a 59, eagling the 72nd hole to edge Steve Pate by one. After several near misses at Augusta, claimed first Major title at the 2001 British Open, winning by three over Niclas Fasth at Royal Lytham & St Annes. Logged 61 top-10 finishes in 161 starts (37.9%) from 1995-2001. Back problems which began in 2000 soon led to a slump of epic proportion, resulting in a disappearance from the world's top 250 by late 2003, and out of the top 800 by late 2007. Nearly scored a comeback for the ages by tying for 2nd at the 2009 U.S. Open at Bethpage (two shots behind Lucas Glover), then lost in sudden death (to Dustin Johnson) at the 2010 AT&T Pro-Am. Save for finishing 106th in 2010, hasn't cracked the PGA Tour's top 125 in $$$ since 2002. **Awards:** Vardon Trophy: 1998. **Teams:** Walker Cup: 1991 (2-1-0). Eisenhower Trophy (2): 1990-92. Ryder Cup (2): 1999-02 (O: 1-3-2, S: 1-0-1). Presidents Cup (3): 1996-98-00 (7-6-1). World Cup (2): 2000-01 (won in '00 w/T.Woods). **OWR Best:** 1 - Mar, 1999.

PGA Tour Wins (13): 1997: Michelob Championship, Walt Disney Classic (Oldsmobile), Tour Championship **1998:** Tucson Open (Chrysler), Houston Open (Shell), World Series of Golf (NEC), Michelob Championship **1999:** Mercedes Championships, Bob Hope Classic (90H), Players Championship, Atlanta Classic (BellSouth) **2000:** Buick Challenge **2001:** British Open.
Japan Tour Wins (1): 2001: Dunlop Phoenix.
Other Wins: 2 Web.com (1993)   +   Fred Meyer Challenge: 1998 (w/J.Furyk)   Shark Shootout: 1999 (w/F.Couples).
Amateur Wins: Porter Cup: 1992   –   U.S. Junior Am: 1989   Northeast Am: 1992.

	90	91	92	93	94	95	96	97	98	99	00	01	02	03	04	05	06	07	08	09	10	11	12	13
Masters	-	-	-	-	-	-	T18	MC	T2	T6	T3	2	MC	MC	-	MC	MC	-	-	MC	-	-	-	-
US Open	T56	-	MC	-	-	T28	T67	T48	T7	T7	T8	T16	MC	MC	MC	MC	T16	-	-	T2	T70	-	-	-
British	-	-	-	-	-	T20	T14	T33	T11	T62	T11	Win	T22	MC	-	MC	T56	-	T39	MC	MC	MC	MC	MC
PGA	-	-	-	-	-	MC	T41	T13	MC	T10	-	T10	T34	WD	MC	MC	MC	-	-	-	-	-	-	-
Money (A)	Am	Am	Am	-	-	11	10	2	1	2	7	8	80	212	210*	260	172	222*	219	130	106	152	233	251*
OWR	614	-	472	454	436	33	19	12	3	2	3	3	15	242	527	494	403	684	802	193	214	489	-	-

	14
Masters	-
US Open	-
British	MC
PGA	-
Money (A)	207
OWR	1065

2014: PGA: 15 st / 3 ct / 0 t10. (T25 New Orleans). Ranked 202nd in FedEx Cup points playing on Past Champion status and sponsor exemptions.
OUTLOOK: Still only 43, and shows the occasional flash of his former brilliance - but those flashes are becoming fewer and further between, and his Past Champion opportunities to build on them are limited. With his raw talent, he may still be able to compete. Occasionally.

STATS: Driving Distance: C+   Driving Accuracy: C-   GIR: D   Short Game: C-   Putting: B-

---

Dyson, Simon (England) (37)   b. York, England 12/21/1977. 6'0" 170 lbs. TP: 1999. Began his professional career in 2000 on the Asian Tour, where he scored victories in the Macau Open, the China Open and the Hong Kong Open and finished 1st in the Order of Merit. Made it through E Tour Q School that autumn but initially found only limited success before eventually winning the 2006 Indonesia and Dutch Opens. Enjoyed a career-best season in 2009, when he won another Dutch Open as well as the Dunhill Links Championship (by three over Rory McIlroy and Oliver Wilson), and finished 7th in the Order of Merit. Nearly matched it in 2011 when he finished 10th in $$$ and again won twice, claiming the Irish Open and, for the third time, the Dutch Open, beating David Lynn by one. Was DQ'd from the 2013 BMW Masters following an odd ball-marking incident which generated much controversy among his peers. **Teams:** Walker Cup: 1999 (0-2-1). Seve Trophy (3): 2007-09-11. **OWR Best:** 26 - Jan, 2012.

European Tour Wins (6): 2006: Indonesia Open, Dutch Open **2009:** Dutch Open, Dunhill Links Championship **2011:** Irish Open, Dutch Open (KLM).
Asian Tour Wins (3): 2000: Macau Open, China Open, Hong Kong Open.
Amateur Wins: Hampshire Salver: 1998   –   Finnish Am: 1999.

	00	01	02	03	04	05	06	07	08	09	10	11	12	13	14
Masters	-	-	-	-	-	-	-	-	-	-	MC	-	MC	-	-
US Open	-	-	-	-	-	MC	-	-	MC	-	MC	-	T51	-	-
British	MC	MC	-	-	MC	T34	T48	-	MC	-	T48	T9	T23	-	-
PGA	-	-	-	-	-	-	-	T6	MC	-	T12	T51	MC	-	-
Money (E)	-	87	60	127	80	58	21	26	55	7	33	10	50	72	41
Money (As)	1	-	-	-	8*	-	-	-	-	-	-	-	-	-	-
OWR	272	264	247	384	309	198	88	64	129	43	64	28	63	171	117

2014: E: 29 st / 18 ct / 7 t10. (2 KLM, T3 Dunhill Champ, T5 BMW PGA, T5 BMW Int'l, T7 Italian, etc.). Failed to win in 29 starts but appeared recovered from his 2013 controversies, logging seven top 10s and climbing back to 41st in $$$.
OUTLOOK: Has always been an up-and-down sort, but with a limited range of variance; his "good" years involve multiple victories, his "bad" years usually resulting in top-60 finishes on the $$$ list. Limited length-wise but hits a ton of greens, which likely accounts for his now having 11 straight seasons ranked among the top 80 in earnings. And from a results perspective, at least, the disciplinary conflict seems now to be behind him.

STATS: Driving Distance: C+   Driving Accuracy: B+   GIR: A   Short Game: C   Putting: B-

---

Edberg, Per Oscar ("Pelle") (Sweden) (35)   b. Jönköping, Sweden 4/13/1979. 5'9" 160 lbs. TP: 1997. Long hitter who spent the better part of a decade playing mini-tours and the Challenge circuit before eventually reaching the E Tour in 2005. Struggled initially before hitting stride in 2007 and '08, finding a form which he has sought to rediscover ever since. Never an E Tour winner, his best finishes being T2s at the 2008 Scandinavian Masters and the 2002 Saint-Omer Open. **OWR Best:** 143 - Sep, 2007.

Edberg, Per Oscar, Cont'd

Other Wins: 4 Nordic League (2003-2006).

	05	06	07	08	09	10	11	12	13	14
Masters	-	-	-	-	-	-	-	-	-	-
US Open	-	-	-	-	-	-	-	-	-	-
British	-	-	T12	MC	-	-	-	-	-	-
PGA	-	-	-	-	-	-	-	-	-	-
Money (E)	176	236*	51	85	132	119	320*	162*	217*	-
OWR	692	689	156	262	358	317	315	378	578	508

2014: Played full-time on the Challenge Tour, where he finished 44th in $$$ before playing his way back to the E Tour via Q School.

OUTLOOK: Though entering his prime years age-wise, has little on his recent résumé to suggest that a 2015 E Tour resurgence is imminent.

STATS (LTD): Driving Distance: A   Driving Accuracy: C-   GIR: C   Short Game: C+   Putting: B

Edfors, Johan (Sweden) (39)

b. Varberg, Sweden 10/10/1975. 6'0" 175 lbs. College: U of Texas-San Antonio. TP: 1997. Initially struggled to find his place in European golf, failing even to crack the top 100 earners on the Challenge Tour prior to topping its Order of Merit (with two wins) in 2003. Exploded on the E Tour in 2006, however, claiming three official wins: the TCL Classic (played in China), the venerable British Masters (where he edged three players by a shot at The Belfry) and the Scottish Open, where a closing 63 helped better the trio of Luke Donald, Andrés Romero and Charl Schwartzel by two. Thereafter, remained a steady $$$ winner since through 2012 but logged only one additional win, a three-stroke triumph over Prayad Marksaeng at the Asian Tour's 2009 Black Mountain Masters. Lost his card, however, in 2013 and narrowly failed to regain it via the Challenge Tour at the close of 2014. **OWR Best:** 44 - Jan, 2007.

European Tour Wins (3): 2006: TCL Classic, British Masters, Scottish Open.

Asian Tour Wins (1): 2009: Black Mountain Masters.

Sunshine Tour Wins (1): 2003: Zambia Open (54H).

Other Wins: 3 Euro Challenge (2003-2014)   +   1 Nordic League (2004)   Black Mountain Inv (Korea): 2013.

	03	04	05	06	07	08	09	10	11	12	13	14
Masters	-	-	-	-	MC	-	-	-	-	-	-	-
US Open	-	-	-	-	MC	MC	T27	-	T19	-	-	-
British	-	-	-	MC	MC	MC	T52	-	-	-	-	-
PGA	-	-	-	MC	MC	-	MC	-	T39	-	-	-
Money (E)	-	147	-	10	67	65	32	59	40	113	155	206*
OWR	296	395	410	48	123	170	123	132	109	301	749	435

2014: Played on the Challenge Tour (18th in $$$) and sparingly on the E Tour, where he managed a T7 at the co-sanctioned Madeira Islands Open.

OUTLOOK: Though never quite matching his knockout 2006, remained a strong earner through 2011 before sliding in 2012, then crashing in 2013. Offers an above-the-median tee-to-green power game but struggles thereafter. Can win on the Challenge Tour, however, so he may yet be back.

STATS: Driving Distance: B+   Driving Accuracy: C+   GIR: B+   Short Game: C   Putting: C+

Els, Theodore Ernest (South Africa) (45)

b. Johannesburg, South Africa 10/17/1969. 6'4" 240 lbs. TP: 1989. Junior tennis star before turning full-time to golf. In 1992, joined Gary Player as only man to win the South African Open, PGA and Masters in a single season. A dominant player in his homeland before breaking onto the world stage at age 24 by winning the 1994 U.S. Open in a three-way playoff with Colin Montgomerie and Loren Roberts at Oakmont. Again defeated Montgomerie at Congressional in 1997 for a second U.S. Open victory. Got halfway to his goal of winning the career Grand Slam by beating Steve Elkington, Stuart Appleby and Thomas Levet in a four-man playoff for the 2002 British Open, ultimately eliminating Levet in sudden death with a memorable sand save at Muirfield's historic 18th green. A truly international player who has won more than 70 titles worldwide, including 53 on four major tours. Awarded a lifetime European Tour membership in 1998, eventually winning that tour's 2003 and '04 Orders of Merit. Seven-time winner of the World Match Play (1994-95-96-02-03-04-07) and has twice claimed WGC titles: the 2004 WGC-American Express (by one over Thomas Bjørn) and 2010's WGC-CA Championship (where he routed Charl Schwartzel by four). Had 2005 season shortened by a knee injury, with his form remaining spotty until 2010, when he won back-to-back starts at the WGC-CA Championship and the Arnold Palmer Invitational, then added his fifth South African Open, nipping Retief Goosen by one at Durban CC. After several strong starts in the U.S., emerged to claim the 2012 British Open (Royal Lytham & St Annes), closing with a 68, then winning as Adam Scott collapsed down the stretch. Ranked among year-end top 5 in the OWR for a remarkable 15 straight years (1994-2008). **Awards:** World Golf Hall of Fame Member (2011). E Tour Golfer of the Year (3): 1994-02-03. Euro Vardon Trophy (2): 2003-04. PGA Tour Rookie of the Year: 1994. **Teams:** Presidents Cup (8): 1996-98-00-03-07-09-11 (20-18-2). World Cup (5): 1992-93-96-97-01 (won in '96 w/W.Westner and '01 w/R.Goosen). **OWR Best:** 1 - Apr, 1998.

PGA Tour Wins (19): 1994: U.S. Open **1995:** Byron Nelson Classic (GTE) **1996:** Westchester Classic (Buick) **1997:** U.S. Open, Westchester Classic (Buick) **1998:** Bay Hill Inv **1999:** Los Angeles Open (Nissan) **2000:** The International (Stableford) **2002:** Doral Open (Genuity), British Open **2003:** Mercedes Championships, Hawaiian Open (Sony) **2004:** Hawaiian Open (Sony), Memorial Tournament, WGC-American Express **2008:** Honda Classic **2010:** WGC-CA Championship, Bay Hill Inv **2012:** British Open.

European Tour Wins (22): 1994: Dubai Classic **1995:** South African PGA **1997:** Johnnie Walker Classic **1998:** South African Open **1999:** South African PGA **2000:** Loch Lomond Inv **2002:** Heineken Classic, Dubai Classic, **2003:** Heineken Classic, Johnnie Walker Classic, Scottish Open, European Masters **2004:** Heineken Classic, World Match Play **2005:** Dubai Classic, Qatar Masters, BMW Asian Open **2006:** Alfred Dunhill Championship, South African Open ('07) **2007:** World Match Play **2010:** South African Open ('11) **2013:** BMW International.

Japan Tour Wins (1): 1993: Dunlop Phoenix.

Sunshine Tour Wins (11): 1991: Amatola Classic **1992:** South Africa Open, South African PGA, South African Masters, Royal Swazi Sun Classic, Players Championship, Goodyear Classic **1995:** South African PGA, Bell's Cup **1996:** South African Open **2001:** SA Players Championship.

Other Wins: World Match Play (England) (5): 1994-95-96-01-03   Johnnie Walker Championship (Jamaica): 1994   Sarazen World Open (USA): 1994   Family House Inv (USA): 1995   World Cup (Individual) (2): 1996-97   Johnnie Walker Super Tour: 1996   PGA Grand Slam (2): 1997-2010   Dunhill Cup (2): 1997-98 (both w/D.Frost & R.Goosen)   Million Dollar Challenge (SA) (3): 1999-00-01   Ernie Els Inv (2): 2002-07   Nelson Mandela Inv: 2004 (w/V.Tshabalala)   Hassan II Trophy (Morocco): 2008.

Amateur Wins: South African Am: 1986   –   Junior World (13-14): 1984   South African Boys: 1986   South African Am Stroke Play: 1989.

Els, Theodore Ernest, Cont'd

	89	90	91	92	93	94	95	96	97	98	99	00	01	02	03	04	05	06	07	08	09	10	11	12
Masters	-	-	-	-	-	T8	MC	T12	T17	T16	T27	2	T6	T5	T6	2	47	T27	MC	MC	MC	T18	T47	-
US Open	-	-	-	-	T7	Win	MC	T5	Win	T49	MC	T2	T66	T24	T5	T9	T15	T26	T51	T14	MC	3	MC	9
British	MC	-	-	T5	T6	T24	T11	T2	T10	T29	T24	T2	T3	Win	T18	2P	T34	3	T4	T7	T8	MC	MC	Win
PGA	-	-	-	MC	MC	T25	T3	T61	T53	T21	MC	T34	T13	T34	T5	T4	-	T16	3	T31	T6	T18	MC	T48
Money (A)	-	-	274*	213*	190*	19	14	14	9	36	15	3	15	5	9	2	47*	28	20	20	36	3	93	16
Money (E)	-	-	-	75	34	10	-	-	8	12	3	4	3	1	1	18	5	2	42	11	7	51	-	
Money (SA)	-	-	1	2	3	1	-	-	-	-	-	-	-	-	-	-	-	-	-	-	5*	-	-	
OWR	385	381	413	40	20	6	3	4	4	5	5	2	4	3	3	3	5	5	4	9	17	12	56	24

	13	14
Masters	T13	MC
US Open	T4	T35
British	T26	MC
PGA	MC	T7
Money (A)	74	55
Money (E)	20	37
Money (SA)	-	-
OWR	27	63

2014: PGA: 24 st / 18 ct / 3 t10. (4 WGC-Match Play, T5 Barclays, T7 PGA). Improved modestly from 2013, finishing 41st in FedEx Cup points.

OUTLOOK: Has seen his game fluctuate considerably in recent years. At age 45, he seems able to still compete at the highest levels but no longer, it seems, on a regular basis. Has seen his Total Driving numbers plunge over the years (from 36 in 2009 to 158 on 2014) but a bigger concern is a nosedive in GIR, from 7 in 2011 to 159 in 2014. Having already used the short putter sporadically, he may not be too bothered by the 2016 anchoring ban; as it is, his putting is more inconsistent than it is truly terrible. Likely to still contend occasionally, but no longer on a frequent basis.

STATS: Driving Distance: B+   Driving Accuracy: C-   GIR: C+   Short Game: B+   Putting: C+

English, Harris (USA) (25)
b. Valdosta, GA 7/23/1989. 6'3" 185 lbs. Two-time All-American at U of Georgia. TP: 2011. Won the 2007 Georgia Amateur at age 18, becoming the event's third youngest winner (behind Bobby Jones and Charlie Yates). Also won the 2011 Southern Amateur. Won the Web.com Tour's 2011 Children's Hospital Invitational while still an amateur, then added a playoff loss (to Danny Lee at the WNB Classic) and a T3 in subsequent Web.com starts after turning pro. Broke through for his maiden PGA Tour victory at the 2013 Memphis Classic (beating Phil Mickelson and Scott Stallings by two), then claimed a second 2013 victory with a four-shot walkaway at November's Mayakoba Classic (officially a 2014 event). **Teams**: Walker Cup: 2011 (2-2-0). **OWR Best**: 36 - Feb, 2014.

PGA Tour Wins (2): 2013: Memphis Classic (FedEx), Mayakoba Classic (OHL)('14).
Other Wins: 1 Web.com (2011)* + Shark Shootout: 2013 (w/M.Kuchar).
Amateur Wins: Southern Am: 2011 - Georgia Am: 2007.

	11	12	13	14
Masters	-	-	-	MC
US Open	-	-	-	T48
British	-	T54	T15	MC
PGA	-	-	T61	MC
Money (A)	-	79	27	23
OWR	274	140	53	77

2014: PGA: 28 st / 20 ct / 7 t10. (Won Mayakoba, 4 Hawaii, T7 CIMB, T7 Travelers, 9 Phoenix, etc.). Continued to enjoy high-level success, winning the wraparound segment's Mayakoba Classic, finishing among the top 30 in $$$ for the second straight year and ranking 32nd in FedEx Cup points.

OUTLOOK: Long-hitting player whose skill set extends well beyond simply overpowering the golf course. Has thus far demonstrated a deft putting touch (off slightly in 2014) and utilizes his length to hit a high number of greens. The rare American to win twice on the PGA Tour before turning 25 - a number supported by his ranking 4 in Final Round Scoring in 2014. Seems capable of making the jump to international stardom.

STATS: Driving Distance: A   Driving Accuracy: B-   GIR: A-   Short Game: C+   Putting: B+

Ernst, Derek Alexander (USA) (24)
b. Woodland, CA 5/16/1990. 6'0" 170 lbs. All-American at UNLV. TP: 2012. After winning a Mountain West conference championship while starring at UNLV, turned pro in 2012 and promptly played his way through four stages of Q School, joining the 2013 PGA Tour as an unheralded rookie. Made only one career PGA or Web.com start (T41 at the 2012 Frys.com Open) prior to qualifying. Playing as the fourth alternate, broke through for a surprise playoff victory (over David Lynn) at the 2013 Wells Fargo Championship in only his ninth Tour start - but has essentially struggled ever since. **Teams**: Palmer Cup: 2012. **OWR Best**: 118 - Aug, 2013.

PGA Tour Wins (1): 2013: Wells Fargo Championship.
Amateur Wins: Memorial Am: 2009.

	13	14
Masters	-	MC
US Open	-	-
British	-	-
PGA	MC	-
Money (A)	66	169
OWR	154	462

2014: PGA: 28 st / 12 ct / 0 t10. (T27 Barracuda). Failed to log a single top 25 and fell to 171st in FedEx Cup points.

OUTLOOK: An outstanding driver of the ball (5 in Total Driving) whose overall game drops off markedly thereafter (173 in Proximity To Hole, 128 in GIR, 165 in SGP). Still exempt off his 2013 Wells Fargo win but needs to shore up many aspects of his game to regularly succeed at this level.

STATS: Driving Distance: A   Driving Accuracy: B+   GIR: C+   Short Game: C-   Putting: C

Estes, Bob Alan (USA) (48) b. Graham, TX 2/2/1966. 6'2" 180 lbs. Three-time All-American, Nicklaus (1988) and Haskins (1988) Awards winner at U of Texas. TP: 1988. An AJGA All-American. Regular PGA Tour money winner, only once missing the top 125 from 1989-2007 and ranking five times among the top 50. Finished a career-best 9th in 2001, claiming wins at the FedEx Classic (edging Bernhard Langer by one) and the Las Vegas Classic (beating Tom Lehman, also by one). Added his fourth career win the following year at the 2002 Kemper Open. Began experiencing right wrist problems in late 2010. The problem continued in 2011, delaying his first PGA Tour start until April and ultimately forcing a return to Q School, where he finished T8. Played 2009 on a one-time Top 50 Career Money Winner exemption, but kept his card in both 2012 and '13. Missed nearly all of 2014 (made 2 starts) with a shoulder injury. **OWR Best:** 13 - Aug, 2002.

PGA Tour Wins (4): 1994: Texas Open **2001:** Memphis Classic (FedEx), Las Vegas Classic (Invensys) (90H). **2002:** Kemper Insurance Open.
Amateur Wins: Trans-Mississippi Am: 1985 – LaJet Am: 1987   Texas Am: 1988.

	89	90	91	92	93	94	95	96	97	98	99	00	01	02	03	04	05	06	07	08	09	10	11	12
Masters						MC	T29	T27	-	-	T4	T19	-	45	22	T31	-	-	-	-	-	-	-	-
US Open	-	-	MC	T44	T52	-	MC	-	-	-	T30	MC	T30	MC	MC	MC	T11	MC	T58	-	-	MC	-	T46
British	-	MC	-	-	-	T24	T8	MC	-	T24	T49	T20	T25	T18	T34	T20	-	-	-	-	T76	-	MC	T45
PGA	-	MC	-	T76	T6	T47	T6	MC	-	T34	T6	MC	T37	MC	T57	MC	T28	MC	-	-	T76	-	-	-
Money (A)	102	69	105	80	32	14	41	149	69	28	26	88	9	26	33	74	92	67	117	127	86	132	135*	99
OWR	306	178	205	200	122	37	47	127	130	45	30	62	18	24	40	76	114	133	245	301	200	295	320	165

	13	14
Masters	-	-
US Open	-	-
British	-	-
PGA	-	-
Money (A)	106	191*
OWR	177	639

2014: PGA: 2 st / 1 ct / 1 t10. (T10 Mayakoba). Missed virtually the entire season after injuring his shoulder in November.
OUTLOOK: Has remained competitive into his late 40s, lagging well behind younger power hitters but living off a high-end short game. Begins 2015 on a 24-event medical extension, which seems reasonably clearable. Not likely to win at this point – until 2016 on the Champions Tour.

STATS: Driving Distance: C+   Driving Accuracy: B+   GIR: B-   Short Game: A   Putting: A-

---

Every, Matthew King (USA) (31) b. Daytona Beach, FL 12/4/1983. 5'11" 190 lbs. Three-time All-American and Hogan Award winner (2006) at U of Florida. TP: 2006. A multi-time All-American after walking on at Florida. Finished T28 at the 2005 U.S. Open as an amateur. After playing the Web.com Tour full-time in 2008 and 2009 (winning once in the latter year), joined the PGA Tour in 2010, finishing 160th in earnings. Requalified for 2012 via an 18th-place finish in 2011 Web.com earnings, then made good in 2012, logging six top-10 finishes and finishing 40th in $$$. Broke through for his first PGA Tour win at the 2014 Arnold Palmer Invitational, edging Keegan Bradley by one at Bay Hill. **Teams:** Walker Cup: 2005 (1-2-1). Palmer Cup (2): 2004-05. **OWR Best:** 42 - Mar, 2014.

PGA Tour Wins (1): 2014: Bay Hill Inv.
Other Wins: 1 Web.com (2009).
Amateur Wins: Int'l Junior Masters: 2001.

	05	06	07	08	09	10	11	12	13	14
Masters	-	-	-	-	-	-	-	-	-	MC
US Open	T28	-	-	-	-	-	-	-	-	MC
British	-	-	-	-	-	-	-	-	-	71
PGA	-	-	-	-	-	-	-	71	MC	MC
Money (A)	-	-	-	-	-	160	-	40	73	33
OWR	700	-	-	449	279	306	300	125	133	76

2014: PGA: 26 st / 17 ct / 6 t10. (Won Arnold Palmer, T3 FedEx St Jude, T6 Northern Trust, T7 McGladrey, T8 Hawaii, etc.). Claimed his first PGA Tour win en route to finishing 45th in FedEx Cup points. Tailed off slightly in the second half, having logged six of his seven top 10s prior to The Masters.
OUTLOOK: Capable, somewhat streaky player who's logged 16 top-10 finishes in 79 starts since 2012. Statistically speaking, possesses a balanced game, though his SGP (4) and Total Putting (17) made major jumps in 2014. Has always seemed physically capable of earning a good living at this level, but if he can somehow maintain his improved putting form, the long-term expectations would begin to rise considerably.

STATS: Driving Distance: B   Driving Accuracy: B-   GIR: B   Short Game: B   Putting: A-

---

Farr, Oliver (Wales) (26) b. Redditch, England 3/25/1988. 5'10" 185 lbs. TP: 2011. After turning pro, spent two years on mini-tours, topping the 2013 EuroPro order of merit to gain his 2014 Challenge Tour card. Then made good on the opportunity by winning in May and finishing 10th in earnings to graduate to the European Tour. **Teams:** Eisenhower Trophy: 2010. **OWR Best:** 248 - Nov, 2014.

Other Wins: 1 Euro Challenge (2014)   +   2 EuroPro (2013).
Amateur Wins: Aberconwy Trophy: 2008   HSBC Champion of Champions: 2009   Welsh Golf Cross (2): 2009-11.

	14
Masters	-
US Open	-
British	-
PGA	-
Money (E)	-
OWR	259

2014: Played full-time on the Challenge Tour, where he won once and gained his first E Tour card by finishing 10th in $$$.
OUTLOOK: With only one Challenge Tour season (and one career E Tour start) on his résumé, a high-impact E Tour debut isn't the likeliest.

STATS: Driving Distance: --   Driving Accuracy: --   GIR: --   Short Game: --   Putting: --

Fasth, Niclas Krister (Sweden) (42) b. Gothenburg, Sweden 4/29/1972. 5'11" 175 lbs. TP: 1993. Underrated player who initially struggled with inconsistency upon reaching the E Tour. Made an ill-fated try at the PGA Tour in 1998 (245th in $$$) and actually returned to the Challenge circuit in 1999. Found great European success thereafter, however, winning six times and finishing T2 (three back of David Duval) in the 2001 British Open. Finished 10th in E Tour earnings during a winless 2001, beginning a strong run that included a playoff victory over Angel Cabrera at the 2005 Deutsche Bank Open and a three-shot triumph over Sergio García at the 2006 Mallorca Classic. Claimed his last win at the 2007 BMW International, where he beat homestanding Bernhard Langer and Jose-Filipe Lima by two. Remained a steady earner through 2009 but has slipped markedly since, failing to crack the top 150 in both 2013 and '14. **Teams:** Eisenhower Trophy: 1992. Ryder Cup: 2002 (O: 0-2-1, S: 0-0-1). Seve Trophy (3): 2002-03-05. World Cup (4): 2001-02-03-05. **OWR Best:** 18 - Oct, 2007.

European Tour Wins (6): 2000: Madeira Islands Open **2005:** New Zealand Open, Deutsche Bank Open **2006:** Spanish Open, Mallorca Classic **2007:** BMW Int'l.

Other Wins: 4 Euro Challenge (1993-1999) + Swedish Pro: 1993.

Amateur Wins: Swedish Am: 1992.

	94	95	96	97	98	99	00	01	02	03	04	05	06	07	08	09	10	11	12	13	14
Masters	-	-	-	-	-	-	-	-	MC	MC	-	-	-	T55	T39	-	-	-	-	-	-
US Open	-	-	-	-	-	-	-	-	T37	T48	-	-	MC	4	MC	-	-	-	-	-	MC
British	-	-	-	-	-	-	-	T2	T28	MC	-	-	MC	T35	MC	-	-	-	-	MC	-
PGA	-	-	-	-	-	-	-	T29	MC	T10	T45	MC	MC	T42	T63	-	-	-	-	-	-
Money (E)	123	56	118	36	-	-	45	10	17	22	83	13	15	5	94	56	104	132	136	152	155
OWR	385	260	355	243	385	493	140	38	39	58	156	60	42	20	108	202	294	438	603	740	900

2014: E: 24 st / 9 ct / 0 t10. (T24 Spanish). Had a virtual repeat of 2013, logging only one top 25 in 26 E Tour starts and finishing 155th in $$$.

OUTLOOK: Statistically, he has fallen to below-the-median status nearly across the board, which surely explains why he's dropped from his top form of the mid-2000s. Is neither too old (at 42) nor too far gone to still play some solid golf - but it's tough with such soft numbers around the green

STATS: Driving Distance: C   Driving Accuracy: B   GIR: C   Short Game: C+   Putting: C+

Fathauer, Derek Jay (USA) (28) b. Stuart, FL 1/20/1986. 6'1" 185 lbs. Two-time All-American at U of Louisville. TP: 2008. Surprised many by tying for 2nd at 2008 Q School but struggled badly on the 2009 PGA Tour. Spent the next two seasons playing mini-tours before reaching the Web.com circuit from 2012-2014, finishing 68th, 109th and 13th, with the latter campaign earning a PGA Tour card - a position he enhanced in the Web.com Finals by winning the Tour Championship to finish second on the priority list. **Teams:** Palmer Cup: 2008. **OWR Best:** 152 - Oct, 2014.

Other Wins: 1 Web.com (2014).

	08	09	10	11	12	13	14
Masters	-	-	-	-	-	-	-
US Open	T69	-	-	-	-	-	-
British	-	-	-	-	-	-	-
PGA	-	-	-	-	-	-	-
Money (A)	-	203	-	-	-	-	-
OWR	1105	879	-	-	778	1000	171

2014: Finished 13th in regular season Web.com Tour $$$, then climbed to 2nd on the priority list via the Web.com Finals.

OUTLOOK: Played the PGA Tour in 2009 immediately after college but finished 203rd in $$$. A power-oriented player whose short game and putting numbers jumped markedly in 2014. If he can bring that game to the big stage, stands a chance of faring much better this time around.

STATS (LTD): Driving Distance: A-   Driving Accuracy: C   GIR: B+   Short Game: B   Putting: B ⇑

Fernandez-Castaño, Gonzalo (Spain) (34) b. Madrid, Spain 10/13/1980. 6'1" 185 lbs. TP: 2004. Top Spanish prospect who won the 2003 Spanish Amateur and represented Spain internationally, notably at the 2002 Eisenhower Trophy. Won the Dutch Open during his first full E Tour season, leading to 2005 Rookie of the Year honors. Validated the win early in 2006 by defeating Henrik Stenson in a playoff to take the BMW Asian Open in China. Claimed a significant win in 2008, beating Lee Westwood in sudden death at the British Masters. A consistent present among the E Tour's top 60 money winners and initially peaked at 17th in 2009 and 19th in 2011, winning a rain-shortened Singapore Open in a playoff with Juvic Pagunsan in the latter year. Closed with 64 to claim his sixth E Tour title at the 2012 Italian Open. Won the 2013 BMW Masters in China, edging Francesco Molinari and Thongchai Jaidee by one en route to a career-best 7th in E Tour $$$. **Awards:** E Tour Rookie of the Year: 2005. **Teams:** Eisenhower Trophy: 2002. Palmer Cup (2): 2003-04. Seve Trophy (3): 2007-09-13. World Cup (2): 2006-09. **OWR Best:** 27 - Mar, 2013.

European Tour Wins (7): 2005: Dutch Open **2006:** BMW Asian Open **2007:** Italian Open (54H) **2008:** British Masters **2011:** Singapore Open (54H) **2012:** Italian Open **2013:** BMW Masters.

Other Wins: Madrid Federation (Spain): 2005.

Amateur Wins: Spanish Am: 2003.

	05	06	07	08	09	10	11	12	13	14
Masters	-	-	-	-	-	-	-	61	T20	T26
US Open	-	-	-	-	MC	-	-	MC	T10	MC
British	-	T48	-	-	T47	MC	-	T54	T54	MC
PGA	-	MC	-	T32	T33	-	-	T62	MC	T59
Money (A)	-	-	-	-	-	-	-	-	128	105
Money (E)	57	40	50	34	17	35	19	20	7	85*
OWR	150	129	90	76	63	92	49	33	35	104

2014: PGA: 25 st / 18 ct / 1 t10. (T4 Canadian). Played almost exclusively in America, finishing 82nd in the FedEx Cup points.

OUTLOOK: Has proven himself a top-shelf E Tour player (logging seven wins in nine full seasons) but now appears set on playing more in America. Possesses a solid all-around game which includes the requisite amount of length, but is anchored by a very well-thought-of short game as well as a solid (if somewhat up and down) putter. Is just entering his prime years, but will he stay in America or return to the easier pickings of Europe?

STATS: Driving Distance: B+   Driving Accuracy: B-   GIR: B-   Short Game: A-   Putting: B

Ferrie, Kenneth Andrew (England) (36) b. Ashington, England 9/28/1978. 6'4" 225 lbs. TP: 1999. Established himself on the E Tour at age 25 by beating Peter Lawrie and Peter Hedblom in sudden death to win the 2003 Spanish Open. Stepped up in 2005 by winning the European Open (by two over Graeme Storm and Colin Montgomerie), leading to a career-best 11th place in E Tour $$$. Tied for the 54-hole lead at the 2006 U.S. Open (Winged Foot) before finishing T6. Following a one-time failed attempt at the PGA Tour (182nd in $$$) in 2008, claimed his third career title at the 2011 Austrian Open, beating Simon Wakefield in a playoff. Also in 2011, carded a 10-under-par 60 in the third round of the Open de Andalucia. Lost his card in 2012 before struggling on the Challenge Tour in 2013, and barely playing in 2014. **OWR Best:** 68 - Dec, 2005.

European Tour Wins (3): 2003: Spanish Open **2005:** European Open **2011:** Austrian Open.
Other Wins: 2 Euro Challenge (2000-2001)   +   Northern Rock Masters (England): 2005.
Amateur Wins: British Boys: 1996   Lagonda Trophy: 1998.

	01	02	03	04	05	06	07	08	09	10	11	12	13	14
Masters	-	-	-	-	-	-	MC	-	-	-	-	-	-	-
US Open	-	-	-	-	-	T6	T42	-	-	-	-	-	-	-
British	-	-	MC	T42	MC	WD	-	-	-	-	70	-	-	-
PGA	-	-	-	-	-	MC	-	-	-	-	-	-	-	-
Money (E)	193	112	34	72	11	54	167	-	119	106	76	160	247*	-
OWR	411	422	167	230	68	116	502	622	433	342	219	499	-	774

2014: Played very little competitive golf, making four E Tour starts (best: T13 at Czech Masters) and two on the Challenge circuit.
OUTLOOK: Seems pretty well removed from his peak years of 2005 and '06 – especially if he's not planning on competing very often. While still notably straight off the tee, the remainder of his game has fallen into statistical mediocrity, so an imminent reversal of fortune isn't likely.

STATS: Driving Distance: C-   Driving Accuracy: A   GIR: C   Short Game: C+   Putting: C-

---

Fichardt, Darren Clive (South Africa) (39) b. Pretoria, South Africa 5/13/1975. 5'8" 200 lbs. TP: 1994. International player who has long competed both in Europe and Southern Africa. A four-time E Tour winner including a five-shot runaway at the 2001 Sao Paulo Open, a sudden death victory over countryman James Kingston at the 2003 Qatar Masters, and a two-stroke triumph over Grégory Bourdy and Jaco Van Zyl at the 2013 Africa Open. A twelve-time winner and two-time Order of Merit leader (2000 and '04) on the Sunshine Tour. Mostly played at home from 2009-2011 when he logged a three-win 2009 (including a one-shot triumph over Marc Cayeux at the South African Masters) and a two-win 2011. Claimed a fourth career E Tour title at the 2013 Africa Open, where he beat Grégory Bourdy by two. **Teams:** World Cup: 2000. **OWR Best:** 75 - Mar, 2013.

European Tour Wins (4): 2001: Sao Paulo Open **2003:** Qatar Masters **2012:** St Omer Open **2013:** Africa Open.
Sunshine Tour Wins (12): 1997: Highveld Classic (54H) **2001:** Tour Championship, Zimbabwe Open **2003:** Dimension Data Pro-Am **2006:** Vodacom-Final (54H), Highveld Classic (54H) **2009:** South African Masters, Vodacom-Selborne (54H), Platinum Classic (54H) **2010:** Dimension Data Pro-Am **2011:** Vodacom-Kwazulu Natal (54H), Suncoast Classic (54H).
Other Wins: Sun City Pro-Am (SA): 1999   PGA Cup (SA): 1999   Gold du Bassin Bleu (France): 2000   Trophée des Nations (France): 2002.
Amateur Wins: Northern Transvaal Jr: 1992   Northern Transvaal Am Stroke Play: 1993.

	95	96	97	98	99	00	01	02	03	04	05	06	07	08	09	10	11	12	13	14
Masters	-	-	-	-	-	-	-	-	-	-	-	-	-	-	-	-	-	-	-	-
US Open	-	-	-	-	-	-	-	-	-	-	-	-	-	MC	-	-	-	-	-	-
British	-	-	-	-	-	-	MC	-	MC	-	MC	-	-	MC	MC	-	-	-	-	-
PGA	-	-	-	-	-	-	-	-	-	-	-	-	-	-	-	-	-	-	-	-
Money (E)	-	-	-	-	-	-	102	79	39	68	145	69	146	190	251*	155*	202*	84	48	52
Money (SA)	154*	75	57	37	24	1	8	8	30*	1*	21*	5*	54*	29	3	9	8	7	2	9
OWR	-	899	659	461	494	363	121	209	201	175	242	161	438	692	316	401	430	150	124	163

2014: E: 29 st / 18 ct / 4 t10. (T5 Africa, T6 Tshwane, T7 Spanish, T10 Abu Dhabi).   Playing full-time in Europe, failed to win but recorded another solid campaign, finishing 52nd in E Tour $$$. Also made three non-co-sanctioned Sunshine Tour events, led by a 2nd at the BMG Classic.
OUTLOOK: After seemingly getting caught between being a star at home or a mid-range man in Europe, has stepped his game up in his late 30s to enjoy renewed prominence on the E Tour. Makes his living on and around the green – which is good because his GIR numbers have generally resided below the median. At age 39, likely play to a bit more in Europe, and can still rate among the elite back in South Africa.

STATS: Driving Distance: B   Driving Accuracy: B   GIR: C   Short Game: A-   Putting: A

Finau, Milton Pouha ("Tony") (USA) (25) b. Salt Lake City, UT 9/14/1989. 6'4" 215 lbs. TP: 2007. Cousin of NBA player Jabari Parker and the first man of Samoan and Tongan descent to play the PGA Tour. Along with his brother Gipper (the youngest player ever to make a Web.com cut), turned pro straight out of high school and played mini-tours prior to reaching - and winning on - the Web.com Tour in 2014. An imposingly long hitter who is bound to garner lots of attention on the PGA Tour. **OWR Best:** 144 - Nov, 2014.

Other Wins: 1 Web.com (2014)   +   Provo Open (2): 2012-13   Junior World (11-12): 2002.
Amateur Wins: Junior World (11-12): 2002   Utah Am: 2007   Utah HS: 2006.

	14
Masters	-
US Open	-
British	-
PGA	-
Money (A)	-
OWR	146

2014: Played the Web.com Tour full-time, winning once and clinching a spot on the 2015 PGA Tour by finishing 8th in regular season $$$.
OUTLOOK: An intriguing talent who some may be surprised took this long to reach the PGA Tour. Can absolutely overpower the golf course but is also fairly skilled in the finesse areas. Has climbed step-by-step to this point so he should be ready. Has the talent to make an immediate impact.

STATS (LTD): Driving Distance: A+   Driving Accuracy: C-   GIR: B   Short Game: C   Putting: B-

Finch, Richard (England) (37)
b. Hull, England 6/9/1977. 6'2" 200 lbs. TP: 2003. Enjoyed a longer-than-normal amateur career (which included winning the 2002 English Amateur) before turning professional at age 26. Struggled through three tough E Tour campaigns before breaking through for a pair of 2008 victories, the first being a three-shot triumph at the New Zealand Open (played in December 2007). Five months later, scored an Irish Open victory (by two over Felipe Aguilar) made memorable by his fall into a creek after blasting his approach from it at the 72nd. Though winless since, he has settled in as a steady $$$ earner, thrice cracking the top 75 from 2010-2012 and only once failing to retain his card (2013). **OWR Best:** 127 - Sep, 2008.

European Tour Wins (2): 2007: New Zealand Open ('08). **2008:** Irish Open.

Amateur Wins: Spanish Amateur: 2000   English Amateur: 2002   –   St Andrews Links Trophy: 2003.

	04	05	06	07	08	09	10	11	12	13	14
Masters	-	-	-	-	-	-	-	-	-	-	-
US Open	-	-	-	-	-	-	-	-	-	-	-
British	-	-	-	-	T58	-	-	-	-	-	-
PGA	-	-	-	-	-	-	-	-	-	-	-
Money (E)	-	60	113	110	20	110	64	74	60	125	100
OWR	677	270	367	277	132	331	299	256	245	266	545

2014: E: 22 st / 6 ct / 3 t10. (2 Dunhill Champ, T8 Hong Kong, T8 Irish). Retained his card (100th in $$$) despite missing his final five cuts.

OUTLOOK: Is a skilled and accurate man from tee to green, but his lack of length and below-the-median putting numbers tend to limit his upside. At age 37, he looks good for several more years of steady earnings, though climbing much above his recent level seems less likely.

STATS: Driving Distance: C+   Driving Accuracy: B+   GIR: A-   Short Game: B-   Putting: C

Fisher, Oliver James (England) (26)
b. Chingford, England 9/13/1988. 6'1" 175 lbs. TP: 2006. One of the more touted British prospects in several decades and a junior superstar who became the youngest player ever to participate in the Walker Cup (at age 17) in 2005. As an amateur, finished 5th at the E Tour's 2006 Q School and immediately turned pro. Has experienced an up-and-down ride since, particularly in 2011 when he missed 20 of his first 21 cuts, appeared in danger of losing his card, then saved himself by claiming his lone E Tour win – the Czech Open – in August, beating Mikael Lundberg by two. Enjoyed a resurgent 2014, going winless but finishing 56th in $$$. **Teams:** Walker Cup: 2005 (1-2-1). Eisenhower Trophy: 2006. **OWR Best:** 161 - Aug, 2008.

European Tour Wins (1): 2011: Czech Open.

Amateur Wins: English Under-16s: 2004   Telegraph Jr: 2005   Duke of York Trophy: 2005   St Andrews Links Trophy: 2006.

	07	08	09	10	11	12	13	14
Masters	-	-	-	-	-	-	-	-
US Open	-	-	-	-	-	-	-	MC
British	-	-	MC	-	-	-	T32	MC
PGA	-	-	-	-	-	-	-	-
Money (E)	109	51	125	81	95	95	118	56
OWR	414	215	363	285	314	357	419	223

2014: E: 29 st / 23 ct / 5 t10. (2P Africa, T4 Denmark, T6 NH Collection, T9 French, T9 KLM). Began to climb towards the heights once projected for him, logging high finishes in several light-field events to rank 56th in $$$, his best finish since 2008.

OUTLOOK: His once-touted career began to show signs of life in 2014 - though it should be noted that he'd previously kept his card several more times than he had lost it. Has the necessary length to compete at this level and is capable of hitting a lot of greens. Having started so young, he's still in his mid-20s so there is plenty of time for him to grow, but probably more steadily than steeply.

STATS: Driving Distance: A-   Driving Accuracy: C+   GIR: B+   Short Game: B-   Putting: B-

---

Fisher, Ross Daniel (England) (34)
b. Ascot, England 11/22/1980. 6'3" 170 lbs. TP: 2004. After a relatively quiet amateur career, joined the E Tour full-time in 2006 and broke through for his first victory at the 2007 Dutch Open (beating Joost Luiten by one at the Kennemer GC). Lost a three-way playoff (with Lee Westwood) to Phil Mickelson at the 2007 HSBC Champions (E Tour '08). Rode a first round 63 to a seven-shot win at the 2008 European Open. Lost a three-way playoff (with Martin Kaymer) to Robert Karlsson at the 2008 Dunhill Links Championship. Beat Anthony Kim 4 & 3 to claim the 2009 World Match Play. Managed the rare feat of leading all four of 2009's Major championships at some stage of the competition – but logged only a single top 10 in the end. Won 2010 Irish Open, edging Padraig Harrington by two at Killarney. Peaked monetarily in 2008 and '09 when he finished 6th and 4th in E Tour earnings. Played 15 PGA Tour events in 2013 as a non-member, finishing 161st in $$$. Ended a four-year victory drought by winning the 2014 Tshwane Open in South Africa, where he beat Danie van Tonder and Mike Hoey by three. **Teams:** Ryder Cup: 2010 (O:2-2-0, S: 0-1-0). Seve Trophy (2): 2009-11. World Cup (2): 2008-09. **OWR Best:** 17 - Nov, 2009.

European Tour Wins (5): 2007: Dutch Open (KLM) **2008:** European Open **2009:** World Match Play **2010:** Irish Open **2014:** Tshwane Open.

Amateur Wins: Finnish Am: 2003.

	05	06	07	08	09	10	11	12	13	14
Masters	-	-	-	-	T30	MC	T11	T47	-	-
US Open	-	-	-	MC	5	MC	-	-	-	-
British	-	-	MC	T39	T13	T37	MC	T45	-	MC
PGA	-	-	-	MC	T19	MC	T45	-	-	MC
Money (E)	-	66	43	6	4	16	52	38	40	28
OWR	337	287	84	29	18	33	100	94	71	68

2014: E: 28 st / 19 ct / 6 t10. (Won Tshwane, T2P BMW Masters, T3 Dunhill Champ, T7 Italian, T8 Irish, etc.). After spending time in America in 2013, confined himself to the E Tour in 2014, where he won once and logged his highest $$$ ranking since his halcyon days of 2008-2009.

OUTLOOK: An extremely solid tee-to-greener whose game slips noticeably on and around the putting surface. Remains a very steady presence in Europe (particularly after logging his first win in four years) and seems better suited to playing at home than splitting time in America. Age-wise, he could just be entering his best years, so his upside at this stage is considerable. More E Tour wins could well be in the near future.

STATS: Driving Distance: A-   Driving Accuracy: B+   GIR: A   Short Game: C   Putting: B-

Fisher, Trevor Jr. (South Africa) (35) b. Johannesburg, South Africa 8/6/1979. 5'10" 185 lbs. TP: 2002. A South African domestic star who, after a solid amateur career, took a surprisingly long time to find his legs on the Sunshine Tour. Failed to crack the top 50 in $$$ over his first four seasons but then began improving steadily, eventually cracking the top 10 in both 2011 and '12. A regular winner, but almost exclusively of 54-hole events during the lighter-field winter season. Claimed his first title at the 2003 Botswana Open (nipping Des Terblanche by two) before adding single wins in 2006, '08 and '09. Made a major jump in 2012, winning thrice, including a one-stroke win over Desvonde Botes and Bradford Vaughan at the Nedbank Affinity Cup. Scored a jackpot payday (and his eighth career Sunshine Tour win) in 2014 by claiming both the Investec Cup (by one over Jacques Blaauw) and its associated R3.5 million bonus pool. **OWR Best:** 179 - Mar, 2013.

Sunshine Tour Wins (8): 2003: Botswana Open (54H)   **2006**: Eskom Power Cup (54H)   **2008**: Seekers Travel Pro-Am (54H)   **2009**: Vodacom-Bloemfontein (54H)   **2012**: Wild Waves Challenge (54H), Vodacom-Sishen (54H), Nedbank Affinity Cup (54H)   **2014**: Investec Cup.

Other Wins: Klipdrift Sun Int'l Pro-Am (SA): 2008.

Amateur Wins: Kwazulu Natal Am: 2001   North West Am: 2001   Northern Province Am: 2001   Champion of Champions: 2002.

	03	04	05	06	07	08	09	10	11	12	13	14
Masters	-	-	-	-	-	-	-	-	-	-	-	-
US Open	-	-	-	-	-	-	-	-	-	-	-	-
British	-	-	-	-	-	-	-	-	-	-	-	-
PGA	-	-	-	-	-	-	-	-	-	-	-	-
Money (SA)	76*	52	70	91*	28	16	17	15	9	4	8	7
OWR	-	-	-	-	990	995	707	642	565	256	290	268

2014: SUN: 19 st / 15 ct / 7 t10. (Incl. Won Investec, T3 Vodacom-Arabella, T4 Alfred Dunhill).   Didn't play his absolute best golf, but his win was at the lucrative, select-field Investec Cup, helping him to log a fourth straight top-10 $$$ ranking.

OUTLOOK: Continues to play almost exclusively in Africa, which is somewhat surprising for a talented player in his prime competitive years. But he's certainly established himself as a regular Sunshine Tour winner, and that doesn't look like changing any time soon.

STATS: Driving Distance: --   Driving Accuracy: --   GIR: --   Short Game: --   Putting: --

---

Fitzpatrick, Matthew Thomas (England) (20) b. Sheffield, England 9/1/1994. 5'10" 155 lbs. College: Northwestern U. TP: 2014. In 2013, became the first Englishman in 102 years to win the U.S. Amateur (2013), while also losing in the English Amateur final, and finishing as low amateur (T44) at the British Open. Surprised everyone by leaving Northwestern after one semester and turning pro. Widely rated among England's top recent prospects, though he turned pro prior to accumulating a huge amateur record. Played his way through Q School on his first try, gaining E Tour status for 2015. **Teams:** Walker Cup: 2013 (3-1-0) **OWR Best:** 397 - Oct, 2014.

Amateur Wins: U.S. Amateur: 2013   -   British Boys: 2012   Telegraph Jr: 2012.

	13	14
Masters	-	MC
US Open	-	T48
British	T44	-
PGA	-	-
Money (E)	-	-
OWR	1014	413

2014: After turning pro, split time among the PGA (4 starts), European (6) and Challenge (9) Tours before playing through E Tour Q School.

OUTLOOK: Arrives with an impressive - if short - competitive résumé, and fairly high expectations. Hasn't played a ton of golf against the pros yet (his best finish is a T23 at the 2014 Heritage) but starring at the Walker Cup and successfully negotiating Q School are certainly good signs.

STATS: Driving Distance: --   Driving Accuracy: --   GIR: --   Short Game: --   Putting: --

---

Fleetwood, Tommy (England) (23) b. Southport, England 1/19/1991. 5'10" 170 lbs. TP: 2010. Enjoyed a strong amateur career which, beyond his domestic wins, included runner-up finishes at the 2008 British Amateur, the 2010 European Amateur and the Challenge Tour's 2010 English Challenge. Turned professional in August of 2010 but initially struggled somewhat on the European Tour, having a limited impact through 2012 and only retaining has card for 2013 via a T6 at November's South African Open.   Stepped up with his first victory at the 2013 Johnnie Walker Championship at Gleneagles (beating Stephen Gallacher and Ricardo González in a playoff), the centerpiece of a season in which he jumped to 26th in $$$. Then backed this up with a strong (if winless) 2014 in which he logged three runner-ups and finished 19th in $$$. **Teams:** Walker Cup: 2009 (1-1-0). Seve Trophy: 2013. **OWR Best:** 51 - Dec, 2014.

European Tour Wins (1): 2013: Johnnie Walker Championship.

Other Wins: 1 Euro Challenge (2011)   +   1 EuroPro (2011).

Amateur Wins: Scottish Am Stroke Play: 2009   English Am: 2010.

	10	11	12	13	14
Masters	-	-	-	-	-
US Open	-	-	-	-	-
British	-	-	-	-	MC
PGA	-	-	-	-	MC
Money (E)	252*	148*	109	26	19
OWR	468	133	276	118	51

2014: E: 28 st / 20 ct / 6 t10. (2 Volvo China, T2 Wales, T2 Dunhill Links, T3 Volvo Champ, T5 Czech Masters, etc.).   Continued to grow in his third full E Tour season, thrice finishing second and climbing to a career-best 19th in $$$.

OUTLOOK: After getting his E Tour beginnings as a teenager, began to look like a rising star as a 23-year-old in 2014. Has thus far shown himself a near-elite ball striker in terms of both length and accuracy, and while his putter lags behind, it's not so bad as to be a liability. At present, looks like the best bet among young English players - and if his putter shows noticeable improvement, he could become dangerous.

STATS: Driving Distance: A-   Driving Accuracy: A-   GIR: A   Short Game: B-   Putting: B-

Flesch, Stephen J. (USA) (47) b. Cincinnati, OH 5/23/1967. 5'11" 165 lbs. College: U of Kentucky. TP: 1990. An AJGA All-American. Spent several successful seasons playing the old Asian Tour, thrice ranking among the top 10 in $$$ and winning the 1996 Malaysian Open. Returned to play the Web.com in 1997, where he won the season-ending Tour Championship to jump to 4th place in $$$, gaining PGA Tour privileges. Was named the Tour's first left-handed Rookie-Of-The-Year in 1998 after finishing 35th in $$$. Very steady earner into the new millennium, boosted by wins at the 2003 New Orleans Classic and the 2004 Colonial (where he edged Chad Campbell by one), then a 2007 campaign which included late-season triumphs at the Reno-Tahoe Open (by five shots, wire-to-wire) and the Turning Stone Championship. Has not bettered 124th in $$$ since 2008 and is trending towards a career in broadcasting. **Awards:** PGA Tour Rookie of the Year: 1998. **OWR Best:** 22 - Jun, 2004.

PGA Tour Wins (4): 2003: New Orleans Classic (HP) **2004:** Colonial Inv (Bank of America) **2007:** Reno-Tahoe Open, Turning Stone Championship.
Asian Tour Wins (1): 1996: Malaysian Open.
Other Wins: 1 Web.com (1997) + Kentucky Open (2): 1991-93.
Amateur Wins: Kentucky Jr: 1985 Kentucky Am (2): 1986-88

	93	94	95	96	97	98	99	00	01	02	03	04	05	06	07	08	09	10	11	12	13	14
Masters	-	-	-	-	-	-	-	-	MC	-	-	T17	T29	-	-	T5	T6	T38	-	-	-	-
US Open	84	MC	-	MC	-	-	MC	-	MC	T18	MC	T7	T67	-	-	MC	-	-	-	-	-	-
British	-	-	-	-	-	-	T20	MC	-	MC	T54	77	-	-	-	-	-	-	-	-	-	-
PGA	-	-	-	-	-	T13	T34	MC	T13	T17	MC	T37	T10	T24	T23	6	T32	-	-	-	-	-
Money (A)	-	-	-	-	-	35	75	13	44	52	21	18	95	61	26	87	124	161	134	-	210*	225*
OWR	338	340	452	289	389	73	97	43	53	89	54	36	101	138	91	99	211	453	456	804	-	1129

2014: PGA: 5 st / 2 ct / 0 t10. (T21 Barracuda). In only five starts, made only two cuts and finished 225th in $$$ – a career-worst.
OUTLOOK: Has Past Champion status but is unlikely to play very much. More a broadcaster than a player now – at least until the Champions Tour.

STATS (LTD): Driving Distance: C-   Driving Accuracy: B   GIR: C   Short Game: C+   Putting: C+

Flores, Martin Thomas (USA) (32) b. Fort Worth, TX 2/17/1982. 6'0" 180 lbs. College: U of Oklahoma. TP: 2004. An AJGA All-American and an Academic All-American at the University of Oklahoma. Mini-tour regular before playing his way through Q School in 2009, then finishing 175th in $$$ in 2010. Repaired to the Web.com Tour in 2011 where, despite missing three of his last five cuts, he hung on to finish 24th in $$$, earning a ticket back to the PGA Tour in 2012. Though seldom a contender, retained his card with room to spare from 2012-2014, climbing to 95th in $$$ in the latter year. **OWR Best:** 141 - May, 2014.

	10	11	12	13	14
Masters	-	-	-	-	-
US Open	-	-	MC	-	-
British	-	-	-	-	-
PGA	-	-	-	-	-
Money (A)	175	-	96	103	95
OWR	575	449	270	253	249

2014: PGA: 26 st / 17 ct / 1 t10. (3 Wells Fargo). Kept his card for the third straight year, finishing 112th in FedEx Cup points.
OUTLOOK: Possesses a surprisingly strong statistical arsenal for a player who has thus far lingered around 100th in PGA Tour $$$. Is already in his 30s, which may suggest a bit shallower learning curve going forward – but numerically the tools are in place for at least a modest step upward.

STATS: Driving Distance: A   Driving Accuracy: C   GIR: B   Short Game: B+   Putting: B ⇩

Forsyth, Alastair (Scotland) (38) b. Glasgow, Scotland 2/5/1976. 6'2" 195 lbs. TP: 1998. Former top Scottish prospect who came straight to the E Tour upon turning pro and remained a full-time player there through 2012. Claimed his first two E Tour victories in sudden death, the first over Stephen Leaney at the 2002 Malaysian Open, the second over Hennie Otto at the lighter-field 2008 Madeira Islands Open. Began to struggle near decade's end, and had to play his way back through Q School each year from 2010-2013, the last time getting through directly on the number. **Teams:** World Cup (5): 2002-03-04-08-09. **OWR Best:** 83 - Aug, 2008.

European Tour Wins (2): 2002: Malaysian Open **2008:** Madeira Islands Open.
Other Wins: Scottish Under 25s (2): 1998-99 Scottish Assts (2): 1998-99 St Omer Open (France): 1999 Scottish Closed PGA: 2000.
Amateur Wins: Scottish Amateur Stroke Play: 1996.

	00	01	02	03	04	05	06	07	08	09	10	11	12	13	14
Masters	-	-	-	-	-	-	-	-	-	-	-	-	-	-	-
US Open	-	-	-	-	-	T15	T12	-	T60	-	-	-	-	-	-
British	-	-	-	T59	T47	MC	-	T67	-	-	-	-	-	-	-
PGA	-	-	-	MC	-	-	-	-	T9	79	-	-	-	-	-
Money (E)	46	116	42	19	33	80	82	47	61	103	127	140	133	185*	157
OWR	207	353	222	100	99	218	398	143	122	264	572	488	501	822	918

2014: E: 24 st / 10 ct / 0 t10. (T18 Russia). Finished 157th in $$$ - and failed to play his way through Q School for the first time in five years.
OUTLOOK: His numbers have been trending downward for the better part of six years, and this time he ran out of Q School magic and is thus bound for the Challenge Tour. Statistically, is still a balanced, mid-range player – but at age 38, his window for making a major upward push is narrowing.

STATS: Driving Distance: B   Driving Accuracy: B   GIR: B-   Short Game: B+   Putting: B-

---

Foster, Mark (England) (39) b. Worksop, England 8/1/1975. 6'2" 195 lbs. TP: 1995. A two-time English Amateur winner who struggled with back problems during the early years of his professional career, and took seven years to reach the E Tour. Has since remained a fixture, however, and eventually claimed his first victory at the 2003 Alfred Dunhill Championship in South Africa, where he won a six-man playoff which included Anders Hansen, Trevor Immelman and Paul Lawrie. Enjoyed a career-best year in 2011, finishing 32nd in $$$ while logging four top-5 finishes. His remained stead (if winless) ever since. **Teams:** Walker Cup: 1995 (2-0-2). Seve Trophy: 2011. **OWR Best:** 121 - Aug, 2011.

Foster, Mark, Cont'd

European Tour Wins (1): 2003: Alfred Dunhill Championship.
Other Wins: 3 Euro Challenge (1997-2001).
Amateur Wins: English Am (2): 1994-95   English Am Stroke Play: 1995 (T w/C.Edwards)   English Boys Stroke Play: 1992.

	02	03	04	05	06	07	08	09	10	11	12	13	14
Masters	-	-	-	-	-	-	-	-	-	-	-	-	-
US Open	-	-	-	-	-	-	-	-	-	-	-	-	-
British	-	T28	T63	-	-	T35	-	-	-	-	-	-	-
PGA	-	-	-	-	-	-	-	-	-	-	-	-	-
Money (E)	93	67	98	107	79	52	82	105	91	32	70	100	77
OWR	359	250	330	456	427	221	257	314	348	143	173	328	299

2014: E: 29 st / 16 ct / 2 t10.   (3 Perth, 4 Hong Kong).   Retained his card for the 13th straight year, finishing 77th in $$$.

OUTLOOK: Though he only owns one E Tour victory (11 years ago), continues rolling steadily along, seldom contending (only 21 career top 10s in 371 starts, through 2014) but rarely sweating too much towards season's end. Lacks length but hits enough greens to hold it all together.

STATS: Driving Distance: C+   Driving Accuracy: B+   GIR: B+   Short Game: B   Putting: B-

---

Fowler, Rick Yutaka (Rickie) (USA) (26)   b. Anaheim, CA 12/13/1988. 5'9" 150 lbs. Two-time All-American and Hogan Award winner (2008) at Oklahoma St. TP: 2009. Four-time AJGA All-American (and world #1 amateur) who left Oklahoma State after two seasons. Lost the 2009 Frys.com Open in a three-way playoff (to winner Troy Matteson and Jamie Lovemark) in only his second PGA Tour start. Gained his card at 2009 Q School and made his full-time PGA Tour debut in 2010, logging seven top-10 finishes, including solo 2nds at the Waste Management Open and the Memorial Tournament. Won Rookie of the Year (despite Rory McIlroy's logging a victory) and was a captain's pick for the Ryder Cup in his first full season. Claimed his first major tour title in 2011 on the OneAsia circuit, scoring a six-shot runaway win (over Rory McIlroy) at the Korean Open. Broke through for his first PGA Tour win at the 2012 Wells Fargo Championship, dramatically beating McIlroy and D.A. Points in a playoff. Finished no worse than 40th in $$$ over his first four PGA Tour seasons. Though winless, stepped up in 2014, climbing to 9th in $$$ and becoming the first man ever to log top-5 finishes in all four Major championships without winning one. **Awards:** PGA Tour Rookie of the Year: 2010. **Teams:** Walker Cup (2): 2007-09 (7-1-0). Eisenhower Trophy: 2008. Palmer Cup: 2008. Ryder Cup (2): 2010-14 (O:0-3-4, S: 0-0-2). **OWR Best:** 9 - Nov, 2014.

PGA Tour Wins (1): 2012: Wells Fargo Championship.
OneAsia Tour Wins (1): 2011: Korean Open.
Amateur Wins: Sunnehanna Am (2): 2007-08   –   Western Jr: 2005   California HS : 2006   Players Am: 2007

	08	09	10	11	12	13	14
Masters	-	-	-	T38	T27	T38	T5
US Open	T60	MC	-	MC	T41	T10	T2
British	-	-	T14	T5	T31	MC	T2
PGA	-	-	T58	T51	MC	T19	T3
Money (A)	Am	-	22	36	21	40	8
OWR	-	251	28	32	31	40	10

2014: PGA: 26 st / 19 ct / 10 t10.   (T2 US Open, T2 British Open, 3 WGC-Match Play, 3 PGA, T4 BMW, etc.).   Though winless, recorded his best year to date, finishing 8th in $$$, 9th in FedEx Cup points and, remarkably, logging top-5 finishes in all four Major championships.

OUTLOOK: Has now established himself as rating consistently among the world's best, logging 33 top 10s in 126 professional PGA Tour starts. Has few weaknesses in his game and is well-rounded statistically, but has somehow managed to record but a single domestic victory to date. One possible explanation: he ranked 125, 165 and 124 in fourth round scoring from 2011-2013 - but, perhaps in a glimpse of the future, that number skyrocketed to 8 in 2014. Clearly took a big step forward in 2014 – but can he get over the hump and start winning regularly? The wager here is yes.

STATS: Driving Distance: A-   Driving Accuracy: B-   GIR: B   Short Game: B   Putting: A-

---

Fox, Ryan (New Zealand) (27)   b. Auckland, New Zealand 1/22/1987. 6'1" 2100 lbs. College: U of Auckland. TP: 2012. The son of retired rugby star Grant Fox. Something of a late bloomer who toiled three seasons on the Australasian and OneAsia Tours before breaking through for a six-shot runaway win at the 2014 Western Australia Open. **Teams**: Eisenhower Trophy: 2010. **OWR Best:** 261 - Dec, 2014.

Australasian Tour Wins (1): 2014: Western Australia Open.

	12	13	14
Masters	-	-	-
US Open	-	-	-
British	-	-	-
PGA	-	-	-
Money (O)	103*	81	9
OWR	763	586	261

2014: Split time between the Australasian and OneAsia Tours, winning once on the former, where he also finished 5th in $$$.

OUTLOOK: Is well thought of in New Zealand, and began showing signs in 2014 of potentially having an international impact down the line.

STATS: Driving Distance: --   Driving Accuracy: --   GIR: --   Short Game: --   Putting: --

---

Fraser, Marcus (Australia) (36)   b. Corowa, New South Wales, Australia 7/26/1978. 6'0" 195 lbs. TP: 2002. Wasted little time heading to Europe upon turning pro, where a very strong 2003 debut included two Challenge Tour victories plus the 2003 Russian Open (then sanctioned by both the E and Challenge Tours), which he won in sudden death over Martin Wiegele. Beat a slightly stronger field at the weather-shortened Ballantine's Championship in 2010 (played in Korea) and, despite a potentially severe back injury in 2012, has remained a reliable earner ever since. Has twice finished 2nd in the Asian Order of Merit based solely on $$$ won in E Tour co-sanctioned events. Missed most of 2014 after undergoing wrist surgery.

Fraser, Marcus, Cont'd

Teams: Eisenhower Trophy: 2002. **OWR Best:** 51 - Feb, 2013.

European Tour Wins (2): 2003: Russian Open **2010:** Ballantine's Championship (54H).
Other Wins: 2 Euro Challenge (2003) + 1 von Nida: 2003.
Amateur Wins: New Zealand Am: 2002 – Asia Pacific Am: 2001.

	03	04	05	06	07	08	09	10	11	12	13	14
Masters	-	-	-	-	-	-	-	-	-	-	-	-
US Open	-	-	-	-	T45	-	-	-	-	MC	-	-
British	-	-	MC	T35	-	-	-	-	-	MC	T54	-
PGA	-	-	-	-	-	-	-	-	-	T66	T47	-
Money (E)	-	51	108	65	98	102	73	52	68	25	45	-
Money (As)	-	-	-	-	-	-	-	2*	-	2*	-	-
OWR	190	189	292	255	266	230	224	147	97	55	97	172

2014: E: 6 st / 4 ct / 1 t10. (T5 Hong Kong). Missed nine months (from late February into October) due to wrist surgery, then finished T5 at the Hong Kong Open in his first event back. Also finished T2 in the season-ending Thailand Golf Championship.

OUTLOOK: A very short (though quite straight) hitter whose tee-to-green game can be suspect – but he's clearly able to make up for both on and around the green. Seems to have recovered ably from his wrist issue so at age 36, he figures to be a borderline top 100 player again shortly.

STATS: Driving Distance: D   Driving Accuracy: A-   GIR: C   Short Game: A-   Putting: A

Fraustro Garza, Oscar (Mexico) (32)
b. Mexico City, Mexico 6/14/1982. 6'0" 165 lbs. College: U of South Florida. TP: 2006. Was Mexico's top-ranked amateur from 2003-2005 while playing collegiately in the U.S. at South Florida. After turning pro, was a mini-tour regular in the U.S. while also competing in Mexico. Finished 2nd in $$$ on the 2012 PGA Tour Latinoamérica to gain status on the Web.com Tour, where in 2014 he played his way through the Finals to reach the PGA Tour. **Teams:** World Cup: 2013. **OWR Best:** 384 - Apr, 2013.

Other Wins: Dominican Republic Open (PGATLA): 2012.

	12	13	14
Masters	-	-	-
US Open	-	-	-
British	-	-	-
PGA	-	-	-
Money (A)	-	-	-
OWR	412	440	561

2014: Played full-time on the Web.com Tour, finishing 61st in regular season $$$ before gaining his PGA Tour card through the Finals.

OUTLOOK: With a limited top-shelf competitive résumé, a limited power game, and having reached the PGA Tour via what would seem a Web.com Finals hot streak, he cannot be viewed as one of those most likely to succeed in the rookie class of 2015.

STATS (LTD): Driving Distance: C   Driving Accuracy: B-   GIR: B   Short Game: C   Putting: B-

---

Frazar, Richard Harrison (USA) (43)
b. Dallas, TX 7/29/1971. 6'0" 190 lbs. College: U of Texas. TP: 1996. An AJGA All-American. A three-time Honorable Mention All-American at Texas. Steady player who, after winning once on the 1997 Web.com circuit, finished comfortably among the PGA Tour's top 100 money winners from 1998-2006. Despite four runner-ups, remained winless throughout, then slipped out of the top 100 from 2007-2010. After a 187th-place $$$ ranking in 2010, was planning his golfing retirement when he surprisingly won the 2011 FedEx St Jude Classic (Memphis), beating Robert Karlsson in sudden death. Missed all of 2013 with a back injury, then returned in 2014 to make only four cuts in 15 starts, cutting his season short in July. **OWR Best:** 82 - Jan, 2012.

PGA Tour Wins (1): 2011: Memphis Classic (St Jude).
Other Wins: 1 Web.com (1997) + Callaway Inv: 2011.

	98	99	00	01	02	03	04	05	06	07	08	09	10	11	12	13	14
Masters	-	-	-	-	-	-	-	-	-	-	-	-	-	-	MC	-	-
US Open	-	-	T66	T54	-	-	-	T58	-	-	-	-	MC	T30	-	-	-
British	-	-	-	-	-	-	-	-	-	-	-	-	-	69	-	-	-
PGA	MC	MC	MC	MC	-	-	MC	-	T20	-	-	-	-	T39	-	-	-
Money (A)	63	79	79	66	96	83	48	79	98	131	163	112	187	69	121	-	224
OWR	134	128	116	131	162	171	101	102	150	279	468	330	563	147	211	-	-

2014: PGA: 15 st / 4 ct / 0 t10. (T58 Humana). Returned from 2013 back injury to finish 223rd in FedEx Cup points.

OUTLOOK: Often-injured player (he's had multiple hip surgeries) who begins 2015 on a 10-event medical extension dating to 2013. Considered retirement in 2011 before coming out of nowhere to win in Memphis. But while he's only 43, health is obviously a primary concern going forward.

STATS: Driving Distance: A-   Driving Accuracy: C-   GIR: C   Short Game: C-   Putting: C

Fritsch, Bradley Joseph (Canada) (37)
b. Edmonton, Alberta, Canada 11/9/1977. 5'11" 235 lbs. College: Campbell U. TP: 2000. Summa Cum Laude graduate of Campbell. Is the nephew of TV talk show host Ed Schultz. A late-developer who initially spent six winless years on his native Canadian Tour before joining the Web.com in 2007. After four winless campaigns, finally finished 18th in 2012 $$$ to play his way onto the PGA Tour as a 35-year-old rookie, then returned for year two via the Web.com Finals - a feat he was unable to repeat after a disappointing 2014. **Teams:** World Cup: 2013. **OWR Best:** 234 - Feb, 2013.

Other Wins: Azores Open: 2006.
Amateur Wins: Ottawa Am: 2000.

Fritsch, Bradley Joseph, Cont'd

	12	13	14
Masters	-	-	-
US Open	-	-	-
British	-	-	-
PGA	-	-	-
Money (A)	-	142	140
OWR	296	308	371

2014: PGA: 18 st / 8 ct / 3 t10. (T8 Wyndham, T9 Canadian, T10 Farmers). Despite three top 10s, finished 151st in FedEx Cup points.

OUTLOOK: Has shown himself a solid tee-to-greener over two PGA Tour seasons (48 and 74 in Ball Striking, 62 in 2014 Proximity To Hole) but has been unable to get it in the hole fast enough thereafter. After failing to play through the Web.com Finals, heads back to the Web.com in 2015.

STATS: Driving Distance: A-   Driving Accuracy: B-   GIR: B   Short Game: B   Putting: C+

Fritsch, Florian (Germany) (29)
b. Munich, Germany 10/29/1985. 5'11" 200 lbs. College: at U of South Carolina. TP: 2009. After playing collegiately in the U.S., spent several seasons playing the Challenge Tour and mini-tours, save for 2011 when he struggled on the E Tour after playing through Q School. Has had his career greatly slowed by a fear of flying as he primarily plays only in events that he can reach by car or train. **Teams**: Eisenhower Trophy (2): 2004-06. **OWR Best**: 215 - Oct, 2014.

Other Wins: 4 EPD Tour (2009-2013).

Amateur Wins: European Youths: 2004.

	09	10	11	12	13	14
Masters	-	-	-	-	-	-
US Open	-	-	-	-	-	-
British	-	-	-	-	-	-
PGA	-	-	-	-	-	-
Money (E)	-	-	156	-	-	-
OWR	536	724	559	978	1508	231

2014: Played full-time on the Challenge Tour, where he was thrice a runner-up and finished 11th in $$$, earning a return to the E Tour for 2015.

OUTLOOK: At age 29, may have the game and maturity to compete on the E Tour - if he can overcome his travel issues to play in enough events.

STATS: Driving Distance: --   Driving Accuracy: --   GIR: --   Short Game: --   Putting: --

---

Fujimoto, Yoshinori (Japan) (25)
b. Nara, Japan 10/25/1989. 5'4" 140 lbs. TP: 2012. After winning the individual silver medal at the 2011 World University Games, turned professional to begin 2012 and made an immediate impact on the Japan Golf Tour. After logging top-10 finishes in three of his first four professional starts (including 2nd at the Totoumi Hamamatsu Open), he claimed his first J Tour victory at the 2012 Japan Tour Championship (carding four sub-70 rounds to beat Masamichi Uehara by two) and finished 5th in the Order of Merit. Added a second title in 2013 at the Toshin Golf Tournament, where he ran away from Koumei Oda by four. **OWR Best**: 124 - Dec, 2012.

Japan Tour Wins (2): **2012**: Japan Tour Championship **2013**: Toshin Tournament.

	12	13	14
Masters	-	-	-
US Open	-	-	-
British	T54	-	-
PGA	-	-	-
Money (J)	5	10	12
OWR	124	132	138

2014: JAP: 24 st / 20 ct / 8 t10. (2 Kansai, T2 Heiwa, T3 ANA, T5 Tokai, 7 Nippon, etc.). Though winless, he enjoyed another strong campaign on the Japan Tour, twice finishing second and finishing 12th in $$$ - impressively, a career worst.

OUTLOOK: Has established himself as one of Japan's top young players, with a fairly balanced skill set which, surprisingly, is weakened mostly by his short game and putting. This, plus middling length, won't help him were he to try heading West, but he looks like a long-term player of note in Japan.

STATS: Driving Distance: B+   Driving Accuracy: B+   GIR: A-   Short Game: B   Putting: B-

---

Fujita, Hiroyuki (Japan) (45)
b. Fukuoka, Japan 6/16/1969. 5'7" 150 lbs. TP: 1992. Began as a journeyman on the Japan Tour who won twice on the Japan Challenge Tour (in 1997) while finding his way. Blossomed in his early 30s (winning four J Tour events from 2001-2005) before peaking as he reached age 40. Finished six straight times in the top 10 of the Order of Merit from 2007-2012, including topping the list in 2012. Beat the legendary Jumbo Ozaki by three to claim his first win at the 1997 Suntory Open. Won the 2008 Pine Valley Beijing Open (co-sponsored by the Asian Tour), then a pair of events in 2009: the Sega Sammy Cup and the Kansei Open. Both of his 2010 wins (a playoff at the Tsuruya Open, and the season-ending Golf Nippon Series JT Cup) came at the expense of 16-time J Tour winner Toru Taniguchi. Returned to defend the latter title in 2012, again besting Taniguchi in sudden death. A four-time winner in 2012, including the Tsuruya Open, the Diamond Cup, the ANA Open and, at year's end, a third straight Golf Nippon Series JT Cup to clinch the Order of Merit title. Began his 2014 campaign strongly, winning the Tsuruya Open for the third time, then added a second win at August's KBC Augusta, where he closed with 65 before beating Wen-Chong Liang in a playoff. Claimed a third 2014 win at September's Diamond Cup, beating a trio of players by two. **Teams**: World Cup (2): 1997-09. **OWR Best**: 43 - Dec, 2012.

Japan Tour Wins (18): **1997**: Suntory Open **2001**: Sun Chlorella Classic **2002**: Okinawa Open (54H) **2004**: Token Homemate Cup **2005**: Munsingwear Open **2008**: Pine Valley Beijing Open **2009**: Sega Sammy Cup, Kansei Open **2010**: Tsuruya Open (54H), Nippon Series JT Cup **2011**: Nippon Series JT Cup (54H) **2012**: Tsuruya Open, Diamond Cup, ANA Open, Nippon Series JT Cup **2014**: Tsuruya Open, KBC Augusta, Diamond Cup Golf.

Other Wins: 2 Japan Challenge (1997).

Fujita, Hiroyuki, Cont'd

	93	94	95	96	97	98	99	00	01	02	03	04	05	06	07	08	09	10	11	12	13	14
Masters	-	-	-	-	-	-	-	-	-	-	-	-	-	-	-	-	-	-	MC	-	MC	-
US Open	-	-	-	-	-	-	-	-	-	-	-	-	-	-	-	-	-	T58	MC	T51	MC	-
British	-	-	-	-	-	-	-	-	-	-	-	-	T41	-	-	-	-	MC	MC	MC	MC	-
PGA	-	-	-	-	-	-	-	-	-	-	-	-	-	-	-	T68	T56	MC	MC	MC	MC	-
Money (J)	148	-	68	89	18	39	36	35	12	12	**7**	17	16	14	**8**	**9**	**5**	**2**	**4**	**1**	25	**2**
OWR	711	851	452	431	129	159	266	319	194	107	112	164	165	178	128	83	64	48	68	43	145	113

2014: JAP: 24 st / 20 ct / 6 t10. (Won Tsuruya, Won KBC Augusta, Won Diamond Cup, 2 Bridgestone, T8 ANA, etc.). Bounced back impressively from a down 2013, winning three times and soaring to 2nd in $$$, his seventh top 10 finish in the last eight years.

OUTLOOK: Enjoyed a great resurgence at age 45, seeing most of his numbers (save for Driving Distance) improve as he logged three more wins. It is fair to wonder how long he can keep this up, but with power being far less important on the Japan Tour, perhaps he has a few great years left.

STATS: Driving Distance: C+   Driving Accuracy: A-   GIR: B+   Short Game: B+   Putting: B+

Fukabori, Keiichiro (Japan) (46)   b. Tokyo, Japan 10/9/1968. 5'10" 140 lbs. TP: 1995. Long-running Japan Tour regular whose career began slowly before finding its legs in 1997, when he finished 12th in $$$ and claimed his first victory at the KSB Open. Was only once outside of the tour's top 25 earners through 2008, a run which saw him win seven more times, highlighted by the 2003 Japan Open (where a closing 64 lifted him above Yasuharu Imano by two) and a pair of triumphs in the ANA Open, in 1998 and 2005. Cooled significantly thereafter, though he did record top-50 $$$ rankings in 2012 and '13. Has only rarely competed in the West but did finish 10th at the 2000 Canadian Open. **OWR Best**: 96 - Jan, 2006.

Japan Tour Wins (8): 1997: KSB Open **1998**: ANA Open **2000**: Jyuken Hiroshima, UBE Kosan Open **2001**: Hiroshima Open (54H) **2003**: Japan Open **2005**: Sun Chlorella Classic, ANA Open.

Other Wins: 1 Japan Challenge (1993) + Kanto Open (Japan): 1996.

Amateur Wins: Japan Jr (15-17): 2009.

	94	95	96	97	98	99	00	01	02	03	04	05	06	07	08	09	10	11	12	13	14
Masters	-	-	-	-	-	-	-	-	-	-	-	-	-	-	-	-	-	-	-	-	-
US Open	-	-	-	-	-	-	-	-	-	-	T57	MC	-	-	-	-	-	-	-	-	-
British	-	-	-	MC	-	-	-	-	-	-	T30	-	T56	-	-	-	-	-	-	-	-
PGA	-	-	-	-	-	-	-	-	-	-	-	-	-	-	-	-	-	-	-	-	-
Money (J)	128	154	46	12	15	25	**8**	10	51	13	13	**3**	20	11	26	94*	73	139*	43	44	78
OWR	743	825	355	147	116	185	151	104	235	153	129	100	128	158	220	463	695	-	574	563	836

2014: JAP: 20 st / 16 ct / 0 t10. (T14 PGA Champ). Slipped to 78th in $$$ and failed to log a single top 10 finish.

OUTLOOK: His numbers have dived since age 40 and at age 46, his best golf is almost surely behind him. But with this résumé, you never know.

STATS: Driving Distance: C+   Driving Accuracy: C   GIR: B-   Short Game: C+   Putting: C-

---

Furyk, James Michael (USA) (44)   b. West Chester, PA 5/12/1970. 6'2" 185 lbs. College: U of Arizona. TP: 1992. An AJGA All-American. Finished 78th in PGA Tour earnings as a rookie (1994) and never worse than 17th from 1997-2010 (save for injury-shortened 2004), a period in which he was five times among the top 5. Won the 2003 U.S. Open at Olympia Fields (by three over Stephen Leaney) with a record-tying 272 total after setting new 36- and 54-hole scoring marks. Counts three victories at the lucrative Las Vegas Invitational (1995, '98 and '99) and two at the Canadian Open (2006 and '07) among his 16 career triumphs. Put together several of his best seasons after 2004 wrist surgery, including a two-win 2006 that saw him rise to #2 in the year-end World Ranking. Plays mostly in America but won South Africa's then-unofficial Nedbank Challenge in 2005 and '06. Had a career-best year in 2010, winning three times (the Transitions Championship, the Heritage – in a playoff with Brian Davis – and the Tour Championship at East Lake) and capturing the $10 million 1st prize in the FedEx Cup. Slipped somewhat during a winless 2011 before starring at November's Presidents Cup. Suffered through an agonizing 2012 that including tough final round losses at the U.S. Open, the WGC-Bridgestone and the late-season McGladrey Classic, as well as in singles (vs. Sergio García) at the Ryder Cup. Five weeks after finishing 2nd at the PGA Championship, became the sixth man ever to shoot 59 on the PGA Tour in round two of the 2013 BMW Championship over the par-71 Conway Farms (IL) GC. **Awards**: PGA Tour Player of the Year: 2010. Vardon Trophy: 2006. FedEx Cup Champion: 2010. **Teams**: Ryder Cup (9): 1997-99-02-04-06-08-10-12-14 (O: 10-20-5, S: 4-4-1). Presidents Cup (7): 1998-00-03-05-07-09-11 (20-10-3). World Cup: 2003. **OWR Best**: 2 - Oct, 2006.

PGA Tour Wins (16): 1995: Las Vegas Inv (90H) **1996**: Hawaiian Open **1998**: Las Vegas Inv (90H) **1999**: Las Vegas Inv (90H) **2000**: Doral Open (Ryder) **2001**: Mercedes Championships **2002**: Memorial Tournament **2003**: U.S. Open, Buick Open **2005**: Western Open (Cialis) **2006**: Wachovia Championship, Canadian Open **2007**: Canadian Open **2010**: Transitions Championship, Heritage Classic (Verizon), Tour Championship.

Other Wins: 1 Web.com (1993) + Kapalua International: 1995 Argentine Open: 1997 Family House Inv: 1997 Fred Meyer Challenge: 1998 (w/D.Duval) Gillette Tour Challenge: 1998 (w/ L.Trevino & M.McGann) Wendy's 3-Tour Challenge: 2002 (w/R.Beem & J.Daly) PGA Grand Slam (2): 2003-08 Million Dollar Challenge (SA) (2): 2005-06 Target World Challenge: 2009.

Amateur Wins: Western Jr: 1987.

	94	95	96	97	98	99	00	01	02	03	04	05	06	07	08	09	10	11	12	13	14
Masters	-	-	T29	T28	**4**	T14	T14	T6	**4**	-	28	T13	T33	**T10**	MC	T24	11	T25	T14
US Open	T28	-	**T5**	**T5**	T14	T17	60	T62	MC	**Win**	T48	28	**T2**	**T2**	T36	T27	T16	MC	**T4**	MC	T12
British	-	-	T45	**4**	**T4**	**T10**	T41	MC	MC	MC	MC	**4**	T12	**T5**	T34	MC	T48	T34	MC	**4**
PGA	-	T13	T17	**T6**	MC	**T8**	T72	**T7**	**9**	T18	MC	T34	T29	MC	T29	T63	T24	T39	T42	**2**	**T5**
Money (A)	78	33	26	**4**	**3**	12	17	13	14	**4**	116*	**4**	**2**	**7**	12	**7**	**2**	53	12	15	**3**
OWR	261	78	49	22	12	11	15	15	11	**5**	21	**7**	**2**	**3**	13	**6**	**5**	50	27	19	**7**

2014: PGA: 21 st / 21 ct / 11 t10. (2 Wells Fargo, 2 Players, 2 Canadian, 2 Tour Champ, T4 British Open, etc.). Though winless, enjoyed a stellar 2014, making 100% of his cuts, logging an imposing 11 top 10s and finishing 4th in FedEx Cup points. Not bad for a 44 year old with a funny swing.

OUTLOOK: At age 44, he shows few weaknesses, save for being relatively short (though extremely straight) off the tee. A reliably solid Ball Striker (32) whose Scrambling (1) remains elite and whose putting still rates well above the median. Despite his age, there is little reason to suspect that a drop in form is imminent - but it must be noted that he hasn't won since a three-victory 2010, losing eight consecutive 54-hole leads in the process.

STATS: Driving Distance: C   Driving Accuracy: A+   GIR: A   Short Game: A   Putting: B+

Gainey, Tommy Dale Jr. (USA) (39) b. Darlington, SC 8/13/1975. 6'0" 190 lbs. College: Central Carolina Technical College. TP: 1997. Took the long and scenic route to the PGA Tour, playing on the Gateway, Hooters and eGolf Tours (winning four times on the latter) before tying for 19th at 2007 PGA Tour Q School. Struggled in 2008 and '09, then returned to the Web.com in 2010, where he won twice and finished 4th in $$$. Finally found his sea legs on the PGA Tour in 2011, logging four 3rd-place finishes en route to an impressive 35th place in $$$. Closed an otherwise quieter 2012 on a high note, claiming his first victory at the McGladrey Classic with a closing 60 at Sea Island. **OWR Best:** 85 - Oct, 2011.

PGA Tour Wins (1): 2012: McGladrey Classic.
Other Wins: 2 Web.com (2010) + 1 NGA/Hooters (2007)   3 eGolf Tour (2006-2007)   3 Gateway (2004-2005)   Callaway Inv: 2012.

	08	09	10	11	12	13	14
Masters	-	-	-	-	-	-	
US Open	-	-	-	-	-	-	
British	-	-	-	-	-	-	
PGA	-	-	-	MC	MC	T61	-
Money (A)	148	202	-	35	55	134	147
OWR	360	558	239	96	129	267	531

2014: PGA: 26 st / 11 ct / 1 t10. (T8 New Orleans). Finished 156th in FedEx Cup points, then failed to play his way back via the Web.com Finals.

OUTLOOK: Has used up his exemption for winning the 2012 McGladrey, and thus will be on Past Champion status for 2015. His homemade swing has held up fairly nicely over the last four years, but his overall performance has slipped nonetheless. Will try to fight back in limited starts.

STATS: Driving Distance: A-   Driving Accuracy: C   GIR: B-   Short Game: C   Putting: B

Gallacher, Stephen James (Scotland) (40) b. Dechmont, Scotland 11/1/1974. 6'2" 190 lbs. TP: 1995. Nephew of Ex-Ryder Cup Captain and 11-time E Tour winner Bernard Gallacher. Pedigreed prospect who won the 1992 Scottish Amateur and the 1994 European Amateur among other notable amateur events. After suffering a 1996 back injury, developed into a steady money winner on the E Tour, ranking among the top 100 in the Order of Merit from 1999-2008. Peak year was 2004 when he ranked 15th, powered by a win at the Dunhill Links Championship, taken in sudden death over Graeme McDowell at St Andrews. Missed much of 2009 with a severe viral infection but returned for a strong 2010, which included four top-10 finishes. Logged his second E Tour win at the 2013 Dubai Desert Classic (where he bettered Richard Sterne by three), then returned to defend his title in 2014, this time anchored by a record-tying nine-under-par 28 on the back nine on Saturday. Joined his uncle by participating in his first Ryder Cup in 2014. **Teams:** Walker Cup: 1995 (2-2-0). Ryder Cup: 2014 (O: 0-2-0, S: 0-1-0). Seve Trophy: 2013. World Cup (3): 2005-11-13. **OWR Best:** 31 - Jul, 2014.

European Tour Wins (3): 2004: Dunhill Links Championship **2013**: Dubai Desert Classic **2014**: Dubai Desert Classic.
Other Wins: 1 Euro Challenge (1998).
Amateur Wins: Scottish Am: 1992   European Am: 1994   -   Scottish Boys Stroke Play (2): 1991-92   Scottish Youths: 1994   Scottish Am Stroke Play: 1995   Lytham Trophy: 1995.

	95	96	97	98	99	00	01	02	03	04	05	06	07	08	09	10	11	12	13	14
Masters	-	-	-	-	-	-	-	-	-	-	-	-	-	-	-	-	-	-	-	T34
US Open	-	-	-	-	-	-	-	-	-	-	MC	-	-	-	-	-	MC	-	-	MC
British	MC	-	-	MC	-	-	-	-	-	-	MC	-	-	-	-	T23	T57	-	T21	T15
PGA	-	-	-	-	-	-	-	-	-	-	MC	-	-	-	-	T18	MC	-	T61	MC
Money (E)	-	180	167	-	101	56	65	97	50	15	51	64	84	77	-	26	61	35	19	16
OWR	-	899	858	-	386	259	228	321	231	66	132	257	349	291	441	89	142	98	66	35

2014: E: 27 st / 23 ct / 8 t10. (Won Dubai, 2P Nordea, 3 Italian, T4 Scottish, T5 BMW PGA, etc.).   Remained very much at the top of his game, defending his 2013 title in Dubai, finishing 16th in $$$ and appearing on his first Ryder Cup team.

OUTLOOK: Builds around a strong and powerful tee-to-green game, as he's rather impressively ranked among the E Tour's top 30 in Driving Distance and top 25 in GIR for the last four years. Though he's now 40, his lack of reliance on a hot putter as a centerpiece of his success may extend his high-end shelf life longer than some. Thus while he may not win often, he figures to remain one of Europe's best for the foreseeable future.

STATS: Driving Distance: A-   Driving Accuracy: B-   GIR: A   Short Game: B   Putting: B-

---

García Fernandez, Sergio (Spain) (34) b. Castellon, Spain 1/9/1980. 5'10" 160 lbs. TP: 1999. A genuine golfing prodigy who won his club's men's championship at age 12, made the cut in the 1995 Turespana Open Mediterranea at 14, and was the youngest-ever winner of the European Amateur in 1995. Won the 1998 British Amateur at Muirfield, and the professional Catalonian Open in 1997. Two-time E Tour winner (and runner-up to Tiger Woods at the 1999 PGA Championship) while still a teenager. Was the 1999 E Tour Rookie of the Year and a two-time PGA Tour winner at 21. Made major swing changes in 2003, resulting in a plunge from 6th and 12th (in 2001 and '02) in PGA Tour $$$ to 95th, before rallying for two wins and 9th place in 2004, and steady success thereafter. Battling constant putting problems, switched to the belly putter for the 2007 British Open and lost in a 4-hole playoff to Padraig Harrington after bogeying the 72nd. Also lost the 2008 PGA to Harrington (by two after bogeying the 70th and 72nd) at Oakland Hills. Had earlier ended a three-year victory drought at the 2008 Players Championship (beating Paul Goydos in sudden death) and later closed the year by winning the HSBC Champions (E Tour '09). Prior to 2011, 13 of his 18 major tour victories came before turning 25. Saw a surge of form in October, 2011, winning the Castello Masters (by 11 shots over Gonzalo Fernández-Castaño) and the Andalucia Masters in back-to-back starts. Ended a four-year PGA Tour victory drought by winning the 2012 Wyndham Championship, edging Tim Clark by two. Won Asian Tour's 2012 Iskandar Johor Open with a closing 61. Scored another late-season Asian victory at the 2013 Thailand Championship (beating Henrik Stenson by four), then won again early in 2014 at the Qatar Masters, where he beat Mikko Ilonen in sudden death. Converted to the claw putting grip in 2011 and saw his putting numbers improve substantially over the ensuing few years, stabilizing his overall game. **Awards:** Vardon Trophy: 2008. E Tour Rookie of the Year: 1999. **Teams:** Eisenhower Trophy (2): 1996-98. Ryder Cup (7): 1999-02-04-06-08-12-14 (O: 18-9-5, S: 3-4-0). Seve Trophy (2): 2000-03. World Cup (4): 2001-04-05-09. **OWR Best:** 2 - Nov, 2008.

PGA Tour Wins (8): 2001: Colonial Inv (Mastercard), Westchester Classic (Buick) **2002**: Mercedes Championships **2004**: Byron Nelson Classic (EDS), Westchester Classic (Buick) **2005**: Booz Allen Classic **2008**: Players Championship **2012**: Wyndham Championship
European Tour Wins (11): 1999: Irish Open, German Masters **2001**: Trophée Lancôme **2002**: Spanish Open **2004**: Mallorca Classic **2005**: European Masters **2008**: Costa Azahar Masters, HSBC Champions ('09) **2011**: Costa Azahar Masters, Andalucia Valderrama Masters **2014**: Qatar Masters.
Asian Tour Wins (3): 2002: Korean Open **2012**: Johor Open (54H) **2013**: Thailand Championship.

García Fernandez, Sergio, Cont'd

Other Wins: Catalonian Open: 1997   Dunhill Cup (2): 1999-00 (both w/M.A.Jiménez & J.M.Olazábal)   Million Dollar Challenge (SA) (2): 2001-03.
Amateur Wins: British Amateur: 1998   European Am: 1995   French Am: 1997   Spanish Am (2): 1997-98   –   Spanish Under-21s: 1996   European Am Masters (2): 1997-98   Sherry Cup (2): 1997-98   British Boys: 1997.

	96	97	98	99	00	01	02	03	04	05	06	07	08	09	10	11	12	13	14
Masters	-	-	-	-	T38	T40	MC	8	T28	T4	MC	46	MC	MC	T38	T45	T35	T12	T8	MC
US Open	-	-	-	-	T46	T12	4	-	T25	T20	T3	MC	MC	T18	T10	T22	T7	T38	T45	T35
British	MC	-	T29	MC	T36	T9	T8	T10	MC	T5	T5	2P	T51	T38	T14	T9	MC	T21	T2
PGA	-	-	-	2	T34	MC	T10	MC	MC	T23	T3	DQ	T2	MC	MC	T12	MC	T61	T36
Money (A)	Am	Am	Am	-	42	6	12	95	9	10	49	9	4	74	104	54	29	26	5
Money (E)	Am	Am	Am	3	21	27	6	49	13	6	11	15	9	10	42	8	43	16	6
OWR	899	858	405	12	16	6	4	36	7	6	11	12	2	11	78	17	16	10	5

2014: PGA: 16 st / 15 ct / 10 t10. (2 WGC-Bridgestone, 2 Travelers, 2 British Open, 3 Houston, 3 Players, etc.).   Did everything but win on the PGA Tour, logging an impressive 10 top 10s (and 12 top 25s) in only 16 starts while finishing among the top 5 in $$$ for the sixth time. Did manage a victory at the Qatar Masters, however, in one of his eight non-Major/WGC E Tour starts, and was a regular presence on leaderboards worldwide.

OUTLOOK: Turns 35th in January – and repetitive though it may be, who'd have thought he wouldn't have won a Major by now? Yet he stands today among the most consistently good players of his era, seemingly always contending but, of late, only rarely winning. Has been an up-and-down ball striker over the years but is currently on an upward trend (16 in Ball Striking, 14 in GIR in 2014). Has a reputation as a shaky putter but has improved markedly of late. Still very much in his prime and seems to have found a newfound maturity, so... Can he find that one additional winning gear?

STATS: Driving Distance: A-   Driving Accuracy: B+   GIR: B+   Short Game: B   Putting: B+ ⇧

García Pinto, Jordi (Spain) (24)
b. Girona, Spain 2/14/1990. 6'0" 155 lbs. TP: 2008. A law student who, despite turning pro at age 18, didn't start playing the Challenge Tour full-time until 2012. Logged three full seasons there, winning twice and, in 2014, finishing 7th in earnings to advance to the European Tour. **OWR Best:** 220 - Jun, 2014.

Other Wins: 2 Euro Challenge (2013-2014).
Amateur Wins: Spanish Jr (2): 2007-08   Spanish Under-21: 2008.

	12	13	14
Masters	-	-	-
US Open	-	-	-
British	-	-	-
PGA	-	-	-
Money (E)	-	-	-
OWR	740	482	297

2014: Played full-time on the Challenge Tour, winning once and earning his 2015 E Tour card by finishing 7th in $$$.
OUTLOOK: Is a well-thought-of prospect in Spain, and it is noteworthy that he several times skipped E Tour Q School, feeling that he should qualify off a full season's Challenge Tour work. Has developed steadily, and is obviously smart, but he may lack the experience to thrive immediately in 2015.

STATS: Driving Distance: --   Driving Accuracy: --   GIR: --   Short Game: --   Putting: --

---

Garnett, Brice (USA) (31)
b. Gallatin, MO 9/6/1983. 5'11" 175 lbs. Two-time D2 All-American at Missouri Western St. TP: 2006. Once won seven straight collegiate events while Missouri Western State. Played the Adams Golf Tour for three years after turning pro before splitting time with the Web.com Tour beginning in 2010. In 2013, finished 14th in regular season $$$ and graduate to the PGA Tour, where he retained his card as a rookie by finishing 121st in FedEx Cup points. **OWR Best:** 268 - Apr, 2013.

Other Wins: 1 Adams (2010)   2 eGolf Tour (2011).

	12	13	14
Masters	-	-	-
US Open	MC	-	-
British	-	-	-
PGA	-	-	-
Money (A)	-	-	132
OWR	463	394	370

2014: PGA: 28 st / 20 ct / 1 t10. (T7 Houston). As a rookie finished 121st in FedEx Cup points to narrowly retain his card.
OUTLOOK: Modestly surprised by keeping his card in 2014, relying on a deft short game and above-the-median putting stroke. His numbers suggest that he could either improve with a year's experience, or that his skill set is limited at this level. We'll bet on the latter, but it's a near thing.

STATS (LTD): Driving Distance: B   Driving Accuracy: C+   GIR: B   Short Game: B+   Putting: B+

Garrido Villacieros, Ignacio (Spain) (42)
b. Madrid, Spain 3/27/1972. 5'11" 170 lbs. TP: 1993. The son of five-time E Tour winner and 1979 Ryder Cup player Antonio. Caddied for his father as a youth but would later join him in a more meaningful way, as only the second father-son pair (after Percy and Peter Alliss) to participate in the Ryder Cup. Won the 1996 Hassan Trophy (Morocco) before it became an official E Tour event, later breaking through at the 2007 German Open, where he ran away from Russell Claydon by four. Logged his biggest win at the 2003 BMW PGA where he closed 66-65 at Wentworth, then defeated Trevor Immelman in sudden death. **Teams:** Eisenhower Trophy: 1992. Ryder Cup: 1997 (O: 0-1-3, S: 0-1-0). Seve Trophy: 2003. World Cup (4): 1995-96-97-03. **OWR Best:** 62 - May, 2003.

European Tour Wins (2): 1997: German Open   **2003:** BMW PGA.
Other Wins: 1 Euro Challenge (1993)   +   Hassan Trophy (Morocco): 1996.
Amateur Wins: English Am Stroke Play: 1992.

Garrido Villacieros, Ignacio, Cont'd

	94	95	96	97	98	99	00	01	02	03	04	05	06	07	08	09	10	11	12	13	14
Masters	-	-	-	-	MC	-	-	-	-	-	-	-	-	-	-	-	-	-	-	-	-
US Open	-	-	-	-	MC	-	-	-	-	-	-	-	-	-	-	-	-	-	-	-	-
British	-	-	-	MC	T55	-	-	-	-	MC	T54	MC	-	-	-	-	T14	-	-	-	-
PGA	-	-	-	T41	MC	-	-	-	-	MC	-	-	-	-	-	-	-	-	-	-	-
Money (E)	63	49	27	6	40	31	43	89	65	17	141	124	87	114	59	65	44	97	107	159	-
OWR	280	150	159	82	126	155	162	223	233	84	214	502	323	445	269	205	145	240	398	785	1483

2014: E: 3 st / 0 ct / 0 t10. Made only three competitive starts worldwide in 2014.

OUTLOOK: Is hardly over the hill at 42, and was a top-50 $$$ winner as recently as 2010, but has scarcely played after losing his card in 2013. With limited length and below-the-median Short Game and Putting numbers, a resurgence at this stage seems unlikely.

STATS: Driving Distance: C   Driving Accuracy: A-   GIR: B ⇓   Short Game: C   Putting: C

Garrigus, Robert Ira (USA) (37)
b. Nampa, ID 11/11/1977. 5'11" 190 lbs. College: Scottsdale(AZ)JC. TP: 1997. Son of an Olympic trap shooting silver medallist. Overcame alcohol issues and nearly a decade on mini-tours and the Web.com circuit before playing his way (via Q School) onto the PGA Tour full-time in 2006. Beyond his prodigious length (he led the Tour in Driving Distance in 2009 and '10), first came to note mostly for an epic collapse at 2010 St. Jude Classic (Memphis) where a triple bogey at the 72nd left him a three-way playoff with eventual winner Lee Westwood and Robert Karlsson. Came back to win the season-ending Children's Miracle Network Classic, where he beat Roland Thatcher by three. Missed a short putt to lose a playoff to Jonathan Byrd at 2011's season-opening Hyundai Tournament of Champions. Though winless since, has emerged as a steady money winner, through he's been trending downward since 2012. **OWR Best:** 35 - Apr, 2013.

PGA Tour Wins: 2010: Walt Disney Classic (Children's Miracle).

	04	05	06	07	08	09	10	11	12	13	14
Masters	-	-	-	-	-	-	-	-	MC	T38	-
US Open	MC	-	-	-	MC	-	-	T3	MC	WD	-
British	-	-	-	-	-	-	-	MC	-	MC	-
PGA	-	-	-	-	-	-	-	T62	T21	T25	-
Money (A)	-	-	144	74	138	127	51	56	20	77	94
OWR	-	911	359	169	273	324	151	105	39	80	254

2014: PGA: 25 st / 15 ct / 2 t10. (T4 Valspar, T5 New Orleans). Declined further from a disappointing 2013, logging only two top 10s en route to finishing 99th in FedEx Cup points.

OUTLOOK: More capable than most of overpowering a golf course with his big drives, though his formerly dead-eye wedge game cooled a bit in 2014 (116 in Approaches from 100-125 yards, 132 from 50-125 yards). Further, his GIR has fallen from 7 to 58 to 84 over the last three seasons. May well have peaked in 2012, when his eight top 10s doubled any other season in his nine-year PGA Tour career.

STATS: Driving Distance: A+   Driving Accuracy: C   GIR: B+   Short Game: C+   Putting: C+

Gates, Robert Michael (USA) (29)
b. Gainesville, FL 12/31/1985. 6'5" 230 lbs. College: Texas A&M. TP: 2008. Two-time AJGA All-American. A winner on the Gateway Tour in 2008, then on the Canadian Tour in 2009 and the Web.com in 2010, where a 16th-place $$$ finish graduated him to the PGA Tour for 2011. Fell from 125th to 126th place at the close of the season-ending Children's Miracle Network Classic when he three-putted the final hole, combined with D.J. Trahan's making birdie. Promptly returned to Q School and finished T3, easily keeping his card for 2012. Had to return to Q School again to re-qualify for 2013. Had his 2014 limited to 14 starts due to a hip injury. **OWR Best:** 184 - May, 2011.

Other Wins: 1 Web.com (2010) + 1 Gateway (2008).

	10	11	12	13	14
Masters	-	-	-	-	-
US Open	T40	-	-	-	MC
British	-	-	-	-	-
PGA	-	-	-	-	-
Money (A)	-	126	141	161	250*
OWR	217	377	471	488	975

2014: PGA: 14 st / 1 ct / 0 t10. (T80 Farmers). Limited to 14 starts by a hip injury which required surgery in July. Made only one of 14 cuts prior to the surgery, and finished 258th in Fedex Cup points.

OUTLOOK: Since 2011, has played through two Q Schools and a Web.com Finals, but will begin 2015 on a five-event medical extension, which may prove difficult to clear. Possesses plenty of power (no shock at 6'5", 230 lbs) but the rest of his game has not yet measured up at this level.

STATS: Driving Distance: A-   Driving Accuracy: C   GIR: C+   Short Game: C   Putting: C+

Gay, Joseph Brian (USA) (43)
b. Fort Worth, TX 12/14/1971. 5'10" 155 lbs. Two-time All-American at U of Florida. TP: 1994. Three-time AJGA All-American. Initially a mini-tour regular after college, highlighted by a 1995 campaign which included nine wins on circuits like the Emerald Coast, Gulf Coast, Gary Player and Tommy Armour Tours. Toiled on the Web.com in 1998 before reaching the PGA Tour (via Q School) in 1999. Enjoyed a steady existence for nearly a decade before blossoming with a victory at the 2008 Mayakoba Classic, then scored runaway 2009 wins at the Heritage Classic (by 10 over Briny Baird and Luke Donald) and the Memphis Classic (by five Bryce Molder and David Toms). Following a down 2012 (103rd in $$$), claimed his fourth career PGA Tour win at the 2013 Humana Challenge, beating Charles Howell III and rookie David Lingmerth in a playoff. **Teams:** Walker Cup: 1993 (0-1-1). **OWR Best:** 35 - Jun, 2009.

PGA Tour Wins (4): 2008: Mayakoba Classic **2009:** Heritage Classic (Verizon), Memphis Classic (Stanford St Jude) **2013:** Humana Challenge.
Other Wins: 1 NGA/Hooters (1994).
Amateur Wins: Rice Planters Am: 1992.

Gay, Joseph Brian, Cont'd

	96	97	98	99	00	01	02	03	04	05	06	07	08	09	10	11	12	13	14
Masters	-	-	-	-	-	-	-	-	-	-	-	-	-	-	MC	-	-	T38	-
US Open	MC	-	-	-	MC	-	MC	MC	MC	-	-	-	-	MC	MC	T63	-	-	-
British	-	-	-	-	-	MC	-	-	-	-	-	-	-	MC	MC	-	-	-	-
PGA	-	-	-	-	-	-	T22	T53	T51	-	-	-	T20	MC	T65	MC	-	MC	-
Money (A)	-	-	-	206	102	41	69	137	122	115	88	86	31	13	56	82	103	63	136
OWR	-	507	-	741	249	88	121	245	272	254	200	210	111	46	105	213	303	158	522

2014: PGA: 26 st / 15 ct / 1 t10. (T4 McGladrey). Experienced his worst season since 2003, finishing 140th in FedEx Cup points after logging only one top 10 and making only one cut (T71 at the Travelers) after May.

OUTLOOK: Has long ridden a recipe of a ultra-straight driving (though slightly less so of late) and an elite short game and putter - though of some concern might be an SGP of 17, 4, 22, 45 over the last four seasons. Still, when striking it well, he's capable of competing at a high level.

STATS: Driving Distance: C-   Driving Accuracy: A-   GIR: C   Short Game: A+   Putting: A

Gibson, Rhein (Australia) (28)
b. Lismore, New South Wales, Australia 1/2/1986. 5'8" 160 lbs. A 4-time NAIA All-American at Oklahoma Christian U. TP: 2009. Initially settled in America after turning pro, playing mini-tours and recording several minor victories. Gained a measure of immortality on May 12, 2012 by shooting a non-competitive 16-under-par 55 on the 6,698-yard River Oaks GC in Oklahoma City, the lowest round ever recorded on a regulation-size course. Has shown occasional flashes, such as finishing T4 at the 2013 Australian Open, but he has yet to gain status anywhere but Australia, where he finished 27th in $$$ in 2014. **OWR Best:** 386 - Mar, 2014.

Other Wins: 1 NGA/Hooters (2013)   +   Oklahoma Open: 2010   Brickyard (IN) Open: 2012   Arkansas Open: 2013.
Amateur Wins: Oklahoma Am: 2008.

	13	14
Masters	-	-
US Open	-	-
British	-	72
PGA	-	-
Money (A)	-	-
OWR	534	424

2014: Played primarily on the Australasian Tour, logging two top 10s in nine starts and finishing 27th in $$$.

OUTLOOK: Has spurts which suggest he can play at a high level, and he is clearly capable of going very low when hot. But at age 28, his game has yet to show a level of consistency conducive to finding success in the West – or perhaps even in Asia.

STATS: Driving Distance: --   Driving Accuracy: --   GIR: --   Short Game: --   Putting: --

---

Gillis, Thomas Charles (USA) (46)
b. Pontiac, MI 7/16/1968. 6'0" 200 lbs. College: Oakland (MI) JC. TP: 1900. A true international journeyman who has played in 26 countries and numerous overseas tours and mini-tours during his career. Played the Web.com full-time in 2006 (110th in $$$) and then again in 2009, this time winning once and graduating to the PGA Tour with a 5th-place $$$ ranking. Kept his card via 76th, 106th and 72nd-place finishes from 2010-2012 before slipping in 2013. Landed squarely in the limelight upon finishing T2 (with Tiger Woods) at 2012 Honda Classic, two back of Rory McIlroy. **OWR Best:** 99 - Feb, 2011.

Other Wins: 1 Web.com (2009)   +   2 eGolf Tour (20089)   1 NGA/Hooters (1996)   4 Gateway (2007-2009)   Waterloo (IA) Open: 1992   Jamaican Open: 1994   Michigan Open (2): 1994-08.

	99	00	01	02	03	04	05	06	07	08	09	10	11	12	13	14
Masters	-	-	-	-	-	-	-	-	-	-	-	-	-	-	-	-
US Open	-	-	-	T70	MC	-	-	-	MC	-	-	-	-	-	-	-
British	WD	-	-	-	-	-	-	-	-	T58	-	-	-	-	-	-
PGA	-	-	-	-	-	-	-	-	-	-	-	-	MC	-	-	-
Money (A)	-	-	-	-	139	-	156	-	-	-	76	106	72	158	-	-
OWR	417	214	373	476	258	512	379	676	754	538	189	117	225	144	382	517

2014: Played the Web.com Tour, finishing 54th in regular season $$$, then played his way back via the Web.com Finals.

OUTLOOK: A journeyman who, in his early 40s, retained his card for three straight years on the PGA Tour (2010-2012). Especially at age 46 he would seem a longshot to make much noise in 2015 - but then he seemed a longshot the first time around as well.

STATS: Driving Distance: B-   Driving Accuracy: B+   GIR: C   Short Game: B   Putting: B+

Glover, Lucas Hendley (USA) (35)
b. Greenville, SC 11/12/1979. 6'2" 195 lbs. Two-time All-American at Clemson U. TP: 2001. An AJGA All-American. Played the Web.com Tour in 2002 and '03, joined the PGA Tour in 2004 and claimed his first victory at the 2005 Walt Disney Classic by holing a 100' bunker shot at the final hole. A consistent money winner who ranked comfortably within the top 60 from 2005-2007. Struggled in 2008 before coming out of nowhere to win a rain-soaked 2009 U.S. Open at Bethpage, beating Phil Mickelson, David Duval and Ricky Barnes by two in a Monday finish. Added a 5th-place finish at August's PGA Championship to complete a career-best year that saw him rank 9th on the money list. Following a solid but unspectacular 2010, won the 2011 Wells Fargo Championship in a playoff with ex-Clemson teammate Jonathan Byrd during an up-and-down season that saw him finish 48th in $$$. Made only 16 PGA Tour starts in 2012 after injuring his knee during the first week of the season, and has never really returned to top form since. **Teams:** Walker Cup: 2001 (2-2-0). Palmer Cup (2): 2001-01. Presidents Cup (2): 2007-09 (2-6-1). **OWR Best:** 15 - Aug, 2009.

PGA Tour Wins (3): 2005: Walt Disney Classic (Funai)   **2009:** U.S. Open   **2011:** Wells Fargo Championship.
Other Wins: 1 Web.com (2003)   +   PGA Grand Slam: 2009.
Amateur Wins: South Carolina Am (3): 1998-99-00   Sunnehanna Am: 2001.

Glover, Lucas Hendley, Cont'd

	02	03	04	05	06	07	08	09	10	11	12	13	14
Masters	-	-	-	-	-	MC	T20	-	T36	-	MC	49	T42
US Open	MC	-	-	-	MC	MC	-	Win	T58	T42	MC	MC	MC
British	-	-	-	-	MC	T27	T78	MC	T48	T12	MC	MC	-
PGA	-	-	-	MC	T46	T50	-	5	MC	MC	MC	MC	-
Money (A)	-	-	134	30	21	53	105	9	57	48	216	108	182
OWR	739	459	274	65	38	81	177	20	57	69	259	294	606

2014: PGA: 26 st / 7 ct / 0 t10. (T14 Arnold Palmer). Made only seven of 26 cuts en route to finishing 185th in FedEx Cup points. Logged but a single top-25 finish (T14 at the Arnold Palmer Invitational) and made only one cut after April.

OUTLOOK: Has never really found his game again after suffering a left knee injury while body surfing in Hawaii early in 2012. Relies on a solid power game but his numbers on and around the green have tanked over the last two seasons (175 and 174 in Total Putting, 178 and 177 in SGP). Though his five-year exemption for winning the 2009 U.S. Open has expired, he remains exempt as a multiple tournament winner through 2015.

STATS: Driving Distance: A- Driving Accuracy: B+ GIR: B+ Short Game: C Putting: C

Goggin, Mathew Charles (Australia) (40)
b. Hobart, Tasmania, Australia 6/13/1974. 6'0" 185 lbs. A product of a golfing family, his mom being a three-time Australian Ladies champion. Played several winters on his native Australasian Tour (winning the 1998 Tour Championship in a playoff with Bradley King) while spending the rest of the year in Europe, then headed for the United States in 2000. Though winless, played the PGA Tour full-time from 2000-2003 before repairing to the Web.com in 2004 and '05. Found greater success on the big circuit from 2006-2009, thrice cracking the top 100 in $$$, tying for 5th at the 2009 British Open and peaking with a 40th-place finish on the 2008 money list. Has bounced back and forth between the PGA and Web.com circuits ever since. **OWR Best:** 48 - Jul, 2009.

Australasian Tour Wins (1): 1998: Tour Championship (ANZ).
Other Wins: 4 Web.com (1999-2011) + 2 Euro Challenge (1996-1997) Tasmanian Open: 1994*.
Amateur Wins: Australian Am: 1995 – Tasmanian Am: 1995.

	97	98	99	00	01	02	03	04	05	06	07	08	09	10	11	12	13	14
Masters	-	-	-	-	-	-	-	-	-	-	-	-	MC	-	-	-	-	-
US Open	-	-	-	-	-	-	-	-	-	MC	T36	MC	-	-	-	-	T21	-
British	-	-	-	-	-	T46	MC	-	MC	-	-	T5	MC	-	-	-	-	-
PGA	-	-	-	-	-	-	-	-	-	-	-	MC	MC	-	-	-	-	-
Money (A)	-	-	-	117	148	142	157	-	-	85	103	40	84	159	-	177	-	-
Money (E)	144	117	-															
OWR	530	169	230	290	324	338	309	420	228	124	191	58	78	318	221	376	358	691

2014: Played the Web.com Tour where he finished 62nd in regular season $$$, then failed to play through the Web.com Finals.

OUTLOOK: Despite some moments in the sun (e.g., four career Web.com titles, a T5 at the 2009 British Open) and a run of four years (2006-2009) when he kept his PGA Tour card, has never truly established himself in the U.S. - and will return to the Web.com Tour again in 2015.

STATS (LTD): Driving Distance: B Driving Accuracy: B- GIR: B Short Game: B Putting: B+

Gómez, Fabián Eduardo (Argentina) (36)
b. Chaco, Argentina 10/27/1978. 5'8" 165 lbs. TP: 2002. A regular winner in his native Argentina since 2004, led by triumphs in the 2008 Argentine Masters and the 2009 Abierto del Centro. Came north to play the Web.com Tour in 2007 and settled in for a four-season stay. Won a 2010 Web.com event en route to a 12th-place $$$ finish and his PGA Tour card. Lost his card after 2011, returned to the big stage via a T22 at 2012 Q School, then lost his card again after 2013 and earned it back again via the 2014 Web.com Tour.
Teams: World Cup: 2013. **OWR Best:** 205 - Apr, 2010.

Other Wins: 1 Web.com (2010) + 1 Gateway (2006) Villa Mercedes Grand Prix: 2004 Venezuela Open: 2006 Chaco Open (Arg): 2007 Argentine Masters: 2008 Norpatagonico Open (Arg): 2009 Abierto del Centro (Arg): 2009 Roberto De Vicenzo Classic (Arg): 2009 Buenos Aires Open: 2010 Personal Classic (PGATLA): 2013.

	07	08	09	10	11	12	13	14
Masters	-	-	-	-	-	-	-	-
US Open	-	-	-	-	-	-	-	-
British	-	-	-	-	-	-	-	-
PGA	-	-	-	-	-	-	-	-
Money (A)	-	-	-	-	157	-	129	-
OWR	319	308	303	271	567	636	348	245

2014: Played the Web.com Tour where he clinched a return to the PGA Tour by finishing 23rd in regular season $$$.

OUTLOOK: Will return to the PGA Tour for the third time in 2015, hoping that his now-considerable re-qualifying experience pays dividends. Is a mid-range sort statistically save for his putter - but that's a good place to start.

STATS: Driving Distance: B Driving Accuracy: B+ GIR: B- Short Game: B Putting: A-

---

Gonzales, Andres Duane (USA) (31)
b. Olympia, WA 5/16/1983. 6'2" 225 lbs. All-American at UNLV. TP: 2006. Known for his distinctive long hair and fu manchu mustache. Played multiple mini-tours for several years after turning pro (logging a handful of wins), then added a 2009 victory on the Canadian circuit. Played through Q School (T22) in 2010 and the Web.com (14th in $$$) in 2012 but each time failed to keep his card on the PGA Tour, never bettering 190th in $$$. Prior to 2015, had logged only one top 10 in a PGA Tour event (T8 at the 2013 Wyndham Championship). **OWR Best:** 219 - Apr, 2012.

Other Wins: 1 Web.com (2012) + 2 Gateway (2007-2009) Saskatchewan Open (Canada): 2009.
Amateur Wins: Scratch Players: 2005.

Gonzales, Andres Duane, Cont'd

	11	12	13	14
Masters	-	-	-	-
US Open	MC	-	-	-
British	-	-	-	-
PGA	-	-	-	-
Money (A)	192	-	190	-
OWR	497	374	531	260

2014: Played the Web.com Tour where he clinched a third visit to the PGA Tour by finishing 11th in regular season $$$.

OUTLOOK: Will take another crack at exiting the ranks of those seemingly stuck between starring on the Web.com and not quite making it on the PGA Tour. Has a solid skill set but only one top 10 (T8 at the 2013 Wyndham Championship) in 44 previous PGA Tour starts.

STATS (LTD): Driving Distance: B+   Driving Accuracy: C+   GIR: C   Short Game: B   Putting: B+

González, Ricardo (Argentina) (45)
b. Corrientes, Argentina 10/24/1969. 6'0" 205 lbs. TP: 1986. Long-hitting Argentinean who has played worldwide, initially spending more than a decade primarily in South America before eventually riding a 1998 Kenya Open victory onto the Challenge Tour. A fixture on the European Tour soon thereafter, he broke through with a three-shot win over Søren Hansen at the 2001 European Masters, then added a one-shot triumph over a group that included Padraig Harrington, Paul Casey and Nick O'Hern at the 2003 Madrid Open. His last E Tour win came at the 2009 SAS Masters, where he edged Jamie Donaldson by two. In South America, most of his wins have taken place in his native Argentina, including four at the Abierto del Litoral (the "Coastal Open"). **Teams:** World Cup (4): 1996-98-05-07. **OWR Best:** 62 - Apr, 2004.

European Tour Wins (4): 2001: European Masters **2003:** Madrid Open **2004:** Sevilla Open **2009:** SAS Masters.

Other Wins: 2 Euro Challenge (1990-1998) + Rosario Open (Arg): 1987 Praderas Grand Prix (Arg): 1988 Uruguay Open: 1995 La Plata Open (Arg): 1995 Chile Open: 1996 World Nature Games (Brazil): 1997 Prince of Wales Open (Chile): 1997 JPGA Championship (Arg): 1998 Abierto del Litoral (Arg) (4): 2003-05-09-10 Parana Open (Arg): 2006 Abierto del Norte (Arg): 2007 (T w/A.Romero).

	92	93	94	95	96	97	98	99	00	01	02	03	04	05	06	07	08	09	10	11	12	13	14
Masters	-	-	-	-	-	-	-	-	-	-	-	-	-	-	-	-	-	-	-	-	-	-	-
US Open	-	-	-	-	-	-	-	-	-	-	-	-	-	-	-	-	-	-	-	-	-	-	-
British	-	-	-	-	-	-	-	-	-	-	MC	-	-	-	-	-	-	-	-	-	-	-	-
PGA	-	-	-	-	-	-	-	-	-	-	T10	MC	MC	-	-	-	-	-	-	-	-	-	-
Money (E)	155	-	-	-	-	-	-	61	34	25	28	47	50	78	55	105	83	72	115	99	82	66	131
OWR	668	-	-	-	858	478	268	167	87	74	81	113	207	121	270	239	162	337	245	252	240	404

2014: E: 25 st / 10 ct / 0 t10. (T16 Scottish). Lost his card for the first time in 16 years, then played his way back by finishing 2nd at Q School.

OUTLOOK: Even at age 45, continues to build around his power, which lies at the heart of his always ranking highly in GIR (18 in a down 2014). His putting is another story, however, but as it's never been a key to his success, there's no great damage done by some incremental declining.

STATS: Driving Distance: A-   Driving Accuracy: C-   GIR: A-   Short Game: B-   Putting: C+

Goosen, Retief (South Africa) (46)
b. Pietersburg, South Africa 2/3/1968. 6'0" 175 lbs. TP: 1990. Former top junior prospect (and 1990 South African Amateur champion) whose career was slowed after being struck by lightning as a teenager. Has 27 career wins on four major tours worldwide plus several prominent unofficial titles, including the 2004 Nedbank Million Dollar Challenge. Was a seven-time winner in South Africa and Europe before winning the 2001 U.S. Open at Southern Hills, missing a short putt for victory at the 72nd, then rebounding to beat Mark Brooks in an 18-hole Monday playoff. Claimed a second U.S. Open title in 2004 at Shinnecock Hills, braving an epic USGA course set-up fiasco to defeat Phil Mickelson by two. Went on to win thrice more in '04, including the European Open (in a five-shot romp) and the season-ending Tour Championship (by four over Tiger Woods). The first non-European since Greg Norman (1982) to top the European Order of Merit in 2001 (when he was also named E Tour Golfer of the Year), then repeated the feat in 2002. Also a top-10 money winner in America in 2002 and '03. Slumped badly in 2007-2008 after problems with laser eye surgery, and with swing issues. Returned to form in 2009 with wins at PGA Tour's Transitions Championship and the Africa Open, but slumped to 108th in $$$ in 2011. Had back surgery in August of 2012, missing the remainder of the season before returning in early 2013, then sitting out after May due to lingering problems. **Awards:** E Tour Golfer of the Year: 2001. Euro Vardon Trophy (2): 2001-02. **Teams:** Presidents Cup (6): 2000-03-05-07-09-11 (14-12-3). World Cup (5): 1993-95-00-01-07 (won in '01 w/E.Els). **OWR Best:** 3 - Jan, 2006.

PGA Tour Wins (7): 2001: U.S. Open **2002:** Atlanta Classic (BellSouth) **2003:** Chrysler Championship **2004:** U.S. Open, Tour Championship **2005:** The International (Stableford) **2009:** Transitions Championship.

European Tour Wins (12): 1996: Northumberland Challenge **1997:** Open de France **1999:** Open de France **2000:** Trophée Lancôme **2001:** Scottish Open, Open de Madrid **2002:** Johnnie Walker Classic **2003:** Trophée Lancôme **2004:** European Open **2005:** German Masters, South African Open ('06) **2007:** Qatar Masters.

Sunshine Tour Wins (5): 1992: Spoornet Classic **1993:** Mount Edgecombe Trophy **1995:** South African Open **2002:** Dimension Data Pro-Am **2009:** Africa Open.

Asian Tour Wins (3): 2005: China Masters **2006:** China Masters **2008:** Johor Open.

Other Wins: Kempton Park Open (54H): 1990 Newcastle Classic (SA): 1991 Bushveld Classic (SA) (54H): 1992 Highveld Classic (SA): 1992 Dunhill Cup (2): 1997-98 (w/E.Els & D.Frost) Nelson Mandela Inv (2): 2000 (w/A.Henning)-06 (w/B.Lincoln) Singapore Skins (2): 2002-03 Million Dollar Challenge (SA): 2004 Emirates Airlines Inv (18H): 2011.

Amateur Wins: South African Am: 1990.

	91	92	93	94	95	96	97	98	99	00	01	02	03	04	05	06	07	08	09	10	11	12	13	14
Masters	-	-	-	-	-	-	-	MC	-	T40	MC	T2	T13	T13	T3	T3	T2	T17	MC	T38	MC	-	-	-
US Open	-	-	-	-	-	-	-	MC	MC	T12	Win	MC	T42	Win	T11	MC	MC	T14	T16	T58	T23	T10	-	T45
British	-	-	MC	-	-	76	T10	MC	T10	T41	T13	T8	T10	T7	T5	T14	T23	T32	T5	6	WD	T64	-	-
PGA	-	-	-	-	-	-	T61	MC	MC	MC	T37	T23	MC	-	T6	T34	T23	T24	T51	T55	WD	T48	-	-
Money (A)	-	-	-	-	-	-	-	-	-	10	10	6	8	19	93	72	11	14	108	136*	162*	114
Money (E)	-	-	44	39	94	25	7	33	5	15	1	1	2	4	12	9	15	27	19	14	42	45	-	-
Money (Sa)	-	2	3*	5*	25*	2*	-	-	6*	3*	-	-	-	-	-	-	7*	-	-	-	-	-	-	-
OWR	470	209	86	100	139	110	60	82	33	38	10	5	7	4	4	6	26	45	19	16	53	107	313	205

Goosen, Retief, Cont'd

2014: PGA: 26 st / 21 ct / 2 t10. (T7 Shell, T8 Hawaii). With back surgery seemingly behind him, put together his first full PGA Tour season in three years, finishing 103rd in FedEx Cup points and clearing a medical extension - the latter perhaps being the biggest accomplishment of all.

OUTLOOK: At age 46, and having endured multiple back issues, Goosen must still be considered very much a wildcard. But given his Hall-of-Fame caliber, multi-Major championship résumé, and an ability to hole lots of puts when it matters, it would be unwise to entirely write him off too quickly.

STATS: Driving Distance: B   Driving Accuracy: C   GIR: C+   Short Game: A-   Putting: A

Gore, Jason William (USA) (40)
b. Van Nuys, CA 5/17/1974. 6'0" 245 lbs. College: Pepperdine U, after transferring from U of Arizona. TP: 1997. Journeyman who exploded in 2005, earning a battlefield promotion to the PGA Tour following three Nationwide Tour wins, then winning the 84 Lumber Classic in his 5th start. Finished 94th in $$$ despite making only eight starts. Became only the second player ever to win on both tours in a single season. Came to fame by lingering around the lead for 54 holes at the 2005 U.S. Open before a closing 84 dropped him to T49. Since 2010, has played mostly on the Web.com Tour, where his seven wins are the Tour record. **Teams**: Walker Cup: 1997 (3-0-0). **OWR Best**: 77 - Dec, 2005.

PGA Tour Wins (1): 2005: 84 Lumber Classic.
Other Wins: 7 Web.com (2000-2010) + California Open (2): 1997*-04.
Amateur Wins: Sahalee Players: 1996   Pacific Coast Am: 1997   California Am: 1997.

	98	99	00	01	02	03	04	05	06	07	08	09	10	11	12	13	14
Masters	-	-	-	-	-	-	-	-	-	-	-	-	-	-	-	-	-
US Open	MC	-	-	-	-	-	-	T49	-	-	MC	-	T47	-	-	-	-
British	-	-	-	-	-	-	-	-	-	-	-	-	-	-	-	-	-
PGA	-	-	-	-	-	-	-	-	-	-	-	-	-	-	-	-	-
Money (A)	-	-	-	178	-	177	-	95*	118	88	134	155	212*	223*	239*	-	-
OWR	-	591	500	449	410	433	666	90	130	173	288	500	440	638	709	659	229

2014: Played the Web.com Tour where he clinched a seventh full season on the PGA Tour by finishing 9th in regular season $$$.

OUTLOOK: Few Web.com arrivals have anywhere near as much experience as this man, who has made 222 career starts through 2014. Coming off a highly efficient season on the Web.com Tour, but at age 40, his chances of truly succeeding on the big stage are starting to wear thin.

STATS: Driving Distance: B+   Driving Accuracy: B-   GIR: B+   Short Game: B-   Putting: B

Goya, Carlos Estanislao ("Tano") (Argentina) (26)
b. Alta Gracia, Argentina 6/1/1988. 6'0" 170 lbs. TP: 2007. Was a decorated amateur in his native Argentina before winning the 2008 Abierto del Centro on the old Tour De Las Americas circuit, an event co-sanctioned by the European Challenge Tour. A year later, he would claim his lone European Tour victory at the 2009 Madeira Islands Open, another event co-sanctioned by the Challenge Tour but which included a partial E Tour exemption. Made little noise thereafter, however, and lost his card in both 2012 and '13. Claimed his second major tour win at the Sunshine circuit's 2014 Dimension Data Pro-Am, where he edged four players by one. **Teams**: Eisenhower Trophy: 2006. World Cup: 2009. **OWR Best**: 98 - Mar, 2009.

European Tour Wins (1): 2008: Madeira Islands Open.
Sunshine Tour Wins (1): 2014: Dimension Data Pro-Am.
Other Wins: 2 Euro Challenge (2008) + De Vicenzo Shootout (Arg): 2008   Angel Cabrera Classic (Arg): 2011.

	08	09	10	11	12	13	14
Masters	-	-	-	-	-	-	-
US Open	-	-	-	-	-	MC	-
British	-	-	MC	-	-	MC	-
PGA	-	-	-	-	-	-	-
Money (E)	-	94	99	98	123	174	141
OWR	191	197	333	311	432	848	574

2014: E: 21 st / 12 ct / 0 t10. (T18 Mandela). Lost his card for the third straight year (141st in $$$) but this time failed to return via Q School.

OUTLOOK: In six seasons, has never bettered 94th in E Tour $$$, and there is little numerically to suggest that this is subject to imminent change.

STATS: Driving Distance: B+   Driving Accuracy: C+   GIR: B-   Short Game: B+   Putting: C+

Goydos, Paul David (USA) (50)
b. Long Beach, CA 6/20/1964. 5'9" 190 lbs. College: Long Beach St. TP: 1989. After playing collegiately at hometown Long Beach State, spent two years on the Web.com Tour before reaching the PGA Tour via 1992 Q School. Initially a journeyman who cracked the top 100 money earners five out of six years from 1994-1999, and edged Jeff Maggert by one to win the 1996 Bay Hill Invitational. After missing 2004 with sinus surgery and a hip injury, then missing the top 125 in 2005, finished 2nd in his final 2006 event (October's Chrysler Championship) to keep his card. Opened 2007 by winning the Sony Open in Hawaii (by one over Charles Howell III and Luke Donald), breathing new life into his career. Became the fourth man ever to shoot 59 in a PGA Tour event in the first round of the 2010 John Deere Classic (TPC Deere Run). Had wrist surgery in March of 2012, missing the remainder of the season plus nearly all of 2013 while recovering. **OWR Best**: 39 - Jan, 2007.

PGA Tour Wins (2): 1996: Bay Hill Inv   **2007**: Hawaiian Open (Sony).
Champions Tour Wins (1): 2014.
Other Wins: 1 Web.com (1992) + Long Beach Open: 1990   EA Sports Golf Challenge: 1996.

	93	94	95	96	97	98	99	00	01	02	03	04	05	06	07	08	09	10	11	12	13	14
Masters	-	-	-	MC	-	-	-	-	-	-	-	-	-	-	MC	-	-	-	-	-	-	-
US Open	-	T44	T62	MC	T28	-	T12	MC	MC	MC	-	-	-	-	MC	-	-	MC	-	-	-	-
British	-	-	-	-	-	-	-	-	-	-	-	-	-	-	-	MC	72	MC	-	-	-	-
PGA	-	-	-	-	T73	T29	T34	T31	-	-	-	-	-	-	MC	T31	T67	MC	-	-	-	-
Money (A)	152	75	129	44	61	82	61	121	132	139	88	-	148	97	78	51	53	81	63	220*	-	226
OWR	489	245	252	87	75	132	116	150	292	318	163	334	305	135	105	98	101	160	164	440	-	1407

Goydos, Paul David, Cont'd

2014: PGA: 19 st / 4 ct / 0 t10. Finished 244th in FedEx Cup points but also made 10 Champions Tour starts, winning in Hawaii.

OUTLOOK: Failed to clear a 2014 medical extension and would be playing on Past Champion status now. Based on his 2006-2011 performance pre-wrist surgery, it wouldn't be crazy to suggest that he can still compete on the PGA Tour – but big success on the Champions circuit seems more likely.

STATS: Driving Distance: D   Driving Accuracy: A   GIR: C   Short Game: C   Putting: C+

Grace, Branden John (South Africa) (26)
b. Pretoria, South Africa 5/20/1988. 5'10" 170 lbs. TP: 2007. After winning the 2006 South African Amateur Stroke Play, turned pro in 2007, then spent 2008, 2010 and 2011 on the European Challenge Tour. Claimed his first major tour title in 2010 at the Sunshine Tour's Coca Cola Charity Championship. Took off with a vengeance in 2012 when, fresh out of the 2011 European Tour Q School, he won the Joburg Open on home soil in January, then a week later added the Volvo Golf Champions, where he defeated Ernie Els and Retief Goosen in a play-off. Won for a third time at April's Volvo China Open, where he beat Nicolas Colsaerts by four. Claimed a fourth 2012 win (his third in South Africa) by winning the 54-hole Vodacom Origins of Golf Final, then added the E Tour's Dunhill Links Championship after opening with a spectacular 60 at Kingsbarns. Inevitably cooled in 2013 but still finished 18th in E Tour $$$, then 31st during a winless 2014. Broke the victory drought in the last event of calendar 2014, running away with the Alfred Dunhill Championship by seven shots, in South Africa. **Teams**: Presidents Cup: 2013 (0-4-0). World Cup: 2013. **OWR Best**: 26 - Jul, 2013.

European Tour Wins (5): 2012: Joburg Open, Volvo Golf Champions, China Open (Volvo), Dunhill Links Championship **2014**: Alfred Dunhill Championship (E '15).

Sunshine Tour Wins (2): 2010: Coca-Cola Championship (54H) **2012**: Vodacom-Final (54H).

Amateur Wins: South African Am Stroke play: 2006.

	08	09	10	11	12	13	14
Masters	-	-	-	-	-	T18	MC
US Open	-	-	-	-	T51	MC	-
British	-	T43	-	-	T77	T64	T36
PGA	-	-	-	-	MC	MC	T47
Money (E)	-	148	-	-	6	18	31
Money (SA)	23	11	13	7	1	47*	4*
OWR	386	359	435	271	34	50	82

2014: E: 21 st / 17 ct / 3 t10. (2 Volvo Champ, T6 Mandela, T9 Tour Champ). Took another small step backwards during the official 2014 season (finishing 31st in $$$ without a win) but ended the calendar year by winning the Alfred Dunhill Championship (officially a 2015 event).

OUTLOOK: A impressive talent who mixes plenty of length with a deft putting stroke – always a profitable combination. Even after two relatively "quiet" seasons, this is a young man (still just 26) with four E Tour victories under his belt, and the seeming ability to rank among the game's very best. Got his 2015 off to a good start by winning the Dunhill, so a strong year may lie ahead. Holds long-term breakout potential.

STATS: Driving Distance: A-   Driving Accuracy: C   GIR: B+   Short Game: B-   Putting: A-

---

Green, Nathan Jonathan Currie (USA) (39)
b. Newcastle, New South Wales, Australia 5/13/1975. 5'8" 175 lbs. TP: 1998. After winning minor titles like the New Zealand Under-23s (twice), the Queensland PGA (then on the Von Nida Tour) and an event on the 2000 Canadian Tour, played primarily on the Web.com Tour from 2002-2005. Earned his way onto the PGA Tour for the 2006 season, then won the '06 New Zealand Open during the winter. An up-and-down money winner on the PGA Tour, cracking the top 70 in 2006 (41st), 2007 (66th) and 2009 (59th). Broke through for his first PGA Tour win at the 2009 Canadian Open, where he beat Retief Goosen in a playoff. Struggled in 2011 (168th in $$$) and has worked to right the ship in America ever since. **Teams**: World Cup: 2007. **OWR Best**: 77 - Jan, 2007.

PGA Tour Wins (1): 2009: Canadian Open.

European Tour Wins (1): 2006: New Zealand Open.

Other Wins: New Zealand Under-23s (2): 1996-98   Queensland PGA (Aus): 2000   Benefit Partners/NRCS Classic (Canada): 2000.

	98	99	00	01	02	03	04	05	06	07	08	09	10	11	12	13	14
Masters	-	-	-	-	-	-	-	-	-	-	-	-	48	-	-	-	-
US Open	-	-	-	-	-	-	-	-	MC	-	-	-	-	-	-	-	-
British	-	-	-	MC	-	-	-	-	-	-	-	-	MC	-	-	-	-
PGA	-	-	-	-	-	-	-	-	T49	-	-	T63	-	-	-	-	-
Money (A)	-	-	-	-	-	-	-	-	41	66	113	59	144	168	163	205*	-
OWR	787	741	591	245	544	401	431	341	78	95	189	208	248	476	532	611	688

2014: Played on the Web.com Tour where he made four of 13 cuts and finished 118th in regular season $$$.

OUTLOOK: Will continue to make limited PGA Tour starts on Past Champion status. Has not made a major impact on either U.S. tour since winning the Canadian Open in 2009, and there is little in his 2014 record or his statistical profile to suggest that's about to dramatically reverse.

STATS: Driving Distance: C   Driving Accuracy: C+   GIR: C   Short Game: B+   Putting: B+

Green, Richard George (Australia) (43)
b. Melbourne, Victoria, Australia 2/19/1971. 6'2" 170 lbs. TP: 1992. Left-hander who competed in his native Australia before coming to Europe full-time in the mid-1990s. Scored his biggest victory by defeating Greg Norman and Ian Woosnam in a playoff at the 1997 Dubai Desert Classic. Logged a major homeland win at the 2004 Australian Masters, where he again needed extra holes, this time beating Greg Chalmers and David McKenzie. Later added a two-stroke victory over four men (including Robert Karlsson) at the 2010 Portugal Masters. Made several (non-member) starts in America in 2005, but returned to Europe thereafter, only once finishing worse than 78th in $$$ through 2014. **Teams**: World Cup (3): 1998-08-11. **OWR Best**: 29 - Jul, 2007.

European Tour Wins (3): 1997: Dubai Desert Classic **2007**: BA-CA Open **2010**: Portugal Masters.

Australasian Tour Wins (1): 2004: Australian Masters.

Other Wins: New Caledonian Open (2): 1994-96   Kooringal Pro-Am (Aus): 1994   Indonesian Pro-Am: 1995.

Green, Richard George, Cont'd

	96	97	98	99	00	01	02	03	04	05	06	07	08	09	10	11	12	13	14
Masters	-	-	-	-	-	-	-	-	-	-	-	-	MC	-	-	-	-	-	-
US Open	-	-	-	-	-	-	-	-	-	T52	MC	-	-	-	-	-	-	-	-
British	-	MC	-	MC	-	T42	T59	-	MC	T32	MC	T4	T32	MC	-	T16	-	-	-
PGA	-	-	-	-	-	-	-	-	-	MC	T37	T40	71	T60	-	MC	-	-	-
Money (E)	45	34	165	102	54	49	51	83	17	50	27	22	23	74	21	65	78	112	74
OWR	162	125	291	387	185	116	140	243	61	70	65	40	61	125	60	99	213	346	218

2014: E: 20 st / 11 ct / 2 t10. (T2P Spanish, T9 Perth). Played as a top-40 career money winner, finished 74th in $$$ to easily regain his card.

OUTLOOK: Has enjoyed a long and prosperous E Tour run and, at age 43, may not be anywhere near done yet. A short-but-very-straight type with an above-the-median putter – but it's now been nearly five years since his last win, so he may be more of a check casher at this stage.

STATS: Driving Distance: C   Driving Accuracy: A   GIR: B   Short Game: B-   Putting: B+

Griffin, Matthew (Australia) (31)
b. Melbourne, Australia 7/26/1983. 6'2" 180 lbs. TP: 2008. An Australasian Tour regular who has also found success on the OneAsia circuit. Logged one victory per year on either circuit from 2011-2014, highlighted by a one-shot win at the 2013 SK Telecom Open. Enjoyed a strong 2014, winning the Victorian Open at home and, during a brief Korean visit, the Korean PGA Championship. **Teams**: Eisenhower Trophy: 2008. **OWR Best**: 236 - Feb, 2014.

OneAsia Tour Wins (2): 2012: Charity High 1 Open   **2013**: SK Telecom Open.

Australasian Tour Wins (1): 2011: South Pacific Open   **2014**: Victorian Open.

Other Wins: KPGA Championship (KPGA): 2014.

Amateur Wins: Rice Planters Am: 2008.

	09	10	11	12	13	14
Masters	-	-	-	-	-	-
US Open	-	-	-	-	-	-
British	-	-	-	-	-	-
PGA	-	-	-	-	-	-
Money (O)	54	7	31	3	-	27
OWR	-	-	-	476	283	266

2014: ONE: 7 st / 4 ct / 0 t10. (T22 Indonesia PGA). Also played regularly on the Australasian Tour (where he won once and finished 8th in $$$) and sporadically around Asia, including in Korea where he emerged as a surprise winner at the Korean PGA Championship.

OUTLOOK: At age 31 he's likely not moving westward in the years ahead, but he's shown plenty of regional game, winning on three different Far Eastern tours over the last three seasons. Figures to maintain something resembling this successful pace for several more years to come.

STATS: Driving Distance: --   Driving Accuracy: --   GIR: --   Short Game: --   Putting: --

---

Grillo, Emiliano (Argentina) (22)
b. Resistencia, Argentina 9/14/1992. 5'9" 145 lbs. TP: 2011. Two-time AJGA All-American. Argentine prospect who, as a teenager, first moved to Buenos Aires, then to the IMG Academy in Bradenton, FL to work on his game. Had a relatively thin amateur résumé (though he did win the 2011 Terra Cotta Invitational, in Florida) before turning pro and heading off to the European Tour in 2012. Kept his card for two straight years before making some noise (44th in $$$) in 2014, when he eagled the 72nd hole but still finished one behind Stephen Gallacher in Dubai. **Teams**: Eisenhower Trophy (2): 2008-10. World Cup: 2013. **OWR Best**: 128 - Dec, 2014.

Amateur Wins: Junior World (15-17): 2009   Terra Cotta Inv: 2011.

	12	13	14
Masters	-	-	-
US Open	-	-	-
British	-	-	-
PGA	-	-	-
Money (E)	94	89	44
OWR	406	277	128

2014: E: 26 st / 18 ct / 4 t10. (2 Dubai, T5 Africa, T8 BMW Int'l, T8 BMW Masters). Climbed to 44th in $$$ after very nearly winning in Dubai, where he eagled the 72nd hole but was pipped at the wire by Stephen Gallacher.

OUTLOOK: Despite his limited size, is a powerful and accurate ball striker who seems destined to be among any tour's GIR leaders for years to come. His putter clearly lags behind but has shown incremental improvement, suggesting that he will likely be around for a while. Plays a very strong game for a 22-year-old and has caught many an eye in Europe. Thus, it takes little great insight to suggest that he is ready to win in 2015.

STATS: Driving Distance: A-   Driving Accuracy: A-   GIR: A   Short Game: B-   Putting: C

Grönberg, Mathias David (Sweden) (44)
b. Stockholm, Sweden 3/12/1970. 6'0" 185 lbs. TP: 1990. After several years playing the Challenge Tour, joined the E Tour full-time in 1994 where his first two wins came at the 1995 European Masters (by two over Constantino Rocca and Barry Lane) and the 1998 European Open, where he triumphed in a 10-shot runaway over Miguel Ángel Jiménez and Phillip Price. Later added the 2000 South African Open (by one over Nick Price, Darren Fichardt and Ricardo González) and the 2003 Italian Open. Tried PGA Tour Q School seven times before winning medalist honors in 2004, then went on to play full-time in America for six years with limited success. Has played only a handful of E Tour events annually since 2004. **Teams**: Eisenhower Trophy: 1990. Seve Trophy: 2002. World Cup (2): 1998-00. **OWR Best**: 65 - Oct, 2003.

European Tour Wins (4): 1995: European Masters   **1998**: European Open   **2000**: South African Open   **2003**: Italian Open.

Other Wins: 1 Euro Challenge (1991)   +   1 Web.com (2009)   Swedish Open: 1991.

Amateur Wins: Swedish Boys: 1988   Eisenhower Trophy (Individual): 1990   British Youths: 1990.

Grönberg, Mathias David, Cont'd

	94	95	96	97	98	99	00	01	02	03	04	05	06	07	08	09	10	11	12	13	14
Masters	-	-	-	-	-	-	-	-	-	-	-	-	-	-	-	-	-	-	-	-	-
US Open	-	-	-	-	MC	-	-	T74	-	-	-	-	-	-	-	-	-	-	-	-	-
British	-	MC	-	-	MC	-	MC	MC	T18	T47	-	-	-	-	-	-	-	-	-	-	-
PGA	-	-	-	-	-	MC	MC	-	MC	-	-	-	-	-	-	-	-	-	-	-	-
Money (A)	-	-	-	-	-	-	-	-	-	-	132	160	124	125	192	-	174	-	-	-	-
Money (E)	86	22	71	108	10	73	20	16	84	26	-	-	-	-	-	-	-	-	-	-	272*
OWR	433	166	199	323	113	157	99	74	136	72	165	338	302	341	569	327	426	701	723	-	-

2014: E: 12 st / 2 ct / 0 t10. (T61 Russia). Finished 272nd in $$$ in limited starts, but generally appeared overmatched when he did tee it up.

OUTLOOK: His best years clearly seem behind him, but with four E Tour wins on his résumé, he must be respected for as long as he opts to play.

STATS: Driving Distance: --   Driving Accuracy: --   GIR: --   Short Game: --   Putting: --

---

Guthrie, Lukas Mitchell (USA) (24)

b. Quincy, IL 1/31/1990. 6'0" 175 lbs. Two-time All-American at U of Illinois. TP: 2012. An AJGA All-American. Turned pro after graduating from Illinois and hit the ground running, losing a playoff (to Ben Kohles) in his first Web.com start, then logging three straight top 10s (plus one MC) before winning back-to-back events in Boise, ID and Midland, TX. Ultimately finished 2nd in $$$ (in only 10 starts), graduating to the PGA Tour, where he retained his card in both 2013 and '14. **OWR Best**: 58 - Mar, 2013.

Other Wins: 2 Web.com (2012).

Amateur Wins: Illinois HS (2): 2006-07.

	12	13	14
Masters	-	-	-
US Open	-	MC	MC
British	-	MC	-
PGA	-	T47	-
Money (A)	-	83	111
OWR	114	82	255

2014: PGA: 26 st / 18 ct / 2 t10. (T5 Shriners, T8 Memorial). Slipped slightly from 2013 but still finished 106th in FedEx Cup points.

OUTLOOK: Has adjusted to the PGA Tour fairly well after winning twice in only 10 Web.com starts in 2012. His around-the-green numbers suggest that he could have some staying power but his overall Ball Striking (145) needs to improve if his frequently-cited potential is to be reached.

STATS: Driving Distance: B-   Driving Accuracy: B-   GIR: C+   Short Game: A-   Putting: B+

Haas, William Harlan (USA) (32)

b. Charlotte, NC 05/24/1982. 6'2" 185 lbs. Three-time All-American, Nicklaus (2004) and Haskins (2004) Awards winner at Wake Forest U. TP: 2004. Son of nine-time PGA Tour winner Jay, and nephew of ex-Tour player Jerry. Played one year (2005) on the Web.com, where a 23rd-place finish graduated him to the PGA Tour for 2006. Steady but unimposing player prior to 2010, when he broke through with a birdie at the final hole to beat Tim Clark, Matt Kuchar and Bubba Watson by one at the Bob Hope Classic. Continued rolling near season's end by winning the Fall Series Viking Classic (played opposite the Ryder Cup), then a week later finishing 2nd at the McGladrey Classic. Won the 2011 Tour Championship (East Lake) in a playoff over Hunter Mahan, saving par at the second extra hole by famously blasting out of water adjacent to the 17th hole. Winner of the 2011 season-long FedEx Cup points race in a year when he finished a career-best 7th in PGA Tour $$$. Won his fourth career title at the 2012 Northern Trust Open, beating Keegan Bradley and Phil Mickelson on the second hole of sudden death. Added a 2013 victory to his ledger at the AT&T National, closing with a 66 (at Congressional) to beat Roberto Castro by three. **Awards**: FedEx Cup Champion: 2011. **Teams**: Walker Cup: 2003 (2-2-0). Palmer Cup (2): 2002-03. Presidents Cup (2): 2011-13 (3-5-2). **OWR Best**: 12 - Feb, 2012.

PGA Tour Wins (5): **2010**: Bob Hope Classic (90H), Viking Classic **2011**: Tour Championship **2012**: Los Angeles Open (Northern Trust) **2013**: AT&T National.

Other Wins: CVS Charity Classis: 2004 (w/Ja.Haas).

Amateur Wins: Players Am: 2002.

	03	04	05	06	07	08	09	10	11	12	13	14
Masters	-	-	-	-	-	-	-	T26	T42	T37	T20	T20
US Open	MC	T40	-	-	-	-	-	-	T23	MC	MC	T35
British	-	-	-	-	-	-	-	MC	T57	T19	MC	T51
PGA	-	-	-	-	-	-	-	MC	T12	T32	T25	T27
Money (A)	Am	-	-	99	104	104	61	20	7	33	14	26
OWR	-	332	325	237	229	252	199	61	27	35	29	39

2014: PGA: 28 st / 27 ct / 5 t10. (T2 Wyndham, T6 Humana, T6 WGC-Cadillac, T8 Memorial, T9 Deutsche Bank). Though rarely contending to win, made 27 of 28 cuts, logged 17 top 25s (61% of his starts) and five top 10s en route to finishing 16th in FedEx Cup points.

OUTLOOK: Has emerged as one of America's most consistent players, winning at least once each year from 2010-2013, and logging 28 top-10 finishes in 127 starts since 2010. Possesses a consistent, well-balanced game that shows little sign of weakening and at age 32, he should just be entering his most productive years. Still seems capable of becoming a top-shelf star, though the absence of a single top-10 finish in 21 career Major championship starts might suggest that he's settled into a safe, highly productive comfort zone instead.

STATS: Driving Distance: B+   Driving Accuracy: B+   GIR: A   Short Game: A-   Putting: B+

Hadley, Chesson Tyler (USA) (27)

b. Raleigh, NC 7/5/1987. 6'4" 170 lbs. All-American at Georgia Tech. TP: 2010. An AJGA All-American. Spent two years playing mini-tours (winning once on the 2012 eGolf Tour) prior to joining the Web.com Tour in 2013, where he won twice, including at the Rex Hospital Open – an event sponsored by the hospital he was born in. Won season-ending Web.com Tour Championship, clinching PGA Tour status for 2014, then claimed his first victory at the Puerto Rico Open (played opposite the WGC-Cadillac) in his 11th start. **Awards**: PGA Tour Rookie of the Year: 2014. **Teams**: Palmer Cup: 2008. **OWR Best**: 56 - Mar, 2014.

Hadley, Chesson Tyler, Cont'd

PGA Tour Wins (1): 2014: Puerto Rico Open.
Other Wins: 2 Web.com (2013) + 1 eGolf Tour (2008).
Amateur Wins: NC Independent HS (2): 2004-06.

	13	14
Masters	-	-
US Open	-	-
British	-	MC
PGA	-	MC
Money (A)	-	58
OWR	103	120

2014: PGA: 29 st / 13 ct / 4 t10. (Won Puerto Rico, T5 Shriners, T9 Deutsche Bank, T10 AT&T Pro-Am). Enjoyed an up-and-down debut season, winning in Puerto Rico and finishing 49th in FedEx Cup points, but also missing 16 of 29 cuts including 10 of 11 from Wells Fargo to Wyndham.

OUTLOOK: Despite a relatively limited collegiate résumé, made good by winning in Puerto Rico as a rookie. But he also missed 16 cuts, so there's room for improvement in terms of consistency. His statistical sample is limited - but the talent, it seems, is there.

STATS (LTD): Driving Distance: B   Driving Accuracy: C   GIR: C   Short Game: C+   Putting: B+

Hadwin, Adam Jerald (Canada) (27)

b. Moose Jaw, Saskatchewan, Canada 11/2/1987. 5'9" 155 lbs. College: U of Louisville. TP: 2009. After turning pro, spent two years playing in his native Canada, where he was named Rookie Of The Year in 2010, won two Canadian Tour events, and also took six titles on a local Vancouver area circuit. Finished T4 at the 2011 Canadian Open. Ranked 30th in Web.com $$$ in 2012 and missed gaining his PGA Tour card by a single shot when James Hahn birdied the final hole of the Tour Championship. Finished 66th in $$$ in 2013 before catching fire in 2014, winning twice and clinching his PGA Tour card for 2015. **OWR Best:** 164 - Oct, 2014.

Other Wins: 2 Web.com (2014) + 1 Gateway (2009)   Desert Dunes Classic (Canada): 2010   Pacific Colombia Tour Champ (Canada): 2011.

	11	12	13	14
Masters	-	-	-	-
US Open	T39	-	MC	-
British	-	-	-	-
PGA	-	-	-	-
Money (A)	-	-	-	-
OWR	238	320	622	180

2014: Played full-time on the Web.com Tour where he won twice and clinched his PGA Tour card by finishing 4th in regular season $$$.

OUTLOOK: Despite his limited size, plays a power-oriented game that may translate well to the PGA Tour. Also, has made eight of 11 PGA Tour cuts prior to 2015, including two top 10s, all of which rates him as one of the more likely members of the 2015 rookie class to stick.

STATS: Driving Distance: --   Driving Accuracy: --   GIR: --   Short Game: --   Putting: --

---

Hahn, James (USA) (33)

b. Seoul, South Korea 11/2/1981. 6'1" 180 lbs. College: U of California-Berkeley. TP: 2003. Born in Korea but raised in the United States. After graduating from UC-Berkeley, played several seasons on the Korean Tour, the Canadian Tour and multiple U.S. mini-tours, winning twice in Canada in 2009. Eventually landed on the Web.com in 2010 and broke through for his lone victory there in 2012, leading to 5th-place finish in $$$ and a ticket (as a 31-year-old rookie) to the PGA Tour. **OWR Best:** 133 - Feb, 2013.

Other Wins: 1 Web.com (2012) + Edmonton Open (Canada): 2009   Riviera Nyarit Classic (Canada): 2009.

	09	10	11	12	13	14
Masters	-	-	-	-	-	-
US Open	-	-	-	MC	-	-
British	-	-	-	-	-	-
PGA	-	-	-	-	-	-
Money (A)	-	-	-	-	98	123
OWR	394	327	696	240	255	363

2014: PGA: 27 st / 14 ct / 2 t10. (T5 Byron Nelson, T6 FedEx St Jude). Finished 123rd in FedEx Cup points to retain his card for the second time.

OUTLOOK: Power-oriented player who slipped somewhat in his sophomore year but still retained PGA Tour privileges for the second straight time. Though he hits a fair number of greens, it will be tough to raise his stock without improving his game on and around them.

STATS: Driving Distance: B+   Driving Accuracy: C+   GIR: B-   Short Game: C   Putting: C+

Hahn, John (USA) (25)

b. Columbus, OH 2/6/1989. 5'11" 185 lbs. College: Kent St. TP: 2011. Was three times an honorable mention All-American at Kent State before qualifying for the E Tour in 2014. Failed to keep his card but twice showed flashes of brilliance, shooting a second round 61 at the Africa Open, then a stunning 12-under-par 58 during an unsuccessful return to Q School in Spain. **OWR Best:** 486 - Jul, 2014.

Amateur Wins: Western Am: 2009.

	13	14
Masters	-	-
US Open	MC	-
British	-	-
PGA	-	-
Money (E)	-	120
OWR	907	542

Hahn, John, Cont'd

2014: E: 22 st / 12 ct / 2 t10. (T3 Africa, T6 Mandela). Despite showing flashes, lost his card after finishing 122nd in $$$.

OUTLOOK: Has yet to find a major tour he can stick on - but if he can ever fully harness his proven ability to go low...

STATS (LTD): Driving Distance: C+   Driving Accuracy: B-   GIR: C   Short Game: B   Putting: A-

---

Haig, Anton Jason (South Africa) (28)
b. Johannesburg, South Africa 5/8/1986. 6'4" 180 lbs. TP: 2004. Began his career as a touted, long-hitting South African teenager who, soon after turning professional, won (at age 19) at the Sunshine Tour's Seekers Travel Pro-Am. In 2006, added a second Sunshine title (the Namibia PGA) as well as a victory in the Asian Tour's Malaysian Masters, then broke through worldwide in 2007 by claiming the E Tour's Johnnie Walker Classic in Thailand, where he defeated Richard Sterne and Oliver Wilson in sudden death. Was soon afflicted with a serious back/neck problem and, after struggling for several years, announced his retirement in 2011. Began a comeback on U.S. mini-tours in 2012 (where he won once), then made spot starts in Africa and Asia in 2013. **OWR Best:** 81 - Apr, 2007.

European Tour Wins (1): 2007: Johnnie Walker Classic.
Asian Tour Wins (1): 2006: Malaysian Masters.
Sunshine Tour Wins (2): 2005: Seekers Travel Pro-Am (54H) **2006**: Namibia PGA (54H).
Other Wins: 1 eGolf Tour (2012) + 1 Big Easy (2013).
Amateur Wins: South African Am: 2003 – Vodacom Champions: 2001 South African Boys: 2003.

	04	05	06	07	08	09	10	11	12	13	14
Masters	-	-	-	-	-	-	-	-	-	-	-
US Open	-	-	-	-	-	-	-	-	-	-	-
British	-	-	-	-	-	-	-	-	-	-	-
PGA	-	-	-	-	-	-	-	-	-	-	-
Money (E)	-	-	-	58	139	235	153	-	-	-	-
Money (SA)	39	36	41*	-	-	94*	66*	-	-	136*	-
OWR	-	758	292	198	543	-	738	-	848	-	-

2014: Did not make a 2014 start after showing signs of a comeback in 2013.

OUTLOOK: Appeared destined for relatively big things before his back injury, and it has thus far been a struggle trying to come back. Still, he's only 28 and his talent level is well documented, so no one should be too quick to write him off – if he's healthy.

STATS: Driving Distance: --   Driving Accuracy: --   GIR: --   Short Game: --   Putting: --

---

Hamilton, William Todd (USA) (49)
b. Galesburg, IL 10/18/1965. 6'1" 195 lbs. Three-time All-American at U of Oklahoma. TP: 1987. Two-time AJGA All-American. Canadian and Web.com Tour player before starring on the Asian and Japan circuits between 1992-2002. Initially won seven times in Japan during the 1990s, including twice in 1994 when he finished 6th in $$$. However, his Japanese career peaked during a four-win 2003, a season in which he finished a career-best 2nd in $$$. Qualified for the PGA Tour (on his eighth try) in late 2003. Proceeded to win in his sixth start (the Honda Classic) before shocking the world by defeating Ernie Els in a four-hole playoff to capture the British Open at Royal Troon. Has struggled since, finishing no better than 133rd in earnings since 2005, and making only limited starts (on Past Champion status) since 2011. **Awards**: PGA Tour Rookie of the Year: 2004. **OWR Best:** 16 - Jul, 2004.

PGA Tour Wins (2): 2004: Honda Classic, British Open.
Japan Tour Wins (11): 1992: Maruman Open **1993**: Acom Int'l **1994**: PGA Philanthropy, Japan Match Play **1995**: Token Cup **1996**: PGA Philanthropy **1998**: Gene Sarazen Jun Classic **2003**: Fujisankei Classic, Diamond Cup, Mizuno Open, Japan Match Play.
Asian Tour Wins (2): 1992: Maruman Open **1995**: Thailand Open.
Asian Wins (4): 1992: Singapore Masters, Thailand Open, Korean Open, Maekyung Open (Korea).
Other Wins: Oklahoma Open: 1999.

	92	93	94	95	96	97	98	99	00	01	02	03	04	05	06	07	08	09	10	11	12	13	14
Masters	-	-	-	-	-	-	-	-	-	-	-	-	40	T39	MC	MC	T36	T15	MC	-	-	-	-
US Open*	-	-	-	-	-	-	-	-	-	-	-	-	MC	MC	MC	MC	T36	T36	-	T60	-	-	-
British	MC	-	-	T45	-	-	-	-	-	-	-	MC	Win	MC	T68	MC	T32	MC	MC	MC	MC	T73	MC
PGA	-	-	-	-	-	-	-	-	-	-	-	T29	T37	T47	MC	T66	MC	-	-	-	-	-	-
Money (A)	-	-	-	-	-	-	-	-	-	-	-	-	11	134	198	212	150	133	211	210*	184*	244*	252*
Money (J)	13	6	6	19	10	37	28	47	78	44	42	2	-	-	-	-	-	-	-	-	-	-	-
OWR	113	91	80	96	77	132	164	206	387	313	288	82	16	97	553	928	365	315	578	689	691	886	1438

* Also MC at 1988 U.S. Open

2014: PGA: 4 st / 1 ct / 0 t10. (T59 John Deere). Finished 246th in FedEx Cup points. Also played 10 Web.com events, finishing 207th in $$$.

OUTLOOK: At age 49, he's far, far removed from his 2004 British Open title. Mostly treading water now, likely awaiting the Champions Tour.

STATS (LTD): Driving Distance: C   Driving Accuracy: B   GIR: C   Short Game: B-   Putting: B-

---

Hansen, Anders Rosenbjerg (Denmark) (44)
b. Sonderborg, Denmark 9/16/1970. 6'0" 170 lbs. TP: 1995. All-American at U of Houston. TP: 1995. Steady Danish player who has toiled primarily on the E Tour since 1997. His first two wins came in the flagship BMW PGA Championship, first in 2002 (by five over Eduardo Romero and Colin Montgomerie), then in 2007, in sudden death over Justin Rose. Despite playing collegiately in America, only tried the PGA Tour once (after getting through 2006 Q School), finishing 153rd on the 2007 money list in only 17 starts. Though not a regular in South Africa, won the 2009 Sunshine Tour Order of Merit, largely on the strength of two early season wins in five starts: the Joburg Open (co-sponsored by the E Tour) and the Tour Championship. While winless, was thrice a runner-up during a 2011 season that saw him finish a career-best 7th in $$$. Slipped a bit in his mid-40s, finishing 83rd and 92nd in $$$ in 2013 and '14. **Teams**: Eisenhower Trophy: 1994 Seve Trophy (2): 2009-11. World Cup (8): 1999-02-03-04-05-07-08-11. **OWR Best:** 23 - Aug, 2011.

European Tour Wins (3): 2002: BMW PGA **2007**: BMW PGA **2009**: Joburg Open.

Hansen, Anders Rosenbjerg, Cont'd

Sunshine Tour Wins (1): 2009: Tour Championship.

Amateur Wins: Danish Am Stroke Play (2): 1992-94.

	97	98	99	00	01	02	03	04	05	06	07	08	09	10	11	12	13	14
Masters	-	-	-	-	-	-	-	-	-	-	-	MC	-	MC	MC	T24	-	-
US Open	-	-	-	-	-	-	-	-	-	-	T55	-	-	-	-	-	MC	-
British	-	-	MC	-	-	T77	MC	MC	-	-	T57	T19	MC	MC	T22	MC	-	-
PGA	-	-	-	-	-	MC	MC	-	-	T24	T12	MC	MC	MC	3	MC	-	-
Money (A)	-	-	-	-	-	-	-	-	-	-	153	-	-	-	-	-	-	-
Money (E)	163	-	107	53	39	16	57	30	35	33	18	47	24	19	7	39	83	92
OWR	771	787	458	251	160	59	126	100	121	105	50	89	40	70	34	61	156	292

2014: E: 15 st / 8 ct / 2 t10. (T2 Laguna, T5 Volvo China).   Retained his card but once again recorded his worst $$$ ranking (92nd) since 1999.

OUTLOOK: Has made 398 E Tour starts through 2014 and may be beginning to wind down. A very straight hitter with a reliable tee-to-green game, but hasn't won since 2009. Was a runner up (at the light-field Laguna National) in 2014, however, so there could still be a win or two left in the bag.

STATS: Driving Distance: C   Driving Accuracy: A-   GIR: A-   Short Game: B+   Putting: B+

Hansen, Joachim B. ("J.B.") (Denmark) (24)
b. Hillerod, Denmark 8/18/1990. 6'1" 160 lbs. TP: 2010. Turned professional after winning medalist honors at the 2010 Eisenhower Trophy. Spent 2011 playing Scandinavian mini-tours before finishing 4th in 2012 Challenge Tour $$$ to move on to the E Tour. After enjoying a strong rookie campaign, struggled a bit in 2014, finishing 137th in $$$ and losing his card. **Teams**: Eisenhower Trophy: 2010. **OWR Best**: 172 - Jul, 2013.

Amateur Wins: Finnish Am: 2010   Eisenhower Trophy (Individual): 2010.

	12	13	14
Masters	-	-	-
US Open	-	-	-
British	-	-	-
PGA	-	-	-
Money (E)	274*	79	137
OWR	223	237	525

2014: E: 32 st / 16 ct / 0 t10.   (T18 Russia).   Had a tough sophomore campaign, making only half his cuts and finishing 137th in $$$.

OUTLOOK: A long-hitting youngster who, with experience, figures to have a solid future. Lost his card after 2014 but his statistics - though limited in depth - suggest a well-rounded game capable of thriving on the E Tour. Failed to return via Q School so he'll mostly play the Challenge Tour in 2015.

STATS: Driving Distance: A-   Driving Accuracy: B   GIR: B+   Short Game: B+   Putting: B-

---

Hansen, Søren (Denmark) (40)
b. Copenhagen, Denmark 3/21/1974. 6'0" 195 lbs. TP: 1997. Unrelated to countryman Anders but has followed his namesake's success eerily, with the timing of his first two E Tour victories and several of his year-end Order of Merit rankings walking nearly in lockstep. Claimed his first E Tour win at the 2002 Irish Open in a four-way playoff with Richard Bland, Niclas Fasth and Darren Fichardt. Finished a career-best 8th in the Order of Merit in 2007, the year in which he claimed his second title at the Mercedes-Benz Championship in Germany. Aside from Majors, has seldom played in America. Made only 10 starts (all MCs) in 2012 due to a cracked rib, then had his worst-ever year in 2013 before rebounding somewhat to retain his card in 2014. **Teams**: Eisenhower Trophy: 1996. Ryder Cup: 2008 (O: 0-2-1, S: 0-1-0). Seve Trophy (2): 2007-09. World Cup (8): 1998-01-02-05-06-07-08-09. **OWR Best**: 39 - Jul, 2008.

European Tour Wins (2): 2002: Irish Open   **2007**: Mercedes-Benz Championship.

Other Wins: 1 Euro Challenge (1998).

Amateur Wins: Danish Am Stroke Play: 1997.

	99	00	01	02	03	04	05	06	07	08	09	10	11	12	13	14
Masters	-	-	-	-	-	-	-	-	-	MC	MC	MC	-	-	-	-
US Open	-	-	-	-	-	-	-	-	-	T53	T6	MC	-	-	-	-
British	-	-	MC	T8	MC	-	T41	-	-	T64	T8	MC	-	-	-	-
PGA	-	-	-	T43	-	-	-	-	-	MC	T36	MC	-	-	-	-
Money (E)	112	73	37	20	55	67	36	34	8	14	22	60	109	-	131	101
OWR	673	321	175	95	146	210	200	157	46	47	47	119	325	523	498	512

2014: E: 31 st / 17 ct / 1 t10.   (6 Dunhill Champ).   Playing as a career top-40 $$$ winner, bounced back to finish 101st in $$$ and retain his card.

OUTLOOK: A longish hitter with a strong all-around tee-to-green game whose already limited putting numbers bottomed out in 2013 and '14. At age 40, there should be plenty left in the tank, but little has happened since 2011 to suggest that a massive turnaround is in the offing.

STATS: Driving Distance: B+   Driving Accuracy: B   GIR: A   Short Game: C+   Putting: C

Hanson, Peter (Sweden) (37)
b. Svedala, Sweden 10/4/1977. 6'3" 185 lbs. TP: 1998. Consistent Swede whose strong amateur career included three minor professional titles in his home country and the 1998 Emirates Amateur. Initially earned his place on the E Tour through 2000 Q School, then through the 2001 Challenge Tour when, having failed to qualify for the British Open, he traveled to Germany and won the Günther Hamburg Classic, clinching a spot among the year's top 15 money winners. Eventually cracked the E Tour Order of Merit top 50 in 2004, then won the Spanish Open (in a playoff with Peter Gustafson) in 2005. Later added the 2008 Scandinavian Masters prior to winning twice in 2010, at the Iberdrola Open (in a playoff with Alejandro Cañizares) and the Czech Open (in a playoff with Gary Boyd and Peter Lawrie). Enjoyed a career-best 2012, led by his fifth career E Tour win at the KLM (Dutch) Open, then a sixth title at the late-season BMW Masters (China), where he edged Rory McIlroy by one. Had his 2014 shortened somewhat by lingering back problems. **Teams**: Eisenhower Trophy: 1998. Ryder Cup (2): 2010-12 (O: 1-4-0, S: 0-2-0). Seve Trophy (4): 2005-07-09-11. World Cup (2): 2007-13. **OWR Best**: 17 - Oct, 2012.

Hanson, Peter, Cont'd

European Tour Wins (6): 2005: Spanish Open **2008**: SAS Masters **2010**: Open Cala Milor Mallorca, Czech Open **2012**: Dutch Open (KLM), BMW Masters.
Other Wins: 1 Euro Challenge (2001) + 1 Nordic League (2000) Vacisteras Open (Sweden) (2): 1997*-98* Husqvarna (Sweden): 1998* Telia Grand Prix (Sweden): 1999.
Amateur Wins: English Am Stroke Play: 1998 Emirates Am: 1998.

	01	02	03	04	05	06	07	08	09	10	11	12	13	14
Masters	-	-	-	-	-	-	-	-	-	-	MC	T3	T50	MC
US Open	-	-	-	-	MC	-	T30	-	-	T16	T7	MC	MC	-
British	-	-	-	-	T34	-	T69	T58	T24	T37	MC	T23	WD	-
PGA	-	-	-	T59	-	-	T23	T52	MC	T58	T64	T7	T33	-
Money (A)	-	-	-	-	-	-	-	-	-	-	-	-	125	169
Money (E)	120	139	-	42	23	57	20	16	16	17	13	4	49*	134*
OWR	283	407	337	195	108	166	54	55	54	40	42	19	48	242

2014: PGA: 13 st / 7 ct / 0 t10. (T11 New Orleans). Finished 169th in PGA Tour $$$ but made only 13 starts due to lingering back problems. Also appeared in eight non-Major/WGC events in Europe, making five cuts and logging only one top 10, a T10 at Abu Dhabi.
OUTLOOK: Coming off an injury-bothered season in which he continued to seemingly spread himself thin, splitting time between America and Europe but having little real success on either side. His 2012 may have been a high watermark but his game seems to travel well and at age 37, there's no reason (beyond injury) to suggest that he doesn't have lots of good golf ahead of him. When healthy, he appears capable of winning in America.

STATS: Driving Distance: A- Driving Accuracy: C+ GIR: B Short Game: B+ Putting: B+

Harding, Justin (South Africa) (28)

b. Somerset West, South Africa 2/9/1986. 6'0" 175 lbs. College: Lamar U. TP: 2010. Decorated South African amateur who finished 3rd at the 2009 Sunshine Tour Q School as an amateur and turned pro shortly thereafter. Has played almost exclusively on his native circuit ever since, initially winning the 2010 Vodacom Origins of Golf Final as a rookie (by one over Ulrich van den Berg), then adding the Lombard Insurance Classic in 2011 (by one over Neil Cheetham) and the Zambia Open in 2012. **OWR Best**: 462 - Jun, 2013.

Sunshine Tour Wins (3): 2010: Vodacom-Final (54H) **2011**: Lombard Insurance Classic (54H) **2012**: Zambia Open.
Amateur Wins: Cape Province Am: 2005 Western Province Am Stroke Play: 2005 Northwest Am: 2005 Southern Cape Am: 2006.

	10	11	12	13	14
Masters	-	-	-	-	-
US Open	-	-	-	-	-
British	-	-	-	MC	-
PGA	-	-	-	-	-
Money (SA)	47	35	26	36	14
OWR	-	985	579	672	495

2014: SUN: 20 st / 14 ct / 4 t10. (Incl. T2 Zambia Open, 4 BMG). Logged four top 10s en route to finishing a career-best 14th in $$$.
OUTLOOK: Thus far a purely domestic player with three wins in five years, a steadily growing wallet and no apparent plans to try playing abroad.

STATS: Driving Distance: -- Driving Accuracy: -- GIR: -- Short Game: -- Putting: --

---

Harman, Brian Eric (USA) (27)

b. Savannah, GA 1/19/1987. 5'7" 150 lbs. Two-time All-American at U of Georgia. TP: 2009. Three-time AJGA All-American and two-time AJGA Player Of The Year (2003 and '04). Won 2003 U.S. Junior Amateur and the 2007 Porter Cup and was a two-time Walker Cup player (2005 and '09), becoming the U.S.'s youngest-ever participant in '05, at age 18. Upon turning pro, mostly played the eGolf Tour before tying for 8th at 2011 PGA Tour Q School. Established himself as a solid money winner over his first two seasons before breaking through for his first win at the 2014 John Deere Classic, where he edged Zach Johnson by one. **Teams**: Walker Cup (2): 2005-09 (4-1-2). Palmer Cup (2): 2006-07. **OWR Best**: 65 - Aug, 2014.

PGA Tour Wins (1): 2014: John Deere Classic.
Other Wins: 1 eGolf Tour (2010).
Amateur Wins: Porter Cup: 2007 - U.S. Junior Am: 2003 Georgia Am: 2005 Players Am: 2005 Dogwood Inv: 2009.

	12	13	14
Masters	-	-	-
US Open	MC	-	-
British	-	-	T26
PGA	-	-	T41
Money (A)	87	92	34
OWR	160	173	86

2014: PGA: 32 st / 23 ct / 6 t10. (Won John Deere, T3 Northern Trust, T6 FedEx St Jude, T7 Frys.com, T7 Heritage, etc.). Broke through for his first PGA Tour win at the John Deere while also logging career bests in $$$ (34th) and FedEx Cup points (36th).
OUTLOOK: Small-of-stature sort who, after keeping his card for two seasons, stepped it up in 2014, winning once. Is surprisingly long and falls above the median in the great majority of statistical categories, with his major 2014 gain coming in Strokes Gained Tee To Green (from 146 to 111). Doesn't appear to have sparkling talent at this level but gets the job done. Thus he will likely continue his slow, steady advance going forward.

STATS: Driving Distance: B+ Driving Accuracy: B+ GIR: B- Short Game: B+ Putting: B+

Harrington, Padraig Peter (Ireland) (43)

b. Dublin, Ireland 8/31/1971. 6'1" 195 lbs. TP: 1995. A former top Irish prospect who, after becoming the rare modern professional to have appeared in three Walker Cups, blossomed into a consistent earner, finishing no worse than 7th in the European Order of Merit from 1999-2004 (including 2nd in 2001 and '02). Shed an early reputation as a bridesmaid before becoming a regular E Tour

Harrington, Padraig Peter, Cont'd

winner. Also captured titles in South America and Asia (and logged prominent back-to-back runner-ups at the 2003 and '04 Players Championships) before winning on the 2005 PGA Tour at the Honda Classic (in a playoff with Vijay Singh) and at The Barclays, where he edged Jim Furyk by one. Won 2006 Dunlop Phoenix (Japan Tour) in a playoff over Tiger Woods and has twice claimed the Dunhill Links Championship (2002 and '06). After making double-bogey at the 72nd, became the first Irishman in 60 years to win the British Open by defeating Sergio García in a four-hole playoff at Carnoustie in 2007. Successfully defended the title in 2008 at Royal Birkdale, playing the last six holes in four under par to pull away, then followed it up with a victory at the 2008 PGA Championship, where he closed with 66-66 at Oakland Hills to beat García and Ben Curtis by two. Endured a significant drop in form in 2010 and '11 (his lone victory coming in the Asian circuit's light-field 2010 Johor Open), with 2012 and '13 doing little to reverse the trend. Broke a four-year victory drought by scoring a late-season win on the 2014 Asian Tour at the Indonesia Open, where he edged Thanyakon Khrongpha by two. Even with the win, he closed the year ranked 265th in the OWR, his worst-ever year-end standing. **Awards:** PGA Tour Player of the Year: 2008. E Tour Golfer of the Year (2): 2007-08. Euro Vardon Trophy: 2006. **Teams:** Walker Cup (3): 1991-93-95 (3-5-1). Ryder Cup (6): 1999-02-04-06-08-10 (O: 9-13-3, S: 3-3-0). Seve Trophy (4): 2000-02-03-05. World Cup (11): 1996-97-98-99-00-01-02-03-04-05-06 (won w/P.McGinley in '97). **OWR Best:** 3 - Jul, 2008.

PGA Tour Wins (5): 2005: Honda Classic, Westchester Classic (Barclays) **2007:** British Open **2008:** British Open, PGA Championship.
European Tour Wins (12): 1996: Spanish Open **2000:** Sao Paulo 500 Years Open, Turespaña Masters **2001:** Volvo Masters (54H) **2002:** Dunhill Links Championship, BMW Asian Open ('03) **2003:** Deutsche Bank Open, Hong Kong Open ('04) **2004:** German Masters **2006:** Dunhill Links Championship **2007:** Irish Open.
Japan Tour Wins (1): 2006: Dunlop Phoenix.
Asian Tour Wins (2): 2010: Johor Open **2014:** Indonesia Open.
Other Wins: Irish Pro (4): 1998-04-05-07   Target World Challenge: 2002   Hassan Trophy (Morocco):2007   PGA Grand Slam: 2012.
Amateur Wins: Irish Am: 1995   –   Sherry Cup: 1991   West of Ireland Am: 1994   Irish Closed Am: 1995.

	96	97	98	99	00	01	02	03	04	05	06	07	08	09	10	11	12	13	14
Masters	-	-	-	-	T19	T27	T5	MC	T13	MC	T27	T7	T5	T35	MC	MC	T8	MC	-
US Open	-	MC	T32	-	T5	T30	T8	T10	T31	MC	5	MC	T36	MC	T22	T46	T4	T21	-
British	T18	T5	MC	29	T20	T37	T5	T22	MC	-	MC	Win	Win	T65	MC	MC	T39	T54	MC
PGA	-	MC	-	-	T58	MC	T17	T29	T45	MC	MC	T42	Win	T10	MC	T64	T18	MC	MC
Money (A)	232*	166*	238*	224*	-	-	-	-	14	68	21	8	20	64	107	53	116	187	
Money (E)	11	8	29	7	7	2	2	3	3	32	1	3	2	15	20	67	34	68	97
OWR	95	78	105	50	24	11	7	8	6	17	8	8	4	5	23	85	59	131	265

2014: PGA: 16 st / 7 ct / 0 t10. (T22 Byron Nelson).   Endured his weakest season to date in America, making only 16 starts, never approaching the top 10, and finishing 188th in FedEx Cup points (missed three of his last four cuts and did not play in the FedEx Cup playoffs). E: 13 st / 10 ct / 1 t10. (T5 Volvo Champ). Fared only slightly better in Europe (97th in $$$) where his best finish was a T5 at the Volvo Golf Champions.
OUTLOOK: Has slipped a long way from 2008, with fewer moments of flash (e.g., nearly stealing the 2012 U.S. Open) to suggest that better things lie ahead. Has seen across-the-board declines numerically, most notably the putter, with his PGA Tour SGP dropping from 25 in 2009 to 160 in 2014. Perhaps his late-2014 victory in Indonesia will give him the confidence to begin reversing that trend.

STATS: Driving Distance: B   Driving Accuracy: C   GIR: C   Short Game: B-   Putting: C+

Hart, Howard Dudley (USA) (46)
b. Rochester, NY 4/4/1968. 5'10" 190 lbs. All-American at U of Florida. TP: 1990. Two-time AJGA All-American. PGA Tour journeyman who was 12 times among the top 100 $$$ winners from 1992-2008, peaking at 29th in both 1999 and 2008. Claimed his biggest win at the 1996 Canadian Open, edging David Duval by one at Glen Abbey. Also won the 2000 Honda Open, as well as the 1998 Sarazen World Open, an unofficial event on the E Tour schedule played near Atlanta. Missed the majority of 2007 to attend to an illness in the family. Underwent career-threatening back surgery during an injury-shortened 2009 and has played on a very limited basis since. **Awards:** PGA Tour Comeback Player of the Year: 2008. **OWR Best:** 21 - Apr, 2000.

PGA Tour Wins (2): 1996: Canadian Open (54H) **2000:** Honda Classic.
Int'l Wins (1): 1998: Sarazen World Open.
Other Wins: Florida Open: 1990   Louisiana Open: 1990   CVS Classic: 2002 (w/C.DiMarco).

	91	92	93	94	95	96	97	98	99	00	01	02	03	04	05	06	07	08	09	10	11	12	13	14
Masters	-	-	-	MC	-	-	-	MC	-	T28	T43	-	-	-	-	-	-	-	T44	-	-	-	-	-
US Open	-	T23	-	-	-	-	-	WD	T17	MC	T62	T12	MC	T53	-	-	-	-	-	-	-	-	-	-
British	-	-	-	-	-	-	MC	81	T37	WD	T37	MC	MC	-	-	-	-	-	-	-	-	-	-	-
PGA	-	MC	T6	T55	-	-	MC	T44	MC	WD	T16	MC	-	WD	T10	WD	-	-	-	-	-	-	-	-
Money (A)	120	61	52	135	148	47	60	53	29	43	53	54	144	92	71	112	-	29	-	-	-	-	-	227*
OWR	336	186	134	195	384	132	79	58	34	41	62	67	164	138	118	218	448	54	206	-	-	-	-	1331

2014: PGA: 4 st / 2 ct / 0 t10. (T35 AT&T Pro-Am).   Made four starts (228th in FedEx Cup points) after a long absence due to back surgery. His MC at Humana was his first start since missing the cut at the 2012 AT&T Pebble Beach Pro-Am.
OUTLOOK: Begins 2015 on an eight-event medical extension dating to 2012. Has now made a total of five starts since 2009 so relevant statistics are unavailable. At age 46, a full comeback seems unlikely but he was, at least, a steady earner (in the top 60 from 1996-2002) before the injuries.

STATS: Driving Distance: --   Driving Accuracy: --   GIR: --   Short Game: --   Putting: --

---

Hartø, Andreas (Denmark) (26)
b. Copenhagen, Denmark 7/26/1988. 6'3" 175 lbs. TP: 2010. Initially came to international note upon winning his first Challenge Tour title (the 2010 ECCO Tour Championship) while still an amateur, then later claiming his second Challenge win in only his fourth career start. Failed to retain his card in each of his first four E Tour seasons, however, and played through E Tour Q School in both 2010 and 2013. Became a YouTube sensation after stripping down to his underwear to play a recovery shot from a water hazard at the 2013 Trophée Hassan II. **OWR Best:** 251 - May, 2013.

Other Wins: 3 Euro Challenge (2010-2012).
Amateur Wins: Danish Am Stroke Play: 2009   Welsh Am Stroke Play.

Hartø, Andreas, Cont'd

	10	11	12	13	14
Masters	-	-	-	-	-
US Open	-	MC	-	-	-
British	-	-	-	-	-
PGA	-	-	-	-	-
Money (E)	-	194	192*	119	163
OWR	308	448	279	411	659

2014: E: 26 st / 6 ct / 1 t10. (T7 Italian). Failed to retain his card for the fourth straight year, finishing 163rd in $$$.

OUTLOOK: A long-but-wild hitter who, at age 26, seems stuck at the developmental tour level, with few of the signs pointing up.

STATS: Driving Distance: B+   Driving Accuracy: C-   GIR: C   Short Game: C   Putting: B-

---

Hatton, Tyrrell (England) (23)
b. High Wycombe, England 10/14/1991. 5'8" 160 lbs. TP: 2011. After a solid amateur career (including an MC at the 2010 British Open), spent 2012 playing the Challenge and EuroPro tours before finishing 10th in Challenge Tour $$$ in 2013. Surprised some by enjoying a very strong rookie campaign on the 2014 E Tour, finishing 36th in $$$. **OWR Best**: 132 - Nov, 2014.

Other Wins: 1 EuroPro (2013).
Amateur Wins: Czech Am: 2010.

	10	11	12	13	14
Masters	-	-	-	-	-
US Open	-	-	-	-	-
British	MC	-	-	-	MC
PGA	-	-	-	-	-
Money (E)	-	-	-	-	36
OWR	-	-	907	376	132

2014: E: 30 st / 19 ct / 5 t10. (T2 Joburg, T3 Euro Masters, T4 Scottish, T6 Tour Champ, T10 Abu Dhabi). Enjoyed a very strong rookie season, logging five top 10s (including an early runner-up in Johannesburg) and finishing 36th in $$$.

OUTLOOK: Somewhat touted prospect who took several years to reach the big stage. In a limited sample, showed a very balanced skill set heavy on precision and a some deft putting. This year should be interesting to watch as he's set the bar high, but many expect him to further blossom.

STATS (LTD):   Driving Distance: B   Driving Accuracy: A-   GIR: A-   Short Game: B+   Putting: A-

---

Havret, Grégory (France) (38)
b. La Rochelle, France 11/25/1976. 6'2" 180 lbs. TP: 1999. A three-time French Amateur winner who claimed his first E Tour victory as a rookie at the 2001 Italian Open before encountering leaner times early in the millennium. Waited six years to win again before beating world #3 Phil Mickelson in a playoff for the 2007 Scottish Open. Also added the 2008 Johnnie Walker Championship (by one over Graeme Storm) before finishing 2nd in the 2010 U.S. Open at Pebble Beach, one behind Graeme McDowell. Through 2014, had retained his card 11 times in 12 years, dating to 2003. **Teams**: Eisenhower Trophy: 1998. Seve Trophy: 2007. World Cup (2): 2007-08. **OWR Best**: 82 - Sep, 2008.

European Tour Wins (3): **2001**: Italian Open **2007**: Scottish Open **2008**: Johnnie Walker Championship.
Other Wins: National Omnium (France): 1998*.
Amateur Wins: European Am: 1999   French Am (3): 1997-98-99.

	01	02	03	04	05	06	07	08	09	10	11	12	13	14
Masters	-	-	-	-	-	-	-	-	-	-	MC	-	-	-
US Open	-	-	-	-	-	-	-	-	-	2	T30	-	-	-
British	-	-	-	-	-	-	MC	T19	-	MC	T57	MC	-	-
PGA	-	-	-	-	-	-	MC	-	-	-	-	-	-	-
Money (E)	60	134	102	61	45	92	19	33	138	27	27	100	71	84
OWR	199	326	410	234	155	351	135	103	292	113	90	233	280	280

2014: E: 25 st / 14 ct / 1 t10. (2P BMW Int'l). Slipped to 84th in $$$ and lost a four-way playoff to Fabrizio Zanotti at the BMW International.

OUTLOOK: At age 38, he remains an infrequent winner but a steady earner, annually retaining his card with regularity and relative ease. A shorter-and-straighter type (which limits his upside in today's game) who is reliable enough to perhaps win again before reaching the finish line.

STATS: Driving Distance: C+   Driving Accuracy: A   GIR: B+   Short Game: B   Putting: B

Hearn, David Geoffrey (Canada) (35)
b. Brampton, Ontario, Canada 6/17/1979. 6'1" 170 lbs. College: U of Wyoming. TP: 2001. After graduating from Wyoming, played his native Canadian Tour from 2002-2004, winning once. Played the Web.com Tour in 2004 and '06, and the PGA Tour in 2005, where he struggled to finish 196th in $$$. Made his way back to the big stage by finishing 21st on the 2010 Web.com, then retained his card by placing 104th on the 2011 money list, and has climbed to 97th, 75th and 92nd since. **Teams**: World Cup: 2013. **OWR Best**: 88 - May, 2014.

Other Wins: 1 Web.com (2004)   +   Times Colonist Open (Canada): 2004.
Amateur Wins: Ontario Match Play: 1997.

	04	05	06	07	08	09	10	11	12	13	14
Masters	-	-	-	-	-	-	-	-	-	-	-
US Open	-	MC	-	-	MC	-	-	-	T21	-	-
British	-	-	-	-	-	-	-	-	-	-	T32
PGA	-	-	-	-	-	-	-	T47	MC	-	-
Money (A)	-	196	-	-	-	-	-	104	97	75	92
OWR	292	411	490	460	579	757	328	254	224	138	126

Hearn, David Geoffrey, Cont'd

2014: PGA: 28 st / 20 ct / 3 t10. (T6 Honda, T6 Players, T8 Valspar). Finished 74th in FedEx Cup points.

OUTLOOK: Steady Canadian who bears the statistical oddity of having his GIR numbers decline (21 to 63 to 101) from 2011-2013 while his $$$ ranking moved almost inversely - a trend perhaps offset by his SGP rising from 71 to 43 to 15 over the same period. But with his GIR climbing back to 55 and his SGP holding nicely at 29 in 2014, he has emerged as a steady earner who looks capable of doing this for several more years.

STATS: Driving Distance: C+   Driving Accuracy: A-   GIR: A-   Short Game: B+   Putting: A-

---

Hebert, Benjamin (France) (27)
b. Brive, France 2/19/1987. 6'2" 165 lbs. TP: 2009. Spent nearly five teenage years living in Tahiti before returning to his native France. After winning the European Amateur in 2007, made a significant splash by winning three times on the 2011 Challenge Tour before losing his E Tour card a year later. In 2014 became the first man ever to win three times on the Challenge Tour in two different years, giving him a third try at the E Tour in 2015. **Teams:** Eisenhower Trophy: 2008. **OWR Best:** 118 - Dec, 2014.

Other Wins: 6 Challenge (2011-2014) + 1 Alps (2009).

Amateur Wins: European Am: 2007   -   Grand Prix de Niort: 2006   La Coupe Mouchy: 2007   Grand Prix de Bordeaux-Lac: 2007   Grand Pix Palmola: 2007   Grand Prix de St Cyprien: 2007.

	08	09	10	11	12	13	14
Masters	-	-	-	-	-	-	-
US Open	-	-	-	-	-	-	-
British	MC	-	-	-	-	-	-
PGA	-	-	-	-	-	-	-
Money (E)	-	-	142	195*	176	-	-
OWR	1381	703	559	188	415	1180	119

2014: Played full-time on the Challenge Tour where he won three times and finished 2nd in $$$, clinching a return to the E Tour for 2015.

OUTLOOK: A shorter-but-straighter type who's failed to make an E Tour impact in the past, but arrives better prepared/more experienced in 2015. Was borderline dominant on the Challenge Tour in 2014, so he may well be ready to at least keep his card this time around.

STATS: Driving Distance: --   Driving Accuracy: --   GIR: --   Short Game: --   Putting: --

---

Hedblom, Peter Mikael (Sweden) (44)
b. Gayle, Sweden 1/20/1970. 6'0" 190 lbs. TP: 1988. Up-and-down player who twice labored extensively on the Challenge Tour (1992-1993 and 1999-2001) before eventually settling into the European circuit. Claimed his maiden E Tour win at the 1996 Moroccan Open (edging Eduardo Romero by one) but then waited nearly 11 years to win a second E Tour title, the 2007 Malaysian Open. Added a third victory in 2009 at the Johnnie Walker Championship, a lighter-field event played at Gleneagles. Missed most of 2002 with a broken leg, and most of 2011 after shoulder surgery. Has mostly struggled since the latter injury, failing to crack the E Tour's top 140 $$$ winners since 2011, and playing without status since 2013. **OWR Best:** 77 - Nov, 2008.

European Tour Wins (3): 1996: Moroccan Open **2007**: Malaysian Open **2009**: Johnnie Walker Championship.

Other Wins: 4 Euro Challenge (1991-2001) + Danish Open: 1991   Alvkarleby Open (Sweden): 2003.

Amateur Wins: Scandinavian Am: 1986   Swedish Boys: 1986.

	90	91	92	93	94	95	96	97	98	99	00	01	02	03	04	05	06	07	08	09	10	11	12	13
Masters	-	-	-	-	-	-	-	-	-	-	-	-	-	-	-	T11	T21	-	-	-	-	-	-	T65
US Open	-	-	-	-	-	-	-	-	-	-	-	-	-	-	-	MC	-	MC	-	MC	-	-	-	-
British	MC	T96	-	-	-	-	T7	MC	MC	-	-	-	-	-	-	-	-	-	MC	-	-	-	-	-
PGA	-	-	-	-	-	-	-	-	-	-	-	-	-	-	-	-	-	-	-	-	-	-	-	-
Money (E)	176	142	-	-	36	45	50	72	140	-	-	-	-	35	66	42	89	56	29	50	89	-	143	164
OWR	-	514	770	-	178	169	168	224	469	741	960	310	445	131	218	167	264	161	86	131	236	685	755	751

	14
Masters	-
US Open	-
British	-
PGA	-
Money (E)	-
OWR	747

2014: E: 9 st / 3 ct / 1 t10. (T9 Czech Masters). Made nine starts without status, logging a top 10 at the light-field Czech Masters.

OUTLOOK: At age 44, has become a below-the-median ball striker and statistically, his short game and putting stroke are not quite strong enough to compensate. Is apparently fully recovered from a 2011 shoulder injury so despite his three-win résumé, his best golf is likely behind him now.

STATS: Driving Distance: C-   Driving Accuracy: C+   GIR: C   Short Game: B   Putting: B-

---

Hend, Scott Robert (Australia) (41)
b. Townsville, Queensland, Australia 8/15/1973. 5'11" 180 lbs. TP: 1998. Long-hitting Australian who has played primarily at home and in Asia, save for a two-year stint (2004-2005) on the PGA Tour. Won several times domestically around the millennium but claimed his biggest wins several years later on the Asian Tour, first at the 2008 Indonesia President Invitational (by one over Wen-Tang Lin), then at the 2012 Singapore Classic. Enjoyed something of a breakout year in 2013 (at age 40), winning the inaugural Chiangmai Classic, the Taiwan Masters (in a four-shot runaway) and the Macau Open, where he beat Anirban Lahiri by three. A year later, won the E Tour-Co-sanctioned Hong Kong Open (in a playoff over Angelo Que), gaining him E Tour status for 2015. **OWR Best:** 96 - Dec, 2014.

European Tour Wins (1): 2014: Hong Kong Open.

Asian Tour Wins (5): 2008: Indonesia President Inv (Pertamina) **2012**: Singapore Classic (ISPS Handa)(54H) **2013**: Chiangmai Classic, Taiwan Masters, Macau Open.

Other Wins: South Australian PGA: 1999   Victoria Open (Canada): 2002   Queensland Open (Aus): 2003   Southern Classic (Aus) (2): 2000-03.

Hend, Scott Robert, Cont'd

	02	03	04	05	06	07	08	09	10	11	12	13	14
Masters	-	-	-	-	-	-	-	-	-	-	-	-	-
US Open	-	-	MC	-	T32	-	-	-	-	MC	-	-	-
British	-	-	-	MC	-	-	-	-	-	-	-	-	-
PGA	-	-	-	-	-	-	-	-	-	-	-	-	-
Money (A)	-	-	136	170	-	-	-	-	-	-	-	-	-
Money (As)	-	-	-	-	-	4	20	4	22	28	13	2	4
OWR	274	320	284	366	618	285	227	271	265	406	262	123	96

2014: ASIA: 12 st / 9 ct / 5 t10. (Incl. Won Hong Kong, T2 Macau). Enjoyed another strong campaign on the Asian Tour, winning once and finishing 4th in $$$ in only 12 events. Also made spot starts in Europe, Australia and Japan, and on the Web.com.

OUTLOOK: One of the longest hitters in Asia, and while the rest of his game lags somewhat behind statistically, it has seen improvements as he enters his 40s. His Hong Kong win has gained him status in Europe for 2015, where he seems capable of enjoying one or two successful moments.

STATS: Driving Distance: A+   Driving Accuracy: C-   GIR: B+   Short Game: B-   Putting: B

Hendry, Michael (New Zealand) (35)
b. Auckland, New Zealand 10/15/1979. 6'1" 210 lbs. TP: 2005. Initially toiled on the Australasian Tour before joining the OneAsia circuit, where he finished among the top 10 in $$$ in 2010 and '11, and claimed victory (in a seven-shot runaway) at the 2010 Indonesia Open. Spent most of 2013 playing in Japan and on the Australasian Tour, where he beat Scott Strange in a playoff to win the New Zealand PGA Championship. Played full-time in Japan in 2014, finishing 51st in $$$. **Teams**: World Cup (2): 2011-13. **OWR Best**: 143 - Mar, 2013.

OneAsia Tour Wins (1): 2010: Indonesia Open.
Australasian Tour Wins (2): 2012: New Zealand PGA Pro-Am **2013**: New Zealand PGA Championship.
Other Wins: Fiji Open: 2010.

	06	07	08	09	10	11	12	13	14
Masters	-	-	-	-	-	-	-	-	-
US Open	-	-	-	-	-	-	-	-	-
British	-	-	-	-	-	-	-	-	-
PGA	-	-	-	-	-	-	-	-	-
Money (J)	-	-	-	-	-	-	-	71	51
Money (O)	-	-	-	3	6	16	-	20*	
OWR				389	585	271	213	353	

2014: JAP: 16 st / 12 ct / 2 t10. (T3 Tsuruya, T6 Mizuno). Climbed modestly to 51st in $$$ in his second full season in Japan. Also made spot starts on his native Australasian Tour, having less impact than in 2012 and '13 but finishing second at the Victorian PGA.

OUTLOOK: A power-oriented player who has proven himself of star caliber on the Australasian Tour but is still figuring things out on the Japan circuit. Seems capable of finding success there but based on two full seasons, Japan would appear to represent his competitive ceiling.

STATS: Driving Distance: A-   Driving Accuracy: C-   GIR: A-   Short Game: B-   Putting: B-

---

Henley, Russell Chapin (USA) (25)
b. Macon, GA 4/12/1989. 6'0" 180 lbs. Three-time All-American and Haskins Award winner (2010) at U of Georgia. TP: 2011. Never won a major amateur event but claimed the 2010 Haskins award as a junior. Became the second amateur ever to win a Web.com Tour event, taking the 2011 Stadion Classic (played over University of Georgia's home course). Won twice more on the Web.com Tour in 2012, finishing 3rd in $$$ and graduating to the PGA Tour. Won his first professional PGA Tour start, carding a blazing 256 aggregate to beat Tim Clark by three at the 2013 Sony Open In Hawaii. Added a bigger triumph at the 2014 Honda Classic, where he birdied the first extra hole to beat Russell Knox, Rory McIlroy and Ryan Palmer. **Teams**: Walker Cup: 2011 (1-2-0). Palmer Cup (2): 2010-11. **OWR Best**: 43 - Apr, 2014.

PGA Tour Wins (2): 2013: Hawaiian Open (Sony) **2014**: Honda Classic.
Other Wins: 3 Web.com (2011-2012).
Amateur Wins: Georgia Am (2): 2008-09   Georgia HS (3): 2004-05-06   Georgia-South Carolina Cup: 2006.

	10	11	12	13	14
Masters	-	-	-	MC	T31
US Open	T16	T42	-	MC	T60
British	-	-	-	T73	MC
PGA	-	-	-	MC	MC
Money (A)	Am	-	-	33	31
OWR	676	428	131	89	60

2014: PGA: 29 st / 17 ct / 3 t10. (Won Honda, T2 Deutsche Bank, T7 Houston). Enjoyed a strong second season, winning for the second time (in a four-way playoff at the Honda Classic) and finishing 19th in FedEx Cup points.

OUTLOOK: With two wins before turning 25, has the potential to emerge as one of America's top young players. Though his statistical sampling is somewhat limited, he seems to possess a nice mix of power and accuracy off the tee (22 in Total Driving) as well as a very fine putting stroke (28 in SGP) - an attribute he needs after ranking 130 in Proximity To Hole. Has an obviously high upside, but can become far more consistent.

STATS: Driving Distance: B+   Driving Accuracy: A-   GIR: C+   Short Game: B-   Putting: A

Henry, Ronald III ("J.J.") (USA) (39)
b. Fairfield, CT 4/2/1975. 6'3" 190 lbs. All-American at Texas Christian. TP: 1998. Won three Connecticut Amateurs (1994, '95 and '98) as well as the 1998 New England Amateur before spending 1999 and 2000 on the Web.com Tour, winning once. Initially mostly a check casher on the PGA Tour, remaining comfortably among the top 125 in $$$ but logging only six top-3 finishes in his first 214 career starts. Scored his maiden victory on home turf at the 2006 Greater Hartford Open, beating Hunter Mahan and Ryan Moore by three. Claimed a second career title at the 2012 Reno-Tahoe Open, edging Alexandre Rocha by one point in the event's first playing under the Modified Stableford scoring system. Stumbled a bit in 2013 (107th in $$$) before falling out of the top 125 for the first time in his career in 2014. **Teams**:

Henry, Ronald III, Cont'd

Palmer Cup: 1998. Ryder Cup: 2006 (O: 0-0-3, S: 0-0-1). World Cup (1): 2006. **OWR Best:** 58 - Jan, 2007.

PGA Tour Wins (2): 2006: Greater Hartford Open (Travelers) **2012**: Reno-Tahoe Open (Stableford).
Other Wins: 1 Web.com (2000) + CVS Classic: 2007 (w/S.Cink).
Amateur Wins: Connecticut Am (3): 1994-95-98 New England Am: 1998.

	01	02	03	04	05	06	07	08	09	10	11	12	13	14
Masters	-	-	-	-	-	-	T37	-	-	-	-	-	-	-
US Open	-	-	-	64	T57	MC	T26	-	MC	MC	T54	-	-	-
British	-	-	-	-	-	MC	T27	-	-	-	-	-	-	-
PGA	-	63	-	-	-	T41	MC	MC	T63	-	MC	T42	T40	-
Money (A)	49	116	96	93	87	29	89	111	80	84	103	65	107	143
OWR	142	179	217	206	189	70	113	275	237	234	233	179	179	398

2014: PGA: 28 st / 18 ct / 0 t10. (T13 FedEx St Jude). Fell from the top 125 in $$$ for the first time, ending an impressive career-long streak of 13 straight times above the line. Also finished 128th in FedEx Cup points.

OUTLOOK: There have been few more consistent PGA Tour money winners in the new millennium; indeed, he finished between 80th-120th in 10 of 12 seasons since 2002. Played his back via the Web.com Finals for 2015, and while it seems like he's been around forever, he's only 39 – so the possibility of his winning again is still a legitimate one, especially since he still hits greens at a pace matched by very, very few.

STATS: Driving Distance: B   Driving Accuracy: A-   GIR: A+   Short Game: C+   Putting: B-

---

Herman, James Robert (USA) (37)
b. Cincinnati, OH 11/5/1977. 6'0" 170 lbs. College: U of Cincinnati. TP: 2000. Former club pro who didn't reach the PGA Tour until his early 30s. Spent three years (2008-2010) on the Web.com circuit, graduating to the PGA Tour by finishing 19th in $$$ in 2010. Finished 189th in PGA Tour $$$ and fell to the Web.com in 2012, but returned to the big stage (barely) after ranking 25th in $$$. Came closer in 2013 (141st in $$$) but still required the Web.com Finals to return for both 2014 and 2015. **OWR Best:** 280 - Sep, 2013.

Other Wins: 1 Web.com (2010) + New Jersey Asst Pro (2): 2006-07.

	10	11	12	13	14
Masters	-	-	-	-	-
US Open	T47	-	MC	T67	-
British	-	-	-	-	-
PGA	-	-	-	-	-
Money (A)	-	189	-	141	185
OWR	375	618	418	334	386

2014: PGA: 21 st / 11 ct / 0 t10. (T26 Frys.com). Finished 182nd in FedEx Cup points but once again played his way back via the Web.com Finals.

OUTLOOK: Statistically a very sound ball striker (25 in Total Driving, 35 in Ball Striking) but he has thus far been unable to parlay this into major PGA Tour success. Did improve markedly from 2011 to 2013 but seemed to hit a wall in 2014. Only 37, but he obviously needs to hole more putts.

STATS: Driving Distance: A-   Driving Accuracy: B+   GIR: A-   Short Game: C   Putting: C

Herron, Timothy Daniel (USA) (44)
b. Minneapolis, MN 2/6/1970. 5'10" 250 lbs. Two-time All-American at U of New Mexico. TP: 1993. Father and grandfather both played in U.S. Opens, sister Alissa won 1999 U.S. Women's Mid-Am. Beat Tiger Woods head-to-head in the second round of the 1992 U.S. Junior Amateur. Played one season on the Web.com Tour (1995) before reaching the PGA Tour via Q School and never looking back, finishing no worse than 67th in $$$ from 1996-2006. As a rookie, won the 1996 Honda Classic wire-to-wire, by four over Mark McCumber. Added victories at the 1997 Texas Open and the 1999 Bay Hill Invitational (in a playoff with Tom Lehman). Though remaining a big money earner, went winless until 2006, when he captured his fourth PGA Tour title by beating Richard S. Johnson in a playoff at Colonial. Has slipped noticeably since 2007, and hasn't bettered 100th in earnings since finishing 94th in 2008. **Teams:** Walker Cup: 1993 (3-0-0). **OWR Best:** 29 - Feb, 2000.

PGA Tour Wins (4): 1996: Honda Classic **1997**: Texas Open (LaCantera) **1999**: Bay Hill Inv **2006**: Colonial Inv (Crown Plaza).

	95	96	97	98	99	00	01	02	03	04	05	06	07	08	09	10	11	12	13	14
Masters	-	MC	-	MC	T44	MC	-	-	-	MC	T11	T36	T37	-	-	-	-	-	-	-
US Open	MC	MC	-	T53	6	MC	T40	T50	-	T13	T33	63	-	-	-	-	MC	-	-	-
British	-	MC	-	-	T30	MC	-	-	-	MC	T41	MC	-	-	-	-	-	-	-	-
PGA	-	T31	T13	75	MC	MC	MC	MC	T14	MC	MC	T14	T66	-	-	-	-	-	-	-
Money (A)	-	39	33	54	22	65	57	67	25	32	28	37	106	94	131	170	102	124	168	181
OWR	711	99	70	83	31	61	133	123	50	65	49	66	162	164	263	479	273	313	442	724

2014: PGA: 15 st / 10 ct / 0 t10. (T22 Byron Nelson). Finished 181st in FedEx Cup points; failed to clear an eight-event medical extension.

OUTLOOK: One of the Tour's steadiest $$$ winners from 1996-2006, but has only once cracked the top 100 since. Statistically his game has held steady for several years – save for the rather crucial aspect of his GIR plunging from 35 to 177 in 2013, then remaining at 170 in 2014. There have been relatively few signs of an imminent resurgence in recent years, and he will make only limited 2015 starts on Past Champion status.

STATS: Driving Distance: B-   Driving Accuracy: C   GIR: C+   Short Game: B+   Putting: B-

---

Hicks, Justin Douglas (USA) (40)
b. Wyandotte, MI 10/28/1974. 6'3" 220 lbs. College: U of Michigan. TP: 1997. After graduating from Michigan, spent nearly a decade playing mini-tours, where he was a regular winner. Joined the Web.com Tour in 2007 and stayed there through 2010, graduating to the PGA Tour by finishing 25th in 2010 $$$. Finished 179th in 2011 PGA Tour $$$ and returned to the Web.com in 2012. Then rode an 11th-place $$$ ranking there back to the big tour where, approaching 40, he managed to retain his card for 2014, then score something of a breakthrough by finishing 66th in $$$. **OWR Best:** 135 - Aug, 2014.

Other Wins: 2 Web.com (2008-2010) + 1 eGolf Tour (2007)   4 Gateway (2006-2008).

Hicks, Justin Douglas, Cont'd

	04	05	06	07	08	09	10	11	12	13	14
Masters	-	-	-	-	-	-	-	-	-	-	-
US Open	MC	-	-	-	T74	-	-	T60	MC	MC	-
British	-	-	-	-	-	-	-	-	-	-	-
PGA	-	-	-	-	-	-	-	-	-	-	-
Money (A)	-	-	-	-	-	-	-	179	-	111	66
OWR				652	377	510	458	593	283	261	185

2014: PGA: 30 st / 21 ct / 3 t10. (2 Barracuda, 3 Canadian, T6 Mayakoba). Enjoyed his best year yet, finishing 75th in FedEx Cup points.

OUTLOOK: Bears the odd statistical quirk of being a big man who's relatively short - but extremely accurate - off the tee. Arrived on Tour late (as a 37-year-old 2011 rookie) and has made great strides. His SGP jumped from 137 to 84 in 2014 - a gain he must hold if he is to continue at this pace.

STATS: Driving Distance: C+   Driving Accuracy: A+   GIR: A   Short Game: C+   Putting: B-

---

Higginbottom, Jake (Australia) (21)
b. Sydney, New South Wales, Australia 10/15/1993. 6'0" 185 lbs. TP: 2012. A touted prospect domestically who came to international attention in 2012 upon becoming the first amateur since Harry Berwick in 1956 to win the New Zealand Open. Wasted little time in turning professional (at age 19) several days later and has played on the Australasian and Asian Tours since. Perhaps surprisingly, he remains winless as a pro. **OWR Best:** 275 - May, 2013.

Australasian Tour Wins (1): 2012: New Zealand Open (BMW): 2012*.

Other Wins: 1 eGolf Tour (2014).

Amateur Wins: China Am: 2010   New South Wales Am: 2010   Queensland Am: 2011   Keperra Bowl: 2011   Handa Jr Masters: 20011   Riversdale Cup: 2012.

	12	13	14
Masters	-	-	-
US Open	-	-	-
British	-	-	-
PGA	-	-	-
Money (As)	-	60	53
OWR	360	370	278

2014: ASIA: 9 st / 6 ct / 3 t10. (Incl. 4 Dubai, T7 Indonesia Open, T9 Selangor Masters). Split time between the Asian circuit and the Australasian Tour, making eight starts on the latter (including three top 10s) and finishing sixth in the Order of Merit.

OUTLOOK: One of Australia's higher-rated recent prospects who stepped up somewhat in 2014. He appears to possess a solid mix of length and above-average skills on the greens, and is young enough to have plenty of time to develop. Still a player to watch, at least regionally.

STATS: Driving Distance: B+   Driving Accuracy: B-   GIR: B   Short Game: B+   Putting: B+

Hiratsuka, Tetsuji (Japan) (43)
b. Kyoto, Japan 11/6/1971. 5'8" 175 lbs. TP: 1999. A late bloomer who didn't win his first major tour event until his early 30s. Claimed this breakthrough win at the 2003 Golf Nippon Series JT Cup (by two over Toshi Izawa) before later adding a pair of Mitsubishi Diamond Cups (2004 and 2006) and the most prestigious of his domestic triumphs, the 2009 Crowns, where he ran away to a seven-shot victory. In recent years has also played extensively on the Asian Tour, notably in 2010 when he finished 5th in their Order of Merit and won three times: the Myanmar Open (in a 10-shot runaway from Prayad Marksaeng) and a pair of events played in Thailand, the Queens Cup and the Black Mountain Masters. Won a Japan/Asian Tour co-sponsored event in 2011, the Asia Pacific Panasonic Open. Slipped noticeably in 2014, recording his worst $$$ ranking (81st) since his rookie season of 1999. **Teams:** World Cup (3): 2006-07-11. **OWR Best:** 65 - Dec, 2010.

Japan Tour Wins (6): 2003: Golf Nippon Series JT Cup **2004:** Mitsubishi Diamond Cup **2006:** Hiroshima Open **2007:** Mitsubishi Diamond Cup **2009:** The Crowns **2011:** Panasonic Open.

Asian Tour Wins (3): 2010: Myanmar Open, Queens Cup, Black Mountain Masters.

	99	00	01	02	03	04	05	06	07	08	09	10	11	12	13	14
Masters	-	-	-	-	-	-	-	-	-	-	-	-	-	-	-	-
US Open	-	-	-	-	-	-	-	-	-	-	-	-	-	-	-	-
British	-	-	-	-	-	T36	-	-	-	-	-	-	MC	-	-	-
PGA	-	-	-	-	-	MC	-	-	-	-	-	MC	MC	-	-	-
Money (E)	-	-	-	-	-	-	-	-	-	-	-	-	144	182*	-	-
Money (J)	108	53	32	29	1	17	24	5	12	55	14	13	9	39	26	81
Money (As)	-	-	-	-	-	-	-	-	-	-	-	54	5	2*	96*	-
OWR	741	379	275	253	90	121	174	122	140	362	167	65	88	217	269	498

2014: JAP: 15 st / 7 ct / 2 t10. (6 Kansai, T7 Tour Champ). Fell to 81st in $$$ but missed the Tour's final nine events for undisclosed reasons.

OUTLOOK: At age 43, he seems to be trending towards the downside now, and is likely settling in for his final run. Though seemingly not the player he was in his late 30s, his career has ventured through several peaks and valleys – and he's surely not too old to make one more climb.

STATS: Driving Distance: C+   Driving Accuracy: B-   GIR: C+   Short Game: A-   Putting: B+

Hoey, Michael George (Northern Ireland) (35)
b. Ballymoney, Northern Ireland 2/13/1979. 6'0" 170 lbs. College: Clemson U. TP: 2002. A once-touted prospect who played collegiately in America and won the 2001 British Amateur. Took far longer to develop than many expected, toiling for four full seasons on the Challenge Tour (where he was thrice a winner) before ultimately sticking on the E Tour in 2009. Claimed his first victory that season at the 2009 Portuguese Open, where he beat Gonzalo Fernandez-Castaño in a play-off. Enjoyed a breakout year in 2011, winning the Madeira Islands Open and the Dunhill Links Championship, the latter by two over countryman Rory McIlroy at St Andrews. Added the 2012 Trophée Hassan II, beating Damien McGrane by three shots. Broke a minor slump by winning the light-field Russian Open in 2013. **Teams:** Walker Cup: 2001 (3-1-0). Palmer Cup: 1999. World Cup: 2007. **OWR Best:** 74 - Mar, 2012.

Hoey, Michael George, Cont'd

European Tour Wins (5): 2009: Portuguese Open **2011**: Madeira Islands Open, Dunhill Links Championship **2012**: Trophée Hassan II **2013**: Russian Open (M2M).
Other Wins: 3 Euro Challenge (2005-2008).
Amateur Wins: British Am: 2001.

	01	02	03	04	05	06	07	08	09	10	11	12	13	14
Masters	-	MC	-	-	-	-	-	-	-	-	-	-	-	-
US Open	-	-	-	-	-	-	-	-	-	-	-	-	-	-
British	MC	-	-	-	-	-	-	-	-	-	-	MC	-	WD
PGA	-	-	-	-	-	-	-	-	-	-	-	DQ	-	-
Money (E)	-	-	-	-	-	187	-	-	93	90	25	56	92	57
OWR	593	506	848	438	432	765	578	379	246	361	102	138	247	206

2014: E: 30 st / 21 ct / 6 t10. (T2 Tshwane, 7 French, T8 Volvo China, T8 Irish, T8 Port Masters, etc.). Though winless, put together one of his strongest seasons to date, logging six top 10s and finishing 57th in $$$.

OUTLOOK: A strong tee-to-greener (especially with his irons) with five E Tour wins since 2009 – though twice (Madeira and Russia) against notably light fields. Arrived with high expectations upon him and is within range of reaching them, but does he have one more gear to win a big one?

STATS: Driving Distance: B   Driving Accuracy: C+   GIR: A   Short Game: C+   Putting: B-

---

Hoffman, Charley Lindley (USA) (38)
b. San Diego, CA 12/27/1976. 6'0" 200 lbs. College: UNLV. TP: 2000. An AJGA All-American. Late-arriving professional who began playing the Web.com Tour in 2002 – and missed his first 14 cuts in succession. Logged one Web.com win in 2004 before earning his way to the PGA Tour in 2006, where he finished 82nd in earnings. Broke through for his maiden victory at the 2007 Bob Hope Classic by eagling the par-5 finisher to force a playoff with John Rollins, which he won with a birdie at the first extra hole. Claimed a bigger title at the 2010 Deutsche Bank (part of the FedEx Cup playoffs) where he routed Jason Day, Luke Donald and Geoff Ogilvy by five. Broke a four-year drought by winning the 2014 Mayakoba Classic, where he edged Jason Bohn by one. **OWR Best:** 46 - Oct, 2010.

PGA Tour Wins (3): 2007: Bob Hope Classic (90H) **2010**: Deutsche Bank Championship **2014**: Mayakoba Classic (OHL)('15).
Other Wins: 1 Web.com (2004) + 2 Gateway (2004).

	06	07	08	09	10	11	12	13	14
Masters	-	-	-	-	-	T27	-	-	-
US Open	T48	-	-	-	-	T46	-	T45	-
British	-	T35	-	MC	-	MC	-	-	T67
PGA	-	MC	-	MC	-	MC	MC	T40	MC
Money (A)	82	50	110	41	25	58	69	57	46
OWR	202	130	345	121	52	84	164	102	74

2014: PGA: 25 st / 21 ct / 5 t10. (T3 Quicken Loans, 4 Shriners, T5 New Orleans, T7 Farmers, T9 Humana). Recorded his sixth consecutive top-75 $$$ ranking (and ninth consecutive top 125), logging a solid 10 top-25 finishes en route to finishing 53rd in FedEx Cup points.

OUTLOOK: Has ranked among the Tour's steadiest/most proficient earners for nearly a decade, yet has not contended quite as much as one might expect for a powerful, highly consistent player. Has seen his SGP climb from 181 to 72 to 44 since 2012, approaching the sort of putting numbers that he produced in his two best seasons, 2009 and '10. If that trend continues, he may return to the winner's circle sooner rather than later.

STATS: Driving Distance: A   Driving Accuracy: B-   GIR: A-   Short Game: B-   Putting: B+

Hoffmann, Morgan (USA) (25)
b. Franklin Lakes, NJ 8/11/1989. 6'1" 180 lbs. Two-time All-American at Oklahoma St. TP: 2011. An AJGA All-American. Ranked as the world's #1 amateur during 2009 despite never winning a major amateur event. Made only 13 starts on the 2012 Web.com Tour but still finished 19th in $$$, earning his way onto the PGA Tour, where he cracked the top 100 $$$ winners as a rookie in 2013, then solidified his position in 2014. **Teams:** Walker Cup: 2009 (2-0-1). Palmer Cup: 2009. **OWR Best:** 97 - Oct, 2014.

	10	11	12	13	14
Masters	-	-	-	-	-
US Open	MC	-	T29	MC	-
British	-	-	-	-	-
PGA	-	-	-	-	-
Money (A)	-	-	-	96	64
OWR	903	876	247	175	124

2014: PGA: 32 st / 20 ct / 2 t10. (3 BMW, T9 Barclays). Stood 128th in $$$ / 124th in FedEx Cup points through the Wyndham Championship, then recorded two Playoffs top 10s (including 3rd at the BMW Championship) to rocket up to 26th in FedEx Cup points.

OUTLOOK: A former highly touted amateur and collegian who played up-and-down golf as rookie, then barely made the FedEx Cup top 125 through the 2014 Wyndham (he stood 124th) before catching fire during the Playoffs. Has a somewhat limited statistical sampling but as he possesses the valuable combination of high-end length and a deft putting stroke, his upside appears high. Still very much into his learning curve.

STATS: Driving Distance: A-   Driving Accuracy: C   GIR: C+   Short Game: B   Putting: A

Hoge, Thomas Robert (USA) (25)
b. Statesville, NC 5/25/1989. 6'1" 175 lbs. College: Texas Christian. TP: 2011. Though born in North Carolina, grew up in Fargo, ND. Was co-medalist at the 2010 Western Amateur. After turning pro, spent 2011 largely on the Canadian Tour (where he won once) before joining the Web.com circuit in 2012. Was winless in three full campaigns before a hot finish allowed him to reach the 2015 PGA Tour via the 2014 Web.com Finals. **OWR Best:** 462 - Nov, 2014.

Other Wins: Players Cup (Canada): 2011.
Amateur Wins: Minnesota Am (2): 2009-10.

Hoge, Thomas Robert, Cont'd

	14
Masters	-
US Open	-
British	-
PGA	-
Money (A)	-
OWR	518

2014: Played full-time on the Web.com Tour, finishing 65th in regular season $$$ but riding a hot streak through the Finals to a PGA Tour card.

OUTLOOK: With a limited amateur résumé and three-year regular season Web.com $$$ rankings of 87th, 57th and 65th, he would appear to fall comfortably into the lower half of the 2015 rookie class. And six career top 10s in 69 career Web.com does little to suggest otherwise.

STATS: Driving Distance: B+   Driving Accuracy: B   GIR: C   Short Game: B-   Putting: B+

Holmes, John Bradley ("J.B.") (USA) (32)
b. Campbellsville, KY 4/26/1982. 5'11" 190 lbs. Three-time All-American at U of Kentucky. TP: 2005. Also an Academic All-American. Ultra-powerful hitter despite utilizing a three-quarter backswing. After participating in the 2005 Walker Cup, was PGA Tour Q School medalist. Won the 2006 Phoenix Open in only his sixth PGA Tour start, overwhelming the TPC Scottsdale with a 21-under-par 263 total that won by seven shots. Returned in 2008 to win the Phoenix Open again, this time defeating Phil Mickelson in sudden death. Lost the 2009 Houston Open (to Paul Casey) in a playoff after finishing early, waiting 2 hours and 40 minutes for the playoff, then hitting his first drive into a pond. Began feeling vertigo-like symptoms in May of 2011 and eventually underwent September brain surgery at Johns Hopkins University to repair Chiari malformations. Missed the remainder of 2011 but returned in 2012 (finishing 80th in $$$), then missed nearly all of 2013 with a broken ankle. Broke a six-year victory drought by edging Jim Furyk by one to claim the 2014 Wells Fargo Championship. **Teams**: Walker Cup: 2005 (2-1-0). Palmer Cup: 2005. Ryder Cup: 2008 (O: 2-0-1, S: 1-0-0). **OWR Best**: 42 - May, 2008.

PGA Tour Wins (3): **2006**: Phoenix Open (FBR) **2008**: Phoenix Open (FBR) **2014**: Wells Fargo Championship.

Amateur Wins: Kentucky Am (2): 2002-04 Kentucky Open: 2004.

	03	04	05	06	07	08	09	10	11	12	13	14
Masters	-	-	-	-	-	T25	-	-	-	-	-	-
US Open	MC	-	-	T48	-	MC	T27	-	-	-	-	T17
British	-	-	-	MC	-	MC	69	T14	MC	-	-	MC
PGA	-	-	-	T37	-	T29	WD	T24	WD	-	-	T65
Money (A)	Am	Am	-	59	118	32	72	31	62	80	246*	35
OWR	-	-	-	90	208	75	127	73	108	128	475	66

2014: PGA: 24 st / 19 ct / 2 t10. (Won Wells Fargo, T10 Arnold Palmer).   Returned from a broken ankle to clear his medical extension in style, claiming his third career PGA Tour victory (but his first outside of Phoenix) at the Wells Fargo Championship and finishing 42nd in FedEx Cup points.

OUTLOOK: Has run into some terrible breaks physically over the last three years but showed once again in 2014 that when healthy, he can be a force to be reckoned with. Capable of overpowering a course with his immense length, with all three of his victories coming on layouts that favor longer hitters. If he can remain healthy, he possesses enough skill on and around the greens to win more regularly.

STATS: Driving Distance: A+   Driving Accuracy: C-   GIR: C+   Short Game: B-   Putting: B-

---

Homa, John Maxwell ("Max") (USA) (24)
b. Burbank, CA 11/19/1990. 6'1" 180 lbs. Two-time All-American at U. of California-Berkeley. TP: 2013. Was Cal's first-ever NCAA champion in 2013 and also won the Pac 12 individual title, notable for including a 61 over the North Course at the Los Angeles Country Club, site of the 2023 U.S. Open. Was a member of the victorious 2013 U.S. Walker Cup team before playing the Web.com Tour in 2014, where a 17th-place finish on the regular season money list earned him his PGA Tour card for 2015. **Teams**: Walker Cup: 2013 (2-1-0). **OWR Best**: 287 - Aug, 2014.

Other Wins: 1 Web.com (2014).

Amateur Wins: NCAA Individual: 2013.

	13	14
Masters	-	-
US Open	MC	-
British	-	-
PGA	-	-
Money (A)	-	-
OWR	767	349

2014: Played full-time on the Web.com Tour, winning once and finishing 17th in regular season $$$ to clinch his 2015 PGA Tour card.

OUTLOOK: Though less experienced than some, has shown the ability to post some impressive numbers and to compete at a high level (T9 at the 2013 Frys.com Open). Thus while the overall body of work is comparatively brief, he appears likely to rank among the top rookies in the class.

STATS (LTD): Driving Distance: A-   Driving Accuracy: C+   GIR: B-   Short Game: B+   Putting: B

Horne, Keith Weller (South Africa) (43)
b. Durban, South Africa 9/6/1971. 6'1" 190 lbs. TP: 1996. An Army veteran who didn't turn pro until his mid 20s after working with Hugh Baiocchi at Prince's Grant Golf Estate. Played several years on developmental circuits before sticking on the Sunshine Tour in the new millennium. Began playing semi-regularly in Europe in 2006 but has found little success there. Stepped up his domestic profile thereafter, however, winning the 2010 Royal Swazi Sun Open (by one point over Christiaan Basson, at Stableford) and the 2012 Telkom PGA Championship, where he beat three players by three. End a two-and-a-half-year drought by winning the 2014 Vodacom Origins of Golf event at St. Francis Bay, then later took the Vodacom Series Final for his seventh career Sunshine Tour victory. **OWR Best**: 173 - Mar, 2012.

Sunshine Tour Wins (7): **1998**: Vodacom-Kwazulu Natal (54H) **2007**: Namibia PGA (MTC) (54H) **2008**: Nashua Golf Challenge (54H) **2010**: Royal Swazi Open (Investec)(Stableford) **2012**: Telkom PGA Championship **2014**: Vodacom-St Francis Bay (54H), Vodacom-Final (54H).

Horne, Keith Weller, Cont'd

Other Wins: Wild Coast Sun Pro-Am (SA): 2003   Royal Swazi Sun Pro-Am (SA): 2003   Klipdrift Sun Int'l Pro-Am (SA): 2009.

	02	03	04	05	06	07	08	09	10	11	12	13	14
Masters	-	-	-	-	-	-	-	-	-	-	-	-	-
US Open	-	-	-	-	-	-	-	-	-	-	-	-	-
British	-	-	-	-	-	-	-	-	-	-	-	-	-
PGA	-	-	-	-	-	-	-	-	-	-	-	-	-
Money (E)	-	-	-	-	145	186	179*	187*	94	113	92	137	178*
Money (SA)	47	24	6	7	8	15	8	33	3	22*	8	24	13
OWR	681	847	457	275	474	546	551	347	275	362	221	548	380

2014: SUN: 18 st / 13 ct / 9 t10. (Incl. Won Vodacom-St. Francis, Won Vodacom-Final, T3 Investec). Played primarily at home in 2014, winning a pair of 54-hole winter events and finishing 13th in $$$. Also made played in five non-co-sanctioned E Tour events, missing four cuts.

OUTLOOK: Seems to have reprioritized away from the European Tour as he reaches his mid-40s, which may make sense as he has never bettered 92nd in $$$ there. Is clearly capable of winning regularly at home, so perhaps that's his best route going forward.

STATS: Driving Distance: C+   Driving Accuracy: B   GIR: B   Short Game: B   Putting: B

Horschel, William John (USA) (28)
b. Grant, FL 12/7/1986. 6'0" 175 lbs. Four-time All-American at U of Florida. TP: 2009. Played his way through 2009 Q School after turning pro but had his rookie 2010 season limited to four starts by a left wrist injury which required surgery. Returned in 2011 and made a late rush in keeping his card (T7 at Frys.com, the halfway lead at McGladrey) but fell apart on Sunday at McGladrey (shot 75 for a T20) and missed the cut at the season-ending Children's Miracle Network Classic. Played on conditional status in 2012 before T4 at 2012 Q School. After three straight top 10s, rode a final round 64 to his first PGA Tour victory at the 2013 Zurich Classic of New Orleans, edging D.A. Points by one. Though he was quiet for much of 2014, landed a big second win in September's BMW Championship (beating Bubba Watson by two at Cherry Hills), then clinched overall victory in the FedEx Cup Playoffs (and the $10 million prize) the following week by winning the Tour Championship, where he beat Jim Furyk and Rory McIlroy by three. **Awards:** FedEx Cup Champion: 2014. **Teams:** Walker Cup: 2007 (3-1-0). Eisenhower Trophy: 2008. Palmer Cup (2): 2007-08. **OWR Best:** 12 - Nov, 2014.

PGA Tour Wins (3): 2013: Zurich Classic (New Orleans) **2014:** BMW Championship, Tour Championship.

Other Wins: 1 eGolf Tour (2009).

	06	07	08	09	10	11	12	13	14
Masters	-	-	-	-	-	-	-	-	T37
US Open	MC	-	-	-	-	-	-	T4	T23
British	-	-	-	-	-	-	-	MC	MC
PGA	-	-	-	-	-	-	-	MC	T59
Money (A)	-	-	-	-	-	140	147	13	7
OWR	-	-	-	-	-	359	312	41	13

2014: PGA: 27 st / 20 ct / 5 t10. (Won BMW, Won Tour Champ, T2 Deutsche Bank, T6 T of C, T6 FedEx St Jude). After plodding quietly along for eight months (only two top 10s in 24 starts) caught fire in the Playoffs, winning the final two events and claiming the $10 million FedEx Cup title.

OUTLOOK: Emerged as one of the PGA Tour's elite ball strikers in 2013 which, combined with his SGP climbing from 113 to 28, added up to a breakout year. Produced more of the same in 2014 (including ranking 3 in Ball Striking) and exploded late in the year to win the FedEx Cup. As stated a year ago, he'll remain a high-level player on his ball striking alone – but if his putting remains strong, the sky's the limit.

STATS: Driving Distance: B+   Driving Accuracy: A   GIR: A+   Short Game: C+   Putting: B+

Horsey, David (England) (29)
b. Stockport, England 4/14/1985. 5'10" 170 lbs. TP: 1999. After a mid-range amateur career, won twice on the 2008 Challenge Tour to play his way onto the European circuit. Finished 76th in $$$ as a rookie, then cracked the top 50 over the next two seasons behind a pair of wins: the 2010 BMW International and the 2011 Trophée Hassan II, where he beat Rhys Davies and Jaco Van Zyl in a playoff. Struggled badly in 2012, slipping to 129th in $$$, but rebounded effectively in 2013, then claimed his third career win at the light-field 2014 Russian Open, where he edged Damian McGrane in a playoff. **Teams:** Walker Cup: 2007 (3-1-0). Seve Trophy: 2011. **OWR Best:** 77 - Sep, 2010.

European Tour Wins (3): 2010: BMW International Open **2011:** Trophée Hassan II **2014:** Russian Open (M2M).

Other Wins: 2 Euro Challenge (2008).

Amateur Wins: Greek Am: 2005.

	08	09	10	11	12	13	14
Masters	-	-	-	-	-	-	-
US Open	-	-	-	-	-	-	-
British	T67	-	-	-	-	-	-
PGA	-	-	T28	MC	-	-	-
Money (E)	-	76	32	43	129	57	69
OWR	128	230	86	121	332	231	155

2014: E: 25 st / 14 ct / 5 t10. (Won Russia, 2 Italian, T3 Africa, T8 Hassan, T9 Lyoness). Continued his solid E Tour career path by winning for the third time (at the light-field Russian Open) and recording a career-high five top 10s en route to finishing 69th in $$$.

OUTLOOK: A short-but-very-straight hitter whose bread and butter is a deft putting touch. If one ignores his 2012 as an outlier, has put together a solid E Tour résumé for a man not yet 30. May never win a significantly larger event, but figures to remain on his present, lucrative path.

STATS: Driving Distance: C   Driving Accuracy: A   GIR: B-   Short Game: B   Putting: A-

---

Howell, Charles Gordon III (USA) (35)
b. Augusta, GA 6/20/1979. 6'1" 190 lbs. Three-time All-American, NCAA individual champion (2000), Nicklaus (2000) and Haskins (2000) Awards winner at Oklahoma St. TP: 2000. Four-time AJGA All-American and 1996 AJGA Player of the Year. A highly thought-of prospect who was named PGA Tour Rookie of the Year in 2001. Scored an early PGA Tour win at the 2002 Michelob Classic

Howell, Charles Gordon III, Cont'd

(beating Scott Hoch and Brandt Jobe by two), a season in which he finished a career-best 9th on the money list. Has always been a steady earner (no worse than 69th in PGA Tour $$$ over his first 14 seasons) but has had trouble winning. Broke a five-year victory drought by beating Phil Mickelson in sudden death at the 2007 Nissan Open but has managed only four runner-ups in the years since. **Awards:** PGA Tour Rookie of the Year: 2001. **Teams:** Palmer Cup: 1998. Presidents Cup (2): 2003-07 (5-4-0). **OWR Best:** 15 - Feb, 2003.

PGA Tour Wins (2): 2002: Michelob Championship **2007:** Los Angeles Open (Nissan).
Amateur Wins: NCAA Individual: 2000.

	01	02	03	04	05	06	07	08	09	10	11	12	13	14
Masters	-	T29	T28	T13	MC	MC	T30	MC	-	-	-	T19	-	-
US Open	MC	T18	T53	T36	T75	T37	T51	MC	-	-	-	MC	-	-
British	-	-	T65	T42	MC	-	MC	MC	MC	-	T28	T64	-	-
PGA	T22	T17	T10	T31	T15	MC	T42	T47	MC	-	T26	MC	MC	MC
Money (A)	33	9	14	33	29	52	18	69	46	60	25	67	38	45
OWR	45	20	18	57	55	82	42	141	142	158	76	117	78	135

2014: PGA: 29 st / 24 ct / 6 t10. (T3 Byron Nelson, T5 Shriners, T6 Mayakoba, T6 Phoenix, T7 CIMB, etc.). Continued his status as a rarely winning earnings machine, quietly logging 10 top 25s, six top 10s and ranking 45th in $$$ and 34th in FedEx Cup points.

OUTLOOK: A remarkably steady player in terms of both $$$ and statistics, plus he possesses the desired mix of power and around-the-greens finesse - so it's a fair question why he hasn't won more. Has never finished worse than 69th in $$$ in 14 years on Tour, and has 71 top 10s in 419 career starts. Still, with the nature of his record, it's hard to predict a rash of upcoming victories - though at age 35, the door could still swing open.

STATS: Driving Distance: A   Driving Accuracy: C   GIR: A   Short Game: A   Putting: B+

Howell, David Alexander (England) (39)

b. Swindon, England 6/23/1975. 6'1" 190 lbs. TP: 1995. A top-25 caliber player on the European Tour early in the new millennium, with career best Order of Merit rankings of 10th, 7th and 3rd from 2004-2006. Claimed his maiden win far abroad at the 1998 Australian PGA (in a seven-shot romp) before breaking through on the E Tour with a four-shot triumph (over Lee Westwood) at the 1999 Dubai Desert Classic. Later added a three-shot win over Tiger Woods at the 2005 HSBC Championship (an '06 E Tour event) and a five-shot runaway victory at the flagship BMW PGA Championship in 2006. After a one-time run at the PGA Tour in 2006 (96th in $$$), a 2007 back injury led to a drastic loss of form, from which he finally began to recover in 2012 with a 62nd-place finish in $$$. Ended a seven-year victory drought by beating Peter Uihlein in a playoff to claim the 2013 Dunhill Links Championship, boosted by a third round 63 at St Andrews. **Teams:** Walker Cup: 1995 (2-0-1). Ryder Cup (2): 2004-06 (O: 3-1-1, S: 1-1-0). Seve Trophy (3): 2000-03-05. World Cup (2): 2005-06. **OWR Best:** 9 - Jun, 2006.

European Tour Wins (5): 1999: Dubai Classic **2005:** BMW Int'l, HSBC Championship ('06) **2006:** BMW PGA **2013:** Dunhill Links Championship.
Australasian Tour Wins (1): 1998: Australian PGA.
Amateur Wins: British Boys: 1993   Midland Am Stroke Play: 1994.

	96	97	98	99	00	01	02	03	04	05	06	07	08	09	10	11	12	13	14
Masters	-	-	-	-	-	-	-	-	-	T11	T19	T44	-	-	-	-	-	-	-
US Open	-	-	-	-	-	MC	-	-	WD	T16	-	-	-	-	MC	-	T65	-	-
British	-	MC	T44	T45	-	MC	MC	MC	MC	-	MC	T53	T7	T52	-	-	-	-	T15
PGA	-	-	-	-	-	-	-	-	T45	MC	67	MC	-	T48	-	-	-	-	-
Money (E)	54	47	32	22	40	14	74	16	10	7	3	142	45	156	96	103	62	21	53
OWR	202	213	161	113	169	115	150	111	43	11	14	165	167	350	391	317	258	93	131

2014: E: 27 st / 17 ct / 2 t10. (2 Italian, T9 Nordea). This wasn't the launchpad season he was surely looking for after his impressive comeback year of 2013, but he did play steady enough golf to finish 53rd in $$$.

OUTLOOK: A healthy back has his career back on track, and his combination of a strong short game and a deft putting touch has proven successful over time. Continued health is an obvious key, but his record suggests that a return to the top 50, and more wins, are both realistic possibilities.

STATS: Driving Distance: C   Driving Accuracy: B-   GIR: B-   Short Game: B+   Putting: A

Hu, Mu (China) (25)

b. Shenzhen, China 10/8/1989. 5'10" 165 lbs. College: U of Florida. TP: 2010. Three-time AJGA All-American. China's best-ever prospect who spent time studying with David Leadbetter in the U.S. (and was twice named AJGA All-American) before staying for one year at the University of Florida. At age 11, skipped two age groups to win the China Junior Open (15-18 division). At age 14, qualified for the U.S. Amateur and for the Asian Tour's Sanya Open, where he tied for 11th. Played the OneAsia Tour and China's developmental circuit in 2011 and '12 before qualifying for the Asian Tour in 2013, where he has thus far made only a limited impact. **OWR Best:** 426 - May, 2013.

Other Wins: 1 China Challenge Tour (2012).
Amateur Wins: Dixie Am: 2006.

	10	11	12	13	14
Masters	-	-	-	-	-
US Open	-	-	-	-	-
British	-	-	-	-	-
PGA	-	-	-	-	-
Money (As)	-	-	-	67	125*
Money (O)	-	86	34	11*	35*
OWR	-	-	837	581	521

2014: After seemingly establishing himself there in 2013, essentially bypassed the Asian circuit this year, instead opting to play domestically on the PGA Tour China. He finished a solid 12th in $$$ there, but that wasn't enough to earn a coveted Web.com status for 2015.

OUTLOOK: An intriguing prospect given his roots, and his time spent in America. Appears to have enough length to hold his own on the bigger tours but has thus far struggled to have a major international impact. Seems destined to remain in the Far East for the foreseeable future.

STATS: Driving Distance: --   Driving Accuracy: --   GIR: --   Short Game: --   Putting: --

Hubbard, Mark Atwell (USA) (25) b. Denver, CO 5/24/1989. 6'0" 175 lbs. College: San Jose St. TP: 2012. An academic All-American at San Jose State. After turning pro, spent 2013 on the PGA Tour Canada, where he won once and finished among top five in $$$. Thus graduated to the 2014 Web.com Tour, where he finished 18th-place finish in regularly season $$$ to reach the 2015 PGA Tour. **OWR Best:** 312 - Aug, 2014.

Other Wins: Wildfire Invitational (Canada): 2013.
Amateur Wins: Colorado Am: 2007   Colorado Stroke Play: 2007.

	13	14
Masters	-	-
US Open	-	-
British	-	-
PGA	-	-
Money (A)	-	-
OWR	729	375

2014: Played full-time on the Web.com Tour, finishing 18th in regular season $$$ to secure his card for the 2015 PGA Tour.
OUTLOOK: Had a somewhat limited amateur résumé before finding success on both the Canadian and Web.com Tours, so his degree of high-level competitive experience is limited. That, plus a lack of length, figure to make him something of a longshot in 2015.

STATS (LTD): Driving Distance: C   Driving Accuracy: B+   GIR: A-   Short Game: B-   Putting: B-

---

Hugo, Victor Jean (South Africa) (39) b. Stellenbosch, South Africa 12/3/1975. 5'9" 190 lbs. College: University of Stellenbosch. TP: 1999. Highly successful on his home Sunshine Tour and played three mostly unsuccessful seasons in Europe from 2001-2003, returning to his native tour thereafter. A 15-time Sunshine Tour winner, including 13 titles since 2006 – but all of his victories have come during the lighter-field winter season. Claimed his first title at the 1999 Zimbabwe Open, and has enjoyed huge success in the Vodacom Origins series, winning nine times - but again, primarily against lighter fields. A three-time winner in 2011, but his biggest domestic title to date was a playoff win over Titch Moore at the 2007 Nashua Masters. **Teams:** Eisenhower Trophy: 1998. **OWR Best:** 148 - Jan, 2002.

Sunshine Tour Wins (15): 1999: Zimbabwe Open **2000:** Western Cape Classic **2006:** Vodacom-Arabella (54H), South African Airways Pro-Am (54H) **2007:** Nashua Masters **2008:** Royal Swazi Open (Stableford), Vodacom-Selborne (54H) **2010:** Vodacom-Gardener Ross (54H), Vodacom-Stellenbosch, Platinum Classic (54H) **2011:** Vodacom-Pretoria (54H), Vodacom-Simola (54H), Vodacom-Final (54H) **2013:** Vodacom-Langebaan (54H) **2014:** Vodacom-Arabella (36H).
Other Wins: 1 Euro Challenge (2000)   +   Wild Coast Sun Pro-Am (SA): 2005.
Amateur Wins: South African Am: 1998   –   South African Stroke Play: 1999.

	99	00	01	02	03	04	05	06	07	08	09	10	11	12	13	14
Masters	-	-	-	-	-	-	-	-	-	-	-	-	-	-	-	-
US Open	-	-	-	-	-	-	-	-	-	-	-	-	-	-	-	-
British	MC	-	MC	-	-	-	-	-	-	-	MC	-	-	-	-	-
PGA	-	-	-	-	-	-	-	-	-	-	-	-	-	-	-	-
Money (E)	-	-	34	120	161	-	-	-	-	-	-	-	-	260*	220*	-
Money (SA)	12*	30*	29*	9*	65*	28	23	15	25	6	13	17	6	26*	17	11
OWR	289	247	156	277	443	796	781	473	483	602	642	-	437	589	400	351

2014: SUN: 24 st / 23 ct / 8 t10.   (Incl. Won Vodacom-Arabella, T2 Dimension Data, T3 Vodacom-Vaal de Grace).   Logged his 15th career Sunshine Tour win (good for 8th all-time) and finished among the top 30 in $$$ for the 15th time in 16 years.
OUTLOOK: A domestic star who hasn't made a meaningful venture off the Sunshine Tour in more than a decade. Knows how to win at this level and at age 39 – and seemingly with eyes only on playing at home – he'll almost certainly bag several more before he hangs it up.

STATS: Driving Distance: --   Driving Accuracy: --   GIR: --   Short Game: --   Putting: --

---

Huh, John CS (USA) (24) b. New York, NY 5/21/1990. 6'0" 190 lbs. College: Cal State-Northridge. TP: 2008. Attended California State University at Northridge but didn't play golf. An under-the-radar prospect who spent 2009-2011 playing primarily on the Korean Tour, where he finished 47th, 7th and 14th in earnings. Highlight came in 2010 when he won the Shinhan Donghae Open, beating K.J. Choi and Seung-Yul Noh by two and three strokes respectively. Despite never having played a single Web.com or PGA Tour event, successfully navigated 2011 Q School, finishing T24 to earn his 2012 card. Quickly proved his presence no fluke, first with a T6 at the Farmers Insurance Open, then by winning the 2012 Mayakoba Classic in a massive eight-hole playoff with Robert Allenby. Has slowed incrementally since, however, dropping from 28th in $$$ in 2012 to 99th in 2014. **Awards:** PGA Tour Rookie of The Year: 2012. **OWR Best:** 62 - Jan, 2013.

PGA Tour Wins (1): 2012: Mayakoba Classic.
Other: Shinhon Donghae Open (KPGA): 2010.

	10	11	12	13	14
Masters	-	-	-	T11	MC
US Open	-	-	-	T17	-
British	-	-	MC	MC	-
PGA	-	-	T68	MC	MC
Money (A)	-	-	28	58	99
OWR	777	543	66	99	167

2014: PGA: 28 st / 16 ct / 2 t10.   (T3 Heritage, T3 Barracuda).   Had a another slightly disappointing year – but again, only relative to his sparkling rookie campaign of 2012. Still managed five top 25s and a 96th-place finish in FedEx Cup points - numbers plenty of guys would covet.
OUTLOOK: A consistently accurate ball striker (62 in Total Driving) who, when his putter heats up, can move quickly into contention. But his putting has been on the decline since his rookie year, with his SGP dropping from 65 to 141 to 132. Further, his GIR nosedived from 45 to 106 in 2014; hopefully that will prove an outlier. These inconsistencies might suggest a performance decline but at 24, he still has lots of room to improve.

STATS: Driving Distance: C+   Driving Accuracy: A+   GIR: B+   Short Game: B-   Putting: B-

Hur, In-Hoi (South Korea) (27) b. Seoul, South Korea 7/24/1987. 5'11" 150 lbs. TP: 2006. After turning pro while still a teenager, spent several years playing domestically on the Korean Tour (eventually winning twice) before starting to play in Japan in 2009. Made little noise abroad until winning the J Tour's 2014 Toshin Golf Tournament, where he ran away by four. **OWR Best:** 160 - Dec, 2014.

Japan Tour Wins (1): 2014: Toshin Tournament.

Other Wins: 1 Japan Challenge (2012) + Philos Open (KPGA): 2008 KYJ Tour Championship (KPGA): 2013.

	09	10	11	12	13	14
Masters	-	-	-	-	-	-
US Open	-	-	-	-	-	-
British	-	-	-	-	-	-
PGA	-	-	-	-	-	-
Money (J)	96*	66	91	-	90	15
OWR	924	618	729	813	528	161

2014: JAP: 18 st / 13 ct / 6 t10. (Won Toshin, 2 Fujisankei, 4 Tokai, 5 Mizuno, 5 Dunlop Phoenix, etc.). Scored a breakthrough in his fourth full season on the Japan Tour, winning once and recording top-10 finishes in 33% of his starts. Also made sporadic starts elsewhere around Asia.

OUTLOOK: For one year at least, he proved he could ride his power game to compete at a high level on the Japan Tour. At age 27 his best years seem likely to remain ahead of him, but with only a middling short game, another year like 2014 would be as significant success.

STATS: Driving Distance: A-   Driving Accuracy: C-   GIR: B   Short Game: C   Putting: B

Hur, Suk-Ho ("S.K. Ho") (South Korea) (41) b. Pusan, South Korea 8/20/1973. 5'10" 170 lbs. TP: 1995. One of the first Korean players to compete primarily (and successfully) in Japan, where he won eight times from 2002-2008 and finished 5th, 4th and 8th in the order of Merit from 2004-06. His biggest victories came in back-to-back triumphs at the Japan PGA Championship, edging Keiichiro Fukabori by one in 2004 and Hideto Tanihara by two in 2005. After slipping in 2007, returned to form during a two-win 2008 which saw him claim the inaugural Championship by Lexus and climb back to 6th place in $$$. Has remained winless since but still cashes regular paychecks in both Japan and Korea. Has not appeared in a non-Major/WGC PGA Tour event. **Teams:** World Cup (3): 2002-03-06. **OWR Best:** 65 - Jun, 2005.

Japan Tour Wins (8): 2002: Juken Sangyou **2004**: Japan PGA Championship (54H), Tour Championship **2005**: Japan PGA, JCB Classic **2006**: Mizuno Open **2008**: Tsuruya Open, Championship by Lexus.

Asian Tour Wins (1): 2002: Shinhan Donghae Open.

Other Wins: 3 Japan Challenge (2001).

	02	03	04	05	06	07	08	09	10	11	12	13	14
Masters	-	-	-	-	-	-	-	-	-	-	-	-	-
US Open	-	-	-	-	-	-	-	-	-	-	-	-	-
British	-	T28	MC	T74	T11	-	-	-	-	-	-	-	-
PGA	-	-	T55	MC	MC	-	-	-	-	-	-	-	-
Money (J)	17	38	5	4	8	47	6	58	40	21	37	19	43
OWR	128	148	88	89	93	233	118	244	355	222	291	260	357

2014: JAP: 22 st / 13 ct / 3 t10. (T2 Diamond Cup, T6 ABC, T7 Kansai). Slipped to his lowest Japan Tour money rank (43rd) in five seasons.

OUTLOOK: Continues to remain relevant on the Japan Tour despite a notable lack of power and only mid-range short game and putting numbers. He's slipped noticeably from his peak years of 2004-2008, and hasn't won since 2008, but he shows enough flashes not to be entirely written off yet.

STATS: Driving Distance: C   Driving Accuracy: B+   GIR: B   Short Game: B-   Putting: B

Hurley, Willard Jeremiah III ("Billy") (USA) (32) b. Leesburg, VA 7/9/1982. 5'10" 170 lbs. College: U.S. Naval Academy. TP: 2006. Comes from an atypical competitive golfing background. After majoring in Quantitative Economics at the Naval Academy, served his mandatory five-year hitch (including time on a destroyer in the Persian Gulf) before pursuing a professional golf career. Won on several mini-tours in 2010, finished 25th in Web.com Tour $$$ in 2011, and just missed earning conditional status on the PGA Tour in 2012 (151st in $$$). Regained his card via the 2013 Web.com Finals, then finished 91st in 2014 PGA Tour $$$. **Teams:** Walker Cup: 2005 (0-2-0). Palmer Cup: 2004. **OWR Best:** 167 - Jul, 2014.

Other Wins: 1 eGolf Tour (2006) + 1 NGA/Hooters (2010).
Amateur Wins: Mid-Atlantic Am: 2004   Virginia Am (2): 2004-05.

	11	12	13	14
Masters	-	-	-	-
US Open	-	-	-	T48
British	-	-	-	T64
PGA	-	-	-	-
Money (A)	-	151	-	91
OWR	349	387	417	182

2014: PGA: 26 st / 17 ct / 4 t10. (T4 Greenbrier, 5 Honda, T8 Quicken Loans, T9 Frys.com). Kept his card and finished 97th in FedEx Cup points.

OUTLOOK: Made good in his second full-time run at the PGA Tour, relying on accurate driving and a strong short game and putter to log four top 10s in his sophomore campaign. Has the advantage of some PGA Tour experience now, and is one of the Tour's more interesting stories, bar none.

STATS (LTD): Driving Distance: C-   Driving Accuracy: A   GIR: B   Short Game: B+   Putting: B+

Hutsby, Sam (England) (26) b. Portsmouth, England 10/29/1988. 5'9" 155 lbs. TP: 2009. A Walker Cup player who, in addition to winning the 2006 Spanish Amateur, lost in the 2009 British Amateur final to Matteo Manassero. Turned pro after the Walker Cup and quickly played through Q School, but struggled to find a regular place on the E Tour thereafter. A strong one-win challenge 2014 Tour campaign will send him back to the big stage for a third full-season try. **Teams:** Walker Cup: 2009 (2-2-0). Eisenhower Trophy: 2008. **OWR Best:** 229 - Sep, 2014.

Other Wins: 1 Euro Challenge (2014).

Hutsby, Sam, Cont'd

Amateur Wins: Spanish Am: 2006   Douglas Johns Trophy: 2004   Duke of York Trophy: 2006   European Nations Cup: 2009.

	10	11	12	13	14
Masters	-	-	-	-	-
US Open	-	-	-	-	-
British	-	-	-	-	-
PGA	-	-	-	-	-
Money (E)	118	234*	206	296*	174*
OWR	427	617	805	774	243

2014: Played full-time on the Challenge Tour, claiming his first professional win (in Kazakhstan) and earning his E Tour card by finishing 6th in $$$.

OUTLOOK: Came close to keeping his card during his one genuinely full E Tour season, and he's shuttled between the E and Challenge circuits ever since. As an ex-Walker Cupper, he arrived with some fanfare. With a 2014 Challenge Tour win under his belt, perhaps he's ready to justify that now.

STATS (LTD):   Driving Distance: B   Driving Accuracy: C+   GIR: C+   Short Game: B+   Putting: C

Hwang, Jung-Gon (South Korea) (22)

b. Seoul, South Korea 5/16/1992. 5'9" 165 lbs. TP: 2009. Korean prospect who turned pro at age 18, qualified for the Japan Tour, then came out of nowhere to win the 2011 Mizuno Open (and gain a spot in the British Open) at age 19. Validated this win in 2012 when he beat Kunihiro Kamii by three to claim the Casio World Open en route to finishing 6th in the Japan Order of Merit and looking like an up-and-coming star. Stepped back somewhat thereafter, however, going winless in 2013 and '14. **OWR Best**: 154 - Nov, 2012.

Japan Tour Wins (2): 2011: Mizuno Open   **2012**: Casio World Open.
Other Wins: Maeil Dairies Open (KPGA): 2014.

	11	12	13	14
Masters	-	-	-	-
US Open	-	-	MC	-
British	T71	-	-	-
PGA	-	-	-	-
Money (J)	27	6	36	34
OWR	237	156	204	263

2014: JAP: 21 st / 19 ct / 2 t10.   (T2 Tokai, T8 ABC).   Stagnated a bit in Japan (34th in $$$) but also won once on his native Korean circuit.

OUTLOOK: Saw significant improvement in many of his Japan Tour statistics, yet witnessed little overall improvement scoring-wise. On raw talent alone, he seems capable of competing among the best in Asia - and at age 22, he has lots of time to figure out how to put it all together.

STATS: Driving Distance: B+   Driving Accuracy: A-   GIR: B+ ⇧   Short Game: B   Putting: C+

Ikeda, Yuta (Japan) (29)

b. Chiba, Japan 12/22/1985. 5'8" 170 lbs. College: Tohoku Fukushi University. TP: 2008. Won the 2003 Junior World Championship (San Diego) and the Japan Junior Championship in 2002 and '03. Earned his college degree before turning pro. After winning once on the Japan Challenge Tour, joined the Japan Golf Tour in 2009 where he exploded, winning four times (including the Japan PGA Championship and the Bridgestone Open), earning Rookie-of-the-Year honors and finishing 2nd (behind Ryo Ishikawa) in both earnings and scoring. Largely repeated the performance in 2010, winning four more times including a successful defense of his Bridgestone Open title and a victory at the Dunlop Phoenix (by two over Kyung-Tae Kim). Slipped somewhat in 2011, falling to 11th in Japan Tour $$$ and managing only a single victory. After a quiet beginning, rallied late in 2012, winning October's Canon Open by three shots, then followed a similar pattern in 2013, winning the Mynavi ABC Championship (in a playoff with S.K. Ho) in November. Claimed his biggest win yet at the 2014 Japan Open, where he edged Shingo Katayama and Satoshi Kodaira by one. **Teams**: Eisenhower Trophy (2): 2004-06.   World Cup: 2011.   **OWR Best**: 33 - Nov, 2009.

Japan Tour Wins (12): 2009: Japan PGA Championship, KBC Augusta, Canon Open (54H), Bridgestone Open   **2010**: Toshin, ANA Open, Bridgestone Open, Dunlop Phoenix   **2011**: Sun Chlorella Classic   **2012**: Canon Open   **2013**: Mynavi ABC Championship   **2014**: Japan Open.
Other Wins: 1 Japan Challenge (2008)   +   Legend Charity Pro-Am (Japan): 2011.
Amateur Wins: Junior World (15-17): 2003   Japan Jr (2): 2002-03   Japan Collegiate (2): 2005-06.

	08	09	10	11	12	13	14
Masters	-	-	29	MC	-	-	-
US Open	-	-	T58	-	-	-	-
British	-	MC	MC	T38	-	-	-
PGA	-	-	MC	T45	-	-	-
Money (J)	-	2	4	11	4	9	7
OWR	389	33	41	75	102	121	106

2014: JAP: 24 st / 20 ct / 6 t10.   (Won Japan Open, T4 Fujisankei, T4 ABC, T5 Tokai, T7 Token Homemate, etc).   Remained among the top 10 in $$$ (for the fifth time in six seasons) and recorded his biggest win to date at the Japan Open.

OUTLOOK: At age 29, he remains something of an enigma. Looked capable of international stardom after winning eight times over his first two seasons, and his statistics have not plummeted from those early days. It may be mostly a matter of finding a different mental gear (he was 10 and 11 in Round 4 Scoring in 2009 and '10, 40 and 38 in 2013 and '14) but for now he remains entrenched at a very successful – but not quite elite – level.

STATS: Driving Distance: B+   Driving Accuracy: B-   GIR: B+   Short Game: B-   Putting: B

Ilonen, Mikko (Finland) (35)

b. Lahti, Finland 12/18/1979. 6'2" 185 lbs. TP: 2001. Finland's first major golfing prospect who served notice by claiming the 2000 British Amateur at Hoylake, then logging a top-10 finish at his first British Open. Enjoyed only E Tour journeyman status through 2005 (actually repairing to the Challenge Tour briefly in '06) before becoming Finland's first-ever E Tour winner in 2007 at the Asian Tour co-sanctioned Indonesia Open. Claimed a second '07 win at the Scandinavian Masters, where he edged five players (including a young Martin Kaymer) by two. Missed much of 2011 with a foot injury. Broke a five-year drought during a resurgent 2013 by winning for the second time at the (Nordea)

Ilonen, Mikko, Cont'd

Scandinavian Masters, beating Jonas Blixt by three. Added a fourth career win at the 2014 Irish Open, going wire-to-wire in his 300th career E Tour start, the a fifth by defeating top seed Henrik Stenson at the World Match Play Championship. **Teams:** Eisenhower Trophy (2): 1998-00. Seve Trophy (2): 2007-13. World Cup: 2007. **OWR Best:** 37 - Oct, 2014.

European Tour Wins (5): 2007: Indonesia Open, Scandinavian Masters **2013:** Scandinavian Masters (Nordea) **2014:** Irish Open, World Match Play.
Amateur Wins: British Amateur: 2000 — Eisenhower Trophy (Individual): 1998   West of Ireland Am: 1999.

	01	02	03	04	05	06	07	08	09	10	11	12	13	14
Masters	MC	-	-	-	-	-	-	-	-	-	-	-	-	-
US Open	-	-	-	-	-	-	-	-	-	MC	-	MC	-	-
British	T9	T50	-	-	-	T16	-	-	-	-	-	-	T79	MC
PGA	-	-	-	-	-	-	-	-	-	-	-	-	MC	T7
Money (E)	119	103	104	100	154	-	34	91	92	68	-	91	23	18
OWR	311	255	324	396	577	355	62	218	297	194	471	354	84	47

2014: E: 26 st / 20 ct / 7 t10.   (Won Irish, Won World Match Play, 2P Qatar, T5 Dubai, T7 PGA Champ, etc.).   Followed a very strong 2013 with an even stronger 2014, winning twice, losing a playoff in Qatar, and finishing a career-best 18th in $$$.
OUTLOOK: Secured his status as one of Europe's best with a second straight high-end season. Surprisingly, he sustained the large statistical gains in putting that he demonstrated in 2013, a key point as the remainder of his numbers are mostly mid-range. At age 35, he could well be heading into his best years right now - but a more cautious view would be that his stats generally suggest that he is playing his best golf already.

STATS: Driving Distance: B   Driving Accuracy: C+   GIR: B   Short Game: C+   Putting: A-

---

Imada, Ryuji (Japan) (38)

b. Mihara, Japan 10/19/1976. 5'8" 150 lbs. All-American at U of Georgia. TP: 1999. Top Japanese junior whose family moved to America when he was 14. Three-time AJGA All-American and 1995 AJGA Player Of The Year. The winner of several major amateur events, including the 1995 Porter Cup and the 1996 Dixie Amateur. Left the University of Georgia after two All-American seasons, then spent five years on the Web.com Tour (logging two wins) before ultimately graduating in 2004. Remained a regular top-125 money winner on the PGA Tour from 2005-2011, though only twice did he crack the top 75: 65th in 2007 and 13th in 2008, when he won the Atlanta Classic in a playoff with Kenny Perry. Has struggled since 2012, and began playing some Japan Tour events in 2013. **Teams:** World Cup (2): 2008-09. **OWR Best:** 49 - May, 2008.

PGA Tour Wins (1): 2008: Atlanta Classic (AT&T).
Other Wins: 2 Web.com (2000-2004).
Amateur Wins: Porter Cup: 1995 — Orange Bowl Jr: 1994   Azalea Inv: 1996   Dixie Am: 1995   Lakewood Inv: 1996   Southeastern Am: 1997   Florida Azalea: 1998.

	00	01	02	03	04	05	06	07	08	09	10	11	12	13	14
Masters	-	-	-	-	-	-	-	-	-	T20	-	-	-	-	-
US Open	MC	-	-	-	-	T15	T12	MC	T18	MC	-	-	-	-	-
British	-	-	-	-	-	-	-	-	MC	64	-	-	-	-	-
PGA	-	-	-	-	-	-	-	MC	MC	MC	-	MC	-	-	-
Money (A)	-	-	-	-	-	121	92	65	13	118	86	90	181	230*	209*
OWR	-	532	561	898	633	387	202	181	180	66	173	190	224	577	792	903

2014: PGA: 9 st / 5 ct / 0 t10.   (T20 Sony).   Also made 11 starts on the Web.com Tour, where he finished 152nd in $$$.
OUTLOOK: Retained his card for the first seven years of his PGA Tour career but has struggled since, playing the last three years on Past Champion status. His major statistics haven't changed too much since his peak year of 2008, but the downward momentum now appears tough to reverse.

STATS: Driving Distance: C-   Driving Accuracy: B-   GIR: C   Short Game: B+   Putting: B+

Immelman, Trevor John (South Africa) (35)

b. Cape Town, South Africa 12/16/1979. 5'9" 180 lbs. TP: 1999. Two-time AJGA All-American. The son of former Sunshine Tour Commissioner Johan Immelman. Runner-up in 1997 British Amateur (at Royal St George's) and played junior/amateur golf worldwide (was a 1st-team AJGA All-American in 1996). Claimed back-to-back South African Opens in 2003 and '04 (the first man to successfully defend since Gary Player) and four top-20 finishes in the European Tour Order of Merit before age 25. Joined the PGA Tour full-time in 2006, logging several high finishes before defeating Tiger Woods and Mathew Goggin by two to win the 2006 Western Open. Was named 2006 PGA Tour Rookie of the Year. Missed the end of 2007 after having a benign tumor removed from his back. Roared back four months later to win his first Major championship at the 2008 Masters, beating Tiger Woods by three. Had his 2009 season limited to 13 PGA Tour starts due to tendonitis in his left wrist, which required surgery in October and limited his game into 2010. Still slowed in early 2011 but eventually climbed back to 81st in PGA Tour $$$. Has struggled since, however, missing the top 125 in $$$ each year. **Awards:** PGA Tour Rookie of the Year: 2006. **Teams:** Eisenhower Trophy: 1998. Presidents Cup (2): 2005-07 (1-6-1). World Cup (4): 2003-04-05-07 (won in '03 w/R.Sabbatini). **OWR Best:** 12 - Sep, 2006.

PGA Tour Wins (2): 2006: Western Open (Cialis) **2008:** Masters Tournament.
European Tour Wins (3): 2003: South African Open **2004:** South African Open, Deutsche Bank Open.
Sunshine Tour Wins (3): 2000: Vodacom Players Championship **2003:** Dimension Data Pro-Am **2007:** Million Dollar Challenge.
Other Wins: 1 Web.com (2013) + Kenya Open: 2000.
Amateur Wins: South African Am: 1997 — U.S. Amateur Public Links: 1998   South African Am Stroke Play: 1998.

	99	00	01	02	03	04	05	06	07	08	09	10	11	12	13	14
Masters	T56	-	-	-	-	MC	T5	MC	T55	Win	T20	T14	T15	60	T50	MC
US Open	-	-	-	-	MC	T55	-	T21	MC	T65	-	MC	MC	MC	-	-
British	-	-	-	T43	T53	T42	T15	-	T60	T19	-	T23	T38	MC	-	-
PGA	-	-	-	-	T48	T37	T17	T34	T6	MC	-	MC	T12	T27	-	-
Money (A)	-	-	-	-	-	-	7	46	19	156*	163	81	129	157	153	-
Money (E)	-	-	88	14	14	16	30	-	-	-	-	-	-	-	-	-
Money (SA)	-	5	36*	1*	-	-	-	-	-	-	-	-	-	-	-	-
OWR	516	209	176	101	55	49	62	13	19	20	133	270	130	200	234	473

Immelman, Trevor John, Cont'd

2014: PGA: 28 st / 13 ct / 1 t10. (T10 Farmers). Finished 145th in FedEx Cup points, then failed to regain his card via the Web.com Finals.

OUTLOOK: Has never fully regained the injury-depleted form of his peak Masters-winning years (2002-2008) and has now out of exemptions, leaving him with conditional status for 2015. Rated among the world's most touted young players a decade ago, and while his statistics have declined predictably (especially putting), he is still only 35 and seemingly capable of returning to the top. But it time feels like its running out.

STATS: Driving Distance: B   Driving Accuracy: C+   GIR: B+   Short Game: B-   Putting: C

Ishikawa, Ryo (Japan) (23)
b. Saitama, Japan 9/17/1991. 5'9" 155 lbs. TP: 2008. Top Japanese prospect who won the J Tour's 2007 Munsingwear Open as a 15-year-old amateur. Turned pro soon thereafter and validated his status by winning the 2008 ABC Championship. Youngest player ever to reach the top 100 of the World Golf Ranking (in November, 2008, age 17). Blossomed fully in 2009, winning four J Tour titles and sweeping both the Order of Merit and scoring titles at age 17. Those 2009 victories included the Fujisankei Classic and the Tokai Classic. Made his American debut on a sponsor exemption at the 2009 Northern Trust Open (MC). Added three more J Tour wins in 2010, led by an historical triumph at The Crowns, where he closed with a 12-under-par 58 to overcome a six-shot 54-hole deficit and win by five. Also defended his Fujisankei title (in a playoff with former high school teammate Shunsuke Sonoda) and won the Taiheiyo Masters (by two over Australian Brendan Jones). Went winless worldwide in 2011, slipping to 6th in Japan Tour $$$. Though still somewhat quiet in 2012, broke a two-year victory drought by winning the Taiheiyo Masters, setting the stage for a transition to the PGA Tour in 2013. After having only sporadic success in America, returned to Japan to win the 2014 Sega Sammy Cup, beating Koumei Oda in a playoff. **Teams**: Presidents Cup (2): 2009-11 (5-4-0). World Cup: 2013. **OWR Best**: 29 - Nov, 2009.

Japan Tour Wins (11): 2007: Munsingwear Open* **2008**: ABC Championship **2009**: Mizuno Open, Sun Chlorella Classic, Fujisankei Classic, Tokai Classic **2010**: The Crowns, Fujisankei Classic, Taiheiyo Masters **2012**: Taiheiyo Masters **2014**: Sega Sammy Cup.

Amateur Wins: Japan Jr (15-17): 2009.

	07	08	09	10	11	12	13	14
Masters	-	-	MC	MC	T20	MC	T38	-
US Open	-	-	-	T33	T30	MC	-	-
British	-	-	MC	T27	MC	MC	-	MC
PGA	-	-	T56	MC	MC	T59	T29	MC
Money (A)	-	-	-	-	-	-	151	76
Money (J)	Am	5	1	3	6	7	65*	19*
OWR	434	60	30	36	51	75	83	102

2014: PGA: 24 st / 14 ct / 3 t10. (T2 Shriners, T7 Farmers, T8 Arnold Palmer). Finally seemed to establish himself on the PGA Tour, finishing 72nd in FedEx Cup points. Also won the Sega Sammy Cup during one of several visits to his homeland.

OUTLOOK: Japan's most touted prospect ever hasn't seen his game travel West very effectively, as he has yet to log a top-25 Major championship finish - but he has now found exempt status on the PGA Tour. Has also recorded only two wins on the Japan Tour since 2010 – a far cry from his seven domestic titles of 2009-2010. To his credit, he has not taken the easy (and lucrative) path of returning home, and he's still only 23 years old, so time remains on his side. Has established himself as a legitimate top 100 player, but the lofty predictions of his teens seem a tad less likely now.

STATS: Driving Distance: B   Driving Accuracy: C   GIR: B-   Short Game: C+   Putting: B+

Iwata, Hiroshi (Japan) (33)
b. Miyagi, Japan 1/31/1981. 5'8" 165 lbs. TP: 2004. After turning pro, played part-time on the Japan Tour for two years before settling in in 2006. Proved himself a steady, if unspectacular, earner over the ensuing years, remaining among the Tour's top 60 from 2007 onward. Was twice a runner-up through 2013, including a playoff loss to Toyokazu Fujishima at the 2008 Fujisankei Classic. Claimed his first victory at the 2014 Fujisankei Classic (where edged In-Hoi Hur by one) in a breakout season with an imposing 11 top-10 finishes. Surprised many by contending late before tying for 3rd at the 2014 WGC-HSBC Champions. **OWR Best**: 63 - Nov, 2014.

Japan Tour Wins (1): 2014: Fujisankei Classic.

	06	07	08	09	10	11	12	13	14
Masters	-	-	-	-	-	-	-	-	-
US Open	-	-	-	-	-	-	-	-	-
British	-	-	MC	-	-	-	-	-	MC
PGA	-	-	-	-	-	-	-	-	-
Money (J)	62	16	21	39	30	50	59	43	4
OWR	492	204	193	317	303	483	646	461	67

2014: JAP: 23 st / 20 ct / 11 t10. (Won Fujisankei, 2 Token Homemate, 2 Dunlop Phoenix, T2 Fukushima, 4 Crowns, etc.). Enjoyed the biggest breakout season on the Japan Tour, claiming his first win, soaring to 4th in $$$ and playing impressively consistent golf throughout the year.

OUTLOOK: After years as a steady, quiet earner, broke out in 2014, primarily due to marked improvements in GIR, Short Game and Putting. That's a tall set of gains to sustain going forward, so despite the consistency of his entire 2014, some decline appears very likely in the year ahead.

STATS: Driving Distance: A-   Driving Accuracy: B-   GIR: B   Short Game: B+   Putting: A-

---

Izawa, Toshimitsu ("Toshi") (Japan) (46)
b. Kanagawa, Japan 3/2/1968. 5'6" 150 lbs. TP: 1989. Leading Japanese professional who, after three steady-but-winless seasons, came into his own around the millennium, winning 12 Japan Tour titles between 1999-2003. Finished four times among the top four in the Order of Merit during this period, including 1st in 2001. Claimed his first win at the 1995 Japan Open (where he edged Kazuhiko Hosokawa by one) and later added the 2007 Japan PGA Championship, where he nosed out Satoru Hirota by the same margin. In between, won two Tokai Classics (1998 and '01), two KBC Augustas (1999 and '05) and back-to-back Taiheiyo Masters in 2000 and '01. Has seen his form slip noticeably since 2007, only once cracking the top 100 in $$$ since, and may be on the verge of retirement. Like many a Japanese star before him, has seldom ventured abroad, but did lose (to Robert Allenby) in a six-man playoff at the 2001 Los Angeles Open. **Teams**: World Cup (2): 2001-02 (won in '02 w/S.Maruyama). **OWR Best**: 17 - Dec, 2001.

Japan Tour Wins (16): 1995: Japan Open **1998**: Tokai Classic **1999**: Aiful Cup, NST Nigita Open **2000**: Players Championship (54H), KBC Augusta, Taiheiyo Masters **2001**: Diamond Cup, Taiheiyo Masters, Tokai Classic, Bridgestone Open, Philip Morris KK Championship **2003**: Tour Championship, Woodone Open **2005**: KBC Augusta **2007**: Japan PGA Championship.

Izawa, Toshimitsu, Cont'd

	95	96	97	98	99	00	01	02	03	04	05	06	07	08	09	10	11	12	13	14
Masters	-	-	-	-	-	-	T4	MC	MC	MC	-	-	-	-	-	-	-	-	-	-
US Open	-	-	-	-	-	-	T44	WD	-	MC	-	-	-	-	-	-	-	-	-	-
British	-	-	-	-	-	-	-	T22	-	-	-	-	MC	-	-	-	-	-	-	-
PGA	-	-	-	-	MC	T39	-	T53	T18	-	-	-	-	-	-	-	-	-	-	-
Money (J)	33	45	50	11	3	4	1	14	4	32	9	78	13	108	90	110	172	159	-	-
OWR	116	166	183	106	75	55	17	49	49	83	119	298	273	566	814	769	-	-	-	-

2014: Did not make a competitive start worldwide.

OUTLOOK: One of the most successful Japan Tour players of his era, but after missing all of 2013 and '14, retirement may be in the offing.

STATS: Driving Distance: C+   Driving Accuracy: C-   GIR: C-   Short Game: C   Putting: B

Jacobson, Fredrik Ulf Yngve ("Freddie') (Sweden) (40)   b. Gothenburg, Sweden 9/26/1974. 6'1" 180 lbs. TP: 1994. A fine all-around athlete who, after slowly building into the new millennium, exploded on the European Tour in 2003 with three wins: the 2002 Hong Kong Open (an official E Tour '03 event), the Portuguese Open and the Volvo Masters. Also finished a career-best 4th in the E Tour Order of Merit and 17th in the year-end OWR. Moved full-time to America thereafter with mixed success, proving himself a regular money winner and occasional contender before ultimately breaking through for his maiden win at the 2011 Travelers Championship, where he edged Ryan Moore and John Rollins by one. Has since remained a steady earner, retaining his card with room to spare, only twice failing to finish among the top 100. **Teams**: Eisenhower Trophy: 1994. Seve Trophy: 2003. World Cup (2): 2003-04. **OWR Best**: 16 - Nov, 2003.

PGA Tour Wins (1): 2011: Travelers Championship.
European Tour Wins (3): 2002: Hong Kong ('03)   **2003**: Portuguese Open, Volvo Masters.
Amateur Wins: Swedish Boys: 1992   European Jr Masters: 1992   Doug Sanders Jr Int'l: 1992   British Youths: 1994.

	95	96	97	98	99	00	01	02	03	04	05	06	07	08	09	10	11	12	13	14
Masters	-	-	-	-	-	-	-	-	-	T17	MC	-	-	-	-	-	-	T19	T25	-
US Open	-	-	-	-	-	-	-	-	T5	MC	-	-	-	MC	-	-	T14	T15	MC	-
British	-	-	-	76	-	MC	MC	MC	T6	MC	T52	-	-	T19	T70	-	T16	T54	T44	MC
PGA	-	-	-	-	-	-	-	-	MC	T17	T34	-	-	T24	-	MC	MC	T36	MC	T70
Money (A)	-	-	-	-	-	-	-	-	-	59	96	108	63	54	77	44	26	104	71	48
Money (E)	174	-	84	75	127	25	38	30	4	54	-	-	-	-	-	-	44	-	-	-
OWR	-	899	304	225	311	144	109	83	17	40	128	146	82	67	120	131	39	62	92	107

2014: PGA: 27 st / 19 ct / 4 t10.   (T2 Wyndham, T3 Colonial, T9 Shriners, T10 Arnold Palmer).   Completed another strong PGA Tour campaign, climbing to 66th in FedEx Cup points, logging an imposing 10 top 10s and keeping his card for the 11th straight year.

OUTLOOK: Looks like he plans on playing out his career in America – and why not? Though only claiming one PGA Tour win, he's ridden his short game-oriented arsenal to strong and steady earnings, averaging 68th place over 11 years. Despite an obvious lack of length (and an associated low GIR average) he certainly has it within him to win again, especially on weeks when his ball striking heats up.

STATS: Driving Distance: C+   Driving Accuracy: C+   GIR: C   Short Game: A-   Putting: A-

---

Jacquelin, Raphael (France) (40)   b. Lyon, France 5/8/1974. 6'0" 165 lbs. TP: 1995. Ex-French junior and amateur champion who enjoyed further success on the Challenge Tour before making a slow climb up the E Tour ladder. Claimed his first E Tour win at the 2005 Madrid Open (beating Paul Lawrie by three) before cementing his status by claiming the 2007 BMW Asian Open in China. Didn't win again until the light-field 2011 Sicilian Open, then took his fourth E Tour title in a record-tying nine-hole playoff (with Felipe Aguilar and Max Kieffer) at the 2013 Spanish Open. **Teams**: Seve Trophy (4): 2002-03-07-11. World Cup (7): 2001-02-03-04-05-06-11. **OWR Best**: 55 - Jul, 2007.

European Tour Wins (4): 2005: Madrid Open   **2007**: BMW Asian Open   **2011**: Sicilian Open   **2013**: Spanish Open.
Other Wins: 2 Euro Challenge (1997)   +   French Pro: 1997.
Amateur Wins: French Jr: 1993   French Am: 1995   French Int'l Nations: 1995.

	97	98	99	00	01	02	03	04	05	06	07	08	09	10	11	12	13	14
Masters	-	-	-	-	-	-	-	-	-	-	-	-	-	-	-	-	-	-
US Open	-	-	-	-	-	-	-	-	-	-	-	MC	-	-	T21	-	-	-
British	MC	-	-	T13	MC	T53	T54	-	-	T65	-	MC	-	8	MC	-	-	-
PGA	-	-	-	-	-	-	MC	-	-	MC	-	-	MC	MC	-	-	-	-
Money (E)	-	88	104	80	28	72	20	29	37	45	25	71	37	39	36	41	37	78
OWR	858	437	379	285	120	196	123	92	96	106	88	216	134	99	106	119	120	248

2014: E: 25 st / 15 ct / 3 t10.   (T5 Volvo Champ, T8 Laguna, T9 Hong Kong).   Winless but finished a solid 78th in $$$.

OUTLOOK: It speaks to his great consistency that 2014's 78th-place $$$ ranking was his worst since 2000. Is also notably durable, having logged 491 career starts (with 42 top 10s) through 2014. Is statistically a mid-range sort across the board, and his wins have mostly been of only middling prestige – but at age 40, with his putting numbers still holding nicely, there's nothing to suggest he's about to slow down in the immediate future.

STATS: Driving Distance: C+   Driving Accuracy: B+   GIR: B   Short Game: B+   Putting: B+

Jaidee, Thongchai (Thailand) (45)   b. Lopburi, Thailand 11/8/1969. 5'9" 160 lbs. TP: 1999. Ex-army paratrooper and Thailand's best-ever international player who didn't turn professional until age 30. Became the first Thai golfer to win on a non-Asian tour by capturing the European Tour co-sanctioned Malaysian Open in 2004. Won the Asian Tour Order of Merit in 2001, '04 and '09, and finished 2nd on three other occasions. Has logged five E Tour wins but didn't claim his first played outside of Asia until 2012, capturing the Wales Open at age 42. Has added nine additional Asian Tour victories including the then-flagship Volvo Masters of Asia in 2003 and '06. At age 44, won the E Tour's Nordea Masters in a playoff with Victor Dubuisson and Stephen Gallacher, his 15th major tour win worldwide. **Teams**: World Cup (4): 2007-08-09-11. **OWR Best**: 33 - Jul, 2014.

Jaidee, Thongchai, Cont'd

European Tour Wins (6): 2004: Malaysian Open **2005**: Malaysian Open **2009**: Indonesia Open, Ballantine's Championship **2012**: Wales Open **2014**: Nordea Masters.

Asian Tour Wins (9): 2000: Korean Open **2001**: Indian Open **2002**: Myanmar Open **2003**: Asian Masters **2004**: Myanmar Open **2006**: Asian Masters **2008**: Vietnam Masters, Cambodian Open **2010**: Cambodian Open.

Other Wins: Bangkok Open (Thailand): 2000   Singha Championship (Thailand): 2001   Maekyung LG Open (Korea): 2001.

Amateur Wins: Pakistan Am: 1995   Thailand Am: 1998   Singapore Am: 1998.

	99	00	01	02	03	04	05	06	07	08	09	10	11	12	13	14
Masters	-	-	-	-	-	-	-	MC	-	-	-	WD	-	-	-	T37
US Open	-	-	T74	-	-	-	-	-	-	-	-	T47	-	-	MC	MC
British	-	-	-	WD	-	-	T52	-	-	-	T13	MC	MC	T77	T32	T39
PGA	-	-	-	-	-	MC	MC	-	MC	-	T36	MC	-	MC	T47	MC
Money (E)	-	-	-	-	125	43	54	37	59	68	19	29	85	27	9	22
Money (As)	18	6	1	2*	3*	1*	2	2*	8*	14*	1*	6*	10*	15	11*	-
OWR	-	420	157	204	150	95	111	75	96	91	58	68	151	80	46	37

2014: E: 26 st / 24 ct / 7 t10.   (Won Nordea, T2 French, T5 BMW Int'l, T8 Port Masters, 9 Nedbank, etc.).   Won for the sixth time on the E Tour and followed up a career-best 2013 by finishing 22nd in $$$. Made three additional non-co-sanctioned starts in Asia, all top 10s.

OUTLOOK: Ageless competitor who rolled onward in 2014, claiming his 15th major tour win worldwide and showing no sign of letting up. Though a short hitter, relies on a very solid tee-to-green game and a surprisingly good putter (for age 45) to still compete toe-to-toe with the world's best. Has a limited record in the Majors (generally played on bigger, tougher layouts) but according to the OWR at least, is playing the best golf of his life.

STATS: Driving Distance: C+   Driving Accuracy: B-   GIR: A-   Short Game: B-   Putting: A-

---

Jamieson, Scott Gemmell (Scotland) (31)
b. Glasgow, Scotland 11/28/1983. 6'1" 175 lbs. College: Augusta St. TP: 2006. Initially spent the three years on the Challenge Tour, graduating to the E Tour following 2012. Finished among the top 60 in $$$ in both 2011 and 2012 before claiming his first win at the rain-shortened 2013 Nelson Mandela Championship (played in late, 2012) in South Africa. Slipped a bit in 2014, but retained his card comfortably. **Teams**: Eisenhower Trophy: 2006. Palmer Cup: 2005. Seve Trophy (2): 2011-13. **OWR Best**: 68 - Feb, 2013.

European Tour Wins (1): 2012: Nelson Mandela Championship (36H) ('13).

Other Wins: 2 EuroPro (2009).

Amateur Wins: Scottish Boys Stroke Play: 2001.

	10	11	12	13	14
Masters	-	-	-	-	-
US Open	-	-	-	-	-
British	-	MC	-	MC	MC
PGA	-	-	-	T29	-
Money (E)	-	59	53	31	76
OWR	431	214	101	112	239

2014: E: 29 st / 17 ct / 4 t10. (3 Russia, T7 Port Masters, T8 Scottish, T9 Czech Masters).   Not surprisingly he slipped a little in 2014 - but not very much. Only contended at the light-field Russian Open but strung together four top 10s and finished 76th in $$$.

OUTLOOK: Having paid his Challenge Tour dues coming up, has plenty of foundation beneath him. Adds up as an upper mid-range type statistically, which may suggest that he's already topped out - but despite lacking a thoroughbred pedigree, he's done pretty well so far.

STATS: Driving Distance: B+   Driving Accuracy: B   GIR: B-   Short Game: B   Putting: B+

Jang, Dong-Kyu (South Korea) (26)
b. Seoul, South Korea 10/22/1988. 5'11" 150 lbs. TP: 2006. A somewhat off-the-radar prospect who spent his first four seasons as a pro competing on the Korean Tour, where he was winless but cracked the top 25 in $$$ in both 2009 and '10. Began playing the Japan Tour in 2012 and made little impact through 2013 before heating up dramatically in 2014, logging four top-5 finishes in a row from the Kansai Open through the Japan Tour Championship, including his maiden victory at the Mizuno Open. **OWR Best**: 201 - Jun, 2014.

Japan Tour Wins (1): 2014: Mizuno Open.

Other Wins: 2 Japan Challenge (2013).

	12	13	14
Masters	-	-	-
US Open	-	-	-
British	-	-	MC
PGA	-	-	-
Money (J)	98	73	13
OWR	479	605	232

2014: JAP: 23 st / 19 ct / 5 t10.   (Won Mizuno, T3 Kansai, T3 Tour Champ, 4 Japan PGA, T4 Toshin).   Enjoyed easily his best year as a pro, winning the Mizuno Open (and thus qualifying for the British Open) and jumping all the way to 13th in $$$. Also finished 26th in $$$ on the Korean Tour.

OUTLOOK: A still-young player who made a major jump in class in 2014, driven by improvements in several statistical categories. These jumps were mostly incremental in nature and thus might be sustainable, but simply retaining his current level of play would make 2015 a successful year.

STATS: Driving Distance: B   Driving Accuracy: A   GIR: B+   Short Game: B-   Putting: B-

---

Jang, Ik-Jae ("I.J.") (South Korea) (41)
b. Busan, South Korea 2/14/1973. 5'7" 165 lbs. College: Kyung Hee University. TP: 1998. A four-time winner on his native Korean Tour but a full-time player in Japan since 2005. Won there as a rookie at the Mitsubishi Diamond Cup (beating Shingo Katayama and Ryoken Kawagishi by three) before playing through seven seasons in which he never bettered 41st in Japan Tour $$$. Climbed

Jang, Ik-Jae, Cont'd

to a career-best 17th-place $$$ ranking in 2012, however, led by his second victory, a two-shot triumph over Steve Conran and Yoshikazu Haku at The Crowns. Began playing the Web.com Tour part-time in 2013. **Teams:** Eisenhower Trophy: 1994. World Cup: 2005. **OWR Best:** 193 - Dec, 2012.

Japan Tour Wins (2): 2005: Mitsubishi Diamond Cup **2012**: The Crowns.

Other Wins: Pocari Sweat Open (KPGA): 2003   Unrecorded KPGA Event (KPGA): 2003   Samsung Benest Open (KPGA): 2005   Kumho Asiana Open (KPGA): 2005.

	05	06	07	08	09	10	11	12	13	14
Masters	-	-	-	-	-	-	-	-	-	-
US Open	-	-	-	-	-	-	-	-	-	-
British	-	-	-	-	-	-	-	-	-	-
PGA	-	-	-	-	-	-	-	-	-	-
Money (J)	22	55	43	86	46	51	41	17	30	22
OWR	203	297	401	598	521	420	408	194	215	290

2014: JAP: 23 st / 20 ct / 5 t10. (2 Crowns, T5 Tsuruya, T8 Sega Sammy, T8 ANA, T9 Casio). Logged five top 10s and finishing 22nd in Japan Tour $$$.

OUTLOOK: At age 41, continues his steady course on the Japan Tour, where it seems any sort of sharply upward trend is at this point unlikely. Maintains a Southern California residence, so he may continue trying to play the Web.com (where he has conditional status) on a seasonal basis.

STATS: Driving Distance: B   Driving Accuracy: B-   GIR: B-   Short Game: B+   Putting: B

Janzen, Lee MacLeod (USA) (50)

b. Austin, MN 8/28/1964. 6'0" 175 lbs. Three-time All-American and Division II individual champion (1986) at Florida Southern. TP: 1986. A steady PGA Tour player (never worse than 72nd in earnings from 1991-2003) who has twice risen to win the U.S. Open, first in 1993 at Baltusrol, then in 1998 at the Olympic Club. Both victories came over Payne Stewart, the latter from five strokes off the 54-hole pace with a closing 68. Also won the 1995 Players Championship (by one over Bernhard Langer) during a career-best three-win 1995. Claimed additional prestige wins at the 1994 Buick Classic (by three over Ernie Els) and, in 1995, both the Kemper Open and the International. With eight Tour victories overall, one of the more underrated players of his time – though all eight titles came within a six-year period, and he has only once cracked the top 125 in $$$ since 2004. **Teams:** Ryder Cup (2): 1993-97 (O: 2-3-0, S: 1-1-0). Presidents Cup: 1998 (1-1-2). **OWR Best:** 13 - Nov, 1995.

PGA Tour Wins (8): 1992: Tucson Open (Northern Telecom) **1993**: Phoenix Open, U.S. Open **1994**: Westchester Classic (Buick) **1995**: Players Championship, Kemper Open, The International (Sprint)(Stableford) **1998**: U.S. Open.

Other Wins: 2 NGA/Hooters (1989) + Shark Shootout: 2000 (w/R.Mediate).

	90	91	92	93	94	95	96	97	98	99	00	01	02	03	04	05	06	07	08	09	10	11	12	13
Masters	-	-	T54	T39	T30	T12	T12	T26	T33	T14	MC	T31	MC	MC	-	-	-	-	-	-	-	-	-	-
US Open*	-	MC	MC	Win	MC	T13	T10	T52	Win	T46	T37	MC	MC	T55	T24	T57	MC	T13	MC	-	-	-	-	-
British	-	-	T39	T48	T35	T24	MC	MC	T24	70	MC	-	T80	MC	-	-	-	-	-	-	-	-	-	-
PGA	-	-	T21	T22	T66	T23	T8	4	MC	MC	T19	MC	T53	T34	-	MC	-	-	-	-	-	-	-	-
Money (A)	115	72	9	7	35	3	31	24	20	48	62	59	56	64	96	155	146	160	152	99	147	185	178*	234*
OWR	297	183	70	22	32	17	32	34	23	39	82	103	103	95	127	252	276	332	430	248	366	675	473	892

	14
Masters	-
US Open	-
British	-
PGA	-
Money (A)	216*
OWR	1297

* Also MC at 1985 U.S. Open

2014: PGA: 8 st / 5 ct / 0 t10. (T27 Barracuda). Finished 220th in FedEx Cup points. Also made two Champions Tour starts upon turning 50.

OUTLOOK: Hasn't bettered 147th in PGA Tour $$$ since 2009, and played only on the Champions Tour once eligible, so…

STATS: Driving Distance: C-   Driving Accuracy: B-   GIR: C   Short Game: B+   Putting: B+

Jeong, Yeon-Jin ("Jin") (South Korean) (24)

b. Busan, South Korea 2/2/1990. 5'8" 150 lbs. TP: 2011. Born in South Korea but moved to Melbourne, Australia in 2006. Enjoyed a fine amateur career highlighted by 2010 wins in the British Amateur (becoming the event's first Asian champion) and the Tasmanian Open, as well as low amateur honors (with a T14) at the British Open. After turning pro, spent 2012 primarily on the Australasian Tour. Began 2013 there as well before playing in some Challenge Tour events, then unexpectedly winning the European/Australasian co-sanctioned 2013 Perth International, edging Ross Fisher on the first hole of sudden death. **OWR Best:** 189 - Feb, 2014.

European Tour Wins (1): 2013: Perth International (ISPS Handa).

Other Wins: Tasmanian Open: 2010*.

Amateur Wins: British Am: 2010   -   Port Phillip Am: 2008   Riversdale Cup: 2010   Boroondara Cup: 2010.

	10	11	12	13	14
Masters	-	MC	-	-	-
US Open	-	-	-	-	-
British	T14	-	-	-	MC
PGA	-	-	-	-	-
Money (E)	-	233*	271*	93*	122
OWR	650	854	-	249	431

2014: E: 24 st / 7 ct / 1 t10. (T2 Joburg). Struggled in his first full E Tour season (122nd in $$$) but remains exempt off his 2013 Perth win.

OUTLOOK: He's still young but at this point, his victory at Perth looks very much an outlier. Had a far-below-the-median statistical year on the 2014 E Tour, but one assumes at least some adjustment factor there. Obviously needs to step it up - a lot - before his exemption expires.

STATS (LTD): Driving Distance: C   Driving Accuracy: C-   GIR: C-   Short Game: C+   Putting: C

Jiménez Rodriguez, Miguel Ángel (Spain) (50) b. Malaga, Spain 1/5/1964. 5'10" 165 lbs. TP: 1982. Popular, highly successful veteran with 21 career E Tour wins in 643 career starts (through 2014). Twice a two-time winner before exploding for five titles in 2004, including the BMW Asian Open and the Hong Kong Open (officially an '05 E Tour event). Very solid tee-to-green player whose previous top victory had come in the 1999 Volvo Masters, where he edged Bernhard Langer, Retief Goosen and Padraig Harrington by two. Won a second Hong Kong Open in 2007 (E Tour '08) and the E Tour's flagship BMW PGA Championship (in a playoff with Oliver Wilson) in 2008. Only an occasional visitor to the PGA Tour. Logged five Major championship top 10s from the 1999 PGA through the 2002 Masters. Rose up at age 46 for a vintage 2010 season, claiming victories at the Dubai Desert Classic (in a playoff with Lee Westwood), the French Open (in a playoff with Alejandro Cañizares and Francesco Molinari) and the European Masters (by three over Edoardo Molinari). Following a quiet 2011, captured a third Hong Kong Open in 2012, at age 48. Missed the early part of 2013 after breaking his leg skiing, yet still managed to finish 22nd in E Tour $$$. Began the 2014 E Tour season by defending his Hong Kong Open title (played in December 2013), thus stretching his record as the circuit's oldest-ever winner (49 years, 337 days). Became the E Tour's first-ever 50-year-old winner by claiming the 2014 Spanish Open (in a playoff with Thomas Pieters and Richard Green), his first victory in 27 tries at his native championship. Also made a debut start on the U.S. Champions Tour, winning the Greater Gwinnett Championship (by two over Bernhard Langer) the week after The Masters. Long known as the "Mechanic," and is widely recognized for his distinctive ponytail and unflappable demeanor.
Teams: Ryder Cup (4): 1999-04-06-10 (O: 4-8-3, S: 1-3-0). Seve Trophy (8): 2000-02-03-05-07-09-11-13. World Cup (14): 1990-92-93-94-00-01-03-04-05-06-07-08-11-13. **OWR Best:** 12 - Dec, 2004.
European Tour Wins (21): 1992: Belgian Open **1994:** Dutch Open **1998:** Turespaña Masters, Trophée Lancôme **1999:** Turespaña Masters, Volvo Masters **2003:** Mallorca Classic (54H) **2004:** Johnnie Walker Classic, Portuguese Open, BMW Asian Open, BMW Int'l, Hong Kong Open ('05) **2005:** Wales Open **2007:** Hong Kong Open ('08) **2008:** BMW PGA **2010:** Dubai Classic, French Open, European Masters **2012:** Hong Kong Open **2013:** Hong Kong Open ('14) **2014:** Spanish Open.
Champions Tour Wins (1): 2014.
Other Wins: Open de L'infloratique (France): 1988   Benson & Hedges Trophy (England): 1989 (w/X.Wunach-Ruiz)   Dunhill Cup (2): 1999-00 (both w/S.García & J.M.Olazábal)   Oki-Telepizza-Olivia Nova (Spain): 1999.

	89	90	91	92	93	94	95	96	97	98	99	00	01	02	03	04	05	06	07	08	09	10	11	12
Masters	-	-	-	-	-	-	MC	-	-	-	MC	T49	T10	T9	MC	-	T31	T11	T44	T8	T46	T12	T27	56
US Open	-	-	-	-	-	-	T28	-	-	-	T23	T2	MC	-	-	MC	MC	T16	-	T6	MC	MC	MC	MC
British	-	-	T80	-	T51	MC	T88	MC	MC	DQ	MC	T26	T3	MC	-	T47	T52	T41	T12	MC	T13	T27	T25	T9
PGA	-	-	-	-	-	-	T13	T24	-	-	T10	T64	MC	-	-	T31	T40	T65	MC	MC	T36	MC	T64	T27
Money (E)	85	54	51	14	35	5	23	19	37	4	4	11	20	66	23	4	14	23	21	4	23	9	12	28
OWR	408	230	154	102	103	42	48	71	108	53	21	27	57	168	94	12	40	73	38	22	49	27	44	54

	13	14
Masters	-	4
US Open	-	MC
British	T13	MC
PGA	T29	MC
Money (E)	22	21
OWR	37	40

2014: E: 26 st / 20 ct / 6 t10. (Won Hong Kong, Won Spanish, 4 Masters, T4 Turkish, T5 Lyoness, etc.). The World's Most Interesting Golfer never slows down, winning twice, setting a new E Tour record for oldest winner, finishing 21st in $$$ and even winning a U.S. Champions Tour event on the side.
OUTLOOK: At age 50, he stands among the game's most engaging stories. Palpably lacks length but he still manages to utilize his great skills on and around the green – combined with lots of veteran guile – to remain top-shelf competitive. At some point he may turn to dominating senior golf, but why take that plunge when he can still compete with the big boys? We'll miss him when the inevitable slowdown comes - but when will that be?

STATS: Driving Distance: C   Driving Accuracy: A   GIR: C+   Short Game: A-   Putting: A-

---

Jobe, Brandt William (USA) (49) b. Oklahoma City, OK 8/1/1965. 5'11" 180 lbs. All-American and member of the 1988 national championship team at UCLA. TP: 1988. After one season in Canada (where he won once and topped the money list), played his way through 1990 Q School but finished 189th in 1991 PGA Tour earnings. Then headed off to Asia for several profitable seasons, where he won four times on the old Asian circuit (records mostly unavailable) and, more prominently, six times in Japan (including the 1998 Japan PGA Championship) between 1995-1998. Returned to the PGA Tour as special temporary member in September 1999 and has earned a sporadically good living domestically ever since. Winless in the U.S. but has been four times a runner-up, most recently at the 2011 Memorial Tournament. Played healthy in 2011 for the first time in several years and climbed to 51st in $$$, his best finish since 2005. Saddled by a herniated disk, he made only 18 starts in 2012 and began 2013 on a medical extension which he did not clear. **OWR Best:** 29 - Sep, 1998.
Japan Tour Wins (6): 1995: Mitsubishi Galant **1997:** Tokai Classic, Golf Digest Classic **1998:** Japan PGA Championship, Ube Kosan Open, Mizuno Open.
Asian Wins (4): 1994: Thailand Open, Mak-Young Classic, Malaysian Classic **1995:** Bali Open.
Other Wins: 1 NGA/Hooters (1994)   +   British Columbia Open (Canada): 1990

	90	91	92	93	94	95	96	97	98	99	00	01	02	03	04	05	06	07	08	09	10	11	12	13
Masters	-	-	-	-	-	-	-	-	-	T14	48	-	-	-	-	-	T32	-	-	-	-	-	-	-
US Open	MC	-	MC	-	T39	T62	MC	-	-	-	MC	T52	-	T35	-	T33	MC	-	T18	-	-	T23	-	MC
British	-	-	-	-	-	MC	-	-	T52	MC	-	-	-	-	-	-	T41	-	-	-	-	-	-	-
PGA	-	-	-	-	-	-	-	-	MC	T16	-	-	-	-	-	-	MC	-	-	-	-	T45	-	-
Money (A)	-	189	257*	-	258*	313*	-	-	177*	141*	120	124	62	91	178*	27	106	252*	179	177*	-	51	169	165
Money (J)	-	-	-	-	-	25	20	6	3	41	-	-	-	-	-	-	-	-	-	-	-	-	-	-
OWR	446	498	498	305	226	71	73	66	35	61	136	268	132	120	251	42	99	562	353	301	307	127	280	473

	14
Masters	-
US Open	-
British	-
PGA	-
Money (A)	-
OWR	655

2014: Lacking PGA Tour status, played four Web.com events (including the first two Finals events) with little success.

Jobe, Brandt William, Cont'd

OUTLOOK: At age 49, begins 2015 with a 10-even non-exempt medical extension - but perhaps he'll mostly be preparing for August eligibility on the Champions Tour. When healthy, he can still drive it with the best, which could be highly advantageous with the 50-and-overs.

STATS: Driving Distance: A-   Driving Accuracy: A-   GIR: B+   Short Game: C+   Putting: B+

Johnson, Dustin Hunter (USA) (30)
b. Columbia, SC 6/22/1984. 6'4" 190 lbs. Three-time All-American and a Walker Cup player at Coastal Carolina U. TP: 2007. Very long hitter who wasted little time making a name for himself, scoring his maiden PGA Tour victory at the 2008 Turning Stone Championship, by one over Robert Allenby. Validated this win by claiming the rain-shortened (54-holes) 2009 AT&T Pebble Beach Pro-Am, beating Mike Weir by four. Successfully defended his AT&T win in 2010 (edging David Duval and J.B. Holmes by one) but several months later suffered a dramatic final round Pebble Beach collapse in the U.S. Open, closing with an 82 after leading by three through 54 holes. Endured an even more painful Major defeat at the 2010 PGA when, leading by one going to the 72nd, he was penalized for grounding his club in a bunker, missing the Watson-Kaymer playoff and ultimately tying for 5th. Came back resiliently one month later to beat Paul Casey by one at the BMW Championship (aka the Western Open). In 2011, continued his streak of winning every year on the PGA Tour by claiming the Hurricane Irene-shortened Barclays, beating Matt Kuchar by two. Had minor right knee surgery after the 2011 season, then missed much of the Spring of 2012 with a back injury before returning to win the 2012 FedEx St Jude Classic. Became the first player since Tiger Woods to win events in his first six seasons directly out of college by claiming the rain-shortened Hyundai Tournament of Champions to kick off 2013, then extended that streak by winning his first WGC event at the 2013 HSBC Champions in China (officially a part of the PGA Tour's 2014 schedule). Began a six-month "leave of absence" from the PGA Tour in August, 2014, with some published reports indicating the cause to be a failed drug test. **Teams:** Walker Cup: 2007 (1-1-1). Palmer Cup: 2007. Ryder Cup (2): 2010-12 (O: 3-3-0, S: 2-0-0). Presidents Cup: 2011 (1-3-1). **OWR Best:** 4 - Aug, 2011.

PGA Tour Wins (8): 2008: Turning Stone Championship   **2009:** AT&T Pro-Am (54H)   **2010:** AT&T Pro-Am, Western Open (BMW)   **2011:** The Barclays (54H)   **2012:** Memphis Classic (St Jude)   **2013:** Tournament of Champions (Hyundai)(54H), WGC-HSBC Champions ('14).
Other Wins: Shark Shootout: 2010 (w/I.Poulter).
Amateur Wins: Northeast Am: 2007   Monroe Inv: 2007.

	08	09	10	11	12	13	14
Masters	-	T30	T38	T38	-	T13	MC
US Open	T48	T40	T8	T23	MC	55	T4
British	-	MC	T14	T2	T9	T32	T12
PGA	-	T10	T5	MC	T48	T8	-
Money (A)	42	15	4	5	19	19	12
OWR	143	53	14	7	23	16	19

2014: PGA: 17 st / 14 ct / 7 t10.   (Won WGC-HSBC, 2 AT&T Pro-Am, 2 Northern Trust, T4 WGC-Cadillac, T4 US Open, etc.).   Won the WGC-HSBC Champions during the 2013 wraparound and finished 30th in FedEx Cup points despite leaving the Tour under cloudy circumstances in August.

OUTLOOK: Remains among the most talented young players in the game with a level of consistency – even with injuries – that is impressive. Has the tools to physically overpower most courses, and while he has been statistically inconsistent on and around the greens, his percentage of made cuts and top 10s, plus a very solid record in Majors, demonstrates his ability to regularly play top-shelf golf. He'll likely mature through the sort of mental mistakes that derailed those Major efforts, but can he get his life/head in order enough to become the truly dominant player so many expect?

STATS: Driving Distance: A+   Driving Accuracy: C   GIR: A   Short Game: C   Putting: B

Johnson, Carl Richard Stanley ("Richard S.") (Sweden) (38)
b. Stockholm, Sweden 10/15/1976. 5'7" 145 lbs. TP: 1998. Comes from American (his grandfather) and Swedish lineage. Played the E Tour for three early seasons, winning the 2002 ANZ Championship in Australia (beating Scott Laycock and Craig Parry by two, at Stableford). Came to America full-time thereafter (via 2002 Q School), eventually winning the 2008 U.S. Bank Championship (Milwaukee) when a closing 64 edged Ken Duke by one. Won the 2010 Scandinavian Masters (in a rare E Tour visit), birdieing the last to edge Rafa Echenique by one. **OWR Best:** 94 - May, 2006.

PGA Tour Wins (1): 2008: US Bank Championship.
European Tour Wins (2): 2002: ANZ Championship   **2010:** Scandinavian Masters.
Other Wins: 1 Euro Challenge (1999)   +   1 Nordic League (1999).

	00	01	02	03	04	05	06	07	08	09	10	11	12	13	14
Masters	-	-	-	-	-	-	-	-	-	-	-	-	-	-	-
US Open	-	-	-	MC	-	-	-	-	-	-	-	-	-	-	-
British	-	-	-	-	-	-	-	-	-	T9	T74	-	-	-	-
PGA	-	-	-	-	-	MC	MC	-	MC	-	-	-	-	-	-
Money (A)	-	-	-	120	148	116	50	165	119	119	135	186	209*	-	-
Money (E)	96	112	64	-	-	-	-	-	-	-	-	139	-	-	-
OWR	314	365	276	199	262	235	112	363	334	235	184	422	590	628	668

2014: Spent the entire year on the Web.com Tour, finishing 57th in regular season $$$, then failing to play through the Web.com Finals.

OUTLOOK: Will return to the Web.com in 2015, and perhaps make some PGA Tour starts as a Past Champion. Very short driver of the ball who tries to make up for it via GIRs and a good short game. At age 38, and seemingly locked into the Web.com Tour, we've very likely seen his best golf.

STATS: Driving Distance: D   Driving Accuracy: A-   GIR: B   Short Game: B+   Putting: C+

Johnson, Zachary Harris (USA) (38)
b. Iowa City, IA 2/24/1976. 5'11" 160 lbs. College: Drake U. TP: 1998. Mini-tour veteran who won the last three events of the 2001 Hooters Tour. Two-time winner and leading earner on 2001 Web.com Tour before winning the Atlanta Classic (BellSouth) as a PGA Tour rookie in 2004. Consistent player whose first three victories all came in the state of Georgia. After playing in the 2006 Ryder Cup, solidified his position on the world stage by claiming the 2007 Masters under trying conditions, his winning score of 289 (the highest of the modern era) besting Tiger Woods, Retief Goosen and Rory Sabbatini by two. Won again in Atlanta in 2007 (six weeks after his Masters triumph) and has twice claimed the Texas Open (2008 and '09). Won the 2010 Crowne Plaza Invitational at Colonial with a tournament record 259 total. Won a second time at Colonial in 2012, edging Jason Dufner by one after incurring a two-stroke penalty at the last for failing to properly re-mark his ball on the putting surface. Also claimed the 2012 John Deere Classic in his native Iowa, beating Troy Matteson on the second hole of sudden death. Logged

Johnson, Zachary Harris, Cont'd

his 10th career PGA Tour win at the 2013 BMW Championship (née Western Open), closing with 65 to beat Nick Watney by two. Began 2014 in continued good form, winning the 30-man Tournament of Champions by one over Jordan Spieth. Save for 2008 (53rd), has ranked among the top 50 money winners for the entirety of his PGA Tour career. **Teams:** Ryder Cup (4): 2006-10-12-14 (O: 6-6-2, S: 2-1-1). Presidents Cup (3): 2007-09-13 (7-6-0). World Cup: 2005. **OWR Best:** 6 - Jan, 2014.

PGA Tour Wins (11): 2004: Atlanta Classic (BellSouth) **2007**: Masters Tournament, Atlanta Classic (BellSouth) **2008**: Texas Open (Valero) **2009**: Hawaiian Open (Sony), Texas Open (Valero) **2010**: Colonial Inv (Crown Plaza) **2012**: Colonial Inv (Crown Plaza), John Deere Classic **2013**: BMW Championship **2014**: Tournament of Champions (Hyundai).
Other Wins: 2 Web.com (2003) + 4 NGA/Hooters (2001-2002)   Wendy's 3-Tour Challenge: 2006 (w/S.Cink & S.Verplank)   Northwestern Mutual World Challenge: 2013.

	03	04	05	06	07	08	09	10	11	12	13	14
Masters	-	-	MC	T32	Win	T20	MC	42	MC	T32	T35	MC
US Open	-	T48	MC	MC	T45	MC	MC	T77	T30	T41	MC	T40
British	-	MC	MC	MC	T20	T51	T47	T76	T16	**T9**	**T6**	T47
PGA	-	T37	T17	MC	MC	MC	**T10**	**T3**	T59	70	**T8**	T70
Money (A)	-	19	39	24	**8**	53	**4**	19	44	**6**	**9**	19
OWR	207	44	57	54	15	46	22	22	37	25	**9**	18

2014: PGA: 26 st / 24 ct / 5 t10. (Won T of C, 2 John Deere, T3 Humana, T6 Texas, T8 Hawaii). Cooled a bit after opening 2014 with a win and two top 10s but still finished 18th in FedEx Cup points, and among the top 25 in $$$ for the eighth time in 11 seasons.
OUTLOOK: The rare short-but-straight type to rank among the modern golf world's best – a feat accomplished behind a first-class iron game (12 in proximity to Hole) and a short game and putting stroke to match. Notably, his SGP has slipped in both 2013 and '14 (from 8 to 31 to 79) while his Total Putting went from 10 to 79 to 62. Still very much in his prime so if his putting holds its ground, there's no reason for the beat not to go on.

STATS: Driving Distance: C-   Driving Accuracy: A+   GIR: A-   Short Game: A   Putting: A

Johnston, Andrew (England) (25)
b. London, England 2/18/1989. 5'11" 225 lbs. TP: 2009. Known as "Beef" for his stocky frame. After a solid junior career (but no major amateur wins), spent three years on mini-tours before parlaying a 2011 Challenge Tour hot streak (amidst limited starts) into an E Tour card for 2012. Lost his card but made a steadier ascent in 2014, winning twice and topping the Challenge Tour money list to return to the big stage. **Teams: OWR Best:** 112 - Dec, 2014.

Other Wins: 2 Challenge (2014).

	11	12	13	14
Masters	-	-	-	-
US Open	-	-	-	-
British	MC	-	-	-
PGA	-	-	-	-
Money (E)	-	163	-	-
OWR	374	530	615	112

2014: Played full-time on the Challenge Tour where he won twice, had nine top 10s and topped the $$$ list, earning an E Tour card for 2015.
OUTLOOK: Another young player returning to the E Tour after a successful Challenge Tour run. The experience should boost his chances this time.

STATS: Driving Distance: --   Driving Accuracy: --   GIR: --   Short Game: --   Putting: --

---

Jones, Brendan Mark (Australia) (39)
b. West Wyalong, New South Wales, Australia 3/3/1975. 6'2" 200 lbs. TP: 1999. After winning the 1999 Australian Amateur, turned professional and soon became a regular on the Japan Tour, where he has logged 13 career victories and seven top-10 Order of Merit finishes since 2002. Won twice in 2004 (including the Mizuno Open) but peaked in a career-best 2007, wherein he finished 3rd in earnings and won three times: at the Tsuruya Open (his third victory there in four years), the long-running Taiheiyo Masters and, most notably, at the Nippon Series JT Cup, where a closing 61 edged Toru Taniguchi by one. Made a one-time run at the PGA Tour in 2005, finishing 2nd at the B.C. Open but ranking 144th in $$$. Back in Japan, also claimed the prestigious Crowns in 2011 (defeating Korea's I.J. Jang in a playoff), then won twice in 2012 at the Token Homemate Cup and the Sun Chlorella Classic in July. Won the 2013 Mizuno Open (by three over Kyung-Tae Kim) to gain a late berth at the British Open before cutting his year short due to wrist problems - an injury which caused him to miss several more events early in 2014. **Teams:** Eisenhower Trophy: 1998. World Cup (2): 2008-11. **OWR Best:** 52 - Dec, 2008.

Japan Tour Wins (13): 2002: Philip Morris KK **2003**: Sun Chlorella **2004**: Tsuruya Open, Mizuno Open **2006**: Tsuruya Open **2007**: Tsuruya Open, Taiheiyo Masters, Nippon Series JT Cup **2010**: Panasonic Open (54H) **2011**: The Crowns **2012**: Token Homemate Cup, Sun Chlorella **2013**: Mizuno Open.
Other Wins: 1 Web.com: 2004 + Tasmanian Open: 1999*.
Amateur Wins: Australian Am: 1999 — Riversdale Cup: 1998   Master of the Amateurs: 1999.

	01	02	03	04	05	06	07	08	09	10	11	12	13	14
Masters	-	-	-	-	-	-	-	-	-	-	-	-	-	-
US Open	-	-	-	MC	-	-	-	-	-	-	-	MC	-	-
British	-	-	-	MC	-	-	T70	-	-	-	T72	MC	-	-
PGA	-	-	-	MC	-	-	MC	T24	-	MC	MC	-	-	-
Money (J)	49	**7**	**6**	9	-	29	**3**	**10**	12	**7**	15	**3**	29	37
OWR	340	167	102	116	243	263	59	53	77	54	80	73	141	293

2014: JAP: 14 st / 11 ct / 3 t10. (3 Fujisankei, T3 Dunlop Phoenix, T6 ABC). Aside from one early MC, didn't begin his Japan Tour season until July due to recovering from 2013 wrist problems. Still managed to finish 37th in $$$ in only 14 starts.
OUTLOOK: One of the Japan Tour's longer hitters, which has allowed him to prosper there despite sketchy Short Game and Putting Numbers. Seems recovered from his wrist problems, so he should continue to prosper in Japan (while completely ignoring Western tours) for the foreseeable future.

STATS: Driving Distance: A-   Driving Accuracy: C   GIR: A-   Short Game: B   Putting: B-

Jones, Matthew Paul (Australia) (34)
b. Sydney, New South Wales, Australia 4/19/1980. 6'0" 170 lbs. All-American at Arizona St. TP: 2001. Played briefly on his native Australasian Tour before settling in the U.S. Played the Web.com Tour from 2004-2007, drawing little attention prior to a breakout 2007 in which he logged four runner-up finishes and 7th place in $$$, and graduated to the PGA Tour. Has mostly lingered just outside the PGA Tour top 125 since 2008 (though he did reach 72nd in a 2010 campaign which included five top-10 finishes) but stepped up in 2013, logging five more top 10s and finishing a career-best 48th in $$$. Broke through for his first PGA Tour win at the 2014 Shell Houston Open, where he holed a 40-yard chip to beat Matt Kuchar on the first hole of sudden death. **OWR Best:** 41 - Apr, 2014.

PGA Tour Wins (1): 2014: Houston Open (Shell).

	07	08	09	10	11	12	13	14
Masters	-	-	-	-	-	-	-	MC
US Open	-	-	WD	-	-	-	-	MC
British	-	-	-	-	-	-	-	T54
PGA	-	-	-	MC	-	-	T40	T47
Money (A)	-	135	134	72	133	172	48	47
OWR	214	269	334	122	236	459	88	78

2014: PGA: 25 st / 17 ct / 1 t10. (Won Houston). Broke through for his first PGA Tour victory in Houston, and finished 67th in FedEx Cup points.

OUTLOOK: After taking a quantum leap in 2013, his performance dropped in 2014 - but his overall year remained strong due to a breakthrough win in Houston. Unfortunately, he gave back most of the huge statistical gains he made in 2013 (save, perhaps tellingly, for SGP), which suggests that the victory may end up being something of an outlier. But while he may slip in 2015, he's now exempt through 2016.

STATS: Driving Distance: A-   Driving Accuracy: C+   GIR: C+   Short Game: B-   Putting: B

Jonzon, Michael (Sweden) (42)
b. Skara, Sweden 4/21/1972. 6'2" 225 lbs. TP: 1991. Began his E Tour career on a high note, finishing a career-best 36th in $$$ in his rookie season of 1995. Finished among the top 75 for three straight years (1997-1999) but has only once cracked the top 100 since (69th in 2009). Claimed his first major tour victory at the 1997 Portuguese Open, where he beat Ignacio Garrido by three. Claimed a second win in Spain at the 2009 Castello Masters Costa Azahar, edging Martin Kaymer and Christian Nilsson by one. **OWR Best:** 159 - Jan, 1996.

European Tour Wins (2): 1997: Portuguese Open **2009**: Castello Masters Costa Azahar.
Other Wins: 2 Euro Challenge (2003) + Sundvall Open (Sweden): 1993 Kinnaborg Open (Sweden): 1994 Open Novotel Perrier (France): 1997 (w/A. Forsbrand) Rosén Open (Sweden): 2006.

	95	96	97	98	99	00	01	02	03	04	05	06	07	08	09	10	11	12	13	14
Masters	-	-	-	-	-	-	-	-	-	-	-	-	-	-	-	-	-	-	-	-
US Open	-	-	-	-	-	-	-	-	-	-	-	-	-	-	-	-	-	-	-	-
British	-	T59	-	-	-	MC	-	-	-	-	-	-	-	-	-	-	-	-	-	-
PGA	-	-	-	-	-	-	-	-	-	-	-	-	-	-	-	-	-	-	-	-
Money (E)	36	107	45	71	68	169	185	-	-	153	179	285*	115	104	69	150	105	165	179	228*
OWR	164	262	227	252	264	407	716	735	355	559	614	980	347	267	203	460	466	570	753	666

2014: Made 11 starts on the Challenge Tour (finishing 68th in $$$) and seven on the E Tour (best: T41 at NH Collection).

OUTLOOK: Is on the verge of falling completely from the mix, but with two career wins, may still pop up from time to time.

STATS: Driving Distance: C+   Driving Accuracy: C   GIR: C+   Short Game: C+   Putting: C

Kamte, James Bongani (South Africa) (32)
b. Queenstown, South Africa 07/20/1982. 5'7" 175 lbs. TP: 2003. Nicknamed "Cobra." Ex-soccer player who rates among the first black golfers to win regularly on the Sunshine Tour. A four-time winner at home who also has played semi-regularly in Asia, where he claimed his first overseas victory in at the 2009 Asian Tour International in Thailand. Claimed his biggest home win at the 2008 Dimension Data Pro-Am, where he beat James Kingston by three to become the first native-born black to win on the tougher Sunshine summer tour. Did not crack the top 30 in Sunshine Tour $$$ from 2011-2014. **OWR Best:** 174 - Feb, 2009.

Asian Tour Wins (1): 2009: Asian Tour International.
Sunshine Tour Wins (4): 2007: Seekers Travel Pro-Am (54H) **2008**: Dimension Data Pro-Am, Highveld Classic (54H) **2011**: BMG Classic (54H).
Amateur Wins: Gauteng North Open: 2002.

	04	05	06	07	08	09	10	11	12	13	14
Masters	-	-	-	-	-	-	-	-	-	-	-
US Open	-	-	-	-	-	MC	-	-	-	-	-
British	-	-	-	-	-	-	-	-	-	-	-
PGA	-	-	-	-	-	-	-	-	-	-	-
Money (E)	-	-	-	-	138	170	157	-	-	-	-
Money (SA)	32	25	21	22	11	16*	12	32	34	33	45
Money (As)	-	-	-	-	-	-	27	-	-	-	-
OWR	-	-	591	442	371	337	541	878	651	701	1041

2014: SUN: 19 st / 15 ct / 1 t10. (T4 Wild Waves). Remained in something of a second-tier niche, finishing 45th in Sunshine Tour $$$.

OUTLOOK: Has regressed significantly over the last three years (he ended 2014 outside of the OWR top 1000) after showing significant early promise. At age 32, and with four Sunshine Tour wins under his belt, seems capable of doing more. Seems due for an uptick in 2015.

STATS (LTD): Driving Distance: A-   Driving Accuracy: C-   GIR: C+   Short Game: C   Putting: C+

Kang, Anthony (USA) (42)
b. Seoul, South Korea 11/30/1972. 6'1" 185 lbs. College: Oregon St. TP: 1996. Born in South Korea but moved to America at age 10. Has played most of his career on the Asian Tour, where he won the Philippine Open in 1999, then backed that up with a two-shot win (over Charlie Wi) at the Myanmar Open in 2001. Beat four players by one shot to win the 2009 Malaysian Open, whose sanctioned status earned him an exemption on the European Tour (where he briefly enjoyed marginal success) – and whose E Tour-enhanced purse pushed him to a career-best 3rd place in the Asian Order of Merit. **OWR Best:** 135 - Mar, 2009.

Kang, Anthony, Cont'd

European Tour Wins (1): 2009: Malaysian Open (Maybank).
Asian Tour Wins (2): 1999: Philippine Open **2001**: Myanmar Open.

	98	99	00	01	02	03	04	05	06	07	08	09	10	11	12	13	14
Masters	-	-	-	-	-	-	-	-	-	-	-	-	-	-	-	-	-
US Open	-	-	-	T74	-	-	-	-	-	-	-	-	-	-	-	-	-
British	-	-	-	-	-	-	-	-	-	-	-	-	-	-	-	-	-
PGA	-	-	-	-	-	-	-	-	-	-	-	-	-	-	-	-	-
Money (E)	-	-	-	-	-	-	-	-	-	-	-	83	111	157	289*	-	-
Money (AS)	77	17	20	11	9	43	27	24	15	13	31	3	13	48*	78	71	83
OWR	-	-	680	498	444	623	598	571	309	280	317	267	447	480	823	910	847

2014: ASIA: 14 st / 8 ct / 0 t10. (T29 Thailand Champ). Failed to crack top 70 in $$$ for the third straight year after a long run in the top 50.

OUTLOOK: At age 42, has fallen statistically well below the median in all major areas save Driving Distance, and is surely on the downside now.

STATS: Driving Distance: B   Driving Accuracy: C+   GIR: C   Short Game: C   Putting: C+

Kang, Sung-Hoon (South Korea) (27)

b. Jejudo, South Korea 6/4/1987. 5'8" 170 lbs. College: Yonsei University. TP: 2007. Korean prospect who initially remained in his home country after turning pro, playing the Korean circuit while earning his degree at Yonsei University. First came to international light upon losing a three-way playoff (to winner Thongchai Jaidee and Gonzalo Fernández-Castaño) at the E Tour's 2009 Ballantine's Championship. Played through PGA Tour Q School in 2010, then, as a 2011 rookie, saved his card by tying for 3rd at the season-ending Children's Miracle Network Classic. Lost it after 2012, however, and returned to Asia in 2013, where he won the 2013 C.J. Invitational in Korea, and the Korean Open on the OneAsia circuit. **Teams**: Eisenhower Trophy: 2006. **OWR Best**: 153 - Oct, 2011.

Asian Tour Wins (1): 2013: C.J. Invitational.
OneAsia Tour Wins (1): 2013: Korea Open.
Other Wins: SBS Lotte Sky Hill Open (KPGA): 2006   Eugene Open (KPGA): 2010.

	10	11	12	13	14
Masters	-	-	-	-	-
US Open	-	T39	-	-	-
British	-	-	-	-	-
PGA	-	-	-	-	-
Money (A)	-	120	194	-	-
OWR	523	160	454	282	383

2014: Spent most of the year playing the Web.com Tour (64th in regular season $$$) but made spot starts around the Far East and Australia.

OUTLOOK: Has yet to prove he's got the game to stick on the PGA Tour and will thus remain on the Web.com – unless he opts to stay to Asia.

STATS: Driving Distance: B   Driving Accuracy: B   GIR: B-   Short Game: B-   Putting: B-

---

Kang, Wook-Soon (South Korea) (48)

b. Seoul, South Korea 6/2/1966. 5'8" 155 lbs. TP: 1989. One of Korea's first male players to make a big impact internationally. A six-time winner on his native Korean Tour but also a seven-time champion on the old Asian circuit, highlighted by the 1998 Hong Kong Open (by two over England's Edward Fryatt) in the years prior to it being co-sanctioned by the European Tour. Twice topped the Asian Order of Merit (1996 and '98) and also topped the Korean circuit in 2002. Played 2003 PGA Tour Q School and missed getting his card by one shot. Made six Web.com starts in 2004 (tying for 9th at the Knoxville Open) before returning to Asia. Hasn't played regularly on the Asian Tour since 2008 but still makes at least a handful of annual appearances on the Korean Tour. **Teams:** World Cup: 1999. **OWR Best:** 346 - Aug, 1997.

Asian Tour Wins (7): 1996: Tournament Players Championship, Kuala Lumpur Open **1998**: Hong Kong Open, Omega PGA Championship **1999**: Taiwan Open **2000**: Maekyung Open **2001**: Thailand Masters.
Other Wins: Bukyung Open (KPGA): 1999   Lance Field Open (KPGA): 1999   Asian Nations Cup: 1999 (w/W.T. Kim)   SBS Open (Korea): 2001   Pocari Sweat Open (KPGA): 2002   Bukyung Open (KPGA): 2003.

	95	96	97	98	99	00	01	02	03	04	05	06	07	08	09	10	11	12	13	14
Masters	-	-	-	-	-	-	-	-	-	-	-	-	-	-	-	-	-	-	-	-
US Open	-	-	-	-	-	-	-	-	-	-	-	-	-	-	-	-	-	-	-	-
British	-	-	-	-	-	-	-	-	-	-	-	-	-	-	-	-	-	-	-	-
PGA	-	-	-	-	-	-	-	-	-	-	-	-	-	-	-	-	-	-	-	-
Money (AS)	34*	1	16	1*	4	10*	8	13	-	43*	28	-	-	-	-	-	-	-	-	-
OWR	-	366	464	787	591	442	409	404	644	624	378	717	909	974	951	-	-	-	798	1240

2014: Played exclusively on his native Korean Tour, making 12 starts and finishing 70th in $$$.

OUTLOOK: Bordering on being a ceremonial player now, though making 12 starts shows he's taking it at least somewhat seriously.

STATS: Driving Distance: --   Driving Accuracy: --   GIR: --   Short Game: --   Putting: --

---

Kapur, Shiv (India) (32)

b. New Delhi, India 2/12/1982. 5'10" 165 lbs. College: Purdue U. TP: 2004. Two-time honorable mention All-American while playing collegiately in the U.S. Claimed his lone major tour victory as a rookie on the Asian Tour, beating countryman Jyoti Randhawa by two at the Volvo Masters of Asia. Began playing regularly in Europe in 2006, finding little consistent success while simultaneously limiting his starts in Asia. Has several times fallen just outside the year-end OWR top 200. Won the first and last events on the 2013 Challenge Tour (finishing 4th in $$$) to return to the E Tour in 2014. **Teams:** Eisenhower Trophy (2): 2000-02. **OWR Best:** 137 - Mar, 2006.

Asian Tour Wins (1): 2005: Volvo Masters of Asia.
Other Wins: 2 Euro Challenge (2013).
Amateur Wins: Malaysian Am: 2000   Indiana Am: 2000   Asian Games (Individual): 2002.

Kapur, Shiv, Cont'd

	05	06	07	08	09	10	11	12	13	14
Masters	-	-	-	-	-	-	-	-	-	-
US Open	-	-	-	-	-	-	-	-	-	T23
British	-	-	-	-	-	-	-	T73	-	-
PGA	-	-	-	-	-	-	-	-	-	-
Money (E)	-	116	97	116	113	97	121	126	156*	87
Money (As)	4	8	12*	34*	59*	16*	24*	8	10	26*
OWR	192	184	274	411	226	269	426	278	143	233

2014: E: 26 st / 17 ct / 0 t10. (T12 Hong Kong). Rode eight top 25s to a career-best 87th-place finish in $$$ on the E Tour. Also played in three non-co-sanctioned events on the Asian Tour (best: 8th at Macau), where he ranked 26th in $$$ in limited starts.

OUTLOOK: Has long been handicapped at the highest level by a lack of length – and unlike many shorter hitters, he lacks the elite short game and putter to readily compensate. Stardom seems unlikely on the E Tour but as he enters his prime years, there's a decent chance he might last awhile.

STATS: Driving Distance: C   Driving Accuracy: A-   GIR: B+ ⇧   Short Game: C+   Putting: B-

---

Karlberg, Rikard (Sweden) (28)
b. Gothenburg, Sweden 12/1/1986. 5'11" 160 lbs. TP: 2006. After topping the 2007 Nordic League Order of Merit, played the Asian Tour full-time in 2010, claiming victories at the SAIL Open (in a five-shot runaway) and the Indian Open, where he edge Seuk-Hyun Baek by two. Has since split time between the Asian and Challenge Tours, with his best golf more often played on the former. Finished among the E Tour's top 130 in $$$ from 2012-2014 as a part-time player. **OWR Best:** 167 - Jan, 2011.

Asian Tour Wins (2): 2010: SAIL Open, Indian Open (Hero Honda).
Other Wins: Landmann Open (Sweden) (2): 2006-07   St Ibb Open (Sweden): 2007   Unibake Masters (Sweden): 2007   Stenungsund Open (Sweden): 2009.
Amateur Wins: Duke Of York Trophy: 2003.

	10	11	12	13	14
Masters	-	-	-	-	-
US Open	MC	-	-	MC	-
British	-	-	-	-	-
PGA	-	-	-	-	-
Money (As)	3	15	24	15	15
OWR	172	230	364	379	235

2014: ASIA: 10 st / 9 ct / 2 t10. (3 SAIL-SBI, T5 Malaysian Open). Finished 15th in Asian Tour $$$ for the second straight year, this time in only 10 starts. Also played eight non-co-sanctioned E Tour events (best: T9 Denmark) and finished 124th in European earnings.

OUTLOOK: Has spent several solid years on the Asian Tour, proving himself a capable earner while also taking advantage of the numerous events the circuit co-sanctions with Europe to edge his way closer to the E Tour. Has a strong all-around skill set so his best golf likely remains in front of him.

STATS: Driving Distance: A-   Driving Accuracy: B   GIR: A-   Short Game: B+   Putting: B

Karlsson, Jan Robert (Sweden) (45)
b. Katrineholm, Sweden 9/3/1969. 6'5" 200 lbs. TP: 1989. One of Europe's tallest competing professionals, a well-known free spirit and possessor of one of the E Tour's most admired swings. For much of his early career, something of an underachiever who suffered through a wildly inconsistent stretch from 2000-04. Re-emerged in 2006, setting an E Tour 54-hole scoring record (189) in winning the 2006 Wales Open and posting a 25-under-par 263 (with a double-bogey at the 72nd) in claiming the 2006 Deutsche Bank Open. A two-time winner in 2008, when he became the first Swede ever to top the E Tour Order of Merit and claimed the Mercedes-Benz Championship and the Dunhill Links Championship, where a closing 65 over the Old Course set up a playoff victory over Ross Fisher and Martin Kaymer. Also logged top 10s in the year's first three Majors, then led the PGA Championship after round one. Had his 2009 season shortened by a macular degenerative condition in his left eye which required surgery. Returned for a strong 2010 which saw him win the Qatar Masters early (by three over Álvaro Quirós) and the season-ending Dubai World Championship late (in a playoff over Ian Poulter). Played the PGA Tour full-time in 2011, finishing 49th in $$$ – but then plummeted thereafter (to 160th in 2012), initially due to a bizarre case of the swing yips encountered at the 2012 British Open, and which he was still coming to grips with during 2013. Found some element of form again in 2014, however, as he made 20 of 22 E Tour cuts while finishing 34th in $$$. **Awards:** E Tour Vardon Trophy: 2008. **Teams:** Ryder Cup (2): 2006-08 (O: 1-2-4, S: 1-1-0). Seve Trophy (4): 2000-02-07-09. World Cup (5): 2001-07-08-09-11 (won in '08 w/H.Stenson). **OWR Best:** 6 - Oct, 2008.

European Tour Wins (11): 1995: Open Mediterrania   **1997:** BMW Int'l   **1999:** Belgacom Open   **2001:** Spanish Open   **2002:** European Masters   **2006:** Wales Open, Deutsche Bank Open   **2008:** Mercedes-Benz Championship, Dunhill Links Championship   **2010:** Qatar Masters, Dubai World Championship.

	91	92	93	94	95	96	97	98	99	00	01	02	03	04	05	06	07	08	09	10	11	12	13	14
Masters	-	-	-	-	-	-	-	-	-	-	-	-	-	-	-	-	T30	T8	MC	T43	T27	T50	-	-
US Open	-	-	-	-	-	-	-	MC	-	-	-	T45	-	-	MC	-	MC	T4	-	T27	T46	T29	71	-
British*	-	T5	MC	-	MC	-	MC	MC	MC	MC	MC	MC	-	-	-	T35	MC	T7	-	T14	MC	-	MC	T12
PGA	-	-	-	-	-	-	-	T65	T41	-	MC	-	-	-	-	T29	T57	T20	-	T16	T4	MC	-	T47
Money (A)	-	-	-	-	-	-	-	305*	196*	-	-	-	-	-	-	-	-	-	-	49	160	145	-	-
Money (E)	62	22	43	56	41	102	10	17	19	114	15	33	48	116	38	4	27	1	98	6	37	68*	-	34
OWR	223	97	99	117	135	245	80	66	67	158	70	62	117	328	216	31	41	6	27	17	24	121	276	98

* Also T77 at 1989 British Open

2014: E: 22 st / 20 ct / 5 t10. (T4 French, T6 Nordea, T6 Tour Champ, T8 Abu Dhabi, T8 Scottish). Played full-time in Europe for the first time since 2011 and did well, finishing 34th in $$$. Also made five PGA Tour starts, finishing T6 at Mayakoba and T10 at McGladrey.

OUTLOOK: After losing his PGA Tour card in 2013, has apparently decided to spend his last competitive years back home in Europe. Statistically, his game has slipped nearly across the board from his halcyon days of 2001-2010, though his putting took an unexpected leap forward in 2014. Has enough pure talent - and a much-admired swing - to still win in Europe, but will his putter remain as cooperative as he nears 50?

STATS: Driving Distance: B+   Driving Accuracy: B-   GIR: B-   Short Game: B-   Putting: B+ ⇧

Katayama, Shingo (Japan) (41) b. Ibaraki, Japan 1/31/1973. 5'6" 155 lbs. TP: 1995. Popular, diminutive player, and the winningest Japan Tour member of his time, claiming 26 titles from 1998-2008, and finishing no worse than 4th in the Order of Merit from 2000-2008. A five-time Order of Merit winner, including three straight from 2004-2006. Twice captured the Japan Open, first in 2005 (by two over Ryoken Kawagishi and Craig Parry at Hirono GC), then in 2008 when he routed Ryo Ishikawa by four. Also won two Japan PGA Championships including 2003 (edging S.K. Ho by one) and a six-shot runaway in 2008. Claimed numerous other prestige titles on the Japan Tour including the 2000 Dunlop Phoenix (by four over American Bob May), the 2004 and '06 Crowns and the 2008 Taiheiyo Masters. Also claimed multiple titles at the ABC Championship (2003, '05 and '06) and the Suntory Open (2001 and '02). Logged his biggest international moments with 4th-place finishes at the 2001 PGA Championship and the 2009 Masters. After a five-year drought, claimed his 27th J Tour title at the 2013 Tokai Classic (beating Hidemasa Hoshino and Satoshi Tomiyama in a playoff), then added a 28th at the 2014 Casio World Open. Has occasionally appeared in non-Major, non-WGC PGA Tour events (his best finish being a T34 at the 2002 Houston Open) and has also made the rare E Tour start. **Teams:** Eisenhower Trophy: 1994. **OWR Best:** 23 - Jan, 2007.

Japan Tour Wins (28): 1998: Sanko Championship **1999**: JCB Classic Sendai **2000**: Kirin Open, Munsingwear Open, Dunlop Phoenix, Nippon Series, FANCL Open in Okinawa **2001**: Token Cup (54H), Kirin Open, Suntory Open **2002**: Nippon Series, Suntory Open **2003**: Japan PGA Championship, ABC Championship **2004**: The Crowns, Woodone Open **2005**: Japan Open, ABC Championship **2006**: The Crowns, Fujisankei Classic, ABC Championship **2007**: Tour Championship, Bridgestone Open **2008**: Japan PGA Championship, Japan Open, Taiheiyo Masters **2013**: Tokai Classic **2014**: Casio World Open.

Other Wins: 2 Japan Challenge (1993-1995).
Amateur Wins: Japan Collegiate: 1994.

	97	98	99	00	01	02	03	04	05	06	07	08	09	10	11	12	13	14
Masters	-	-	-	-	T40	MC	T37	-	T33	T27	T44	MC	4	MC	-	-	-	-
US Open	-	-	-	-	MC	T35	-	-	MC	MC	T36	MC	-	-	-	-	-	-
British	-	-	71	MC	MC	T50	T34	-	-	MC	-	-	-	-	-	-	T44	-
PGA	-	-	-	MC	T4	MC	MC	MC	T62	T23	-	T50	-	MC	-	-	-	-
Money (J)	55	22	8	1	4	3	3	1	1	1	2	1	16	16	12	18	4	6
OWR	326	129	101	53	37	47	59	54	39	24	39	32	56	130	112	159	77	79

2014: JAP: 18 st / 16 ct / 7 t10. (Won Casio, T2 Japan Open, T5 Tsuruya, T6 Bridgestone, T9 Diamond Cup, etc.).   Remained in his customary spot among the Japan Tour elite, scoring a late victory at the Casio World Open and finishing 6th in $$$.

OUTLOOK: At age 41, he has recovered from several down seasons and is again a regular presence in the Japan Tour top 10 and the OWR top 100. His statistics actually climbed a bit in 2014 and as his 28 career victories indicate, this is a man who knows very well how to find the winner's circle. May not be all that he once was, but he just may have a few more good years (and wins) left in him after all.

STATS: Driving Distance: B   Driving Accuracy: B   GIR: A-   Short Game: B+   Putting: B+

Kawamura, Masahiro (Japan) (21) b. Mie, Japan 6/25/1993. 5'8" 150 lbs. TP: 2011. Well-thought-of prospect who debuted on the Japan Tour in 2012 as a teenager and promptly tied for 3rd at the Tsuruya Open in his second career start. Added three more top 10s as a rookie, then fought through an early season thumb injury in 2013 before breaking through for his maiden win at the Asia-Pacific Panasonic Open, where he edged Sung-Joon Park by one. **Teams:** Eisenhower Trophy: 2010. **OWR Best:** 169 - Jan, 2014.

Japan Tour Wins (1): 2013: Asia-Pacific Panasonic Open.

	12	13	14
Masters	-	-	-
US Open	-	-	-
British	-	-	-
PGA	-	-	-
Money (J)	32	11	80
Money (As)	-	-	44
OWR	393	170	310

2014: JAP: 17 st / 9 ct / 0 t10. (T14 Dunlop Phoenix). Collapsed badly from 2013, failing to log a top 10 and tumbling to 80th in $$$.

OUTLOOK: Following two years which suggested great promise, he crashed and burned in 2014, seeing multiple statistical declines of significance (e.g., 18 to 53 in GIR) and failing ever to contend. Was widely considered an up-and-comer, so some bounce back improvement seems likely in 2015.

STATS: Driving Distance: C+   Driving Accuracy: B+   GIR: B   Short Game: B-   Putting: C+

Kaymer, Martin (Germany) (30) b. Dusseldorf, Germany 12/28/1984. 6'0" 165 lbs. TP: 2005. Ex-elite German amateur who won twice on the E Challenge Tour (and shot a 59 in a Satellite EPD Tour event) in 2006 before joining the E Tour full-time in 2007, promptly winning Rookie of the Year. Finished his next two seasons ranked among the top 25 in the world, and among the E Tour Order of Merit's top 10. Opened 2008 beating Henrik Stenson and Lee Westwood by four for his first win in Abu Dhabi. Later added the 2008 BMW International in his homeland, beating Anders Hansen in a playoff. Won back-to-back E Tour events immediately prior to the 2009 Open Championship, beating Lee Westwood in a playoff at the French Open, then claiming the Scottish Open a week later. Broke four bones in his foot in a go cart accident following the 2009 Open Championship, missing two months. Returned to enjoy a strong 2010, a season in which he won the E Tour Order of Merit and also claimed his first Major title, the PGA Championship, in a three-hole playoff with Bubba Watson. Also won his second Abu Dhabi Championship early (edging Ian Poulter by one) as well as both the KLM Open and the Dunhill Links Championship immediately after the PGA. Had an up-and-down 2011, initially winning his third Abu Dhabi Championship (and moving to #1 in the OWR for eight weeks – Feb 27-April 14), then flattening out before claiming a late win at the WGC HSBC Champions in China. Ended a disappointing 2012 season by holing the clinching putt at the Ryder Cup at Medinah, then winning the unofficial Nedbank Golf Challenge (12-player field) in South Africa. Went winless in 2013, however, and made little earnings headway, finishing 24th in the Order of Merit. Came back strongly to win the 2014 Players Championship, keyed by a sweeping 28-foot par putt at the 71st hole. Then took another great leap a month later by claiming the U.S. Open in an eight-shot runaway victory at Pinehurst. **Awards:** E Tour Golfer of the Year: 2010 (w/G.McDowell). Euro Vardon Trophy: 2010. E Tour Rookie of the Year: 2007. **Teams:** Eisenhower Trophy: 2004. Ryder Cup (3): 2010-12-14 (O: 4-3-3, S: 2-1-0). World Cup (4): 2007-08-09-11. **OWR Best:** 1 - Feb, 2011.

PGA Tour Wins (3): 2010: PGA Championship **2014**: Players Championship, U.S. Open.
European Tour Wins (9): 2008: Abu Dhabi Championship, BMW International **2009**: French Open, Scottish Open **2010**: Abu Dhabi Championship, Dutch Open (KLM), Dunhill Links Championship **2011**: Abu Dhabi Championship, WGC-HSBC Champions.

Kaymer, Martin, Cont'd

Sunshine Tour Wins (1): 2012: Million Dollar Challenge.
Other Wins: 2 Euro Challenge (2006) + 6 EPD Tour (2005-2006)   PGA Grand Slam: 2014.
Amateur Wins: Austrian Am: 2004   German Closed Am: 2004   German Am Stroke Play: 2005   German Am Match Play: 2005.

	06	07	08	09	10	11	12	13	14
Masters	-	-	MC	MC	MC	MC	T44	T35	T31
US Open	-	-	T53	MC	T8	T39	T15	T59	Win
British	-	-	80	T34	T7	T12	MC	T32	70
PGA	-	-	MC	T6	Win	MC	MC	T33	MC
Money (A)	-	-	-	-	-	-	-	94	10
Money (E)	-	41	8	3	1	3	30	24	15
OWR	164	76	25	13	3	4	28	39	12

2014: PGA: 19 st / 15 ct / 4 t10. (Won Players, Won US Open, T7 Deutsche Bank, T8 WGC-HSBC).   Ended what many called a slump with a vengeance, winning both the Players and the U.S. Open, and finishing 16th in FedEx Cup points. Were it not for McIlroy, he'd have been the year's biggest story.
OUTLOOK: Though his statistics continued not to overwhelm, he firmly repositioned himself among the world elite in 2014, having played through his recent swing issues. It's actually hard to equate his numerical profile with so strong a season, but during his two dominant victories, he looked very much like the machine-like star of 2009-2011. The reality is that for him to challenge Rory McIlroy for the world number one spot, a greater level of consistency will be required. But with his confidence likely now matching his talent again, plenty of great golf should still lie ahead.

STATS: Driving Distance: B+   Driving Accuracy: B   GIR: B+   Short Game: B-   Putting: B

Kelly, Jerome Patrick (USA) (48)
b. Madison, WI 11/23/1966. 5'11" 165 lbs. College: U of Hartford. TP: 1989. All-city hockey selection in high school who attended the University of Hartford on a hockey scholarship, then turned to golf after the school dropped the winter sport. The 1995 Web.com Tour Player of the Year after winning twice. Joined PGA Tour full-time in 1996 and became a steady performer, cracking the top 60 money winners from 2000-2009, including a career-best 6th in 2002. Won the 2002 Hawaiian Open (beating John Cook by one in his 200th career start) and the 2002 Western Open (by two over Davis Love III). Broke a seven-year drought by winning the 2009 New Orleans Classic, edging three players by a shot. A rare winner but an ironman (560 career starts through 2014) and an earnings machine, having pocketed just over $26 million.
Teams: Presidents Cup: 2003 (2-2-0). **OWR Best:** 18 - Mar, 2003.
PGA Tour Wins (3): 2002: Hawaiian Open (Sony), Western Open (Advil)   **2009:** New Orleans Classic (Zurich).
Other Wins: 2 Web.com (1995) + Wisconsin Open: 1992   Shark Shootout (2): 2006 (w/R.Pampling)-09 (w/S.Stricker).

	96	97	98	99	00	01	02	03	04	05	06	07	08	09	10	11	12	13	14
Masters	-	-	-	-	-	-	T20	48	T31	T20	-	T5	MC	-	T12	MC	-	-	-
US Open	-	-	T57	T37	-	MC	MC	T40	83	-	T7	MC	-	T63	-	-	T41	-	-
British	-	T44	-	-	-	MC	T28	WD	T47	MC	T26	T49	MC	-	MC	MC	-	-	-
PGA	-	MC	WD	T26	MC	T44	MC	MC	MC	T34	48	MC	MC	MC	MC	T26	-	-	T27
Money (A)	59	103	87	77	59	35	6	26	17	58	39	36	50	23	79	61	126	99	73
OWR	143	173	192	185	130	79	27	33	32	66	95	63	102	80	144	132	254	212	123

2014: PGA: 23 st / 17 ct / 4 t10. (3 Hawaii, 3 John Deere, T6 Texas, T9 Puerto Rico).   Finished 62nd in FedEx Cup points.
OUTLOOK: Remains remarkably consistent at age 48, building around a very accurate driving game and a short game which is also upper-tier. He's bound to slow down one of these years, but as his putting numbers actually improved in 2014, it's hard to really know when.

STATS: Driving Distance: D   Driving Accuracy: A   GIR: B+   Short Game: A   Putting: A-

---

Kelly, Troy Edward (USA) (36)
b. Tacoma, WA 8/2/1978. 6'2" 225 lbs. All-American at U of Washington. TP: 2003. Spent several years toiling on the Gateway, Spanos and Golden State Tours before making 17 PGA Tour starts in 2009, and finishing 238th in $$$. Played semi-regularly on the Web.com in 2009 and '10, then made 19 Web.com starts in 2011, finishing 11th in $$$ to return to the PGA Tour for 2012. Rode a playoff loss (to Ted Potter Jr.) at the Greenbrier Classic to 116th place in $$$, but then struggled during an injury-shortened 2013. **OWR Best:** 167 - Jul, 2012.
Other Wins: 2 Gateway (2005-2006).

	05	06	07	08	09	10	11	12	13	14
Masters	-	-	-	-	-	-	-	-	-	-
US Open	MC	-	-	-	-	-	-	-	-	-
British	-	-	-	-	-	-	MC	-	-	-
PGA	-	-	-	-	-	-	-	-	-	-
Money (A)	-	-	-	-	238	-	-	116	228*	-
OWR	-	-	-	-	507	606	342	250	596	-

2014: PGA: 2 st / 0 ct / 0 t10. Played only twice coming back from knee surgery, while also making seven Web.com starts (177th in $$$).
OUTLOOK: Begins 2015 on a 12-event medical extension. Has thus far made little impact on the PGA Tour with one career top-10 finish in 54 career starts. Statistically, his mix of length and a quality short game is intriguing – but thus far it has yielded only limited results.

STATS: Driving Distance: A   Driving Accuracy: D   GIR: C   Short Game: B+   Putting: B-

---

Kennedy, Brad (Australia) (40)
b. Sydney, New South Wales, Australia 6/18/1974. 5'11" 180 lbs. TP: 1994. Longtime Australasian Tour journeyman who found his form well into his 30s, winning thrice at home, including a playoff triumph over Craig Parry at the 2011 New Zealand Open. Began playing the Japan Tour full-time in 2011 and a year later broke through for his biggest career win, closing in 66 to claim the Mizuno Open – and a late bid to the British Open. Added a second Japan Tour win at the 2013 Kansai Open, where he beat Sung-Joon Park by one, and he now appears locked in to a lucrative career in the Land Of The Rising Sun. **OWR Best:** 118 - Jun, 2012.
Japan Tour Wins (2): 2012: Mizuno Open   **2013:** Kansai Open.

Kennedy, Brad, Cont'd

Australasian Tour Wins (3): 2010: Western Australia Open **2011**: New Zealand Open (BMW) **2013**: Queensland PGA Championship.
Other Wins: Queensland Trainee (Aus): 1996   Wynnum Open (Aus) (2): 1999-00   Bargara Classic (Aus) (2): 2000-01.

	01	02	03	04	05	06	07	08	09	10	11	12	13	14
Masters	-	-	-	-	-	-	-	-	-	-	-	-	-	-
US Open	-	-	-	-	-	-	-	-	-	-	-	-	-	-
British	-	-	-	-	-	-	-	-	-	-	MC	MC	-	-
PGA	-	-	-	-	-	-	-	-	-	-	-	-	-	-
Money (J)	-	-	-	-	-	-	-	-	-	-	29	23	18	29
Money (As)	65*	19	5*	11*	66*	10	63	95	-	-	-	-	-	-
OWR	800	562	414	219	459	329	400	683	668	584	128	141	155	189

2014: JAP: 21 st / 16 ct / 5 t10. (Incl. T3 Kansai, 5 Heiwa, T5 Crowns, T6 Japan Open). Had a solid follow-up season to his career best 2013, logging five top 10s and finishing 29th in Japan Tour $$$.

OUTLOOK: Statistically a solid, balanced player who's established himself as a consistent competitor on the Japan circuit, winning in both 2012 and '13. Having turned 40, he's probably just looking down from his peak, but the descent might be slow and easy.

STATS: Driving Distance: B-   Driving Accuracy: A-   GIR: B+   Short Game: B+   Putting: B+

Khan, Rashid (India) (23)

b. New Delhi, India 2/15/1991. 5'11" 155 lbs. TP: 2010. Former Delhi GC caddie who logged four victories on his native Indian Tour before narrowly missing out on his first Asian Tour win at the 2013 SAIL-SBI Open, where he lost a playoff on his home course. Returned a year later to win the same event, beating Siddikur Rahman in sudden death after opening the event with a dazzling 11-under-par 61. Claimed a second 2014 win at the Chiangmai Classic, where he edged Jyoti Randhawa and Thanyakon Khrongpha by one.   **Teams**: Eisenhower Trophy (2): 2008-10. **OWR Best**: 200 - Dec, 2014.

Asian Tour Wins (2): 2014: SAIL-SBI Open, Chiangmai Classic.
Other Wins: Nepal Masters: 2011   Players Championship (PGTI) (2): 2012-13   Bilt Open (PGTI): 2013   PGTI Eagleburg Masters (PGTI): 2014.
Amateur Wins: Faldo Series Asia (2): 2007-09.

	12	13	14
Masters	-	-	-
US Open	-	-	-
British	-	-	-
PGA	-	-	-
Money (As)	117*	41*	10
OWR	1393	600	200

2014: ASIA: 16 st / 11 ct / 5t10. (Incl. Won SAIL-SBI, Won Chiangmai). Enjoyed a breakout year, winning twice on the Asian Tour, once early (March's SAIL-SBI Open) and once late (November's Chiangmai Classic). Ended the year a career-best 10th in $$$.

OUTLOOK: At age 23 he rates among the top up-and-coming talents on the Asian Tour, utilizing a strong all-around game which is nicely balanced statistically. Though it's early, he appears to have the potential to succeed in Europe, though to date he has toiled strictly at home.

STATS: Driving Distance: A-   Driving Accuracy: B   GIR: B+   Short Game: B+   Putting: B

Khan, Simon (England) (42)

b. Epping, England 6/16/1972. 6'3" 195 lbs. TP: 1991. Journeyman E Tour player whose first win – at the 2004 Wales Open – came in sudden death over Paul Casey, and featured an opening-round 61. After several steady years earnings-wise, has bounced noticeably up and down since 2009, with the high point being a stunning second victory at 2010 BMW PGA Championship, where he rolled in a 20' birdie at the last to edge Luke Donald and Fredrik Andersson Hed by one after entering play ranked 471st in the OWR. Obviously likes Wentworth as he nearly won another BMW PGA title in 2013, losing in a playoff. **Teams**: Seve Trophy: 2013. **OWR Best**: 69 - Aug, 2006.

European Tour Wins (2): 2004: Wales Open **2010**: BMW PGA.
Other Wins: Essex Open (England) (2): 1996-00   East Region Championship (England): 1999.

	00	01	02	03	04	05	06	07	08	09	10	11	12	13	14
Masters	-	-	-	-	-	-	-	-	-	-	-	-	-	-	-
US Open	-	-	-	-	-	-	-	-	MC	MC	-	-	72	-	-
British	MC	-	-	-	T41	T31	-	T39	-	T55	T38	T45	-	-	
PGA	-	-	-	-	-	-	MC	-	-	-	T24	-	-	-	-
Money (E)	-	-	165	86	27	40	25	49	84	127	25	120	116	55	164*
OWR	710	781	984	263	136	117	83	151	279	385	129	257	470	168	478

2014: E: 14 st / 5 ct / 0 t10. (T14 Irish). On limited starts, made only five of 14 cuts and finished 164th in $$$.

OUTLOOK: If Wentworth didn't exist, he'd have likely probably retired years ago. He has at times proven himself a cat of nine lives, but given his statistical profile, it seems likely that his days of making serious runs on the E Tour are behind him - but then many thought that before 2010 as well.

STATS: Driving Distance: C+   Driving Accuracy: B-   GIR: A-   Short Game: C   Putting: C-

---

Kieffer, Maximilian (Germany) (24)

b. Bergisch-Gladbach, Germany 6/25/1990. 5'11" 165 lbs. College: U of Florida. TP: 2010. After several years with the German national team, spent one year at the University of Florida before turning pro. Played the Challenge Tour full-time in 2011 and '12, finishing 14th in $$$ in the latter campaign to earn E Tour status. As a rookie, lost the 2013 Spanish Open in a record-tying nine-hole playoff with winner Raphaël Jacquelin and Felipe Aguilar. **Teams**: Eisenhower Trophy: 2010. World Cup: 2013. **OWR Best**: 224 - Jun, 2014.

Other Wins: 1 Euro Challenge (2012).

Kieffer, Maximilian, Cont'd

	12	13	14
Masters	-	-	-
US Open	-	-	MC
British	-	-	-
PGA	-	-	-
Money (E)	-	73	106
OWR	366	242	339

2014: E: 28 st / 18 ct / 2 t10. (T5 Spanish, T8 Russia). Slipped somewhat as a sophomore, falling to 106th in $$$ but narrowly keeping his card.

OUTLOOK: A well-thought-of prospect who nearly won as a rookie. Despite slipping a bit in year two, he has a nice mix of power and accuracy from tee to green, with the putter lagging somewhat behind. Will try to chart a better course in year three, when he figures to be more of a regular factor.

STATS: Driving Distance: B+   Driving Accuracy: A-   GIR: B+   Short Game: B-   Putting: B-

---

Kim, Anthony Ha-Jin (USA) (29)
b. Los Angeles, CA 6/19/1985. 5'10" 160 lbs. Three-time All-American at U of Oklahoma. TP: 2006. Three-time AJGA All-American who turned pro after three years of college. T2 at the 2006 Texas Open (on a sponsor's exemption) in his first PGA Tour start. Won twice in 2008 to establish himself among the game's rising young stars, taking the Wachovia Championship (in a five-shot romp over Ben Curtis) and the AT&T National (by two over Fredrik Jacobson). Won the 2010 Shell Houston Open (in a playoff with Vaughn Taylor) before undergoing surgery on his left thumb in May, shortening his season to 14 starts. Slipped somewhat in 2011, making only 14 of 26 cuts and falling to a career-low 87th in $$$. Had Achilles tendon surgery in June of 2012 and hasn't played since. **Teams:** Walker Cup: 2005 (2-1-1). Ryder Cup: 2008 (O: 2-1-1, S: 1-0-0). Presidents Cup: 2009 (3-1-0). **OWR Best:** 6 - Sep, 2008.

PGA Tour Wins (3): 2008: Wachovia Championship, AT&T National **2010:** Houston Open (Shell).
Other Wins: Kiwi Challenge (New Zealand): 2009.
Amateur Wins: Junior World (15-17): 2001   Northeast Am: 2004.

	07	08	09	10	11	12	13	14
Masters	-	-	T20	3	MC	-	-	-
US Open	T20	T26	T16	-	T54	-	-	-
British	-	T7	MC	-	T5	-	-	-
PGA	T50	T55	T51	MC	MC	-	-	-
Money (A)	60	6	39	24*	87	232*	-	-
Money (E)	-	-	38	-	-	-	-	-
OWR	75	11	24	31	78	300	-	-

2014: Sat out all of 2014, theoretically still recovering from May, 2012 surgery on his left Achilles tendon.

OUTLOOK: Can begin 2015 on a 16-event medical extension - if he chooses to play. Appeared on his way to stardom after winning twice in 2008 (at age 22) and again in 2010. Initially had some perceived attitude issues but as hindrances go, those were trumped by a serious 2012 Achilles injury that required surgery. After so long an absence, the state of his game would be impossible to predict - but the point may be moot as he reportedly has a $10 million insurance policy against career-ending injury and thus may choose to retire and collect.

STATS (LTD): Driving Distance: A ⇩   Driving Accuracy: C- ⇩   GIR: B ⇩   Short Game: B+   Putting: A- ⇩

Kim, Bi-o (South Korea) (24)
b. Seoul, South Korea 8/21/1990. 6'0" 180 lbs. College: Yonsei University. TP: 2009. After scoring a rare double of winning the Japan and Korean Amateurs in the same season, turned professional while still a teenager and won his first Korean Tour event (the 2010 Johnnie Walker Open) while still 19. Played through 2010 PGA Tour Q School but lost his card in 2011, repairing to the OneAsia circuit where, in back-to-back weeks, he claimed two of the 2012 Tour's bigger events, the Caltex Maekyung Open (in a five-shot runaway) and the SK Telecom Open, while also topping the Order of Merit. Currently splitting time between the OneAsia and Web.com Tours. **Teams:** Eisenhower Trophy: 2008. **OWR Best:** 200 - May, 2012.

OneAsia Tour Wins (3): 2011: China Masters (Nanshan) **2012:** Caltex Maekyung Open, SK Telecom Open.
Other: Johnnie Walker Open (KPGA): 2010.
Amateur Wins: Japan Am: 2008   Korean Am: 2008.

	10	11	12	13	14
Masters	-	-	-	-	-
US Open	-	-	-	T45	-
British	-	-	-	-	-
PGA	-	-	-	-	-
Money (A)	-	162	-	-	-
Money (O)	12*	-	1	43	46
OWR	539	368	350	704	1145

2014: Played mostly in Korea where he finished a disappointing 64th in $$$. Also made several more One-Asia starts, finishing 47th in $$$ there.

OUTLOOK: A young-but-experienced Korean who did little in the West in 2011 but would seem a stronger prospect than his record in Asia shows. Was only 20 when he began his 2011 PGA Tour campaign, so he may well be better prepared for international action going forward.

STATS (LTD): Driving Distance: B+   Driving Accuracy: C   GIR: C+   Short Game: C+   Putting: B-

---

Kim, Dae-Hyun (South Korea) (26)
b. Daegu-si, South Korea 4/8/1988. 5'9" 165 lbs. College: Daegu University. TP: 2007. Nicknamed "Bigfoot." Korean prospect who spent the first several years of his professional career splitting time amidst the Asian, OneAsia and Korean Tours, along with spot visits to Japan. Enjoyed his best season in 2010 when he finished second in OneAsia $$$ (despite starting only four of the circuit's 10 official events) while also winning the Caltex Maekyung Open (by four over Kyung-Tae Kim) en route to topping the Korean Tour's Order of Merit. Bounced around Asia in 2012 before having limited success on the Web.com Tour in 2013. **OWR Best:** 226 - May, 2010.

Kim, Dae-Hyun, Cont'd

Other Wins: KEB Invitational (KPGA): 2009   Caltex Maekyung Open (KPGA): 2010.

	07	08	09	10	11	12	13	14
Masters	-	-	-	-	-	-	-	-
US Open	-	-	-	-	MC	-	-	-
British	-	-	-	-	-	-	-	-
PGA	-	-	-	-	-	-	-	-
Money (As)	-	-	57	-	-	-	-	-
Money (O)	-	-	66*	2*	27	13	-	-
OWR	-	-	422	309	341	297	571	971

2014: Played almost entirely in Korea, where he finished 36th in $$$.

OUTLOOK: Another Korean prospect with eyes on the West – but thus far he has yet to truly establish himself around Asia. One of the Korean Tour's longer hitters (#1 in Driving Distance in 2011) so he'll bring the needed length if the time comes.

STATS: Driving Distance: --   Driving Accuracy: --   GIR: --   Short Game: --   Putting: --

---

Kim, Do-Hoon ("#752" or "Daegu") (South Korea) (25)

b. Daegu-si, South Korea 3/12/1989. 5'8" 170 lbs. TP: 2010. Is generally listed as Do-Hoon Kim #752 or Do-Hoon Kim (Daegu) to distinguish him from his namesake (who hails from Busan) on the Asian and Japan Tours. Enjoyed a strong 2010 rookie season in Japan, finishing 11th in $$$ and logging nine top-10 finishes in his final 13 starts, including a playoff loss (to Michio Matsumura) at the Casio World Open. Posted two more solid years in 2011 and '12 but slipped noticeably thereafter. Has only one professional victory, claiming 2010 Dongbu Promi Cup on the Korean Tour. **OWR Best:** 114 - Jan, 2011.

Other Wins: Dongbu Promi Cup (KPGA): 2010.

	10	11	12	13	14
Masters	-	-	-	-	-
US Open	-	-	-	-	-
British	-	-	-	-	-
PGA	-	-	-	-	-
Money (J)	11	22	20	68	86
OWR	128	150	215	422	748

2014: JAP: 19 st / 8 ct / 0 t10. (T12 Tokai, T12 Toshin). As he reaches an age where experience should begin to become an advantage, he's been backsliding on the Japan Tour, failing to log a top 10 and finishing 86th in $$$.

OUTLOOK: Initially appeared destined for Japan Tour stardom, but his power game is somewhat offset by below-the-median short game and putting numbers, both of which have recently declined. Is young enough to turn it around but at present, he looks like a mid-range J Tour player.

STATS: Driving Distance: A-   Driving Accuracy: C+   GIR: B   Short Game: C+   Putting: C+

Kim, Hyung-Sung (South Korea) (34)

b. Seoul, South Korea 5/12/1980. 5'9" 160 lbs. TP: 2005. A three-time winner during his first three seasons on his native Korean circuit, but has played the Japan Tour full-time since 2009. After finishing 31st in $$$ as a J Tour rookie, was relatively quiet for two years before climbing to 8th in $$$ in a 2012 campaign which included a victory at the Vana H Cup KBC Augusta. Claimed his biggest win to date in 2013, closing with a 65 to overcome an eight-shot deficit and win the Japan PGA Championship en route to finishing 2nd in the Order of Merit. Also won the 2013 Korean PGA Championship, and was thrice a runner-up in Japan. Won for the third straight year in Japan in 2014, taking the Crowns by four. **Teams:** World Cup: 2011. **OWR Best:** 62 - Dec, 2013.

Japan Tour Wins (3): **2012:** KBC Augusta **2013:** Japan PGA Championship **2014:** The Crowns.

Other Wins: KPGA Championship (KPGA): 2006   SBS Tomato Open (KPGA): 2008   Ace Bank Montvert Open (KPGA): 2008   KPGA Championship (KPGA): 2013

	08	09	10	11	12	13	14
Masters	-	-	-	-	-	-	-
US Open	-	-	-	-	-	-	MC
British	-	-	-	-	-	MC	MC
PGA	-	-	-	-	-	-	MC
Money (J)	-	31	60	45	8	2	9
OWR	688	260	287	316	116	62	110

2014: JAP: 19 st / 15 ct / 7 t10. (Won Crowns, T2 Tokai, T3 KBC Augusta, T3 ANA, T3 Casio, etc.). Won for the third consecutive year on the Japan Tour, logged four top 5s in one five-event mid-season stretch and ranked among the top 10 $$$ earners for the third straight time.

OUTLOOK: Possesses a very reliable tee-to-green game and saw his putting jump significantly in 2015. The latter point, if sustained, might suggest future success beyond just Asia, and with three non-major PGA Tour starts on his 2014 ledger (best: T34 WGC-Cadillac), the notion has obviously crossed his mind. But for now he figures to remain a force in Japan (and domestically) while looking for a path westward.

STATS: Driving Distance: B+   Driving Accuracy: B+   GIR: A   Short Game: B+   Putting: B+⇧

Kim, Hyung-Tae ("#404") (South Korea) (37)

b. Seoul, South Korea 9/27/1977. 5'7" 160 lbs. TP: 1999. Is now often listed as Hyung-Tae Kim #404 to distinguish him from a far lesser-ranked namesake. A Korean Tour veteran who has made semi-regular forays onto the Japan circuit, notably from 2009-2012. Though winless in Japan, he has seen more success at home, claiming five wins between 2006-2013, led by the 2013 KPGA Championship. **OWR Best:** 236 - Nov, 2011.

Other Wins: KPGA Tour Championship (KPGA): 2006   Nonghyup Open (KPGA): 2007   Meritz Solmoro Open (KPGA): 2008   KEB Invitational (KPGA): 2010   KPGA Championship (KPGA): 2013.

Kim, Hyung-Tae, Cont'd

	07	08	09	10	11	12	13	14
Masters	-	-	-	-	-	-	-	-
US Open	-	-	-	-	-	-	-	-
British	-	-	-	-	-	-	-	MC
PGA	-	-	-	-	-	-	-	-
Money (J)	76	-	66	34	31	82	-	60
OWR	495	566	565	290	248	609	392	483

2014: JAP: 18 st / 9 ct / 2 t10. (T3 Mizuno, T5 Japan PGA). Returned to Japan full-time and was competitive, finishing 60th in $$$.

OUTLOOK: Though a proven mid-range earner in Japan, his tee-to-green numbers have never been inspiring, and his short game uncharacteristically plunged in 2014. Still a top-flight putter, but he's unlikely to win outside of Korea if his ball striking remains at this level.

STATS: Driving Distance: B-   Driving Accuracy: C   GIR: C   Short Game: B⇩   Putting: A

Kim, Kyung-Tae ("K.T.") (South Korea) (28)

b. Kangwon Province, South Korea 9/2/1986. 5'10" 160 lbs. College: Yonsei University. TP: 2006. Touted young Korean who won two events on his home tour prior to turning pro, then added two more as a professional in 2007 before claiming his first major tour victory, the Asian Tour's 2007 Caltex Maekyung Open (in a five-shot rout over Wen-Chong Liang). Has played primarily in Japan since, where he climbed into 8th place in the Order of Merit during a winless 2009, then exploded to dominate the J Tour in 2010. After winning the 2010 Diamond Cup, became the second Korean (following Hon Chang Sang in 1972) ever to claim the Japan Open (where he edged Hiroyuki Fujita by two), then scored a late-season triumph at the ABC Mynavi Championship. Spent more time on the fledgling OneAsia Tour in 2011, winning the Caltex Maekyung Open in an eight-shot runaway and finishing 2nd in $$$. Reached a new level of international prominence by playing in the 2011 Presidents Cup in Melbourne, going 2-2-0 for the International side. Won for the third straight year in Japan in 2012, edging Yuta Ikeda by one at the Fujisankei Classic. **Teams**: Eisenhower Trophy: 2006. Presidents Cup: 2011 (2-2-0). World Cup: 2008. **OWR Best**: 18 - Aug, 2011.

Japan Tour Wins (5): 2010: Diamond Cup, Japan Open, Mynavi ABC Championship **2011**: Sega Sammy Cup **2012**: Fujisankei Classic.

Asian Tour Wins (1): 2007: Caltex Maekyung Open.

OneAsia Tour Wins (1): 2011: Caltex Maekyung Open.

Other Wins: Pocari Enerzen Open (KPGA): 2006*   Samsung Benest Open (KPGA)*: 2006   SBS Tomato Open (KPGA): 2007   Apple City Open (KPGA): 2007.

Amateur Wins: Korean Am: 2006   Japan Am: 2005-06.

	06	07	08	09	10	11	12	13	14
Masters	-	-	-	-	-	T44	MC	-	-
US Open	-	-	-	-	-	T30	67	-	-
British	-	-	-	-	T48	MC	MC	T73	-
PGA	-	-	-	-	T48	T59	61	-	-
Money (J)	-	-	48	8	1	13	9	20	35
Money (O)	-	-	-	-	-	9	2	-	-
OWR	795	268	265	110	29	25	72	151	284

2014: JAP: 20 st / 16 ct / 3 t10. (6 Tour Champ, T6 Bridgestone, T8 ANA). Remained a notch below his internationally prominent level of 2009-2012, going winless for the second straight year and falling to 35th in Japan Tour $$$.

OUTLOOK: A medium-range ball striker but a very serviceable hand on and around the green. Played in the 2011 Presidents Cup so his upside is manifest, and a putting stroke like his can turn good rounds great in a hurry. Thus a bounce back year seems to be in order.

STATS: Driving Distance: C+   Driving Accuracy: B-   GIR: B   Short Game: B+   Putting: A-

---

Kim, Seung-Hyuk (South Korea) (28)

b. Busan, South Korea 4/5/1986. 5'9" 150 lbs. TP: 2005. Spent his first seven professional years toiling relatively quietly on the Korean Tour before joining the Japanese circuit in 2013. Took a quantum leap in 2014 when he broke through to win the Tokai Classic (edging countrymen Jung-Gon Hwang and Hyung-Sung Kim by one) while also dominating back in Korea, where he topped the Order of Merit and won twice. **OWR Best**: 121 - Dec, 2014.

Japan Tour Wins (1): 2014: Tokai Classic.

OneAsia Tour Wins (2): 2014: S.K. Telecom Open, Korea Open (Kolon).

	11	12	13	14
Masters	-	-	-	-
US Open	-	-	-	-
British	-	-	-	-
PGA	-	-	-	-
Money (J)	-	-	99	16
Money (O)	-	-	-	1*
OWR	615	790	748	121

2014: JAP: 18 st / 16 ct / 4 t10. (Won Tokai, 2 Toshin, T7 Token Homemate, T9 Nippon). Enjoyed a breakout year, winning once (and finishing 16th in $$$) on the Japan Tour while also winning twice and topping the order of merit on his native Korean Tour.

OUTLOOK: Was his 2014 breakthrough a fluke? There was little on his résumé previously to support this degree of success, but his statistics are solid enough to suggest that if a retrenchment takes place in 2015, it might only be a modest one.

STATS: Driving Distance: B+   Driving Accuracy: B   GIR: B   Short Game: A-   Putting: B+

Kim, Si-Hwan ("Sihwan") (South Korea) (26)

b. Seoul, South Korea 12/4/1988. 6'1" 210 lbs. All-American at Stanford. TP: 2011. Four-time AJGA All-American. Born in South Korea but moved to Buena Park, CA with his family at age 12. Was the 2004 U.S. Junior Amateur champion and an All-American at Stanford as a freshman, but never bettered honorable mention thereafter. Took his game to Europe upon turning

Kim, Si-Hwan, Cont'd

pro but reached only the Challenge Tour over his first two seasons, then the E Tour in 2014 where he finished 132nd in $$$, then missed regaining his card at Q School by a single shot. **OWR Best:** 220 - Sep, 2013.

Amateur Wins: U.S. Junior Am: 2004   Orange Bowl Jr: 2006.

	12	13	14
Masters	-	-	-
US Open	-	-	-
British	-	-	-
PGA	-	-	-
Money (E)	-	-	132
OWR	498	258	429

2014: E: 30 st / 15 ct / 2 t10   (T9 Lyoness, T9 Perth).   Lost his card (132nd in $$$) despite making a brave late run at Perth.

OUTLOOK: Beginning to look like a candidate for the Eddie Pearce Peaked-To-Early award after losing his E Tour card as a rookie. But the talent he showed at his teens is likely still in there somewhere; he just needs to find a major tour to stick on to give it an extended chance to develop.

STATS (LTD):   Driving Distance: B-   Driving Accuracy: B-   GIR: B+   Short Game: B   Putting: C+

Kim, Si-Woo (South Korea) (19)

b. Seoul, South Korea 6/28/1995. 5'9" 180 lbs. TP: 2012. While still attending Shinsung HS in Seoul, turned professional and played his way through all three initial stages of PGA Tour Q School, then finished T20 at PGA West to become the youngest player ever (17 years, 5 months, 6 days) to earn his card. Was not eligible to officially join the Tour until he turned 18 the following June. Finished 3rd in the OneAsia Tour's 2012 SK Telecom Open as an amateur. Failed to keep his PGA Tour card after 2013 (when he failed to make a cut in eight starts) and moved to the Web.com thereafter. **Teams:** Eisenhower Trophy: 2012. **OWR Best:** 711 - Jun, 2014.

	13	14
Masters	-	-
US Open	-	-
British	-	-
PGA	-	-
Money (A)	-	-
OWR	-	819

2014: Played full-time on the Web.com Tour, where he made four of 19 cuts and finished 96th in regular season $$$.

OUTLOOK: A talented youngster whose underage status limited him in trying to keep his PGA Tour card in 2013. Remains a major mystery because beyond his eight PGA Tour starts, he's made precious few major tour appearances worldwide. Thus still a big X factor, wherever he plays.

STATS: Driving Distance: --   Driving Accuracy: --   GIR: --   Short Game: --   Putting: --

---

Kim, Meen-Whee ("Whee") (South Korea) (22)

b. Seoul, South Korea 2/22/1992. 5'11" 170 lbs. College: Yonsei University. TP: 2010. Won the 2010 Korean Amateur as well as an individual gold medal in the 2010 Asian Games. After turning pro, initially played on the OneAsia Tour as well as his native Korean circuit, where he won the Shinhan Donghae Open (in a playoff with Kevin Na) and was named Rookie Of The Year. Led 2012 PGA Tour Q School after the second and third round before fading, ending up on the Web.com Tour, where he played his way through the Finals in 2014 to earn his PGA Tour card. **Teams:** Eisenhower Trophy: 2010. **OWR Best:** 281 - May, 2013.

Other Wins: Shinhan Donghae (KPGA): 2012.
Amateur Wins: Korean Am: 2010   Asian Games (Individual): 2010.

	11	12	13	14
Masters	-	-	-	-
US Open	-	-	-	-
British	-	-	-	-
PGA	-	-	-	-
Money (O)	8	19	-	-
OWR	535	310	383	621

2014: Played full-time on the Web.com Tour, finishing 72nd in regular season $$$ but gaining his 2015 PGA Tour card via the Finals.

OUTLOOK: After proving himself one of Asia's stronger prospects in his late teens, spent two middling years on the Web.com before slipping through the Finals to gain his card. His long-term potential is significant but his American résumé to date suggests that he may not be ready quite yet.

STATS (LTD):   Driving Distance: C+   Driving Accuracy: B   GIR: B-   Short Game: B+   Putting: B+

Kingston, James Hubert (South Africa) (49)

b. Ottosdal, South Africa 11/30/1965. 6'0" 160 lbs. TP: 1988. Top South African player who initially toiled on the Sunshine Tour, then added the Asian circuit in 1998 before joining the E Tour in 2003. Four times among the top 10 in the Asian Order of Merit (including three straight from 1999-2001) and a regular top-10 earner at home. Claimed his first Sunshine win (by four over John Fourie) at the 1992 Lombard Tyres Classic. Two-time Sunshine winner in 1995, '96 and '01. Biggest victory came at the 2007 South African Open (a 2008 event on the E Tour), where he nipped England's Oliver Wilson by one. Later added a second E Tour triumph at the 2009 Mercedes-Benz Championship, edging Anders Hansen in a playoff in Germany. At age 47, broke a near-three-year victory drought by claiming his 11th Sunshine Tour title at the Sunshine Tour's Royal Swazi Open, beating Ruan de Smidt in a Stableford playoff. **OWR Best:** 65 - Oct, 2008.

European Tour Wins (2): 2007: South African Open ('08)   **2009:** Mercedes-Benz Championship.
Asian Tour Wins (4): 1998: Thailand Open   **1999:** Maekyung Daks Open   **2000:** Myanmar Open, Ericsson Classic.
Sunshine Tour Wins (11): 1992: Lombard Tyres Classic (54H)   **1995:** FNB Series-Swaziland (54H), Namibia Open (54H)   **1996:** Bushveld Classic (54H), FNB Series-Namibia (54H)   **2001:** Randfontein Classic (54H), Atlantic Beach Classic (54H)   **2002:** Royal Swazi Sun Classic (54H)   **2008:** Tour Championship   **2010:** Vodacom-Selborne (54H)   **2013:** Royal Swazi Open (Stableford).

Kingston, James Hubert, Cont'd

Amateur Wins: Western Transvaal Closed Am: 1987   Transvaal Am Match Play: 1987.

	92	93	94	95	96	97	98	99	00	01	02	03	04	05	06	07	08	09	10	11	12	13	14
Masters	-	-	-	-	-	-	-	-	-	-	-	-	-	-	-	-	-	-	-	-	-	-	-
US Open	-	-	-	-	-	-	-	-	-	-	-	-	-	-	-	-	-	-	-	-	-	-	-
British	-	-	-	-	-	-	-	-	-	-	MC	-	T57	-	-	-	MC	T27	-	-	-	-	-
PGA	-	-	-	-	-	-	-	-	-	-	-	-	-	-	-	-	T55	-	-	-	-	-	-
Money (E)	-	-	-	-	-	-	-	-	-	-	-	66	59	94	106	83	17	51	79	75	135	111	185
Money (As)	-	-	-	-	-	-	14	5	9	7	16	-	-	8*	-	-	-	-	-	-	-	-	-
Money (SA)	-	11	33*	21	14	6	16*	26*	39*	5	26*	8*	17*	24*	28*	1	5*	10*	18*	10*	43*	11	56
OWR	622	257	346	467	567	420	366	389	361	386	311	219	171	179	349	155	72	81	148	196	435	331	603

2014: E: 16 st / 6 ct / 0 t10.   (T16 Dunhill Champ).   Finished 185th in $$$ while still making spot starts on his native Sunshine Tour.

OUTLOOK: Long a reliable hand both in Africa and Europe but as he nears 50, his best is now behind him – until he's senior tour-eligible in 2015.

STATS: Driving Distance: B-   Driving Accuracy: B+   GIR: C+   Short Game: B+   Putting: B-

Kirk, Christopher Brandon (USA) (29)

b. Atlanta, GA 5/8/1985. 6'3" 175 lbs. Three-time All-American, Hogan Award winner (2007) and a Walker Cup player while at U of Georgia. TP: 2007. Two-time AJGA All-American. Played three Web.com Tour seasons beginning in 2008, with a strong 2010 yielding two wins, a 2nd-place finish on the $$$ list and a ticket to the PGA Tour. Enjoyed a fine rookie campaign in 2011, claiming a one-stroke victory at the Viking Classic and finishing 45th in $$$. Validated this by logging four top 10s and finishing 78th in $$$ in 2012. Recorded his second win at the 2013 McGladrey Classic (part of the Tour's 2013-14 schedule), beating Briny Baird and Tim Clark by two. Later added his biggest win to date at the 2014 Deutsche Bank Championship, beating Geoff Ogilvy, Russell Henley and Billy Horschel by two. **Teams**: Walker Cup: 2007 (1-1-0). Palmer Cup (2): 2006-07. **OWR Best**: 18 - Nov, 2014.

PGA Tour Wins (3): 2011: Viking Classic **2013**: McGladrey Classic ('14) **2014**: Deutsche Bank Championship.
Other Wins: 2 Web.com (2010).

	08	09	10	11	12	13	14
Masters	-	-	-	-	-	-	T20
US Open	T78	MC	-	-	-	-	T28
British	-	-	-	-	-	-	T19
PGA	-	-	-	T34	-	T57	MC
Money (A)	-	-	-	45	78	47	6
OWR	579	864	146	98	115	60	20

2014: PGA: 28 st / 26 ct / 5 t10. (Won McGladrey, Won Deutsche Bank, 2 Hawaii, T4 Memorial, T4 Tour Champ). Enjoyed a career-best campaign, winning the McGladrey early and the Deutsche Bank during the FedEx Cup Playoffs, while also finishing 6th in $$$ and 2nd in FedEx Cup points

OUTLOOK: Took his game to new levels in 2014, and he'll no longer be operating under the radar going forward. Oddly, his GIR declined from 69 to 129, but this was more than offset by his ability to sustain 2013's huge gains in Scrambling (9) and SGP (22). If these numbers hold going forward, his solid ball striking may allow him to carve a more permanent place among America's best as he approaches the peak years of his 30s.

STATS: Driving Distance: B+   Driving Accuracy: B-   GIR: B+   Short Game: A   Putting: A-

Kisner, Kevin James (USA) (30)

b. Aiken, SC 2/15/1984. 5'10" 165 lbs. College: U of Georgia. TP: 2006. An AJGA All-American. After being named an Honorable Mention All-American for four straight years at Georgia, spent 2007-2009 playing mini-tours, where he won thrice. Began playing the Web.com Tour full-time in 2010, promptly winning once, finishing 11th in $$$ and graduating to the PGA Tour. Finished 181st in 2011 $$$ but retained his card via Q School. Finished 168th in 2012 and returned to the Web.com Tour where he won once and finished 13th in regular season $$$, returning him to the PGA Tour where he finished 100th in $$$ in 2014. **OWR Best**: 212 - Oct, 2014.

Other Wins: 2 Web.com (2010-2013)   +   2 eGolf Tour (2007-2008)   1 NGA/Hooters (2008)   Callaway Inv: 2013.
Amateur Wins: North Carolina HS (2): 2004-06.

	10	11	12	13	14
Masters	-	-	-	-	-
US Open	-	-	-	-	MC
British	-	-	-	-	-
PGA	-	-	-	-	-
Money (A)	-	181	168	-	100
OWR	235	394	500	354	236

2014: PGA: 26 st / 17 ct / 3 t10. (T6 Wells Fargo, T8 Wyndham, T9 Canadian). Made good in his third PGA Tour go-round (104th in FedEx Cup points).

OUTLOOK: Had easily his best year in 2014 after playing his way back from the Web.com. Hit far more GIR (76) than he did in either of his previous two PGA Tour campaigns, with his usually strong putter regularly converting. But can he maintain this across-the-board form going forward?

STATS: Driving Distance: B-   Driving Accuracy: B   GIR: B   Short Game: B-   Putting: A-

Kjeldsen, Søren Panum (Denmark) (39)

b. Århus, Denmark 5/17/1975. 5'7" 145 lbs. TP: 1995. Steady, underrated Dane who finished among the top 70 in the E Tour Order of Merit from 1999-2013. Claimed his first win at the 2003 Johnnie Walker Championship (at Gleneagles), beating Alastair Forsyth by two. Scored his biggest victory at the 2008 Volvo Masters at Valderrama, where he edged Martin Kaymer and Anthony Wall by two, and ended the season by becoming the second Dane (after Thomas Bjørn) to play in the Ryder Cup. Added a third win at the 2009 Open de Andalucia but slipped modestly thereafter, then more significantly in 2014 when he fell to 103rd in $$$. **Teams**: Eisenhower Trophy: 1994. Ryder Cup: 2008 (0-2-1). Seve Trophy: 2009. World Cup (5): 1998-99-03-04-09. **OWR Best**: 31 - Jul, 2009.

European Tour Wins (3): 2003: Johnnie Walker Championship **2008**: Volvo Masters **2009**: Open de Andalucia.

Kjeldsen, Søren Panum, Cont'd

Other Wins: 1 Euro Challenge (1997).

	98	99	00	01	02	03	04	05	06	07	08	09	10	11	12	13	14
Masters	-	-	-	-	-	-	-	-	-	-	-	MC	T30	-	-	-	-
US Open	-	-	-	-	-	-	-	T52	-	MC	-	-	T33	-	MC	-	-
British	-	-	-	MC	-	MC	-	-	T41	-	MC	T27	T37	-	-	-	-
PGA	-	-	-	-	-	-	-	-	-	-	MC	T6	MC	-	-	-	-
Money (E)	115	56	66	50	67	27	49	55	36	17	10	13	43	69	42	61	103
OWR	458	354	328	221	215	139	172	191	137	69	50	35	84	195	158	205	335

2014: E: 27 st / 18 ct / 1 t10. (T3 Czech Masters). Fell out of the top 100 in $$$ for the first time since his rookie season of 1998, dropping to 103rd but still retaining his card for an impressive 16th straight year.

OUTLOOK: One of the shorter hitters in Europe but makes up for it in lots of other ways, resulting in a consistency which must be admired. Has only logged three wins (against 53 top 10s) in 479 career starts but figures to continue as a $$$ machine for several more years to come.

STATS: Driving Distance: D   Driving Accuracy: B+   GIR: B+   Short Game: B+   Putting: A-

---

Knost, Colt (USA) (29)
b. Garrettsville, OH 6/26/1985. 5'9" 225 lbs. All-American at Southern Methodist. TP: 2007. Born in Ohio but grew up in Pilot Point, Texas, where he was the Class 3A state champion in 2003. Won three USGA events in 2007, joining Bobby Jones (1930) and Jay Sigel (1983) as the only players ever to do so. Won the U.S. Amateur Public Links (6 & 4 over Cody Paladino) and the U.S. Amateur (2 & 1 over Michael Thompson), and was a part of the winning 2007 Walker Cup side in September. Was also #1 in the World Amateur Ranking for five weeks. As a pro, graduated from the Web.com Tour in both 2008 (6th) and 2010 (15th), but finished 193rd and 174th in the PGA Tour seasons that followed. Retained his card in 2012 but lost it in 2013, finishing 184th in FedEx Cup points. **Teams:** Walker Cup: 2007 (2-0-2). **OWR Best:** 206 - Apr, 2012.

Other Wins: 2 Web.com (2008).
Amateur Wins: U.S. Amateur: 2007   –   Dixie Am: 2005   U.S. Amateur Public Links: 2007.

	08	09	10	11	12	13	14
Masters	-	-	-	-	-	-	-
US Open	-	-	-	-	MC	-	-
British	-	-	-	-	-	-	-
PGA	-	-	-	-	-	-	-
Money (A)	-	193	-	174	109	191	-
OWR	214	492	331	435	318	682	360

2014: Played full-time on the Web.com Tour, finishing 37th in regular season $$$, then returning to the PGA Tour via the Web.com Finals.

OUTLOOK: Notably short hitter who has never quite found his place on the PGA Tour. Statistically speaking, he hits it very straight and can make a lot of putts, but from fairway to green he is numerically weak. Will give it a fifth try in 2015.

STATS: Driving Distance: D   Driving Accuracy: A   GIR: C-   Short Game: C+   Putting: A-

---

Knox, Russell Colin (Scotland) (29)
b. Inverness, Scotland 6/21/1985. 5'10" 155 lbs. College: U of Jacksonville. TP: 2007. Scottish native who came to America for college. After turning pro, spent four years playing mini-tours, most regularly the Hooters circuit. Stepped up to the Web.com in 2011, where one win and a 12th-place $$$ finish graduated him to the PGA Tour for 2012. Finished 143rd in $$$ and thus had only conditional status in 2013. Shot 59 in the second round of the Web.com Tour's 2013 Albertson's Boise Open before returning to the PGA Tour, where he solidified his position by finishing 68th in $$$ in 2014. **OWR Best:** 81 - Oct, 2014.

Other Wins: 1 Web.com (2011)   +   1 eGolf Tour (2010)   2 NGA/Hooters (2009-2010).

	11	12	13	14
Masters	-	-	-	-
US Open	-	-	T45	-
British	-	-	-	-
PGA	-	-	-	MC
Money (A)	-	143	166*	68
OWR	308	328	245	100

2014: PGA: 26 st / 20 ct / 3 t10. (T2 Honda, T9 Heritage, T10 Farmers). After struggling in both 2012 and '13, took a gigantic leap forward in 2014, when he recorded only three top 10s but climbed to 68th in $$$ and 40th in FedEx Cup points.

OUTLOOK: After two less lucrative seasons, stepped up in 2014, combining a strong tee-to-green game (23 in Ball Striking, 38 in Total Driving, 22 in GIR) with a strong short game to crack the top 70 in $$$. Is capable of going low (as a 2013 Web.com Tour 59 attests) but also possesses the sort of steady ball striking that weathers nicely on the PGA Tour. Turned some heads in 2014 and that steady climb figures to continue in the year ahead.

STATS: Driving Distance: B-   Driving Accuracy: A   GIR: A   Short Game: B+   Putting: B-

---

Kobayashi, Masanori (Japan) (38)
b. Chiba, Japan 2/14/1976. 6'1" 180 lbs. TP: 1998. Late-developing player who won twice on the 2000 Japan Challenge Tour, struggled for several years on the Japan Tour, then bounced back to the developmental circuit. Returned to the Japan Tour full-time in 2011 and made good, beating Ryo Ishikawa in a playoff to take May's Totoumi Hamamatsu Open. Validated that victory by taking the 2012 Asia-Pacific Panasonic Open (co-sanctioned with the Asian Tour), where he edged Koumei Oda by one. Took another big step by winning a weather-delayed Japan Open in 2013 (pulling away from Koumei Oda, this time by three) on his way to a career-best 14th place in $$$. Followed that up by plummeting to 107th in $$$ during a hapless 2014. **OWR Best:** 163 - Dec, 2013.

Japan Tour Wins (3): 2011: Totoumi Hamamatsu Open **2012:** Asia-Pacific Panasonic Open **2013:** Japan Open.
Other Wins: 2 Japan Challenge (2000).

Kobayashi, Masanori, Cont'd

	00	01	02	03	04	05	06	07	08	09	10	11	12	13	14
Masters	-	-	-	-	-	-	-	-	-	-	-	-	-	-	-
US Open	-	-	-	-	-	-	-	-	-	-	-	-	-	-	-
British	-	-	-	-	-	-	-	-	-	-	-	-	-	-	MC
PGA	-	-	-	-	-	-	-	-	-	-	-	-	-	-	-
Money (J)	87	103	62	59	128	-	-	-	-	79	154*	24	25	14	107
OWR	479	651	549	517	740	-	-	-	-	728	968	296	229	163	409

2014: JAP: 20 st / 4 ct / 0 t10. (T16 Japan Open). Lost form completely, plunging to 107th in $$$ and only making four cuts.

OUTLOOK: It took 12 years to win his first Japan Tour event and crack the top 50 in $$$, but in 2014 he abruptly reversed course. His stats are decidedly mid-range and, not surprisingly, took a beating last year. Is at something of a crossroads, and the bet here is for only a limited recovery.

STATS: Driving Distance: B+   Driving Accuracy: C-   GIR: C+ ⇩   Short Game: C+   Putting: C+

Kodaira, Satoshi (Japan) (25)
b. Tokyo, Japan 9/11/1989. 5'8" 150 lbs. TP: 2011. A little-known prospect outside of Japan who toiled in relative obscurity during 2011 and '12, logging but a single top 10: a T10 at the 2011 Japan Open. Initially drew attention by winning on the 2010 Japan Challenge Tour as an amateur, then won again there in 2012. But after his indifferent 2011 and '12 campaigns, he enjoyed a strong Japan Tour season in 2013, logging three straight top 10s and landing his first victory, a one-shot triumph over Thailand's Kiradech Aphibarnrat and Korean veteran S.K. Ho at the Japan Golf Tour Championship. Returned to the winner circle with a two-shot victory at the 2014 Fukushima Open. **Teams**: Eisenhower Trophy: 2010. **OWR Best**: 153 - Oct, 2014.

Japan Tour Wins (2): 2013: Japan Tour Championship **2014**: Fukushima Open.

Other Wins: 2 Japan Challenge (2010-2012).

	11	12	13	14
Masters	-	-	-	-
US Open	-	-	-	-
British	-	-	MC	-
PGA	-	-	-	-
Money (J)	78	87	12	21
OWR	697	760	223	160

2014: JAP: 22 st / 11 ct / 4 t10. (Won Fukushima, T2 Japan Open, T3 Casio, T9 Nippon). Though he fell from 20 made cuts to 11, he did a decent job of maintaining his 2013 gains, winning for the second time and finishing 21st in $$$.

OUTLOOK: A reliably powerful and solid ball striker who struggles comparatively around the green. By largely validating his fine 2013 performance in 2014, he looks a solid bet to settle into the Japan Tour's upper tier - but real stardom will require some measurable improvement around the greens.

STATS: Driving Distance: A-   Driving Accuracy: B+   GIR: B+   Short Game: C+   Putting: B-

---

Koepka, Brooks (USA) (24)
b. Wellington, FL 5/3/1990. 6'0" 185 lbs. Two-time All-American at Florida St. TP: 2012. After college, opted to take his game to the 2012 European Challenge Tour, where he began playing at mid-season and promptly won in his eighth start. Exploded during 2013, winning thrice by the end of June and earning immediate promotion to the European Tour. Among these victories, the Fred Olsen Challenge de España featured a 24-under-par 260 aggregate (and a 10-shot margin of victory), and he thrice carded rounds of 62 during 2013. Playing on a sponsor exemption, T3 at the PGA Tour's Frys.com Open (after leading through 54 holes) in October. Broke through for his first major tour win at the 2014 Turkish Airlines Open, the penultimate event in the E Tour's Final Series. **OWR Best**: 33 - Dec, 2014.

European Tour Wins (1): 2014: Turkish Airlines Open.

Other Wins: 4 Euro Challenge (2012-2013).

Amateur Wins: Rice Planters Inv: 2009.

	12	13	14
Masters	-	-	-
US Open	MC	-	T4
British	-	MC	T67
PGA	-	T70	T15
Money (E)	-	113*	8
OWR	436	86	34

2014: PGA: 16 st / 12 ct / 2 t10. (T3 Frys.com, T4 US Open). E: 15 st / 10 ct / 5 t10. (Won Turkey, T3 Dubai, T3 Euro Masters, T9 Dunhill Links). Earned enough non-member PGA Tour $$$ to gain Temporary Membership, then gained 2015 privileges by finishing among the top 125 in non-member $$$. In Europe, broke through for his first major tour win at the Finals Series Turkish Airlines Open, jumping him to 8th in $$$ for the year.

OUTLOOK: Having clawed his way onto the PGA Tour via non-member earnings, this powerful, aggressive player seems poised to have a major impact in America in the years ahead. His ball striking numbers have been imposing both in Europe (where he held full status is 2014) and at home, and it will be interesting to see how much he still plays abroad going forward. Young and slightly unpolished, but an impressive talent.

STATS: Driving Distance: A+   Driving Accuracy: C   GIR: B+   Short Game: B-   Putting: B

Kofstad, Espen (Norway) (27)
b. Oslo, Norway 8/11/1987. 6'2" 175 lbs. College: U of Denver. TP: 2010. After playing collegiately in the U.S., spend two successful years on the Challenge Tour, winning twice (and topping the Order of Merit) in 2012 to gain E Tour status for 2013. Lost his card at season's end, missed playing through Q School by a single shot, then missed nearly all of 2014 with a spinal injury. **Teams**: Eisenhower Trophy (2): 2008-10. World Cup: 2013. **OWR Best**: 180 - Oct, 2012.

Other Wins: 2 Euro Challenge (2012).

Amateur Wins: Norwegian Am (2): 2008-10.

Kofstad, Espen, Cont'd

	12	13	14
Masters	-	-	-
US Open	-	-	-
British	-	-	-
PGA	-	-	-
Money (E)	-	135	243*
OWR	191	345	776

2014: E: 3 st / 1 ct / 0 t10. (T24 Hong Kong). Missed the great majority of the year due to a serious spinal injury.

OUTLOOK: At age 27, with plenty of power and tee-to-green accuracy, still seems a viable E Tour prospect. But after recovering from his injury, he will spend 2015 back on the Challenge Tour where, if healthy, he figures to rank among the favorites to crack the year-end top 15.

STATS (LTD): Driving Distance: A-   Driving Accuracy: B-   GIR: A-   Short Game: C-   Putting: C-

---

Kokrak, Jason Kenneth (USA) (29)
b. North Bay, Ontario, Canada 5/22/1985. 6'4" 225 lbs. College: Xavier (OH) U. TP: 2008. Though raised in America, was born in Canada, while his mother was visiting her homeland, eventually becoming a U.S. citizen at age 14. A two-time Ohio state high school champion who played collegiately miles off the big-time golfing radar at Ohio's Xavier University. Spent two seasons playing mini-tours (winning four times on the eGolf circuit) before joining the Web.com in 2011. Ranked 70th in $$$ entering September before winning two of his next four starts (the Albertson's Boise Open and the Miccosukee Championship) to jump to 4th and earn PGA Tour privileges for 2012. Very long hitter who led the 2011 Web.com in driving distance at an eye-popping 318.6 yards, and has since ranked among the PGA Tour's top 15 in each of his three seasons. Has now retained his card for three consecutive years. **OWR Best**: 87 - Apr, 2014.

Other Wins: 2 Web.com (2011) + 4 eGolf Tour (2010-2011).

	07	08	09	10	11	12	13	14
Masters	-	-	-	-	-	-	-	-
US Open	MC	-	-	-	-	-	-	-
British	-	-	-	-	-	-	-	-
PGA	-	-	-	-	-	-	MC	MC
Money (A)	-	-	-	-	-	119	70	86
OWR	-	-	-	-	191	236	161	156

2014: PGA: 19 st / 13 ct / 2 t10. (4 Arnold Palmer, T10 McGladrey). Despite recording only two top 10s in a relatively light 19 starts, finished 73rd in FedEx Cup points to keep his card for the third straight year.

OUTLOOK: Big, strong player who can overwhelm the golf course when he's on. Statistically he has an above-the-median short game, and while his putter has been a question mark at times, his SGP made a major jump in 2014 (122 to 54). Given his obvious advantages in today's power-based game, a continuation of that improvement figures to result in a win or two, perhaps sooner rather than later.

STATS: Driving Distance: A+   Driving Accuracy: C   GIR: B+   Short Game: B   Putting: B

Kondo, Tomohiro (Japan) (37)
b. Tokai, Japan 6/17/1977. 5'6" 135 lbs. TP: 1999. A consistently strong Japan Tour regular who cracked the top 30 in the Order of Merit in 2001 and has never finished worse than 43rd since. Has ranked four times among the top 10, including finishing 10th during a two-win 2006 that included his maiden victory, a playoff triumph over Katsuyoshi Tomori at the Japan PGA Championship. Added the ANA Open title that same year, then took the JCB Classic (by one, over four players) during a career-best 2007 that saw him finish 4th in $$$. Won the 2008 Crowns in a playoff over Hiroyuki Fujita, then claimed a fifth career Japan Tour title in a four shot walkaway at the 2011 Tsuruya Open. Ended a three-and-a-half-year drought at the 2014 Heiwa PGM Championship, cruising home to a four-shot victory en route to a career-best 3rd-place finish in $$$. **Teams**: Eisenhower Trophy: 1998. **OWR Best**: 89 - Dec, 2014.

Japan Tour Wins (6): **2006**: Japan PGA Championship, ANA Open **2007**: JCB Classic **2008**: The Crowns **2011**: Tsuruya Open **2014**: Heiwa PGM Championship.

Amateur Wins: Asian Games (Individual): 1998   Japan Jr (15-17): 1994   Japan Collegiate: 1998.

	00	01	02	03	04	05	06	07	08	09	10	11	12	13	14
Masters	-	-	-	-	-	-	-	-	-	-	-	-	-	-	-
US Open	-	-	-	-	-	-	-	-	-	-	-	-	-	-	-
British	-	-	-	-	-	-	MC	-	MC	-	-	-	-	-	MC
PGA	-	-	-	-	-	-	-	-	-	-	-	-	-	-	-
Money (J)	123*	29	18	41	12	33	10	4	18	11	43	7	24	17	3
OWR	800	236	183	290	196	212	160	110	131	100	226	114	187	220	90

2014: JAP: 22 st / 19 ct / 8 t10. (Won Heiwa, 3 Toshin, T3 Mizuno, T3 Taiheiyo, T3 Casio, etc.). Jumped to a career-best 3rd-place finish in $$$, driven by his sixth career win and a quartet of third-place finishes.

OUTLOOK: Players of this consistency tend to build around rock-solid tee-to-green games, and thus tend to age well – and thus far, Kondo is no different. But 2014 also saw his putting numbers jump noticeably - gains not likely to be maintained at age 37. The rest of his arsenal figures to remain steady, however, so there's no reason to expect more than an incremental decline in the near future.

STATS: Driving Distance: B+   Driving Accuracy: B+   GIR: A-   Short Game: B+   Putting: B+

Korhonen, Mikko (Finland) (34)
b. Mäntsälä, Finland 7/23/1980. 5'10" 170 lbs. TP: 2004. Took the slow-and-steady route upward, turning pro at age 24, spending three years on mini-tours, then five on the Challenge circuit before reaching the E Tour (via Q School) in 2011. Failed to keep his card three times thereafter and remains winless as a pro, but he has thrice returned via Q School, including as medalist in 2014. **Teams**: Eisenhower: 2004. World Cup: 2008-13. **OWR Best**: 297- Sep, 2013.

Amateur Wins: Finnish Boys Stroke Play: 1998   Finnish Boys Match Play: 1998   Nordic Boys: 1998.

Korhonen, Mikko, Cont'd

	08	09	10	11	12	13	14
Masters	-	-	-	-	-	-	-
US Open	-	-	-	-	-	-	-
British	-	-	-	-	-	-	-
PGA	-	-	-	-	-	-	-
Money (E)	-	-	-	166	-	124	128
OWR	541	645	624	611	347	353	410

2014: E: 21 st / 13 ct / 0 t10. (T12 Russia). Logged seven top 25s but finished 124th in $$$, regained his card via Q School, where he was medalist.

OUTLOOK: One of a number of players seemingly stuck atop the fence between the E and Challenge Tours. He generally hasn't missed keeping his card by much and at 34, experience may be on his side - but there is no shortage of young, up-and-coming talent in Europe either.

STATS: Driving Distance: B- Driving Accuracy: A GIR: B+ Short Game: B Putting: B-

---

Kruger, James Barry ("Jbe'") (South Africa) (28)

b. Kimberley, South Africa 6/23/1986. 5'5" 135 lbs. TP: 2007. Former South African Amateur Of The Year (2006) who climbed steadily as a pro, claiming his first win at the 2009 Zambia Open (by three over Titch Moore), then backing that up by taking the 2010 Zimbabwe Open, where he edged Jaco Van Zyl by two. Has since played regularly in both Europe and Asia, winning the co-sanctioned 2012 Avantha Masters in India (by two over Jorge Campillo and Marcel Siem), gaining him full E Tour status for two years. Won a second Zimbabwe Open in 2014, closing with 65 to edge Jacques Blaauw by one. **OWR Best:** 109 - Feb, 2012.

European Tour Wins (1): 2012: Avantha Masters.

Sunshine Tour Wins (3): 2009: Zambia Open (54H) **2010**: Zimbabwe Open (Africom) **2014**: Zimbabwe Open (Golden Pilsener).

	07	08	09	10	11	12	13	14
Masters	-	-	-	-	-	-	-	-
US Open	-	-	-	-	-	-	-	-
British	-	-	-	-	-	MC	-	-
PGA	-	-	-	-	-	-	-	-
Money (E)	-	-	-	-	92	47	132	86
Money (As)	-	-	64	19	4	3	40*	32
Money (SA)	48	36	22	4	13	-	5*	15
OWR	-	-	587	136	155	189	229	188

2014: E: 28 st / 14 ct / 1 t10. (T2 South African). Playing on an exemption from his 2012 Avantha Masters win, bounced back from an terrible 2013 by finishing 86th in E Tour $$$. Also made spot starts in Asia and his native South Africa, winning the Zimbabwe Open on the Sunshine Tour.

OUTLOOK: Is a surprisingly long hitter for so diminutive a man, and he rebuilt several statistical categories that fell during his disappointing 2013. Looks capable of earning a living in Europe for the long haul, though how often he'll be able to win there is a slightly murkier question.

STATS: Driving Distance: A- Driving Accuracy: C GIR: A- Short Game: B- Putting: B+

Kuboya, Kenichi (Japan) (42)

b. Kanagawa, Japan 3/11/1972. 5'9" 150 lbs. College: Meiji University. TP: 1995. An up-and-down Japan Tour veteran who initially grabbed the limelight with a two-win 1997, the victories coming at the Fujisankei Classic (by one over Jumbo Ozaki and Yoshinori Kaneko) and the Daikyo Open. Slipped in 1998 and '99 but re-emerged in 2002, when he captured the Japan PGA Championship (in a playoff with Shingo Katayama) and the Munsingwear Open. Later scored a five-shot runaway at the 2011 Canon Open and, after losing in a playoff to Sang-Moon Bae in 2011, came back to win the Japan Open in 2012, beating Juvic Pagunsan by one. **OWR Best:** 73 - Nov, 2009.

Japan Tour Wins (6): 1997: Fujisankei Classic, Daikyo Open **2002**: Japan PGA Championship, Munsingwear Open **2011**: Canon Open **2012**: Japan Open.

	96	97	98	99	00	01	02	03	04	05	06	07	08	09	10	11	12	13	14
Masters	-	-	-	-	-	-	-	-	-	-	-	-	-	-	-	-	-	-	-
US Open	-	-	-	-	-	-	-	-	-	-	-	-	-	-	-	T68	-	-	-
British	-	-	-	-	-	T59	-	-	-	-	-	T27	-	-	-	-	MC	-	-
PGA	-	-	-	-	-	-	-	-	-	-	-	-	-	-	-	-	-	-	-
Money (J)	113	14	77	95	24	28	8	95*	86	73	49	40	11	7	31	10	15	72	88
OWR	899	185	237	418	270	242	153	237	539	490	577	513	172	73	169	146	130	384	950

2014: JAP: 13 st / 6 ct / 1 t10. (T9 Casio). played only one event in the spring half of the schedule (for reasons undisclosed) and closed the year with a top 10 as the Casio World Open, but still finished 88th in $$$.

OUTLOOK: After cracking the top 40 in $$$ from 2007-2012, has seen a significant drop in his GIR and short game, an awkward mix. Still, at age 42, he's put enough good golf in the record books that he may well have some stronger moments left – but he needs to turn things around relatively fast.

STATS: Driving Distance: C+ Driving Accuracy: C+ GIR: C+ Short Game: B- Putting: B-

---

Kuchar, Matthew Gregory (USA) (36)

b. Winter Park, FL 6/21/1978. 6'4" 195 lbs. Two-time All-American and Haskins Award winner (1998) at Georgia Tech. Won 1997 U.S. Amateur at Cog Hill, 2 & 1 over Joel Kribel. TP: 2000. Two-time AJGA All-American. Logged rare amateur top-25 finishes at both the Masters and U.S. Open in 1998. Has experienced an up-and-down ride on the PGA Tour after initially winning his card off sponsor exemptions in 2001. Claimed his first victory at the 2002 Honda Classic. After returning to the Web.com Tour in 2006, secured his second PGA Tour win at the late-season Turning Stone Championship in 2009, where he beat Vaughn Taylor in a playoff. After finishing 24th in earnings in 2009, took his career to new heights in 2010, logging 11 top 10s in 26 PGA Tour starts, winning The Barclays in August (in sudden death over Martin Laird) and winning both the money title and the Vardon Trophy. Followed it up with a winless but strong 2011 which included nine top-10 finishes and 6th place in $$$. Claimed his biggest win at the 2012 Players Championship, where he edged four players by two, then backed it up by beating Hunter Mahan 2 & 1 to take the 2013 WGC-Match Play. Beat Kevin Chappell by two to win the 2013 Memorial Tournament. Won for the seventh time on the PGA Tour at the 2014 RBC Heritage, holing from a bunker at the 72nd hole to edge Luke Donald by one. **Awards:** Vardon Trophy: 2010.
Teams: Walker Cup: 1999 (0-3-0). Eisenhower Trophy: 1998. Palmer Cup (2): 1998-99. Ryder Cups (3): 2010-12-14 (O: 4-5-2, S: 1-2-0).

Kuchar, Matthew Gregory, Cont'd

Presidents Cup (2): 2011-13 (4-5-1). World Cup (2): 2011-13 (won in '11 w/G.Woodland). **OWR Best:** 4 - Jun, 2013.

PGA Tour Wins (7): 2002: Honda Classic **2009:** Turning Stone Championship **2010:** The Barclays **2012:** Players Championship **2013:** WGC-Match Play, Memorial Tournament **2014:** Heritage (RBC).

Other Wins: 1 Web.com (2006) + Shark Shootout: 2013 (w/H.English).

Amateur Wins: U.S. Amateur: 1997 – Terra Cotta Inv: 1997.

	98	99	00	01	02	03	04	05	06	07	08	09	10	11	12	13	14
Masters	T21	T50	-	-	MC	-	-	-	-	-	-	-	T24	T27	T3	T8	T5
US Open	T14	MC	-	-	MC	-	-	MC	MC	-	T48	MC	T6	T14	T27	T28	T12
British	MC	-	-	-	MC	-	-	-	-	MC	MC	MC	T27	MC	T9	T15	T54
PGA	-	-	-	-	MC	-	-	-	-	-	-	MC	T10	T19	MC	T22	-
Money (A)	Am	Am	-	-	49	182	139	159	241*	115	70	24	1	6	11	3	9
OWR	332	389	634	206	87	301	320	322	189	202	135	61	13	11	21	7	11

2014: PGA: 24 st / 22 ct / 11 t10. (Won Heritage, 2 Houston, T4 Texas, T4 Canadian, T5 Masters, etc.). Enjoyed another elite season, winning once, making 92% of his cuts, logging 17 top 25s and finishing 8th in FedEx Cup points.

OUTLOOK: Has emerged as America's most consistently good top-tier player, riding a flat, effective swing to become a veritable money-making and top-10 machine (48 in his last 119 PGA Tour starts). For the most part, his statistics are similarly consistent; he has, for example, finished 25, 25, 26 and 15 in SGP since 2011. At age 36, he figures to remain highly productive for several more years, with his primary challenges now being to win more regularly and, of course, to win a Major. The former could easily happen, but his career record suggests the latter might be a tougher nut.

STATS: Driving Distance: C+   Driving Accuracy: A-   GIR: A-   Short Game: A+   Putting: A

Kuehne, Henry August II ("Hank") (USA) (39)

b. Dallas, TX 9/11/1975. 6'2" 205 lbs. Two-time All-American at Southern Methodist after transferring from Oklahoma St. TP: 1999. An AJGA All-American. Brother of former OSU All-American Trip and two-time U.S. Women's Amateur winner Kelli. Immensely long hitter who won the 1998 U.S. Amateur while starring at SMU. Played briefly in Europe and Canada early in his career before finding middling PGA Tour success in 2004 and '05. Back injuries have derailed his career since, however, though 2011 treatments in Germany have made it possible for him to at least begin competing again. **Teams:** Eisenhower Trophy: 1998. **OWR Best:** 102 - May, 2003.

Other Wins: Texas Challenge (Canada): 2002   Quebec Open (Canada): 2002   Shark Shootout (2): 2003-04 (both w/J. Sluman)

Amateur Wins: U.S. Amateur: 1998.

	99	00	01	02	03	04	05	06	07	08	09	10	11	12	13	14
Masters	MC	-	-	-	-	-	-	-	-	-	-	-	-	-	-	-
US Open	65	-	-	-	-	-	-	-	-	-	-	-	-	-	-	-
British	-	-	-	-	-	-	-	-	-	-	-	-	-	-	-	-
PGA	-	-	-	-	MC	-	-	-	-	-	-	-	-	-	-	-
Money (A)	-	-	-	-	-	99	104	244*	-	-	-	-	241*	219*	-	-
OWR	516	494	646	299	149	163	196	419	1369	-	-	-	-	1492	986	1504

2014: Did not make a start on either the PGA or Web.com Tours.

OUTLOOK: Begins 2015 on a longshot one-event medical extension based on back problems dating to 2006. Was widely acclaimed as the longest hitting touring pro in the game prior to his injuries, but wasn't able to parlay his power into PGA Tour success - and that's unlikely to change now.

STATS: Driving Distance: --   Driving Accuracy: --   GIR: --   Short Game: --   Putting: --

---

Lafeber, Maarten (Netherlands) (40)

b. Eindhoven, Netherlands 12/11/1974. 6'3" 165 lbs. TP: 1997. Enjoyed a decorated amateur career around continental Europe before beginning a long and steady run on the European Tour. Remained among the top 100 in $$$ from 2002-2010, peaking at 29th in 2003. Made his lone E Tour victory a big one, edging Søren Hansen and Mathias Gronberg by one to become the first native in 56 years to win the Dutch Open. Has struggled since 2010, narrowly keeping his card in 2012 but losing it again in 2013, then struggling on the Challenge Tour in 2014. **Teams:** Eisenhower Trophy: 1994-96. Seve Trophy: 2005. World Cup (5): 1999-01-04-05-07. **OWR Best:** 88 - Jul, 2005.

European Tour Wins (1): 2003: Dutch Open (KLM).

Other Wins: 1 Euro Challenge (1999).

Amateur Wins: Spanish Am: 1997   Dutch Am: 1997   Swiss Am: 1997 – Dutch Am Stroke Play: 1995.

	98	99	00	01	02	03	04	05	06	07	08	09	10	11	12	13	14
Masters	-	-	-	-	-	-	-	-	-	-	-	-	-	-	-	-	-
US Open	-	-	-	-	MC	-	-	MC	-	-	-	-	MC	-	-	-	-
British	-	-	MC	-	-	MC	T41	-	-	-	-	-	-	-	-	-	-
PGA	-	-	-	-	-	-	-	MC	-	-	-	-	-	-	-	-	-
Money (E)	194	144*	85	103	49	29	69	25	70	92	66	96	96	149	114	180	260*
OWR	626	405	344	369	184	107	182	103	182	329	311	329	386	621	560	810	974

2014: Played full-time on the Challenge Tour, where he finished 60th in $$$. Also made three E Tour starts (best: T28 at NH Collection).

OUTLOOK: Sits a long way from his 2003 peak (notably with the putter, which was never elite to begin with) and may be nearing the end of the line.

STATS: Driving Distance: B-   Driving Accuracy: B   GIR: C+   Short Game: B+   Putting: C+

Lahiri, Anirban (India) (27)

b. Bangalore, India 6/29/1987. 5'9" 155 lbs. TP: 2007. Strong Indian prospect who was a regular winner on the Professional Golf Tour of India in his early 20s, claiming seven titles through his first five seasons. Began playing the Asian Tour full-time in 2008, where his first three wins all came in playoffs. Claimed his first title at the 2011 Panasonic Open India, then added back-to-back victories at the SAIL SBI Open (the first in sudden death with Prom Meesawat) in 2012 and '13. Cracked the top 10 in the Asian Order of Merit for the first time in 2012 (10th), then climbed to 3rd in 2013. Claimed his first win outside of India at the 2014 Indonesian Masters (eagling the 72nd hole to edge Seuk-Hyun

Lahiri, Anirban, Cont'd

Baek by one), then added a second at the 2014 Macau Open. **Teams:** Eisenhower Trophy: 2006. World Cup: 2013. **OWR Best:** 64 - May, 2014.

Asian Tour Wins (5): 2011: Panasonic Open India **2012:** SAIL SBI Open **2013:** SAIL SBI Open **2014:** Indonesian Masters (CIMB Niaga), Macau Open (Venetian).

Other Wins: Haryana Open (PGTI): 2009   Bilt Open (PGTI) (2): 2009-10   PGTI-Amby Valley (PGTI): 2010   PGI-Oxford (PGTI): 2010   PGTI-Tollygunge (PGTI): 2011   PGTI-Panchkula (PGTI): 2011   Ahmedabad Masters (PGTI): 2014

	08	09	10	11	12	13	14
Masters	-	-	-	-	-	-	-
US Open	-	-	-	-	-	-	-
British	-	-	-	-	T31	-	MC
PGA	-	-	-	-	-	-	MC
Money (As)	111	24	56	33	10	3	2
OWR	-	419	432	365	203	111	64

2014: ASIA: 18 st / 16 ct / 9 t10.   (Incl. Won Indonesian Masters, Won Macau,, T2 Kings Cup).   Backed up a very strong 2013 with an even stronger 2014, winning twice, logging top 10s in half of his Asian Tour starts and finishing 2nd in $$$.

OUTLOOK: A power-oriented player who has seen a significant improvement in nearly all statistical areas in recent years, though his putter is still the weakest part of his arsenal. Looks ready to succeed on a bigger stage, but has yet to make his way to Europe for more than co-sanctioned events.

STATS: Driving Distance: A-   Driving Accuracy: B+   GIR: B-   Short Game: B+   Putting: B-

---

Laird, Martin Charles Campbell (Scotland) (32)

b. Glasgow, Scotland 12/29/1982. 6'2" 190 lbs. All-American at Colorado St. TP: 2004. Initially played two years on the Web.com Tour, winning once. Joined the PGA Tour in 2008 and kept his card by finishing 125th in earnings. Won the 2009 Justin Timberlake Shriners Hospital Open (Las Vegas) where he beat Chad Campbell and George McNeill in a playoff. Followed up with a strong 2010 season which included playoff losses at both The Barclays and the Justin Timberlake. Climbed further in 2011, winning the Bay Hill Invitational (edging Steve Marino by one) and finishing a career-best 23rd in $$$. Won the 2013 Valero Texas Open (with a scorching final round 63, to beat Rory McIlroy by two) before struggling in 2014, falling to 138th in $$$. **Teams:** World Cup (2): 2011-13. **OWR Best:** 21 - Mar, 2011.

PGA Tour Wins (3): 2009: Justin Timberlake Open **2011:** Bay Hill Inv **2013:** Texas Open (Valero).
Other Wins: 1 Web.com (2007)   +   2 Gateway (2006)   Denver Open: 2004   San Juan Open: 2006.

	07	08	09	10	11	12	13	14
Masters	-	-	-	-	T20	T57	MC	-
US Open	MC	-	MC	-	MC	MC	T21	-
British	-	-	MC	MC	MC	T72	T44	-
PGA	-	-	-	T48	MC	T42	MC	-
Money (A)	-	125	65	35	23	36	45	138
OWR	251	268	104	50	47	71	85	170

2014: PGA: 20 st / 13 ct / 1 t10.   (T6 Barracuda).   After ranking among the top 65 in PGA Tour $$$ for five straight seasons, unexpectedly stumbled in 2014, logging only one top 10 en route to finishing 138th in $$$ and 127th in FedEx Cup points.

OUTLOOK: Encountered a speed bump or two in 2014, missing the FedEx Cup Playoffs but skipping the Web.com Finals as he's exempt through 2015 via his 2013 Texas Open win. A reliably strong and accurate driver (25 in Total Driving) whose GIR actually climbed (back to 58) despite it being a down year. Given the consistency of his track record, the bet here is that he'll right the ship in 2014 and get back to his comfortably exempt ways.

STATS: Driving Distance: A   Driving Accuracy: B-   GIR: B+   Short Game: B-   Putting: B-

---

Lampert, Moritz Horst (Germany) (22)

b. Schwetzingen, Germany 5/14/1992. 5'11" 150 lbs. TP: 2012. Quickly joined the E Tour after a fine amateur career but struggled in 2013, finishing 184th in $$$. Won three of 11 Challenge Tour starts in 2014, thus earning a battlefield promotion back to the big circuit through 2015. **Teams:** Eisenhower Trophy: 2012. **OWR Best:** 146 - Aug, 2014.

Other Wins: 3 Euro Challenge (2014)   +   1 EPD Tour (2014).
Amateur Wins: German Am: 2012   Portuguese Am: 2012   French Jr: 2010   German Boys: 2010.

	13	14
Masters	-	-
US Open	-	-
British	-	-
PGA	-	-
Money (E)	184	252*
OWR	1018	195

2014: Won a remarkable three of 11 starts on the Challenge Tour, earning a battlefield promotion to the E Tour, where he made one of six cuts.

OUTLOOK: Well-thought-of German prospect who made four of 22 E Tour cuts during a washout 2013, then dominated the Challenge Tour in 2014. He certainly figures to stick on the big circuit this time but as he cools down from last summer's hot streak, having a major impact seems less likely.

STATS (LTD): Driving Distance: C   Driving Accuracy: B-   GIR: C   Short Game: C+   Putting: C+

Langley, Scott Alexander (USA) (25)

b. Barrington, IL 3/28/1989. 5'10" 155 lbs. All-American and NCAA individual champion (2010) at U of Illinois. TP: 2011. An AJGA All-American. T16 at the 2010 U.S. Open while still an amateur. With only limited PGA or Web.com Tour experience, finished T17 at 2012 Q School to gain PGA Tour status for 2013. Finished 127th in $$$ as a rookie but benefited from the Tour's switch to FedEx Cup points (where he finished 122nd) in order to keep his card. **Teams:** Eisenhower Trophy: 2010. Palmer Cup: 2010 **OWR Best:** 166 - Aug, 2014.

Amateur Wins: NCAA Individual: 2010.

Langley, Scott Alexander, Cont'd

	10	11	12	13	14
Masters	-	-	-	-	-
US Open	T16	-	T29	T41	T54
British	-	-	-	-	-
PGA	-	-	-	-	-
Money (A)	Am	-	-	127	90
OWR	576	-	861	341	203

2014: PGA: 29 st / 19 ct / 1 t10. (3 Valspar). After narrowly keeping his card (122nd in FedEx Cup points) in 2013, stepped up significantly in his sophomore year, recording six top 25s and finishing 77th in FedEx Cup points.

OUTLOOK: Still in his formative stages but has acquitted himself nicely over two years, particularly as he lacked professional competitive experience prior to playing his way through Q School. Thus far has relied on his short game and putter, but so far so good.

STATS (LTD): Driving Distance: C   Driving Accuracy: B-   GIR: B-   Short Game: A-   Putting: B+

Lara, José Manuel (Spain) (37)
b. Valencia, Spain 5/21/1977. 6'1" 190 lbs. TP: 1997. Mostly a journeyman European Tour player who put together a run of five straight top-65 Order of Merit finishes from 2004-2008. Won his first E Tour title at the 2006 Hong Kong Open (E Tour '07), edging Juvic Pagunsan by one. Claimed a second E Tour win at the 2010 Austrian Open (beating David Lynn in a playoff) before slipping in 2012 and '13, losing his status after the latter campaign. **Teams:** Eisenhower Trophy: 1996. World Cup: 2007. **OWR Best:** 76 - Dec, 2006.

European Tour Wins (2): 2006: Hong Kong Open ('07)   **2010:** Austrian Open.
Other Wins: 1 Euro Challenge (1996)   +   Peugeot Loewe Tour de Maioris (France): 2008   Peugeot Loewe Golf El Escorpion (France): 2009.
Amateur Wins: Spanish Am: 1996   –   European Jr: 1998.

	99	00	01	02	03	04	05	06	07	08	09	10	11	12	13	14
Masters	-	-	-	-	-	-	-	-	-	-	-	-	-	-	-	-
US Open	-	-	-	-	-	-	-	-	-	-	MC	-	-	-	-	-
British	-	-	-	-	-	-	-	-	-	-	-	MC	-	-	-	-
PGA	-	-	-	-	-	-	-	-	-	-	-	-	-	-	-	-
Money (E)	-	-	158	164	93	47	33	30	65	56	95	93	77	112	154	195
OWR	741	504	495	703	273	200	154	76	194	240	299	229	198	399	626	980

2014: E: 15 st / 2 ct / 1 t10. (T5 Hong Kong). Coming off declining years in 2012 and '13, made only two of 15 cuts (and missed his last 12) en route to falling to a career-worst (easily) 195th place in $$$.

OUTLOOK: A short and not-altogether-straight hitter who has not, in recent years, made up for it on or around the greens. At age 37, and with only nine made cuts in his last 43 E Tour starts, his chances of catching up with the young bombers look smaller with each passing day.

STATS: Driving Distance: C-   Driving Accuracy: C   GIR: B   Short Game: B   Putting: C

Larrazábal, Pablo (Spain) (31)
b. Barcelona, Spain 05/15/1983. 5'10" 170 lbs. TP: 2004. Spaniard who spent a year of HS in the United States. Saw only limited success on the Challenge Tour prior to joining the E Tour in 2008, then promptly won the French Open, by four over Colin Montgomerie. Claimed a second E Tour title at the 2011 BMW International, where he beat Sergio García in sudden death. Though winless, he remained highly competitive, and among the top 40 in $$$, in both 2012 and '13. Kicked off 2014 by logging his third career win at the Abu Dhabi Championship, where he bested Rory McIlroy and Phil Mickelson by one. **Awards:** E Tour Rookie of the Year: 2008. **Teams:** Eisenhower Trophy: 2000. Seve Trophy: 2011. World Cup: 2008. **OWR Best:** 53 - Jan, 2014.

European Tour Wins (3): 2008: French Open   **2011:** BMW International   **2014:** Abu Dhabi Championship.
Other Wins: 1 Alps Tour (2012)   +   E Tour Q School: 2007.

	08	09	10	11	12	13	14
Masters	-	-	-	-	-	-	-
US Open	-	-	-	-	-	-	MC
British	T23	MC	-	T30	T45	-	MC
PGA	-	-	-	T45	MC	MC	MC
Money (E)	18	86	88	17	37	34	29
OWR	96	283	364	77	85	101	71

2014: E: 28 st / 21 ct / 6 t10. (Won Abu Dhabi, T5 KLM, T5 World Match Play, T7 BMW PGA, T8 Malaysian, etc.). Continues to run on the edge of the E Tour elite, claiming his third career victory in Abu Dhabi and making more than 20 cuts for the fourth time while finishing 29th in $$$.

OUTLOOK: A balanced player who hits a lot of greens (though less of late) and makes up for the ones he misses with a well-thought-of short game. Well established as a regular E Tour contender and his 2014 victory in Abu Dhabi suggests that he may now be ready to reach the winner's circle more often. Further, he figures to just now be entering his peak years, so continued success - with, perhaps, a larger sprinkling of wins - seems most likely.

STATS: Driving Distance: B   Driving Accuracy: B-   GIR: B ⇩   Short Game: A-   Putting: A-

---

Lascuña, Antonio (Philippines) (44)
b. Manila, Philippines 12/26/1970. 5'9" 175 lbs. TP: 1997. Didn't turn professional until age 27, four years after winning the Philippine Amateur. Though reportedly an 18-time winner in domestic events on the Philippines Tour, has done everything but win an Asian Tour title. Has been a steady earner for years before experiencing a surge in form in his early 40s, recording his top three finishes in the Order of Merit since 2012. Despite a closing 63, lost the 2014 Selangor Master in sudden death to Chapchai Nirat - an event he won in 2007 prior to its becoming an official Asian Tour stop. **Teams:** Eisenhower Trophy: 1996. World Cup (2): 2007-13. **OWR Best:** 136 - Oct, 2014.

Other Wins: 1 Asian Developmental (2014)   +   Selangor Masters (Malaysia): 2007   Sabah Masters (Malaysia): 2013.
Amateur Wins: Canlubang Open: 1992   Putra Cup: 1996   Philippine Am: 1993   DHL Amateur Open: 1994.

Lascuña, Antonio, Cont'd

	07	08	09	10	11	12	13	14
Masters	-	-	-	-	-	-	-	-
US Open	-	-	-	-	-	-	-	-
British	-	-	-	-	-	-	-	-
PGA	-	-	-	-	-	-	-	-
Money (As)	48	55	47	48	60	12	23	**9**
OWR	486	443	617	797	716	293	284	157

2014: ASIA: 17 st / 14 ct / 5 t10. (Incl. 2 Selangor Masters, T2 Taiwan Masters). Put together his third straight notably strong Asian Tour campaign, finishing a career-best 9th in $$$ and logging four top-3 finishes, including three straight during the autumn.

OUTLOOK: A long-running Asian Tour player who, after many years in the middle of the pack, found vastly improved form over the last three seasons. At age 44, his time near the top is surely limited - but he just might be able to sustain it long enough to land that elusive first Asia Tour win.

STATS: Driving Distance: C-   Driving Accuracy: A-   GIR: B+   Short Game: B+   Putting: C+

Lawrie, Paul Stewart, M.B.E. (Scotland) (46)
b. Aberdeen, Scotland 1/1/1969. 5'11" 200 lbs. TP: 1986. Initially a workman-like E Tour player who gained a measure of immortality by winning the 1999 British Open at Carnoustie, defeating Justin Leonard and Jean Van de Velde in a four-hole playoff after Van de Velde famously let apparent victory get away at the last. Four times a top-10 finisher in the E Tour Order of Merit thereafter. Widely viewed as a flukish champion but has claimed seven additional E Tour titles, including a seven-shot runaway at the 1999 Qatar Masters and a one-shot triumph over Ernie Els at the inaugural 2001 Dunhill Links Championship. Saw his fortunes fall in the new millennium before ending a 232-event, nine-year drought by winning the light-field 2011 Open de Andalucia. Closed 2011 strongly with a 2nd-place finish (two behind Álvaro Quirós) at the Dubai World Championship, then struck early in 2012 with a four-shot win at the wind-shortened Qatar Masters. Later added the Johnnie Walker Championship (rolling past Brett Rumford by four) en route to his first top-10 $$$ ranking in a decade. **Teams**: Ryder Cup (2): 1999-12 (O: 4-3-1, S: 2-0-0). Seve Trophy (4): 2000-02-03-13. World Cup (4): 1996-00-02-03. **OWR Best**: 26 - Oct, 2012.

PGA Tour Wins (1): 1999: British Open.
European Tour Wins (7): 1996: Open de Catalonia (36H) **1999**: Qatar Masters **2001**: Dunhill Links Championship **2002**: Wales Open **2011**: Open de Andalucia **2012**: Qatar Masters, Johnnie Walker Championship.
Other Wins: Scottish Assts: 1990   UAP Under-25s: 1992   Scottish PGA (2): 1992-05   Scottish Match Play: 2002.

	92	93	94	95	96	97	98	99	00	01	02	03	04	05	06	07	08	09	10	11	12	13	14
Masters	-	-	-	-	-	-	-	-	MC	MC	MC	T15	T37	-	-	-	-	-	-	-	T24	T38	-
US Open	-	-	-	-	-	-	-	-	-	MC	T30	MC	MC	-	-	-	-	-	-	-	-	T32	-
British	T22	T6	T24	T58	MC	-	MC	**Win**	MC	T42	T59	MC	MC	T52	MC	MC	MC	T47	MC	T66	T34	T26	MC
PGA	-	-	-	-	-	-	-	T34	T22	MC	MC	-	-	-	-	-	-	-	-	T48	MC	-	-
Money (E)	83	57	76	107	21	52	62	**6**	26	**9**	**10**	51	140	48	61	72	40	82	69	18	**10**	63	117
OWR	274	217	222	291	102	155	241	44	56	56	42	74	293	169	192	231	166	201	244	83	29	109	322

2014: E: 16 st / 10 ct / 0 t10. (T11 Qatar). Made only 16 starts and failed to retain his card for the first time in a decade, finishing 117th in $$$.

OUTLOOK: At age 46, he is clearly on the downside now, following an impressive two-year run in 2011 and '12. Still hits lots of green but declining putting numbers make it a challenge from there. Hosting his own new event on the 2015 calendar is another sign that he's winding things down.

STATS: Driving Distance: B   Driving Accuracy: B-   GIR: A   Short Game: B-   Putting: B-

---

Lawrie, Peter (Ireland) (40)
b. Dublin, Ireland 3/22/1974. 6'0" 160 lbs. College: University College Dublin. TP: 1997. Reached the European Tour after finishing 4th in $$$ on the 2002 Challenge Tour and quickly emerged as a very consistent earner, missing the top 70 of the Order of Merit only once (89th in 2004) from 2003-2012. Claimed his lone E Tour win at the 2008 Spanish Open, where he defeated homestanding Ignacio Garrido in a playoff. Grabbed the final exempt spot for 2014 by finishing 110th in 2013 earnings, but after finishing 172nd in $$$, missed regaining his card at 2014 Q School by one shot. Has never appeared in a non-Major championship PGA Tour event. **Awards**: E Tour Rookie of the Year: 2003. **Teams**: Palmer Cup: 1997. **OWR Best**: 105 - Oct, 2010.

European Tour Wins (1): 2008: Spanish Open.
Other Wins: 1 Euro Challenge (2002).
Amateur Wins: Irish Closed Am: 1996.

	03	04	05	06	07	08	09	10	11	12	13	14
Masters	-	-	-	-	-	-	-	-	-	-	-	-
US Open	-	-	-	-	-	-	-	-	MC	-	-	-
British	-	-	MC	-	-	-	-	MC	-	-	-	-
PGA	-	-	-	-	-	-	-	-	-	-	-	-
Money (E)	56	89	53	67	66	38	43	36	58	48	110	172
OWR	232	335	234	274	275	179	159	106	153	155	300	896

2014: E: 30 st / 6 ct / 0 t10. (T20 Laguna). Lost his card by miles (a career-worst 172nd in $$$) but only narrowly missed regaining it at Q School.

OUTLOOK: Saw nearly all of his ball-striking numbers collapse (especially driving accuracy) during a disastrous 2014, reducing his GIR numbers and adding pressure to a lower-mid-range putting stroke. At age 40, needs to reverse things quickly - but will be doing so on the Challenge Tour.

STATS: Driving Distance: C   Driving Accuracy: B- ⇩   GIR: C   Short Game: B-   Putting: B-

---

Leaney, Stephen John (Australia) (45)
b. Busselton, Western Australia 3/10/1969. 6'0" 170 lbs. TP: 1992. Won the 1991 Western Australian Open while still an amateur. Primarily an Australasian and European Tour player who, after logging multiple victories at home, claimed four E Tour victories in a five-year span, led by an eight-shot runaway (over Robert Karlsson) at the 1998 Moroccan Open. Also logged a pair of wins at the Dutch Open, beating Darren Clarke by one in 1998 and Bernhard Langer by four in 2000. Played the PGA Tour full-time from 2002-2008, peaking

Leaney, Stephen, Cont'd

with a second-place finish at the 2003 U.S. Open, finishing three behind Jim Furyk. Toiled largely on the Web.com Tour from 2009-2011 before returning to the Far East. **Teams:** Eisenhower Trophy: 1992. Presidents Cup: 2003 (1-2-1). World Cup (2): 2003-04. **OWR Best:** 22 - Jul, 2003.

European Tour Wins (4): 1998: Moroccan Open, Dutch Open **2000:** Dutch Open **2002:** German Masters.
Australasian Tour Wins (3): 1995: Victorian Open **1997:** Victorian Open **1998:** ANZ Players Championship.
Other Wins: Western Australian Mixed Foursomes: 1989 (w/S.Waugh)   Western Australian Open (3): 1991*-94-97   Western Australian Foursomes: 1995   Western Australia PGA: 1997.
Amateur Wins: Western Australian Jr: 1988   Victorian Champion of Champions (2): 1990-91   Western Australian Am: 1992   Malaysian Am: 1992   Lake Maquarie Am: 1992.

	95	96	97	98	99	00	01	02	03	04	05	06	07	08	09	10	11	12	13	14
Masters	-	-	-	-	-	-	-	-	T17	-	-	-	-	-	-	-	-	-	-	-
US Open	-	-	-	-	MC	-	-	-	2	T40	-	-	-	-	-	-	-	-	-	-
British	MC	-	-	MC	MC	MC	MC	T37	T65	MC	-	-	-	-	-	-	-	-	-	-
PGA	-	-	-	68	MC	-	-	-	MC	MC	MC	-	MC	-	-	-	-	-	-	-
Money (A)	-	-	-	-	-	-	-	68	105	68	105	116	97	208	-	-	-	-	-	-
Money (E)	151	11	33	28	90	15	13	-	31	60	160	201	168	456	803	893	903	844	804	925
OWR	277	246	137	57	89	105	174	60	31	60	160	201	168	456	803	893	903	844	804	925

2014: JAP: 12 st / 5 ct / 0 t10. (T25 Japan Open). Finished 113th in Japan Tour $$$. Also made seven Australasian starts (71st in $$$).
OUTLOOK: Seems to be done in the West and, after failing to make an impact at home or in Japan in 2014, he's likely well onto the downside now.

STATS: Driving Distance: --   Driving Accuracy: --   GIR: --   Short Game: --   Putting: --

---

Lee, Craig (Scotland) (37)
b. Stirling, Scotland 5/9/1977. 5'11" 175 lbs. TP: 1996. Turned pro as a teenager but was unsuccessful, and entered the club pro ranks. Played one E Tour campaign in 2008 before repairing to mini-tours, and the Challenge Tour, graduating back to the E Tour in 2012. Lost a playoff to Thomas Bjørn at the 2013 European Masters after carding a third round 61. **OWR Best:** 190 - Jan, 2014.

Other Wins: Scottish Assts: 2000   Northern Open (Scotland): 2009.
Amateur Wins: Scottish Boys Stroke Play: 1995.

	08	09	10	11	12	13	14
Masters	-	-	-	-	-	-	-
US Open	-	-	-	-	-	-	-
British	-	-	-	-	-	-	-
PGA	-	-	-	-	-	-	-
Money (E)	186	-	-	-	115	59	107
OWR	773	-	634	416	409	208	319

2014: E: 31 st / 19 ct / 1 t10. (T10 Abu Dhabi). Fell back towards his normal career path - but narrowly retained his card by finishing 107th in $$$.
OUTLOOK: His 2014 season suggests that his upstart 2013 was indeed an outlier, with pullbacks recorded in a wide range of statistical categories. The question now is can he maintain this current level going forward - but looking over his career body of work, the bet here is a cautious no.

STATS: Driving Distance: B+   Driving Accuracy: B-   GIR: C+   Short Game: B   Putting: B+

Lee, Danny Jin-Myung (New Zealand) (24)
b. Incheon, South Korea 07/24/1990. 6'0" 160 lbs. TP: 2009. Korean native who grew up in New Zealand. Won the 2008 U.S. Amateur at Pinehurst, becoming, at 18 years, 1 month, the event's then-youngest-ever champion. Also won the 2008 Western Amateur, and was ranked the #1 amateur in the world. While still an amateur, became the youngest-ever winner of an E Tour event upon claiming the 2009 Johnnie Walker Classic in Australia, a record later broken by Matteo Manassero. After turning pro, played on several circuits (including 11 starts on the 2009 PGA Tour), then failed to stick in a full shot at the PGA Tour in 2012. Returned in 2014 and this time retained his card with room to spare (88th in FedEx Cup points). **Teams:** Eisenhower Trophy: 2008. World Cup: 2009. **OWR Best:** 114 - Aug, 2009.

European Tour Wins (1): 2009: Johnnie Walker Classic*.
Other Wins: 1 Web.com (2011).
Amateur Wins: U.S. Amateur: 2008   New Zealand Am: 2007   Western Am: 2008   -   Lake Maquarie Am: 2008.

	09	10	11	12	13	14
Masters	MC	-	-	-	-	-
US Open	-	-	-	-	-	-
British	-	-	-	-	-	-
PGA	-	-	-	-	-	-
Money (A)	-	-	-	166	-	120
Money (E)	164	159	84	-	-	-
OWR	143	490	152	253	357	220

2014: PGA: 28 st / 12 ct / 1 t10. (2 Puerto Rico). Finished 88th in FedEx Cup points to keep his PGA Tour card for the first time.
OUTLOOK: Former world #1 amateur who, prior to 2014, had largely disappointed as a pro (his lone major tour victory coming as an amateur in 2009). His limited statistical sample suggests middle-of-the-road numbers across the board, but his raw talent is well-documented.

STATS (LTD):   Driving Distance: B-   Driving Accuracy: B-   GIR: B-   Short Game: B   Putting: B

Lee, Dong-Hwan (D.H.) (South Korea) (27)
b. Seoul, South Korea 4/9/1987. 5'10" 175 lbs. College: Korea University. TP: 2005. A touted Korean prospect who claimed 18 amateur titles around Asia before initially plying his professional trade on the Japan Tour. Finished 6th in $$$ in 2007, when he claimed maiden victory at the rain-shortened Mizuno Open (beating six men in a four-shot runaway). Missed all of 2009 and '10

Lee, Dong-Hwan, Cont'd

while fulfilling his two-year military commitment but returned to win the Toshin Tournament in 2011. Birdied the final three holes to beat Ross Fisher for medalist honors at 2012 PGA Tour Q School, gaining status for 2013, then had his 2014 limited by a neck injury. **OWR Best:** 123 - Oct, 2007.

Japan Tour Wins (2): 2007: Mizuno Open (54H) **2011:** Toshin Golf Tournament.
Other Wins: 1 Japan Challenge (2006) + PGA Tour Q School: 2012.
Amateur Wins: Japan Am: 2004   Korean Am: 2004.

	06	07	08	09	10	11	12	13	14
Masters	-	-	-	-	-	-	-	-	-
US Open	-	-	-	-	-	-	MC	-	-
British	-	MC	-	-	-	-	-	-	-
PGA	-	-	-	-	-	-	-	-	-
Money (A)	-	-	-	-	-	-	-	95	195
Money (J)	43	6	19	-	-	19	34	-	-
OWR	435	129	162	-	-	182	234	244	657

2014: PGA: 20 st / 8 ct / 0 t10.   (T20 John Deere).   Missed several starts due to a neck injury but finished 193rd in FedEx Cup points.

OUTLOOK: Came out of left field to play through 2012 Q School, then made good for a year before struggling in 2014. Will begin 2015 on a three-event medical extension that figures to be hard to clear. Seemed a longshot to begin with, and figures to regroup this year on the Web.com.

STATS: Driving Distance: C   Driving Accuracy: A   GIR: C   Short Game: B   Putting: B

Lee, Han (USA) (37)
b. Seoul, South Korea 9/2/1977. 6'3" 200 lbs. College: U of California-Berkeley. TP: 2000. Born in South Korea but moved to America in HS. Spent three years on the Web.com Tour before returning to Asia where he spent 2007, then settled in on the Japan Tour. Claimed his first professional win at the 2012 Mynavi ABC Championship, where he closed with a splendid 63. **OWR Best:** 156 - Oct, 2010.

Japan Tour Wins (1): 2012: Mynavi ABC Championship.
Amateur Wins: Canadian Am (2): 1999-00.

	06	07	08	09	10	11	12	13	14
Masters	-	-	-	-	-	-	-	-	-
US Open	-	-	-	-	-	-	-	-	-
British	-	-	-	-	-	-	-	-	-
PGA	-	-	-	-	-	-	-	-	-
Money (J)	-	-	65	29	19	54	14	35	44
Money (AS)	-	102	-	-	-	-	-	-	-
OWR	-	792	399	231	165	332	184	259	359

2014: JAP: 20 st / 14 ct / 2 t10.   (T3 Taiheiyo, T8 Sega Sammy).   Maintained his steady earning status, finishing 44th in $$$.

OUTLOOK: A power-oriented player with above-the-median short game and putting numbers – normally a lethal combination, and one which has made him a consistent earner (if not winner) on the Japan Tour. Has played the Web.com Tour in the past but seems rooted in Japan now.

STATS: Driving Distance: B+   Driving Accuracy: B-   GIR: B-   Short Game: B+   Putting: B+

Lee, Kyoung-Hoon (South Korea) (23)
b. Seoul, South Korea 8/4/1991. 5'9" 180 lbs. TP: 2011. Joined the OneAsia Tour at age 20, then the Japan Tour at 21. Finished 10th in $$$ as a J Tour rookie and also claimed his first victory at the Sega Sammy Cup. Followed it up with strong (if winless) seasons in 2013 and '14, regularly contending and finishing 13th and 24th in $$$. **OWR Best:** 148 - Dec, 2013.

Japan Tour Wins (1): 2012: Sega Sammy Cup.

	11	12	13	14
Masters	-	-	-	-
US Open	-	-	-	MC
British	-	-	-	-
PGA	-	-	-	-
Money (J)	-	10	13	24
Money (O)	39	-	-	-
OWR	767	172	149	215

2014: JAP: 21 st / 18 ct / 5 t10.   (T2 Japan PGA, T5 Diamond Cup, 8 Crowns, T8 ANA, T8 ABC).   Went winless but finished 24th in $$$.

OUTLOOK: Plays a strong and balanced game, hitting greens at a high clip and rating above the median in nearly every major statistical area - though his putting slipped a tad in 2014. As a result, he's off to a strong start in Japan – but can he begin winning on a regular basis?

STATS: Driving Distance: B+   Driving Accuracy: A-   GIR: A-   Short Game: B+   Putting: B

Lee, Richard Hee (USA) (27)
b. Chicago, IL 5/4/1987. 5'9" 170 lbs. All-American at U of Washington. TP: 2010. Spent 2011 on the Web.com Tour after missing earning his PGA Tour card at Q School by one stroke. Returned to 2011 Q School and birdied the last two holes to qualify by a shot, then played his way through Q School again in 2012 before retaining his card with a solid 2013 campaign. **OWR Best:** 189 - Aug, 2013.

	12	13	14
Masters	-	-	-
US Open	-	-	-
British	-	-	-
PGA	-	-	-
Money (A)	138	89	131
OWR	333	238	379

Lee, Richard Hee, Cont'd

2014: PGA: 27 st / 13 ct / 2 t10. (T4 Puerto Rico, T10 AT&T Pro-Am). Finished 138th in FedEx Cup points.

OUTLOOK: Saw a huge decline in his tee-to-green numbers during a disappointing 2014, including his GIR (52 to 171), Driving Accuracy (24 to 77) and Ball Striking (63 to 157) - so it's easy to see where his problems lie. Still strong around the greens but he'll only have conditional status in 2015.

STATS: Driving Distance: C+   Driving Accuracy: A-   GIR: B   Short Game: B+   Putting: A-

---

Lee, Richard T. (Canada) (24)
b. Toronto, Ontario, Canada 10/29/1990. 5'10" 180 lbs. TP: 2007. The son of a golf professional who was runner-up at the 2006 U.S. Junior Amateur, and was the second youngest U.S. Open participant ever after qualifying at age 16. Turned pro immediately afterwards. Played mini-tours prior to joining the Asian circuit in 2013, where he broke through for his maiden win at the 2014 Solaire Open, beating Chawalit Plaphol by one after finishing runner-up there a year earlier. **OWR Best**: 255 - Apr, 2014.

Asian Tour Wins (1): 2014: Solaire Open.
Other Wins: 1 Gateway (2012).
Amateur Wins: Junior World (13-14): 2005.

	07	08	09	10	11	12	13	14
Masters	-	-	-	-	-	-	-	
US Open	-	-	-	-	-	-	-	
British	WD	-	-	-	-	-	-	
PGA	-	-	-	-	-	-	-	
Money (As)	-	-	-	-	-	-	32	28
OWR	1375	1381	1106	802	1096	-	492	379

2014: ASIA: 13 st / 8 ct / 2 t10. (Won Solaire, T6 Queens Cup). Claimed his first major tour win and finished 28th in Asian Tour $$$.

OUTLOOK: His days as an apparent phenom are well in the past but at age 24, he still has plenty of time to build his game going forward. Appears to possess the combination of length and touch that suggests a bigger upside than just Asia. Could be a man to watch in 2015 and '16.

STATS (LTD): Driving Distance: B+   Driving Accuracy: B-   GIR: B-   Short Game: B+   Putting: A-

---

Leishman, Marc (Australia) (31)
b. Warrnambool, Victoria, Australia 10/24/1983. 6'2" 210 lbs. TP: 2005. A former top Australian junior prospect who, after turning pro, won once on the Korean Tour and three times on Australia's developmental Von Nida circuit. A 19th-place finish on the 2008 Web.com Tour graduated him to the PGA Tour where, though winless for his first three seasons, he proved himself a strong earner, particularly in a rookie year which saw him finish 47th in $$$. Finished T2 at the 2009 BMW Championship and the 2010 Farmers Insurance Open before claiming his first PGA Tour win at the 2012 Travelers Championship, closing with 62 to edge Charley Hoffman and Bubba Watson by one. **Awards**: PGA Tour Rookie of the Year: 2009. **Teams**: Presidents Cup: 2013 (2-2-0). **OWR Best**: 39 - Aug, 2014.

PGA Tour Wins (1): 2012: Travelers Championship.
Other Wins: 1 Web.com (2008)   +   SBS Jissan Resort Open (KPGA): 2006   Queensland Cairns Classic (Aus): 2006   Toyota Southern Classic (Aus) (2): 2006-07.
Amateur Wins: Victorian Jr Masters: 2001   South Australian Jr Masters: 2001   Victorian Boys: 2001   Lake Maquarie Am: 2005.

	08	09	10	11	12	13	14
Masters	-	-	MC	-	-	T4	MC
US Open	-	-	MC	T51	-	MC	-
British	-	-	T60	-	MC	MC	T5
PGA	-	-	T48	-	T27	T12	T47
Money (A)	-	47	59	100	41	60	32
OWR	217	98	101	171	87	72	46

2014: PGA: 24 st / 18 ct / 6 t10. (T2 Farmers, 3 WGC-Bridgestone, 3 Byron Nelson, 5 Hawaii, 5 British Open, etc.). Continued establishing himself as a well-above-average PGA Tour player, finishing 58th in FedEx Cup points and a career-best 32nd in $$$.

OUTLOOK: Other then 2011 (which wasn't terrible), has been a very consistent earner since joining the PGA Tour in 2009. Regained some of his lost driving distance (32) in 2014 (17 and 31 in 2009 and '10, 102 in 2013) which helped jump his Ball Striking from 130 to 79. Remains solidly above the median in numerous areas and has become more consistently relevant week-to-week. Seems about ready to win again.

STATS: Driving Distance: B+   Driving Accuracy: C+   GIR: B   Short Game: B+   Putting: B-

---

Leonard, Justin Charles Garrett (USA) (42)
b. Dallas, TX 6/15/1972. 5'9" 170 lbs. Four-time All-American, Nicklaus (1994) and Haskins (1994) Awards winner, and NCAA individual champion (1994) at U of Texas. Won 1992 U.S. Amateur (8 & 7 over Tom Scherrer) at Muirfield Village GC. TP: 1994. Three-time AJGA All-American. Highly skilled shotmaker who played his way onto the Tour in 1994 without visiting Q School, earning enough money in 13 starts to qualify off the Non-Member $$$ list – a path previously taken only by Gary Hallberg, Scott Verplank and Phil Mickelson. Won the 1997 British Open at Troon with a brilliant closing 65, beating Jesper Parnevik and Darren Clarke by three. Nearly claimed a second Claret Jug at Carnoustie in 1999, losing a three-way playoff to winner Paul Lawrie and Jean Van de Velde, who'd tragically melted down at the 72nd. Holed clinching putt in the 1999 Ryder Cup at The Country Club, sparking a controversial/overzealous American celebration. Won the 1998 Players Championship (beat Glen Day and Tom Lehman by two). Lost 2004 PGA Championship in three-way playoff with winner Vijay Singh and Chris DiMarco. Slumped in 2006 but came on towards the close of 2007, winning the Texas Open and lifting himself back into the world top 50 by early '08. Has become proficient at retaining his card but hasn't won since 2008. **Teams**: Walker Cup: 1993 (3-0-0). Eisenhower Trophy: 1992. Ryder Cup (3): 1997-99-08 (O: 2-4-6, S: 0-1-2). Presidents Cup (5): 1996-98-03-05-09 (8-11-4). World Cup (2): 1997-03. **OWR Best**: 6 - May, 1998.

PGA Tour Wins (12): 1996: Buick Open **1997**: Kemper Open, British Open **1998**: Players Championship **2000**: Texas Open (Westin) **2001**: Texas Open **2002**: Heritage Classic (Worldcom) **2003**: Honda Classic **2005**: Bob Hope Classic (90H), Memphis Classic (FedEx) **2007**: Texas Open (Valero) **2008**: Memphis Classic (Stanford St Jude).
Other Wins: CVS Classic: 2000 (w/D.Love III).
Amateur Wins: U.S. Amateur: 1992   Western Am (2): 1992-93   Southern Am (2): 1992-93   –   NCAA Individual: 1994.

Leonard, Justin Charles Garrett, Cont'd

	93	94	95	96	97	98	99	00	01	02	03	04	05	06	07	08	09	10	11	12	13	14
Masters	MC	-	-	T27	**T7**	T8	T18	T28	T27	T20	MC	T35	T13	T39	-	T20	MC	MC	-	-	-	-
US Open	T68	-	-	T50	T36	T40	T15	T16	MC	T12	T20	MC	T23	MC	MC	T36	MC	T14	-	-	-	59
British	MC	-	T58	MC	**Win**	T57	**T2P**	T41	MC	T14	MC	T16	T52	-	MC	T16	**T8**	MC	MC	MC	T13	MC
PGA	-	-	**T8**	**T5**	**2**	MC	MC	T41	**T10**	**T4**	MC	**T2P**	MC	MC	MC	T58	T67	T39	-	-	-	-
Money (A)	Am	126*	22	11	**5**	**8**	**8**	14	25	**8**	17	42	12	109	33	**10**	30	87	91	140	119	117
OWR	621	351	54	29	11	15	13	18	40	17	20	39	33	126	89	23	45	120	204	340	221	334

2014: PGA: 22 st / 16 ct / 2 t10. (T3 Humana, T6 Mayakoba). Finished 120th in FedEx Cup points, hanging on despite missing his last three cuts.

OUTLOOK: Has forever been a short-but-straight type with an elite wedge and a very strong short game. Interestingly, even at age 42, his putting numbers remain among the elite (8 in SGP, 13 in Total Putting) - which is good because most of his long game numbers lie near the very bottom. Those putting numbers tend to fade in one's 40s, but on shorter, accuracy-oriented layouts, he can still be a factor.

STATS: Driving Distance: C-   Driving Accuracy: A-   GIR: C   Short Game: A   Putting: A-

---

Levet, Thomas Jean Roget (France) (46)
b. Paris, France 9/5/1968. 5'9" 160 lbs. TP: 1988. France's top golfer since the long-ago days of Arnaud Massy. Unsuccessfully played the PGA Tour in 1994 (the first Frenchman to try, making 10 starts) and became the first native to win an open major event on French soil since 1969 by taking the 1998 Cannes Open. Stepped up in class by winning the 2001 British Masters in a four-way playoff. Lost the 2002 British Open in another four-man playoff (plus sudden death) to Ernie Els. After returning to America for a tough four-year run (from 2003-2006), then suffering a severe bout with vertigo in 2006, ended a four-year E Tour drought at the 2008 Open de Andalucia. Claimed a long-coveted victory in the French Open in 2011, beating Mark Foster and Thorbjørn Olesen by one. **Teams**: Eisenhower Trophy: 1988. Ryder Cup: 2004 (O: 1-2-0, S: 1-0-0). Seve Trophy (2): 2002-05. World Cup (8): 1998-00-01-02-03-04-05-09. **OWR Best**: 41 - Jan, 2005.

European Tour Wins (6): 1998: Cannes Open   **2001**: British Masters   **2004**: Scottish Open   **2008**: Open de Andalucia   **2009**: Spanish Open   **2011**: French Open.

Other Wins: 1 Euro Challenge (1993)   +   French Pro (3): 1988-91-92   National Omnium (France): 1990   Toulouse Open (France): 1997   French Masters: 1997.

	92	93	94	95	96	97	98	99	00	01	02	03	04	05	06	07	08	09	10	11	12	13	14
Masters	-	-	-	-	-	-	-	-	-	-	-	MC	-	T13	MC	-	-	-	-	-	-	-	-
US Open	-	-	-	-	-	-	-	-	-	-	T18	-	MC	T52	-	-	MC	T45	-	MC	-	-	-
British	-	-	-	-	-	-	MC	T49	-	T66	**T2P**	T22	**T5**	T34	-	-	T38	MC	-	-	-	-	-
PGA	-	-	-	-	-	-	-	-	-	-	71	-	MC	MC	-	-	-	T51	-	-	-	-	-
Money (A)	-	-	-	-	-	-	-	-	-	-	133	-	150	200	-	-	-	-	-	-	-	-	-
Money (E)	103	110	88	98	191	-	69	83	88	19	25	78	**5**	66	-	79	60	28	110	45	96	136	221
OWR	492	428	432	358	531	858	256	287	340	97	79	124	42	87	450	343	151	107	257	161	207	425	936

2014: E: 25 st / 3 ct / 0 t10. (T17 South African). Crashed to a disastrous 221st in $$$, making only three cuts and posting only one top 25.

OUTLOOK: Has reached the age where both his power and putting stroke have gone around the bend, making the entire game a major challenge. A sustained charge back seems unlikely at this point, but the record does suggest that he may still be able to rise to the occasion on French soil.

STATS: Driving Distance: C-   Driving Accuracy: C   GIR: B-   Short Game: B   Putting: D

Levin, Spencer Joseph (USA) (30)
b. Sacramento, CA 6/15/1984. 5'10" 155 lbs. Two-time All-American at U of New Mexico (after transferring from UCLA). TP: 2005. Two-time AJGA All-American. Father, Don, was a three-time All-American at San Jose State and played the PGA Tour in the early 1980s. Following a strong amateur run, played the Canadian Tour in 2007 (winning twice) and the Web.com Tour in 2008 before joining the PGA Tour full-time in 2009. Progressed steadily each year, with 2011 including 13 top 25s, six top 10s and a playoff loss to Johnson Wagner at the Mayakoba Classic. Lost another chance to secure his first PGA Tour win at the 2012 Waste Management Phoenix Open, where he led by six through 54 holes, then shot 75 to finish 3rd. Missed nearly all of 2013 after having thumb surgery, with the injury popping up to somewhat limit his 2014 as well. **Teams**: Palmer Cup: 2005. **OWR Best**: 60 - Jun, 2012.

Other Wins: Iberostar Riviera Maya Open (Canada): 2007   Times Colonist Open (Canada): 2007.

Amateur Wins: Porter Cup: 2004   –   Northern California Am (2): 2002-04   Azalea Inv: 2003   California Am: 2004   Scratch Players: 2004.

	04	05	06	07	08	09	10	11	12	13	14
Masters	-	-	-	-	-	-	-	-	-	-	-
US Open	T13	MC	-	-	-	-	-	MC	-	-	-
British	-	-	-	MC	-	-	-	T44	-	-	-
PGA	-	-	-	-	-	-	-	T26	MC	-	-
Money (A)	-	-	-	-	-	141	74	31	68	-	174
OWR	-	538	856	381	211	391	245	93	133	312	390

2014: PGA: 20 st / 9 ct / 0 t10. (T12 Frys.com). Finished 163rd in FedEx Cup points while still affected by a 2012 thumb injury.

OUTLOOK: Was coming off three strong PGA Tour campaigns when he injured his thumb in October, 2012 and hasn't been the same since. The big problem: His GIR averaged 31 from 2009-2011 but fell to 109 in 2014. Will begin 2015 on an eight-event medical extension which he appears to have a good chance of clearing. When healthy he looked a very solid young player...so at the moment, it all comes down to his thumb.

STATS: Driving Distance: C   Driving Accuracy: B+   GIR: B   Short Game: B+   Putting: B

Levy, Alexander (France) (24)
b. Orange, CA 8/1/1990. 6'2" 190 lbs. TP: 2011. Despite being born abroad, is a French citizen who played on that nation's victorious 2010 Eisenhower Trophy team. Also won the 2009 French Amateur before beginning a professional career which commenced with two years on the Challenge Tour before he reached the E Tour (via Q School) for 2013. Kept his card by finishing 109th in 2013 $$$ but solidified his status by winning the 2014 Volvo China Open, riding a second round 62 to a four-shot victory over Tommy Fleetwood. Again went low (63-61) at the 2014 Portugal Masters, winning by three after rain washed out the final two rounds. Went on to finish 9th in E Tour $$$, establishing himself as a young man to watched. **Teams**: Eisenhower Trophy: 2010. **OWR Best**: 52 - Dec, 2014.

Levy, Alexander, Cont'd

European Tour Wins (2): 2014: China Open (Volvo), Portugal Masters (36H).
Amateur Wins: French Am: 2009 - French International Am: 2010.

	13	14
Masters	-	-
US Open	-	-
British	-	-
PGA	-	T30
Money (E)	109	9
OWR	226	53

2014: E: 30 st / 25 ct / 3 t10. (Won Volvo China, Won Port Masters, T2P BMW Masters). Experienced a truly impressive breakout year, winning early in China, late in Portugal, and losing in a four-way playoff at the BMW Masters. Also finished 9th in $$$, a surprise to even his most ardent boosters.

OUTLOOK: Not surprisingly, his numbers skyrocketed in 2014, cementing his place as a powerful player whose tee-to-green skills appear destined to rank among Europe's best. Though his putter looks to be his weakest link, it is hardly terrible - plus, as his occasional bursts of low scoring show, he is clearly capable of holing a bunch. Was 2014 something of a stretch? Maybe, but the bet here is that he won't slip too much in 2015.

STATS: Driving Distance: A   Driving Accuracy: B   GIR: A-   Short Game: B+   Putting: B

Lewis, Tom (England) (23)

b. Welwyn Garden City, England 1/5/1991. 5'10" 165 lbs. TP: 2011. Son of ex-E Tour journeyman Bryan Lewis. Quit school at 16 to concentrate on golf. Made an international splash with an opening 65 at the 2011 Open Championship (while paired with Tom Watson), the lowest Major championship round ever shot by an amateur. Turned pro several months later and quickly broke through for his maiden E Tour win at the 2011 Portugal Masters (beating Rafael Cabrera-Bello by two) before settling in as a steady earner, climbing slowly through 2013, then retaining his card 104th in $$$) in 2014. **Awards**: E Tour Rookie of the Year: 2011. **Teams**: Walker Cup: 2011 (1-2-1). Eisenhower Trophy: 2010. **OWR Best**: 162 - May, 2012.

European Tour Wins (1): 2011: Portugal Masters.
Amateur Wins: British Boys: 2009   St Andrews Links Trophy: 2011.

	11	12	13	14
Masters	-	-	-	-
US Open	-	-	-	MC
British	T30	-	-	-
PGA	-	-	-	-
Money (E)	66*	117	94	104
OWR	172	275	408	405

2014: E: 27 st / 21 ct / 1 t10. (T8 Hassan). Played steady golf (21 made cuts) but little more, logging only one top 10 and finishing 104th in $$$.

OUTLOOK: On the plus side, while he's yet to live up to the promise shown in 2011 at Royal St. George's, he seems more comfortable playing at this level than many a 23 year old. On the minus, he shows little sign of blossoming into anything beyond a journeyman - but he's hardly out of time.

STATS: Driving Distance: B+   Driving Accuracy: C   GIR: B   Short Game: C+   Putting: B-

---

Lewton, Stephen Michael (England) (31)

b. Northampton, England 5/5/1983. 6'4" 185 lbs. All-American at North Carolina St. TP: 2008. After a solid collegiate career in America, joined the 2011 European Tour via Q School but lost his card. Headed to Asia thereafter where, after two middling seasons, he broke through to win the 2014 Mercuries Taiwan Masters, where he beat veterans Adilson da Silva and Antonio Lascuña by two. **Teams**: Palmer Cup: 2006. **OWR Best**: 288 - Oct, 2014.

Asian Tour Wins (1): 2014: Taiwan Masters.
Amateur Wins: New South Wales Medal (Australia): 2006   Avondale Medal (Australia): 2006.

	11	12	13	14
Masters	-	-	-	-
US Open	-	-	-	-
British	-	-	-	-
PGA	-	-	-	-
Money (E)	209	-	-	-
Money (As)	-	86	58	13
OWR	1094	1020	521	298

2014: ASIA: 16 st / 11 ct / 3 t10. (Incl. Won Taiwan Masters, T4 Solaire). Claimed his first win and finished a career-best 13th in Asian Tour $$$.

OUTLOOK: Seems to have found a niche for himself on the Asian circuit, where he has now won once and seen his earnings climb for three straight seasons. Has the necessary length to potentially succeed in Europe, but for now seems rooted in the Far East.

STATS: Driving Distance: A-   Driving Accuracy: C   GIR: C   Short Game: C   Putting: B+

Li, Hao-Tong (China) (19)

b. Hunan, China 8/3/1995. 6'0" 175 lbs. TP: 2011. Among the highest rated of China's crop of young talent, he turned pro at age 16, began playing professionally on the OneAsia Tour at age 18, then ranked among the elite of the new PGA Tour China circuit in 2014 as a 19-year-old. Won three of the final four events on the latter tour and topped its Order of Merit, but gained more attention for his victory at the OneAsia's 2014 Nanshan China Masters, where he ran away to a four-shot triumph. His PGA China finish made him exempt on the Web.com Tour in 2015. **OWR Best**: 189 - Dec, 2014.

OneAsia Tour Wins (1): 2014: Nanshan China Masters.
Other Wins: Henan Open (PGA-China): 2014   Hainan Open (PGA-China): 2014   CTS Tycoon Championship (PGA-China): 2014.

Li, Hao-Tong, Cont'd

	13	14
Masters	-	-
US Open	-	-
British	-	-
PGA	-	-
Money (O)	58	2
OWR	730	192

2014: At age 19, topped the inaugural PGA Tour China Order of Merit, exploding for three victories in the circuit's final four events. Drew greater attention by also winning the OneAsia Tour's Nanshan Masters, and climbing into the OWR top 200.

OUTLOOK: One of the game's more intriguing prospects who few in the West have actually seen play. A T35 at November's WGC-HSBC Champions suggests that he may not be overmatched against the big boys. Is exempt on the 2015 Web.com Tour, so we may start to get a firsthand look.

STATS: Driving Distance: --   Driving Accuracy: --   GIR: --   Short Game: --   Putting: --

---

Liang, Wen-Chong (China) (36)
b. Zhongshan, China 8/02/1978. 5'7" 135 lbs. TP: 1999. Heir apparent to Liang-Wei Zhang as China's top player, despite an odd, baseball-like swing. Played three winless seasons in Japan beginning in 2004, but initially was a regular winner on the minor (now-defunct) Chinese Tour. Scored his first major win at the European/Asian co-sanctioned 2007 Singapore Masters, leading to a first-place finish in the '07 Asian Order of Merit. Added the Asian Tour's 2009 Indian Open before starring on the new OneAsia circuit, winning three of the tour's first 15 events and claiming its 2010 Order of Merit title. Won again on the Asian Tour in 2013 at the Manila Masters, beating Prom Meesawat in a playoff. Spent most of 2014 playing in Japan. **Teams**: World Cup (6): 2001-07-08-09-11-13. **OWR Best**: 57 - Aug, 2010.

European Tour Wins (1): 2007: Singapore Masters.
Asian Tour Wins (2): 2008: Indian Open **2013**: Manila Masters.
OneAsia Tour Wins (4): 2009: Midea China Classic **2010**: Luxehills Chengdu Open, Thailand Open **2012**: China Masters.
Other Wins: Kunming Classic (China) (2): 1999-05   Dalian Classic (China) (2): 1999-02   Beijing Classic (2): 1999-00   Shenzhen Classic (China): 1999   Shanghai Classic (2): 2000-01   Davidoff Nation's Cup (China) (w/L.W.Zhang): 2001   Hainan (China): 2006   Omega (China): 2006.
Amateur Wins: China Am (3): 1996-97-98.

	02	03	04	05	06	07	08	09	10	11	12	13	14
Masters	-	-	-	-	-	-	MC	-	-	-	-	-	-
US Open	-	-	-	-	-	-	-	-	-	-	-	-	MC
British	-	-	-	-	-	T64	MC	-	-	-	-	-	-
PGA	-	-	-	-	-	MC	-	-	T8	MC	-	-	-
Money (E)	-	-	-	-	-	88	127	54	72	-	101*	78	-
Money (J)	-	-	53	49	21	-	-	-	-	-	-	-	32
Money (As)	12*	-	-	-	-	1	4	2*	-	-	-	6*	-
Money (O)	-	-	-	-	-	-	-	-	1	42*	6*	-	-
OWR	492	583	258	195	140	86	107	82	67	251	190	104	174

2014: JAP: 14 st / 12 ct / 5 t10. (2 KBC Augusta, T3 ANA, 5 Taiheiyo, T8 Indonesia, T9 Diamond Cup). His round-the-Far-East odyssey landed him primarily in Japan in 2014, where he logged top 10s in more than one-third of his starts and finished 32nd in $$$.

OUTLOOK: Primarily confines himself to the Far East but he's clearly shown that he can compete with most of the E Tour's best. There are few signs that he plans on coming West – or that he won't continue on his present successful course for several more years to come.

STATS (LTD): Driving Distance: B   Driving Accuracy: B   GIR: A-   Short Game: B+   Putting: A-

---

Lima, José-Filipe (France/Portugal) (33)
b. Versailles, France 11/26/1981. 5'10" 170 lbs. TP: 2002. Portuguese national who was born and raised in France, where his father was a club professional. Got off to a fast professional start by winning back-to-back on the 2004 Challenge Tour, with the latter event (the St. Omer Open) being co-sanctioned by the European Tour, thus earning him immediate status. Retained his card from 2005-2007 but spent 2011-2013 back on the Challenge Tour, eventually playing his way back for 2014 - and then falling back once again. **Teams**: World Cup (2): 2005-13. **OWR Best**: 183 - Jun, 2005.

European Tour Wins (1): 2004: St. Omer Open.
Other Wins: 3 Euro Challenge (2004-2009) +   Masters 13 (France): 2004   Masters 13 (France): 2005.
Amateur Wins: French Open Stroke Play: 2000.

	04	05	06	07	08	09	10	11	12	13	14
Masters	-	-	-	-	-	-	-	-	-	-	-
US Open	-	MC	-	-	-	-	-	-	-	-	-
British	-	-	-	MC	T70	-	-	-	-	-	-
PGA	-	-	-	-	-	-	-	-	-	-	-
Money (E)	131	73	63	85	122	160*	161	225*	315*	-	156
OWR	280	261	244	330	427	190	438	450	520	225	497

2014: E: 24 st / 11 ct / 1 t10. (T10 Madeira). Returned from three years in the wilderness but finished 156th in $$$, losing his card once more.

OUTLOOK: After three years on the Challenge Tour, he did very little to suggest he's ready for the big stage in 2014, struggling from tee to green (and thereafter) and recording his lone top 10 at the Tour's lightest-field event. Realistically, it's difficult to be optimistic at this point...

STATS (LTD): Driving Distance: B   Driving Accuracy: C   GIR: C   Short Game: B-   Putting: C+

Lin, Wen-Tang (Taiwan) (40)
b. Hsinchu City, Taiwan 06/28/1974. 5'7" 165 lbs. TP: 1996. Comes from a well-known Taiwanese golfing family, his father, uncle and two brothers all being professionals. Found his game in his early 30s, claiming his first win at the 2006 Taiwan Open, then winning on the Asian Tour in each of the following three seasons. Finished 2nd in the Asian Order of Merit in 2008 after winning the Asian Tour

Lin, Wen-Tang, Cont'd

International by five shots. Won the 2008 Hong Kong Open in a thrilling playoff over Rory McIlroy and Francesco Molinari. Was eligible for E Tour membership thereafter, but rarely played. **Teams:** Eisenhower Trophy: 1992. World Cup (2): 2008-09. **OWR Best:** 47 - Jan, 2009.

European Tour Wins (1): 2008: Hong Kong Open ('09).
Asian Tour Wins (5): 2006: Taiwan Open **2007**: Brunei Open **2008**: Asia Tour Int'l **2009**: Taiwan Masters **2013**: Solaire Open.
Other Wins: 1 Asian Dev (2010) + Hsin Fong Open (Taiwan): 1998 Taiwan PGA: 2004.

	98	99	00	01	02	03	04	05	06	07	08	09	10	11	12	13	14
Masters	-	-	-	-	-	-	-	-	-	-	-	MC	-	-	-	-	-
US Open	-	-	-	-	-	-	-	-	-	-	-	-	-	-	-	-	-
British	-	-	-	-	-	-	-	-	-	-	-	-	-	-	-	-	-
PGA	-	-	-	-	-	-	-	-	-	-	-	-	-	-	-	-	-
Money (As)	-	54	-	-	-	-	-	-	26	28	2	12*	26*	55	66	47	76
OWR	-	-	-	-	-	577	517	465	231	171	49	99	277	447	701	478	536

2014: ASIA: 13 st / 6 ct / 1 t10. (T5 Indonesia Masters). Had a disappointing year, making only six cuts and falling to 76th in Asian Tour $$$.

OUTLOOK: Though clearly still capable of contending in Asia, is well off his peak of the late 2000s. At age 39, is certainly still capable of producing some better golf but a lack of length and limited ball striking numbers don't bode well. Seems unlikely to venture out of Asia at this point.

STATS: Driving Distance: C   Driving Accuracy: B+   GIR: C+   Short Game: B-   Putting: B-

---

Lingmerth, David Thomas (Sweden) (27)
b. Tranas, Sweden 7/22/1987. 5'7" 175 lbs. Division 2 All-American at U of West Florida before transferring to Arkansas. TP: 2010. Moved directly from college to the Web.com Tour where he narrowly missed graduating to the PGA Tour in 2011 (finishing 27th in $$$), then qualified a year later by winning once and finishing 10th in $$$. Wasted little time competing on the PGA Tour, losing a three-way playoff (to Brian Gay) at the 2013 Humana Challenge in his second career start, and later tying for second at the Player's Championship. **Teams:** Palmer Cup: 2010. **OWR Best:** 76 - Jul, 2013.

Other Wins: 1 Web.com (2012).
Amateur Wins: Dixie Am: 2007.

	12	13	14
Masters	-	-	-
US Open	-	T17	-
British	-	-	-
PGA	-	MC	-
Money (A)	-	46	128
OWR	237	115	169

2014: PGA: 26 st / 14 ct / 2 t10. (T5 Colonial, T8 Honda). Fell to 134th in FedEx Cup points but played his way back via the Web.com Finals.

OUTLOOK: Following a strong rookie year, stumbled a bit in 2014 before saving himself in the Web.com Finals. Has thus far demonstrated a steady all-around skill set with few great strengths, and the combination of 137 in Ball Striking with 130 in Total Putting is hardly ideal. But he showed flashes in 2013, and his Web.com Finals performance was clutch, so he seems ready for some incremental improvement in 2015.

STATS: Driving Distance: B   Driving Accuracy: B   GIR: C+   Short Game: B-   Putting: B

Lipsky, David (USA) (25)
b. Los Angeles, CA 7/14/1988. 5'10" 160 lbs. College: Northwestern U. TP: 2011. After being named Honorable Mention All-American at Northwestern, was medalist at Asian Tour Q School and finished 11th in earnings as a rookie, highlighted by a win at the 2012 Handa Faldo Cambodia Classic (in a playoff with Elmer Salvador) in his third start. Despite being exempt in Asia, opted to play the Web.com Tour in 2013, but finished 179th in $$$. Returned to Asia in 2014 but played in several co-sanctioned E Tour events, tying for 2nd at the Championship at Laguna National, one behind Felipe Aguilar. Scored a breakthrough win at the Omega European Masters (where he edged Graeme Storm on the first extra hole), allowing him to top the Asian Tour Order of Merit. **OWR Best:** 130 - Oct, 2014.

European Tour Wins (1): 2014: European Masters (Omega).
Asia Tour Wins (1): 2012: Faldo Cambodia Classic.

	12	13	14
Masters	-	-	-
US Open	-	-	-
British	-	-	-
PGA	-	-	-
Money (E)	-	-	58*
Money (As)	11	70	1
OWR	248	519	131

2014: ASIA: 14 st / 12 ct / 4 t10. (Incl. Won European Masters, T2 Laguna National, T4 Selangor Masters). Broke through in a big way upon winning the co-sanctioned Omega European Masters in Switzerland, and winning the Asian Tour Order of Merit.

OUTLOOK: After a solid-but-unspectacular college career, has spent three productive years in Asia including something of a breakout campaign in 2014. A lack of length may be a concern, but we'll get a better sense of his upside in 2015 when he'll begin playing regularly in Europe.

STATS: Driving Distance: C+   Driving Accuracy: B   GIR: B   Short Game: B   Putting: B+

Loar, James Edward III (USA) (37)
b. Dallas, TX 11/15/1977. 6'4" 215 lbs. Four-time All-American at Oklahoma St. TP: 2000. Two-time AJGA All-American. Former top prospect who dominated the amateur and collegiate ranks and played on the 1999 Walker Cup team before packing off for part-time excursions onto the Asian Tour from 2002-2006. Won the 2003 Thailand Open and the 2004 Korean Open before eventually returning to play the Web.com Tour in 2007, where he struggled to finish 102nd in $$$. T2 at the 2006 Dunhill Links Championship (five behind

Loar, James Edward III, Cont'd

Padraig Harrington), in a year where he made 10 European Tour starts. Finally joined the PGA Tour (via Q School) in 2012 but made only seven of 23 cuts to finish 210th in $$$. Rallied on the 2013 Web.com Tour, however, winning once and finishing 4th in regular season $$$ - but then fared even worse on the 2014 PGA Tour. **Teams:** Walker Cup: 1999 (2-1-0). Palmer Cup: 1998. **OWR Best:** 171 - Oct, 2006.

Asian Tour Wins (2): 2003: Thailand Open **2004:** Korean Open.
Other Wins: 2 Web.com (2012-2013) + 1 Adams (2011) 6 Gateway (2008-2009).
Amateur Wins: Southern Am: 1999 Sunnehanna Am (2): 1999-00 – Southwestern Am: 1997 Southwestern Am: 1997.

	05	06	07	08	09	10	11	12	13	14
Masters	-	-	-	-	-	-	-	-	-	-
US Open	-	-	-	-	-	-	-	MC	T32	-
British	-	-	-	-	-	-	-	-	-	-
PGA	-	-	-	-	-	-	-	-	-	-
Money (A)	-	-	-	-	-	-	-	210	-	233
OWR	249	172	382	-	-	-	-	491	207	579

2014: PGA: 19 st / 3 ct / 0 t10. (T53 Canadian). Finished 233rd in Fedex Cup points after making only three of 19 cuts,.
OUTLOOK: Despite having lots of international experience and length, has not demonstrated the ability to compete successfully on the PGA Tour. At age 37, he lacks status on the PGA or Web.com Tours, so it will be interesting to see where he appears in 2015.

STATS (LTD): Driving Distance: A-   Driving Accuracy: C   GIR: B   Short Game: C   Putting: B-

---

Lonard, Peter Lawrence (Australia) (47)
b. Sydney, New South Wales, Australia 7/17/1967. 6'0" 225 lbs. TP: 1989. After some fairly quiet beginnings in Europe, emerged from a bout with Ross River Fever to establish himself as one of Australia's top new millennium players. Was a regular winner at home for several years, highlighted by back-to-back Australian Open titles in 2003 and 2004 (the latter by one over Stuart Appleby). Also claimed three Australian PGAs in a seven-year span, led by a three-shot win over David Smail in 2007. Played the PGA Tour full-time from 2002-2009, where he won the 2005 Heritage Classic, beating four players (including Darren Clarke, Jim Furyk and Davis Love III) by two. With nothing more than Past Champion status on the PGA Tour, has opted to play mostly on the Web.com Tour in recent years, but hasn't come close to regaining his PGA Tour card. **Teams:** Presidents Cup (2): 2003-05 (4-4-0). World Cup: 2005. **OWR Best:** 25 - Apr, 2005.

PGA Tour Wins (1): 2005: Heritage Classic (MCI).
Australasian Tour Wins (10): 1997: Ericsson Masters **2000:** Ford Open **2001:** ANZ Championship **2002:** Australian PGA (T w/J.Moseley), Australian Masters **2003:** Australian Open **2004:** New South Wales Open, Australian Open, Australian PGA **2007:** Australian PGA.
Other Wins: Hyundai Team: 2002 (w/R.Beem).

	91	92	93	94	95	96	97	98	99	00	01	02	03	04	05	06	07	08	09	10	11	12	13	14
Masters	-	-	-	-	-	-	-	-	-	-	-	-	MC	MC	MC	MC	-	MC	-	-	-	-	-	-
US Open	-	-	-	-	-	-	-	-	-	-	T66	11	T20	T31	T42	-	-	-	-	-	-	-	-	-
British	-	-	-	-	-	-	T24	-	T49	-	T47	T14	T59	MC	66	T16	-	-	-	-	-	-	-	-
PGA	-	-	-	-	-	-	MC	MC	-	-	T17	T29	MC	MC	MC	-	-	T68	-	-	-	-	-	-
Money (A)	-	-	-	-	-	-	-	-	-	-	41	50	119	34	103	75	66	164	-	-	-	-	-	-
Money (E)	143*	127	-	-	-	-	48	51	75	94	54	40	18	48	-	-	-	-	-	-	-	-	-	-
OWR	198	267	467	735	425	161	65	99	138	175	119	43	28	37	46	86	58	115	418	847	575	683	858	986

2014: Played the Web.com Tour, finishing 155th in $$$. Also made five autumn starts in Australia (best: T18 Australian PGA).
OUTLOOK: Clearly prefers the more lucrative Web.com Tour to returning to Australia, but at age 47 it's a struggle on either side of the ocean now.

STATS: Driving Distance: --   Driving Accuracy: --   GIR: --   Short Game: --   Putting: --

---

Lorenzo-Vera, Michael (France) (29)
b. Bayonne, France 1/28/1985. 5'10" 150 lbs. TP: 2005. After turning pro, played his way onto the Challenge Tour via the Alps circuit, then earned his 2008 E Tour card by winning the final Challenge event of 2007 after opening with a 62. Retained his card (barely) after 2008 but lost it in 2009, and has been battling back ever since. **OWR Best:** 128 - Apr, 2008.

Other Wins: 1 Euro Challenge (2007) + 4 Alps Tour (2005-2009) Open de Landes (France): 2006 Schweppes Grand Prix (France): 2009.

	07	08	09	10	11	12	13	14
Masters	-	-	-	-	-	-	-	-
US Open	-	-	-	-	-	-	-	-
British	-	-	-	-	-	-	-	-
PGA	-	-	-	-	-	-	-	-
Money (E)	-	108	131	188	-	277*	-	-
OWR	141	246	370	574	622	509	940	285

2014: Played full-time on the Challenge Tour, where he regained E Tour privileges (for the first time in four years) by finishing 9th in $$$.
OUTLOOK: Showed flashes in 2007 but is now coming off four winless years on the Challenge Tour - so keeping his card in 2015 is a reasonable goal.

STATS: Driving Distance: --   Driving Accuracy: --   GIR: --   Short Game: --   Putting: --

---

Loupe, Andrew Gravolet (USA) (26)
b. Baton Rouge, LA 11/22/1988. 6'1" 185 lbs. College: Louisiana St. TP: 2011. Twice an Honorable Mention All-American pick at LSU. HS basketball star who also won the 2005 Louisiana Junior and the 2009 Louisiana Am. Had surgery on his left shoulder in June of 2010. After turning pro, spent a year playing mini-tours before joining the Web.com Tour in 2013, where a T6 in the Tour Championship clinched his PGA Tour card. A long hitter who finished 2nd in Web.com Driving Distance in 2013. **OWR Best:** 293 - Apr, 2014.

Amateur Wins: Louisiana Jr: 2005 Louisiana Am: 2009.

Loupe, Andrew Gravolet, Cont'd

	13	14
Masters	-	-
US Open	-	-
British	-	-
PGA	-	-
Money (A)	-	142
OWR	656	412

2014: PGA: 22 st / 10 ct / 1 t10. (T4 Texas). Finished 137th in FedEx Cup points, then failed to play through the Web.com Finals.

OUTLOOK: Will have conditional status in 2015. Has the necessary length to compete at this level, but it looks as though he's a year or two away.

STATS (LTD): Driving Distance: A+   Driving Accuracy: C-   GIR: C+   Short Game: B-   Putting: B+

Love, Davis Milton III (USA) (50)
b. Charlotte, NC 4/13/1964. 6'3" 185 lbs. Three-time All-American at U of North Carolina. TP: 1985. Son of prominent teacher/Tour player Davis Love II. Prodigiously long hitter and hugely consistent money winner, finishing no worse than 33rd in PGA Tour $$$ from 1990-2006. Finished 10 times among the top 10 and five times among the top 5 while logging 20 official Tour victories. Also ranked among the top 10 in the year-end OWR for nine straight years from 1996-2004. Broke a long string of frustrating Major championship losses at the 1997 PGA Championship, winning by five over Justin Leonard at Winged Foot. Five-time winner of the Heritage Classic, including his first PGA Tour triumph (by one over Steve Jones in 1987) and back-to-back titles in 1991 and '92. Also a two-time winner at the AT&T Pebble Beach Pro-Am (2001 and '03) and the old International (1990 and 2003). More importantly, also a two-time victor at the Players Championship, including 2003, when a closing 64 led to a six-shot runaway. From 1995-2005, recorded 19 top-10 finishes in 44 Major championship starts. Missed the close of 2007 and early '08 seasons after injuring his left ankle. His play has steadily declined in his late 40s, and he missed much of early 2013 with neck surgery for spinal stenosis. **Awards**: Bob Jones Award (2013). **Teams**: Walker Cup: 1985 (2-0-1). Ryder Cup (6): 1993-95-97-99-02-04 (O: 9-12-5, S: 3-1-2). Presidents Cup (6): 1994-96-98-00-03-05 (16-8-4). World Cup (5): 1992-93-94-95-97 (won 1992-95 w/F.Couples). **OWR Best**: 2 - Jul, 1998.

PGA Tour Wins (20): 1987: Heritage Classic (MCI) **1990**: The International (Stableford) **1991**: Heritage Classic (MCI) **1992**: Players Championship, Heritage Classic (MCI), Greater Greensboro Open (KMart) **1993**: Tournament of Champions, Las Vegas Inv (90H) **1995**: New Orleans Classic (Freeport-McMoran) **1996**: San Diego Open (Buick Inv) **1997**: PGA Championship, Buick Challenge **1998**: Heritage Classic (MCI) **2001**: AT&T Pro-Am **2003**: AT&T Pro-Am, Players Championship, Heritage Classic (MCI), The International (Stableford) **2006**: Greater Greensboro Open **2008**: Walt Disney Classic (Children's Miracle).

Japan Tour Wins (1): 1998: The Crowns.

Other Wins: JCPenney Mixed Team (2): 1990-95 (both w/B.Daniel)   Kapalua International (2): 1992-97   Shark Shootout: 1992 (w/T.Kite)   World Cup (Individual): 1995   Wendy's 3-Tour Challenge: 1996 (w/F.Couples & P.Stewart)   CVS Classic: 2000 (w/J.Leonard)   Target World Challenge (2): 2000-03   Williams World Challenge: 2000.

Amateur Wins: North & South Am: 1984   –   Middle Atlantic Am: 1984.

	86	87	88	89	90	91	92	93	94	95	96	97	98	99	00	01	02	03	04	05	06	07	08	09
Masters	-	-	MC	-	-	T42	T25	T54	MC	2	T7	T7	T33	2	T7	MC	T14	T15	T6	MC	T22	T27	-	-
US Open	-	-	MC	T33	-	T11	T60	T33	T28	T4	T2	T16	MC	T12	MC	T7	T24	MC	MC	T6	MC	MC	T53	-
British	-	MC	MC	T23	MC	T44	MC	MC	T38	T98	MC	T10	8	T7	T11	T21	T14	T4	T5	MC	MC	MC	T19	T27
PGA	T47	MC	-	T17	T40	T32	T33	T31	MC	MC	MC	Win	T7	T49	T9	T37	T48	MC	T4	T34	MC	MC	MC	MC
Money (A)	77	33	35	44	20	8	2	12	33	6	7	3	11	3	9	5	21	3	10	13	16	96	48	52
OWR	147	60	90	64	44	23	10	9	25	20	9	5	4	4	7	5	9	4	9	19	16	67	80	79

	10	11	12	13	14
Masters	-	MC	-	-	-
US Open	T6	T11	T29	-	-
British	MC	T9	MC	-	-
PGA	T55	T72	MC	MC	MC
Money (A)	73	88	100	167	173
OWR	115	129	151	335	423

2014: PGA: 22 st / 15 ct / 0 t10. (T26 Arnold Palmer). Finished 162nd in FedEx Cup points before debuting on the Champions Tour in September.

OUTLOOK: Though still able to launch the driver with most of the youngsters, has seen his overall skills diminish predictably in his later 40s. Its debatable how competitive he can be on the PGA Tour at this point - but he'll likely be spending most of his time on the Champions Tour anyway.

STATS: Driving Distance: A   Driving Accuracy: C+   GIR: B   Short Game: C   Putting: C-

---

Lovemark, Jamie (USA) (26)
b. Rancho Santa Fe, CA 1/23/1988. 6'4" 210 lbs. Two-time All-American, NCAA individual champion (2007), Nicklaus (2007) and Haskins (2007) Awards winner at USC. TP: 2009. Three-time AJGA All-American who played two years at USC before turning pro. Lost a 2007 Web.com Tour event to Chris Riley in a playoff while still an amateur. Lost a three-way playoff at the 2009 Frys.com Open (to Troy Matteson) in his fourth start as a pro. Web.com Player-of-the-Year as a rookie, winning once and becoming the tour's youngest-ever $$$ leader. Rookie season of 2011 (and much of 2012) was plagued by back problems. Despite considerable talent, continued to struggle through 2014, when he finished 168th in PGA Tour $$$. **Teams**: Walker Cup: 2007 (3-0-0). Eisenhower Trophy: 2008. Palmer Cup: 2007. **OWR Best**: 120 - Oct, 2010.

Other Wins: 1 Web.com (2010).

Amateur Wins: Western Am: 2005   –   Western Jr: 2004   NCAA Individual: 2007.

	09	10	11	12	13	14
Masters	-	-	-	-	-	-
US Open	-	-	-	-	-	-
British	-	-	-	-	-	-
PGA	-	-	-	-	-	-
Money (A)	-	-	231*	-	-	168
OWR	444	133	465	624	391	491

Lovemark, Jamie, Cont'd

2014: PGA: 20 st / 13 ct / 0 t10. (T12 Canadian). Finished 172nd in FedEx Cup points, then failed to play his way back via the Web.com Finals.

OUTLOOK: Highly touted prospect whose fast professional start was sidetracked by back problems. A tall, powerful player whose talent level seems to suggest big things, but whose short game and putting have yet to reach a PGA Tour standard. He's only 26, but the clock is ticking.

STATS (LTD):   Driving Distance: A   Driving Accuracy: C   GIR: C+   Short Game: C+   Putting: B-

---

Lowry, Shane (Ireland) (27)

b. Clara, Ireland 4/2/1987. 6'0" 225 lbs. College: Athlone Institute of Technology. TP: 2009. The son of a well-known Gaelic football player who made a major splash in 2009 by becoming the third amateur in history to win a European Tour event, opening 67-62 en route to claiming the Irish Open (in a playoff with Robert Rock) at the County Louth GC. Enjoyed steady E Tour success upon turning pro, proving himself a strong earner and claiming his second victory at the 2012 Portuguese Masters, where a closing 66 erased a four-stroke 54-hole deficit and proved enough to edge Ross Fisher by one. Seemed on the verge of becoming a second-tier E Tour sort before stepping up noticeably in 2014, finishing 2nd at the BMW PGA Championship, logging an impressive seven top 10s and ranking a career-best 10th in $$$. **Teams**: Eisenhower Trophy: 2008. World Cup: 2013. **OWR Best**: 44 - Dec, 2014.

European Tour Wins (2): 2009: Irish Open*   **2012**: Portugal Masters.

Amateur Wins: Irish Am Closed: 2007   West of Ireland: 2008   North of Ireland: 2008   Mullingar Cup: 2008   Lee Valley Cup: 2009.

	09	10	11	12	13	14
Masters	-	-	-	-	-	-
US Open	-	-	MC	-	-	MC
British	-	T37	-	-	T32	T9
PGA	-	MC	-	-	T57	T47
Money (E)	153	62	41	29	36	10
OWR	135	161	119	52	76	44

2014: E: 27 st / 19 ct / 7 t10. (2 BMW PGA, T2 Wales, T4 Scottish, T6 Dunhill Links, T9 British Open, etc.). Though he failed to win, enjoyed a breakout season overall, logging seven top 10s and 13 top 25s en route to a 10th-place finish in $$$.

OUTLOOK: After firmly establishing himself as a top-40 type over the last five years, stepped up in class in 2014. Keyed his year by finishing 2nd at the flagship BMW PGA and was a regular threat thereafter. The obvious question now is whether he can translate his improved across-the-board form into more victories, with the sense here being that he can, perhaps fairly early in 2015. Also looks like a potential force in match play.

STATS: Driving Distance: B+   Driving Accuracy: A-   GIR: B+   Short Game: B-   Putting: A

Luiten, Willibrordus Adrianus Maria ("Joost") (Netherlands) (28)

b. Bleiswijk, Netherlands 1/7/1986. 5'10" 155 lbs. TP: 2006. Touted Dutch prospect who won the 2005 Dutch, Spanish and German Amateurs, as well as Dutch Boys and Youths titles in 2004. Led The Netherlands to a surprise victory at the 2006 Eisenhower Trophy. Mostly played the Challenge Tour in 2007 but managed a near storybook finish at the KLM (Dutch) Open, where he finished 2nd, one back of Ross Fisher. Battled a significant wrist injury for much of 2008 and '09 but returned to health for a successful 2010 that saw him finish 28th in the E Tour Order of Merit and log four top-10 finishes. Claimed his first major tour victory in late 2011, beating Daniel Chopra by one at the rain-shortened Johor Open (E Tour/Asian Tour). Added the light-field Lyoness Open in 2013 before breaking through to win his coveted Dutch Open in September, beating Miguel Ángel Jiménez in a playoff. Added a fourth E Tour win at the 2014 Wales Open, where he edged Tommy Fleetwood and Shane Lowry by one en route to finishing a career-best 11th in $$$. **Teams**: Eisenhower Trophy: 2006. Palmer Cup: 2006. Seve Trophy: 2013. World Cup: 2011. **OWR Best**: 28 - Nov, 2014.

European Tour Wins (4): 2011: Iskandar Johor Open (54H)   **2013**: Lyoness Open, Dutch Open (KLM)   **2014**: Wales Open (ISPS Handa).

Other Wins: 2 Euro Challenge (2007)   +   1 Alps Tour (2009).

Amateur Wins: Dutch Am: 2005   Spanish Am: 2005   German Am: 2005   –   Dutch Boys: 2004   Dutch Youths: 2004.

	07	08	09	10	11	12	13	14
Masters	-	-	-	-	-	-	-	T26
US Open	-	-	-	-	-	-	-	MC
British	-	-	-	T63	T65	-	-	MC
PGA	-	-	-	-	-	T21	MC	T26
Money (E)	-	124	-	28	24	44	12	11
OWR	102	226	794	97	64	108	49	29

2014: E: 27 st / 24 ct / 9 t10. (Won Wales, 3 Lyoness, 3 World Match Play, T3 Volvo Champ, 4 Spanish, etc.). Continued settling in among the E Tour's elite, winning at the Wales Open, frequently contending and finishing a career-best 11th in $$$.

OUTLOOK: Has emerged in his late 20s as the star many predicted he would be. A steady and very accurate ball striker who has yet to seriously branch out beyond the E Tour, making limited U.S. starts, always in advance of a Major or WGC. Given his age and steadiness, there is little reason to think he won't continue to improve incrementally, and a genuinely prominent international victory could well be reached in 2015.

STATS: Driving Distance: B   Driving Accuracy: A-   GIR: A-   Short Game: B-   Putting: B+

Lunde, William Jeremiah (USA) (39)

b. San Diego, CA 11/18/1975. 6'1" 220 lbs. Two-time All-American at UNLV. TP: 1998. After starring on UNLV's 1998 national championship team, began his professional career on mini-tours, and also spent time overseas (T2 at the 2004 New Zealand PGA) before eventually joining the Web.com for 2004 and '05. Fell back to the mini-tours for two more seasons before a 5th-place finish on the 2008 Web.com earned a PGA Tour card for 2009. Though largely a journeyman on Tour, won the 2010 Turning Stone Classic (in his 53rd career start) by closing with 66 to edge J.J. Henry by one. Fell from the top 125 in $$$ in 2011 and '12, before plunging (playing on conditional status) in 2013 and playing the Web.com in 2014. **OWR Best**: 154 - Mar, 2009.

PGA Tour Wins (1): 2010: Turning Stone Championship.

Other Wins: 1 Web.com (2008)   +   1 NGA/Hooters (2002)   1 Gateway (2003).

Amateur Wins: Monroe Inv: 1998.

Lunde, William Jeremiah, Cont'd

	03	04	05	06	07	08	09	10	11	12	13	14
Masters	-	-	-	-	-	-	-	-	-	-	-	-
US Open	MC	-	-	-	-	-	-	-	-	MC	-	-
British	-	-	-	-	-	-	-	-	-	-	-	-
PGA	-	-	-	-	-	-	-	MC	T39	-	-	-
Money (A)	-	-	-	-	-	-	102	83	130	133	183*	-
OWR	-	643	842	-	-	232	265	258	299	375	495	388

2014: Played the Web.com Tour full-time, clinching a return to the PGA Tour by finishing 22nd in regular season $$$.

OUTLOOK: Despite winning in 2010, has never proven himself consistently capable of thriving on the PGA Tour. Will return in 2015 but playing from 44th on the Web.com priority list, his opportunities to achieve major success may be numerically limited.

STATS: Driving Distance: B   Driving Accuracy: C+   GIR: B   Short Game: B-   Putting: C+

Lundberg, Mikael (Sweden) (41)
b. Helsingborg, Sweden 8/13/1973. 5'11" 200 lbs. College: Wallace (AL) JC. TP: 1997. Spent one year at an American junior college, then most of his professional career bouncing back and forth between the E and Challenge Tours. Won twice on the latter circuit over a 10-year span but claimed his two E Tour victories in an unlikely location, taking the Russian Open both in 2005 (when it was co-sanctioned by the Challenge Tour) and 2008, when he beat Jose Manuel Lara by two. Ended a six-year drought by winning the light-field 2014 Lyoness Open in Austria, beating Bernd Wiesberger on the first hole of a playoff. **Teams**: Eisenhower Trophy: 1994. **OWR Best**: 145 - Jan, 2009.

European Tour Wins (3): 2005: Russian Open **2008**: Russian Open **2014**: Lyoness Open.

Other Wins: 2 Euro Challenge (1997-2007) + Slovenian Open: 1995 Husqvarna Open (Sweden): 1995.

	01	02	03	04	05	06	07	08	09	10	11	12	13	14
Masters	-	-	-	-	-	-	-	-	-	-	-	-	-	-
US Open	-	-	-	-	-	-	-	-	-	-	-	-	-	-
British	-	-	-	-	-	-	-	-	-	-	-	-	-	-
PGA	-	-	-	-	-	-	-	-	-	-	-	-	-	-
Money (E)	63	96	137	261*	155*	156	-	63	144	125	135*	128	168	96
OWR	230	328	460	594	326	409	263	146	366	664	374	343	675	341

2014: E: 24 st / 12 ct / 2 t10. (Won Lyoness, T9 Denmark). After losing his card for five straight years, actually made only incremental improvement over the entire season, but took one giant leap in winning the Lyoness Open, leading to a 96th-place finish in $$$ and an exempt 2015.

OUTLOOK: Appears about five years removed from his best golf, but was experienced enough to turn his best week into a 2014 win, at least somewhat reinvigorating his career. Even with a strong putter, it's unlikely that he can sustain such play, but he'll have all of 2015 to try.

STATS: Driving Distance: C-   Driving Accuracy: B-   GIR: C-   Short Game: B   Putting: A-

---

Lyle, Jarrod (Australia) (33)
b. Shepparton, Victoria, Australia 8/21/1981. 6'2" 235 lbs. TP: 2004. After recovering from acute myeloid leukemia as a teenager, enjoyed great amateur success (finishing 2nd at the 2004 Australian and New Zealand Amateurs) before turning professional. Named the 2005 Rookie of the Year on his native Australasian Tour before twice playing (and graduating from) the Web.com Tour, finishing 18th in 2006 and 4th during a two-win 2008. Has since played regularly on the PGA Tour but has never finished among the top 125 in PGA Tour $$$, playing his way through Q School multiple times. Had a recurrence of his Leukemia after seven 2012 starts, returned to competitive play in the fall in Australia, and will play on a medical extension upon his U.S. return in 2014. **Teams**: Eisenhower Trophy: 2004. **OWR Best**: 142 - Apr, 2006.

Other Wins: 2 Web.com (2008).

Amateur Wins: Lake Maquarie Am (2): 2003-04.

	05	06	07	08	09	10	11	12	13	14
Masters	-	-	-	-	-	-	-	-	-	-
US Open	-	-	-	T48	-	-	-	-	-	-
British	-	MC	-	-	-	-	-	-	-	-
PGA	-	-	-	-	-	-	-	-	-	-
Money (A)	-	-	164	-	175	162	167	164*	-	-
OWR	295	179	346	243	375	347	390	385	-	893

2014: Made four Web.com starts (including a T11 and three MCs) after recovering from his second bout with leukemia.

OUTLOOK: Will return to the PGA Tour in 2015 on a 20-event medical extension. A popular - and obviously gutsy - player who has long seemed determined to play in America. Has yet to have an impact on the PGA Tour but will certainly be a huge sentimental favorite going forward.

STATS (LTD): Driving Distance: B+   Driving Accuracy: C+   GIR: B-   Short Game: B   Putting: B-

---

Lynn, David Anthony (England) (41)
b. Billinge, England 10/20/1973. 6'3" 170 lbs. TP: 1995. Longtime E Tour player who graduated off the Challenge Tour in 1997, lost his E Tour card in '98 (after missing eight cuts by a single shot), regained it via Q School and became a mainstay on the big circuit thereafter. Finished eight times among the E Tour's top 70 $$$ winners from 2001-2008. Won the 2004 Dutch Open (by three over Paul McGinley and Richard Green) the week after he lost a lucky ball marker that he'd used his entire career. In 2012, lifted himself enormously with one great week of golf, finishing 2nd (eight shots behind Rory McIlroy) at the PGA Championship in his second Major start. The runner-up finish earned enough non-member money to qualify for full status on the 2013 PGA Tour. Lost in sudden death (to Derek Ernst) at the 2013 Wells Fargo Championship, but later won on the E Tour with a closing 63 at the Portugal Masters. **Teams**: Seve Trophy: 2013. **OWR Best**: 34 - Oct, 2013.

European Wins (2): 2004: Dutch Open (KLM) **2013**: Portugal Masters.

Other Wins: 1 Euro Challenge (1997).

Amateur Wins: Greek Amateur: 1994.

Lynn, David Anthony, Cont'd

	98	99	00	01	02	03	04	05	06	07	08	09	10	11	12	13	14
Masters	-	-	-	-	-	-	-	-	-	-	-	-	-	-	-	T46	MC
US Open	-	-	-	-	-	-	-	-	-	-	-	-	-	-	-	-	-
British	-	-	-	-	-	T53	-	-	-	-	-	-	-	-	-	MC	-
PGA	-	-	-	-	-	-	-	-	-	-	-	-	-	-	2	T22	-
Money (A)	-	-	-	-	-	-	-	-	-	-	-	-	-	-	-	53	184*
Money (E)	125	185*	63	40	78	41	26	28	46	68	35	89	84	35	18	52	112
OWR	698	581	283	161	232	185	114	91	125	201	145	217	209	91	46	45	227

2014: E: 14 st / 10 ct / 0 t10. (T21 Euro Masters). Spent most of the year playing in Europe, where his form was off just enough to finish 112th in $$$. Also made seven non-Major/WGC starts in America, finishing 184th in $$$ - and thus has 2015 status only in Europe.

OUTLOOK: Was something of a surprising (if brief) success on the PGA Tour, and the run of form that got him there may now be over. Thus seems destined to ply his trade in Europe, where he won as recently as 2013 - but 2015 figures to be a challenge across the board.

STATS: Driving Distance: C   Driving Accuracy: C   GIR: C-   Short Game: A   Putting: A-

---

MacKenzie, William Ruggles (Will) (USA) (40)
b. Greenville, NC 9/28/1974. 5'11" 170 lbs. TP: 2000. A free spirit who gave up golf for 10 years as a teenager, is a professional kayaker and once spent several years living out of his van in Montana. Successfully competed on mini- and Canadian tours before initially joining the PGA Tour in 2005, losing his card, then re-qualifying (via Q School) for 2006. Landed an unexpected victory by making birdie at the 72nd hole to edge Bob Estes by one at the 2006 Reno-Tahoe Open. Claimed a second title at the 2008 Viking Classic, defeating Marc Turnesa and Brian Gay in a playoff. Regained PGA Tour status via the 2013 Web.com finals, then enjoyed his strongest season ever, finishing 51st in earnings. **OWR Best**: 84 - Mar, 2014.

PGA Tour Wins (2): 2006: Reno-Tahoe Open **2008**: Viking Classic.

Other Wins: 3 NGA/Hooters (2003).

	05	06	07	08	09	10	11	12	13	14
Masters	-	-	-	-	-	-	-	-	-	-
US Open	-	-	-	-	-	-	-	-	-	-
British	-	-	-	-	-	-	-	-	-	-
PGA	-	-	T57	-	MC	-	-	-	-	MC
Money (A)	179	100	85	114	126	152	-	224*	-	51
OWR	412	246	203	225	232	402	624	765	317	109

2014: PGA: 27 st / 14 ct / 5 t10. (T2 Texas, T4 Valspar, T6 Honda, T7 Farmers, T9 Frys.com). Returned to the PGA Tour with a vengeance, logging five top 10s and finishing 65th in FedEx Cup points. Did most of his damage early, however, as he missed 11 of 12 cuts from April through August.

OUTLOOK: A streaky sort who, as two career wins testifies, has the skills to compete at the highest level. The secret of his 2014 success is easy to find: His SGP jumped to 64 - a quantum leap above his career average. Can he repeat this in 2015? Well, he does get hot sometimes...

STATS (LTD): Driving Distance: B+   Driving Accuracy: B+   GIR: B+   Short Game: B-   Putting: C+ ⇑

Madsen, Morten Ørum (Denmark) (26)
b. Silkeborg, Denmark 4/9/1988. 6'3" 210 lbs. College: Oregon St. TP: 2011. Twice represented Denmark in the Eisenhower Trophy and played collegiately in the United States. Upon turning pro, won twice in 2011 on the Nordic League mini-tour, then finished 19th on the 2012 Challenge Tour to earn E Tour status for 2013. After retaining his card comfortably as a rookie, claimed his maiden victory at the season-opening South African Open in November (an official 2014 event), beating Jbe' Kruger and Hennie Otto by two. **Teams**: Eisenhower Trophy (2): 2008-10. **OWR Best**: 107 - Jan, 2014.

European Tour Wins (1): 2013: South African Open ('14).

Other Wins: 3 Nordic League (2011-2013).

Amateur Wins: Houborg Open: 2008   Wibroe Cup: 2008   Danish Am Stroke Play: 2009.

	12	13	14
Masters	-	-	-
US Open	-	T28	-
British	MC	-	-
PGA	-	-	-
Money (E)	237*	81	67
OWR	364	119	204

2014: E: 29 st / 16 ct / 2 t10. (Won South African, T3 Port Masters). Wasted little time in stepping up during his sophomore year, winning the South African Open in his first start. Only logged a single top 10 thereafter but still finished a solid 67th in $$$.

OUTLOOK: An intriguing prospect who, in a limited statistical sampling, has shown a profitable blend of power, decent accuracy and an above-the-median putting stroke. His South African win didn't spark a jackpot 2014 but he appears skilled enough to stick around for a while.

STATS: Driving Distance: A   Driving Accuracy: B-   GIR: B-   Short Game: C+   Putting: B+

Maggert, Jeffrey Allan (USA) (50)
b. Columbia, MO 2/20/1964. 5'9" 165 lbs. All-American at Texas A&M. TP: 1986. Two-time AJGA All-American. Began his professional career playing frequently overseas, logging wins on the old Asian Tour and the Australasian circuit. Joined the Web.com Tour in 1990 where, after winning twice and placing 1st in $$$, he graduated to the PGA Tour. Immediately began a run of 11 straight top-75 money finishes between 1991-2001, and remained among the top 100 through 2004. Claimed his first victory at the 1993 Walt Disney Classic, but his biggest win came at the inaugural WGC Match Play (1999), where he beat Andrew Magee at the 38th hole. Consistently strong Major championship player who has logged eight top-5 finishes, including three at the U.S. Open. Slipped a bit beginning in 2005, but claimed his third career PGA Tour victory at the 2006 FedEx St Jude Classic, beating Tom Pernice Jr. by three. Finished 216th in $$$ in 2011, but retained playing privileges with a T13 at Q School, then retained his card in both 2012 and '13 before fading - as he turned 50 - in 2014. **Teams**: Ryder Cup (3):

Maggert, Jeffrey Allan, Cont'd

1995-97-99 (O: 6-5-0, S: 1-2-0). Presidents Cup: 1994 (2-2-0). **OWR Best:** 13 - May, 1999.

PGA Tour Wins (3): 1993: Walt Disney Classic (Oldsmobile) **1999**: WGC-Match Play **2006**: Memphis Classic (FedEx).
Asian Wins (1): 1989: Malaysian Open.
Australasian Tour Wins (1): 1990: Vines Classic.
Other Wins: 2 Web.com (1990) + Texas Jr: 1980   Texas State Open (2): 1988-90   Louisiana Open: 1989   Diners Club Matches (2): 1994 (w/J.McGovern)-97 (w/S.Elkington).

	86	87	88	89	90	91	92	93	94	95	96	97	98	99	00	01	02	03	04	05	06	07	08	09
Masters	-	-	-	-	-	-	-	T21	T50	MC	T7	MC	T23	MC	MC	T20	-	5	MC	T20	-	-	-	-
US Open	MC	MC	-	-	-	-	-	T52	T9	T4	T97	4	T7	T7	MC	T44	3	MC	3	T78	-	-	-	-
British	-	-	-	-	-	MC	MC	T24	T68	T5	T51	MC	T30	T41	MC	T47	-	-	-	-	MC	-	-	-
PGA	-	-	-	-	-	-	6	T51	MC	T3	T73	3	T44	MC	MC	MC	MC	MC	-	MC	T62	-	-	-
Money (A)	-	-	-	-	-	68	38	11	9	34	23	26	27	9	39	72	94	86	43	106	60	123	162	128
OWR	-	-	-	211	162	133	91	50	27	32	27	29	30	17	37	102	120	132	58	122	159	255	437	403

	10	11	12	13	14
Masters	-	-	-	-	-
US Open	-	-	-	-	MC
British	-	-	-	-	-
PGA	-	-	-	-	-
Money (A)	121	216	123	80	166
OWR	312	728	372	218	369

2014: PGA: 19 st / 8 ct / 1 t10. (T7 Travelers). Despite turning 50 in February, made 19 PGA Tour starts and finished 174th in FedEx Cup points. Also made eight Champions Tour starts, logging five top 10s including winning his Tour debut at the Mississippi Golf Resort Classic.

OUTLOOK: Would seem a potential star on the Champions Tour, but in 2014 at least, he chose to compete primarily against the under-50s. His skills have shown very little decline with age (he's still quite solid tee to green) - but surely he'll play with people his own age in 2015?

STATS: Driving Distance: C-   Driving Accuracy: A   GIR: B+   Short Game: B   Putting: C-

---

Mahan, Hunter Myles (USA) (32)

b. Orange, CA 5/17/1982. 5'11" 175 lbs. All-American at USC, two-time All-American, Nicklaus (2003), Haskins (2003) and co-Hogan (2003, with Ricky Barnes) Awards winner at Oklahoma State. TP: 2003. Three-time AJGA All-American and 1999 AJGA Player of the Year. The 1999 U.S. Junior Amateur winner and runner-up in 2002 U.S. Amateur (Oakland Hills) to Ricky Barnes. Went through Q School twice (2003 and '05) before getting his sea legs with an 83rd-place finish in 2006 PGA Tour $$$. Claimed his first win at 2007 Travelers Championship (Hartford), birdieing the 72nd to force sudden death with Jay Williamson, then sticking a wedge to 2' to clinch victory on the first extra hole. Shot 62 three times during 2007. Won the 2010 Waste Management Phoenix Open (by one over Rickie Fowler), then won again in August at the WGC Bridgestone Invitational, where he beat Ryan Palmer by two. Claimed his second career WGC win at the 2012 WGC Match Play, beating Rory McIlroy 2 & 1. Won the 2012 Shell Houston Open, edging Carl Pettersson by one. Broke a 30-month drought by winning the 2014 Barclays, where he beat Stuart Appleby, Jason Day and Cameron Tringale by two. **Teams:** Eisenhower Trophy: 2002. Palmer Cup: 2002. Ryder Cup (3): 2008-10-14 (O: 4-4-4, S: 0-1-2). Presidents Cup (4): 2007-09-11-13 (10-7-1). **OWR Best:** 4 - Apr, 2012.

PGA Tour Wins (6): 2007: Greater Hartford Open (Travelers) **2010**: Phoenix Open (Waste Management), WGC-Bridgestone Inv **2012**: WGC-Match Play, Houston Open (Shell) **2014**: The Barclays.
Amateur Wins: U.S. Junior Am: 1999   Western Jr: 1999.

	03	04	05	06	07	08	09	10	11	12	13	14
Masters	T28	-	-	-	-	MC	T10	T8	MC	T12	MC	T26
US Open	MC	-	-	-	T13	T18	T6	MC	MC	T38	T4	MC
British	-	T36	-	T26	T6	MC	MC	T37	MC	T19	T9	T32
PGA	-	-	MC	-	T12	MC	T16	T39	T19	MC	T57	T7
Money (A)	-	100	131	83	16	30	16	10	15	9	18	22
OWR	454	133	240	219	34	44	29	19	19	26	31	22

2014: PGA: 25 st / 20 ct / 6 t10. (Won Barclays, T4 Phoenix, 6 AT&T Pro-Am, T7 PGA, T9 WGC-Match Play, etc.). Had a strong, steady year highlighted by his sixth career win at The Barclays, a 6th-place finish in FedEx Cup points and a captain's selection by Tom Watson to the U.S. Ryder Cup team.

OUTLOOK: One of the top ball strikers in the game (18 in Ball Striking, 3 in Total Driving) and has a fine putting touch as well. Indeed, from a statistical standpoint, there is little room to grow, so the prospects of him joining the ranks of the world elite hinge more on the mental side. Has ranked 112 and 88 in Final Round Scoring the last two years - but then he ranked 91 during his two-win 2012 season, so perhaps this means little.

STATS: Driving Distance: A-   Driving Accuracy: A   GIR: A   Short Game: B-   Putting: A-

---

Mallinger, John Charles (USA) (35)

b. Escondido, CA 9/25/1979. 6'0" 165 lbs. College: Long Beach St. TP: 2002. After spending 2005 on the Canadian Tour, played 15 Web.com events in 2006 before reaching the PGA Tour via (Q School) in 2007. Finished 91st or better in PGA Tour earnings from 2007-2009. Slipped to 195th (in only 15 starts) in 2011 but also claimed the 14th spot on the Web.com money list (in just nine events) to regain PGA Tour status. Retained his card in 2012 but had his 2013 season shortened by a shoulder injury. **OWR Best:** 85 - Aug, 2009.

Other Wins: Callaway Inv: 2010.

	05	06	07	08	09	10	11	12	13	14
Masters	-	-	-	-	-	-	-	-	-	-
US Open	T67	MC	-	T65	T45	T22	-	-	-	-
British	-	-	-	-	-	-	-	-	-	-
PGA	-	-	-	T60	T60	-	-	-	-	-
Money (A)	-	-	51	91	50	133	195	86	196*	-
OWR	589	444	164	171	115	208	216	174	508	608

Mallinger, John Charles, Cont'd

2014: PGA: 14 st / 7 ct / 0 t10. (T12 Phoenix). Made only four starts after failing to clear a medical extension.

OUTLOOK: Has proven himself able to earn a good living when healthy, but he needs to get back on the big circuit in order to do that.

STATS: Driving Distance: C+   Driving Accuracy: A-   GIR: B-   Short Game: B+   Putting: B-

---

Mamat, Mardan (Singapore) (47)
b. Kuala Lumpur, Singapore 10/31/1967. 6'0" 175 lbs. TP: 1994. After a Singapore PGA title while still an amateur, became a mainstay of the Asian Tour who also spent three years in Europe (2006-2008) and one in Japan (83rd in $$$ in 2011). Was the first player from Singapore to win on the Asian Tour (the 2004 Indian Open) and the E Tour (the co-sanctioned 2006 Singapore Masters), and to play in the British Open (MC in 1997). Has only cracked the top 10 in the Asian Order of Merit once (8th in 2010). Scored a surprise six-shot triumph at the 2014 Manila Masters. **Teams**: Eisenhower Trophy: 1992. World Cup (5): 2002-05-06-09-11. **OWR Best**: 201 - Apr, 2011.

European Tour Wins (1): **2006**: Singapore Masters (OSIM).
Asian Tour Wins (3): **2004**: Indian Open **2012**: Philippine Open (ICTSI) **2014**: Manila Masters.
Other Wins: 1 Asian Dev (2012)   +   Singapore PGA (4): 1993*-94*-97-98   PFP Classic (Malaysia): 2001   Singapore Masters: 2009   Malaysian Masters: 2010   PGA A'Famosa Masters (Singapore): 2013.
Amateur Wins: Putra Cup: 1993   Malaysian Am: 1994.

	95	96	97	98	99	00	01	02	03	04	05	06	07	08	09	10	11	12	13	14
Masters	-	-	-	-	-	-	-	-	-	-	-	-	-	-	-	-	-	-	-	-
US Open	-	-	-	-	-	-	-	-	-	-	-	-	-	-	-	-	-	-	-	-
British	-	-	MC	-	-	-	-	-	-	-	MC	-	-	-	-	-	-	-	-	-
PGA	-	-	-	-	-	-	-	-	-	-	-	-	-	-	-	-	-	-	-	-
Money (E)	-	-	-	-	-	-	-	-	-	-	-	138	116	165	159*	136*	239*	178*	-	-
Money (As)	27	34	48	69	36	41	13	44	34	12	36	11	42	24	11	8	57	16	34	12
OWR	-	899	858	787	741	931	590	708	589	415	499	336	507	484	389	219	286	321	570	428

2014: ASIA: 21 st / 10 ct / 1 t10. (Won Manila Masters). Logged only one top 10 in 21 Asian starts - a win at the Manila Masters.

OUTLOOK: The numbers suggest that he is well onto the downside now, but as 2014 proved, he can still catch lighting on any given week.

STATS: Driving Distance: C+   Driving Accuracy: B+   GIR: B   Short Game: B   Putting: C+

Manassero, Matteo (Italy) (21)
b. Verona, Italy 4/19/1993. 6'0" 170 lbs. TP: 2010. Top Italian prospect who won the 2009 British Amateur (the youngest ever to win it at age 16) en route to being ranked the #1 Amateur in the world. Low amateur (T13) at the 2009 British Open at Turnberry. Turned pro in 2010 and became the youngest-ever winner on the European Tour, claiming the 2010 Costa Azahar Masters (by four over Ignacio Garrido) at 17 years, 188 days (breaking Danny Lee's record, set in 2009). Also the then-youngest-ever player to make the cut at the Masters, where he was low amateur in 2010, at 16 years, 11 months. Validated his breakthrough victory with an early 2011 win at the Malaysian Open, beating Grégory Bourdy by one. Hardly intimidated by coming to America, making five of six cuts on U.S. soil in 2011, plus T9 at WGC Match Play. Made it three wins in three years by taking the 2012 Barclays Singapore Open, beating Louis Oosthuizen in a playoff. Stepped up in class at age 20, winning the 2013 BMW PGA Championship in a playoff with Simon Khan and Marc Warren, and finished a career-best 11th in E Tour $$$. **Awards**: E Tour Rookie of the Year: 2010. **Teams**: Seve Trophy (2): 2011-13. World Cup: 2013. **OWR Best**: 25 - Jun, 2013.

European Tour Wins (4): **2010**: Costa Azahar Masters **2011**: Malaysian Open **2012**: Singapore Open **2013**: BMW PGA Championship.
Amateur Wins: British Amateur: 2009   –   Italian Jr: 2008   European Team Championship (Individual): 2009   Italian Jr Stroke Play: 2009.

	09	10	11	12	13	14
Masters	-	T36	-	-	MC	MC
US Open	-	-	T54	T46	MC	-
British	T13	-	MC	-	MC	T19
PGA	-	-	T37	MC	T72	MC
Money (E)	Am	31	31	13	11	60
OWR	570	62	58	44	43	147

2014: E: 24 st / 17 ct / 2 t10. (T4 Scottish, T10 Volvo Champ). Took an unexpected step back in 2014, going winless and finishing 60th in $$$.

OUTLOOK: Witnessed significant drop offs in both driving accuracy and putting in 2014, uncharacteristic slides that had much to do with his failing to build on the momentum generated by his 2013 BMW PGA win. Still, he's proven decisively that he can win at this level (no player has ever logged four major tour victories so young) so for now, 2014 will be viewed as a mere bump in the road. Should return to form in 2015 - but it's not quite a lock.

STATS: Driving Distance: C-   Driving Accuracy: B ⇩   GIR: B   Short Game: B+   Putting: B+ ⇩

Manley, Stuart (Wales) (35)
b. Mountain Ash, Wales 1/16/1979. 6'0" 180 lbs. College: Division 2 All-American at West Florida. TP: 2011. Though fairly quiet as an American collegiate player, was a member of the 2003 Walker Cup team. Played three full seasons on the E Tour between 2005-2011, never bettering 147th in $$$. Won once on the 2013 Challenge Tour en route to finishing 19th in $$$ and regaining his E Tour card, only to lose it again at the end of 2014. **Teams**: Walker Cup: 2003 (2-0-1). Palmer Cup: 2002. World Cup: 2013. **OWR Best**: 191 - Feb, 2014.

Other Wins: 1 Euro Challenge (2013)   +   1 EuroPro (2012).
Amateur Wins: Welsh Am: 2003.

	05	06	07	08	09	10	11	12	13	14
Masters	-	-	-	-	-	-	-	-	-	-
US Open	-	-	-	-	-	-	-	-	-	-
British	-	-	-	-	-	-	-	-	-	-
PGA	-	-	-	-	-	-	-	-	-	-
Money (E)	147	-	-	150	-	-	185	-	125	-
OWR	744	687	344	540	592	365	656	-	195	403

Manley, Stuart, Cont'd

2014: E: 29 st / 12 ct / 2 t10. (2P Hong Kong, T9 Denmark). Despite losing a playoff in Hong Kong, finished 125th in $$$ and lost his card.

OUTLOOK: A short but very straight type who at age 35 appears destined to reside in that gray area between the European and Challenge Tours - though he came closer than ever before to retaining his E Tour card in 2014.

STATS (LTD):	Driving Distance: C	Driving Accuracy: A	GIR: C	Short Game: B-	Putting: B+

Marino, Stephen Paul Jr. (USA) (34)
b. Altus, OK 3/10/1980. 6'0" 180 lbs. College: U of Virginia. TP: 2002. In 2006, played both the Gateway mini-tour (winning twice) and the Web.com Tour (42nd in $$$) before earning his way onto the PGA Tour for 2007 via Q School. Finished a solid 80th in rookie-year earnings and then became a money machine, ranking 34th, 35th, 61st and 39th in earnings. Seldom a contender to win (only four top-3 finishes through 2010) prior to recording runner-ups at the Sony Open and the Arnold Palmer Invitational in 2011. Made only six PGA Tour starts in 2012 due to a torn meniscus in his left knee, then only 12 in 2013 and 13 in 2014 due to the same injury. **OWR Best:** 54 - Mar, 2011.

Other Wins: 3 Gateway (2006).
Amateur Wins: Virginia Am: 1999   Virginia HS: 1998.

	07	08	09	10	11	12	13	14
Masters	-	-	-	T14	T42	-	-	-
US Open	MC	MC	-	T63	-	MC	-	-
British	-	-	T38	T55	MC	-	-	-
PGA	-	T60	MC	MC	MC	-	-	-
Money (A)	80	34	35	61	39	212*	194*	170*
OWR	199	109	86	108	95	461	976	645

2014: PGA: 13 st / 7 ct / 0 t10. (T11 Greenbrier). Was limited to 13 starts due to a lack of status upon failing to clear a nine-event medical extension. Thus finished 169th in FedEx Cup points, then failed to play through the Web.com Finals.

OUTLOOK: Though winless on the PGA Tour, had blossomed into a very steady earner prior to his 2012 knee injury. Statistically, his talent level suggests that once healthy, he'll be back, but he failed to clear his lingering medical extension and he's now four years removed from playing high-level golf. As his ball striking had slipped considerably in 2010 and 2011 pre-injury, it's now tough to envision too fast a comeback here.

STATS:	Driving Distance: A-	Driving Accuracy: C+	GIR: B-	Short Game: B	Putting: B+

Marksaeng, Prayad (Thailand) (48)
b. Hua Hin, Thailand 1/30/1966. 5'4" 160 lbs. TP: 1991. Smooth-swinging Thai star who has proven himself something of a late-bloomer, and who didn't claim his first major tour win (the Asian Circuit's China Open) until age 30. Evolved into a regular new millennium winner in Asia, highlighted by a one-shot victory over Juvic Pagunsan and Chris Rodgers at the prestigious 2007 Asian Masters. Began playing regularly in Japan in 2001 where, after seven solid seasons and at age 42, he exploded with a three-win 2008, highlighted by a one-shot triumph over Ryo Ishikawa at the Dunlop Phoenix and a third-place finish in the Order of Merit. At age 47, and seemingly on the down side, enjoyed a big bounce-back year in 2013, winning both the Japan Tour-sanctioned Thailand Open (by two over Scott Strange) and the Asian Tour's Queen's Cup, then added the 2014 King's Cup (officially a 2013 Asian Tour event) for his 12th career major tour victory. **Teams:** World Cup (5): 1994-07-08-09-13. **OWR Best:** 47 - Mar, 2009.

Japan Tour Wins (4): 2008: Mitsubishi Diamond Cup, Mizuno Open, Dunlop Phoenix **2013:** Thailand Open.
Asian Tour Wins (8): 1996: China Open **1997:** Singapore PGA, Thai International **2000:** Philippine Open **2005:** Crowne Plaza Open **2007:** Asian Masters **2013:** Queen's Cup **2014:** King's Cup ('13).
Other Wins: Singha E San Open (Thailand): 2007.

	95	96	97	98	99	00	01	02	03	04	05	06	07	08	09	10	11	12	13	14
Masters	-	-	-	-	-	-	-	-	-	-	-	-	-	WD	MC	-	-	-	-	-
US Open	-	-	-	-	-	-	-	-	-	-	-	-	-	-	-	-	-	-	-	-
British	-	-	-	-	MC	-	-	-	-	-	-	-	-	MC	MC	-	MC	MC	-	-
PGA	-	-	-	-	-	-	-	-	-	-	-	-	-	T15	MC	-	-	-	-	-
Money (E)	-	-	-	-	-	-	-	-	-	-	-	-	-	-	-	-	-	-	-	-
Money (J)	-	-	-	-	-	-	53	30	26	46	35	26	10	3	36*	74*	39	36	23	17
Money (As)	56	6	2	-	14	7	-	-	11*	6*	18	13	5	12	9	9	11*	56	7*	74*
OWR	825	688	616	461	375	342	286	287	186	180	194	156	72	52	94	216	192	288	160	136

2014: JAP: 17 st / 15 ct / 6 t10. (2 Nippon, 4 Japan Open, 5 Tour Champ, T8 Sega Sammy, T8 ANA, etc.). Split time between the Japan and Asian Tours, but managed a solid 17th-place $$$ finish in Japan, where he made the lion's share of his starts.

OUTLOOK: Still rolling along at age 48, based on a balanced range of skills led, not surprisingly, by an elite short game. One wonders how much longer he can keep winning at this level, but he's lost surprisingly little length, and he seems to have found a different mental gear since his mid-40s. Thus given the lesser talent pools of the Japan and Asian Tours, perhaps he can remain this successful until he's Champions Tour eligible at age 50.

STATS:	Driving Distance: B+	Driving Accuracy: A-	GIR: B	Short Game: A	Putting: B+

Martin, Benjamin Walter (USA) (27)
b. Greenwood, SC 8/26/1987. 5'11" 175 lbs. College: Clemson U. TP: 2010. Lost in the final of the 2009 U.S. Amateur (7 & 5 to Byeong-Hun An at Southern Hills) while playing collegiately at Clemson. After turning pro, spent one year on the eGolf mini-tour (winning once) before playing his way through Q School, then making 12 of 25 cuts on the 2011 PGA Tour en route to finishing 164th in $$$. Played the Web.com Tour in 2012 and '13, winning twice during the latter season to finish 2nd in regular season $$$. Returned to the PGA Tour in 2014 and easily kept his card, then wasted little time in landing his first win at the Shriners Hospitals Open (Las Vegas) in the second event of the 2014-15 wraparound schedule. **OWR Best:** 57 - Oct, 2014.

PGA Tour Wins (1): 2014: Las Vegas Classic (Shriners)('15).
Other Wins: 2 Web.com (2013)   +   1 eGolf Tour (2010).
Amateur Wins: Palmetto Am: 2006.

Martin, Benjamin Walter, Cont'd

	09	10	11	12	13	14
Masters	-	MC	-	-	-	-
US Open	MC	MC	-	-	-	-
British	-	-	-	-	-	T26
PGA	-	-	-	-	-	MC
Money (A)	Am	-	164	-	-	70
OWR	-	-	579	555	157	65

2014: PGA: 26 st / 13 ct / 3 t10. (3 Puerto Rico, 3 Heritage, 3 Quicken Loans). Made good in his second PGA Tour go-round, ranking 76th in Fedex Cup points, logging three top-3 finishes and generally making good on some strong pre-season predictions.

OUTLOOK: Has proven himself both a solid ball striker (especially off the tee, where he ranked 20 in Total Driving) and well above average on and around the greens, his numbers on the Web.com Tour having translated nicely to the big stage. Didn't have a glowing amateur record but blossomed on the Web.com, and now seems capable of growing into a PGA Tour star. Another victory in 2015 would not be surprising.

STATS: Driving Distance: B+   Driving Accuracy: A-   GIR: B+   Short Game: B+   Putting: A-

---

Martin Benavides, Pablo (Spain) (28)
b. Malaga, Spain 04/20/1986. 5'11" 175 lbs. Two-time All-American, Nicklaus (2006) and Haskins (2006) Awards winner at Oklahoma St. TP: 2007. Made an early name for himself when, four years after leading the 2003 Spanish Open through 54 holes at age 17, he became the first amateur to win an E Tour event at the 2007 Portuguese Open, where he edged Raphaël Jacquelin by one. Surprisingly struggled thereafter until late 2009, when he edged Charl Schwartzel by one to win the Alfred Dunhill Championship (a '10 E Tour event). Returned a year later to successfully defend his title, beating three players by two even after triple-bogeying the 71st hole. Slipped badly during 2012, then scarcely teed it up – by choice – in 2013, and played only slightly more often in 2014. **Teams:** Eisenhower Trophy (2): 2002-06. Palmer Cup (2): 2005-06. **OWR Best:** 163 - Apr, 2011.

European Tour Wins (3): 2007: Portuguese Open* **2009:** Alfred Dunhill Championship ('10) **2010:** Alfred Dunhill Championship ('11).
Amateur Wins: Spanish Am: 2003   Porter Cup: 2005   –   British Boys: 2001   European Under 16s: 2002   Spanish Closed Am: 2002   Orange Bowl Jr: 2003   English Boys Stroke Play; 2004.

	07	08	09	10	11	12	13	14
Masters	-	-	-	-	-	-	-	-
US Open	T30	-	-	T82	-	-	-	-
British	-	-	-	-	-	-	-	-
PGA	-	-	-	-	-	-	-	-
Money (E)	178	182	118	66	72	164	-	-
OWR	286	525	240	183	258	782	-	-

2014: E: 8 st / 1 ct / 0 t10. (T58 Mandela). Chose to play limited golf in 2013, making only eight E Tour starts and four on the Challenge Tour.

OUTLOOK: Moved to Sweden with his girlfriend in 2013, playing little competitive golf. Though he struggled badly in 2012, the combination of his age and demonstrated talent still suggests not writing him off too quickly - but his future is looking a bit chancy at this juncture.

STATS: Driving Distance: B+   Driving Accuracy: C-   GIR: C   Short Game: B   Putting: B

Maruyama, Shigeki (Japan) (45)
b. Chiba, Japan 9/12/1969. 5'7" 185 lbs. College: Nihon University. TP: 1992. Well established as Japan's most successful PGA Tour player, claiming three victories from 2001-2003 during a nine-year stretch in which he played in America full-time. Though a regular winner in Japan beginning in 1993, came to international fame by going 5-0 for the victorious International team at the 1998 Presidents Cup in Melbourne. Logged his first U.S. win at the 2001 Greater Milwaukee Open (in a playoff with Charles Howell III), then added the 2001 Byron Nelson Classic (by three over Ben Crane) and the 2003 Chrysler Classic of Greensboro, where he routed Brad Faxon by five. Slumped badly in 2007 and '08 before returning to Japan in 2009, where he claimed his 10th J Tour win at the season-ending Nippon Series JT Cup and finished 6th in the Order of Merit. Also won the 1997 Japan PGA, and is a three-time winner of the Bridgestone Open (1995, '96 and '99). Shot 58 at Woodmont (MD) CC during a scouting round for the 2000 U.S. Open. **Teams:** Eisenhower Trophy: 1990. Presidents Cup (2): 1998-00 (6-2-0). World Cup (5): 2000-01-02-03-04 (won in '02 w/T.Izawa). **OWR Best:** 20 - Feb, 2004.

PGA Tour Wins (3): 2001: Greater Milwaukee Open **2002:** Byron Nelson Classic (Verizon) **2003:** Chrysler Classic.
Japan Tour Wins (10): 1993: Pepsi Ube **1995:** Bridgestone Open **1996:** Bridgestone Open **1997:** Japan PGA Championship, Yomiuri Open, PGA Match Play, Nippon Series **1998:** PGA Philanthropy **1999:** Bridgestone Open **2009:** Nippon Series.
Amateur Wins: Japan Jr (12-14): 1984   Japan Jr (15-17): 1987   Japan Collegiate (2): 1990-91.

	93	94	95	96	97	98	99	00	01	02	03	04	05	06	07	08	09	10	11	12	13	14
Masters	-	-	-	-	MC	T31	T46	MC	T14	MC	MC	MC	MC	-	-	-	-	-	-	-	-	-
US Open	-	-	-	-	-	-	-	MC	-	T16	MC	T4	T33	-	-	-	-	-	-	-	-	-
British	-	-	-	T14	T10	T29	MC	T55	MC	T5	MC	T30	MC	-	-	-	-	-	-	-	-	-
PGA	-	-	-	-	T23	T65	MC	T46	T22	T43	T48	MC	MC	MC	-	-	-	-	-	-	-	-
Money (J)	20	24	3	5	2	7	3	-	-	-	-	-	-	-	6	22	118	105	150*	-		
Money (A)	-	-	-	-	-	-	-	37	37	16	37	23	32	79	105	207	-	-	-	-	-	-
OWR	200	184	82	56	33	42	62	49	63	29	39	28	44	108	230	260	129	166	459	-	-	-

2014: JAP: 2 st / 0 ct / 0 t10. Made only two starts, missing the cut at both the Sega Sammy Cup and the Dunlop Phoenix.

OUTLOOK: Has witnessed a marked decline in his ball striking since returning to Japan Tour at age 40, and now seems semi-retired.

STATS: Driving Distance: C-   Driving Accuracy: C   GIR: C+   Short Game: B-   Putting: B+

Matsumura, Michio (Japan) (31)
b. Saitama, Japan 7/22/1983. 5'8" 150 lbs. TP: 2006. A two-time winner on the 2007 Japan Challenge Tour before stepping up to the big tour in 2008 and quickly making good. After two solid campaigns, exploded in 2010 when he finished 5th in the Order of Merit behind wins at the Tokai Classic (in a playoff with Hiroyuki Fujita and Takashi Kanemoto) and the Casio World Open (in a playoff with

Matsumura, Michio, Cont'd

Do-Hoon Kim). After slipping somewhat in 2012, claimed a strong third win at the 2013 Crowns, edging Hideki Matsuyama by one. Wasted little time winning in 2014, taking the season-opening Indonesia PGA by birdieing six of his final eight holes. Opened the 2014 Crowns with a 10-under-par 60 at the Nagoya Golf Club. **OWR Best:** 82 - Dec, 2010.

Japan Tour Wins (4): 2010: Tokai Classic (Coca-Cola), Casio World Open **2013**: The Crowns **2014**: Indonesia PGA.

Other Wins: 2 Japan Challenge (2007).

	07	08	09	10	11	12	13	14
Masters	-	-	-	-	-	-	-	-
US Open	-	-	-	-	-	-	-	-
British	-	MC	-	-	-	-	-	-
PGA	-	-	-	-	-	-	-	-
Money (J)	85*	27	33	5	17	45	22	25
OWR	787	290	293	82	122	295	323	308

2014: JAP: 24 st / 15 ct / 3 t10. (Won Indonesia, T3 Nippon, T6 Taiheiyo). Logged a second straight season with a win and a top-25 $$$ ranking.

OUTLOOK: A mid-range player statistically whose improved ball striking complimented his above-the-median putting in 2014. Well-established as an occasional winner and a regular earner, but there remains little in his record or numbers to suggest an impending quantum leap.

STATS: Driving Distance: B+   Driving Accuracy: C+   GIR: B+   Short Game: C   Putting: B+

Matsuyama, Hideki (Japan) (22)

b. Ehime, Japan 2/25/1992. 5'11" 170 lbs. College: Tohoku Fukushi University. TP: 2013. Japan's strongest prospect since Ryo Ishikawa...or maybe longer. Two-time Asian Amateur winner with each victory earning an exemption to The Masters, where he was low amateur in 2011. Won the Japan Tour's 2011 Taiheiyo Masters while still an amateur (edging Toru Taniguchi by two) and reached #1 in the World Amateur Ranking in August, 2012. Ranked 127th in 2012's year-end OWR while still an amateur. After turning pro, won his second start on the Japan Tour, the 2013 Tsuruya Open (where a closing 66 edged American David Oh by one) before dominating the circuit while essentially only playing it part-time, logging four victories and winning the Order-of-Merit despite spending considerable time abroad and making only 13 domestic starts. Broke through for his first PGA Tour victory at the 2014 Memorial Tournament, birdieing the 72nd hole to tie Kevin Na, then winning on the first hole of sudden death. Returned home to claim the strong-field Dunlop Phoenix in November, beating Hiroshi Iwata in sudden death. **Teams:** Eisenhower Trophy (2): 2008-12. Presidents Cup: 2013 (1-3-1). **OWR Best:** 13 - Jun, 2014.

PGA Tour Wins (1): 2014: Memorial Tournament.

Japan Tour Wins (6): 2011: Taiheiyo Masters (54H)* **2013**: Tsuruya Open, Diamond Cup Golf, Fujisankei Classic, Casio World Open **2014**: Dunlop Phoenix.

Amateur Wins: Asian Am (2): 2010-11 – Japan Jr (15-17): 2009   Japan Collegiate (2): 2011-12   World University Games (Individual): 2011.

	11	12	13	14
Masters	T27	T54	-	MC
US Open	-	-	T10	T35
British	-	-	T6	T39
PGA	-	-	T19	T36
Money (A)	Am	Am	-	27
Money (J)	Am	Am	1	26*
OWR	201	127	23	16

2014: PGA: 24 st / 20 ct / 4 t10. (Won Memorial, T3 Frys.com, T4 Phoenix, T10 Colonial). Confirmed his ability to star in America by claiming his first PGA Tour win (at Memorial) and finishing 27th in $$$. Later returned home to win November's Dunlop Phoenix, Japan's strongest OWR event.

OUTLOOK: One of the game's bright young stars and arguably Japan's best international prospect of all time. Is a very solid tee-to-greener with a faintly mechanical swing who clearly knows how to win. Based on initial results, his game appears to travel West far better than most Japanese players who've tried the PGA Tour before him. Looks capable of winning quite a bit more, and eventually taking a regular place in the OWR top 25.

STATS: Driving Distance: B+   Driving Accuracy: B+   GIR: A   Short Game: B+   Putting: B+

Matteson, Troy Jason (USA) (35)

b. Rockledge, FL 11/8/1979. 6'0" 200 lbs. Three-time All-American, NCAA individual champion (2002) and Byron Nelson Award (2003) at Georgia Tech. TP: 2003. Also a two-time Academic All-American in college. Played the Web.com Tour in 2004 and '05, winning twice and finishing 1st in $$$ in 2005, thus graduating to the PGA Tour. Promptly won as a rookie at the 2006 Las Vegas Invitational, where he edged Daniel Chopra and Ben Crane by one. Followed that up with a 2009 victory at the Frys.com Open when, after bogeying the 71st and 72nd holes, he beat touted rookies Rickie Fowler and Jamie Lovemark in sudden death. Lost a playoff to Zach Johnson at the 2012 John Deere. Lost his card at the end of 2013 but regained it via the Web.com finals. **OWR Best:** 73 - Feb, 2007.

PGA Tour Wins (2): 2006: Las Vegas Classic (Fry's.com) **2009**: Fry's.com Open.

Other Wins: 2 Web.com (2005).

Amateur Wins: NCAA Individual: 2002.

	05	06	07	08	09	10	11	12	13	14
Masters	-	-	MC	-	-	-	-	-	-	-
US Open	-	-	-	-	-	-	-	-	-	-
British	-	-	-	-	-	-	T39	-	-	-
PGA	-	-	T66	-	-	T28	-	-	-	-
Money (A)	-	36	73	89	56	128	94	77	177	159
OWR		336	81	100	185	182	232	266	183	265 664

2014: PGA: 23 st / 7 ct / 1 t10. (T5 Shriners). Finished 165th in FedEx Cup points, then failed to play his way back via the Web.com Finals.

OUTLOOK: Logged both of his wins in years whose statistical numbers he has never matched since. Still, he'd emerged as a steady earner with a fairly balanced, power-oriented game prior to 2013. Will see limited action off Past Champion status, so the Web.com may be his best way back.

STATS: Driving Distance: A   Driving Accuracy: C-   GIR: C+   Short Game: C+   Putting: B-

Mattiace, Leonard Earl (USA) (48)
b. Mineola, NY 2/14/1986. 6'1" 185 lbs. College: Wake Forest. TP: 1990. Web.com Tour player before making good on the PGA Tour, ranking among the top 100 money winners from 1996-2003, with career-best 18th in 2002. Claimed both of his victories in 2002, first edging three players by one at the Los Angeles Open, then beating Tim Petrovic by one at the Memphis Classic. Just missed achieving immortality by losing the 2003 Masters in a playoff with Mike Weir after closing with a splendid 65. Began to slide in 2004 and hasn't played a full PGA Tour season since 2006. **Teams:** Walker Cup: 1987 (2-1-0). **OWR Best:** 24 - May, 2003.

PGA Tour Wins (2): 2002: Los Angeles Open (Nissan), Memphis Classic (FedEx).
Amateur Wins: Southern Am: 1985 - Dixie Am (2): 1984-89.

	93	94	95	96	97	98	99	00	01	02	03	04	05	06	07	08	09	10	11	12	13	14
Masters	-	-	-	-	-	-	-	-	-	2P	MC	-	-	-	-	-	-	-	-	-	-	-
US Open	-	-	-	-	T24	-	T42	-	-	T68	T57	-	MC	-	-	-	-	-	-	-	-	-
British	-	-	-	-	-	-	T30	-	-	T69	T65	-	-	-	-	-	-	-	-	-	-	-
PGA	-	-	-	-	MC	MC	-	-	MC	T48	T51	-	-	-	-	-	-	-	-	-	-	-
Money (A)	160	-	-	92	77	68	100	61	84	18	56	188	191	226	-	237*	228*	235*	-	250*	-	246*
OWR	477	-	-	256	176	176	189	145	155	51	70	233	570	898	1302	843	770	1049	1357	1492	737	1179

2014: PGA: 4 st / 2 ct / 0 t10. (T49 Mayakoba). Also made 18 Web.com starts, making six cuts and finishing 159th in regular season $$$.
OUTLOOK: Seems unlikely to have much of an impact at this stage of the game - but the Champions Tour lies only two years in the distance.

STATS: Driving Distance: B+ Driving Accuracy: A- GIR: B Short Game: B Putting: A-

---

Maybin, Gareth (Northern Ireland) (34)
b. Belfast, Northern Ireland 9/14/1980. 5'9" 175 lbs. College: U of South Alabama. TP: 2005. After playing collegiately in America, traveled U.S. mini-tours (winning twice on the Hooters Tour) before returning to the European Challenge Tour in 2007, and winning there in late 2008. Joined the E Tour in 2009 and, though winless in Europe, he did reach a playoff at the 2008 South African Open, where he lost to homestanding Richard Sterne. Cracked the top 60 in E Tour $$$ in 2009 and '10 but has since taken a step back, ranking no better than 95th (2013). **Teams:** Palmer Cup: 2004. World Cup: 2007. **OWR Best:** 84 - Feb, 2009.

Other Wins: 1 Euro Challenge (2008) + 2 NGA/Hooters (2006-2007).

	08	09	10	11	12	13	14
Masters	-	-	-	-	-	-	-
US Open	-	-	T63	-	-	-	-
British	-	-	MC	-	-	MC	-
PGA	-	-	-	-	-	-	-
Money (E)	-	53	40	117	111	95	123
OWR	90	124	110	261	552	390	450

2014: E: 25 st / 12 ct / 3 t10. (T7 Spanish, T9 Denmark, T9 Euro Masters). Lost his card after finishing a career-worst 123rd in $$$.
OUTLOOK: A shorter hitter of only middling accuracy – a tough combination when one's short game isn't quite high-end enough to cover. At 34, winless on the E Tour and with only conditional status in 2015, he cannot be considered a likely star going forward.

STATS: Driving Distance: C- Driving Accuracy: B GIR: B- Short Game: B Putting: B

Mayfair, William Fred (USA) (48)
b. Phoenix, AZ 8/6/1966. 5'8" 175 lbs. Three-time All-American and collegiate player of the Year (1987) at Arizona St. Won 1987 U.S. Amateur (4 & 3 over Eric Rebmann). TP: 1988. Four-time AJGA All-American. Former elite junior and amateur prospect who, after turning pro, enjoyed 15 consecutive seasons among the PGA Tour's top 125 money winners between 1989-2003. Career peaked in 1995 when he edged four players by one to win the Western Open, beat Steve Elkington and Corey Pavin by three at the Tour Championship, and finished 2nd in $$$. Defeated Tiger Woods in sudden death at the 1998 Los Angeles Open (Valencia CC). Holds a piece of the PGA Tour's nine-hole scoring record with a nine-under-par 27 posted in the final round of the 2001 Buick Open. After slipping out of the top 125 in 2003 and '04, utilized a new putting stroke to climb back to 22nd in $$$ in 2005. After finishing 142nd in 2010, played his way back onto the Tour as medalist at Q School (22 years after his initial visit). Made only limited PGA Tour starts in 2013 and '14. **Teams:** Walker Cup: 1987 (3-0-0). **OWR Best:** 25 - Jun, 1996.

PGA Tour Wins (5): 1993: Greater Milwaukee Open **1995:** Western Open (Motorola), Tour Championship **1998:** Los Angeles Open (Nissan), Buick Open.
Amateur Wins: U.S. Amateur: 1987 – Junior World (9-10): 2976 Junior World (11-12): 1979 PGA Junior: 1982 Arizona Jr: 1983 U.S. Amateur Public Links: 1986 Pacific Coast Am (2): 1987-88.

	88	89	90	91	92	93	94	95	96	97	98	99	00	01	02	03	04	05	06	07	08	09	10	11
Masters	MC	-	-	T12	T42	-	MC	-	MC	MC	-	-	T32	T37	-	-	T14	59	-	MC	-	-	-
US Open	T25	T33	MC	T37	T23	-	MC	-	T32	-	T10	MC	-	T5	T10	66	-	MC	-	-	T40	-	-
British	-	-	-	-	-	-	T45	-	-	T52	MC	-	T3	MC	-	-	-	-	-	-	T52	-	-
PGA	-	-	T5	MC	MC	T28	T39	T23	T52	T53	T7	T34	T74	MC	MC	T61	-	MC	T37	T60	T47	-	-
Money (A)	-	116	12	89	79	30	113	2	55	79	16	58	106	29	75	79	140	22	65	44	44	157	142	109
OWR	-	231	67	116	169	121	166	30	43	120	41	52	112	58	86	145	254	72	92	111	92	290	416	348

	12	13	14
Masters	-	-	-
US Open	-	-	-
British	-	-	-
PGA	-	-	-
Money (A)	128	199*	230*
OWR	330	643	945

2014: PGA: 4 st / 2 ct / 0 t10. (T27 Barracuda). Also made 16 Web.com starts, finishing 125th in $$$ and not qualifying for the Finals.
OUTLOOK: Has Past Champion status but evidently felt his best way back was via the Web.com Tour in 2014. Enjoyed a very long run as a highly consistent earner before slipping noticeably since 2010, and sharply in 2013. One obvious reason is a sharp decline in GIR from 2011 onward (23, 123, 96 and 152) but at age 48, he's likely just starting to tune up for a potentially lucrative Champions Tour run starting in 2016.

STATS: Driving Distance: C+ Driving Accuracy: A GIR: B-⇩ Short Game: B- Putting: C-

McCarron, Scott Michael (USA) (49)
b. Sacramento, CA 7/10/1965. 5'10" 170 lbs. College: UCLA. TP: 1992. Gave up golf for several years after college before qualifying for PGA Tour (via Q School) in 1995. Finished 128th in $$$ his rookie year but was never out of the top 125 for 10 years thereafter (with three appearances among the top 30) before missing half of 2006 and all of '07 with elbow surgery. All three of his Tour victories have come in the deep South, beginning with the 1996 New Orleans Classic, where he ran away from Tom Watson by five. Later added two triumphs at the Atlanta Classic, beating a trio of players by three shots in 1997, then edging Mike Weir by the same margin in 2001. Missed most of 2012 with left thumb surgery and played on a medical extension through 2014. **OWR Best:** 20 - Feb, 2002.

PGA Tour Wins (3): 1996: New Orleans Classic (Freeport-McDermott) **1997:** Atlanta Classic (BellSouth) **2001:** Atlanta Classic (BellSouth).
Other Wins: Shark Shootout (3): 1998 (w/B.Lietzke)-00-01 (both w/B.Faxon)   Fred Meyer Challenge: 2002 (w/B. Henninger).

	95	96	97	98	99	00	01	02	03	04	05	06	07	08	09	10	11	12	13	14
Masters	-	**T10**	T30	T16	T18	-	-	MC	T23	-	-	-	-	-	-	-	-	-	-	-
US Open	-	T82	**T10**	T40	-	-	-	T30	MC	-	MC	-	-	-	-	-	-	-	-	-
British	-	-	MC	-	-	-	-	T18	T34	-	-	-	-	MC	-	-	-	-	-	-
PGA	-	T47	**T10**	MC	-	-	T66	T39	T14	MC	T59	-	-	-	T24	-	-	-	-	-
Money (A)	128	49	25	69	101	97	23	29	54	105	81	196	-	108	92	141	145	-	254*	237*
OWR	346	103	44	74	172	210	54	30	64	125	147	379	-	241	195	356	393	734	-	-

2014: PGA: 12 st / 2 ct / 0 t10.   (T75 New Orleans).   Made only 12 starts after failing to clear a medical extension dating to 2012.
OUTLOOK: At age 49, he may well have his mind focused more on a broadcasting career - until becoming Champions Tour eligible in July.

STATS: Driving Distance: B-   Driving Accuracy: B+   GIR: C-   Short Game: B   Putting: B+⇩

McDowell, Graeme, M.B.E. (Northern Ireland) (35)
b. Portrush, Northern Ireland 7/30/1979. 5'11" 165 lbs. Two-time All-American and Haskins Award winner (2002) at U of Alabama-Birmingham. TP: 2002. Two-time Irish Youth champion (1999 and '00) who starred for the 2001 Great Britain & Ireland Walker Cup side before joining the European Tour full-time in 2002. Won the 2002 Scandinavian Masters (by one over Trevor Immelman) in only his fourth professional start. Won the 2004 Italian Open (in a playoff over Thomas Levet) and, at season's end, shot a final round 62 at St Andrews before losing in a playoff (to Stephen Gallacher) at the Dunhill Links Championship. A breakout 2008 included victories at the Ballantine's Championship (in a playoff with Jeev Milkha Singh) and the Scottish Open (by two over James Kingston), as well as a 5th-place finish in E Tour $$$. Scored a breakthrough victory at the 2010 U.S. Open, edging Grégory Havret by one at Pebble Beach. Completed an elite season by also claiming the Wales Open (with a scorching 64-63 close), the Andalucia Valderrama Masters and the unofficial Chevron World Challenge, where he came from four back to defeat Tiger Woods in sudden death. Honored with an M.B.E. in 2011. Claimed his first regular PGA Tour win at the 2013 Heritage, beating Webb Simpson in a playoff. Five weeks later, won the World Match Play (2 & 1 over Thongchai Jaidee) in Bulgaria, then added the French Open (by four, over Richard Sterne) in July. Returned to defend his French Open title in 2014, beating Thongchai Jaidee and Kevin Stadler by three. **Awards:** E Tour Golfer of the Year: 2010 (w/M.Kaymer). **Teams:** Walker Cup: 2001 (2-2-0). Palmer Cup (2): 2000-01. Ryder Cup (4): 2008-10-12-14 (O: 8-5-2, S: 3-1-0). Seve Trophy (2): 2005-09. World Cup (4): 2008-09-11-13. **OWR Best:** 4 - Jan, 2011.

PGA Tour Wins (2): 2010: U.S. Open **2013:** Heritage (RBC).
European Tour Wins (9): 2002: Scandinavian Masters **2004:** Italian Open (54H) **2008:** Ballantine's Championship, Scottish Open **2010:** Wales Open, Andalucia Valderrama Masters **2013:** World Match Play, French Open **2014:** French Open.
Other Wins: Chevron World Challenge: 2010.
Amateur Wins: Irish Youths (2): 1999-00   Irish Closed Am: 2000   South of Ireland Am: 2000.

	02	03	04	05	06	07	08	09	10	11	12	13	14
Masters	-	-	-	MC	-	-	-	T17	MC	MC	T12	MC	MC
US Open	-	-	-	T80	T48	T30	-	T18	**Win**	T11	**T2**	MC	T28
British	-	-	MC	T11	T61	MC	T19	T34	T23	MC	**T5**	T58	**T9**
PGA	-	-	MC	MC	T37	-	T15	**T10**	MC	MC	T11	T12	T47
Money (A)	-	-	-	-	169	-	-	-	50*	86	31	28	41
Money (E)	56	96	**6**	34	58	37	**5**	33	**2**	16	**9**	**4**	14
OWR	185	234	55	56	132	106	33	39	**6**	13	15	14	15

2014: PGA: 17 st / 16 ct / 8 t10.   (3 WGC-HSBC, T5 WGC-Match Play, T7 AT&T Pro-Am, T8 WGC-Bridgestone, T9 WGC-Cadillac, etc.).   Won only once (at the French Open) but was far more consistent than in 2013, finishing 56th in FedEx Cup points and playing in his fourth straight Ryder Cup.
OUTLOOK: Statistically, 2014 saw his GIR climb back to 65 (from an outlying 144) while for the second straight year, his SGP took a giant leap (160 to 71 to 1 since 2012). Not a long hitter but the precision of his ball striking (21 in Proximity to Hole) can generally offset that. Has at times stood on the edge of superstardom, but at this point seems destined to remain a long-term world top-25 - which definitely isn't bad.

STATS: Driving Distance: C   Driving Accuracy: A+   GIR: B+   Short Game: B+   Putting: B+⇧

McGinley, Paul Noel (Ireland) (48)
b. Dublin, Ireland 12/16/1966. 5'7" 160 lbs. TP: 1991. Journeyman who cracked the top 100 in E Tour $$$ every year from 1992-2008, peaking with a pair of top-10 finishes in 2001 and '05. Won two lesser events (the 1996 Austrian Open and the 1997 Oki Pro-Am) as well as the weather-shortened Wales Open in 2001. Claimed his biggest triumph in 2005 at the Volvo Masters, where he beat Sergio García by two. Three-time Ryder Cup player who holed clinching putt in 2002 at the Belfry. Captained the victorious European Ryder Cup Team in 2014. **Teams:** Walker Cup: 1991 (1-2-0). Ryder Cup (3): 2002-04-06 + Capt in 2014 (O: 2-2-5, S: 1-0-2). Seve Trophy (2): 2002-05 + Capt in 2009 & '11. World Cup (13): 1993-94-97-98-99-00-01-02-03-04-05-06-08 (won in '97 w/P.Harrington). **OWR Best:** 18 - Oct, 2005.

European Tour Wins (4): 1996: Austrian Open **1997:** Oki Pro-Am **2001:** Wales Open (36H) **2005:** Volvo Masters.
Other Wins: Irish Pro (4): 1997-00-02-03.
Amateur Wins: Irish Youths: 1988   Scottish Youths Stroke Play: 1988   Irish Closed Am: 1989   South of Ireland Am: 1991.

	92	93	94	95	96	97	98	99	00	01	02	03	04	05	06	07	08	09	10	11	12	13	14
Masters	-	-	-	-	-	-	-	-	-	-	T18	-	-	-	MC	-	-	-	-	-	-	-	-
US Open	-	-	-	-	-	-	-	-	-	-	-	-	-	MC	T42	MC	-	-	-	-	-	-	-
British	MC	MC	MC	-	T14	T66	MC	MC	T20	T54	MC	T28	T57	T41	MC	19	-	T43	-	-	-	-	-
PGA	-	-	-	-	-	-	-	-	MC	T22	MC	MC	**T6**	T23	WD	T60	-	-	-	-	-	MC	-
Money (E)	97	38	46	52	15	21	30	37	18	**8**	58	33	22	**3**	52	74	26	104	123	152	83	127	167*
OWR	388	170	161	161	81	102	146	127	68	35	99	157	68	21	71	207	104	222	448	472	292	412	585

McGinley, Paul Noel, Cont'd

2014: E: 13 st / 6 ct / 0 t10.   (T15 Spanish).   Was a part-time player in 2014, partially due to serving as European Ryder Cup Captain.

OUTLOOK: With a victorious Ryder Cup captaincy behind him, he now looks like a man biding his time to make a run at the senior tours in 2016.

| **STATS**: | Driving Distance: C- | Driving Accuracy: A | GIR: C | Short Game: B- | Putting: B- ⇧ |

McGirt, William Curtis III (USA) (35)
b. Lumberton, NC 6/21/1979. 5'8" 200 lbs. College: Wofford College. TP: 2004. After starring at Wofford, spent several years playing on mini-tours, notably the eGolf (where he was a winner), Hooters and Gateway circuits. Reached the Web.com Tour in 2010 and finished 34th, then qualified for the 2011 PGA Tour by finishing T2 at Q School – and earned his way back a second time with a T13 a year later. Settled in nicely thereafter, cracking the top 100 in $$$ (and FedEx Cup points) from 2012 onward. **OWR Best:** 118 - Aug, 2014.

Other Wins: 1 eGolf Tour (2007).

Amateur Wins: Cardinal Am: 2003.

	11	12	13	14
Masters	-	-	-	-
US Open	-	-	-	-
British	-	-	-	-
PGA	-	MC	-	-
Money (A)	141	74	97	84
OWR	444	196	187	149

2014: PGA: 29 st / 19 ct / 4 t10. (T5 Barclays, T6 Northern Trust, T8 Wyndham, T9 Heritage).   Logged a career-best four top 10s (and eight top 25s) en route to finishing 61st in FedEx Cup points, and comfortably keeping his card for the third straight season.

OUTLOOK: Winless above the mini-tour level but has earned steadily on the PGA Tour. Statistically, has remained fairly consistent, with a strong two-year rise in Driving Accuracy (107 to 79 to 33) perhaps offset by a corresponding drop in GIR (65 to 88 to 105). A reliably strong putter may allow him to remain at this level, but he'll likely need to improve his tee-to-green game to climb much further.

| **STATS**: | Driving Distance: C | Driving Accuracy: B+ | GIR: B+ | Short Game: B+ | Putting: A- |

McGowan, Ross Ian Thomas (England) (32)
b. Basildon, England 04/23/1982. 5'11" 190 lbs. All-American at U of Tennessee. TP: 2006. Ex-American college star who won twice on the Challenge Tour in 2007, earning his way onto the E Tour. Scored a breakthrough win (behind a third round 60) at the 2009 Madrid Masters, where he beat Mikko Ilonen by three. Begin suffering wrist problems in 2010, fell of significantly in 2011 as a result, and was limited to four E Tour starts in 2012 and five in 2013. **Teams**: Eisenhower Trophy: 2006. **OWR Best**: 63 - Feb, 2010.

European Tour Wins (1): 2009: Madrid Masters.

Other Wins: 2 Euro Challenge (2007)   +   Abu Dhabi Citizen Open: 2012.

Amateur Wins: English Am: 2006.

	07	08	09	10	11	12	13	14
Masters	-	-	-	-				
US Open	-	77	-	T41	-	-	-	-
British	-	-	-	MC	-			
PGA	-	-	-	70	-	-		
Money (E)	-	70	12	77	151	285*	207*	266*
OWR	109	198	68	150	578	-	915	491

2014: Played mostly on the Challenge Tour, finishing 73rd in $$$. Also made four E Tour starts (best: T48 at Lyoness).

OUTLOOK: His first two seasons (especially 2009, when he finished 12th in E Tour $$$) suggested a bright future, but he has since been derailed by recurring wrist problems. Has the raw talent to compete at a high level but as far removed as he currently is, it would be a very long road back.

| **STATS (LTD)**: | Driving Distance: B | Driving Accuracy: B | GIR: B | Short Game: B | Putting: B- |

McGrane, Damien (Ireland) (43)
b. Meath, Ireland 04/13/1971. 5'8" 165 lbs. TP: 1991. Journeyman E Tour player who didn't crack the circuit's top 100 in $$$ until age 35. Improved his stock thereafter and eventually enjoyed a career campaign in 2008, finishing 2nd at the Indian Masters before winning the Volvo China Open in a nine-shot runaway over Simon Griffiths, Michael Lorenzo-Vera and Oliver Wilson. Save for a slightly disappointing 2011, has remained a steady earner ever since. **OWR Best**: 119 - Jan, 2011.

European Tour Wins (1): 2008: China Open (Volvo).

Other Wins: Irish Assistants (2): 1993-94   Irish PGA Southern: 1999   Wynyard Hall Open (Ireland): 1999.

Amateur Wins: Irish Boys: 1988   Kilkenny Cup: 1991.

	03	04	05	06	07	08	09	10	11	12	13	14
Masters	-	-	-	-	-	-	-	-				
US Open	-	-	-	-	-	-	-	-				
British	-	-	-	-	-	MC	MC	-	-	-		
PGA	-	-	-	-	-	-	-	-				
Money (E)	140	101	59	56	73	30	60	41	115	76	81	95
OWR	339	323	257	223	320	174	179	125	239	351	338	342

2014: E: 32 st / 18 ct / 2 t10.   (2 Russia, T9 Africa).   Logged both of his top 10s in light-field events, but finished 95th in $$$ to easily secure his card.

OUTLOOK: A steady $$$ winner but seldom a serious contender – which is often a low-stress recipe that can last a while. At age 43, a run of victories seems beyond his grasp. But as he actually improved in several key 2014 statistical categories, he may well have several good years left.

| **STATS**: | Driving Distance: C | Driving Accuracy: A- | GIR: B ⇧ | Short Game: B- | Putting: B- |

McGuigan, Douglas Gordon (South Africa) (44) b. Durban, South Africa 8/7/1970. 6'0" 190 lbs. TP: 1989. Long-running Sunshine Tour veteran who virtually never leaves home. Played for more than a decade before winning the 2003 Platinum Classic (by one over Ashley Roestoff), then became a consistent winner thereafter. Beat Desvonde Botes and Jean Hugo by two at the 2006 Telkom PGA Pro-Am and Jaco Van Zyl by one at the 2008 BMG Classic. Later beat Hugo in a playoff at the 2011 Zambia Open, and claimed the 2012 ISPS Handa Match Play, defeating Jaco Ahlers one up. Has only once cracked the Sunshine $$$ top 10, though he's knocked on the door several times. **OWR Best:** 236 - May, 2013.

Sunshine Tour Wins (6): 2003: Platinum Classic **2006**: Telkom PGA Pro-Am **2008**: BMG Classic (54H) **2009**: Nashua Golf Challenge (54H) **2011**: Zambia Open (KCM) **2012**: ISPS Handa Match Play Championship.

	00	01	02	03	04	05	06	07	08	09	10	11	12	13	14
Masters	-	-	-	-	-	-	-	-	-	-	-	-	-	-	-
US Open	-	-	-	-	-	-	-	-	-	-	-	-	-	-	-
British	-	-	-	-	-	MC	-	MC	MC	-	-	-	-	-	-
PGA	-	-	-	-	-	-	-	-	-	-	-	-	-	-	-
Money (SA)	19	11	11	6	35	38	11	14	37	23	35	19	12	43	63
OWR	426	371	459	506	803	686	684	767	-	-	818	385	241	415	967

2014: SUN: 17 st / 13 ct / 1 t10. (T6 Sun Boardwalk). Continued a three-year downward trend, finishing 63rd in Sunshine Tour $$$.

OUTLOOK: Still rambling along on the Sunshine Tour at age 44, though his 2013 and '14 earnings may suggest he is now on the decline.

STATS: Driving Distance: --   Driving Accuracy: --   GIR: --   Short Game: --   Putting: --

---

McIlroy, Rory, M.B.E. (Northern Ireland) (25) b. Holywood, Northern Ireland 5/4/1989. 5'11" 160 lbs. TP: 2007. Left Sullivan Upper School at age 16 to concentrate on his golf career. Precocious talent who shot 61 at Royal Portrush at age 16, won the European Amateur at 17 and was ranked the #1 amateur in the world before turning pro at age 18. Finished 3rd in his second pro event (2007 Dunhill Links Championship). Broke through for his maiden victory (at age 19) at the 2009 Dubai Desert Classic, edging Justin Rose by one. Youngest player ever to finish in the top 10 of a year-end Official World Ranking (9th in 2009, at age 20). Scored first U.S. triumph at 2010 Quail Hollow Championship, utilizing a record-setting final round 62 to beat a very strong international field. T3 at the 2010 British Open after firing a stunning first round 63 at St Andrews. Also T3 at the 2010 PGA Championship at Whistling Straits, missing the Kaymer-Watson playoff by one. In 2011, suffered an epic collapse at Augusta after dominating The Masters for 63 holes, then broke through at the US Open, where he shattered numerous scoring records en route to a thunderous eight-shot win over Jason Day. Later added wins at the Hong Kong Open and the unsanctioned Shanghai Masters to close out a breakthrough season. Awarded an M.B.E. at the end of 2011. After losing the final of the 2012 WGC Match Play, assumed the #1 spot in the OWR a week later by winning the Honda Classic. Fell out of the top spot shortly thereafter but reclaimed it via an eight-stroke runaway win at the 2012 PGA Championship (Kiawah Island), his second eight-stroke Major triumph in 14 months. Three weeks later, added the Deutsche Bank Championship (by one over Louis Oosthuizen), then won again the following week at the 70-man BMW Championship. Closed out 2012 by winning the E Tour's season-ending DP World Tour Championship, finishing with five straight birdies to edge Justin Rose by two. Joined Luke Donald (2011) as the only men to lead both the PGA and European Tours in earnings in the same season. Salvaged an otherwise disappointing 2013 by defeating Adam Scott on the final green to win the Australian Open. In the week in which he terminated his on-again, off-again marriage plans with tennis star Caroline Wozniacki, roared home with a closing 66 to win the E Tour's flagship 2014 BMW PGA Championship. Took a big step towards immortality eight weeks later by winning the British Open at Hoylake (by two over Sergio García and Rickie Fowler), joining Jack Nicklaus and Tiger Woods as the only men to win three legs of the career Grand Slam by age 25. Added his first WGC win at the Bridgestone Invitational in his next start, then established himself as the game's next superstar by coming from three shots behind over the final nine to win the PGA Championship, edging Phil Mickelson by one. **Awards:** PGA Tour Player of the Year: 2012. E Tour Player of the Year: 2012. Vardon Trophy: 2012. **Teams:** Walker Cup: 2007 (1-2-1). Eisenhower Trophy: 2006. Ryder Cup (3): 2010-12-14 (O: 6-4-4, S: 2-0-1). Seve Trophy: 2009. World Cup (2): 2009-11. **OWR Best:** 1 - Mar, 2012.

PGA Tour Wins (9): 2010: Quail Hollow Championship (Wachovia) **2011**: U.S. Open **2012**: Honda Classic, PGA Championship, Deutsche Bank Championship, BMW Championship **2014**: British Open, WGC-Bridgestone, PGA Championship.
European Tour Wins (4): 2009: Dubai Classic **2011**: Hong Kong Open **2012**: Dubai World Championship **2014**: BMW PGA Championship.
Australasian Tour Wins (1): 2013: Australian Open (Emirates).
Other Wins: Shanghai Masters: 2011.
Amateur Wins: European Am: 2006   –   Irish Youths: 2004   Irish Boys: 2004   Ulster Boys (2): 2003-04   Irish Closed Am (2): 2005-06   Faldo Junior Series: 2006   Sherry Cup: 2007.

	07	08	09	10	11	12	13	14
Masters	-	-	T20	MC	T11	T40	T25	T8
US Open	-	-	T10	MC	Win	MC	T41	T23
British	T42	-	T47	T3	T25	T60	MC	Win
PGA	-	-	T3	T3	T64	Win	T8	Win
Money (A)	-	-	-	26	-	1	41	1
Money (E)	-	36	2	13	2	1	35*	1
OWR	232	39	9	10	3	1	6	1

2014: PGA: 17 st / 17 ct / 12 t10. (Won British Open, Won WGC-Bridgestone, Won PGA, T2 Honda, T2 Tour Champ, etc.). Bounced back dramatically from a disappointing 2013 to firmly reclaim the world number one spot. Also won the E Tour's flagship BMW PGA Championship, logged five top 10s in non Major/WGC E Tour events and led the circuit in earnings, making him the obvious runaway choice for Player Of The Year.

OUTLOOK: With his equipment, his personal life and, shortly, his business affairs now apparently in order, it's hard to envision him falling from his perch anytime soon. Utilizes almost surrealistic power to construct a dominant tee-to-green game (6 in GIR, 7 in Ball Striking), and in 2014 both his short game and putting were up to the task of capitalizing. An elite generational talent, his four Major wins by age 25 have elevated him to the point where he's now playing against history - and in this regard, it will be interesting how far he has climbed, say, by the time he turns 30. One caveat: His jackpot years of 2012 and '14 are the only times his SGP has bettered 100, so there's potential for at least some modest regression there.

STATS: Driving Distance: A+   Driving Accuracy: B-   GIR: A   Short Game: B   Putting: B+

McNeill, George William Jr. (USA) (39) b. Naples, FL 10/2/1975. 6'1" 180 lbs. College: Florida St. TP: 1998. Spent one year (2003) on the Web.com Tour and several on mini-tours before breaking through at 2006 Q School (where he was medalist by five shots) in his ninth try. Logged his first PGA Tour victory as a rookie, beating D.J. Trahan by four at the 2007 Las Vegas Invitational (Frys.com). Save for a disappointing 2010, finished no worse than 91st on the $$$ list through 2012 before slipping slightly during a quiet 2013. Claimed his second career PGA Tour win

McNeill, George William Jr., Cont'd

at the 2012 Puerto Rico Open, birdieing the last three holes to beat Ryo Ishikawa by two. **OWR Best:** 67 - Mar, 2008.

PGA Tour Wins (2): 2007: Las Vegas Classic (Fry's.com) **2012:** Puerto Rico Open.
Other Wins: Waterloo (IA) Open: 2001.

	02	03	04	05	06	07	08	09	10	11	12	13	14
Masters	-	-	-	-	-	-	-	-	-	-	-	-	-
US Open	MC	-	-	-	MC	63	-	MC	-	-	-	-	-
British	-	-	-	-	-	-	-	-	MC	-	-	-	MC
PGA	-	-	-	-	-	-	MC	-	MC	-	T62	-	MC
Money (A)	-	-	-	-	-	61	76	57	138	59	91	136	43
OWR	-	-	-	-	-	-	115	140	136	238	166	161	275	114

2014: PGA: 24 st / 16 ct / 4 t10. (2 Greenbrier, T6 Northern Trust, 7 Valspar, 7 Frys.com).   Finished a career-best 46th in FedEx Cup points.
OUTLOOK: Though winless since 2012, put together his career-best season in 2014. Statistically, a solid all-around player with few real weaknesses, but also little in the way of high-end strengths. Still, he can heat up on a moment's notice, as two 62s and a 61 in 2014 indicate. His putting has been a tad less consistent than the rest of his game, but if he could normalize his stronger years, more wins would surely lie in his near future.

STATS: Driving Distance: B   Driving Accuracy: B+   GIR: B   Short Game: B   Putting: B+

Meesawat, Prom (Thailand) (29)

b. Hua Hin, Thailand 7/21/1984. 6'2" 210 lbs. TP: 2004. Nicknamed the "Blue Dolphin." Son of the 1991 Thailand open champion (the first native to win the title) and was a major amateur star in his homeland. Planned to play amateur golf in the U.S. but was convinced by Vijay Singh to turn pro and play the Asian circuit. Enjoyed initial success, cracking the Order of Merit top 10 in 2006 and '07, and winning the 2006 SK Telecom Open. Spent limited time in Europe from 2006-2010 and played regularly in Japan in 2008-2009. Battled injuries in 2010 and '11 but showed a return to form in 2012, finishing 6th in Asian $$$. Won for the second time at the 2014 Tournament Players Championship, beating 19-year-old Miguel Tabuena in sudden death. **Teams:** Eisenhower Trophy: 2010. **OWR Best:** 140 - Feb, 2008.

Asian Tour Wins (2): 2006: SK Telecom Open **2014:** Yeangder TPC.
Other Wins: Singha Pattaya Open (Thailand) (3): 2006-11-12.
Amateur Wins: Thailand Am (3): 2001-02-03   Junior World (13-14): 1997   Junior World (15-17): 2002

	04	05	06	07	08	09	10	11	12	13	14
Masters	-	-	-	-	-	-	-	-	-	-	-
US Open	-	-	-	-	-	-	-	-	-	-	-
British	-	-	-	-	-	-	-	MC	-	-	-
PGA	-	-	-	-	-	-	-	-	-	-	-
Money (E)	-	-	-	-	-	-	-	-	-	160	135*
Money (J)	-	-	-	150	125	-	-	-	-	-	-
Money (As)	55	15	3	7	46	60	68	34	6	8	3
OWR	924	386	185	152	433	830	710	378	162	211	129

2014: ASIA: 18 st / 17 ct / 6 t10. (Incl. Won Yeangder TPC, T2 Macau, 3 Manila Masters). Enjoyed a fine year on the Asian Tour, making 17 of 18 cuts (the last was a WD), winning for the second time (in Taiwan) and finishing 3rd in $$$.
OUTLOOK: After struggling in Europe in 2013, proved once more that he can compete at the highest level in Asia in 2014. A lack of distance is, as ever, an issue, but the rest of his game mostly measures up well. Once looked capable of climbing higher, but Asia may be his best bet now.

STATS: Driving Distance: C-   Driving Accuracy: B+   GIR: B+   Short Game: A-   Putting: B+

Merrick, John Sampson (USA) (32)

b. Long Beach, CA 3/20/1982. 6'1" 170 lbs. College: UCLA. TP: 2004. In 2001, became the youngest player since Tiger Woods to win the Southern California Amateur (at age 19). A mini-tour player in 2004 and '05 before a 21st-place finish on the 2006 Web.com Tour earned PGA Tour playing privileges for 2007. Though winless over his first six seasons, he twice cracked the top 100 in $$$, peaking at 58th in 2009. Broke through for his maiden win in 2013 at his hometown Northern Trust Open, beating Charlie Beljan on the second hole of sudden death. **Teams:** World Cup: 2009. **OWR Best:** 73 - Feb, 2013.

PGA Tour Wins (1): 2013: Northern Trust Open.
Other Wins: 1 Web.com (2006).
Amateur Wins: Southern California Am 2001.

	05	06	07	08	09	10	11	12	13	14
Masters	-	-	-	-	T6	MC	-	-	MC	-
US Open	MC	-	-	T6	MC	-	-	-	-	-
British	-	-	-	-	-	-	-	-	-	-
PGA	-	-	-	T52	T10	MC	-	-	T47	-
Money (A)	-	-	135	83	58	140	119	93	34	144
OWR	-	332	359	173	152	319	357	228	91	325

2014: PGA: 25 st / 20 ct / 0 t10. (T19 Phoenix). Remarkably, made 20 of 25 cuts yet still finished 133rd in FedEx Cup points.
OUTLOOK: Has slipped noticeably since winning at Riviera in 2013. Statistically, he recovered some of his Total Driving loss from 2012 to 2013 (13 to 155 to 36) but his SGP slipped from 82 in 2013 to 166 in 2014. Exempt through this season but will need to solidify things in 2015.

STATS: Driving Distance: B-   Driving Accuracy: A   GIR: A   Short Game: C   Putting: C

Merritt, Troy Brian (USA) (29)

b. Osage, IA 10/25/1985. 6'0" 160 lbs. All-American at Boise St. after transferring from Winona (MN) St., where he was a Division 2 All-American. TP: 2008. After spending 2009 on the Web.com Tour, was a rare wire-to-wire winner at 2009 Q School, then kept his card by finishing 125th in PGA Tour $$$ in 2010. Lost it after 2011, however, and returned to the Web.com for 2012 and '13 before

Merritt, Troy Brian, Cont'd

enjoying more success on the PGA Tour in 2014. **OWR Best:** 236 - Apr, 2010.

Other Wins: 1 Web.com (2009).

	10	11	12	13	14
Masters	-	-	-	-	-
US Open	-	-	-	-	-
British	-	-	-	-	-
PGA	-	-	-	-	-
Money (A)	125	202	-	-	107
OWR	388	680	793	762	286

2014: PGA: 20 st / 10 ct / 1 t10. (2 FedEx St Jude). Logged only a single PGA Tour top 10, but as it was a second (at FedEx St Jude), he was able to retained his PGA Tour card for the first time since 2010, finishing 101st in FedEx Cup points.

OUTLOOK: Will be fully exempt for the first time since 2011. Has had a limited PGA Tour impact to date, logging two top 10s (including last year's FedEx St Jude runner-up) in 72 career starts. Has little that truly stands out statistically, and seems a longshot to explode going forward.

STATS: Driving Distance: C+   Driving Accuracy: B   GIR: B-   Short Game: C+   Putting: B

Micheel, Shaun Carl (USA) (45)

b. Orlando, FL 1/5/1969. 6'0" 180 lbs. College: All-American at Indiana U. TP: 1992. An AJGA All-American. After college, embarked on a professional career that was domestically unproductive for the better part of a decade – though overseas forays did produce a victory in the 1998 Singapore Open on the old Asian Tour. Then, with but a single 3rd-place finish over 163 PGA Tour starts on his résumé, he won the 2003 PGA Championship at Oak Hill after nearly holing a 7 iron approach to the 72nd, beating Chad Campbell by two. Experienced several up-and-down seasons thereafter (finishing 46th in $$$ in 2006 and 88th in 2010) before slipping significantly since 2011. Underwent heart surgery to unclog arteries in April, 2014 but was competing again days afterward. **OWR Best:** 34 - Feb, 2004.

PGA Tour Wins (1): 2003: PGA Championship.

Asian Wins (1): 1998: Singapore Open.

Other Wins: 1 Web.com (1999).

	94	95	96	97	98	99	00	01	02	03	04	05	06	07	08	09	10	11	12	13	14
Masters	-	-	-	-	-	-	-	-	-	-	T22	MC	MC	MC	MC	-	-	-	-	-	-
US Open	-	-	-	-	MC	-	T40	-	-	-	T28	MC	MC	MC	-	-	T22	-	-	-	-
British	-	-	-	-	-	-	-	-	-	-	T47	MC	MC	T35	-	-	-	-	-	-	-
PGA	-	-	-	-	-	-	-	-	-	Win	T24	MC	2	T32	-	MC	T48	T74	MC	MC	MC
Money (A)	247	-	-	250	286*	-	104	136	105	32	82	146	46	108	209	180	88	188	208*	-	-
OWR	-	-	-	858	787	467	269	278	245	46	73	222	57	103	424	531	179	498	833	-	-

2014: PGA: 1 st / 0 ct / 0 t10. Only PGA Tour start was the PGA Championship (plus eight Web.com starts) after having heart surgery.

OUTLOOK: Is limited to Past Champion status these days. Has battled injuries seemingly forever, most recently nursing a shoulder, plus his heart surgery. Seems to be winding it all down – perhaps in anticipation of a recuperative break prior to becoming Champions Tour eligible in 2019.

STATS: Driving Distance: C+   Driving Accuracy: C   GIR: C-   Short Game: C+   Putting: B+

Mickelson, Philip Alfred (USA) (44)

b. San Diego, CA 6/16/1970. 6'2" 190 lbs. Four-time All-American, three-time Nicklaus (1990-1992) and three-time Haskins (1990-1992) Awards winner, and three-time NCAA individual champion (1989, '90 and '92) at Arizona St. Won 1990 U.S. Amateur (5 & 4 over Manny Zerman) at Cherry Hills CC. TP: 1992. Four-time AJGA All-American and three-time AJGA Player Of The Year (1986-1988). Last player to win a PGA Tour event as an amateur (1991 Tucson Open). Has enjoyed one of contemporary golf's elite professional careers, winning PGA Tour events in all but two seasons since 1993, and scoring multiple titles in 14 of them. Was 0-for-46 in Major championships (including nine top-5 finishes) prior to winning the 2004 Masters in great style, carding a 72nd-hole birdie to edge Ernie Els by one. Validated this at the 2005 PGA at Baltusrol, where a clutch up-and-down at the 72nd preserved a one-shot victory over Thomas Bjørn and Steve Elkington. Won his second Masters in 2006, where a closing 69 stood him two clear of Tim Clark, then claimed a third Green Jacket in 2010 in similar fashion, closing with a fine 67 to beat Lee Westwood by three. Has suffered several heartbreaking Major losses, especially at the U.S. Open where he three-putted from five feet at the 71st to lose in 2004, double-bogeyed the 72nd to lose by one in '06, bogeyed the 68th and 71st to lose in 2009, and was nipped at the wire by Justin Rose in 2013. Had his 2007 season affected by a lingering wrist injury. A natural right-hander who long ago surpassed New Zealand's Bob Charles as golf's greatest lefty. Diagnosed in late 2010 with Psoriatic Arthritis, in response to which he became a vegetarian. Lipped out a putt for 59 in first round of 2013 Waste Management Phoenix Open before going on to win by four shots. Won his first title on a links course at the 2013 Scottish Open (in a playoff with Branden Grace), then came back a week later to win his first British Open, carding a spectacular closing 66 at Muirfield to win by three. Nearly salvaged a disappointing 2014 by finishing second at the PGA Championship (one behind Rory McIlroy) but on the whole the year matched 2003 for his worst season as a professional. **Awards:** World Golf Hall of Fame Member (2012). **Teams:** Walker Cup (2): 1989-91 (4-2-2). Eisenhower Trophy: 1990. Ryder Cup (10): 1995-97-99-02-04-06-08-10-12-14 (O: 16-19-6, S: 5-5-0). Presidents Cup (10): 1994-96-98-00-03-05-07-09-11-13 (20-16-11). World Cup: 2002. **OWR Best:** 2 - Feb, 2001.

PGA Tour Wins (42): 1991: Tucson Open (Northern Telecom)* **1993:** San Diego Open (Buick Inv), The International (Stableford) **1994:** Mercedes Championships **1995:** Tucson Open (Northern Telecom) **1996:** Tucson Open (Nortel), Phoenix Open, Byron Nelson Classic (GTE), World Series of Golf (NEC) **1997:** Bay Hill Inv, The International (Sprint) **1998:** Mercedes Championships, AT&T Pro-Am (54H) **2000:** San Diego Open (Buick Inv), Atlanta Classic (BellSouth) (54H), Colonial Inv (Mastercard), Tour Championship **2001:** San Diego Open (Buick Inv), Greater Hartford Open (Canon) **2002:** Bob Hope Classic (90H), Greater Hartford Open (Canon) **2004:** Bob Hope Classic (90H), Masters Tournament **2005:** Phoenix Open (FBR), AT&T Pro-Am, Atlanta Classic (BellSouth), PGA Championship **2006:** Atlanta Classic (BellSouth), Masters Tournament **2007:** AT&T Pro-Am, Players Championship, Deutsche Bank Championship **2008:** Northern Trust Open, Colonial Inv (Crown Plaza) **2009:** Northern Trust Open, WGC-CA Championship, Tour Championship **2010:** Masters Tournament **2011:** Houston Open (Shell) **2012:** AT&T Pro-Am **2013:** Phoenix Open (Waste Management), British Open.

European Tour Wins (3): 2007: HSBC Champions ('08) **2009:** WGC-HSBC Champions **2013:** Scottish Open (Barclays).

Other Wins: 1 Euro Challenge (1993)   +   Dunhill Cup: 1996 (w/M.O'Meara & S.Stricker)   Ernst Championship: 1996   Wendy's 3-Tour Challenge (2): 1997 (w/F.Couples & T.Lehman)-00 (w/N.Begay III & R.Mediate)   TELUS Skins (Canada): 2004   PGA Grand Slam (36): 2004.

Amateur Wins: U.S. Amateur: 1990   Porter Cup: 1990   Western Am: 1991   –   NCAA Individual (3): 1989-90-92   Junior World (9-10): 1980.

Mickelson, Philip Alfred, Cont'd

	90	91	92	93	94	95	96	97	98	99	00	01	02	03	04	05	06	07	08	09	10	11	12	13
Masters	-	T46	-	T34	-	T7	3	MC	T12	T6	T7	3	3	3	Win	10	Win	T24	T5	5	Win	T27	T3	T54
US Open	T29	T55	MC	-	T47	T4	T94	T43	T10	2	T16	T7	2	T55	2	T33	T2	MC	T18	T2	T4	T54	T65	T2
British	-	T73	-	-	MC	T40	T41	T24	79	MC	T11	T30	T66	T59	3	T60	T22	MC	T19	-	T48	T2	MC	Win
PGA	-	-	-	T6	3	MC	T8	T29	T34	T57	T9	2	T34	T23	T6	Win	T16	T32	T7	73	T12	T19	T36	T72
Money (A)	Am	Am	90*	22	15	28	2	11	6	14	2	2	2	38	3	3	6	2	3	3	6	12	8	4
OWR	462	147	145	47	22	24	7	6	10	9	4	2	2	15	5	3	3	2	3	2	4	14	17	5

	14
Masters	MC
US Open	T28
British	T23
PGA	2
Money (A)	38
OWR	14

2014: PGA: 21 st / 18 ct / 1 t10. (2 PGA). Finished 68th in FedEx Cup points. Made the same number of starts and cuts as 2013 but dropped from seven top 10s to one (also T2 at Abu Dhabi on the E Tour). A down year, but he played his way onto a 10th consecutive Ryder Cup team.

OUTLOOK: At age 44, did we see the first sign of a decline in 2014? Has seen his SGP fluctuate over the last five years (133, 134, 10, 5, 50) as well as his GIR (155, 51, 120, 43, 79), so it can reasonably be argued that he's simply more streaky than slipping. Has also witnessed a real drop in Driving Distance (13 in 2009 and '10, 93 and 70 in 2013 and '14) but there is no question that at least some of this was by design. And where does his Psoriatic Arthritis fit into this mix? As he's still chasing a U.S. Open, he's surely still motivated - but maybe not as often as before.

STATS: Driving Distance: B+   Driving Accuracy: C   GIR: B+   Short Game: A   Putting: A-

---

Miyamoto, Katsumasa (Japan) (42) b. Shizuoka, Japan 8/28/1972. 5'8" 165 lbs. TP: 1996. A highly successful Japan Tour player who has five times finished among the circuit's top 10 money winners. Broke through for his first victory at the 1998 Tsuruya Open (where he edged Australian Peter McWhinney by one) and later that season won the first of his three Nippon Series JT Cups, beating the legendary Jumbo Ozaki in a playoff. Also a two-time winner of the Japan Tour Championship, running away from Jeev Milkha Singh by seven shots in 2001, then edging Hiroyuki Fujita by three in 2010. After finishing 9th in 2010 earnings, slipped significantly for three straight seasons before breaking a four-year drought by winning the 2014 ANA Open, where he downed Hideto Tanihara in sudden death. Made 2014 his first multi-win season since 2001 by claiming the season-ending Nippon Series JT Cup for the third time. **Teams**: Eisenhower Trophy (2): 1992-94. **OWR Best**: 89 - Feb, 1999.

Japan Tour Wins (10): 1998: Tsuruya Open, Nippon Series JT Cup **2001**: Japan Tour Championship, Nippon Series JT Cup **2003**: Nigata Open **2007**: KBC Augusta **2008**: Token Homemate Cup **2010**: Japan Tour Championship **2014**: ANA Open, Nippon Series JT Cup.

	97	98	99	00	01	02	03	04	05	06	07	08	09	10	11	12	13	14
Masters	-	-	-	-	-	-	-	-	-	-	-	-	-	-	-	-	-	-
US Open	-	-	-	-	-	-	-	-	-	-	-	-	-	MC	-	-	-	-
British	-	-	-	-	-	-	-	-	-	-	-	-	-	-	-	-	-	-
PGA	-	-	-	-	-	-	-	-	-	-	-	-	-	-	-	-	-	-
Money (J)	53	4	102	12	7	24	11	19	32	16	7	16	25	9	44	35	46	5
OWR	321	94	188	189	110	138	119	141	187	176	163	186	196	95	210	334	423	154

2014: JAP: 24 st / 14 ct / 8 t10. (Won ANA, Won Nippon, T3 Bridgestone, T7 Token Homemate, T7 Kansai, etc.). Played notably up-and-down golf, missing 10 of 24 cuts but logging eight top 10s as he finished 5th in Japan Tour $$$.

OUTLOOK: A steady, above-the-median ball striker who witnessed the odd statistical blend of a marked decrease in Driving Accuracy with a pronounced increase in GIR in 2014. At 42, he may not maintain his current highs much longer, but he should remain competitive for a while.

STATS: Driving Distance: B+   Driving Accuracy: B+ ⇩   GIR: B+ ⇧   Short Game: B-   Putting: B+

Miyazato, Yusaku (Japan) (34) b. Higashi, Japan 6/19/1980. 5'7" 150 lbs. College: Tohoku Fukushi University. TP: 2003. The older brother of LPGA star Ai Miyazato. Won the 2001 Japan Amateur, the 1998 Japan Junior and three Japan Collegiate titles (2000, '01 & '02). Spent his first decade as a professional occupying journeyman status on the Japan Tour, only once bettering 27th in earnings (14th in 2007) and going winless. Broke through for his maiden victory at 2013's season-ending Golf Nippon Series JT Cup (edging China's Ashun Wu by three), then validated that win by claiming the Token Homemate Cup (by two over Hiroshi Iwata) in his second start of 2014. Managed the astonishing feat of recording two holes-in-one in a single PGA Tour round, carding aces at the Montreux G&CC's 7th and 12th holes during the second round of the 2006 Reno-Tahoe Open. **Teams**: Eisenhower Trophy (3): 1998-00-02. **OWR Best**: 147 - Apr, 2014.

Japan Tour Wins (2): 2013: Nippon Series **2014**: Token Homemate Cup.
Other Wins: Kyusu Open (Japan): 2013.
Amateur Wins: Japan Amateur: 2001   Japan Junior: 1998   Orange Bowl Jr: 1998   Japan Collegiate (3): 2000-01-02.

	03	04	05	06	07	08	09	10	11	12	13	14
Masters	-	-	-	-	-	-	-	-	-	-	-	-
US Open	-	-	-	-	-	-	-	-	-	-	-	-
British	-	-	-	-	-	-	-	-	-	-	-	MC
PGA	-	-	-	-	-	-	-	-	-	-	-	-
Money (J)	54	49	43	27	14	32	30	55	20	30	7	11
OWR	218	295	348	252	197	253	261	362	255	238	178	166

2014: JAP: 24 st / 18 ct / 7 t10. (Won Token Homemate, T3 KBC Augusta, T5 Japan PGA, T6 Dunlop Phoenix, T9 Diamond Cup, etc.). Did a strong job of holding his 2013 gains, winning early at the Token Homemate Cup and contending often enough to finish 11th in $$$.

OUTLOOK: Arrived with an elite Japanese amateur pedigree, then took a full decade to find his footing on the Japan Tour. Solid, strong ball striker who can hit a lot of greens. His putting holds him back, but his overall talent level suggest he can hold his gains in the peak years of his mid-30s.

STATS: Driving Distance: A-   Driving Accuracy: B+   GIR: A-   Short Game: B   Putting: C+

Molder, Bryce Wade (USA) (35) b. Harrison, AR 1/27/1979. 6'0" 180 lbs. Four-time All-American, two-time Nicklaus (1998 and 2001) and Haskins (2001) Awards winner at Georgia Tech. TP: 2000. Three-time AJGA All-American. Followed David Duval, Phil Mickelson and Gary Hallberg as the then-only four-time first-team All-Americans in NCAA history. Struggled significantly for a decade after turning pro, winning once on the Web.com Tour (2006) but never retaining a spot on the PGA Tour until 2009. Strung together three straight top-65 $$$ rankings from 2009-2011, however, and also broke through for his first win at the 2011 Frys.com Open, beating another previous non-winner, Briny Baird, in a six-hole playoff. **Teams:** Walker Cup (2): 1999-01 (3-3-2). Eisenhower Trophy: 2000. Palmer Cup (3): 1998-99-01. **OWR Best:** 64 - Aug, 2010.

PGA Tour Wins (1): 2011: Frys.com Open.

Other Wins: 1 Web.com (2006).

	99	00	01	02	03	04	05	06	07	08	09	10	11	12	13	14
Masters	-	-	-	-	-	-	-	-	-	-	-	-	-	-	-	-
US Open	MC	-	T30	-	MC	-	-	-	-	-	T43	-	-	-	-	-
British	-	-	-	-	-	-	-	-	-	-	-	-	-	-	-	-
PGA	-	-	-	-	-	-	-	-	-	-	-	T12	T56	MC	-	-
Money (A)	-	-	-	-	-	-	-	-	185	-	63	63	40	82	102	113
OWR	-	-	397	240	590	751	-	323	441	382	106	85	115	149	214	228

2014: PGA: 25 st / 14 ct / 2 t10. (T6 Northern Trust, T10 AT&T Pro-Am). Kept his card for the sixth straight year, finishing 109th in FedEx Cup points.

OUTLOOK: It took him nine years to stick on the PGA Tour but emerged as a steady earner thereafter, riding a straight driver and an elite short game. Seems to have slipped from a career peak but as he's only 35, it's possible that some of his best golf could very well still lie ahead.

STATS: Driving Distance: C   Driving Accuracy: B+   GIR: B-   Short Game: A   Putting: A

Molinari, Edoardo (Italy) (33) b. Turin, Italy 02/11/1981. 5'11" 165 lbs. College: University of Torino. TP: 2006. In 2005, became the first European since Harold Hilton (1911) to win the U.S. Amateur, beating Dillon Dougherty 4 & 3 at Merion. Postponed turning pro until after college (where he earned an Engineering degree), then became a five-time winner on the Challenge Tour from 2007-09. Claimed his first major tour win at the 2009 Dunlop Phoenix in Japan, where he edged Robert Karlsson in a playoff. Teamed with brother Francesco to log Italy's first-ever win in the World Cup in 2009, in Shenzhen, China. Enjoyed a very strong 2010 season, which saw him win both the Barclays Scottish Open (beating Darren Clarke by three on the eve of the Open Championship) and the Johnnie Walker Championship (by one over Brett Rumford) while also finishing 11th in the E Tour Order of Merit. Slipped a bit during a winless 2011, finishing 46th in $$$. Had surgery on his left wrist in June of 2012, limiting him to 17 E Tour starts. Had his 2013 season cut short by August surgery to his left thumb, limiting him to 14 starts. **Teams:** Eisenhower Trophy (4): 1998-00-02-04. Ryder Cup: 2010 (O: 0-1-2, S: 0-0-1). World Cup (4): 2007-08-09-11 (won in '09 w/F.Molinari). **OWR Best:** 14 - Oct, 2010.

European Tour Wins (2): 2010: Scottish Open, Johnnie Walker Championship.

Japan Tour Wins (1): 2009: Dunlop Phoenix.

Other Wins: 5 Euro Challenge (2007-2009).

Amateur Wins: U.S. Amateur: 2005   Italian Am: 2001   –   English Under-16s: 1996   Italian Am Foursomes (2): 2002-04 (both w/F.Molinari)   Turkish Am: 2003.

	05	06	07	08	09	10	11	12	13	14
Masters	-	MC	-	-	-	MC	T11	T57	-	-
US Open	-	MC	-	-	-	T47	T54	-	-	-
British	T60	T68	-	-	-	T27	T66	-	-	T7
PGA	-	-	-	-	-	T33	T69	-	T33	T47
Money (E)	Am	258	-	147	-	11	46	86	91*	40
OWR	944	960	292	653	48	18	65	235	285	103

2014: E: 31 st / 23 ct / 5 t10. (2 Irish, T4 Wales, T7 British Open, T9 Dubai, T10 Tshwane). Returned to good health for the first time in three years and, though winless, recorded five top 10s (including a runner-up at the Irish Open) and ranked 40th in $$$, his best finish since 2011.

OUTLOOK: Prior to his injuries, climbed as high as #14 in the world (2010) and was a winner both in Europe (twice) and Japan – so when healthy, he can compete effectively at a high level. Very straight off the tee and has improved both his GIR and his short game, making him a far more well-rounded player. Assuming continued good health, he should be pushing to get back among the OWR top 50 sometime in 2015.

STATS: Driving Distance: B-   Driving Accuracy: A-   GIR: B+   Short Game: B+   Putting: B+

Molinari, Francesco (Italy) (32) b. Turin, Italy 11/08/1982. 5'8" 160 lbs. TP: 2004. Younger brother of Edoardo (and his caddy during the 2005 U.S. Amateur) but turned professional sooner. Italian Boys (2000) and Amateur (2004) champion who has represented Italy as an amateur (the 2002 and '04 Eisenhower Trophies) and a professional (six World Cups beginning in 2006). Gained his first E Tour win at the 2006 Italian Open, riding a dramatic final round 65 to beat Anders Hansen and Jarmo Sandelin by four shots and become the first native since Massimo Mannelli (1980) to claim the national title. Teamed with Edoardo to log Italy's first ever win in the World Cup in 2009, in Shenzhen, China. Blossomed in 2010, logging 10 top 10s in 18 E Tour starts and claiming a prominent victory at November's WGC HSBC Champions in China, where he won a head-to-head battle with #1-ranked Lee Westwood, by one. Won for the third time on the E Tour at the 2012 Spanish Open, riding a closing 65 to a three-shot triumph. **Teams:** Eisenhower Trophy (2): 2002-04. Palmer Cup: 2004. Ryder Cup (2): 2010-12: 0-4-2, S: 0-1-1). Seve Trophy (3): 2009-11-13. World Cup (6): 2006-07-08-09-11-13 (won in '09 w/F.Molinari). **OWR Best:** 14 - Nov, 2010.

European Tour Wins (3): 2006: Italian Open **2010**: WGC-HSBC Champions **2012**: Spanish Open.

Other Wins: Italian PGA: 2009.

Amateur Wins: Italian Am: 2004   –   Italian Am Stroke Play (2): 2002-04   Italian Am Foursomes (2): 2002-04 (both w/E.Molinari)   Sherry Cup (Spain): 2004   Italian Boys: 2000.

	05	06	07	08	09	10	11	12	13	14
Masters	-	-	-	-	-	T30	MC	T19	MC	50
US Open	-	-	-	-	T27	MC	MC	T29	MC	T23
British	-	-	MC	-	T13	MC	MC	T39	T9	T15
PGA	-	-	-	-	T10	T33	T34	T54	-	T59
Money (E)	86	38	60	24	14	5	21	8	13	35
OWR	311	147	177	79	38	15	41	30	38	55

Molinari, Francesco, Cont'd

2014: E: 25 st / 21 ct / 2 t10. (4 Volvo China, T7 BMW PGA). Actually took a small step backwards, logging his worst $$$ ranking (35th) since 2007. Also made six non-Major/WGC starts in America, led by a T5 at the Arnold Palmer Invitational and a T6 at the Players Championship.

OUTLOOK: A short but extremely straight hitter (he's finished no worse than 11th in Driving Accuracy since 2007) and owns a place among the E Tour's most consistent earners. Three career wins is nothing to sneeze at, but aside from an obvious lack of length, he certainly seems capable of potentially winning more regularly. But regardless, at age 32, he figures as a safe bet to stay among Europe's best for at least another decade.

STATS: Driving Distance: C+   Driving Accuracy: A+   GIR: A-   Short Game: B-   Putting: B-

---

Moore, Jonathan (USA) (29)
b. Oceanside, CA 4/17/1985. 6'1" 180 lbs. All-American and NCAA individual champion (2006) at Oklahoma St. TP: 2007. Three-time AJGA All-American. After winning the NCAA individual title as a redshirt freshman, left college early and played on multiple mini-tours before joining the Asian Tour full-time in 2011. Finished 2nd (to Sergio García) at the 2012 Iskandar Johor Open after carding a final round 61 but has otherwise had only a limited impact. **Teams**: Walker Cup: 2007 (2-0-1). Eisenhower Trophy: 2006. **OWR Best**: 205 - Jan, 2013.

Other Wins: 1 Asian Dev (2011) + 1 Adams (2009) 1 eGolf Tour: 2008.
Amateur Wins: Oregon Am: 2001   Western Jr: 2001   NCAA Individual: 2006   Players Am: 2006.

	06	07	08	09	10	11	12	13	14
Masters	-	-	-	-	-	-	-	-	-
US Open	MC	-	-	-	-	-	-	-	-
British	-	-	-	-	-	-	-	-	-
PGA	-	-	-	-	-	-	-	-	-
Money (AS)	-	-	-	-	-	72	7	75	-
OWR	-	-	-	-	-	706	212	449	746

2014: Made only one major tour start worldwide, finishing T6 on a sponsor exemption at the Thailand Golf Championship.

OUTLOOK: Began 2013 ranked 212th in the OWR and looking capable of playing his way back to the West - but it's been all downhill since. A statistically average player, but he's still in his 20s so there's time left to get things turned around.

STATS: Driving Distance: B+   Driving Accuracy: C+   GIR: B-   Short Game: B   Putting: B

Moore, Patrick Joseph (USA) (44)
b. Austin, MN 4/28/1970. 5'11" 160 lbs. College: All-American at U of North Carolina. TP: 1993. After playing the Canadian Tour, eventually qualified for the 2002 Web.com Tour where, somewhat out of left field, he won three times (the first as a Monday qualifier) to become the fifth player in the circuit's history to earn an immediate battlefield promotion. Made only three PGA Tour starts in 2003 before being besieged with back problems which have severely curtailed his schedule since. **OWR Best**: 249 - Nov, 2002.

Other Wins: 3 Web.com (2002).

	04	05	06	07	08	09	10	11	12	13	14
Masters	-	-	-	-	-	-	-	-	-	-	-
US Open	-	-	-	-	-	-	-	-	-	-	-
British	-	-	-	-	-	-	-	-	-	-	-
PGA	-	-	-	-	-	-	-	-	-	-	-
Money (A)	248*	-	-	-	-	-	-	-	-	-	-
OWR	-	-	-	-	-	-	-	-	-	-	-

2014: Once again failed to make a PGA Tour start due to ongoing back issues. Can anyone out there actually remember seeing him play?

OUTLOOK: Begins 2014 with four events left on the game's all-time longest medical extension, which dates to his rookie year of 2003. Hasn't played in a Tour event since 2010; a return to any sort of exempt status might cause the Tour to reinstate the Comeback Player Award – and then retire it.

STATS: Driving Distance: --   Driving Accuracy: --   GIR: --   Short Game: --   Putting: --

---

Moore, Ryan David (USA) (32)
b. Tacoma, WA 12/5/1982. 5'9" 170 lbs. Four-time All-American, NCAA individual champion (2004), Nicklaus (2005), Haskins (2005) and Hogan (2005) Awards winner at UNLV. Won 2004 U.S. Amateur (2 up over Luke List) at Winged Foot. TP: 2005. Two-time AJGA All-American. In 2004, also won his second U.S. Public Links (previously won it in 2002) and the Western Amateur. Turned pro in the spring of 2005, then earned over $680,000 in 12 fall events, making him the first player since Tiger Woods to jump from college to the PGA Tour in a single season without going to Q School. Emerged as a consistent money earner, climbing to 31st and 32nd in winnings in 2009 and '10. Claimed his first PGA Tour victory at the 2009 Wyndham Championship (Greensboro), beating Jason Bohn and Kevin Stadler on the third hole of sudden death. Won for the second time in 2012 in Las Vegas, edging Brendon de Jonge by one at the Justin Timberlake Shriners Open. Claimed his third win in Malaysia, edging Gary Woodland in a playoff at the 2013 CIMB Classic, then returned a year later to defend his title, beating a trio of players by three. **Teams**: Walker Cup: 2003 (0-2-0). Eisenhower Trophy: 2004. Palmer Cup: 2003. **OWR Best**: 27 - Nov, 2014.

PGA Tour Wins (4): **2009**: Greater Greensboro (Wyndham) **2012**: Las Vegas Classic (Shriners) **2013**: CIMB Classic ('14) **2014**: CIMB Classic ('15).
Amateur Wins: U.S. Amateur: 2004   Western Am: 2004   –   U.S. Amateur Public Links (2):2002-04   NCAA Individual: 2004   Sahalee Players: 2004.

	02	03	04	05	06	07	08	09	10	11	12	13	14
Masters	-	T45	-	T13	-	-	-	-	T14	T35	-	T38	MC
US Open	MC	-	-	T57	-	MC	-	T10	T33	MC	-	MC	T48
British	-	-	-	-	-	T42	-	-	MC	T28	-	T32	T12
PGA	-	-	-	-	T9	MC	MC	-	T65	T56	MC	T55	T41
Money (A)	Am	Am	Am	-	81	59	88	31	32	42	26	61	21
OWR	-	-	793	718	142	79	74	158	51	45	57	40	33	30

2014: PGA: 24 st / 20 ct / 7 t10. (Won CIMB, T5 Travelers, T6 Phoenix, T7 John Deere, T8 WGC-Bridgestone, etc.). In addition to claiming his third PGA Tour win, logged seven top 10s and finished a career-best 21st in $$$ and 39th in FedEx Cup points.

Moore, Ryan David, Cont'd

OUTLOOK: Only thrice a winner but remains one of the PGA Tour's most consistent earners. Has seen his ball striking numbers bounce around (but move generally upward) over the last few years, particularly his GIR (155, 61, 114, 23) and Ball Striking (122, 36, 73, 24). On the downside, his SGP, which stood firmly among the top 50 from 2009-2012 has slipped to 110 and 91 since. It is probably reasonable to ask why he doesn't win more, but at age 32 he's likely just entering his best years – and meanwhile, his bank account continues to grown at a very fast clip.

STATS: Driving Distance: C+   Driving Accuracy: A   GIR: B+ ⇧   Short Game: B-   Putting: B+

Moore, Trevor Richard ("Titch") (South Africa) (38)
b. Port Elizabeth, South Africa 2/18/1976. 5'11" 200 lbs. TP: 1997. Notably long hitter who enjoyed a dominant amateur career, winning the 1996 South African Amateur and Stroke Play titles, as well as multiple provincial crowns. Initially made several unsuccessful forays onto the European Tour (failing to keep his card over three full seasons from 2003-2006) as well as an early visit to several U.S. mini-tours. Has been a steady winner at home, however, notably at the 2001 Royal Swazi Sun Classic (in a playoff over Keith Horne), a pair of Platinum Classics (2002 and '04) and the 2007 Coca-Cola Charity Championship, where he beat James Kingston, Louis Oosthuizen and Steve Basson by four. Missed most of 2011 with a torn tendon in his elbow, but rebounded well in 2012 and '13. Broke a six-year victory drought by beating Ulrich van den Berg on the fifth hole of sudden death at the 2014 Telkom PGA Championship, then added a second 2014 title at the inaugural Sun Boardwalk Challenge. **OWR Best**: 195 - Mar, 2002.

Sunshine Tour Wins (9): **2000**: Cock O' The North **2001**: Royal Swazi Sun Classic **2002**: Highveld Classic, Platinum Classic **2004**: Platinum Classic **2007**: Vodacom-Final (54H), Coca-Cola Charity Championship **2014**: Telkom PGA Championship, Sun Boardwalk Challenge (36H).

Other Wins: 1 Euro Challenge (2003).

Amateur Wins: South African Am: 1996 – World Under-17: 1993   Western Province Am: 1993   Transvaal Am: 1993   Eastern Province Am: 1993   World Int'l Masters: 1995   South African Am Stroke Play: 1996.

	98	99	00	01	02	03	04	05	06	07	08	09	10	11	12	13	14
Masters	-	-	-	-	-	-	-	-	-	-	-	-	-	-	-	-	-
US Open	-	-	-	-	-	-	-	-	-	-	-	-	-	-	-	-	-
British	-	-	-	-	-	-	-	-	-	-	-	-	-	-	-	-	-
PGA	-	-	-	-	-	-	-	-	-	-	-	-	-	-	-	-	-
Money (E)	-	-	-	-	200	186*	121	159	-	-	-	-	-	-	-	-	-
Money (SA)	92	39	29	7	16	13*	5*	4	13*	9	59	14	36	-	48	23	20
OWR	-	741	411	332	301	413	393	255	429	526	927	411	716	-	896	466	358

2014: SUN: 24 st / 17 ct / 4 t10. (Incl. Won Telkom PGA, Won Sun Boardwalk, T4 Sun City).   Despite missing his first four cuts, posted another solid Sunshine Tour campaign, winning twice (including at the Telkom PGA) and finishing 20th in $$$.

OUTLOOK: A long-term domestic star in South Africa who never gained much foothold in brief new millennium forays abroad. Returned to the winner's circle twice in 2014, completing a comeback from 2011 elbow surgery. At age 38, should have plenty of good golf left in the tank.

STATS: Driving Distance: --   Driving Accuracy: --   GIR: --   Short Game: --   Putting: --

---

Morrison, James Ian (England) (29)
b. Chertsey, England 1/24/1985. 5'11" 170 lbs. College: U of South Carolina. TP: 2006. Former youth cricket star who played collegiate golf in the U.S. After turning pro, spent three seasons on the Challenge Tour before earning his way onto the E Tour for 2010, then won the lighter-field Madeira Islands Open (by one over Oliver Fisher) in his sixth start and finished 2nd in the Spanish Open in his seventh. Enjoyed three solid campaigns earnings-wise before struggling markedly in 2013, then reestablishing himself (finishing 88th in $$$) in 2014. Has suffered from Crohn's disease since his teens. **OWR Best**: 132 - May, 2010.

European Tour Wins (5): **2010**: Madeira Islands Open.

Amateur Wins: Victorian Open Am (Australian): 2005   Italian Am Stroke Play: 2006.

	10	11	12	13	14
Masters	-	-	-	-	-
US Open	MC	-	-	-	-
British	-	-	T23	-	-
PGA	-	-	-	-	-
Money (E)	61	57	80	139	88
OWR	175	178	231	470	394

2014: E: 28 st / 21 ct / 1 t10. (T4 Perth).   Though recording only one top 10, made 21 of 28 E Tour cuts en route to retaining his card for the fourth time in five years, finishing 88th in $$$.

OUTLOOK: Never a long hitter but he hits plenty of greens. During 2014 he saw an across-the-board return to many of the higher statistical levels present in 2010 and '11, which obviously bodes well going forward. His only win came at the Madeira Islands Open, but such light-field or opposite events may again prove healthy hunting grounds before he's finished. Still in his 20s, he certainly still has time to grow.

STATS: Driving Distance: C+   Driving Accuracy: A-   GIR: B+   Short Game: B   Putting: B

Mulroy, Garth David (South Africa) (36)
b. Durban, South Africa 7/8/1978. 6'1" 200 lbs. College: North Carolina St. TP: 2002. Initially based his professional career mostly in America while regularly playing a short winter schedule in his homeland. Played several U.S. mini-tours after turning pro before joining the Web.com from 2007-2009, finishing 14th (with one win) in '09 to reach the PGA Tour. Lost his card after 2010 but regained it via the Web.com again in 2011. Was twice a Sunshine Tour winner during 2008, claiming the Vodacom Origins of Golf – Arabella title (by four over Richard Sterne) and the Coca-Cola Charity Championship in a seven-shot runaway. Biggest win to date came at the E Tour co-sanctioned Alfred Dunhill Championship in 2011. Began spending more time in Europe and America (again) in 2013. **OWR Best**: 124 - Mar, 2013.

European Tour Wins (1): **2011**: Alfred Dunhill Championship.

Sunshine Tour Wins (2): **2008**: Vodacom-Arabella (54H), Cola-Cola Championship.

Other Wins: 1 Web.com (2009) + Gary Player Inv (SA): 2008 (w/B. Lincoln).

Mulroy, Garth David, Cont'd

	08	09	10	11	12	13	14
Masters	-	-	-	-	-	-	-
US Open	-	-	-	-	-	-	T40
British	-	-	-	-	T64	-	-
PGA	-	-	-	-	-	-	-
Money (A)	-	-	181	-	175	-	-
Money (E)	-	-	-	-	-	60	-
Money (SA)	2*	44*	76*	1*	9*	6*	73*
OWR	300	298	553	168	167	174	392

2014: Made only three starts on African soil (best: T34 Africa Open). Made seven Web.com starts, finishing 90th in regular season $$$.

OUTLOOK: A powerful player whose short game and putting are below-the-median in America – though the latter improved noticeably in Europe in 2013. Would seem to have enough game to succeed overseas – but like most South Africans, seems a much greater threat to win on home soil.

STATS (LTD): Driving Distance: A-   Driving Accuracy: C+   GIR: B   Short Game: C   Putting: B

Murless, Mark (South Africa) (38)
b. Johannesburg, South Africa 3/29/1976. 6'0" 165 lbs. TP: 1995. Former South African Stroke Play champion who has seldom ventured off the Sunshine Tour since turning pro. A four-time winner there, highlighted by the 2007 Nedbank Affinty Cup (where he beat James Kingston and T.C. Charamba by one) and the 2008 Mt. Edgecomb Trophy, where he defeated Darren Fichardt in a playoff. Peaked in earnings during those two seasons (7th and 4th in the Order of Merit) but began trending downward in 2010. **OWR Best**: 288 - Feb, 2007.

Sunshine Tour Wins (4): 1996: Platinum Classic **2004**: Namibian PGA Championship **2007**: Nedbank Affinity Cup **2008**: Mt. Edgecomb Trophy.
Amateur Wins: Transvaal Stroke Play: 1994   South African Stroke Play: 1995.

	97	98	99	00	01	02	03	04	05	06	07	08	09	10	11	12	13	14
Masters	-	-	-	-	-	-	-	-	-	-	-	-	-	-	-	-	-	-
US Open	-	-	-	-	-	-	-	-	-	-	-	-	-	-	-	-	-	-
British	-	-	-	-	-	-	-	-	-	-	-	-	-	-	-	-	-	-
PGA	-	-	-	-	-	-	-	-	-	-	-	-	-	-	-	-	-	-
Money (SA)	31	44	46	28	62	30	21	13	11	17	7	4	30	69	70	76	68	67
OWR	570	716	741	881	554	390	597	571	479	520	549	661	765	843	954	-	-	1348

2014: SUN: 18 st / 9 ct / 0 t10. (T11 Wild Waves). Failed to crack the top 60 in $$$ for the fifth consecutive season, finishing 67th.

OUTLOOK: Though hardly over the hill at 38, settling in outside of the top 60 $$$ winners suggests his days as a star may now be behind him.

STATS: Driving Distance: --   Driving Accuracy: --   GIR: --   Short Game: --   Putting: --

---

Muto, Toshinori (Japan) (36)
b. Gunma Prefecture, Japan 3/10/1978. 5'7" 170 lbs. TP: 2003. A five-time Japan Tour winner who played through several mediocre seasons before breaking through for a victory at the Munsingwear Open (and finishing 17th in the Order of Merit) in 2006. Has since established himself as a regular J Tour winner and money earner (including top-10 $$$ finishes in 2008 and '11), claiming the 2008 Tokai Classic (by one over Yuta Ikeda), the 2009 Championship by Lexus (a three-shot triumph over up-and-coming Kyung-Tae Kim) and the 2011 Dunlop Phoenix, where he beat Gonzalo Fernández-Castaño (among several other visiting Europeans) by four. Won the 2012 at the Kansai Open, opening 64-65 before hanging on to edge Hyung-Sung Kim by one. **OWR Best**: 102 - Dec, 2012.

Japan Tour Wins (5): 2006: Munsingwear Open **2008**: Tokai Classic **2009**: Championship by Lexus **2011**: Dunlop Phoenix (54H) **2012**: Kansai Open.

	03	04	05	06	07	08	09	10	11	12	13	14
Masters	-	-	-	-	-	-	-	-	-	-	-	-
US Open	-	-	-	-	-	-	-	-	-	-	-	-
British	-	-	-	MC	MC	-	-	-	-	T72	-	-
PGA	-	-	-	-	-	-	-	-	-	-	-	-
Money (J)	175	206	80	17	50	9	18	52	8	12	32	20
OWR	-	-	-	700	208	298	120	137	315	113	103	228	202

2014: JAP: 19 st / 15 ct / 6 t10. (2 Taiheiyo, T3 KBC Augusta, T3 Nippon, T6 Dunlop Phoenix, T9 Crowns, etc.). After a somewhat slow start, played his best golf at year's end, closing with four straight top 10s to finish 20th in $$$.

OUTLOOK: A solid, consistent tee-to-greener whose earnings have climbed near or into the top 10 in the five seasons when he has logged a victory. At age 36, is likely in his prime, and the steadiness of his numbers suggests that he'll continue along at this pace for several years to come.

STATS: Driving Distance: B+   Driving Accuracy: B-   GIR: A-   Short Game: B   Putting: B

Na, Kevin Sangwook (USA) (31)
b. Seoul, South Korea 9/15/1983. 5'11" 165 lbs. TP: 2001. Three-time AJGA All-American. Korean-born player raised in Diamond Bar, CA after moving to America at age eight. Came to note by turning pro after junior year of high school. Failed to qualify for PGA Tour but played six 2002 events in Asia, scoring his first major tour win at the season-ending Volvo Masters. Played in Asia and Europe in 2003 before getting through PGA Tour Q School and becoming the Tour's youngest player (at age 20) in 2004. Played an abbreviated 2006 schedule (including a victory on the Web.com Tour) after injuring his hand, then came back to crack the top 125 in 2007. Climbed significantly in 2009 and '10, finishing 19th and 37th in earnings and logging nine top-10s in 2009. Broke through for his maiden U.S. victory at the 2011 Justin Timberlake Open – six months after achieving notoriety by carding a 16 on the par-4 9th hole during the first round of the Texas Open. Was affected by a bizarre inability to take the club back during the 2012 Players Championship, causing repeated false starts to his swing, then missed of much of 2013 with back problems. Rebounded impressively in 2014, climbing back to 20th in PGA Tour $$$. **OWR Best**: 25 - Sep, 2014.

PGA Tour Wins (1): 2011: Las Vegas Classic (Shriners).
Asian Tour Wins (1): 2002: Asian Masters (Volvo).

Na, Kevin Sangwook, Cont'd

Other Wins: 1 Web.com (2006).

Amateur Wins: Orange Bowl Jr: 2000.

	02	03	04	05	06	07	08	09	10	11	12	13	14
Masters	-	-	-	-	-	-	-	-	MC	MC	T12	59	-
US Open	-	-	-	-	-	-	-	-	MC	MC	T29	-	T12
British	-	-	-	-	-	-	-	-	T27	MC	MC	-	T54
PGA	-	-	-	MC	-	-	-	T43	T58	T10	WD	-	MC
Money (A)	-	-	87	67	205*	122	100	19	37	30	38	199*	20
Money (As)	6*	-	-	-	-	-	-	-	-	-	-	-	-
OWR	426	295	178	172	245	183	233	69	66	70	68	233	25

2014: PGA: 27 st / 20 ct / 6 t10. (2 Valspar, 2 Memorial, T3 Frys.com, T4 AT&T Pro-Am, T8 Hawaii, etc.). After making only eight starts due to back issues in 2013, bounced back strongly, tying a career best with six top 10s and finishing 24th in FedEx Cup points.

OUTLOOK: Cleared a 13-event medical extension in 2014 and now moves forward again. Only once a PGA Tour winner but, if healthy, is clearly capable of more. Strives to rate above the median from tee to green but possesses an elite short game and a largely comparable putting stroke, allowing to him to soar during better ball striking weeks. In his early 30s, still looks capable of blossoming into a more frequent winner.

STATS: Driving Distance: C   Driving Accuracy: A-   GIR: B-   Short Game: A+   Putting: A

Nirat, Chapchai (Thailand) (31)   b. Bangkok, Thailand 6/5/1983. 5'8" 180 lbs. TP: 1998. The son of a professional golfer who himself turned professional at age 15. Joined the Asian Tour in 2005 where, two years later, he would finish 2nd in $$$ and also win both the Vietnam Masters and the TCL Classic, the latter an E Tour co-sanctioned event which earned him exempt status in Europe in 2008 and '09. In 2009, opened with back-to-back 62s en route to winning the SAIL Open by 11 shots, his 256 total setting an Asian Tour record. Though seldom appearing in Europe since 2013, has remained a regular on the Asian Tour - save for a one-year semi-commitment to the Japan circuit in 2012, which saw him finish 111th in J Tour $$$. Broke a five-year drought by winning the Selangor Masters, where he beat Antonio Lascuña in a playoff. **OWR Best:** 135 - Apr, 2009.

European Tour Wins (1): 2007: TCL Classic.

Asian Tour Wins (2): 2007: Vietnam Masters (Hana Bank)   **2009**: SAIL Open   **2014**: Selangor Masters (Worldwide Holdings).

Other Wins: Genting Masters (Malaysia): 2004.

	05	06	07	08	09	10	11	12	13	14
Masters	-	-	-	-	-	-	-	-	-	-
US Open	-	-	-	-	-	-	-	-	-	-
British	-	-	-	-	-	-	-	-	-	-
PGA	-	-	-	-	-	-	-	-	-	-
Money (E)	-	-	165*	136	116	154	174*	131*	-	-
Money (As)	29	21	2	13	8	32	12	9	12	18
OWR	474	345	139	209	209	430	434	341	321	197

2014: ASIA: 19 st / 15 ct / 5 t10. (Incl. Won Selangor Masters, T6 Dubai). Claimed his fourth career win and finished a solid 18th in $$$.

OUTLOOK: A reliably strong tee-to-greener whose putting remains a bit below the median. His best years may well still lie ahead, and he'll surely make additional runs at the more lucrative European Tour. Seems capable of winning more frequently, but his established level isn't a bad one.

STATS: Driving Distance: B   Driving Accuracy: B-   GIR: A-   Short Game: B   Putting: B-

---

Nixon, Matthew (England) (25)   b. Manchester, England 6/12/1989. 6'0" 150 lbs. TP: 2010. Was something of a touted amateur prospect after winning the 2006 British Boys, and eventually turned pro after playing his way through Q School while still an amateur at age 21. Requalified via Q School in 2011 and '12 before narrowly keeping his card in 2013, then retaining it by an even narrower margin (after finishing 109th in earnings) in 2014. **OWR Best**: 355 - Jul, 2014.

Amateur Wins: British Boys: 2006.

	11	12	13	14
Masters	-	-	-	-
US Open	-	-	-	-
British	-	-	-	-
PGA	-	-	-	-
Money (E)	183	191*	105	109
OWR	828	643	414	442

2014: E: 31 st / 17 ct / 1 t10. (T4 NH Collection). Narrowly retained his card for the second straight year, finishing 109th in $$$.

OUTLOOK: After two failed attempts, has now quietly retained his playing privileges for two straight years. Though his statistical samples are a tad limited, his lack of length combined with a sometimes-balky putter is an awkward combination, and figures to limit his upside going forward.

STATS: Driving Distance: C-   Driving Accuracy: A   GIR: B+   Short Game: B   Putting: C+

Noh, Seung-Yul (South Korea) (23)   b. Seoul, South Korea 5/29/1991. 6'1" 165 lbs. TP: 2007. Won both the Korean Junior and the Korean Amateur in 2005. Widely touted prospect who became the third youngest winner in Asia Tour history (at age 17) when he defeated Terry Pilkadaris by one at the 2008 Midea China Classic – this after thrice finishing 2nd earlier in the year. Asian Tour 2008 Rookie of the Year. Mixed it up between the Asian and European Tours from 2009-2011, claiming his first E Tour victory at the 2010 Malaysian Open (where he edged K.J. Choi by one) while also winning the Asian Order of Merit despite limited starts. Finished 86th in E Tour $$$ in 2011 but secured PGA Tour privileges soon thereafter by tying for 3rd at Q School, then finished 49th in U.S. winnings as a rookie. Struggled in 2013 but retained his playing privileges by winning a Web.com Finals event in Columbus, OH, then broke through for his first PGA Tour win at the 2014 Zurich Classic of New Orleans, edging Andrew Svoboda and Robert Streb by two. **OWR Best**: 61 - Jan, 2011.

Noh, Seung-Yul, Cont'd

PGA Tour Wins (1): 2014: Zurich Classic (New Orleans).
European Tour Wins (1): 2010: Malaysian Open.
Asian Tour Wins (1): 2008: Midea China Classic.
Other Wins: 1 Web.com (2013).
Amateur Wins: Korean Junior: 2005   Korean Am: 2005.

	07	08	09	10	11	12	13	14
Masters	-	-	-	-	-	-	-	-
US Open	-	-	-	T41	T30	-	-	T52
British	-	-	-	MC	T30	-	-	-
PGA	-	-	-	T28	T45	T21	-	MC
Money (A)	-	-	-	-	-	49	155	39
Money (E)	-	-	-	34	86	-	-	-
Money (As)	-	10	20	1*	31*	-	-	-
OWR	-	180	241	63	107	95	176	105

2014: PGA: 27 st / 20 ct / 3 t10. (Won New Orleans, T9 Deutsche Bank, T10 Farmers). Bounced back from a major sophomore slump, claiming his first PGA Tour win in New Orleans, finishing 35th in FedEx Cup points, and making himself exempt through 2016.

OUTLOOK: Touted prospect who stumbled in 2013 but roared back for a career-best 2014. Has always been a surprisingly long hitter but is less consistent around the greens, particularly with his putter (though his SGP rose from 167 to 123 in 2014). Still his, 2013 issues trace more to ball striking (his three-year GIR: 33, 115, 38) and that problem seemed to be solved in 2014. Seems capable of winning more regularly.

STATS: Driving Distance: A   Driving Accuracy: C   GIR: A-   Short Game: B+   Putting: C+

Noren, Alexander (Sweden) (32)
b. Stockholm, Sweden 07/12/1982. 5'11" 170 lbs. All-American at Oklahoma St. TP: 2005. Played one successful season (including one victory) on the Challenge Tour before joining the E Tour full-time in 2007. Claimed his first major tour victory at the 2009 European Masters, edging Bradley Dredge by two at Crans-sur-Sierre. Finished 31st and 25th in the Order of Merit in 2008 and '09 before slipping to 85th in a winless 2010 that included only two top-10 finishes. Stepped up significantly in 2011, however, finishing a career-best 14th in $$$ and winning at both the Wales Open and the Scandinavian Masters where, after leading by 11 through 54 holes, a closing 77 left him seven shots clear of Richard Finch. Underwent surgery on his left wrist in late 2013, which effectively wiped out his entire 2014 season. **Teams**: Eisenhower Trophy: 2004. Palmer Cup (2): 2004-05. Seve Trophy: 2011. World Cup: 2011. **OWR Best**: 48 - Oct, 2012.

European Tour Wins (3): 2009: European Masters **2011**: Wales Open, Scandinavian Masters (Nordea).
Other Wins: 1 Euro Challenge (2006).

	06	07	08	09	10	11	12	13	14
Masters	-	-	-	-	-	-	-	-	-
US Open	-	-	-	-	-	T51	MC	-	-
British	-	-	T19	-	MC	MC	T9	WD	-
PGA	-	-	-	-	-	T34	T66	MC	-
Money (E)	-	63	31	25	85	14	24	56	271*
OWR	188	187	97	55	141	66	56	95	653

2014: After having left wrist surgery in late 2013, missed all but two E Tour events in 2014, making his season a near-complete washout.

OUTLOOK: With all-around above-the-median statistics and a far-above-the-median putting stroke, consistently ranked among the top 60 in E Tour $$$ prior to his wrist surgery. At age 32, he should just be entering his best years, but health is now an obvious question mark. Previously, he looked capable of being a regular E Tour winner, and he may well return to that level - but after losing nearly all of 2014, how quickly can that happen?

STATS: Driving Distance: B+   Driving Accuracy: C   GIR: B+   Short Game: B+   Putting: A

Norlander, Henrik Anders (Sweden) (27)
b. Stockholm, Sweden 3/25/1987. 6'4" 210 lbs. Two-time All-American at Augusta (GA) St. TP: 2011. Part of back-to-back NCAA championship teams (2010 and '11) at Augusta State. After graduating, returned home and struggled on the Challenge Tour (137th in 2011 $$$), then on U.S. mini-tours in 2012 before playing himself through all three stages of 2012 Q School (plus pre-qualifying) to gain status for 2013. **Teams**: Eisenhower Trophy (2): 2008-10. Palmer Cup (2): 2011-12. **OWR Best**: 393 - Jul, 2014.

	13	14
Masters	-	-
US Open	-	MC
British	-	-
PGA	-	-
Money (A)	151	-
OWR	494	617

2014: Played full-time on the Web.com Tour, finishing 50th in regular season $$$ before failing to play his way through the Finals.

OUTLOOK: Appears capable of playing his way back from the Web.com, but one wonders if, at some point, he opts to head back to Europe instead.

STATS (LTD): Driving Distance: B+   Driving Accuracy: B   GIR: B-   Short Game: C+   Putting: B-

---

O'Hair, Sean Marc (USA) (32)
b. Lubbock, TX 7/11/1982. 6'2" 180 lbs. TP: 1999. An AJGA All-American. Turned professional prior to graduating from high school, and endured a much-publicized estrangement from his father. Starred as a 2005 PGA Tour rookie (18th in earnings) despite seldom dominating at the Web.com (one top 10 in 19 total starts) or mini-tour levels. Victory at the 2005 John Deere Classic came in only his 18th Tour start. Won the 2008 PODS Championship by two over six players with the highest winning total on tour (284) since the 2007 U.S. Open. Also won the strong-field 2009 Quail Hollow Championship (by one over Lucas Glover and Bubba Watson) during a career-best year which saw him

O'Hair, Sean Marc, Cont'd

finish 6th in earnings and log nine top-10 finishes. Despite slipping to 41st and 57th in $$$ in 2010 and '11, claimed his fourth career title in the latter season by edging Kris Blanks in a playoff at the Canadian Open. Struggled in 2013 and '14 but kept his card via the Web.com Finals each year. **Awards:** PGA Tour Rookie of the Year: 2005. **Teams:** Presidents Cup: 2009 (2-2-1). **OWR Best:** 12 - May, 2009.

PGA Tour Wins (4): 2005: John Deere Classic **2008:** PODS Championship **2009:** Quail Hollow Championship **2011:** Canadian Open.
Other Wins: Shark Shootout: 2012 (w/K. Perry).

	05	06	07	08	09	10	11	12	13	14
Masters	-	MC	-	T14	T10	T30	MC	T32	-	-
US Open	-	T26	MC	-	T23	T12	-	-	-	-
British	T15	T14	T67	82	T65	T7	MC	-	-	-
PGA	T59	T12	T42	T31	75	MC	T64	WD	-	-
Money (A)	18	62	38	35	6	41	57	84	174	156
OWR	37	67	65	59	15	43	79	137	352	474

2014: PGA: 25 st / 14 ct / 1 t10. (T10 Arnold Palmer). Finished 160th in FedEx Cup points, but played his way back via the Web.com Finals.

OUTLOOK: Failed to keep his PGA Tour card for the second straight year and needed a last-minute T3 in the Web.com Tour Championship to return for 2015. Statistically inconsistent for several seasons now but one clear downer is his Total Driving, which has gone from 46 to 83 to 106 since 2012.

STATS: Driving Distance: A Driving Accuracy: C GIR: C+ Short Game: B- Putting: C+

O'Hern, Nicholas Simon (Australia) (43)

b. Perth, Western Australia 10/18/1971. 6'0" 160 lbs. TP: 1991. Prominent international left-hander who has proven himself a steady earner worldwide (including five top-100 PGA Tour $$$ finishes from 2006-2011) but has never won outside of his native Australia. Spent seven mostly productive seasons in Europe before coming to America in the latter part of 2005. His homeland wins came on the same golf course (the Hyatt Regency Resort at Coolum) seven years apart, but in different events. The first was the 1999 Coolum Classic while the second was the more prominent Australian PGA, where he defeated Peter Lonard in a playoff. Missed most of 2010 after having surgery on both of his knees before returning to a full U.S. schedule in 2011. Slipped markedly in 2012 and '13, logging only two top 10s and losing his status. **Teams:** Presidents Cup (2): 2005-07 (3-7-0). World Cup (2): 2004-07. **OWR Best:** 16 - Jan, 2007.

Australasian Tour Wins (2): 1999: Coolum Classic (54H) **2006:** Australian PGA.
Other Wins: Port Hedland Classic (Aus) (2): 1997-98 South West Open (Aus): 1998.
Amateur Wins: Mt Lawley Am: 1991.

	99	00	01	02	03	04	05	06	07	08	09	10	11	12	13	14
Masters	-	-	-	-	-	-	T45	T19	MC	MC	-	-	-	-	-	-
US Open	-	-	-	-	-	-	T49	T6	T23	-	-	-	MC	-	-	-
British	-	T41	-	-	-	MC	-	T15	MC	MC	T32	-	-	-	-	-
PGA	-	-	MC	-	-	T31	MC	MC	T50	MC	-	-	-	-	-	-
Money (A)	-	-	-	-	-	-	-	94	68	75	88	168*	96	145	170	-
Money (E)	108	42	42	71	37	12	21	26	40	-	-	-	-	-	-	-
OWR	141	109	137	180	103	45	24	21	37	95	122	170	136	257	405	837

2014: Played full-time on the Web.com Tour but struggled badly, finishing 138th in regular season $$$.

OUTLOOK: Begins his second year without any PGA Tour status of any type. A short but very straight ball striker whose overall performance level has never quite recovered after his duel knee surgeries of 2010. At age 43, he may look to return to Asia or Oz if 2015 fails to yield a U.S. comeback.

STATS: Driving Distance: D Driving Accuracy: A+ GIR: C+ Short Game: A Putting: C

Oberholser, Arron Matthew (USA) (39)

b. San Luis Obispo, CA 2/2/1975. 6'0" 180 lbs. Two-time All-American at San Jose St. TP: 1998. Ex-collegiate star who was Canadian Tour Rookie of the Year in 1999 (winning the Ontario Open by a record 11 shots), a Web.com Tour star in 2002 and a PGA Tour regular by 2003. Highly thought-of talent who has occasionally been bothered by disc problems in his back. Logged his first PGA Tour win at the 2006 AT&T Pro-Am, running away from Rory Sabbatini by five. Soon beset by hand problems and had two surgeries following the 2007 season, then several more (plus hip surgery) in 2010. Has been on a medical extension ever since. **OWR Best:** 22 - Sep, 2007.

PGA Tour Wins (1): 2006: AT&T Pro-Am.
Other Wins: 2 Web.com (2002) + Ontario Open (Canada): 1999 Eagle Creek Classic (Canada): 1999 Shinhan Korea Championship: 2004.
Amateur Wins: Sahalee Players: 1997 Eastern Am: 1998.

	03	04	05	06	07	08	09	10	11	12	13	14
Masters	-	-	-	T14	58	T25	-	-	-	-	-	-
US Open	-	-	T9	T16	MC	-	-	-	-	-	-	-
British	-	-	-	MC	T45	-	-	-	-	-	-	-
PGA	-	T13	T28	MC	T4	-	-	-	-	-	-	-
Money (A)	103	52	88	23	47	-	-	-	-	-	-	-
OWR	196	91	99	44	30	124	679	-	-	-	1457	-

2014: Did not make a start anywhere during 2014, while still recovering from 2010 hand and hip surgeries.

OUTLOOK: Begins 2015 on a 10-event medical extension that dates to 2009, but will likely spend far more time broadcasting than playing.

STATS: Driving Distance: -- Driving Accuracy: -- GIR: -- Short Game: -- Putting: --

---

Oda, Koumei (Japan) (36)

b. Tagawa, Japan 6/7/1978. 5'9" 185 lbs. TP: 2000. A somewhat late-arriving Japan Tour star who never bettered 80th in the Order of Merit until his late 20s. Also didn't log his first victory until age 30, but that was a significant title: the 2008 Casio World Open, where he beat Kenichi Kuboya by three. Successfully defended his Casio title in 2009 (this time edging Ryo Ishikawa by three) and also claimed

Oda, Koumei, Cont'd

back-to-back victories at the 2009 and 2010 Token Homemate Cup, both in sudden death. Won his fifth J Tour title in four seasons at the 2011 Diamond Cup, a four-shot triumph over Toshinori Muto and Kaname Yokoo. After a quieter run, won the 2013 ANA Open in a four-shot runaway, then added the 2014 Kansai Open, winning by two via an eagle at the par-5 72nd hole. Claimed his eight J Tour win at the 2014 Bridgestone Open, where he birdied the 72nd to edge Hiroyuki Fujita by one, capping a year in which he finished first in earnings. **OWR Best:** 53 - Dec, 2014.

Japan Tour Wins (8): 2008: Casio World Open **2009:** Token Homemate Cup, Casio World Open **2010:** Token Homemate Cup **2011:** Diamond Cup **2013:** ANA Open **2014:** Kansai Open, Bridgestone Open.

	03	04	05	06	07	08	09	10	11	12	13	14
Masters	-	-	-	-	-	-	-	-	-	-	-	-
US Open	-	-	-	-	-	-	-	-	-	-	-	-
British	-	-	-	-	-	-	MC	MC	-	MC	-	T39
PGA	-	-	-	-	-	-	-	MC	-	-	-	T41
Money (J)	84	95	149	81	9	12	3	12	5	11	3	1
OWR	657	492	749	712	176	139	72	102	81	100	67	56

2014: JAP: 23 st / 19 ct / 9 t10. (Won Kansai, Won Bridgestone, 2 Sega Sammy, T2 Japan PGA, T2 ABC). Enjoyed another outstanding season in which he added two more victories and topped the Japan Tour money list for the first time.

OUTLOOK: Has an imposing record since 2007, utilizing some very solid ball striking and an all-around strong skill set to achieve great consistency. Saw further statistical improvements in 2014, thus he may well continue for several more seasons at something resembling his present lucrative pace.

STATS: Driving Distance: A- Driving Accuracy: B GIR: A Short Game: B Putting: A-

---

Oda, Ryuichi (Japan) (38)

b. Kagoshima, Japan 12/12/1976. 5'9" 200 lbs. TP: 2002. After not finding his stride until his late 20s, emerged as a steady money winner on the Japan Tour, with his career initially peaking around two significant victories. In 2009, he defeated Ryo Ishikawa and Yasuharu Imano in a playoff to take the Japan Open, highlighting a year in which he finished a career-best 5th in earnings. Five years later, he claimed the Mynavi ABC Championship in a five-shot runaway, anchoring a campaign in which he finished 23rd. **OWR Best:** 110 - Jan, 2010.

Japan Tour Wins (2): 2009: Japan Open **2014:** Mynavi ABC Championship.

	02	03	04	05	06	07	08	09	10	11	12	13	14
Masters	-	-	-	-	-	-	-	-	-	-	-	-	-
US Open	-	-	-	-	-	-	-	-	-	-	-	-	-
British	-	-	-	-	-	-	-	-	MC	-	-	-	-
PGA	-	-	-	-	-	-	-	-	-	-	-	-	-
Money (J)	148	101	41	28	36	53	60	5	21	42	26	107	23
OWR	1262	705	290	227	272	426	613	114	163	307	265	598	313

2014: JAP: 24 st / 16 ct / 1 t10. (Won ABC). Logged exactly one top 10 finish - his second career win - en route to finishing a solid 23rd in $$$.

OUTLOOK: Has proven himself a very steady player/earner over the last decade, but with below-the-median Driving Accuracy and GIR, it is probably asking too much to expect him to rise much further. A similarly mediocre short game doesn't help.

STATS: Driving Distance: B+ Driving Accuracy: C+ GIR: C+ Short Game: C+ Putting: B+

Ogilvy, Geoff Charles (Australia) (37)

b. Adelaide, South Australia 6/11/1977. 6'2" 180 lbs. TP: 1998. Son of an English father (who emigrated to Australia) and an Australian mother, and is a distant relative of Britain's Royal Family. Played two full seasons in Europe (1999-00) prior to coming to America (via the 2000 Q School). Eight-time PGA Tour winner highlighted by the 2006 U.S. Open, where he chipped in for par at the 71st, then got up-and-down at the 72nd to edge Jim Furyk and the imploding Phil Mickelson by one. A three-time WGC winner, including the WGC Accenture Match Play in 2006 (beat Davis Love III 3 & 2 at La Costa) and 2009 (4 & 3 over Paul Casey at Ritz-Carlton GC), plus the 2008 WGC CA Championship (by one over Jim Furyk, Retief Goosen and Vijay Singh). Claimed his first PGA Tour win at the 2005 Tucson Open (in a playoff with Mark Calcavecchia and Kevin Na) and also won the season-opening Mercedes/SBS Championship in both 2009 and 2010. Returned home to win the 2008 Australian PGA Championship (beating Mathew Goggin by two) and the 2010 Australian Open (by four over Matt Jones and Alistair Presnell), the latter allowing him to claim the Australasian Order of Merit title despite playing full-time in America. After struggling for much of 2012 and '13, returned to the winner's circle at the 2014 Barracuda Championship (Reno-Tahoe), beating Justin Hicks by five points under modified Stableford scoring. **Teams:** Presidents Cup (3): 2007-09-11 (7-6-1). **OWR Best:** 3 - Jun, 2008.

PGA Tour Wins (8): 2005: Tucson Open (Chrysler) **2006:** WGC-Match Play, U.S. Open **2008:** WGC-CA Championship **2009:** Mercedes Championships, WGC-Match Play **2010:** SBS Championship **2014:** Reno-Tahoe Open (Barracuda).

Australasian Tour Wins (2): 2008: Australian PGA **2010:** Australian Open.

Amateur Wins: Australian Foursomes: 1994 Lake Macquarie Am: 1997.

	99	00	01	02	03	04	05	06	07	08	09	10	11	12	13	14
Masters	-	-	-	-	-	-	-	T16	T24	T39	T15	T26	T4	T19	-	-
US Open	-	-	-	MC	-	T28	Win	T42	T9	T47	MC	MC	MC	T32	MC	
British	MC	-	MC	-	-	T5	T16	MC	MC	MC	MC	MC	T9	T44	-	-
PGA	-	-	-	T27	T24	T6	T9	T6	T31	T43	MC	MC	T11	MC	T47	
Money (A)	-	-	95	64	45	61	33	5	14	15	8	29	43	71	93	54
Money (E)	65	48	-	-	-	-	-	-	-	6	-	-	-	-	-	-
OWR	174	155	134	131	76	70	50	10	13	12	14	26	36	51	122	94

2014: PGA: 26 st / 16 ct / 2 t10. (Won Barracuda, T2 Deutsche Bank). After another slow start (141st in $$$ through the Canadian Open), won the Barracuda Championship, closed strongly in the FedEx Cup Playoffs, and finished 54th in $$$ and 29th in FedEx Cup points.

OUTLOOK: Cited improved putting for sparking his bounceback, but this was only true late in the year; overall, his SGP now has a five-year run of 30, 20, 43, 155, 150, while his Scrambling has ranked 6, 132 and 137 since 2012. Combing that with mediocre Ball Striking (121) and his slump isn't hard to understand, but... All of those numbers improved late, and this is still an experienced, talented hand, so things may well trend upward in 2015.

STATS: Driving Distance: B+ Driving Accuracy: B- GIR: C+ Short Game: B- Putting: B-

Oh, David (USA) (33) b. Los Angeles, CA 3/28/1981. 5'11" 180 lbs. College: USC. TP: 2004. An AJGA All-America who, after turning pro, played only sporadically on major tours until joining the OneAsia for 2010-2011, then moving onto the Japan Tour in 2012. Struggled initially but climbed to 31st in J Tour winnings, then 18th during a 2014 season which saw him log his first professional win at the Taiheiyo Masters, where he birdied the last to edge Toshinori Muto by one. **OWR Best:** 214 - Nov, 2014.

Japan Tour Wins (1): 2014: Taiheiyo Masters.
Amateur Wins: Junior World (13-14): 1995.

	05	06	07	08	09	10	11	12	13	14
Masters	-	-	-	-	-	-	-	-	-	-
US Open	MC	MC	-	-	-	-	-	-	-	MC
British	-	-	-	-	-	-	-	-	-	-
PGA	-	-	-	-	-	-	-	-	-	-
Money (J)	-	-	-	-	-	-	-	94	31	18
Money (O)	-	-	-	-	-	26	36	-	-	42*
OWR	1182	742	746	1178	775	607	710	561	361	119

2014: JAP: 22 st / 16 ct / 2 t10. (Won Taiheiyo, 5 Sega Sammy). In his third Japan Tour season, recorded only two top 10s en route to finishing a career-best 18th in $$$ - but one of them was his first career major tour win, at the stronger-field Taiheiyo Masters.
OUTLOOK: Took a while to get here but proved himself a capable player at age 33. Aside from some deft short game skills, his numbers are all mid-range, suggesting that 2014 was more likely a peak than a beginning - but with everything trending upwards for three years, you never know.

STATS: Driving Distance: B-   Driving Accuracy: B   GIR: B   Short Game: A-   Putting: B-

---

Olazábal Menterola, José Maria (Spain) (48) b. Fuenterrabia, Spain 2/5/1966. 5'10" 160 lbs. Top junior prospect who won 1984 British Amateur at Formby, as well as the 1983 British Boys, the 1985 British Youths and national Amateurs of Spain (1983 and '85) and Italy (1983). Occasionally erratic driver whose superb shotmaking and iron skills have long made up the difference. As a professional, starred in Europe from 1986-2000, logging 10 top-10 Order of Merit finishes and 18 official victories during this period, as well as the 1986 E Tour Rookie of the Year award. Biggest E Tour wins included the 1994 BMW PGA Championship (by one over Ernie Els at Wentworth), the 1990 Trophée Lancôme (by one over Colin Montgomerie) and a pair of Benson & Hedges Internationals (1990 and 2000). Enjoyed seven multiple win seasons in Europe between 1986-1994. Announced his American presence in 1990 with a record 12-shot victory (over Lanny Wadkins) at the World Series of Golf. Won a second World Series of Golf in 1994, by one over Scott Hoch. Scored his first Major championship at the 1994 Masters, beating Tom Lehman by two while following Seve Ballesteros as the second Spaniard to don the Green Jacket. Added a second Masters title in 1999 after overcoming an arthritic foot condition (initially misdiagnosed as back problems) which had left him bedridden in 1995. Like his mentor Ballesteros, a Ryder Cup demon, the pair having amassed a remarkable 11-2-2 record together in foursomes/four ball play. In twilight of his career, has only cracked the top 100 in E Tour $$$ once since 2006.
Awards: World Golf Hall of Fame Member (2009). E Tour Rookie of the Year: 1986. **Teams:** Eisenhower Trophy (2): 1982-84. Ryder Cup (7): 1987-89-91-93-97-99-06 (O: 18-8-5, S: 2-4-1) + Capt in 2012. Seve Trophy (4): 2000-02-03-05. World Cup (2): 1989-00. **OWR Best:** 2 - Mar, 1991.
PGA Tour Wins (6): 1990: World Series of Golf (NEC) **1991:** The International (Stableford) **1994:** Masters Tournament, World Series of Golf (NEC) **1999:** Masters Tournament **2002:** San Diego Open (Buick Inv).
European Tour Wins (21): 1986: European Masters – Swiss Open, Sanyo Open **1988:** Belgian Open, German Masters **1989:** Tenerife Open, Dutch Open **1990:** Benson & Hedges Int'l, Irish Open, Trophée Lancôme **1991:** Open Catalonia, Grand Prix of Europe **1992:** Open de Tenerife, Open Mediterrania **1994:** Open Mediterrania, BMW PGA **1997:** Turespaña Masters **1998** Dubai Classic **2000:** Benson & Hedges Int'l **2001:** French Open, Hong Kong Open ('02) **2005:** Mallorca Classic.
Japan Tour Wins (2): 1989: Taiheiyo Masters **1990:** Taiheiyo Masters.
Other Wins: Tournoi Perrier de Paris: 1995 (w/S.Ballesteros)   Dunhill Cup (2): 1999-00 (both w/M.A.Jiménez & S.García).
Amateur Wins: British Amateur: 1984   Italian Am: 1983   Spanish Am (2): 1983-85   –   British Boys: 1983   Belgian Int'l Youths: 1984   British Youths: 1985.

	84	85	86	87	88	89	90	91	92	93	94	95	96	97	98	99	00	01	02	03	04	05	06	07
Masters	-	MC	-	MC	-	T8	13	2	T42	T7	Win	T14	-	T12	T12	Win	MC	T15	4	T8	30	MC	T3	T44
US Open	-	-	-	T68	-	T9	T8	T8	MC	MC	T28	-	-	T16	T18	WD	T12	MC	T50	MC	-	-	T21	T45
British	MC	T25	T16	T11	T36	T23	T16	T80	3	MC	T38	T31	-	T20	T15	MC	T31	T54	MC	MC	-	T3	T56	-
PGA	-	-	-	MC	-	MC	T14	MC	MC	T56	T7	T31	-	MC	MC	MC	T4	T37	69	T51	MC	T47	T55	MC
Money (A)	Am	-	-	-	-	-	38	43	161	174	7	87	-	126	133	46	-	110	24	132	142	41	31	101
Money (E)	Am	-	2	17	3	2	3	7	6	18	4	-	-	9	7	32	9	35	13	52	81	10	28	-
OWR	-	-	43	49	20	7	3	3	4	15	5	13	-	42	25	26	34	46	38	93	126	26	18	71

	08	09	10	11	12	13	14
Masters	MC	MC	-	MC	MC	T50	T34
US Open	-	-	-	-	MC	-	-
British	-	-	-	-	-	-	-
PGA	-	-	-	MC	MC	-	-
Money (A)	-	-	-	-	-	-	-
Money (E)	-	158	-	169	88	126	162
OWR	418	395	568	591	431	453	734

2014: E: 20 st / 5 ct / 0 t10. (T34 Masters). Made just 25% of his cuts en route to finishing 162nd in $$$.
OUTLOOK: Though he did make 20 E Tour starts in 2014, one senses that he is now primarily a ceremonial player. The difference lies mostly in his ball striking which, though always somewhat erratic, has tailed off from his halcyon days. The big question: Will he want to play senior golf in 2016?

STATS: Driving Distance: C-   Driving Accuracy: D   GIR: D   Short Game: B   Putting: B+

Olesen, Jacob Thorbjørn (Denmark) (25) b. Fureso, Denmark 12/21/1989. 5'9" 150 lbs. TP: 2008. Originally an under-the-radar Danish prospect who won four times in the Nordic League in 2008-2009, plus a Challenge Tour event in 2010. Came seemingly out of nowhere to finish 2nd at the December, 2010 Alfred Dunhill Championship, the first official event on the 2011 E Tour schedule. Added 2nd-place finishes at the 2011 Italian and French Opens before breaking through for his first major tour win at the 2012 Sicilian Open (where he edged England's Chris Wood

Olesen, Jacob Thorbjørn, Cont'd

by one), the anchor of a season in which he finished a career-best 15th in E Tour $$$. Ended an otherwise disappointing 2014 campaign on a high note by winning the Perth International in Australia. **Teams:** Seve Trophy: 2013. World Cup (2): 2011-13. **OWR Best:** 33 - Apr, 2013.

European Tour Wins (2): 2012: Sicilian Open **2014:** Perth International (ISPS Handa).
Other Wins: 1 Euro Challenge (2010) + 4 Nordic League (2008-2009).

	09	10	11	12	13	14
Masters	-	-	-	-	T6	T44
US Open	-	-	-	-	MC	-
British	-	-	MC	T9	MC	T64
PGA	-	-	-	T27	T40	T30
Money (E)	-	-	48	15	32	32
OWR	529	114	163	50	65	80

2014: E: 22 st / 19 ct / 5 t10. (Won Perth, T3 Qatar, T5 Dubai, T6 WGC HSBC Champ, T7 Denmark). Initially seemed bound for a moderately disappointing year before turning things around with a late victory in Perth, helping him to finish 32nd in $$$ for the second straight season.

OUTLOOK: Remains one of the game's more intriguing young players as he has frequently demonstrated the potential to play among the elite, but hasn't completely pieced it together yet. Has few statistical weaknesses in his game and is both surprisingly powerful and a particularly dangerous iron player when he's on. Based on his 2014 finish - and his considerable talent - he could be in for an international breakout year in 2015.

STATS: Driving Distance: A-   Driving Accuracy: C   GIR: A-   Short Game: B   Putting: B+

Oosthuizen, Lodewicus Theodorus ("Louis") (USA) (32)

b. Mossel Bay, South Africa 10/19/1982. 5'10" 160 lbs. TP: 2002. The most famous beneficiary of Ernie Els' foundation, which helps fund less privileged South African golfing prospects. Shot a non-competitive 57 over his home Mossel Bay GC in 2002, and teamed with Charl Schwartzel to win the World Amateur Team Championship the same year. Well-traveled South African who won five times on the Sunshine Tour from 2004-2008, and regularly finished in the Order of Merit top 10, often in limited starts. Blossomed in 2007 with three homeland victories (headed by the Dimension Data Pro-Am and his first Telkom PGA Championship), then narrowly missed the tour's all-time scoring record (with a 260 aggregate) during a 14-shot runaway win while defending the Telkom PGA in 2008. Played full-time in Europe from 2004-2010 before taking a PGA Tour membership for 2011. Won his first E Tour title with a three-shot triumph at the 2010 Open de Andalucia, then stepped up four months later to win the British Open at St Andrews in an impressive seven-shot runaway. Won the 2011 Africa Open, then defended the title to start 2012. Lost the 2012 Masters on the second hole of sudden death to Bubba Watson, then flew halfway around the world to win the E Tour's Malaysian Open the following week. Opened 2013 by winning the Volvo Golf Champions, marking the third straight season that he won his first event of the calendar year. After struggling with injuries in the latter half of 2013, defended the title (and extended the streak to four years) in 2014. **Teams:** Eisenhower Trophy: 2002. Presidents Cup: 2013 (1-3-1). World Cup: 2011. **OWR Best:** 5 - Dec, 2012.

PGA Tour Wins (1): 2010: British Open.
European Tour Wins (6): 2010: Open de Andalucia **2011:** Africa Open **2012:** Africa Open, Malaysia Open **2013:** Volvo Golf Champions **2014:** Volvo Golf Champions.
Sunshine Tour Wins (5): 2004: Vodacom-Arabella (54H) **2007:** Dimension Data Pro-Am, Telkom PGA Championship, Platinum Classic (54H) **2008:** Telkom PGA Championship.
Other Wins: Southern Cape Open (SA) (2): 2001-02.
Amateur Wins: Irish Am: 2002 – Southern Cape Closed Am: 2000   Karen Challenge (2): 2000-01   George Silver Vase: 2000   Transvaal Am Stroke Play: 2001   Silver Salver: 2001   Kwazulu-Natal Stroke Play: 2002.

	02	03	04	05	06	07	08	09	10	11	12	13	14
Masters	-	-	-	-	-	-	-	MC	MC	MC	2P	MC	25
US Open	-	-	-	-	-	-	-	-	MC	T9	MC	WD	T40
British	-	-	MC	-	MC	-	-	MC	Win	T54	T19	WD	T36
PGA	-	-	-	-	-	-	73	MC	MC	MC	T21	-	T15
Money (A)	-	-	-	-	-	-	-	-	-	117	15	139*	101
Money (E)	-	-	74	139	93	64	62	31	10	15	3	47	17
Money (SA)	20*	4*	15*	3*	2*	2*	19*	-	5*	5*	-	-	6*
OWR	-	512	244	251	337	112	134	89	20	40	6	34	45

2014: PGA: 16 st / 10 ct / 1 t10. (T5 WGC-Match Play). Finished 124th in Fedex Cup points. Not entirely recovered from a recurring problem in his neck and side, he still managed to defend his title at the E Tour's Volvo Golf Champions, winning his first start for the fourth consecutive year.

OUTLOOK: When he's on (and not in pain), still one of the world's finest tee-to-greeners, generating tremendous power for someone of middling stature and measuring up well in most key statistical categories (e.g., 18 in Total Driving, 30 in Ball Striking). The lingering effects of his injuries are a serious concern but when he's right, he's a threat to win at any time - and when he's hot, he can leave the field behind like few in the game.

STATS: Driving Distance: A   Driving Accuracy: B+   GIR: A-   Short Game: C+   Putting: B-

---

Ormsby, Wade (Australia) (34)

b. Adelaide, South Australia 3/31/1980. 5'9" 160 lbs. College: U of Houston. TP: 2001. After spending three years at the University of Houston, played several seasons at home before heading off to Europe, where he found only middling success during an eight-year, on-and-off run through 2011. Moved to the Asian Tour thereafter and settled in effectively, logging his first win at the 2013 Panasonic Open India, where he edged 56-year-old veteran Boonchu Ruangkit by one. **OWR Best:** 148 - Dec, 2014.

Asian Tour Wins (1): 2013: Panasonic Open India.

	04	05	06	07	08	09	10	11	12	13	14
Masters	-	-	-	-	-	-	-	-	-	-	-
US Open	-	-	-	-	-	-	-	-	-	-	-
British	-	-	-	-	-	-	-	-	-	-	-
PGA	-	-	-	-	-	-	-	-	-	-	-
Money (E)	112	71	133	145	-	166	-	182	-	-	51
Money (As)	-	-	-	-	-	-	-	39	14	-	-
OWR	323	294	235	474	592	651	681	800	687	239	148

Ormsby, Wade, Cont'd

2014: E: 28 st / 22 ct / 4 t10. (T4 Turkey, T5 Hassan, T8 Hong Kong, T9 Perth). Returned successfully to the E Tour, finishing 51st in $$$.

OUTLOOK: A shortish hitter who lives off a quality short game. Such a defensive approach can often lack consistency, so it will be interesting to see if he can sustain his 2013 and '14 performance level going forward. Plays surprisingly little on his native Australasian circuit.

STATS (LTD): Driving Distance: C   Driving Accuracy: B+   GIR: B   Short Game: A-   Putting: B

Ortiz Becerra, Carlos (Mexico) (23)

b. Guadalajara, Mexico 4/24/1991. 6'0" 150 lbs. College: U of North Texas. TP: 2013. Mexican native who followed in Lorena Ochoa's footsteps at the Guadalajara Country Club. After an unspectacular collegiate career, played his way through Web.com Q School in 2013 (T15) to fully exempt status, then surprised many observers by dominating the Tour in 2014. Won three times in his first 16 starts, earning a late-August battlefield promotion to the PGA Tour.   **Teams**: Eisenhower Trophy (2): 2010-12.   **OWR Best**: 121 - Aug, 2014.

Other Wins: 3 Web.com (2014).

	14
Masters	-
US Open	-
British	-
PGA	-
Money (A)	-
OWR	142

2014: Played full-time on the Web.com Tour and was surprisingly dominant, winning thrice to gain immediate exempt status on the PGA Tour.

OUTLOOK: There is little on his résumé to suggest immediate PGA Tour stardom - but that's how most viewed his Web.com chances a year ago, so...

STATS: Driving Distance: --   Driving Accuracy: --   GIR: --   Short Game: --   Putting: --

---

Otaegui, Adrian (Spain) (22)

b. San Sebastian, Spain 11/21/1992. 6'0" 175 lbs. TP: 2011. Mentored by his Hall-of-Famer countryman Jose Maria Olazábal. Enjoyed a strong amateur career led by wins at the 2010 British Boys and the 2011 Spanish Closed Amateur. After splitting time between the European and Challenge Tours in 2012, graduated from the latter in 2013 (via a 7th-place $$$ ranking), then failed to retain his card in 2014 before returning via Q School.   **Teams**: Eisenhower Trophy: 2010.   **OWR Best**: 263 - Oct, 2013.

Amateur Wins: British Boys: 2010   Spanish Closed Am: 2011   Faldo Series Under-16: 2008.

	13	14
Masters	-	-
US Open	-	-
British	-	-
PGA	-	-
Money (E)	-	118
OWR	304	434

2014: E: 32 st / 5 ct / 1 t10. (T6 NH Collection). Logged but a single top 10 in finishing 118th in $$$, then played his way back through Q School.

OUTLOOK: Under Jose Maria Olazábal's tutelage, was considered one of Spain's top prospects, and he has shown the ability both to reach the E Tour quickly and to return (via Q School) after narrowly losing his card. Hasn't won yet as a pro but still appears to have a bright future.

STATS (LTD): Driving Distance: B   Driving Accuracy: A   GIR: B   Short Game: B+   Putting: B

Otto, Hendrik Johannes ("Hennie") (South Africa) (38)

b. Boksburg, South Africa 6/25/1976. 5'8" 180 lbs. TP: 1997. Strong South African domestic player who was thrice a top-10 finisher in Sunshine Tour $$$ before turning 25. Was a multiple winner in 1999 and 2002 prior to beating Trevor Immelman by two to claim the Sunshine circuit's 2003 Tour Championship. Began playing in Europe in 2000 but didn't break through for his first E Tour victory until the 2008 Italian Open, where he edged Oliver Wilson by one. Claimed his biggest-ever win at the 2011 South African Open, beating Bernd Wiesberger by one in this E Tour co-sanctioned event. Had earlier claimed both the Dimension Data Pro-Am and the Platinum Classic in a year in which he'd finish 2nd in Sunshine Tour $$$ and 116th in the year-end OWR. Ended a three-year victory drought when, in his second start after 2014 back surgery, he rode a second round 62 to his second career triumph at the Italian Open. Has never played in a non-Major, non-WGC PGA Tour event.   **Teams**: Eisenhower Trophy: 1996.   **OWR Best**: 73 - Jun, 2008.

European Tour Wins (3): 2008: Italian Open **2011**: South African Open **2014**: Italian Open.

Sunshine Tour Wins (11): 1999: Limpopo Classic (54H), Vodacom-Kwazulu-Natal (54H) **2002**: Limpopo Classic (54H), Nashua Masters **2003**: Tour Championship **2005**: Vodacom-Erinvale (54H), Vodacom-Pretoria (54H) **2009**: Namibia PGA (54H) **2010**: Tour Championship **2011**: Dimension Data Pro-Am, Platinum Classic (54H).

Other Wins: 1 Euro Challenge (1999).

	97	98	99	00	01	02	03	04	05	06	07	08	09	10	11	12	13	14
Masters	-	-	-	-	-	-	-	-	-	-	-	-	-	-	-	-	-	-
US Open	-	-	-	-	-	-	-	-	-	-	-	-	-	-	-	-	-	-
British	-	-	-	-	-	-	T10	MC	-	-	-	MC	-	-	-	-	-	-
PGA	-	-	-	-	-	-	-	-	-	-	-	MC	-	-	-	-	-	-
Money (E)	-	-	-	135	147	-	73	145	-	-	-	37	152	108	53	89	90	46
Money (SA)	38	6	8	4	33*	3	22*	19	16	3	4	18*	-	7*	2*	36*	4*	10*
OWR	659	588	317	395	348	269	127	293	443	410	390	94	255	298	116	181	125	101

2014: E: 23 st / 17 ct / 3 t10. (Won Italian, T2 South African, 5 Tshwane). Overcame minor back surgery to win in Italy in his second post-recovery start, while also adding two other top 10s and finishing 46th in $$$. Also make three non-co-sanctioned starts on his native Sunshine circuit.

OUTLOOK: A highly competitive sort whose game is built around accuracy, hitting lots of greens and, of late, an improved putter. Is still at an age where at least some of his best golf may yet lie ahead of him - and he remains capable of winning regularly on South African soil.

STATS: Driving Distance: B-   Driving Accuracy: A-   GIR: A-   Short Game: B-   Putting: B+

Overton, Jeffrey Laurence (USA) (31) b. Evansville, IN 5/28/1983. 6'4" 195 lbs. Two-time All-American at Indiana U. TP: 2005. A two-time Indiana Amateur champion (2003 and '04) who rose steadily on the PGA Tour, culminating in selection to the 2010 Ryder Cup team in a year where he finished 12th in Tour $$$. Remains winless as a professional but logged three 2nd-place finishes (New Orleans, Byron Nelson and The Greenbrier Classic) during 2010. Has slipped slightly since but remained a steady earner through 2014. **Teams:** Walker Cup: 2005 (3-1-0). Palmer Cup: 2006. Ryder Cup: 2010 (O: 2-2-0, S: 1-0-0). **OWR Best:** 45 - Aug, 2010.

Amateur Wins: Indiana Am (2): 2003-04.

	06	07	08	09	10	11	12	13	14
Masters	-	-	-	-	-	T44	-	-	-
US Open	-	-	-	-	-	T63	-	-	-
British	-	-	T70	T13	T11	T38	-	-	-
PGA	-	-	-	T32	71	MC	MC	-	-
Money (A)	136	99	118	76	12	74	52	112	93
OWR	316	249	247	186	53	74	99	182	302

2014: PGA: 24 st / 17 ct / 3 t10. (4 New Orleans, 7 Hawaii, T9 Shriners). Improved modestly from 2013, finishing 92nd in FedEx Cup points.

OUTLOOK: Former Ryder Cup player appeared on the verge of stardom in 2010 (12th in $$$) but hasn't approached those heights since. At age 31 he certainly has time on his side, but his three-year numbers in several ball striking categories (43, 121 and 164 in Total Driving, 42, 109 and 118 in Ball Striking) aren't trending well. Has also witnessed moderate fall-offs in his putting numbers as well, so winning seems a bit of reach at present.

STATS: Driving Distance: B   Driving Accuracy: C+   GIR: B+   Short Game: B   Putting: B+

Owen, Gregory Clive (USA) (42) b. Mansfield, England 2/19/1972. 6'4" 205 lbs. TP: 1992. Played the E Tour full-time from 1998-2004, finishing among the top 40 money winners from 2000-2003 and claiming a significant win at the 2003 British Masters, where he beat Christian Cevaer and Ian Poulter by three. T4 at 2004 PGA Tour Q School and came to America thereafter, playing five of six seasons on the PGA Tour from 2005-2010 (2008 was spent on the Web.com), wherein he thrice retained his card. Spent 2011 on the Web.com (52nd in $$$ over 23 starts) but finished T18 at 2011 Q School to return to the big Tour in 2012. Struggled thereafter, failing to retain his card in 2013 and '14. **OWR Best:** 49 - Apr, 2006.

European Tour Wins (1): 2003: British Masters (Daily Telegraph).
Other Wins: 1 Euro Challenge (1996)   +   1 Web.com (2014)   +   World Sand Championship (Abu Dhabi): 2004.

	98	99	00	01	02	03	04	05	06	07	08	09	10	11	12	13	14
Masters	-	-	-	-	-	-	-	-	-	-	-	-	-	-	-	-	-
US Open	-	-	-	-	-	-	-	-	-	-	-	-	-	-	-	-	-
British	-	MC	T55	T23	MC	MC	-	-	T22	-	-	-	-	-	T54	-	-
PGA	-	-	-	-	MC	MC	-	T47	MC	-	-	-	-	-	-	-	-
Money (A)	-	-	-	-	-	-	-	57	69	157	-	109	183	-	85	147	206*
Money (E)	89	64	39	32	37	21	94	-	-	-	-	-	-	-	-	-	-
OWR	457	275	177	126	125	115	168	88	94	334	256	253	621	623	214	331	345

2014: PGA: 8 st / 6 ct / 0 t10. (T24 Puerto Rico). Also played 12 Web.com events, including regaining his PGA Tour card via the Web.com finals.

OUTLOOK: Will play the 2015 PGA Tour from the 21st spot off the Web.com priority list. Has long ridden a solid power game but has seen his GIR drop from 17 to 77 to 116 (in limited starts) since 2012. Is obviously determined to keep playing in the U.S. despite the potential to find more success back in Europe, but at 42 - and with a sometimes uncooperative putter - his opportunities for big success here may be dwindling.

STATS: Driving Distance: B+   Driving Accuracy: B   GIR: A-   Short Game: C+   Putting: C-

---

Pagunsan, Juvic (Philippines) (36) b. Manila, Philippines 5/11/1978. 6'0" 170 lbs. TP: 2006. The son of a golf professional but didn't turn pro himself until age 27, first enjoying a strong amateur career that included a 2nd-place finish at the 2004 Philippine Open and three national amateur titles a year later. Finished 7th in $$$ in his Asian Tour debut in 2006 and would win the Order of Merit in 2011 – but his lone major tour win came at the circuit's Indonesia President Invitational (where he edged Gaganjeet Bhullar by one) in 2007. Began playing in Japan – thus far with moderate success – in 2012. **Teams:** Eisenhower Trophy (3): 2000-02-04. **OWR Best:** 104 - Oct, 2012.

Asian Tour Wins (1): 2007: Indonesia President Inv (Pertamina).
Other Wins: 1 Asian Dev (2010)   +   Country Club Inv (Philippines) (3): 2006-08-12   Negeri Masters (Malaysia): 2007   ICTSI-Riviera Classic (Philippines): 2010   Mercedes-Benz Masters (Thailand): 2010   ICTSI Philippine Tour: 2011.
Amateur Wins: Philippine Am: 2005   Thailand Am: 2005   Malaysian Am: 2005   Kuala Lumpur SEA: 2001

	06	07	08	09	10	11	12	13	14
Masters	-	-	-	-	-	-	-	-	-
US Open	-	-	-	-	-	-	-	-	-
British	-	-	-	-	-	-	T72	-	MC
PGA	-	-	-	-	-	-	-	-	-
Money (J)	-	-	-	-	-	-	29	37	33
Money (As)	7	17	51	16	39	1	-	-	-
OWR	227	179	287	346	371	157	111	274	380

2014: JAP: 19 st / 14 ct / 3 t10. (2 Mizuno, T2 Indonesia, T9 Diamond Cup). Logged two of his top 10s in his first four starts; finished 33rd in $$$.

OUTLOOK: After six often-successful years on the Asian Tour, has transitioned with moderate success to the tougher Japan circuit, cracking the top 40 in $$$ in each of his first three years. Needs to tee-to-green it a bit better to win in Japan, but he's certainly capable of earning a living there.

STATS: Driving Distance: B+   Driving Accuracy: C   GIR: C+   Short Game: B+⇧   Putting: B+

Palmer, Jason (England) (30) b. Melton Mowbray, England 10/8/1984. 6'1" 155 lbs. College: Birmingham University. TP: 2009. After turning pro, spent several seasons splitting time between the Alps mini-tour (where he won four times) and the Challenge Tour, where he claimed his first victory in 2014 en route to earning his E Tour card. Is well known for chipping and hitting bunker shots with only his right hand after suffering

Palmer, Jason, Cont'd

short game yips in 2008. **OWR Best:** 265 - Nov, 2014.

Other Wins: 1 Euro Challenge (2014) + 1 Alps Tour (2010-2013).
Amateur Wins: Italian Am: 2006 Midland Amateur (England): 2008 South of England Am: 2010.

	11	12	13	14
Masters	-	-	-	-
US Open	-	-	-	-
British	-	-	-	-
PGA	-	-	-	-
Money (E)	-	-	-	-
OWR	959	1333	-	267

2014: Played full-time on the Challenge Tour, winning once and clinching his first E Tour card by finishing 8th in $$$.
OUTLOOK: With only two E Tour starts on his résumé, it's difficult to envision glowing results on the big circuit as a 30-year-old rookie.

STATS: Driving Distance: -- Driving Accuracy: -- GIR: -- Short Game: -- Putting: --

---

Palmer, Ryan Hunter (USA) (38)
b. Amarillo, TX 9/19/1976. 5'11" 175 lbs. College: Texas A&M. TP: 2000. After toiling on mini-tours and the Web.com Tour (2003), made a major splash as a 2004 PGA Tour rookie, winning the Walt Disney Classic in his 34th Tour start and finishing 37th in earnings. Was somewhat up-and-down thereafter, following a disappointing 2007 with a win at the 2008 Ginn Sur Mer Classic (beating five players by one shot), then rebounding from an equally flat 2009 with a win at the 2010 Sony Open in Hawaii, where he edged Robert Allenby by one. Lost the 2011 Byron Nelson Championship in sudden death to Keegan Bradley. Generally not a frequent contender but stepped his game up in 2014, logging a career-best eight PGA Tour top 10s, and finishing among the top 60 in $$$ for the fifth straight year. **OWR Best:** 38 - Oct, 2014.

PGA Tour Wins (3): 2004: Walt Disney Classic (Funai) **2008:** Ginn Sur Mer Classic **2010:** Hawaiian Open (Sony).
Other Wins: 1 Web.com (2003).
Amateur Wins: Southwestern Am: 1999.

	98	99	00	01	02	03	04	05	06	07	08	09	10	11	12	13	14
Masters	-	-	-	-	-	-	-	T39	-	-	-	-	MC	10	MC	-	-
US Open	MC	-	-	-	-	-	-	-	-	MC	-	-	-	T21	-	MC	MC
British	-	-	-	-	-	-	-	-	-	-	-	-	-	T30	-	-	T58
PGA	-	-	-	-	-	-	T47	T49	-	-	MC	T33	T19	MC	T47	T5
Money (A)	Am	Am	-	-	-	-	37	60	84	144	68	150	17	47	58	59	24
OWR	-	-	-	-	-	304	93	80	145	410	201	276	59	73	118	126	42

2014: PGA: 23 st / 20 ct / 8 t10. (2 Humana, 2 Honda, T4 BMW, T5 Colonial, T5 PGA, etc.). Though once again winless, enjoyed what can arguably be considered a career-best year with 10 top 25s, eight top 10s and a 14th-place finish in FedEx Cup points.
OUTLOOK: Has won three times (all in relatively light-field events) and utilizes a nice balance of power (he hasn't ranked worse than 26 in Driving Distance since 2008) and an effective putter (24, 37, 35 in SGP since 2012) to a highly consistent record. Has seen his GIR improve for four straight years (139, 94, 56, 46) which, with that sort of putting, explains much of his recent success. At age 38, he seems capable of climbing a bit higher still.

STATS: Driving Distance: A Driving Accuracy: C+ GIR: B+ Short Game: B Putting: A

Pampling, Rodney (Australia) (45)
b. Redcliffe, Western Australia 9/23/1969. 5'10" 175 lbs. TP: 1994. Initially played for several seasons in his homeland, yielding a win at the 1999 Canon Challenge, where he fended off a young Geoff Ogilvy by three. Came to America full-time in 2000 and played two Web.com campaigns, the latter including a 4th-place $$$ ranking and a ticket to the PGA Tour. Became a rare historical footnote at the 1999 British Open (Carnoustie), being the first round leader (with 71), then shooting a second round 86 to miss the cut. Established himself as a reliable earner in America while winning twice, first edging Alex Cejka at the 2004 International, then beating Greg Owen by one at the 2006 Bay Hill Invitational. Began to slip in 2009, later failing to keep his card from 2012-2014. **OWR Best:** 22 - Jun, 2006.

PGA Tour Wins (2): 2004: The International (Stableford) **2006:** Bay Hill Inv.
European Tour Wins (1): 2008: Australian Masters ('09).
Australasian Tour Wins (1): 1999: Canon Challenge.
Other Wins: Shark Shootout (w/J.Kelly): 2006

	98	99	00	01	02	03	04	05	06	07	08	09	10	11	12	13	14
Masters	-	-	-	-	-	-	-	T5	T16	T37	-	-	-	-	-	-	-
US Open	-	-	-	-	MC	-	MC	T32	MC	T14	MC	-	-	70	-	MC
British	-	MC	-	-	-	-	T27	T78	T35	T27	MC	MC	-	-	-	-	-
PGA	-	-	-	-	-	T14	T55	MC	MC	T42	MC	MC	-	-	-	-	-
Money (A)	-	-	-	89	68	31	48	17	62	47	94	180	124	127	200	193*
Money (E)	-	-	-	-	-	-	-	-	-	-	71	-	-	-	-	-
OWR	214	161	332	264	175	110	50	47	30	52	56	92	346	340	216	433	252

2014: PGA: 7 st / 4 ct / 1 t10. (5 Barracuda). Also made 16 Web.com starts (38th in $$$) and failed to play through the Web.com Finals.
OUTLOOK: Enjoyed a long and profitable run in America but at 45 and relying solely on Past Champion status for limited PGA Tour starts, he might be nearing the end of that road. Has seen his SGP slip slowly over the past few seasons, but he's otherwise held fairly firm statistically.

STATS: Driving Distance: C+ Driving Accuracy: B+ GIR: B- Short Game: B- Putting: C

Paratore, Renato (Italy) (18)
b. Rome, Italy 12/14/1996. 5'7" 140 lbs. TP: 2014. Arrives on the E Tour as a fascinating prospect, having been only 17 when he led the 2014 Q School for five rounds before finishing 6th. Has a somewhat short amateur résumé but his talent has shown on one or two occasions beyond Q School. Is mentored by Matteo Manassero. **Teams:** Eisenhower Trophy: 2012. **OWR Best:** 1447 - Sep, 2012.

Paratore, Renato, Cont'd

Amateur Wins: Portuguese Am: 2014 - Youth Olympic Games: 2014   Orange Bowl Jr: 2013.

	14
Masters	-
US Open	-
British	-
PGA	-
Money (E)	-
OWR	-

2014: Made two E Tour starts as an amateur (best: T57 in the Spanish Open) before finishing sixth at Q School to gain his E Tour card.

OUTLOOK: Is very well thought of in Italy and showed why at Q School, putting on quite a show for a then-17 year old. But at only 18, is he really ready to seriously compete on the E Tour? The bet is that he isn't, but hopefully will play well enough to gain (rather then crash) from the experience.

STATS: Driving Distance: --   Driving Accuracy: --   GIR: --   Short Game: --   Putting: --

---

Park, Sang-Hyun (South Korea) (31)
b. Seoul, South Korea 4/23/1983. 5'6" 155 lbs. TP: 2004. Veteran Korean Tour player who joined the circuit in 2004 and scored his best year in 2009, when he won the SK Telecom Open (in its final year before becoming a OneAsia event) and the South Sea Open. Began playing the Japan Tour part-time in 2013, then increased his presence there in 2014 - a season in which he added two more wins (and finished 2nd in $$$) on the Korean circuit. **OWR Best:** 171 - Oct, 2014.

Other Wins: SK Telecom Open (KPGA): 2009   South Sea Open (KPGA): 2009   Vainer Pineridge Open (KPGA): 2014   K.J. Choi Invitational (KPGA): 2014.

	09	10	11	12	13	14
Masters	-	-	-	-	-	-
US Open	-	-	-	-	-	-
British	-	-	-	-	-	-
PGA	-	-	-	-	-	-
Money (J)	-	-	-	-	-	41
OWR	-	1322	294	317	487	183

2014: JAP: 15 st / 11 ct / 3 t10.   (2 Tsuruya, T7 KBC Augusta, T8 Tokai).   Settled in nicely during first official season in Japan (finishing 41st in $$$) while also starring domestically, winning twice and finishing 2nd in the KPGA Order of Merit.

OUTLOOK: A shorter-but-straight type who can hit lots of green and convert with an above-the-median putting stroke. Given his success in Korea, one has to believe he is capable of winning in Japan, but given his limited statistical sampling, his 2014 form may prove difficult to sustain.

STATS (LTD): Driving Distance: B-   Driving Accuracy: A-   GIR: B+   Short Game: C+   Putting: B+

Park, Sung-Joon (South Korea) (27)
b. Seoul, South Korea 6/9/1986. 5'9" 160 lbs. TP: 2008. Initially played almost exclusively in Japan, first on the developmental Challenge circuit (where he won once in 2010), then on the Japan Tour. Was a quiet presence (only two career top 10s) through 2012 but blossomed in 2013, winning a rain-shortened KBC Augusta (by two over Jung-Gon Hwang), then losing a three-way playoff (to Hideki Matsuyama) at the Fujisankei Classic a week later. Began playing the Web.com Tour in 2014 and played his way through the Finals to gain PGA Tour status for 2015. **Teams:** World Cup: 2011. **OWR Best:** 92 - Oct, 2013.

Japan Tour Wins (1): 2013: KBC Augusta.
Other Wins: 1 Japan Challenge (2010).

	10	11	12	13	14
Masters	-	-	-	-	-
US Open	-	-	-	-	-
British	-	-	-	-	-
PGA	-	-	-	-	-
Money (J)	89	40	76	5	103*
OWR	825	441	628	96	209

2014: Made 15 Web.com starts, finishing 73rd in regular season $$$ before playing through the Finals, taking 45th place on the priority list.

OUTLOOK: With a T11 at the Web.com Tour Championship, became one of the least likely qualifiers in the incoming PGA Tour class. While his skills around the green should hold up well, his tee-to-green game may not measure up well at this level. From the 45th priority slot, a real longshot.

STATS: Driving Distance: B   Driving Accuracy: B   GIR: B-   Short Game: A-   Putting: B+

Parnevik, Jesper Bo (Sweden) (49)
b. Stockholm, Sweden 3/7/1965. 6'0" 175 lbs. TP: 1986. Colorful player who became Sweden's first male golfer to succeed widely in America. Began splitting time between Europe and the U.S. in 1994, becoming a regular top-50 money earner (and five time tournament winner) on the PGA Tour into the new millennium. Finished 2nd at the 1994 and '97 British Opens, leading the former until being overtaken by Nick Price at the 71st. Scored his first major tour win at the 1993 Scottish Open, beating Payne Stewart by five. Twice a winner of the E Tour's Scandinavian Masters (1995 and '98), the first time in a five-shot runaway over Colin Montgomerie. His first U.S. win was a three-shot triumph at the 1998 Phoenix Open. Despite his Nordic background, all five of his PGA Tour wins have come in southern or desert locales. Recovered from a minor slump by finishing 40th in PGA Tour earnings during a winless 2004, then slipped again in '05. Battled multiple injuries from 2007 onward, including serious back problems in 2010. Hasn't been a full-time Tour player since 2008. **Teams:** Eisenhower Trophy (2): 1984-86. Ryder Cup (3): 1997-99-02 (O: 4-3-4, S: 0-2-1). World Cup (2): 1994-95. **OWR Best:** 7 - May, 2000.

PGA Tour Wins (5): 1998: Phoenix Open   **1999:** Greater Greensboro Open (Chrysler)   **2000:** Bob Hope Classic (90H), Byron Nelson Classic (GTE)   **2001:** Honda Classic.

European Tour Wins (4): 1993: Scottish Open   **1995:** Scandinavian Masters   **1996:** Trophée Lancôme   **1998:** Scandinavian Masters.

Parnevik, Jesper Bo, Cont'd
Other Wins: Odense Open (Sweden): 1988   Ramlosa Open (Sweden): 1988   Open Passing Shot (France): 1988   Swedish Open: 1990   Johnnie Walker Super Tour (Sweden): 1997.
Amateur Wins: Dixie Am (USA): 1986.

	89	90	91	92	93	94	95	96	97	98	99	00	01	02	03	04	05	06	07	08	09	10	11	12
Masters	-	-	-	-	-	-	-	-	T21	T31	MC	T40	T20	T29	-	-	MC	-	-	-	-	-	-	-
US Open	-	-	-	-	-	-	-	-	T48	T14	T17	MC	T30	T54	MC	-	-	-	-	T74	-	-	-	-
British	-	-	-	T21	2	T24	T45	T2	T4	T10	T36	T9	T28	DQ	-	-	-	-	-	-	-	-	-	-
PGA	-	-	-	-	-	MC	T20	T5	T45	MC	T10	T51	T13	MC	T34	MC	T28	MC	-	-	-	-	-	-
Money (A)	-	-	-	-	-	120	84	53	12	14	36	8	31	63	118	40	109	71	90	143	219*	245*	229*	253*
Money (E)	50	72	48	73	17	26	17	-	-	-	-	-	-	-	-	-	-	-	-	-	-	-	-	-
OWR	216	219	161	196	72	39	37	39	18	14	15	11	32	81	181	75	107	97	178	292	614	-	-	-

	13	14
Masters	-	-
US Open	-	-
British	-	-
PGA	-	-
Money (A)	220*	254*
OWR	-	154

2014: PGA: 3 st / 1 ct / 0 t10. (T65 Puerto Rico). Was scarcely playing prior to a summer rib injury which ended his season.
OUTLOOK: Has been rendered a shadow of his former self by back and neck injuries that saw him begin 2013 on a medical extension. At age 49, and now playing as a Past Champion, he's likely just biding his time until he becomes Champions Tour-eligible in March.
STATS: Driving Distance: C-   Driving Accuracy: C+   GIR: D   Short Game: B-   Putting: B

Parry, John Anthony (England) (28)   b. Harrogate, England 11/17/1986. 5'7" 145 lbs. TP: 2009. After playing on the 2007 Walker Cup team, graduated the 2009 Challenge Tour to reach the E Tour. Won as a rookie there as well, claiming the Vivendi Classic when he edged Johan Edfors by two. Repaired to the Challenge Tour for 2012 but regained E Tour status for 2013 by winning the 2012 Q School. Kept his card easily in 2013 but had to return via Q School after a disastrous campaign in 2014. **Teams:** Walker Cup: 2007 (1-1-0). **OWR Best:** 114 - Jan, 2011.

European Tour Wins (1): 2010: Vivendi Cup.
Other Wins: 1 Euro Challenge (2009)   +   2 EuroPro (2008).
Amateur Wins: Spanish Am: 2007   -   Peter McEvoy Trophy: 2004   Danish Am: 2005   Welsh Am Stroke Play: 2007.

	09	10	11	12	13	14
Masters	-	-	-	-	-	-
US Open	-	-	-	-	T28	-
British	-	-	-	-	-	-
PGA	-	-	-	-	-	-
Money (E)	-	51	126	218*	77	171
OWR	270	126	235	594	302	661

2014: E: 29 st / 5 ct / 0 t10. (T25 Dunhill Links). Made only one of his first 22 cuts in finishing 171st in $$$, then regained his card via Q School.
OUTLOOK: Saw marked declines in most ball-striking categories during a disastrous 2014, though he showed plenty of grit by playing his best golf late, and finishing 6th at Q School. Still, he lacks length and fails to offset it anywhere else, so consistent contending seems unlikely.
STATS: Driving Distance: C+   Driving Accuracy: C+   GIR: C   Short Game: B+   Putting: B

Pavan, Andrea (Italy) (25)   b. Rome, Italy 4/27/1989. 6'3" 185 lbs. College: All-American at Texas A&M. TP: 2010. Was dominant as a junior player in Italy, then starred on a national championship-winning Texas A&M team in 2009. Won twice on the 2011 Challenge Tour to finish 2nd in $$$ and graduate to the E Tour. After losing his card in 2012, once again dominated the Challenge circuit in 2013 (winning twice more) before again failing to retain his E Tour card in 2014. **Teams:** Eisenhower Trophy (2): 2009-10. Palmer Cup: 2010. **OWR Best:** 173 - Nov, 2011.

Other Wins: 4 Euro Challenge (2011-2013).
Amateur Wins: Italian Am Stroke Play (2): 2005-07   Italian Omnium: 2007.

	11	12	13	14
Masters	-	-	-	-
US Open	-	-	MC	-
British	-	-	-	-
PGA	-	-	-	-
Money (E)	-	158	-	119
OWR	181	382	183	304

2014: E: 31 st / 14 ct / 4 t10. (T8 Hong Kong, T8 Russia, T9 Wales, T9 Perth). Finished 119th in $$$ but regained his card via Q School.
OUTLOOK: Arrived for his second E Tour try as the 2013 Challenge Tour's leading $$$ winner, lost his card (despite two late top 10s) but then quickly regained it at Q School. Thus despite some limited stats, he likely has enough to stick this time around - but stardom remains beyond the horizon.
STATS (LTD): Driving Distance: C+   Driving Accuracy: C   GIR: B   Short Game: B   Putting: B-

---

Pepperell, Eddie (England) (23)   b. Oxford, England 1/22/1991. 6'1" 180 lbs. TP: 2011. Enjoyed a solid amateur career (was runner-up in the 2009 British Boys) before turning pro, then failed to secure even a Challenge Tour card. But playing on a special invite, he won the Allianz Open Cotes d'Armor Bretagne to gain full Challenge Tour status for the rest of 2012, then played his way onto the E Tour by finishing 13th in $$$. Though

Pepperell, Eddie, Cont'd

winless, climbed nicely over his first two seasons, finishing 49th in $$$ in 2014. **Teams:** Eisenhower Trophy: 2010. **OWR Best:** 151 - Nov, 2014.

Other Wins: 1 Euro Challenge (2012).

Amateur Wins: Portuguese Am: 2011 – Berkshire Trophy: 2010 Welsh Am Stroke Play: 2010.

	12	13	14
Masters	-	-	-
US Open	-	MC	-
British	-	-	-
PGA	-	-	-
Money (E)	-	76	49
OWR	322	256	151

2014: E: 27 st / 14 ct / 6 t10. (4 KLM, T4 Denmark, T4 Wales, T5 Czech Masters, T6 Nordea, etc.). Stepped up nicely in year two, finishing 49th in $$$.

OUTLOOK: Saw significant year two improvement in his GIR, short game and putting - though the samples remains too small to reach long-term conclusions. Still, he's bettered expectations so far, seemingly without reaching. Remains winless, however, and that may not change right away.

STATS: Driving Distance: B   Driving Accuracy: B-   GIR: B+   Short Game: B+   Putting: B+

Percy, Cameron Blair (Australia) (40)

b. Chelsea, Victoria, Australia 5/5/1974. 6'0" 180 lbs. TP: 1998. Spent the early years of his career playing mostly in his native Australia (where he won back-to-back Tasmanian Opens on the old Von Nida developmental tour) and around Asia. Played the Web.com Tour full-time in 2005, '08 and '09, finishing 8th in $$$ in '09 to graduate to the PGA Tour. Bounced between the two tours for two seasons before a 13th-place finish in Web.com $$$ returned him to the big stage for 2013. **OWR Best:** 182 - Jan, 2010.

Other Wins: 1 Web.com (2014) + Tasmanian Open (2): 1997-98 Victorian PGA (Aus): 2005 Queensland PGA (Aus): 2006 Queensland Masters (Aus): 2006.

Amateur Wins: Malaysian Am: 1998.

	03	04	05	06	07	08	09	10	11	12	13	14
Masters	-	-	-	-	-	-	-	-	-	-	-	-
US Open	-	-	-	-	-	-	-	-	-	-	-	-
British	MC	-	-	-	-	-	-	MC	-	-	-	-
PGA	-	-	-	-	-	-	-	-	-	-	-	-
Money (A)	-	-	-	-	-	-	-	145	176*	-	169	-
OWR	705	-	763	722	734	477	185	247	401	202	315	347

2014: Played the Web.com Tour full-time, regaining his PGA Tour card by finishing 14th in regular season $$$.

OUTLOOK: A long-hitting Australian who has failed to keep his PGA Tour card through two full seasons (2011 and '13) but fought his way back for a third try via the 2014 Web.com Tour. Following this strong 2014 campaign, now faces his best-ever chance at American success.

STATS: Driving Distance: A-   Driving Accuracy: B-   GIR: B+   Short Game: B-   Putting: B+

Perez, Patrick A. (USA) (38)

b. Phoenix, AZ 3/1/1976. 6'0" 180 lbs. College: Arizona St. TP: 1997. An AJGA All-American. A touted junior who, in 1993, claimed both the Junior World (at Torrey Pines) and the Maxfli PGA Junior (at Pinehurst). Was a member of Arizona State's 1996 national championship team before spending two seasons playing the Web.com Tour, winning once in 2000. Has finished among the top 125 $$$ winners for the entirety of his PGA Tour career but has never bettered the 40th-place finish achieved as a rookie. Lone PGA Tour win came at the 2009 Bob Hope Chrysler Classic, where he beat John Merrick by three after opening with Tour record rounds of 61-63. **OWR Best:** 48 - Mar, 2009.

PGA Tour Wins (1): 2009: Bob Hope Chrysler Classic (90H).

Other Wins: 1 Web.com (2000) + Champions Challenge: 2002 (w/J.Daly).

Amateur Wins: Junior World (15-17): 1993 PGA Junior: 1993.

	02	03	04	05	06	07	08	09	10	11	12	13	14
Masters	-	T45	-	-	-	-	-	MC	-	-	-	-	-
US Open	MC	-	T40	-	-	MC	T36	-	-	-	-	-	-
British	-	-	-	T67	-	T20	MC	-	-	-	-	-	-
PGA	70	-	-	T6	MC	T18	T58	MC	-	-	T21	-	T47
Money (A)	40	117	111	62	117	52	43	49	101	73	94	84	82
OWR	108	188	205	116	173	70	82	90	191	185	142	190	207

2014: PGA: 25 st / 18 ct / 3 t10. (T2 Farmers, T7 AT&T Pro-Am, T8 Hawaii). Kept his card for a 13th straight year, finishing 98th in FedEx Cup points.

OUTLOOK: Despite a famously combustible temper, has emerged as a reliable player who posts his share of top 10s (three more in 2014) and has emerged as an ultra-consistent money winner. Has a statistically balanced and relatively consistent game, with a 2014 tail off in Total Driving (61 to 147) being offset by a similar improvement in SGP (110 to 48). Not likely to explode, but he's bound to win again one of these days.

STATS: Driving Distance: B   Driving Accuracy: B+   GIR: B   Short Game: B+   Putting: B+

Peterson, John Herring (USA) (25)

b. Fort Worth, TX 4/18/1989. 5'11" 175 lbs. All-American and individual national champion (2011) at Louisiana St. TP: 2011. As an amateur, held the 54-hole lead at the Web.com Tour's Children's Hospital Invitational before losing at the 72nd to fellow amateur Harris English. Drew great attention after tying for 4th at the 2012 U.S. Open at the Olympic Club. Won the 2013 Web.com Finals, cementing PGA Tour status for 2014, then lost his card before returning via the Web.com Finals. **OWR Best:** 129 - Oct, 2013.

Other Wins: Adams (2012).

Amateur Wins: NCAA Individual: 2011   Jones Cup: 2011.

Peterson, John Herring, Cont'd

	12	13	14
Masters	-	60	-
US Open	T4	T67	-
British	-	-	-
PGA	-	-	-
Money (A)	-	-	179
OWR	344	147	272

2014: PGA: 25 st / 7 ct / 0 t10. (T19 FedEx St Jude). Struggled as a rookie, finishing 179th in FedEx Cup points but returning via the Web.com Finals.

OUTLOOK: Arrived in 2014 as a touted prospect, partially due to having finished T4 at the 2012 U.S. Open. But perhaps tellingly, he had never won beyond the mini-tour level, and he struggled to compete on the big stage. Likely to see some improvement this second time around.

STATS: Driving Distance: B   Driving Accuracy: A-   GIR: B+   Short Game: B-   Putting: C

Petrovic, Timothy J. (USA) (48)
b. Northampton, MA 8/16/1966. 6'2" 195 lbs. College: U of Hartford. TP: 1988. Former Web.com and overseas player who generally remained a fixture among the PGA Tour's top 100 $$$ winners from 2002-2010. Claimed his lone Tour victory at the 2005 Zurich (New Orleans) Classic, where he defeated fellow Massachusetts native James Driscoll in a playoff. Slipped significantly in 2011, and has played on conditional and Past Champion status since. **OWR Best:** 65 - May, 2005.

PGA Tour Wins (1): 2005: New Orleans Classic (Zurich).
Amateur Wins: New England Am: 1986   Connecticut Am: 1988.

	01	02	03	04	05	06	07	08	09	10	11	12	13	14
Masters	-	-	-	T41	-	-	-	-	-	-	-	-	-	-
US Open	T62	-	T15	T24	-	-	MC	-	-	-	WD	-	-	-
British	-	MC	-	-	MC	-	-	MC	-	MC	-	-	-	-
PGA	-	-	MC	MC	MC	-	-	-	MC	MC	-	-	-	-
Money (A)	-	86	36	65	44	132	92	107	54	85	146	137	185*	200*
OWR	413	237	86	104	112	232	265	280	170	178	384	453	516	821

2014: PGA: 10 st / 4 ct / 0 t10. (T14 Puerto Rico). Finished 192nd in FedEx Cup points, then failed to play through the Web.com Finals.

OUTLOOK: At age 48, and set to play on Past Champion status, he seems unlikely to be a central player on the PGA Tour. Steady declines in several of his bread-and-butter areas (71 to 124 in Driving Accuracy, 53 to 99 to 136 in SGP) don't bode well. A strong Champions Tour candidate for 2016.

STATS: Driving Distance: C-   Driving Accuracy: B   GIR: C   Short Game: B+   Putting: B

Pettersson, Carl (Sweden) (37)
b. Gothenburg, Sweden 8/29/1977. 5'11" 195 lbs. All-American and two-time national champion at Central(AL)JC before transferring to North Carolina St. TP: 2000. An AJGA All-American. Swedish native whose family moved to North Carolina when he was 14. After turning pro, spent two years on the European Tour, enjoying a strong 2002 in which he placed 26th in $$$ and won the Portuguese Open in a playoff with David Gilford. Played through PGA Tour Q School in late 2002 and has remained a Tour fixture since 2003, only once finishing worse than the 74th place of his rookie year (136th in 2009) through 2012. Broke through for his first U.S. victory at the 2005 Chrysler Championship, then logged a prestigious win at the 2006 Memorial, where he beat Zach Johnson and Brett Wetterich by two. Ended a two-year victory drought at the 2010 Canadian Open, where he shot 60 in the third round (St. George's G&CC). Claimed his fifth PGA Tour win at the 2012 RBC Heritage, beating Zach Johnson by five at Harbour Town. Cooled noticeably in 2013 but righted the ship somewhat with a stronger 2014. **Teams**: Eisenhower Trophy: 2000. World Cup (2): 2002-06. **OWR Best:** 23 - Jul, 2006.

PGA Tour Wins (5): 2005: Chrysler Championship   **2006**: Memorial Tournament   **2008**: Wyndham Championship   **2010**: Canadian Open   **2012**: Heritage.
European Tour Wins (1): 2002: Portuguese Open (36H).
Amateur Wins: National JC (2): 1997-98   European Am: 2000.

	01	02	03	04	05	06	07	08	09	10	11	12	13	14
Masters	-	-	-	-	-	T27	T52	-	MC	-	MC	-	61	-
US Open	-	-	-	-	MC	MC	T17	T6	T36	-	-	MC	T41	-
British	-	T43	-	T57	-	T8	T45	-	-	-	-	T23	T54	-
PGA	-	MC	MC	54	-	MC	-	T47	MC	T24	-	T3	MC	-
Money (A)	-	-	74	51	31	9	18	34	136	39	52	13	110	79
Money (E)	61	26	-	-	-	-	62	-	-	-	-	-	-	-
OWR	159	114	118	87	53	36	61	62	212	109	110	32	105	173

2014: PGA: 28 st / 17 ct / 4 t10. (T3 FedEx St Jude, T4 Puerto Rico, T7 Travelers, T9 Deutsche Bank).   Recovered somewhat from a flat 2013, logging eight top 25s and climbing back to 63rd in FedEx Cup points.

OUTLOOK: Bounced back somewhat in 2013 but it's difficult to ignore that his putting has slipped, with his five-year SGP reading 2, 24, 20, 112, 125; some of this has been due to switching back to the short putter - but regardless, that's not an optimistic sign going forward. On the positive side, he's added a bit of length over the last three years (47 in Driving Distance) which helps. Still capable of winning, but is his best golf behind him?

STATS: Driving Distance: A-   Driving Accuracy: C+   GIR: B- ⇧   Short Game: B-   Putting: B+

Piercy, Scott (USA) (36)
b. Las Vegas, NV 11/6/1978. 6'0" 185 lbs. College: San Diego St. TP: 2001. After college, spent seven years playing mini-tours (mostly the Hooters) before finishing 9th in $$$ during a two-win 2008 season on the Web.com Tour. Aside from a disappointing 2010, has climbed steadily in PGA Tour earnings, initially drawing attention by finishing 75th in a 2011 campaign which included his first win, a one-shot triumph over Pat Perez at the Reno-Tahoe Open. Gained his second PGA Tour victory in the summer of 2012, edging Robert Garrigus and William McGirt by one at the Canadian Open. Struggled during an injury-shortened 2014. **OWR Best:** 36 - Mar, 2013.

Piercy, Scott, Cont'd

PGA Tour Wins (2): 2011: Reno-Tahoe Open **2012**: Canadian Open (RBC).
Other Wins: 2 Web.com (2008) + 1 NGA/Hooters (2006).

	08	09	10	11	12	13	14
Masters	-	-	-	-	-	T54	-
US Open	MC	-	-	T51	MC	MC	-
British	-	-	-	-	-	MC	-
PGA	-	-	-	T26	T48	**T5**	MC
Money (A)	-	90	136	75	27	39	155*
OWR	196	176	376	175	41	55	184

2014: PGA: 12 st / 7 ct / 0 t10. (T12 Wyndham). Had his season shortened by right arm surgery in February, limiting him to 12 starts (166th in Fedex Cup points), plus two July rehab starts on the Web.com.
OUTLOOK: Will begin 2015 on a 14-event medical extension. Has never finished worse than 21st in Driving Distance over a full season, but also possesses a strong short game and putter. That's a combination that suggests a nice bounceback campaign in 2015.

STATS: Driving Distance: A+   Driving Accuracy: C-   GIR: B-   Short Game: B+   Putting: B+

Pieters, Thomas (Belgium) (22)

b. Antwerp, Belgium 1/27/1992. 6'5" 190 lbs. A two-time All-American and NCAA individual champion (2012) at U of Illinois. TP: 2013. Belgium's highest-rated prospect since Nicolas Colsaerts. After turning pro, had time for only six Challenge and three E Tour starts in 2013, requiring him to earn his 2014 card at Q School. Made some noise as a rookie, losing (along with Richard Green) to Miguel Ángel Jiménez in a playoff at the 2014 Spanish Open. **Teams:** Eisenhower Trophy: 2010. Palmer Cup: 2012. **OWR Best:** 237 - Oct, 2014.
Amateur Wins: NCAA Individual: 2012   Jack Nicklaus Inv: 2011   Monroe Inv: 2012.

	13	14
Masters	-	-
US Open	-	-
British	-	-
PGA	-	-
Money (E)	-	83
OWR	1122	240

2014: E: 27 st / 10 ct / 3 t10. (T2P Spanish, T6 Russia, T8 Malaysian). Enjoyed a surprisingly strong rookie year, finishing 83rd in $$$.
OUTLOOK: Arrived as something of a longshot in 2013 but so far has made good, relying on a power game and an above-the-median putting stroke to nearly win the Spanish Open and excel overall as a rookie. Now 2015 will tell us if those numbers hold up, but the bet here is a cautious yes.

STATS (LTD): Driving Distance: A   Driving Accuracy: C   GIR: C   Short Game: B+   Putting: B+

Pinckney, Scott D. (USA) (25)

b. Orem, UT 3/13/1989. 6'0" 165 lbs. College: Arizona St. TP: 2011. Won the 2010 Trans-Mississippi Amateur. Upon turning pro, spent 2012 on both the European and Challenge Tours, then moved to the Web.com where he played his way through the 2014 finals to gain PGA Tour status. Is a longtime friend of Rory McIlroy's, dating to their junior tournament days. **OWR Best:** 473 - Oct, 2014.
Amateur Wins: Trans-Mississippi Am: 2010.

	11	12	13	14
Masters	-	-	-	-
US Open	MC	-	-	-
British	-	MC	-	-
PGA	-	-	-	-
Money (A)	-	-	-	-
OWR	1401	982	1274	504

2014: Played full-time on the Web.com Tour, finishing 37th in regular season $$$ before gaining 2015 PGA Tour status via the Finals.
OUTLOOK: Another 2015 rookie whose PGA Tour status is based far more on a timely Web.com hot streak than an accumulated body of work.

STATS (LTD): Driving Distance: B+   Driving Accuracy: B   GIR: B-   Short Game: B-   Putting: B+

Plaphol, Chawalit (Thailand) (40)

b. Chon Buri, Thailand 8/30/1974. 5'9" 170 lbs. TP: 1996. A steady (if unspectacular earner) since 1996. Claimed his first win (by five over Boonchu Ruangkit) at the 1998 Orient Masters, and would later capture the Japan Tour's ANA Open during his first season there. After a quiet period in 2009-2010, emerged to beat Prayad Marksaeng by two at the 2011 Queen's Cup before adding the season-opening Myanmar Open (by one over Mithun Perera) in 2013. **Teams:** World Cup: 2000. **OWR Best:** 178 - Jan, 2012.
Japan Tour Wins (1): 2004: ANA Open.
Asian Tour Wins (4): 1998: Orient Masters **2006**: Bangkok Airways Open **2011**: Queen's Cup **2013**: Myanmar Open (Zykabar).
Other Wins: Hugo Boss Foursomes (China): 1998 (w/J.Rutledge)   Mt. Malarayat Championship (Philippines): 2010.
Amateur Wins: Southeast Asian Games (Individual): 1995.

	96	97	98	99	00	01	02	03	04	05	06	07	08	09	10	11	12	13	14
Masters	-	-	-	-	-	-	-	-	-	-	-	-	-	-	-	-	-	-	-
US Open	-	-	-	-	-	-	-	-	-	-	-	-	-	-	-	-	-	-	-
British	-	-	-	-	-	-	-	-	-	-	-	-	-	-	-	-	-	-	-
PGA	-	-	-	-	-	-	-	-	-	-	-	-	-	-	-	-	-	-	-
Money (J)	-	-	-	-	-	-	39	64	72	49	56	104	-	43	92	-	-	-	-
Money (As)	55	36	11	33	52	26	47	20	13*	7	33	27	26	72	51	19	53*	21	48
OWR	688	771	787	422	571	697	915	720	227	244	280	267	276	514	749	179	413	522	636

Plaphol, Chawalit, Cont'd

2014: ASIA: 19 st / 12 ct / 1 t10. (2 Solaire). Had a moderately disappointing year in Asia, slipping to 48th in $$$.

OUTLOOK: A mediocre tee-to-greener who thrives on and around the putting surface. Still competitive on the Asian circuit as he hits 40, and while he likely won't be making an major excursions abroad anymore, he should remain a solid regional for the immediate future.

STATS: Driving Distance: B-   Driving Accuracy: C   GIR: C-   Short Game: B+   Putting: A-

---

Points, Darren Andrew ("D.A.") (USA) (38)

b. Pekin, IL 12/1/1976. 6'1" 195 lbs. All-American at U of Illinois. TP: 1999. Two-time AJGA All-American. A three-time Illinois Amateur champion. Reached the quarter-finals of the 1996 U.S. Amateur (Pumpkin Ridge) where he was eliminated by Tiger Woods. Played six full seasons (logging four wins) on the Web.com Tour, graduating to the PGA Tour in both 2004 (two wins and 2nd place in $$$) and 2008 (16th in $$$). Has settled into a solid money earning role since 2009, led by a 2011 campaign which included his first PGA Tour win, a two-shot triumph over Hunter Mahan at the AT&T Pebble Beach Pro-Am. As the cornerstone of a career-best 23rd-place $$$ ranking, won the 2013 Houston Open by holing a 13-foot par putt at the last to edge Billy Horschel and Henrik Stenson by one. **OWR Best:** 45 - May, 2013.

PGA Tour Wins (2): 2011: AT&T Pro-Am **2013**: Houston Open (Shell).

Other Wins: 4 Web.com (2001-2008).

Amateur Wins: Illinois Am (3): 1995-98-99.

	05	06	07	08	09	10	11	12	13	14
Masters	-	-	-	-	-	-	MC	-	T38	MC
US Open	-	-	-	T69	-	-	MC	MC	MC	MC
British	-	-	-	-	-	MC	-	-	MC	T32
PGA	-	-	-	-	-	T16	T10	MC	T40	-
Money (A)	161	162	-	-	66	93	37	56	23	165
OWR	347	476	449	282	187	205	120	148	61	344

2014: PGA: 27 st / 12 ct / 0 t10. (T18 Wyndham). Stumbled badly, making only five cuts after mid-March and finishing 173rd in FedEx Cup points.

OUTLOOK: Despite crashing in 2014, he'll remain exempt in 2015 due to his Houston Open victory. Statistically, his game is something of an oddity as he is a short-but-accurate driver of the ball, yet he hits relatively few greens and is a below-the-median putter. Still, his very steady earnings from 2009-2013 can't be ignored, and at age 38, he should still have more than enough in the tank to climb back among the top 125.

STATS: Driving Distance: C+   Driving Accuracy: A-   GIR: C+   Short Game: B-   Putting: C+

Porteous, Haydn (South Africa) (20)

b. Johannesburg, South Africa 7/8/1994. 5'9" 150 lbs. TP: 2013. A domestically touted prospect who, after claiming the 2012 South African Amateur (and numerous other domestic amateur titles), turned pro and began splitting time between Europe and the Sunshine Tour. Logged multiple high finishes domestically, several times losing events in their latter stages - but his obvious ability to contend bodes well for the future. **Teams:** Eisenhower Trophy: 2012. **OWR Best:** 306 - Oct, 2014.

Other Wins: Northern Cape Open (South Africa): 2010*   Boland Open (South Africa): 2011*.

Amateur Wins: South African Am: 2012   -   Open Free State: 2010   South African Stroke Play (2): 2012-13   Kwa Zulu Natal Match Play: 2012   Limpopo Stroke Play: 2012   Harry Oppenheimer Cup: 2012   Boland Am: 2012   Prince's Grant Am: 2013   Northern Am Stroke Plat: 2012   Cape Province Am: 2012.

	14
Masters	-
US Open	-
British	-
PGA	-
Money (SA)	25
OWR	336

2014: SUN: 17 st / 12 ct / 7 t10. (Incl. 2 Sun City, 3 Zimbabwe, 3 BMG). Got his feet wet nicely as a rookie, logging seven top 10s in 17 starts.

OUTLOOK: Is viewed domestically as one of South Africa's stronger young prospects, and while he's thus far won only at home, a rookie season with so many top 10s (including a one-shot loss at the Sun City Challenge) did nothing to refute that notion.

STATS: Driving Distance: --   Driving Accuracy: --   GIR: --   Short Game: --   Putting: --

---

Potter, Theodore Charles Jr. (USA) (31)

b. Ocala, FL 11/9/1983. 5'11" 185 lbs. TP: 2002. Turned professional directly out of high school. A longtime mini-tour veteran who was named Hooters Tour Player of the Year in 2006. Made a memorably futile debut on the Web.com Tour in 2004, missing all 24 cuts (!) and earning nothing. Returned to the Web.com in 2007 and 2010, finishing 189th and 148th respectively. Caught fire in 2011, however, winning twice (including the season-opening South Georgia Classic) and finishing 2nd in Web.com $$$, graduating to the 2012 PGA Tour. Completed a remarkable early career arc by winning as a rookie at the 2012 Greenbrier Classic, beating Troy Kelly on the third extra hole. Found slightly less success in 2013 and '14, failing to keep his card in the latter year. **OWR Best:** 83 - Jul, 2012.

PGA Tour Wins (1): 2012: Greenbrier Classic.

Other Wins: 2 Web.com (2011)   +   7 NGA/Hooters (2006-2011).

	11	12	13	14
Masters	-	-	MC	-
US Open	-	-	MC	-
British	-	T60	-	-
PGA	-	MC	-	-
Money (A)	-	62	100	160
OWR	174	112	219	440

Potter, Theodore Charles Jr., Cont'd

2014: PGA: 24 st / 9 ct / 0 t10.   (T13 FedEx St Jude).   Fell to 154th in FedEx Cup points in a year slightly shortened by late-summer ankle surgery.

OUTLOOK: Declined further off his rookie year peak, but will still have a (small) chance to keep his card via a two-event medical extension at the start of 2015. A short but fairly steady ball striker whose putting slipped badly in 2014 (50 to 140 in SGP). Seems headed back to the Web.com.

STATS: Driving Distance: C   Driving Accuracy: A   GIR: B-   Short Game: B+   Putting: B

Poulter, Ian James (England) (38)
b. Stevenage, England 1/10/1976. 6'1" 190 lbs. TP: 1994. Well known in the golfing world for his offbeat fashion and wild hair styles. Established European star whose back-to-back top-10 Order of Merit finishes in 2003 and '04 landed him on his first Ryder Cup team. A 10-time E Tour winner (and 2000 E Tour Rookie of the Year) whose early résumé was led by a sudden-death victory over Sergio García at the 2004 Volvo Masters, and a pair of wins (2000 and 2002) in the Italian Open. Also claimed the 2007 Dunlop Phoenix in Japan, beating Gonzalo Fernández-Castaño by three. Runner-up at the 2008 British Open, finishing four behind Padraig Harrington at Royal Birkdale. Closed 2009 on a high note, winning the E Tour co-sanctioned Singapore Open (by one over Wen-Chong Liang) in November. Scored a major victory on the world stage at the 2010 WGC Match Play, defeating countryman Paul Casey 4 & 2 in the final. Five times among the E Tour Order of Merit top 10 from 2003-2009. Became a PGA Tour member in 2005, earning big money prior to a disappointing 2011 in which he slipped all the way to 115th – though the season did include a victory in the World Match Play, where he beat Luke Donald 2 & 1 in the final. After a quiet 2012, went undefeated in Ryder Cup play to spark a European comeback win at Medinah, then won his second career WGC title at the WGC-HSBC Champions in China, where he beat a quartet including Jason Dufner, Ernie Els and Phil Mickelson by two. **Awards**: E Tour Rookie of the Year: 2000. **Teams**: Ryder Cup (5): 2004-08-10-12-14 (O: 12-4-2, S: 4-0-1). Seve Trophy (3): 2003-05-11. World Cup (5): 2001-07-08-09-11. **OWR Best**: 5 - Feb, 2010.

PGA Tour Wins (2): **2010**: WGC-Match Play   **2012**: WGC-HSBC Champions.
European Tour Wins (10): **2000**: Italian Open   **2001**: Moroccan Open   **2002**: Italian Open (54H)   **2003**: Wales Open, Nordic Open   **2004**: Volvo Masters   **2006**: Madrid Open   **2009**: Singapore Open   **2010**: Hong Kong Open   **2011**: World Match Play.
Japan Tour Wins (1): **2007**: Dunlop Phoenix.
Australasian (1): **2011**: Australian Masters.
Other Wins: 1 Euro Challenge (1999)   +   Shark Shootout: 2010 (w/D.Johnson).

	99	00	01	02	03	04	05	06	07	08	09	10	11	12	13	14
Masters	-	-	-	-	-	T31	T33	-	T13	T25	T20	T10	T27	7	MC	T20
US Open	-	-	-	-	-	MC	T57	T12	T36	-	T18	T47	MC	T41	T21	T17
British	-	T64	-	T50	T46	T25	T11	MC	T27	2	MC	T60	MC	T9	T3	MC
PGA	-	-	MC	-	T61	T37	T47	T9	T23	T31	T19	-	T39	T3	T61	T59
Money (A)	-	-	-	-	-	-	86	51	64	65	25	36	115	45	49	63
Money (E)	30	31	24	24	5	9	19	8	24	19	9	4	23	5	2	13
OWR	-	160	77	76	42	35	59	34	22	26	12	11	16	12	12	27

2014: PGA: 17 st / 13 ct / 2 t10.   (2 WGC-HSBC, T6 FedEx St Jude).   Recorded his second straight winless season worldwide but remained a solid earner, finishing 63rd in PGA Tour $$$ (and 78th in FedEx Cup points) in only 17 starts. As a captain's pick, played in his fifth Ryder Cup.

OUTLOOK: As he nears 40, he's been slowed of late by a recurring wrist problem, which at least partially explains a moderate loss of form. Has seen recent modest declines in his SGP (62 to 91), Driving Accuracy (39 to 71 to 87) and the new Strokes Gained Tee To Green (58 to 118) but his strong short game and often-clutch putting can at least somewhat overcome that. Still a strong threat when healthy - especially at match play.

STATS: Driving Distance: C+   Driving Accuracy: B+   GIR: C   Short Game: B+   Putting: B+

Pratt, Kieran (Australia) (26)
b. Melbourne, Victoria, Australia 5/14/1988. 5'11" 165 lbs. TP: 2010. Has spent his first professional years playing primarily at home and on the Asian circuit, where he claimed his first victory at the 2012 Myanmar Open, beating Kiradech Aphibarnrat and Adam Blyth in sudden death. **Teams**: Eisenhower Trophy: 2010. **OWR Best**: 247 - Apr, 2012.

Asian Wins (1): **2012**: Myanmar Open (Zykabar).
Amateur Wins: Victorian Match Play: 2009   Dunes Medal: 2009   Port Phillip Am: 2009   Lake Macquarie Am: 2010.

	11	12	13	14
Masters	-	-	-	-
US Open	-	-	-	-
British	-	-	-	-
PGA	-	-	-	-
Money (As)	85	37	55	54
OWR	519	269	607	745

2014: ASIA: 19 st / 12 ct / 1 t10.   (9 Macau).   Logged but a single top 10 en route to finishing 54th in Asia Tour $$$.

OUTLOOK: A mostly median-level player statistically who reached the Asian Tour at a young age but looks like only a regional golfer at this point.

STATS: Driving Distance: B   Driving Accuracy: B-   GIR: B-   Short Game: B   Putting: C+

Presnell, Alistair Steven (Australia) (35)
b. Melbourne, Victoria, Australia 3/26/1979. 6'3" 210 lbs. TP: 2004. Long hitter who began his career playing on the Australasian and Asian Tours. Won the 2009 Web.com Tour's season-opening Moonah Classic (played in Australia) before playing the circuit full-time through 2012, eventually reaching the PGA Tour via a 23rd-place finish in $$$ in 2012. Won the Australasian Tour's 2010 Victorian PGA Championship by shooting a closing 12-under-par 60 at the Sandhurst Club in Melbourne. Has played mostly in America since, reaching the PGA Tour in 2013 but failing to keep his card. **OWR Best**: 203 - Feb, 2011.

Australasian Tour Wins (1): **2010**: Victorian PGA Championship.
Other Wins: 1 Web.com (2009).
Amateur Wins: Dunes Medal: 2003.

Presnell, Alistair Steven, Cont'd

	04	05	06	07	08	09	10	11	12	13	14
Masters	-	-	-	-	-	-	-	-	-	-	-
US Open	-	-	-	-	-	-	-	-	T29	T67	-
British	-	-	-	-	-	-	-	-	-	-	-
PGA	-	-	-	-	-	-	-	-	-	-	-
Money (A)	-	-	-	-	-	-	-	-	191	-	
Money (As)	60	57	87	-	-	-	-	-	-	-	-
OWR	494	567	823	-	-	377	231	387	335	450	625

2014: Played full-time on the Web.com Tour, finishing 49th in regular season $$$ and failing to play through the Finals.

OUTLOOK: Is ticketed for the Web.com Tour once more, where he has proven himself a steady earner. Like several other Australians, shows little interest in returning home to the far less lucrative Australasian Tour, save for its December slate of bigger events.

STATS (LTD): Driving Distance: B-   Driving Accuracy: C+   GIR: C   Short Game: B   Putting: B-

---

Price, John Phillip (Wales) (48)
b. Pontypridd, Wales 10/21/1966. 5'11" 180 lbs. TP: 1989. Journeyman European player who has twice cracked the Order of Merit top 10, including a career-best 8th in 2000. Scored his first two E Tour wins at the Portuguese Open, initially beating a trio of players (including Retief Goosen) by four in 1994, then edging Padraig Harrington and Sven Struver by two in 2001. Also defeated Mark McNulty and Alistair Forsyth by one at the 2003 European Open. Has tailed off in his 40s, and hasn't cracked the top 100 in $$$ since 2006. **Teams**: Ryder Cup: 2002 (O: 1-1-0, S: 1-0-0). Seve Trophy (2): 2000-03. World Cup (10): 1991-94-95-97-98-99-00-01-04. **OWR Best**: 41 - Jul, 2003.

European Tour Wins (3): **1994**: Portuguese Open   **2001**: Portuguese Open   **2003**: European Open.
Other Wins: Welsh Pro: 1993.

	90	91	92	93	94	95	96	97	98	99	00	01	02	03	04	05	06	07	08	09	10	11	12	13
Masters	-	-	-	-	-	-	-	-	-	-	-	-	-	-	T35	-	-	-	-	-	-	-	-	-
US Open	-	-	-	-	-	-	-	-	-	T53	-	-	-	-	T57	-	-	-	-	-	-	-	-	-
British	-	-	-	-	-	-	-	MC	T58	MC	T30	MC	T10	MC	-	MC	-	-	-	-	-	-	-	
PGA	-	-	-	-	-	-	-	-	-	-	MC	T59	MC	MC	MC	-	-	-	-	-	-	-	-	-
Money (E)	169	71	96	60	34	110	73	39	15	36	8	21	48	10	45	-	121	111	164	198	100	118	103	157
OWR	614	350	351	247	144	200	320	237	109	104	51	60	127	48	82	240	357	420	790	-	488	395	478	680

	14
Masters	-
US Open	-
British	-
PGA	-
Money (E)	-
OWR	951

2014: E: 12 st / 3 ct / 0 t10.   (T24 Madeira).   Played part-time at age 47, and had very little impact here, or in five Challenge Tour starts.

OUTLOOK: Another older player whose lack of length, combined with declining putting numbers, means he's now waiting for the senior tour.

STATS: Driving Distance: D   Driving Accuracy: A+   GIR: B   Short Game: B   Putting: C+

Pride, Richard Fletcher III ("Dicky") (USA) (45)
b. Tuscaloosa, AL 7/15/1969. 6'0" 175 lbs. College: U of Alabama. TP: 1992. After walking on at Alabama as a sophomore, was a semi-finalist at the 1991 U.S. Amateur. Made a gigantic splash as a PGA Tour rookie by winning the 1994 Memphis Classic, holing a 20-foot birdie putt at the 72nd hole to force sudden death with Gene Sauers and Hal Sutton, then winning on the first extra hole with another birdie. Virtually disappeared thereafter, only twice cracking the top 125 (125th in 2006 and 109th in 1999) before repairing to the Web.com Tour in the latter half of the 2000s. Playing as a Past Champion, made a storybook comeback in 2012, logging three top 10s in his first seven starts (including 2nd at the Byron Nelson) and launching himself back to one year's worth of prominence. **OWR Best**: 181 - May, 2012.

PGA Tour Wins (1): **1994**: Memphis Classic (FedEx St Jude).

	92	93	94	95	96	97	98	99	00	01	02	03	04	05	06	07	08	09	10	11	12	13	14
Masters	-	-	-	MC	-	-	-	-	-	-	-	-	-	-	-	-	-	-	-	-	-	-	-
US Open	MC	-	-	-	-	-	-	-	-	MC	-	T28	-	-	-	-	-	-	-	-	-	-	-
British	-	-	-	-	-	-	-	-	-	-	-	-	-	-	-	-	-	-	-	-	-	-	-
PGA	-	-	T73	-	-	-	-	-	-	-	-	-	-	-	-	-	-	-	-	-	-	-	-
Money (A)	-	-	57	161	125	207	234	109	153	170	190	127	184	234*	197*	159	200*	187*	227*	220*	70	140	178*
OWR	-	-	204	256	332	458	625	227	301	489	478	270	367	536	711	540	528	663	433	633	198	387	585

2014: PGA: 13 st / 3 ct / 1 t10.   (T7 Canadian).   Playing on conditional status, finished 178th in FedEx Cup points in only 13 PGA Tour starts.

OUTLOOK: Will be limited to Past Champion status in 2015, which will greatly limited his chances at a major comeback. Following an early 40s resurgence in 2012, has fallen off badly since; at this stage of the game, he may soon be counting down the years until he's Champions Tour-eligible.

STATS: Driving Distance: C-   Driving Accuracy: A-   GIR: B-   Short Game: B+   Putting: B+

Prugh, Alexander William (USA) (30)
b. Spokane, WA 9/1/1984. 5'10" 175 lbs. All-American at U of Washington. TP: 2007. After winning the 2005 Pacific and Washington State Amateurs, turned pro and spent one year on mini-tours before joining the Web.com full-time. Won the Web.com's New Zealand Open in 2009, leading to a 16th-place $$$ finish and a place on the 2010 PGA Tour. Finished 70th in $$$, but struggled in 2011, finishing 175th. Returns to the PGA Tour for 2014 after finishing 11th in 2013 Web.com regular season $$$. **OWR Best**: 172 - Mar, 2010.

Other Wins: 1 Web.com (2009).
Amateur Wins: Pacific Coast Am: 2005   Washington Am: 2005.

Prugh, Alexander William, Cont'd

	07	08	09	10	11	12	13	14
Masters	-	-	-	-	-	-	-	-
US Open	MC	-	-	-	-	-	-	-
British	-	-	-	-	-	-	-	-
PGA	-	-	-	-	-	-	-	-
Money (A)	-	-	-	70	175	-	-	208
OWR	-	483	305	240	631	827	385	447

2014: PGA: 16 st / 4 ct / 0 t10. (T29 New Orleans). Finished 206th in FedEx Cup points. Also made 11 Web.com starts, returning via the Finals.

OUTLOOK: Enjoyed a strong PGA Tour rookie year in 2010 before falling to the Web.com after 2011. Finished 36th in regular season Web.com $$$ but saved himself via the Finals. Has the requisite power for the PGA Tour but his remaining numbers suggest it will still be a struggle.

STATS (LTD): Driving Distance: A-   Driving Accuracy: C+   GIR: B+   Short Game: C   Putting: C+

Putnam, Andrew David (USA) (25)

b. Tacoma, WA 1/25/1989. 6'1" 170 lbs. College: Pepperdine U. TP: 2011. An AJGA All-American. The younger brother of PGA Tour player Michael Putnam. After winning the 2010 Pacific Coast Amateur and thrice being named honorable mention All-American at Pepperdine, spent 2012 playing mini-tours, then two years on the Web.com Tour. In 2014, won once and clinched a 2015 PGA Tour card by finishing 2nd in regular season earnings. **OWR Best:** 192 - Jul, 2014.

Other Wins: 1 Web.com (2014).
Amateur Wins: Pacific Coast Am: 2010.

	10	11	12	13	14
Masters	-	-	-	-	-
US Open	MC	-	-	-	-
British	-	-	-	-	-
PGA	-	-	-	-	-
Money (A)	-	-	-	-	-
OWR	1322	-	1492	657	287

2014: Played full-time on the Web.com Tour, winning once and earning a 2015 PGA Tour card by finishing 2nd in regular season $$$.

OUTLOOK: Though never a superstar at the amateur level, played two strong campaigns on the Web.com Tour to get here, plus having a brother on Tour figures to make his transition easier than some. Still, he doesn't seem the most likely rookie to make a major splash in 2015.

STATS (LTD): Driving Distance: B-   Driving Accuracy: B+   GIR: B+   Short Game: B   Putting: B+

Putnam, Michael John (USA) (31)

b. Tacoma, WA 6/1/1983. 6'4" 215 lbs. Two-time All-American at Pepperdine U. TP: 2005. Won the 2004 Pacific Coast Amateur and played on the 2005 Walker Cup team. Became a Web.com Tour regular after turning pro, winning thrice and graduating to the PGA Tour in both 2006 (17th in $$$) and 2010 (24th). Struggled in both turns on the big tour, finishing 158th in $$$ in 2007 and 153rd in 2011. Rebounded on the 2013 Web.com Tour, re-gaining full PGA Tour status by winning twice and topping the regular season money list. **Teams:** Walker Cup: 2005 (1-2-1). Palmer Cup: 2006. **OWR Best:** 111 - Aug, 2013.

Other Wins: 3 Web.com (2010-2013).
Amateur Wins: Pacific Coast Am: 2004.

	05	06	07	08	09	10	11	12	13	14
Masters	-	-	-	-	-	-	-	-	-	-
US Open	MC	-	T55	-	-	-	T45	-	-	-
British	-	-	MC	-	-	-	-	-	-	-
PGA	-	-	-	-	-	-	-	-	-	-
Money (A)	-	-	158	-	-	-	153	-	-	116
OWR	428	233	417	614	782	351	356	373	169	222

2014: PGA: 30 st / 23 ct / 1 t10. (T4 Canadian). Finished 93rd in FedEx Cup points to easily retain his card for the first time.

OUTLOOK: Established a PGA Tour beachhead in 2014, and certainly possesses both the length (65 in Driving Distance - 41 in 2011) and overall Ball Striking (44) to survive here, but... Which is his "real" SGP, 25 in 2011 or 157 in 2014? Either way, he looks like he can stick around for a bit.

STATS (LTD): Driving Distance: A-   Driving Accuracy: B-   GIR: A-   Short Game: B   Putting: C+

Que, Angelo (Philippines) (36)

b. Manila, Philippines 12/3/1978. 5'9" 150 lbs. TP: 2003. Two-time Philippine Amateur champion who claimed his maiden Asian Tour victory (by two over Thongchai Jaidee) at the 2004 Carlsberg Masters Vietnam, and later added the 2008 Philippine Open and the 2010 Selangor Masters, where he beat England's Chris Rodgers in a playoff. Enjoyed a career-best 13th-place $$$ ranking in 2013, then topped it by climbing to a 6th in 2014. **Teams:** Eisenhower Trophy (2): 1998-02. World Cup (3): 2008-09-13. **OWR Best:** 220 - Nov, 2014.

PGA Tour Wins (3): 2004: Carlsberg Masters Vietnam **2008:** Philippine Open **2010:** Selangor Masters (Worldwide Holdings).
Other Wins: Mt. Malarayat Championship (Philippines) (2): 2008-09.
Amateur Wins: Philippine Am (2): 2001-02.

	03	04	05	06	07	08	09	10	11	12	13	14
Masters	-	-	-	-	-	-	-	-	-	-	-	-
US Open	-	-	-	-	-	MC	-	-	-	-	-	-
British	-	-	-	-	MC	-	-	-	-	-	-	-
PGA	-	-	-	-	-	-	-	-	-	-	-	-
Money (As)	82	56	39	45	50	40	22	27	25	22	13	6
OWR	-	555	593	653	648	426	443	357	482	380	268	225

Que, Angelo, Cont'd

2014: ASIA: 16 st / 12 ct / 4 t10. (Incl. 2 Hong Kong, T8 CIMB). Though winless, finished a career-best 6th in Asia Tour $$$.

OUTLOOK: Veteran player whose above-the-median short game and putting are his meal ticket. At age 36 he's trending upwards, his career-best 6th-place $$$ ranking being his sixth straight year among the top 30. May not very often, but figures to keep collecting checks for good while longer.

STATS: Driving Distance: B+   Driving Accuracy: C-   GIR: C   Short Game: B+   Putting: B+

Quesne, Julien (France) (34)
b. Le Mans, France 8/16/1980. 6'1" 200 lbs. TP: 2003. After turning pro, bounced back and forth between the Alps and Challenge Tours until eventually reaching the E Tour in 2010 (when he finished 156th in $$$) and again in 2012, when he finished 63rd. Claimed his first E Tour win at the 2012 Open de Andalucia, where he edged Matteo Manassero by two. Validated it a year later by winning the 2013 Italian Open, playing the final nine in 31 to beat David Higgins and Steve Webster by one. **OWR Best**: 115 - Jan, 2014.

European Tour Wins (2): 2012: Open de Andalucia **2013**: Italian Open.

Other Wins: 2 Challenge Tour (2009-2011) + Maroc Telecom (France): 2004   Normandie Open (France): 2007   Open de Bussy (France): 2007   Open Stade Francais (France): 2007.

	09	10	11	12	13	14
Masters	-	-	-	-	-	-
US Open	-	-	-	-	-	-
British	-	-	-	-	-	-
PGA	-	-	-	-	-	-
Money (E)	-	156	267*	63	42	80
OWR	242	487	326	188	130	211

2014: E: 23 st / 16 ct / 2 t10. (T5 Malaysian, T8 Volvo Champ). Slipped somewhat to an 80th-place finish in $$$, but comfortably retained his card.

OUTLOOK: Something of a late bloomer who won in 2012 and '13 to establish himself as an E Tour presence. Has a mid-range game statistically and will likely never rate among the elite, but with a number of prime years ahead of him, he should remain a solid earner for the foreseeable future.

STATS: Driving Distance: B+   Driving Accuracy: C+   GIR: B+   Short Game: B   Putting: B+

Quirós García, Alvaro (Spain) (31)
b. Guadiaro, Spain 1/21/1983. 6'3" 185 lbs. TP: 2004. Arguably the longest hitter in professional golf, leading the E Tour in driving distance in 2007, '08, '09 and '11 (finished 39th in accuracy in '09). Played his way onto the E Tour at age 23 via the Challenge circuit. Won the 2007 Alfred Dunhill Championship (played in late '06) by one over Charl Schwartzel in only his fifth career start. Missed much of 2007 with a wrist injury, but returned to win the 2008 Portuguese Master, then edged Luis Oosthuizen and Henrik Stenson by two to claim the 2009 Qatar Masters. Won his native Spanish Open in 2010, defeating Jamie Morrison in a playoff. Completed the "Dubai Double" in 2011, winning the Dubai Desert Classic (with a final round that included an eagle on a par 4, a triple bogey and a hole-in-one) and the lucrative, season-ending Dubai World Championship, where he beat Paul Lawrie by two. Missed the first third of 2013 after undergoing surgery on his right wrist, and has yet to return to his pre-surgery form through 2014. **Teams**: Seve Trophy: 2009. World Cup: 2011. **OWR Best**: 21 - Feb, 2011.

European Tour Wins (6): 2006: Alfred Dunhill Championship ('07) **2008**: Portugal Masters **2009**: Qatar Masters **2010**: Spanish Open **2011**: Dubai Desert Classic, Dubai World Championship.

Other Wins: 1 Euro Challenge (2006) + Seville Open (Spain): 2006.

Amateur Wins: Biarritz Cup: 2004.

	06	07	08	09	10	11	12	13	14
Masters	-	-	-	MC	MC	T27	MC	-	-
US Open	-	-	-	MC	MC	T54	MC	-	T35
British	-	-	-	MC	T11	MC	MC	MC	-
PGA	-	-	-	T24	MC	MC	MC	-	-
Money (E)	-	102	25	20	14	6	73	104	79
OWR	175	291	73	52	49	22	90	278	251

2014: E: 19 st / 13 ct / 3 t10. (3 Volvo China, T5 Joburg, T6 Nordea). Played his best golf early before eventually finishing 79th in $$$.

OUTLOOK: When healthy, a gargantuan hitter who can overpower any layout, yet he's also skilled enough to parlay his length into victories. At age 31 he should just be entering his best years, but despite some gaudy power and GIR numbers, he has struggled to return to his pre-injury form.

STATS: Driving Distance: A+   Driving Accuracy: C   GIR: A-   Short Game: B-   Putting: C

Rahman, Mohammad Siddikur (Bangladesh) (30)
b. Dhaka, Bangladesh 11/20/1984. 5'4" 150 lbs. TP: 2005. Bangladesh's first world-class golfer. Is generally referred to only as Siddikur. Won multiple smaller amateur titles around Asia before turning pro, and was a regular winner on the region's lesser tours before joining the Asian circuit in 2009. Has since established himself as a strong earner and occasional winner, taking his maiden Asia Tour victory at the 2010 Brunei Open, where he beat South African Jbe' Kruger in a playoff. Claimed his second title by edging Anirban Lahiri and S.S.P. Chowrasia by one at the 2013 Indian Open en route to finishing 3rd in $$$. Missed much of 2014 with lower back problems. **Teams**: World Cup: 2013. **OWR Best**: 117 - May, 2011.

Asian Tour Wins (2): 2010: Brunei Open **2013**: Indian Open (Hero).

Other Wins: 1 Asian Dev (2011) + Unitech Hryana Open (PGTI): 2008   PGTI-Poona (PGTI): 2008   Bangalore Open (PGTI): 2009   Bangladesh Open: 2010   Negeri Masters (Malaysia): 2011.

	09	10	11	12	13	14
Masters	-	-	-	-	-	-
US Open	-	-	-	-	-	-
British	-	-	-	-	-	-
PGA	-	-	-	-	-	-
Money (As)	84	7	8	17	4	36
OWR	-	199	158	206	166	226

Rahman, Mohammad Siddikur, Cont'd

2014: ASIA: 12 st / 7 ct / 4 t10. (Incl. 2 SAIL-SBI, T2 Philippine Open). Was limited to 12 starts by lower back problems (but still finished 36th in $$$).

OUTLOOK: Came from the least likely of golfing beginnings but has blossomed into a regional star. A short-but-straight type who rates among the best in Asia on and around the green. At age 30, he should just be hitting his peak - but lets see how he recovers from his back issues in 2015.

STATS: Driving Distance: C+   Driving Accuracy: A-   GIR: C+   Short Game: A-   Putting: A-

---

Ramsay, Richie (Scotland) (31) b. Aberdeen, Scotland 06/15/1983. 5'9" 155 lbs. McLennan (TX) JC / U of Stirling. TP: 2007. Became the first native Scot to win the U.S. Amateur since Findlay Douglas (1898) when he claimed the 2006 title, beating John Kelly 4 & 2 at Hazeltine National. Played one year of junior college golf in Texas before completing his studies in his native Scotland. After winning twice on the 2008 Challenge Tour, joined the E Tour in 2009 and won before year's end, taking the South African Open by beating Shiv Kapur in a playoff. Added a second title at the 2012 European Masters, beating a quartet of players by four shots at Crans-sur-Sierre. **Teams:** Walker Cup: 2005 (1-1-0). Eisenhower Trophy: 2006. Palmer Cup: 2006. **OWR Best:** 52 - Oct, 2012.

European Tour Wins (2): 2009: South African Open ('10)   **2012:** European Masters.

Other Wins: 2 Euro Challenge (2008).

Amateur Wins: U.S. Amateur: 2006 – Scottish Am Stroke Play: 2004   Irish Am Stroke Play: 2005.

	06	07	08	09	10	11	12	13	14
Masters	-	MC	-	-	-	-	-	-	-
US Open	-	MC	-	-	-	-	-	-	-
British	-	MC	MC	-	-	MC	T58	-	-
PGA	-	-	-	-	-	-	-	MC	-
Money (E)	Am	-	-	97	47	28	26	70	43
OWR	827	432	161	117	142	103	57	136	92

2014: E: 22 st / 14 ct / 6 t10. (T2 NH Collection, T2 Dunhill Links, T4 Italian, T5 Spanish, 8 Euro Masters, etc.).   Retrenched somewhat after a down 2013, logging six top 10s (including a pair of runner-ups) and climbing back to 43rd in $$$.

OUTLOOK: A rare player who finds success despite well-below-the-median length and a limited putter, though his once-mediocre numbers on the greens have improved in recent seasons. Is just heading into his best years, but may not climb too much beyond what we've seen already.

STATS: Driving Distance: C   Driving Accuracy: A-   GIR: A   Short Game: B   Putting: B

Randhawa, Jyoti Singh (India) (42) b. New Delhi, India 5/4/1972. 6'1" 180 lbs. TP: 1994. Indian star who won once on the old (pre-2009) Indian tour before playing in Asia and, eventually, Europe. Regular winner in Asia with his first title coming at the 1998 Honda Masters (where he beat Jeev Milkha Singh by four), a title he would successfully defend a year later. Also won back-to-back titles at the Indian Open in 2006 and '07. Played the Japan Tour semi-full-time in 2003 and '04, winning the 2003 Suntory Open. A frequent presence among the top 10 in the Asian Tour Order of Merit (including winning it in 2002) but has only once cracked the top 60 in Europe (33rd in 2007). Also continues to play on India's PGTI circuit. **Teams:** Eisenhower Trophy: 1992. World Cup (4): 2005-07-08-09. **OWR Best:** 70 - Mar, 2008.

Japan Tour Wins (1): 2003: Suntory Open.

Asian Tour Wins (8): 1998: Honda Masters **1999:** Honda Masters **2000:** Indian Open, Singapore Open **2004:** Asian Masters **2006:** Indian Open **2007:** Indian Open **2009:** Thailand Open.

Other Wins: DLF Masters (PGTI): 2007   Players Championship (PGTI) (2): 2011-12   CG Open (PGTI): 2011.

	95	96	97	98	99	00	01	02	03	04	05	06	07	08	09	10	11	12	13	14
Masters	-	-	-	-	-	-	-	-	-	-	-	-	-	-	-	-	-	-	-	-
US Open	-	-	-	-	-	-	-	-	-	-	-	MC	-	-	-	-	-	-	-	-
British	-	-	-	-	-	MC	-	-	MC	T27	-	-	-	-	-	-	-	-	-	-
PGA	-	-	-	-	-	-	-	-	-	-	-	-	-	WD	MC	-	-	-	-	-
Money (E)	-	-	-	-	-	-	-	-	-	85	68	33	67	100	164	206*	-	-	-	-
Money (J)	-	-	-	-	-	-	-	-	28	54	-	-	-	-	-	-	-	-	-	-
Money (As)	-	-	49	22	6	2	24	1	16*	2*	3*	6*	-	11*	5*	-	36	30	17	17
OWR	-	533	616	-	467	293	453	211	133	115	123	84	87	147	218	456	502	562	395	288

2014: ASIA: 17 st / 12 ct / 3 t10. (Incl. T2 Chiangmai). Went winless for the fifth straight year but again cracked the top 20 in $$$.

OUTLOOK: Though not quite the player he was in the early 2000s (he hasn't won since 2009), remains a decent earner in Asia as he climbs into his 40s. Actually saw improvement in most statistical categories in 2014, so he could still have a win or two left in the bag.

STATS: Driving Distance: B-   Driving Accuracy: B   GIR: B+   Short Game: B   Putting: B

Randolph, Jonathan Evan (USA) (26) b. Brandon, MS 8/10/1988. 6'0" 210 lbs. All-American at U. of Mississippi. TP: 2011. A semi-finalist at the 2011 U.S. Public Links. Upon turning pro, spent two seasons playing on the NGA Pro Golf Tour, winning twice and being named the circuit's Rookie Of The Year in 2012. Joined the Web.com Tour for 2014, where he ranked 16th in regular season earnings to earn his PGA Tour card. **Teams:** Palmer Cup: 2010. **OWR Best:** 298 - Aug, 2014.

Other Wins: 2 NGA/Hooters (2012-2013).

Amateur Wins: Mississippi Am: 2009.

	13	14
Masters	-	-
US Open	-	-
British	-	-
PGA	-	-
Money (A)	-	-
OWR	1001	343

Randolph, Jonathan Evan, Cont'd

2014: Played full-time on the Web.com Tour, where he finished 16th in regular season $$$ to secure his PGA Tour card for 2015.

OUTLOOK: With two years of successful mini-tour golf prior to the Web.com Tour, he might be somewhat better prepared to survive as a PGA Tour rookie. Perhaps notably, he has finished T21 and T14 in two early professional appearances at the PGA Tour's Sanderson Farms Championship.

STATS (LTD): Driving Distance: B+ Driving Accuracy: B- GIR: C Short Game: B Putting: B+

Reavie, William Chesney ("Chez") (USA) (33)
b. Wichita, KS 11/12/1981. 5'9" 160 lbs. All-American at Arizona St. TP: 2004. The 2001 U.S. Public Links champion. Also a former AJGA All-American who spent two full seasons on mini-tours and the Web.com circuit before leading the Web.com money list in 2007. Joined the PGA Tour full-time in 2008 and logged his only victory to date as a rookie, beating Billy Mayfair by three to claim the Canadian Open. Struggled with a knee injury during 2010, and began 2011 on a medical extension – then made good by logging five top 10s en route to a career-best 34th in $$$. Played through Q School to regain his card for 2013. **OWR Best:** 65 - Sep, 2011.

PGA Tour Wins (1): 2008: Canadian Open.
Other Wins: 1 Web.com (2007) + 1 Gateway (2005).
Amateur Wins: U.S. Amateur Public Links: 1986 – Mesa City Am: 2001.

	02	03	04	05	06	07	08	09	10	11	12	13	14
Masters	MC	-	-	-	-	-	-	MC	-	-	MC	-	-
US Open	-	MC	T62	-	-	-	-	-	-	-	MC	-	-
British	-	-	-	-	-	-	-	-	-	-	MC	-	-
PGA	-	-	-	-	-	-	T60	-	-	-	T62	-	-
Money (A)	Am	Am	-	-	-	-	71	146	204	34	135	126	249*
OWR	-	-	711	952	587	310	208	386	758	67	178	369	797

2014: PGA: 2 st / 1 ct / 0 t10. (T51 Frys.com). Made two pre-New Years starts before having season-ending surgery on his left wrist.

OUTLOOK: Begins 2015 on a 24-event medical exemptions - essentially a full season to compete against last year's numbers. A shortish but reliable ball striker who struggles with the putter. Has struggled of late, but he's only 33, and his career-best year was only four years ago, in 2011.

STATS: Driving Distance: B- Driving Accuracy: A+ GIR: A- Short Game: B Putting: C+

Reed, Patrick Nathaniel (USA) (24)
b. San Antonio, TX 8/5/1990. 6'0" 200 lbs. Two-time All-American at Augusta (GA) St. TP: 2011. Spent one year at the U of Georgia before transferring to Augusta State, where he led the team to back-to-back national championships in 2010 and 2011. Without PGA Tour status, Monday qualified six times in 2012 before playing through Q School at season's end. Broke through for his first Tour win as a rookie, beating Jordan Spieth in sudden death to claim the 2013 Wyndham Championship, en route to a strong 35th-place $$$ ranking. Claimed his second victory at the 2014 Humana Challenge, where he set a new PGA Tour 54-hole scoring-relative-to-par record (-27 after carding three straight 63s) before holding on to win by two. Took a giant step by winning (for the third time in 14 starts) at the WGC-Cadillac Championship, where he beat a field including the entire OWR top 50 wire-to-wire. Quieted down somewhat after becoming a father but rose up again at the 2014 Ryder Cup, where he was clearly the USA's best player. **Teams:** Ryder Cup: 2014 (O: 3-0-1, S: 1-0-0). **OWR Best:** 20 - Mar, 2014.

PGA Tour Wins (3): 2013: Wyndham Championship **2014:** Humana Challenge, WGC-Cadillac Championship.
Amateur Wins: Junior British Open: 2006 Louisiana HS: 2007 Jones Cup: 2010.

	12	13	14
Masters	-	-	MC
US Open	-	-	T35
British	-	-	MC
PGA	-	-	T59
Money (A)	-	35	14
OWR	586	73	23

2014: PGA: 28 st / 20 ct / 4 t10. (Won Humana, Won WGC-Cadillac, T4 WGC-Bridgestone, T9 Barclays). Established himself as one of the world's top young stars, winning twice, finishing 21st in FedEx Cup points and starring in his first appearance on the U.S. Ryder Cup team.

OUTLOOK: Seems on his way to worldwide stardom after managing the rare feat of winning three times in his first 51 PGA Tour starts. Blends a nice mix of power with a deft touch on and around the greens, as well as some highly creative shotmaking ability. Throw in some obvious moxy (see his 2014 Ryder Cup performance) and there is precious little not to like. His lone significant weakness is a mediocre iron game (118 in Proximity To Hole, 124 in GIR) but with a short game like his, that becomes only a modest hindrance. A potential superstar.

STATS: Driving Distance: A- Driving Accuracy: C GIR: B- Short Game: A- Putting: A-

---

Reifers, Kyle Robert (USA) (31)
b. Columbus, OH 10/13/1983. 6'2" 175 lbs. All-American at Wake Forest U. TP: 2006. Enjoyed a very solid amateur career, which included being runner-up at 2006 NCAA Championship and playing on the 2005 Walker Cup squad. After turning pro, won his first start on the Web.com Tour (as a Monday qualifier) and later played through Q School, but struggled as a 2007 PGA Tour rookie and has never quite been able to find his circa-2006 magic since. **Teams:** Walker Cup: 2005 (0-2-0). **OWR Best:** 297 - Apr, 2007.

Other Wins: 1 Web.com (2006) + 1 eGolf Tour (2006).
Amateur Wins: Monroe Inv: 2004 Ohio Am: 2004 Northeast Am: 2005.

	06	07	08	09	10	11	12	13	14
Masters	-	-	-	-	-	-	-	-	-
US Open	-	-	-	-	-	-	-	-	-
British	-	-	-	-	-	-	-	-	-
PGA	-	-	-	-	-	-	-	-	-
Money (A)	-	181	-	-	-	-	154	-	-
OWR	472	529	574	590	545	470	443	618	399

Reifers, Kyle Robert, Cont'd

2014: Played full-time on the Web.com Tour, finishing 25th in regular season $$$ to regain PGA Tour status for the third time.

OUTLOOK: Comes back for a third try at the PGA Tour, bringing a game that was fairly strong across the board on the 2014 Web.com circuit, but which has struggled on the big stage previously. Maturity/experience may help but the bet here is that his 2015 success will be fairly limited.

STATS (LTD): Driving Distance: B   Driving Accuracy: B   GIR: B+   Short Game: B   Putting: B-

---

Renner, James Eric (USA) (31)
b. Boston, MA 10/31/1983. 6'1" 210 lbs. NAIA All-American, Player of the Year (2005) and individual champion (2005) at Johnson & Wales (FL) U (after transferring from U of Oklahoma). TP: 2007. Spent several seasons playing mini-tours after turning pro, and was a dominant force in New England. Finished 155th in $$$ in 2011, necessitating a return to the Web.com circuit. Returned to the PGA Tour in 2014 and retained his card by the skin of his teeth. **OWR Best:** 254 - Apr, 2014.

Other Wins: 2 NGA/Hooters (2008-2010)   Massachusetts Open: 2008   Vermont Open: 2008   Rhode Island Open: 2008   Maine Open: 2009.
Amateur Wins: New England Am: 2005   Massachusetts Am: 2001   Massachusetts HS: 2002.

	11	12	13	14
Masters	-	-	-	-
US Open	-	-	-	MC
British	-	-	-	-
PGA	-	-	-	-
Money (A)	155	-	-	121
OWR	532	585	539	426

2014: PGA: 25 st / 6 ct / 1 t10.   (T2 AT&T Pro-Am). Finished 147th in FedEx Cup points; stayed exempt as a top 125 in $$$ through the Wyndham.

OUTLOOK: Long-hitting player who, statistically speaking, seems to have enough tee-to-green game to succeed on the PGA Tour, but whose short game and putting lag significantly behind. Was fortunate to remain exempt via the top 125-after-Wyndham route, but may not improve much in 2015.

STATS (LTD): Driving Distance: B+   Driving Accuracy: C+   GIR: B-   Short Game: C   Putting: C

Ridings, Taggart Twain (USA) (40)
b. Oklahoma City, OK 9/7/1974. 6'1" 200 lbs. College: U of Arkansas. TP: 1997. Journeyman PGA Tour player who has reverted back to the Web.com circuit multiple times. Logged lone professional win at the Web.com's 2002 Permian Basin Open, where he holed a 138-yard wedge to beat Mark Hensby on the first hole of sudden death. **OWR Best:** 119 - Mar, 2006.

Other Wins: 1 Web.com (2002).

	00	01	02	03	04	05	06	07	08	09	10	11	12	13	14
Masters	-	-	-	-	-	-	-	-	-	-	-	-	-	-	-
US Open	MC	-	-	-	-	MC	-	-	-	-	-	-	-	-	-
British	-	-	-	-	-	-	-	-	-	-	-	-	-	-	-
PGA	-	-	-	-	-	-	-	-	-	-	-	-	-	-	-
Money (A)	-	-	-	-	125	91	149	168	147	161	-	156	-	149	221*
OWR	-	-	449	511	166	137	289	394	387	429	261	491	637	486	905

2014: PGA: 12 st / 4 ct / 0 t10.   (T45 New Orleans).   Finished 219th in FedEx Cup points, then failed to play through the Web.com Finals.

OUTLOOK: Very long hitter who seems perennially stuck in that gray area between the bottom of the PGA Tour and the top of the Web.com. Begins 2015 with a one-event medical extension which he's highly unlikely to clear, so.....back to the Web.com once again.

STATS: Driving Distance: A   Driving Accuracy: C   GIR: C+   Short Game: B-   Putting: B-

---

Riley, Chris J. (USA) (41)
b. San Diego, CA 12/8/1973. 5'11" 160 lbs. Three-time All-American at UNLV. TP: 1996. Two-time AJGA All-American. Initially appeared destined for stardom, finishing no worse than 56th in earnings from 2001-04, winning the 2002 Reno-Tahoe Open (in a playoff over Jonathan Kaye) and qualifying for the 2004 Ryder Cup team. But largely crashed thereafter, failing to better 150th in earnings and losing his PGA Tour status, save for a 90th-place finish in 2010. A three-time Q School graduate but is currently playing on Past Champion status - and scarcely choosing to utilize that. **Teams:** Walker Cup: 1995 (1-1-1). Ryder Cup: 2004 (O: 1-1-1, S: 0-1-0). **OWR Best:** 22 - Feb, 2004.

PGA Tour Wins (1): 2002: Reno-Tahoe Open.
Other Wins: 1 Web.com (2007).
Amateur Wins: Junior World (11-12): 1986.

	99	00	01	02	03	04	05	06	07	08	09	10	11	12	13	14
Masters	-	-	-	-	T23	44	49	-	-	-	-	-	-	-	-	-
US Open	MC	-	-	-	MC	T48	-	-	-	-	-	-	-	-	-	-
British	-	-	-	T22	MC	MC	T67	-	-	-	-	-	-	-	-	-
PGA	-	-	T51	3	MC	T4	T66	T41	-	-	-	-	-	-	-	-
Money (A)	112	71	45	23	23	56	184	150	161	166	129	90	154	195*	233*	-
OWR	244	183	88	44	27	46	201	381	260	347	318	241	419	515	868	1473

2014: PGA: 2 st / 0 ct / 0 t10.   Made only two starts, missing both cuts. Did not play on the Web.com Tour.

OUTLOOK: Former touted prospect and Ryder Cup player seems, by choice, to be past the point of PGA Tour relevance.

STATS (LTD): Driving Distance: C-   Driving Accuracy: A   GIR: B   Short Game: B   Putting: C

Rocha, Alexandre Nardy (Brazil) (37)
b. Sao Paulo, Brazil 11/21/1977. 6'0" 175 lbs. College: All-American at Mississippi St. TP: 2000. International player who labored in South America, Europe and Canada, on first- and second-tier tours, prior to reaching the PGA Tour in 2011. Won the 2001 Rabobank Masters on the old Tour de Las Americas, as well as multiple domestic events in his native Brazil. Had full-season shots at the PGA

Rocha, Alexandre Nardy, Cont'd

Tour in 2011 and '12 but failed to keep his card either time. **Teams:** World Cup: 2013. **OWR Best:** 323 - Sep, 2008.

Other Wins: San Fernando Open (Brazil): 2000   Rabobank Masters (Chile): 2001   Rio de Janeiro Pro-Am: 2002   Brasilia DF Open: 2003   Club de Campo Open (Brazil): 2003   Curtiba Open (Brazil): 2003   Casino de Charlevoix Cup (w/B. Parry)(Canada): 2003   Marbella Open (Chile): 2008.

Amateur Wins: South American Am (2): 1992-95   Brazil Am (2): 1994-97   Brazil Jr (2); 1993-95.

	06	07	08	09	10	11	12	13	14
Masters	-	-	-	-	-	-	-	-	-
US Open	-	-	-	-	-	T68	-	-	-
British	-	-	-	-	-	-	-	-	-
PGA	-	-	-	-	-	-	-	-	-
Money (A)	-	-	-	-	-	184	131	236*	-
Money (E)	125	159	-	211	-	-	-	-	-
OWR	391	479	363	640	-	673	411	407	760

2014: Played the Web.com Tour full-time, finishing 98th in $$$ and failing to reach the Finals.

OUTLOOK: A star in his native South America but, at age 37, seems more suited to the Web.com than the PGA Tour.

STATS: Driving Distance: C+   Driving Accuracy: B+   GIR: A   Short Game: C+   Putting: C+

Rock, Robert (England) (37)

b. Armitage, England 4/6/1977. 5'10" 170 lbs. TP: 1998. Rose to prominence from a Midlands PGA teaching pro with an impressive performance at the 2003 British Masters (T4). Was a long-struggling journeyman thereafter, never bettering 111th in E Tour earnings (or logging any top-three finishes) until 2009. Was thrice 2nd that season (including a playoff loss to amateur Shane Lowry at the Irish Open) on his way to a career-best 29th in $$$. Broke through for his first win at the 2011 Italian Open (holding off Gary Boyd and Thorbjørn Olesen – who closed with 62 – by one), then stepped up in class by claiming the 2012 Abu Dhabi Championship, where he edged Rory McIlroy by one and Sunday playing partner Tiger Woods, Thomas Bjørn and Graeme McDowell by two. **Teams:** Seve Trophy (2): 2009-11. **OWR Best:** 55 - Jan, 2012.

European Tour Wins (2): 2011: Italian Open (BMW)   **2012:** Abu Dhabi Championship (HSBC).

	03	04	05	06	07	08	09	10	11	12	13	14
Masters	-	-	-	-	-	-	-	-	-	-	-	-
US Open	-	-	-	-	-	-	-	-	T23	MC	-	-
British	-	-	T67	T16	-	-	MC	T7	T38	MC	-	-
PGA	-	-	-	-	-	-	-	-	-	MC	-	-
Money (E)	116*	125	177	114	128	111	29	57	34	33	85	93
OWR	363	397	732	333	357	244	149	134	123	104	301	373

2014: E: 28 st / 16 ct / 2 t10.   (T5 Dubai, T9 Wales).   Remains well off his top seasons of 2009-2012, but still finished 93rd in $$$.

OUTLOOK: One of the longer shots in recent E Tour history, but enjoyed a nice run from 2009-2012. A very solid ball striker who hits tons of greens, and has made enough putts to prosper. But given the trajectory of many longshot careers, he's likely on the downside now.

STATS: Driving Distance: B+   Driving Accuracy: B-   GIR: A-   Short Game: C+   Putting: B-

---

Rollins, John H. (USA) (39)

b. Richmond, VA 6/25/1975. 6'0" 200 lbs. College: Virginia Commonwealth U. TP: 1997. Two-time winner of the Virginia Amateur who initially bounced back and forth between the Web.com and PGA Tours before settling in on the latter, remaining among the top 125 money winners (often with much room to spare) from 2002-2013. After graduating Q School for the second time, won the 2002 Canadian Open in sudden death over Justin Leonard and Neal Lancaster. In 2006, won the final playing of the B.C. Open (where he edged Bob May by one), which was played opposite the British Open. His third win, a three-shot triumph at the 2009 Reno-Tahoe Open, was also a light-field event, being played opposite the WGC Bridgestone Invitational. Faltered badly in 2014, losing his card for the first time. **OWR Best:** 40 - Apr, 2007.

PGA Tour Wins (3): 2002: Canadian Open   **2006:** B.C. Open   **2009:** Reno-Tahoe Open.

Other Wins: 1 Web.com (2001).

Amateur Wins: Virginia Am (2): 1996-97.

	00	01	02	03	04	05	06	07	08	09	10	11	12	13	14
Masters	-	-	-	47	MC	-	-	T20	MC	-	MC	-	-	-	-
US Open	-	-	-	T53	T48	MC	MC	T42	T48	-	MC	-	-	-	-
British	-	-	-	70	-	-	-	MC	T70	-	-	-	-	-	-
PGA	-	-	MC	MC	-	T40	MC	MC	-	T24	-	T51	MC	-	-
Money (A)	171	-	25	39	109	99	57	24	103	28	75	64	59	76	172
OWR	551	447	77	63	124	180	127	65	175	87	164	175	147	202	430

2014: PGA: 28 st / 14 ct / 0 t10.   (T19 Phoenix).   Finished 164th in FedEx Cup points, then failed to play his way back via the Web.com Finals.

OUTLOOK: Crashed uncharacteristically in 2014 and will now play on Past Champion status as a result. Has actually seen his ball striking (long the backbone of his game) slip since 2012, notably in Ball Striking (32, 41, 114), Total Driving (9, 61, 127) and Driving Distance (47, 31, 86). At age 39, he still has some time to turn things around, but barring a crazy week or two, his route back is likely via the Web.com Tour.

STATS: Driving Distance: B+   Driving Accuracy: B   GIR: B+   Short Game: B-   Putting: C

Romero, Andrés Fabian (Argentina) (33)

b. Tucumen, Argentina 5/8/1981. 5'11" 145 lbs. TP: 1998. Argentine who won thrice in South America before heading to Europe full-time in 2006. Gained immediate international fame at the 2007 British Open where, having tied for 8th as an unknown at Royal St George's in '06, he lost the title with a 6-5 finish after leading outright through 70 holes. Responded wonderfully by claiming his maiden E Tour victory the very next week at the Deutsche Bank Open, defeating Søren Hansen and Oliver Wilson by three. Won his first PGA Tour title in only his 12th U.S. start, the 2008 New Orleans Classic, where he edged Peter Lonard by one. Now plays primarily in America, but also visits to his native South America. **Awards:** PGA Tour Rookie of the Year: 2008. **Teams:** World Cup (2): 2006-07. **OWR Best:** 21 - Mar, 2008.

Romero, Andrés Fabian, Cont'd

PGA Tour Wins (1): 2008: New Orleans Classic (Zurich).
European Tour Wins (1): 2007: Deutsche Bank Open.
Other Wins: 1 Euro Challenge (2005) + Cable & Wireless Masters Panama: 2003   Abierto del Norte (Arg) (4): 2003-06-08 (T w/R.González)-99   Masters Personal Cup (Arg): 2006   Abierto de Medelin (Colombia): 2003   Roberto De Vicenzo Classic (Arg): 2005   Tourneo de Maestros (Arg) (2): 2006-10   Abierto del Litoral (Arg) (2): 2006-09   Abierto del Centro (Arg): 2010.

	06	07	08	09	10	11	12	13	14
Masters	-	-	T8	T49	-	-	-	-	-
US Open	-	-	T36	T47	-	-	-	-	-
British	T8	3	T32	T13	-	-	83	-	-
PGA	MC	MC	T7	MC	-	T45	-	-	-
Money (A)	-	-	36	106	92	70	101	115	119
Money (E)	35	7	39	-	-	-	-	-	-
OWR	109	28	30	112	174	125	135	222	270

2014: PGA: 26 st / 16 ct / 1 t10. (T5 Quicken Loans). A career-worst $$$ year but he finished 100th in FedEx Cup points, easily retaining his card.

OUTLOOK: Long-hitting Argentinean who has retained his card every season he's played in America. Has cut it a little fine the last couple of years, slowed a bit by an inconsistent putter (his last four SGPs: 23, 141, 73, 23) but he's young enough to rise again, and he's due for a good year.

STATS: Driving Distance: A-   Driving Accuracy: C-   GIR: C-   Short Game: B   Putting: B+

Roos, Jakobus ("Jake") (South Africa) (34)

b. Pretoria, South Africa 10/20/1980. 6'2" 170 lbs. College: University of Stellenbosch. TP: 2005. Spent multiple years playing California's Golden State Tour (winning six times) before settling into a career back in South Africa. Managed the remarkable feat of capturing his first five Sunshine Tour wins in playoffs, including a trio of titles during a career-best 2012: the Platinum Classic, the Lombard Insurance Classic and the inaugural Cape Town Open. Claimed his first regulation victory at the 2013 Zimbabwe Open, where he edged Darren Fichardt and Francesco Laporta by one. **OWR Best:** 159 - Apr, 2013.

Sunshine Tour Wins (6): 2008: Suncoast Classic (54H)   **2009:** Nedbank Affinity Cup (54H)   **2012:** Platinum Classic (54H), Lombard Insurance Classic (54H), Cape Town Open (Lion of Africa)   **2013:** Zimbabwe Open (Golden Pilsener).
Other Wins: Zurich Open (Switzerland): 2010.
Amateur Wins: Los Logartos (Argentina): 2004   Zone Six (Namibia): 2004.

	06	07	08	09	10	11	12	13	14
Masters	-	-	-	-	-	-	-	-	-
US Open	-	-	-	-	-	-	-	-	-
British	-	-	-	-	-	-	-	-	-
PGA	-	-	-	-	-	-	-	-	-
Money (SA)	122*	57	14	39	33	52	13	14	39*
OWR	-	-	696	855	608	671	263	306	311

2014: Played primarily on the Challenge Tour and the gamble paid off, as he finished 14th in $$$ to gain an E Tour card for 2015. Also made nine starts on home soil, with his best result being 2nd at the Vodacom-Vaal de Grace event.

OUTLOOK: Initially an Africa-only player who has emerged in his early 30s as a frequent Sunshine Tour contender – though generally in lighter-field winter events that lack an E Tour presence. Is 5-0 in playoffs, however, so he knows how to win. Could possibly stick in Europe in 2015.

STATS: Driving Distance: --   Driving Accuracy: --   GIR: --   Short Game: --   Putting: --

---

Rose, Justin Peter (England) (34)

b. Johannesburg, South Africa 7/30/1980. 6'2" 180 lbs. TP: 1998. Arrived on the golfing scene by tying for 4th in the 1998 British Open at Royal Birkdale as a 17-year-old amateur, famously holing a long pitch at the final green. Turned pro the next day but made only 14 of his first 42 European Tour cuts through 2000. Arrived for a second time in 2002 when he won twice on the E Tour (at the Alfred Dunhill Championship and the British Masters) as well as the Japan Tour's Crowns and the Sunshine Tour's Nashua Masters. Later won twice more in Europe, notably at the 2007 British Masters, which clinched the top spot in the '07 Order of Merit. Won his first PGA Tour title at the 2010 Memorial Tournament, closing with 66 to beat Rickie Fowler by three. After losing a fourth round lead at the Travelers Championship in his next start, came back to win the AT&T National, edging Ryan Moore by one. Though slightly quieter in 2011, still finished 18th in PGA Tour $$$ and won the BMW Championship (née the Western Open) by two over John Senden. Won his first WGC title at the 2012 WGC Cadillac Championship, edging Bubba Watson by one at Doral. Broke through for his first Major championship at the 2013 U.S. Open, holding up under intense pressure to beat Phil Mickelson and Jason Day by two at Merion. After nursing shoulder tendinitis early in 2014, beat Shawn Stefani in sudden death at the Quicken Loans National, then won the Scottish Open (by two over Kristoffer Broberg) in his next start. Was also a 2014 Ryder Cup stalwart, going undefeated in five matches to lift his career record to 9-3-2. **Awards:** Euro Vardon Trophy: 2007. **Teams:** Walker Cup: 1997 (2-2-0). Ryder Cup (3): 2008-12-14 (O: 9-3-2, S: 2-0-1). Seve Trophy (2): 2003-07. World Cup (4): 2002-03-07-11. **OWR Best:** 3 - Mar, 2013.

PGA Tour Wins (6): 2010: Memorial Tournament, AT&T National   **2011:** Western Open (BMW)   **2012:** WGC-Cadillac Championship   **2013:** U.S. Open   **2014:** Quicken Loans National.
European Tour Wins (5): 2002: Alfred Dunhill Champ, British Masters   **2006:** Australian Masters ('07)   **2007:** Volvo Masters   **2014:** Scottish Open.
Japan Tour Wins (1): 2002: The Crowns.
Sunshine Tour Wins (1): 2002: Nashua Masters.
Amateur Wins: English Boys Stroke Play: 1995   English Under-16s: 1995   St Andrews Links Trophy: 1997   Telegraph Jr: 1997

	98	99	00	01	02	03	04	05	06	07	08	09	10	11	12	13	14
Masters	-	-	-	-	-	T37	T22	-	-	T5	T36	T20	-	T11	T8	T25	T14
US Open	-	-	-	-	T5	MC	-	-	T10	MC	MC	-	MC	T21	Win	T12	
British	T4	MC	-	T30	T22	MC	-	-	T12	T70	T13	MC	T44	MC	MC	T23	
PGA	-	-	-	-	T23	MC	MC	-	T41	T12	T9	MC	MC	T3	T33	T24	
Money (A)	-	-	-	-	-	-	62	55	47	19	99	83	9	18	7	8	15
Money (E)	-	197	122	33	9	25	93	-	-	1	81	52	-	55	2	3	3
OWR	256	345	439	162	37	52	71	86	51	6	19	70	30	18	4	4	6

Rose, Justin Peter, Cont'd

2014: PGA: 19 st / 17 ct / 8 t10. (Won Quicken Loans, T4 Players, T4 WGC-Bridgestone, T4 Tour Champ, 5 WGC-HSBC, etc.).   Shook off early season shoulder tendinitis to claim his sixth PGA Tour win, finish 11th in FedEx Cup points (in just 19 starts) and star on the European Ryder Cup side.

OUTLOOK: Likely due to early rustiness, slipped a bit in Ball Striking (3 to 47) but still remains a much-admired tee-to-greener. A very difficult man to beat until the ball is on the putting surface, where he is little beyond average in most statistical areas - though his SGP did edge upward in 2014 (133 to 108). At age 34, he seems well positioned to remain among the world elite for the foreseeable future, especially since putting – the most volatile component for most – is a secondary aspect of his arsenal. Could easily have another Major or two lying in his future.

STATS: Driving Distance: A-   Driving Accuracy: B+   GIR: A   Short Game: A-   Putting: B-

---

Rumford, Brett Michael (Australia) (37)   b. Perth, Western Australia 7/27/1977. 5'11" 150 lbs. TP: 2000. Won the Australasian Tour's 1999 Players Championship as an amateur, beating Craig Spence in a playoff. Has spent virtually his entire professional career playing primarily in Europe, where he logged solid early wins at the 2004 Irish Open (by four over Padraig Harrington and Raphaël Jacquelin) and the 2007 European Masters, where he edged Phillip Archer in sudden death. After struggling somewhat in 2011 and '12, re-emerged in 2013 by claiming back-to-back E Tour victories at the Ballantine's Championship (eagling the first hole of a playoff with Marcus Fraser and Peter Whiteford) and the Volvo China Open (by four over Mikko Ilonen) en route to a career-best 17th-place $$$ ranking. **Teams:** Eisenhower Trophy: 1998. **OWR Best:** 74 - May, 2013.

European Tour Wins (5): 2003: St-Omer Open **2004**: Irish Open **2007**: European Masters **2013**: Ballantine's Championship, China Open (Volvo).
Australasian Tour Wins (1): Players Championship (ANZ): 1999*.
Amateur Wins: Australian Am: 1998   –   Western Australian Jr: 1994   Lake Macquarie Am: 1998.

	99	00	01	02	03	04	05	06	07	08	09	10	11	12	13	14
Masters	-	-	-	-	-	-	-	-	-	-	-	-	-	-	-	-
US Open	-	-	-	-	-	-	-	-	-	-	-	-	-	-	-	-
British	-	-	MC	-	-	-	-	T16	-	-	-	-	-	-	MC	MC
PGA	-	-	-	-	-	-	-	-	-	-	-	-	-	-	MC	-
Money (E)	Am	-	57	132	112	37	61	51	48	-	99	45	110	61	17	115
OWR	306	148	143	324	284	152	164	152	145	329	365	111	229	217	75	176

2014: E: 23 st / 10 ct / 1 t10.   (T10 Volvo Champ).   Logged only one top 10 in slumping to 117th in $$$ - miles off his peak 2013 form.

OUTLOOK: After exploding during a career-best 2013 campaign, crashed back to earth during a down 2014. The problem, as ever, is that he relies on his elite talent inside of 50 yards to survive, and very few ball strikers of his below-the-median level have enjoyed high levels of success long-term.

STATS: Driving Distance: C+   Driving Accuracy: C-   GIR: C-   Short Game: A-   Putting: A

Ryu, Hyun-Woo (South Korea) (33)   b. Seoul, South Korea 9/8/1981. 5'7" 180 lbs. TP: 2002. Spent most of his 20s playing on his native Korean Tour before moving full-time to the OneAsia circuit in 2010. Also began playing the Japan Tour in 2012, where he claimed his first professional win at the Tokai Classic, beating Shingo Katayama in a playoff. Added OneAsia's Caltex Maekyung Open (a Korean Tour co-sanctioned event) in 2013, edging Do-Hoon Kim #753 and Hyung-Sung Kim by one. **OWR Best:** 155 - Dec, 2012.

Japan Tour Wins (1): 2012: Tokai Classic (Coca-Cola).
OneAsia Tour Wins (1): 2013: Caltex Maekyung Open.

	10	11	12	13	14
Masters	-	-	-	-	-
US Open	-	-	-	-	-
British	-	-	-	-	-
PGA	-	-	-	-	-
Money (J)	-	-	21	86	31
Money (O)	107	55	7*	2	-
OWR	-	508	157	230	327

2014: JAP: 20 st / 18 ct / 2 t10.   (T2 Heiwa, T10 Taiheiyo).   Climbed to 31st in Japan Tour $$$ while also ranking 25th in Korean Tour earnings.

OUTLOOK: Seems to be trending more towards the Japan Tour (after making only six Korean starts in 2014) which makes economic sense if he can maintain his current form. Has mid-range numbers nearly across the board, but is capable of hitting enough greens to earn a good living.

STATS: Driving Distance: B-   Driving Accuracy: B+   GIR: B+   Short Game: B-   Putting: B

Sabbatini, Rory Mario Trevor (South Africa) (38)   b. Durban, South Africa 4/2/1976. 5'10" 160 lbs. Two-time All-American at U of Arizona. TP: 1998. The rare South African who did not play the Sunshine and/or European Tours, instead going straight from college to the PGA Tour. Claimed his first win at the 2000 Air Canada Championship, leading to a 36th-place finish on the money list. Never finished worse than 90th in earnings from 2000-2013. Added prestige wins in 2006 at the Nissan Los Angeles Open (by one over Adam Scott) and 2007 at Colonial (in a playoff with Bernhard Langer and Jim Furyk). Ended a two-year drought by edging Y.E. Yang by one at the 2011 Honda Classic. Confident sort who's been known to rattle cages with his speed of play and his attitude, but few PGA Tour players were consistently better from 2000-2010. **Teams:** Palmer Cup: 1998. Presidents Cup: 2007 (0-3-1). World Cup (6): 2002-03-04-06-08-09 (won in '03 w/T.Immelman). **OWR Best:** 8 - Sep, 2007.

PGA Tour Wins (6): 2000: Air Canada Championship **2003**: Kemper Open (FBR Capital) **2006**: Los Angeles Open (Nissan) **2007**: Colonial Inv (Crown Plaza) **2009**: Byron Nelson Classic (EDS) **2011**: Honda Classic.
Amateur Wins: Int'l Junior Masters: 1993.

	99	00	01	02	03	04	05	06	07	08	09	10	11	12	13	14
Masters	-	-	MC	MC	-	-	MC	T36	T2	MC	T20	MC	MC	MC	-	-
US Open	-	MC	-	-	MC	MC	T71	MC	T51	T58	MC	MC	T30	-	MC	-
British	-	-	T54	-	T53	T66	MC	T26	MC	MC	MC	-	T54	-	-	MC
PGA	-	77	MC	MC	68	MC	T74	MC	MC	T39	T67	MC	T74	MC	-	MC
Money (A)	108	36	52	68	41	16	89	12	6	56	18	54	27	90	67	96
OWR	221	84	69	90	75	34	71	39	11	34	67	94	71	134	127	181

Sabbatini, Rory Mario Trevor, Cont'd

2014: PGA: 26 st / 16 ct / 3 t10. (T3 Mayakoba, T8 Wells Fargo, T9 Heritage).   Well off his peak years of 2006 and '07, he logged five top 25s and finished 108th in FedEx Cup points Cup points, but easily retained his card for an imposing 16th straight season.

OUTLOOK: At age 38, he might be onto the downside but he still remains competitive at the highest level. Though his ball striking was hardly terrible, he experienced declines in GIR (23 to 74), Ball Striking (38 to 110) and Proximity to Hole (7 to 120), so his marginal drop in performance isn't hard to explain. Though hardly over the hill, the declining numbers and growing time since his last win suggest no great resurgence is imminent.

STATS: Driving Distance: B+   Driving Accuracy: C   GIR: B   Short Game: B-   Putting: C

Saddier, Adrien (France) (22) b. Annamasse, France 9/15/1992. 6'0" 155 lbs. TP: 2013. Turned pro upon completing his schooling in France. T55 at the 2012 European Masters while still an amateur. Made four 2013 Challenge Tour starts before playing his way through three stages of E Tour Q School, then lost his card upon finishing 127th in $$$ in 2014. **OWR Best:** 493 - May, 2014.

Amateur Wins: Nations Cup Individual: 2013.

	14
Masters	-
US Open	
British	
PGA	
Money (E)	127
OWR	564

2014: PGA: 27 st / 15 ct / 1 t10. (4 Mandela).   Logged but a single top 10 as an E Tour rookie en route to finishing 127th in $$$.

OUTLOOK: Came in as something of a wildcard in 2014 and remains so - though in 2015, he'll be doing it mostly on the Challenge Tour.

STATS (LTD): Driving Distance: A-   Driving Accuracy: B-   GIR: A   Short Game: B-   Putting: C-

---

Sainz, Carlos Jr. (USA) (29) b. Chicago, IL 11/7/1985. 5'11" 185 lbs. College: Mississippi St. TP: 2010. Spent several years on mini-tours before finishing 9th in $$$ on the 2013 PGA Tour Canada. Joined the Web.com Tour in 2014, where he barely made the Finals after finishing 74th in regular season earnings – and then barely qualified for the PGA by finishing 49th after the Finals. **OWR Best:** 456 - Nov, 2014.

Other Wins: Players Cup (Canada): 2013   Chicago Open: 2013.

	13	14
Masters	-	-
US Open	-	-
British	-	-
PGA	-	-
Money (A)	-	-
OWR	673	477

2014: Played full-time on the Web.com Tour, where he finished 74th in regular season $$$ before reaching the 2015 PGA Tour via the Finals.

OUTLOOK: Reaches the PGA Tour with a somewhat limited résumé, and by remarkably narrow margins, having slipped into the Web.com Finals in the 74th spot, then onto the Tour in the 49th spot on the priority list. At this stage of the game, an obvious longshot.

STATS (LTD): Driving Distance: B   Driving Accuracy: B   GIR: B+   Short Game: B-   Putting: B-

---

Santos, Ricardo (Portugal) (32) b. Faro, Portugal 9/7/1982. 6'1" 200 lbs. TP: 2006. Spent most of his 20s on the Challenge Tour before finishing 4th in 2011 $$$, earning E Tour status for 2012. Won the Madeira Islands Open in his eleventh start (beating Magnus Carlsson by four), and went on to win the Henry Cotton Rookie-Of-The-Year award, then raised his stock during a winless 2013 which saw him jump to 65th in $$$.

Awards: E Tour Rookie Of The Year: 2012.   **Teams**: Eisenhower Trophy: 2004. World Cup (3): 2008-11-13. **OWR Best:** 137 - Mar, 2013.

European Tour Wins (1): 2012: Madeira Islands Open.

Other Wins: 1 Euro Challenge (2011)   +   PT Masters (Portugal): 2006   Algarve Championship (Portugal): 2008   Pestana Sives (Portugal): 2010   Pestana Alto (Portugal): 2011.

Amateur Wins: Swiss Am: 2004.

	11	12	13	14
Masters	-	-	-	-
US Open	-	-	-	-
British	-	-	-	-
PGA	-	-	-	-
Money (E)	-	90	65	116
OWR	269	277	203	550

2014: E: 29 st / 17 ct / 1 t10. (T10 NH Collection). After two solid campaigns, plunged to 116th in $$$, giving him only conditional status in 2015.

OUTLOOK: Aside from being notably wild off the tee, a statistically balanced player whose results began tailing off in late 2013, a trend which carried over to 2014. With his win being at the light-field Madeira Islands Open, his ability to succeed long-term on the E Tour remains open to question.

STATS: Driving Distance: B+   Driving Accuracy: D   GIR: B+   Short Game: A   Putting: B⇩

Saunders, Samuel Palmer (USA) (27) b. Orlando, FL 7/30/1987. 6'0" 175 lbs. College: Clemson U. TP: 2009. The grandson of Hall-of-Famer Arnold Palmer (whom he caddied for in Palmer's final Masters appearance in 2004). Former Florida HS champion who turned pro after three unspectacular seasons at Clemson, relying on sponsor exemptions to compete in events above the mini-tour level. Played the Web.com Tour full-time

Saunders, Samuel Palmer, Cont'd

beginning in 2012, graduating to the PGA Tour via a dash through the 2014 Web.com Finals. **OWR Best:** 402 - Oct, 2014.

Amateur Wins: Florida HS: 2004.

	11	12	13	14
Masters	-	-	-	-
US Open	MC	-	-	-
British	-	-	-	-
PGA	-	-	-	-
Money (A)	-	-	-	-
OWR	772	538	855	443

2014: Played full-time on the Web.com Tour, finishing 45th in regular season $$$ before earning his PGA Tour card via the Finals.

OUTLOOK: Despite making 22 PGA Tour starts through 2014 (including eight made cuts and two top 25s), his record over three full Web.com seasons does little to suggest that he's ready to succeed on the big stage. Is a veteran at Bay Hill, having played in his grandfather's event five times.

STATS (LTD): Driving Distance: B+   Driving Accuracy: C+   GIR: B-   Short Game: B   Putting: B

Schwartzel, Charl Adriaan (South Africa) (30)

b. Johannesburg, South Africa 8/31/1984. 5'11" 160 lbs. TP: 2002. Elite South African prospect who claimed numerous local and regional junior titles, several prominent amateur wins, and was South Africa's #1 ranked amateur in 2002. Secured his E Tour card at 18 years, 81 days (second youngest ever, after countryman Dale Hayes) and won the Alfred Dunhill Championship at 21, in a playoff over Neil Cheetham. Won three straight Southern Africa Tour Orders of Merit from 2004-06, despite making less than 10 homeland starts each season. In addition to six South African events co-sanctioned by the European Tour, has also won twice on European soil, taking the 2007 Spanish Open and the inaugural 2008 Madrid Masters. Finished 8th in the E Tour Order of Merit in 2010, led by back-to-back victories at the inaugural Africa Open (by one over Thomas Aiken) and the Joburg Open, where he ran away by six. Scored breakthrough victory at the 2011 Masters, beating Jason Day and Adam Scott by two after closing with a 66 and becoming the only man ever to birdie the last four holes to clinch a Major. Also defended his title in the Joburg Open, highlighted by a second round 61. Bailed out a winless 2012 by claiming the Thailand Golf Championship by a stunning 11 shots, then scored a second runaway win the next week at the Alfred Dunhill Championship, routing the field by 12. Followed much the same pattern in 2013, not winning until claiming the OneAsia Tour's China Masters in October, then defending his Alfred Dunhill title a month later. **Teams:** Eisenhower Trophy: 2002. Presidents Cup (2): 2011-13 (5-4-1). World Cup: 2011. **OWR Best:** 6 - Mar, 2012.

PGA Tour Wins (1): 2011: The Masters.
European Tour Wins (8): 2004: Alfred Dunhill Championship ('05) **2007:** Spanish Open **2008:** Madrid Masters **2010:** Africa Open, Joburg Open **2011:** Joburg Open **2012:** Alfred Dunhill Championship ('13) **2013:** Alfred Dunhill Championship ('14).
Asian Tour Wins (1): 2012: Thailand Championship.
Sunshine Tour Wins (1): 2006: Tour Championship.
OneAsia Tour Wins (1): 2013: China Masters.
Amateur Wins: Transvaal Am (2): 2001-02   Indian Am: 2002   –   Transvaal Am Stroke Play: 2001   English Am Stroke Play: 2002   National Am Inv: 2002   English Am Stroke Play: 2002.

	03	04	05	06	07	08	09	10	11	12	13	14
Masters	-	-	-	-	-	-	-	T30	Win	T50	T25	MC
US Open	-	-	-	T48	T30	-	MC	T16	T9	T38	14	MC
British	MC	-	MC	T22	MC	-	MC	T14	T16	MC	T15	T7
PGA	-	-	-	MC	MC	T52	T43	T18	T12	T59	MC	T15
Money (A)	-	-	-	-	-	-	-	-	24	89	25	44
Money (E)	71	103	52	18	35	28	26	8	4	16	27*	24
Money (SA)	-	1*	1*	1*	17*	9*	2*	1*	3*	-	1*	49*
OWR	228	193	143	55	83	68	65	34	9	14	18	31

2014: PGA: 18 st / 15 ct / 5 t10. (T4 WGC-Bridgestone, 5 Northern Trust, T7 British Open, T8 Memorial, T9 WGC-Cadillac). Endured his first winless year worldwide since 2009, recording 11 top-25 PGA Tour finishes and finishing 43rd in FedEx Cup points.

OUTLOOK: At times can rate among the game's worldwide elite, particularly when his streaky putter heats up, allowing him to run the table on some big stages, and win by big margins. Also one of the game's longer straight drivers (though he dropped from 27 to 54 in Total Driving in 2014), which sets up a strong overall tee-to-green game and a statistically sharp short game. The result was his second consecutive year ranking 5 in Birdie Average but, overall, a season which represented a minor step back. Barring any health issues, expect a rebound in 2015.

STATS: Driving Distance: A   Driving Accuracy: B   GIR: B-   Short Game: A-   Putting: B+

Scott, Adam Derek (Australia) (34)

b. Adelaide, South Australia 7/16/1980. 6'0" 170 lbs. College: UNLV. TP: 2000. Attended UNLV but turned pro after one season. Quickly established himself internationally, claiming victories on four continents prior to turning 25. His biggest early victory was the 2004 Players Championship, where a clutch up-and-down at the 72nd (after pulling his approach into the water) secured a one-shot triumph over Padraig Harrington. Claimed 2003 Deutsche Bank Championship (by four over Rocco Mediate) at age 23. Also won the 2006 Tour Championship, by three over Jim Furyk at East Lake. Shot a scorching final round 61 to win the 2008 Qatar Masters on the European Tour, beating Henrik Stenson by three. Logged an unofficial win at the 36-hole, rain-shortened 2005 Nissan Open. After struggling for most of the year, won the 2009 Australian Open (in a five-shot runaway) in December. Claimed his first U.S. win in four years at the 2010 Valero Texas Open, rallying from four back on a 36-hole Sunday to edge Fredrik Jacobson by one. T2 (with countryman Jason Day) at the 2012 Masters, looking much like a winner until Charl Schwartzel reeled off four closing birdies. Scored one of 2011's more memorable victories at the WGC Bridgestone Invitational, beating Luke Donald and Rickie Fowler by four with ex-Tiger Woods caddie Steve Williams on his bag. Finished 2nd at 2012 British Open (Royal Lytham) after leading through 68 holes, then bogeying the final four. Salvaged his 2012 season with a November win at the Australian Masters, then broke through in 2013 to become Australia's first-ever Masters champion, memorably defeating Angel Cabrera on the second hole of sudden death. Also won the 2013 Barclays, coming from six shots back with a closing 66 at Liberty National. In November, beat Rickie Fowler by four to win the 2013 Australian PGA (becoming only the sixth man to win the Australian PGA, Open and Masters), then defended his Australian Masters title the following week at Royal Melbourne. Took over the #1 spot in the Official World Ranking on May 19, 2014 (largely due to Tiger Woods' absence due to injury), then validated it the next weekend by defeating Jason Dufner in sudden death to win at Colonial. **Teams:** Presidents Cup (6): 2003-05-07-09-11-13 (12-15-3). World Cup (3): 2001-02-13 (won in 2013 w/J. Day). **OWR Best:** 1 - May, 2014.

Scott, Adam Derek, Cont'd

PGA Tour Wins (11): 2003: Deutsche Bank Championship **2004**: Players Championship, Booz Allen Classic **2006**: Tour Championship **2007**: Houston Open (Shell) **2008**: Byron Nelson Classic (EDS) **2010**: Texas Open (Valero) **2011**: WGC-Bridgestone Inv **2013**: The Masters, The Barclays **2014**: Colonial Inv (Crown Plaza).
European Tour Wins (7): 2001: Alfred Dunhill Championship **2002**: Qatar Masters, Scottish PGA **2003**: Scandinavian Masters **2005**: Johnnie Walker Classic **2008**: Qatar Masters **2010**: Singapore Open.
Asian Tour Wins (2): 2005: Singapore Open (54H) **2006**: Singapore Open (54H).
Australasian Tour Wins (4): 2009: Australian Open **2012**: Australian Masters **2013**: Australian PGA, Australian Master (Talisker).
Other Wins: Los Angeles Open (Nissan)(36H): 2005 PGA Grand Slam (36): 2013.
Amateur Wins: Australian Boys (2): 1997-98 Queensland Jr (2): 1996-97 New Zealand Jr: 1996 Doug Sanders Jr Int'l: 1997.

	00	01	02	03	04	05	06	07	08	09	10	11	12	13	14
Masters	-	-	T9	T23	MC	T33	T27	T27	T25	MC	T18	T2	T8	Win	T14
US Open	-	-	MC	MC	MC	T28	T21	MC	T26	T36	MC	MC	T15	T45	T9
British	MC	T47	MC	MC	T42	T34	T8	T27	T16	MC	T27	T25	2	T3	T5
PGA	-	MC	T23	T23	T9	T40	T3	T12	MC	MC	T39	7	T11	T5	T15
Money (A)	-	-	-	55*	7	15	3	11	39	108	28	11	25	6	13
Money (E)	102	13	7	11	36	24	-	-	43	36	-	-	-	-	-
OWR	166	48	40	25	11	9	4	7	17	34	24	5	5	2	3

2014: PGA: 17 st / 17 ct / 10 t10. (Won Colonial, 3 Arnold Palmer, T4 Memorial, T5 British Open, T6 T of C, etc.). Though he only won once (at Colonial) in 2014, he still enjoyed a memorable season, recording 10 top 10s in 17 U.S. starts and ascending to the number one spot in the OWR in May.
OUTLOOK: At age 34, he opens 2015 firmly entrenched among the world elite, having established himself as the most consistently excellent tee-to-greener in the game. Maintained these lofty standards in 2014 by ranking 13 in Driving Distance, 10 in GIR, 6 in Strokes Gained Tee To Green, 10 in Total Driving and 6 in Ball Striking - a remarkable array of numbers. Still has to contend with the 2016 anchored putter ban, and it will be interesting to see if he makes the switch during 2015. A superstar whose rock-solid tee-to-green foundation suggests there may still be room for improvement.

STATS: Driving Distance: A+   Driving Accuracy: B   GIR: A   Short Game: B   Putting: B

Scrivener, Jason (Australia) (25)

b. Perth, Western Australia 4/18/1989. 5'10" 155 lbs. TP: 2011. Spent time on the Australasian and OneAsia Tours, as well as the 2013 PGA Tour Canada. Played his way through the 2014 E Tour Q School where, after playing his first four holes four over par, he closed with a final round 66 (including five birdies in his last seven holes) to gain his 2015 card. **OWR Best**: 587 - Dec, 2014.

Amateur Wins: Australian Boys: 2007.

	13	14
Masters	-	-
US Open	-	-
British	-	-
PGA	-	-
Money (O)	46	26
OWR	659	588

2014: Appeared on the Australasian (7 starts), European (2), OneAsia (2) and Japan (1) Tours before playing dramatically through E Tour Q School.
OUTLOOK: Well thought of in Australian circles but he's not played long enough on any major tour to leave many measurable footsteps. Showed some Q School flash in closing with 66 to gain his E Tour card for 2015 - and it wouldn't be surprising if he logs a notable moment or two as a rookie.

STATS: Driving Distance: --   Driving Accuracy: --   GIR: --   Short Game: --   Putting: --

---

Senden, John Gerard (Australia) (43)

b. Brisbane, Queensland, Australia 4/20/1971. 6'3" 195 lbs. TP: 1992. After playing in Australia, Asia and Europe, settled full-time on the PGA Tour in 2002. Though a winner of the 1995 Indonesian PGA, didn't become a notable presence until the new millennium, establishing himself as a consistent $$$ earner in America and ranking among the top 125 every year since 2002. Stepped up in 2006, winning in America at the John Deere Classic and scoring his biggest victory, at the Australian Open during a winter visit home. After slumping somewhat in 2013, came back to claim his second PGA Tour win at the 2014 Valspar Championship, where he edged Kevin Na by one. Widely noted as a superior ball striker whose fortunes are ultimately settled with the putter. **Teams**: World Cup (1): 2006. **OWR Best**: 28 - Mar, 2012.

PGA Tour Wins (2): 2006: John Deere Classic **2014**: Valspar Championship.
Asian Tour Wins (1): 1995: Indonesian PGA.
Australasian Tour Wins (1): 2006: Australian Open.
Other Wins: 2 Euro Challenge (1998)   +   Queensland Closed (Aus): 1993.

	95	96	97	98	99	00	01	02	03	04	05	06	07	08	09	10	11	12	13	14
Masters	-	-	-	-	-	-	-	-	-	-	-	-	-	-	-	MC	-	MC	T35	T8
US Open	-	-	-	-	-	-	-	MC	-	-	-	-	MC	-	MC	T30	T10	T15	MC	
British	-	-	-	-	-	MC	-	-	-	T35	T45	-	MC	T48	-	T34	MC	T58		
PGA	-	-	-	-	-	-	-	-	-	MC	T4	T42	MC	MC	T19	T32	T70	MC		
Money (A)	-	-	-	-	-	114	108	114	97	45	39	86	27	69	33	42	120	25		
Money (E)	-	-	-	69	71	81	-	-	-	-	-	-	-	-	-	-	-	-	-	-
OWR	362	400	616	532	282	260	258	242	223	197	115	68	55	106	76	83	43	38	108	49

2014: PGA: 27 st / 22 ct / 5 t10. (Won Valspar, T4 McGladrey, T5 Colonial, T5 Deutsche Bank, T8 Masters). Rebounded impressively from a down 2013, recording his second PGA Tour win in Tampa, recording his best-ever $$$ ranking and finishing 23rd in FedEx Cup points.
OUTLOOK: Moved back towards ranking among the PGA Tour's strongest tee-to-greeners in 2014, climbing from 99 to 49 in Total Driving, 68 to 25 in GIR and 80 to 32 in Ball Striking. But far more impressive was an epic leap in SGP (125 to 13); with that level of putting even a far lesser ball striker could find success. But even with his tee-to-green game, a modest decline in putting could result in at least something of a decline in 2015.

STATS: Driving Distance: B+   Driving Accuracy: A-   GIR: A   Short Game: B-   Putting: B+ ⇧

Siem, Marcel (Germany) (34) b. Mettmann, Germany 7/15/1980. 6'2" 165 lbs. TP: 2000. Was initially overshadowed by Martin Kaymer among younger German players. After two years spent mostly on the Challenge Tour, made a big splash in early 2004 when he won the E Tour's Alfred Dunhill Championship, defeating Grégory Havret and Raphaël Jacquelin in a playoff. Took eight years to claim a second title, winning the 2012 French Open by one over Francesco Molinari. Won the 2013 Trophée Hassan II in Morocco but narrowly missed moving into the OWR top 50 and thus failed to garner an invite to The Masters. Won for the third straight year in 2014 but waited until the lucrative E Tour Final Series to do it, beating Ross Fisher and Alexander Levy in sudden death to claim the BMW Masters in China. **Teams:** Eisenhower Trophy (2): 1998-00. World Cup (4): 2003-04-06-13 (won in 2006 w/B. Langer). **OWR Best:** 48 - Apr, 2013.

European Tour Wins (4): 2004: Alfred Dunhill Championship **2012**: French Open **2013**: Trophée Hassan II **2014**: BMW Masters.

Amateur Wins: Spanish Am: 1999   –   Sherry Cup: 1999.

	02	03	04	05	06	07	08	09	10	11	12	13	14
Masters	-	-	-	-	-	-	-	-	-	-	-	-	-
US Open	-	-	-	-	-	-	-	-	-	T60	-	T59	T12
British	-	-	-	-	-	-	-	-	T27	-	MC	MC	-
PGA	-	-	-	-	-	-	-	-	-	-	T36	MC	-
Money (E)	131	95	39	99	50	129	96	79	80	87	14	53	7
OWR	421	302	148	248	220	425	383	259	268	253	60	90	61

2014: E: 22 st / 19 ct / 3 t10. (Won BMW Masters, T7 BMW PGA, T8 Turkey). Turned a moderately disappointing year positive in its late stages, winning the BMW Masters in November and finishing T8 in Turkey - all of which led to a career-best 7th-place finish in $$$.

OUTLOOK: Statistically, he possesses the ideal contemporary mix of length off the tee and some increasingly fine putting numbers; only driving accuracy (which is common) and a slightly below-the-median short game work against him. At age 34, has proven himself capable of winning regularly, and has fared well in limited appearances in America. Seems to have the necessary tools to win even more, at least in Europe.

STATS: Driving Distance: A-   Driving Accuracy: C   GIR: B+   Short Game: B-   Putting: A-

---

Sim, Michael (Australia) (30) b. Aberdeen, Scotland 10/23/1984. 6'0" 155 lbs. TP: 2005. Born in Scotland but moved to Australia (whom he has always represented) at age 5. After ranking as the world #1 amateur in 2005, turned pro as a touted prospect but saw most of his 20s sidetracked by injuries. Had his PGA Tour rookie year of 2007 derailed by a spinal fracture. Showed his potential by winning thrice (and topping the $$$ list) on the 2009 Web.com Tour, then finishing 65th in 2010 PGA Tour $$$ in 20 starts, tying for 2nd at the Farmer's Insurance Open. Reached #34 in the OWR in January of 2010, mostly due to his Web.com success. Has since battled a shoulder injury which limited him to 12 Web.com starts in 2012, then only sporadic appearances on the Australasian circuit in 2013. **Teams:** Eisenhower Trophy: 2004. **OWR Best:** 34 - Jan, 2010.

Other Wins: 4 Web.com (2006-2009).

Amateur Wins: Southern Am: 2004   –   Western Australia Am: 2002   Riversdale Cup: 2004   Sunnehanna Am: 2005   Monroe Inv: 2005   New Zealand Am Stroke Play: 2005   Western Australia Match Play: 2005.

	06	07	08	09	10	11	12	13	14
Masters	-	-	-	-	-	-	-	-	-
US Open	-	-	-	T18	MC	-	-	-	-
British	-	-	-	-	MC	-	-	-	-
PGA	-	-	-	T51	MC	-	-	-	-
Money (A)	-	162	-	-	65	225	-	-	-
OWR	275	215	312	44	81	460	-	-	977

2014: Played primarily on the Australasian Tour, where he finished 41st in $$$. Also T6 at the OneAsia's Nanshan China Masters.

OUTLOOK: Has had a very promising career steamrolled by injuries. At his 2009 peak, showed a relatively powerful tee-to-green game (5 in 2009 Web.com GIR) and a solid putting stroke (1 in Web.com Putting Average) – but at this point, it's chancy if he'll ever return to that level.

STATS: Driving Distance: --   Driving Accuracy: --   GIR: --   Short Game: --   Putting: --

---

Simpson, James Fredrick Webb (USA) (29) b. Raleigh, NC 8/8/1985. 6'2" 175 lbs. College: Wake Forest U. TP: 2008. Four-time AJGA All-American. After thrice being named honorable mention All-American, played his way through Q School after graduation and had little trouble making money on the PGA Tour, finishing 70th and 94th in earnings over his first two seasons. Suffered two crushing 2011 defeats, first at the Transitions Championship (losing to Gary Woodland by one after bogeying the 72nd), then at New Orleans, where he fell to Bubba Watson on the second extra hole after incurring a controversial moving ball penalty on the 15th hole. Bounced back resiliently, however, to claim his first PGA Tour victory at the Wyndham Championship, then added the Deutsche Bank Championship (in a playoff with Chez Reavie) en route to finishing 2nd in $$$ – and then only because of Luke Donald's spectacular victory at the season-ending Children's Miracle Network. Broke through for his first Major championship at the 2012 U.S. Open, edging Michael Thompson and Graeme McDowell by one at Olympic. Claimed his fourth career win with a six-shot runaway at the 2013 Shriners Hospitals Open (Las Vegas), and seems firmly set among the elite of young American golf. **Teams:** Walker Cup: 2007 (0-2-1). Palmer Cup: 2007. Ryder Cup (2): 2012-14 (O: 2-3-1, S: 0-1-1). Presidents Cup (2): 2011-13 (5-3-2). **OWR Best:** 5 - Jun, 2012.

PGA Tour Wins (4): 2011: Wyndham Championship, Deutsche Bank Championship **2012**: U.S. Open **2013**: Las Vegas Classic (Shriners)('14).

Amateur Wins: Southern Am (2): 2005-07   –   Azalea Inv (2): 2004-07   Sunnehanna Am: 2006   Dogwood Am: 2007.

	08	09	10	11	12	13	14
Masters	-	-	-	-	T44	MC	MC
US Open	-	-	-	T14	Win	T32	T45
British	-	-	-	T16	-	T64	MC
PGA	-	-	-	MC	MC	T25	MC
Money (A)	-	70	94	2	17	20	17
OWR	332	146	213	10	11	21	43

2014: PGA: 25 st / 19 ct / 9 t10. (Won Shriners, 3 Greenbrier, 3 T of C, 3 FedEx St Jude, T5 Wyndham, etc.). His long-ago 2013 Las Vegas served as an anchor to his 2014 season - a year in which he finished 25th in FedEx Cup points and ranked among the top 20 in $$$ for the fourth straight time.

OUTLOOK: Though not quite the player he was in 2011 and '12, he remains among America's top young stars, regularly contending and banking significant $$$. A solid ball striker but one who's witnessed a four-year decline in his GIR (8, 32, 43, 77) and a similar drop in his Scrambling numbers

Simpson, James Fredrick Webb, Cont'd

(16, 56, 86, 77) - all of which, combined with a dismal showing at the 2014 Ryder Cup, injects at least an element of doubt going forward. But when one looks at his six-year body of work, it seems more likely that he'll iron out the ripples and continue playing well for the foreseeable future.

STATS: Driving Distance: B Driving Accuracy: B+ GIR: A- ⇩ Short Game: B+ Putting: A-

---

Singh, Chiranjeev Milkha ("Jeev") (India) (43)
b. Chandigarh, India 12/15/1971. 6'0" 165 lbs. Two-time D2 All-American and NCAA individual champion (1993) at Abilene (TX) Christian. TP: 1993. Was the first Indian to gain playing privileges on the E Tour where he initially found only minor success, settling back onto the Asian and Japan circuits in 2003. Enjoyed a breakthrough season in 2006, returning to Europe to win twice (including a one-shot victory over Luke Donald, Sergio García and Padraig Harrington at the Volvo Masters) while also claiming the Casio World Open and Nippon Series finale back-to-back in Japan. Won the 2006 and '08 Asian Tour Orders of Merit. Broke a four-year winless drought by capturing the 2012 Scottish Open, edging Francesco Molinari in a playoff, but largely struggled thereafter. **Teams:** Eisenhower Trophy (2): 1988-92. World Cup (2): 2008-09. **OWR Best:** 28 - Mar, 2009.

European Tour Wins (4): 2006: China Open (54H), Volvo Masters **2008:** BA-CA Open (54H) **2012:** Scottish Open.
Japan Tour Wins (4): 2006: Casio World Open, Nippon Series **2008:** Sega Sammy Cup, Nippon Series.
Asian Tour Wins (5): 1995: Philippine Classic, Asia Match Play **1996:** Asia Cup **1999:** Lexus Int'l (Thailand) **2008:** Singapore Open.
Other Wins: Southern Oklahoma Open: 1993 Bukit Kaira Championship (Malaysia): 1993 Shinhan Donghae Open (Korea): 1994 Northern India Open: 1994 Thailand PGA: 1995 Mahindra BPGC Open (India): 1995 Toyota Crown Open (Thailand): 1995.

	95	96	97	98	99	00	01	02	03	04	05	06	07	08	09	10	11	12	13	14
Masters	-	-	-	-	-	-	-	-	-	-	-	-	T37	T25	MC	-	-	-	-	-
US Open	-	-	-	-	-	-	-	T62	-	-	-	T59	T36	-	MC	-	-	-	-	-
British	-	-	-	-	-	-	-	-	-	-	-	-	-	MC	-	-	-	T69	-	-
PGA	-	-	-	-	-	-	-	-	-	-	-	-	MC	T9	T67	-	-	MC	-	-
Money (A)	-	-	-	-	-	-	-	-	-	-	-	-	-	-	-	164	-	-	-	-
Money (E)	-	-	-	104	50	-	108	152	-	-	-	16	46	12	34	74	94	32	133	179
Money (J)	-	-	-	-	-	-	34	76	74	45	51	2	-	-	-	-	-	-	-	-
Money (As)	3*	33	5*	-	-	-	-	-	-	-	21	1	-	1*	-	-	13*	-	62*	-
OWR	676	832	400	322	169	279	179	356	550	356	377	37	77	35	59	168	187	96	287	1190

2014: E: 24 st / 9 ct / 0 t10. (T38 Irish). Extended a sharp two-year decline, failing to log even one top 25 en route to finishing 179th in $$$.

OUTLOOK: At age 43, he is clearly in something of a decline, with his strong 2012 now looking like an outlier. Statistically, he still has the short game and putting numbers to remain competitive, but his long game - never his strength to begin with - is limiting his ability to seriously compete.

STATS: Driving Distance: B- Driving Accuracy: C- GIR: C Short Game: A- Putting: B+

Singh, Vijay (Fiji) (51)
b. Lautoka, Fiji 2/22/1963. 6'2" 210 lbs. TP: 1982. Fijian who played his way up through various golfing backwaters, claiming early wins like the Malaysian PGA, an Ivory Coast Open and two Nigerian Opens. By 1990 he cracked the top 20 in the European Order of Merit (rising as high as 6th in 1994) and by the end of 1994, he was a six-time winner there, including the 1994 Trophée Lancôme. Began playing in America in 1993, when he won the Buick Classic (Westchester) as a 30-year-old rookie. By 1995 he was winning regularly and finished 9th on the money list, but this was just a prelude for a remarkable run of golf which saw him occupy a spot in the top 5 on the PGA Tour money list, and the top 10 in the year-end OWR, from 1998-2008. Won 19 events (including two Majors) during this period and topped the PGA Tour in earnings in 2003, during an epic, nine-win 2004, and in 2008. Ended the 2004 season ranked #1 in the OWR. Won the 1998 PGA Championship at Sahalee, shooting 271 to beat Steve Stricker by two. Won the 2000 Masters with a 278 total, beating Ernie Els by three. Took his second PGA Championship in 2004 at Whistling Straits, defeating Chris DiMarco and Justin Leonard in a playoff. Swept the PGA Player of the Year, Vardon Trophy and E Tour Golfer of the Year awards in 2004. His 34 career PGA Tour wins is most by a non-American. Won 23 PGA Tour events after turning 40 (most ever). Appeared on the verge of irrelevance after finishing 68th and 66th in $$$ in 2009 and '10 before climbing back to 28th in 2011, at age 48. An occasionally controversial sort who has perhaps not received his due as a player in consequence. His 2013 decision to sue the PGA Tour after admitting publicly to using a banned performance-enhancing substance won't help. **Awards:** World Golf Hall of Fame Member (2006). PGA Tour Player of the Year: 2004. E Tour Golfer of the Year: 2004. Vardon Trophy: 2004. PGA Tour Rookie of the Year: 1993. FedEx Cup Champion: 2008. **Teams:** Eisenhower Trophy: 1980. Presidents Cup (8): 1994-96-98-00-03-05-07-09 (16-15-9). World Cup (3): 2001-02-13. **OWR Best:** 1 - Sep, 2004.

PGA Tour Wins (34): 1993: Westchester Classic (Buick) **1995:** Phoenix Open, Westchester Classic (Buick) **1997:** Memorial Tournament (54H), Buick Open **1998:** PGA Championship, The International (Sprint)(Stableford) **1999:** Honda Classic **2000:** Masters Tournament **2002:** Houston Open (Shell), Tour Championship **2003:** Phoenix Open, Byron Nelson Classic (EDS), John Deere Classic, Walt Disney Classic (Funai) **2004:** AT&T Pro-Am, Houston Open (Shell), New Orleans Classic (HP), Buick Open, PGA Championship, Deutsche Bank Championship, Canadian Open, 84 Lumber Classic, Chrysler Championship **2005:** Hawaiian Open (Sony), Houston Open (Shell), Wachovia Championship, Buick Open **2006:** Westchester Classic (Barclays) **2007:** Mercedes Championships, Arnold Palmer Inv **2008:** WGC-Bridgestone Inv, The Barclays, Deutsche Bank Championship.
European Tour Wins (9): 1989: Open di Firenze **1990:** El Bosque Open **1992:** Turespaña Masters, German Open **1994:** Scandinavian Masters, Trophée Lancôme **1997:** South African Open **2001:** Malaysian Open, Singapore Masters.
Asian Tour Wins (2): 1995: Passport Open **2000:** Taiwan Open.
Asian Wins (1): 1992: Malaysian Open.
Sunshine Tour Wins (1): 1993: Bells Cup.
Other Wins: Malaysian PGA: 1984 Nigerian Open (2): 1988-89 Swedish Pro: 1988 Ivory Coast Open: 1989 Zimbabwe Open: 1989 Hassan Trophy (Morocco): 1991 World Match Play (England): 1997 Johnnie Walker Super Tour: 1998 TELUS Skins (Canada): 2003 Korean Open (KPGA): 2007 Chevron World Challenge: 2008.

	89	90	91	92	93	94	95	96	97	98	99	00	01	02	03	04	05	06	07	08	09	10	11	12
Masters	-	-	-	-	-	T27	MC	T39	T17	MC	T24	Win	T18	7	T6	T6	T5	T8	T13	T14	T30	MC	MC	T27
US Open	-	-	-	-	MC	-	T10	T7	T77	T25	T3	T8	T7	T30	T20	T28	T6	T6	T20	T65	T27	T41	-	MC
British	T23	T12	T12	T51	T59	T20	T6	T11	T38	T19	MC	T11	T13	MC	T2	T20	T5	MC	T27	MC	T38	T37	WD	T9
PGA	-	-	-	T48	4	MC	MC	T5	T13	Win	T49	MC	T51	8	T34	Win	T10	MC	MC	MC	T16	T39	MC	T36
Money (A)	-	-	-	-	19*	52	9	17	16	2	4	5	2	4	3	1	1	2	4	3	1	68	66	28	51
Money (E)	24	13	13	9	39	6	54	-	-	-	-	-	-	-	-	-	-	-	-	-	-	-	-	-
OWR	86	76	77	38	16	15	16	20	15	9	7	9	8	8	2	1	2	7	10	5	26	91	63	82

414

Singh, Vijay, Cont'd

	13	14
Masters	T38	T37
US Open	-	-
British	MC	-
PGA	T68	T36
Money (A)	164	97
Money (E)	-	-
OWR	135	262

2014: PGA: 25 st / 16 ct / 1 t10. (2 Frys.com). Though Champions Tour eligible (where he opted to make only three starts), remained a full-time PGA Tour player - but to little avail. Did finish second at Frys.com but otherwise logged only three top 25s and finished 87th in FedEx Cup points.

OUTLOOK: He still moves the ball fairly effectively (73 in GIR, 97 in Ball Striking) but at age 51, his always-suspect putting isn't likely to become a strength to counter declining ball striking. Figures to dominate on the Champions Tour, but will 2015 be the year he makes the transition?

STATS: Driving Distance: B   Driving Accuracy: B   GIR: B+   Short Game: B   Putting: C-

---

Sjöland, Patrik (Sweden) (43)
b. Boras, Sweden 5/13/1971. 5'9" 165 lbs. TP: 1990. Played the Challenge circuit for several years before reaching the E Tour (via Q School) in 1996. Quickly proved himself a capable earner before breaking through for his first win at the 1998 Italian Open, where he beat José María Olazábal and Joakim Haeggman by three. Edged Ian Woosnam by one to claim the 1999 Hong Kong Open (then sanctioned only by the Asian Tour) and made it three wins in three years by taking the 2000 Irish Open, where he beat Fredrik Jacobson by two. Saw his form decline markedly after 2004, and ceased competing regularly on the E Tour after 2010, only to return (via a 16th-place finish at Q School) for 2014. **Teams**: World Cup (3): 1996-98-99. **OWR Best**: 47 - Sep, 1998.

European PGA Tour Wins (2): 1998: Italian Open **2000**: Irish Open (Murphy's).

Asian Tour Wins (1): 1999: Hong Kong Open.

Other Wins: 1 Euro Challenge (1995)   +   2 Nordic League (2004-2013).

	96	97	98	99	00	01	02	03	04	05	06	07	08	09	10	11	12	13	14
Masters	-	-	-	MC	-	-	-	-	-	-	-	-	-	-	-	-	-	-	-
US Open	-	-	-	MC	-	-	-	-	-	-	-	-	-	-	-	-	-	-	-
British	-	-	T38	T18	MC	-	MC	-	-	73	-	-	-	-	-	-	-	-	-
PGA	-	-	MC	MC	-	-	-	-	-	-	-	-	-	-	-	-	-	-	-
Money (E)	58	17	5	43	23	93	86	97	55	149	-	133	119	181	171	-	-	-	168
OWR	296	133	50	86	93	244	348	370	237	372	416	573	516	591	752	-	-	-	1208

2014: E: 17 st / 9 ct / 0 t10. (T26 Wales). Finished 168th in $$$ in his first full E Tour campaign since 2010.

OUTLOOK: With his 2014 comeback coming up empty, he seems a longshot to find any real continuing success at this stage of the game.

STATS (LTD): Driving Distance: C-   Driving Accuracy: B   GIR: C-   Short Game: B+   Putting: B

Slattery, Lee Andrew (England) (36)
b. Southport, England 8/3/1978. 5'11" 175 lbs. TP: 1998. Was a three-time winner on the EuroPro mini-tour before winning twice on the Challenge Tour, the victories coming six years apart. Joined the E Tour in 2005 and lost his card in 2007 – by only €77. Twice played his way back via Q School before claiming his first E Tour victory at the 2011 Madrid Masters (where he beat Lorenzo Gagli by one) and retaining his card each year thereafter prior to finishing an agonizing 111th in $$$ in 2014. **OWR Best**: 160 - Oct, 2012.

European Tour Wins (1): 2011: Madrid Masters (Bankia).

Other Wins: 2 Euro Challenge (2004-2010)   +   3 EuroPro (2001-2004).

	04	05	06	07	08	09	10	11	12	13	14
Masters	-	-	-	-	-	-	-	-	-	-	-
US Open	-	-	-	-	-	-	-	-	T73	-	-
British	-	-	T26	-	-	-	-	-	T64	-	-
PGA	-	-	-	-	-	-	-	-	-	-	-
Money (E)	-	144	91	118	107	136	239*	82	59	99	111
OWR	-	286	368	301	318	454	506	323	180	176	314	414

2014: E: 29 st / 14 ct / 3 t10. (4 Lyoness, T7 Italian, T9 Euro Masters). Missed three of his last four cuts to finish a heartbreaking 111th in $$$.

OUTLOOK: Will have only conditional status in 2015 and failing to keep his card by one spot. Is saddled with below-the-median numbers in both GIR and Short Game, a combination which obviously puts massive pressure on one's putter. Seems an E/Challenge borderline player going forward.

STATS: Driving Distance: B-   Driving Accuracy: B-   GIR: C+   Short Game: C+   Putting: B

Sloan, Roger Brandon (Canada) (27)
b. Calgary, Alberta, Canada 5/15/1987. 6'2" 175 lbs. College: U of Texas-El Paso. TP: 2009. Initially played the Canadian Tour for three seasons, winning twice in 2011. Joined the Web.com Tour in 2013 and missed 11 of his first 13 cuts before ultimately finishing the regular season ranked 87th in earnings. Returned in 2014 to win once and finish 24th in regular season earnings to clinch his PGA Tour status for 2015. **OWR Best**: 370 - Jul, 2014.

Other Wins: 1 Web.com (2014)   +   Western Championship (Canada): 2011.

	11	12	13	14
Masters	-	-	-	-
US Open	-	-	-	-
British	-	-	-	-
PGA	-	-	-	-
Money (A)	-	-	-	-
OWR	572	748	742	516

Sloan, Roger Brandon, Cont'd

2014: Played full-time on the Web.com Tour, where he won once and finished 24th in regular season $$$ to clinch his 2015 PGA Tour card.

OUTLOOK: Has played multiple seasons in Canada and the Web.com Tour, but only narrowly graduated the latter, largely on the strength of a July win in Nova Scotia which was his only top 10 of the season. Thus a longshot for the PGA Tour in 2015.

STATS (LTD): Driving Distance: B-   Driving Accuracy: B   GIR: B   Short Game: B   Putting: B

Slocum, Tyler Heath (USA) (40)
b. Baton Rouge, LA 2/3/1974. 5'8" 150 lbs. Three-time All-American at U of South Alabama. TP: 1996. Played on the same Milton (FL) HS team as Boo Weekley (Bubba Watson would follow immediately thereafter). After playing the 1997 season on the Web.com Tour, spent the better part of two years recovering from a bout with colitis. Returned to the Web.com in 2001, winning thrice and becoming the second player to receive an in-season battlefield promotion to the PGA Tour. Beginning in 2002, became a very steady money winner, never ranking worse than 80th in PGA Tour winnings until slipping to 112th in 2011. Claimed his first Tour win in 2004, edging Aaron Baddeley by one at the Chrysler Classic (Tucson). Closed with 64-66 to win the 2005 Southern Farm Bureau Classic, then waited four years to collect his biggest win, the 2009 Barclays, where he beat Ernie Els, Padraig Harrington, Steve Stricker and Tiger Woods by one. Won the inaugural (2010) McGladrey Classic, edging Bill Haas by one, before steadily slipping from 2011-2014. **Teams**: World Cup: 2007. **OWR Best**: 52 - Oct, 2010.

PGA Tour Wins (4): 2004: Tucson Open (Chrysler) **2005**: Southern Farm Classic **2009**: The Barclays **2010**: McGladrey Classic.

Other Wins: 3 Web.com (2001).

Amateur Wins: Spirit of America: 1995.

	02	03	04	05	06	07	08	09	10	11	12	13	14
Masters	-	-	-	-	-	-	T33	-	T18	MC	-	-	-
US Open	MC	-	-	-	-	-	T9	MC	MC	T11	-	-	-
British	-	-	-	-	-	-	T32	-	T60	-	-	-	-
PGA	22	-	MC	T47	T29	T23	MC	-	T33	MC	-	-	-
Money (A)	76	80	52	50	77	30	64	32	30	112	142	206*	141
OWR	161	194	203	105	110	73	100	71	56	155	349	564	338

2014: PGA: 23 st / 12 ct / 1 t10. (4 Wyndham). Missed the FedEx Cup Playoffs (129th in points) but played through the Web.com Finals.

OUTLOOK: Returns to the PGA Tour via the Web.com Finals (with the 33rd spot on the priority list) for the second straight year. Well established as one of the straightest drivers on Tour (6, 2, 2, 1, 5 in Driving Accuracy since 2010) and annually hits a ton of greens. His putter is the obvious fly in the ointment (149, 169, 182, 180 and 113 in SGP since 2010) but as a four-time Tour winner, he can clearly make some when he needs to.

STATS: Driving Distance: C-   Driving Accuracy: A+   GIR: A   Short Game: A-   Putting: C

Smith, Byron Jay (USA) (33)
b. Palm Springs, CA 3/31/1981. 6'0" 185 lbs. College: Pepperdine U. TP: 2003. Never got into an actual collegiate match at Pepperdine and quit before his junior year. Initially played on mini-tours and in Canada, where he ultimately won four times. Joined the Web.com full-time in 2013 before finishing 21st in regular season $$$ in 2014 to get his PGA Tour card. **OWR Best**: 302 - Jun, 2014.

Other Wins: 1 Web.com (2014) + Jane Rogers Championship (Canada): 2007   Mazatlan Classic (Canada): 2007   Times Colonist Open (Canada): 2009   Desert Dunes Classic (Canada): 2011.

	07	08	09	10	11	12	13	14
Masters	-	-	-	-	-	-	-	-
US Open	-	-	-	-	-	-	-	-
British	-	-	-	-	-	-	-	-
PGA	-	-	-	-	-	-	-	-
Money (A)	-	-	-	-	-	-	-	-
OWR	397	482	483	849	756	982	537	484

2014: Played full-time on the Web.com Tour, winning once and finishing 21st in regular season $$$ to clinch his 2015 PGA Tour card.

OUTLOOK: Has taken the scenic route to the PGA Tour, and proven himself capable of winning by taking four titles in Canada, then one on the Web.com, but... He never played in a single PGA Tour event prior to earning his card, so he must be considered a major longshot at this juncture.

STATS (LTD): Driving Distance: B   Driving Accuracy: B-   GIR: B-   Short Game: B-   Putting: B-

---

Smith, Cameron (Australia) (21)
b. Brisbane, Australia 8/18/1993. 6'0" 155 lbs. TP: 2013. Touted prospect who made a name for himself by winning both the Australian Boys and Stroke Play in 2012, then the Australian Amateur a year later. Turned pro soon thereafter and made a fast 2014 impact around the far east, putting together a run of seven straight top-10 finishes on three tours, highlighted by a T5 at the PGA Tour co-sanctioned CIMB Classic in Malaysia. **Teams**: Eisenhower Trophy: 2012. **OWR Best**: 211 - Nov, 2014.

Amateur Wins: Australian Am: 2013   -   Handa Jr Masters: 2009   Australian Boys: 2011   Australian Stroke Play: 2012   Nomura Cup: 2011.

	13	14
Masters	-	-
US Open	-	-
British	-	-
PGA	-	-
Money (As)	-	5*
OWR	899	190

2014: ASIA: 9 st / 8 ct / 7 t10. (T2 Indonesian Masters, T4 Selangor Masters). In only nine starts, made a significant impact on the Asian Tour, closing the season with six straight top 10s. Also made six starts in Australia, managing to finish 20th in $$$.

OUTLOOK: Though a limited statistical sampling may not reflect it, he did much to live up to some strong regional billing in 2014, especially on the Asian Tour. Might need some length to compete effectively on the bigger circuits, but it's very early yet. A regional prospect to watch.

STATS (LTD): Driving Distance: C+   Driving Accuracy: C+   GIR: A-   Short Game: B-   Putting: C+

Snedeker, Brandt (USA) (34) b. Nashville, TN 12/8/1980. 6'1" 185 lbs. College: Two-time All-American at Vanderbilt U. TP: 2004. 1998 U.S. Public Links champion who played his way up from the Web.com Tour to the PGA Tour in 2006, then cashed numerous checks en route to a 17th-place $$$ finish and Rookie of the Year honors in 2007. Claimed his first victory at the 2007 Wyndham Championship (Greensboro) when a closing 63 left him two clear of Billy Mayfair, Jeff Overton and Tim Petrovic. Also shot 61 over Torrey Pines' North Course during that season's Buick Invitational, including a 9-under-par 27 on the back nine (his outward half). Missed the latter part of 2009 with a wrist injury. A very steady money winner since 2007, finishing between 48th and 59th from 2008-2010, then climbing to 14th in 2011. Logged his second career win at the 2011 Heritage, where he beat Luke Donald in sudden death. Had post-season surgery to correct a degenerative condition in his right hip (had his left-hip done a year earlier). Got lucky in landing his third career win (the 2012 Farmers Insurance Open) when Kyle Stanley triple-bogeyed the 72nd, allowing Snedeker into a playoff, which he won on the second hole. Closed 2012 out with a bang, winning the Tour Championship at East Lake (by three over Justin Rose) and clinching 1st place in the $10 million FedEx Cup playoffs. After recording back-to-back 2nds (behind Tiger Woods and Phil Mickelson) in San Diego and Phoenix, won the 2013 ATT&T National Pebble Beach Pro-Am to climb to a career-best 4th in the OWR. Won again in 2013 at the Canadian Open, where he walked away from a quartet of players by three. **Awards:** PGA Tour Rookie of the Year: 2007. FedEx Cup Champion: 2012. **Teams:** Palmer Cup: 2003. Ryder Cup: 2012 (O: 1-2-0, S: 0-1-0). Presidents Cup: 2013 (2-3-0). World Cup: 2008. **OWR Best:** 4 - Feb, 2013.

PGA Tour Wins (6): 2007: Wyndham Championship **2011:** Heritage Classic **2012:** San Diego Open (Farmers), Tour Championship **2013:** AT&T Pro-Am, Canadian Open (RBC).
Other Wins: 2 Web.com (2006).
Amateur Wins: U.S. Amateur Public Links: 2003 — Tennessee HS (2): 1997-98   Dixie Am: 2003.

	04	05	06	07	08	09	10	11	12	13	14
Masters	T41	-	-	-	T3	MC	-	T15	T19	T6	T37
US Open	-	MC	-	T23	T9	MC	T8	T11	-	T17	T9
British	-	-	-	-	MC	MC	-	MC	T3	T11	T58
PGA	-	-	-	T18	T24	MC	T39	MC	MC	T66	T13
Money (A)	-	-	-	17	59	55	48	14	3	5	60
OWR	412	512	243	47	64	96	87	38	10	13	58

2014: PGA: 25 st / 20 ct / 3 t10.   (T5 Wyndham, T8 Arnold Palmer, T9 US Open).   Logged a career-low three top 10s, never seriously contended and finished a career-worst 86th in FedEx Cup points and 60th in $$$.
OUTLOOK: Is coming off the worst year of his PGA Tour career, a campaign in which he saw noticeable drops in his GIR (79 to 136), Strokes Gained Tee To Green (55 to 82), Proximity To Hole (13 to 67) and, more importantly (for him), his Scrambling (33 to 67), Total Putting (22 to 56) and SGP (4 to 27). At age 34, one would expect him to be entering his best years, so this may well prove just an off year, but so broad a numerical decline is a cause for concern. The smart money still sees him among America's best - but his 2015 season will bear close watching to see if this holds up.

STATS: Driving Distance: C+   Driving Accuracy: B+   GIR: B-   Short Game: A⇩   Putting: A+⇩

Snyder, Joseph Andrew III (Joey) (USA) (41) b. Springville, NY 6/7/1973. 6'2" 225 lbs. College: Arizona St. TP: 1996. Web.com Tour player in 1998 and '99, then played overseas and in Canada before getting his PGA Tour card via 2004 Q School. Enjoyed a fine rookie season in 2005 (72nd in $$$) before being afflicted by back and neck injuries which have imperiled his career since, limiting him to 14 starts from 2007-2012. Is still playing on his 2007 medical extension. **OWR Best:** 124 - Jan, 2006.

Amateur Wins: Porter Cup: 1996.

	05	06	07	08	09	10	11	12	13	14
Masters	-	-	-	-	-	-	-	-	-	-
US Open	-	-	-	-	-	-	-	-	-	-
British	-	-	-	-	-	-	-	-	-	-
PGA	-	-	-	-	-	-	-	-	-	-
Money (A)	72	253*	-	-	-	-	-	206*	204	-
OWR	133	360	-	-	-	-	-	973	847	1371

2014: PGA: 1 st / 0 ct / 0 t10.   Made only one PGA Tour start, missing the cut in Phoenix.
OUTLOOK: Begins 2015 with one event left on a medical extension that dates to back and neck injuries in 2007. Other than a seemingly anomalous 2005, has never cracked the top 200 in PGA Tour $$$ – and there's little to suggest that even healthy, he might do so now.

STATS (LTD): Driving Distance: B+   Driving Accuracy: B-   GIR: C+   Short Game: C-   Putting: C

Sonoda, Shunsuke (Japan) (25) b. Tokyo, Japan 9/26/1989. 5'10" 190 lbs. College: Meiji University. TP: 2010. Spent his junior high school years studying in Australia before returning to Japan for HS, where he was a teammate of Ryo Ishikawa at the Suginami-Gakuin School. Began playing the Japan Tour in 2010, soon winning the Mizuno Open (by three over Toru Taniguchi) to earn a berth in the British Open. Later that season, lost in playoffs at the Sega Sammy Cup (to Mamo Osanai) and the Fujisankei Classic (to ex-teammate Ishikawa). Took his second title at the 2013 Sega Sammy Cup, winning by three behind a third round 61. **Teams:** Eisenhower Trophy: 2008. **OWR Best:** 89 - Jan, 2011.

Japan Tour Wins (2): 2010: Mizuno Open (54H) **2013:** Sega Sammy Cup.

	10	11	12	13	14
Masters	-	-	-	-	-
US Open	-	-	-	-	-
British	MC	-	-	-	-
PGA	-	-	-	-	-
Money (J)	10	30	42	15	45
OWR	90	199	361	193	295

2014: JAP: 22 st / 11 ct / 3 t10.   (T3 Bridgestone, T6 Sega Sammy, T7 Heiwa).   Continued to play up-and-down golf while finishing 45th in $$$.
OUTLOOK: A talented but streaky young player who, despite mostly mid-range statistics, has demonstrated the ability to win when he heats up. He may gain a measure of consistency with maturity but for the moment, less-than-ideal putting numbers figure to keep him below Japan's top tier.

STATS: Driving Distance: B+   Driving Accuracy: C+   GIR: B-   Short Game: B   Putting: C+

Spieth, Jordan Alexander (USA) (21) b. Dallas, TX 7/27/1993. 6'1" 185 lbs. College: All-American at U of Texas. TP: 2012. Three-time AJGA All-American and 2009 AJGA Player Of The Year. Joined Tiger Woods as the only player to capture multiple U.S. Junior Amateur titles, winning in 2009 (at Trump National, NJ) and 2011 (at Gold Mountain, WA). As a 16-year-old amateur, T16 at 2010 Byron Nelson (on sponsor's exemption) after being T7 through 54 holes. After starring at the collegiate level, turned pro in late 2012 and began playing the PGA Tour without status, but quickly gained Special Temporary Membership after logging two top-10 finishes (including T2 at the Puerto Rico Open). Gained full status in July upon winning the John Deere Classic, where he beat David Hearn and Zach Johnson in a five-hole playoff (and became, at age 19, the Tour's youngest winner in 82 years). Was a regular contender thereafter and ended the year as a Captain's pick for the Presidents Cup team. Though winless in the U.S. in 2014, he won November's Australian Open in a six-shot runaway via a dazzling final-round 63, then scored a noteworthy unofficial win by taking the limited-field Hero World Challenge by a resounding 10 shots. **Awards:** PGA Tour Rookie of the Year: 2013. **Teams:** Walker Cup: 2011 (2-0-1). Ryder Cup: 2014 (O: 2-1-1, S: 0-0-1). Presidents Cup: 2013 (2-2-0). **OWR Best:** 7 - Apr, 2014.

PGA Tour Wins (1): 2013: John Deere Classic.
Australasian Tour Wins (1): 2014: Australian Open.
Other Wins: Hero World Challenge: 2014.
Amateur Wins: U.S. Junior Am (2): 2009-11   —   Texas HS (3): 2009-10-11.

	12	13	14
Masters	-	-	T2
US Open	T21	MC	T17
British	-	T44	T36
PGA	-	MC	MC
Money (A)	-	10	11
OWR	809	22	9

2014: PGA: 27 st / 24 ct / 8 t10. (2 T of C, T2 Masters, T4 AT&T Pro-Am, T4 Players, T5 WGC-Match Play, etc.). Though winless at home, backed up his splendid rookie year nicely, logging six top 10s in his first 14 starts, finishing 15th in Fedex Cup points and playing effectively on his first Ryder Cup team. Then scored a classic win at the Australian Open, where a closing 63 (which beat the field by three) sparked a six-shot victory.
OUTLOOK: Statistically, he possesses a well-rounded game, especially on and around the greens. It must be noted, however, that his ball striking dropped noticeably in 2014 (17 to 156 in Ball Striking, 8 to 146 in Total Driving, 37 to 152 in GIR) - though this may be partially due to in-season swing changes that hardly seemed an issue in the fall. Still, to remain as competitive as he was despite this says a lot; the only pressing question now is can he turn all of this highly impressive talent into a long ledger of victories? The bet here is yes, though perhaps not overnight.

STATS: Driving Distance: B   Driving Accuracy: B+ ⇩   GIR: B ⇩   Short Game: A   Putting: A-

---

Sriroj, Thammanoon (Thailand) (45) b. Bangkok, Thailand 6/24/1969. 5'8" 165 lbs. TP: 1991. One of Thailand's first international players who won five times on the old Asian Tour from 1996-2004. Also played the Japan Tour full-time from 2004-2007, never finishing better than 57th in $$$. Has played sporadically in Asian events co-sanctioned by the E Tour but never entered a PGA Tour-sanctioned event, save for an MC at the 2005 British Open. **Teams:** World Cup: 2000. **OWR Best:** 247 - Jan, 2005.

Asian Tour Wins (5): 1996: Bangkok Open, Tugu Pratama PGA **1997:** Pakistan Masters **1999:** Tianjin TEDA Open **2004:** Tianjin TEDA Open.
Other Wins: 1 Japan Challenge: 2003   +   Thailand PGA Championship: 1996.

	95	96	97	98	99	00	01	02	03	04	05	06	07	08	09	10	11	12	13	14
Masters	-	-	-	-	-	-	-	-	-	-	-	-	-	-	-	-	-	-	-	-
US Open	-	-	-	-	-	-	-	-	-	-	-	-	-	-	-	-	-	-	-	-
British	-	-	-	-	-	-	-	-	-	-	MC	-	-	-	-	-	-	-	-	-
PGA	-	-	-	-	-	-	-	-	-	-	-	-	-	-	-	-	-	-	-	-
Money (AS)	48	3	13	48	10	55	18	5	7	18	14	35	29	92	60	79	98	76	73	115
Money (J)	-	-	-	-	-	-	-	-	-	57	70	64	119	-	-	-	-	-	-	-
OWR	-	899	858	787	741	-	-	488	366	256	321	424	674	944	453	636	-	875	638	1249

2014: ASIA: 16 st / 6 ct / 0 t10. (T24 Dubai). Slipped significantly, failing to log a top 10 and finishing a career-worst 115th in $$$.
OUTLOOK: Plays a shortish schedule (has only once made 20 Asian Tour starts in the last decade) and, at 45, now appears on the downside.

STATS: Driving Distance: B-   Driving Accuracy: D   GIR: D   Short Game: B+   Putting: A

Stadler, Kevin (USA) (34) b. Reno, NV 2/5/1980. 5'10" 250 lbs. College: USC. TP: 2002. An AJGA All-American who followed in his father's footsteps by playing collegiately at USC. Won twice on the Web.com Tour in both 2004 and 2006 but first came to international note by edging Nick O'Hern by two to claim the E-Tour co-sanctioned 2006 Johnnie Walker Classic in Australia. Also won the 2005 Argentine Open, where he edged homestanding Angel Cabrera by two. After finishing 168th in earnings in 2005, has remained a full-time PGA Tour player since 2007, finishing a career-best 36th in earnings in 2014. Claimed his first PGA Tour win at the 2014 Waste Management Phoenix Open, edging Bubba Watson and Graham DeLaet by one. **OWR Best:** 52 - Apr, 2014.

PGA Tour Wins (1): 2014: Phoenix Open (Waste Management) .
European Tour Wins (1): 2006: Johnnie Walker Classic.
Int'l Wins (2): 2005: Argentine Open.
Other Wins: 4 Web.com (2004-2006)   +   1 Euro Challenge (2006)   Colorado HS: 1997   Champions Challenge (w/C. Stadler): 1999   Colorado Open: 2002.
Amateur Wins: Junior World (15-17): 1997.

	04	05	06	07	08	09	10	11	12	13	14
Masters	-	-	-	-	-	-	-	-	-	-	T8
US Open	65	-	MC	-	-	-	-	-	-	-	T63
British	-	-	-	T51	T58	-	-	-	-	-	T39
PGA	-	-	-	-	-	-	MC	-	-	MC	T65
Money (A)	-	168	-	124	145	97	105	111	54	68	36
OWR	361	266	118	167	309	278	246	330	126	113	70

Stadler, Kevin, Cont'd

2014: PGA: 26 st / 21 ct / 3 t10. (Won Phoenix, T8 Masters, T10 McGladrey). Scored his first PGA Tour win and finished 38th in FedEx Cup points.

OUTLOOK: After bouncing around abroad for several years, has found success on the PGA Tour, cracking the top 75 in $$$ the last three seasons. A very strong tee-to-greener (9 in GIR, 10 in Ball Striking, 24 in Total Driving) who struggles comparatively around the greens. Like many a top ball striker, his putter may limit his upside, but on weeks when it gets hot, he's likely to contend. May climb a little further before he's reached his peak.

STATS: Driving Distance: B+   Driving Accuracy: A-   GIR: A+   Short Game: C   Putting: C

Stal, Gary (France) (22)
b. Decines, France 2/9/1992. 5'10" 150 lbs. TP: 2012. French prospect who has been somewhat overlooked due to the presence of Dubuisson, Levy, Wattel, etc. Spent 2012 and '13 on the Challenge Tour, where he won twice in the former year but narrowly missed earning his E Tour card after finishing 17th in $$$. Eventually moved up to the big circuit for 2014 via Q School, then kept his card by finishing 89th in $$$ as a rookie. **OWR Best:** 279 - Aug, 2012.

Other Wins: 2 Euro Challenge (2012) + French Professional: 2012.

Amateur Wins: French Am: 2011.

	12	13	14
Masters	-	-	-
US Open	-	-	-
British	-	-	-
PGA	-	-	-
Money (E)	-	-	89
OWR	325	630	435

2014: E: 25 st / 21 ct / 1 t10. (T8 Irish). Though he logged only one top-10 finish, kept his card as a rookie by finishing 89th in $$$.

OUTLOOK: Continues to play largely under the radar, partially because he never contended as a rookie, instead playing steady (if unspectacular) golf en route to retaining his card. A very limited statistical sampling suggests a skilled iron player who can hit greens - but it's very early.

STATS (LTD): Driving Distance: B-   Driving Accuracy: B   GIR: A-   Short Game: C+   Putting: B-

---

Stallings, Scott Robert (USA) (29)
b. Worcester, MA 3/25/1985. 6'0" 195 lbs. College: Tennessee Tech. TP: 2007. Spent three years playing mini-tours after turning pro before missing his 2010 PGA Tour card by a single shot at 2009 Q School. After spending 2010 on the Web.com circuit, began 2011 playing PGA Tour events on sponsor exemptions before finishing 3rd at the Transitions Championship, then eventually landing his first Tour victory (in his 21st start) at the Greenbrier Classic, where he defeated Bob Estes and Bill Haas in sudden death. Claimed his second Tour win at the 2012 True South Classic (played opposite the British Open) where he edged Jason Bohn by two. Took his third win on a larger stage, edging five players with a 72nd-hole birdie at the 2014 Farmers Insurance Open at Torrey Pines. **OWR Best:** 53 - Jan, 2014.

PGA Tour Wins (3): 2011: Greenbrier Classic **2012:** True South Classic **2014:** San Diego Open (Farmers).

	11	12	13	14
Masters	-	T27	-	MC
US Open	-	-	T53	-
British	-	-	MC	MC
PGA	MC	MC	T55	MC
Money (A)	41	66	54	75
OWR	145	123	106	125

2014: PGA: 28 st / 12 ct / 1 t10. (Won Farmers). Won in San Diego (his lone top 10 of the year) and finished 84th in FedEx Cup points.

OUTLOOK: A very streaky player who actually missed more cuts (59) than he's made (50) over his first four seasons, yet has three victories and four top-75 $$$ rankings to his credit. A power-oriented sort, but he saw multiple declines in ball striking in 2014, including 76 to 123 in Ball Striking, 50 to 92 in Total Driving and 104 to 140 in GIR. Nothing catastrophic, but his consistency surely won't begin to improve with those types of numbers.

STATS: Driving Distance: A   Driving Accuracy: C   GIR: B ⇓   Short Game: C   Putting: C+

Stankowski, Paul Francis (USA) (45)
b. Oxnard, CA 12/2/1969. 6'1" 185 lbs. College: U of Texas-El Paso. TP: 1991. Initially looked destined for a strong PGA Tour career, winning the 1996 Atlanta Classic (in a playoff with Brandel Chamblee) and the 1997 Hawaiian Open (also in sudden death, over Jim Furyk and Mike Reid), and finishing among the top 125 $$$ winners for nine of his first 10 seasons. Missed later half of 2004 and all of '05 with wrist injury, and was later afflicted by shoulder problems, with his form never returning thereafter. Currently plays a very limited schedule off of Past Champion status. **OWR Best:** 25 - Sep, 1997.

PGA Tour Wins (2): 1996: Atlanta Classic (BellSouth) **1997:** Hawaiian Open.
Japan Tour Wins (1): 1996: Casio World Open.
Other Wins: 1 Web.com (1996) + 1 Gateway (2009)   Kapalua International: 1996.

	94	95	96	97	98	99	00	01	02	03	04	05	06	07	08	09	10	11	12	13	14
Masters	-	-	MC	T5	T39	-	-	-	-	-	-	-	-	-	-	-	-	-	-	-	-
US Open	MC	-	-	T19	MC	-	-	-	T62	-	-	-	-	-	-	-	-	-	-	-	-
British	-	-	-	-	MC	-	-	-	-	-	-	-	-	-	-	-	-	-	-	-	-
PGA	-	MC	T47	T67	MC	-	T41	74	-	-	-	-	-	-	-	-	-	-	-	-	-
Money (A)	106	133	52	21	96	113	70	69	118	89	150*	-	-	171	178	210*	206*	137	177	225*	-	257*
OWR	329	293	59	31	76	190	120	125	230	193	222	673	573	552	676	878	396	539	-	-	-

2014: PGA: 3 st / 1 ct / 0 t10. (T72 Puerto Rico). Made only three starts, all in light-field events.

OUTLOOK: Playing (sparingly) on Past Champion status. At age 45, seems to have little intention of expanding his schedule regardless.

STATS (LTD): Driving Distance: B-   Driving Accuracy: C   GIR: B-   Short Game: C   Putting: B+

Stanley, Kyle Matthew (USA) (27)   b. Gig Harbor, WA 11/19/1987. 5'11" 165 lbs. Two-time All-American and Hogan Award winner (2009) at Clemson U. TP: 2009. Two-time AJGA All-American and a star at Clemson, where he played in the 2007 Walker Cup. Turned pro after finishing 53rd at the 2009 US Open. Played the Web.com Tour in 2010 (35th in $$$) before moving to the PGA Tour via Q School. Then enjoyed a strong 2011 rookie campaign in which he finished 55th in $$$. Suffered a heartbreaking loss at the 2012 Farmers Insurance Open (San Diego) when he led by three going to the last, made a triple-bogey 8 on the 18th, then lost a playoff to Brandt Snedeker. Amazingly, rebounded to win the Waste Management Phoenix Open the next week, beating Ben Crane by one. **Teams:** Walker Cup: 2007 (0-3-0). **OWR Best:** 47 - Mar, 2012.

PGA Tour Wins (1): 2012: Phoenix Open (Waste Management).

Amateur Wins: Southern Am (2): 2006-08   –   Sahalee Players: 2006   Jones Cup: 2009.

	08	09	10	11	12	13	14
Masters	-	-	-	-	MC	-	-
US Open	MC	53	-	-	MC	73	-
British	-	-	-	T44	T39	MC	-
PGA	-	-	-	-	MC	MC	-
Money (A)	-	-	-	55	32	62	148
OWR	-	571	358	148	76	128	352

2014: PGA: 28 st / 16 ct / 1 t10. (T8 Barracuda). Had a career-worst year, finishing 158th in FedEx Cup points, then failed in the Web.com Finals.

OUTLOOK: One of the Tour's more powerful-yet-controlled ball strikers (28 in Ball Striking, 20 in Total Driving) but has to work a bit harder around the greens. Seemed on the verge of stardom when he won at Phoenix in 2012 (after giving away the Farmers a week earlier) but fell apart in 2014. Is still comfortably in his 20s but if he's to going to develop into the player of his potential, he needs to get things turned around pretty quickly.

STATS: Driving Distance: A   Driving Accuracy: B-   GIR: A   Short Game: C   Putting: C-

---

Steele, Brendan (USA) (31)   b. Idyllwild, CA 4/5/1983. 6'2" 175 lbs. College: U of California-Riverside. TP: 2005. A two-time Academic All-American who began his professional career by claiming four titles on the 2005 Golden State Tour. Next spent two years in Canada, then three on the Web.com Tour before finishing 6th in $$$ during a one-win 2010, which graduated him to the PGA Tour for 2011. Wasted little time finding success, breaking through to victory in just his 12th start with a one-shot triumph over Charley Hoffman and Kevin Chappell at the Texas Open. Has leveled off – but annually retained his card – ever since. **OWR Best:** 102 - Jun, 2014.

PGA Tour Wins (1): 2011: Texas Open (Valero).

Other Wins: 1 Web.com (2010).

Amateur Wins: Shark Shootout (w/K. Bradley): 2011.

	10	11	12	13	14
Masters	-	-	MC	-	-
US Open	-	-	-	MC	-
British	-	-	-	-	MC
PGA	-	T19	-	-	T59
Money (A)	-	38	110	82	78
OWR	192	126	204	184	152

2014: PGA: 26 st / 18 ct / 4 t10. (T5 Travelers, T5 Quicken Loans, T6 Phoenix, T10 Northern Trust). Finished 79th in FedEx Cup points.

OUTLOOK: Statistically a mid-range player who won as a rookie and has developed into a steady earner ever since. A solid ball striker (48 in Total Driving, 45 in Ball Striking, 53 in GIR) who may have the tools to climb a little higher. Should be just about ready to win again.

STATS: Driving Distance: B+   Driving Accuracy: B+   GIR: B+   Short Game: B-   Putting: B

Stefani, Shawn Anthony Peter (USA) (33)   b. Baytown, TX 12/2/1981. 6'2" 205 lbs. College: Lamar U. TP: 2005. A mini-tour player for several years after turning pro (where he won three times in 2009-2010). Joined the Web.com Tour in 2012, won twice and finished 6th in $$$ to graduate to the PGA Tour. Flirted with keeping his card in 2013 (a season shortened slightly by an August neck injury) before doing so in a strong 2014 in which he climbed to 77th in earnings. **OWR Best:** 110 - Nov, 2014.

Other Wins: 2 Web.com (2012)   +   2 Adams (2007-2010)   1 NGA/Hooters (2011)   Texas State Open: 2011.

	09	10	11	12	13	14
Masters	-	-	-	-	-	-
US Open	MC	-	-	-	T59	-
British	-	-	-	-	-	MC
PGA	-	-	-	-	-	69
Money (A)	-	-	-	-	136	77
OWR	-	-	-	199	288	115

2014: PGA: 17 st / 13 ct / 2 t10. (2 Quicken Loans, 5 Houston). Finished 83rd in FedEx Cup points, making good in his second PGA Tour try.

OUTLOOK: Cleared a two-event medical extension to begin 2014 and played quite well thereafter. Has the requisite power to compete but he saw large jumps in several categories (129 to 60 in GIR, 108 to 6 in Total Driving, 125 to 29 in Ball Striking) which may not prove sustainable. On the other hand, his SGP dropped from 37 to 126, so perhaps these offset? It will be interesting to see if he can maintain this level of play in 2015.

STATS: Driving Distance: A   Driving Accuracy: B   GIR: B   Short Game: B   Putting: B-

---

Stenson, Henrik (Sweden) (38)   b. Gothenburg, Sweden 4/5/1976. 6'1" 175 lbs. TP: 1999. Sweden's highest-ranked male pro ever (4th, May, 2009 and 3rd, November, 2013). Spent 15 months as a fixture in the OWR top 10, from August 2008 through all of 2009. A top-10 finisher in the E Tour Order of Merit from 2005-2008. Won the 2006 BMW International by closing with 68, then beating Retief Goosen and Padraig Harrington with an eagle on the first playoff hole. Jumped into the OWR top 10 for the first time after beating Tiger Woods and Ernie Els at the 2007 Dubai Desert Classic, then defeating Geoff Ogilvy 2 & 1 to win the WGC Match Play in February. Climbed still another notch by winning the 2009 Players

Stenson, Henrik, Cont'd

Championship, closing with 66 to beat Ian Poulter by four. Gained worldwide attention after stripping to his underwear in order to keep his clothes clean while blasting from a water hazard at the 2009 WGC-CA Championship. Struggled through a tough 2010 wherein he slipped to 134th in PGA Tour $$$ (in 15 starts) and sunk even lower in 2011, spurred by financial problems stemming from investing through swindler Allen Stanford. Finally broke a three-and-a-half year slump by claiming the 2012 South African Open, cruising past George Coetzee by four. Added a third PGA Tour win at the 2013 Deutsche Bank Championship (where he beat Steve Stricker by two), then claimed the season-ending Tour Championship and with it the FedEx Cup, with its $10 million bonus. A month later, completed a unique double by winning the E Tour's four-event Final Series, led by a spectacular six-shot triumph at the season-ending Tour Championship in Dubai, in which his GIR for the week was 94%. Remained winless throughout an otherwise solid 2014 until successfully defending his title at the Tour Championship in Dubai, where he birdied the last two to beat Dubuisson, Rose and McIlroy by two. **Awards:** FedEx Cup Champion: 2013. **Teams:** Eisenhower Trophy: 1998. Ryder Cup (3): 2006-08-14 (O: 5-4-2, S: 1-2-0). Seve Trophy (2): 2005-09. World Cup (4): 2005-06-08-09. **OWR Best:** 2 - May, 2014.

PGA Tour Wins (4): 2007: WGC-Match Play **2009:** Players Championship **2013:** Deutsche Bank Championship, Tour Championship.

European Tour Wins (8): 2001: Benson & Hedges Int'l **2004:** The Heritage **2006:** Qatar Masters, BMW Int'l **2007:** Dubai Classic **2012:** South African Open **2013:** Dubai World Championship **2014:** Dubai World Championship.

Sunshine Tour Wins (1): 2008: Million Dollar Challenge.

Other Wins: 3 Euro Challenge (2000).

Amateur Wins: Italian Am Stroke Play: 1996   Greek Am Stroke Play: 1997.

	00	01	02	03	04	05	06	07	08	09	10	11	12	13	14
Masters	-	-	-	-	-	-	MC	T17	T17	T38	MC	MC	T40	T18	T14
US Open	-	-	-	-	-	-	T26	MC	MC	9	T29	T23	-	T21	T4
British	-	MC	-	-	-	T34	T48	MC	T3	T13	T3	68	-	2	T39
PGA	-	-	-	-	-	T47	T14	MC	T4	T6	MC	-	-	3	T3
Money (A)	-	-	-	-	-	-	-	40	-	-	134	166	115	2	49
Money (E)	-	44	176	68	32	8	6	4	7	18	49	136	40	1	2
OWR	178	82	336	316	145	32	12	16	8	8	51	207	53	3	2

2014: PGA: 15 st / 14 ct / 3 t10.   (T3 PGA, T4 US Open, T5 Arnold Palmer).   E: 11 st / 10 ct / 8 t10.   (Won Tour Champ, 2P BMW Int'l, 2 World Match Play, 3 Turkey, 4 Nedbank, etc.).   Though not quite the player he was in 2013, still enjoyed a fine year, successfully defending his title at the DP World Tour Championship and finishing 2nd in E Tour $$$. Remained an elite ball striker and stayed among the OWR top 5 for the entire year.

OUTLOOK: Has emerged over the last two years as one of the game's elite ball strikers (1 in Ball Striking for the second straight year, 8 in GIR, 2 in Total Driving) who held up fairly well following his epic 2013. At age 38, has recovered from his 2011 financially related doldrums and now appears ready to hang around the top for a while. For the second straight year, we'll suggest that his ball striking has to cool off at some point (he was 87 in GIR in 2012) but his all-around game has become strong enough that he should be able to weather the storm when that time comes.

STATS: Driving Distance: B+   Driving Accuracy: A   GIR: A   Short Game: B   Putting: B

Sterne, Richard (South Africa) (33)

b. Pretoria, South Africa 8/27/1981. 5'7" 150 lbs. TP: 2001. Dominant South African amateur who met with early success in Europe, winning his first E Tour event at the 2004 Madrid Open. Added the Wales Open in 2007, edging four players by one at Celtic Manor. Having already won the 2005 Nashua Masters, exploded on home soil in 2008, claiming the 2008 Sunshine Order of Merit behind an early win at the Joburg Open and back-to-back late-season triumphs at the Alfred Dunhill Championship and the South African Open. Missed the most of 2010 and '11 with a disc problem in his back but returned to form with a vengeance in 2013, winning a second Joburg Open title (in a seven-shot runaway over Charl Schwartzel), finishing a career-best 8th in E Tour $$$ and winning a spot on the Presidents Cup team. **Teams:** Presidents Cup: 2013 (0-4-0). World Cup (3): 2006-08-09. **OWR Best:** 29 - Jan, 2008.

European Tour Wins (6): 2004: Madrid Open **2007:** Wales Open **2008:** Joburg Open, Alfred Dunhill Championship ('09), South African Open ('09) **2013:** Joburg Open

Sunshine Tour Wins (2): 2005: Nashua Masters **2007:** Tour Championship.

Other Wins: Rye Hill Championship (England): 2001.

Amateur Wins: South African Am: 1999   Indian Am: 2001   –   South African Jr: 1999   Southern Cross (Australia): 2000   South African Am Stroke Play: 2001.

	01	02	03	04	05	06	07	08	09	10	11	12	13	14
Masters	-	-	-	-	-	-	-	T25	MC	-	-	-	T25	-
US Open	-	-	-	-	-	-	-	-	MC	-	-	-	-	-
British	-	-	-	-	-	MC	MC	MC	T34	-	-	T39	T21	MC
PGA	-	-	-	-	-	-	WD	-	-	-	-	-	MC	T36
Money (E)	-	-	76	70	44	78	14	75	42	-	-	-	8	48
Money (SA)	35	10	26*	12*	27*	6*	5*	1*	6*	23*	-	11*	4*	-
OWR	514	385	313	213	130	196	44	43	93	413	-	154	51	87

2014: E: 17 st / 12 ct / 2 t10.   (T4 WGC-Cadillac, T6 Dunhill Links,).   After a healthy 2013, missed four months (March-June) with a torn labrum, then returned to finish 48th in E Tour $$$. Then played through the Web.com Finals to gain PGA Tour status (for the first time) in 2015.

OUTLOOK: Appeared capable of achieving greatness prior to his back problems, so little he does going forward can really be considered a surprise. Plays a very well-rounded game, utilizing considerable length for a smallish man, very consistent overall ball striking and a deft touch around the green. The only question is his health; if his back and shoulder hold up, he may soon once hold a regular spot among the world's top 50.

STATS: Driving Distance: B+   Driving Accuracy: B   GIR: A-   Short Game: B-   Putting: A-

---

Stolz, Andre Pierre (Australia) (44)

b. Brisbane, Queensland, Australia 5/10/1970. 5'11" 180 lbs. TP: 1992. Three-time winner on his home Australasian Tour (including a two-shot triumph over Brett Rumford at the 2000 Tour Championship) before coming to America and surprising everyone by winning the 2004 Las Vegas Classic (edging three players by one stroke) in his 21st PGA Tour start. Only returned for 13 events in 2005 following a significant wrist injury. Later retired for three years before returning to the limelight Down Under with a win at the 2009 Victorian PGA. Further emerged as a star on the OneAsia circuit, where he won twice, and topped the Order of Merit, in 2011. Won the Australasian Tour's 2013 South Pacific Open, beating Michael Wright on the fifth hole of sudden death. **OWR Best:** 53 - Apr, 2003.

Stolz, Andre Pierre, Cont'd

PGA Tour Wins (1): 2004: Las Vegas Classic (Michelin).
Japan Tour Wins (1): 2003: Token Homemate Cup.
Australasian Tour Wins (5): 2000: Tour Championship **2002:** Queensland PGA, Victorian Open **2009:** Victorian PGA **2013:** South Pacific Open.
OneAsia Tour Wins (2): 2011: Indonesia PGA, Thailand Open.
Other Wins: 1 Web.com (2003).

	00	01	02	03	04	05	06	07	08	09	10	11	12	13	14
Masters	-	-	-	-	-	-	-	-	-	-	-	-	-	-	-
US Open	-	-	-	-	-	-	-	-	-	-	-	-	-	-	-
British	-	-	-	-	-	-	-	-	-	-	-	-	-	-	-
PGA	-	-	-	MC	-	-	-	-	-	-	-	-	-	-	-
Money (A)	-	-	-	-	101	215*	-	-	-	-	-	-	-	-	-
Money (O)	-	-	-	-	-	-	-	-	-	-	8	1	54*	50	-
OWR	228	479	133	101	149	250	-	-	663	816	360	232	597	687	1048

2014: Made only six starts all year, five on the Australasian Tour where he made two cuts and finished 146th in $$$.
OUTLOOK: Has had an up-and-down, injury-affected career that has likely seen its best days – but he still might make a splash or two at home.

STATS: Driving Distance: --   Driving Accuracy: --   GIR: --   Short Game: --   Putting: --

---

Storm, Graeme Raymond (England) (36)

b. Hartlepool, England 3/13/1978. 5'11" 175 lbs. TP: 2000. The 1999 British Amateur champion initially struggled as a professional, playing three unsuccessful years on the E Tour before spending two years rebuilding on the Challenge circuit. A two-win 2004 helped him return to the E Tour where he would claim his first victory at the 2007 French Open, edging Søren Hansen by one.
Teams: Walker Cup: 1999 (2-2-0). Seve Trophy: 2007. **OWR Best:** 102 - Aug, 2008.

European Tour Wins (1): 2007: French Open.
Other Wins: 2 Euro Challenge (2004).
Amateur Wins: British Am: 1999   –   English Under-16: 1994   European Jr: 1996   English Boys Stroke Play: 1996.

	99	00	01	02	03	04	05	06	07	08	09	10	11	12	13	14
Masters	-	MC	-	-	-	-	-	-	-	-	-	-	-	-	-	-
US Open	-	-	-	-	-	-	MC	-	-	-	-	-	-	-	-	MC
British	MC	-	-	-	-	T78	-	MC	T39	T52	-	MC	-	-	-	
PGA	-	-	-	-	-	-	-	-	T62	-	-	-	-	-	-	-
Money (E)	Am	214*	121	211	-	-	31	53	16	50	49	83	101	87	75	72
OWR	741	676	367	693	682	299	162	186	149	137	150	254	297	336	303	289

2014: E: 30 st / 15 ct / 1 t10.   (2 Euro Masters).   Finished 2nd at the European Masters - his lone top 10 - en route to ranking 72nd in $$$.
OUTLOOK: Statistically is a slightly below-the-median player, with no particular area of strength to anchor his game. Still, he has, for a decade now, been a very steady E Tour earner and at age 36, there is little reason to think he won't continue quietly strumming along.

STATS: Driving Distance: C+   Driving Accuracy: B+   GIR: B-   Short Game: B-   Putting: B-

---

Strange, Scott (Australia) (37)

b. Perth, Western Australia 04/07/1977. 6'0" 170 lbs. TP: 2000. Australian player who found only limited success at home before winning twice on the Asian Tour, first at the 2005 Myanmar Open, then in a five-shot runaway at the 2006 Philippine Open. Joined the E Tour in 2006 and, after two difficult seasons, won the 2008 Wales Open (by four over Robert Karlsson) and the 2009 Volvo China Open, moving himself far more into the international spotlight. Also played several OneAsia events in 2009, winning the tour's first-ever Order of Merit. Returned to Europe (with limited success) from 2010-2012 before bouncing around Asia and Japan in 2013. **OWR Best:** 81 - Jun, 2008.

European Tour Wins (2): 2008: Wales Open **2009:** China Open (Volvo).
Asian Tour Wins (2): 2005: Myanmar Open **2006:** Philippine Open.
Other Wins: Vanuatu Open (Aus): 2002   Port Hedland Classic (Aus): 2003.
Amateur Wins: Western Australia Am: 1998   Lake Macquarie Am: 2000.

	00	01	02	03	04	05	06	07	08	09	10	11	12	13	14
Masters	-	-	-	-	-	-	-	-	-	-	-	-	-	-	-
US Open	-	-	-	-	-	-	-	-	-	-	-	-	-	-	-
British	-	-	-	-	-	-	-	MC	-	-	-	-	-	-	-
PGA	-	-	-	-	-	-	-	MC	-	-	-	-	-	-	-
Money (E)	-	-	-	-	-	149	106	32	41	148	125	188	-	-	-
Money (J)	-	-	-	-	-	-	-	-	-	-	-	-	-	-	63
Money (As)	-	-	-	-	17	14	22	9*	-	-	-	-	-	-	-
Money (O)	-	-	-	-	-	-	-	-	-	1	40*	-	33*	4	19*
OWR	-	-	682	841	-	367	224	239	117	91	300	458	780	248	364

2014: JAP: 19 st / 12 ct / 2 t10.   (T8 Sega Sammy, T9 Diamond Cup).   Made only a limited impact in his first full season in Japan, finishing 63rd in $$$.
OUTLOOK: Found a place on the Japan Tour after years in Europe and elsewhere, but his combination of limited length and below-the-median Short Game and Putting numbers likely limits his upside. Probably still has a win or two left in him, likely on the Asian or Australasian circuits.

STATS: Driving Distance: B-   Driving Accuracy: B+   GIR: B-   Short Game: C+   Putting: C+

Streb, Robert Charles (USA) (27)

b. Chickasha, OK 4/7/1987. 5'10" 165 lbs. College: Kansas St. TP: 2009. A mini-tour player for two years after turning pro, then played the Web.com circuit in 2012, where a 7th-place $$$ ranking moved him to the PGA Tour. Lost his card after 2013 but, playing on conditional status, retained it following a far more successful 2014. Ended the year by winning the 2015 McGladrey Classic (officially a

Streb, Robert Charles, Cont'd

2015 event) in a two-hole playoff with Brendon de Jonge and Will MacKenzie after shooting a Sunday 63. **OWR Best:** 87 - Nov, 2014.

PGA Tour Wins (1): 2014: McGladrey Classic.
Other Wins: 1 Web.com (2012)   +   Oklahoma Open (2): 2009-11.

	12	13	14
Masters	-	-	-
US Open	-	-	-
British	-	-	-
PGA	-	-	-
Money (A)	-	143	83
OWR	245	356	91

2014: PGA: 21 st / 17 ct / 2 t10.   (T2 New Orleans, T9 Deutsche Bank).   Easily retained his card for the first time, finishing 71st in FedEx Cup points.

OUTLOOK: Surprised many by comfortably retaining his card in 2014 off of conditional status. Another long-hitting youngster, but one with enough all-around game to rank 69 in GIR (82 in 2013) and 49 in Proximity To Hole. Very much a mid-range putter (75 in SGP, 111 in Total Putting) but is by no means poor, suggesting that with a bit more experience, he may begin to contend on a more regular basis.

STATS: Driving Distance: A   Driving Accuracy: B-   GIR: B+   Short Game: B   Putting: B

Streelman, Kevin Garrett (USA) (36)

b. Winfield, IL 11/4/1978. 5'10" 175 lbs. College: Duke U. TP: 2001. After turning pro, played all manner of mini-tours (but not the Web.com), logging four wins prior to getting through Q School in 2007. Initially proved himself a consistent earner, finishing between 62nd and 91st from 2008-2011 before slipping to 107th in 2012. T4 at the 2008 Barclays, where he missed a 16-foot birdie putt at to join the Vijay Singh-Sergio García-Kevin Sutherland playoff. Broke through for his maiden Tour victory at the 2013 Tampa Bay Championship (beating Boo Weekley by two) in his 153rd PGA Tour start. Broke a 58-year-old PGA Tour record by birdieing his final seven holes to win the 2014 Travelers Championship (Hartford). **Teams:** World Cup: 2013. **OWR Best:** 36 - May, 2013.

PGA Tour Wins (2): 2013: Tampa Bay Championship **2014**: Greater Hartford Open (Travelers).
Other Wins: 1 NGA/Hooters (2005)   +   3 Gateway (2007).

	08	09	10	11	12	13	14
Masters	-	-	-	MC	-	MC	T42
US Open	T53	-	-	67	-	MC	MC
British	-	-	-	MC	-	T79	T54
PGA	-	MC	-	T62	-	T12	MC
Money (A)	78	91	62	72	107	17	40
OWR	123	204	140	137	225	44	52

2014: PGA: 24 st / 17 ct / 2 t10.   (Won Travelers, T3 T of C).   Though somewhat less consistent than in 2013, followed up his breakout year nicely, winning for the second time (in Hartford) and finishing a solid 44th in FedEx Cup points.

OUTLOOK: Has climbed from the farthest reaches of mini-tour purgatory to the top of the PGA Tour. Statistically a very balanced player who traded Driving Distance (63 in 2012, 97 in 2014) for Driving Accuracy (89 to 16), with palpably good results (17 in Total Driving). However, his iron game fell in 2014 (54 to 137 in GIR) and his SGP (which has always fluctuated) fell from 501 to 102. At age 36, figures to hold this level for a few more years.

STATS: Driving Distance: B   Driving Accuracy: A-   GIR: B   Short Game: B+   Putting: B+

Stricker, Steven Charles (USA) (47)

b. Edgerton, WI 2/23/1967. 6'0" 190 lbs. Two-time All-American at U of Illinois. TP: 1990. Up-and-down career on the PGA Tour, peaking first in 1996 (when he finished 4th on the money list and won twice), then in early 2010 when he climbed to #2 in the Official World Ranking. Won the 1996 Western Open in an eight-shot waltz over Billy Andrade and Jay Don Blake at Cog Hill. Won 2001 WGC Match Play title in Australia, defeating Pierre Fulke 2 &1 in the event's only non-American playing. Returned from three-year stretch (2003-05) outside the top 150 in earnings with a solid 2006 (34th in $$$). Climbed even further in '07, including a win at the Barclays (Westchester) in the PGA Tour's first-ever FedEx Cup playoff event. As a result, won the PGA Tour's Comeback player of the Year award for two straight years (2006 and '07). Soared with a banner 2009 that included wins at Colonial, the John Deere and the Deutsche Bank Championship and a year-end #3 OWR ranking. Won the 2010 Northern Trust Open, where a remarkable second round 65 (in a driving rain) sparked a two-shot victory over Luke Donald. Was the only player in the field to post four rounds in the 60s en route to winning the 2011 Memorial Tournament by one over Brandt Jobe and Matt Kuchar. Two weeks later, birdied the 72nd hole to claim his third straight John Deere Classic. Following off-season concerns regarding a neck injury, began 2012 with his 12th PGA Tour win at the Hyundai Tournament of Champions, beating Martin Laird by three. Began 2013 by announcing that he would only be a part-time player thereafter – and promptly finished 7th in PGA Tour $$$ in only 13 starts. **Awards:** PGA Tour Comeback Player of the Year (2): 2006-07. **Teams:** Ryder Cup (3): 2008-10-12 (O: 3-7-1, S: 1-2-0). Presidents Cup (5): 1996-07-09-11-13 (14-10-0). **OWR Best:** 2 - Sep, 2009.

PGA Tour Wins (12): 1996: Kemper Open, Western Open (Motorola) **2001**: WGC-Match Play **2007**: Westchester Classic (Barclays) **2009**: Colonial Inv (Crown Plaza), John Deere Classic, Deutsche Bank Championship **2010**: Los Angeles Open (Northern Trust), John Deere Classic **2011**: Memorial Tournament, John Deere Classic **2012**: Tournament of Champions (Hyundai).
Int'l Wins (1): 1993: Canadian PGA.
Other Wins: Wisconsin Open (5): 1987*-90-91-98-00   Victorian Open (Canada): 1990   Dunhill Cup: 1996 (w/P.Mickelson & M.O'Meara)   Shark Shootout: 2009 (w/J.Kelly).
Amateur Wins: Wisconsin Jr (2): 1984-85   Wyoming Am Stroke Play: 1985   Wisconsin Am Stroke Play: 1985.

	93	94	95	96	97	98	99	00	01	02	03	04	05	06	07	08	09	10	11	12	13	14
Masters	-	-	-	MC	MC	-	T38	T19	T10	MC	-	-	-	-	MC	MC	T6	T30	T11	T47	T20	T31
US Open	83	-	T13	T60	T36	T5	5	T27	MC	T16	-	MC	-	T6	T13	T29	T23	T58	T19	T15	T8	T21
British	-	-	-	T22	T62	T52	MC	MC	T42	T59	-	-	-	-	T8	T7	T52	T55	T12	T23	-	-
PGA	-	-	T23	T26	MC	2	MC	MC	T66	MC	-	-	T7	T23	T39	MC	T18	T12	T7	T12	T7	
Money (A)	-	50	40	4	130	13	64	113	30	88	189	151	162	34	4	23	2	5	8	18	7	89
OWR	338	133	75	12	43	26	29	91	55	92	285	300	338	63	5	15	3	7	6	18	8	41

Stricker, Steven Charles, Cont'd

2014: PGA: 11 st / 11 ct / 2 t10. (T6 Memorial, T7 PGA).   The magic of his eight-top-10s-in-13-starts 2013 wore off, as he logged only two top 10s in 11 starts, finished 89th in $$$ and 116th in FedEx Cup points.

OUTLOOK: At age 47, he's finally starting to look like a part-time player, witnessing some huge declines in his ball striking numbers (2 to 162 in GIR, 5 to 178 in Ball Striking, 19 to 178 in Total Driving, etc.) as he ceased to contend seemingly on a weakly basis. But even going into his late 40s, his general accuracy and much-envied putting stroke remain intact, so one should not be surprised if he contends a few more times going forward.

STATS: Driving Distance: C+   Driving Accuracy: A-   GIR: A- ⇩   Short Game: A   Putting: A+

Stroud, Christopher James (USA) (32)
b. Nederland, TX 2/3/1982. 6'2" 180 lbs. Two-time All-American at Lamar U. TP: 2004. Winner of the 2003 North & South Amateur. After turning pro, played mini-tours (mostly the Hooters and Tight Lies) from 2004-2006 before tying for 16th at the 2006 Q School. Though winless, has steadily improved on Tour, cracking the top 100 in $$$ (85th) in 2011, then jumping to 55th in 2013 and 53rd in 2014. **Teams**: Palmer Cup: 2004. **OWR Best**: 74 - Apr, 2014.

Amateur Wins: North & South Am: 2003.
Other Wins: 1 NGA/Hooters (2005).

	07	08	09	10	11	12	13	14
Masters	-	-	-	-	-	-	-	-
US Open	MC	MC	MC	T47	-	-	-	-
British	-	-	-	-	-	-	-	MC
PGA	-	-	-	-	-	MC	MC	T65
Money (A)	133	155	113	102	85	105	55	53
OWR	342	417	351	278	205	260	81	108

2014: PGA: 25 st / 19 ct / 4 t10. (T3 CIMB, T3 Mayakoba).   Finished a career-best 53rd in $$$, and 47th in FedEx Cup points.

OUTLOOK: Shortish but fairly accurate ball striker who maintained his gains of 2013, mostly behind continued improvement in GIR (113 to 80), Total Driving 161 to 85) and Ball Striking (148 to 82). More of a check casher than contender to date, and the numbers suggest this is unlikely to change.

STATS: Driving Distance: B-   Driving Accuracy: B+   GIR: B   Short Game: A-   Putting: A-

---

Stuard, Brian Glen (USA) (32)
b. Jackson, MI 12/10/1982. 5'10" 175 lbs. College: Oakland (MI) U. TP: 2005. Began his career with two seasons of mini-tour golf before playing the Web.com Tour in 2008 and '09. Played through 2009 Q School but lost his card at the end of 2010 despite tying for 2nd at the Mayakoba Classic. Spent two more years on the Web.com, finishing 20th in 2012 to return to the PGA Tour, where he then made good, finishing 79th and 52nd in $$$ in 2013 and '14. **OWR Best**: 110 - May, 2014.

	10	11	12	13	14
Masters	-	-	-	-	-
US Open	-	-	-	MC	MC
British	-	-	-	-	-
PGA	-	-	-	-	MC
Money (A)	154	-	-	79	52
OWR	451	654	460	181	177

2014: PGA: 29 st / 17 ct / 4 t10. (2 Mayakoba, 5 Humana, 5 Heritage, 6 Hawaii).   Retained his card by finishing 51st in FedEx Cup pts.

OUTLOOK: Failed on his first PGA Tour try (2010) but seems to have established himself the second time around. Having largely maintained his statistical profile in year three, there is little to suggest that he can't continue playing at this level. Though well below the median lengthwise, if his short game and putting hold up, the idea of his winning - likely in a lighter-field event - becomes worthy of discussion.

STATS: Driving Distance: C+   Driving Accuracy: A   GIR: B-   Short Game: A-   Putting: A-

---

Sucher, Zachary Albert (USA) (28)
b. Atlanta, GA 10/2/1986. 6'0" 210 lbs. All-American at U of Alabama-Birmingham. TP: 2009. Was an All-State basketball player and led a four-time state golf championship team at St. Paul's Episcopal HS in Mobile, AL. Spent three years playing mini-tours before joining the Web.com circuit full-time in 2014, where he won once and finished 3rd in regular season. **OWR Best**: 186 - Aug, 2014.

Other Wins: 1 Web.com (2014).
Amateur Wins: Cardinal Am (2): 200708   Azalea Inv: 2008.

	13	14
Masters	-	-
US Open	-	-
British	-	-
PGA	-	-
Money (A)	-	-
OWR	726	216

2014: Played full-time on the Web.com Tour, where he won once and clinched a 2015 PGA Tour card by finishing 3rd in regular season $$$.

OUTLOOK: Coming off a strong Web.com campaign (six top 10s and 11 top 25s in 25 starts) and has thus far put up solid numbers with the putter, but his overall competitive record makes it hard to rate him above the middle of the pack within the 2015 rookie class.

STATS (LTD): Driving Distance: B+   Driving Accuracy: C   GIR: B   Short Game: B+   Putting: A-

---

Sullivan, Andrew (England) (28)
b. Nuneaton, England 5/19/1986. 5'9" 160 lbs. TP: 2011. Finished 3rd at 2011 E Tour Q School shortly after turning pro, then returned to take 3rd again in 2012 after finishing 145th in E Tour earnings and losing his card. Retained it, somewhat narrowly, in 2013, then soared in 2014, recording five top 10s and finishing 33rd in $$$. **Teams**: Walker Cup: 2011 (2-2-0). **OWR Best**: 147 - Nov, 2014.

Sullivan, Andrew, Cont'd

Amateur Wins: Scottish Am Stroke Play: 2011.

	12	13	14
Masters	-	-	-
US Open	-	-	-
British	-	-	-
PGA	-	-	-
Money (E)	145	98	33
OWR	394	364	150

2014: E: 31 st / 21 ct / 5 t10. (2 Hassan, 3 KLM, T4 Turkey, T5 Joburg, T8 Volvo China).   Climbed significantly for the third straight year, logging five top 10s and finishing a career-best 33rd in $$$.

OUTLOOK: Is a long and surprisingly accurate driver of the ball, and hits a large number of greens as a result. However, his putting numbers, while improved, still fall below the median, and therein lies the question. But given his overall ball striking, he figures to hang around for a while.

STATS: Driving Distance: A-   Driving Accuracy: A   GIR: B+   Short Game: B+   Putting: C+

Summerhays, Daniel Rich (USA) (31)
b. Farmington, UT 12/2/1983. 5'8" 185 lbs. All-American at Brigham Young U. TP: 2007. Nephew of former PGA Tour player Bruce Summerhays. Shot a 10-under-par 60 at Williamsburg, VA's Golden Horseshoe GC to tie the NCAA single-round scoring record while at Brigham Young. While still in school, became the first amateur to win a Web.com Tour event, claiming the Children's Hospital Invitational in Columbus, OH. Turned pro upon winning and became a Web.com regular through 2010, a season in which he twice finished 2nd and placed 5th in $$$. Struggled as a 2011 PGA Tour rookie (171st in $$$) but returned for 2012 via Q School to finish 92nd in $$$, then improved to 69th during a strong 2013 campaign. **OWR Best:** 92 - Aug, 2014.

Other Wins: 1 Web.com (2007).
Amateur Wins: Sahalee Players: 2007   Utah Am (2): 2000-01.

	10	11	12	13	14
Masters	-	-	-	-	-
US Open	MC	-	-	-	-
British	-	-	-	-	-
PGA	-	-	-	-	T33
Money (A)	-	171	92	69	69
OWR	256	429	232	136	139

2014: PGA: 27 st / 22 ct / 2 t10. (T2 Texas, T10 McGladrey).   Maintained his gains made in year three by finishing 57th in FedEx Cup points.

OUTLOOK: Is building around a solid, balanced game which has improved annually. Statistically, the big story is his putter, which has improved dramatically over the last four years (152, 120, 56, 9 in SGP, 156, 88, 42, 42 in Total Putting). If he can sustain most of these gains and hold his up-and-down ball striking numbers steady (150, 28, 108, 42 in GIR), he'll likely win (perhaps in a lighter-field event) sometime fairly soon.

STATS: Driving Distance: C+   Driving Accuracy: B+   GIR: B+   Short Game: B-   Putting: A-

---

Sutherland, Kevin John Woodward (USA) (50)
b. Sacramento, CA 4/4/1964. 6'1" 185 lbs. College: All-American at Fresno St. TP: 1987. Former collegiate walk-on whose brother David is a former PGA Tour player. Steady player who finished no worse than 67th on the money list from 1997-2003, and remained within the top 125 through 2010. Won 2002 WGC Match Play event after being seeded 62nd in a field of 64, beating Scott McCarron 1 up in the final. Finished 18th in $$$ in 2008 behind two 2nd-place finishes, losing in playoffs at both The Barclays and the Frys.com Open. Suffered neck and back injuries in 2011 which have limited him since, and he began 2013 on a medical extension. Shot the first 59 in Champions Tour history in the second round of the 2014 Dick's Sporting Goods Open. **OWR Best:** 32 - Feb, 2002.

PGA Tour Wins (1): 2002: WGC-Match Play.
Other Wins: Pebble Beach Inv: 2000.
Amateur Wins: California State Fair: 1984.

	96	97	98	99	00	01	02	03	04	05	06	07	08	09	10	11	12	13	14
Masters	-	-	-	-	-	-	MC	T33	-	-	-	-	-	T46	-	-	-	-	-
US Open	MC	-	MC	-	-	T44	T37	T28	MC	-	-	T58	-	T27	-	-	-	T67	MC
British	-	-	-	-	-	T9	MC	-	-	-	-	-	-	T60	-	-	-	-	-
PGA	-	T76	T44	MC	MC	MC	T43	T18	MC	77	-	T9	T63	T32	MC	-	-	-	-
Money (A)	135	52	66	63	66	32	36	67	85	101	115	67	18	73	118	178*	244*	178*	-
OWR	408	128	114	119	102	66	65	97	137	183	241	150	51	84	228	503	-	662	1047

2014: PGA: 1 st / 0 ct / 0 t10. MC at the U.S. Open. Also made seven Champions Tour starts in the latter half of the season.

OUTLOOK: Looks like he'll play regularly on the Champions Tour where, like most 50-year-olds PGA Tour veterans who've aged well, he'll be a threat.

STATS (LTD):   Driving Distance: B-   Driving Accuracy: A-   GIR: A   Short Game: B+   Putting: C-

---

Svoboda, Andrew Robert (USA) (35)
b. New Rochelle, NY 10/2/1979. 5'9" 200 lbs. College: St Johns U. TP: 2004. After winning both the Metropolitan Open and Amateur, turned pro and played mini-tours (winning once) prior to joining the Web.com Tour in 2010. Finished 21st in $$$ in 2012 (behind two runner-up finishes) to regain his PGA Tour card for 2013, then retained his card for 2014 by also playing enough Web.com events to finish 25th in regular season earnings. **OWR Best:** 143 - Jun, 2014.

Other Wins: 1 Web.com (2013)   +   Metropolitan (NY) Open: 2003*.
Amateur Wins: Metropolitan Am: 2004.

Svoboda, Andrew Robert, Cont'd

	06	07	08	09	10	11	12	13	14
Masters	-	-	-	-	-	-	-	-	-
US Open	MC	-	T71	MC	-	-	-	MC	-
British	-	-	-	-	-	-	-	-	-
PGA	-	-	-	-	-	-	-	-	-
Money (A)	-	-	-	-	-	-	-	209	88
OWR	-	-	-	-	514	644	483	251	178

2014: PGA: 24 st / 14 ct / 2 t10. (T2 New Orleans, T6 FedEx St Jude). Kept his card in year two, finishing 94th in FedEx Cup points.

OUTLOOK: Fared far better in his second year on the PGA Tour, due to marked increases in several ball striking categories (70 to 18 in GIR, 71 to 26 in Ball Striking). With those numbers he might have the stuff to stick around - but the short-off-the-tee/mediocre-putter recipe is seldom a great one.

STATS: Driving Distance: B   Driving Accuracy: B+   GIR: A-   Short Game: C+   Putting: B

Swafford, James Hudson (USA) (27)
b. Lakeland, FL 9/9/1987. 6'3" 200 lbs. College: Two-time All-American at U of Georgia. TP: 2011. An AJGA All-American. Redshirted his senior year at Georgia due to shoulder surgery. AJGA All-American. Played at Georgia with fellow PGA Tour players Brian Harman, Russell Henley and Harris English. Won Web.com's 2012 Stadion Classic (played over Georgia's home course) via a final-round 62. After an otherwise quiet season, gained 2014 PGA Tour status via a hot 2013 Web.com Finals. **OWR Best:** 290 - Oct, 2014.

Other Wins: 1 Web.com (2012).
Amateur Wins: Dogwood Inv: 2006.

	10	11	12	13	14
Masters	-	-	-	-	-
US Open	MC	-	-	-	MC
British	-	-	-	-	-
PGA	-	-	-	-	-
Money (A)	-	-	-	-	146
OWR	-	-	444	527	314

2014: PGA: 26 st / 11 ct / 1 t10. (T8 Hawaii). Finished 146th in FedEx Cup points as a rookie, but saved himself via the Web.com Finals.

OUTLOOK: Has shown himself a long, surprisingly accurate driver of the ball (4 in Total Driving) who can hit a lot of greens in regulation. Did little of distinction as a PGA Tour rookie but if he ever finds some magic with the putter, he could be a force to be reckoned with.

STATS (LTD): Driving Distance: A   Driving Accuracy: A-   GIR: A   Short Game: C   Putting: C

Tabuena, Miguel Luis (Philippines) (20)
b. Manila, Philippines 10/13/1994. 5'3" 130 lbs. TP: 2011. A touted prospect who, after claiming a silver medal at the 2010 Asian Games, played his way through 2010 Asian Tour Q School as a 16-year-old amateur, turning pro thereafter. Failed to make a major impact over his first two seasons, logging three top 10s but seldom contending – though he did win twice, with impressive performances, in domestic events in the Philippines. Is still widely viewed as the nation's best-ever prospect. **OWR Best:** 395 - Nov, 2014.

Other Wins: Splendido Classic (Philippines): 2012   Eastridge Classic (Philippines): 2012.

	11	12	13	14
Masters	-	-	-	-
US Open	-	-	-	-
British	-	-	-	-
PGA	-	-	-	-
Money (As)	62	82	107	37
OWR	797	724	744	406

2014: ASIA: 13 st / 8 ct / 2 t10. (2 Yeanger TPC, T7 Solaire). Climbed to a career-best 37th in $$$ in only 13 Asian Tour starts.

OUTLOOK: A highly rated prospect as a mid-teen but who initially struggled but is now showing signs as he reaches 20. Is a short-but-straight type (in part due to his limited size) who has thus far not adequately compensated with his longer irons and putter.

STATS: Driving Distance: C+   Driving Accuracy: A-   GIR: C   Short Game: B+   Putting: C+

Takayama, Tadahiro (Japan) (36)
b. Wakayama, Japan 2/12/1978. 5'9" 1705 lbs. TP: 1999. Won two smaller professional events before beginning full-time play on the Japan Tour in 2002. Appeared to be on his way into the circuit's upper ranks after a 2005 campaign which saw him finish 13th in $$$ and win both the Token Homemate Cup (beating Nozomi Kawahara in a playoff) and the late-season Okinawa Open (a part of the 2006 Order of Merit). Stepped back somewhat thereafter, however, before climbing again in 2010, when he claimed the Sun Chlorella Classic and finished 14th in $$$. Enjoyed a very strong 2011, finishing 2nd in $$$ and adding wins at the Token Homemate Cup (where he beat Shingo Katayama by two) and the Casio World Open. Backed off somewhat thereafter but remained a solid money winner through 2013. **OWR Best:** 103 - Dec, 2005.

Japan Tour Wins (5): 2005: Token Homemate Cup, Okinawa Open **2010**: Sun Chlorella Classic **2011**: Token Homemate Cup, Casio World Open.
Other Wins: PGA Rookie (Japan): 2001   Sankei Sports Open (Japan): 2002.

	00	01	02	03	04	05	06	07	08	09	10	11	12	13	14
Masters	-	-	-	-	-	-	-	-	-	-	-	-	-	-	-
US Open	-	-	-	-	-	-	MC	-	-	-	-	MC	-	-	-
British	-	-	-	-	T23	-	-	-	-	-	MC	MC	-	-	-
PGA	-	-	-	-	-	-	-	-	-	-	-	-	-	-	-
Money (J)	-	-	54	32	38	13	31	44	46	34	14	2	66	40	27
OWR	888	-	434	227	287	110	247	508	493	348	176	135	302	530	348

Takayama, Tadahiro, Cont'd

2014: JAP: 24 st / 23 ct / 5 t10. (6 Token Homemate, T6 Taiheiyo, T7 Kansai, T9 Mizuno, T9 Dunlop Phoenix).   Though winless, enjoyed an impressively consistent season, making 23 of 24 Japan Tour cuts on his way to recording his best $$$ ranking (27th) since 2011.

OUTLOOK: Statistically has generally been a below-the-median player, though his Short Game and Putting numbers have crept above it over the last few years. His 2011 campaign was clearly an outlier, but his five wins and very consistent earnings suggest a number of good years left to come.

STATS: Driving Distance: B   Driving Accuracy: B-   GIR: B-   Short Game: B+   Putting: B+

Takeya, Yoshitaka (Japan) (34)
b. Yamaguchi, Japan 1/27/1980. 5'5" 145 lbs. TP: 2005. A late-arriving presence on the Japan Tour, where he played only one full season and never logged a top 10 finish prior to blossoming in 2014. Came out of nowhere to win the Japan Tour Championship (by two over Sang-Hee Lee), then showed that performance not to be an outlier by posting four top 10s (plus an 11th) in five starts from the Diamond Cup to the Bridgestone Open. **OWR Best**: 198 - Dec, 2014.

Japan Tour Wins (1): 2014: Japan Tour Championship.

Other Wins: 1 Japan Challenge (2013).

	08	09	10	11	12	13	14
Masters	-	-	-	-	-	-	-
US Open	-	-	-	-	-	-	-
British	-	-	-	-	-	-	-
PGA	-	-	-	-	-	-	-
Money (J)	159*	134*	-	-	-	151	10
OWR	1381	1368	1322	1401	-	1508	199

2014: JAP: 21 st / 17 ct / 5 t10. (Won Tour Champ, T3 Bridgestone, T4 Toshin, T5 Diamond Cup, T8 Tokai).   Enjoyed one of the top breakout years anywhere on earth, winning once, logging four top 10s in a five-event autumn run, and rocketing from 151st to 10th in $$$.

OUTLOOK: It is virtually impossible to view the full body of work and not view his breakout 2014 as a one-time thing. Numerically, he lived and died with his putter, but if he can sustain the high-end stroke he demonstrated in 2014, perhaps he'll prove that conclusion wrong.

STATS (LTD): Driving Distance: B-   Driving Accuracy: B-   GIR: C+   Short Game: B+   Putting: A-

---

Tanaka, Hidemichi (Japan) (43)
b. Hiroshima, Japan 3/29/1971. 5'6" 135 lbs. TP: 1991. Diminutive player who was an elite performer on the Japan Tour prior to a semi-successful five-year stint in America from 2002-2006. Claimed 10 Japan Tour titles before leaving, including the 1998 Japan Open (a one-stroke triumph over Joe Ozaki), the 1999 Acom International (a five-shot runaway) and the 2000 Crowns, where he again left the field behind by that same five-stroke margin. Retained his card for four straight years in the U.S. but seldom contended, twice tying for third (at the 2004 B.C. Open and the 2005 Chrysler Championship). Has struggled in Japan since returning, and played limited schedules in recent years, making six, two and three starts annually from 2011-2013. **Teams**: World Cup (3): 2000-03-04. **OWR Best**: 59 - Jul, 1996.

Japan Tour Wins (10): 1995: Philip Morris **1996**: Pepsi Ube-Kosan **1998**: Aiful Cup, Japan Open, Okinawa Open **1999**: Acom Int'l **2000**: Dydo Shizuoka Open, The Crowns **2001**: Tsuruya Open, Mizuno Open.

Other Wins: 2 Japan Challenge (1995) +   Hirao Masaaki Pro-Am (Japan) (2): 1996-98   Hawaii Pearl Open: 2001.

	94	95	96	97	98	99	00	01	02	03	04	05	06	07	08	09	10	11	12	13	14
Masters	-	-	-	-	-	-	-	-	-	-	-	-	-	-	-	-	-	-	-	-	-
US Open	-	-	-	-	-	-	-	-	T37	T15	T36	-	-	-	-	-	-	-	-	-	-
British	-	-	T33	-	-	MC	-	MC	-	-	-	-	-	-	-	-	-	-	-	-	-
PGA	-	-	-	-	-	MC	79	MC	-	-	T55	-	-	-	-	-	-	-	-	-	-
Money (J)	242	6	16	44	3	12	5	6	-	-	-	-	-	178	-	77	87	111*	-	-	-
Money (A)	-	-	-	-	-	-	-	-	92	69	104	117	224	-	-	-	-	-	-	-	-
OWR	-	94	76	193	79	85	64	59	105	116	158	197	564	-	-	797	740	974	-	-	-

2014: JAP: 2 st / 0 ct / 0 t10.   Made only two starts in 2014, missing cuts at the Crowns and the Japan PGA Championship.

OUTLOOK: Appears unlikely to seriously compete going forward, but he's not too old to at least regain his competitiveness if he does.

STATS: Driving Distance: --   Driving Accuracy: --   GIR: --   Short Game: --   Putting: --

---

Tangkamolprasert, Pavit (Thailand) (25)
b. Bangkok, Thailand 5/2/1989. 5'7" 145 lbs. TP: 2007. After turning pro, played a full slate of Asian Tour events in 2008 but failed to retain his card. Has remained primarily on the Asian Developmental Tour since, winning once in 2013, then exploding via a three-win 2014 that saw him climb into the OWR 250, and which returned him to the big circuit. **OWR Best**: 214 - Dec, 2014.

Other Wins: 4 Asian Developmental (2013-2014)   +   SAT Thailand: 2011   Singha Gassan Championship (Thailand): 2012   Singha Gassan Classic (Thailand): 2102   Singha Artitaya Championship (Thailand): 2012   Singha Open (Thailand): 2014.

	08	09	10	11	12	13	14
Masters	-	-	-	-	-	-	-
US Open	-	-	-	-	-	-	-
British	-	-	-	-	-	-	-
PGA	-	-	-	-	-	-	-
Money (As)	125	117*	125*	-	165*	116*	103*
OWR	1381	1080	1191	1401	1492	865	214

2014: Starred on the Asian Developmental Tour, winning thrice to receive a late-season battlefield promotion to the Asian Tour.

OUTLOOK: A force on the second tier but has logged only one top-25 finish (T15 at the 2009 King's Cup) in nearly 50 career Asian Tour starts. He's young enough to still be growing, of course, and his confidence will be much higher, but keeping his card is probably a realistic 2015 goal.

STATS: Driving Distance: --   Driving Accuracy: --   GIR: --   Short Game: --   Putting: --

Taniguchi, Toru (Japan) (46) b. Nara, Japan 2/10/1968. 5'5" 155 lbs. TP: 1992. A leading Japanese star of his era and the winner of 19 Japan Tour titles since 1998. His most prestigious victories include the 2004 Japan Open (in a four-shot walkaway), the 2007 Japan Open (by two over Shingo Katayama), the 2005 Casio World Open (by two over Korea's J.D. Kim), plus a pair of Japan PGA Championships in 2010 and 2012. Also a three-time winner of the Bridgestone Open (2004, '11 and '12) and has recorded five multi-win seasons in his homeland (including four victories in 2002 and three in 2007). Won the Order of Merit in 2002 and '07, finished 2nd in 2000 and '04. Has made occasional PGA Tour appearances, including a 3rd–place finish at the 2001 WGC Match Play and 5th at the 2002 Los Angeles Open. Two-time winner in 2012, taking both his second Japan PGA Championship and his third Bridgestone Open. Declined incrementally in 2013 and '14, leaving him still highly relevant but not quite the force he used to be. **Teams:** World Cup: 2008. **OWR Best:** 27 - Dec, 2007.

Japan Tour Wins (19): 1998: Mitsubishi Galant **2000:** Acom Int'l, Philip Morris **2002:** Token Cup, Yomiuri Open, Acom Int'l (54H), Tokai Classic **2004:** Japan Open, Bridgestone Open **2005:** Casio World Open **2006:** Omaezaki Open **2007:** Hiroshima Open, Sega Sammy Cup, Japan Open **2009:** ANA Open **2010:** Japan PGA Championship **2011:** Bridgestone Open **2012:** Japan PGA Championship, Bridgestone Open.

	94	95	96	97	98	99	00	01	02	03	04	05	06	07	08	09	10	11	12	13	14
Masters	-	-	-	-	-	-	-	-	MC	MC	-	-	-	-	MC	-	-	-	-	-	-
US Open	-	-	-	-	-	-	-	MC	-	MC	-	MC	MC	MC	MC	-	T63	-	MC	-	67
British	-	-	-	MC	-	-	-	T37	T69	MC	-	MC	-	T60	-	-	T60	-	MC	MC	-
PGA	-	-	-	-	-	-	-	MC	MC	MC	-	MC	-	MC	MC	-	-	-	T68	-	-
Money (J)	109	-	67	59	18	11	2	5	1	33	2	7	3	1	34	19	6	3	2	38	50
OWR	743	-	409	271	143	122	58	49	50	104	62	92	80	27	93	158	58	61	77	246	441

2014: JAP: 15 st / 11 ct / 3 t10. (T7 Japan PGA, T8 Sega Sammy, T9 Crowns). Finished 50th in $$$, his worst ranking since 1997.

OUTLOOK: One of the elite Japanese stars of his era but at age 46, he seems to be on the downside now. Suffers from a significant lack of length but has long relied on his short game and putter to see him through – though the latter has slipped a bit in recent days. It's hardly inconceivable that he could catch fire and record a 20th career win, but the consistently excellent golf of his heyday is now likely a thing of the past.

STATS: Driving Distance: C-   Driving Accuracy: B+   GIR: B   Short Game: A-   Putting: B

Tanihara, Hideto (Japan) (36) b. Onomichi, Japan 11/16/1978. 5'10" 170 lbs. TP: 2001. One of the new millennium's stronger entries on the Japan Tour, particularly from 2004-2008, when he won seven times and was four times among the top 10 in $$$. The lone exception was 2005, when he played the PGA Tour full-time, but with little success. Claimed his first win in a weather-shortened 2003 Yomiuri Open, then won twice in both 2006 and '07, including a five-shot runaway (over Shingo Katayama) at the 2006 JCB Classic. Played in several Major championships during his peak years, tying for fifth at the 2006 British Open at Hoylake. Struggled somewhat in 2011 but rebounded to finish 13th in $$$ in 2012, then claimed his 10th career win in 2013 by logging a one-shot victory at the Taiheiyo Masters. **Teams:** World Cup (3): 2006-07-13. **OWR Best:** 68 - Dec, 2007.

Japan Tour Wins (10): 2003: Yomiuri Open **2004:** Okinawa Open **2006:** JCB Classic, Sun Chlorella Classic **2007:** Fujisankei Classic, Suntory Open **2008:** Munsingwear Open, Asia Pacific Open (Panasonic) **2010:** KBC Augusta **2013:** Taiheiyo Masters.
Other Wins: 1 Japan Challenge (2002).

	02	03	04	05	06	07	08	09	10	11	12	13	14
Masters	-	-	-	-	-	MC	-	-	-	-	-	-	-
US Open	-	-	-	-	-	-	-	-	-	-	-	-	-
British	-	MC	-	-	T5	MC	MC	-	-	-	-	-	-
PGA	-	-	-	-	-	T55	-	-	-	-	-	-	MC
Money (J)	78	16	7	42*	6	5	4	27	18	65	13	6	8
Money (A)	-	-	-	224	-	-	-	-	-	-	-	-	-
OWR	689	135	134	231	96	68	77	153	202	389	186	94	88

2014: JAP: 21 st / 19 ct / 8 t10. (2 ANA, T2 ABC, T2 Heiwa, T3 Tsuruya, T3 Tour Champ, etc.). Though winless, put together his second very strong year in succession, logging eight top 10s (after posting nine in 2013) and finishing 8th in $$$.

OUTLOOK: With his ball striking coming on strong over the last two years, has returned to Japan's top tier, winning in 2013 and cracking the top 10 in $$$ in 2013 and '14. Has long possessed one of the top short games and putters in Japan, so for as long as his ball striking holds...

STATS: Driving Distance: B-   Driving Accuracy: B ⇑   GIR: B+ ⇑   Short Game: A   Putting: A

Taylor, Nicolas Alexander (Canada) (26) b. Winnipeg, Manitoba, Canada 4/17/1988. 6'0" 170 lbs. Two-time All-American and Hogan Award winner (2010) at U of Washington. TP: 2010. After winning the 2006 Canadian Junior (by a record 11 shots) and the 2007 Canadian Amateur, spent 21 weeks as the world's number one ranked amateur during 2009. After turning pro, spent three years playing on the Canadian Tour/PGA Tour Canada with surprisingly light results. Played the 2014 Web.com Tour, making his way through the Finals to gain 2015 PGA Tour status - then won the light-field Sanderson Farms Championship in his fourth start of the season. **Teams:** Eisenhower Trophy: 2008. **OWR Best:** 207 - Dec, 2014.

PGA Tour Wins (1): 2014: Sanderson Farms Championship ('15).
Amateur Wins: Canadian Am: 2007 - Canadian Jr: 2006 - Sahalee Players: 2009.

	08	09	10	11	12	13	14
Masters	-	-	-	-	-	-	-
US Open	MC	T36	-	-	-	-	-
British	-	-	-	-	-	-	-
PGA	-	-	-	-	-	-	-
Money (A)	-	-	-	-	-	-	-
OWR	1381	862	1138	1233	1112	718	208

2014: Had a relatively quiet first year on the Web.com Tour (69th in regular season $$$) before heating up in the Finals to earn his PGA Tour card, then won the Sanderson farms Championship in his fourth start to become exempt through 2017.

OUTLOOK: Though highly touted as a junior and collegian, had accomplished fairly little as a pro prior to the 2014 Web.com Finals, and his surprise Sanderson Farms win. Perhaps he's found something in his mid-20s but for the moment, the bet here is that this recent form is a relative outlier.

STATS: Driving Distance: --   Driving Accuracy: --   GIR: --   Short Game: --   Putting: --

Taylor, Vaughn Joseph (USA) (48) b. Roanoke, VA 3/9/1976. 6'0" 150 lbs. College: Augusta St. TP: 1999. After turning pro, spent several seasons developing on mini-tours (where he won four times) and the Web.com circuit, eventually finishing 11th in 2003. As PGA Tour rookie, won a playoff over Scott McCarron, Hunter Mahan and Steve Allan at the 2004 Reno-Tahoe Open. Successfully defended his title a year later in wire-to-wire fashion, beating Jonathan Kaye by three. Though winless since, remained a strong earner through 2010, finishing no worse than 98th in $$$ and losing in playoffs at the 2009 Turning Stone Championship (to Matt Kuchar) and the 2010 Houston Open (Anthony Kim). Played on conditional status in 2012 and '13. **Teams:** Ryder Cup: 2006 (O: 0-1-1, S: 0-1-0). **OWR Best:** 37 - Apr, 2007.

PGA Tour Wins (2): 2004: Reno-Tahoe Open **2005:** Reno-Tahoe Open.

Other Wins: 1 Web.com (2003)   +   4 NGA/Hooters (2001-2002).

	98	99	00	01	02	03	04	05	06	07	08	09	10	11	12	13	14
Masters	-	-	-	-	-	-	-	-	MC	T10	MC	-	-	-	-	-	-
US Open	MC	-	-	-	-	-	-	-	-	MC	-	-	-	-	-	-	-
British	-	-	-	-	-	-	-	-	T66	MC	-	-	-	-	-	-	-
PGA	-	-	-	-	-	-	T28	MC	MC	MC	MC	-	MC	-	-	-	-
Money (A)	-	-	-	-	-	-	67	36	35	70	98	79	42	148	139	154	242*
OWR	-	-	777	-	-	418	139	74	69	99	228	233	107	327	522	430	569

2014: PGA: 3 st / 2 ct / 0 t10. (T61 Travelers). Made 20 Web.com starts, finishing 47th in $$$ and narrowly failing to play through the Finals.

OUTLOOK: At age 48, and having only Past Champion status, he has smartly looked to better his position via the Web.com Tour. Still a fairly solid tee-to-greener, but at this stage he seems unlikely to have a major impact prior to becoming Champions Tour-eligible in 2016.

STATS: Driving Distance: B-   Driving Accuracy: B+   GIR: B+   Short Game: B   Putting: B+

Teater, Joshua Bain (USA) (35) b. Danville, KY 4/6/1979. 5'10" 180 lbs. College: Morehead St. TP: 2001. Spent his first seven years as a professional plying his trade on mini-tours, particularly the Hooters and eGolf circuits. In his seventh try at Q School (2008), finished with two double bogeys and a triple in his last four holes (!) to fall below the line, but landed on the 2009 Web.com Tour. A 7th-place finish there (with one win) then graduated him to the PGA Tour, where he retained his card from 2010-2013. **OWR Best:** 98 - Mar, 2013.

Other Wins: 1 Web.com (2009).

	09	10	11	12	13	14
Masters	-	-	-	-	-	-
US Open	-	-	-	-	T56	-
British	-	-	-	-	82	-
PGA	-	-	-	-	T47	-
Money (A)	-	89	110	98	65	164
OWR	188	221	295	201	167	564

2014: PGA: 28 st / 17 ct / 0 t10. (T23 Mayakoba). Finished 148th in FedEx Cup points, then failed to play his way back via the Web.com finals.

OUTLOOK: After four solid campaigns, fell apart in 2014, and will now (barely) have conditional status in 2015. Builds his game around power/ball striking but saw moderate declines in these numbers across the board. Likely a Web.com regular this year as he tries to turn things around.

STATS: Driving Distance: A-   Driving Accuracy: B   GIR: B+   Short Game: B-   Putting: C+

Terblanche, Desmond ("Des") (South Africa) (49) b. Vryburg, South Africa 10/27/1965. 6'3" 275 lbs. TP: 1987. A huge man who has been a regular winner in his native South Africa since the late 1980s while also playing regularly in Asia and Australia. Has never played the PGA Tour, and most of his E Tour appearances have come in co-sanctioned African and Asian events. A multiple winner at home in 1989, 1991, 1993 and 1996. Despite this lofty regional status, has never played in a Major championship or cracked the top 200 in the OWR. Did win three times on the old Asian Tour, however, including twice in 1997 at the Sabah Masters and the Volvo Asian Match Play. **OWR Best:** 220 - Jan, 2001.

Asian Tour Wins (3): 1997: Sabah Masters, Volvo Asian Match Play **2000:** Thailand Open.

Sunshine Tour Wins (14): 1989: Bloemfontein Classic, Iscor Newcastle Classic **1991:** Kalahari Classic, S.A. Winter Championships, Sun City Pro-Am (T w/J.Hobday) **1993:** Highveld Classic (54H), Sun Leopard Park Classic (54H) **1994:** Royal Swazi Sun Classic (54H) **1996:** Highveld Classic (54H), FNB Pro Series: Botswana (54H) **1997:** Vodacom-Eastern Cape (54H) **2000:** Emfuleni Classic (54H) **2003:** Royal Swazi Sun Open (Stableford) **2007:** Royal Swazi Sun Open (Stableford).

Other Wins: Royal Swazi Sun Pro-Am (SA): 2006   Nashua Shootout (SA) (18H): 2009.

Amateur Wins: Junior World (15-17): 1983   South African Jr: 1983   South African Under-23s: 1985

	91	92	93	94	95	96	97	98	99	00	01	02	03	04	05	06	07	08	09	10	11	12	13	14
Masters	-	-	-	-	-	-	-	-	-	-	-	-	-	-	-	-	-	-	-	-	-	-	-	-
US Open	-	-	-	-	-	-	-	-	-	-	-	-	-	-	-	-	-	-	-	-	-	-	-	-
British	-	-	-	-	-	-	-	-	-	-	-	-	-	-	-	-	-	-	-	-	-	-	-	-
PGA	-	-	-	-	-	-	-	-	-	-	-	-	-	-	-	-	-	-	-	-	-	-	-	-
Money (SA)	2	44*	51*	47*	36*	8	25	36	48	14	26*	24*	40*	15	9	41	21	110	86	63	69	71	94*	-
OWR	361	540	607	693	517	431	570	626	566	257	343	483	713	644	623	654	821	-	-	-	-	-	-	1489

2014: Made only one Sunshine Tour start in 2014, missing the cut (at Stableford Scoring) at the Royal Swazi Open.

OUTLOOK: Hasn't won since 2007 and is largely a ceremonial player now, mostly entering lighter-field Sunshine Tour winter-season events.

STATS: Driving Distance: --   Driving Accuracy: --   GIR: --   Short Game: --   Putting: --

---

Teshima, Taichi (Japan) (46) b. Fujuoka, Japan 10/16/1968. 5'8" 150 lbs. TP: 1993. After spending half of his 1995 season on the Japan Challenge circuit (where he won twice), quickly became a mainstay of the Japan Tour, where he remained among the top 50 earners for 15 straight seasons, four times cracking the top 10. Scored his first major victory at the 2001 Japan Open (where he cruised to a four-shot win) in a season in which he finished a career-best 3rd in $$$. Nearly matched that in 2006 when he finished 4th and claimed victories at the KBC Augusta (by one shot over Tetsuji Hiratsuka) and, two months later, the Bridgestone Open. Broke a seven-year drought at the 2014 Japan PGA Championship,

Teshima, Taichi, Cont'd

edging Koumei Oda and Kyoung-Hoon Lee by one. **Teams:** World Cup: 1997. **OWR Best:** 69 - Jan, 2002.

Japan Tour Wins (7): 1999: Okinawa Open **2001:** Japan Open **2003:** Aiful Cup **2006:** KBC Augusta, Bridgestone Open **2007:** Casio World Open **2014:** Japan PGA Championship.

Other Wins: 2 Japan Challenge (1995).

	95	96	97	98	99	00	01	02	03	04	05	06	07	08	09	10	11	12	13	14
Masters	-	-	-	-	-	-	-	-	-	-	-	-	-	-	-	-	-	-	-	-
US Open	-	-	-	-	-	-	-	-	-	-	-	-	-	-	-	-	-	-	-	-
British	-	-	-	-	-	-	MC	MC	-	-	-	-	-	-	-	-	-	-	-	-
PGA	-	-	-	-	-	-	-	MC	-	-	-	-	-	-	-	-	-	-	-	-
Money (J)	136	47	31	50	6	22	3	29	5	29	17	4	27	17	32	33	52	33	70	14
OWR	-	253	203	269	140	179	71	130	121	174	149	91	146	138	221	314	371	326	511	282

2014: JAP: 23 st / 17 ct / 5 t10. (Won Japan PGA, 6 Heiwa, T8 ANA, T8 Tokai, T9 Mizuno). Enjoyed something of a revival at age 46, winning for the first time since 2007 (at the Japan PGA Championship) and logging his highest $$$ ranking (14th) since 2006.

OUTLOOK: A short but very straight driver of the ball who hits lots of greens but has never wielded a high-end putter. Such players often age nicely in golf and he is certainly a walking example - but at 46, one expects he'll have a tough time maintaining all of his 2014 form going forward.

STATS: Driving Distance: C+   Driving Accuracy: A   GIR: B+   Short Game: B   Putting: B

Thomas, Justin Louis (USA) (21)

b. Louisville, KY 4/29/1993. 5'10" 150 lbs. Two-time All-American, NCAA individual champion (2013), Nicklaus (2012), Haskins (2012) & Mickelson (2012) Award winner at U of Alabama. TP: 2013. Two-time AJGA All-American before playing two years at Alabama. As a 16-year-old, shot 65 in his first PGA Tour round at the Wyndham Championship (finished T78). Won the Web.com's 2014 Nationwide Hospitals Championship at age 21, becoming that circuit's fourth youngest winner. On a sponsor exemption, finished T10 at the 2014 Farmers Insurance Open. **Teams:** Walker Cup: 2013 (2-0-1). Eisenhower Trophy: 2012. Palmer Cup (2): 2012-13. **OWR Best:** 122 - Nov, 2014.

Other Wins: 1 Web.com (2014).

Amateur Wins: NCAA Individual: 2013   Terra Cotta Inv: 2010   Jones Cup Inv: 2012   Kentucky HS: 2009.

	14
Masters	-
US Open	MC
British	-
PGA	-
Money (A)	-
OWR	122

2014: Played full-time on the Web.com Tour, winning once and clinching 2015 PGA Tour status by finishing 5th in regular season $$$.

OUTLOOK: Beginning at age 16, made three of four cuts as an amateur in PGA Tour events, and five of 11 as a pro through 2014. Arrives as a touted prospect who has won (and quickly) at every level. The adjustment is always huge, but his chances of success rank with any rookie in 2015.

STATS: Driving Distance: --   Driving Accuracy: --   GIR: --   Short Game: --   Putting: --

---

Thompson, Michael Hayes (USA) (29)

b. Tucson, AZ 4/16/1985. 6'0" 185 lbs. All-American at U of Alabama after transferring from Tulane. TP: 2008. Runner-up at the 2007 U.S. Amateur (lost 2 & 1 to Colt Knost at the Olympic Club) and in voting for the 2008 Ben Hogan Award (behind Rickie Fowler). Upon turning pro, played mini-tours (being named 2010 Rookie of the Year on the Hooters Tour) before playing his way through 2010 Q School, where he tied for 16th. Made 15 of 25 cuts as a 2011 PGA Tour rookie, peaking late with a solo 3rd at the McGladrey. Tied for 2nd at the 2012 U.S. Open (Olympic) after leading with a first round 66. Claimed his first PGA Tour victory at the 2013 Honda Classic (where he beat Geoff Ogilvy by two) en route to a career-best 52nd in $$$. **Teams:** Palmer Cup: 2008. **OWR Best:** 43 - Mar, 2013.

PGA Tour Wins (1): 2013: Honda Classic.

Other Wins: 1 NGA/Hooters (2010).

Amateur Wins: Arizona HS: 2001   Greystone Inv: 2007.

	08	09	10	11	12	13	14
Masters	MC	-	-	-	-	T25	-
US Open	T29	-	-	-	T2	MC	-
British	-	-	-	-	MC	MC	-
PGA	-	-	-	-	MC	T22	-
Money (A)	-	-	-	98	60	52	103
OWR	768	-	-	131	86	79	238

2014: PGA: 22 st / 15 ct / 1 t10. (T10 Colonial). Slipped from a career-best 2013, finishing 117th in FedEx Cup pts.

OUTLOOK: A curious player statistically as little among the basic numbers stands out, save for his putting stroke – particularly after his SGP bounced back dramatically (121 to 14) in 2014. Also saw a major jump in GIR (162 to 68) but as his two previous rankings were 104 and 101, one is skeptical as to his ability to maintain that gain. Tough to see a huge resurgence here, but as Willie Park Jr. once said: "A good putter is a match for anyone."

STATS: Driving Distance: B-   Driving Accuracy: B   GIR: B-⇧   Short Game: B   Putting: A-

---

Thompson, Nicholas David (USA) (32)

b. Plantation, FL 12/25/1982. 6'0" 185 lbs. Two-time All-American at Georgia Tech. TP: 2005. Two-time AJGA All-American. Brother of up-and-coming LPGA star Lexi Thompson. Began his career in up-and-down fashion, playing the PGA Tour in four of five years from 2006-2010 (peaking with a 41st-place $$$ ranking in 2008) before losing his card and repairing to the Web.com Tour. A 22nd-place finish on the 2012 Web.com brought him back to the PGA Tour for 2013 where he comfortably retained his card, before 2014 saw him keep it by ranking 123rd in $$$ after the Wyndham Championship. **Teams:** Walker Cup: 2005 (1-1-0). **OWR Best:** 139 - Nov, 2008.

Thompson, Nicholas David, Cont'd

Other Wins: 1 Web.com (2007).
Amateur Wins: Jones Cup: 2005.

	06	07	08	09	10	11	12	13	14
Masters	-	-	-	-	-	-	-	-	-
US Open	MC	-	-	-	-	-	T51	T56	-
British	-	-	-	-	-	-	-	-	-
PGA	-	-	T24	-	-	-	-	-	-
Money (A)	180	-	41	123	153	-	-	87	125
OWR	559	327	156	300	474	720	353	201	212

2014: PGA: 30 st / 12 ct / 1 t10. (T3 Colonial). Finished 126th in FedEx Cup points; kept his card by ranking 123 in $$$ after Wyndham.

OUTLOOK: Has had an up and (mostly) down PGA Tour career. A strong ball striker (35 in Ball Striking, 46 in GIR) who is one of the straighter long drivers on Tour (34 in Total Driving). His short game and putting, however, have never followed suit, limiting his upside considerably.

STATS: Driving Distance: B+   Driving Accuracy: A-   GIR: A-   Short Game: C+   Putting: C

Thornton, Simon (Ireland) (37)

b. Bradford, England 3/18/1977. 6'2" 160 lbs. TP: 2005. Born in England but moved to Ireland as a young man, where he worked at Royal County Down GC. Didn't turn pro until age 28. First played the E Tour (via Q School) in 2010, fell back to the Challenge Tour for 2011, then finished 12th in $$$ and returned to the bigger stage. Fell back again after 2012 but broke through via a win at the Challenge/E Tour co-sanctioned Najeti Hotels Open in 2013 to gain an exemption through 2014. **OWR Best:** 264 - Jan, 2014.

European Tour Wins (1): 2013: Najeti Hotels Open.
Other Wins: Ulster PGA: 2005   Bovey Castle (Ireland): 2008   Irish PGA: 2011.

	06	07	08	09	10	11	12	13	14
Masters	-	-	-	-	-	-	-	-	-
US Open	-	-	-	-	-	-	-	-	-
British	-	-	-	-	-	-	-	-	-
PGA	-	-	-	-	-	-	-	-	-
Money (E)	283*	317*	-	-	141	197*	161	128*	146
OWR	-	-	-	742	501	319	527	297	511

2014: E: 28 st / 13 ct / 0 t10. (T14 Lyoness). Struggled throughout the year, failing to log a top 10 and finishing 146th in $$$.

OUTLOOK: Given his overall résumé, his down 2014 largely confirms that his 2013 win at the light-field Najeti Hotels Open was an outlier. Aside from being a particularly straight driver, has little else statistically to build around - but how many golfers can say they won on the E Tour?

STATS: Driving Distance: C   Driving Accuracy: A-   GIR: B-   Short Game: B-   Putting: C

Todd, Brendon Dean (USA) (29)

b. Pittsburgh, PA 7/22/1985. 6'3" 180 lbs. Two-time All-American at U of Georgia. TP: 2007. Two-time AJGA All-American. After turning pro, won on both the eGolf and Hooters Tours before finishing 20th (with one win) on the 2008 Web.com circuit. Finished 186th in $$$ as a 2009 PGA Tour rookie, then struggled on the 2010 Web.com when he missed the cut in all 13 events entered. Eventually played himself back onto the PGA Tour by claiming medalist honors at 2011 Q School. Logged holes-in-one on the same par 3 on back-to-back days of the Web.com's 2009 Athens Regional Foundation Classic, acing the 17th at the Jennings Mill CC in both the first and second rounds. Claimed his first PGA Tour victory at the 2014 Byron Nelson Championship in his 77th start, beating Mike Weir by two. **OWR Best:** 40 - Jul, 2014.

PGA Tour Wins (1): 2014: Byron Nelson Championship.
Other Wins: 2 Web.com (2008-2013)   +   1 eGolf Tour (2007)   1 NGA/Hooters (2007).

	08	09	10	11	12	13	14
Masters	-	-	-	-	-	-	-
US Open	-	-	-	-	-	-	T17
British	-	-	-	-	-	-	T39
PGA	-	-	-	-	-	-	73
Money (A)	-	186	-	-	150	142*	18
OWR	266	407	972	859	606	186	54

2014: PGA: 29 st / 25 ct / 7 t10. (Won Byron Nelson, T4 Greenbrier, T5 Colonial, T5 Quicken Loans, T6 Humana, etc.). Made good in his third try at the PGA Tour, logging 12 top-25 finishes, seven top 10s and finishing 27th in FedEx Cup points.

OUTLOOK: After previously struggling in two full seasons, suddenly looks like an up-and-coming PGA Tour star. Despite standing 6'3", is by no means a power-oriented player, and his overall tee-to-green game (119 in GIR, 119 in Ball Striking) is barely above the median. On and around the greens he stands among the best (7 in Scrambling, 6 in SGP) but unless his long game improves, the numbers suggest he can't climb too much higher.

STATS: Driving Distance: C   Driving Accuracy: B↑   GIR: B-   Short Game: A   Putting: A

Toms, David Wayne (USA) (47)

b. Monroe, LA 1/4/1967. 5'10" 160 lbs. Two-time All-American at Louisiana St. TP: 1989. An AJGA All-American. A two-time Web.com Tour winner who eventually cracked the PGA Tour's top 50 money winners in 1997, then finished four times in the top 10 (including 3rd in 2001) from 1999-2003. Won the 1999 International, birdieing the last two holes to beat David Duval by three points (modified Stableford scoring). During a career-best three-win campaign, won the 2001 PGA Championship at the Atlanta AC, holing a 12' putt on the last green (after laying up his second shy of a fronting lake) to beat Phil Mickelson by one. Won back-to-back Michelob Championships (at Kingsmill) in 2000 and '01. Won the inaugural Wachovia Championship (2003) by two shots despite carding a quadruple-bogey eight at the 72nd. Underwent wrist surgery in late 2003 but, after an up-and-down 2004, was back on form in 2005, winning the WGC Match Play (6 & 5 over Chris DiMarco) at La Costa. Also won back-to-back FedEx St Jude Classics (Memphis) in 2003 and '04. After a something of a dry spell, returned to form in 2011, first losing a playoff to K.J. Choi at the Players Championship (by three-putting the first extra hole), then opening with 62-62 en route to winning Colonial a week later. **Teams:** Ryder Cup (3): 2002-04-06 (O: 4-6-2, S: 1-2-0). Presidents Cup (4): 2003-05-07-11 (9-8-1). World Cup: 2002. **OWR Best:** 5 - Nov, 2002.

Toms, David Wayne, Cont'd

PGA Tour Wins (13): 1997: Quad Cities Open **1999:** The International (Sprint)(Stableford), Buick Challenge **2000:** Michelob Championship **2001:** New Orleans Classic (Compaq), PGA Championship, Michelob Championship **2003:** Wachovia Championship, Memphis Classic (FedEx) **2004:** Memphis Classic (FedEx) **2005:** WGC-Match Play **2006:** Hawaiian Open (Sony) **2011:** Colonial Inv (Crowne Plaza).
Int'l Wins (1): 1999: Hassan II Trophy (Morocco).
Other Wins: 2 Web.com (1995) + 1 NGA/Hooters (1990) CVS Charity Classic (w/N. Price): 2009.
Amateur Wins: Louisiana Jr: 1983 Junior World (15-17): 1984 PGA Junior: 1984.

	92	93	94	95	96	97	98	99	00	01	02	03	04	05	06	07	08	09	10	11	12	13	14
Masters	-	-	-	-	-	-	T6	MC	T49	T31	T36	**T8**	MC	MC	MC	**9**	T42	-	T14	T24	T50	T13	-
US Open	-	-	-	-	MC	WD	-	MC	T16	T66	T45	**T5**	T20	T15	WD	**T5**	T60	MC	T33	MC	**T4**	MC	MC
British	-	-	-	-	-	-	-	**T4**	MC	83	MC	T30	DQ	-	MC	-	MC	-	-	**T4**	-	-	-
PGA	-	-	-	-	-	MC	MC	MC	T41	**Win**	MC	T29	T17	**T10**	T16	T42	T15	T36	T33	**T4**	T42	7	-
Money (A)	101	123	164	-	105	49	44	**10**	15	**3**	**4**	**8**	22	**5**	11	32	131	14	49	**10**	47	123	118
OWR	273	287	418	303	303	101	70	24	23	**7**	**6**	**9**	20	15	19	43	116	42	79	26	42	117	175

2014: PGA: 20 st / 13 ct / 2 t10. (T4 Puerto Rico, T5 Colonial). Finished 118th in FedEx Cup points, avoiding Past Champion status for 2015.
OUTLOOK: At age 47 he still seems capable of competing at a high level, but not quite as well as during his halcyon days. Power is not his forte (81 in Total Driving despite ranking 1 in Driving Accuracy) but his recently inconsistent GIR surged from 130 to 13, driven by ranking 15 in Proximity To Hole. Still has moments but as these numbers may prove hard to maintain, his next victory celebration will likely come on the Champions Tour.

STATS: Driving Distance: C- Driving Accuracy: A+ GIR: B+ ⇧ Short Game: A- Putting: B-

---

Trahan, Donald Roland Jr. ("D.J.") (USA) (34)

b. Atlanta, GA 12/18/1980. 6'3" 185 lbs. Two-time All-American, Nicklaus (2002) and Hogan (2002) Awards winner at Clemson U. TP: 2003. Former junior star who also won the 2000 U.S. Public Links, where he beat Bubba Watson in a 37-hole final. Helped lead Clemson to the 2003 NCAA championship and played on the 2001 Walker Cup team. Played one year on the Web.com Tour (2004) before a T11 at Q School earned him PGA Tour privileges for 2005. Logged his first win at the 2006 Southern Farm Bureau Classic (defeating Joe Durant in sudden death), then added a second title by shooting a closing 65 to overtake Justin Leonard at the 2008 Bob Hope Chrysler Classic. Stole the 125th spot on the 2011 money list via a clutch 72nd-hole par at the season-ending Children's Miracle Network Classic, but failed to retain his card in both 2012 and '13. **Teams:** Walker Cup: 2001 (1-3-0). Eisenhower Trophy: 2002. Palmer Cup: 2002. **OWR Best:** 62 - Oct, 2008.

PGA Tour Wins (2): 2006: Southern Farm Classic **2008:** Bob Hope Chrysler Classic (90H).
Other Wins: 1 Web.com (2004).
Amateur Wins: U.S. Amateur Public Links: 2000 Jones Cup: 2001 Azalea Inv: 2002 Monroe Inv: 2002.

	01	02	03	04	05	06	07	08	09	10	11	12	13	14
Masters	MC	-	-	-	-	-	-	MC	T44	-	-	-	-	-
US Open	-	-	-	-	-	MC	-	**T4**	MC	-	-	-	-	-
British	-	-	-	-	-	-	-	-	MC	-	-	-	-	-
PGA	-	-	-	-	-	-	MC	T31	MC	67	MC	-	-	-
Money (A)	Am	Am	-	-	103	89	87	26	87	47	125	132	169	248*
OWR	-	-	-	516	221	193	211	74	178	143	223	329	566	898

2014: PGA: 5 st / 1 ct / 0 t10. Also made 16 Web.com starts, finishing 132nd in $$$ and failing to qualify for the Web.com Finals.
OUTLOOK: Still has Past Champion status to fall back on. Remains a solid ball striker but has been held back by his struggles on and around the greens. Has fallen a long way from his 2008-2010 peak and will likely need the Web.com Tour (more than sporadic PGA Tour starts) to get back.

STATS: Driving Distance: B+ Driving Accuracy: B- GIR: A- Short Game: C Putting: C-

---

Tringale, Cameron Joseph (USA) (27)

b. Mission Viejo, CA 8/24/1987. 6'2" 185 lbs. Two-time All-American at Georgia Tech. TP: 2009. The increasingly rare player to skip mini-tours and the Web.com Tour completely, instead tying for 19th at the 2009 PGA Tour Q School shortly after turning pro. Lost his card after finishing 179th in 2010 $$$ but once more played through Q School, then made good in 2011 by logging four top 10s and finishing 68th in earnings, and backing that up with a 75th-place finish in 2012. Climbed significantly in 2014 when, despite logging only three top 10s, he finished 37th in $$$. **Teams:** Walker Cup: 2009 (1-1-1). Palmer Cup: 2009. **OWR Best:** 69 - Sep, 2014.

	09	10	11	12	13	14
Masters	-	-	-	-	-	-
US Open	MC	-	-	-	-	-
British	-	-	-	-	-	MC
PGA	-	-	MC	72	-	T33
Money (A)	-	179	68	75	86	37
OWR	-	534	197	169	198	85

2014: PGA: 31 st / 25 ct / 3 t10. (T2 Barclays, 4 Houston, 4 Greenbrier). Finished a career-best 20th in FedEx Cup points.
OUTLOOK: Despite remaining winless as a pro, stepped up nicely in 2014, further establishing himself as a strong young player capable of competing. Is a solid enough ball striker who hits plenty of greens (though his tee-to-green numbers mostly declined somewhat in 2014) and a well above average player around the greens. He certainly seems ready to win - and after five full seasons one wonders what is holding him back.

STATS: Driving Distance: B- Driving Accuracy: A- GIR: A- Short Game: A- Putting: B+

Tullo, Mark (Chile) (36)

b. Santiago, Chile 2/9/1978. 5'7" 150 lbs. College: North Carolina St. TP: 2003. Won a reported 16 amateur titles in his native Chile while also playing collegiate golf in America. Is also credited with more than 20 domestic professional wins including back-to-back Chile Opens in 2005 and '06. Began playing in Europe in 2007 and has bounced between the Challenge Tour (where he has three victories) and the E Tour ever since. **Teams:** Eisenhower Trophy: 2002. World Cup (2): 2008-13. **OWR Best:** 182 - Jul, 2011.

Tullo, Mark, Cont'd

Other Wins: 3 Euro Challenge (2010-2014) + Chile Open (2): 2005-06.

	08	09	10	11	12	13	14
Masters	-	-	-	-	-	-	-
US Open	-	-	-	-	-	-	-
British	-	-	-	-	-	-	-
PGA	-	-	-	-	-	-	-
Money (E)	-	-	-	119	-	114	-
OWR	570	604	185	262	389	378	241

2014: Played full-time on the Challenge Tour, winning once and finishing 5th in $$$ to clinch his E Tour card for the third time.

OUTLOOK: Has twice narrowly missed keeping his E Tour card and, following another strong season on the Challenge Tour, will try a third time in 2015. Little suggest that he'll blossom out there but with greater experience, he might retain his privileges this time around.

STATS (LTD): Driving Distance: B   Driving Accuracy: A-   GIR: C   Short Game: B   Putting: B+

Turnesa, Marc Brian (USA) (36)
b. Rockville Centre, NY 3/19/1978. 6'0" 190 lbs. College: North Carolina St. TP: 2001. A product of New York's legendary Turnesa family; his grandfather/great uncles won a combined 21 PGA Tour titles, 1 Major championship, 2 U.S. Amateurs and 1 British Amateur. After a relatively quiet amateur and mini-tour career, joined the PGA Tour in 2008 and, after losing the Viking Classic in a playoff (to Will MacKenzie) won a month later, edging Matt Kuchar by one at the Las Vegas Classic. Had his 2010 season limited to seven starts by a back injury and, in limited appearances, has seldom been a factor since. **OWR Best:** 138 - Oct, 2008.

PGA Tour Wins (1): 2008: Las Vegas Classic (Justin Timberlake).

Other Wins: 1 Web.com (2007).

	07	08	09	10	11	12	13	14
Masters	-	-	-	-	-	-	-	-
US Open	-	-	-	-	MC	-	-	-
British	-	-	-	-	-	-	-	-
PGA	-	-	MC	-	-	-	-	-
Money (A)	-	81	190	243*	173	205*	246*	236*
OWR	247	148	378	962	566	871	1472	-

2014: PGA: 6 st / 3 ct / 0 t10 (T47 Barracuda). Strictly a part-time player, with limited starts available on Past Champion status.

OUTLOOK: Though still making limited starts, he seems a longshot to have a major PGA Tour impact at this stage of the game.

STATS: Driving Distance: --   Driving Accuracy: --   GIR: --   Short Game: --   Putting: --

---

Uihlein, Peter (USA) (25)
b. New Bedford, MA 8/29/1989. 6'1" 190 lbs. Two-time All-American and Hogan Award winner (2011) at Oklahoma St. TP: 2011. Four-time AJGA All-American and two-time AJGA Player Of The Year (2005 & '07). Son of Titleist Chairman and CEO Wally Uihlein. Attended David Leadbetter's/IMG Golf Academy in Bradenton, FL. Won all four of his matches for the victorious 2009 American Walker Cup team. Spent much of 2010 as the world's #1-ranked amateur after winning the U.S. Amateur on his 21st birthday, beating David Chung 4 & 2 at Chambers Bay. Without PGA Tour status, went to Europe in 2013, where he broke through for his first E Tour victory at the 2013 Madeira Islands Open, beating Morten Madsen and Mark Tullo by two. Became the first American ever to win E Tour Rookie of the Year honors. **Awards:** E Tour Rookie of the Year: 2013. **Teams:** Walker Cup (2): 2009-11 (6-2-0). Eisenhower Trophy: 2010. **OWR Best:** 60 - Oct, 2013.

European Tour Wins (1): 2013: Madeira Islands Open.

Amateur Wins: U.S. Amateur: 2010   –   St Augustine Am: 2006   Terra Cotta Inv: 2007   Dixie Am (2): 2009-10   Sahalee Players: 2010   Northeast Am: 2011.

	11	12	13	14
Masters	T75	-	-	-
US Open	MC	-	-	-
British	T48	-	-	MC
PGA	-	-	MC	-
Money (E)	-	-	14	65
OWR	883	384	63	143

2014: E: 23 st / 14 ct / 2 t10. (T9 Perth, T10 Nedbank). Slumped badly in his second E Tour season, logging only two top 10s and falling to 65th in $$$. Also made five non-Major/WGC PGA Tour starts: four MCs and a late T4 at Sanderson Farms. It was not the year most expected.

OUTLOOK: His march to stardom via the European Tour hit a stumbling block in 2014, though his form was far better late in the season. While his stats inevitably suffered a bit, he still reads as a player with more strengths than weaknesses. Unlike his buddy Brooks Koepka, he came nowhere near qualifying for the 2015 PGA Tour via Non-Member Money, so his rebuild figures to take place in Europe. But the talent is still very much there.

STATS: Driving Distance: A   Driving Accuracy: C-   GIR: B⇩   Short Game: B-   Putting: A-

---

Van Aswegen, Tyrone (South Africa) (32)
b. Johannesburg, South Africa 1/6/1982. 6'0" 170 lbs. College: Three-time NAIA All-American and individual national champion (2002) at Oklahoma City U. TP: 2004. After turning professional, spent several years playing overseas, including on his native South African Sunshine Tour, where he won twice in 2008 and finished 7th in the 2009 Order of Merit. Though still competing part-time at home, began playing the Web.com Tour full-time in 2011, eventually reaching the PGA Tour in 2014 - then retaining his status via the season-ending Web.com Finals. **OWR Best:** 368 - Jun, 2014.

Sunshine Tour Wins (2): 2008: Vodacom-Pretoria (54H), Nedbank Affinity Cup.

Other Wins: Long Beach (CA) Open: 2009.

Amateur Wins: Transvaal Stroke Play: 1999.

Van Aswegen, Tyrone, Cont'd

	07	08	09	10	11	12	13	14
Masters	-	-	-	-	-	-	-	-
US Open	-	-	-	-	-	-	-	-
British	-	-	-	-	-	-	-	-
PGA	-	-	-	-	-	-	-	-
Money (A)	-	-	-	-	-	-	-	151
Money (SA)	37	33	7	30	-	-	-	-
OWR	771	-	533	680	724	405	469	451

2014: PGA: 25 st / 15 ct / 0 t10.   (T16 Byron Nelson).   Considering his résumé, he actually acquitted himself nicely in his first PGA Tour season, finishing 144th in FedEx Cup points, then returning for 2015 via the Web.com Finals.

OUTLOOK: Arrived last year with more international experience than most rookies but still struggled. Returns for another try in 2015 with early numbers suggesting a mid-range game across the board. The experience of 2014 will help but he still seems a longshot to make a significant impact.

STATS (LTD):   Driving Distance: B   Driving Accuracy: C-   GIR: B-   Short Game: B-   Putting: B+

Van den Berg, Ulrich (South Africa) (39)
b. East London, South Africa 1/13/1975. 6'0" 180 lbs. TP: 1999. Veteran Sunshine Tour player who has seldom gone abroad, save for two part-time ventures onto the E Tour in 2008 and '09. A regular winner on the Sunshine Tour, however (though only in the lighter-field winter season), where his earnings peaked with four consecutive top-10 finishes in the Order of Merit from 2004-2007. His $$$ declined from 2008 onward but he logged wins in 2010 and 2013, the latter a five-shot runaway at the BMG Classic. Went winless in 2014 but played well enough to log his best $$$ finish (12th) in seven season. **OWR Best**: 228 - Aug, 2014.

Sunshine Tour Wins (7): **2000**: Riviera Resort Classic (36H) **2001**: Vodacom Trophy (54H) **2004**: Seekers Travel Pro-Am (54H) **2005**: Parmalat Classic (54H) **2007**: Vodacom-Bloemfontein (54H) **2010**: Vodacom-Humewood (54H) **2013**: BMG Classic (54H).

Amateur Wins: South African Stroke Play: 1997   Transvaal Amateur: 1997   Western Province Stroke Play: 1997.

	00	01	02	03	04	05	06	07	08	09	10	11	12	13	14
Masters	-	-	-	-	-	-	-	-	-	-	-	-	-	-	-
US Open	-	-	-	-	-	-	-	-	-	-	-	-	-	-	-
British	-	-	-	-	-	-	-	-	-	-	-	-	-	-	-
PGA	-	-	-	-	-	-	-	-	-	-	-	-	-	-	-
Money (SA)	22	28	41	43	10	10	6	10	57	20	29	29	28	20	12
OWR	554	782	-	-	681	457	652	907	776	596	685	692	596	388	270

2014: SUN: 22 st / 20 ct / 12 t10.   (Incl. 2 Telkom PGA, 2 Vodacom-Final, T2 Wild Waves).   Perhaps the most consistent golfer among full-time Sunshine players, as he logged an impressive 12 top-10 finishes (including a trio of runner-ups) for the second consecutive season.

OUTLOOK: Is now the closest thing the domestic circuit has to a cut-making, top 10-logging machine. Some may suggest that he could win more but if he continues at anything resembling his current pace, several more victories should come along in due time.

STATS: Driving Distance: --   Driving Accuracy: --   GIR: --   Short Game: --   Putting: --

---

Van der Walt, Isak Dawid ("Dawie") (South Africa) (31)
b. Paarl, South Africa 2/11/1983. 6'5" 260 lbs. Two-time All-American at Lamar U. TP: 2007. An enormous man who, after college, spent time on multiple U.S. mini-tours (winning five times) before dividing his time between his native Sunshine Tour and the Web.com circuit. Was a second-tier player at home prior to breaking through in 2013 for a two-shot victory over Darren Fichardt at the European Tour co-sanctioned Tshwane Open, then validating that win at year's end by adding the rain-shortened Nelson Mandela Championship (a part of the 2014 E Tour schedule). **Teams**: Eisenhower Trophy (2): 2004-06. **OWR Best**: 172 - Jun, 2014.

European Tour Wins (2): 2013: Tshwane Open, Nelson Mandela Championship (54H)('14).

Other Wins: 4 Adams (2008-2011)   +   1 NGA/Hooters (2009).

	08	09	10	11	12	13	14
Masters	-	-	-	-	-	-	-
US Open	-	-	-	-	-	-	-
British	-	-	-	-	-	MC	-
PGA	-	-	-	-	-	-	-
Money (SA)	40*	27	31*	53*	18*	1*	48*
OWR	-	657	687	584	414	194	281

2014: SUN: 7 st / 5 ct / 1 t10.   (T6 Investec).   Followed up his big 2013 by playing mostly on the Web.com Tour, where he finished 53rd in regular season $$$ and 81st after the Finals. Had only a limited impact in his handful of domestic outings.

OUTLOOK: While he failed to reach the PGA Tour via the 2014 Web.com circuit, he didn't miss by all that much. One of the game's more imposing physical specimens who, not surprisingly, builds his game off the tee. His biggest question going forward involves where he'll opt to play, as he enters 2015 fully exempt on both the European and Web.com Tours - but only the latter offers a manageable path to the PGA Tour.

STATS (LTD):   Driving Distance: A-   Driving Accuracy: B   GIR: B   Short Game: C   Putting: C+

Van der Walt, Tjaart Nicolaas (South Africa) (40)
b. Pretoria, South Africa 9/25/1974. 6'1" 190 lbs. JC All-American at Alexander (AL) JC. TP: 1996. Following a three-year stint playing junior college golf in America, has played professionally all over the world, spending considerable time on the Web.com Tour (where he has logged multiple runner-up finishes) as well as on the PGA Tour from 2004-2006. Played through Asian Tour Q School in 2010 and E Tour Q School (for the second time) in late 2011. At age 39, broke through for his first major tour victory at the Sunshine circuit's Cape Town Open, where he ran away by six. **OWR Best**: 198 - Jan, 2006.

Sunshine Tour Wins (1): 2013: Cape Town Open.

Amateur Wins: Willow Point Inv (USA): 1995.

Van der Walt, Tjaart Nicolaas, Cont'd

	97	98	99	00	01	02	03	04	05	06	07	08	09	10	11	12	13	14
Masters	-	-	-	-	-	-	-	-	-	-	-	-	-	-	-	-	-	-
US Open	-	-	-	-	-	-	-	-	-	-	-	-	-	-	-	-	-	-
British	-	-	-	-	-	-	T36	-	-	-	-	-	-	-	-	-	-	-
PGA	-	-	-	-	-	-	-	-	-	-	-	-	-	-	-	-	-	-
Money (A)	-	-	-	-	-	-	-	204*	135	185	-	-	-	-	-	-	-	-
Money (E)	-	-	-	-	206*	-	-	-	-	218*	-	-	-	-	143*	120	129	176*
Money (SA)	45	7	18	3*	15*	31*	12*	-	20*	35*	-	-	70*	16	14	5*	12*	29*
OWR	400	234	375	347	368	514	440	445	204	435	465	733	549	462	347	408	299	367

2014: E: 12 st / 7 ct / 0 t10. (T12 Madeira Islands). Played a very limited schedule, almost entirely in Europe. His lone non-co-sanctioned Sunshine appearance was in defense of his 2013 Cape Town Open title (T7). Also finished T8 at December's Alfred Dunhill Championship (E Tour '15).

OUTLOOK: A world traveling player but he's got no place where he's successfully rooted these days. Outside of his homeland, he's never found major success, and as he moves into his 40s, it's not terribly logical to assume that he suddenly will now.

STATS (LTD): Driving Distance: B+   Driving Accuracy: C   GIR: B+   Short Game: C+   Putting: C

Van Pelt, Robert Jr. ("Bo") (USA) (39)
b. Richmond, IN 5/16/1975. 6'4" 200 lbs. All-American at Oklahoma St. TP: 1998. Lost his card after one season and spent three of the next four years on the Web.com Tour where, in 2003, he won once and regained his PGA Tour card by finishing 5th in earnings. Was far more successful the second time around, only once finishing worse than 64th in $$$ (115th in 2008) through 2012 and winning the 2009 U.S. Bank Championship where, after a closing 64, he beat John Mallinger on the second hole of sudden death. Followed this up with a very successful (if winless) 2010 which saw him finish 13th in earnings and log eight top 10s. Won an unofficial PGA Tour event, the Asian Tour-sponsored Asia Pacific Classic, in 2011, running away from Jeff Overton by six. Returned to the Far East the next year to win the E Tour's inaugural ISBS Handa Perth International, edging Jason Dufner by two. **Teams**: Palmer Cup: 1997. **OWR Best**: 20 - Oct, 2012.

PGA Tour Wins (1): 2009: US Bank Championship (Milwaukee).
European Tour Wins (1): 2012: Perth International.
Asian Tour Wins (1): 2011: CIMB Classic.
Other Wins: 1 Web.com (2003).
Amateur Wins: Northern Am: 1995   Indiana Jr (2): 1991-93.

	99	00	01	02	03	04	05	06	07	08	09	10	11	12	13	14
Masters	-	-	-	-	-	-	MC	-	-	-	-	-	T8	T17	T20	-
US Open	-	-	-	-	-	T31	-	T40	-	-	MC	T40	T14	T59	T21	T63
British	-	-	-	-	-	T30	T52	MC	-	-	-	T44	T57	-	T44	-
PGA	-	-	-	-	-	T31	T17	-	MC	-	MC	T28	MC	T18	WD	-
Money (A)	210	-	-	191	-	39	51	64	58	115	40	13	29	23	88	98
OWR	-	736	534	541	428	109	82	104	126	250	157	44	29	22	57	201

2014: PGA: 25 st / 16 ct / 1 t10. (T7 John Deere). Continued a modest two-year slide, finishing 81st in FedEx Cup points.

OUTLOOK: Continued somewhat below his ultra-consistent work of 2010-2012, logging only one top 10 in 2014 (vs. 23 from 2010-2012). Did see a resurgence in his GIR number (to 16, after tumbling to 81 in 2013), with his Ball Striking (26) and Proximity To Hole (6) following in kind. But such numbers might've suggested better overall results, which makes one wonder if his best golf is now behind him. Still, if his putter heats up…

STATS: Driving Distance: B+   Driving Accuracy: A-   GIR: A-   Short Game: B-   Putting: B-

---

Van Tonder, Daniel ("Danie") (South Africa) (23)
b. Boksburg, South Africa 3/12/1991. 5'10" 175 lbs. TP: 2011. Highly thought of amateur who, upon turning pro in 2011, won 10 out of 18 events on South Africa's IGT mini-tour. Joined the Sunshine Tour in 2012 and was named Rookie Of The Year after finishing 20th in $$$. Broke through for his first Sunshine win at the 2014 Royal Swazi Sun Open (beating Jacques Blaauw and Jared Harvey in a playoff), then took the Vodacom Origins event at Euphoria six weeks later. Highly touted domestically but has yet to venture abroad. **OWR Best**: 168 - Jun, 2014.

Sunshine Tour Wins (2): 2014: Royal Swazi Sun Open (Investec), Vodacom-Euphoria (54H).
Amateur Wins: Ekerhuleni Open: 2009   African Int'l Team: 2009 (T w/D.Burmester)   Mpumalanga Open: 2010   Eastern Province Open: 2010
Central Open: 2010.

	12	13	14
Masters	-	-	-
US Open	-	-	-
British	-	-	-
PGA	-	-	-
Money (SA)	20	26	1
OWR	633	602	191

2014: SUN: 24 st / 23 ct / 13 t10. (Incl. Won Royal Swazi, Won Vodacom-Euphoria, T2 Tshwane, T2 Zambia Open, T2 Nedbank Affinity). Took a step towards the stardom that many predict for him, winning twice, missing only one cut and posting an impressive 13 top 10s

OUTLOOK: Has something of an unorthodox swing but has proven himself of star caliber on his home turf. Entering 2015 at age 23, time is largely on his side, but it will be interesting to see how long he waits to try and make the jump to Europe, or Asia.

STATS: Driving Distance: --   Driving Accuracy: --   GIR: --   Short Game: --   Putting: --

---

Van Zyl, Phillipus Jacobus ("Jaco") (South Africa) (35)
b. Kokstad, South Africa 2/23/1979. 5'10" 170 lbs. TP: 2001. Former South African Amateur champion who has been a regular – if streaky – winner on the Sunshine Tour. Won thrice on home soil in 2009 and four times in 2010, cementing his status as one of South Africa's strongest domestic players. Reached the 2007 PGA Tour via Q School but made only four of 21

Van Zyl, Phillipus Jacobus, Cont'd

cuts and finished 227th in $$$. Became the first golfer on record to card a professional level 58, doing so en route to winning the sixth event on South Africa's Diner's Club mini-tour in 2003. Won three times in four domestic starts in Feb/March 2013, including triumphs in the Dimension Data Pro-Am, the Telkom PGA Championship and a playoff victory over Hennie Otto at the select-field Investec Cup. Had his 2014 shortened by problems with both of his knees. **Teams:** Eisenhower Trophy: 2000. **OWR Best:** 68 - Mar, 2013.

Sunshine Tour Wins (13): 2005: Platinum Classic **2008:** Vodacom-Final (54H) **2009:** Telkom PGA Championship, Royal Swazi Sun Open (Stableford), Telkom PGA Pro-Am **2010:** Vodacom-Sishen (54H), Nashua Golf Challenge (54H), Telkom PGA-Pro-Am, SAA Pro-Am Inv **2011:** Telkom PGA Pro-Am **2013:** Dimension Data Pro-Am, Telkom PGA Championship, Investec Cup.
Other Wins: Diner's Club #6 (SA): 2003.
Amateur Wins: South African Am: 2000.

	02	03	04	05	06	07	08	09	10	11	12	13	14
Masters	-	-	-	-	-	-	-	-	-	-	-	-	-
US Open	-	-	-	-	-	-	-	-	-	-	-	MC	-
British	-	-	-	-	-	-	-	-	-	-	-	-	-
PGA	-	-	-	-	-	-	-	-	-	-	-	MC	-
Money (E)	-	-	-	-	-	-	-	-	-	-	-	86	
Money (SA)	18	45	-	8	10	51	17	4	6	5	3	3	17*
OWR	453	775	-	509	502	623	863	401	332	104	146	144	362

2014: E: 9 st / 8 ct / 1 t10. (T5 Africa). Was limited to nine E Tour starts (and four non-co-sanctioned Sunshine events) because of problems with both of his knees, derailing the considerable momentum he might have brought forward from his strong 2013 campaign.
OUTLOOK: One of South Africa's top domestic stars who, for several years, teetered on the edge of making the jump to the more lucrative foreign circuits before heading for Europe in 2013, then getting injured. He begins 2015 on an E Tour medical extension.

STATS (LTD): Driving Distance: C   Driving Accuracy: B+   GIR: B   Short Game: B   Putting: B+

Vaughan, Bradford (South Africa) (39)

b. Johannesburg, South Africa 6/14/1975. 6'3" 220 lbs. TP: 1995. Won the 1994 South African Amateur before embarking on a successful professional career played almost entirely on his native Sunshine Tour. Has enjoyed an uncommon level of success at two particular golf courses, first winning the 1999 and 2004 Royal Swazi Sun Classics and the 2001 Royal Swazi Sun Open (in an eight-shot runaway) at the Royal Swazi Sun Country Club. Later enjoyed a similar dominance at the Polokwane Golf Club, where he won the 2004, '05 and '06 Limpopo Classics, the last in a playoff with Warren Abery. **Teams:** Eisenhower Trophy: 1994. **OWR Best:** 188 - Apr, 2002.

Sunshine Tour Wins (8): 1997: Turstbank Gauteng Classic **1999:** Royal Swazi Sun Classic **2001:** Investec Royal Swazi Sun Open **2004:** Royal Swazi Sun Classic, Limpopo Classic (54H) **2005:** Highveld Classic, Limpopo Classic **2006:** Limpopo Classic.
Amateur Wins: South African Am: 1994.

	97	98	99	00	01	02	03	04	05	06	07	08	09	10	11	12	13	14
Masters	-	-	-	-	-	-	-	-	-	-	-	-	-	-	-	-	-	-
US Open	-	-	-	-	-	-	-	-	-	-	-	-	-	-	-	-	-	-
British	-	-	-	-	MC	-	-	-	-	-	-	-	-	-	-	-	-	-
PGA	-	-	-	-	-	-	-	-	-	-	-	-	-	-	-	-	-	-
Money (SA)	58	16	23	16	2	22	4	57*	22	12	24	24	42	27	26	61	61	178
OWR	659	626	494	688	193	339	411	825	316	273	568	689	824	853	594	699	852	1345

2014: SUN: 9 st / 1 ct / 0 t10. (49 Lombard). Plunged to 178th in $$$ in a dismal season in which he made only nine starts and never broke 70.
OUTLOOK: Well removed from his peak years, and 2014 was a washout – but he's still young enough not to be written of entirely.

STATS: Driving Distance: --   Driving Accuracy: --   GIR: --   Short Game: --   Putting: --

---

Vegas, Jhonattan Luis (Venezuela) (30)

b. Maturin, Venezuela 8/19/1984. 6'3" 230 lbs. College: U of Texas. TP: 2008. Venezuela's best-ever golf prospect who learned the game on a rudimentary nine-hole course built for oil workers. Played four seasons at the U of Texas, during which time he won the 2006 Venezuela Amateur and was a 2007 semi-finalist at the U.S. Amateur. After turning pro, played through two Web.com seasons with the second (2010) yielding one win and a 7th-place $$$ ranking. Wasted no time in establishing himself on the PGA Tour, winning the Bob Hope Classic (his second event) in a playoff over Gary Woodland and Bill Haas. Followed this with a T3 at the Farmers Insurance Open before cooling off, and has not returned to such prominence since. Recovered from a 2013 left shoulder injury to retain his card in 2014. **Teams:** Eisenhower Trophy: 2002. World Cup: 2009. **OWR Best:** 69 - Jan, 2011.

PGA Tour Wins (1): 2011: Bob Hope Classic (90H).
Int'l Wins: Argentine Open: 2010.
Other Wins: 1 Web.com (2010) + TELUS World Skins Game (Canada): 2011.
Amateur Wins: Venezuela Am: 2006.

	10	11	12	13	14
Masters	-	MC	-	-	-
US Open	-	-	-	-	-
British	-	-	-	-	-
PGA	-	T51	-	-	-
Money (A)	-	46	113	-	122
OWR	182	111	249	606	275

2014: PGA: 23 st / 16 ct / 2 t10. (T3 John Deere, T8 Wyndham). Cleared a 21-event medical extension and finished 115th in FedEx Cup points.
OUTLOOK: Purely a power-oriented player who briefly looked like a world beater upon arriving on the PGA Tour in 2011, but leveled off thereafter. Utilizes his power to hit an especially high number of greens, but things become somewhat less predictable thereafter. Still, he has yet to lose his card and he's still fairly young; if his ball striking numbers hold, the potential is there for him to improve considerably, and certainly to win again.

STATS: Driving Distance: A+   Driving Accuracy: C   GIR: A   Short Game: C+   Putting: C

Verplank, Scott Rachal (USA) (50) b. Dallas, TX 7/9/1964. 5'9" 165 lbs. Four-time All-American and 1986 NCAA individual champion at Oklahoma St. TP: 1986. Two-time AJGA All-American and AJGA Player Of The Year (1982). Won 1984 U.S. Amateur (4 & 3 over Sam Randolph) at Oak Tree GC while enjoying one of the stronger amateur careers of the modern era. Won 1985 Western Open, becoming the first amateur in 29 years to claim a PGA Tour event when he beat Jim Thorpe in sudden death. Has had his PGA Tour career twice interrupted by elbow surgeries (1992 and '96), with the former leading to a run of 37 missed cuts in 39 starts. Battled back with great perseverance and thereafter logged three wins and numerous top-50 finishes on the money list, peaking at 10th place in 2001. Won the 2000 Reno-Tahoe Open in a playoff with Jean Van de Velde, then added the 2001 Canadian Open in the event's return to Royal Montreal GC. Scored an emotional victory at the 2007 Byron Nelson Classic, edging Luke Donald by one in the event's first playing after Nelson's death. Despite his injuries, a long-running performer who finished no worse than 82nd in $$$ through 2011 (age 47). **Awards:** PGA Tour Comeback Player of the Year: 1998. **Teams:** Walker Cup: 1985 (3-0-1). Eisenhower Trophy: 1984. Ryder Cup (2): 2002-06 (O: 4-1-0, S: 2-0-0). Presidents Cup (2): 2005-07 (6-2-1). World Cup (2): 1998-04. **OWR Best:** 11 - Oct, 2001.

PGA Tour Wins (5): 1985: Western Open* **1988:** Buick Open **2000:** Reno-Tahoe Open **2001:** Canadian Open **2007:** Byron Nelson Classic (EDS).
Int'l Wins (1): 1998: World Cup (Individual).
Other Wins: Wendy's 3-Tour Challenge: 2006 (w/S.Cink & Z.Johnson).
Amateur Wins: U.S. Amateur: 1984   Porter Cup (2): 1983-85   Western Am: 1985   –   Texas Jr: 1981   Texas Am (3): 1982-84-85   LaJet Am (4): 1982-83-84-85   Sunnehanna Am (2): 1984-85   NCAA Individual: 1986.

	85	86	87	88	89	90	91	92	93	94	95	96	97	98	99	00	01	02	03	04	05	06	07	08
Masters	MC	MC	MC	MC	-	-	-	-	-	-	-	-	-	-	MC	-	MC	43	T8	29	T20	T16	T30	MC
US Open	T34	T15	MC	-	-	T61	-	-	-	T18	T21	-	-	T49	T17	T46	T22	MC	T10	T40	MC	MC	T7	T29
British	-	MC	-	MC	-	-	-	-	-	-	-	-	-	-	T15	MC	T30	T37	MC	T7	T23	T31	T57	T58
PGA	-	-	-	MC	MC	T31	-	-	-	-	MC	-	-	T54	T34	MC	T7	MC	MC	T62	T34	MC	T9	MC
Money (A)	Am	177*	173	31	141	47	266	309*	-	97	55	171*	159	18	82	22	10	50	19	20	16	40	12	77
OWR		127	184	87	159	106	233	369	-		275	108	182	347	49	73	50	16	33	24	22	28	52	25	63

	09	10	11	12	13	14
Masters	-	T18	-	T54	-	-
US Open	-	T47	-	-	-	-
British	-	T76	-	-	-	-
PGA	MC	MC	T4	WD	-	-
Money (A)	38	45	79	235*	213*	251*
OWR	60	71	92	400	-	1444

2014: PGA: 12 st / 1 ct / 0 t10. (T72 Hawaii). Had little PGA Tour impact in 12 starts, then fared little better in four Champions Tour entries.
OUTLOOK: At age 50, still a straight driver but the rest of his skills have declined, likely due to injuries and age. Played only on the Champions Tour (in the form of four uninspiring starts) upon turning 50 so it is fair to assume that he'll be focusing his interests there, especially if 100% healthy.
STATS: Driving Distance: C-   Driving Accuracy: B+   GIR: C-   Short Game: B-   Putting: C

Versfeld, Allan (South Africa) (23) b. Johannesburg, South Africa 2/21/1991. 5'9" 145 lbs. TP: 2011. Solid amateur prospect who won the second-tier Botswana and Mpumalanga Opens in 2010, prior to turning pro. Was named Sunshine Tour Rookie Of The Year in 2011 after logging four top-5 finishes and placing 16th in $$$. Broke through for his maiden win at the 2012 Vodacom Origins – Western Cape event, where he beat Ockie Strydom by three, before taking a modest step back in 2013, and a bigger one in 2014. **OWR Best:** 341 - Jan, 2013.

Sunshine Tour Wins (1): 2012: Vodacom-Western Cape (54H).
Other Wins: Botswana Open: 2010*   Mpumalanga Open (SA): 2010*   Telkom PGA Pro-Am (SA): 2012.
Amateur Wins: Central Gauteng Under 23: 2010   Central Gauteng Am: 2010.

	11	12	13	14
Masters	-	-	-	-
US Open	-	-	-	-
British	-	-	-	-
PGA	-	-	-	-
Money (SA)	16	19	31	80
OWR	810	345	632	1115

2014: SUN: 22 st / 12 ct / 0 t10. (T16 Zambia Open). Had just the year he didn't need, logging zero top 10s and falling to 80th in $$$.
OUTLOOK: At age 23 he has plenty of time to develop, but has been trending the wrong way since 2012. Needs a big turnaround in 2015.
STATS: Driving Distance: --   Driving Accuracy: --   GIR: --   Short Game: --   Putting: --

---

Villegas Restrepo, Camilo (Colombia) (32) b. Medellin, Colombia 1/7/1982. 5'9" 160 lbs. Four-time All-American at U of Florida. TP: 2004. Easily Colombia's highest-ranked and most prominent golf professional ever. Won the 2001 Colombian Open while still an amateur. Played his way onto the PGA Tour by finishing 13th on the 2005 Web.com Tour money list. Claimed his first major tour win in Japan, at the 2007 Tokai Classic, beating Toyokazu Fujishima in a playoff. After finishing 38th and 41st in PGA Tour earnings in 2006 and '07, broke through in 2008 to claim two victories during the FedEx Cup playoffs, the BMW Championship (where he edged Dudley Hart by two at Bellerive) and, three weeks later, at the Tour Championship, where a closing 66 led to a victory over Sergio Garcia on the first hole of sudden death. Logged his third U.S. victory at the 2010 Honda Classic (where he ran away from Anthony Kim by five) but quieted considerably thereafter, slipping to 77th and 144th in $$$ in 2011 and '12. Broke a four-year drought by winning the 2014 Wyndham Championship, closing with a 63 to edge Bill Haas and Freddie Jacobson by one. **Teams:** Eisenhower Trophy (3): 1998-00-02. Presidents Cup: 2009 (0-4-0). World Cup (2): 2006-11. **OWR Best:** 7 - Sep, 2008.

PGA Tour Wins (4): 2008: Western Open (BMW), Tour Championship **2010:** Honda Classic **2014:** Wyndham Championship.
Japan Tour Wins (1): 2007: Tokai Classic.
Other Wins: 1 NGA/Hooters (2005)   Colombian Open: 2001*.
Amateur Wins: Players Am: 2003   Colombia Am: 1998   Colombia Jr Match Play: 1998   Colombia Jr Stroke Play: 1998   Orange Bowl Jr: 1999.

Villegas Restrepo, Camilo, Cont'd

	04	05	06	07	08	09	10	11	12	13	14
Masters	-	-	-	MC	MC	T13	T38	49	-	-	-
US Open	MC	-	T59	T26	T9	T33	T70	MC	-	-	-
British	-	-	-	-	T39	T13	T44	MC	-	MC	-
PGA	-	-	MC	T23	T4	T51	T8	MC	-	-	-
Money (A)	-	-	38	41	7	45	16	77	144	117	62
Money (E)	-	-	-	-	-	30	-	-	-	-	-
OWR	390	303	117	56	7	23	37	89	251	292	145

2014: PGA: 29 st / 20 ct / 1 t10. (Won Wyndham). Completed a two-year comeback from the edge of the abyss, winning for the first time in four years and finished 62nd in FedEx Cup pts - though it must be noted that his victory was his lone top 10 finish of the year.

OUTLOOK: Did his Wyndham victory signal a return to the upper ranks or was it a one-off fluke? Oddly, his GIR skyrocketed to 4 in 2012 and has remained high (40 and 39) since. Even stranger, his ball striking numbers are generally *better* than they were during 2008, and while his putting has slipped, it's hardly catastrophic (97 in Total Putting). Logically his overall results should be better - so a return to the elite may have to wait a while.

STATS: Driving Distance: B+   Driving Accuracy: B-   GIR: A-   Short Game: B-   Putting: C+

Vongvanij, Arnond (USA/Thailand) (26)

b. Honolulu, HI 12/15/1988. 5'5" 140 lbs. All-American at U of Florida. TP: 2011. Two-time AJGA All-American. Nicknamed (and widely known as) "Bank." Born in Hawaii but spent his first 12 years in Thailand before moving back to the states to study under David Leadbetter in Bradenton, FL. A four-time AJGA All-American. Joined the Asian Tour as a 2012 rookie, where he logged five top-10 finishes and, in his 18th start, won the King's Cup, beating Mardan Mamat and Thaworn Wiratchant by two. Surprisingly, saw a steady decline in form in both 2013 and '14. **Teams:** Palmer Cup: 2011. **OWR Best:** 219 - Jun, 2013.

Asian Tour Wins (1): 2012: King's Cup.

Amateur Wins: St. Augustine Am: 2005   Terra Cotta Inv: 2006   Eastern Am: 2009.

	12	13	14
Masters	-	-	-
US Open	-	-	-
British	-	-	-
PGA	-	-	-
Money (As)	18	24	51
OWR	268	252	546

2014: ASIA: 19 st / 8 ct / 1 t10. (T2 Philippine Open). Slipped in earnings for the second straight year, falling to 51st.

OUTLOOK: A well-thought-of junior prospect in America who has not yet really found his stride as a pro – though he has shown signs. Is a short hitter and, statistically speaking, a mediocre ball striker, but can largely make up for it around the greens. Needs to reverse things quickly.

STATS: Driving Distance: C+   Driving Accuracy: B+   GIR: C-   Short Game: B+   Putting: A-

---

Wagner, Montford Johnson (USA) (34)

b. Amarillo, TX 3/23/1980. 6'3" 230 lbs. College: All-American at Virginia Tech. TP: 2002. A native Texan who maintained an unprecedented dominance of New York area amateur golf, winning the 2001 and '02 Metropolitan Amateurs, the 2002 Met Amateur Stroke play ("The Ike") and both the 2001 and '02 Metropolitan Opens, the latter as a pro. Played four seasons on the Web.com Tour (2002-2006) before hitting stride with a two-win 2006 that included a 2nd-place $$$ finish. Broke through for his first PGA Tour title at the 2008 Houston Open, edging Chad Campbell and Geoff Ogilvy by two. After slipping earnings-wise in 2009 and '10, returned to the limelight in 2011 by beating Spencer Levin in a playoff to win the Mayakoba Classic (played opposite the WGC Match Play). Began 2012 on a similarly high note, winning the Sony Open in Hawaii in his second start, then rolling to a career-best 35th in $$$. Cooled off significantly in 2013. **OWR Best:** 60 - Apr, 2012.

PGA Tour Wins (3): 2008: Houston Open (Shell)   **2011:** Mayakoba Classic   **2012:** Hawaiian Open (Sony).

Other Wins: 2 Web.com (2006)   +   Metropolitan (NY) Open: 2002.

Amateur Wins: Metropolitan Am (2): 2001-02.

	02	03	04	05	06	07	08	09	10	11	12	13	14
Masters	-	-	-	-	-	-	T36	-	-	-	MC	-	-
US Open	-	-	MC	-	MC	-	-	-	-	-	-	-	-
British	-	-	-	-	-	-	-	-	-	-	MC	T58	-
PGA	-	-	-	-	-	-	MC	-	-	T51	MC	-	-
Money (A)	-	-	-	-	-	98	73	153	126	78	35	104	158
OWR	-	-	837	630	251	237	149	352	389	220	109	264	411

2014: PGA: 24 st / 11 ct / 1 t10. (T7 John Deere). Finished 150th in FedEx Cup points, then failed to play his way through the Web.com Finals.

OUTLOOK: Appeared on the verge of stardom in late 2011/early 2012 but has fallen off badly since, and will play 2015 on conditional status (by the skin of his teeth). A surprisingly short hitter given his size - a significant problem given that his Driving Accuracy has fallen to 149. Has proven himself a streaky type so a comeback is hardly out of the question, but barring a crazy-hot week or two, it wil most likely start on the Web.com Tour.

STATS: Driving Distance: C+   Driving Accuracy: B-   GIR: B-   Short Game: B-   Putting: B+

Wakefield, Simon (England) (40)

b. Newcastle-under-Lyme, England 4/14/1974. 6'2" 180 lbs. TP: 1997. Long-running E Tour veteran who has bounced back and forth to the Challenge Tour, causing him to return to Q School an impressive nine times. Logged his lone major win at the Sunshine Tour's 2005 Dimension Data Pro-Am, where he beat homestanding Nic Henning by three. Retained his E Tour card for much of the 2000s, but has now not had fully exempt status since 2008. **OWR Best:** 189 - Sep, 2006.

Sunshine Tour Wins (1): 2005: Dimension Data Pro-Am.

Other Wins: 1 Euro Challenge (2002).

Amateur Wins: Tillman Trophy: 1996.

Wakefield, Simon, Cont'd

	00	01	02	03	04	05	06	07	08	09	10	11	12	13	14
Masters	-	-	-	-	-	-	-	-	-	-	-	-	-	-	-
US Open	-	-	-	-	-	-	-	-	-	-	-	-	-	-	-
British	-	-	-	MC	MC	-	T48	-	T19	-	-	-	-	-	-
PGA	-	-	-	-	-	-	-	-	-	-	-	-	-	-	-
Money (E)	196	-	-	99	118	75	60	54	88	174	-	122	199*	134	142
OWR	-	705	462	497	533	256	226	244	320	589	721	334	227	435	658

2014: E: 26 st / 11 ct / 3 t10. (T7 Dunhill Champ, T9 Lyoness, T9 Denmark). Lost his card for the fourth straight year, finishing 142nd in $$$.

OUTLOOK: Has played through an on-again, off-again career which has never quite reached a level of stability on the European Tour. At age 40, winless on the E Tour, and carrying both limited length and putting numbers, he would appear to be solidly on the downside now.

STATS: Driving Distance: C-   Driving Accuracy: A   GIR: B-   Short Game: B+   Putting: C

Walker, Jimmy M. (USA) (35)

b. Oklahoma City, OK 1/16/1979. 6'2" 1805 lbs. All-American at Baylor U. TP: 2001. Took a long and persistent road to PGA Tour success, having twice graduated from Web.com Tour from (and from both ends of the spectrum: 1st in 2004 and 25th in 2007) and also qualified via a T11 at 2008 Q School. A three-time winner on the Web.com, including twice during his #1-ranked 2004 campaign. Has maintained a spot on the PGA Tour since 2009, climbing steadily in earnings through 2013, when he claimed his maiden victory at the Frys.com Open (the first event on the Tour's new wraparound schedule), beating a 50-year-old Vijay Singh by two. Won again three months later at the Sony Open in Hawaii (edging Chris Kirk by one), then made it three triumphs in eight start by taking the 2014 AT&T Pebble Beach Pro-Am by one. Finished 2014 ranked 4th in $$$, and made his first Ryder Cup appearance. **Teams**: Ryder Cup: 2014 (O: 1-1-3, S: 1-0-0). **OWR Best**: 17 - May, 2014.

PGA Tour Wins (3): 2013: Frys.com Open ('14) 2014: Hawaiian Open (Sony), AT&T Pro-Am.
Other Wins: 3 Web.com (2004-2007).

	01	02	03	04	05	06	07	08	09	10	11	12	13	14
Masters	-	-	-	-	-	-	-	-	-	-	-	-	-	T8
US Open	T52	MC	-	-	-	-	-	-	-	-	-	-	-	T9
British	-	-	-	-	-	-	-	-	-	-	-	-	MC	T26
PGA	-	-	-	-	-	-	-	-	MC	-	T21	MC	T7	
Money (A)	-	-	-	-	-	202	-	185	125	103	67	48	30	5
OWR	924	577	450	329	435	597	477	563	398	259	165	120	47	21

2014: PGA: 27 st / 23 ct / 10 t10. (Won Frys.com, Won Hawaii, Won AT&T Pro-Am, 6 CIMB, 6 Players, etc.). Climaxed his steady climb with a meteoric season, winning thrice, logging 19 top 25s, finishing 4th in $$$ and 7th in Fedex Cup points, and making his first Ryder Cup appearance.

OUTLOOK: Blossomed into a major star in 2014, riding an enviable mix of power and a strong short game to a top-20 spot in the OWR. Has seen some imposing four-year improvements in his game, especially in GIR (136, 116, 61 and 28), Ball Striking (145, 129, 92 and 69) and, to a lesser degree, SGP (49, 16, 45, 11). As solid as his 2014 was, it can be suggested that he'll be hard pressed to maintain such form. But given that his rise has been statistically methodical, the sense here is that he can continue this form - if not, perhaps, so many wins - at least into 2015.

STATS: Driving Distance: A   Driving Accuracy: C-   GIR: B+⇧   Short Game: B+   Putting: A

Wall, Anthony David (England) (39)

b. London, England 5/29/1975. 6'2" 195 lbs. TP: 1995. A very steady earner on the European Tour, finishing 90th in $$$ as a rookie in 1998 and never failing to better that all the way through 2012. Won his lone E Tour title at the 2000 Alfred Dunhill Championship in South Africa, beating Phillip Price and Gary Orr by two. Finished a career-best 13th in $$$ in a 2006 campaign which saw him thrice finish a runner-up. Missed much of 2013 with an unspecified injury. **Teams**: Seve Trophy: 2009. **OWR Best**: 59 - Dec, 2006.

European Tour Wins (1): 2000: Alfred Dunhill Championship.
Amateur Wins: Golf Illustrated Gold Vase: 1993   Sunningdale Foursomes: 1994 (w/S. Webster).

	98	99	00	01	02	03	04	05	06	07	08	09	10	11	12	13	14
Masters	-	-	-	-	-	-	-	-	-	-	-	-	-	-	-	-	-
US Open	-	-	-	-	-	-	-	-	-	MC	-	-	-	-	-	-	-
British	-	-	-	-	T46	-	-	T11	MC	T51	T43	-	-	-	-	-	-
PGA	-	-	-	-	-	-	-	-	MC	WD	-	MC	-	-	-	-	-
Money (E)	90	59	44	48	80	87	86	63	13	57	22	40	76	70	65	-	110
OWR	288	237	218	180	252	328	340	265	59	131	110	83	207	218	210	367	418

2014: E: 30 st / 16 ct / 1 t10. (T10 Joburg). Returned from an injury-shortened year to finish 110th in $$$ - and claim the last exempt spot.

OUTLOOK: Never a big winner, but he has ridden a steady tee-to-green game, plus a strong short game, to a long run of E Tour monetary success. Now healthy again, he'll try to extend his career into his 40s - preferably more comfortably than his by-skin-of-his-teeth 2014.

STATS: Driving Distance: B   Driving Accuracy: B+   GIR: A-   Short Game: A-   Putting: C+

Walters, Justin Jeremy (South Africa/England) (34)

b. Johannesburg, South Africa 10/23/1980. 6'0" 230 lbs. All-American and NAIA individual champion (2201) at Huntington (AL) College, two-time All-American at North Carolina St. after transferring. TP: 2003. Has represented England in team play as his mother is English. Initially played U.S. mini-tours (winning once), the Web.com circuit and in his native South Africa, where he claimed the 2004 Parmalat Open and, in 2011, the bigger Royal Swazi Open (played at Stableford). Played the European Challenge Tour in 2012, finishing 15th in $$$ to earn E Tour privileges for 2013. Retained his card as a rookie but then narrowly lost it during a disappointing 2014. **Teams**: Palmer Cup: 2002. **OWR Best**: 181 - Mar, 2014.

Sunshine Tour Wins (2): 2004: Parmalat Classic (54H) 2011: Royal Swazi Open (Investec)(Stableford).
Amateur Wins: Puerto Rico Classic: 2003.

Walters, Justin Jeremy, Cont'd

	04	05	06	07	08	09	10	11	12	13	14
Masters	-	-	-	-	-	-	-	-	-	-	-
US Open	-	-	-	-	-	-	-	-	-	-	-
British	-	-	-	-	-	-	-	-	-	-	MC
PGA	-	-	-	-	-	-	-	-	-	-	-
Money (E)	-	-	-	-	-	-	-	-	-	64	126
Money (SA)	118*	36*	38*	41*	35*	87*	41	30	24	30*	8*
OWR	-	921	634	713	750	-	-	396	290	196	354

2014: E: 29 st / 11 ct / 1 t10. (T2 Joburg). After turning some heads with a strong rookie campaign on the E Tour, fell to 126th in $$$ in his sophomore year, then failed (by two shots) to play his way back via Q School.

OUTLOOK: Though never quite a top-shelf star in South Africa, transitioned nicely to the E Tour in 2013, then fell in his sophomore campaign. Has demonstrated enough power to serve him well on the big stage – but it appears he'll primarily be back on home soil in 2015.

STATS: Driving Distance: A-   Driving Accuracy: C   GIR: B   Short Game: C   Putting: B-

---

Wang, Jeung-Hun (South Korea) (19)

b. Seoul, South Korea 9/7/1995. 5'9" 160 lbs. TP: 2012. After a solid amateur career (which included several smaller wins), became an Asian Tour regular where he began to hit stride in 2014, finishing runner-up to Arjun Atwal at the season-ending Dubai Open and finishing 21st in $$$. Also claimed his first professional victory in 2014, winning the Mission Hills Haikou Open on the PGA Tour China circuit. **OWR Best:** 269 - Dec, 2014.

Other Wins: Haikou Open (PGA-China): 2014.

Amateur Wins: Philippine Am: 2011.

	13	14
Masters	-	-
US Open	-	-
British	-	-
PGA	-	-
Money (As)	76	15
OWR	727	269

2014: ASIA: 16 st / 16 ct / 4 t10. (2 Dubai Open, T6 Queens Cup, T8 Philippine Open). Enjoyed something of a breakout year, winning on the PGA Tour China and very nearly winning on the Asian circuit in Dubai. Finished 21st in Asian Tour $$$.

OUTLOOK: Has made a name for himself around Asia in his teens, riding a power-oriented game to what looks like a strong future. His samplings are limited but his putting numbers improved in 2014; if he can hold those gains going forward, bigger things seem possible. Might well have been exempt on the 2015 Web.com Tour as a top-5 earner on the PGA Tour China but he only played in six of 12 events, finishing 10th in $$$.

STATS (LTD):   Driving Distance: A-   Driving Accuracy: A   GIR: B-   Short Game: B+   Putting: B

Waring, Paul James (England) (29)

b. Birkenhead, England 2/2/1985. 5'11" 175 lbs. TP: 2007. Played his way through the 2007 E Tour Q School and retained his card for three consecutive years thereafter, peaking during 2010 when he finished 93rd in $$$. Suffered an injury to his right wrist at the 2011 BMW PGA which required surgery, with his recovery extending through all of 2012. Began 2013 on a medical extension but made good, logging five top 10s en route to finishing 69th in $$$. **OWR Best:** 159 - Mar, 2014.

Amateur Wins: English Am: 2005   –   English Under-16s: 2001   English Public GCs Under 18: 2002.

	08	09	10	11	12	13	14
Masters	-	-	-	-	-	-	-
US Open	-	-	-	-	-	-	-
British	T19	MC	-	-	-	-	-
PGA	-	-	-	-	-	-	-
Money (E)	105	115	95	-	-	69	94
OWR	278	354	359	627	595	180	250

2014: E: 25 st / 15 ct / 1 t10. (T8 Hassan). Fell moderately off of his career-best 2013 but still comfortably retained his card, making 15 of 25 cuts on his way to finishing 94th in E Tour $$$.

OUTLOOK: A powerful and fairly skilled player from tee-to-green, though things are a tad less certain from there. His 2013 was probably an outlier but his initial post-injury returns suggest that he can earn a living at this level - and, perhaps, win in a lighter-field or opposite event.

STATS: Driving Distance: A-   Driving Accuracy: B   GIR: B+   Short Game: C   Putting: B-

---

Warren, Marc (Scotland) (33)

b. East Kilbride, Scotland 1/4/1981. 5'11" 170 lbs. TP: 2002. First came to fame by holing the winning putt at the 2001 Walker Cup at Sea Island, GA, Great Britain & Ireland's second Cup win on U.S. soil. Initially struggled as a pro, placing no better that 79th in Challenge Tour earnings prior to leading the tour's Order of Merit with a two-win 2005. Recorded his first E Tour win at the 2006 Scandinavian Masters, defeating homestanding Robert Karlsson in a playoff. The following year, added the Johnnie Walker Championship (beating Simon Wakefield in a playoff at Gleneagles) and teamed with Colin Montgomerie to record Scotland's first-ever win in the World Cup, in China. Lost the 2013 BMW PGA Championship in a playoff with winner Matteo Manassero and Simon Khan. Broke a seven-year victory drought by claiming the E Tour's inaugural Made In Denmark event in 2014, beating Bradley Dredge by two. **Awards:** E Tour Rookie of the Year: 2006. **Teams:** Walker Cup: 2001 (2-1-0). Seve Trophy (2): 2007-13. World Cup (2): 2006-07 (won in '07 w/C.Montgomerie). **OWR Best:** 64 - Sep, 2014.

European Tour Wins (3): 2006: Scandinavian Masters **2007:** Johnnie Walker Championship **2014:** Made In Denmark.

Other Wins: 2 Euro Challenge (2005).

Amateur Wins: English Am: 1996   –   Doug Sanders World Boys: 1994

Warren, Marc, Cont'd

	02	03	04	05	06	07	08	09	10	11	12	13	14
Masters	-	-	-	-	-	-	-	-	-	-	-	-	-
US Open	-	-	-	-	-	-	-	-	-	-	T65	-	-
British	-	-	-	-	-	-	-	-	-	-	-	MC	T39
PGA	-	-	-	-	-	-	-	-	-	-	-	T12	T15
Money (E)	-	-	-	-	42	42	97	84	124	114	55	33	26
OWR	832	989	826	302	120	153	272	328	469	367	182	114	69

2014: E: 30 st / 23 ct / 4 t10. (Won Denmark, 3 Scottish, T4 Wales, T6 NH Collection). Won once and finished a career-best 26th in E Tour $$$.

OUTLOOK: Has risen from earning a nice E Tour living to being a top-50 money winner, riding a very desirable mix of power and a strong short game. His victories have been in lighter-field events but as he continues to contend more consistently, something bigger may well be in the offing.

STATS: Driving Distance: A-   Driving Accuracy: C+   GIR: B   Short Game: B+   Putting: A-

---

Watney, Nicholas Alan (USA) (33)
b. Sacramento, CA 4/25/1981. 6'2" 180 lbs. Three-time All-American at Fresno St. TP: 2003. Nephew of ex-PGA Tour player Mike Watney, his college coach at Fresno St. Top ball striker who has climbed steadily in his professional career, winning once on the Web.com Tour in 2004 before moving permanently to the PGA Tour in 2005. Broke through for his first PGA Tour victory at the 2007 New Orleans Classic, where he beat Ken Duke by three. Claimed his second Tour win at the 2009 Buick Invitational (San Diego) where two late birdies edged John Rollins by one at Torrey Pines. Led the 2010 PGA Championship (Whistling Straights) through 54 holes but closed with an 81, ultimately tying for 18th. Began to emerge as a star in 2011, winning the WGC Cadillac Championship (by two over Dustin Johnson) and the AT&T National, where he shot 62-66 on the weekend to win by two over K.J. Choi. Closed a moderately disappointing 2012 by winning The Barclays, beating Brandt Snedeker by three at Bethpage. Later added an unofficial win by closing with a 61 at the Asia Tour's CIMB Classic in Malaysia. Maintained form in a winless 2013 before stumbling a bit in 2014, finishing 106th in $$$. **Teams**: Palmer Cup: 2002. Presidents Cup: 2011 (2-1-1). World Cup: 2009. **OWR Best**: 9 - Jul, 2011.

PGA Tour Wins (5): 2007: New Orleans Classic (Zurich) **2009**: San Diego Open (Buick Inv) **2011**: WGC-Cadillac Championship, AT&T National **2012**: The Barclays.

Asian Tour Wins (1): 2011: CIMB Classic.

Other Wins: 1 Web.com (2004) + Lewis Chitengwa Memorial (Canada): 2003   Callaway Inv: 2005   Wendy's 3-Tour Challenge: 2012 (w/J.Day & D.Love III).

Amateur Wins: Southwestern Am: 2002.

	05	06	07	08	09	10	11	12	13	14
Masters	-	-	-	T11	19	7	46	T32	T13	T44
US Open	-	-	MC	T60	MC	76	MC	T21	MC	MC
British	-	-	T35	-	T27	T7	MC	T23	MC	MC
PGA	-	-	MC	-	MC	T18	T12	MC	MC	T33
Money (A)	127	75	43	121	12	27	3	22	24	106
OWR	259	171	137	203	32	35	12	20	30	127

2014: PGA: 25 st / 17 ct / 2 t10. (T5 Wyndham, T8 Barracuda). Slipped noticeably, finishing 105th in FedEx Cup points and 106th in $$$.

OUTLOOK: After a strong five-year run, fell somewhat abruptly in 2014, this despite actually scoring modest statistical gains in areas like Total Driving (26 to 12) and Driving Distance (63 to 45), and holding dead steady in Ball Striking (15). And while he did lose ground in GIR (13 to 32) and SGP (99 to 115), neither would seem enough to explain his decline. Thus a bounce back year - and perhaps his sixth PGA Tour win - seems in order.

STATS: Driving Distance: A-   Driving Accuracy: B   GIR: A   Short Game: B-   Putting: B-

---

Watson, Gerry Lester Jr. ("Bubba") (USA) (36)
b. Bagdad, FL 11/5/1978. 6'3" 180 lbs. College: Faulkner(AL)JC/U of Georgia. TP: 2003. A two-time AJGA All-American and a Junior College All-American at Faulkner (AL) JC before attending Georgia. Tremendously long hitting left-hander who led the PGA Tour in Driving Distance from 2006-2008, and in 2012, and finished 2nd (behind Robert Garrigus twice, then J.B. Holmes) in 2009, '10 and '11. Spent three seasons on the Web.com Tour before reaching the PGA Tour in 2005. Though a touted junior, he never won either a collegiate or developmental tour event. First PGA Tour victory came at the 2010 Travelers Championship, where he beat veterans Corey Pavin and Scott Verplank in sudden death. Lost a three-hole playoff to Martin Kaymer at the 2010 PGA Championship, but earned enough points to clinch a spot on the Ryder Cup team. Reached stardom in 2011 by winning twice, edging Phil Mickelson by one to take the Farmers Insurance Open at Torrey Pines, then adding the Zurich Classic of New Orleans where he beat Webb Simpson in a playoff after Simpson incurred a hard-luck moving ball penalty on the 15th. Closed out 2011 by shooting a non-competitive 58 at the Estancia Club in Scottsdale. Broke through for his first Major championship at the 2012 Masters, defeating Louis Oosthuizen on the second hole of sudden death. Ended a 41-event post-Masters victory drought by winning the 2014 Northern Trust Open, shooting 64-64 on the weekend at Riviera, then claimed his second Green Jacket in two years by cruising to a three-shot victory at The Masters. Ended 2014 in style by claiming the WGC-HSBC Champions in China, holing a 72nd-hole bunker shot to tie Tim Clark, then winning in a playoff. **Teams**: Ryder Cup (3): 2010-12-14 (O: 3-8-0, S: 0-3-0). Presidents Cup: 2011 (3-2-0). **OWR Best**: 3 - Jun, 2014.

PGA Tour Wins (7): 2010: Greater Hartford Open (Travelers) **2011**: San Diego Open (Farmers), New Orleans Classic (Zurich) **2012**: Masters Tournament **2014**: Northern Trust Open, Masters Tournament, WGC-HSBC Champions ('15).

Other Wins: Wendy's 3-Tour Challenge: 2010 (w/D.Johnson & B.Weekley).

	04	05	06	07	08	09	10	11	12	13	14
Masters	-	-	-	-	T20	42	-	T38	Win	T50	Win
US Open	MC	-	-	T5	MC	T18	-	T63	MC	T32	MC
British	-	-	-	-	-	-	MC	MC	T30	T23	T32	MC
PGA	-	-	-	-	MC	70	MC	2P	T26	T11	MC	T65
Money (A)	-	-	90	55	58	60	15	16	5	44	2
OWR	-	534	219	168	107	125	97	32	21	8	28	4

2014: PGA: 21 st / 18 ct / 8 t10. (Won Northern Trust, Won Masters, 2 BMW, 2 Phoenix, 2 WGC-Cadillac, etc.). Returned to form with a vengeance early in the year, winning at Riviera, then winning his second Masters, en route to finishing a career-best 2nd in $$$ and 5th in FedEx Cup points.

Watson, Gerry Lester Jr., Cont'd

OUTLOOK: Is widely known both for his elite power (finished 1 or 2 in Driving Distance every year but one since 2006) and the range of his shotmaking, allowing him to finish among the top 10 in GIR from 2011-2013 (24th in 2014) and 5 in Proximity To Hole in 2014. Consistency (in terms of both scoring and attitude) is an issue, however, and may well be tied to Attention Deficit Hyperactivity Disorder, which he acknowledges having but apparently chooses not to medicate. Thus more of the same - some major (or Major) highs mixed with some bizarre lows - seems likely in 2015.

STATS: Driving Distance: A+   Driving Accuracy: B-   GIR: A+   Short Game: C+   Putting: B-

---

Wattel, Romain (France) (23)
b. Montpelier, France 1/10/1991. 5'9" 160 lbs. TP: 2010. One of France's more touted new millennium prospects who gained early notice first via strong 2009 amateur campaign, then, in 2010, by becoming only the fifth amateur to win on the Challenge Tour when he claimed the Allianz European Strasbourg event by three shots. After starring on France's winning team at the Eisenhower Trophy, played his way through 2010 Q School and has since established himself as a steady earner on the E Tour. Though still winless, stepped up somewhat in 2014, finishing 28th in E Tour $$$. **Teams:** Eisenhower Trophy: 2010. **OWR Best:** 95 - Dec, 2014.

Other Wins: 1 Euro Challenge (2010).
Amateur Wins: Argentine Am: 2009   French Under-18: 2009   French Am Stroke Play: 2009   Orange Bowl Jr: 2009   Scottish Am Stroke Play: 2010   Scratch Players: 2010.

	11	12	13	14
Masters	-	-	-	-
US Open	-	-	-	-
British	-	-	-	-
PGA	-	-	-	-
Money (E)	90	51	84	28
OWR	242	168	172	97

2014: E: 28 st / 21 ct / 8 t10. (T3 Dunhill Champ, T3 Dubai, T3 Port Masters, 4 Mandela, T5 KLM, etc.). Took a significant step up in class by doubling his previous best for top 10s (logging eight of them) and climbing to 28th in $$$.

OUTLOOK: Though his statistical sample is somewhat limited, has thus far demonstrated a solid mix of power with impressive putting numbers, all of which was boosted by a significant improvement in GIR in 2014. It seems surprising that he hasn't won yet, and that is a fair question to raise entering his fifth full E Tour season. But he still seems to be in the climbing phase of his career, so a breakthrough victory could well be imminent.

STATS: Driving Distance: A   Driving Accuracy: B   GIR: B+   Short Game: B-   Putting: A-

---

Webster, Steven (England) (39)
b. Nuneaton, England 1/17/1975. 5'8" 155 lbs. TP: 1995. Veteran Englishman who has survived as a steady earner on the E Tour, remaining among the top 100 $$$ winners since 1997. Claimed his first win during a career-best 2005 (29th in $$$) beating a trio of players by three at the Italian Open. Validated the victory by claiming the 2007 Portuguese Masters, where he edged Robert Karlsson by two. Has existed primarily as a steady (if unspectacular) earner since. **Teams:** Seve Trophy (2): 2002-09. **OWR Best:** 72 - Jan, 2008.

European Tour Wins (2): 2005: Italian Open **2007:** Portugal Masters.
Amateur Wins: English Under-16s: 1992   Peter McEvoy Trophy: 1993.

	95	96	97	98	99	00	01	02	03	04	05	06	07	08	09	10	11	12	13	14
Masters	-	-	-	-	-	-	-	-	-	-	-	-	-	-	-	-	-	-	-	-
US Open	-	-	-	-	-	-	-	-	-	-	-	-	-	-	-	-	-	-	-	-
British	T24	-	-	-	-	MC	-	-	-	T41	-	-	MC	-	-	-	-	-	-	-
PGA	-	-	-	-	-	-	-	-	-	-	T59	-	-	MC	MC	-	-	-	-	-
Money (E)	-	129	63	37	48	69	30	68	98	64	29	81	31	49	47	92	62	99	67	108
OWR	536	460	252	171	133	191	117	151	317	253	124	205	80	112	126	218	227	209	197	324

2014: E: 19 st / 11 ct / 2 t10. (T5 Qatar, T5 Dubai). Started fast in the desert (his habit) before barely retaining his card, finishing 108th in $$$.

OUTLOOK: Has long ridden a strong tee-to-green game to earn a good European Tour living, but his short game and putting have kept him from winning more regularly. Is liable to steal another title one of these days - and recent form suggests the winter desert swing as the most likely time.

STATS: Driving Distance: B+   Driving Accuracy: B   GIR: A   Short Game: C+   Putting: B-

---

Weekley, Thomas Brent ("Boo") (USA) (41)
b. Milton, FL 7/23/1973. 6'0" 210 lbs. College: Baldwin Agricultural College. TP: 1997. Played high school golf with PGA Tour member Heath Slocum (Bubba Watson later also attended Milton High School). After playing multiple mini-tours in the late 1990s, spent four full years on the Web.com circuit (2003-2006), his 7th-place money finish in 2006 qualifying him for the PGA Tour. Finished 23rd in earnings as a rookie highlighted by a victory at the Heritage Classic, where he edged Ernie Els by one. Returned in 2008 to defend his Heritage crown, this time beating Aaron Baddeley and Anthony Kim by three. Finished 25th in 2008 $$$ and played on the U.S. Ryder Cup team. Failed to better 85th for the next four years (slipping to 180th during an injury-bothered 2011) before returning to the winner's circle at Colonial – and logging a career-best 22nd place in $$$ – in 2013. **Teams:** Ryder Cup: 2008 (O: 2-0-1, S: 1-0-0). World Cup: 2007. **OWR Best:** 23 - Apr, 2008.

PGA Tour Wins (3): 2007: Heritage Classic (Verizon) **2008:** Heritage Classic (Verizon) **2013:** Colonial Inv (Crown Plaza).
Other Wins: Wendy's 3-Tour Challenge: 2010 (w/D.Johnson & B.Watson).

	02	03	04	05	06	07	08	09	10	11	12	13	14
Masters	-	-	-	-	-	-	T20	MC	-	-	-	MC	-
US Open	-	-	-	-	-	T26	T26	MC	-	-	MC	66	-
British	-	-	-	-	-	T35	MC	T13	-	-	T58	MC	-
PGA	-	-	-	-	-	T9	T20	T36	MC	-	T12	WD	-
Money (A)	200	-	-	-	23	25	85	111	180	108	22	112	
OWR	814	-	-	204	45	48	116	242	529	299	54	118	

2014: PGA: 24 st / 16 ct / 1 t10. (T5 Byron Nelson). Fell from a very strong 2013, finishing 111th in FedEx Cup points and never really contending.

Weekley, Thomas Brent, Cont'd

OUTLOOK: Still one of the game's top ball strikers. Ranked 12 in Ball Striking, 15 in Total Driving and 20 in GIR – and that was in an obviously down year. Always a shaky putter, however, and his short game has not been significantly better. Curiously, despite big power numbers, his three career victories have come at shorter, shotmaking-oriented courses (Harbour Town and Colonial). But it's tough to regularly prosper with so balky a putter.

STATS: Driving Distance: B+   Driving Accuracy: A   GIR: A+   Short Game: C   Putting: D

Weir, Michael Richard (Canada) (44)
b. Sarnia, Ontario, Canada 5/12/1970. 5'9" 155 lbs. All-American at Brigham Young U. TP: 1992. Three-time recipient (2000, '01 and '03) of Lionel Conacher Award, given to Canada's Male Athlete of the Year. Canada's greatest-ever golfer, having equaled George Knudson's eight PGA Tour wins, but with a Major championship included. After playing for several years in Canada, joined the PGA Tour full-time in 1998, winning eight times over nine seasons and five times cracking the Tour's top 25 money winners. First PGA Tour win came on home soil when he beat Fred Funk by two at the 1999 Air Canada Championship. Won the 2001 Tour Championship in a four-man playoff, defeating Ernie Els, Sergio García and David Toms at Champions GC. Gained immortality by winning the 2003 Masters in sudden death over Len Mattiace, highlighting a career-best season in which he won thrice and finished 5th in earnings. Claimed back-to-back Los Angeles Opens in 2003 (in sudden death over Charles Howell III) and 2004 (edging Shigeki Maruyama by one). Hasn't won since 2007 but remained a consistent money earner prior to being handicapped by a partial ligament tear in his right elbow in 2010 (ultimately required surgery in August of 2011). Finally regained his card in 2014 (at age 44), narrowly requalifying by ranking among the top 125 in regular season PGA Tour $$$. Canada's only Major champion. **Teams:** Presidents Cup (5): 2000-03-05-07-09 (13-9-2). World Cup (6): 1997-00-01-02-06-07. **OWR Best:** 3 - Jun, 2003.

PGA Tour Wins (8): 1999: Air Canada Championship **2000**: WGC-American Express **2001**: Tour Championship **2003**: Bob Hope Classic (90H), Los Angeles Open (Nissan), Masters Tournament **2004**: Los Angeles Open (Nissan) **2007**: Fry's.com Open.

Other Wins: Canadian TPC: 1993   Canadian Masters: 1997   B.C. Tel Open (Canada): 1997   Champions Challenge (2): 2003-04 (both w/D.Wilson).

Amateur Wins: Canadian Juvenile: 1986   Ontario Jr: 1988   Ontario Am (2): 1990-92.

	98	99	00	01	02	03	04	05	06	07	08	09	10	11	12	13	14
Masters	-	-	T28	T27	T24	Win	MC	T5	T11	T20	T17	T46	T43	MC	MC	MC	T44
US Open	-	MC	T16	T19	MC	T3	T4	T42	T6	T20	T18	T10	T80	-	-	T28	-
British	-	T37	T52	MC	T69	T28	T9	MC	T56	T8	T39	MC	MC	-	-	-	-
PGA	-	T10	T30	T16	T34	T7	MC	T47	6	MC	T42	MC	MC	-	-	-	-
Money (A)	131	23	6	11	78	5	14	56	33	35	14	26	151	240	-	186	109
OWR	309	57	21	12	46	6	8	48	45	35	21	36	171	898	-	631	326

2014: PGA: 25 st / 9 ct / 1 t10. (2 Byron Nelson). Had his best year since 2010 (again) but despite ranking 109th in $$$, was 139th in FedEx Cup points, only keeping his card by ranking among the top 125 in $$$ after the Wyndham Championship.

OUTLOOK: Had his career sidetracked by a 2010 ligament tear in his right elbow. Has now used up his Career Top-50 and Top-25 Money Winner exemptions but narrowly regained his card by ranking 104th in $$$ after Wyndham. Has never recovered his tee-to-green game since the injury, and while 2014 showed some modest incremental improvement, at age 44, a huge resurgence seems highly unlikely at this point.

STATS: Driving Distance: D   Driving Accuracy: C-   GIR: C-   Short Game: B-   Putting: B+

Westwood, Lee John, O.B.E. (England) (41)
b. Worksop, England 4/24/1973. 6'0" 205 lbs. TP: 1993. A true international golfer who has won events on six major tours. Hailed in the late 1990s as Europe's answer to Tiger Woods, and has since enjoyed a flashy but up-and-down ride. Won 15 European Tour events between 1996-2000, ending Colin Montgomerie's seven-year perch atop the Order of Merit in 2000. In 2001, suffered a baffling loss of form that saw him go winless internationally for the next two seasons while plunging as low as 75th in the E Tour Order of Merit. Recovered to win the 2003 BMW International and the Dunhill Links Championship, and climbed to 7th in the Order of Merit for both 2003 and '04 before dropping again (to 27th and 24th) during winless 2005 and '06 campaigns. 2007 victories at the Andalucia Open and the British Masters got the ball rolling again, leading to a 3rd-place finish at the 2008 U.S. Open (Torrey Pines), then a breakout 2009 which included wins at the Portuguese Masters and, with a closing 64, the season-ending Dubai World Championship. 2009 also featured a 1st-place finish in the E Tour Order of Merit and T3s at both the British Open (where a 72nd-hole bogey left him one shy of the Watson-Cink playoff) and the PGA, plus a career-best 4th in the year-end OWR. 2010 included his 2nd PGA Tour win at the FedEx St Jude Classic (where Robert Garrigus' triple-bogey at the 72nd famously set up a three-way playoff), solo 2nds at both the Masters (three behind Phil Mickelson, after leading through 54 holes) and the British Open and a climb to the #1 spot in the OWR on November 1st. Is the second winningest Englishman (behind Nick Faldo) in E Tour history. Lost the OWR #1 to Martin Kaymer early in 2011 but picked things up with a win at the Asian Tour's Indonesian Masters, then added the jointly sponsored (Europe and Asia) Ballantine's Championship several weeks later. Near season's end, won the short-field Nedbank Golf Challenge in South Africa and the inaugural Thailand Golf Championship, where rounds of 60-64 staked him to a stunning 11-shot halfway lead. Claimed his first win of 2012 by defending his Indonesian Masters title, then won the E Tour's Scandinavian Masters in a five-shot walkaway. Ended a two-year victory drought with a runaway seven-shot win at the 2014 Malaysian Open, then returned to Asia late in the year to win his second Thailand Golf Championship. **Awards:** E Tour Golfer of the Year (3): 1998-00-09. Euro Vardon Trophy (2): 2000-09. **Teams:** Ryder Cup (9): 1997-99-02-04-06-08-10-12-14 (O: 20-15-6, S: 3-6-0). Seve Trophy (4): 2000-02-03-11. **OWR Best:** 1 - Oct, 2010.

PGA Tour Wins (2): 1998: New Orleans Classic (Freeport-McDermott) **2010**: Memphis Classic (St Jude).

European Tour Wins (23): 1996: Scandinavian Masters **1997**: Volvo Masters (54H) **1998**: Deutsche Bank Open, English Open, Loch Lomond Inv, Belgacom Open **1999**: Dutch Open, European Open, European Masters **2000**: Deutsche Bank Open, European Grand Prix, European Open, Scandinavian Masters, Belgacom Open **2003**: BMW Int'l, Dunhill Links Championship **2007**: Open de Andalucia, British Masters **2009**: Portugal Masters, Dubai World Championship **2011**: Ballantine's Championship **2012**: Scandinavian Masters (Nordea) **2014**: Malaysian Open (Maybank).

Japan Tour (4): 1996: Taiheiyo Masters (54H) **1997**: Taiheiyo Masters **1998**: Taiheiyo Masters, Dunlop Phoenix.

Asian Tour Wins (6): 1997: Malaysian Open **1999**: Macau Open **2011**: Indonesian Masters, Thailand Golf Championship **2012**: Indonesian Masters **2014**: Thailand Golf Championship.

Sunshine Tour Wins (3): 2000: Dimension Data Pro-Am **2010**: Million Dollar Challenge **2011**: Million Dollar Challenge.

Australasian Tour Wins (1): 1997: Australian Open.

Other Wins: Didata Better Ball (South Africa): 1999   World Match Play (England): 2000   Nelson Mandela Inv (SA): 2003 (w/S.Hobday)   Million Dollar Challenge (SA): 2010

Amateur Wins: St George's Challenge Cup: 1992   –   Peter McEvoy Trophy: 1991   English County Champions: 1992   Prince of Wales Challenge Cup: 1992   Lagonda Trophy: 1992   British Youths: 1993   Leven Gold Medal: 1993.

Westwood, Lee John, O.B.E., Cont'd

	94	95	96	97	98	99	00	01	02	03	04	05	06	07	08	09	10	11	12	13	14
Masters	-	-	-	T24	44	T6	MC	-	44	-	-	MC	MC	T30	T11	43	2	T11	T3	T8	7
US Open	-	-	-	T19	T7	MC	T5	MC	-	-	T36	T33	-	T36	3	T23	T16	T3	T10	T15	MC
British	-	T96	MC	T10	T64	T18	T64	T47	MC	MC	4	MC	T31	T35	T67	T3	2	MC	T45	T3	MC
PGA	-	-	-	T29	MC	T16	T15	T44	MC	MC	MC	T17	T29	T32	MC	T3	-	T8	MC	T33	T15
Money (A)	-	-	288*	-	138*	46*	106*	-	-	-	-	142	130*	177*	57*	-	-	-	24	31	85
Money (E)	43	75	6	3	3	2	1	52	75	7	7	27	24	10	3	1	3	5	12	15	27
OWR	252	258	64	23	8	6	5	28	182	65	24	41	49	23	10	4	1	2	7	25	26

2014: PGA: 18 st / 12 ct / 2 t10. (T6 Players, 7 Masters). Played primarily in America for the third straight year and endured another disappointing campaign by his standards, finishing 85th in money and failing to contend in a Major. Made six additional non-Major/WGC E Tour starts, led by a victory at the Malaysian Open. Also ended the year nicely by winning December's Thailand Golf Championship on the Asian circuit.

OUTLOOK: At age 41, he continues to play a powerful but fairly accurate tee-to-green game, then rides a sometimes streaky putter on the greens. Has taken up PGA Tour membership (and a Florida residence) for the last three years, but it is debatable if that move has paid tangible dividends. Given the massive body of work, one can be reasonably optimistic that he's capable of turning things around and winning many more times worldwide in the future - but landing that elusive Major title is looking less and less likely with each passing year.

STATS: Driving Distance: A-   Driving Accuracy: B   GIR: B+↓   Short Game: B-   Putting: B

Wheatcroft, Steven John (USA) (36)
b. Indiana, PA 2/21/1978. 6'3" 225 lbs. College: Indiana U. TP: 2001. A non-recruited walk-on at Indiana. A mini-tour veteran but also a regular on the Web.com circuit, where he has won twice and thrice lifted himself up to the PGA Tour. Notably, his 2011 Web.com win at the Prince George's County Open came by a resounding 12 shots. **OWR Best:** 234 - Mar, 2010.

Other Wins: 2 Web.com (2011-2014)   +   Pennsylvania Open: 2003.
Amateur Wins: Northern Am: 2001.

	07	08	09	10	11	12	13	14
Masters	-	-	-	-	-	-	-	-
US Open	-	-	-	T63	-	-	-	-
British	-	-	-	-	-	-	-	-
PGA	-	-	-	-	-	-	-	-
Money (A)	206	-	-	166	-	199	-	-
OWR	861	806	296	394	366	537	574	489

2014: Played full-time on the Web.com Tour, finishing 19th in regular season $$$ to earn a fourth try at the PGA Tour.

OUTLOOK: Will try the PGA once again in 2015, with a recent Web.com win and, presumably, a bit of confidence under his belt. Has demonstrated elements of the ever-reliable length-and-putting touch combination, so perhaps the fourth time will be the charm.

STATS (LTD): Driving Distance: B+   Driving Accuracy: C   GIR: C   Short Game: B   Putting: B+

Whiteford, Peter William (Scotland) (34)
b. Kirkaldy, Scotland 8/3/1980. 5'11" 160 lbs. TP: 2002. After winning twice on the Europro mini-tour, spent five of six years from 2004-2009 on the Challenge Tour where he won three times. Was a steady presence on the E Tour thereafter, placing a career-best 63rd in $$$ in 2011, and - though remaining winless - retaining his card for four straight campaigns through 2013 before slumping to 144th in $$$ in 2014. **OWR Best:** 189 - Jul, 2011.

Other Wins: 3 Euro Challenge (2007-2009)   +   2 EuroPro (2002-2003).
Amateur Wins: Scottish Under 16: 1996.

	07	08	09	10	11	12	13	14
Masters	-	-	-	-	-	-	-	-
US Open	-	-	-	-	-	-	-	-
British	-	-	-	-	MC	-	-	-
PGA	-	-	-	-	-	-	-	-
Money (E)	-	145	289*	86	63	110	88	144
OWR	304	495	338	289	234	324	327	571

2014: E: 30 st / 11 ct / 1 t10. (5 Russia). After keeping his card every year since 2010, struggled significantly in 2014, making only 11 of 30 cuts (including only four of his first 20) on his way to finishing 144th in $$$.

OUTLOOK: Despite earning a solid living, has never truly established himself as a regular factor on the E Tour. Saw a significant drop off in GIR in 2014 and he will be playing on conditional status in 2015, so there's little in the numbers that suggest more than an incremental comeback.

STATS: Driving Distance: B+   Driving Accuracy: C-   GIR: B-   Short Game: B-   Putting: B+

Wi, Charlie (South Korea) (42)
b. Seoul, South Korea 1/3/1972. 5'10" 160 lbs. All-American at U of California-Berkeley. TP: 1995. The 1990 California Amateur champion (at age 17) and the 1995 Southern California Amateur winner. International veteran who has enjoyed success in Asia among attempts at gaining a foothold in Europe and/or America. Thrice among the Asian Tour's top 10 in earnings, and also logged seven wins on smaller regional circuits. Gained PGA Tour playing privileges in 2005 (via Q School) but lost them at season's end. After winning the E Tour's Malaysian Open, played through Q School again in 2006 and this time found success, finishing no worse than 84th in PGA Tour $$$ (and logging four runner-up finishes) through 2012 before fading thereafter. **Teams:** World Cup (2): 2006-09. **OWR Best:** 82 - Apr, 2009.

European Tour Wins (1): 2006: Malaysian Open (54H).
Other Wins: Kuala Lumpur Open: 1997   SK Telecom Open (KPGA) (2): 2001-02   Shinhan Donghae Open (KPGA): 2001   China Open: 2001   Taiwan Open: 2004   Pocari Sweat Open (KPGA): 2004   Caltex Masters (KPGA): 2005.
Amateur Wins: California Am: 1990   Southern California Am: 1995.

Wi, Charlie, Cont'd

	97	98	99	00	01	02	03	04	05	06	07	08	09	10	11	12	13	14
Masters	-	-	-	-	-	-	-	-	-	-	-	-	-	-	-	-	-	-
US Open	-	-	-	-	-	-	-	-	-	-	-	-	MC	-	-	T29	-	-
British	-	-	-	-	-	-	-	-	-	-	-	-	-	-	-	-	-	-
PGA	-	-	-	-	-	-	-	-	-	-	-	T9	T56	MC	MC	MC	-	-
Money (A)	-	-	-	-	-	-	-	-	186	-	84	61	64	53	80	43	121	161
Money (E)	-	-	-	-	-	88	123	-	-	-	-	-	-	-	-	-	-	-
Money (As)	17	-	-	-	2	-	-	9*	-	4*	-	-	-	-	-	-	-	79*
OWR	-	787	741	661	220	216	378	273	374	191	182	114	147	137	154	106	224	417

2014: PGA: 25 st / 11 ct / 0 t10. (T12 Frys.com). Continued a two-year decline by falling to 149th in FedEx Cup points.

OUTLOOK: Begins 2015 on a one-event medical extension. Never a PGA Tour winner but he managed to retain his card for a solid seven-year run (2007-2013). A shorter hitter and is limited tee-to-green (173 in Ball Striking), opening the door for a 2014 decline in putting numbers to sink him.

STATS: Driving Distance: C   Driving Accuracy: C+   GIR: C-   Short Game: A   Putting: A-

---

Wiesberger, Bernd Klaus (Austria) (29)
b. Vienna, Austria 10/8/1985. 6'2" 190 lbs. TP: 2006. Austria's top modern prospect who took until 2009 to reach the European Tour, then fell back to the Challenge circuit where he won twice in 2010. Found his sea legs on the E Tour by finishing 64th in $$$ in 2011, then blossomed in 2012 by claiming wins at the lucrative Ballantine's Championship (in a five-shot runaway) and in his native Austrian Open, where he beat Thomas Levet and Shane Lowry by three. Added his first Asian Tour triumph at the 2013 Indonesian Masters, where he held off Ernie Els by one, then contended at the 2014 PGA Championship, where he trailed Rory McIlroy by one through 54 holes before fading to a T15 on Sunday. **Teams:** Eisenhower Trophy (2): 2004-06. World Cup: 2013. **OWR Best:** 52 - Nov, 2013.

European Tour Wins (2): 2012: Ballantine's Championship, Austrian Open (Lyoness).
Asian Tour Wins (1): 2013: Indonesian Masters (CIMB Niaga).
Other Wins: 2 Euro Challenge (2010)   +   Zurich Open: 2012.
Amateur Wins: Austrian Am: 2004   Austrian Am Stroke Play (3): 2004-05-096   Austrian Boys: 1997   Austrian Youths (2): 2005-06.

	09	10	11	12	13	14
Masters	-	-	-	-	-	-
US Open	-	-	-	-	-	MC
British	-	-	-	-	T64	MC
PGA	-	-	-	MC	MC	T15
Money (E)	172	-	64	22	28	39
OWR	678	227	162	65	52	71

2014: E: 26 st / 19 ct / 4 t10. (2P Lyoness, T2 Malaysian, T4 Italian, T9 Dubai). Continued to settle in among the second tier of Europe's best, losing a playoff in his native Austria, contending at the PGA Championship (before fading on Sunday) and finishing 39th in $$$.

OUTLOOK: A powerful ball striker whose driving accuracy and GIR have climbed significantly in the last two years. At age 28, has established himself as a strong player, but can he climb to real stardom? The numbers are a bit chancy there, but continued E Tour success seems a safe bet.

STATS: Driving Distance: A-   Driving Accuracy: B ⇧   GIR: A ⇧   Short Game: C+   Putting: B-

---

Wilcox, William Ferdinand IV ("Will") (USA) (28)
b. Birmingham, AL 6/2/1986. 6'1" 150 lbs. College: Two-time D2 All-American at Clayton (GA) St after transferring from U of Alabama-Birmingham. TP: 2009. Won the 2008 Alabama Amateur before turning pro, then spending multiple years playing mini-tours and the Canadian circuit, where he won the Dakota Dunes Casino Open in 2010. Played on the Web.com Tour from 2011-2013, finishing 7th in $$$ (with one win) in the latter year. In 2013, also became the fourth player in Web.com history to break 60, carding a 12-under-par 59 in the final round of the Utah Championship. **OWR Best:** 233 - Sep, 2014.

Other Int'l Wins (1): 2010: Dakota Dunes Open (Canada).
Other Wins: 1 Web.com (2013).
Amateur Wins: Alabama Am: 2008.

	11	12	13	14
Masters	-	-	-	-
US Open	MC	-	-	-
British	-	-	-	-
PGA	-	-	-	-
Money (A)	-	-	-	137
OWR	403	607	326	279

2014: PGA: 16 st / 10 ct / 2 t10. (T4 Greenbrier, T8 Hawaii). Finished 142nd in FedEx Cup points, then failed to play through the Web.com Finals.

OUTLOOK: A long and relatively straight driver of the ball (he led the 2013 Web.com Tour in Total Driving) who might well have kept his card had there been 20+ starts on his docket. Has conditional status in 2015, so the Web.com Tour may prove his most realistic route forward.

STATS (LTD): Driving Distance: A-   Driving Accuracy: B   GIR: B   Short Game: B   Putting: C+

Wilkinson, Timothy David (New Zealand) (36)
b. Palmerston North, New Zealand 7/28/1978. 5'8" 155 lbs. College: St. Peters College. TP: 2003. Spent 2005-2007 on the Web.com Tour, never bettering 49th in $$$ but qualifying for the PGA Tour via Q School in 2007. Finished 92nd in 2008 PGA Tour earnings (including a T2 at the Texas Open) to retain his card but eventually lost it when a 2009 thumb injury necessitated a medical extension that ran into 2010. Returned to the Web.com in 2011 and remained there for three years before finishing 10th (in only 16 starts) in $$$ during 2013. **Teams:** Eisenhower Trophy: 2002. World Cup: 2013. **OWR Best:** 233 - Jan, 2009.

Amateur Wins: New Zealand Stroke Play: 2000   SBS inv (New Zealand): 2002.

Wilkinson, Timothy David, Cont'd

	08	09	10	11	12	13	14
Masters	-	-	-	-	-	-	-
US Open	-	-	-	-	-	-	-
British	-	-	-	-	-	-	-
PGA	-	-	-	-	-	-	-
Money (A)	92	173*	-	-	-	-	115
OWR	234	309	467	647	738	318	346

2014: PGA: 25 st / 18 ct / 3 t10. (T7 AT&T Pro-Am, T8 Barracuda, T10 Mayakoba).   Did a fine job of retaining his card in his first full PGA Tour season in six years, riding top 10s in lighter-field events like Mayakoba and Barracuda (Reno-Tahoe) to a 119th-place finish in FedEx Cup points.

OUTLOOK: Veteran who has played in the U.S. since 2005. A short hitter who thrives on and around the greens. Kept his PGA Tour card in 2008 (though largely due to two hot weeks) and narrowly retained it again in 2014. Numerically, it's tough to project a major step forward here.

STATS (LTD):   Driving Distance: C+   Driving Accuracy: B   GIR: C   Short Game: A+   Putting: B+

Willett, Daniel John (England) (27)
b. Sheffield, England 10/03/1987. 5'11" 180 lbs. TP: 2008. Former #1 rated amateur in the world who has seen mixed success since joining the E Tour in late 2008. Save for 2011, he has trended well, finishing 23rd in E Tour $$$ in both 2010 and '12, and claiming his first victory in the latter year at the BMW International Open, where he beat Marcus Fraser in a playoff. Found a higher gear in the latter stages of 2014 when, following a run of strong golf, he claimed his second E Tour win at the select-field 2014 Nedbank Golf Challenge in South Africa, where he walked away by four. Cracked the year-end OWR top 50 (sitting on 50th) for the first time. **Teams:** Walker Cup: 2007 (0-2-2). World Cup: 2013. **OWR Best:** 50 - Dec, 2014.

European Tour Wins (2): 2012: BMW International   **2014**: Nedbank Challenge ('15).

Amateur Wins: English Am: 2007   –   Australian Am Stroke Play: 2008   Spanish Am: 2008.

	08	09	10	11	12	13	14
Masters	-	-	-	-	-	-	-
US Open	-	-	-	-	-	-	T45
British	-	-	-	MC	-	T15	MC
PGA	-	-	MC	-	-	T40	T30
Money (E)	-	58	23	91	23	62	25
OWR	616	138	74	190	93	116	50

2014: E: 27 st / 22 ct / 7 t10. (T3 Irish, T4 Turkey, T5 Malaysian, T5 Euro Masters, T8 BMW Int'l, etc.).   Came back effectively from a quiet 2013, recording seven top 10s (including three in his final eight starts) and climbing to 25th in $$$.

OUTLOOK: Has a ton of experience for a young player (167 E Tour starts at age 27) and at times appeared on the verge of reaching the circuit's upper tier during 2014. Has always been a long driver capable of hitting lots of greens, but 2014 also witnessed sizeable improvement in both driving accuracy and his putting numbers. If those gains are largely sustained going forward, more wins (and stardom) could lie just around the corner.

STATS: Driving Distance: A-   Driving Accuracy: B ⇧   GIR: A   Short Game: B+   Putting: B+ ⇧

Williams, Deveraux Lee Jr. (USA) (36)
b. Anderson, SC 1/27/1978. 6'4" 215 lbs. All-American at Auburn U. TP: 2005. A rare modern two-time Walker Cup player who toiled for multiple seasons on mini-tours before reaching the Web.com for 2012. A victory in the Mexican Open helped him to a 16th-place $$$ finish and a PGA Tour card for 2013 - a season he would end by playing himself back through the Web.com Finals. **Teams:** Walker Cup (2): 2003-05 (3-2-2). Eisenhower Trophy: 2004. **OWR Best:** 331 - Jul, 2012.

Other Wins: 1 Web.com (2012)   +   1 NGA/Hooters (2007).

Amateur Wins: Southern Am: 2002   –   Greystone Inv (2): 2001-03   Dogwood Inv: 2003   Alabama HS: 2000.

	05	06	07	08	09	10	11	12	13	14
Masters	-	-	-	-	-	-	-	-	-	-
US Open	MC	T40	MC	-	-	-	-	-	-	-
British	-	-	-	-	-	-	-	-	-	-
PGA	-	-	-	-	-	-	-	-	-	-
Money (A)	-	-	-	-	-	-	-	-	198	215*
OWR	-	901	798	-	-	-	-	391	594	1086

2014: PGA: 13 st / 5 ct / 0 t10. (T43 Puerto Rico). Made only 13 PGA Tour starts due to a back injury, putting the clubs away after June's FedEx St Jude Classic, having missed four of his last five cuts. Finished the season ranked 204th in FedEx Cup points.

OUTLOOK: Begins 2015 on a six-event medical extension. Remains a limited tee-to-greener (178 in Ball Striking) who earns his money with a numerically strong short game and a fairly straight driver. The numbers suggest that he's in somewhat over his head at this level.

STATS (LTD):   Driving Distance: C+   Driving Accuracy: B+   GIR: B-   Short Game: A-   Putting: B

Wilson, Jack (Australia) (24)
b. Echuca, Victoria, Australia 12/10/1990. 6'1" 180 lbs. TP: 2011. Touted Australian prospect who, after winning the 2010 Victoria Amateur, turned professional in 2011 and won multiple trainee events around Australia. Grabbed national attention upon winning the 2013 Western Australia PGA, becoming the first trainee to win an Australasian Tour event. Grabbed international attention at year's end by finishing third (behind Adam Scott and Rickie Fowler) at the Australian PGA. So armed, he stumbled badly in 2014, finishing 84th in the Australasian Order of Merit. **OWR Best:** 363 - Mar, 2014.

Australasian Tour Wins (1): 2013: Western Australia PGA.

Other Wins: Royal Melbourne Purse: 2013

Amateur Wins: Victoria Am: 2010.

Wilson, Jack, Cont'd

	13	14
Masters	-	-
US Open	-	-
British	-	-
PGA	-	-
Money (O)	-	109*
OWR	386	624

2014: Split time among multiple Far Eastern tours but made little headway, finishing 105th in OneAsia $$$ (five starts) and 84th in Australia.

OUTLOOK: Initially looked capable of great things but after a splashy 2013, lost all of his momentum in 2014. He's obviously young enough to turn things around but first he needs to succeed at home...and then find another tour to expand on abroad.

STATS: Driving Distance: --   Driving Accuracy: --   GIR: --   Short Game: --   Putting: --

---

Wilson, Mark Joseph (USA) (40)
b. Menomonee Falls, WI 10/31/1974. 5'8" 145 lbs. College: U of North Carolina. TP: 1997. An AJGA All-American. Two-Academic All-American and a journeyman Web.com/PGA Tour player who, after a decade of gaining little traction, surprised everyone by breaking through, in a four-man playoff (Jose Coceres, Camilo Villegas and Boo Weekley) to win the 2007 Honda Classic. Emerged as a consistent top-60 money winner thereafter and added a second victory at the 2009 Mayakoba Classic (played opposite the WGC-Match Play) where he beat J.J. Henry by two. Slipped to 123rd in 2010 earnings before exploding in 2011 when he won twice early in the season, first at the Sony Open in Hawaii (by two over Tim Clark and Steve Marino), then at the Phoenix Open, in a playoff over Jason Dufner. Got off to another strong winter start in 2012, winning the Humana Challenge by two over Robert Garrigus, Jeff Maggert and John Mallinger, before cooling off somewhat in 2013, then plummeting to a career-worst 192nd in $$ in 2014. **OWR Best:** 24 - Feb, 2012.

PGA Tour Wins (5): 2007: Honda Classic **2009**: Mayakoba Classic **2011**: Hawaiian Open (Sony), Phoenix Open (Waste Management) **2012**: Humana Challenge.

Other Wins: 3 NGA/Hooters (1998-2001) + Champions Challenge (2): 2003-04 (both w/M.Weir).

	98	99	00	01	02	03	04	05	06	07	08	09	10	11	12	13	14
Masters	-	-	-	-	-	-	-	-	-	-	-	-	-	MC	MC	-	-
US Open	MC	-	-	-	-	-	-	-	-	-	-	-	-	MC	MC	-	MC
British	-	-	-	-	-	-	-	-	-	-	-	-	-	T63	MC	-	-
PGA	-	-	-	-	-	MC	-	MC	-	-	-	-	-	T26	MC	-	-
Money (A)	-	-	-	-	-	128	167	133	156	56	55	44	123	19	37	91	192
OWR	787	741	-	657	-	351	353	225	270	124	119	103	230	62	97	206	462

2014: PGA: 25 st / 9 ct / 0 t10. (T23 Wells Fargo). Plunged to 183rd in FedEx Cup points but remains exempt as a past multiple event winner.

OUTLOOK: After a long, steady run, he took a tumble upon turning 40, hitting career lows in both $$$ and FedEx Cup points. Has seen his SGP go from major strength (22 and 34 in 2008 and '09) to below the median (134 and 164 in 2013 and '14). Also saw his GIR crash from 56 to 137 last year, so there are multiple issues here. All five of his wins have come during the winter so if he's going to turn it around, it figures to happen early.

STATS: Driving Distance: C   Driving Accuracy: A   GIR: B ⇩   Short Game: B+   Putting: C+

Wilson, Oliver John (England) (34)
b. Mansfield, England 9/14/1980. 5'11" 170 lbs. College: Augusta (GA) St. TP: 2003. After playing collegiately in America, became the rare player to be selected for Ryder Cup play despite never having won a tournament as a professional (though he was four times an E Tour runner-up in 2008) or any major amateur titles. Widely viewed as a major up-and-comer in the mid-2000s as he climbed the E Tour Order of Merit, peaking at 11th and 8th in 2008 and '09. Slipped a bit in 2010 before crashing thereafter. Played the Challenge Tour in 2013 before finally breaking through for his first E Tour win in 2014, edging Rory McIlroy, Richie Ramsay and Tommy Fleetwood by one at the Dunhill Links Championship in his 228th career start. **Teams**: Walker Cup: 2003 (2-0-1). Palmer Cup (3): 2001-02-03. Ryder Cup: 2008 (O:1-1-0, S: 0-1-0). Seve Trophy (2): 2007-09. **OWR Best:** 35 - Oct, 2009.

European Tour Wins (1): 2014: Dunhill Links Championship.

	03	04	05	06	07	08	09	10	11	12	13	14
Masters	-	-	-	-	-	-	MC	MC	-	-	-	-
US Open	-	-	-	MC	-	T36	T23	MC	-	-	-	-
British	-	-	-	-	MC	MC	T24	MC	-	-	-	-
PGA	-	-	-	-	-	MC	T19	MC	-	-	-	-
Money (E)	-	-	97	71	30	11	8	48	130	137	236*	54
OWR	-	541	280	368	101	40	41	88	352	482	507	164

2014: E: 9 st / 6 ct / 1 t10. (Won Dunhill Links). Spent most of the year on the Challenge Tour (16 starts) but was also able to make nine E Tour starts, using the latter to break through for a long-awaited first victory at the Dunhill Links Championship.

OUTLOOK: Has dropped a long way from his Ryder Cup-playing peak of 2008 and '09, but potentially turned his entire career around by wining the Dunhill Links. His numbers do little to suggest more greatness lies ahead, but he's still fairly young, and now he's exempt through 2016.

STATS: Driving Distance: C   Driving Accuracy: C   GIR: B   Short Game: B+   Putting: C

Wiratchant, Thaworn (Thailand) (48)
b. Nakhon Prathorn, Thailand 12/28/1966. 6'0" 160 lbs. TP: 1987. One of the Asian Tour's top native performers in the new millennium, winning 17 times (plus an 18th European Tour co-sanctioned event) overall and 16 times since 2001. Though often a part-timer on the E Tour, has rarely been outside of the Asian Order of Merit top 10 since 2001, finishing 1st in both 2005 (with four wins) and 2012, when he was named the tour's Player Of The Year. Biggest win came at the 2005 Indonesia Open (where he ran away from Raphaël Jacquelin by five), though he also logged a six-shot triumph (over Gaganjeet Bhullar) at the 2009 Macau Open. Won three times in 2012, including a playoff victory (over Richie Ramsay) at the Indian Open. Added a 16th Asian Tour triumph (including his 2005 co-sanctioned E Tour win) in 2013 by claiming a second Yeangder TPC title at age 46. Won the 2014 Queen's Cup to cement his status as the Asian Tour's all-time winningest player, then added the King's Cup five months later, allowing him to finish 2014 with five more wins than his closest pursuer, Thongchai Jaidee. Possesses a stylish,

Wiratchant, Thaworn, Cont'd

stylish, much-photographed swing. **Teams:** Eisenhower Trophy: 1984. World Cup (2): 1989-90. **OWR Best:** 68 - Jan, 2013.

European Tour Wins (1): 2005: Indonesia Open.

Asian Tour Wins (18): 1996: Sabah Masters **2001:** Singapore Open, Asian Masters **2004:** Taiwan Masters **2005:** Taiwan Open, Indian Open, Vietnam Masters **2007:** China Classic **2008:** Bangkok Airways Open **2009:** Macau Open **2010:** Yeangder TPC (54H) **2012:** Queen's Cup, Selangor Masters, Indian Open **2013:** Yeangder TPC **2014:** Queen's Cup, King's Cup.

Other Wins: Australian Foursomes: 1985 PTT Performa (Thailand): 1995 TPC Championship (Thailand): 2001 Indonesia Open: 2011.

Amateur Wins: Asian Jr (2): 1984-85 Putra Cup (2): 1985-86 Thailand Am: 1987 Singapore Am: 1987 Southeast Asian Games: 1987.

	95	96	97	98	99	00	01	02	03	04	05	06	07	08	09	10	11	12	13	14
Masters	-	-	-	-	-	-	-	-	-	-	-	-	-	-	-	-	-	-	MC	-
US Open	-	-	-	-	-	-	-	-	-	-	-	-	-	-	-	-	-	-	-	-
British	-	-	-	-	-	-	-	-	-	-	T31	-	-	-	-	-	-	-	MC	-
PGA	-	-	-	-	-	-	-	-	-	-	-	-	-	-	-	-	-	-	-	-
Money (E)	-	-	-	-	-	-	-	-	-	-	133	80	176	-	-	-	-	-	-	-
Money (As)	29	17	60	68	60	49	4	25	4	4	1	9	11	8	14	11	5	1	20	7
Money (O)	-	-	-	-	-	-	-	-	-	-	-	-	-	-	27*	3*	44*	-	-	-
OWR	891	899	858	-	741	-	416	520	438	221	131	163	199	160	215	155	186	69	142	159

2014: ASIA: 20 st / 18 ct / 6 t10. (Incl. Won Queens Cup, Won Kings Cup, T4 Taiwan Masters, T4 Dubai). Rebounded from a slightly down 2013 to claim two Asian Tour victories (his native Thailand's Queen's and King's Cups) and finish 7th in $$$.

OUTLOOK: Has been one of Asia's most reliably effective players since the mid-1990s, showing few effects of age into his late 40s. Tough to say what's left in the tank at this point, but two more 2014 wins suggest that he very likely isn't done adding trophies to the mantle yet.

STATS: Driving Distance: C-   Driving Accuracy: B   GIR: C   Short Game: A-   Putting: A-

---

Wood, Christopher James (England) (27)

b. Bristol, England 11/26/1987. 6'5" 195 lbs. TP: 2008. Among the tallest E Tour players of his era at 6'5". Announced himself to the world by tying for 5th at the 2008 British Open as a 20-year-old amateur, then returned as a professional in 2009 to tie for 3rd, one stroke out of the Watson-Cink playoff. Initially established himself as a steady European Tour player but claimed his first win abroad, beating Dong-Kyu Jang by two at the OneAsia Tour's 2012 Thailand Open. Broke through in style for his maiden E Tour triumph at the 2013 Qatar Masters where, having blown a lead and trailing by one, he eagled the par-5 18th to steal the trophy. **Awards:** E Tour Rookie of the Year: 2009. **Teams:** Seve Trophy (2): 2009-13. World Cup: 2013. **OWR Best:** 57 - Aug, 2009.

European Tour Wins (1): 2013: Qatar Masters (Commercial Bank).

OneAsia Tour Wins (1): 2012: Thailand Open.

Amateur Wins: Russian Am: 2007 Welsh Am Stroke Play: 2008.

	08	09	10	11	12	13	14
Masters	-	-	MC	-	-	-	-
US Open	-	-	-	-	-	-	-
British	T5	T3	MC	-	-	T64	T23
PGA	-	T76	MC	-	-	MC	T47
Money (E)	162*	44	53	89	46	29	64
OWR	194	74	103	212	139	74	141

2014: E: 24 st / 16 ct / 6 t10. (5 Laguna, T6 Tshwane, T5 Malaysian, T5 Euro Masters, T8 BMW Int'l, etc.). Failed to follow his career-best 2013 with the continued improvement many expected, but he still logged a career-best six top 10s and finished 64th in $$$.

OUTLOOK: An intriguing talent as he plays a very solid tee-to-green game, and appears capable of running with the world's best when he's on. But perhaps held back by his putter, he failed to reach stardom in 2014 - though his year hardly represented a big step backwards. At age 27, he still possesses the raw talent to step up as his best years approach - but consistency still remains an issue until further notice.

STATS: Driving Distance: B   Driving Accuracy: B-   GIR: A-   Short Game: C+   Putting: B⇧

Woodland, Gary Lynn (USA) (30)

b. Topeka, KS 5/21/1984. 6'1" 195 lbs. College: U of Kansas. TP: 2007. Strong all-around athlete who played one year of basketball at Washburn (KS) University before transferring to the University of Kansas to play golf. Reached the PGA Tour via 2008 Q School, then had his rookie season (2009) cut short by a shoulder injury after 18 events. Following surgery and a medical extension, played a 2010 schedule split between the PGA and Web.com Tours, eventually returning to Q School at the close of the year and regaining his card for 2011. Played career-best golf during a successful early season run that included a playoff loss to Jhonattan Vegas at the Bob Hope Classic and his first career win at the Transitions Championship, where he edged Webb Simpson by one. Ended a two-year slump by winning the 2013 Reno-Tahoe Open (contested with modified Stableford scoring). **Teams:** World Cup: 2011 (won w/M.Kuchar). **OWR Best:** 36 - Jul, 2011.

PGA Tour Wins (2): 2011: Transitions Championship **2013:** Reno-Tahoe Open (Stableford).

Amateur Wins: Kansas Am (2): 2005-07.

	09	10	11	12	13	14
Masters	-	-	T24	WD	-	T26
US Open	T47	MC	T23	MC	-	T52
British	-	-	T30	T34	-	T39
PGA	-	-	T12	T42	74	MC
Money (A)	204	-	17	134	37	29
OWR	962	591	52	152	56	48

2014: PGA: 25 st / 23 ct / 5 t10. (2 CIMB, T7 Byron Nelson, T8 Valspar, T9 Tour Champ, T10 Farmers). Though winless, continued his comeback from a down 2012, losing in a playoff (to Ryan Moore) at the fall's CIMB Classic and finishing 22nd in FedEx Cup pts.

OUTLOOK: An overpowering player who, after making a big rookie splash in 2011, battled wrist problems and swing changes during a disappointing

Woodland, Gary Lynn, Cont'd

2012. Came back strong in 2013 and continued that form in 2014, however, riding his considerable length (9 in Driving Distance) and the ability to hit lots of green to thrust himself back into the top-shelf mix. There are few more imposing natural talents among younger American players, and now that he's back on track – and assuming he stays healthy – the breakout year we anticipated in 2014 remains eminently possible this time around.

STATS: Driving Distance: A+   Driving Accuracy: C+   GIR: A-   Short Game: B-   Putting: C+

Woods, Eldrick Tont ("Tiger") (USA) (39)
b. Cypress, CA 12/30/1975. 6'1" 185 lbs. Two-time All-American, NCAA individual champion (1996), Nicklaus (1996) and Haskins (1996) Awards winner at Stamford U. Won U.S. Amateur in 1994 (at TPC Sawgrass), '95 (Newport GC) and '96 (Pumpkin Ridge GC). TP: 1996. Four-time AJGA All-American and two-time AJGA Player Of The Year (1991 & '92). Won 1991, '92 and '93 U.S. Junior Amateurs (first multi-time winner in the event's history). The youngest-ever U.S. Amateur winner and the only man to win it three years straight. Joined the PGA Tour by winning twice in eight starts in late 1996, launching an unprecedented run of domination which saw him win 37 times between 1997-2003. Won the 1997 Masters in record fashion, routing Tom Kite by 12. An eight-win 1999 included the PGA Championship at Medinah, claimed in a memorable duel with Sergio García. Won the 2000 U.S. Open at Pebble Beach by 15 shots, breaking Old Tom Morris's Major championship margin-of-victory record set in 1864. Added the British Open at St Andrews (by eight shots) to complete the career Grand Slam, and his second PGA Championship (outdueling Bob May in a three-hole playoff) to join Ben Hogan as the only men to win three professional Majors in a single season. Won 2001 Masters (by two over David Duval) and thus held all four Major titles simultaneously. Added a third Masters in 2002, then backed it with a three-shot victory over Phil Mickelson at the U.S. Open at Bethpage. Despite becoming a far less accurate player, defeated Chris DiMarco in sudden death at the 2005 Masters, then eased to a five-shot victory at the British Open. Defended that title a year later at Royal Liverpool (hitting one driver all week en route to a two-shot triumph), then routed the field a month later too win the PGA Championship by five at Medinah. Won his 13th Major at the 2007 PGA Championship (Southern Hills) behind a record 63 in the second round, and his 14th at the 2008 U.S. Open (Torrey Pines) by holing a tying birdie putt at the 72nd, then beating Rocco Mediate in a Monday playoff – all on a broken leg which required season-ending surgery thereafter. Won seven times in 2009 before having his career derailed by epic scandal, beginning with his November 27, 2009 car accident. Returned to the Tour in April 2010 and, despite brief flashes of solid play (T4s at the 2010 and '11 Masters and the 2010 U.S. Open) went through a prolonged slump lasting through most of 2011. Finally broke his 107-week victory drought in December at his own unofficial Chevron World Challenge, where he birdied the final two holes to edge Zach Johnson by one. Later recorded his first official PGA Tour win since 2009 by claiming the 2012 Arnold Palmer Invitational (by five over Graeme McDowell), then tied Jack Nicklaus's PGA Tour career victory total (73) by capturing Jack's Memorial Tournament. Claimed his 75th career PGA Tour win at the 2013 Farmer's Insurance Open. Went on to add four more PGA Tour wins in 2013 but again faltered in the Majors, though he ended the year once again ranked #1 in the OWR. After struggling in early 2014, underwent surgery in April to alleviate a pinched nerve in his back, then cut his late season short due to back problems and all manner of swing issues. Closed the year by firing swing coach Sean Foley and replacing him with little-known Chris Como, who was tactfully introduced as a "swing consultant." **Awards:** AP Male Athlete of the Year (4): 1997-99-00-06. PGA Tour Player of the Year (11): 1997-99-00-01-02-03-05-06-07-09-13. Vardon Trophy (9): 1999-00-01-02-03-05-07-09-13. PGA Tour Rookie of the Year: 1996. FedEx Cup Champion (2): 2007-09. **Teams:** Walker Cup: 1995 (2-2-0). Eisenhower Trophy: 1994. Ryder Cup (7): 1997-99-02-04-06-10-12 (O: 13-17-3, S: 4-1-2). Presidents Cup (8): 1998-00-03-05-07-09-11-13 (24-15-1). World Cup (3): 1999-00-01 (won in '99 w/M.O'Meara and '00 w/D.Duval). **OWR Best:** 1 - Jun, 1997.

PGA Tour Wins (79): 1996: Las Vegas Inv (90H), Walt Disney Classic (Oldsmobile) **1997:** Mercedes Championships (54H), Masters Tournament, Byron Nelson Classic (GTE), Western Open (Motorola) **1998:** Atlanta Classic (BellSouth) **1999:** San Diego Open (Buick Inv), Memorial Tournament, Western Open (Motorola), PGA Championship, WGC-NEC Inv, Walt Disney Classic (National Car), Tour Championship, WGC-American Express **2000:** Mercedes Championships, AT&T Pro-Am, Bay Hill Inv, Memorial Tournament, U.S. Open, British Open, PGA Championship, WGC-NEC Inv, Canadian Open **2001:** Bay Hill Inv, Players Championship, Masters Tournament, Memorial Tournament, WGC-NEC Inv **2002:** Bay Hill Inv, Masters Tournament, U.S. Open, Buick Open, WGC-American Express **2003:** San Diego Open (Buick Inv), WGC-Match Play, Bay Hill Inv, Western Open, WGC-American Express **2004:** WGC-Match Play **2005:** San Diego Open (Buick Inv), Doral Open (Ford), Masters Tournament, British Open, WGC-NEC Inv, WGC-American Express **2006:** San Diego Open (Buick Inv), Doral Open (Ford), British Open, Buick Open, PGA Championship, WGC-Bridgestone Inv, Deutsche Bank Championship, WGC-American Express **2007:** San Diego Open (Buick Inv), WGC-CA Championship, Wachovia Championship, WGC-Bridgestone Inv, PGA Championship, Western Open (BMW), Tour Championship **2008:** San Diego Open (Buick Inv), WGC-Match Play, Bay Hill Inv, U.S. Open **2009:** Bay Hill Inv, Memorial Tournament, AT&T National, Buick Open, WGC-Bridgestone Inv, Western Open (BMW) **2012:** Bay Hill Inv, Memorial Tournament, AT&T National **2013:** San Diego Open (Farmers), WGC Cadillac Championship, Arnold Palmer Inv. Players Championship, WGC-Bridgestone Inv.

European Tour Wins (8): 1998: Johnnie Walker Classic **1999:** Deutsche Bank Open **2000:** Johnnie Walker Classic ('01) **2001:** Deutsche Bank Open **2002:** Deutsche Bank Open **2006:** Dubai Desert Classic **2008:** Dubai Desert Classic **2009:** Australian Masters.

Japan Tour Wins (2): 2004: Dunlop Phoenix **2005:** Dunlop Phoenix.

Asian Tour Wins (1): 1997: Asian Honda Classic.

Other Wins: PGA Grand Slam (MP)(2): 1998-99   World Cup (Individual): 1999   PGA Grand Slam(5): 00-01-02-05-06   Chevron World Challenge (5): 2001-04-06-07-11.

Amateur Wins: U.S. Amateur (3): 1994-95-96   Western Am: 1994   –   U.S. Junior Am (3): 1991-92-93   Junior World (9-10)(2): 1984-85   Junior World (11-12): 1988   Junior World (13-14)(2): 1989-90   Junior World (15-17): 1991   Orange Bowl Jr: 1991   Pacific Northwest Am: 1994   Southern California Am: 1994   NCAA Individual: 1996.

	95	96	97	98	99	00	01	02	03	04	05	06	07	08	09	10	11	12	13	14
Masters	T41	MC	Win	T8	T18	5	Win	Win	T15	T22	Win	T3	T2	2	T6	T4	T4	T40	T4	-
US Open	WD	T82	T19	T18	T3	Win	T12	Win	T20	T17	2	MC	T2	Win	T6	T4	-	T21	T32	-
British	T68	T22	T24	3	T7	Win	T25	T28	T4	T9	Win	Win	T12	-	MC	T23	-	T3	T6	69
PGA	-	-	T29	T10	Win	Win	T29	2	T39	T24	T4	Win	Win	-	2	T28	MC	T11	T40	MC
Money (A)	Am	24*	1	4	1	1	1	1	2	4	1	1	1	2*	1	68*	128*	2	1	201*
OWR	517	33	2	1	1	1	1	1	1	2	1	1	1	1	1	2	23	3	1	32

2014: PGA: 7 st / 5 ct / 0 t10. (T25 WGC-Cadillac). After struggling early, had his season shortened by back surgery, then shortened again by back pain/bad golf. Was never a factor in any of his seven starts, logging only one top 25 (T25 at the WGC-Cadillac), withdrawing during the final round at Honda and the WGC-Bridgestone, and only completing 72 holes three times. A complete washout of a year.

OUTLOOK: Where to begin? After winning five times in 2013, his swing became balky enough last year that he fired Sean Foley at season's end - but what other cards were there left to play? After several more reliable years, his driver once again dropped anchor (178 in Total Driving), his Proximity To Hole dove to 178 and his SGP (a bright spot over the previous three years) sunk to 98. But beyond this litany of problems, the constant parade of injuries is a question (as is their root cause), with his chances of catching Jack Nicklaus's Major championships record looking slimmer and slimmer. At age 39 he's at an all-time low, and while the talent is legendary, there may just be too many issues - both physical and mental - to ever soar again.

STATS: Driving Distance: A-   Driving Accuracy: C+   GIR: B+ ⇩   Short Game: A-   Putting: B+

Wu, Ashun (China) (29)

b. Zangzhou, China 6/22/1985. 6'0" 185 lbs. TP: 2007. Began his professional career by playing two full seasons (2008 and '09) on the Asian Tour where he had limited success. Finished 19th in earnings on the OneAsia Tour in 2011 before qualifying for the Japan Tour in 2012, where he finished 27th in $$$ and became the first Chinese player to win in Japan, taking the weather-shortened Toshin Tournament (in a playoff with Yuta Ikeda) in September. Validated it a year later by jumping out to four-stroke 54-hole lead, then barely holding on to win the 2013 Heiwa PGM Championship. **Teams:** World Cup: 2013. **OWR Best:** 127 - Jan, 2014.

Japan Tour Wins (2): 2012: Toshin Golf Tournament (54H) **2013:** Heiwa PGM Championship.
Amateur Wins: All-China Games (Individual): 2006.

	08	09	10	11	12	13	14
Masters	-	-	-	-	-	-	-
US Open	-	-	-	-	-	-	-
British	-	-	-	-	-	MC	MC
PGA	-	-	-	-	-	-	-
Money (J)	-	-	100	-	27	8	46
Money (As)	78	44*	-	-	-	-	-
Money (O)	-	-	-	19	117*	-	-
OWR	753	515	762	931	170	129	186

2014: JAP: 16 st / 13 ct / 2 t10. (4 Indonesia, T6 Taiheiyo). Fell off his career-best 2013 numbers but still finished 46th in $$$.
OUTLOOK: Has established himself as the best of China's newer wave of young professionals, and has won twice in Japan in four full seasons there. Has average length and below-the-median putting numbers, however, which will likely hinder his ability to succeed at a level higher than this.

STATS: Driving Distance: B   Driving Accuracy: B+   GIR: B+   Short Game: B   Putting: B-

Yamashita, Kazuhiro (Japan) (41)

b. Osaka, Japan 11/5/1973. 5'7" 155 lbs. TP: 1998. A long-running Japan Tour veteran who has never won a professional event in Japan - his nearest miss being a playoff loss in a Japan Challenge Tour event in 2004. Didn't establish himself until his mid-30s, finishing 42nd in Japan Tour $$$ in 2008 and remaining a steady earner thereafter, peaking at 15th during a 2009 season which included eight top 10s and a runner-up finish at the ANA Open. **OWR Best:** 180 - Jan, 2010.

	00	01	02	03	04	05	06	07	08	09	10	11	12	13	14
Masters	-	-	-	-	-	-	-	-	-	-	-	-	-	-	-
US Open	-	-	-	-	-	-	-	-	-	-	-	-	-	-	-
British	-	-	-	-	-	-	-	-	-	-	-	-	-	-	-
PGA	-	-	-	-	-	-	-	-	-	-	-	-	-	-	-
Money (J)	239	-	-	-	-	-	220*	212*	42	15	39	51	22	16	30
OWR	1042	1201	1262	-	-	1182	1309	1375	517	181	250	401	255	199	244

2014: JAP: 23 st / 15 ct / 5 t10. (T2 Fukushima, T3 Sega Sammy, T6 Taiheiyo, T8 Toshin, T9 Diamond Cup). Finished a solid 30th in $$$.
OUTLOOK: A short-but-straight type who has ridden above average iron play, plus a solid short game and putter, to a fairly lucrative Japan Tour career. Has lack of winning stands out like a sore thumb, however, and realistically it's hard to predict that will change given his consistency to date.

STATS: Driving Distance: C+   Driving Accuracy: A-   GIR: B+   Short Game: B+   Putting: B+

Yang, Yong-Eun (South Korea) (42)

b. Seoul, South Korea 1/15/1972. 5'9" 195 lbs. TP: 1996. Korean Tour 1999 Rookie-of-the-Year (at age 27) who played primarily in Japan from 2001-06, winning four times and finishing in the Order of Merit top 10 from 2004-06. Shot a closing 63 to win the 2006 Suntory Open by six shots. Surprised a world-class field (including Tiger Woods and Retief Goosen) to claim the 2006 (E Tour '07) HSBC Champions event, taking up E Tour membership upon winning. Came to America full-time in 2008 and broke through for his first PGA Tour victory at the 2009 Honda Classic, beating John Rollins by one. Validated it emphatically (and became Asia's first-ever men's Major champion) by beating Tiger Woods head-to-head at Hazeltine at the 2009 PGA Championship. Played both in the U.S. and Europe in 2010, winning the latter circuit's Volvo China Open, where he edged Rhys Davies and Stephen Dodd by two. A solid 2011 included finishing 32nd in PGA Tour $$$ and T3 at the U.S. Open, before he slipped badly thereafter. **Teams:** Presidents Cup (2): 2009-11 (3-5-1). World Cup: 2009. **OWR Best:** 19 - May, 2010.

PGA Tour Wins (2): 2009: Honda Classic, PGA Championship.
European Tour Wins (2): 2006: HSBC Champions ('07) **2010:** China Open (Volvo).
Japan Tour Wins (4): 2004: Sun Chlorella Classic, Asahi-Ryokuken Memorial **2005:** Tokai Classic **2006:** Suntory Open.
Asian Tour Wins (1): 2006: Korean Open.
OneAsia Tour Wins (1): 2010: Korean Open.
Other Wins: SBS Open (KPGA): 2002   Korean Open (KPGA): 2006.

	00	01	02	03	04	05	06	07	08	09	10	11	12	13	14
Masters	-	-	-	-	-	-	-	T30	-	MC	T8	T20	T57	MC	MC
US Open	-	-	-	-	-	MC	-	-	-	-	MC	T3	MC	MC	MC
British	-	-	-	-	-	MC	-	MC	-	-	T60	T16	MC	T32	MC
PGA	-	-	-	-	-	T47	-	MC	-	Win	MC	T69	T36	MC	MC
Money (A)	-	-	-	-	-	-	-	-	157	10	67	32	153	176	177
Money (E)	-	-	-	-	-	-	-	28	-	-	37	33	-	-	-
Money (J)	-	-	117	-	3	10	9	-	-	-	-	-	-	-	-
OWR	684	536	657	684	77	106	33	94	478	31	42	45	105	320	638

2014: PGA: 28 st / 12 ct / 0 t10. (T23 Wells Fargo). Made his most PGA Tour starts since 2008 but still failed to crack the top 150 in $$$ for the third straight season. Finished 167th in FedEx Cup points, then failed to play through the Web.com Finals.
OUTLOOK: Has fallen so far from his 2009 prime that he'll be playing on Past Champion status in 2015. Other than a rise in Driving Accuracy (34), there are precious few positive numbers in his game these days. The bottom line is that when your Ball Striking ranks 130 and your Total Putting 131, high-level success is unlikely. Past his competitive prime in the U.S., it appears – but he might still prosper in the Far East were he to return home.

STATS: Driving Distance: C+   Driving Accuracy: B+ ⇧   GIR: C   Short Game: B   Putting: B ⇩

Yokoo, Kaname (Japan) (42) b. Tokyo, Japan 7/24/1972. 5'9" 170 lbs. College: Nihon University. TP: 1995. One of only a handful of period Japanese players to try the PGA Tour full-time, where he played – with only middling success – from 2001-2003. Thrice a winner (and thrice a top-10 finisher in the Order of Merit) on the Japan Tour before heading to America, highlighted by a one-shot triumph over Vijay Singh at the 1999 Tokai Classic and a 2 & 1 victory over Toru Taniguchi at the 2000 Japan PGA Match Play. Claimed another prestige win at the 2002 Dunlop Phoenix, where he edged Sergio García by one. Slipped slightly beginning in 2010 but remained competitive (if seldom winning) in his homeland through 2013 before fading to a career-worst 2014. **OWR Best:** 105 - Apr, 2001.

Japan Tour Wins (5): 1998: Acom Int'l **1999:** Tokai Classic **2000:** Japan PGA Match Play **2002:** Dunlop Phoenix **2006:** Mitsubishi Diamond Cup.

Amateur Wins: Japan Collegiate: 1993.

	96	97	98	99	00	01	02	03	04	05	06	07	08	09	10	11	12	13	14
Masters	-	-	-	-	-	-	-	-	-	-	-	-	-	-	-	-	-	-	-
US Open	-	-	-	T57	-	-	MC	-	-	-	-	MC	-	MC	MC	-	-	-	-
British	-	-	-	-	-	-	-	-	-	-	-	-	-	-	-	-	-	-	-
PGA	-	-	-	-	-	-	-	-	-	-	-	-	-	-	-	-	-	-	-
Money (A)	-	-	-	-	-	105	130	225	-	-	-	-	-	-	-	-	-	-	-
Money (J)	30	25	8	9	10	-	-	103*	21	15	12	23	24	20	44	61	46	57	118
OWR	207	238	138	110	113	185	117	252	255	157	180	236	242	177	301	530	513	584	1159

2014: JAP: 21 st / 7 ct / 0 t10. (T41 Heiwa). Collapsed hard, never topping 41st, missing 66% of his cuts and finishing a career-worst 118th in $$$.

OUTLOOK: As a shortish driver who struggles to hit a sizeable number of greens, he needs far better numbers around the putting surface to seriously compete deeper into his 40s. Given his obvious 2014 struggles, this does not seem like a good bet going forward.

STATS: Driving Distance: C+   Driving Accuracy: C+   GIR: C-   Short Game: C+   Putting: B-

---

Zanotti, Fabrizio (Paraguay) (31) b. Asuncion, Paraguay 5/21/1983. 5'7" 150 lbs. TP: 2003. Paraguay's top amateur for several years, then starred on the old Tour de las Americas (topping the 2006 Order of Merit) and won a Challenge Tour event in Mexico in 2006 (counted on 2007 schedule). Graduated to the European Tour in 2008 and, though going winless, managed to retain his card from 2009-2012. Returned for 2014 via a 2nd-place finish at Q School, then broke through for his first major tour victory by closing 65-65, then winning a four-man, five-hole playoff at the BMW International Open in Germany. **Teams:** Eisenhower Trophy (2): 2000-02. World Cup: 2007. **OWR Best:** 90 - Aug, 2014.

European Tour Wins (1): 2014: BMW International.

Other Wins: 1 Euro Challenge (2006) + Carlos Franco Inv (Paraguay): 2011.

	08	09	10	11	12	13	14
Masters	-	-	-	-	-	-	-
US Open	-	-	-	-	-	-	-
British	-	-	-	-	-	-	-
PGA	-	-	-	-	-	T47	-
Money (E)	153	63	75	100	69	140	38
OWR	575	258	200	241	264	514	99

2014: E: 26 st / 17 ct / 5 t10. (Won BMW Int'l, T3 Madeira, T5 Lyoness, T9 French, T10 BMW Masters). Enjoyed something of a breakout year, winning a four-man playoff (that included Henrik Stenson) at the BMW International and finishing a career-best 38th in $$$.

OUTLOOK: Statistically, the key to his 2014 was an improvement in putting numbers of a sort that often cannot be sustained long-term. Thus while he clearly seems capable of sticking around for a while, the higher-percentage play says he corrects downward a bit during 2015.

STATS: Driving Distance: B-   Driving Accuracy: B   GIR: B+   Short Game: C   Putting: B⇧

Zhang, Lian-Wei (China) (49) b. Zhuhai, China 5/2/1965. 6'0" 165 lbs. TP: 1994. Became first Chinese player to win a European Tour event, his 72nd-hole birdie beating Ernie Els at the 2003 Singapore Masters. A four-time winner on the old Asian circuit, highlighted by a playoff victory over Nick Price at the 2002 Macau Open. The first Chinese player to be invited to the Masters (2004), missing the cut by a single stroke. Has made no other Major championship appearances. Has never entered more than 12 E Tour events in a season and, approaching 50, he's now mostly a spot starter in Asia. **Teams:** World Cup (6): 1994-96-01-07-08-09. **OWR Best:** 93 - May, 2003.

European Tour Wins (1): 2003: Singapore Masters.

Asian Tour Wins (4): 1996: Asian Match Play **2001:** Macau Open **2002:** Macau Open **2003:** China Open.

Other Wins: Volvo Masters (Malaysia)(2): 1995-96   Volvo Masters (Thailand)(2): 1995-96   Volvo Open (China): 1995   Blue Ribbon Open (China): 1996   Founder Open (China): 1997   Hong Kong PGA: 1998   Ontario Open (Canada): 2000   Davidoff Nation's Cup (China) (w/W.C.Liang): 2001   Guangzhou (China) (2): 2007-08.

Amateur Wins: China Am (3): 1989-91-94.

	95	96	97	98	99	00	01	02	03	04	05	06	07	08	09	10	11	12	13	14
Masters	-	-	-	-	-	-	-	-	-	MC	-	-	-	-	-	-	-	-	-	-
US Open	-	-	-	-	-	-	-	-	-	-	-	-	-	-	-	-	-	-	-	-
British	-	-	-	-	-	-	-	-	-	-	-	-	-	-	-	-	-	-	-	-
PGA	-	-	-	-	-	-	-	-	-	-	-	-	-	-	-	-	-	-	-	-
Money (As)	-	-	-	18*	-	16*	16*	18*	3*	17*	19	-	55	63	75*	-	105*	-	-	110*
OWR	603	688	464	405	450	296	297	146	160	314	267	422	533	679	607	683	931	900	880	1076

2014: Made six starts on the Asia Tour and four on the OneAsia circuit (best: T17 Yeangder TPC).

OUTLOOK: Was something of a trailblazer in his day, but is largely a ceremonial player now. Still figures to make spot starts, even nearing 50.

STATS: Driving Distance: --   Driving Accuracy: --   GIR: --   Short Game: --   Putting: --

Printed in Great Britain
by Amazon